PENGUIN REFERENCE BOOKS

# THE PENGUIN CONCISE DICTIONARY OF BIOGRAPHICAL QUOTATION

Justin Wintle was educated at Stowe and Magdalen College, Oxford. After graduating in Modern History he joined the Inter-Action Community Arts Trust, and, with Ed Berman, compiled *The Fun Art Bus*, an account of the Inter-Action experimental theatre project. Since then he has worked in London, New York and Bangkok as a freelance writer and editor. His other publications include: *The Pied Pipers*, a collection of interviews with leading British and American children's writers, and, most recently, *Makers of Modern Culture* (1981), a guide to the ideas and arts of the twentieth century which he devised and edited. In addition he has contributed to a variety of publications including *The Times*, *New Society*, *The Times Educational Supplement*, *Architectural Design* and *Kodomo no Yakata* (Tokyo).

Richard Kenin was born in Portland, Oregon, and was educated at Reed College, the London School of Economics and Magdalen College, Oxford, where he took a Doctorate in Modern History in 1973. After leaving Oxford he was attached to the United States Embassy in London for three years, before becoming a Research Historian at the National Portrait Gallery of the Smithsonian Institution. He is a Fellow of the Royal Society of Arts and is currently Picture Editor for Time-Life Books Inc. in Washington D.C. His most recent book is *Return to Albion: Americans in England 1760–1940* (1979).

# THE PENGUIN CONCISE DICTIONARY OF BIOGRAPHICAL QUOTATION

Justin Wintle was educated at Stowe and Magdalen College, Oxford. After graduating in Modern History he joined the Inter-Action Community Arts Trust and, with Ed Berman, compiled *The Fun Art Bus*, an account of Inter-Action's experimental theatre project. Since then he has worked in London, New York and Bangkok as a freelance writer and editor. His other publications include: *The Pied Pipers*, a collection of interviews with leading British and American children's writers, and, most recently, *Makers of Modern Culture* (1981), a guide to the ideas and arts of the twentieth century which he devised and edited. In addition he has contributed to a variety of publications including *The Times*, *New Society*, *The Times Educational Supplement*, *Architectural Design* and [illegible] in Tokyo.

Richard Kenin was born in Portland, Oregon, and was educated at Reed College, the London School of Economics and Magdalen College, Oxford, where he took a Doctorate in Modern History in 1973. After leaving Oxford he was attached to the United States Embassy in London for three years, before becoming a Research Historian at the National Portrait Gallery of the Smithsonian Institution. He is a Fellow of the Royal Society of Arts and is currently Picture Editor for Time-Life Books Inc. in Washington D.C. His most recent book is *Return to Albion: Americans in England 1760–1940* (1979).

THE PENGUIN CONCISE

# DICTIONARY OF BIOGRAPHICAL QUOTATION

EDITED BY JUSTIN WINTLE
AND RICHARD KENIN

PENGUIN BOOKS

Penguin Books Ltd, Harmondsworth, Middlesex, England
Penguin Books, 625 Madison Avenue, New York, New York 10022, U.S.A.
Penguin Books Australia Ltd, Ringwood, Victoria, Australia
Penguin Books Canada Ltd, 2801 John Street, Markham, Ontario, Canada L3R 1B4
Penguin Books (N.Z.) Ltd, 182–190 Wairau Road, Auckland 10, New Zealand

—

First published by Routledge & Kegan Paul Ltd as
*The Dictionary of Biographical Quotation* 1978

Abridged edition first published by Penguin Books 1981



—

Typeset, printed and bound in Great Britain by
Hazell Watson & Viney Ltd,
Aylesbury, Bucks
Set in Monotype Times

For our parents

# Contents

# Research Team

Julian Barnes  John Baxter  Dr Joan Hart
Amy Henderson  Robert Hewison
Dr May Hofman  Sally Issler  Jonathan Keates
Sarah Maitland  Deirdre McKenna
Ivan Pichardo  Martha Sandweiss  Basil Thesiger
Giles Waterfield  William Waterfield
Charlotte Willson-Pepper  Peter Yapp

# Acknowledgements

The editors are entirely indebted to the industry and enthusiasm of each member of the research team which produced a mountain of biographical quotation from which the final selection was made. In addition, the editors wish to express their gratitude to the following: Mrs Anne Francis, Harriett Gilbert, Sebastian Lucas, Jennifer Martin, Claudia Still, Christopher and Sarah Wintle, and the staff of the London Library.

Where they have drawn extensively from works which are still in copyright the editors would like to make the following acknowledgements:

For excerpts from Lloyd Morris, *Not So Long Ago*, used by permission of Random House, Inc.; for excerpts from W. H. Auden, *The Dyer's Hand and other Essays*, used by permission of Random House, Inc. and Faber and Faber Ltd; from Ezra Pound, *Personae* (Copyright 1926 by Ezra Pound), reprinted by permission of New Directions and of Faber and Faber Ltd; from *Selected Letters 1907–1941 of Ezra Pound*, ed. D. G. Paige (Copyright 1950 by Ezra Pound), reprinted by permission of New Directions and of Faber and Faber Ltd; from *Selected Letters of Dylan Thomas*, ed. Constantine Fitzgibbon (Copyright 1965, 1966 by the Trustees for the Copyrights of Dylan Thomas), reprinted by permission of New Directions and of J. M. Dent and Sons Ltd; from William Carlos Williams, *Collected Later Poems* (Copyright 1944 by William Carlos Williams), reprinted by permission of New Directions; from *Agee on Film, Volume I* by James Agee (Copyright © 1946, 1949, 1958 by the James Agee trust), used by permission of Grosset and Dunlap, Inc. and of Peter Owen Ltd, London; from *It All Started With Columbus* by Richard Armour (Copyright 1961 by Richard Armour), used by permission of McGraw-Hill Book Company; for four lines from Olive Dargan, 'To William Blake', reprinted by permission of Charles Scribner's Sons; for excerpts from T. S. Eliot, *Murder in the Cathedral* (Copyright T. S. Eliot 1963), reprinted by permission of Harcourt Brace Jovanovich, Inc. and of Faber and Faber Ltd; from Carl Sandburg, *The People, Yes* (Copyright 1936 by Harcourt Brace Jovanovich, Inc., renewed 1964 by Carl Sandburg), reprinted by permission of the publishers; from Edgar Lee Masters, 'At Sagamore Hill' from *Starved Rook*, published by the Macmillan Publishing Company, Inc., reprinted by the permission of Ellen C. Masters; for four lines from 'Blood and the Moon' and sixteen lines from 'In Memory of Major Robert Gregory' from W. B. Yeats, *Collected Poems* (Copyright the Macmillan Publishing Company 1933, renewed by Bertha Georgia Yeats 1961 and 1947 respectively), reprinted with the permission of the Macmillan Publishing Company and of A. P. Watt Ltd; for ten lines from 'Bryan, Bryan, Bryan, Bryan' from Vachel Lindsay, *Collected Poems* (Copyright the Macmillan Publishing Company, Inc. 1920, renewed 1948 by Elizabeth C. Lindsay), reprinted with permission of the Macmillan Publishing Company Ltd; for nine lines from 'The Raft', twelve lines from 'Our Mother Pocahontas', eight lines from 'The Knight in Disguise' and eleven lines from 'General William Booth Enters into Heaven' from Vachel Lindsay, *Collected Poems* (Copyright by the Macmillan Publishing Company, Inc. 1917, renewed 1945 by Elizabeth C. Lindsay), reprinted by permission of the Macmillan Publishing Company, Inc.; from Eleanor Ruggles, *Prince of Players: Edwin Booth* (Copyright 1963 by W. W. Norton & Company, Inc.), reprinted with permission of W. W. Norton & Company, Inc.; from Stephen Vincent Benét, *John Brown's Body* (published by Holt, Rinehart and Winston, Inc., copyright 1927, 1928 by Stephen Vincent Benét, renewed 1955, 1956 by Rosemary Carr Benét), reprinted with permission of Brandt & Brandt, Literary Agency, Inc.; from 'Captain Kidd', 'Daniel Boone', 'John James Audubon' and 'Cotton Mather' from Rosemary and Stephen Vincent Benét, *A Book of Americans* (published by Holt, Rinehart and Winston, Inc., copyright 1933 by Stephen Vincent Benét, renewed 1961 by Rosemary Carr Benét), reprinted by permission of Brandt & Brandt, Literary Agency, Inc.; from Otis Ferguson, *The Film Criticism of Otis Ferguson*, edited by Robert Wilson (Copyright 1971), reproduced by permission of Temple University Press; from Harold Nicolson's *Diaries and Letters*, 3 vols (© 1956, 1967, 1968 by William Collins Ltd), reprinted by permission of William Collins, Sons & Co. Ltd, and of Atheneum Publishers; for nine lines from 'H. L. Mencken Meets a Poet in the West Side YMCA' from E. B. White, *The Fox of Peapack and Other Poems* (Copyright 1936 by E. B. White), reprinted by permission of Harper & Row, Publishers, Inc.; for excerpts from T. S. Eliot, *The Sacred Wood*, reproduced by permission of Barnes & Noble/Harper & Row Publishers, Inc.; from Janet Flanner, *Paris Was Yesterday, 1925–9* (Copyright 1925–1939 (inclusive) © 1972 by the New Yorker Magazine, Inc.), used by permission of the Viking Press and of Angus and Robertson (UK) Ltd; from Malcolm Cowley, *The Second Flowering* (Copyright © 1956, 1967, 1968, 1970, 1973 by Malcolm Cowley), used by permission of the Viking Press; for four lines from Dorothy Parker, 'Sunset Gun', used by permission of the Viking Press, and of Gerald Duckworth & Co.; from 'Steiglitz' by Gertrude Stein from *America and Alfred Steiglitz* (Copyright 1934 by Doubleday & Company, Inc.), used by permission of the publisher; from Adela Rogers St Johns, *The Honeycomb* (Copyright 1969 by Adela Rogers St Johns), used by permission of Doubleday and Company, Inc.; for seven Clerihews from W. H. Auden, *Academic Grafitti* (Copyright W. H. Auden), used by permission of Random House, Inc. and of Faber and Faber Ltd; for twelve lines from 'New Year Letter' from W. H. Auden, *Collected Poems*, ed. Edward Mendelson, used by permission of Random House, Inc. and of Faber and Faber Ltd; for eight lines from 'To T. S. Eliot on His Sixtieth Birthday' from W. H. Auden, *Collected Poems*, ed. Edward Mendelson, used by permission of Random House, Inc. and of Faber and Faber Ltd; from Eero Saarinen, *Eero Saarinen, on His Work*, ed. Aline Saarinen (Copyright © 1962, 1968 Yale University Press), used by permission of Yale University; from 'Elegiacs for T. S. Eliot' from George Barker, *Dreams of a Summer Night*, used by permission of Faber and Faber Ltd; for seven lines from 'Five-finger Exercises' and sixteen lines from 'Whispers of Immortality' from T. S. Eliot, *Collected Poems 1909–1962* (Copyright 1936 by Harcourt Brace Jovanovich, Inc., Copyright © 1963, 1964 by T. S. Eliot), used by permission of Faber and Faber Ltd and of Harcourt Brace Jovanovich, Inc.; from Walter de la Mare, 'Epitaph for William Blake', used by permission of The Literary Trustees of Walter de la Mare and the Society of Authors as their representatives; from Leo Sherley-Price's translation of Bede's *A History of the English Church and People* (Copyright © Leo Sherley-Price 1955, 1968), used by permission of Penguin Books Ltd; from A. P. Herbert, 'To B-P', used by permission of The Estate of the Late Sir Alan Herbert; from G. K. Chesterton, 'Ballad of the White Horse', reprinted by permission of The Estate of the Late G. K. Chesterton; from Brendan Kennelly, 'Yeats', used by permission of Brendan Kennelly, and for excerpts from *On Native Grounds* (Copyright 1942, 1970 by Alfred Kazin), reprinted by permission of Harcourt Brace Jovanovich, Inc.

# Introduction

Somewhere between Alexander Pope's dictum that 'The Proper study of Mankind is Man' and the popular adage 'there's nowt so queer as folk' lies the key to the world's most intriguing subject: the individual.

The idea of 'Proper study' implies method, and there has never been a shortage of invented means for dealing systematically with human character. If today we are mildly incredulous of Good and Bad Angels, of the Four Humours or the Ruling Passions; or if perhaps we smile at the alchemical endeavours of Physiognomy, or Astrology, that is because we have, in modern psychology and psychoanalysis, our own interpretative devices. But method is predisposed toward finding stereotypes, toward reducing its materials to instances of common rules, and is often impervious to the essential queerness, the unclassifiable peculiarities of the individual personality. We adopt method in our search for similarities in human behaviour, forgetting that what originally attracts us to the task are the differences.

This book, *The Dictionary of Biographical Quotation*, has been compiled to keep the differences alive, to give an impression of the rich diversity of the things people have written and said about one another. First and foremost we hope that, in this respect, it is a repository of linguistic use. But it has also been our intention that it should have a practical value, as a source of reference for students of all disciplines that are concerned with human endeavour. For this reason the compilation has been made according to historical principles.

Millions of observations have been made about millions of people. Somehow we had to impose some limitations on the undertaking if it was to have any coherent, feasible shape. We began therefore by restricting ourselves for our subjects to those deceased Britons and Americans whose contributions to their respective cultures (and sometimes to both) have, over the years, attracted most attention, be it fame or notoriety; while for quotations about them we decided that both contemporaneous and post-contemporaneous sources should be used, so that each individual might appear in the lights of his or her own times, as well as under the scrutiny of posterity. We considered including living subjects as well, but felt this would not have been entirely ethical.

When preparing our lists of subjects we aimed to represent all walks of life, without any bias toward one particular group, although we later discovered natural biases in the sense that poets, for example, have tended to attract rather more lively comment than, say, scientists. To do this we used such standard authorities as the *Dictionary of National Biography* and the *Dictionary of American Biography*. But we had to be careful. The *DNB* is unduly strong on staunch Victorian clerics and pedagogues, and somewhat less accommodating toward women. The *DAB* shares these prejudices, and is perhaps over-hospitable to soldiers. Where we were aware of this kind of weighting, we tried to redress the imbalance. This said, it would be presumptuous for us to claim that this Dictionary is without its contours. As Britain is an older nation than the United States, there are inevitably more British names, particularly from the period when Great Britain was the world power; but as we move into the twentieth century, the proportion changes in favour of the Americans.

The overwhelming advantage of these parameters was that they ensured the Dictionary would have the right balance between cultural unity and cultural diversity. The contrasting histories of Britain and the United States are indissolubly linked, and their shared language, English, has been modified by each without becoming incomprehensible to the other.

There were also disadvantages. Mainly it meant excluding such figures as Jesus Christ, Napoleon and others whose influence on English and American communities is obvious. But to have made any exceptions would simply have been to involve ourselves further in decisions of an arbitrary nature. To have included Napoleon would have entailed including Hitler; but would it have entailed including Bismarck? Our list of subjects, itself an arbitrary selection, threatened to over-extend, and so we chose to stick by our guns.

Having thus established our boundaries, we then sought ways of achieving flexibility within them. There was the question of what kind of quotation should find its way into the Dictionary, and our answer was: every kind. This included criticism of our subjects' achievements. 'Every man's work,' wrote Samuel Butler in *The Way of All Flesh*, 'whether it be literature or music or portraits or architecture or anything else, is always a portrait of himself.' And, still bearing with the generous spirit of this remark, we also extended the brief to our researchers to cover autobiographical quotations.

These were the principles by which we measured and cast our net. When, more than a year later, we examined the landed catch, we discovered there was no necessary correlation between, on the one hand, the quality and quantity of comment about a given individual, and, on the other, his or her received stature. For this reason we do not pretend that *The Dictionary of Biographical Quotation*, through the number of quotations pertaining to each subject, provides a gauge to the subject's relative importance; although we do content ourselves that the hundred or so indisputably major figures have been accorded justice. Certain persons, not of the first rank, but still of acknowledged significance, have been omitted altogether for want of appealing material. Conversely, when irresistibly attractive material relating to acknowledged insignificants surfaced during the research our inclination was not to exclude it. It would, for example, have been unforgivable to have overlooked Pope's caricature of Lord Hervey ('Let Sporus tremble'), even though other, more important courtiers of Hervey's generation have not been so fortunate in their condemnations. We would have been unduly fastidious had we said No Butts.

In making a final selection of quotations we were concerned, wherever possible, with exhibiting a balance of views relating to each subject, so that the insights of both a man's detractors and his admirers might be shown side by side. But even these, when they are plentiful on both sides, do not constitute a balanced portrait of a personality, and we should emphasize that *The Dictionary of Biographical Quotation* offers no short cuts to the understanding of historical and cultural figures, which can only be attained through detailed study of their lives and achievements. But having studied, the quotations here should oil the shift from knowledge to interpretation.

There is, of course, one crucial complexity. When one person evaluates another, he inevitably reveals something of his own values. Of this we were mindful, and we very often included a quotation precisely on account of what it seemed to be telling us about its author. Thus William Hone, the Regency propagandist, is represented by two comments reflecting the diametrically opposed reactions to his trial on the parts of John Keats and William Wordsworth. To get the best out of this book we suggest that the reader who is anxious to find out about, for instance, Lord Byron, should first turn to the quotations about him, and then see what he has said about other subjects. To this end we have provided an index of authors. Those marked q.v. are also featured in the main body of the Dictionary, which is arranged alphabetically according to subject.

However, our principal criteria for selection lay in the quotations themselves. The qualities we looked for were critical or psychological acuity, lively satire, ingenious wit or good humour, articulate calumny or delicious malice, transparent flattery or veiled defamation, for fine reflection and original perspective. Most of all we sought the magic that comes when insight and expression are married into a new amalgam of content and form. This is the *raison d'être* of all books of quotations. But because we had an overall purpose, the specifically biographical quest, we have been able to take some liberties with tradition. It will be seen that whereas many entries are succinct and concise, thereby conforming to the normal concept of a 'good quote', others are longer, more passage-like. These we opted to keep for two reasons. First, to have performed pruning operations on what are often classic statements of character analysis would have been a travesty, while to have excluded them altogether would have been a denial of our aims. Second, there was a tendency, though by no means absolute, for the seriousness of a comment to increase in proportion to its length, and we were determined that there should be an equal distribution of fun and thoughtfulness. Again, we have sometimes incorporated two- or three-word phrases which would not stand up as quotations elsewhere; but taken in context with the other quotations relating to the same subject they met our purposes. And the same is true of course of some of the longer quotations as well.

Finally, our materials have been drawn from a great number of sources: not only from the standard lives, biographies, and biographical collections, but also from anecdotes, epigrams, epitaphs, eulogies, obituaries, reminiscences, memoirs, reviews, essays, critical works, letters, diaries, volumes of poetry, verse, ballads and songs, pamphlets, tracts, broadsheets, sermons, newspapers, broadcasts, institutional reports, chronicles, histories, as well as from entendus, slogans, graffitti, and from at least one horoscope. Out of this diversity we hope we have been able to assemble a representative reflection of the many aspects of the human character as mirrored by itself.

Justin Wintle, London
Richard Kenin, Washington

# Guidelines

They only who live with a man can write his life with any genuine exactness and discrimination, and few people who have lived with a man know what to remark about him.

James Boswell, *Life of Johnson*

A biography, at best, is a series of photographs, taken from a limited number of positions, on a selectively sensitive plate, by a photographer whose presence affects the expression of the sitter in a characteristic way.

C. D. Broad, *Ethics and the History of Philosophy*

I wonder how the deuce any body could make such a world; for what purpose Dandies, for instance, were ordained – and kings – and fellows of colleges – and women of 'a certain age' – and many men of any age – and myself, most of all.

Lord Byron, Journal, 14 February 1814 – Midnight

History is the essence of innumerable biographies.

Thomas Carlyle, *Essay on History*

We know life is futile. A man who considers that his life is of very wonderful importance is awfully close to a padded cell.

Clarence Seward Darrow, in a lecture at the University of Chicago, 1929, on 'Facing Life Fearlessly: Omar Khayyám and A. E. Housman'

There is nothing more unfair to persons of mark than the attempts of those who know them but slightly to portray their characters or descant on their manners. Few men are to be seen through at a single or even a double glance, particularly those who are observed and waylaid, so to say, by the professional sketchers, who lie in wait for, and suddenly pounce upon them. The 'Eminent Individuals' soon acquire a knack of keeping on their guard, of almost sleeping with their eyes open. They learn to assume a conventional air, adopt certain set phrases, sometimes lay themselves out for effect, and too often display but a 'counterfeit resemblance' of their real nature. The lion-hunters teach the lions how to baffle them, and the latter shake the mane, or lash the tail, or growl or grin, according to a regular stereotyped plan for deceiving the tribe they are beset by.

Thomas Colley Grattan, *Beaten Paths and Those Who Trod Them*

History may be formed from permanent monuments and records; but Lives can only be written from personal knowledge, which is growing every day less and in a short time is lost for ever. What is known can seldom be immediately told; and when it might be told, it is no longer known. The delicate features of the mind, the nice discriminations of character, and the minute peculiarities of conduct, are soon obliterated; and it is surely better that caprice, obstinacy, frolic and folly, however they might delight in the description, should be silently forgotten, than that, by wanton merriment, and unseasonable detection, a pang should be given to a widow, a daughter, a brother, or a friend.

Samuel Johnson, *Lives of the Poets*: 'Addison'

The remedies of all our diseases will be discovered long after we are dead; and the world will be made a fit place to live in, after the death of most of those by whose exertions it will have been made so. It is to be hoped that those who live in those days will look back with sympathy to their known and unknown benefactors.

John Stuart Mill, Diary, 15 April 1854

The man who makes no mistakes does not usually make anything.

E. J. Phelps, Speech at Mansion House, 1899

One cannot define in a sentence a man whom it has taken God several millions of years to make.

Arthur Ransome, *Oscar Wilde, A Critical Study*

A Character differeth from a Picture only in this, every Part of it must be like, but it is not necessary that every Feature should be comprehended in it as in a Picture, only some of the most remarkable.

George Savile, Marquis of Halifax, *A Character of King Charles the Second*

Every great man nowadays has his disciples, and it is usually Judas who writes the biography.

Oscar Wilde, in the *Court and Society Review*, 20 April 1887

Most people are other people. Their thoughts are someone else's opinions, their life a mimicry, their passions a quotation.

Oscar Wilde, Letter to Lord Alfred Douglas, in *De Profundis*

When we meet, all the world to nothing we shall laugh; and, in truth Sir this world is worthy of nothing else.

Sir Henry Wotton, Letter to Sir Edmund Bacon, 21 March 1614

# 'A'

## ABERDEEN, EARL OF (GEORGE HAMILTON GORDON)

1784–1860 Statesman

His grief was such that at times he felt as if every drop of blood that would be shed would rest upon his head.

On himself, concerning the Crimean War, in conversation with John Bright, 22 March 1854, Bright, Diary

You complain'd of Lord Aberdeen's unceasing conversation, but with his knowledge and cleverness it was not such a bad substitute for a book.

Lady Bessborough, Letter to Lord Granville Leveson-Gower, November 1812

His temper naturally morose, has become licentiously peevish. Crossed in his Cabinet, he insults the House of Lords, and plagues the most eminent of his colleagues with the crabbed malice of a maundering witch.

Benjamin Disraeli, Letter to the Press, 1853

*See also* Queen Victoria

## ABERNETHY, JOHN

1764–1831 Surgeon

One of the brightest points in Abernethy's character, was, that, however he might sometimes forget the courtesy due to his private patients, he was never unkind to those whom charity had confided to his care. One morning, leaving home for the hospital, when some one was desirous of detaining him, he said: 'Private patients, if they do not like me, can go elsewhere; but the poor devils in the hospital I am bound to take care of'.

George Macilwain, *Memoirs of John Abernethy, F.R.S.*

Many years after this, I met him coming into the hospital one day, a little before two (the hour of lecture), and seeing him rather smartly dressed, with a white waistcoat, I said;

'You are very gay to-day, Sir?'

'Ay,' said he; 'one of the girls was married this morning'.

'Indeed, Sir,' I said. 'You should have given yourself a holiday on such an occasion, and not come down to lecture'.

'Nay,' returned he. 'Egad! I came down to lecture the day I was married myself!'

*Ibid.*

He is reported to have been consulted by the late Duke of York; and he stood before his royal highness, whistling, with his hands in his breeches-pockets, as usual. The duke, astonished at his conduct, said, 'I suppose you know who I am?' 'Suppose I do,' said he, 'what of that?' And his advice to his royal highness was given thus: 'Cut off the *supplies*, as the Duke of Wellington did in his campaigns, and the enemy will leave the citadel.'

Thomas Joseph Pettigrew, *Medical Portrait Gallery*

A man of rank consulted Mr Abernethy, and was received by him with remarkable rudeness. Upon some severe remark being made, the patient lost his temper, and told Mr A. he would make him *eat his words*. 'It will be of no use', said Mr A., coolly, 'for they will be sure to come up again!'

*Ibid.*

When Abernethy was canvassing for the office of surgeon to St Bartholomew Hospital, he called upon such a person,

– a rich grocer, one of the governors. The great man behind the counter seeing the great surgeon enter, immediately assumed the grand air towards the supposed suppliant for his vote. 'I presume, sir, you want my vote and interest at this momentous epoch of your life'. Abernethy, who hated humbugs, and felt nettled at the tone, replied: 'No, I don't: I want a pennyworth of figs; come, look sharp and wrap them up: I want to be off!'

Samuel Smiles, *Self-help*

## ACHESON, DEAN G.

1893–1971 Government Official

I am something of a stoic both by nature and by inheritance. And I learned from the example of my father that the manner in which one endures what must be endured is more important than the thing that must be endured.

On himself, in Merle Miller, *Plain Speaking, An Oral Biography of Harry S. Truman*

I will undoubtedly have to seek what is happily known as gainful employment, which I am glad to say does not describe holding public office.

On himself, on leaving his post as Secretary of State, in *Time*, 22 December 1952

I watch his smart-aleck manner and his British clothes and that New Dealism, everlasting New Dealism in everything he says and does, and I want to shout 'Get out, get out. You stand for everything that has been wrong with the United States for years.'

Senator Hugh Butler, in Merle Miller, *Plain Speaking, An Oral Biography of Harry S. Truman*

Not only did he not suffer fools gladly, he did not suffer them at all.

Lester Pearson, in *Time*, 25 October 1971

*See also* Harry S. Truman

## ACTON, LORD, JOHN EMERICH EDWARD DALBERG

1834–1902 Historian

I think our studies ought to be all but purposeless. They want to be pursued with chastity like mathematics. This . . . is my profession of faith.

On himself, Letter to Richard Simpson, 19 January 1859

. . . such men [as Acton] are all vanity: they have the inflation of German professors, and the ruthless talk of undergraduates.

Cardinal Manning, comment, 1870, in Lytton Strachey, *Eminent Victorians*

. . . a historian to whom learning and judgment had not been granted in equal proportions . . . that laborious and scrupulous scholar, that life-long enthusiast for liberty, that almost hysterical reviler of priestcraft and persecution, trailing his learning so discrepantly along the dusty Roman way . . . there are some who know how to wear their Rome with a difference; and Lord Acton was one of these.

Lytton Strachey, *Eminent Victorians*

## ADAM, ROBERT

1728–92 Architect

I am a very promising young man.

On himself, Letter to his family, 1756

Mr Adam's success arose chiefly from his knowledge of detail and his minute and elaborate taste – but he was not an artist of any force nor of very sound judgement – he began with details and adapted them to the necessary lines. I am sure his ideas first assembled in ornament & decorations – his plans are a labyrinth . . .

C. R. Cockerell, Diary, July 1821

The chief merit of the Adam variation of the classical style was its recognition of the ancillary trades and crafts. It had,

moreover, the attraction of being economical while retaining the appearance of being costly.
Sir Albert Richardson, *An Introduction to Georgian Architecture*

Adam, our most admired [architect], is all gingerbread, filigraine, and fan-painting.
Horace Walpole, Letter to Sir Horace Mann, 22 April 1775

Mr Adam has published the first number of his Architecture. In it is a magnificent gateway and screen for the Duke of Northumberland at Sion, which I see erecting every time I pass. It is all lace and embroidery, and as croquant as his frames for tables; consequently most improper to be executed in the high road to Brentford. From Kent's mahogany we are dwindled to Adam's filigree. Grandeur and simplicity are not yet in fashion. In his Preface he seems to tax Wyatt with stealing from him; but Wyatt has employed the antique with more judgement, and the 'Pantheon' is still the most beautiful edifice in England. What are the Adelphi Buildings? warehouses laced down the seams, like a soldier's trull in a regimental lace coat.
Horace Walpole, Letter to the Rev. W. Mason, 29 July 1773

## ADAMS, FRANKLIN PIERCE

1881–1960 Journalist

As I often have said, I am easily influenced. Compared with me a weather vane is Gibraltar.
On himself, in Robert E. Drennan ed., *Wit's End*

## ADAMS, HENRY BROOKS

1838–1918 Historian

I want to look like an American Voltaire or Gibbon, but am slowly settling down to be a third-rate Boswell hunting for a Dr Johnson.
On himself, in Ernest Samuels, *Henry Adams, The Major Phase*

. . . with the wings of a beautiful but ineffectual conscience beating vainly in a vacuum jar.
T. S. Eliot, in J. C. Levenson, *The Mind and Art of Henry Adams*

. . . the only man in America who could sit on a fence and see himself go by.
Ed Howe, in Ernest Samuels, *Henry Adams, The Major Phase*

In these great stresses, friendship reaches out to the making of an image of the friend who has suffered assault – and I make one of you thus according to my sense of your rich and ingenious mind and your great resources of contemplation, speculation, resignation – a curiosity in which serenity is yet at home.
Henry James, in a 1912 letter to Adams after the latter's stroke, in J. C. Levenson, *The Mind and Art of Henry Adams*

Adams, in brief, did not care for truth, unless it was amusing; for he was a modern nihilist, and hence a hedonist or nothing.
Yvor Winters, *The Anatomy of Nonsense*

## ADAMS, JOHN

1735–1826 Second United States President

Vanity, I am sensible, is my cardinal vice and cardinal folly.
On himself, in J. T. Morse, *John Adams*

See Johnny at the helm of State, / Head itching for a crowny, / He longs to be like Georgy, great, / And pull Tom Jeffer downy. /
Anon., in Arthur Styron, *The Last of the Cocked Hats*

Ali Baba among his Forty Thieves is no more deserving of sympathy than John Adams shut up within the seclusion of his Cabinet room with his official family of secret enemies.

Claude G. Bowers, *Jefferson and Hamilton*

. . . he was the founder of a dynasty and belonged to his descendants rather than to his ancestors.

Gilbert Chinard, *Honest John Adams*

. . . an imagination sublimated and eccentric, propitious neither to the regular display of sound judgment nor to steady perseverance in a systematic plan of conduct.

Alexander Hamilton, in Page Smith, *John Adams, 1784–1826*

He is vain, irritable, and a bad calculator of the force and probable effect of the motives which govern men. This is all the ill which can possibly be said of him. He is as disinterested as the Being who made him.

Thomas Jefferson, Letter to James Madison, 1787

His Rotundity.

William Maclay, in Page Smith, *John Adams, 1784–1826*

It has been the political career of this man to begin with hypocrisy, proceed with arrogance, and finish with contempt.

Tom Paine, *Open Letter To The Citizens Of The United States*, 22 November 1802

*See also* John Quincy Adams

## ADAMS, JOHN QUINCY

1767–1848 Sixth United States President

I am a man of reserved, cold, austere, and forbidding manners: my political adversaries say, a gloomy misanthropist, and my personal enemies, an unsocial savage.

On himself, Diary, 4 June 1819

Well has he been called 'The Massachusettes Madman.' He boasts that he places all his glory in independence. If independence is synonymous with obstinacy, he is the most independent statesman living.

Anon., in *New York Times* on the Emancipation debates, in L. Falkner, *The President Who Wouldn't Retire*

John Quincy Adams was the second Adams to become president. He is not to be confused with his father, John Adams, who was the first Adams but the second president, or with his Uncle Sam Adams (who was not the real Uncle Sam, except to his nieces and nephews). It was fortunate for us, if not for the second John Adams, that he had the Quincy, which the first John did not.

Richard Armour, *It All Started With Columbus*

Like George Washington he did not believe in parties or in sections, the essential realities of American politics – and they did not believe in him.

S. F. Bemis, *John Quincy Adams and the Union*

In politics he was an apostate, and in private life a pedagogue, and in everything but amiable and honest.

De Witt Clinton, in R. V. Remini, *Martin Van Buren and the Making of the Democratic Party*

When they talk about his old age and venerableness and nearness to the grave, he knows better. He is like one of those old cardinals, who as quick as he is chosen Pope, throws away his crutches and his crookedness, and is as straight as a boy. He is an old roué, who cannot live on slops, but must have sulphuric acid in his tea.

Ralph Waldo Emerson, *Journals*

The cub is a greater bear than the old one.

John Randolph of Roanoke, in Alfred Steinberg, *The First Ten*

John Quincy Adams was a short, stout, bald, brilliant and puritanical twig off a short, stout, bald, brilliant, and puritanical tree. Little wonder, then, that he took the same view of the office of President as had his father.

Alfred Steinberg, in *ibid.*

## ADAMS, SAMUEL

1722–1803 Revolutionary Statesman

The whole continent is ensnared by that Machiavel of chaos.

Anon. letter to Governor Thomas Hutchinson, 14 September 1776

Sam Adams was born with a silver spoon in his mouth, but once it was removed he became a fine orator.

Richard Armour, *It All Started With Columbus*

Every dip of his pen stung like a horned snake.

Governor Sir Francis Bernard, in J. C. Miller, *Samuel Adams, Pioneer in Propaganda*

Mr Samuel Adams, although not fluent of elocution, was so rigorously logical, so clear in his views, abundant in good sense, and master always of his subject, that he commanded the most profound attention whenever he arose in an assembly by which the froth of declamation was heard with the most sovereign contempt.

Thomas Jefferson, in Stewart Beach, *Samuel Adams, The Fateful Years, 1764–1776*

Truly the Man of the Revolution.

Thomas Jefferson, in John C. Miller, *Sam Adams, Pioneer in Propaganda*

*See also* John Quincy Adams

## ADDAMS, JANE

1860–1935 Social Reformer

Jane Addams is to Chicago what Joan of Arc was to her people, she is sacrificing all for the masses.

Anon., in *Springfield Caxton*, August 1910, in Allen F. Davis, *American Heroines, The Life and Legend of Jane Addams*

She simply inhabits reality, and everything she says necessarily expresses its nature. *She can't help writing truth.*

William James, in *American Journal of Sociology*, 1909

Remember Botticelli's Fortitude / In the Uffizi? – The worn, waiting face; / The pale, fine-fibred hands upon the mace; / The brow's serenity, the lips that brood, / The vigilant, tired patience of her mood? / There was a certain likeness I could trace / The day I heard her in a country place, / Talking to knitting women about Food. / Through cool statistics glowed the steady gleam / Of that still undismayed, interned desire; / But – strength and stay, and deeper than the dream – / The two commands that she is pledged to keep / In the red welter of a world on fire, / Are, 'What is that to thee?' and 'Feed my sheep!'

Ruth Comfort Mitchell, 'Jane Addams', in *Atlantic Monthly*, November 1918

The crowning irony of Jane Addams' life . . . was that she compromised her intellect for the sake of human experiences which her nature prevented her from having. Life, as she meant the term, forever eluded her.

William L. O'Neill, *Everyone was brave*

## ADDINGTON, HENRY, VISCOUNT SIDMOUTH

1757–1844 Statesman, Prime Minister

I stand before your Lordships charged with having used my best endeavours to stop the progress of blasphemy and sedition. To that charge I plead guilty, and while I live I shall be proud to have such a charge brought against me.

On himself, on his action to curb the cheap press, House of Lords debate, 12 May 1817

I hate liberality . . . nine times out of ten it is cowardice, and the tenth time lack of principle.

On himself, in John Mitford's MS notebook, 'Sayings of Lord Sidmouth'

This is the true and lamentable story of the rise and progress of the Doctor and Co., who, like Bazilio in the Barbier de Seville, works his way in and then, piano, piano, spreads and dilates and gathers strength from the weakness or necessities of those around him.

Lady Bessborough, Letter to Lord Granville Leveson-Gower, 27 September 1806

The Duke of Wellington upon home service.

George IV, comment on Addington's conduct of the Cato Street operation, in Sir Benjamin Bloomfield, Letter to Addington, 12 March 1820

The indefinable air of a village apothecary inspecting the tongue of the State.

Lord Rosebery, *Life of Pitt*

[Pitt] exclaiming, 'I am delighted to have got amongst you, for we have had the Doctor travelling with his own horses for the last hour and a half, and we thought he would never arrive at the end of the stage.' In those days gentlemen's postillions used to drive with long whips and velvet caps with silver tassels to them, which played up and down in conformity with the measured and slow action of the postillions on their horses. And one can conceive Addington's pompous delivery, measured phraseology, and monotonous intonation, affording a capital likeness of a gentleman's own horses during a long stage.

The Duke of Rutland, Letter to John Wilson Croker, 2 March 1847

Clothed with the Bible, as with light, / And the shadows of the night, / Like Sidmouth, next Hypocrisy / On a crocodile rode by.

Percy Bysshe Shelley, *The Mask of Anarchy*

. . . two vultures sick for battle, / Two scorpions under one wet stone, / Two bloodless wolves whose dry throats rattle, / Two crows perched on the murrained cattle, / Two vipers tangled into one.

Percy Bysshe Shelley, *Similes for two Political Characters*

## ADDISON, JOSEPH

1672–1719 Poet, Statesman

Thus I live in the world rather as a Spectator of mankind, than as one of the species, by which means I have made myself a speculative statesman, soldier, merchant, and artisan, without ever meddling with any practical part of life.

On himself, in *Spectator*, no. 1, March 1711

I have sent for you that you may see how a Christian can die.

On himself, last words, addressed to Lord Warwick, his prodigal step-son

Addison was responsible for many of the evils from which English prose has since suffered. He made prose artful and whimsical, he made it sonorous when sonority was not needed, affected when it did not require affectation . . . He was the first Man of Letters. Addison had the misuse of an extensive vocabulary and so was able to invalidate a great number of words and expressions; the quality of his mind was inferior to the language which he used to express it.

Cyril Connolly, *Enemies of Promise*

In him / Humour in holiday and slightly trim / Sublimity and Attic taste, combin'd, / To polish, furnish, and delight the mind.

William Cowper, *Table Talk*

No whiter page than Addison remains. / He from the taste obscene reclaims our youth, / And sets the passions on the side of Truth, / Forms the soft bosom with the gentlest Art, / And pours each human virtue in the heart.

Alexander Pope, *Imitations of Horace: Epistles; Book II, epistle i*

Statesman, yet friend to truth! of soul sincere, / In action faithful, and in honour clear; / Who broke no promise, served no private end, / Who gained no title, and who lost no friend.

Alexander Pope, *Moral Essays, epistle vii*, 'To Mr Addison'

Blest with each talent and each art to please, / And born to write, converse, and live with ease: / Should such a man, too fond to rule alone, / Bear, like the Turk, no brother near the throne; / View him with scornful, yet with jealous eyes, / And hate for arts that caus'd himself to rise; / Damn with faint praise, assent with civil leer, / And without sneering, teach the rest to sneer; / Willing to wound, and yet afraid to strike, / Just hint a fault, and hesitate dislike; / Alike reserv'd to blame, or to commend, / A tim'rous foe, and a suspicious friend; / Dreading ev'n fools, by Flatterers besieg'd, / And so obliging, that he ne'er oblig'd; / Like *Cato*, give his little Senate laws, / And sit attentive to his own applause; / While Wits and Templars ev'ry sentence raise, / And wonder with a foolish face of praise: – / Who must but laugh, if such a man there be? / Who would not weep, if ATTICUS were he?

Alexander Pope, *Epistle to Dr Arbuthnot*

Mr Addison could not give out a common order in writing, from his endeavouring always to word it too finely. – He had too beautiful an imagination to make a man of business.

Alexander Pope, in Joseph Spence, *Anecdotes*

There still remains the fact that the essays of Addison are perfect essays ... Whether it was a high thing, or whether it was a low thing, whether an epic is more profound or a lyric more passionate, undoubtedly it is due to Addison that prose is now prosaic – the medium which makes it possible for people of ordinary intelligence to communicate their ideas to the world.

Virginia Woolf, *The Common Reader*

*See also* Henry Fielding, Alexander Pope

## ADRIAN IV (NICHOLAS BREAKSPEAR)

– d. 1159 Pope

He held his place four years, *eight months*, and *eight and twenty dayes*: and Anno 1158 [sic], as he was drinking, was choakt with a *Fly*: which in the large Territory of St *Peters patrimony* had no place but his Throat to get into.

Thomas Fuller, *The History of the Worthies of England*

## AIDAN, SAINT

– d. 651 First Bishop of Lindisfarne

King Oswin ... had given Aidan a very fine horse, in order that he could ride whenever he had to cross a river or undertake any difficult or urgent journey, although the bishop ordinarily travelled on foot. Not long afterwards, when a poor man met the bishop and asked for alms, the bishop immediately dismounted and ordered the horse with all its royal trappings to be given to the beggar; for he was most compassionate, a protector of the poor and a father to the wretched. When this action came to the king's ears, he asked the bishop as they were going in to dine; 'My lord bishop, why did you give away the royal horse which was necessary for your own use?' . . . The bishop at once answered, 'What are you saying, Your Majesty? Is this child of a mare more valuable to you than this child of God?' . . . As he stood by the fire, the king turned over in his mind what the bishop had said; then suddenly unbuckling his sword and handing it to a servant, he impulsively knelt at the bishop's feet and begged his forgiveness. At the bishop's request, the king sat down and began to be merry; but Aidan on the contrary grew so sad that he began to shed tears. His chaplain asked him in his own language, which the king and his servants did not understand, why he wept. Aidan replied: 'I know that the king will not live very long; for I have never before seen a humble king' . . . Not very long afterwards, as I have related, the bishop's foreboding was borne out by the king's death.

Bede, *Ecclesiastical History of the English People,* translated by Leo Sherley-Price

## AIKIN, LUCY

1781–1864 Author

Miss Lucy Aikin . . . pert as a pearmonger.

Robert Southey, Letter to Caroline Bowles, 8 February 1835

## AILRED OF RIEVAULX, SAINT

1109–66 Cistercian Abbot

I shall not omit to tell how he had built a small chamber of brick under the floor of the novice house, like a little tank, into which water flowed from hidden rills. Its opening was shut by a very broad stone in such a way that nobody would notice it. Ailred would enter this contrivance, when he was alone and undisturbed, and immerse his whole body in the icy cold water, and so quench the heat in himself of every vice.

Walter Daniel, *The Life of Ailred of Rievaulx*, translated from the Latin by F. M. Powicke

Perfect in every part of his body, the dead father shone like a carbuncle, was fragrant as incense, pure and immaculate in the radiance of his flesh as a child. I was not able to restrain the kisses which I gave his feet, although I chose his feet lest feeling rather than pure affection should reproach me; the beauty of one who sleeps rather than the love of one who lies as he lay.

*Ibid.*

## AITKEN, WILLIAM MAXWELL, *see* BEAVERBROOK, LORD

## AKENSIDE, MARK

1721–70 Poet

I see they have published a splendid edition of Akenside's works. One bad Ode may be suffered, but a number of them together makes one sick.

Samuel Johnson, in James Boswell, *Life of Johnson*

Another of these tame genius's, a Mr Akinside.

Horace Walpole, Letter to Sir Horace Mann, 29 March 1745

## ALBERT FRANCIS CHARLES AUGUSTUS

1819–61 Prince Consort to Victoria

I do not cling to life. You do: but I set no store by it . . . I am sure that if I had a severe illness I should give up at

once, I should not struggle for life. I have no tenacity of life.
On himself, in conversation with Queen Victoria, circa November 1861

I have had wealth, rank and power, but, if these were all I had, how wretched I should be.
On himself, attributed last words

. . . When in doubt about 'who's to blame', play Prince Albert, it is always a trump card, and ten to one it takes the trick.
'F. Airplay Esq.', *Prince Albert: Why is he unpopular?*

. . . His Royal Highness ought to be considered . . . *as an Alter Ego, and not as a Privy Councillor,* and [that] this communication was the inevitable result of a female being on the throne.
Lord Campbell, Statement to the Lords, 1854

The Queen talked freely of the Prince: he *would* die: he seemed not to care to live. Then she used these words 'He died from want of what they call pluck'.
Benjamin Disraeli, *Reminiscences*

The Prince had wit. There was a picture at Balmoral; all the children introduced, game birds &c: one said where is Princess Helena; reply, there with a Kingfisher. 'A very proper bird for a Princess', said Albert.
*Ibid.*

. . . His character always comes out *honest*. I take it that he governs us really, in everything.
Emily Eden, Letter to Mrs Drummond, January 1848

He has, I think, that average stock of energy, which enables men to do that which they cannot well avoid doing, or that which is made ready to their hands: but he has not the rare supply of it, which enables a man to make duty, and so win honour and confidence.
W. E. Gladstone, Letter to Earl Granville, December 1870

The Prince is become so identified with the Queen, that they are one person, and as He likes and She dislikes business, it is obvious that while she has the title he is really discharging the functions of the Sovereign. He is King to all intents and purposes.
Charles Greville, *Memoirs*

As for his sense of fun . . . I never could discover it. He went into immoderate fits of laughter at anything like a practical joke; for instance, if anyone caught his foot in a mat, or nearly fell into the fire . . . the mirth of the whole Royal Family, headed by the Prince, knew no bounds. His original jokes were heavy and lumbered.
M. Ponsonby, *Mary Elizabeth, Lady Ponsonby, A Memoir*

. . . she is inclined to think it will be better for her, instead of attempting an Enactment by Parliament, with its attendant discussions, to do merely as much as her Prerogative will enable her . . . and to content herself by simply giving her husband by Letters Patent the title of 'Prince Consort' which can injure no one while it will give him an *English title* consistent with his position, & avoid his being treated by Foreign Courts as a *junior Member* of the house of *Saxe Coburg*.
Queen Victoria, Letter to Lord Palmerston, 15 March 1857

*None* of you can *ever* be proud enough of being the *child* of SUCH a Father who has not his *equal* in this world – so great, so good, so faultless. Try, all of you to follow in his footsteps and don't be discouraged, for to be *really* in everything like him *none* of you, I am sure, will ever be. Try, therefore, to be like him in *some* points, and you will have *acquired a great deal.*
Queen Victoria, Letter to the Prince of Wales, 26 August 1857

*See also* Queen Victoria, Duke of Wellington

## ALCOTT, AMOS BRONSON

1799–1888 Educator, Author, Mystic

The good Alcott, with his long, lean face and figure, with his grey worn temples and mild radiant eyes; all bent on saving the world by a return to acorns and the golden age.

Thomas Carlyle, in Marjorie Worthington, *Miss Alcott of Concord*

The tedious archangel.

Ralph Waldo Emerson, in Florence Whiting Brown, *Alcott and the Concord School of Philosophy*

## ALCOTT, LOUISA MAY

1832–88 Author

Now I am beginning to live a little and feel less like a sick oyster at low tide.

On herself, in Ednah D. Cheney, *Louisa May Alcott, Her Life, Letters and Journals*

When I don't look like the tragic muse, I look like a smoky relic of the great Boston Fire.

On herself, in Katharine Anthony, *Louisa May Alcott*

If I think of my woes I fall into a vortex of debts, dishpans, and despondency awful to see.

On herself, in Gamaliel Bradford, *Portraits and Personalities*

[She] resolved to take fate by the throat and shake a living out of her.

Ednah D. Cheney, *Louisa May Alcott, Her Life, Letters and Journals*

If Miss Alcott's experience of human nature has been small, as we should suppose, her admiration of it is nevertheless great.

Henry James, in Katharine Anthony, *Louisa May Alcott*

Living almost always among intellectuals, she preserved to the age of fifty-six that contempt for ideas which is normal among boys and girls of fifteen.

Odell Shepard, 'Mother of Little Women', in *North American Review*

## ALDRICH, THOMAS BAILEY

1836–1907 Poet, Editor

His language is so clean, so free from vulgar suggestion, that one almost sees the author wearing gloves as he writes.

Alexander Cowie, *The Rise of the American Novel*

When it came to making fun of a folly, or silliness, a windy pretense, a wild absurdity, Aldrich the brilliant, Aldrich the sarcastic, Aldrich the ironical, Aldrich the merciless, was a master.

Mark Twain, in Bernard De Voto ed., *Mark Twain in Eruption*

Aldrich was always brilliant, he couldn't help it; he is a fire-opal set round with rose diamonds; when he is not speaking, you know that his dainty fancies are twinkling and glimmering around in him; when he speaks, the diamonds flash.

Mark Twain, in Charles E. Samuels, *Thomas Bailey Aldrich*

## ALEXANDER, HAROLD RUPERT LEOFRIC GEORGE, EARL ALEXANDER OF TUNIS

1891–1969 Soldier

I have had a good weathering in this war, and I am going to get the fruits of it if I can. You can bet your life that I shall have a good try.

On himself, Letter to his Aunt Margaret, 22 November 1918

He did not issue an order. He sold the . . . general the idea, and made him think that he had thought of it all himself. This system, which he invariably pursued, made Alexander particularly fit to command an Allied army . . . in the Italian campaign controlling the troops of many countries, he developed this method into a remarkable technique. If Montgomery was the Wellington, Alexander was certainly the Marlborough of this war.

Harold Macmillan, *The Blast of War, 1939–45*

He had almost every quality you could wish to have, except that he had the average brain of an average English gentleman. He lacked that little extra cubic centimetre which produces genius. If you recognise that, it's perhaps a greater tribute to what he did achieve by leadership, courage and inspiring devotion in those who served under him.

Earl Mountbatten, in Nigel Nicolson, *Alex*

Alex wouldn't do any work, except when he had to, and when he had to, it was on big exercises . . . He was ambitious to do his duty. He was lazy, but not over the essentials. He relied on his staff. If they did something wrong he would pull them up. His laziness was a virtue. It meant a capacity to delegate, and in wartime it became a tremendous asset, because it meant that he could relax and unhook.

Field Marshal Sir Gerald Templer, in *ibid.*

The Dominion's most industrious gadabout.

*Time*, October 1946

## ALEXANDER, SIR WILLIAM, EARL OF STIRLING

1567?–1640 Poet, Statesman

His minor pieces are elegant and musical. There is less of conceit in the merely conceitful sense than was common with contemporaries, and if you only persevere, opalescent hues edge long passages otherwise comparable with mist and fog.

Alexander Balloch Grosart, in *Dictionary of National Biography*

## ALEXANDRA CAROLINE MARY CHARLOTTE LOUISE JULIA

1844–1925 Queen Consort to Edward VII

I may be pale, but it is from anger at being obliged to see the King of Prussia, and not from cold.

On herself, retort to Sir William Knollys, 11 October 1867, in Philip Magnus, *King Edward the Seventh*

Alex, good as she is, is not worth the price we have to pay for her in having such a family connection [the Queen of Denmark].

Queen Victoria, Letter to her daughter, the Crown Princess of Prussia, 11 October 1864

## ALFRED

849–901 King of England

Then king Alfred ordered warships to be built to meet the Danish ships: they were almost twice as long as the others, some had sixty oars, some more; they were both swifter, steadier, and with more freeboard than the others; they were built neither after the Frisian design nor after the Danish, but as it seemed to himself that they could be most serviceable.

*Anglo-Saxon Chronicle*, translated by G. N. Garmonsway

And from his cradle a longing for wisdom before all things and among all the pursuits of this present life, combined with his noble birth, filled the noble temper of his mind; but alas, by the unworthy carelessness of his parents and tutors he remained ignorant of letters until his twelfth year, or even longer. But he listened attentively to Saxon poems day and night, and hearing them often repeated by others committed them to his retentive memory . . . When therefore, his mother one day was showing him and his brothers a certain book of Saxon poetry which she held in her hand she said: 'I will give this book to whichever of you can learn it most quickly.' And moved by these words, or rather by divine inspiration, and attracted by the beauty of the initial letter of the book, Alfred said in reply to his mother, forestalling his brothers, his elders in years though not in grace: 'Will you really give this book to one of us, to the one who can soonest understand and repeat it to you?' And, smiling and rejoicing she confirmed it. . . Then taking the book from her hand he immediately went to his master, who read it. And when it was read, he went back to his mother and repeated it.

Asser, *Life of King Alfred*, translated by L. C. Jane

There was not English Armour left, / Nor any English thing, / When Alfred came to Athelney / To be an English King. /

G. K. Chesterton, *Ballad of the White Horse*, Book I

There is a story that King Arthur once burnt some cakes belonging to Mrs Girth, a great lady of the time, at a place called Atheling. As, however, Alfred could not have been an Incendiary King *and* a Good King, we may dismiss the story as absurd, and in any case the event is supposed to have occurred in a marsh where the cakes would not have burnt properly. Cf. the famous lines of poetry about King Arthur and the cakes: 'Then slowly answered Alfred from the marsh –' *Arthur, Lord Tennyson.*

W. C. Sellar and R. J. Yeatman, *1066 and All That*

Truth-teller was our England's Alfred named.

Alfred, Lord Tennyson, *Ode on the Death of the Duke of Wellington*

Thus cruel ages pass'd; and rare appear'd / White mantled Peace, exulting o'er the vale, / As when, with Alfred, from the wilds she came / To policed cities and protected plains. /

James Thomson, *Liberty: Britain*

Not long after venturing from his concealment, he hazarded an experiment of consummate art. Accompanied only by one of his most faithful adherents, he entered the tent of the Danish King under the disguise of a minstrel; and being admitted as a professor of the mimic art, to the banqueting room, there was no object of secrecy that he did not minutely attend to both with eyes and ears. Remaining there several days, till he had satisfied his mind on every matter which he wished to know, he returned to Ethelingai: and assembling his companions, pointed out the insolence of the enemy and the easiness of their defeat.

William of Malmesbury, *History of the Kings of England*, translated by J. Sharpe

*See also* Hengist and Horsa

## ALGER, HORATIO

1834–99 Author

He helped make success a quasi-religious moral idea that leaves people who fail (whether in spelling or in something bigger) with the conviction they are unloved. He stands for trying harder, wanting more, and contributing to the community chest. The people who want to distribute Sears, Roebuck catalogs to Russians to persuade them of America's superiority are his disciples, too.

Richard Fink, in John Tebbel, *From Rags to Riches*

Horatio Alger wrote the same novel 135 times and never lost his audience.

George Juergens, *Joseph Pulitzer and the New York World*

## ALLEN, FRED (JOHN FLORENCE SULLIVAN)

1894–1956 Comedian

Eventually I have high hopes I'll be able to retire from the human race.

On himself, in Maurice Zolotow, *No People Like Show People*

I don't have to look up my family tree, because I know that I'm the sap.

On himself, *Much Ado About Me*

You can count on the thumb of one hand the American who is at once a comedian, a humorist, a wit and a satirist, and his name is Fred Allen.

James Thurber, in Joe McCarthy ed., *Fred Allen's Letters*

## ALLEN, THOMAS

1542–1632 Mathematician

In those dark times, Astrologer, Mathematician, and Conjurer were accounted the same things; and the vulgar did verily beleeve him to be a Conjurer. He had a great many Mathematicall Instruments and Glasses in his Chamber, which did also confirme the ignorant in their opinion, and his servitor (to impose on Freshmen and simple people) would tell them that sometimes he should meet the Spirits comeing up his staires like Bees. Now there is to some men a great Lechery in Lying, and imposing on the understandings of beleeving people, and he thought it for his credit to serve such a Master.

John Aubrey, *Brief Lives*

## ALLEN, WILLIAM

1770–1843 Philanthropist

All the world is a little queer save thee and me, and even thou art a little queer.

Robert Owen, attributed, 1828

## ALLENBY, EDMUND HENRY HYNMAN, VISCOUNT

1861–1936 Soldier

The last of the Paladins.

Sir Ronald Storrs, *Orientations*

## ALLEYN, EDWARD

1566–1626 Actor

The Tradition concerning the Occasion of the Foundation [of Dulwich College], runs thus; that Mr *Alleyne*, being a Tragedian, and one of the Original Actors in many of the celebrated *Shakespear*'s Plays, in one of which he played a Daemon, with six others, and was in the midst of the Play surpriz'd by an *Apparition* of the *Devil*, which so worked on his Fancy, that he made a Vow, which he perform'd at this place.

John Aubrey, *The Natural History and Antiquities of the County of Surrey*

Alleyne's fortune proceeded no doubt from marrying three wives, each of whom brought a handsome fortune, partly from the success of his theatre, partly from his being keeper of the King's wild beasts, and master of the Royal Bear Garden, and partly from his being a most rigid and penurious economist, which character he so strictly enjoined himself, that he was the first pensioner in his own charity.

C. Dibdin, in Clark Russell, *Representative Actors*

He was bred a stage-player; a calling which many have condemned, more have questioned, some few have excused, and far fewer conscientious people have commended. He was the Roscius of our age, so acting to the life, that he made any part (especially a majestick one) to become him. He got a very great estate, and in his old age, following Christ's counsel (on what forcible motive belongs not to me to inquire), 'he made friends of his unrighteous Mammon,' building therewith a fair college at Dulwich in Kent, for the relief of poor people.

Some I confess count it built on a foundered foundation, seeing in a spiritual sense none is good and lawful money, save what is honestly and industriously gotten. But perchance such who condemn Master Allin herein, have as bad shillings in the bottom of their own bags, if search was made therein. Sure I am, no hospital is tied with better or stricter laws, that it may not *sagg* from the intention of the founder. The poor of his native parish, Saint Botolph, Bishopsgate, have a privilege to be provided for therein, before others. Thus he, who out-acted others in his life, out-did himself before his death, which happened Anno Domini 1626.

Thomas Fuller, *The History of the Worthies of England*

Edward Allen, alias Allein, of Dullwich, Esquire, at this time builded a very faire Hospitall at Dulwich, in *Surrey*, for six poore men and six poore women, and for 12 poore children from the age of 4 or 6 yeares, to be there kept, maintained and taught, untill they come to the age of 14 or 16 yeares: their schoolemaster to have his diet, lodging, and a competent stipend. He intends also to have a Master to reside in the same Hospitall, whose name shall be Allen or Alleyne, and by that name to be chosen to that Government of his Hospitall for ever, as the place shall grow vacant.

Edmund Howe, *Continuation of Stow's Annales or Generall Chronicle*

Weare this renowne. 'Tis just, that who did give / So many *Poets* life, by one should live. /

Ben Jonson, *Epigrammes*

## ALLSTON, WASHINGTON

1779–1843 Artist, Author

The calm and meditative ease of these pictures, the ideal beauty that shone *through* rather than *in* them, and the harmony of coloring were as unlike anything else I saw, as the Vicar of Wakefield to Cooper's novels. I seemed to recognise in painting that self-possessed elegance, that transparent depth, which I most admired in literature; I thought with delight that such a man as this had been able to grow up in our bustling, reasonable community, that he had kept his foot upon the ground, yet never lost sight of the rose-clouds of beauty floating above him. I saw, too, that he had not been troubled, but possessed his own soul with the blandest patience; and I hoped, I scarce know what, probably the *mot d'enigme* for which we are all looking. How the poetical mind can live and work in peace and good faith! how it may unfold to its due perfection in an unpoetical society!

Margaret Fuller, in *Dial*, 1839

One man may sweeten a whole town. I never pass through Cambridge Port without thinking of Allston. His memory is the quince in the drawer, and perfumes the atmosphere.

Henry Wadsworth Longfellow, in Longfellow MSS

I go to Allston as a comet goes to the sun, not to add to his material, but to imbibe light from him.

Samuel F. B. Morse, in Harry B. Wehle, *Samuel F. B. Morse*

## ANDERSON, ELIZABETH GARRETT

1836–1917 Doctor

I was a young woman living at home with nothing to do in what authors call 'comfortable circumstances.' But I was wicked enough not to be comfortable. I was full of energy and vigour and of the discontent that goes with unemployed activities. Everything seemed wrong to me.

On herself, MS draft for a speech

But for Miss Garrett, I must say of her that I gained more from her than from any other doctor, for she not only repeated what all of the others had said, but entered much more into my mental state and way of life than they could do, because I was able to *tell* her so much more than I ever could or would tell to any *man*.

Josephine Butler, in E. M. Bell, *Josephine Butler*

She was neither a brilliant nor a born doctor. She made no outstanding contribution to medical science; although she read widely her temperament was not suited to laboratory work and she had neither time nor ambition to undertake original research. If one regards medicine as a pure science her claims to distinction are not high. If one regards it as a skilled exercise in personal relationships one must rate her very high indeed. It was as a general practitioner that she excelled, with all the qualities of character that calling demands – courage, sense of duty, good judgement and warm humanity. By these she disarmed a hostile profession and won the trust of a whole generation of women patients.

Naomi Mitchison, *Revaluations – Studies in Biography*

Mrs Anderson was not the woman to let the grass grow under her feet, nor was she one to consider unduly the effects of overwork or fatigue on herself and her colleagues. She was a persistent, shameless and highly successful beggar.

Mary Scharlieb, *Reminiscences*

## ANDERSON, SHERWOOD

1876–1941 Author

And so in my inner self I have accepted my own Mid-American as a walled-in place. There are walls everywhere, about individuals, about groups. The houses are mussy. People die inside the walls without ever having seen the light. I want the houses cleaned, the doorsteps washed, the walls broken away. That can't happen in my time. Culture is a slow growth.

On himself, Letter to Paul Rosenfeld, 24 October 1921, in Mark Schorer, *Sherwood Anderson*

I'm for anything crooked but like to be approached as a fellow crook.

On himself, Letter to Ben Hecht, in Ben Hecht, *Letters from Bohemia*

Anderson, his life and his writings, epitomize for me the pilgrimage of a poet and dreamer across this limited stage called life, whose reactions to the mystery of our being and doings here . . . involved tenderness, love and beauty, delight in the strangeness of our will-less reactions as well as pity, sympathy and love for all things both great and small.

Theodore Dreiser, 'Sherwood Anderson', in Paul P. Appel ed., *Homage to Sherwood Anderson*

If a girl was with us, I was sure to hear Swatty open up as a searcher for deep truths. You could tell how smitten he was with a girl by how ardently he started praising himself. He called it self-revelation.

Ben Hecht, *Letters from Bohemia*

Anderson seemed the archetype of all those writers who were trying to raise themselves to art by sheer emotion and sheer will, who suspected intellect as a cosmopolitan snare that would destroy their gift for divining America's mystic essence, and who abominated the society which had formed them but knew no counterpoise of value by which to escape its moral dominion.

Irving Howe, *Sherwood Anderson*

Anderson more than others, in fact, gave to a younger generation growing up in the twenties a sense of curiosity, an unashamed acceptance of their difficulties and yearnings, that was to remain with them long after he had come to seem a curiously repetitive and even confused figure.

Alfred Kazin, *On Native Grounds*

He seemed to have the real, the authentic American voice. The style was as free and natural, I thought then, as the glass of ice water which stands on every table in every home and restaurant. Later I learned that it was not so free and natural, that it had been acquired through long apprenticeship.

Henry Miller, 'Anderson the Storyteller', in Paul P. Appel ed., *Homage to Sherwood Anderson*

... On November 27, 1912, a successful manufacturer in the town of Elyria, Ohio, dreaming of becoming a great benevolent tycoon, chafing more often at the stultifying routines of promotion and salesmanship, Sherwood Anderson, aged thirty-six, walked out of his office and away from his wife and family into the freedom of a wandering literary life, never to return to business.

Mark Schorer, 'Sherwood Anderson', in Perry Miller ed., *Major Writers of America*, vol. 2

At his best, Sherwood Anderson functions with a natural ease and beauty on a plane in the depths of life – as if under a diving-bell submerged in the human soul – which makes the world of the ordinary novelist seem stagy and superficial.

Edmund Wilson, *The Shores of Light*

## ANDREWES, LANCELOT

1555–1626 Bishop of Winchester

The world, Wanted Learning to know how learned this man was, so skilled in all (especially oriental) languages, that some conceived he might (if then living) have almost served as an interpreter-general at the Confusion of Tongues.

Thomas Fuller, *Church History of Britain*

Truth however, compels us to add, that in some points Andrewes was not in advance of his age.

John Henry Overton, in *Dictionary of National Biography*

## ANNE

1665–1714 Queen of England

. . . as long as I live it shall be my endeavour to make my country and my friends easy and though those that come after me may be more capable of so great a trust as it has pleased God to put into my hands, I am sure they can never discharge it more faithfully than her that is sincerely your humble servant.

On herself, Letter to Sidney Godolphin, 1707

I believe sleep was never more welcome to a weary traveller than death was to her.

Dr John Arbuthnot, Letter to Jonathan Swift, 12 August 1713

Queen Anne was one of the smallest people ever set in a great place.

Walter Bagehot, *The English Constitution*

I have tried here to render comprehensible some of the Inarticulates of this world by setting down my own reading of that Queen of Inarticulates – Anne Stuart.

Beatrice Curtis Brown, *Anne Stuart, Queen of England*

If it were in my power, I would not be a favourite, which few will believe . . . as fond as people are of power, I fancy that anybody that had been shut up so many tedious hours as I have been, with a person that had no conversation, and yet must be treated with respect, would feel something of what I did, and be very glad, when their circumstances did not want it, to be freed from such a slavery, which must be uneasy at all times, though I do protest that upon the account of her loving me and trusting me so entirely as she did, I had a concern for her which was more than you will easily believe, and I would have served her with the hazard of my life upon any occasion; but after she put me at liberty by using me ill, I was very easy, and liked better that anybody should have her favour than myself at the price of flattery, without which I believe nobody can be well with a King or a Queen.

Sarah Churchill, Duchess of Marlborough, Letter, 23 April 1711

Queen Anne had a person and appearance not at all ungraceful, till she grew exceeding gross and corpulent. There was something of Majesty in her look, but mixed with a sullen and constant frown, that plainly betrayed a gloominess of soul and a cloudiness of disposition within. She seemed to inherit a good deal of her father's moroseness which naturally produced in her the same sort of stubborn positiveness in many cases, both ordinary and extraordinary, as well as the same sort of bigotry in religion.

Sarah Churchill, *Character of Queen Anne*

Her friendships were flames of extravagant passion ending in aversion.

*Ibid.*

She moved on broad, homely lines. She was devoted to her religion, to her husband, and to friends whose fidelity she had proved. It cannot be doubted at all that she would have faced poverty, exile, imprisonment, or even death with placid, unconquerable resolution for the sake of any of them. Once she got set, it took years to alter her. She was not very wise, nor clever, but she was very like England.

Winston Churchill, *Marlborough, His Life and Times*

Anne . . . when in good humour, was meekly stupid, and when in bad humour, was sulkily stupid.

T. B. Macaulay, *History of England*

Nature had made her a bigot. Such was the constitution of her mind that to the religion of her nursery she could not but adhere, without examination and without doubt, till she was laid in her coffin. In the Court of her father she had been deaf to all that could be urged in favour of transubstantiation and auricular confession. In the Court of her brother in law, she was equally deaf to all that could be urged in favour of a general union among Protestants. This slowness and obstinacy made her important. It was a great thing to be the only member of the Royal Family who regarded Papist and Presbyterian with impartial aversion.

*Ibid.*

In religion narrow, constant, and sincere, she gave the rest of her small mind to determining the rival claims of her favourites upon her preference and her affections. If she had been born to a private station, she would have passed almost unnoticed as a good woman and a regular churchgoer, with a singular incapacity for rearing the numerous children to whom she gave birth. The tempests that rocked the world in which, from no choice of her own, she played a conspicuous, if not an

important part, scarcely stirred the dull shallows of her soul.
Herbert Paul, *Queen Anne*

Close by those meads, for ever crowned with flowers, / Where Thames with pride surveys his rising towers, / There stands a structure of majestic frame, / Which from the neighb'ring Hampton takes its name. / Here Britain's statesmen oft the fall foredoom / Of foreign tyrants and of nymphs at home; / Here thou, great *Anna*! whom three realms obey, / Dost sometimes counsel take – and sometimes tea. /
Alexander Pope, *The Rape of the Lock*, canto iii

The Queen, from the Variety of Hands she had employed and Reasonings she had heard since her coming to the Crown, was grown very fond of moderating Scheams, which, as things then stood, were by no means reduceable to Practice. She had likewise a good Share of that Adherence to her Own Opinions which is usually charged upon her Sex. And lastly . . . having received some Hints that she had formerly been too much governed, she grew very difficult to be advised . . . The Queen was by no means inclined to make many changes in Employments, she was positive in her Nature, and extremely given to Delay.
Jonathan Swift, *Enquiry into the Behaviour of the Queen's last Ministry*

For all her simplicity the wisest and most triumphant of her race.
G. M. Trevelyan, *England in the Reign of Queen Anne*

The Church's wet-nurse, Goody Anne.
Horace Walpole, Letter to William Mason, 1778

*See also* John Arbuthnot, Wiillam III

## ANSELM, SAINT

1033–1109 Archbishop of Canterbury, Statesman

In truth, had your divine Anselm, your divine Pope Gregory have had their way, the results had been very notable. Our Western World had all become a European Thibet, with one Grand Lama sitting at Rome; our one honourable business that of singing mass, all day and night. Which would not in the least have suited us!
Thomas Carlyle, *Past and Present*

In so far as Anselm lived in yesterday, Anselm was what we now call a liberal and even a freethinker.
G. K. Chesterton, Introduction to Carlyle's *Past and Present*

This Riculfus, whom I have mentioned, held the office of sacrist in the monastery. One night, when he was walking through the cloister waiting for the moment when he would waken the brethren for vigils, he happened to pass the door of the chapter house. He looked in and saw Anselm standing in prayer in the midst of a great ball of blazing light.
Eadmer, *Life of St Anselm*, translated by R. W. Southern

## ANSON, GEORGE, LORD

1697–1762 Voyager

Stay, traveller, awhile and view / One who has travelled more than you. / Quite round the globe, through each degree, / Anson and I have ploughed the sea, / Torrid and frigid zones have passed, / And safe ashore arriv'd at last. / In ease, with dignity, appear / He in the House of Lords, I here. /

Inscription on the pedestal of the figurehead of Anson's flagship *Centurion*

His popularity among the settlers of South Carolina was very great. They gave his name to districts, towns and mines; and we still find, on our maps, Anson County, Anson Ville, Anson's Mines.

Sir John Barrow, *Life of Admiral Lord Anson*

It was a melancholy day for human nature when that stupid Lord Anson, after beating about for three years, found himself again at Greenwich. The circumnavigation of our globe was accomplished, but the illimitable was annihilated & a fatal blow dealt to all imagination.

Benjamin Disraeli, *Reminiscences*

Lord Anson was reserved and proud, and so ignorant of the world, that Sir Charles Williams said he had been round it, but never in it.

Horace Walpole, *Memoirs*

## ANTHONY, SUSAN BROWNELL

1820–1906 Suffragette

Susan is lean, cadaverous and intellectual, with the proportions of a file and the voice of a hurdy-gurdy.

Anon., in *New York World*, 1866, in Ida Husted Harper, *Life and Work of Susan B. Anthony*, vol. 1

Imagine her then in a full black satin frock cut off at the knee, with Turkish trousers of the same material, her wrap a double broche shawl, and on her head the hideous great bonnet then in fashion. I have seen scarecrows that did credit to farmers' boys' ingenuity, but never one better calculated to scare all birds, beasts and human beings.

Mary Bull, in Andrew Sinclair, *The Better Half*

## ARBUCKLE, ROSCOE CONKLING 'FATTY'

1887–1933 Actor

Roscoe had been a poor boy, abandoned as a kid by his father, who was an alcoholic. So I guess he had to make up for his impoverished childhood. He spent money wildly. He was the first star to have the entourage. Roscoe bought me a Rolls-Royce, the first one in Hollywood with a genuine silver radiator. And jewels, my darling, like you've never seen. He was the most generous man on earth. I never knew a man as generous as he was, not only to me but to everybody. He couldn't say no to anyone. Roscoe used to give me all the money he didn't spend himself. My dear, I've sat with thousands and thousands of dollars in my purse. Roscoe always said 'I'll make it, darlin', and you spend it'.

Minta Durfee Arbuckle, in Walter Wagner, *You Must Remember This*

As a comedy star, Fatty Arbuckle had contributed nothing but laughter, maybe a little comfort to those others who had been told that nobody loves a fat man. But my father [lawyer Earl Rogers] had said at once that, though he was innocent, beyond question he would be publicly castigated because it was repulsive to think of a fat man in the role of a rapist.

Adela Rogers St Johns, *The Honeycomb*

In spite of his suet [Arbuckle] was an agile man – the kind of fat man known as light on his feet – [and] became a superb pie pitcher. Arbuckle was ambidextrous and had double vision like a T-formation quarterback. He could throw two pies at once in different directions, but he was not precise in this feat.

Mack Sennett, *King of Comedy*

## ARBUTHNOT, JOHN

1667–1735 Physician, Wit

His imagination was almost inexhaustible . . . it was at anybody's service, for as soon as he was exonerated he did not care what became of it;

insomuch that his sons, when young, have frequently made kites of his scattered papers of hints, which would have furnished good matter for folios.

Lord Chesterfield, *Letters*, Mahon ed., 1845

This leach Arbuthnot was yclept, / Who many a night not once had slept, / But watch'd our gracious Sovereign still; / For who could rest when she was ill? / Oh, mayst thou henceforth sweetly sleep. / Shear, swains, oh shear your softest sheep / To swell his couch; for well I ween, / He saved the Realm who saved the Queen. /

John Gay, Prologue to *The Shepherd's Week*

The grating scribbler! Whose untuned Essays / Mix the Scotch Thistle with the English Bays; / By either Phoebus preordained to ill, / The hand prescribing, or the flattering quill, / Who doubly plagues, and boasts two Arts to kill. /

James Moore Smythe, *One Epistle to Mr Alexander Pope, occasion'd by Two Epistles lately published*

The Doctor is the King of Inattention!

Jonathan Swift, Letter to John Gay, 10 July 1732

*See also* Jonathan Swift

## ARKWRIGHT, SIR RICHARD

1732–92 Inventor

The fact is too strikingly characteristic not to be mentioned, that he separated from his wife not many years after their marriage, because she, convinced that he would starve his family by scheming when he should have been shaving, broke some of his experimental models of machinery.

Edward Baines, *History of the Cotton Manufacture in Great Britain*

Arkwright was a tremendous worker, and a man of marvellous energy, ardor, and application in business. At one period of his life he was usually engaged, in the severe and continuous labors involved by the organization and conduct of his numerous manufactories, from four in the morning until nine at night. At fifty years of age he set to work to learn English grammar, and improve himself in writing and orthography. When he travelled, to save time, he went at great speed, drawn by four horses. Be it for good or for evil, Arkwright was the founder in England of the modern factory system, a branch of industry which has unquestionably proved a source of immense wealth to individuals and to the nation.

Samuel Smiles, *Self-help*

## ARLEN, MICHAEL

1895–1956 Novelist

Arlen, for all his reputation, is not a bounder. He is every other inch a gentleman.

Alexander Woollcott, in Robert E. Drennan ed., *Wit's End*

## ARLINGTON, EARL OF (HENRY BENNETT)

1618–85 Statesman

. . . the inkhorn Lord.

John Ayloffe, *The Dream of the Cabal*

He had learned during a life passed in travelling and negotiating, the art of accommodating his language and deportment to the society in which he found himself. His vivacity in the closet amused the King; his gravity in debates and conferences imposed on the public; and he had succeeded in attaching to himself, partly by services and partly by hopes, a considerable number of personal retainers.

T. B. Macaulay, *History of England*

On the 14 of Mar. 1664 Sir Henry Benet, sometimes student of Ch. Ch. was created 'lord Arlington of Arlington', and the reason why he would not be called 'lord Benet' was, as 'tis said, 1, because the name did not sound well, and 2dly, because there was an old bawd at Westminster called 'lady Benet.'

Anthony à Wood, *Life and Times*, 14 March 1663/4

## ARMOUR, PHILIP DANFORTH

1832–1901 Captain of Industry

I like to turn bristles, blood, and the inside and outside of pigs and bullocks into revenue.

On himself, in Matthew Josephson, *The Robber Barons*

. . . the premier 'pork baron' who taught mankind how to use 'all the pig but the squeal.'

Harper Leech and John Charles Carroll, *Armour and His Times*

## ARMSTRONG, LOUIS DANIEL

1900–71 Musician

To me wherever you go – even behind the Iron Curtain – it's just another city. All hotels are alike – bed, bureau, two pillows. Maybe after a show, you try to make one or two joints, have a ball, get stoned, and that's it for the night. That's my life.

On himself, in Richard Merryman, *Louis Armstrong – A Self-Portrait*

## ARNE, THOMAS AUGUSTINE

1710–78 Composer

Hark! Hark! What notes enchant my Ears / Sweet as the musick of the Spheres? / 'Tis ARNE – the Gods' Viceregent comes, / Now vanish Rackets, Routs, and Drums; / And with him come the Muses Hand in Hand, / To see fulfilled Apollo's great command. / See Taste with Joy its Head uprears, / Rais'd by Arne's heav'nly Airs; / Skill'd with equal Pow'r t'inspire / Irene's youth with martial Fire, / And lull to Rest, with Soul-delighting Sounds, / The Pains of Grief, and heal Love's bleeding Wounds. /

Anon., in *Faulkner's Journal*, January 1756

During his residence at Ditton, near Hampton Court, he received a visit from Mr Garrick . . . 'Tommy (said he, in his usual familiar way), you should consider that music is, at best, but pickle to my roast-beef.' 'By ——, Davy (replied the Doctor, in a strain of equal jocularity), your beef shall be well pickled before I have done.'

*Biographia Dramatica*, ed. Baker, Jones and Reed

Dr Arne died on the 5th of March 1778, of a spasm on his lungs; retaining his faculties to the last moment of his existence. He had originally been instructed in the principles of the Romish Church: these however he had for many years wholly neglected, as inconsistent with a life of ease and gallantry, in which he indulged to the full extent of his purse and constitution. In his last stage, the dormant seeds of early maxims and prejudices (as is usually the case) revived in his bosom, too strong to be checked, or perhaps discriminated by sound reason. The complicated train of doubts, hopes and fears, operated so forcibly on the Doctor's feelings, at this awful period, that a priest was sent for, by whom he was soon awed into a state of most submissive repentance. In thus renewing the duties of a Christian, those of his professional line were not forgotten: for about an hour before his death, he sung an harmonious Halleluja; a flight of fancy calculated, as it were, to usher him into the other world.

*Ibid.*

Thoughtless, dissipated and careless, he neglected or rather scoffed at all other but musical reputation. And he was so little scrupulous in his ideas of propriety, that he took pride, rather than shame in being publicly classed, even in the decline of life, as a man of pleasure. Such a character was ill qualified to form or protect the morals of a youthful pupil, and it is probable that not a notion of duty occurred to Dr Arne, so happy was his self-complacency in the fertility of his invention and the ease of his compositions, and so dazzled by the brilliancy of his success in the powers of melody – which, in truth, for the English stage, were in sweetness and variety unrivalled – that, satisfied and flattered by the practical exertions and the popularity of his fancy, he had no ambition, or rather, no thought concerning the theory of his art.

Fanny Burney, *A Memoir of Dr Burney*

Let Tommy Arne, with usual pomp of style, / Whose chief, whose only merit's to compile, / Who, meanly pilfering here and there a bit, / Deals music out, as Murphy deals out wit; / Publish proposals, laws for taste prescribe, / And chaunt the praise of an Italian tribe; / Let him reverse Kind Nature's first decrees, / And teach e'en Brent a method not to please: / But never shall a truly British age / Bear a vile race of eunuchs on the stage: / The boasted work's called national in vain / If one Italian voice pollute the strain. /

Charles Churchill, *The Rosciad*

He further managed to acquire some proficiency on the violin, and soon contrived to get some lessons from the accomplished and eminent violinist, Michael Festing . . . Calling in King Street one day for this purpose, Festing found Arne diligently practising with his music supported on the lid of a coffin. Horrified with the sight, he declared he could not play under such circumstances, as he would be constantly imagining there might be a corpse in the coffin beneath. 'So there is,' said Arne, and gave proof by removing the lid.

W. H. Cummings, *Dr Arne and Rule, Britannia*

I have read your play and rode your horse, and do not approve of either. They both want particular spirit which alone can give pleasure to the reader and the rider. When the one wants wits, and the other the spur, they both jog on very heavily. I must keep the horse, but I have returned you the play. I pretend to some little knowledge of the last; but as I am no jockey, they cannot say that the knowing one is taken in.

David Garrick, undated letter endorsed 'Designed for Dr Arne, who sold me a horse, a very dull one; and sent me a comic opera, ditto'

## ARNOLD, MATTHEW

1822–88 Poet, Critic

My poems represent, on the whole, the main movement of mind of the last quarter of a century, and thus they will probably have their day as people become conscious to themselves of what that movement of mind is, and interested in the literary productions which reflect it. It might be fairly urged that I have less poetical sentiment than Tennyson, and less intellectual vigour and abundance than Browning; yet, because I have perhaps more of a fusion of the two than either of them . . . I am likely enough to have my turn, as they have had theirs.

On himself, Letter to his Mother, 5 June 1869

Mr Arnold, to those who cared for him at all, was the most *useful* poet of his day. He lived much nearer us than poets of his distinction usually do. He was neither a prophet nor a recluse. He lived neither above us nor away from us. There are two ways of being a recluse – a poet may live remote from men, or he may live in a crowded street but remote from their thoughts. Mr Arnold did neither, and consequently his verse tells and tingles. None of it is thrown away. His readers feel that he bore the same yoke as themselves.

Augustine Birrell, in *Scribner's Magazine*, November 1888

'Is there a God?' asks the reader. 'Oh yes,' replies Mr Arnold, 'and I can verify him in experience.' 'And what is he then?' cries the reader. 'Be virtuous, and as a rule you will be happy,' is the answer. 'Well, and God?' 'That is God,' says Mr Arnold; 'there is no deception, and what more do you want?' I suppose we do want a good deal more. Most of us, certainly the public which Mr Arnold addresses, want something they can worship; and they will not find that in any hypostasized copybook heading, which is not much more adorable than 'Honesty is the best policy', or 'Handsome is that handsome does', or various other edifying maxims, which have not yet come to an apotheosis.

F. H. Bradley, *Ethical Studies*

You are a fortunate man. The young men read you; they no longer read me. And you have invented phrases which everyone quotes – such as 'Philistinism' and 'Sweetness and Light'.

Benjamin Disraeli, to Arnold, *circa* 1880, in G. W. E. Russell, *Collections and Recollections*

Mat Arnold when at college bathed in a river in front of a village. The clergyman came to remonstrate. Mat quite naked waved the towel gracefully and with quiet seriousness said, Is it possible that you see anything indelicate in the human form divine?

George Eliot, Diary, 10 April 1878

In a society in which the arts were seriously studied, in which the art of writing was respected, Arnold might have become a critic . . . Arnold was not so much occupied in establishing a criticism as in attacking the uncritical. The difference is that while in constructive work something can be done, destructive work must incessantly be repeated; and furthermore Arnold, in his destruction, went for game outside of the literary preserve altogether, much of it political game untouched and inviolable by ideas . . . Arnold is not to be blamed: he wasted his strength, as men of superior ability sometimes do, because he saw something to be done and no one else to do it. The temptation, to any man who is interested in ideas and primarily in literature, to put literature into the corner until he has cleaned up the whole country first, is almost irresistible.

T. S. Eliot, *The Sacred Wood*

I met Matthew Arnold and had a few words with him. He is not as handsome as his photographs – or as his poetry.

Henry James, Letter to Charles Eliot Norton, 31 March 1873

In his absence the whole tone of discussion would have seemed more stupid, more literal. Without his irony to play over its surface, to clip it here and there of its occasional fustiness, the life of our Anglo-Saxon race would present a much greater appearance of insensibility.

Henry James, in *English Illustrated Magazine*, January 1884

Arnold gives distinction to everything he touches. His style reminds one of a very well-bred and cultured lady, somewhat advanced in years so that the passions of life are more than half forgotten, and of such exquisite manners as to suggest a bygone day, yet with humour and vivacity such that

the thought never occurs to one that she belongs to an older generation.
Somerset Maugham, *A Writer's Notebook*

Arnold is a dandy Isaiah, a poet without passion, whose verse, written in a surplice, is for freshmen and for gentle maidens who will be wooed to the arms of these future rectors.
George Meredith, in *Fortnightly Review*, July 1909

When Abraham Lincoln was murdered / The one thing that interested Matthew Arnold / Was that the assassin shouted in Latin / As he leapt from the stage. / This convinced Matthew / There was still hope for America. /
Christopher Morley, *Point of View*

Poor Matt, he's gone to Heaven, no doubt – but he won't like God.
Robert Louis Stevenson, on hearing of Arnold's death

[Wordsworth's] Immortality Ode . . . is no more than moderately good . . . I put by its side the poems of Matthew Arnold, and think what a delightfully loud splash the two would make if I dropped them into a river.
Dylan Thomas, Letter to Pamela Hansford Johnson, 1933

An English saint in side whiskers.
Oscar Wilde, in L. Levinson ed., *Bartlett's Unfamiliar Quotations*

*See also* Phineas Barnum, John Dryden

## ARNOLD, THOMAS

1795–1842 Headmaster

My love for any place, or person, or institution, is exactly the measure of my desire to reform them; a doctrine which seems to me as natural now, as it seemed strange when I was a child.
On himself, Letter to Dean Stanley, 4 March 1835

My object will be, if possible, to form Christian men, for Christian boys I can scarcely hope to make.
On himself, Letter written at the time of his appointment to the Headship of Rugby, 1828

Dr Arnold was almost indisputably an admirable master for a common English boy, – the small, apple eating animal whom we know. He worked, he pounded, if the phrase may be used, into the boy a belief, or at any rate a floating, confused conception, that there are great subjects, that there are strange problems, that knowledge has an indefinite value, that life is a serious and solemn thing. The influence of Arnold's teaching on the majority of his pupils was probably very vague, but very good. To impress on the ordinary Englishman a general notion of the importance of what is intellectual and the reality of what is supernatural, is the greatest benefit which can be conferred upon him . . . But there are a few minds which are very likely to think too much of such things. A susceptible, serious, intellectual boy may be injured by the incessant inculcation of the awfulness of life and the magnitude of great problems. It is not desirable to take this world too much *au sérieux*; most persons will not; and the one in a thousand who will, should not.
Walter Bagehot, *Essay on Clough*

There are men – such as Arnold – too intensely, fervidly practical to be literally, accurately, consistently theoretical; too eager to be observant, too royal to be philosophical, too fit to head armies and rule kingdoms to succeed in weighing words and analysing emotions; born to do, they know not what they do.
A. H. Clough, *Poems and Prose Remains*

*See also* A. H. Clough

## ARTHUR, PRINCE OF WALES

1486–1502

Robert viscount Fitzwater deposed, the prince was then about 15, and queen Catherine elder; and that, the next day after being in bed together (which he remembered after they entered to be solemnly blessed) he waited at breakfast on prince Arthur, where Maurice St John did carve, and he the lord Fitzwater give drink; at which time the said Maurice demanding of the prince how he had done that night? The prince answered, I have been in Spain this night . . . Anthony Willoughby, knight, deposed that being the morrow after the Marriage in the prince's privy-chamber, the said prince spake afore divers witnesses these words, 'Willoughby, give me a cup of ale, for I have been this night in the midst of Spain.' After which he said, 'Masters, it is a good pastime to have a wife'.

William Cobbett, *State Trials* (the evidence at a divorce hearing between Henry VIII and Catherine of Aragon that her marriage with Prince Arthur had been consummated)

## ARTHUR, CHESTER ALAN

1830–86 Twenty-First United States President

First in ability on the list of second rate men.

Anon., in *New York Times*, 20 February 1872

. . . a creature for whose skin the romancist ought to go with carving knife.

Henry Adams, in George Frederick Howe, *Chester Arthur: A Quarter of a Century of Machine Politics*

## ASHMOLE, ELIAS

1617–92 Antiquary

Born in Litchfield, critically skilled in ancient coins, chemistry, heraldry, mathematicks, and what not?

Thomas Fuller, *The History of the Worthies of England*

## ASQUITH, HERBERT HENRY, EARL OF OXFORD AND ASQUITH

1852–1928 Prime Minister

You were, in the world above, almost a classical example of *Luck*. You were endowed at birth with brains above the average. You had, further, some qualities of temperament which are exceptionally useful for mundane success – energy under the guise of lethargy; a faculty for working quickly, which is more effective in the long run than plodding perseverance; patience (which is one of the rarest of human qualities); a temperate but persistent ambition; a clear mind, a certain quality and lucidity of speech; intellectual, but not moral, irritability; a natural tendency to understand & appreciate the opponent's point of view: and, as time went on, & your nature matured, a growing sense of proportion, which had its effect upon both friends and foes, and which, coupled with detachment from any temptation to intrigue, and, in regard to material interests & profits, an unaffected indifference, secured for you the substantial advantage of personality and authority . . . you were what is called in the slang vocabulary of your time a 'good get out'.

On himself, from his private sketch imagining the assessment of the Judge of the Infernal Tribunal, March 1915, in Roy Jenkins, *Asquith*

For twenty years he has held a season ticket on the line of least resistance, and gone wherever the train of events has carried him, lucidly justifying his position at whatever point he has happened to find himself.

L. S. Amery, in the House of Commons, *circa* 1916

Asquith's mind is a perfect instrument, and he takes points after the manner of a trained lawyer. But he lacks some element of character; perhaps hardiness, I should say he was a soft man; and his chin *recedes* when an attack is possible or imminent.

Lord Esher, Diary, 28 November 1907

My colleagues tell military secrets to their wives, except X who tells them to other people's wives.

Lord Kitchener, in Philip Magnus, *Kitchener*

The criticism which is directed against the govt. and against yourself is chiefly based on this – that as Prime Minister you have not devoted yourself absolutely to co-ordinating all the moves of the war because so much of your time and energy has been devoted to control of the political machine.

Andrew Bonar Law, Letter to Asquith, 2 November 1915

Asquith worries too much about small points. If you were buying a large mansion he would come to you and say 'Have you thought that there is no accommodation for the cat.'

David Lloyd George, Letter to Lord Riddell, 1915

. . . A forensic gladiator who never made a heart beat quicker by his words, and who never by any possibility brought a lump into his hearers' throats.

W. T. Stead, in *Review of Reviews*, January 1906

. . . the P.M. is absolutely devoid of all principles except one – that of retaining his position as Prime Minister. He will sacrifice everything except No. 10 Downing St. D[avid Lloyd George] says he is for all the world like a Sultan with his harem of 23, using all his skill and wiles to prevent one of them from eloping.

Frances Stevenson, Diary, 30 November 1916

His public career suggests a parallel with Walpole. But one gathers that under all Sir Robert's low-minded opportunism there was a certain grandeur, and that his actual capacity was supreme. In Asquith's case the inveterate lack of ideals and imagination seems really unredeemed; when one has peeled off the brown-paper wrapping of phrases and compromises, one finds – just nothing at all.

Lytton Strachey, in M. Holroyd, *Lytton Strachey*

## ASQUITH, EMMA ALICE MARGARET (MARGOT), COUNTESS OF OXFORD AND ASQUITH

1864–1945 Society Woman

. . . black and wicked and with only a nodding acquaintance with the truth.

Lady Cunard, in Henry Channon, Diary, 7 January 1944

The affair between Margot Asquith and Margot Asquith will live as one of the prettiest love stories in all literature.

Dorothy Parker, in Robert Drennan ed., *Wit's End*

## ASTON, SIR ARTHUR

– d. 1649 Soldier

September 1644. – Sir Arthur Aston was governour of Oxon at what time it was garrison'd for the king, a testy, forward, imperious and tirannical person, hated in Oxford and elsewhere by God and Man. Who kervetting on horseback in Bullington green before certaine ladies, his horse flung him and broke his legge: so that it being cut off and he therupon rendred useless for employment, one coll. Legge succeeded him. Soon after the country people coming to market would be ever and anon asking the sentinell, 'who was governor of Oxon?' They answered

'one Legge.' Then replied they: 'A pox upon him! Is he governor still?'
Anthony à Wood, *Life and Times*

## ASTOR, NANCY WITCHER, VISCOUNTESS

1879–1964 First Woman Member of Parliament

The Wait and See Policy has changed me into a fighting woman.
On herself, sentence omitted from the final version of a Letter to Margot Asquith, 1915

I am a Virginian, so naturally I am a politician.
On herself, Acceptance speech, Autumn 1919

Nobody wants me as a Cabinet Minister and they are perfectly right. I am an agitator, not an administrator.
On herself, Address to a women's luncheon, *circa* 1929

Am I dying or is this my birthday?
On herself, at the sight of all her children assembled in her last illness, April 1964

*Nancy:* Winston, if I were married to you, I'd put poison in your coffee.
*Churchill:* Nancy, if you were my wife, I'd drink it.
Exchange at Blenheim Palace, *circa* 1912, in Elizabeth Langhorne, *Nancy Astor and her friends*

When I married Nancy, I hitched my wagon to a star and when I got into the House of Commons in 1910, I found that I had hitched my wagon to a shooting star. In 1919 when she got into the House, I found that I had hitched my wagon to a sort of V-2 rocket.
Viscount Astor, Speech to a women's organization dinner, December 1944

Here England buries her grudge against Columbus.
Kensal Green (Colin Hurry), *Premature Epitaphs*

Viscount Waldorf Astor owned Britain's two most influential newspapers, *The Times* and the *Observer*, but his American wife, Nancy, had a wider circulation than both papers put together.
Emery Kelen, *Peace in Their Time*

I shall not soon forget the sight of Lady Astor's trim little figure dressed in appropriate black, advancing from the bar of the House of Commons flanked by Mr Balfour and Mr Lloyd George . . . That was your second conquest of Britain.
Lord Lothian, British Ambassador, to the Virginia Legislature, 1939

Nannie was a devout Christian Scientist, but not a good one. She kept confusing herself with God. She didn't know when to step aside and give God a chance.
Mrs Gordon Smith, in Elizabeth Langhorne, *Nancy Astor and her friends*

## ATTERBURY, FRANCIS

1662–1732 Bishop of Rochester

. . . a mind inexhaustibly rich in all the resources of controversy, and familiar with all the artifices which make falsehood look like truth and ignorance like knowledge.
T. B. Macaulay, *Life of Atterbury*

Atterbury goes before, and sets everything on fire. I come after him with a bucket of water.
George Smalridge, Bishop of Bristol, in T. B. Macaulay, *Life of Atterbury*

He never attempts your passions until he has convinced your reason. All the objections which he can form are laid open and dispersed, before he uses the least vehemence in his sermon; but when he thinks he has your head, he very soon wins your heart; and never pretends to show the beauty of holiness, until he hath convinced you of the truth of it.

Richard Steele, in *Tatler*, no. 66

## ATTLEE, CLEMENT RICHARD, EARL ATTLEE

1883–1967 Prime Minister

I am a very diffident man. I find it hard to carry on a conversation. But if any of you wish to come and see me, I will welcome you.

On himself, speaking to junior Labour ministers, June 1945

I have none of the qualities which create publicity.

On himself, in Harold Nicolson, Diary, 14 January 1949

He seems determined to make a trumpet sound like a tin whistle . . . He brings to the fierce struggle of politics the tepid enthusiasm of a lazy summer afternoon at a cricket match.

Aneurin Bevan, in *Tribune*, 1945

[*As it Happened*] is a good title. Things happened to him. He never *did* anything.

Aneurin Bevan, on Attlee's *Autobiography*, in Michael Foot, *Aneurin Bevan*

He is a sheep in sheep's clothing.

Winston Churchill, attributed, 1945

Anyone can respect him, certainly, but admire – no!

Winston Churchill, in Henry Channon, Diary, 20 July 1948

We all understand his position. 'I am their leader, I must follow them'.

Winston Churchill, attributed

A modest little man with much to be modest about.

Winston Churchill, in Michael Foot, *Aneurin Bevan*

Attlee is a charming and intelligent man, but as a public speaker he is, compared to Winston [Churchill], like a village fiddler after Paganini.

Harold Nicolson, Diary, 10 November 1947

*See also* Winston Churchill

## AUBREY, JOHN

1626–97 Antiquary, Biographer

My Memoires of Lives is now a booke of 2 quires, close written: and after I had begun it I had such an impulse in my spirit that I could not be at quiet till I had done it. I Beleeve never any in England were delivered so faithfully and with so good authority.

On himself, Letter to Anthony à Wood

Mild of spirit; mightily susceptible of Fascination. My Idea very cleer; Phansie like a Mirrour, pure chrystal water which the least wind does disorder and unsmooth. Never riotous or prodigall; but (as Sir E. Leech said) Sloath and carelessness are equivalent to all other vices.

On himself, his schooldays, *Brief Lives*

About as credulous an old goose as one could hope to find out of Gotham.

B. G. Johns, 'John Aubrey of Wilts', in *Gentleman's Magazine*, 1893

His insatiable passion, for singular odds and ends had a meaning in it; he was groping towards a scientific ordering of phenomena; but the twilight of his age was too confusing, and he could rarely distinguish between a fact and a fantasy. He was clever enough to understand the Newtonian system, but he was not clever enough to understand that a horoscope was an absurdity; and so, in his crowded curiosity shop of a brain, astronomy and astrology both found a place, and were given equal values.

Lytton Strachey, *John Aubrey*

He was a shiftless person, roving and magotis-headed, and sometimes little better than crased. And being exceedingly credulous, would stuff his many letters sent to A.W. with fooleries, and misinformations, which sometimes would guid him into the paths of errour.

Anthony à Wood, *Life and Times*

## AUDEN, WYSTAN HUGH

1907–73 Poet

It is a sad fact about our culture that a poet can earn much more money writing or talking about his art than he can by practicing it. All the poems I have written were written for love; naturally, when I have written one, I try to market it, but the prospect of a market played no role in its writing. On the other hand, I have never written a line of criticism except in response to a demand by others for a lecture, an introduction, a review, etc.; though I hope that some love went into their writing, I wrote them because I needed the money.

On himself, Foreword to *The Dyer's Hand*

Most people enjoy the sight of their own handwriting as they enjoy the smell of their own farts. Much as I loathe the typewriter, I must admit that it is a help in self-criticism. Typescript is so impersonal and hideous to look at that, if I type out a poem, I immediately see defects which I missed when I looked through it in manuscript.

On himself, *The Dyer's Hand*

The son of book-loving, Anglo-Catholic parents of the professional class . . . I was . . . mentally precocious, physically backward, shortsighted, a rabbit at all games, very untidy and grubby, a nail-biter, a physical coward, dishonest, sentimental, with no community sense whatever, in fact a typical little highbrow and difficult child.

On himself, in Dennis Davison, *W. H. Auden*

A face like a wedding cake left out in the rain.

Anon., in L. Levinson, *Bartlett's Unfamiliar Quotations*

In a century of the symbolist, surreal, and absurd, W. H. Auden is essentially a poet of the reasonable.

James D. Brophy, *W. H. Auden*

Later, standing in the wings, / I heard you read: no dramatics, / More interested in what you said / Than how you said it; / Airless Stateside vowels / Ricocheting off the kippered panelling / Like custard pies, yet more telling / Than bullets or blood transfusions. /

Charles Causley, *Letter from Jericho*

Poetry is highly explosive, but no good poet since Eliot can but perceive the extreme difficulty of writing good poetry . . . We have one poet of genius in Auden, who is able to write prolifically, carelessly, and exquisitely, nor does he seem to have to pay any price for his inspiration. It is as if he worked under the influence of some mysterious drug which presents him with a private vision, a mastery of form and of vocabulary.

Cyril Connolly, *Enemies of Promise*

The youthful Auden . . . was tall and slim, with a mole on his upper lip, rather untidy tow-coloured hair in a loop over his forehead, with extraordinary greenish eyes suggesting that iceberg glare he liked to claim from his Norse ancestors . . . My feelings towards him were entirely platonic . . . but my subconscious demanded more and I was put out by a dream (based on his ballad) in which, stripped to the waist beside a basin ('O plunge your hands in water') he indicated to me two small firm breasts: 'Well, Cyril, how do you like my lemons?'

Cyril Connolly, in *Encounter*, March 1975

Auden is . . . something of an intellectual jackdaw, picking up bright pebbles of ideas so as to fit them into exciting conceptual patterns.

Richard Hoggart, *W. H. Auden*

Auden is, and always has been, a most prolific writer. Problems of form and technique seem to bother him very little. You could say to him: 'Please write me a double ballade on the virtues of a certain brand of toothpaste, which also contains at least ten anagrams on the names of well-known politicians, and of which the refrain is as follows . . .' Within twenty-four hours your ballade would be ready – and it would be good.

Christopher Isherwood, in *New Verse*, November 1937

One never steps twice into the same Auden.

Randall Jarrell, *The Third Book of Criticism*

. . . an engaging, bookish, American talent, too verbose to be memorable and too intellectual to be moving.

Philip Larkin, in George T. Wright, *W. H. Auden*

He is all ice and woodenfaced acrobatics.

Percy Wyndham Lewis, *Blasting and Bombardiering*

[At Oxford] Auden, then as always, was busy getting on with the job. Sitting in a room all day with the blinds down, reading very fast and very widely – psychology, ethnology, *Arabia Deserta*. He did not seem to *look* at anything, admitted he hated flowers and was very free with quasi-scientific jargon, but you came away from his presence always encouraged; here at least was someone to whom ideas were friendly – they came and ate out of his hand – who would always have an interest in the world and always have something to say.

Louis MacNeice, *The Strings are False*

Wystan Auden reads us some of his new poem in the evening . . . It interests me particularly as showing, at last, that I belong to an older generation. I follow Auden in his derision of patriotism, class distinctions, comfort, and all the ineptitudes of the middle-classes. But when he also derides the other soft little harmless things which make my life comfortable, I feel a chill autumn wind. I feel that were I a communist the type of person whom I should most wish to attack would not be the millionaire or the imperialist, but the soft, reasonable, tolerant, secure, self-satisfied intellectual like Vita and myself. A man like Auden with his fierce repudiation of half-way houses and his gentle integrity makes one feel terribly discontented with one's own smug successfulness. I go to bed feeling terribly Edwardian and back-number, and yet, thank God, delighted that people like Wystan Auden should actually exist.

Harold Nicolson, Diary, 4 August 1933

Mr Auden's brand of amoralism is only possible if you are the kind of person who is always somewhere else when the trigger is pulled. So much of left-wing thought is a kind of playing with fire by people who don't even know that fire is hot.

George Orwell, *Inside the Whale*

I personally do *not* share the Auden craze, it isn't as much as a craze anyhow; it is merely that Auden is so large a part of what little they've got. Mutatis mutandis, another J. E.

Flecker, I mean about that general mule-power.

Ezra Pound, Letter to Harriet Monroe, 27 March 1931.

Surely, at some deep level . . . Auden's notorious rudeness and his despotic directives – go easy with the lavatory paper; bring your own cigarettes – were efforts to be *interesting*. Lurking somewhere was the demand for love, and the fear of being boring. Somehow, though, in later life, he was less and less able to work the trick to his own satisfaction. His many friends went on loving him in spite of his cantankerous behaviour: Auden evidently wished to be loved because of it. At the touch of pity he withdrew inside the famous carapace.

Craig Raine, in *New Statesman*, 28 March 1975

People sometimes divide others into those you laugh at and those you laugh with. The young Auden was someone you could laugh-at-with.

Stephen Spender, Valedictory Address, 27 October 1973, at Auden's memorial service at Christ Church, Oxford

Few understand the works of Cummings, / And few James Joyce's mental slummings, / And few young Auden's coded chatter; / But then it is the few that matter. /

Dylan Thomas, Letter to Pamela Hansford Johnson, 1933

I sometimes think of Mr Auden's poetry as a hygiene, a knowledge and practice, based on a brilliantly prejudiced analysis of contemporary disorders, relating to the preservation and promotion of health, a sanitary science and a flusher of melancholies. I sometimes think of his poetry as a great war, admire intensely the mature, religious, and logical fighter, and deprecate the boy bushranger.

Dylan Thomas, in *New Verse*, November 1937

Auden often writes like Disney. Like Disney, he knows the shape of beasts (and incidentally he, too, might have a company of artists producing his lines); unlike Lawrence, he does not know what shapes or motivates those beasts. He's a naturalist who looks for beasts that resemble himself, and, failing that, he tries to shape them in his own curious image. The true naturalist, like Gilpin, offers his toe to the vampire bat; Auden would suck the bat off.

Dylan Thomas, Letter to Henry Treece, 1938

Mr Auden himself has presented the curious case of a poet who writes an original poetic language in the most robust English tradition, but who seems to have been arrested at the mentality of an adolescent schoolboy. His technique has seemed to mature, but he has otherwise not grown up. His mind has always been haunted, as the minds of boys at prep school still are, by parents and uncles and aunts. His love poems seem unreal and ambiguous as if they were the products of adolescent flirtations and prep-school homosexuality . . . The seizure of power he dreams of is an insurrection in the schoolroom.

Edmund Wilson, *The Shores of Light*

*See also* Edith Sitwell

## AUDUBON, JOHN JAMES LEFOREST

1785–1851 Artist, Ornithologist

Some men live for warlike deeds, / Some for women's words. / John James Audubon / Lived to look at birds . . ./

Coloured them and printed them / In a giant book / 'Birds of North America' – / All the world said, 'Look!' /

Stephen Vincent Benét, *John James Audubon*

## AUSTEN, JANE

1775–1817 Novelist

What dreadful hot weather we have! It keeps me in a continual state of inelegance.

On herself, Letter, September 1796

I think I may boast myself to be, with all possible vanity, the most unlearned and uninformed female who ever dared to be an authoress.

On herself, Letter to the Rev. James Clarke, 1815

The little bit (two inches wide) of Ivory on which I work with so fine a Brush, as produces little effect after much labour.

On herself, describing her own work, Letter to Edward Austen, 1816

What became of that Jane Austen (if she ever existed) who set out bravely to correct conventional notions of the desirable and virtuous? From being their critic (if she ever was) she became their slave. That is another way of saying that her judgement and her moral sense were corrupted. *Mansfield Park* is the witness of that corruption.

Kingsley Amis, *What Became of Jane Austen?*

Beside her Joyce seems innocent as grass. / It makes me most uncomfortable to see / An English spinster of the middle class / Describe the amorous effects of 'brass', / Reveal so frankly and with such sobriety / The economic basis of society. /

W. H. Auden, *Letter to Lord Byron*, part 1

She supported, during two months, all the varying pain, irksomeness, and tedium, attendant on decaying nature, with more than resignation, with a truly elastic cheerfulness. She retained her faculties, her memory, her fancy, her temper, and her affections, warm, clear, and unimpaired, to the last . . . She wrote whilst she could hold a pen, and with a pencil when a pen was become too laborious. The day preceding her death she composed some stanzas replete with fancy and vigour. Her last voluntary speech conveyed thanks to her medical attendant; and to the final question asked of her, purporting to know her wants, she replied, 'I want nothing but death.'

Henry Austen, *Biographical Notice*

I had not seen *Pride and Prejudice* till I read that sentence of yours, and then I got the book. And what did I find? An accurate daguerreotyped portrait of a commonplace face; a carefully fenced, highly cultivated garden, with neat borders and delicate flowers; but no glance of a bright, vivid physiognomy, no open country, no fresh air, no blue hill, no bonny beck. I should hardly like to live with her ladies and gentlemen, in their elegant but confined houses.

Charlotte Brontë, Letter to G. H. Lewes, 12 January 1848

Her business is not half so much with the human heart as with the human eyes, mouth, hands, and feet; what sees keenly, speaks aptly, moves flexibly, it suits her to study; but what throbs fast and full, though hidden, what the blood rushes through, what is the unseen seat of Life and the sentient target of death – *this* Miss Austen ignores . . . Jane Austen was a complete and most sensible lady, but a very incomplete and rather insensible (*not senseless*) woman. If this is heresy, I cannot help it.

Charlotte Brontë, Letter to W. S. Williams, 1850

Jane Austen is slandered if she is called either a miniaturistic or a naturalistic novelist. Her books are domestic in the sense that *Oedipus Rex* is domestic. Her moral dilemmas are often drawn in precisely oedipal terms.

Brigid Brophy, *Don't Never Forget*

Too washy; water-gruel for mind and body at the same time were too bad.

Jane Welsh Carlyle (anticipating her uncle's reply if offered a novel by Jane Austen to read), Letter to Helen Walsh, March 1843

My uncle Southey and my father had an equally high opinion of her merits, but Mr Wordsworth used to say that though he admitted that her novels were an admirable copy of life, he could not be interested in productions of that kind; unless truth to nature were presented to him clarified, as it were, by the pervading light of imagination, it had scarce any attractions in his eyes.

Sara Coleridge, Letter to Emily Trevenen, August 1834

I am at a loss to understand why people hold Miss Austen's novels at so high a rate, which seem to me vulgar in tone, sterile in artistic invention, imprisoned in the wretched conventions of English society, without genius, wit, or knowledge of the world. Never was life so pinched and narrow. The one problem in the mind of the writer in both the stories I have read . . . is marriageableness. All that interests in any character introduced is still this one, Has he or [she] the money to marry with, and conditions conforming? 'Tis the 'nympholepsy of a fond despair', say, rather, of an English boarding-house. Suicide is more respectable.

Ralph Waldo Emerson, *Journal*, 1861

Scott misunderstood it when he congratulated her for painting on a square of ivory. She is a miniaturist, but never two-dimensional. All her characters are round, or capable of rotundity.

E. M. Forster, *Aspects of the Novel*

She has given us a multitude of characters, all in a certain sense, commonplace, all such as we meet every day. Yet they are all as perfectly discriminated from each other as if they were the most eccentric of human beings.

T. B. Macaulay, in *Edinburgh Review*, January 1843

Nothing very much happens in her books, and yet, when you come to the bottom of a page, you eagerly turn it to learn what will happen next. Nothing very much does and again you eagerly turn the page. The novelist who has the power to achieve this has the most precious gift a novelist can possess.

Somerset Maugham, *Ten Novels and Their Authors*

I have discovered that our great favourite, Miss Austen, is my countrywoman . . . with whom mamma before her marriage was acquainted. Mamma says that she was then the prettiest, silliest, most affected, husband-hunting butterfly she ever remembers.

Mary Russell Mitford, Letter to Sir William Elford, 3 April 1815

. . . A friend of mine, who visits her now, says that she has stiffened into the most perpendicular, taciturn piece of single-blessedness that ever existed, and that, till *Pride and Prejudice* showed what a precious gem was hidden in that unbending case, she was no more regarded in society than a poker or fire-screen . . . She is still a poker, but a poker of whom everybody is afraid.

Mary Russell Mitford, *Life of Mary Russell Mitford*

I have been reading *Emma*. Everything Miss Austen writes is clever, but I desiderate something. There is a want of *body* to the story. The action is frittered away in over-little things . . . Miss Austen has no romance – none at all. What vile creatures her parsons are!

John Henry Newman, Letter to Mrs John Mozley, 10 January 1837

Read again, and for the third time at least, Miss Austen's very finely written novel of *Pride and Prejudice* ... The Big Bow-wow strain I can do myself like any now going; but the exquisite touch, which renders ordinary commonplace things and characters interesting, from the truth of the description and the sentiment, is denied to me.

Sir Walter Scott, *Journal*, 14 March 1826

When I take up one of Jane Austen's books ... I feel like a barkeeper entering the kingdom of heaven. I know what his sensation would be and his private comments. He would not find the place to his taste, and he would probably say so.

Mark Twain, in Q. D. Leavis, *Fiction & the Reading Public*

*See also* Rudyard Kipling

## AUSTIN, ALFRED

1835–1913 Poet Laureate

Mr Alfred Austin has a clearly-defined talent, the limits of which are by this time generally recognized.

Anon., in *Daily Telegraph*, 22 May 1908

Mr Austin is neither an Olympian nor a Titan, and all the puffing in Paternoster Row cannot set him on Parnassus.

Oscar Wilde, in *Pall Mall Gazette*, 1887

## AUSTIN, JAMES LANGASHAW

1911–60 Philosopher

You are like a greyhound who doesn't want to run himself, and bites the other greyhounds, so they cannot run either.

A. J. Ayer, in Sir Isaiah Berlin, 'Austin and the Early Beginnings of Oxford Philosophy', in Berlin *et al.*, *Essays on J. L. Austin*

He wanted us to think of philosophy as more like a science than an art, as a matter of finding things out and getting things settled, not of creating a certain individual effect. And certainly not as one of the *performing* arts; once, when I saw him in the audience of a very distinguished philosophical performer, he found the spectacle so manifestly intolerable to him that he had to go away – and was not himself play-acting in doing so. He could not bear histrionics.

G. J. Warnock, 'Saturday Mornings', in *ibid.*

# 'B'

## BABBAGE, CHARLES

1792–1871 Mathematician

He once tried to investigate statistically the credibility of the biblical miracles. In the course of his analysis he made the assumption that the chance of a man rising from the dead is 1 in $10^{12}$.

B. V. Bowden, *Faster than Thought*

Shortly before his death he told a friend that he could not remember a single completely happy day in his life: 'He spoke as if he hated mankind in general, Englishmen in particular, and the English Government and Organ Grinders most of all'.

*Ibid.*

I remember a funny dinner at my brother's, where, amongst a few others, were Babbage and Lyell, both of whom liked to talk. Carlyle, however, silenced every one by haranguing during the whole dinner on the advantages of silence. After dinner, Babbage, in his grimmest manner, thanked Carlyle for his very interesting lecture on silence.

Charles Darwin, *Autobiography*

I knew Mr Babbage, and am quite sure that he was not the man to say anything on the topic of calculating machines which he could not justify.

T. H. Huxley, in L. Huxley, *Life and Letters of Thomas Henry Huxley*

## BACON, FRANCIS, VISCOUNT ST ALBANS

1561–1626 Philosopher, Statesman

Lastly, I confess that I have as vast contemplative ends, as I have moderate civil ends: for I have taken all knowledge to be my province;...

On himself, Letter to Lord Burghley, 1591

It is my act, my hand, my heart: I beseech your lordships to be merciful to a broken reed.

On himself, identifying his confession at his Trial, 1621

He had a delicate, lively, hazel Eie; Dr Harvey tolde me it was like the Eie of a viper.

John Aubrey, *Brief Lives*

Mr Hobbs told me that the cause of his Lordship's death was trying an experiment; viz. as he was taking the aire in a Coach with Dr Witherborne . . . towards High-gate, snow lay on the ground, and it came into my Lord's thoughts, why flesh might not be preserved in snow, as in Salt. They were resolved they would try the Experiment presently. They alighted out of the Coach and went into a poore woman's house at the bottom of Highgate hill, and bought a Hen, and made the woman exenterate it, and then stuffed the body with Snow, and my Lord did help to doe it himselfe. The Snow so chilled him that he immediately fell so extremely ill, that he could not returne to his Lodging . . . but went to the Earle of Arundel's house at High-gate, where they putt him in a good bed warmed with a Panne, but it was a damp bed that had not been layn-in in about a yeare before, which gave him such a colde that in 2 or 3 days as I remember Mr Hobbes told me, he dyed of Suffocation.

*Ibid.*

When their lordships asked Bacon / How many bribes he had taken / He had at least the grace / To get very red in the face. /

Edmund Clerihew Bentley, *Baseless Biography*

In Bacon see the culminating prime / Of British intellect and British crime. / He died, and Nature, settling his affairs, / Parted his powers among us, his heirs: / To each a pinch of common-sense for seed, / And, to develop it, a pinch of greed. / Each frugal heir, to make the gift suffice, / Buries the talent to manure the vice. /

Ambrose Bierce, 'Sir Francis Bacon', in *Lantern*, 1874

An Atheist pretending to talk against Atheism!

William Blake, *Annotations to Bacon*

It is evident that he was a sincere if unenthusiastic Christian of that sensible school which regards the Church of England as a branch of the Civil Service, and the Archbishop of Canterbury as the British Minister for Divine Affairs.

C. D. Broad, *Ethics and the History of Philosophy*

There is a skeleton in the cupboard of Inductive Logic, which Bacon never suspected and Hume first exposed to view . . . May we venture to hope that when Bacon's next centenary is celebrated the great work which he set going will be completed; and that Inductive Reasoning, which has long been the glory of Science, will have ceased to be the scandal of Philosophy?

*Ibid.*

Bacon, like Moses, led us forth at last; / The barren Wilderness he past, / Did on the very Border stand / Of the blest promis'd Land, / And from the mountain's Top of his Exalted Wit / Saw it himself, and shew'd us it. /

Abraham Cowley, *To the Royal Society*

The word *wisdom* characterises him more than any other. It was not that he did so much himself to advance the knowledge of man or nature, as that he saw what others had done to advance it, and what was still wanting to its full accomplishment . . . He was master of the comparative anatomy of the mind of man, of the balance of power among the different faculties.

William Hazlitt, *Lectures on the Age of Elizabeth: Character of Lord Bacon's Works*

His strength was in reflection, not in production: he was the surveyor, not the builder of science.

*Ibid.*

It is not easy to make room for him and his reputation together. This great and celebrated man in some of his works recommends it to pour a bottle of claret into the ground of a morning, and to stand over it inhaling the perfumes. So he sometimes enriched the dry and barren soil of speculation with the fine aromatic spirit of his genius.

William Hazlitt, Footnote to 'On Persons one Would Wish to have Seen', in *New Monthly Magazine*, January 1826

He not only made a scientific philosophy out of the practice of artisans: he also secularized their age-old chiliastic dreams, and suggested the possibility of getting back behind the Fall on earth before the millennium. This made possible new attitudes towards history – progress without chiliasm, change without apocalypse, reformation without tarrying for the Second Coming.

Christopher Hill, *Intellectual Origins of the English Revolution*

In his adversity I ever prayed, that God would give him strength; for greatness he could not want.

Ben Jonson, *Timber, or Discoveries*

His faults were – we write it with pain – coldness of heart, and meanness of spirit. He seems to have been incapable of feeling strong affection, of facing great dangers, of making great sacrifices. His desires were set on things below; titles, patronage, the mace, the seals, the coronet, large houses, fair gardens, rich manors, many services of plate, gay hangings, curious cabinets, had as great attraction for him as for any of the courtiers who dropped on their knees in the dirt when Elizabeth went by, and then hastened home to write to the King of Scots that her Grace seemed to be breaking fast.

T. B. Macaulay, *Essays*: 'Lord Bacon'

The difference between the soaring angel and the creeping snake was but a type of the difference between Bacon the philosopher and Bacon the Attorney-General, Bacon seeking for truth, and Bacon seeking for the Seals.

*Ibid.*

In Plato's opinion man was made for philosophy; in Bacon's opinion philosophy was made for man.

*Ibid.*

Lo! Rome herself, proud mistress now no more / Of arts, but thund'ring against heathen lore; / Her grey-hair's Synods damning books unread, / And Bacon trembling for his brazen head. /

Alexander Pope, *The Dunciad*, book 3

If Parts allure thee, think how Bacon shin'd, / The wisest, brightest, meanest of mankind. /

Alexander Pope, *Essay on Man*, epistle 4

We ought, he says, to be neither like spiders, which spin things out of their own insides, nor like ants, which merely collect, but like bees, which both collect and arrange. This is somewhat unfair to the ants, but it illustrates Bacon's meaning.

Bertrand Russell, *History of Western Philosophy*

Francis Bacon has been described more than once with the crude vigour of antithesis; but in truth such methods are singularly inappropriate to his most unusual case. It was not by the juxtaposition of a few opposites, but by the infiltration of a multitude of highly varied elements, that his mental composition was made up. He was not striped frieze; he was shot silk.

Lytton Strachey, *Elizabeth and Essex*

The great Secretary of Nature and all learning, Sir Francis Bacon.

Izaak Walton, *Life of Herbert*

Bacon's task, it may be said, was to prove that natural science was Promethean and not Mephistophelean.

Basil Willey, *The Seventeenth Century Background*

Sir Francis Bacon, in Parliament, after a very fair speech made, said: I should willingly assent to your former speech, if we were not come hither rather for physic, than music.

Sir Henry Wotton, *Table Talk*

The splendid fault of Lord Bacon . . . is being too beautiful and too entertaining, in points that require reasoning alone.

Edward Young, in Joseph Spence, *Anecdotes*

*See also* Roger Bacon, James I

## BACON, ROGER

1214?–94 Scientist

He speculated on lenses which would focus the sun and so burn up enemies at long range, 'for the perfect experimenter could destroy any hostile force by this combustion', and he foresaw that 'machines for navigating rivers' were 'possible without rowers.' 'Likewise,' he wrote, 'cars may be made so that without a draft animal they may be moved with inestimable impetus . . . And flying machines are possible so that a man may sit in the middle turning some device by which artificial wings may beat the air in the manner of a flying bird.'

John Bowle, *England, A Portrait*

The neglect of observation and experiment, the abuse of syllogistic reasoning, the blind deference to authority in science and philosophy as well as in religion – on all these points Roger Bacon, writing in the thirteenth century, is as vigorous a censor of the ordinary, scholastic methods as Francis Bacon in the seventeenth, even though he sometimes illustrates the very defects which he condemns.

H. Rashdall, *The Universities of Europe in the Middle Ages*

## BADEN-POWELL, ROBERT STEPHENSON SMYTH

1857–1941 Soldier, Founder of the Boy Scouts and Girl Guides

I know my weak points and am only thankful that I have managed to get along in spite of them! I think that's the policy for this world: Be glad of what you have got, and not miserable about what you would like to have had, and not over-anxious about what the future will bring.

On himself, Letter to Mrs Juliette Low, 4 July 1911

Man, matron, maiden / Please call it Baden. / Further for Powell, / Rhyme it with Noel. /

On himself, in William Hillcourt, *Baden-Powell: the two lives of a hero*

Chief Scout of the World.

Title awarded by the boy scouts assembled at the first Boy Scout International Jamboree, 7 August 1920

Few pioneers live long enough to see / what they have done; / Most men are glad if they can leave / the world a single son; / Did ever man, before he died, see / such a dream come true? / Did any leave so many living / monuments as you? /

A. P. Herbert, *To B-P, 12 January 1941*

## BAGEHOT, WALTER

1826–77 Economist, Journalist

He had a very fine skin, very white near where the hair started, and a high colour . . . Such a colour is associated with soft winds and a moist air, cider-growing orchards, and very green, wet grass. His eyelids were thin, and of singularly delicate texture, and the white of his eyeballs was a blue white. He would pace a room when talking, and, as the ideas framed themselves in words, he would throw his head back as some animals do when sniffing the air.

Mrs Russell Barrington, *Life of Bagehot*

More than any of his contemporaries he excelled in the art of informal criticism – of what it would be tempting to call talkative criticism, if that didn't suggest the maundering velvet-jacketed causerie of a later date. His occasional excursions into the uplands of literary theory, such as his well-known tripartite division of poetry into the Pure, the Ornate, the Grotesque, are the least rewarding part of his work. Luckily they *are* only occasional. For the rest, he generalizes cheerfully but undogmatically: he is a master of the disposable aphorism, the working classification which he knows when to jettison.

John Gross, *The Rise and Fall of the Man of Letters*

## BALDWIN, STANLEY, EARL OF BEWDLEY

1867–1947 Prime Minister

I speak not as the man in the street even, but as a man in a field-path, a much simpler person steeped in tradition and impervious to new ideas.

On himself, speaking during his first ministry, in *Dictionary of National Biography*

He is the grandson of a blacksmith . . . It is an instinct of the blood to protect the offspring of our kind. Baldwin talks a lot about pigs, but he really means pig-iron.

Lord Beaverbrook, Letter to Lord Melchett, 11 November 1930

The Flying Scotsman is no less splendid a sight when it travels north to Edinburgh than when it travels south to London. Mr Baldwin denouncing sanctions was as dignified as Mr Baldwin imposing them. At times it seemed that there were two Mr Baldwins on the stage, a prudent Mr Baldwin, who scented the danger in foolish projects, and a reckless Mr Baldwin, who plunged into them head down, eyes shut. But there was, in fact, only one Mr Baldwin, a well-meaning man of indifferent judgement, who, whether he did right or wrong, was always sustained by a belief that he was acting for the best.

Lord Beaverbrook, in *Daily Express*, 29 May 1937

It is medicine man talk. It lifts the discussion on to so abstract a plane that the minds of the hearers are relieved of the effort of considering the details of the immediate problems. It imposes no intellectual strain because thought drifts into thought, assembling and dissolving like clouds in the upper air, having no connection with earthly obstacles. It flatters, because it appears to offer intimate companionship with a rare and noble spirit. It pleases the unsceptical, because it blurs the outline of unpleasant fact in a maze of meaningless generalities. Over and over again I have been amazed by the ease with which even Labour members are deceived by this nonsense. Murmurs of admiration break out as this second-rate orator trails his tawdry wisps of mist over the parliamentary scene.

Aneurin Bevan, in *Tribune*, 1937

I see no point in swapping donkeys when crossing a stream.

Lord Birkenhead, comment to F. W. Hirst on a pre-election proposal to replace Baldwin

I think Baldwin has gone mad. He simply takes one jump in the dark; looks round; and then takes another.

Lord Birkenhead, Letter to Austen Chamberlain, August 1923

. . . Not dead. But the candle in that great turnip has gone out.

Winston Churchill, on Baldwin's retirement, in Harold Nicolson, Diary, 17 August 1950

Not even a public figure.

Lord Curzon, in Harold Nicolson, *Curzon*

Had he been a greater man, either he would have been all right, or so unpopular that he could have been soon defeated; had he been completely incompetent, he could never have kept his high position; it was that fatal touch of talent . . . and England and the Empire and the world are suffering now in consequence.

J. L. Garvin, in Henry Channon, Diary, 24 March 1942

His fame endures; we shall not forget / The name of Baldwin until we're out of debt.

Kensal Green (Colin Hurry), *Premature Epitaphs*

The conspirators got, instead of him [Lord Curzon] Stanley Baldwin, the Prime Minister they preferred. And that might have been possible to bear, had it not been for the fact that the people – who had played no part in this squalid comedy – got Stanley Baldwin too.

Leonard Mosley, *The Glorious Fault*

*See also* John Locke

## BALFOUR, ARTHUR JAMES, EARL

1848–1930 Prime Minister

You put a pistol to my head – yes.

On himself, remark on Lloyd George's offer of the foreign secretaryship, December 1916

The difference between Joe [Chamberlain] and me is the difference between youth and age: I am age.

On himself, in Denis Judd, *Balfour and the British Empire*

We are none of us infallible – not even the youngest of us.

Dr W. H. Thompson, Master of Trinity, in G. W. E. Russell, *Collections and Recollections*

*See also* Nancy Astor

## BANCROFT, GEORGE

1800–91 Historian, Diplomat

He needs a great deal of cutting and pruning, but we think him an infant Hercules.

Ralph Waldo Emerson, in Michael Kraus, 'George Bancroft', in *New England Quarterly*, December 1934

Bancroft has simply taken phrases and sentences here and there from a long document and rearranged, combined, and in some cases, actually paraphrased them in his own way. Logically and rhetorically, the work is his own. Like Thucydides he composed speeches for his heroes, but unlike the Greek historian he did not have the privilege of participating in the events described.

Thomas Wentworth Higginson, in Harvey Wish, *The American Historian*

## BANKHEAD, TALLULAH BROCKMAN

1903–68 Actress

I'm as pure as driven slush.

On herself, in *Observer*, 24 February 1957

A day away from Tallulah Bankhead is like a month in the country.

Anon., in *Show Business Illustrated*, 17 October 1961

Watching Tallulah Bankhead on the stage is like watching somebody skating over very thin ice – and the English want to be there when she falls through.

Mrs Patrick Campbell, in Gavin Lambert, *On Cukor*

Dorothy Parker gave a party one night at the Algonquin, and guest Tallulah Bankhead, slightly inebriated, carried on in a wild indecorous manner. After Miss Bankhead had been escorted out, Mrs Parker called in from an adjoining room, 'Has Whistler's Mother left yet?'

The next day at lunch Tallulah took out a pocket mirror, examined herself painfully, and said, with a glance at Mrs Parker, 'The less I behave like Whistler's Mother the night before, the more I look like her the morning after.'

Robert E. Drennan, *Wit's End*

And of the many 'images' which have since fascinated the public, Tallulah's was archetypally modern. She informed people, through her own projectile, that she was an open, wayward, free, cosmopolitan, liberated, sensuous human being. In thus systematically invading her own privacy, she was the first of the modern personalities.

Lee Israel, *Miss Tallulah Bankhead*

## BANKS, SIR JOSEPH

1743–1820 President of the Royal Society

Sir Joseph was so exceedingly shy that we made no sort of acquaintance at all. If instead of going round the world he had only fallen from the moon, he could not appear less versed in the usual modes of a tea-drinking party. But what, you will say, has a tea-drinking party to do with a botanist, a man of science, a president of the Royal Society?

Fanny Burney, Diary, March 1788

The Great Southern Caterpillar transformed into a Bath Butterfly – This insect first crawled into notice from among the weeds and mud of the Southern Seas and being afterwards placed in a warm situation by the Royal Society was changed by the heat of the sun into its present form. It is noticed and valued solely on account of the powerful red which encircles its body and the shining spot on its breast, a distinction which never fails to render caterpillars valuable.

James Gillray, in H. C. Cameron, *Sir Joseph Banks*

To give a breakfast in Soho, / Sir Joseph's very bitterest foe / Must certainly allow him peerless merit; / Where, on a wagtail and tomtit, / He shines, and sometimes on a nit, / Displaying powers few Gentlemen inherit. /

I grant he is no intellectual lion / Subduing everything he darts his eye on; / Rather, I ween, an intellectual flea, / Hopping on Science's broad, bony back / Poking its pert proboscis of attack, / Drawing a drop of blood, and fancying it a sea! /

Peter Pindar (John Wolcot), *On A Report in the Newspapers that Sir Joseph Banks was made A Privy Counsellor*

Butler, the author of *Hudibras*, might as well be employed to describe a solemn funeral, in which there was nothing ridiculous. This, however, is better than his going to draw naked savages, and be scalped, with that wild man Banks, who is poaching in every ocean for the fry of little islands that escaped the drag-net of Spain.

Horace Walpole, Letter to Sir Horace Mann, 20 September 1772

## BARA, THEDA

1890–1955 Actress

Theda Bara was another dream-world figure. Surrounded by potted palms, silken hangings and blackamoors and other dust collectors, Miss Bara was Pestilence herself, her monumental wickedness would not have been tolerated by Caligula in his beatnik depths for one moment. She was divinely, hysterically, insanely malevolent. The public fell at Miss Bara's feet. She climbed from option to option while thousands cheered.

Bette Davis, *The Lonely Life*

By 1920 Bara's screen career was at an end. Her contribution to the art of the film was negligible, but her contribution to the making of the sex symbol – a major figure in screen history – was considerable. Bara laid most of the ground rules. She was the first popular star whose primary attraction was her sexuality. She proved conclusively that audiences paid vast sums of money to see women projecting a highly sexual image. She showed the industry that a star can be built from the publicity man's head and through the media. She showed that *true* sex symbols have a bisexual appeal in that they attract equally the fantasies of the opposite sex and the vanity of their own. Men adored, women emulated.

Clyde Jeavons and Jeremy Pascall, *A Pictorial History of Sex in the Movies*

Miss Bara made voluptuousness a common American commodity, as accessible as chewing gum.

Lloyd Morris, *Not So Long Ago*

. . . a pyrogenic half pint . . . who immortalized the vamp just as Little Egypt, at the World's Fair of 1893, had the hoochie-coochie.

S. J. Perelman, 'Cloudland Revisited: The Wickedest Woman in Larchmont', in *The Most of S. J. Perelman*

Theda Bara vamped at a rate that makes the mind boggle. She made dotty pictures in which she seduced unwitting men, her ample bosom heaving, her curvaceous figure draped with semi-transparent silks, her undulating walk an invitation to unbridled passion. Once the men were won away from wives or lovers and completely under Theda's spell, she began to reverse her course, scorning the advances of her conquests, driving them mad with frustration. Daggers, poison, fire and flame – by one device or another their lives came to an end. As one observer put it, an enterprising undertaker could have made a fortune simply by camping on her trail.

Norman Zierold, *The Moguls*

*See also* Marilyn Monroe

## BARBIROLLI, SIR JOHN

1899–1970 Conductor

If you want a cure for a cold, put on two pullovers, take up a baton, poker or pencil, tune the radio to a symphony concert, stand on a chair, and conduct like mad for an hour or so and the cold will have vanished. It never fails. You know why conductors live so long? Because we perspire so much.

On himself, in Leslie Ayre, *The Wit of Music*

I prefer to face the wrath of the police rather than the wrath of Sir John Barbirolli.

A member of the Hallé Orchestra, to a magistrate, on being fined for parking his car outside Huddersfield Town Hall in order not to be late for rehearsal

## BARING, EVELYN, EARL OF CROMER

1841–1917 Statesman

His temperament, all in monochrome, touched in with cold blues and indecisive greys, was eminently unromantic. He had a steely colourlessness, and a steely pliability, and a steely strength. Endowed beyond most men with the capacity of foresight, he was endowed as very few men have ever been with that staying-power which makes the fruit of foresight attainable. His views were long, and his patience was even longer. He progressed imperceptibly; he constantly withdrew; the art of giving way he practised with the refinement of a virtuoso. But, though the steel recoiled and recoiled, in the end it would spring forward.

Lytton Strachey, *Eminent Victorians*

His ambition can be stated in a single phrase; it was, to become an institution; and he achieved it.

*Ibid.*

## BARKER, HARLEY GRANVILLE

1877–1946 Actor, Dramatist

He extended the format of the well-made drawing-room play to attack drawing-room values; he brought hard-headed political debate onto the English stage; and he championed female independence with unstrident sympathy. Combining radical ideas with a feeling of upholstered solidity, his plays are rather like time-bombs secreted on a luxury liner.

Michael Billington, in *Guardian*, 3 October 1975

Oh G.B. you are a very clever and interesting youth of 30; but you are an atrocious manager. You don't know where to put your high light and where to put your smudge.

George Bernard Shaw, Letter to Granville Barker, 18 September 1907

When will you understand that what has ruined you as a manager is your love for people who are 'a little weak perhaps, but just the right tone'. The right tone is never a little weak perhaps; it is always devastatingly strong. Keep your worms for your own plays; and leave me the drunken, stagey, brass-bowelled barnstormers my plays are written for.

George Bernard Shaw, Letter to Granville Barker, 19 January 1908

## BARNUM, PHINEAS TAYLER

1810–91 Impresario

You and I, Mr Arnold, ought to be acquainted. You are a celebrity, I am a notoriety.

On himself, Letter to Matthew Arnold, in R. Werner, *Barnum*

I am not in the show business alone to make money. I feel it my mission, as long as I live, to provide clean, moral, and healthful recreation for the public to which I have so long catered.

On himself, in Neil Harris, *Humbug*

This is a trading world and men, women and children, who cannot live on gravity alone, need something to satisfy their gayer, lighter moods and hours, and he who ministers to this want is in a business established by the Author of our nature. If he worthily fulfils his mission and amuses without corrupting, he need never feel that he has lived in vain.

On himself, in Irving Wallace, *The Fabulous Showman*

He will ultimately take his stand in the social rank . . . among the swindlers, blacklegs, pickpockets, and thimble-riggers of his day.

Anon., in *Tait's Edinburgh Magazine*, 1855

The Prometheus of the Pleasure Principle.

Popular soubriquet, quoted in Neil Harris, *Humbug*

What was it, after all, that made Barnum a showman? We know, of course, what made him one of the *greatest* showmen in history. This was talent, or a kind of genius, if you will – the gift of chromosomes or his Maker – the instinctive understanding of what startled, amazed, astonished, titillated, thrilled, the special extra sense of knowing what Everyman was curious about and finding the means by which to exploit this curiosity.

Charles Godfrey Leland, in Irving Wallace, *The Fabulous Showman*

*See also* Aimee Semple McPherson

## BARRETT, LAWRENCE

1838–91 Actor

His face with its craggy Celtic cheek-bones and bulging forehead looked like a monk's, but the hunger in his unhappy eyes was not for God. Fate was unjust, for [Edwin] Booth, who had been born to fame, could have been happy if the world had never heard of him, and here was Barrett whose unique desire was to be recognized by the world as a great, a *great* actor.

Eleanor Ruggles, *Prince of Players: Edwin Booth*

## BARRIE, SIR JAMES MATTHEW

1860–1937 Playwright, Novelist

I am not young enough to know everything.

On himself, in A. K. Adams, *The Home Book of Humorous Quotations*

A little child whom the Gods have whispered to.

Mrs Patrick Campbell, Letter to Bernard Shaw, January 1913

The cheerful clatter of Sir James Barrie's cans as he went round with the milk of human kindness.

Philip Guedalla, *Some Critics*

Barrie struck twelve once – with *Peter Pan* – a subtly unwholesome sweetmeat, like most of his books.

Florence Becker Lennon, *Lewis Carroll*

Mr Barrie is a born storyteller; and he sees no further than his stories – conceives any discrepancy between them and the world as a shortcoming on the world's part, and is only too happy to be able to re-arrange matters in a pleasanter way. The popular stage, which was a prison to Shakespeare's genius, is a playground to Mr Barrie's. At all events he does the thing as if he liked it, and does it very well. He has apparently no eye for human character; but he has a keen sense of human qualities, and he produces highly popular assortments of them. He cheerfully assumes, as the public wish him to assume, that one endearing quality implies all endearing qualities, and one repulsive quality, all repulsive qualities; the exceptions being comic characters, who are permitted to have 'weaknesses' or stern and terrible souls who are at once understood to be saving up some enormous sentimentality for the end of the last act but one.

George Bernard Shaw, in *Saturday Review*, 13 November 1897

I like Barrie and his work; but someday a demon in the shape of Alice will sit by the fire in hell and poke up the flames in which he is consuming.

George Bernard Shaw, Letter to Ellen Terry, November 1905

*See also* H. G. Wells

## BARRINGTON, GEORGE

b. 1755 Pickpocket, Author

From distant climes, o'er widespread seas we come / Tho' not with much *éclat* or beat of drum; / True Patriots we, for be it understood, / We left our country for our country's good. / No private views disgraced our generous zeal, / What urged our travels was our country's weal; / And none will doubt but that our emigration / Has proved most useful to the British nation. /

On himself, writing from Australia, Prologue to *Dr Young's Revenge*, January 1796

The coarse, incompetent, and generally cowardly highwaymen of the early part of the eighteenth century have undeservedly become the heroes of schoolboys, and the lay-figures of romance-makers. But here we have a veritable villain who disdained force, and practised to perfection urbanity and refinement; who penetrated the society of princes and peers, and was accepted as their companion and equal; who pursued theft with the same persistence and versatility as another man might pursue trade; and who never made an enemy, and never admitted defeat.

Richard S. Lambert, *The Prince of Pickpockets*

## BARRY, ELIZABETH

1658–1713 Actress

This fine Creature was not handsome, her Mouth opening most on the Right side, which she strove to draw t'other

Way, and at Times, composing her Face, as if sitting to have her Picture drawn, – Mrs *Barry* was middle-sized, and had darkish Hair, light Eyes, dark Eye-brows, and was indifferently plump: – Her Face somewhat preceded her Action, as the latter did her Words, her Face ever expressing the Passions; not like the Actresses of late Times, who are afraid of putting their Faces out of the Forms of Non-meaning, lest they should crack the Cerum, White-wash, or other Cosmetic, trowel'd on.

Anthony Aston, *A Brief Supplement to Colley Cibber's Lives*

## BARRY, JAMES

1741–1806 Painter

Barry was another instance of those who scorn nature, and are scorned by her. He could not make a likeness of any one object in the universe: when he attempted it, he was like a drunken man on horseback; his eye reeled, his hand refused its office, – and accordingly he set up for an example of the *great style* in art, which, like charity, covers all other defects.

William Hazlitt, in *Edinburgh Review*, August 1820

## BARRYMORE, ETHEL

1879–1959 Actress

For an actress to be a success she must have the face of Venus, the brains of Minerva, the grace of Terpsichore, the memory of Macaulay, the figure of Juno, and the hide of a rhinoceros.

On herself, in George Jean Nathan, *The Theatre in the Fifties*

Miss Barrymore . . . did what came naturally to her; took the stage, filled it, and left the rest of us to stage rear.

Edward G. Robinson, *All My Yesterdays*

## BARRYMORE, JOHN

1882–1942 Actor

My only regret in the theatre is that I could never sit out front and watch me.

On himself, in Eddie Cantor, *The Way I See It*

John Barrymore was Icarus who flew so close to the sun that the wax on his wings melted and he plunged back to earth – from the peak of classical acting to the banalities of show business.

Brooks Atkinson, *Broadway*

## BARTON, ELIZABETH, 'MAID OF KENT'

1506?–34 Heretic

Now began Elizabeth Barton to play her tricks, commonly called 'the holy maid of Kent'; though at this day OF KENT alone is left unto her, as whose *maidenship* is vehemently suspected, and *holiness* utterly denied.

Thomas Fuller, *Church History of Britain*

## BARUCH, BERNARD MANNES

1870–1965 Financier

We can't always cross a bridge until we come to it; but I always like to lay down a pontoon ahead of time.

On himself, in A. K. Adams, *The Home Book of Humorous Quotations*

## BASKERVILLE, JOHN

1706–75 Printer

O BASKERVILLE! the anxious wish was thine / Utility with beauty to combine; / To bid the O'erweening thirst of gain subside; / Improvement all thy care and all thy pride; / When Birmingham – for riots and for crimes / Shall meet the long reproach of future times, / Then shall she find amongst our honour'd race, / One name to save her from entire disgrace. /

Anon., in J. H. Benton, *Baskerville*

Although constructed with the light timber of a frigate, his movement was solemn as a ship of the line.

William Hutton, in *European Magazine*, November 1785

## BASS, SAM

1851–78 Desperado

I've lived a dog's life, Parson. And I'll die a dog's death.

On himself (as he lay dying), in Harold Preece, *Lone Star Man: Ira Aten, Last of the Old Texas Rangers*

## BAXTER, RICHARD

1615–91 Presbyterian Divine

I was but a pen, and what praise is due to a pen?

On himself, *Reliquiae Baxterianae*

I had rather to be a Martyr for love, than for any other article of the Christian Creed.

*Ibid.*

As to myself, my faults are no disgrace to any university; for I was of none. I have little but what I had out of books, and inconsiderable helps of country tutors. Weakness and pain helped me to study how to die; that set me on studying how to live; and that on studying the doctrine from which I must fetch my motives and comforts. Beginning with necessities I proceeded by degrees, and now am going to see that for which I have lived and studied.

On himself, Letter to Anthony à Wood, in *Athenae Oxonienses*

He had a very moving and pathetical way of writing, and was his whole life long a man of great zeal and much simplicity; but was most unhappily subtle and metaphysical in every thing.

Gilbert Burnet, *History of His Own Time*

Baxter often expresses himself so as to excite a suspicion that he was inclined to Sabellianism.

Samuel Taylor Coleridge, *Notes on English Divines*

I can deal with saints as well as sinners. There stands Oates on one side of the pillory; and, if Baxter stood on the other, the two greatest rogues in the kingdom would stand together . . . This is an old rogue, a schismatical knave, a hypocritical villain. He hates the Liturgy. He would have nothing but longwinded cant without book: . . . Richard, thou art an old knave. Thou hast written books enough to load a cart, and every book as full of sedition as an egg is full of meat.

Judge Jeffreys, at Baxter's trial, 1685

## BEACONSFIELD, *see under* DISRAELI, BENJAMIN

## BEARDSLEY, AUBREY VINCENT

1872–98 Artist, Author

My favourite authors are Balzac, Voltaire, and Beardsley.

On himself, from an interview with him in *Idler*, March 1897

I have one aim – the grotesque. If I am not grotesque I am nothing.

On himself, in Stanley Weintraub, *Aubrey Beardsley*

I make a blot upon the paper and begin to shove the ink about and something comes.

*Ibid.*

Awfully Weirdly.

Popular nickname, quoted in Stanley Weintraub, *Aubrey Beardsley*

B is for Beardsley, the idol supreme, / Whose drawings are not half so bad as they seem. /
Gelett Burgess, *Our Clubbing List*, an alphabetical guide to the nineties, 1896

A peal of morning dew.
Roy Campbell, *Flowering Rifle*, part 2

The Fra Angelico of Satanism.
Roger Fry, in Stanley Weintraub, *Aubrey Beardsley*

It was an inner existence that Beardsley had put down on paper, of sexual images and fantastic literary reveries. He had a sort of innocent familiarity with evil, he communed with the leering dwarfs, the bloated, epicene figures that peopled the depraved landscapes and grotesque interiors designed by his pen, as a child might talk with fairies.
William Gaunt, *The Aesthetic Adventure*

Beware the Yallerbock, my son! / The aims that rile, the art that racks, / Beware the Aub-Aub bird, and shun / The stumious Beerbomax! /
Mostyn Piggott, burlesque of Lewis Carroll's *Jabberwock*, in Haldane MacFall, *Aubrey Beardsley*

With the art of Beardsley we enter the realm of pure intellect; the beauty of the work is wholly independent of the appearance of the thing portrayed.
Ezra Pound, in *Forum*, April 1912

Daubaway Weirdsley.
*Punch*, February 1895

He is the satirist of essential things; it is always the soul, and not the body's discontent only, which cries out of these insatiable eyes, that have looked on all their lusts, and out of these bitter mouths, that have eaten the dust of all their sweetnesses, and out of these hands, that have laboured delicately for nothing, and out of these feet, that have run after vanities. They are so sorrowful because they have seen beauty, and because they have departed from the line of beauty.
Arthur Symons, *Aubrey Beardsley*

There were great possibilities always in the cavern of his soul, and there is something macabre and tragic in the fact that one who added another terror to life should have died at the age of a flower.
Oscar Wilde, Letter to Leonard Smithers, March 1898

Absinthe is to all other drinks what Aubrey's drawings are to other pictures; it stands alone; it is like nothing else; it shimmers like southern twilight in opalescent colouring; it has about it the seduction of strange sins. It is stronger than any other spirit and brings out the subconscious self in man. It is just like your drawings, Aubrey; it gets on one's nerves and is cruel.
Oscar Wilde, in conversation, reported in Frank Harris, *Oscar Wilde*

A monstrous orchid.
Oscar Wilde, in conversation, quoted in Stanley Weintraub, *Aubrey Beardsley*

I invented Aubrey Beardsley.
*Ibid.*

. . . a face like a silver hatchet, with grass-green hair.
Oscar Wilde, in Richard Le Gallienne, *The Romantic '90s*

## BEAUMONT, FRANCIS

1584–1616 Dramatist

They [Beaumont and Fletcher] lived together on the Banke side, not far from the Play-house, both batchelors; lay together; had one Wench in the house between them, which they did so admire; the same cloathes and cloake, &c.; betweene them.

John Aubrey, *Brief Lives*

On Death, thy murderer, this revenge I take: / I slight his terror, and just question make / Which of us two the best precedence have, / Mine to this wretched world, thine to the grave. / Thou should'st have followed me, but Death, to blame, / Miscounted years, and measured age by fame. /

Sir John Beaumont, *Epitaph on His Brother*

In Shakespeare the mere generalities of sex, mere words oftenest, seldom or never distinct images – all head-work, and fancy-drolleries – no sensation supposed in the Speaker, no itchy wriggling. In B. and F. the minutiae of a lecher.

Samuel Taylor Coleridge, Annotation to Stockdale's edition of Beaumont and Fletcher's Works, 1811

B. & F. always write as if Virtue or Goodness were a sort of Talisman or Strange Something that might be lost without the least fault on the part of the Owner. In short, their chaste Ladies value their Chastity as a material thing, not as an act or state of being – and this mere *thing* being merely imaginary, no wonder that all his [sic] Women are represented with the minds of Strumpets, except a few irrational Humorists far less capable of exciting our sympathy than a Hindoo, who had had a basin of Cow-broth thrown over him – for this, though a debasing superstition is still real, and we might pity the poor wretch, though we cannot help despising him. But B. & F.'s Lucinas are clumsy *Fictions*. It is too plain that the authors had no one idea of Chastity as a virtue – but only such a conception as a blind man might have of the power of seeing by handling an Ox's Eye.

*Ibid.*

I have never been able to distinguish the presence of Fletcher during the life of Beaumont, nor the absence of Beaumont during the survival of Fletcher.

Samuel Taylor Coleridge, *Notes for Lecture on Beaumont and Fletcher*

Their plots were generally more regular than Shakespeare's ... and they understood and imitated the conversation of gentlemen much better; whose wild debaucheries, and quickness of wit in repartees, no poet can ever paint as they have done. Humour, which Ben Jonson derived from particular persons, they made it not their business to describe; they represented all the passions very lively, but above all, love. I am apt to believe that the English language in them arrived to its highest perfection.

John Dryden, *An Essay of Dramatic Poesy*

The blossoms of Beaumont and Fletcher's imagination draw no sustenance from the soil, but are cut and slightly withered flowers stuck into sand...

T. S. Eliot, *Essays*: 'Ben Jonson'

They are not safe teachers of morality; they tamper with it, like an experiment tried *in corpore vili*; and seem to regard the decomposition of the common affections, and the dissolution of the strict bonds of society, as an agreeable study, and a careless pastime.

William Hazlitt, *Lectures on the Age of Elizabeth: On Beaumont and Fletcher*

How I doe love thee *Beaumont*, and thy *Muse* / That unto me dost such religion use! / How I doe feare my selfe, that am not worth / The least indulgent thought thy pen drops forth! / At once thou mak'st me happie, and unmak'st; / And giving largely to me, more thou tak'st. / What fate is mine, that so it selfe bereaves? / What art is thine, that so thy friend deceives? / When even there, where most thou praysest mee, / For writing better, I must envie thee. /

Ben Jonson, *Epigrammes*

Bards of Passion and of Mirth / Ye have left your souls on earth! / Have ye souls in heaven too, / Double lived in regions new? /

John Keats, *Ode* inscribed in his copy of *The Fair Maid of the Inn*

I confess to a condescending tolerance for Beaumont and Fletcher . . . The pair wrote a good deal that was pretty disgraceful; but at all events they had been educated out of the possibility of writing Titus Andronicus.

George Bernard Shaw, in *Saturday Review*, 19 February 1898

*Beaumont* bringing the Ballast of Judgement, *Fletcher* the Sail of Phantasie, but compounding a Poet to admiration . . . It is reported of them, that meeting once in a tavern, to contrive the rude Draught of a Tragedy, *Fletcher* undertook to *kill the King* therein, whose words being overheard by a Listener (though his loyalty was not to be blamed herein) he was accused of High Treason, till the Mistake soon appearing, that the Plot was only against a Dramatick and Scenicall King, all wound off in Merriement.

William Winstanley, *Lives of the Most Famous English Poets*

*See also* John Fletcher, Shakespeare

## BEAVERBROOK, LORD (WILLIAM MAXWELL AITKEN)

1879–1964 Newspaper Magnate

My principle is – take a trick while you can and go on with the game.

On himself, Letter to F. B. Edwards, 6 March 1930

I can give it and I can take it.

On himself, Letter to Tom Driberg, 3 December 1952

. . . a Maxi-millionaire.

On himself, comment to William Gerhardie, in A. J. P. Taylor, *Beaverbrook*

. . . there are many other people to whom it will be easy to talk. Chief among these is Beaverbrook. He is a magnet to all young men, and I warn you if you talk to him no good will come of it. Beware of flattery.

Clement Attlee, speaking to junior Labour ministers, June 1945

Beaverbrook is so pleased to be in the Government that he is like the town tart who has finally married the Mayor!

Beverley Baxter, in Henry Channon, Diary, 12 June 1940

. . . he likes me and I like him, but that would not prevent him doing me in.

David Lloyd George, in A. J. Sylvester, Diary, 2 January 1932

. . . so long as there is a battle on, B[eaverbrook] will behave as a great and loyal fighter. But once the battle is over and victory is assured, B. will get bored and will create battles, if necessary in his own party. His pugnacity destroys both his judgment and his decent feeling. If they ally themselves with B. they must think of some bone to give him later which will keep him busy. He lives only by opposition: if he cannot find an opposition he creates one.

Harold Nicolson, advice to Sir Oswald Mosley, Diary, 6 November 1930

If Max gets to Heaven he won't last long. He will be chucked out for trying to pull off a merger between Heaven and Hell . . . after having secured a controlling interest in key subsidiary companies in both places, of course.

H. G. Wells, in A. J. P. Taylor, *Beaverbrook*

## BECKET, *see under* THOMAS À BECKET

## BECKFORD, WILLIAM

1759–1844 Novelist, Art Collector

. . . On Hartford Bridge, we changed horses at an Inn where the great Apostle of Paederasty Beckford! sojourned for the night, we tried in vain to see the Martyr of Prejudice, but could not.

Lord Byron, Letter to Francis Hodgson, 25 June 1809

Restless, half-sincere charlatans, like d'Annunzio, have an undying attraction for those whose day-dreams need stimulating; and myth always gathers round very rich men. Beckford has both appeals, and it is not surprising that fascinated historians have made him an influence on the Gothic Revival. This suggestion was made in Beckford's day, and was not well received. 'No,' he said, 'I have enough sins to answer for without having that laid to my charge.'

Kenneth Clark, *The Gothic Revival*

Mr Beckford has undoubtedly shown himself an industrious *bijoutier*, a prodigious virtuoso, an accomplished patron of unproductive labour, an enthusiastic collector of expensive trifles . . . The author of Vathek is a scholar; the proprietor of Fonthill has travelled abroad, and has seen all the finest remains of antiquity and boasted specimens of modern art. Why not lay his hands on some of these? He had power to carry them away . . . Hardly an article of any consequence that does not seem to be labelled to the following effect – 'This is mine, and there is no one else in the whole world in whom it can inspire the least interest, or any feeling beyond a momentary surprise!'

William Hazlitt, *Fonthill Abbey*

A male Horace Walpole.

J. G. Lockhart, in *Quarterly Review*, June 1834

He lived a strictly secluded life. A wall twelve feet high surrounded his estate [at Fonthill], and, at the heavy double gates, servants were stationed with orders to exclude strangers. It was a rare mark of favour to be invited inside the entrance, and it is said that even George IV was denied a sight of the Abbey. Strange stories began to circulate of what went on there, but the truth is that Beckford lived absorbed in his books and his building, with only his doctor and one or two artists for company, and an Italian dwarf as his personal attendant. We are told that the sight of this hideous little creature opening the Abbey doors, thirty feet high, provided another of those contrasts that so delighted his master.

Osbert Sitwell and Margaret Barton, *Sober Truth*

## BEDE, THE 'VENERABLE'

673–735 Historian

Northumbria was fortunate . . . in having in this twilight scene a chronicler . . . whose words have descended to us out of the long silence of the past. Bede, a monk of high ability, working unknown in the recesses of the Church, now comes forward as the most effective and almost the only audible voice from the British islands in these dim times . . . He alone attempts to paint for us, and, so far as he can, explain the spectacle of Anglo-Saxon England in its first phase.

Winston Churchill, *History of the English-Speaking People*

O venerable Bede! / The saint, the scholar from a circle freed / Of toil stupendous, in a hallowed seat / Of learning where thou heard'st the billows beat / On a wild coast, rough monitors to feed / Perpetual industry. Sublime Recluse! / The recreant soul, that dares to shun the debt / Imposed on human kind, must first forget / Thy diligence, thy unrelaxing use / Of a long life; and in the hour of death, / The last dear service of thy passing breath! /

William Wordsworth, *Ecclesiastical Sonnets*

## BEDLOE, WILLIAM

1650–80 Perjurer

The Lord is pleased when Man does cease to sin; / The Divil is pleased when he a soul does win; / The World is pleased when every Rascal dies: / So all are pleased, for here Will Bedloe lies. /

Anon., *Epitaph*

Sad fate! our valiant Captain Bedloe / In earth's cold bed lies with his head low; / Who to his last made out the Plot / And swearing, di'd upon the spot. / Sure Death was Popishly affected / She had our witness else protected; / Or downright Papist, or the jade / A Papist is in masquerade. /

Richard Duke, *Funeral Tears upon the Death of Captain William Bedloe*

One *Bedlow*, a man of inferior note.

John Eveyln, Diary, 18 July 1679

## BEECHAM, THOMAS

1820–1907 Industrialist

Hark! the Herald Angels sing, / Beecham's Pills are just the thing. /

Anon., *circa* 1892, subsequently used by Beecham in his advertising campaigns

There is a small house next to the stables on the Lawn Farm, Cropredy, where Thomas Beecham of Beecham's Pill Fame, used to live as a shepherd, and where he used to make the knitting sheaths that he gave to some of his old friends . . . According to the old tales he experimented while he was there, and when he got on in the world a bit, he used to send some of the old people in the village a box of his famous pills with a guinea at the bottom. That is how they came to be known to 'be worth a guinea a box.'

Anon., in *Banbury Guardian*, 29 December 1932

It seems he owed his success to a single phrase. As he stood in the market place at St Helens selling his pills, a woman came to him to buy, saying they were worth a guinea a box.

Anon., in *Witney Gazette*, 13 April 1907

## BEECHAM, SIR THOMAS

1879–1961 Conductor

Indeed I was the most ordinary and, in some ways, the most satisfactory kind of youngster any parents could wish to have. I disliked noise of any sort, never indulged in it myself, was a model of taciturnity and gentle melancholy, and altogether an embryonic hero for a Bulwer-Lytton novel.

On himself, *A Mingled Chime*

I have always been noted for my instability. I am a very, very low brow.

On himself, reported by Adam Bell, in *Evening Standard*, 8 March 1961

I am not the greatest conductor in this country. On the other hand I'm better than any damned foreigner.

On himself, as reported by Noel Goodwin, in *Daily Express*, 9 March 1961

At a rehearsal I let the orchestra play as they like. At the concert I make them play as *I* like.

On himself, in Neville Cardus, *Sir Thomas Beecham*

He conducted like a dancing dervish.
Sir John Barbirolli, in Charles Reid, *John Barbirolli*

One day there was a face strange to him among the woodwind. 'Er, Mr—?' 'Ball' came the reply. 'I beg your pardon?' 'Ball, Sir Thomas.' 'Ball? Ah – *Ball*. Very singular.'
Neville Cardus, *Sir Thomas Beecham*

. . . I never heard him refer to religion. To women he referred once, saying that none of them was worth the loss of a night's sleep.
*Ibid.*

Occasionally his conducting was as slapdash as well could be; to such a level of unconscious bluff on the rostrum could he descend that often I have blushed for him. The finale of the Seventh Symphony of Beethoven acted on him as red rag to a bull.
*Ibid.*

. . . For the impish joy he brought to music, the martinet Arturo Toscanini dismissed him as *pagliaccio* – 'buffoon'.
Gerald Jackson, in *Reader's Digest*, July 1972

He would address a choir: 'Ladies and gentlemen, if you will make a point of singing *All we, like sheep, have gone astray* with a little less satisfaction, we shall meet the aesthetical as well as the theological requirements.'
*Liverpool Echo and Evening Express*, 8 March 1961

At a dinner given in honour of his seventieth birthday, when messages of congratulation from great musicians all over the world were being read out, he was heard to murmur: 'What, nothing from Mozart?'
Patricia Young, *Great Performers*

*See also* Frederick Delius

## BEECHER, HENRY WARD

1813–87 Clergyman, Abolitionist

He slapped the backs of all men, he tickled the ribs of almost all the current ideas, and he kissed a surprising proportion of the women.
Sinclair Lewis, Introduction to Paxton Hibben, *Henry Ward Beecher: An American Portrait*

He came out for the right side of every question – always a little too late.
*Ibid.*

As a preacher he is a landscape painter of Christianity.
Sen. Oliver H. Smith, *Early Indiana Trials and Reminiscences*

In Boston the human race is divided into 'the Good, the Bad, and the Beechers.'
The Rev. W. M. Taylor, in *Scottish Review*, October 1859

## BEERBOHM, SIR HENRY MAXIMILIAN (MAX)

1872–1956 Author, Cartoonist

I was a modest, good-humoured boy. It is Oxford that has made me insufferable.
On himself, *More*

Very little gold has come the way of Sir Max. Although few writers have acquired his réclame – he has since his first success had a legendary quality – yet his books were sold in very small quantities and today are out of print. It is rather terrible to know that the successful Somerset Maugham criticized Max as being someone whose shirt-cuffs were generally dirty.
Cecil Beaton, *The Strenuous Years*

It always makes me cross when Max is called 'The Incomparable Max'. He is not incomparable at all, and in fact compares very poorly with Harold Nicolson, as a stylist, a wit, and an observer of human nature. He is a shallow, affected, self-conscious fribble – so there.

Vita Sackville-West, Letter to Harold Nicolson, 9 December 1959

He has the most remarkable and seductive genius – and I should say about the smallest in the world.

Lytton Strachey, Letter to Clive Bell, 4 December 1917

We went to tea with Max Beerbohm who is in a little house near Stroud. A delicious little old dandy, very quick in mind still. A touch of Ronnie Knox and of Harold Acton. 'The tongue has, correct me if I am wrong, seven follicles in adult life.' Much of what he said would have been commonplace but for his exquisite delivery.

Evelyn Waugh, Diary, 17 May 1947

Tell me, when you are alone with Max, does he take off his face and reveal his mask?

Oscar Wilde, in W. H. Auden, *Forewords and Afterwords*

The Gods bestowed on Max the gift of perpetual old age.

Oscar Wilde, in Vincent O'Sullivan, *Aspects of Wilde*

Max like a Cheshire cat. Orbicular. Jowled. Blue eyed . . . all curves.

Virginia Woolf, *A Writer's Diary*, 1 November 1928

*See also* Aubrey Beardsley

## BELL, ALEXANDER GRAHAM

1847–1922 Inventor

Mr Thomas A. Watson, Bell's assistant, relates that it was on March 10, 1876, over a line extending between two rooms in a building at No. 5 Exeter Place, Boston, that the first complete sentence was ever spoken by Bell and heard by Watson, who recorded it in his notebook at the time. It consisted of these words: 'Mr Watson, come here; I want you.' Thus the telephone was born.

John J. Carty, in *The Smithsonian Report for 1922*

## BELLOC, JOSEPH HILAIRE PIERRE RENÉ

1870–1953 Author, Historian

When I am dead, I hope it may be said: / 'His sins were scarlet, but his books were read.' /

On himself, *On His Books*

Mr Hilaire Belloc / Is a case for legislation ad hoc. / He seems to think nobody minds / His books being all of different kinds. /

E. C. Bentley, *Biography for Beginners*

You, Mister Belloc, thought it fine / To put one's faith in God and Wine; / You see the Pickle I am in / Who put my faith in Men and Gin. /

W. Bridges-Adams, *Reproach*

In so far as he is a traditionalist, he is an English traditionalist. But when he was specially a revolutionist, he was in the very exact sense a French Revolutionist. And it might be roughly symbolised by saying that he was an English poet but a French soldier.

G. K. Chesterton, *Autobiography*

Two buttocks of one bum.

T. Sturge Moore, on Belloc and Chesterton, in Stephen Potter, *Sense of Humour*

Wells and I, contemplating the Chesterbelloc, recognize at once a very amusing pantomime elephant, the front legs being that very exceptional and un-English individual Hilaire Belloc, and the hind legs that extravagant freak of French nature, G. K. Chesterton.

George Bernard Shaw, 'The Chesterbelloc', in *New Age*, 15 February 1908

Poor Mr Belloc looked as though the grave were the only place for him. He has grown a splendid white beard and in his cloak, which with his hat he wore indoors and always, he seemed an archimandrite. He lost and stole and whatever went into his pockets, toast, cigarettes, books never appeared, like the reverse of a conjuror's hat. He talked incessantly, proclaiming with great clarity the grievances of 40 years ago . . . At times he was coaxed by the women to sing and then with face alight with simple joy and many lapses of memory, he quavered out old French marching songs and snatches from the music halls of his youth. He is conscious of being decrepit and forgetful, but not of being a bore.

Evelyn Waugh, Diary, 1 May 1945

*See also* G. K. Chesterton, P. G. Wodehouse

## BELLOWS, GEORGE

1882–1925 Painter, Lithographer

Perhaps the ingredients of his art can best be suggested by the story told of his small daughter Anne, who, at the age of four, was serving tea with a set of child's china to three invisible guests. Asked who they were, she replied solemnly, 'God, Rembrandt, and Emma Goldman.'

Charles H. Morgan, *George Bellows*

George was six feet tall and weighed around one hundred and eighty pounds; he looked and moved like an athlete, which he was. He had a rich baritone voice, took vocal lessons, and liked to sing for his friends. He had a wonderful sense of humor and a quick wit as demonstrated in his already well-known retort to Joseph Pennell. When the latter accused him of being a slacker for having painted the execution of Edith Cavell without having witnessed it, Bellows replied that, though he had not witnessed the execution, neither had Leonardo da Vinci been present at the Last Supper!

Eugene Speicher, *A Personal Reminiscence*

## BENCHLEY, ROBERT CHARLES

1889–1945 Humorist, Critic, Actor

I do most of my work sitting down; that's where I shine.

On himself, in *The Treasury of Humorous Quotations*

I haven't been abroad in so long that I almost speak English without an accent.

On himself, in Robert E. Drennan ed., *Wit's End*

A friend once told Benchley that a particular drink he was drinking was slow poison, to which Benchley replied, 'So who's in a hurry?'

*Ibid.*

It took me fifteen years to discover that I had no talent for writing, but I couldn't give it up because by that time I was too famous.

*Ibid.*

Drawing on my fine command of language I said nothing.

On himself, in A. K. Adams, *The Home Book of Humorous Quotations*

Arriving home with a group of friends one rainy evening Benchley suggested (though some have attributed the remark to Aleck Woollcott), 'Let's get out of these wet clothes and into a dry martini.'

Robert E. Drennan ed., *Wit's End*

Robert Benchley has a style that is weak and lies down frequently to rest.

Max Eastman, *Enjoyment of Laughter*

When he died, one of them said, 'They're going to have to stay up late in heaven now.'

James Thurber, *Credos and Curios*

## BENJAMIN, JUDAH PHILIP

1811–84 Confederate Politician, Lawyer

Mr Benjamin was a brilliant lawyer, but he knew as much about war as an Arab knows of the Sermon on the Mount.

Anon. Confederate soldier, in Alexander Hunter, *Johnny Reb and Billy Yank*

Judah P. Benjamin, the dapper Jew, / Seal-sleek, black-eyed, lawyer and epicure, / Able, well-hated, face alive with life, / Looked round the council-chamber with the slight / Perpetual smile he held before himself / Continually like a silk-ribbed fan. / Behind the fan, his quick, shrewd fluid mind / Weighed Gentiles in an old balance . . . / The mind behind the silk-ribbed fan / Was a dark prince, clothed in an Eastern stuff, / Whose brown hands cupped about a crystal egg / That filmed with coloured cloud. The egg stared searching. /

Stephen Vincent Benét, *John Brown's Body*

. . . the Mephistopheles of the Southern Confederacy.

James G. Blaine, in S. I. Nieman, *Judah Benjamin*

## BENNETT, ENOCH ARNOLD

1867–1931 Novelist

I cannot conceive that any author should write, as the de Goncourts say they wrote, 'for posterity' . . . I would not care a bilberry for posterity. I should be my own justest judge, from whom there would be no appeal; and having satisfied him (whether he was right or wrong) I should be content – as an artist. As a *man*, I should be disgusted if I could not earn plenty of money and the praise of the discriminating.

On himself, *Journal*, 28 January 1897

When Arnold Bennett lay dying in his luxury flat at Chiltern Court, with the straw spread lavishly across the width of Marylebone Road, I reflected, as sadly I stood and looked up at his windows, that the astute A.B., were he conscious, would have been the first to point out how obsolete in our day of pneumatic tyres and smooth roads, with no sound but the hooting of horns and the changing of gear, is a custom designed to deaden the noise of wooden wheel and iron hoof on cobblestones. Presently, I hoped, he would come to and expose the archaism in an article in the *Evening Standard.* When I passed again the straw had been removed, and Arnold Bennett was dead.

William Gerhardie, *Memoirs of a Polyglot*

'Twas Arnold Bennett's habit to deplore / That younger writers did not publish more / And yet it would be easier to assess / His own position had he written less. /

Kensal Green (Colin Hurry), *Premature Epitaphs*

The psychology of an artist cannot be reduced to the simple contrasts of a morality play. Bennett's naked careerism may have done him lasting damage as a writer, yet without it, would he have had any career at all? *Psychologiser, c'est tout pardonner* – but there is surely a very good case for supposing that Bennett's cruder ambitions were bound up with his stamina, his curiosity, his appetite for experience, with qualities which were indispensable to him as a novelist.

John Gross, *The Rise and Fall of the Man of Letters*

Bennett – sort of pig in clover.

D. H. Lawrence, Letter to Aldous Huxley, 27 March 1928

The Hitler of the book-racket.

Percy Wyndham Lewis (on

Bennett's powers as literary editor of *Evening Standard*), *Blasting and Bombardiering*

I remember that once, beating his knee with his clenched fist to force the words from his writhing lips, he said: 'I am a nice man.' He was.

Somerset Maugham, *The Vagrant Mood*

1908 saw a stirring. By 1912 it was established, at least in Ormond St, that Arnold Bennett was inadequate, that British impressionism was too soft.

Ezra Pound, in *Criterion*, 1937

Arnold Bennett knew his eggs. Whatever his interest in good writing, he never showed the public anything but his AVARICE. Consequently they adored him.

Ezra Pound, Letter to Laurence Pollinger, May 1936

Nickel cash-register Bennett.

Ezra Pound, Letter to Michael Roberts, July 1937

Never have I known anyone else so cheerfully objective as Bennett. His world was as bright and hard surfaced as crockery – his *persona* was, as it were, a hard, definite china figurine. What was not precise, factual and contemporary, could not enter into his consciousness. He was friendly and self-assured; he knew quite clearly that we were both on our way to social distinction and incomes of several thousands a year . . . He had a through ticket and a time-table – and he proved to be right.

H. G. Wells, *Experiment in Autobiography*

The trouble is, whenever I do a thing, Arnold does it too, but twice as posh.

H. G. Wells, in Osbert Sitwell, *Noble Essences*

He can make a book so well constructed and solid in its craftmanship that it is difficult for the most exacting of critics to see through what chink or crevice decay can creep in. And yet – if life should refuse to live there?

Virginia Woolf, *The Common Reader*

Arnold Bennett died last night, which leaves me sadder than I should have supposed. A loveable genuine man: impeded, somehow a little awkward in life; well meaning; ponderous; kindly; coarse; knowing he was coarse; dimly floundering and feeling for something else; glutted with success; wounded in his feelings . . . Some real understanding power, as well as gigantic absorbing power. Queer how one regrets the dispersal of anybody who seemed – as I say – genuine: who had direct contact with life – for he abused me; and yet I rather wished him to go on abusing me; and me abusing him.

Virginia Woolf, *A Writer's Diary*, 28 March 1931

*See also* Virginia Woolf

## BENNETT, HENRY, *see under* ARLINGTON

## BENNETT, JAMES GORDON JR

1841–1918 Editor

He is a human paradox. Always a patrician, he is frequently a buffoon. To him the whole world is a joke, but to no one else will he permit the privilege of looking upon it in any but a serious manner.

Leo L. Redding, 'Bennett of the Herald', in *Everybody's Magazine*, June 1914

He it was who originated the definition of a great editor as one who knows where hell is going to break loose next and how to get a reporter first on the scene – a definition attributed to various others, but belonging to him and reflecting some light upon his methods of thought.

*Ibid.*

Under the tigerish proprietor Bennett, with his fickleness and brutality, men were unjustly fired or demoted. Even the most deserving staff members were reduced in rank or in pay through young Bennett's erratic and contemptible conduct. Serving his evil system of ill-usage was as desperate as serving in the French Foreign Legion.

R. W. Stallmann, *Stephen Crane*

## BENNY, JACK (BENJAMIN KUBELSKY)

1894–1974 Comedian

I was born in Waukegan a long, long *long* time ago. As a matter of fact, our rabbi was an Indian . . . he used a tomahawk . . . I was eight days old . . . what did I know?

On himself, in Irving A. Fein, *Jack Benny*

I'm not able to sleep any more. You probably ask, 'Why can't he sleep? He has money, beauty, talent, vigor and many teeth' – but the possession of all these riches has nothing to do with it. I see Bund members dropping down my chimney, Comrades under my bed, Fifth Columnists in my closets, a bearded dwarf, called Surtax, doing a gavotte on my desk with a little lady known as Confiscation. I'm setting aside a small sum for poison which I'm secreting in a little sack under my mattress.

On himself, Letter to Arthur Sheekman, 12 June 1940

I don't want to say that Jack Benny is cheap, but he's got short arms and carries his money low in his pockets.

Fred Allen, in Irving A. Fein, *Jack Benny*

When Jack Benny plays the violin, it sounds as if the strings are still back in the cat.

*Ibid.*

Is Mr Benny tight? Well, a little snug, perhaps . . . If he can't take it with him, he ain't gonna go.

Eddie 'Rochester' Anderson, in *ibid.*

## BENTHAM, JEREMY

1748–1832 Political Theorist

It seems to me, all deniers of Godhood, and all lip-believers of it, are bound to be Benthamites, if they have courage and honesty. Benthamism is an *eyeless* Heroism: the Human Species, like a hapless blinded Samson grinding in the Philistine Mill, clasps convulsively the pillars of its Mill; brings huge ruin down, but ultimately deliverance withal.

Thomas Carlyle, *On Heroes and Hero Worship*

Hunt told me after of the prodigious power of Bentham's mind. 'He proposed,' said Hunt, 'a reform in the handle of battledores!' 'Did he?' said I with awful respect. 'He did,' said Hunt, 'taking in everything, you see, like the elephant's trunk, which lifts alike a pin or twelve hundredweight. Extraordinary mind!'

Benjamin Haydon, *Autobiography and Memoirs*

His eye is quick and lively, but it glances not from object to object, but from thought to thought. He is evidently a man occupied with some train of fine and inward association. He regards people as no more than flies of a summer. He meditates the coming age. He hears and sees only what suits his purpose, or some 'foregone conclusion'; and looks out for facts and passing occurrences in order to put them into his logical machinery and grind them into the dust and powder of some subtle theory, as the miller looks out for grist to his mill.

William Hazlitt, *The Spirit of the Age*

The universal admission of Mr Bentham's great principle would, as far as we can see, produce no other effect than those orators who, while waiting for a meaning, gain time (like bankers paying in sixpences during a run) by uttering words that mean nothing, would substitute 'the greatest happiness', or rather, as the longer phrase, 'the greatest happiness of the greatest number', for 'under existing circumstances', – 'now that I am on my legs', – and 'Mr Speaker, I, for one, am free to say'. In fact principles of this sort resemble those forms which are sold by law-stationers, with blanks for the names of parties, and for special circumstances of every case – mere customary headings and conclusions which are equally at the command of the most honest and of the most unrighteous claimant.

T. B. Macaulay, *Miscellaneous Writings*: 'Westminster Reviewer's Defence of Mill'

The arch-philistine Jeremy Bentham was the insipid, pedantic, leather-tongued oracle of the bourgeois intelligence of the Nineteenth Century.

Karl Marx, *Das Kapital*

The father of English innovation, both in doctrines and in institutions, is Bentham: he is the great *subversive*, or, in the language of continental philosophers, the great *critical*, thinker of his age and country.

John Stuart Mill, *Dissertations*: 'Bentham'

It is the introduction into the philosophy of human conduct, of this method of detail – of this practice of never reasoning about wholes till they have been resolved into their parts, nor about abstractions till they have been translated into realities – that constitutes the originality of Bentham in philosophy, and makes him the great reformer of the moral and political branch of it.

*Ibid.*

Bentham and the utilitarians interpret 'justice' as 'equality': when two men's interests clash, the right course is that which produces the greatest total of happiness, regardless of which of the two enjoys it, or how it is shared among them. If more is given to the better man than to the worse, that is because, in the long run, the general happiness is increased by rewarding virtue and punishing vice, not because of an ultimate ethical doctrine that the good deserve more than the bad.

Bertrand Russell, *History of Western Philosophy*

Bentham's adoption of the principle of 'the greatest happiness of the greatest number' was no doubt due to democratic feeling, but it involved opposition to the doctrine of the rights of man, which he bluntly characterized as 'nonsense'.

*Ibid.*

There is an obvious lacuna in Bentham's system. If every man always pursues his own pleasure, how are we to secure that the legislator shall pursue the pleasure of mankind in general? Bentham's own instinctive benevolence (which his psychological theories prevented him from noticing) concealed the problem from him.

*Ibid.*

Apparently Bentham thought that human beings had but two desires, gain and pleasure, and he accepted those desires as the facts of our condition (he hated St Paul) and tried to make of them a philosophy whose keystone was an eloquent defence of usury. He would have been at home in New York.

Gore Vidal, *Burr*

*See also* John Stuart Mill

## BENTINCK, WILLIAM, EARL OF PORTLAND

1649–1709 Politician

The Earl of Sunderland had a very mean opinion of the Earl of Portland; and said, upon Keppel's being sent to him by the king upon some business, 'This young man brings and carries a message well; but Portland is so dull an animal that he can neither fetch nor carry.'

Speaker Arthur Onslow, Note in the Oxford edition of Burnet, *A History of My Own Time*

## BENTLEY, RICHARD

1662–1742 Scholar

The special glory of England in classical scholarship.

G. N. Clark, *The Seventeenth Century*

While Bentley, long to wrangling schools confin'd, / And, but by books, acquainted with mankind, / Dares, in the fulness of the pedant's pride, / Rhyme, tho' no genius; though no judge, decide; / Yet he, prime pattern of the captious arts, / Out-tibbalding poor Tibbald, tops his parts, / Holds high the scourge o'er each fam'd author's head; / Nor are their graves a refuge for the dead. /

David Mallet, *On Verbal Criticism*

As many quit the streams that murm'ring fall / To lull the sons of Marg'ret and Clare-hall, / Where Bentley late tempestuous wont to sport / In troubled waters, but now sleeps in Port. / Before them march'd that awful Aristarch; / Plough'd was his front with many a deep Remark: / His Hat, which never vail'd to human pride, / Walker with rev'rence took, and laid aside. / Low bow'd the rest: He, kingly, did but nod, / So upright Quakers please both Man and God. / Mistress! dismiss that rabble from your throne: / Avaunt – is Aristarchus yet unknown? / Thy mighty Scholiast, whose unweary'd pains / Made Horace dull, and humbled Milton's strains. /

Alexander Pope, *The Dunciad*, book 4

Tall, but without Shape and Comeliness; Large, but without strength or Proportion. His Armour was patch'd up of a thousand incoherent Pieces; and the Sound of it, as he march'd, was loud and dry, like that made by the Fall of a Sheet of Lead, which an *Etesian* Wind blows suddenly down from the Roof of some Steeple. His Helmet was of old rusty Iron, but the Vizard was Brass, which tainted by his Breath, corrupted into Copperas, nor wanted Gall from the same Fountain; so that whenever provoked by Anger or Labour, an atramentous Quality, of most malignant Nature, was seen to distil from his Lips.

Jonathan Swift, *Battle of the Books*

## BENTON, THOMAS HART

1792–1858 Politician

Mr President, sir . . . I never quarrel, sir. But sometimes I fight, sir; and whenever I fight, sir, a funeral follows, sir.

On himself, in John F. Kennedy, *Profiles in Courage*

. . . the doughty knight of the stuffed cravat.

John Quincy Adams, in Alfred Steinberg, *The First Ten*

If he ever forgot or forgave an intended injury, only his creator knew it.

James Birch, in William M. Meigs, *The Life of Thomas Hart Benton*

. . . a temporary people's man, remarkable chiefly for his pomposity – swelling amidst his piles of papers and books, [looked] like a being designed by nature to be a good-humored barber (!) but forced by fate to make himself into a mock-heroic senator.

Harriet Martineau, in William Nisbet Chambers, *Old Bullion Benton: Senator from the New West*

## BENTON, THOMAS HART

1889–1975 Artist

A little, swarthy and cocky man. Benton resembles a well-nourished Sicilian bootblack rather than a mid-west oldstock American. When I first got acquainted with him, I called upon him frequently, apparently always in time to help him carry about the studio his 400 lb. murals which he was painting for the New School of Social Research. (I posed for the negro with the drill and learned egg-tempera as a reward.) The time was summer and it was amusing to watch Benton, muscular in his underwear, sit low in an arm-chair, survey the mural, suddenly load his brush with a lot of tempera goo, crouch like a cat, spring across the room in a flying tackle, scrub the brush around in great circles, catch his breath, and then resume his place in the chair.

Benton is a colorful, scrappy, uncouth person, with a demonic energy and a strong tendency to publicize himself. All this is to his credit. If he were to hibernate or vegetate or dress like Fred Astaire, he would be hamstrung undoubtedly. Let him have his flash-bulbs, his harmonicas, his windmills, his mules, his little Pickaninnies and Persephones, it's all part of his constitution.

Reginald Marsh, 'Thomas Benton', *Demcourier*

## BERENSON, BERNARD

1865–1959 Art Historian

Life has taught me that it is not for our faults that we are disliked and even hated but for our qualities.

On himself, *The Passionate Sightseer*, from the diaries, 1957

He was supposed to have invented a trick by which one could tell infallibly the authorship of any Italian painting, and he made an enemy of every owner of a picture he would not ascribe to Raphael, Giorgione, Tintoretto or Titian. He ranked with astrologers, palmists and fortune-tellers, while he was a pet of rich collectors.

Van Wyck Brooks, *The Confident Years: 1885–1915*

. . . a little tiny man, more of a genial fox than roaring lion, spruce and grey, so formally and neatly dressed that he looked like a miniature banker in Wall Street; though his voice was gentler.

Eric Linklater, *The Art of Adventure*

Little wonder that the last years of his life had become so precious to him that, as he said, he would willingly stand at 'street corners hat in hand begging passers-by to drop their unused minutes into it.'

John Walker, Introduction to Hanna Kiel ed., *The Bernard Berenson Treasury*

## BERESFORD, WILLIAM CARR

1768–1854 General

Wellington paid the greatest tribute to him when he declared that if he were removed by death or illness he would recommend Beresford to succeed him, not because he was a great general, but because he alone could 'feed an army'.

Henry Morse Stephens, in *Dictionary of National Biography*

## BERKELEY, GEORGE, BISHOP

1685–1753 Philosopher

observed that though we are satisfied his doctrine is not true, it is impossible to refute it. I never shall forget the alacrity with which Johnson answered, striking his foot with mighty force against a large stone, till he rebounded from it, 'I refute it *thus*.'

James Boswell, *Life of Johnson*

When Bishop Berkeley said 'there was no matter', / And proved it – 'twas no matter what he said: / They say his system 'tis in vain to batter, / Too subtle for the airiest human head; / And yet who can believe it? I would shatter / Gladly all matters down to stone or lead, / Or adamant, to find the world a spirit, / And wear my head, denying that I wear it. /

What a sublime discovery 'twas to make the / Universe universal egotism, / That all's ideal – *all ourselves*! /

Lord Byron, *Don Juan*, canto xi

There was a young man who said, 'God / Must think it exceedingly odd / If he finds that this tree / Continues to be / When there's no one about in the Quad.' /

Ronald Knox, *Limerick*

Dear Sir:
Your astonishment's odd: / *I* am always about in the quad. / And that's why the tree / Will continue to be, / Since observed by, / *Yours faithfully*, / GOD. /

Anon., Rejoinder

And God-appointed Berkeley that proved all things a dream, / That this pragmatical, preposterous pig of a world, its farrow / that so solid seem, / Must vanish on the instant if the mind but change its theme. /

William Butler Yeats, *Blood and the Moon*

## BESSBOROUGH, LADY (HENRIETTA FRANCES PONSONBY)

1761–1821 Society Woman

. . . good-natured tumultuous Lady Bessborough.

Lady Granville, Letter to Lady Morpeth, 17 August 1820

## BETTERTON, THOMAS

1635–1710 Actor, Dramatist

For who can hold to see the Foppish Town / Admire so bad a Wretch as Betterton? / Is't for his Legs, his Shoulders or his Face, / His formal Stiffness, or his awkward Grace, / A Shop for Him had been the fittest place? / But Brawn Tom the Playhouse needs must chuse / The Villains Refuge, and Whores Rendezvouse: / Where being Chief, each playing Drab to swive, / He takes it as his chief prerogative. /

Anon., *Satyr on the Players, circa* 1684

When I acted the Ghost with Betterton, instead of my awing him, he terrified me. But divinity hung round that man.

Barton Booth, in Thomas Davies, *Dramatic Miscellanies*

*Betterton* had so just a sense of what was true or false Applause, that I have heard him say, he never thought any kind of it equal to an attentive Silence; that there were many ways of deceiving the Audience into a loud one; but to keep them husht and quiet was an Applause which only Truth and Merit could arrive at: of which Art there never was an equal Master to himself. From these various Excellencies, he had so full a possession of the Esteem and Regard of his Auditors, that upon his Entrance into every Scene, he seem'd to seize upon the Eyes and Ears of the giddy and inadvertent! To have talk'd or look'd another way would then have been thought Insensibility or Ignorance. In all his Soliloquies of Moment, the strong Intelligence of his Attitude and Aspect drew you into such an impatient Gaze, and eager Expectation, that you almost imbib'd the Sentiment with your Eye before the Ear could reach it.

Colley Cibber, *Apology for the Life of Colley Cibber*

Archbishop Tillotson was very well acquainted with Betterton, and continued that acquaintance, even after he was in that high station. One day, when Betterton came to see him at Lambeth, that prelate asked him how it came about that after he had made the most moving discourse that he could, was touched deeply with it himself, and spoke it as feelingly as he was able, yet he could never move people in the Church near so much as the other did on stage? 'That,' says Betterton, 'I think is easy to be accounted for: 'tis because you are only *telling* them a story, and I am *showing* them facts.'

Joseph Spence, *Anecdotes*

## BETTY, WILLIAM HENRY WEST

1791–1874 Actor

Betty is performing here, I fear, very ill, his figure is that of a hippopotamus, his face like the bull and *mouth* on the pannels of a heavy coach, his arms are fins fattened out of shape, his voice the gargling of an alderman with the quinsy, and his acting altogether ought to be natural, for it certainly is like nothing that *Art* has ever yet exhibited on the stage.

Lord Byron, Letter to Lady Melbourne, September 1812

## BEVAN, ANEURIN

1897–1960 Politician

Bevan Done and lost his friends – one-quarter Bloody Revolution one-quarter Pacifist one-half Same policy as Tories but with jobs.

Lord Beaverbrook, April 1958, in A. J. P. Taylor, *Beaverbrook*

He was like a fire in a room on a cold winter's day.

Constance Cummings, in Michael Foot, *Aneurin Bevan*

The outrageous ranter started so softly; his wit was delicate; he dealt in paradox and satire. His sentences were uttered with the perfect, if unconscious, timing of an actor. He seemed to wrestle with the problem of his audience, and, as the argument mounted in intensity, the language became direct and simple. As he spoke, a glowing clarity pierced the clouds and the story ended in a blaze of sunshine . . . He was always primarily a debater; his perorations might rise to a tremendous emotional climax, but the argument always came from the intellect.

Michael Foot, *Aneurin Bevan*

Nye was born old and died young.

Jennie Lee, in *ibid.*

He enjoys prophesying the imminent fall of the capitalist system, and is prepared to play a part, any part, in its burial, except that of mute.

Harold Macmillan, addressing the House of Commons, 1934

Goebbels, though not religious, must thank Heaven / For dropping in his lap Aneurin Bevan; / And, doubtless, this pious mood invokes / An equal blessing on the trusty Stokes. / How well each does his work as a belittler / Of Germany's arch-enemy! Heil Hitler. /

A. A. Milne, on Bevan's opposition to Churchill, in the *News Chronicle*, Autumn 1942

## BEVIN, ERNEST

1881–1951 Statesman

. . . When I took this job on I knew it wouldn't be a daisy. In fact, no Foreign

Secretary has had to keep so many plates in the air at the same time. But what I said to my colleagues at the time was this: 'I'll take on the job. But don't expect results before three years.' Now it's patience you want in this sort of thing. I'm not going to throw my weight about 'ere in Paris. I'm just going to sit sturdy 'ere and 'elp.

On himself, at the Paris Peace Conference, 1946, in Harold Nicolson, Diary

A turn-up in a million.

On himself, in *Dictionary of National Biography*

A speech from Ernest Bevin on a major occasion had all the horrific fascination of a public execution. If the mind was left immune, eyes and ears and emotions were riveted.

Michael Foot, *Aneurin Bevan*

. . . His public character had a curious duality. Capable of great suppleness in negotiation and sensitive to the mutual interests which made industrial co-operation desirable, he presented in public an image which was dogmatic, over-bearing, uncompromising, and egotistical. In negotiation he was a realist who understood the need for compromise. On the public platform he permitted himself every licence of venom, innuendo, and the grossest partiality.

Lord Francis-Williams, in the *Dictionary of National Biography*

The familiar saying that Bevin always treated the Soviet Union as if it were a breakaway faction of the Transport and General Workers' Union . . .

Kingsley Martin, *Harold Laski*

He objected to ideas only when others had them.

A. J. P. Taylor, *English History 1914–1945*

Bevin thought he was Palmerston wearing Keir Hardie's cloth cap, whereas he was really the Foreign Office's Charlie McCarthy.

Konni Zilliacus, in Kingsley Martin, *Harold Laski*

## BEWICK, THOMAS

1753–1828 Wood Engraver, Author, Naturalist

The nobles of his day left him to draw the frogs, and pigs, and sparrows – of his day, which seemed to him, in his solitude, the best types of its Nobility. No sight or thought of beautiful things was ever granted him; – no heroic creature, goddess-born – how much less any native Deity – ever shone upon him. To his utterly English mind, the straw of the sty, and its tenantry, were abiding truth; – the cloud of Olympus, and its tenantry, a child's dream. He could draw a pig, but not an Aphrodite.

John Ruskin, *Ariadne Florentina*

## BIERCE, AMBROSE GWINETT

1842–1914? Journalist, Author

I have the supremest contempt for my books – as books. As a journalist I believe I am unapproachable in my line; as an author, a slouch!

On himself, in Richard O'Connor, *Ambrose Bierce*

Born in a log cabin, he defied [Horatio] Alger's law and did not become President.

Clifton Fadiman, *The Selected Writings of Clifton Fadiman: Portrait of a Misanthrope*

He made a business of cracking skulls and ideas. Product of three disillusioning experiences, pioneer life, war, and journalistic uproars, he ended up with almost nothing that he could regard as sacred. He was an all-inclusive cynic.

C. Hartley Grattan, *Bitter Bierce*

He was close on to six feet tall, of military bearing, and of such extraordinary vitality that young ladies asserted they could feel him ten feet away.

*Ibid.*

Bierce would bury his best friend with a sigh of relief, and express satisfaction that he was done with him.

Jack London, in Paul Fatout, *Ambrose Bierce, The Devil's Lexicographer*

There was no more discretion in Bierce than you will find in a runaway locomotive.

H. L. Mencken, 'Ambrose Bierce', in *The American Scene*, selected and edited by Huntington Cairns

More than war wounds, more than asthma contracted in graveyards, more than bitterness engendered by domestic strife, more than disillusionment with an imperfect world, frontier journalism, through its unusual freedom, created the satirist who was later to be hailed as its anathema.

Franklin Walker, *San Francisco's Literary Frontier*

## BILLINGTON, ELIZABETH

1768–1818 Singer

Her face was beautiful and expressive, her figure graceful; her voice possessed a peculiar sweetness of tone, and was of great extent, but wanted what Dr Burney would call *calibre*. The most scientific songs she executed with bewitching taste and affecting pathos; and though her voice was not overpowerful, it possessed great variety, and a most perfect shake.

Anon., *The Manager's Note-Book*, 1837–8

When Haydn, the composer, called on Sir J. Reynolds, as he was engaged in painting the portrait of Mrs Billington, 'I like the portrait,' said Haydn, 'much; but you have painted Billington listening to the angels; you should rather have made the angels listening to her.'

George Raymond, *Memoirs of R. W. Elliston*

Her voice was powerful, and resembled the tone of a clarionet.

W. Clark Russell, *Representative Actors*

## BILLY THE KID (WILLIAM H. BONNEY)

1859–81 Desperado

All who ever knew Billy will testify that his polite, cordial and gentlemanly bearing invited confidence and promised protection – the first of which he never betrayed and the latter he was never known to withhold. Those who knew him best will tell you that in his most savage and dangerous moods his face always wore a smile. He eat [sic] and laughed, drank and laughed, rode and laughed, talked and laughed, fought and laughed, and killed and laughed.

Pat F. Garrett, *The Authentic Life of Billy the Kid*

## BINGHAM, GEORGE CALEB

1811–79 Painter

To Bingham's way of thinking, it always became necessary to leave the secluded life. He was an Aristotelian: he believed that there are a thousand ways to be wrong, but only one way to be right.

Albert Christ-Janer, *George Caleb Bingham of Missouri*

## BIRKENHEAD, EARL OF (FREDERICK EDWIN SMITH)

1872–1930 Statesman

The trouble with Lord Birkenhead is that he is so un-Christlike.

Margot Asquith, in C. M. Bowra, *Memories*

Your father fought hard and clean. He never concealed that he wanted the prizes of life. When they came to him he took them with dignity and without any illusions about their value. When hard knocks came he met them with great high spirits. He bore no man a grudge, and he never struck a foul blow.

Lord Beaverbrook, Letter to the second Lord Birkenhead, 21 September 1934

. . . this dark Hermes.

Henry Channon, Diary, 1 May 1934

. . . a man with the vision of an eagle but with a blind spot in his eye.

Andrew Bonar Law, 1917, in A. J. P. Taylor, *Beaverbrook*

## BLACK HAWK

1767–1838 War Chief of the Sauk Nation

I fought hard. But your guns were well aimed. The bullets flew like birds in the air, and whizzed by our ears like the wind through the trees. My warriors fell around me; it began to look dismal. I saw my evil day at hand. The sun rose dim on us in the morning, and at night it sank in a dark cloud, and looked like a ball of fire. That was the last sun that shone on Black Hawk. His heart is dead, and no longer beats quick in his bosom. He is now a prisoner to the white men; they will do with him as they wish. But he can stand torture and is not afraid of death. He is no coward. Black Hawk is an Indian.

On himself (upon his surrender in 1832), in T. C. McLuhan, *Touch the Earth*

I – am – a man – and you – are – another.

On himself (after his surrender upon meeting President Andrew Jackson), in Carl Sandburg, *Abraham Lincoln, The Prairie Years*

## BLACK, JOSEPH

1728–79 Scientist

In one department of his lecture he exceeded any I have ever known, the neatness and unvarying success with which all the manipulations of his experiments were performed. His correct eye and steady hand contributed to the one; his admirable precautions, foreseeing and providing for every emergency, secured the other. I have seen him pour boiling water or boiling acid from a vessel that had no spout into a tube, holding it at such a distance as made the stream's diameter small, and so vertical that not a drop was spilt . . . The long table on which the different processes had been carried out was as clean at the end of the lecture as it had been before the apparatus was planted upon it. Not a drop of liquid, not a grain of dust remained.

Henry, Lord Brougham, *Lives of Men of Letters and Science who flourished in the Time of George III*

He has less nonsense in his head than any man living.

Adam Smith, in Henry, Lord Brougham, *ibid.*

## BLACKMORE, SIR RICHARD

1653–1729 Poet

See who ne'er was nor will be half-read! / Who first sung Arthur, then sung Alfred; / Praised great Eliza in God's anger, / Till all true Englishmen cried, 'Hang her!' . . . / Maul'd human wit in one thick satire; / Next in three books sunk human nature: / Undid Creation at a jerk, / And of Redemption made damn'd work. / Then took his Muse at once, and dipt her / Full in the middle of the Scripture. /

John Gay, *Verses to be Placed Under the Picture of England's Arch-Poet*

He said, the criticks had done too much honour to Sir Richard Blackmore, by writing so much against him.
Samuel Johnson, in James Boswell, *Life of Johnson*

Remains a difficulty still, / To purchase fame by writing ill. / From Flecknoe down to Howard's time / How few have reached the low sublime! / For when our high-born Howard died, / Blackmore alone his place supplied. /
Jonathan Swift, *Poetry: A Rhapsody*

## BLACKSTONE, SIR WILLIAM

1723–80 Jurist

Any lawyer who writes so clearly as to be intelligible . . . is an enemy to his profession.
Francis Hargrave, in Croake James, *Curiosities of Law and Lawyers*

This legal classic is the poetry of the law, just as Pope is logic in poetry.
Judge John Marshall, in Albert J. Beveridge, *Life of John Marshall*

## BLAINE, JAMES GILLESPIE

1830–93 Statesman

Wallowing in corruption like a rhinoceros in an African pool.
E. L. Godkin, in Allen Churchill, *The Roosevelts*

No man in our annals has filled so large a space and left it so empty.
Charles Edward Russell, in D. S. Muzzey, *James G. Blaine*

*See also* Theodore Roosevelt

## BLAIR, ERIC, *see under* ORWELL, GEORGE

## BLAKE, ROBERT

1599–1657 Admiral

His life can show no private irregularities, no scandals to excite the curiosity of the prurient or the avaricious; nor has it any lessons in intrigue or finesse. It thus lacks the stimulus of sex, wealth, and power . . . And how typically were his qualities those which Englishmen like to claim as their own – reticence, aversion to publicity, abhorrence of the theatrical, and the sense that, in the great moments of life, it should be thought only to do faithfully, leaving glory to follow good deeds.
Roger Beadon, *Robert Blake*

**R** est here in peace the sacred dust
**O** f valiant Blake, the good, the just,
**B** elov'd of all on every side;
**E** ngland's honour, once her pride,
**R** ome's terror, Dutch annoyer,
**T** ruth's defender, Spain's destroyer.

**B** ring no dry eyes unto this place;
**L** et not be seen in any case,
**A** smiling or an unsad face.
**K** indle desires in every breast
**E** ternally with him to rest.
George Harrison, *Epitaph Acrostic, . . . on board the Dunbar in the Downs*, 11 August 1657

I do not reckon myself equal to Blake.
Horatio Nelson, Letter to Earl of St Vincent, 1797

## BLAKE, WILLIAM

1757–1827 Poet, Artist

Having spent the Vigour of my Youth & Genius under the Opression of S[r] Joshua [Reynolds] & his Gang of Cunning Hired Knaves Without Employment & as much as could possibly be Without Bread, The Reader must expect to Read in all my Remarks on these Books Nothing but Indignation & Resentment. While S[r] Joshua was rolling in Riches, Barry was Poor & Unemploy'd except by his own Energy; Mortimer was call'd a Madman, & only Portrait Painting applauded & rewarded by the Rich & Great. Reynolds & Gainsborough Blotted & Blurred one against the other & Divided all the English World between them. Fuseli, indignant, almost hid himself. I am hid.

On himself, *Annotations to Reynolds's Discourses*

I do not pretend to Paint better than Rafael or Mich. Angelo or Julio Romano or Alb. Durer, but I do Pretend to Paint finer than Rubens or Remb[t]. or Correggio or Titian.

On himself, 'Public Address', from *Note Book*, 1810

Self-educated *William Blake* / Who threw his spectre in the lake, / Broke off relations in a curse / With the Newtonian Universe, / But even as a child would pet / The tigers Voltaire never met, / Took walks with them through Lambeth, and / Spoke to Isaiah in the Strand, / And heard inside each mortal thing / Its holy emanation sing. /

W. H. Auden, *New Year Letter*

Blake saw a treeful of angels at Peckham Rye, / And his hands could lay hold on the tiger's terrible heart, / Blake knew how deep is Hell, and Heaven how high, / And could build the universe from one tiny part. /

William Rose Benét, *Mad Blake*

Be a god, your spirit cried; / Tread with feet that burn the dew; / Dress with clouds your locks of pride; / Be a child, God said to you. /

Olive Dargan, *To William Blake*

I lived; I toiled – day in, day out, /Endless labour, shafts of bliss, / For three score years and ten, / And then; / I watched, with speechless joy and grief, / My last and loveliest spring / Take wing. /

Think you, I grudged the travailing? / I, who am come to this. /

Walter de la Mare, *A Lifetime: Epitaph for William Blake*

Blake . . . knew what interested him, and he therefore presents only the essential, only, in fact, what can be presented, and need not be explained. And because he was not distracted, or frightened, or occupied in anything but exact statements, he understood. He was naked, and saw man naked, and from the centre of his own crystal. To him there was no more reason why Swedenborg should be absurd than Locke. He accepted Swedenborg, and eventually rejected him, for reasons of his own. He approached everything with a mind unclouded by current opinions. There was nothing of the superior person about him. This makes him terrifying.

T. S. Eliot, *The Sacred Wood*

Blake is damned good to steal from!

Henry Fuseli, in Alexander Gilchrist, *Life of Blake*

I was having these Blake visions. So. The thing I understood from Blake was that it was possible to transmit a message through time which could reach the enlightened, that poetry had a definite effect, it wasn't just pretty, or just beautiful, as I had understood pretty beauty before . . . But anyway the impression I got was that it was like a kind of time machine through which he could transmit, Blake could transmit, his basic consciousness and communicate it to somebody else after he was dead – in other words, build a time machine.

Allen Ginsberg, in *Paris Review*

This seer's ambition soared too far; / He sank, on pinions backward blown; / But, tho' he touched nor sun nor star, / He made a world his own. /

Edmund Gosse, *William Blake*

He has no sense of the ludicrous, and, as to God, a worm crawling in a privy is as worthy an object as any other, all being to him indifferent. So to Blake the Chimney Sweeper etc. He is ruined by vain struggles to get rid of what presses on his brain – he attempts impossibles.

William Hazlitt, in Henry Crabb Robinson, Diary, 1811

For me the most poetical of all poets is Blake. I find his lyrical note as beautiful as Shakespeare's and more beautiful than anyone else's; and I call him more poetical than Shakespeare, even though Shakespeare has so much more poetry, because poetry in him preponderates more than in Shakespeare over everything else, and instead of being confounded in a great river can be drunk pure from a slender channel of its own.

A. E. Housman, *The Name and Nature of Poetry*

Blake is the only painter of imaginative pictures, apart from landscape, that England has produced. And unfortunately there is so little Blake, and even in that little the symbolism is often artificially imposed. Nevertheless, Blake paints with real intuitional awareness and solid instinctive feeling. He dares handle the human body, even if he sometimes makes it a mere ideograph. And no other Englishman has even dared handle it with alive imagination.

D. H. Lawrence, *Introduction to his Paintings*

His eye was the finest I ever saw: brilliant, not roving, clear and intent; yet susceptible; it flashed with genius or melted with tenderness. It could also be terrible. Cunning and falsehood quailed under it, but it was never busy with them. It pierced them and turned away. Nor was the mouth less expressive; the lips flexible and quivering with feeling. I yet recall it when, on one occasion, dwelling upon the exquisite parable of the Prodigal, he began to repeat a part of it; but at the words: 'When he was yet a great way off, his father saw him', could go no further; his voice faltered and he was in tears.

Samuel Palmer, Letter to Alexander Gilchrist, 1855

He died on Sunday Night at 6 Oclock in a most glorious manner. He said He was going to that Country he had all His life wished to see & expressed Himself Happy hoping for Salvation through Jesus Christ. Just before he died his Countenance became fair. His eyes Brighten'd and he burst out singing of the things he saw in Heaven.

George Richmond, Letter to Samuel Palmer, 15 August 1827

He is not so much a disciple of Jacob Böhmen and Swedenborg as a fellow Visionary. He lives, as they did, in a world of his own, enjoying constant intercourse with the world of spirits. He receives visits from Shakespeare, Milton, Dante, Voltaire, etc. etc. etc., and has given me repeatedly their very words in their conversations. His paintings are copies of what he saw in his Visions. His books (and his MSS. are immense in quantity) are dictations from the spirits. He told me yesterday that when he writes it is for the spirits only; he sees the words fly about the room the moment he has put them on paper, and his book is then published. A man so favoured, of course, has sources of wisdom peculiar to himself.

Henry Crabb Robinson, Letter to Dorothy Wordsworth, 1826

Blake, in the hierarchy of the inspired, stands very high indeed. If one could strike an average among poets, it would probably be true to say that, as far as inspiration is concerned, Blake is to the average poet, as the average poet is to the man in the street. All poetry, to be poetry at all, must have the power of making one, now and then, involuntarily ejaculate: 'What made him think of that?' With Blake, one is asking the question all the time.

Lytton Strachey, *Books and Characters*

Blake is the only poet who sees all temporal things under a form of eternity. To him reality is merely a symbol, and he catches at its terms, hastily and faultily, as he catches at the lines of the drawing-master, to represent, as in a faint image, the clear and shining outlines of what he sees with the imagination, through the eye, not with it, as he says. Where other poets use reality as a spring-board into space, he uses it as a foothold on his return from flight.

Arthur Symons, *William Blake*

There is no doubt that this poor man was mad, but there is something in the madness of this man which interests me more than the sanity of Lord Byron and Walter Scott.

William Wordsworth, in Henry Crabb Robinson, *Reminiscences*

That William Blake / Who beat upon the wall / Till Truth obeyed his call. /

William Butler Yeats, *An Acre of Grass*

*See also* Thomas Gainsborough, William Butler Yeats

## BLESSINGTON, MARGUERITE, COUNTESS

1789–1849 Hostess, Author

Miladi seems highly literary . . . She is also very pretty even in a morning, – a species of beauty on which the sun of Italy does not shine so frequently as the chandelier. Certainly, English women wear better than their continental neighbours of the same sex.

Lord Byron, *Letters and Journals*, 2 April 1823

Hospitable heart / Whom twenty summers more and more endear'd; / Part on the Arno, part where every clime / Sent its most grateful sons, to kiss thy hand, / To make the humble proud, the proud submiss, / Wiser the wisest, and the brave more brave. /

Walter Savage Landor, *In Memoriam Lady Blessington*

Unlike all other beautiful faces that I have seen, hers was at the time of which I speak [sc. 1822], neither a history nor a prophecy . . . but rather a star to kneel before and worship . . . an end and a consummation in itself, not a promise of anything else.

P. G. Patmore (on seeing her standing before her portrait by Sir Thomas Lawrence at the Royal Academy Exhibition), in R. H. Stoddard, *Personal Recollections of Lamb, Hazlitt, and Others*

## BLOOMER, AMELIA JENKS

1818–94 Social Reformer

We all felt that the dress was drawing attention from what we thought to be of far greater importance – the question of woman's right to better education, to a wider field of employment, to better remuneration for her labour, and to the ballot for the protection of her rights. In the minds of some people the short dress and woman's rights were inseparably connected. With us, the dress was but an incident, and we were not willing to sacrifice greater questions to it.

On herself, in Charles N. Gattey, *The Bloomer Girls*

## BLOW, JOHN

1648–1708 Composer

It does not appear that Purcell, whom he did himself the honour to call his scholar, . . . ever threw notes about at random, in his manner, or insulted the ear with lawless discords, which no concords can render tolerable.

Dr Charles Burney, *A General History of Music*

## BOADICEA, QUEEN

– d. 62 Warrior

The Greek historian Dio Cassius, who lived about a century after Boadicea, when her fame and figure were already legendary, describes her as fierce and lofty, with a harsh voice and huge masses of fair hair. Those who remember Florence Austral as Brünhilde will be immediately struck by the resemblance.

Nicolas Bentley, *Golden Sovereigns*

The citizens of London implored Suetonius to protect them, but when he heard that Boadicea, having chased Cerialis towards Lincoln, had turned and was marching south, he took the hard but right decision to leave them to their fate.

Winston Churchill, *History of the English-Speaking Peoples*

Although, as a Stoic, Seneca officially despised riches, he amassed a huge fortune . . . Much of this he acquired by lending money in Britain; according to Dio, the excessive rates of interest that he exacted were among the causes of revolt in that country. The heroic Queen Boadicea, if this is true, was heading a rebellion against capitalism as represented by the philosophic apostle of austerity.

Bertrand Russell, *History of Western Philosophy*

Julius Caesar advanced very energetically, throwing his cavalry several thousands of paces over the River Flumen; but the Ancient Britons, though all well over military age, painted themselves true blue or *woad*, and fought as heroically under their dashing queen, Woadicea, as they did later in thin red lines under their good queen Victoria.

W. C. Sellar and R. J. Yeatman, *1066 and All That*

Boadicea, with her daughters before her in a chariot, went up to tribe after tribe, protesting that it was indeed unusual for Britons to fight under the leadership of a woman. 'But now,' she said, 'it is not as a woman descending from noble ancestry, but as one of the people that I am avenging lost freedom, my scourged body, the outraged chastity of my daughters. Roman lust has gone so far that not our very persons, not even age or virginity, are left unpolluted . . . This is a woman's resolve; as for men, they may live and be slaves' . . . Great glory, equal to that of our old victories, was won on that day. Some indeed say that there fell little less than eighty thousand of the Britons, with a loss to our soldiers of about four hundred, and only as many wounded. Boadicea put an end to her life by poison.

Tacitus, *Annals*, translated by A. J. Church and W. J. Brodribb

*See also* Hengist and Horsa

## BODLEY, SIR THOMAS

1545–1613 Scholar, Diplomat

Thy treasure was not spent on *Horse* and *Hound*, / Nor that new *Mode*, which doth old States confound . . . / Th'hast made us all thine *Heirs*: whatever we / Hereafter write, 'tis thy *Posterity*. / *This* is thy *Monument*! here thou shalt stand / Till the times fail in their last grain of Sand. / And whereso'er thy silent *Reliques* keep, / This Tomb will never let thine honour sleep. / Still we shall think upon thee; all our fame / Meets here to speak one *Letter* of thy name. / Thou cans't not dye! Here thou art more than safe / When every *Book* is thy large *Epitaph*.

Henry Vaughan, *On Sir Thomas Bodley's Library*

## BOGART, HUMPHREY DE FOREST

1899–1957 Actor

Bogie was a curious mixture. He wasn't cynical. He didn't expect too much, he never realized he would leave the kind of mark he has left. He never tried to impress anyone. I've never known anyone who was so completely his own man. He could not be led in any direction unless it was the direction he chose to go . . . He didn't think he owed anybody anything except good work.

Lauren Bacall, in Earl Wilson, *The Show Business Nobody Knows*

Bogart is so much better than any other tough-guy actor. [He] can be tough *without* a gun. Also he has a sense of humor that contains that grating undertone of contempt.

Raymond Chandler, *Raymond Chandler Speaking*

Humphrey Bogart is probably the most subtle bad man (genus American) the films have produced.

Otis Ferguson, *The Films of Otis Ferguson*

His yes meant yes, his no meant no; . . . there was no bunkum about Bogart.

Katharine Hepburn, in Joe Hyams, *Bogie*

Bogie and I were good friends, and he gave me some good advice. He said 'Whatever it is, be against it'. I told him 'I've got a lot of scars already from being an againster'. He said 'You've got a lot of scars, but you're still alive'.

Robert Mitchum, in Earl Wilson, *The Show Business Nobody Knows*

Probably no other actor of his era has fit a detective part so perfectly. Humphrey Bogart. Wry, detached, anti-Establishment, a man with the sure masculinity of whiskey straight . . . Bogart was unflinching, outspoken, cynical and a realist; a tough guy in a trenchcoat, a man's man.

David Zinman, *Fifty Classic Motion Pictures*

## BOLEYN, ANNE

1507–36 Queen Consort to Henry VIII

Neither did I at any time so far forget myself in my exaltation, or received queenship, but that I always looked for such an alteration as now I find; for the ground of my preferment being on no surer foundation than your grace's fancy, the least alteration was fit and sufficient (I know) to draw that fancy to some other subject. You have chosen me from a low estate to be your queen and companion, far beyond my desert or desire.

On herself, Last Letter to Henry VIII (attributed by Bishop Burnet, in his *History of the Reformation*)

At the opening of the year 1536 Anne Boleyn's position rested on two supports: the life of Catherine of Aragon and the prospect of a prince. Never was fortune more cruel. On January 7th Catherine died, and on the twenty-ninth, the day of the funeral, Anne gave premature birth to a male child. She had miscarried of her saviour. The tragedy must obviously move to a close; and it moved swiftly. On May 2nd she was arrested and sent to the tower, accused of adultery with five men, one of whom was her brother. In the subsequent trials all were found guilty, and the law took its course. Anne herself was executed on May 18th. Whether she was guilty or not, no human judgement can now determine, and contemporaries differed. In all probability she had been indiscreet. If she had gone further, if she had really committed adultery – and that possibility cannot be lightly dismissed –

then it is likely that a desperate woman had taken a desperate course to give England its prince and save herself from ruin. Whatever the truth, she had played her game and lost.

J. E. Neale, *Queen Elizabeth*

For something like five years she succeeded in holding him [Henry VIII] at arms' length, a remarkable performance, all things considered, and probably indicative that there was considerably more of cold calculation than of passion in Anne's attitude.

Conyers Read, *The Tudors*

## BOLINGBROKE, VISCOUNT (HENRY ST JOHN)

1678–1751 Statesman

Whilst I loved much, I never loved long, but was inconstant to them all for the sake of all.

On himself, Letter to Charles Wyndham, 26 December 1735

He has been a most mortifying instance of the violence of human passions, and of the weakness of the most improved and exalted human reason. His virtues and his vices, his reason and his passions, did not blend themselves by a gradation of tints, but formed a shining and a sudden contrast. Here the darkest, there the most splendid colours; and both rendered more striking from their proximity.

Lord Chesterfield, *Letters*, vol. 4, 12 December 1749

It was his inspiring pen that . . . eradicated from Toryism all those absurd and odious doctrines which Toryism had adventitiously adopted, clearly developed its essential and permanent character . . . and in the complete reorganization of the public mind laid the foundation for the future accession of the Tory party to power.

Benjamin Disraeli, *Vindication of the British Constitution*

When he was appointed Minister, a woman of the streets was said to have cried . . . 'Seven thousand guineas a year, my girls, and all for us!'

Michael Foot, *The Pen and the Sword*

Those who were most partial to him could not but allow that he was ambitious without fortitude, and enterprising without resolution; that he was fawning without insinuation, and insincere without art; that he had admirers without friendship, and followers without attachment; parts without probity, knowledge without conduct, and experience without judgement.

Lord Hervey, *Memoirs*, vol. 1

Sir, he was a scoundrel and a coward; a scoundrel for charging a blunderbuss against religion and morality; a coward because he had not resolution to fire it off himself, but left half a crown to a beggarly Scotchman to draw the trigger after his death.

Samuel Johnson, in James Boswell, *Life of Johnson*

. . . it is to be noted that it was not until he had most signally failed as a statesman that he began to acquire a reputation as a political philosopher, and had he been able to make up his mind during the last few weeks of Anne's reign, he could have presented the country with a Patriot King in the person of James III instead of merely a volume on the need for one.

Sir Charles Petrie, *The Four Georges*

Lord Bolingbroke quitted the Pretender, because he found him incapable of making a good prince. He himself, if in power, would have been the best of ministers. – These things will be proved one of these days. The proofs are ready, and the world *will* see them.

Alexander Pope, in Joseph Spence, *Anecdotes*

Lord Bolingbroke's father said to him on his being made a lord, 'Ah, Harry, I ever said you would be hanged, but now I find you will be beheaded.'
Joseph Spence, *ibid.*

*See also* Jonathan Swift

## BOONE, DANIEL

1734–1820 Pioneer

I had not been two years at the licks before a d----d Yankee came, and settled down *within an hundred miles of me*!!
On himself, in Henry Nash Smith, *Virgin Land*

As Daniel Boone himself used to say, all you needed for happiness was 'a good gun, a good horse, and a good wife'.
John E. Bakeless, *Daniel Boone*

When Daniel Boone goes by, at night, / The phantom deer arise / And all lost, wild America / Is burning in their eyes. /
Stephen Vincent Benét, *Daniel Boone*

'Tis true he shrank from men even of his nation / When they built up unto his darling trees, – / He moved some hundred miles off, for a station / Where there were fewer houses and more ease. /
Lord Byron, *Don Juan*, canto viii

A Nimrod by instinct and physical character, his home was in the range of woods, his beau ideal the chase, and forests full of buffaloes, bear and deer. More expert at their own arts than the Indians themselves, to fight them, and foil them, gave scope to the exulting consciousness of the exercise of his own appropriate and peculiar powers.
Timothy Flint, *Indian Wars of the West*

*See also* Gary Cooper

## BOOTH, JOHN WILKES

1838–65 Actor, Assassin

I have too great a soul to die like a criminal.
On himself, in A. K. Adams, *The Home Book of Humorous Quotations*

What he was after was to be '*the* Booth', to shoulder his way ahead of his brothers, to approach the level of his father's fame, and it was this ambition that kept him in the North even after war broke out and the South he loved was fighting gloriously. When Edwin sailed for England John saw his chance. He starred in St Louis, in Chicago, then in Baltimore; and here in the city most intimately associated with all the Booths his posters proclaimed defiantly: I AM MYSELF ALONE!
Eleanor Ruggles, *Prince of Players: Edwin Booth*

*See also* Carl Sandburg

## BOOTH, 'GENERAL' WILLIAM

1829–1912 Founder of the Salvation Army

. . . This vehement person who . . . unroofed the slum to Victorian respectability, and spoke of himself as a moral scavenger netting the very sewers, was of a singularly delicate constitution . . . It was this extreme sensitiveness to squalor and suffering which made him so effective in unveiling the dark places of civilization. He saw sharply what others scarcely saw at all, and he felt as an outrage what others considered to be natural.
Harold Begbie, in *Dictionary of National Biography*

Booth led boldly with his big brass drum – / (Are you washed in the blood of the Lamb?) / The Saints smiled gravely and they said: 'He's come.' / (Are you washed in the blood of the Lamb?) / Walking Lepers followed, rank on rank, / Lurching bravos from the ditches dank, / Drabs from the alleyways and drug fiends pale – / Minds still passion-ridden, soul-power frail: – /Vermin-eaten saints with moldy breath, / Unwashed Legions with the ways of Death – / (Are you washed in the blood of the Lamb?) /

Vachel Lindsay, *General William Booth Enters Into Heaven*

It was William Booth who explained the authoritarian framework of his Salvation Army by remarking that if Moses had operated through committees, the Israelites never would have got across the Red Sea.

Edward Morello, in *New York World-Telegram and Sun*, 28 July 1965

## BORDEN, LIZZIE ANDREW

1860–1927 Alleged Murderess

Lizzie Borden took an ax / And gave her mother forty whacks; / And when she saw what she had done / She gave her father forty-one. /

Anon., *Lizzie Borden*

## BOSWELL, JAMES

1740–95 Author

I am a being very much consisting of feelings. I have some fixed principles. But my existence is chiefly conducted by the powers of fancy and sensation. It is my business to navigate my soul amidst the gales as steadily and smoothly as I can.

On himself, *Journal*, 26 March 1775

An honest self-portrait is extremely rare because a man who has reached the degree of self-consciousness presupposed by the desire to paint his own portrait has almost always developed an ego-consciousness which paints himself painting himself, and introduces artificial highlights and dramatic shadows. As an autobiographer, Boswell is almost alone in his honesty.

I determined, if the Cyprian Fury
should seize me, to participate my
amorous flame with a genteel girl.

Stendhal would never have dared write such a sentence. He would have said to himself: 'Phrases like *Cyprian Fury* and *amorous flame* are clichés; I must put down in plain words exactly what I mean.' But he would have been wrong, for the Self thinks in clichés and euphemisms, not in the style of the Code Napoléon.

W. H. Auden, *The Dyer's Hand*

I felt a strong sensation of that displeasure which his loquacious communications of every weakness and infirmity of the first and greatest good man of these times has awakened in me, at his first sight; and, though his address to me was courteous in the extreme, and he made a point of sitting next me, I felt an indignant disposition to a nearly forbidding reserve and silence. How many starts of passion and prejudice has he blackened into record, that else might have sunk, for ever forgotten, under the preponderance of weightier virtues and excellences! Angry, however, as I have long been with him, he soon insensibly conquered, though he did not soften me: there is so little of ill-design or ill-nature in him, he is so open and forgiving for all that is said in return, that he soon forced me to consider him in a less serious light, and change my resentment against his treachery into something like commiseration of his levity; and before we parted we became good friends.

Fanny Burney, Letter to Mrs Phillips, June 1792

Silly, snobbish, lecherous, tipsy, given to high-flown sentiments and more than a little of a humbug, Boswell is redeemed by a generosity of mind, a concentration on topics that will always appeal . . . and a naivety that endeared him to the great minds he cultivated. He needed Johnson as ivy needs an oak.

Cyril Connolly, *The Evening Colonnade*

Jamie, you have a light head, but a damned heavy a---; and, to be sure, such a man will run easily down hill, but it would be severe work to get him up.

Lord Eglinton, in Boswell, *London Journal*, 9 May 1763

You have but two topics, yourself and me, and I'm sick of both.

Samuel Johnson, in *ibid.*, May 1776

If general approbation will add anything to your enjoyment, I can tell you that I have heard you mentioned as *a man whom everybody likes*. I think life has little more to give.

Samuel Johnson, Letter to Boswell, 3 July 1778

*Lues Boswelliana*, or disease of admiration.

T. B. Macaulay, *Essays*: 'Earl of Chatham'

He longed passionately to pull himself together. Men who had nobly succeeded had an irresistible attraction for him. With them for a while his better self was uppermost.

Desmond MacCarthy, *Criticism*

See Boswell (but who for such drudg'ry more fit?) / Collect the vile refuse of poor Johnson's wit; / And fir'd with zeal for the scavenger's warm on't, / Indite what Same did, when his wisdom lay dormant. /

Anthony Pasquin (John Williams), *The Children of Thespis*

It would be difficult to find a more shattering refutation of the lessons of cheap morality than the life of James Boswell. One of the most extraordinary successes in the history of civilization was achieved by an idler, a lecher, a drunkard, and a snob. Nor was this success of that sudden explosive kind . . . ; it was the supreme expression of an entire life. Boswell triumphed by dint of abandoning himself, through fifty years, to his instincts. The example, no doubt, is not one to be followed rashly. Self-indulgence is common, and Boswells are rare.

Lytton Strachey, *Portraits in Miniature*

His collected journals make up the most extraordinary biography, the most determined effort of a human being to put himself totally on record, to be found anywhere. Compared with Boswell, Rousseau is evasive, Henry Miller reticent.

John Wain, *Samuel Johnson*

Jemmy had a sycophantish, but a sincere admiration of the genius, erudition and virtue of Ursa-Major, and in recording the noble growlings of the Great Bear, thought not of his own Scotch snivel.

John Wilson, *Noctes Ambrosianae*

*See also* Henry Adams, Samuel Johnson

## BOTTOMLEY, HORATIO WILLIAM

1860–1933 Journalist, Financier

I'm Bottomley . . . I hold the unique distinction of having gone through every court in the country – except one . . . the Divorce Court . . . Although I'm nominally a bankrupt, I *never* had a better time in my *life*.

On himself, speaking to the Business League, Summer 1912

I have not had your advantages, gentlemen. What poor education I have received has been gained in the University of Life.

On himself, speaking at the Oxford Union, 1921

A wire I'll send to a gentleman friend / I'll call him Horatio B. / He's noted today for seeing fair play, / In a country that claims to be free. / If you feel in a plight, to his journal you write / And get reparation in full. / So you'll all say with me, Good luck to H.B. / And continued success to *John Bull.* /

Anon., Pantomime jingle, 1915

At the end of the war Bottomley had the public by the ears, the Government by the hand and his past by the throat.

'Tenax' [Edward Bell], *The Gentle Art of Exploiting Gullibility*

England's Greatest Living Humbug.

Reuben Bigland, Telegram to Bottomley, November 1920

He had two brains, that man. One linked up with his tongue and the other thought while he talked.

Sir Harry Preston, *Leaves from my Unwritten Diary*

An acquaintance finding him stitching mail bags in prison, said: 'Ah, Bottomley, sewing?' Bottomley replied: 'No, reaping.'

A. J. P. Taylor, *English History 1914–1945*

## BOW, CLARA

1905–65 Actress

Elinor Glyn . . . discovered in Clara Bow the epitome of 'It'. 'It was this: a strange magnetism which attracts both sexes . . . there must be a physical attraction but beauty is unnecessary.' Probably Bow as the 'It' Girl was a studio scheme with which Elinor Glyn was happy to comply, but in the founding of the whole silly syndrome, Bow was an entirely worthy centrepiece. Even if the whole thing, including what she did on the screen, was evolved from the sort of girl she was, her life and career still seem to have been dreamed up by one of her scriptwriters.

David Shipman, *The Great Movie Stars*

## BOWIE, JAMES

1796–1838 Adventurer

Colonel [William] Travis died like a hero, gun in hand, stretched across the carriage of a cannon, but the boastful Bowie died like a woman, almost concealed beneath a mattress.

Edward S. Sears, 'The Low Down on Jim Bowie', in Moody C. Boatright and Donald Day eds, *From Hell to Breakfast*

## BOYLE, HON. ROBERT

1627–91 Natural Philosopher

He is very tall (about six foot high) and streight, very temperate, and vertuouse, and frugall: a Batcheler; keepes a Coach; sojournes with his sister, the Lady Ranulagh. His greatest delight is Chymistrey. He haz at his sister's a noble Laboratory, and severall servants (Prentices to him) to looke to it. He is charitable to ingeniose men that are in want, and foreigne Chymists have had large proofe of his bountie, for he will not spare for cost to gett any rare Secret.

John Aubrey, *Brief Lives*

I went to the Society where were divers Experiments in Mr Boyls Pneumatique Engine. We put in a snake but could not kill it, by exhausting the aire, onely make it extreamly sick, but the chick died of Convulsions out right, in a short space.

John Evelyn, Diary, 25 April 1661

I went to Lon: din'd at my Lord Falklands, made visits, & return'd: Mr Boile had now produced his Invention of dulcifying Sea-Water, like to be of mighty consequence.

*Ibid.*

It has plainly astonish'd me to have seen him so often recover when he has not been able to move, or bring his hand to his mouth; and indeed the contexture of his body, during the best of his health, appeared to me so delicate, that I have frequently compar'd him to a crystal or Venice glass; which tho' wrought never so thin and fine, being carefully set up, would outlast the hardier metals of daily use.

John Evelyn, Letter to Henry Wotton, March 1696

I took boat at the Old Swan, and there up the river all alone as high as Putney almost, and then back again, all the way reading, and finishing Mr Boyle's book of Colours, which is so chymical, that I can understand but little of it, but understand enough to see that he is a most excellent man.

Samuel Pepys, Diary, 2 June 1667

A late distinguished professor, indeed, guiltless of any purpose of jesting or playing upon words, once gravely summed up the memorabilia of Boyle's history in the singular epitome, that he was 'the son of the Earl of Cork and the father of modern chemistry'.

George Wilson, in *British Quarterly Review*, 1849

## BRADFORD, JOHN

1510?–55 Gentleman

There, but for the grace of God, goes John Bradford.

On himself, attributed, watching criminals on their way to execution

## BRADLEY, FRANCIS HERBERT

1846–1924 Philosopher

... It seems the greatest sign of friendship that he can give anyone is to take them to see his dog's grave. There are those who would not sit down among the angels, he says in his book, if their dogs were not admitted with them.

Bertrand Russell, Letter to Alys Russell, December 1895

*See also* J. E. McTaggart

## BRADSHAW, JOHN

1602–59 Judge, Regicide

My brother Henry must heir the land / My brother Frank must be at his command / Whilst I, poor Jack, shall do that / Which all the world will wonder at. /

On himself, scribbled on a tombstone in Macclesfield Churchyard, when a boy, according to legend

Bold and resolute, with a small organ of veneration, and a great lack of modesty, and not encumbered with any nice delicacy of feeling.

Edward Foss, *Judges of England*

A stout man, and learned in his profession. No friend to Monarchy.

Bulstrode Whitelocke, *Memorials of the English Affairs*, 31 October 1659

## BRADSTREET, ANNE

*circa* 1612–72 Poet

To be wrenched from the libraries and the courtesies of the Old World to the bleakness of peril of the new was not entirely to the girl's liking, and a pardonable homesickness for England shows now and then through the verses she wrote as a solace for her duties as a homemaker and mother of eight children.

Grant C. Knight, *American Literature and Culture*

Her breast was a brave Pallace, a Broad-street, / Where all heroick ample thoughts did meet, / Where nature such a Tenement had tane, / That other Souls, to hers, dwelt in a lane. /

John Norton, in Helen Campbell, *Anne Bradstreet and Her Time*

## BRANGWYN, SIR FRANK (FRANÇOIS GUILLAUME)

1867–1956 Painter

It is felt abroad that Brangwyn alone in his work symbolises the daring manliness of the British temperament; that he alone represents his time and race, showing courage, indomitable energy, and blending knowledge of the East with an intense sympathy for the grim stress and strain of Western industrialism.

W. Shaw-Sparrow, *Frank Brangwyn and his Art*

If you are sensitive to the throbbing tide of energy in creative work, you will find it a fatigue to follow with dramatic pleasure the constructional workmanship of two or three Brangwyns in a single sitting. I have felt the same fatigue when watching a strong athlete run in a great race, and there is, in fact, a certain resemblance between the nervous energy of the trained athlete and the constructive energy shown by Brangwyn.

*Ibid.*

## BREAKSPEAR, NICHOLAS, *see* ADRIAN IV

## BRIGHT, JOHN

1811–89 Orator, Statesman

It is not my duty to make this country the knight-errant of the human race.

On himself, speaking in 1855, in A. J. P. Taylor, *Beaverbrook*

. . . always ready for a chat and a fulmination, and filling up the intervals of business with 'Paradise Regained' . . . his opinion on men and things . . . is strong, clear, and honest, however one-sided. But he flies off provokingly into pounds, shillings, and pence when one wants him to abide for a little among deeper and less tangible motives, powers and arguments.

Caroline Fox, Letter to Lucy Hodgkin, May 1861

In Bright there was an unlimited self-confidence which amounted to corruption of the soul.

Lord John Morley, in J. H. Morgan, *John Viscount Morley*

It is not personalities that are complained of. A public man is right in attacking persons. But it is his attacks on *classes* that have given offence.

Lord Palmerston, in conversation with Richard Cobden, June 1859

## BRONTË, ANNE

1820–49 Novelist

She had, in the course of her life, been called on to contemplate near at hand and for a long time, the terrible effects of talents misused and faculties abused; hers was naturally a sensitive, reserved, and dejected nature; what she saw sank very deeply into her mind; it did her harm. She brooded over it till she believed it to be a duty to reproduce every detail . . . as a warning to others . . . This well-meant resolution brought on her misconstruction and some abuse, which she bore, as it was her custom to bear whatever was unpleasant, with mild, steady patience. She was a very sincere and practical Christian, but the tinge of religious melancholy communicated a sad shade to her brief, blameless life.

Charlotte Brontë, *Biographical Notice*

A sort of literary Cinderella.

George Moore, *Conversation in Ebury Street*

Anne Brontë serves a twofold purpose in the study of what the Brontës wrote and were. In the first place, her gentle and delicate presence, her sad, short story, her hard life and early death, enter deeply into the poetry and tragedy that have always been entwined with the memory of the Brontës, as women and as writers; in the second, the books and poems that she wrote serve as matter of comparison by which to test the greatness of her two sisters. She is the measure of their genius – like them, but not with them.

Mrs Humphry Ward, Preface to the Haworth edition of the Brontës' Works

## BRONTË, (PATRICK) BRANWELL

1817–48 Artist

I shall never be able to realise the too sanguine hopes of my friends, for at twenty-eight I am a thoroughly *old man* – mentally and bodily. Far more so, indeed, than I am willing to express ... My rude rough acquaintances here ascribe my unhappiness solely to causes produced by my sometimes irregular life because they have no other pains than those resulting from excess or want of ready cash. They do not know that I would rather want a shirt than want a springy mind, and that my total want of happiness, were I to step into York Minster now, would be far, far worse than their want of a hundred pounds when they might happen to need it, and that if a dozen glasses or a bottle of wine drives off their cares, such cures only make me outwardly passable in company but *never* drive off mine.

On himself, Letter to Joseph Leyland, 24 January 1847

A Brother – sleeps he here? – / Of all his gifted race / Not the least-gifted; young, / Unhappy, beautiful; the cause / Of many hopes, of many tears. / O Boy, if here thou sleep'st, sleep well! / On thee too did the Muse / Bright in thy cradle smile: / But some dark Shadow came / (I know not what) and interpos'd. /

Matthew Arnold, *Haworth Churchyard*

The Brontë son did not fulfil his early promise; his great misfortune was that he was a man. If he had been constrained, as were his sisters, by the spirit of the times; if he had been compelled, for want of other outlet, to take up his pen or else burst, he might have been known to-day as rather more than the profligate brother of the Brontës.

Muriel Spark, *The Brontë Letters*

## BRONTË, CHARLOTTE

1816–55 Novelist

She showed that abysses may exist inside a governess and eternities inside a manufacturer.

G. K. Chesterton, *Twelve Types*

I have read *Jane Eyre*, mon ami, and shall be glad to know what you admire in it. All self-sacrifice is good – but one would like it to be in a somewhat nobler cause than that of a diabolical law which chains a man body and soul to a putrefying carcase. However, the book *is* interesting – only I wish the characters would talk a little less like the heroes and heroines of police reports.

George Eliot, Letter to Charles Bray, 11 June 1848

We shall not attempt to resolve the much agitated question of the sex of the author of these remarkable works. All that we shall say on the subject is, that if they are the productions of a woman, she must be a woman pretty nearly unsexed; and Jane Eyre strikes us as a personage much more likely to have sprung ready armed from the head of a man, and that head a pretty hard one, than to have experienced, in any shape, the softening influence of female creation.

James Lorimer, in *North British Review*, August 1849

Had Brontë herself not grown up in a house of half-mad sisters with a domestic tyrant for father, no 'prospects', as marital security was referred to, and with only the confines of governessing and celibacy staring at her from the future, her chief release the group fantasy of 'Angria', that collective dream these strange siblings played all their lives, composing stories about a never-never land where women could rule, exercise power, govern the state, declare night and day, death and life – then we would never have heard from Charlotte . . . Had that been the case, we might never have known what a resurrected soul wished to tell upon emerging from several millennia of subordination.

Kate Millett, *Sexual Politics*

It amuses me to read the author's naïve confession [in *Villette*] of being in love with 2 men at the same time, and her readiness to fall in love at any time. The poor little woman of genius! the fiery little eager brave tremulous homely-faced creature! I can read a great deal of her life as I fancy in her book, and see that rather than have fame, rather than any other earthly good or mayhap heavenly she wants some Tomkins or another to love her and be in love with. But you see she is a little bit of a creature without a penny worth of good looks, thirty years old I should think, buried in the country, and eating up her own heart there, and no Tomkins will come.

W. M. Thackeray, Letter to Lucy Baxter, 11 March 1853

March 21. Read to Albert out of that melancholy, interesting book, *Jane Eyre* . . . May 13. We dined alone and talked and read, going on reading till past 11 in that intensely interesting novel *Jane Eyre* . . . May 21. We remained up reading in *Jane Eyre* till ½ p. 11 – quite creepy . . . August 4. At near 10 we went below and nearly finished reading that most interesting book *Jane Eyre*. A peaceful, happy evening.

Queen Victoria, Diary, 1858

Has it ever been sufficiently recognized that Charlotte Brontë is first and foremost *an Irishwoman*, that her genius is at bottom a Celtic genius? The main characteristics indeed of the Celt are all hers – disinterestedness, melancholy, wildness, a wayward force and passion, for ever wooed by sounds and sights to which other natures are insensible – by murmurs from the earth, by colours in the sky, by tones and accents of the soul, that speak to the Celtic sense as to no other . . . Then, as to the Celtic pride, the Celtic shyness, the Celtic endurance, – Charlotte Brontë was rich in them all.

Mrs Humphry Ward, Preface to the Haworth edition of the Brontës' Works

## BRONTË, EMILY JANE

1818–48 Novelist

She – / (How shall I sing her?) – whose soul / Knew no fellow for might, /

Passion, vehemence, grief, / Daring, since Byron died. /
Matthew Arnold, *Haworth Churchyard*

In Emily's nature the extremes of vigour and simplicity seemed to meet. Under an unsophisticated culture, inartificial tastes, and an unpretending outside lay a secret power and fire that might have informed the brains and kindled the veins of a hero; but she had no worldly wisdom; her powers were unadapted to the practical business of life: she would fail to defend her most manifest rights, to consult her most legitimate advantage. An interpreter ought always to have stood between her and the world.
Charlotte Brontë, Preface to *Wuthering Heights*

Posterity has paid its debt to her too generously, and with too little understanding.
Ivy Compton-Burnett, Letter to Anthony Powell

I've been greatly interested in *Wuthering Heights*, the first novel I've read for an age, and the best (as regards power and sound style) for two ages . . . But it is a fiend of a book, an incredible monster, combining all the stronger female tendencies from Mrs Browning to Mrs Brownrigg. The action is laid in Hell, – only it seems places and people have English names there.
D. G. Rossetti, Letter to William Allingham, 19 September 1854

## BRONTËS (COLLECTIVELY)

Literary criticism of the Brontës has been a long game of masculine prejudice wherein the player either proves they can't write and are hopeless primitives, whereupon the critic sets himself up like a schoolmaster to edit their stuff and point out where they went wrong, or converts them into case histories from the wilds, occasionally prefacing his moves with a few pseudo-sympathetic remarks about the windy house on the moors, or old maidhood, following with an attack on every truth the novels contain, waged by anxious pedants who fear Charlotte might 'castrate' them or Emily 'unman' them with her passion.
Kate Millett, *Sexual Politics*

## BROOKE, RUPERT CHAWNER

1887–1915 Poet

If I should die, think only this of me: / That there's some corner of a foreign field / That is forever England. /
On himself, *The Soldier*

The thoughts to which he gave expression in the very few incomparable war sonnets which he has left behind will be shared by many thousands of young men moving resolutely and blithely forward into this, the hardest, the cruellest, and the least-rewarded of all the wars that men have fought. They are a whole history and revelation of Rupert Brooke himself. Joyous, fearless, versatile, deeply instructed, with classic symmetry of mind and body, he was all that one would wish England's noblest sons to be in days when no sacrifice but the most precious is acceptable, and the most precious is that which is most freely proffered.
Winston Churchill, Obituary in *The Times*, 26 April 1915

The death of Rupert Brooke fills me more and more with the sense of the fatuity of it all. He was slain by bright Phoebus' shaft – it was in keeping with his general sunniness – it was the real climax of his pose. I first heard of him as a Greek god under a Japanese sunshade, reading poetry in his pyjamas, at Grantchester, – at Grantchester upon the lawns where the river goes. Bright

Phoebus smote him down. It is all in the saga.

D. H. Lawrence, Letter to Lady Ottoline Morrell, 30 April 1915

He energized the Garden-Suburb ethos with a certain original talent and the vigour of a prolonged adolescence. His verse exhibits a genuine sensuousness rather like Keats's (though more energetic) and something that is rather like Keats's vulgarity with a Public School accent.

F. R. Leavis, *New Bearings in English Poetry*

He was, in a sense, very neurotic. I think he was very highly-strung. Supposing he had been alive today, his early experiences wouldn't have made him so. But in that day and age, in his class, men knew as little about sex really as women did. He fell in love and induced a woman to live with him and then grew out of love with her. He thought she was with child by him, and then she had a miscarriage, and the whole thing put a terrible guilt complex in him. But once he'd got over that, he seemed extraordinarily sane and balanced.

Cathleen Nesbitt, in *Listener*, 20 January 1972

Rupert had immense charm when he wanted to be charming, and he was inclined to exploit his charm so that he seemed to be sometimes too much the professional charmer. He had a very pronounced streak of hardness, even cruelty, in his character, and his attitude to all other males within a short radius of any attractive female was ridiculously jealous – the attitude of a farmyard cock among the hens.

Leonard Woolf, *Beginning Again*

Yeats talked about you the other night. He thinks you are likely to be a considerable person if you can get rid of what he calls 'languid sensuality' and get in its place 'robust sensuality'. I suppose you will understand this.

William Butler Yeats, reported in St John Ervine, Letter to Brooke, January 1913

He is the handsomest man in England, and he wears the most beautiful shirts.

William Butler Yeats, in conversation, January 1913

## BROOKS, VAN WYCK

1886–1963 Author

Although he turned out to be a critic of divided mind, a man whose life was broken in half, in one respect his career was all of a piece: from first to last he sought to transform America from an industrial jungle into a place fit for the realization of Emerson's Romantic dream.

William Wasserstrom, *Van Wyck Brooks*

## BROUGHAM, HENRY PETER, LORD BROUGHAM AND VAUX

1778–1868 Statesman, Author

Never was there a subject that Grey did not say the Government was gone if I did not speak, and generally if I did not undertake it. All this necessarily led to my *interfering* . . . as to *domineering* it is possibly true. I am of a hasty and violent, at least vehement, nature, and not bred in courts or offices, and never was a subaltern, therefore I am a bad courtier. However I meant no harm and never grudged work; and always, both in and out of Parliament, was working as hard as a horse for the party, and never once for myself or to thwart them.

On himself, Letter to Lord Spencer, January 1835

He was a kind of prophet of knowledge. His voice was heard in the streets. He preached the gospel of the alphabet; he sang the praises of the primer all day long.

Walter Bagehot, *Biographical Studies*: 'Lord Brougham'

If he were a horse, nobody would buy him; with that eye, no one could answer for his temper.

*Ibid.*

Mr Brougham's mountain is delivered, and behold! – the mouse. The wisdom of the reformer could not overcome the craft of the lawyer. Mr Brougham, after all, is not the man to set up a simple, natural, and rational administration of justice against the entanglements and technicalities of our English law proceedings.

Jeremy Bentham, Memorandum: 'On Brougham's Law Reform', after Brougham's speech of 7 February 1828

Beware lest blundering Brougham destroy the sale, / Turn beef to bannocks, cauliflower to kail. /

Lord Byron, *English Bards and Scotch Reviewers*

The fault of Mr Brougham is, that he holds no intellect at present in great dread, and, consequently, allows himself on all occasions to run wild. Few men hazard more unphilosophical speculations; but he is safe, because there is no one to notice them. On all great occasions, Mr Brougham has come up to the mark; an infallible test of a man of genius.

Benjamin Disraeli, *The Young Duke*

This curious and versatile creature . . . after acting Jupiter one day in the House of Lords, is ready to act Scapin anywhere else the next.

Charles Greville, Diary, 9 August 1839

His eye is as fine an eye I ever saw. It is like a lion's, watching for prey. It is a clear grey, the light vibrating at the bottom of the iris, and the cornea shining, silvery and tense. I never before had the opportunity of examining Brougham's face with the scrutiny of a painter, and I am astonished at that extraordinary eye.

Benjamin Haydon, *Autobiography*

He is at home in the crooked mazes of rotten boroughs, is not baffled by Scotch law, and can follow the meaning of one of Mr Canning's speeches.

William Hazlitt, *The Spirit of the Age*

Lo! in Corruption's lumber-room, / The remnants of a wondrous broom; / That walking, talking, oft was seen, / Making stout promise to sweep clean; / But evermore, at every push, / Proved but a stump without a brush. / Upon its handle-top, a sconce, / Like Brahma's, looked four ways at once, / Pouring on king, lords, church and rabble / Long floods of favour-currying gabble; / From four-fold mouth-piece always spinning / Projects of plausible beginning, / Whereof said sconce did ne'er intend / That any one should have an end; / Yet still by shifts and quaint inventions, / Got credit for its good intentions, / Adding no trifle to the store, / Wherewith the devil paves his floor. / Worn out at last, found bare and scrubbish, / And thrown aside with other rubbish, / We'll e'en hand o'er the enchanted stick, / As a choice present for Old Nick, / To sweep, beyond the Stygian lake, / The pavement it has helped to make. /

Thomas Love Peacock, in *Examiner*, August 1831

Bias of honour, place, wealth, worldly good, / Drew all away; he would not so be drawn. / Truth's and Right's soldier from the first he stood, / And in the thickest darkness looked for dawn. /

Tom Taylor, in *Punch*, 30 May 1868

. . . he might have been any *one* of ten first-rate kinds of men, but . . . he tried to be *all* ten, and has failed.
*The Times*, in Walter Bagehot, *Biographical Studies*: 'Sir George Cornewall Lewis'

He was one of those characters in real life who would appear incredible in fiction. He was so marvellously ill-favoured as to possess some of the attractiveness of a gargoyle. He had neither dignity, nor what a Roman would have called gravity. As Lord Chancellor, he distinguished himself by belching from the Woolsack.
Esmé Wingfield-Stratford, in L. Levinson ed., *Bartlett's Unfamiliar Quotations*

*See also* John Cavanagh

## BROUN, HEYWOOD CAMPBELL

1888–1939 Journalist

The trouble with me is that I inherited an insufficient amount of vengeful feeling. Kings, princes, dukes and even local squires rode their horses so that they stepped upon the toes of my ancestors, who did nothing about it except to apologize. I would then have joined more eagerly in pulling down the Bastille, but if anybody had caught me at it and given me a sharp look I'm afraid I would have put it back again.
On himself, in Robert E. Drennan ed., *Wit's End*

No one is so impotent that, meeting Broun face to face, he cannot frighten him into any lie. Any mouse can make this elephant squeal. Yet, I know no more honest being, for, when not threatened, his speech is an innocent emptying of his mind as a woman empties her purse, himself genuinely curious about its contents.
Alexander Woollcott, in Edwin P. Hoyt, *Alexander Woollcott: The Man Who Came to Dinner*

## BROUNCKER, WILLIAM, VISCOUNT

1620?–84 First President of the Royal Society

I perceive he is a rotten-hearted, false man as any else I know, even as Sir W. Pen himself, and, therefore, I must beware of him accordingly, and I hope I shall.
Samuel Pepys, Diary, 29 January 1666–7

## BROWN, FORD MADOX

1821–93 Painter

He would make no concessions and play no tricks, he was obstinate and rancorous, and he is so rare an example of popularity forfeited that by every rule of the game, he should have appeared today in force only to confound the generations that misjudged him. He is, however, not quite up to his part. The sincerity that shines out in him lights up not only the vulgarity of his age, but too many of his own perversities and pedantries.
Henry James, 'Lord Leighton and Ford Madox Brown', in *Harper's Weekly*, 1897

Do you not see that his name never occurs in my books – do you think that would be so if I *could* praise him, seeing that he is an entirely worthy fellow? But pictures are pictures, and things that ar'n't ar'n't.
John Ruskin, Letter to Ellen Heaton, March 1862

## BROWN, JOHN

1800–59 Abolitionist

I am fully persuaded that I am worth inconceivably more to hang than for any other purpose.
On himself, 2 November 1859, in Burton Stevenson, *The Home Book of Quotations*

Nature obviously was deeply intent in the making of him. He is of imposing appearance, personally, – tall, with square shoulders and standing; eyes of deep gray, and couchant, as if ready to spring at the least rustling, dauntless yet kindly; his hair shooting backward from low down on his forehead; nose trenchant and Romanesque; set lips, his voice suppressed yet metallic, suggesting deep reserves; decided mouth; the countenance and frame charged with power throughout . . . I think him about the manliest man I have ever seen, – the type and synonym of the Just.

Amos Bronson Alcott, in *ibid.*

. . . A stone eroded to a cutting edge / By obstinacy failure and cold prayers . . . / And with a certain minor prophet air / That fooled the world to thinking him half-great / When all he did consistently was fail. /

Stephen Vincent Benét, *John Brown's Body*

John Brown's body lies a-mouldering in the grave / But his soul goes marching on.

C. S. Hall, *John Brown's Body*

The death of Brown is more than Cain killing Abel: it is Washington slaying Spartacus.

Victor Hugo, *A Word Concerning John Brown to Virginia*, 2 December 1859

The Portent / Hanging from the beam, / Slowly swaying (such the law), / Gaunt the shadow on your green, / Shenandoah! / The cut is on the crown / (Lo John Brown), / And the stabs shall heal no more. /

Hidden in the cap / Is the anguish none can draw; / So your future veils its face, / Shenandoah! / But the streaming beard is shown / (Weird John Brown), / The meteor of the War. /

Herman Melville, in F. O. Matthiessen ed., *The Oxford Book of American Verse*

I would now sing how an old man, tall with white hair, / mounted the scaffold in Virginia. / (I was at hand, silent I stood with teeth shut close, I watched / I stood very near you old man when cool and indifferent, / but trembling with age and your inheal'd wounds / you mounted the scaffold.) /

Walt Whitman, *Leaves of Grass*

## BROWN, ROBERT

1773–1858 Naturalist

I saw a good deal of Robert Brown, 'facile Princeps Botanicorum', as he was called by Humboldt. He seemed to me to be chiefly remarkable for the minuteness of his observations and their perfect accuracy. His knowledge was extraordinarily great, and much died with him, owing to his excessive fear of ever making a mistake. He poured out his knowledge to me in the most unreserved manner, yet was strangely jealous on some points. I called on him two or three times before the voyage of the *Beagle*, and on one occasion he asked me to look through a microscope and describe what I saw. This I did, and believe now that it was the marvellous currents of protoplasm in some vegetable cell. I then asked him what I had seen; but he answered me, 'That is my little secret'.

Charles Darwin, *Autobiography*

Perhaps no naturalist ever recorded the results of his investigations in fewer words and with greater precision than Robert Brown: certainly no one ever took more pains to state nothing beyond the precise point in question. Indeed we have sometimes fancied that he preferred to enwrap rather than to explain his meaning; to put it into such a form that, unless you follow Solomon's injunction and dig for the wisdom as for hid treasure, you may hardly apprehend it until you have found it all out for yourself, when you will have the satisfaction of perceiving that Mr Brown not only knew all about it, but put it upon record long before.

Asa Gray, in *Nature*, 4 June 1874

## BROWNE, SIR THOMAS

1605–82 Physician, Author

I dare, without usurpation, assume the honourable style of Christian.

On himself, *Religio Medici*, part 1

Lord, deliver me from myself.

On himself, *Religio Medici*, part 2

It would be difficult to describe Browne adequately; exuberant in conception and conceit, dignified, hyper-latinistic, a quiet and sublime enthusiast; yet a fantast, a humourist, a brain with a twist; egotistic like Montaigne, yet with a feeling heart and an active curiosity, which, however, too often degenerates into a hunting after oddities.

Samuel Taylor Coleridge, *Literary Remains*

Sir Thomas Browne seemed to be of opinion that the only business of life was to think, and that the proper object of speculation was, by darkening knowledge, to breed more speculation, and 'find no end in wandering mazes lost'. He chose the incomprehensible and impracticable as almost the only subjects fit for a lofty and lasting contemplation, or for the exercise of a solid faith . . . He pushes a question to the utmost verge of conjecture, that he may repose on the certainty of doubt . . . he delighted in the preternatural and visionary, and he only existed at the circumference of his nature.

William Hazlitt, *Character of Sir T. Browne as a Writer*

His style is, indeed, a tissue of many languages; a mixture of heterogeneous words, brought together from distant regions, with terms originally appropriated to one art, and drawn by violence into the service of another. He must, however, be confessed to have augmented our philosophical diction; and in defence of uncommon words and expressions, we must consider, that he had uncommon sentiments.

Samuel Johnson, *Life of Browne*

Who would not be curious to see the lineaments of a man who, having himself been twice married, wished that mankind were propagated like trees!

Charles Lamb, as reported by William Hazlitt, 'On Persons One Would wish to have Seen', in *New Monthly Magazine*, January 1826

It is interesting – or at least amusing – to consider what are the most appropriate places in which different authors should be read. Pope is doubtless at his best in the midst of a formal garden, Herrick in an orchard, and Shelley in a boat at sea. Sir Thomas Browne demands, perhaps, a more exotic atmosphere. One could read him floating down the Euphrates, or past the shores of Arabia; and it would be pleasant to open the *Vulgar Errors* in Constantinople, or to get by heart a chapter of the *Christian Morals* between the paws of a Sphinx.

Lytton Strachey, *Books and Characters*

His immense egotism has paved the way for all psychological novelists, autobiographers, confession-mongers, and dealers in the curious shades of our private life. He it was who first turned from the contacts of man with man, to their lonely life within.

Virginia Woolf, *The Common Reader*

*See also* Samuel Taylor Coleridge, Robert Louis Stevenson

## BROWNING, ELIZABETH BARRETT

1806–61 Poet

The Greatest Novel Reader in the World.

On herself, Proposed epitaph

The simple truth is that *she* was the poet, and I the clever person by comparison.

Robert Browning, Letter to Isa Blagden, 19 August 1871

Mrs Browning's death is rather a relief to me, I must say. No more Aurora Leighs, thank God! A woman of real genius, I know; but what is the upshot of it all? She and her sex had better mind the kitchen and the children; and perhaps the poor. Except in such things as little novels, they only devote themselves to what men do much better, leaving that which men do worse or not at all.

Edward Fitzgerald, in W. A. Wright, *Letters and Literary Remains of Edward Fitzgerald*

The poetess was everything I did not like. She had great cavernous eyes, glowering out under two big bushes of black ringlets, a fashion I had not beheld before. She never laughed, or even smiled, once, during the whole conversation, and through all the gloom of the shuttered room I could see that her face was hollow and ghastly pale. *Mamma mia*! but I was glad when I got out into the sunshine again.

Mrs Hugh Fraser, *A Diplomatist's Wife in Many Lands*

Her physique was peculiar: curls like the pendant ears of a water spaniel and poor little hands – so thin that when she welcomed you she gave you something like the foot of a young bird.

Frederick Locker, *My Confidences*

She was just like a King Charles Spaniel, the same large soft brown eyes, the full silky curls falling round her face like a spaniel's ears, the same pathetic wistfulness of expression. Her mouth was too large for beauty, but full of eloquent curves and movements. Her voice was very expressive, her manner gentle but full of energy. At times she became intense in tone and gesture, but it was so spontaneous, that nobody could ever have thought it assumed as is the fashion with later poets and poetesses.

Mrs David Ogilvy, *Recollections of Mrs Browning*

## BROWNING, ROBERT

1812–89 Poet

That bard's a Browning; he neglects the form: / But ah, the sense, ye gods, the weighty sense! /

On himself, *The Inn Album*

As to my own Poems – they must be left to Providence and that fine sense of discrimination which I never cease to meditate upon and admire in the public: they cry out for new things and when you furnish them with what they cried for, 'it's *so* new', they grunt.

On himself, Letter to John Ruskin, 10 December 1855

I can have but little doubt that my writing has been, in the main, too hard for many I should have been pleased to communicate with; but I never designedly tried to puzzle people, as some of my critics have supposed. On the other hand, I never pretended to offer such literature as should be a substitute for a cigar, or a game of dominoes, to an idle man. So perhaps, on the whole, I get my deserts and something over – not a crowd, but a few I value more.

On himself, Letter to W. G. Kingsland, 1868

Browning is a man with a moderate gift passionately desiring movement and fulness, and obtaining but a confused multitudinousness.

Matthew Arnold, Letter to A. H. Clough, 1848–9

Robert Browning / Immediately stopped frowning / And started to blush / When fawned on by Flush. /

W. H. Auden, *Academic Graffiti*

He is at once a student of mysticism and a citizen of the world. He brings to the club-sofa distinct visions of old creeds, intense images of strange thoughts: he takes to the bookish student tidings of wild Bohemia, and little traces of the *demi-monde*. He puts down what is good for the naughty, and what is naughty for the good. Over women his easier writings exercise that imperious power which belongs to the writings of a great man of the world upon such matters. He knows women, and therefore they wish to know him.

Walter Bagehot, *Wordsworth, Tennyson, and Browning*

It became a favourite pastime for ingenious brains to construe the craggiest passages in Browning, and to read him was for long in England the mark of a taste for nimble intellectual exercise rather than for a love of poetry . . . His ideas were new, for poetry – and for that reason people thought them at first obscure – but they were quite clear. Only he had as it were a stutter in his utterance.

Rupert Brooke, *Browning*

Browning used words with the violence of a horse-breaker, giving out the scent of a he-goat. But he got them to do their work.

Ford Madox Ford, *The March of Literature*

Other poets say anything – say everything that is in them. Browning lived to realize the myth of the Inexhaustible Bottle.

W. E. Henley, in *Athenaeum*, 22 August 1885

The idea, with Mr Browning, always tumbles out into the world in some grotesque hind-foremost manner; it is like an unruly horse backing out of his stall, and stamping and plunging as he comes. His thought knows no simple stage – at the very moment of its birth it is a terribly complicated affair.

Henry James, in *Nation*, 20 January 1876

Shelley . . . is a light, and Swinburne is a sound – Browning alone is a temperature.

Henry James, 'The Novel in "The Ring and the Book"'

Browning! Since Chaucer was alive and hale, / No man hath walk'd along our roads with step / So active, so inquiring eye, or tongue / So varied in discourse. /

Walter Savage Landor, *To Robert Browning*

Behold him shambling go, / At once himself the showman and the show, / Street preacher of Parnassus, roll on high / His blinking orbs, and rant tautology, / While gaping multitudes around the monk / Much wonder if inspired, or simply drunk. /

William Leech, *The Obliviad*

Old Hippety-Hop o' the accents.

Ezra Pound, *Mesmerism*

Robert Browning is unerring in every sentence he writes of the Middle Ages; always vital, right and profound; so that in the matter of art, with which we have been specially concerned, there is hardly a principle connected with the mediaeval temper, that he has not struck upon in those seemingly careless and too rugged lines of his.

John Ruskin, *Modern Painters*

Mr Browning intends apparently to finish a laborious life in an access or paroxysm of indiscriminate production. He floods acres of paper with brackets and inverted commas. He showers octavos on the public with a facility and grace like that of a conjuror scattering shoulder-knots and comfits out of a confederate's hat. What! we exclaim, all this monstrous quantity of verse out of no more of a poet than can be buttoned into one single-breasted waistcoat!

Robert Louis Stevenson, in *Vanity Fair*, 11 December 1875

Mr Browning has in the supreme degree the qualities of a great debater or an eminent leading counsel; his finest reasoning has in its expression and development something of the ardour of personal energy and active interest which inflames the argument of a public speaker; we feel . . . how many a first rate barrister or parliamentary tactician has been lost in this poet.

A. C. Swinburne, *George Chapman*

To charge him with obscurity is as accurate as to call Lynceus purblind, or complain of the sluggish action of the telegraph wire. He is something too much the reverse of obscure; he is too brilliant and subtle for the ready reader to follow with any certainty the track of an intelligence which moves with such incessant rapidity.

*Ibid.*

*This* bard's a Browning! – there's no doubt of that: / But, ah, ye gods, *the sense!* Are we so sure / If sense be sense unto our common-sense, / Low sense to higher, high to low, no sense, / All sense to those, all sense no sense to these? / That's where your poet tells! – and you've no right / (Insensate sense with sensuous thought being mixed) / To ask analysis! /

Bayard Taylor, in *New York Daily Tribune*, 4 December 1875

He has plenty of music in him, but he cannot get it out.

Alfred, Lord Tennyson, in Hallam Tennyson, *Tennyson: A Memoir by his Son*

Meredith is a prose Browning, and so is Browning. He used poetry as a medium for writing in prose.

Oscar Wilde, *The Critic as Artist*

In art, only Browning can make action and psychology one.

Oscar Wilde, Letter to H. C. Marillier, *circa* November 1885

*See also* Matthew Arnold, John Keats

## BRUCE, JAMES

1730–94 African Traveller

Bruce, drooping, bending in despondency over the fountains of the Nile must ever form a most striking picture, exemplifying the real practical difference which exists between moral and religious exertions; for although, among men, he had gained his prize, it may justly be asked, what was it worth? The course of a river is like the history of a man's life. All of it that is useful to us is worth knowing: but the source of the one is the birth of the other, and the 'hillock of green sod' is 'the infant mewling and puking in the nurse's arms.'

Major F. B. Head, *Life of Bruce*

For several hours every effort was made to restore him to the world; all that is usual, customary, and useless in such cases was performed. There was the bustle, the hurry, the confusion, the grief unspeakable, the village leech, his lancet, his phial, and his little pill; but the lamp was out, – the book was closed, – the lease was up – the game was won – the daring, restless, injured spirit had burst from the covert, and was – away!

*Ibid.*

Someone asked him what musical instruments were used in Abyssinia. Bruce hesitated, not being prepared for the question; and at last said, 'I think I only saw one *lyre* there.' George Selwyn whispered his next man, 'Yes; and there is one less since he left the country.'

John Pinkerton, *Walpoliana*

## BRUCE, LENNY (LEONARD ALFRED SCHNEIDER)

1926–66 Comedian

I'm Super-Jew!

On himself, shouted as he leapt from a window in an apparent, though unsuccessful, suicide attempt

Though he leaves a red-faced litter of bluenoses and blow-hard columnists in his wake, Bruce remains the most powerful after-dinner monologist since Teddy Roosevelt.

Anon., in *Show Business Illustrated*, April 1962

Usually he worked on the rim of danger. He let the weird notions run. When one clicked, it'd lock in in Bruce's mind, and he'd get the rush all comics do who move off the moment. Bruce did it more than other comics did. He took the chances. He was not afraid to fall flat on his arse with new material. There were those that saw him go gurgling down the drain one night and make thunder the next.

Philip Berger, *The Last Laugh*

Instead of working out of phony show-biz 'charm' and cuteness and carefully rehearsed topicality, Lenny Bruce was hitting the late fifties' mainline – the sense of smothered rage.

Albert Goldman, *Ladies and Gentlemen, Lenny Bruce!!*

He always suffered from verbal disabilities: a tendency to singsong, a habit of mumbling, a coy and uncomfortable relation with the mike. Only late at night, when he was working to a very hip crowd and the Methedrine was scalding through his veins could he ever attain the energy level of the parent style. When he did, though, he produced the most dazzling poetry of his entire career.

*Ibid.*

His gospel was freedom, sexual freedom, racial freedom, religious freedom, cliché freedom, hate freedom – in short, happiness through truth. Bruce enraged many people, including some arresting officers and psychiatrists and judges and prosecutors and critics who by the record of their lives and deeds were at least as sick as he was. But wasn't that what his whole *shtick* was about?

Jerry Tallmer, in John Cohen, *The Essential Lenny Bruce*

## BRYAN, WILLIAM JENNINGS

1860–1925 Politician

. . . money-grabbing, selfish, office seeking, favour hunting, publicity-loving, marplot from Nebraska.

Anon., in D. H. Elletson, *Roosevelt and Wilson: A Comparative Study*

. . . a halfbaked glib little briefless jack-leg lawyer . . . grasping with anxiety to collar that $50,000 salary, promising the millennium to everybody with a hole in his pants and destruction to everybody with a clean shirt.

John Hay, in Paolo E. Coletta, 'The Bryan Campaign of 1896', in P. W. Glad, *William Jennings Bryan: A Profile*

One could drive a prairie schooner through any part of his argument and never scrape against a fact.

David Houston, in John A. Garraty, 'A Leader of the People', in *ibid.*

I brag and chant of Bryan, Bryan, Bryan, Bryan, / Candidate for president who sketched a silver zion. /

Vachel Lindsay, *Bryan, Bryan, Bryan, Bryan*

The President of the United States may be an ass, but he at least doesn't believe that the earth is square, and that witches should be put to death, and that Jonah swallowed the whale.

H. L. Mencken, in John A. Garraty, 'Bryan: The Progressives, Part 1', *American Heritage*, December 1961

What a disgusting, dishonest fakir Bryan is! When I see so many Americans running after him, I feel very much as I do when a really lovely woman falls in love with a cad.

Elihu Root, Letter to William M. Laffa, 31 October 1900

His mind was like a soup dish, wide and shallow; it could hold a small amount of nearly anything, but the slightest jarring spilled the soup into somebody's lap.

Irving Stone, *They Also Ran*

*See also* Theodore Roosevelt

## BRYANT, WILLIAM CULLEN

1794–1878 Poet, Editor

Poetry often seems for Bryant something hallowed and set apart, like a best parlor filled with marmoreal statuary that is only opened up on Sundays. It is a little difficult to speak naturally or breathe very deeply in it.

Marius Bewley, in *William Cullen Bryant*, in Perry Miller ed., *Major Writers of America*, vol. I

It has always seemed to me Bryant, more than any other American, had the power to suck in the air of spring, to put it into his song, to breathe it forth again . . . never a wasted word – the last superfluity struck off a clear nameless beauty pervading and overarching all the work of his pen.

Walt Whitman, in Edgar Lee Masters, *Whitman*

## BUCHANAN, GEORGE

1506–82 Scholar, Author

In a conversation concerning the literary merits of the two countries, a Scotchman, imagining that on this ground he should have an undoubted triumph over him, exclaimed, 'Ah, Dr Johnson, what would you have said of Buchanan, had he been an Englishman?' – 'Why, Sir, (said Johnson, after a little pause), I should *not* have said of Buchanan, had he been an *Englishman*, what I will now say of him as a *Scotchman*, – that he was the only man of genius his country ever produced.'

James Boswell, *Life of Johnson*

## BUCHANAN, JAMES

1791–1868 Fifteenth United States President

President James Buchanan is known as The Only President Who Never Married, and thus has become extremely useful in quizzes and crossword puzzles.

Richard Armour, *It All Began With Columbus*

The Constitution provides for every accidental contingency in the Executive – except a vacancy in the mind of the President.

Senator Sherman of Ohio, in A. K. Adams, *The Home Book of Humorous Quotations*

There is no such person running as James Buchanan. *He is dead of lockjaw*. Nothing remains but a platform and a bloated mass of political putridity.

Thaddeus Stevens, in Fawn M. Brodie, *Thaddeus Stevens, Scourge of the South*

## BUCKINGHAM, FIRST DUKE OF (GEORGE VILLIERS)

1592–1628 Statesman, Royal Favourite

Who rules the Kingdom? The King!
Who rules the King? The Duke!

Who rules the Duke? The Devil!
Anon., Contemporary graffiti

But it is generally given to him who is the little god at court, to be the great devil in the country. The commonalty hated him with a perfect hatred; and all miscarriages in Church and state, at home, abroad, at sea and land, were charged on his want of wisdom, valour, or loyalty.

John Felton, a melancholy, malcontented gentleman, and a sullen soldier, apprehending himself injured, could find no other way to revenge his conceived wrongs, than by writing them with a point of a knife in the heart of the Duke, whom he stabbed at Portsmouth, Anno Domini, 1629. It is hard to say how many of this nation were guilty of this murder, either by public praising, or private approving thereof.

His person, from head to foot could not be charged with any blemish, save that some hypercritics conceived his brows somewhat overpendulous, a cloud which in the judgement of others was by the beams of his eyes sufficiently dispelled.
Thomas Fuller, *The History of the Worthies of England*

. . . His ascent was so quick, that it seemed rather a flight than a growth, and he was such a darling of fortune, that he was at the topp, before he was seen at the bottome . . . If he had an immediate ambition, with which hee was charged, and is a weede (if it bee a weede) apt to grow in the best soyles, it does not appeare that it was in his nature, or that he brought it with him to the Courte, but rather found it there, and was a garment necessary for that ayre: nor was it more in his power to be without promotion and titles, and wealth, then for a healthy man to sitt in the sunn, in the brightest dogge days, and remayne without any warmth: he needed no ambition who was so seated in the hertes of two such masters.
Edward Hyde, Earl of Clarendon, *History of the Rebellion*

Christ has his John, and I have my George.
James I, attributed

The King cast a glancing eye towards him, which was easily observed by such as observed their Prince's humour . . . then one gave him his place of Cup-bearer, that he might be in the King's eye; another sent to his Mercer and Taylor to put good cloathes on him; a third to his Sempster for curious linnen, and all as in-comes to obtain offices upon his future rise; then others took upon themselves to be his Braccoes, to undertake his quarrels upon affronts, put upon him by *Somerset's* Faction. So all hands helped to the piecing up this new Favourite.
Anthony Weldon, *Court and Character of James I*

No one dances better, no man runs or jumps better. Indeed he jumped higher than ever Englishman did in so short a time, from a private gentleman to a dukedom.
Arthur Wilson, *The History of Great Britain*

## BUCKINGHAM, SECOND DUKE OF (GEORGE VILLIERS)

1628–87 Statesman

He had no principles of religion, vertue, or friendship. Pleasure, frolick, or extravagant diversion was all that he laid to heart. He was true to nothing, for he was not true to himself. He had no steadiness of conduct: He could keep no secret, nor execute any design without spoiling it. He could never fix his thoughts, nor govern his estate, tho' then the greatest in *England.* He was bred about the King: and for many years he had a great ascendent over him: But he spake of him to all persons with that contempt, that at last he drew a lasting disgrace upon himself.

Gilbert Burnet, *History of My Own Time*

A Duke of Bucks, Is one that has studied the whole Body of Vice. His parts are disproportionate to the whole, and like a Monster he has more of some, and less of others than he should have. He has pulled down all that Fabrick that Nature raised in him, and built himself up again after a model of his own. He has dam'd up all those Lights, that Nature made into the noblest Prospects of the World, and opened other little blind Loopholes backward, by turning Day into Night, and Night into Day. His appetite to his Pleasures is diseased and crazy, like the Pica in a Woman, that longs to eat that, which was never made for food, or a Girl in the Green-sickness that eats Chalk and Mortar . . . He endures Pleasures with less Patience, than other Men do their Pains.

Samuel Butler, *The Character of A Duke of Bucks*

A Man so various, that he seem'd to be, / Not one, but all Mankind's Epitome. / Stiff in Opinions, always in the wrong; / Was Everything by starts and Nothing long: / But, in the course of one revolving Moon, / Was Chymist, Fidler, Statesman, and Buffoon; / Then all for Women, Painting, Rhyming, Drinking, / Besides ten thousand Freaks that died in thinking. / Blest Madman who could every Hour employ / With something New to wish or to enjoy! / Railing and praising were his usual Theams; / And both (to shew his Judgement) in Extreams: / So over Violent or over Civil, / That every Man with him was God or Devil. / In squandring Wealth was his peculiar Art: / Nothing went unrewarded, but Desert. / Begger'd by Fools, whom still he found too late: / He had his Jest, and they had his Estate. /

John Dryden, *Absalom and Achitophel*

Buckingham was a sated man of pleasure who had turned to ambition as a pastime.

T. B. Macaulay, *History of England*

They do tell me here that the Duke of Buckingham hath surrendered himself to Secretary Morrice and is going to the Tower. Mr Fenn at the table says that he hath been taken by the Wach two or three times of late at unseasonable hours, but so disguised that they could not know him (and when I came home, by and by, Mr Lowther tells me that the Duke of Buckingham doth dine publicly this day at Wadlows, at the Sun Tavern and is mighty merry, and sent word to the Lieutenant of the Tower that he would come to him as soon as he had dined): Now, how sad a thing it is when we come to make sport of proclaiming men traitors and banishing them, and putting them out of their offices and Privy Council, and of sending to and going to the Tower. God have mercy on us.

Samuel Pepys, Diary, 28 June 1667

In the worst inn's worst room with mat half-hung, / The floors of plaister and the walls of dung, / On once a flock-bed, but repair'd with straw, / With tape-ty'd curtains, never meant to draw, / The George and Garter dangling from the bed / Where tawdry yellow strove with dirty red, / Great Villiers lies – alas! how chang'd from him, / That life of pleasure, and that soul of whim! / Gallant and gay, in Cliveden's proud alcove, / The bow'r of wanton Shrewsbury and love; / Or just as gay, at Council, in a ring / Of mimick'd Statesmen, and their merry King. / No Wit to flatter left of all his store! / No Fool to laugh at, which he valu'd more. / There, Victor of his health, of fortune,

friends, / And fame, this lord of useless thousands ends. /
Alexander Pope, *Epistle iii, to Allen Lord Bathurst*

The witty Duke of Buckingham was an extreme bad man. His duel with Lord Shrewsbury was concerted between him and Lady Shrewsbury. All that morning she was trembling for her gallant, and wishing the death of her husband; and, after his fall, 'tis said the Duke slept with her in his bloody shirt.
Alexander Pope, in Joseph Spence, *Anecdotes*

But when degrees of Villany we name, / How can we choose but think of B(uckingham)? / He who through all of them has boldly ran, / Left ne're a Law unbroke by God or Man. / His treasur'd sins of Supererrogation, / Swell to a summ enough to damn a Nation: / But he must here, perforce, be left alone, / His acts require a Volumn of their own. /
John Wilmot, Earl of Rochester, *Rochester's Farewell*

## BULL, JOHN
1563?–1628 Composer

The Bull by force / In Field doth Raigne, / But Bull by Skill / Good will doth gayne. /
Anon., from the portrait of Bull in the Oxford Music School, 1589

I have been frequently astonished, in perusing Dr Bull's lessons, at the few new and pleasing passages which his hand suggested to his pen. It has been said, that the late Dr Pepusch preferred Bull's compositions to those of Couperin and Scarlatti, not only for harmony and contrivance, but air and modulation: an assertion which rather proves that the Doctor's taste was *bad*, than Bull's Music *good*. Though I should greatly admire the hand, as well as the patience, of any one capable of playing his compositions; yet, *as Music*, they would afford me no kind of pleasure: *Ce sont des notes, & rien que des notes;* there is nothing in them which excites rapture. They may be heard by a lover of Music with as little emotion as the clapper of a mill, or the rumbling of a post-chaise.
Dr Charles Burney, *A General History of Music*

He made the invention of new difficulties of every kind which could impede or dismay a performer his sole study.
*Ibid.*

Of all the bulls that live, this hath the greatest asses ears.
Elizabeth I, attributed

The queens will being to know the said music, her Grace was at that time at the virginals: whereupon, he, being in attendance, Master Bull did come by stealth to hear without, and by mischance did sprawl into the queens Majesties Presence, to the queens great disturbance. She demanding incontinent the wherefore of such presumption, Master Bull with great skill said that wheresoever Majesty and Music so well combined, no man might abase himself too deeply; whereupon the queen's Majesty was mollified and said that so rare a Bull hath sung as sweet as Byrd.
Peter Philips, *A Briefe Chronicle*

Dr Bull hearing of a famous musician belonging to a certain cathedral at St Omer's, he applied himself as a novice to him, to learn something of his faculty, and to see and admire his works. This musician, after some discourse had passed between them, conducted Bull to a vestry or music-school joining to the cathedral, and shewed to him a lesson or song of forty parts, and then made a vaunting challenge to any person in the world to add one more part to them, supposing it to be so complete and full that it was impossible for any mortal man to correct or add to it; Bull thereupon desiring the use of pen, ink and ruled paper, such as we call musical paper; prayed the musician to lock him up in the said school for two or three hours; which being done, not without great disdain by the musician, Bull in that time or less, added forty more parts to the said lesson or song. The musician thereupon being called in, he viewed it, tried it, and retried it; at length he burst out into a great ecstasy, and swore by the great God that he that added those forty parts must either be the Devil or Dr Bull, etc. Whereupon Bull making himself known, the musician fell down and adored him.

Anthony à Wood, *Fasti Oxonienses*

## BUNYAN, JOHN

1628–88 Religious Writer

I have not for these things fished in other men's waters; my Bible and Concordance are my only library in my writing.

On himself, *To the Christian Reader, Prefaratory to Solomon's Temple Spiritualized*

. . . but yet I did not think / To shew to all the world my pen and ink / In such a mode; I only thought to make / I knew not what; nor did I undertake / Thereby to please my neighbour; no, not I, / I did it mine own self to gratify. /

On himself, 'The Author's Apology for His Book', prefaced to *Pilgrim's Progress*

Nowhere perhaps, except in Homer, is there such perfect description by the use of merely plain words . . . The Elstow tinker produced an original thing, if an original thing was ever produced.

G. K. Chesterton, Introduction to *Pilgrim's Progress*

Bunyan was never, in our received sense of the word, wicked. He was chaste, sober, honest; but he was a bitter blackguard; that is, damned his own, or his neighbour's eyes on slight, or no occasion, and was fond of a row . . . The transmutation of actual reprobates into saints is doubtless possible; but like many recorded facts of corporeal alchemy, it is not supported by modern experiments.

Samuel Taylor Coleridge, *The Literary Remains of Samuel Taylor Coleridge*, 1836–9

Mr Bunyan . . . preached so New-Testament-like, that he made me admire and weep for joy, and give him my affections. And he was the first man that ever I heard preach to my unenlightened understanding and experience, for methought all his sermons were adapted to my condition, and had apt similitudes, being full of the love of God, and the manner of its secret working upon the soul, and of the soul under the sense of it, that I could weep for joy, most part of his sermons.

Charles Doe, *Experiences of Charles Doe*

Put your Shakespearian hero and coward, Henry V and Pistol, or Parolles, beside Mr Valiant, and Mr Fearing, and you have a sudden revelation of the abyss that lies between the fashionable author who could see nothing in the world but personal aims and the tragedy of their disappointment, or the comedy of their incongruity, and the field preacher who achieved virtue and courage by identifying himself with the purpose of the world as he understood it. The contrast is enormous: Bunyan's coward stirs your blood more than Shakespeare's hero, who actually leaves you cold and secretly hostile. You suddenly see that Shakespeare, with all his flashes and divinations, never understood virtue and courage, never conceived how any man who was not a fool, could, like Bunyan's hero, look back from the brink of the river of death, over the strife and labour of his pilgrimage, and say, 'yet do I not repent me'; or, with the panache of a millionaire, bequeath 'my sword to him that shall succeed me in my pilgrimage, and my courage and skill to him that can get it.'

George Bernard Shaw, 'Epistle Dedicatory to A. B. Walkley', Preface to *Man and Superman*

He was greatly served . . . by a certain rustic privilege of his style, which like the talk of strong, uneducated men, when it does not impress by its force, still charms by its simplicity . . . We have to remark in him, not the parts where inspiration fails and is supplied by cold and merely decorated invention, but the parts where faith has grown to incredulity, and his characters become so real to him that he forgets the end of their creation. We can follow him step by step, into the trap which he lays for himself by his own entire good faith and triumphant liberality of vision, till the trap closes and shuts him in an inconsistency.

Robert Louis Stevenson, Introduction to *Pilgrim's Progress*

*Pilgrim's Progress*, about a man that left his family, it didn't say why. I read considerable in it now and then. The statements was interesting but tough.

Mark Twain, *The Adventures of Huckleberry Finn*

He merely told his own story, and said it may be yours also.

Ola Elizabeth Winslow, *John Bunyan*

John Bunyan came into English literature and history by a side door.

*Ibid.*

Why do you call Bunyan a mystic? It is not possible to make a definition of mysticism to include him.

William Butler Yeats, Letter to his father, 24 June 1918

*See also* Daniel Defoe

## BURBAGE, RICHARD

1567?–1619 Actor

He's gone, & with him what a world are dead, / Which he revivd to be revived soe. / No more young Hamlett, ould Heironymoe. / King Leer, the greved Moore, and more beside, / That lived in him, have now for ever dy'de. / Oft have I seene him leape into the grave, / Suiting the person which he seem'd to have / Of a sad lover with so true an eye, / That theer I would have sworne, he meant to dye. / Oft Have I seene him play this part in ieast, / Soe lively, that spectators and the rest / Of his sad crew, whilst he but seem'd to bleed, / Amazed, thought even then hee dyed in deed. /

John Fletcher (?), *An elegie on the death of the famous actor Rich: Burbage who died 13 Martij Ao. 1618*

Whatsoever is commendable in the grave Orator, is most exquisitely perfect in him; for by a full and significant action of body, he charmes our attention: sit in a full Theater, and you will think you see so many lines drawne from the circumference of so many eares, whiles the *Actor* is the *Centre*. He doth not strive to make nature monstrous, she is often seen in the same scaene with him, but neither on Stilts nor Crutches; and for his voice 'tis not lower than the prompter, nor lowder than the Foile and Target. By his action he fortifies morall precepts with example; for what we see him personate we thinke truely done before us; a man of a deepe thought might apprehend the Ghosts of our ancient *Heroes* walk't againe, and take him (at severall times) for many of them. Hee is much affected to painting, and 'tis a question whether that make him an excellent Plaier, or his playing an exquisite painter. Hee adds grace to the Poets labours: for what in the Poet is but ditty, in him is both ditty and musicke . . . All men have beene of his occupation: and indeed, what he doth fainedly, that doe others essentially.

John Webster (ascribed), *Character of an Excellent Actor*, 1615

*See also* Shakespeare

## BURBANK, LUTHER

1849–1926 Horticulturalist

Old man Burbank is gone. Perhaps you remember him. He was a great man in a garden. His wife often said Luther had ten green thumbs. What a witty woman she must have been! Burbank was the wizard who crossed all those fruits and vegetables until he had the poor plants in such a confused and jittery condition that they could never decide whether to enter the dining room on the meat platter or the dessert dish.

Groucho Marx, Undated letter to Warner Brothers Studio

*See also* Thomas Alva Edison

## BURDETT, SIR FRANCIS

1770–1844 Radical

. . . all were agreed that our debts should increase / Excepting the Demagogue Francis. / That rogue! how could Westminster chuse him again / To leaven the virtue of these honest men! /

Lord Byron, *The Devil's Drive*

. . . The general *football* Sir F. Burdett, kicked at by all, and owned by none.

Lord Byron, Letter to John Hanson, 15 January 1809

He saw, that a blaze of talent had burst forth. He saw that, if a Reform really took place, he would be *nothing* in that line of talent. He could not endure the idea of standing amidst a crowd of second or third rates; therefore he began to halt; to consider; to hesitate; to damp. We were going *too fast*; we exceeded *his bounds*, who, before, had *no bounds*. Till now he had been undisputed chief; that pleased him well, and he zealously and sincerely strove for the victory. But, when he found that the victory, if won, would leave him a disputed truncheon, he stopt short, and left us to the mercy of our foes, choosing rather to eke out his life as the *chief* of an unsuccessful, than to live an *associate* in a successful cause.

William Cobbett, *A History of the Last Hundred Days of English Freedom*

It so happened that the French Revolution was coincident with Burdett's appearance in public life, & so in the confusion of circumstances it turned out, that he was looked upon as a Jacobin, when in reality he was a Jacobite.

Benjamin Disraeli, *Reminiscences*

In one of his last speeches in Parliament, (then reformed, & full of quiet middle class people) on the expenses of elections, he greatly denounced them, & observed that he had a right to give an opinion on this subject, as there was a period in his life, when parliamentary contests had reduced him to a state of absolute beggary. There was a murmur of admiring incredulity. 'I assure you, Sir,' he continued, 'I am indulging in no exaggeration. Honourable gentlemen may not believe it, but I can assure them there was a time, when Lady Burdett had only one pair of horses to her carriage!'

The effect of this remark in one of

the early reformed Parliaments full of retired tradesmen, many of whom had amassed wealth, but had never plucked up courage to keep a carriage, may be conceived. It was the most patrician definition of poverty ever made.

*Ibid.*

Sir Francis Burdett has often been left in a minority in the House of Commons, with only one or two on his side. We suspect, unfortunately for his country, that History will be found to enter its protest on the same side of the question!

William Hazlitt, *The Spirit of the Age*

*See also* Horne Tooke

## BURGHLEY, LORD (WILLIAM CECIL)

1520–98 Statesman

The only faithful Watchman for the realme, / That in all tempests never quit the helme, / But stood unshaken in his Deeds and Name, / And labour'd in the worke; not with the fame: / That still was good for goodness' sake, nor thought / Upon reward, till the reward him sought. / Whose Offices and honours did surprize, / Rather than meet him: And, before his eyes / Clos'd to their peace, he saw his branches shoot, / And in the noblest Families tooke root. / Of all the Land, who now, at such a Rate / Of divine blessing, would not serve a State? /

Ben Jonson, *Epigram on William Lord Burghley*

When the treasurer, in the latter part of his life, was much afflicted with gout, the queen always made him sit down in her presence with some obliging expression. 'My Lord,' she would say, 'we make use of you, not for your bad legs, but for your good head.'

John Macdiarmid, *Lives of British Statesmen*

## BURKE, EDMUND

1729–97 Author, Statesman

Burke loved to evade the arbitration of principle. He was prolific of arguments that were admirable but not decisive. He dreaded two-edged weapons and maxims that faced both ways. Through his inconsistencies we can perceive that his mind stood in a brighter light than his language . . . Half of his genius was spent in making the secret that hampered it.

Lord Acton, in the Rev. Robert Murray, *Edmund Burke*

When Johnson was ill and unable to exert himself as much as usual without fatigue, Mr Burke having been mentioned, he said: 'That fellow calls forth all my powers. Were I to eee Burke now, it would kill me.'

James Boswell, *Life of Johnson*

Such Spirit – such Intelligence – so much energy when serious, so much pleasantry when sportive, – so manly in his address, so animated in his conversation, so eloquent in Argument, so exhilarating in trifling – ! O, I shall rave about him till I tire you.

Fanny Burney, Diary

Yet never, Burke, thou drankst Corruption's bowl! / Thee stormy Pity and the cherished lure / Of Pomp and proud Precipitance of soul / Wildered with meteor fires. Ah, Spirit pure! / The error's mist had left thy purged eye: / So might I clasp thee with a Mother's joy. /

Samuel Taylor Coleridge, *Monody on the Death of Chatterton*

Here lies our good Edmund, whose genius was such / We scarcely can praise it, or blame it too much; / Who, born for the Universe, narrowed his mind, / And to party gave up what was meant for mankind. /

Oliver Goldsmith, *Retaliation*

Is he like Burke, who winds into a subject like a serpent?

Oliver Goldsmith, in James Boswell, *Life of Johnson*

He was so fond of arbitrary power that he could not sleep on his pillow unless he thought the king had a right to take it from under him.

Henry Grattan, in R. J. McHugh, *Henry Grattan*

Burke understands everything but gaming and music. In the House of Commons I sometimes think him only the second man in England; out of it he is always the first.

Gerald Hamilton, in James Prior, *Memoir of the Life and Character of the Right Honourable Edmund Burke*

Oft have I wondered that on Irish Ground / No poisonous reptiles ever yet were found; / Reveal'd the secret strands of nature's work, / She sav'd her venom to create a Burke. /

Warren Hastings, in A. M. Davies, *Warren Hastings*

The only specimen of Burke is, *all that he wrote.*

William Hazlitt, *English Literature*, 9, *The Character of Mr Burke*

You could not stand five minutes with that man beneath a shed, while it rained, but you must be convinced you had been standing with the greatest man you had ever seen.

Samuel Johnson, attributed to Mrs Piozzi

As he rose like a rocket, he fell like a stick.

Thomas Paine, *Letter to His Addressors*

## BURNE-JONES, SIR EDWARD COLEY

1833–98 Painter

The Golden Age was with us while he stayed: / For the Seven Ages knew him, and their wings / Were stilled for him to paint; the Wizard Kings / Showed him the Orient treasures which they laid / At the Infant's feet, the Courts of Love obeyed / His incantations; every Myth which brings / Light out of darkness seemed imaginings / Of God, or things that God himself had made. /

Wyke Bayliss, *Five Great Painters of the Victorian Era*

The magician who held in his hand the crystal of romance.

*Ibid.*

It is the art of culture, of reflection, of intellectual luxury, of aesthetic refinement, of people who look at the world and at life not directly, as it were, and in all its accidental reality, but in the reflection and ornamental portrait of it furnished by art itself in other manifestations; furnished by literature, by poetry, by history, by erudition.

Henry James, 'The Picture Season in London', in *Galaxy*, August 1877

Mr Burne-Jones's figures have a way of looking rather sick; but if illness is capable of being amiable – and most of us have had some happy intimation that it is – Mr Burne-Jones accentuates this side of the case.

Henry James, 'London Pictures', in *Atlantic Monthly*, August 1882

His design was a child of the imagination, which had led him into an enchanted land, hidden behind high, rocky mountains, where Knights and Princesses rode through dark forests and wandered dreaming by moated granges, or looked out from towers of brass, and about whose shores mermaids swam and centaurs stamped their hairy hoofs.

William Rothenstein, *Men and Memories*

I generally go and see Burne-Jones when there's a fog. He looks so angelic, painting away there by candlelight.

Ellen Terry, Letter to George Bernard Shaw, 29 October 1896

## BURNET, GILBERT, BISHOP

1643–1715 Historian

There prevailed in those days an indecent custom; when the preacher touched any favourite topick in a manner that delighted his audience [of MPs], their approbation was expressed by a loud *hum*, continued in proportion to their zeal and pleasure. When Burnet preached, part of his congregation *hummed* so loudly and so long, that he sat down to enjoy it, and rubbed his face with his handkerchief.

Samuel Johnson, *Lives of the Poets: Sprat*

Burnet's *History of his own Times* is very entertaining. The style, indeed, is mere chit-chat. I do not believe that Burnet intentionally lied; but he was so much prejudiced that he took no pains to find out the truth. He was like a man who resolves to regulate his time by a certain watch, but will not inquire whether the watch is right or not.

Samuel Johnson, in James Boswell, *Life of Johnson*

*See also* George I, John Wilmot

## BURNEY, FRANCES (FANNY) (MADAME D'ARBLAY)

1752–1840 Novelist, Diarist

Miss Burney is a real wonder. What she is, she is intuitively. Dr Burney told me she had had the fewest advantages of any of his daughters, from some peculiar circumstances. And such has been her timidity, that he himself had not any suspicion of her powers.

Samuel Johnson (in conversation with Mrs Thrale), in Fanny Burney, Diary, 20 June 1779

Was introduced by Rogers to Made. D'Arblay . . . an elderly lady with no remains of personal beauty but a gentle manner and a pleasing expression of countenance. She told me she had wished to see two persons – myself of course being one, the other Geo. Canning. This was really a compliment to be pleased with, a nice little handsome [pat] of butter made up by a neat-handed Phillis of a dairy maid instead of the grease fit only for cart-wheels which one is dozed with by the pound.

Sir Walter Scott, *Journal*, 18 November 1826

The jealousy of accomplished weepers came to a head in Fanny Burney, who became positively cattish about an unfortunate girl called Sophy Streatfield, because the latter was able to cry at will. It was because Fanny herself was probably the second-best weeper in the kingdom, and could not endure to be beaten.

T. H. White, *The Age of Scandal*

## BURNS, ROBERT

1759–96 Poet

I don't well know what is the reason of it, but somehow or other, though I am, when I have a mind, pretty generally beloved, yet I never could get the art of commanding respect: I imagine it is owing to my being deficient in what Sterne calls 'that understrapping virtue of discretion.' I am so apt to a *lapsus linguae*, that I sometimes think the character of a certain great man I have read of somewhere is very much *à-propos* to myself – that he was a compound of great talents and great folly.

On himself, *Journal*, May 1784

Read Burns to-day. What would he have been, if a patrician? We should have had more polish – less force – just as much verse, but no immortality –

a divorce and a duel or two, the which had he survived, as his potations must have been less spirituous, he might have lived as long as Sheridan, and outlived as much as poor Brinsley.

Lord Byron, *Journal*, 16 November 1813

What an antithetical mind! – tenderness, roughness – delicacy, coarseness – sentiment, sensuality – soaring and grovelling, dirt and deity – all mixed up in that one compound of inspired clay!

Lord Byron, *Journal*, 13 December 1813

And rustic life and poverty / Grew beautiful beneath his touch ... / Whose lines are mottoes of the heart, / Whose truths electrify the sage. /

Thomas Campbell, *Ode to the Memory of Burns*

A Burns is infinitely better educated than a Byron.

Thomas Carlyle, *Note Books*, November 1831

It was a curious phenomenon, in the withered, unbelieving, secondhand Eighteenth Century, that of a Hero starting up, among the artificial pasteboard figures and productions, in the guise of Robert Burns. Like a little well in the rocky desert places, – like a sudden splendour of Heaven in the artificial Vauxhall! People knew not what to make of it. They took it for a piece of the Vauxhall fire-work; alas, it *let* itself be so taken, though struggling half-blindly, as in bitterness of death, against that! Perhaps no man had such a false reception from his fellow-men ... You would think it strange if I called Burns the most gifted British soul we had in all that century of his: and yet I believe the day is coming when there will be little danger in saying so.

Thomas Carlyle, *On Heroes and Hero Worship*

His face was deeply marked by thought, and the habitual expression intensely melancholy. His frame was very muscular and well proportioned, though he had a short neck, and something of a ploughman's stoop: he was strong, and proud of his strength. I saw him one evening match himself with a number of masons; and out of five-and-twenty practised hands, the most vigorous young men in the parish, there was only one that could lift the same weight as Burns.

Allan Cunningham, in J. G. Lockhart, *Life of Burns*

He held the plough or the pen with the same firm, manly grasp; nor did he cut out poetry as we cut out watch-papers, with finical dexterity, nor from the same flimsy materials.

William Hazlitt, *Lectures on the English Poets*

Poor unfortunate fellow – his disposition was southern – how sad it is when a luxurious imagination is obliged in self defence to deaden its delicacy in vulgarity, and riot in things attainable that it may not have leisure to go mad after things which are not.

John Keats, Letter to Tom Keats, 7 July 1818

My word, you can't know Burns unless you can hate the Lockharts and all the estimable bourgeois and upper classes as he really did – the narrow-gutted pigeons . . . Oh, why doesn't Burns come to life again, and really salt them!

D. H. Lawrence, Letter to Donald Carswell, 5 December 1927

Burns of all poets is the most a man.

D. G. Rossetti, *On Burns*

I would have taken the poet, had I not known what he was, for a very sagacious country farmer of the old Scotch school, *i.e.* none of your modern agriculturists, who keep labourers for their drudgery, but the *douce gudeman* who held his own plough. There was a strong expression of sense and shrewdness in all his lineaments; the eye alone, I think, indicated the poetical character and temperament.

Sir Walter Scott, in J. G. Lockhart, *Life of Burns*

Notwithstanding the spirit of many of his lyrics, and the exquisite sweetness and simplicity of others, we cannot but deeply regret that so much of his time and talents were frittered away in compiling and composing for musical collections . . . This constant waste of his power and fancy in small and insignificant compositions, must necessarily have had no little effect in deterring him from undertaking any grave or important task.

Sir Walter Scott, in *Quarterly Review*, no. 1

A dreamer of the common dreams, / A fisher in familiar streams, / He chased the transitory gleams / That all pursue; / But on his lips the eternal themes / Again were new. /

William Watson, *The Tomb of Burns*

I mourned with thousands, but as one / More deeply grieved, for he was gone / Whose light I hailed when first it shone, / And showed my youth / How verse may build a princely throne / On humble truth. /

William Wordsworth, *At the Grave of Burns*

*See also* William Wordsworth

## BURR, AARON

1756–1836 Politician

The rule of my life is to make business a pleasure and pleasure my business.

On himself, in A. K. Adams, *The Home Book of Humorous Quotations*

Oh, Aaron Burr, what hast thou done? / Thou hast shooted dead that great Hamilton. / You got behind a bunch of thistle / And shot him dead with a big hoss-pistol. /

Anon., in Bernard Mayo, *Henry Clay, Spokesman of the New West*

. . . the Mephistopheles of politics.

Henry Adams, *History of the United States*, vol. 2

Burr's life, take it altogether, was such as in any country of sound morals his friends would be desirous of burying in profound oblivion. The son and grandson of two able and eminent Calvinistic divinities, he had no religious principles, and little, if any sense of reverence to a moral Governor of the Universe . . . He lived and died as a man of the world – brave, generous, hospitable and courteous, but ambitious, rapacious, faithless and intriguing. This character raised him within a hair's breadth of a gibbett and a halter for treason, and left him, for the last thirty years of his life a blasted monument of Shakespeare's vaulting ambition.

John Quincy Adams, in Samuel H. Wandell, *Aaron Burr in Literature*

Just before the end of his life [Alexander] Hamilton engaged in a duel with Aaron Burr, a disappointed presidential candidate who never got beyond the vice-presidency. It is not known whether Burr shot (1) straighter or (2) sooner, but (3) he was declared the winner, and Hamilton, his time being up, (4) expired. One of the unanswered questions of history is why the ambitious Burr shot Hamilton instead of Jefferson, which would have given him the presidency. It would, however, have established a bad precedent for vice-presidents.

Richard Armour, *It All Started With Columbus*

He is in every sense a profligate; a voluptuary in the extreme, with uncommon habits of expense . . . He is artful and intriguing to an inconceivable degree . . . bankrupt beyond redemption except by the blunder of his country . . . he will certainly attempt to reform the government a la Bonoparte . . . as unprincipled and dangerous a man as any country can boast – as true a Catiline as ever met in midnight conclave.

Alexander Hamilton, Letter to James A. Bayard, 6 August 1800

I never thought him an honest, frank-dealing man, but considered him as a crooked gun or other perverted machine whose aim or shot you could never be sure of.

Thomas Jefferson, Letter to William B. Giles, April 1807

He was always at market, if they had wanted him.

Thomas Jefferson, in Fawn M. Brodie, *Thomas Jefferson, An Intimate History*

Burr was practiced in every art of gallantry; he had made womankind a study. He never saw a beautiful face and form without a sort of restless desire to experiment upon it and try his power over the inferior inhabitant . . . He was one of those persons who systematically managed and played upon himself and others, as a skilled musician on an instrument.

Harriet Beecher Stowe, *The Minister's Wooing*

How misunderstood – how maligned.

Woodrow Wilson to Walter Flavius McCaleb at the grave of Aaron Burr, in F. F. Beirne, *Shout Treason: The Trial of Aaron Burr*

## BURROUGHS, EDGAR RICE

1875–1950 Author

I am sorry that I have not led a more exciting existence, so that I might offer a more interesting biographical sketch; but I am one of those fellows who has few adventures and always gets to the fire after it is out.

On himself, in Richard A. Lupoff, *Edgar Rice Burroughs: Master of Adventure*

## BURTON, SIR RICHARD FRANCIS

1821–90 Explorer

. . . It is a *real* advantage to belong to some parish. It is a great thing, when you have won a battle, or explored central Africa, to be welcomed home by some little corner of the Great World, which takes a pride in your exploits, because they reflect honour upon itself. In the contrary conditions you are a waif, a stray; you are a blaze of light, without a focus. Nobody outside your own fireside cares.

On himself, in Lady Isabel Burton, *The Life of Captain Sir Richard Francis Burton*

I struggled for forty-seven years, I distinguished myself in every way I possibly could. I never had a compliment nor a 'Thank you', nor a single farthing. I translated a doubtful book in my old age, and I immediately made sixteen thousand guineas. Now that I know the tastes of England, we need never be without money.

On himself, in A. Symons, *Dramatis Personae: A neglected genius*

Elizabeth, not Victoria, should have been his queen.

Desmond MacCarthy, *Portraits*

## BURTON, ROBERT

1577–1640 Author

All my joys to this are folly, / Naught so sweet as Melancholy. /

On himself, *Anatomy of Melancholy*

Like a roving spaniel, that barks at every bird he sees, leaving his game, I have followed all, saving that which I should, and may justly complain, and truly, *qui ubique est, nusquam est* [he who is everywhere is nowhere], which Gesner did in modesty, that I have read many books, but to little purpose, for want of good method; I have confusedly tumbled over divers authors in our libraries, with small profit for want of art, order, memory, judgement.
*Ibid.*

He added, that 'Burton's Anatomy of Melancholy' was also excellent, from the quantity of desultory information it contained, and was a mine of knowledge that, though much worked, was inexhaustible.
Lord Byron, in Lady Blessington, *Conversations of Lord Byron*

Burton's *Anatomy of Melancholy*, he said, was the only book that ever took him out of bed two hours sooner than he wished to be.
Samuel Johnson, in James Boswell, *Life of Johnson*

He lived like a king, a despot in the realm of words.
Desmond MacCarthy, *Portraits*

## BUTE, EARL OF (JOHN STUART)

1713–92 Statesman

O Bute, if instead of contempt and of odium, / You wish to obtain universal eulogium, / From your breast to your gullet transfer the blue string, / Our hearts are all yours at the very first swing. /
Anon., in Alan Lloyd, *The Wickedest Age*

Enough of Scotland – let her rest in peace; / The cause removed, effects of course should cease; / Why should I tell how Tweed, too mighty grown, / And proudly swelled with waters not his own, / Burst o'er his banks, and, by Destruction led, / O'er our fair England desolation spread, / Whilst, riding on his waves, Ambition, plumed / In tenfold pride, the port of BUTE assumed, / Now that the river god, convinced, though late, / And yielding, though reluctantly, to Fate, / Holds his fair course, and with more humble tides, / In tribute to the sea, as usual, glides? /
Charles Churchill, *The Candidate*

On the whole the Earl of Bute might fairly be called a man of cultivated mind. He was also a man of undoubted honour. But his understanding was narrow, and his manners cold and haughty. His qualifications for the part of statesman were best described by Prince Frederick . . . 'Bute,' said his Royal Highness, 'you are the very man to be envoy at some small proud German court where there is nothing to do.'
T. B. Macaulay, *Essays*: 'Chatham'

. . . his bottom was that of any Scotch nobleman, proud, aristocratical, pompous, imposing, with a greal deal of superficial knowledge, such as is commonly to be met in France and Scotland, chiefly upon matters of natural philosophy, mines, fossils, a smattering of mechanics, a little metaphysics, and a very false taste in everything.
Lord Shelburne, in Alan Lloyd, *The Wickedest Age*

The fondness he retained for power, his intrigues to preserve it, the confusion he helped to throw into almost every succeeding system, and his impotent and dark attempt to hang on the wheels of Government, which he only clogged, and to which he dreaded even being suspected of recommending drivers, all proved that neither virtue nor philosophy had the honour of dictating his retreat, but that fear, and fear only,

was the immediate, inconsiderate and precipitate cause of his resignation.
Horace Walpole, *Memoirs*

Lord Bute, when young, possessed a very handsome person, of which advantage he was not insensible; and he used to pass many hours, every day as his enemies asserted, occupied in contemplating the symmetry of his own legs, during his solitary walks by the side of the Thames.
Sir Nathaniel Wraxall, *Historical Memoirs Of My Own Time*

## BUTLER, BENJAMIN FRANKLIN

1818–93 Soldier

After outraging the sensibilities of civilized humanity . . . he returns, reeking with crime, to his own people, and they receive him with joy . . . the beastliest, bloodiest poltroon and pickpocket the world ever saw.
Anon., in *Richmond Examiner*, in *Butler's Book*.

A man whom all the waters of Massachusetts Bay cannot wash back into decency.
Anon., in *New York World*, 15 January 1863

If there comes a time when there is an absolute dearth of news, when you can't think of anything to make an interesting letter, there is always one thing you can do, and that is to pitch into Ben Butler.
Murat Halstead, to a group of fellow journalists, in the Washington *Evening Star*, 23 January 1899

## BUTLER, JOSEPH, BISHOP OF DURHAM

1692–1752 Author

Butler, Aristotle, Dante, Saint Augustine – my four doctors.
W. E. Gladstone, *Life of Cardinal Manning*

Others had established the historical and prophetical ground of the Christian religion, and that sure testimony of its truth, which is found in its perfect adaptation to the heart of man. It was reserved for him to develop its analogy to the constitution and course of nature; and laying his strong foundations in the depth of that great argument, there to construct another and irrefragable proof, thus rendering Philosophy subservient to Faith, and finding in outward and visible things the type of those within the veil.
Robert Southey, *Epitaph on Bishop Butler*

## BUTLER, SAMUEL

1612–80 Satirist, Poet

Who can read with pleasure more than a hundred lines or so of *Hudibras* at one time? Each couplet or quatrain is so whole in itself, that you can't connect them. There is no fusion.
Samuel Taylor Coleridge, *Table Talk*, 3 July 1833

Butler's Hudibras is a poem of more wit than any other in the language. The rhymes have as much genius in them as the thoughts; but there is no story in it, and but little humour . . . The fault of Butler's poem is not that it has too much wit, but that it has not an equal quantity of other things. One would suppose that the starched manners and sanctified grimace of the times in which he lived, would of themselves have been sufficiently rich in ludicrous incidents and characters; but they seem rather to have irritated his spleen, than to have drawn forth his powers of picturesque imitation.
William Hazlitt, *Lectures on the English Poets*

If exhaustible wit could give perpetual pleasure, no eye would ever leave half-read the work of Butler; for what poet has ever brought so many remote images so happily together? It is scarcely possible to peruse a page without finding some association of images that was never found before. By the first paragraph the reader is amused, by the next he is delighted, and by a few more strained to astonishment; but astonishment is a toilsome pleasure; he is soon weary of wondering, and longs to be diverted.

Samuel Johnson, *Lives of the Poets*

This kind of stuff – the boisterous and obscure topical satire, the dismally comic mock-heroic poem, the social allusion sustained through hundreds of rhymed couplets, the academic tour de force, and the coy fugitive verses – is something intrinsically inartistic and anti-poetical, since its enjoyment presupposes that Reason is somehow, in the long run, superior to Imagination, and that both are less important than a man's religious or political beliefs.

Vladimir Nabokov, *Commentary to Eugene Onegin*

While Butler, needy wretch, was yet alive, / No generous patron would a dinner give: / See him, when starv'd to death, and turn'd to dust, / Presented with a monumental bust. / The poet's fate is here in emblem shown, / He ask'd for bread, and he receiv'd a stone. /

Samuel Wesley, Lines written on the erection of a monument to Butler in Westminster Abbey, 1681

## BUTLER, SAMUEL
1835–1902 Author

I am the *enfant terrible* of literature and science. If I cannot, and I know I cannot, get the literary and scientific big-wigs to give me a shilling, I can, and I know I can, heave bricks into the middle of them.

On himself, *Notebooks*

Butler's books have worn well, far better than those of more earnest contemporaries like Meredith and Carlyle, partly because he never lost the power to use his eyes and to be pleased by small things, partly because in the narrow technical sense he wrote so well. When one compares Butler's prose with the contortions of Meredith and the affectations of Stevenson, one sees what a tremendous advantage is gained simply by not trying to be clever.

George Orwell, in *Tribune*, 21 July 1944

When I admit neglect of Gissing, / They say I don't know what I'm missing. / Until their arguments are subtler, / I think I'll stick to Samuel Butler. /

Dorothy Parker, *Sunset Gun*

Butler obviously had a need to revolt against authority (as we see not only from his attitude to his own stern clerical father but from his attitude to all father-figures). He also had a need for security (witness his attitude to money, for him the stated root of all *good* – as it was in practice for his less honest contemporaries). He is therefore the most conservative and bourgeois of rebels, next to Dr Johnson. And most of his rebellion seems to be the product of fear and thwarted rage, which resulted in destructiveness and possessiveness – somewhat incompatible qualities.

Allan Rodway, *English Comedy*

Yet Butler, though he could be most amusing about people's mercenary motives, was too much a middle-class man himself to analyze the social system, in which, for all his financial difficulties, he occupied a privileged position . . . For all his satiric insight, he had basically the psychology of the rentier.

Edmund Wilson, *The Shores of Light*

## BYNG, JOHN

1704–57 Admiral

The manner and cause of raising and keeping up the popular clamour and prejudice against me will be seen through – I shall be considered (as now I consider myself) a victim destroyed to divert the indignation and resentment of an injured and deluded people from the proper objects.

On himself, in Dudley Pope, *At Twelve Mr Byng Was Shot*

Dans ce-pays-ci il est bon de tuer de temps en temps un amiral pour encourager les autres.
(In this country it's thought proper to kill an admiral from time to time, to encourage the others.)

Voltaire, *Candide*

I never knew poor Byng enough to bow to.

Horace Walpole, Letter to Sir Horace Mann, 3 March 1757

Some of the more humane officers represented to him, that his face being uncovered might throw reluctance into the executioners, and besought him to suffer a handkerchief. He replied with the same unconcern: 'If it will frighten *them*, let it be done; they would not frighten me.'

Horace Walpole, *Memoirs*

## BYRD, WILLIAM

1543–1623 Composer

Indeed, the best memorials of a professional man's existence are his surviving works; which, from their having been thought worthy of preservation by posterity, entitle him to a niche in the Temple of Fame, among the benefactors of mankind. The physician who heals the diseases, and alleviates the anguish of the body, certainly merits a more conspicuous and honourable place there; but the musician, who eminently soothes our sorrows, and innocently diverts the mind from its cares during health, renders his memory dear to the grateful and refined part of mankind, in every civilized nation.

Dr Charles Burney, *A General History of Music*

Byrd's misfortune is that when he is not first-rate he is so rarely second-rate.

Gustav Holst, 'My Favourite Tudor Composer', in *Midland Musician*, January 1926

There be two whose benefits to us can never be requited: God, and our parents; the one for that He gave us a reasonable soul, the other for that of them we have our being. To these the prince and (as Cicero termeth him) the God of the Philosophers added our masters, as those by whose directions the faculties of the reasonable soul be stirred up to enter into contemplation and searching of more than earthly things, whereby we obtain a second being, more to be wished and much more durable than that which any man since the world's creation hath received of his parents, causing us to live in the minds of the virtuous, as it were, deified to the posterity. The consideration of this hath moved me to publish these labours of mine under your name, both to signify unto the world my thankful mind, and also to notify unto yourself in some sort the entire love and unfeigned affection which I bear unto you.

Thomas Morley, Dedication to *A Plain and Easy Introduction to Practical Music*

## BYRON, GEORGE GORDON NOEL, LORD

1788–1824 Poet

And be the Spartan's epitaph on me – / 'Sparta hath many a worthier son than he.' /

On himself, *Childe Harold*, canto iv

I awoke one morning and found myself famous.

On himself, after the publication of the first cantos of *Childe Harold*, in Thomas Moore, *Life of Byron*

Even I, – albeit I'm sure I did not know it, / Nor sought of foolscap subjects to be king, – / Was reckon'd, a considerable time, / The grand Napoleon of the realms of rhyme. /

On himself, *Don Juan*, canto xi

I perch upon a humbler promontory, / Amidst life's infinite variety: / With no great care for what is nicknamed glory, / But speculating as I cast mine eye / On what may suit or may not suit my story, / And never straining hard to versify, / I rattle on exactly as I'd talk / With anybody in a ride or walk. /

*Ibid.*, canto xv

This morning I *swam* from *Sestos* to *Abydos*, the immediate distance is not above a mile but the current renders it hazardous, so much so, that I doubt whether Leander's conjugal powers must not have been exhausted in his passage to Paradise.

On himself, Letter to Henry Drury, 3 May 1810

Well, – I have had my share of what are called the pleasures of this life, and have seen more of the European and Asiatic world than I have made a good use of . . . At five-and-twenty, when the better part of life is over, one should be *something*; and what am I? nothing but five-and-twenty – and the odd months. What have I seen? the same man all over the world, – ay, and woman too. Give *me* a Mussulman who never asks questions, and a she of the same race who saves one the trouble of putting them.

On himself, *Journal*, 14 November 1813

I am like the tyger (in poesy), if I miss my first Spring, I go growling back to my Jungle. There is no second. I can't correct; I can't, and I won't.

*Ibid.*, 18 November 1820

There is something to me very softening in the presence of a woman, – some strange influence, even if one is not in love with them, – which I cannot at all account for, having no very high opinion of the sex. But yet, – I always feel in better humour with myself and every thing else, if there is a woman within ken. Even Mrs Mule, my firelighter, – the most ancient and withered of her kind, – and (except to myself) not the best-tempered – always makes me laugh.

On himself, *Journal*, 27 February 1814

Now, if I know myself, I should say, that I have no character at all . . . But, joking apart, what I think of myself is, that I am so changeable, being everything by turns and nothing long, – I am such a strange *melange* of good and evil, that it would be difficult to describe me. There are but two sentiments to which I am constant, – a strong love of liberty, and a detestation of cant, and neither is calculated to gain me friends.

On himself, in Lady Blessington, *Conversations with Lord Byron*

I remember reading somewhere . . . a *concetto* of designating different living poets, by the cups Apollo gives them to drink out of. Wordsworth is made to drink from a wooden bowl, and my melancholy self from a skull, chased with gold. Now, I would add the following cups:– To Moore, I would give a cup formed like a lotus flower, and set in brilliants; to Crabbe, a scooped pumpkin; to Rogers, an antique vase, formed of agate; and to Colman, a champagne glass.

*Ibid.*

When Byron's eyes were shut in death, / We bow'd our head and held our breath. / He taught us little: but our soul / Had *felt* him like the thunder's roll. /

Matthew Arnold, *Memorial Verses*

What helps it now, that Byron bore, / With haughty scorn which mock'd the smart, / Through Europe to the Aetolian shore / The pageant of his bleeding heart? / That thousands counted every groan, / And Europe made his woe her own? /

Matthew Arnold, *The Grande Chartreuse*

. . . He had not the intellectual equipment of a supreme modern poet; except for his genius he was an ordinary nineteenth-century English gentleman, with little culture and no ideas.

Matthew Arnold, *Essays in Criticism*: 'Heinrich Heine'

So long as Byron tried to write Poetry with a capital P, to express deep emotions and profound thoughts, his work deserved that epithet he most dreaded, *una seccatura*. As a thinker he was, as Goethe perceived, childish, and he possessed neither the imaginative vision – he could never invent anything, only remember – nor the verbal sensibility such poetry demands . . . His attempts to write satirical heroic couplets were less unsuccessful, but aside from the impossibility of equaling Dryden and Pope in their medium, Byron was really a comedian, not a satirist.

W. H. Auden, *The Dyer's Hand*

I told him that he had rendered the most essential service to the cause of morality by his confessions, as a dread of similar disclosures would operate [more] in putting people on their guard in reposing dangerous confidence in men, than all the homilies that ever were written; and that people would in future be warned by the phrase of 'beware of being *Byroned*', instead of the old cautions used in past times.

Lady Blessington, *Conversations with Lord Byron*

And poor, proud Byron, sad as grave / And salt as life; forlornly brave, / And quivering with the dart he gave. /

Elizabeth Barrett Browning, *A Vision of Poets*

He is the absolute monarch of words, and uses them, as Bonaparte did lives, for conquest, without more regard to their intrinsic value.

Lady Byron, Letter to Lady Anne Barnard, 2 December 1816

If they had said the sun or the moon had gone out of the heavens, it could not have struck me with the idea of a more awful and dreary blank in the creation than the words: Byron is dead.

Jane Welsh Carlyle (on Byron's death), Letter to Thomas Carlyle

A gifted Byron rises in his wrath; and feeling too surely that he for his part is not 'happy', declares the same in very violent language, as a piece of news that may be interesting. It evidently has surprised him much. One dislikes to see a man and poet reduced to proclaim on the streets such tidings.

Thomas Carlyle, *Past and Present*

Close thy Byron, open thy Goethe.

*Ibid.*

The truth is that Byron was one of a class who may be called the unconscious optimists, who are very often, indeed, the most uncompromising conscious pessimists, because the exuberance of their nature demands for an adversary a dragon as big as the world. But the whole of his essential and unconscious being was spirited and confident, and that unconscious being, long disguised and buried under emotional artifices, suddenly sprang into prominence in the face of a cold, hard, political necessity.

In Greece he heard the cry of reality, and at the time that he was dying, he began to live.

G. K. Chesterton, *Twelve Types*

It seems, to my ear, that there is a sad want of harmony in Lord Byron's verses. Is it not unnatural to be always connecting very great intellectual power with utter depravity? Does such a combination often really exist *in rerum natura*?

Samuel Taylor Coleridge, *Table Talk*, 1822

W. Wordsworth calls Lord Byron the mocking bird of our Parnassian ornithology, but the mocking bird, they say, has a very sweet song of its own, in true notes proper to himself. Now I cannot say I have ever heard any such in his Lordship's volumes of warbles: and spite of Sir W. Scott, I dare predict that in less than a century, the Baronet's and the Baron's Poems will lie on the same shelf of oblivion, Scott be read and remembered as a novelist and the founder of a new race of novels, and Byron not remembered at all, except as a wicked lord who, from morbid and restless vanity, pretended to be ten times more wicked than he was.

Samuel Taylor Coleridge, marginalia in his copy of Pepys's *Memoirs*

The world is rid of Lord Byron, but the deadly slime of his touch still remains.

John Constable, Letter to John Fisher, three weeks after Byron's death

He seems to me the most *vulgar-minded* genius that ever produced a great effect in literature.

George Eliot, Letter, 21 September 1869

Of Byron one can say, as of no other English poet of his eminence, that he added nothing to the language, that he discovered nothing in the sounds, and developed nothing in the meaning, of individual words. I cannot think of any other poet of his distinction who might so easily have been an accomplished foreigner writing English . . . Just as an artisan who can talk English beautifully while about his work or in a public bar, may compose a letter painfully written in a dead language bearing some resemblance to a newspaper leader, and decorated with words like 'maelstrom' and 'pandemonium': so does Byron write a dead or dying language.

T. S. Eliot, *Byron*

A coxcomb who would have gone into hysterics if a tailor had laughed at him.

Ebenezer Elliott, *The Village Patriarch*

It is the workers who are most familiar with the poetry of Shelley and Byron. Shelley's prophetic genius has caught their imagination, while Byron attracts their sympathy by his sensuous fire and by the virulence of his satire against the existing social order. The middle classes, on the other hand, have on their shelves only ruthlessly expurgated 'family editions' of these writers. These editions have been prepared to suit the hypocritical moral standards of the bourgeoisie.

Friedrich Engels, *The Condition of the Working Class in England*, translated by W. C. Henderson and W. H. Chaloner

He writes the thoughts of a city clerk in metropolitan clerical vernacular.

Ford Madox Ford, *The March of Literature*

Lord Byron ist nur gross, wenn er dichtet, sobald er reflektiert ist er ein Kind.

(Byron is great in his talk, but a child in his reflections.)

J. W. von Goethe, *Conversations with Eckermann*

Lord Byron is the spoiled child of fame as well as fortune. He has taken a surfeit of popularity, and is not contented to delight, unless he can shock the public. He would force them to admire in spite of decency and common sense . . . He is to be 'a chartered libertine' from whom insults are favours, whose contempt is to be a new incentive to admiration. His Lordship is hard to please: he is equally averse to notice or neglect, enraged at censure and scorning praise. He tries the patience of the town to the very utmost, and when they show signs of weariness or disgust, threatens to *discard* them. He says he will write on, whether he is read or not. He would never write another page, if it were not to court popular applause, or to affect a superiority over it.

William Hazlitt, *The Spirit of the Age*

You speak of Lord Byron and me. There is this great difference between us. He describes what he sees, I describe what I imagine. Mine is the hardest task.

John Keats, Letter to George Keats, 1819

The truth is, that what has put Byron out of favour with the public of late has not been his faults but his excellences. His artistic good taste, his classical polish, his sound shrewd sense, his hatred of cant, his insight into humbug, above all, his shallow pitiable habit of being intelligible – these are the sins which condemn him in the eyes of a mesmerising, table-turning, spirit-rapping, spiritualising, Romanising generation, who read Shelley in secret, and delight in his bad taste, mysticism, extravagance, and vague and pompous sentimentalism. The age is an effeminate one, and it can well afford to pardon the lewdness of the gentle and sensitive vegetarian, while it has no mercy for the sturdy peer proud of his bull neck and his boxing, who kept bears and bulldogs, drilled Greek ruffians at Missolonghi, and 'had no objection to a pot of beer'; and who might, if he had reformed, have made a gallant English gentleman; while Shelley, if once his intense self-opinion had deserted him, would probably have ended in Rome as an Oratorian or a Passionist.

Charles Kingsley, *Thoughts on Shelley and Byron*

Mad – bad – and dangerous to know.

Lady Caroline Lamb, *Journal*, 25 March 1812

So we have lost another poet. I never much relished his Lordship's mind, and shall be sorry if the Greeks have cause to miss him. He was to me offensive, and I can never make out his great *power*, which his admirers talk of. Why a line of Wordsworth's is a lever to lift the immortal spirit! Byron can only move the Spleen. He was at best a Satyrist, – in any other way he was mean enough. I dare say I do him injustice; but I cannot love him, nor squeeze a tear to his memory.

Charles Lamb, Letter to Bernard Barton, 1824

Byron dealt chiefly in felt and furbelow, wavy Damascus daggers, and pocket pistols studded with paste. He threw out frequent and brilliant sparks; but his fire burnt to no purpose; it blazed furiously when it caught muslin, and it hurried many a pretty wearer into an untimely blanket.

Walter Savage Landor, *Imaginary Conversations*

He had a head which statuaries loved to copy, and a foot the deformity of which the beggars in the street mimicked.

T. B. Macaulay, *Essays*: 'Moore's Life of Byron'

From the poetry of Lord Byron they drew a system of ethics, compounded of misanthropy and voluptuousness, in which the two great commandments were, to hate your neighbour, and to love your neighbour's wife.

*Ibid.*

To the Right Honourable Lord Byron . . . with that admiration of his poetic talents which must be universally and inevitably felt for versification undecorated with the meretricious fascinations of harmony, for sentiments unsophisticated by the delusive ardor of philanthropy, for narrative enveloped in all the cimmerian sublimity of the impenetrable obscure.

Thomas Love Peacock, Dedication of *Sir Proteus*

A very interesting day. Rose late; at half-past ten joined Wordsworth in Oxford Road, and we then got into the fields and walked to Hampstead. We talked of Lord Byron. Wordsworth allowed him power, but denied his style to be English. Of his moral qualities we think the same. He adds there is insanity in Lord Byron's family, and that he believes Lord Byron to be somewhat cracked.

Henry Crabb Robinson, Diary, 24 May 1812

Byron wrote, as easily as a hawk flies, and as clearly as a lake reflects, the exact truth in the precisely narrowest terms.

John Ruskin, *Praeterita*

The aristocratic rebel, since he has enough to eat, must have other causes of discontent.

Bertrand Russell, *History of Western Philosophy*

I remember saying to him [in 1815], that I really thought, that if he lived a few years longer, he would alter his sentiments. He answered rather sharply, 'I suppose you are one of those who prophesy that I will turn Methodist.' I replied – 'No. I don't expect your conversion to be of such an ordinary kind. I would rather look to see you retreat upon the Catholic faith, and distinguish yourself by the austerity of your penances.'

Sir Walter Scott, in Thomas Moore, *Notices of the Life of Lord Byron*

Our Lord Byron – the fascinating – faulty – childish – philosophical being – daring the world – docile to a private circle – impetuous and indolent – gloomy and yet more gay than any other.

Mary Shelley, Letter to John Murray, 19 January 1830

O mighty mind, in whose deep streams this age / Shakes like a reed in the unheeding storm, / Why dost thou curb not thine own sacred rage? /

Percy Bysshe Shelley, *Fragment: Addressed to Byron*

The fact is, that first, the Italian women with whom he associates are perhaps the most contemptible of all who exist under the moon – the most ignorant, the most disgusting, the most bigoted; countesses smell so strongly of garlic, that an ordinary Englishman cannot approach them. Well, L.B. is familiar with the lowest sort of these women, the people his gondolieri pick up in the streets. He associates with wretches who seem almost to have lost the gait and physiognomy of man, and who do not scruple to avow practices, which are not only not named, but I believe seldom even conceived in England. He says he disapproves, but he endures.

Percy Bysshe Shelley, Letter to Thomas Love Peacock, 1818

The Coryphaeus of the Satanic School.

Robert Southey, in *London Courier*, replying to an attack by Byron, 1822

Of all remembered poets the most wanting in distinction of any kind, the most dependent for his effects on the most violent and vulgar resources of rant and cant and glare and splash and splutter.

Algernon C. Swinburne, *Wordsworth and Byron*

Ah, what a poet Byron would have been had he taken his meals properly, and allowed himself to grow fat – and not have physicked his intellect with wretched opium pills and acrid vinegar, that sent his principles to sleep, and turned his feelings sour! If that man had respected his dinner, he never would have written *Don Juan*.

W. M. Thackeray, *Memorials of Gormandizing*

There lay the embalmed body of the Pilgrim – more beautiful in death than in life. The contraction of the muscles and skin had effaced every line that time or passion had ever traced on it; few marble busts could have matched its stainless white, the harmony of its proportions, and perfect finish . . . To confirm or remove my doubts as to the cause of his lameness, I uncovered the Pilgrim's feet, and was answered – the great mystery was solved. Both his feet were clubbed, and his legs withered to the knee – the form and features of an Apollo, with the feet and legs of a sylvan satyr.

E. J. Trelawny, *Recollections of the Last Days of Shelley and Byron*

My friend the apothecary o'er the way / Doth in his window Byron's bust display. / Once, at Childe Harold's voice, did Europe bow: / He wears a patent lung-protector now. /

William Watson, *The Fall of Heroes*

I hate the whole race of them, there never existed a more worthless set than Byron and his friends.

Duke of Wellington, in conversation with Lady Salisbury, in Lord David Cecil, *The Cecils of Hatfield House*

*See also* Robert Burns, Isadora Duncan, Lady Caroline Lamb, John Masefield

# 'C'

## CAEDMON

*fl.* 670 Poet

It sometimes happened at a feast that all the guests in turn would be invited to sing and entertain the company; then, when he saw the harp coming his way, he would get up from the table and go home. On one such occasion he had left the house in which the entertainment was being held and went out to the stable, where it was his duty that night to look after the beasts. There when the time came he settled down to sleep. Suddenly in a dream he saw a man standing beside him who called him by name. 'Caedmon,' he said, 'sing me a song.' 'I don't know how to sing,' he replied. 'It is because I cannot sing that I left the feast and came here.' The man who addressed him then said: 'But you shall sing to me.' . . . And Caedmon immediately began to sing verses in praise of God the Creator that he had never heard before . . . When Caedmon awoke, he remembered everything that he had sung in his dream, and soon added more verses in the same style to a song truly worthy of God. Early in the morning he went to his superior the reeve, and told him about this gift that he had received. The reeve took him before the abbess, who ordered him to give an account of his dream and repeat the verses in the presence of many learned men, so that a decision might be reached by common consent as to their quality and origin. All of them agreed that Caedmon's gift had been given him by the Lord.

Bede, *Ecclesiastical History of the English Nation*, translated by Leo Sherley-Price

## CALHOUN, JOHN CALDWELL

1782–1850 Statesman

When Calhoun took snuff, all South Carolina sneezed.

Anon., in Hudson Strode, *Jefferson Davis, American Patriot, 1808–61*

. . . tall, careworn, with furrowed brow, haggard and intensely gazing, looking as if he were dissecting the last abstraction which sprung from metaphysician's brain, and muttering to himself, in half-uttered tones, 'This is indeed a real crisis.'

Henry Clay, in Richard Hofstadter, *The American Political Tradition*

. . . the Marx of the masterclass.

Richard Hofstadter, *The American Political Tradition*

. . . the cast-iron man, who looks as if he had never been born, and never could be extinguished.

Harriet Martineau, *Retrospect of Western Travel*

## CAMDEN, WILLIAM

1551–1623 Antiquary

He is the chaste model of all succeeding antiquaries.

Anon., in *Biographical Magazine*, 1794

Camden, most reverend head, to whom I owe / All that I am in arts, all that I know. / (How nothing's that?) To whom my countrey owes / The great renowne, and name wherewith shee goes. /

Ben Jonson, *Epigrammes*

What name, what skill, what faith hast thou in things! / What sight in searching the most antique springs! / What weight, and what authority in thy speech! / Men scarce can make that doubt, but thou canst teach. /

*Ibid.*

## CAMPBELL, JOHN, BARON

1779–1861 Jurist

Edinburgh is now celebrated for having given us the two greatest bores that have ever yet been known in London, for Jack Campbell in the House of Lords is just what Tom Macaulay is in private society.

Lord Brougham, *circa* 1846, in *Dictionary of National Biography*

If Campbell had engaged as an opera-dancer, I do not say he would have danced as well as Deshayes, but I feel confident he would have got a higher salary.

J. Perry, in *Dictionary of National Biography*

[His biographies] added another sting to death.

Sir Charles Wetherell, on Campbell's *Lives of the Lord Chancellors*, in *Dictionary of National Biography*

## CAMPBELL, MRS PATRICK (BEATRICE STELLA)

1865–1940 Actress

On one occasion after a particularly wild 'tantrum' she walked to the footlights and peered out at Yeats, who was pacing up and down the stalls of the Abbey Theatre. 'I'd give anything to know what you're thinking,' shouted Mrs Pat. 'I'm thinking,' replied Yeats, 'of the master of a wayside Indian railway-station who sent a message to his Company's headquarters saying: "Tigress on the line: wire instructions."'

Gabriel Fallon, *Sean O'Casey: The Man I Knew*

You will tell me no doubt that Mrs Patrick Campbell cannot act. Who said she could? – who wants her to act? – who cares twopence whether she possesses that or any other second-rate accomplishment? On the highest plane one does not act, one *is*. Go and see her move, stand, speak, look, kneel – go and breathe the magic atmosphere that is created by the grace of all those deeds; and then talk to me about acting, forsooth!

George Bernard Shaw, in *Saturday Review*, 7 March 1896

Bah! You have no nerve; you have no brain: you are the caricature of an eighteenth century male sentimentalist, a Hedda Gabler titivated with odds and ends from Burne-Jones's ragbag . . . You are an owl sickened by two days of my sunshine.

George Bernard Shaw, Letter to Mrs Campbell, 11 August 1913

If only you could write a true book entitled WHY, THOUGH I WAS A WONDERFUL ACTRESS, NO MANAGER OR AUTHOR WOULD EVER ENGAGE ME TWICE IF HE COULD POSSIBLY HELP IT, it would be a best seller. But you couldn't. Besides, you don't know. I do.

*Ibid.*, 19 December 1938

An ego like a raging tooth.

William Butler Yeats, in Gabriel Fallon, *Sean O'Casey: The Man I Knew*

## CAMPBELL, THOMAS

1777–1844 Poet

Mr Campbell always seems to me to be thinking how his poetry will look when it comes to be hot-pressed on superfine wove paper, to have a disproportionate eye to points and commas, and dread of errors of the press. He is so afraid of doing wrong, of making the smallest mistake, that he does little or nothing. Lest he should wander irretrievably from the right path, he stands still. He writes according to established etiquette.

He offers the Muses no violence. If he lights upon a good thought, he immediately drops it for fear of spoiling a good thing.

William Hazlitt, *Lectures on the English Poets*

I often wonder how Tom Campbell with so much real genius has not maintained a greater figure in the public eye than he has done of late . . . Somehow he wants audacity – fears the public and, what is worse, fears the shadow of his own reputation. He is a great corrector too which succeeds as ill in composition as in education. Many a clever boy is flogged into a dunce and many an original composition corrected into mediocrity.

Sir Walter Scott, *Journal*, 29 June 1826

*See also* Walter Scott

## CAMPBELL-BANNERMAN, SIR HENRY

1836–1908 Prime Minister

Personally I am a great believer in bed, in constantly keeping horizontal . . . the heart and everything else go slower, and the whole system is refreshed.

On himself, Letter to Mrs Whiteley, 11 September 1906

You'll do, you're cantie and you're couthy.

W. E. Gladstone, on C-B's taking his seat in the Cabinet, February 1886, in John Wilson, *C.B. A life of Sir Henry Campbell-Bannerman*

Mildly nefarious / Wildly barbarious / Beggar that kept the cordite down. /

Rudyard Kipling, recalling 'C-B' at the War Office, June 1901, in John Wilson, *ibid.*

A jolly, lazy sort of man with a good dose of sense.

Sir Alfred Pease, Diary, 13 May 1886

## CAMPION, EDMUND, SAINT

1540–81 Jesuit

It was not our death that ever we feared. But we knew that we were not lords of our own lives, and therefore for want of answer would not be guilty of our deaths. The only thing that we have now to say is, that if our religion do make us traitors, we are worthy to be condemned; but otherwise are, and have been, as good subjects as ever the Queen had.

On himself, Speech at his Trial

## CANNING, GEORGE

1770–1827 Prime Minister

I know and have always known that I am – I would be either yours or nothing.

On himself, Letter to William Pitt, 1803

. . . a heavier charge . . . that I am an adventurer. To this charge, as I understand it, I am willing to plead guilty. A representative of the people, I am one of the people, and I present myself to those who choose me only with the claims of character . . . If to depend directly upon the people, as their representative in parliament; if, as a servant of the crown, to lean on no other support than that of public confidence – if that be to be an adventurer, I plead guilty . . . and I would not exchange that situation, to whatever taunts it may expose me, for all the advantages which might be derived from an ancestry of a hundred generations.

On himself, addressing his Liverpool constituents, 1816

The turning of coats so common is grown, / That no one would think to attack it; / But no case until now was so flagrantly known / Of a schoolboy's turning his jacket. /

Anon., Verse by a Brooks's Club wit on Canning entering Parliament as a Tory, 1794

Yet something may remain perchance to chime / With reason, and what's stranger still, with rhyme. / Even thy genius, Canning, may permit, / Who, bred a statesman, still was born a wit, / And never, even in that dull House, couldst tame / To unleaven'd prose thine own poetic flame; / Our last, our best, our only orator. /
Lord Byron, *The Age of Bronze*

That is a name never to be mentioned ... in the House of Commons without emotion. We all admire his genius; we all, at least most of us, deplore his untimely end; and we all sympathize with him in his fierce struggle with supreme prejudice and sublime mediocrity – with inveterate foes, and with – 'candid friends'.
Benjamin Disraeli, in the House of Commons, 28 February 1845

Very well, gentlemen, since you are determined to have him, take him in God's name, but remember I tell you he will throw you all overboard.
George IV, to his Tory ministers, September 1822, in *Diary and Correspondence of Henry Wellesley 1st Lord Cowley 1790–1846*

Mr Canning has the luckless ambition to play off the tricks of a political rope-dancer, and he chooses to do it on the nerves of humanity!
William Hazlitt, *The Spirit of the Age*, 1824

Canning was the strong man of [Perceval's] government – so strong that the others did not know what to make of him; and he did not know how to get on with them. He was the eagle in the dovecote, or rather among the owls. He fluttered the Volces in their Coriolo so tremendously that we find them heartily wishing that their gates had never shut him in among them ... It seems as if his exuberant activity and boyish petulance and fun made him forget how old and wise he really was.
Harriet Martineau, *History of England 1800–1815*

His absorbing idea was to be the political Atlas of England, to raise her on his shoulders.
Lady Morgan, Diary, August 1827

It was Canning's temper that killed him.
Duke of Wellington, Letter to Lord Bathurst, 10 August 1827

*See also* Lord Brougham, John Cavanagh

## CANNING, STRATFORD, VISCOUNT STRATFORD DE REDCLIFFE
1786–1880 Diplomat

Thou third great Canning, stand among our best / And noblest, now thy long day's work hath ceased, / Here silent in our Minster of the West / Who wert the voice of England in the East. /
Alfred, Lord Tennyson, *Epitaph on Lord Stratford de Redcliffe*, in Westminster Abbey

## CANUTE (CNUT)
994?–1035 King of England

A noble figure he was, that great and wise Canute ... trying to expiate by justice and mercy the dark deeds of his bloodstained youth; trying (and not in vain) to blend the two races over which he ruled; rebuilding the churches and monasteries which his father had destroyed ...; rebuking, as every child has learned, his housecarles' flattery by setting his chair on the brink of the rising tide; and then laying his golden crown, in token of humility, on the high altar of Winchester, never to wear it more.
Charles Kingsley, *Hereward the Wake*

Canute began by being a Bad King on the advice of his Courtiers, who infor-

med him (owing to a misunderstanding of the Rule Britannia) that the King of England was entitled to sit on the sea without getting wet. But finding that they were wrong he gave up this policy and decided to take his own advice in future – thus originating the memorable proverb, 'Paddle your own Canute' – and became a Good King and C. of E., and ceased to be memorable.
W. C. Sellar and R. J. Yeatman, *1066 and All That*

## CAPONE, 'SCARFACE' AL(PHONSE)

1899–1944 Bootlegger

My rackets are run on strictly American lines and they're going to stay that way.
On himself, in Claud Cockburn, *In Time of Trouble*

Don't get the idea that I'm one of these goddam radicals. Don't get the idea that I'm knocking the American system.
*Ibid.*

They talk about me not being on the legitimate. Why, lady, nobody's on the legit., when it comes down to cases; you know that.
On himself, in Fred D. Pasley, *Al Capone, The Biography of a Self-Made Man*

They call Al Capone a bootlegger. Yes, it's bootleg while it's on the trucks, but when your host at the club, in the locker room, or on the Gold Coast hands it to you on a silver tray, it's hospitality. What's Al Capone done, then? He's supplied a legitimate demand. Some call it bootlegging. Some call it racketeering. I call it a business. They say I violate the prohibition law. Who doesn't?
*Ibid.*

A pleasant enough fellow to meet – socially – in a speakeasy – if the proprietor were buying Capone beer: a fervent handshaker, with an agreeable, ingratiating smile, baring a gleaming expanse of dental ivory: a facile conversationalist; fluent as to topics of the turf, the ring, the stage, the gridiron, and the baseball field; what the police reporters call 'a right guy'; generous – lavishly so, if the heart that beat beneath the automatic harnessed athwart the left armpit were touched.
Fred D. Pasley, in *ibid.*

He is Neapolitan by birth and Neanderthal by instinct.
*Ibid.*

Capone bestrode Chicago like the Loop.
Andrew Sinclair, in *ibid.*

Al Capone was to crime what J. P. Morgan was to Wall Street, the first man to exert national influence over his trade.
*Ibid.*

## CAREW, THOMAS

1594/5–1640 Poet

An elegant court trifler.
William Hazlitt, *Lectures on the Literature of the Age of Elizabeth*

Carew, it seems to me, has claims to more distinction than he is commonly accorded; more than he is accorded by the bracket that, in common acceptance, links him with Lovelace and Suckling. He should be, for more readers than he is, more than an anthology poet . . . To say this is not to stress any remarkable originality in his talent; his strength is representative, and he has individual force enough to be representative with unusual vitality.
F. R. Leavis, *Revaluation*

Tom Carew was next, but he had a fault, / That would not well stand with a Laureat; / His Muse was hard bound, and th'issue of's brain / Was seldom brought forth but with trouble and pain. /

John Suckling, *A Session of Poets*

## CARLYLE, JANE BAILLIE WELSH

1801–66 Letter Writer

Jenny kissed me when we met, / Jumping from the chair she sat in; / Time, you thief, who love to get / Sweets into your list, put that in: / Say I'm weary, say I'm sad, / Say that health and wealth have missed me, / Say I'm growing old, but add, / Jenny kissed me. /

Leigh Hunt, in *Monthly Chronicle*

## CARLYLE, THOMAS

1795–1881 Historian, Essayist

Let me have my own way exactly in everything, and a sunnier and pleasanter creature does not exist.

On himself, in A. K. Adams, *The Home Book of Humorous Quotations*

That anyone who dressed so very badly as did Thomas Carlyle should have tried to construct a philosophy of clothes has always seemed to me one of the most pathetic things in literature.

Max Beerbohm, *Works*

I heard him growl a little about the [Crystal Palace] Exposition . . . 'a dreadful sight,' he called it: 'There was confusion enough in the universe, without building a crystal palace to represent it.' How like Carlyle!

Elizabeth Barrett Browning, Letter to Mrs David Ogilvy, 25 July 1851

It is so dreadful for him to try to unite the characters of the prophet and the mountebank; he has keenly felt it; and also he has been haunted by the wonder whether the people were not considering if they had had enough for their guinea.

Jane Welsh Carlyle, of her husband as lecturer, 1840, in *The Journals of Caroline Fox*

Carlyle has led us all out into the desert, and he has left us there.

A. H. Clough, in conversation with R. W. Emerson, in E. E. Hale, *J. R. Lowell and his Friends*

He is like a lover or an outlaw who wraps up his message in a serenade, which is nonsense to the sentinel, but salvation to the ear for which it is meant.

Ralph Waldo Emerson, *Papers from the Dial*: 'Past and Present'

Carlyle has been at issue with all the tendencies of his age. Like a John the Baptist, he has stood alone preaching repentance in a world which is to him a wilderness.

J. A. Froude, *The Oxford Counter-Reformation*

The philosophy of Carlyle is simple, and it hardly changes all through his life. It is a revolt; or rather, a counter-revolution. In a word, it is *anti-mechanism.* Its main tenets are: (1) the universe is fundamentally not an inert automatism, but the expression or indeed incarnation of a cosmic spiritual life; (2) every single thing in the universe manifests this life, or at least could do so; (3) between the things that do and those that do not there is no intermediate position, but a gap that is infinite; (4) the principle of cosmic life is progressively eliminating from the universe everything alien to it; and man's duty is to further this process, even at the cost of his own happiness.

John Holloway, *The Victorian Sage*

The dynasty of British dogmatists, after lasting a hundred years and more, is on its last legs. Thomas Carlyle, third in the line of descent finds an audience very different from those which listened to the silver speech of Samuel Taylor Coleridge and the sonorous phrases of Samuel Johnson . . . We smile at his clotted English.

Oliver Wendell Holmes Sr, *Scholastic and Bedside Teaching*

In the whole tone and temper of his teaching Carlyle is fundamentally the Puritan. The dogma of Puritanism he had indeed outgrown; but he never outgrew its ethics. His thought was dominated and pervaded to the end, as Froude rightly says, by the spirit of the creed he had dismissed . . . It is, perhaps, the secret of Carlyle's imperishable greatness as a stimulating and uplifting power that, beyond any other modern writer, he makes us feel with him the supreme claims of the moral life, the meaning of our responsibilities, the essential spirituality of things, the indestructible reality of religion.

W. H. Hudson, Introduction to the Everyman edition of *Sartor Resartus* and *On Heroes and Hero Worship*

Carlyle is abundantly contemptuous of all who make their intellects bow to their moral timidity by endeavouring to believe in Christianity. But his own creed – that everything is right and good which accords with the laws of the universe – is either the same or a worse perversion. If it is not a resignation of the intellect into the hands of fear, it is the subordination of it by a bribe – the bribe of being on the side of Power – irresistible and eternal Power.

John Stuart Mill, Diary, 22 February 1854

The old Ram Dass with the fire in his belly.

Lord Morley, *Recollections*

At bottom Carlyle is simply an English atheist who makes it a point of honor not to be one.

Friedrich Nietzsche, *The Twilight of the Idols*

Naturally, with his constitutional tendency to antagonism, his delight in strong words, and his unmeasured assumption of superiority, he was ever finding occasion to scorn and condemn and denounce. By use, a morbid desire had been fostered in him to find badness everywhere, unqualified by any goodness. He had a daily secretion of curses which he had to vent on somebody or something.

Herbert Spencer, *An Autobiography*

To be a prophet is to be a moralist, and it was the moral preoccupation in Carlyle's mind that was particularly injurious to his artistic instincts . . . In his history, especially, it is impossible to escape from the devastating effects of his reckless moral sense.

Lytton Strachey, *Portraits in Miniature*

Carlyle is a poet to whom nature has denied the faculty of verse.

Alfred, Lord Tennyson, Letter to W. E. Gladstone, *circa* 1870

Dr Pessimist Anticant was a Scotchman, who had passed a great portion of his early days in Germany . . . He had astonished the reading public by the vigour of his thoughts, put forth in the quaintest language. He cannot write English, said the critics. No matter, said the public; we can read what he does write, and that without yawning. And so Dr Pessimist Anticant became popular. Popularity spoilt him for all further real use, as it has done many another. While, with some diffidence, he confined his objurgations to the occasional follies or shortcomings of mankind . . . it was all well; we were glad to be told our faults and to look forward to the coming millennium, when all men, having sufficiently studied the works of Dr Anticant, would become truthful and energetic. But the doctor mistook the signs of the times and the minds of men, instituted himself censor of things in general, and began the great task of reprobating everything and everybody, without further promise of any millennium at all. This was not so well; and, to tell the truth, our author did not succeed in his undertaking. His theories were all beautiful, and the code of morals that he taught us certainly an improvement on the practices of the age. We all of us could, and many of us did, learn much from the doctor while he chose to remain vague, mysterious, and cloudy: but when he became practical, the charm was gone.

Anthony Trollope, *The Warden*

*See also* Samuel Butler, Samuel Taylor Coleridge, J. A. Froude, Gerard Manley Hopkins, D. H. Lawrence, George Bernard Shaw, Jonathan Swift, Algernon Swinburne, H. G. Wells

## CARNEGIE, ANDREW

1835–1919 Industrialist, Philanthropist

The man who dies thus rich dies disgraced.

On himself, 'Wealth', in *North American Review*, June 1889

Pity the poor millionaire, for the way of the philanthropist is hard.

On himself, Letter to *Independent*, 26 July 1913

He had no ears for any charity unless labelled with his name . . . He would have given millions to Greece had she labelled the Parthenon Carnegopolis.

Poultney Bigelow, *Seventy Summers*, vol. 2

The public library was his temple and the 'Letters to the Editor' column his confessional.

Joseph Frazier Wall, *Andrew Carnegie*

## CAROLINE AMELIA ELIZABETH OF BRUNSWICK

1768–1821 Queen Consort to George IV

No one in fact care for me; and this business has been more cared for as a political affair dan as de cause of a poor forlorn woman.

On herself, in Reginald Coupland, *Wilberforce*

Most Gracious Queen, we thee implore / To go away and sin no more; / But, if that effort be too great, / To go away at any rate. /

Anon., in Lord Colchester, Diary, 15 November 1820

Fate wrote her a most tremendous tragedy, and she played it in tights.

Max Beerbohm, *King George the Fourth*

If she was fit to be introduced as Queen to God she was fit to introduce to men.

Sir Benjamin Bloomfield, on the form of public prayer, in John Wilson Croker, Diary, 6 February 1820

Damn the North! and damn the South! and damn Wellington! the question is, how am I going to get rid of this damned Princess of Wales?

George IV, when Prince of Wales, October 1811, in W. H. Wilkins, *Mrs Fitzherbert and George IV*

'Sir, your bitterest enemy is dead.'
'Is she, by God!' said the tender husband.

George IV's response to Sir E. Nagle's attempt to tell him of Napoleon's death, in *The Journal of Hon. Henry Edward Fox*, 25 August 1821

No proof of her guilt her conduct affords, / She sleeps not with courtiers, she sleeps with the Lords. /

Lord Holland, *Epigram*, 17 August 1819, after Caroline had been observed to sleep during the first day of her trial

Oh! deep was the sorrow and sad was the day, / When death took our gracious old Monarch away, / And gave us a Queen, lost to honour and fame, / Whose manners are folly, whose conduct is shame; / Who with aliens and vagabonds long having stroll'd, / Soon caught up their morals, loose, brazen, and bold. /

Theodore Hook, *Imitation of Bunbury's 'Little Grey Man'*

Well, gentlemen, since you will have it so – 'God save the Queen', and may all your wives be like her!

Duke of Wellington, to the men barring his way to champion the Queen's cause, in G. W. E. Russell, *Collections and Recollections*

## CAROLINE WILHELMINA OF ANSBACH

1683–1737 Queen Consort to George II

She was with regard to power as some men are to their amours, the vanity of being thought to possess what she desired was equal to the pleasure of the possession itself.

Lord Hervey, *Memoirs*

Here lies, wrapt up in forty thousand towels, / The only proof that Caroline had bowels. /

Alexander Pope, *Epigram on Queen Caroline*

What tho' the royal carcase must, / Squeez'd in a coffin, turn to dust? / Those elements her name compose, / Like atoms are exempt from blows. /

Jonathan Swift, *Directions for Making a Birthday Song*

## CARR, ROBERT, EARL OF SOMERSET

– d. 1645 Politician, Courtier

Thou was a man but of compounded part; / Nothing thy own, but thy aspiring heart; / Thy house Raleigh's, Westmoreland's thy land, / Overbury's thy wit, Essex thy wife. So stand, / By Aesop's Law, each bird may pluck his feather, / And thou stript naked art to wind and weather. / Yet care of friends, to shelter thee from cold, / Have mewed thee up in London's strongest hold. / Summer is set, and winter is come on, / Yet Robin Redbreast's chirping voice is gone. /

Anon., *Manuscript in Belvoir Castle*

Blest pair of swans, O may you interbring / Daily new joys, and never sing: / Live till all grounds of wishes fail, / Till honour, yes, till wisdom grow so stale / That new great heights to try, / It must serve your ambition to die. /

John Donne, referring also to Lady Carr, *The Benediction*

## CARROLL, LEWIS (CHARLES LUTWIDGE DODGSON)

1832–98 Children's Writer

In answer to your question, 'What did you mean the Snark was?' will you tell your friend that I meant the Snark was a *Boojum*.

On himself, Letter to May Barber, January 1897

In writing it out, I added many fresh ideas, which seemed to grow of themselves upon the original stock; and many more added themselves when, years afterwards, I wrote it all over again for publication: but (this may interest some readers of 'Alice' to know) every such idea and nearly every word of the dialogue, *came of itself*. Sometimes an idea comes at night, when I have to get up and strike a light to note it down – sometimes when out on a lonely winter walk, when I have had to stop, and with half-frozen fingers jot down a few words which should keep the new-born idea from perishing – but whenever or however it comes, *it comes of itself*.

On himself and the composition of *Alice*, in *Theatre*, April 1887

Carroll's ego, a Humpty Dumpty (egg), was in perpetual peril of falling, never to be put together again. Indeed, Humpty Dumpty is the archetypal image of a Platonic man – seen as the union of white and yolk, yang and yin, enclosed within a thin shell of brittle skin. His defensive hypersensitivity to a little girl's curiosity is a reflection of a boy too long exposed to feminine eyes. It is the anguished cry of a little boy forced to spend the first years of his life in the almost exclusive company of sisters (of which Carroll ultimately had seven).

Judith Bloomingdale, 'Alice as *Anima*: The Image of Woman in Carroll's Classic', in Robert Phillips, *Aspects of Alice*

To make the dream-story from which *Wonderland* was elaborated seem Freudian one has only to tell it.

William Empson, *Some Versions of Pastoral*

The symbolic completeness of Alice's experience is, I think, important. She runs the whole gamut; she is a father in getting down the hole, a fetus at the bottom, and can only be born by becoming a mother and producing her own amniotic fluid. Whether Carroll's mind played the trick of putting this into the story or not, he has the feelings that would correspond to it. A desire to include all sexuality in the girl-child, the least obviously sexed of human creatures, the one that keeps its sex in the safest place, was an important part of their fascination for him.

*Ibid.*

. . . Carroll was not selfish, but a liberal-minded, liberal-handed egotist, but his egotism was all but second childhood.

Harry Furniss, *Confessions of a Caricaturist*

Although the first book has all the trappings of romance, including a quest for identity, a magic garden, magical transformations, and the luxuriance of perpetual springtime and a perpetual beginning, it ends with a trial, and there are no trials in utopias. It is strangely reminiscent of Carroll's experience upon seeing a sign that he thought read 'Romancement', only to discover, upon getting closer, that it actually said 'Roman cement'.

Jan B. Gordon, 'The Alice Books and Metaphors of Victorian Childhood', in Robert Phillips, *Aspects of Alice*

Carroll's superiority over Barrie is that his mawkish writings are his dull ones – he never succeeds in making sentimentality seductive.

Florence Becker Lennon, *Lewis Carroll*

In Lewis Carroll's writings the oral trauma (or the oral situation, to express the same thing more cautiously) is always breaking through the polite superficialities. For example, we attend a 'Mad Tea-Party' with Alice, the March Hare, the Mad Hatter, and the Dormouse. It is a *mad* tea-party. The March Hare *is* as mad as a March Hare, and so is the Mad Hatter; while Dormouse (*dormeuse*), with his continual tendency to fall asleep, represents withdrawal. In view of all this we expect to find a duplication of schizophrenic mechanisms in this part of the narrative, and we are not disappointed.

Géza Róheim, 'Magic and Schizophrenia', in Robert Phillips, *Aspects of Alice*

Carroll's special genius, perhaps, lies in his ability to disguise charmingly the seriousness of his own concern, to make the most playful quality of his work at the same time its didactic crux.

Patricia Spacks, *Logic and Language in Through the Looking-Glass*

His great delight was to teach me his Game of Logic. Dare I say this made the evening rather long, when the band was playing outside on the parade, and the moon was shining on the sea?

Irene Vanbrugh, in Robert Phillips, *Aspects of Alice*

## CARSON, CHRISTOPHER ('KIT')

1809–68 Frontiersman

He was not dressed in the outlandish habiliments with which fancy, since the time of Boone, instinctively invests the hunter and the trapper, but in genteel American costume . . . Carson is rather under the medium height, but his frame exceedingly well knit, muscular, symmetrically proportioned. His hair, a light auburn, and worn long, falls back from a forehead high, broad and indicating more than a common share of intellect. The general contour of his face is not handsome, and yet not unpleasing. But that which at once arrests and almost monopolizes your attention is the eye – such an eye! gray, searching, piercing, as if with every glance he would reach the well-springs of thought, and read your very silent imaginings.

*Arkansas Gazette & Democrat*, 13 June 1851

Kit Carson was one of the famous frontiersmen of his day. He was also a back-woodsman. For this reason he is said to have known the West backwoods and forewoods. As a young man he was a scout; as a boy, he was a boy scout. The daring deeds of Kit Carson are in no way minimized in a book about them which was written by Kit Carson.

Richard Armour, *It All Started With Columbus*

*See also* Gary Cooper

## CARTERET, JOHN, EARL GRANVILLE

1690–1763 Statesman

A careless, lolling, laughing love of self; a sort of Epicurean ease, roused to action by starts and bounds – such was his real character. For such a man to be esteemed really great, he must die early! He must dazzle as he passes, but he cannot bear a close and continued gaze.

Lord Mahon, *History of England, 1713–1783*

Commanding beauty, smooth'd by cheerful grace, / Sat on the open features of his face./ Bold was his language, rapid, glowing, strong,/ And science flow'd spontaneous from his tongue. / A genius, seizing systems, slighting rules, / And void of gall, with boundless scorn of fools,/ Ambition dealt her flambeau to his hand,/ And Bacchus sprinkled fuel on the brand . . ./ Unhurt, undaunted, undisturb'd he fell,/ Could laugh the same, and the same stories tell:/ And more a sage than he who bade await/ His revels till his conquests were complete,/ Our jovial statesman either sail unfurl'd,/ And drank his bottle, tho' he miss'd the world./

Horace Walpole, in Basil Williams, *Carteret and Newcastle*

Like a true Cornishman, indifferent, as is said, to what the rest of England was doing or thinking, he scorned the necessary condescensions of statesmen to secure the co-operation of fellow ministers, parliament, or people.

Basil Williams, *The Whig Supremacy*

## CARUSO, ENRICO

1873–1921 Singer

The Man With the Orchid-Lined Voice.

Edward L. Bernays, Caruso's publicist, in numerous press releases

His records had made him known to millions, including a significant majority of non-opera-goers, but the Caruso cult owed as much to his almost magnetic rapport with the public, both on and off stage . . . The beaming smile, lit by flashing white teeth, radiated an urchin exuberance and *joie de vivre.* Only Caruso would dare to go before the Metropolitan curtain, pat his stomach and implore the audience to go home 'because I'm so hungry and want my supper'.

Stanley Johnson, *Caruso*

## CARVER, GEORGE WASHINGTON

1864–1943 Agricultural Chemist, Educator

Isn't it fantastic that George Washington Carver found over 300 uses for the lowly peanut – but the South never had any use for George Washington Carver?

Dick Gregory, *From the Back of the Bus*

## CASTLEMAINE, COUNTESS OF, *see under* VILLIERS, BARBARA

## CASTLEREAGH, VISCOUNT (ROBERT STEWART, MARQUESS OF LONDONDERRY)

1739–1821 Statesman

A wretch never named but with curses and jeers!

Lord Byron, *The Irish Avatar*

The intellectual eunuch Castlereagh.

Lord Byron, *Don Juan*, canto i (fragment)

That sad inexplicable beast of prey – / That Sphinx, whose words would ever be a doubt, / Did not his deeds unriddle them each day – / That monstrous hieroglyphic – that long spout / Of blood and water, leaden Castlereagh! /

Lord Byron, *Don Juan*, canto ix

Q. Why is a Pump like V-sc--nt C-stl-r--gh?
A. Because it is a slender thing of wood, / That up and down its awkward arm doth sway, / And coolly spout and spout and spout away, / In one weak, washy, everlasting flood! /

Thomas Moore, *A Riddle*

I met Murder on the way – / He had a mask like Castlereagh – / Very smooth he looked, yet grim; / Seven bloodhounds followed him: / All were fat; and well they might / Be in admirable plight, / For one by one, and two by two, / He tossed them human hearts to chew / Which from his wide cloak he drew. /

Percy Bysshe Shelley, *The Mask of Anarchy*

*See also* Henry Addington

## CATHER, WILLA SIBERT

1873–1947 Author

Her style is so deftly a part of her theme that to the uncomprehending, to the seeker after verbal glass jewels, she is not perceivable as a 'stylist' at all.

Sinclair Lewis, 'A Hamlet of the Plains', in James Schroeter ed., *Willa Cather and Her Critics*

The disappearance of the old frontier left Miss Cather with a heritage of the virtues in which she had been bred but with the necessity of finding a new object for them. Looking for the new frontier she found it in the mind.

Lionel Trilling, 'Willa Cather', in Malcolm Cowley ed., *After the Genteel Tradition*

Hers is to move on the sunlit face of the earth, with the gracious amplitude of Ceres, bidding the soil yield richly, that the other kind of artist, who is like Persephone and must spend half of his days in the world under the world, may be refreshed on emergence.

Rebecca West, 'The Classic Artist', in James Schroeter ed., *Willa Cather and Her Critics*

## CATHERINE OF ARAGON

1485–1536 Queen Consort to Henry VIII

I have done England little good, but I should be sorry to do it any harm.

On herself, attributed

A pious woman toward God, (according to her devotion), frequent in prayer, which she always performed on her bare knees, nothing else between her and the earth interposed; little curious in her clothes, being wont to say, she accounted no time lost but what was laid out in dressing of her, though art might be more excusable in her, to whom nature had not been over-bountiful. She was rather staid, than stately; reserved, than proud; grave from her cradle, insomuch that she was a matron before she was a mother. This her natural gravity increased with her apprehended injuries, settled in her reduced age into a habit of melancholy, and that terminated into a consumption of the spirits.

Thomas Fuller, *Church History of Britain*

## CATHERINE OF BRAGANZA

1638–1705 Queen Consort to Charles II

The *Queene* arived, with a traine of Portugueze Ladys in their monstrous fardingals or *Guard-Infantas*: their complexions *olivaster*, & sufficiently unagreeable: *Her majestie* in the same habit, her foretop long & turned aside very strangely: She was yet of the handsomest Countenance of all the rest, & tho low of stature pretily shaped, languishing and excellent Eyes, her teeth wronging her mouth by stiking a little too far out: for the rest sweete & lovely enough.

John Evelyn, Diary, 30 May 1662

Mr Coventry tells me today that the Queene hath a very good night last night; but yet it is strange that she still raves and talks of little more than of her having of children, and fancies now that she hath three children and that the girle is very like the King. And this morning about 5 a-clock, waked (the Physician feeling her pulse, thinking to be better able to judge, she being still and asleep, waked her) and the first word she said was, 'How do the children?'

Samuel Pepys, Diary, 27 October 1663

. . . the Queene is very well again, and the King lay with her on Saturday night last. And that she speaks now very pretty English and makes her sense out now and then with pretty phrases – as, among others, this is mightily cried up – that meaning to say she did not like such a horse so well as the rest, he being too prancing and full of tricks, she said he did 'make too much vanity'.

Samuel Pepys, Diary, 4 January 1664

A little woman, no breeder.

Anthony à Wood, *Life and Times*, 20 May 1662

## CAVANAGH, JOHN

Early Nineteenth-Century Fives Player

He was a fine, sensible, manly player, who did what he could, but that was more than any one else could even affect to do. His blows were not undecided and ineffectual – lumbering like Mr Wordsworth's epic poetry, nor wavering like Mr Coleridge's lyric prose, nor short of the mark like Mr Brougham's speeches, nor wide of it like Mr

Canning's wit, nor foul like the *Quarterly*, nor *let* balls like the *Edinburgh Review*. Cobbett and Junius together would have made a Cavanagh.

William Hazlitt, *Table Talk: The Indian Jugglers*

## CAVENDISH, HON. HENRY

1731–1810 Natural Philosopher

Mr Cavendish received no one at his residence; he ordered his dinner daily by a note which he left at a certain hour on the hall table, where the housekeeper was to take it, for he held no communication with his female domestics, from his morbid shyness. It followed, as a matter of course, that his servants thought him strange, and his neighbours deemed him out of his mind. He hardly ever went into society. The only exceptions I am aware of are an occasional christening at Devonshire or Burlington House, the meetings of the Royal Society, and Sir Joseph Banks' weekly conversaziones. At both the latter places I have met him, and recollect the shrill cry he uttered as he shuffled quickly from room to room, seeming to be annoyed if looked at, but sometimes approaching to hear what was passing among others. His face was intelligent and mild, though, from the nervous irritation which he seemed to feel, the expression could hardly be called calm. It is not likely that he ever should have been induced to sit for his picture; the result therefore of any such experiment is wanting. His dress was of the oldest fashion, a greyish green coat and waistcoat, with flaps, a small cocked hat, and his hair dressed like a wig (which possibly it was) with a thick clubbed tail. His walk was quick and uneasy; of course he never appeared in London unless lying back in the corner of his carriage. He probably uttered fewer words in the course of his life than any man who ever lived to fourscore years, not at all excepting the monks of La Trappe.

Henry, Lord Brougham, *Lives of Men of Letters and Science*

## CAVENDISH, MARGARET, DUCHESS OF NEWCASTLE

1624?–74 Author

A dear favourite of mine, of the last century but one – the thrice noble, chaste, and virtuous, – but again somewhat fantastical, and original-brain'd, generous Margaret Newcastle.

Charles Lamb, *Elia*

She succeeded during her lifetime in drawing upon herself the ridicule of the great and the applause of the learned. But the last echoes of that clamour have now all died away; she lives only in the few splendid phrases that Lamb scattered upon her tomb; her poems, her plays, her philosophies, her orations, her discourses – all those folios and quartos in which, she protested, her real life was shrined – moulder in the gloom of public libraries, or are decanted into tiny thimbles which hold six drops of their profusion. Even the curious student, inspired by the words of Lamb, quails before the mass of her mausoleum, peers in, looks about him, and hurries out again, shutting the door.

Virginia Woolf, *The Common Reader*

## CAVENDISH, RICHARD

Eighteenth-Century Gentleman

Mr Sheridan told us of Mr Richard Cavendish, who had a trick of swinging his arm round when talking, that, walking up Bond Street with a friend, he found, on stopping, that he had drawn seven hackney coaches to him.

Lord Broughton, *Recollections of a Long Life*, 4 June 1810

## CAVENDISH, WILLIAM, DUKE OF NEWCASTLE

1592–1676 Statesman

Newcastle on's horse for entrance next strives / Well stuffd was his cloak-bag, and so were his breeches. / And unbutt'ning the place where Nature's posset-maker lives, / Pulls out his wife's poems plays essays and speeches. /

'Whoop' quoth Apollo, 'What the de'il have we here? / Put up thy wife's trumpery good noble Marquis, / And home again, home again, take thy career / To provide her fresh straw and a chamber that dark is.' /

Anon., *The Session of the Poets*, 1668

## CAXTON, WILLIAM

1422–91 Printer

It was in the year 1474 that our first press was established in Westminster Abbey, by William Caxton: but in the choice of his authors, that liberal and industrious artist was reduced to comply with the vicious taste of his readers; to gratify the nobles with treatises on heraldry, hawking and the game of chess, and to amuse the popular credulity with romances of fabulous knights, and legends of more fabulous saints.

Edward Gibbon, *An Address*

## CECIL, EDGAR ALGERNON ROBERT GASCOYNE, VISCOUNT OF CHELWOOD

1864–1958 Statesman, Co-Founder of the League of Nations

Lord Robert . . . with a permanent stoop . . . gave one the impression when he was denouncing the [Welsh Disestablishment] Bill of a benevolent hawk, if there be such a bird, anxious to swoop upon the Liberal Party to remove it from its evil environment of Radicalism and Nonconformity and secure it body and soul for the Church.

Lord Winterton, *Orders for the Day*

## CECIL, ROBERT, EARL OF SALISBURY

1563–1612 Statesman

Here lieth Robin Crookback, unjustly reckoned / A Richard the Third, he was Judas the Second . . . /

Anon., from a manuscript collection of verses on Robert Cecil's death

Here lies, thrown down for worms to eat, / Little bossive that was so great. / Not Robin Goodfellow, or Robin Hood / But Robin th'encloser of Hatfield Wood, / Who seemed as sent from Ugly Fate / To spoil the Prince, and rot the State, / Owning a mind of dismal ends / As trap for foes and tricks for friends. / But now in Hatfield lies the Fox / Who stank while he lived and died of the Pox. /

Anon., Popular celebration of Salisbury's death

He was no fit counsellor to make affairs better, yet he was fit to stop them from getting worse.

Francis Bacon, in David Cecil, *The Cecils of Hatfield House*

It is an unwholesome thing to meet a man in the morning which hath a wry neck, a crooked back and a splay foot.

John Mylles, servant of the Earl of Essex, in *ibid.*

He had a full mind in an imperfect body . . . In a chair he had both a sweet and a grave presence, as if nature understanding how good a counsellor he would make, gave him no more beauty of person anywhere else, of purpose because it should not move him into action.

Sir Henry Wotton, *The Character of Sir Robert Cecil*

The Queen was wont to call Sir Robert Cecil her register of remembrances.

Sir Henry Wotton, *Table Talk*

*See also* Mary Herbert

## CECIL, WILLIAM, *see under* BURGHLEY, LORD

## CHADWICK, SIR EDWIN

1800–90 Reformer, Philanthropist

He exhibits a curious example of the strictly legal as opposed to the scientific and practical order of mind . . . The legal mind, like Mr Chadwick's, first jumps to a conclusion of theory, in fact makes a case, and then devotes all its powers to support that case, rejects . . . every circumstance, . . . every practical and scientific fact, that contradicts its settled theory . . . Hence it is that reports drawn up by Mr Chadwick's Board of Health ignore the daily instance of choking-up of the pipe sewers, which he declared to be 'self-cleansing' . . . Hence, tables of the cost of sewerage works in various towns are published in the 1854 report, with one-half of the cost omitted, and instances of total failure are cited as triumphant successes. Mr Chadwick settled his system in 1848, and he would rather believe all the world wrong, rather see London made impassable, than permit himself to doubt that his theories, his dry water-works, and choked-up pipes are not perfection.

Anon., *Engineers and Officials*, 1856

. . . he babbled too much, not of green fields, but of sewage. I remember Lord Farrar when president [of the Political Economy Club] calling Mr Chadwick to order and in tones of thunder saying, 'The subject is taxation not drainage.'

Sir J. MacDonnell, Political Economy Club, *Journal*, 5 July 1905

I may say in brief that he is one of the contriving and organizing minds of the age; a class of mind of which there are very few, and still fewer who apply those qualities to the practical business of government. He is, however, one of the few men I have known who has a passion for the public good; and nearly the whole of his time is devoted to it in one form or another.

John Stuart Mill, Letter to James Henderson, August 1868

## CHAMBERLAIN, (ARTHUR) NEVILLE

1869–1940 Prime Minister

. . . You, like the late Bonar Law, always understate your case. That is part of your character. But you do not make headway on this understatement. You make it on character. So do not be deceived.

Lord Beaverbrook, Letter to Chamberlain, 7 June 1934

The worst thing I can say about democracy is that it has tolerated the right hon. Gentleman for four and a half years.

Aneurin Bevan, speaking in Parliament of Chamberlain as Minister of Health, 23 July 1929

Listening to a speech by Chamberlain is like paying a visit to Woolworths; everything in its place and nothing above sixpence.

Aneurin Bevan, in *Tribune*, 1937

Neville Chamberlain is no better than a Mayor of Birmingham, and in a lean year at that. Furthermore he is too old. He thinks he understands the modern world. What should an old hunks like him know of the modern world?

Lord Hugh Cecil, in Lord David Cecil, *The Cecils of Hatfield House*

No man that I know is less tempted than Mr Chamberlain to cherish unreal illusions.

Lord Halifax, February 1939, in Keith Feiling, *Life of Neville Chamberlain*

Well, he seemed such a nice old gentleman, I thought I would give him my autograph as a souvenir.

Adolf Hitler, attributed, in *The Penguin Dictionary of Modern Quotations*

Look at his head. The worst thing Neville Chamberlain ever did was to meet Hitler and let Hitler see him.

David Lloyd George, in conversation in Parliament, 3 September 1939

He has appealed for sacrifice. The nation is prepared for every sacrifice so long as it has leadership. I say solemnly that the Prime Minister should give an example of sacrifice, because there is nothing which can contribute more to victory in this war than that he should sacrifice the seals of office.

David Lloyd George, to the House of Commons, May 1940

He saw foreign policy through the wrong end of a municipal drainpipe.

David Lloyd George, attributed

As Priam to Achilles for his son, / So you, into the night, divinely led, / To ask that young men's bodies, not yet dead, / Be given from the battle not begun. /

John Masefield, in Keith Feiling, *Life of Neville Chamberlain*

I think it is the combination of real religious fanaticism with spiritual trickiness which makes one dislike Mr Chamberlain so much. He has all the hardness of a self-righteous man, with none of the generosity of those who are guided by durable moral standards.

Harold Nicolson, Diary, 26 April 1939

He was a meticulous housemaid, great at tidying up.

A. J. P. Taylor, *English History 1914–1945*

## CHAMBERLAIN, SIR (JOSEPH) AUSTEN

1863–1937 Statesman

Sir Austen Chamberlain said, when he was Foreign Secretary, that he loved France like a mistress. Poor Sir Austen doesn't know anything about mistresses.

Lord Beaverbrook, Letter to Roy Howard, 8 December 1931

Austen always played the game and always lost it.

Lord Birkenhead, comment (undated), in A. J. P. Taylor, *English History 1914–1945*

Austen – alas! is a son of a Father and when the Father is dead, the son's stock will drop heavily.

Rudyard Kipling, 1911, in A. J. P. Taylor, *Beaverbrook*

. . . the mind and manners of a clothes-brush . . .

Harold Nicolson, Diary, 6 June 1936

He was very independent . . . when the post of Chancellor [of the Exchequer] was offered to him – complained that he had not been sent for by the P.M., but that the office had just been thrown at him – like a bone at a dog. 'Stop a minute, Austen,' said the P.M. to him, 'there is a good deal of meat on that bone.'

Frances Stevenson, Diary, 5 March 1919

## CHAMBERLAIN, JOSEPH

1836–1914 Statesman

I have been called the apostle of the Anglo-Saxon race, and I am proud of the title. I think the Anglo-Saxon race is as fine as any on earth.

On himself, 1900, in H. Wickham Steed, *Through Thirty Years*

They see me sitting on the Terrace with a big cigar, and they think me lazy, but when I go back to the Office, I make things hum . . .

On himself, in J. L. Garvin, *Life of Joseph Chamberlain*

Mr Chamberlain is no ephemeron, no mere man of the hour. He is the man of tomorrow, and the day after tomorrow.

*African Review*, 15 March 1902

'Moatlhodi': The Man who Rights Things.

Title conferred on Chamberlain by the Bechuana chiefs, 1895, in J. L. Garvin, *Life of Joseph Chamberlain*

. . . the master of the feast has the manners of a cad and the tongue of a bargee.

H. H. Asquith, Letter to Herbert Gladstone, October 1900

Mr Chamberlain was incomparably the most live, sparkling, insurgent, compulsive figure in British affairs . . . 'Joe' was the one who made the weather. He was the man the masses knew. He it was who had solutions for social problems; who was ready to advance, sword in hand if need be, upon the foes of Britain; and whose accents rang in the ears of all the young peoples of the Empire and of lots of young people at its heart.

Winston Churchill, *Great Contemporaries*

Mr Chamberlain who looked and spoke like a cheesemonger.

Benjamin Disraeli, Letter to Lady Bradford, August 1880

He is a man worth watching and studying: of strong self-consciousness under most pleasing manners and I should think of great tenacity of purpose: expecting to play an historical part, and probably destined to it.

W. E. Gladstone, Letter to Lord Granville, June 1877

I do not see how a dissolution can have any terrors for him. He has trimmed his vessel, and he has touched his rudder in such a masterly way, that in whichever direction the winds of heaven may blow they must fill his sails.

W. E. Gladstone, in a Home Rule speech, House of Commons, 8 June 1886

The peace of shocked Foundations flew / Before his ribald questionings. / He broke the Oracles in two, / And bared the paltry wires and strings. / He headed desert wanderings; / He led his soul, his cause, his clan / A little from the ruck of Things. / *Once on a time there was a Man.* /

Rudyard Kipling, *Things and the Man*

Oh, Joe was a great man. He woke the Colonial Office up and it has been going to sleep ever since.

Sir Henry Lambert, *circa* 1918, in Sir Ralph Furse, *Aucuparius*

. . . Dangerous as an enemy, untrustworthy as a friend, but fatal as a colleague.

Sir Hercules Robinson, Letter to Sir Graham Bower, in Lady Longford, *Jameson's Raid*

The Chamberlain family govern the country as if they were following hounds – where according to hunting conventions it is mean-spirited to look before you leap.

Lord Salisbury, Letter to A. J. Balfour, 21 September 1904

Well, I could live for Balfour, but I could die for Chamberlain. He says what he means to do – and why – and then he does it.

Sir Henry Morton Stanley, Letter to his Wife, *circa* 1900

He was a man full of ambition, bringing the instincts of a commercial traveller to the affairs of the Empire. Pushfulness was to be the watchword of his Colonial administration.

William T. Stead, in *Review of Reviews*, 1899

*See also* A. J. Balfour, Theodore Roosevelt

## CHAMBERS, SIR WILLIAM

1723–96 Architect

WILL CHAMBERS screw'd from Britain's purse, / Five hundred thousand pound, / To raise a pile, when part was rais'd, / It tumbled to the ground. / But let not Scorn annoy the Knight, / Or make his worth her prey; / He sure deserves a nation's thanks, / Who makes the *base* give way. /

Anthony Pasquin (John Williams), *Epigrammatic Apology for Sir William Chambers*

## CHANDLER, RAYMOND THORNTON

1888–1959 Author

Having just read the admirable profile of Hemingway in the *New Yorker* I realize that I am much too clean to be a genius, much too sober to be a champ, and far, far, too clumsy with a shotgun to live the good life.

On himself, in Philip Durham, *Down These Mean Streets a Man Must Go*

Chandler brought together in one personification a representative folk hero; a combination of the American frontier hero, war hero, political hero, athletic hero, and chivalric hero. Although he was only a symbol – albeit a symbol of honor in all things – Raymond Chandler's knight went among the people in the language of the people.

Philip Durham, *ibid.*

The obvious accomplishment of his thrillers is to generate a sort of nervous tension which is the literary analogue to the tension generated by being an American.

George P. Elliott, *A Piece of Lettuce*

## CHANEY, ALONZO ('LON')

1883–1930 Actor

When you hear a person talk you begin to know him better. My whole career has been devoted to keeping people from knowing me. It has taken me years to build up a sort of mystery surrounding myself, which is my stock in trade. And I wouldn't sacrifice it by talking.

On himself, in *New York Times*, 6 July 1930

The Fates . . . dealt with Alonzo Chaney much as they would the hero of a Greek tragedy. The length of the thread when cut was far too short, but it was a golden thread, bright with accomplishment and success, twisted with heartache and hardship, and interwoven with irony. No dramatist could have created a more extraordinary story: that of a man born on April Fools' Day of deaf mute parents, who learned to communicate with his hands and body, and died of throat cancer on the threshold of a new career in which he would have been able to use his expressive voice.

Robert G. Anderson, *Faces, Forms, Films: The Artistry of Lon Chaney*

*See also* Boris Karloff

## CHAPLIN, SIR CHARLES

1889–1977 Actor

Of all the comedians he worked most deeply and most shrewdly within a realization of what a human being is, and is up against. The Tramp is as centrally representative of humanity, as many-sided and as mysterious as Hamlet, and it seems unlikely that any dancer or actor can ever have excelled him in eloquence, variety or poignancy of motion . . . the finest pantomime, the deepest emotion, the richest and most poignant poetry are in Chaplin's work.

James Agee in Theodore Huff, *Charles Chaplin*

The world was his oyster, and he, after his first faltering two-reelers, was its pearl.

John Mason Brown, *Book of the Month Club News*, 1964

Chaplin does not wish to give himself to any emotion, to any situation, to any life. Life draws him too terribly for that. Whatever he feels must immediately arouse its opposite; so that Chaplin may remain untouched – immaculate and impervious in himself.

Waldo Frank, *Scribners Magazine*, September 1929

There were two sides to Charlie, as there are to most clowns. The first was the fantastic cock of the walk who kidded our sacred institutions and solemn paraphernalia with merciless acumen. He kept a slop bucket in a safe and investigated a clock with a can opener. He slapped bankers on the back, and pinched a pretty cheek when he saw one. He had nothing but wit, grace, and agility with which to oppose the awful strength of custom and authority, but his weapons were a good deal more than sufficient.

The other Charlie was a beggar for sympathy and an apostle of pity. He pitied everything that stumbled or whimpered or wagged a tail, particularly he pitied himself. There has never been a portrait of self-pity so vivid or so shocking as Charlie with a rose in his hand.

Robert Hatch, *Reporter*, 25 November 1952

The Zulus know Chaplin better than Arkansas knows Garbo.

Will Rogers, *Atlantic Monthly*, August 1939

## CHAPMAN, GEORGE

1559–1634 Poet, Dramatist

Cloud-grapling *Chapman*, whose Aerial minde / Soares at Philosophy, and strikes it blinde. /

Anon., 'On the Time-Poets', in *Choyce Drollery*

The learned Shepherd of faire Hitching hill.

William Browne, *Britannia's Pastorals*

I have sometimes wondered, in the reading, what was become of those glaring colours which amazed me in *Bussy D'Amboys* upon the theatre; but when I had taken up what I supposed a fallen star, I found I had been cozened with a jelly; nothing but a cold dull mass, which glittered no longer than it was shooting; a dwarfish thought dressed up in gigantic words.

John Dryden, Dedication of *The Spanish Friar*

Oft of one wide expanse had I been told / That deep-brow'd Homer ruled as his demesne; / Yet never did I breathe its pure serene / Till I heard Chapman speak out loud and bold: / Then felt I like some watcher of the skies / When a new planet swims into his ken; / Or like stout Cortez when with eagle eyes / He star'd at the Pacific – and all his men / Look'd at each other with a wild surmise – / Silent, upon a peak in Darien. /

John Keats, *On First Looking into Chapman's Homer*

When one thinks of the donnish insolence and perpetual thick-skinned swagger of Chapman over his unique achievements in sublime balderdash, and the opacity that prevented Webster, the Tussaud Laureate, from appreciating his own stupidity . . . it is hard to keep one's critical blood cold long enough to discriminate in favour of any Elizabethan whatever.

George Bernard Shaw, in *Saturday Review*, 19 February 1898

There is no unity of design in Chapman's plays. Amid the thickets of rhetoric there are sudden clearings where the grimness of his political vision carries all before it. But no proportion is sustained, as if a severe Palladian threshold gave sudden access to a baroque interior.

George Steiner, *The Death of Tragedy*

## CHARLES I

1600–49

As I was going by Charing Cross, / I saw a black man upon a black horse; / They told me it was King Charles the First – / Oh dear, my heart was ready to burst. /

Nursery rhyme, traditional

When I was a Freshman at Oxford 1642, I was wont to go to *Christ Church* to see King *Charles* I at supper: where I once heard him say, 'That as he was hawking in *Scotland*, he rode into the Quarry, and found the covey of Partridges falling upon the Hawk'; and I do remember this expression further, *viz*, and I will swear upon the Book 'tis true. When I came to my Chamber, I told this story to my Tutor; said he, *That Covey was London.*

John Aubrey, *Miscellanies*

There was a Seam in the middle of his Fore-head, (downwards) which is a very ill sign in Metoposcopie.

*Ibid.*

King Charles the First, after he was condemned, did tell Colonel *Tomlinson*, that he believed, *That the English Monarchy was now at an end*: About half an Hour after, he told the Colonel, *That now he had Assurance by a strong impulse on his Spirit, that his Son should reign after him.* This information I had from *Fabian Phillips* Esq of the Inner-Temple, who had good Authority for the truth of it.

*Ibid.*

Never have I beheld features more unfortunate.

Gíovanni Bernini, attributed, on seeing Van Dyck's Charles I in three positions

With Queen Bess for a husband, how happy had it been! There is a real selectness, if little nobleness of nature in him; his demeanor everywhere is that of a man who at least has no doubt that he is able to command. Small thanks to him perhaps; – had not all persons from his very birth been inculcating this lesson on him? He has, if not the real faculty to command, at least the authentic pretension to do it, which latter of itself will go far in this world.

Thomas Carlyle, *Historical Sketches*

Charles knew his power; & Cromwell and Ireton knew it likewise, and knew, that it was the power of a Man who was within a yard's Length of a Talisman, only not within an arm's length, but which in that state of the public mind could he but have once grasped, would have enabled him to blow up Presbyterian and Independent. If ever a lawless act was defensible on the principle of self-preservation, the murther of Charles might be defended.

Samuel Taylor Coleridge, *Notes on the English Divines*, 'Richard Baxter'

His mind was an open book where all who chose might read, and he committed to paper more indiscretions than any ruler in history.

Wilbur Cortez, in W. C. Abbott,

*Writings and Speeches of Oliver Cromwell*

He was the worthyest gentleman, the best husbande, the best father, and the best Christian, that the age in which he lyved had produced, and if he was not the best kinge, if he was without some parts and qualityes which have made some kings greate and happy, no other Prince was ever unhappy, who was possessed of half his virtues and indowments, and so much without any kinde of vice.

Edward Hyde, Earl of Clarendon, *History of The Rebellion*

He said, that if he were necessitated to take any particular profession of life, he could not be a lawyer, adding his reasons: 'I cannot (saith he) defend a bad, nor yield in a good cause'.

Archbishop Laud, Diary, 1 February 1623

He died in the beginning of his climacterical year, fatal many times where killing directions in the nativity threaten.

William Lilly, *Life and Death of Charles The First*

He did not greatly court the ladies, nor had he a lavish affection unto many; he was manly and well fitted for venerial sports, yet rarely frequented illicit beds: I do not hear of above one or two natural children he had or left behind him. He had exquisite judgement by the eye, and *physionomy*, to discover the virtuous from the wanton; he honoured the virtuous; and was very shy and choice in wandering those ways; and when he did it, it was with much cautiousness and secrecy: nor did he prostitute his affection, but unto those of exquisite persons or parts; and this the queen well knew, nor did she wink at it.

William Lilly, *True History of King James I and King Charles I*

We charge him with having broken his coronation oath; and we are told that he kept his marriage vow! We accuse him of having given up his people to the merciless inflictions of the most hot-headed and hard-hearted of prelates; and the defence is, that he took his little son on his knee and kissed him! We censure him for having violated the articles of the Petition of Right, after having, for good and valuable consideration, promised to observe them; and we are informed that he was accustomed to hear prayers at six o'clock in the morning! It is to such considerations as these, together with his Vandyke dress, his handsome face, and his peaked beard, that he owes, we verily believe, most of his popularity with the present generation.

T. B. Macaulay, *Essays*: 'Milton'

He seems to have learned from the theologians whom he most esteemed that between him and his subjects there could be nothing of the nature of mutual contract; that he could not, even if he would, divest himself of his despotic authority; and that in every promise which he made, there was an implied reservation that such promise might be broken in case of necessity, and that of the necessity he was the sole judge.

T. B. Macaulay, *History of England*

He nothing common did nor mean / Upon that memorable scene, / But with his keener eye / The axe's edge did try; / Nor call'd the Gods, with vulgar spite, / To vindicate his helpless right; / But bow'd his comely head / Down, as upon a bed. /

Andrew Marvell, *An Horatian Ode upon Cromwell's Return from Ireland*

A Glorious Prince this Parliament / The King should be, did swear, / But now we understand they meant / In heaven and not here. /

King and no King was once a play / Or fable on the stage. / But see! It is become this day / The moral of our age. /

Marchamont Nedham, *A Short History of the English Rebellion compiled in verse*

King Charles the First walked and talked / Half an hour after his head was cut off. /

'Peter Puzzlewell', *A Choice Collection of Riddles, Charades and Rebuses*

We wish we had rather endured thee (O Charles) than have been condemned to this mean tyrant [Cromwell]: not that we desire any kind of slavery, but that the Quality of the Master something graces the condition of the slave.

Edward Sexby, *Killing No Murder*

Had his active courage equall'd his passive, the rebellious and tumultuous humor of those, who were disloyall to him, probably had been quashed in their first rise: for thro' out the English story it may be observ'd, that the souldier-like spirit in the Prince hath been ever much more fortunate and esteemed, than the pious.

Sir Philip Warwick, *Memoires of the Reigne of King Charles I*

How prophetically he spake, when the first reformers began to take the government asunder, which he resembled to a watch, telling the tamperers with it, that it was easy to disjoin the pieces, but hard to set them together again in good order, and so it proved.

*Ibid.*

*See also* Oliver Cromwell, George II, Lord Strafford

## CHARLES II

1630–85

As Nero once with harp in hand survey'd / His flaming Rome, and as that burn'd he play'd / So our great Prince, when the Dutch fleet arriv'd / Saw his ships burn'd, and, as they burn'd, he swiv'd. / So kind he was in our extremest need / He would those flames extinguish with his seed. / But against Fate all human aid is vain / His pr--- then proved as useless as his chain. /

Anon., *Fourth Advice to a Painter*

*Arise Evans* had a fungous Nose, and said it was revealed to him, that the King's Hand would Cure him: And at the first coming of King Charles II into St James's Park, he kiss'd the King's Hand, and rubbed his Nose with it; which disturbed the King, but Cured him.

John Aubrey, *Miscellanies*

He said once to my self, he was no atheist, but he could not think God would make a man miserable only for taking a little pleasure out of the way. He disguised his popery to the last . . . He was affable and easy and loved to be made so by all about him. The great art of keeping him long was, the being easy, and the making every thing easy to him. He had made such observations on the *French* government, that he thought a King who might be checkt, or have his Ministers called to an account by a Parliament, was but a King in name. He had a great compass of knowledge, tho' he was never capable of much application or study. He understood the Mechanicks and Physick; and was a good Chymist, and much set on several preparations of Mercury, chiefly the fixing it. He understood navigation well: But above all he knew the architecture of ships so perfectly, that in that respect he was exact rather more than became a Prince. His apprehension was quick, and his memory good. He was an everlasting talker. He told his stories with a good grace: But they came in his way too often. He had a very ill opinion both of men and women; and did not think that there was either sincerity or chastity in the world out of principle, but that some had either the one or the other out of humour or vanity. He thought that no body did serve him out of love: And so he was quits with all the world, and loved others as little as he thought they loved him. He hated business, and could not be easily brought to mind any: but when it was necessary, and he was set to it he would stay as long as Ministers had work for him. The ruine of his reign and of all his affairs was occasioned chiefly by his delivering himself up at his first coming over to a mad range of pleasure.

Gilbert Burnet, *History of My Own Time*

He loved to talk over all the stories of his life to every new man that came about him . . . He went over these in a very graceful manner; but so often, and so copiously, that all those who had been long accustomed to them grew weary of them: And when he entered on those stories they usually withdrew: So that he often began them in a full audience, and before he had done there were not above four or five left about him. Which drew a severe jest from *Wilmot*, Earl of *Rochester*. He said, he wondered to see a man have so good a memory as to repeat the same story without losing the least circumstance, and yet not remember that he had told it to the same persons the very day before. This made him fond of strangers; for they hearkened to all his often repeated stories, and went away in a rapture at such an uncommon condescension in a King.

*Ibid.*

There were some moral and social values in his perfection in little things. He could not keep the Ten Commandments, but he kept the ten thousand commandments. His name is unconnected with any great acts of duty or sacrifice, but it is connected with a great many of those acts of magnanimous politeness, of a kind of dramatic delicacy which lie on the dim borderland between morality and art.

G. K. Chesterton, *Essays*: 'Charles II'

He would fain be a Despot, even at the cost of being another's Underling . . . I look on him as one of the moral Monsters of History.

Samuel Taylor Coleridge, *Annotation to Lord Braybrooke's Edition of S. Pepys's Diary*

A prince of many Virtues, & many greate Imperfections, Debonaire, Easy of Accesse, not bloudy or Cruel: his Countenance fierce, his voice greate, proper of person, every motion became him, a lover of the sea, & skillfull in shipping, not affecting other studys, yet he had a laboratory and knew of many Empyrical Medicines, & the easier Mechanical Mathematics: Loved Planting, building, & brought in a politer way of living, which passed to Luxurie and intollerable expense: He had a particular Talent in telling stories & facetious passages of which he had innumerable, which made some bouffounes and vitious wretches too presumptuous, & familiar, not worthy the favours they abused: He tooke delight to have a number of little spaniels follow him, & lie in his bed-Chamber, where often times he suffered the bitches to puppy & give suck, which rendered it very offensive, & indeede made the whole Court nasty and stinking.

John Evelyn, Diary, 6 February 1685

In some of the State Poems, Charles II is ridiculed under the nick-name of Old Rowley, which was an ill-favoured stallion kept in the Meuse, that was remarkable for getting fine colts. – Mrs Holford, a young lady much admired by Charles, was sitting in her apartment and singing a satirical ballad upon 'Old Rowley the King', when he knocked at the door. Upon her asking who was there? he, with his usual good humour replied, 'Old Rowley himself, Madam'.

James Granger, *Biographical History of England*

And art thou borne, brave Babe?

Ben Jonson, *An Epigram on the Princes Birth*

C--t is the mansion house where thou dost swell, / There thou art fix'd as tortoise is to shell, / Whose head peeps out a little now and then / To take the air, and then peeps in again. / Strong are thy lusts, in c--t th'art always diving / And I dare swear thou pray'st to die a-swiving. / How poorly squander'st thou thy seed away / Which should get kings for nations to obey! /

John Lacy, *Satire*

According to him every person was to be bought: but some people haggled more about the price than others; and when this haggling was very obstinate and very skilful, it was called by some fine name. The chief trick by which clever men kept up the price of their abilities, was called integrity. The chief trick by which handsome women kept up the price of their beauty was called modesty. The love of God, the love of country, the love of family, the love of friends, were phrases of the same sort, delicate and convenient synonyms for the love of self. Thinking thus of mankind, Charles naturally cared very little what they thought of him. Honour and shame were scarcely more to him than light and darkness to the blind.

T. B. Macaulay, *History of England*

See in what Glory Charles now sits / With Truth to conquer Treason / And prove he is the King of wits / The world, himself, and Reason . . . /

The King the four great Bills must pass / And none but Saints are free / The Irish and Cavaliers, alas! / Must th'only rebels be . . . /

Thus Royal Charles lets to lease / Lays sword and sceptre down / To shew he values us and Peace / Above a glorious Crown. /

Marchamont Nedham, *A Short History of the English Rebellion compiled in verse*

Upon the Quarter-deck he fell in discourse of his escape from Worcester. Where it made me ready to weep to hear the stories that he told of his difficulties that he had passed through. As his travelling four days and three nights on foot, every step up to the knees in dirt, with nothing but a green coat and a pair of country breeches on and a pair of country shoes, that made him so sore all over his feet that he could scarce stir.

Yet he was forced to run away from a miller and other company that took them for rogues.

His sitting at table at one place, where the master of the house, that had not seen him in eight years, did know him but kept it private; when at the same table there was one that had been of his own Regiment at Worcester, could not know him, but made him drink the King's health and said that the King was at least four inches higher than he.

Another place, he was by some servants of the house made to drink, that they might know him not to be a Roundhead, which they swore he was.

In another place, at his Inn, the master of the house, as the King was standing with his hands on the back of a chair by the fire-side, he kneeled down and kissed his hand privately, saying that he would not ask him who he was, but bid God bless him whither that he was going. Then the difficulty of getting a boat to get into France, where he was fain to plot with the master thereof to keep his design from the four men and a boy (which was all his ship's company), and so got to Feckham in France.

At Roane, he looked so poorly that the people went into the rooms before he went away, to see whether he had not stole something or other.

Samuel Pepys, referring back to Charles's escape from Worcester, Diary, 23 May 1660

In our way discoursing of the wantonness of the Court and how it minds nothing else. And I saying that that would leave the King shortly, if he did not leave it, he told me 'No', for the King doth spend most of his time in feeling and kissing them naked all over their bodies in bed – and contents himself, without doing all the other but as he finds himself inclined; but this lechery will never leave him.

*Ibid.*, 16 October 1665

Mr Pierce did also tell me as a great truth, as being told it by Mr Cowly who was by and heard it, – that Tom Killigrew should publicly tell the King that his matters were coming into a very ill state, but that yet there was a way to help all – which is, says he, 'There is a good honest able man that I could name, that if your Majesty would imploy and command to see all things well executed, all things would soon be mended; and this is one Charles Stuart, – who now spends his time in imploying his lips and his prick about the Court, and hath no other imployment. But if you would give him this imployment, he were the fittest man in the world to perform it.' This he says is most true.

*Ibid.*, 8 December 1666

But Sir H Cholmly tells me that the King hath this good luck: that the next day he hates to have anybody mention what he had done the day before, nor will suffer anybody to gain upon him that way – which is a good quality.

*Ibid.*, 23 September 1667

If love prevailed with him more than any other passion, he had this for excuse, besides that his complexion was of an amorous sort, the women seemed to be the aggressors; and I have since heard the king say that they would sometimes offer themselves to his embrace.

Sir John Reresby, *Memoirs*

He was not an active, busy, or ambitious prince, but perfectly a friend to ease, and fond of pleasure; he seemed to be chiefly desirous of peace and quiet for his own time.

*Ibid.*

So have I seen a King at chess / (His rooks and knights withdrawn / His queen and bishops in distress / Shifting about grow less and less) / With here and there a pawn. /

Charles Sackville, Earl of Dorset, *On the Young Statesmen*

Those who knew his Face, fixed their Eyes there; and thought it of more importance to See than to Hear what he said. His face was as little a blab as most Mens, yet though it could not be called a prattling Face, it would sometimes tell tales to a good Observer. When he thought fit to be angry, he had a very peevish Memory; there was hardly a Blot that escaped him.

George Savile, Marquis of Halifax, *A Character of King Charles the Second*

A Mistress either Dexterous in herself, or well instructed by those that are so, may be very useful to her Friends, not only in the immediate Hours of her

Ministry, but by her Influences and Insinuations at other times. It was resolved generally by others, whom he should have in his Arms, as well as whom he should have in his Councils. Of a Man who was so capable of choosing, he chose as seldom as any Man that ever lived.
*Ibid.*

He lived with his Ministers as he did with his Mistresses; he used them, but he was not in love with them.
*Ibid.*

Kings are not born: they are made by artificial hallucination. When the process is interrupted by adversity at a critical age, as in the case of Charles II, the subject becomes sane and never completely recovers his kingliness.
George Bernard Shaw, 'Maxims for Revolutionists', in *Man and Superman*

I' th' Isle of *Britain*, long since famous grown / For breeding the best C---- in *Christendom*, / There reigns, and oh! long may he reign and thrive, / The easiest King and best bred Man alive. / Him no ambition moves to get Renown / Like the *French* Fool, that wanders up and down / Starving his People, hazarding his Crown. / Peace is his aim, his gentleness is such, / And love he loves, for he loves f------ much. / Nor are his high desires above his strength: / His Scepter and his P---- are of a length; / And she may sway the one who plays with th'other, / And make him little wiser than his Brother. / Poor Prince! thy P----, like thy Buffoons at Court, / Will govern thee because it makes thee sport. / 'Tis sure the sauciest P--- that e'er did swive, / The proudest, peremptoriest P---- alive. / Though Safety, Law, Religion, Life lay on't, / 'Twould break through all to make its way to C---. / Restless he rolls about from Whore to Whore, / A merry Monarch, scandalous and poor. /
John Wilmot, Earl of Rochester, *On King Charles by the Earl of Rochester, for Which he Was Banished the Court and Turned Mountebank*

Here lies our Sovereign Lord the King, / Whose word no man relies on, / Who never said a foolish thing, / Nor ever did a wise one. /
John Wilmot, Earl of Rochester, *Epitaph on Charles II*

Chast, pious, prudent, C(harles) the Second / The miracle of thy Restauration, / May like to that of *Quails* be reckoned / Rain'd on the Israelitick Nation; / The wisht for blessing from Heav'n sent, / Became their curse and Punishment. /
John Wilmot, Earl of Rochester, *The History of Insipids, a Lampoon*

*See also* Second Duke of Buckingham, John Dryden, John Flamsteed, George III, Nell Gwyn, Edward Hyde, Louise de Kerouaille, Duke of Monmouth, William Petty, Samuel Pepys, Frances Stuart, Barbara Villiers

## CHARLOTTE SOPHIA

1744–1818 Queen Consort to George III

Yes, I do think that the *bloom* of her ugliness is going off.
Colonel Disbrowe (her chamberlain), in William Timbs, *A Century of Anecdote*

## CHASE, SALMON PORTLAND

1808–73 Politician

I would rather that the people should wonder why I wasn't President than why I am.
On himself, in Samuel H. Dodson, *Diary and Correspondence of Salmon P. Chase*

. . . like the bluebottle fly, [will] lay his eggs in every rotten spot he can find. I have shut my eyes, as far as possible, to everything of the sort. Mr Chase makes a good secretary and I shall keep him where he is. If he becomes President, all right, I hope we may never have a worse man.

Abraham Lincoln, in T. G. Belden and M. R. Belden, *So Fell the Angels, Salmon Portland Chase*

## CHATHAM, FIRST EARL OF (WILLIAM PITT THE ELDER)

1708–78 Statesman

The atrocious crime of being a young man . . . I shall attempt neither to palliate nor to deny.

On himself, Speech in the Commons, replying to Robert Walpole, January 1741

England has been a long time in labour, but she has at last brought forth a man.

Frederick of Prussia, attributed

Lord Chatham is a greater paradox than ever: – is seen at home by no human creature; – absolutely by none! rides twenty miles every day, – is seen on the road, and appears in perfect good health; but will now speak to no creature he meets. I am much persuaded all is quackery; – he is not mad; that is, no madder than usual.

David Hume, Letter to Sir Gilbert Elliot, July 1768

He was the first Englishman of his time, and he had made England the first country in the world.

T. B. Macaulay, *Essays*: 'The Earl of Chatham'

Pitt, as his sister often said, knew nothing accurately except Spenser's Fairy Queen.

*Ibid.*

Walpole acted decisively. He threw Pitt out of his army commission. 'We must muzzle,' he said, 'this terrible cornet of the horse.' As well might he attempt to stop a hurricane with a hairnet.

J. H. Plumb, *Chatham*

. . . this immaculate man has accepted the Barony of Chatham for his wife, with a pension of three thousand pounds a year for three lives . . . The pension he has left *us* is a war for three thousand lives! perhaps for twenty times three thousand lives! . . . What! to sneak out of the scrape, prevent peace, and avoid the war! blast one's character, and all for the comfort of a paltry annuity, a long-necked peeress, and a couple of Grenvilles!

Horace Walpole, Letter to the Countess of Ailesbury, 10 October 1761

*See also* Adam Smith

## CHATTERTON, THOMAS

1752–70 Poet

An addiction to poetry is very generally the result of 'an uneasy mind in an uneasy body' . . . Chatterton, *I* think, mad.

Lord Byron, Letter to Leigh Hunt, November 1815

O Chatterton! that thou wert yet alive! / Sure thou would'st spread the canvass to the gale, / And love with us the tinkling team to drive / O'er peaceful freedom's undivided dale; / And we, at sober eve, would round thee throng / Hanging, enraptured, on thy stately song! / And greet with smiles the young-eyed Poesy / All deftly masked as hoar Antiquity. /

Samuel Taylor Coleridge, *Monody on the Death of Chatterton*

I cannot find in Chatterton's works any thing so extraordinary as the age at which they were written. They have a facility, vigour, and knowledge, which were prodigious in a boy of sixteen, but which would not have been so in a man of twenty. He did not shew extraordinary powers of genius, but extraordinary precocity. Nor do I believe he would have written better, had he lived. He knew this himself, or he would have lived. Great geniuses, like great kings, have too much to think of to kill themselves.

William Hazlitt, *Lectures on the English Poets*

**C** omfort and joy's forever fled
**H** e ne'er will warble more!
**A** h me! the sweetest youth is dead
**T** hat e'er tun'd reed before.
**T** he Hand of Mis'ry bowed him low,
**E** 'en Hope forsook his brain;
**R** elentless man contemn'd his woe:
**T** o you he sigh'd in vain.
**O** ppressed with want, in wild despair he cried
'**N** o more I'll live', swallowed the draught and died.

(Samuel) William Henry Ireland, *Acrostic on Chatterton*

O Chatterton! How very sad thy fate! / Dear child of sorrow – son of misery! / How soon the film of death obscur'd that eye, / Whence Genius mildly flash'd, and high debate. / How soon that voice, majestic and elate, / Melted in dying numbers! Oh! how nigh / Was night to thy fair morning. Thou didst die / A half blown flow'ret which cold blasts amate. /

John Keats, *Sonnet to Chatterton*

The finest of the Rowley poems . . . rank absolutely with the finest poetry in the language . . . He was an absolute and untarnished hero.

Dante Gabriel Rossetti, Letter to Hall Caine

He was an instance that a complete genius and a complete rogue can be formed before a man is of age.

Horace Walpole, Letter to William Mason, 24 July 1778

I thought of Chatterton, the marvellous Boy, / The sleepless Soul that perished in his pride. /

William Wordsworth, *Resolution and Independence*

## CHAUCER, GEOFFREY

*c.* 1340–1400 Poet

Long had our dull forefathers slept supine, / Nor felt the raptures of the tuneful nine; / Till Chaucer first, a merry bard, arose, / And many a story told in rhyme and prose. /

Joseph Addison, *Account of the Greatest English Poets*

He lacks the high seriousness of the great classics, and therewith an important part of their virtue.

Matthew Arnold, *Essays in Criticism*: 'The Study of Poetry'

And Chaucer, with his infantine / Familiar clasp of things divine; / That mark upon his lip is wine. /

Elizabeth Barrett Browning, *A Vision of Poets*

Grete thankes, laude and honour ought to be gyven unto the clerkes, poetes and historiographs that have wreton many noble bokes of wisdom; . . . emong whom and in especial tofore alle other we ought to gyve a syngular laud unto that noble and grete philosopher Gefferey Chaucer, the whiche for his ornate wrytyng in our tongue may wel have the name of a laureate poete.

William Caxton, Proem to *The Canterbury Tales*

Sunk in a Sea of Ignorance we lay, / Till *Chaucer* rose, and pointed out the Day, / A Joking Bard, whose Antiquated Muse, / In mouldy Words could solid Sense produce. /

Samuel Cobb, *Poetae Britannici*

It may be thought he was unusually likeable, especially to men, because of his wide conversational interests and lively fund of unexpected knowledge. As to women, it is less safe to conjecture. He has the whim in his poetry to represent himself as most unlikely to attract them. This may well be true. He knew too much about them.

Neville Coghill, *The Poet Chaucer*

I take unceasing delight in Chaucer. His manly cheerfulness is especially delicious to me in my old age. How exquisitely tender he is, and yet how perfectly free from the least touch of sickly melancholy or morbid drooping! The sympathy of the poet with the subjects of his poetry is particularly remarkable in Shakespeare and Chaucer; but what the first effects by a strong act of imagination and mental metamorphosis, the last does without any effort, merely by the inborn kindly joyousness of his nature. How well we seem to know Chaucer! How absolutely nothing do we know of Shakespeare!

Samuel Taylor Coleridge, *Table Talk*, 15 March 1834

As he is the Father of *English* Poetry, so I hold him in the same Degree of Veneration as the *Grecians* held *Homer*, or the *Romans Virgil*: He is a perpetual Fountain of good Sense; learned in all Sciences; and therefore speaks properly on all Subjects: As he knew what to say, so he knows also when to leave off; a Continence which is practis'd by few Writers.

John Dryden, *Preface to the Fables*

Chaucer, I confess, is a rough diamond; and must be polished e'er he shines.

*Ibid.*

Chaucer followed Nature everywhere, but was never so bold to go beyond her.

*Ibid.*

Chaucer is glad and erect.

Ralph Waldo Emerson, *Representative Men*: 'Shakespeare'

And gret wel Chaucer whan ye mete, / As mi disciple and mi poete, / For in the floures of his youthe, / In sondri wise, as he wel couthe, / Of Ditees and of songes glade, / The whiche he for mi sake made, / The lond fulfild is overal: / Whereof to him in special / Above all othre I am most holde. /

John Gower, *Confessio Amantis*

Chaucer was the most practical of all the great poets, and the most a man of business and the world.

William Hazlitt, *Lectures on the English Poets*

The history of our language is now brought to the point at which the history of our poetry is generally supposed to commence, the time of the illustrious Geoffrey Chaucer, who may perhaps, with great justice, be styled the first of our versifiers who wrote poetically. He does not, however, appear to have deserved all the praise which he has received, or all the censure he has suffered.

Samuel Johnson, *Dictionary of the English Language*

For many historians of literature, and for all general readers, the great mass of Chaucer's work is simply a background to the *Canterbury Tales*, and the whole output of the fourteenth century is simply a background to Chaucer.

C. S. Lewis, *Allegory of Love*

Sithe of our language he was the lodesterre.

John Lydgate, Prologue to *The Falls of Princes*

[Chaucer] owre englishe gilt with his sawes, / Rude and boistous firste be olde dawes, / That was ful fer from al perfeccioun, / And but of litel reputacioun, / Til that he cam, and, thorugh his poetrie, / Gan oure tonge first to magnifie, / And adorne it with his elloquence, – / To whom honour, laude, and reuerence. /

John Lydgate, *Troy Book*

He is a master of manners, of description, and the first tale-teller in the true enlivened natural way.

Alexander Pope, in Joseph Spence, *Anecdotes*

Chawcer, undoubtedly, did excellently in his *Troilus and Cressid*: of whome, trulie, I knowe not whether to marvaile more, either that hee in that mistie time could see so clearly, or that wee in this cleare age, goe so stumblingly after him.

Sir Philip Sidney, *Defence of Poesie*

Dan Chaucer, well of English undefiled, / On Fame's eternal beadroll worthy to be filed. /

Edmund Spenser, *The Faerie Queene*, book 4

He was a staunch churchman, but he laughed at priests. He was an able public servant and courtier, but his views upon sexual morality were extremely lax. He sympathized with poverty, but did nothing to improve the lot of the poor . . . And yet, as we read him, we are absorbing morality at every pore.

Virginia Woolf, *The Common Reader*

*See also* Robert Browning, William Dunbar, John Gower, Shakespeare, Edmund Spenser

## CHESTERFIELD, EARL OF (PHILIP DORMER STANHOPE)

1694–1773 Politician, Correspondent

Tyrawley and I have been dead these two years; but we don't choose to have it known.

On himself, in old age, in James Boswell, *Life of Johnson*

This man I thought had been a Lord among wits; but, I find, he is only a wit among Lords!

Samuel Johnson, in James Boswell, *Life of Johnson*

They teach the morals of a whore, and the manners of a dancing-master.

*Ibid.*, referring to Chesterfield's Letters

Chesterfield admired, and often quoted, Cardinal de Retz: 'I can truly call him a man of great parts, but I cannot call him a great man. He never was so much as in his retirement'. Was there not a touch of self-identification in that description?

Sir Lewis Namier, *Crossroads of Power*

He had neither creative passion nor unity of purpose, and therefore lacked single-mindedness; and while ready to pursue an interesting line of enquiry or argument, he easily tired of drudgery – 'a half-lazy man'.

*Ibid.*

The only Englishman who ever argued for the art of pleasing as the first duty of life.

Voltaire, Letter to Frederick the Great, 16 August 1774

I was too late for the post on Thursday, and have since got Lord Chesterfield's Letters, which, without being well entertained, I sat up reading last night till between one and two, and devoured above 140. To my great surprise they seem really written from the heart, not for the honour of his head, and in truth do no great honour to the last, nor show much feeling in the first, except in wishing for his son's fine gentlemanhood.

Horace Walpole, Letter to the Countess of Upper Ossory, 9 April 1774

Here is a disillusioned politician, who is prematurely aged, who has lost his office, who is losing his teeth, who, worst fate of all, is growing deafer day by day. Yet he never allows a groan to escape him. He is never dull; he is never boring; he is never slovenly. His mind is as well-groomed as his body. Never for a second does he 'welter in an easy-chair.'

Virginia Woolf, *Essays*: 'Lord Chesterfield's Letters'

## CHESTERTON, GILBERT KEITH

1874–1936 Novelist, Poet, Critic

Apart from vanity or mock modesty (which healthy people always use as jokes) my real judgement of my own work is that I have spoilt a number of jolly good ideas in my time.

On himself, *Autobiography*

This liberal colleague of Mr Shaw's . . . is a sort of caricature of 'a Liberal' as seen by Rowlandson.

Percy Wyndham Lewis, *The Art of Being Ruled*

Two buttocks of one bum.

T. Sturge Moore, on Chesterton and Belloc, in Stephen Potter, *Sense of Humour*

Chesterton is like a vile scum on a pond . . . All his slop – it is really modern catholicism to a great extent, the *never* taking a hedge straight, the mumbo-jumbo of superstition dodging behind clumsy fun and paradox . . . I believe he creates a milieu in which art is impossible. He and his kind.

Ezra Pound, Letter to John Quinn, 21 August 1917

Wells and I, contemplating the Chesterbelloc, recognize at once a very amusing pantomime elephant, the front legs being that very exceptional and un-English individual Hilaire Belloc, and the hind legs that extravagant freak of French nature, G. K. Chesterton.

George Bernard Shaw, 'The Chesterbelloc', in *New Age*, 15 February 1908

Chesterton's resolute conviviality is about as genial as an *auto da fé* of teetotallers.

George Bernard Shaw, *Pen Portraits and Reviews*

Here lies Mr Chesterton, / Who to heaven might have gone, / But didn't when he heard the news / That the place was run by Jews. /

Humbert Wolfe, *Lampoons*

*See also* Hilaire Belloc

## CHRISTIE, DAME AGATHA

1890–1976 Thriller Writer

A sausage machine, a perfect sausage machine.

On herself, in G. C. Ramsey, *Agatha Christie, Mistress of Mystery*

In a Christie, you know, for example, that the corpse is not a real corpse, but merely the pretext for a puzzle. You know that the policeman is not a real policeman, but a good-natured dullard introduced on to the scene to emphasize the much greater intelligence of Poirot or Miss Marple. You know that there will be no loving description of the details of physical violence. You know (or up to a few years ago, used to know) that, although the murderer is going to be hanged, you will be kept well at a distance from this displeasing event. You know that although people may fall in love you will not be regaled with the physical details of what they do in bed. You know, relaxing with a Christie, that for an hour or two you can forget the authentic nastiness of life and submerge yourself in a world where, no matter how many murders take place, you are essentially in never-never land.

Edmund Crispin, in H. R. F. Keating ed., *Agatha Christie, First Lady of Crime*

At her best, Agatha Christie's writing is instantly forgettable; at her worst, she may have forgotten it instantly herself.

Penelope Houston, in *Spectator*, 30 April 1977

As a person she had a quality of elusiveness which stemmed from her earliest days – a defensive resistance to inquisitive probing, an inbuilt armour off which any questionnaire was liable to glance like a spent arrow.

Sir Max Mallowan (Christie's husband), *Mallowan's Memoirs*

Her skill was not in the tight construction of plot, nor in the locked-room mystery, nor did she often make assumptions about the scientific and medical knowledge of readers. The deception in these Christie stories is much more like the conjurer's sleight-of-hand. She shows us the ace of spades face up. Then she turns it over, but we still know where it is, so how has it been transformed into the five of diamonds?

Julian Symons, *Bloody Murder, From the Detective Story to the Crime Novel: a History*

## CHURCHILL, CHARLES

1731–64 Poet

The comet of a season.

Lord Byron, *Churchill's Grave*

Nay, Sir, I am a very fair judge. He did not attack me violently till he found I did not like his poetry; and his attack on me shall not prevent me from continuing to say what I think of him, from an apprehension that it may be ascribed to resentment. No, Sir, I called the fellow a blockhead at first, and I will call him a blockhead still.

Samuel Johnson, in James Boswell, *Life of Johnson*

To be sure, he is a tree that cannot produce true fruit. He only bears crabs. But, Sir, a tree that produces a great many crabs is better than one which produces only a few crabs.

Samuel Johnson, in James Boswell, *London Journal*, 1 July 1763

## CHURCHILL, JENNIE JEROME (LADY RANDOLPH SPENCER-)

1854–1921 Society Lady

I shall never get used to not being the most beautiful woman in the room. It was an intoxication to sweep in and know every man had turned his head. It kept me in form.

On herself, in conversation with her sister Leonie, 1914, in Anita Leslie, *Jennie*

Had Lady Randolph Churchill been like her face, she could have governed the world.

Margot Asquith, *Autobiography*

## CHURCHILL, JOHN, *see under* MARLBOROUGH, DUKE OF

## CHURCHILL, LORD RANDOLPH HENRY SPENCER-

1849–95 Statesman

All great men make mistakes. Napoleon forgot Blücher, I forgot Goschen.

On himself, in Lady Dorothy Nevill, *Leaves from the Notebooks*

He has thrown himself from the top of the ladder, and will never reach it again!

Mr George Moore (civil servant), on hearing of Lord Randolph's resignation as Chancellor of the Exchequer, 1886, in Mrs Cornwallis West, *Reminiscences of Lady Randolph Churchill*

I have four departments – the Prime Minister's, the Foreign Office, the Queen, and Randolph Churchill; the burden of them increases in that order.

Lord Salisbury, 1886, in David Cecil, *The Cecils of Hatfield House*

Did you ever know a man who, having had a boil on his neck, wanted another?

Lord Salisbury, on being pressed to give Lord Randolph office after 1886, in *ibid.*

## CHURCHILL, SIR WINSTON LEONARD SPENCER-

1874–1965 Prime Minister

It's no use sitting upon me, for I am india-rubber – and I bounce!

On himself, to suppressive fellow-subalterns, Meerut 1898, in Lord Baden-Powell, *Indian Memories*

Like a good many other Generals at this time, French disapproved of me. I was that hybrid combination of subaltern and widely-followed war-correspondent which was not unnaturally obnoxious to the military mind.

On himself, recalling the Boer War, *Great Contemporaries*

I would say to the House, as I said to those who have joined the Government: 'I have nothing to offer but blood, toil, tears and sweat.'

On himself, Speech in the Commons, 13 May 1940

Let me, however, make this clear, in case there should be any mistake about it in any quarter. We mean to hold our own. I have not become the King's First Minister in order to preside over the liquidation of the British Empire.

On himself, Speech at the Mansion House, 10 November 1942

I did not suffer from any desire to be relieved of my responsibilities. All I wanted was compliance with my wishes after reasonable discussion.

On himself, in *The Second World War: The Hinge of Fate*

I am ready to meet my Maker. Whether my Maker is prepared for the ordeal of meeting me is another matter.

On himself, on his seventy-fifth birthday, 1949

I have never accepted what many people have kindly said, namely that I inspired the nation. It was the nation and the races dwelling all round the globe that had the lion heart. I had the luck to be called upon to give the roar.

On himself, Eightieth Birthday Speech, November 1954

Always remember, that I have taken more out of alcohol than alcohol has taken out of me.

On himself, in Quentin Reynolds, *By Quentin Reynolds*

Winston's back.

Radio message sent out to the Royal Navy by the Board of Admiralty in September 1939, when Churchill was re-appointed First Lord of the Admiralty

I have always said that the key to Winston is to realize that he is mid-Victorian, steeped in the politics of his father's period, and unable ever to get the modern point of view. It is only his verbal exuberance and abounding vitality that conceal this elementary fact about him.

L. S. Amery, *My Political Life*

Then comes Winston with his hundred-horse-power mind and what can I do?

Stanley Baldwin, in G. M. Young, *Stanley Baldwin*

Churchill is a good judge in every matter which does not concern himself. There, his judgement is hopeless, and he is sure to come to a big crash in time . . . He is born to trouble, for like Jehovah in the hymn – 'He plants his footsteps on the deep and rides upon the storm'.

Lord Beaverbrook, Letter to Sir Robert Borden, 10 June 1925

The weakness in this Indian issue is, that Winston Churchill is making it his ladder for the moment. Churchill has the habit of breaking the rungs of any ladder he puts his foot on.

Lord Beaverbrook, Letter to Arthur Brisbane, 20 October 1932

Churchill on the top of the wave has in him the stuff of which tyrants are made.

Lord Beaverbrook, *Politicians and the War*

I arrived at the conclusion that his chameleon-like character is founded upon a temperamental disability. He fills all the roles with such exceeding facility that his lack of political stability is at once explained.

Aneurin Bevan, Speech in the House of Commons, July 1929

The seven-league-boot tempo of his imagination hastens him on to the 'sunny uplands' of the future, but he is apt to forget that the slow steps of humanity must travel every inch of the weary road that leads there.

Aneurin Bevan, in *Tribune*, 1940

The man who may be the wrecker of the Tory Party, but was certainly saviour of the civilised world.

Henry Channon, Diary, 9 April 1952

Winston may in your eyes and in those with whom he has to work have faults, but he has the supreme quality which I venture to say very few of your present future Cabinet possess – the power, the imagination, the deadliness, to fight Germany.

Clementine Churchill, Letter to H. H. Asquith, May 1915

. . . In private conversation he tries on speeches like a man trying on ties in his bedroom to see how he would look in them.

Lionel Curtis, Letter to Nancy Astor, 1912

. . . full of go, no doubt full of foolishness, but he will like his father make the fur fly.

Mary Kingsley, Letter to John Holt, 10 May 1899

He has spoilt himself by reading about Napoleon.

David Lloyd George, in Frances Stevenson, Diary, 19 May 1917

Winston is an able man, but he is not a leader. He does not want men around him with understanding minds. He would rather not have them. He is intolerant of them. That is bad leadership.

David Lloyd George, in A. J. Sylvester, Diary, 25 June 1940

Winston was nervous before a speech, but he was not shy . . . Winston would go up to his Creator and say that he would very much like to meet His Son, about Whom he had heard a great deal and, if possible, would like to call on the Holy Ghost. Winston *loved* meeting people.

*Ibid.*, 2 January 1937

The first time you meet Winston you see all his faults and the rest of your life you spend in discovering his virtues.

Lady Lytton, in Christopher Hassall, *Edward Marsh*

His passion for the combative renders him insensitive to the gentle gradations of the human mind.

Harold Nicolson, Diary, 19 December 1945

He is a young man who will go far if he doesn't overbalance!

Cecil John Rhodes, 1901, in J. G. McDonald, *Rhodes: A Life*

As history it is beneath contempt, the special pleading of a defence lawyer. As literature it is worthless. It is written in a sham Augustan prose which could only have been achieved by a man who thought always in terms of public speech, and the antitheses clang like hammers in an arsenal.

Evelyn Waugh, on Churchill's *Life of Marlborough*, in David Pryce-Jones, *Evelyn Waugh and His World*

Winston is always expecting rabbits to come out of empty hats.

Field-Marshall Lord Wavell, in Henry Channon, Diary, 30 May 1943

When Mr Attlee is presiding in the absence of the Prime Minister the Cabinet meets on time, goes systematically through its agenda, makes the necessary decisions, and goes home after three or four hours' work. When Mr Churchill presides we never reach the agenda and we decide nothing. But we go home to bed at midnight, conscious of having been present at an historic occasion.

Ellen Wilkinson, during the Second World War, in Kingsley Martin, *Harold Laski*

*See also* Huey Long

## CIBBER, COLLEY

1671–1757 Actor, Dramatist

It may be observable, too, that my Muse and my Spouse were equally prolifick; that the one was seldom the Mother of a Child, but in the same Year, the other made me the Father of a Play; I think we had a Dozen of each Sort between us; of both which kinds, some died in their Infancy, and near an equal number of each were alive when I quitted the Theatre – But it is no wonder, when a Muse is only call'd upon by Family Duty, she should not always rejoice in the Fruit of her Labour.

On himself, *Apology for the Life of Mr Colley Cibber*, 1740

In merry old England it once was a rule / The King had his Poet, and also his Fool. / But now we're so frugal, I'd have you to know it, / That Cibber can serve both for Fool and for Poet. /

Anon., attributed by Cibber to Alexander Pope, before 1742

Colley Cibber was extremely haughty as a theatrical manager, and very insolent to dramatists. When he had rejected a play, if the author desired him to point out the particular parts of it which displeased him, he took a pinch of snuff, and answered in general terms, 'Sir, there is nothing in it to coerce my passions.'

George Colman, *Random Records*

He was known only for some years, by the name of Master Colley. After waiting impatiently for some time for the Prompter's Notice, by good fortune he obtained the honour of carrying a message on the stage, in some play, to Betterton. Whatever was the cause, Master Colley was so terrified, that the scene was disconcerted by him. Betterton asked, in some anger, who the young fellow was that had committed the blunder. Downes replied, 'Master Colley!' – 'Master Colley! then forfeit him!' – 'Why Sir,' said the prompter, 'he has no salary.' – 'No!' said the old man; 'why then put him down 10s. a week, and forfeit him 5s.'

Thomas Davies, *Dramatic Miscellanies*

. . . for that you, not having the Fear of Grammar before your Eyes, on the of at a certain Place, called the *Bath* in the County of Somerset, in *Knightsbridge* in the County of *Middlesex*, in and upon the *English* Language an Assault did make, and then and there, with a certain Weapon, called a Goosequill, value one Farthing, which you in your left Hand then held, several very broad Wounds, but of no Depth at all, on the said *English* Language did make, and so you the said Col. *Apol.* the said *English* Language did murder.

Henry Fielding, in *Champion*, 17 May 1740

Cibber! write all thy Verses upon Glasses, / The only way to save 'em from our A---s.

Alexander Pope, *Epigram Occasioned by Cibber's Verses in Praise of Nash*

Swearing and supperless the Hero sate, / Blasphemed his Gods, the Dice, and damn'd his Fate. / Then gnaw'd his pen, then dash'd it on the ground, / Sinking from thought to thought, a vast profound! / Plunged for his sense, but found no bottom there, / Yet wrote and flounder'd on, in mere despair. / Round him much Embryo, much Abortion lay, / Much future Ode, and abdicated Play; / Nonsense precipitate, like running Lead / That slip'd through cracks and Zig-zags of the Head; / All that on Folly Frenzy could beget, / Fruits of dull Heat, and Sooterkins of Wit. / Next o'er his Books his eyes began to roll, / In pleasing Memory of all he stole, / How here he sipp'd, now there he plundered snug, / And suck'd all o'er like an industrious Bug. /

Alexander Pope, *The Dunciad*, 1742

Me Emptiness and Dulness could inspire, / And were my Elasticity and Fire. / Some Daemon stole my pen (forgive th'offence) / And once betray'd me into common sense: / Else all my prose and verse were much the same; / This, prose on stilts; that, poetry fall'n lame. / Did on the Stage my Fops appear confin'd? / My Life gave ampler lessons to mankind. / Did the dead Letter unsuccessful prove? / The brisk Example never fail'd to move. /

*Ibid.*

The proud Parnassian sneer, / The conscious simper, and the jealous leer, / Mix on his look. /

*Ibid.*

Quoth *Cibber* to *Pope*, tho' in Verse you foreclose, / I'll have the last Word, for by G-d I'll write Prose. / Poor *Colley*, thy Reas'ning is none of the strongest, / For know, the last Word is the Word that lasts longest. /

Alexander Pope, *Epigram, On Cibber's Declaration that he will have the last word with Mr Pope*

*See also* Samuel Foote, James Thomson

## CLARE, JOHN
1793–1864 Poet

I have seen the original document authorizing the admission of poor Clare into the Asylum . . . There is a string of printed questions which the examining Physician answers. To the query whether the malady was preceded by any serious or long continued mental emotion or exertion the answer is – 'After years addicted to *poetical prosing*.'

G. J. de Wilde, Letter to F. Martin, 28 February 1865

How good was Clare? At his best he was very good indeed, with a natural simplicity supported by a remarkable sense of language; meant what he said, considered it well before he wrote it down, and wrote with love. When he was not good, he was no worse, than any other not-good poet of his time.

Robert Graves, in *Hudson Review*, Spring 1955

The principal token of his mental eccentricity was the introduction of prize-fighting, in which he seemed to imagine he was to engage; but the allusion to it was made in the way of interpolation in the middle of the subject on which he was discoursing, brought in abruptly, and abandoned with equal suddenness, and an utter want of connexion with any association of ideas which it could be thought might lead to the subject at any time; as if the machinery of thought were dislocated, so that one part of it got off its pivot . . . This was the only symptom of aberration of mind we observed about Clare.

Cyrus Redding, in *English Journal*, 15 May 1841

## CLARENDON, *see under* HYDE, EDWARD

## CLAY, HENRY

1777–1852 Statesman

I am the most unfortunate man in the history of parties; always run by my friends when sure to be defeated, and now betrayed when I, or any one, would be sure of election.

On himself, in Marquis James, *Andrew Jackson: Portrait of a President*

He wires in and wires out, / And leaves the people still in doubt, / Whether the snake that made the track, / Was going South or coming back. /

Anon., 1844, in Charles Sellars, *James K. Polk – Continentalist, 1843–46*

He prefers the specious to the solid, and the plausible to the true.

John C. Calhoun, in L. A. Harris, *The Fine Art of Political Wit*

. . . [The] ineffable meanness of the lion turned spaniel in his fawnings on the masters whose hands he was licking for the sake of the dirty puddings they might have to toss to him.

Edmund Quincy, in John F. Kennedy, *Profiles in Courage*

. . . like a mackerel in the moonlight; he shines and he stinks.

John Randolph of Roanoke, in Ray Gingers, *Joke book about American History*

Clay could get more men to run after him to hear him speak, and fewer to vote for him, than any man in America.

Mr Shepperd of North Carolina, as reported by Alexander H. Stephens in a letter to his brother, January 1845

He was a chameleon; he could turn any color that might be useful to him. To read of his career one must have cork-screw eyes.

Irving Stone, *They Also Ran*

Henry Clay said 'I would rather be right than be president.' This was the sourest grape since Aesop originated his fable.

*Ibid.*

## CLEVELAND, DUCHESS OF, *see under* VILLIERS, BARBARA

## CLEVELAND, JOHN

1613–58 Poet

Heliconean Dew.

On himself, Anagram of his name

A general artist, pure latinist, exquisite orator, and eminent poet. His epithets were pregnant with metaphysics, carrying in them a difficult plainness, difficult at the hearing, plain at the considering thereof. Never so eminent a poet was interred with fewer (if any remarkable) elegies upon him.

Thomas Fuller, *The History of the Worthies of England*

## CLEVELAND, (STEPHEN) GROVER

1837–1908 Twenty-Second and Twenty-Fourth United States President

I am not concerning myself about what history will think, but contenting myself with the approval of a fellow named Cleveland whom I have generally found to be a pretty good sort of a fellow.

On himself, in D. H. Elletson, *Roosevelt and Wilson: A Comparative Study*

Hurrah for Maria / Hurrah for the kid / I voted for Grover / And am damn glad I did. /

Anon., Cleveland campaign slogan, 1884, referring to the rumour that Cleveland, a bachelor, had fathered the child of Maria Halpin of Buffalo, New York

. . . his whole huge carcass seemed to be made of iron. There was no give in him, no bounce, no softness. He sailed through American history like a steel ship loaded with monoliths of granite.

H. L. Mencken, 'From a Good Man in a Bad Trade', in *American Mercury*, January 1933

## CLIVE, ROBERT, LORD

1725–74 Imperial Administrator

Consider my position. A great prince was dependent on my pleasure; an opulent city lay at my mercy; its richest bankers bid against each other for my smiles; I walked through vaults which were thrown open to me alone, piled on either hand with gold and jewels! By God, Mr Chairman, at this moment I stand astonished at my own moderation.

On himself, Address to Parliament, 1772

Clive, like most men who are born with strong passions and tried by strong temptations, committed great faults. But every person who takes a fair and enlightened view of his whole career must admit that our island, so fertile in heroes and statesmen, has scarcely ever produced a man more truly great either in arms or in council.

T. B. Macaulay, *Essays*: 'Lord Clive'

A savage old Nabob, with an immense fortune, a tawny complexion, a bad liver and a worse heart.

*Ibid.*

## CLOUGH, ARTHUR HUGH

1819–61 Poet

Something of the land-surveyor, one might say, mingles with the poet.

William Allingham, Diary

I never met with anyone who was more thoroughly high-minded. I believe he acted all through life simply from the feeling of what was right. He certainly had great genius, but some want of will or some want of harmony with things around him prevented his creating anything worthy of himself.

Benjamin Jowett, Letter to Florence Nightingale (shortly after Clough's death)

We have a foreboding that Clough, imperfect as he was in many respects, and dying before he had subdued his sensitive temperament to the sterner requirements of his art, will be thought a hundred years hence to have been the truest expression in verse of the moral and intellectual tendencies, the doubt and struggle towards settled convictions, of the period in which he lived. To make beautiful conceptions immortal by exquisiteness of phrase, is to be a poet no doubt; but to be a new poet is to feel and to utter that immanent life of things without which the utmost perfection of mere form is at best only wax or marble.

James Russell Lowell, *My Study Windows*

. . . A grave gentlemanly man, handsome, greyhaired, with an air of fastidious languor about him.

Alfred Munby, Diary, 9 March 1859

At the age of sixteen, he was in the Sixth Form, and not merely a Praepostor, but head of the School House. Never did Dr Arnold have an apter pupil. This earnest adolescent, with the weak ankles and the solemn face, lived entirely with the highest ends in view. He thought of nothing but moral good, moral evil, moral influence, and moral responsibility . . . Perhaps it is not surprising that a young man brought up in such an atmosphere should have fallen a prey, at Oxford, to the frenzies of religious controversy; that he should have been driven almost out of his wits by the ratiocinations of W. G. Ward; that he should have lost his faith; that he should have spent the rest of his existence lamenting that loss, both in prose and verse; and that he should have eventually succumbed, conscientiously doing up brown paper parcels for Florence Nightingale.

Lytton Strachey, *Eminent Victorians*

There was a poor poet named Clough, / Whom his friends all united to puff, / But the public, though dull, / Had not such a skull / As belonged to believers in Clough. /

Algernon C. Swinburne, *Essays and Studies, Matthew Arnold*

## COBBETT, WILLIAM

1763–1835 Polemicist, Author, Agriculturist

I was born under a King and Constitution; but I was not born under the Six Acts.

On himself, *The Last Hundred Days of English Freedom*

Cobbett, through all his life a cheat, / Yet as a rogue was incomplete, / For now to prove a finished knave / To dupe and trick, he robs a grave. /

The radicals seem quite elated, / And soon will be intoxicated / For Cobbett means to turn their brain / With his American Sham Paine. /

Anon., *circa* 1819, in Robert Huish, *Memoirs of the Late Mr Cobbett Esq.*

Mr C--B--T ask'd leave to bring in very soon / A Bill to abolish the Sun and the Moon. / The Honourable Member proceeded to state / Some arguments us'd in a former debate, / On the subject of Sinecures, Taxes, Vexations, / The Army and Navy, and Old Corporations; – / The Heavenly Bodies, like those upon Earth, / Had, he said, been corrupt from the day of their birth, / With reckless profusion expending their light, / One after another, by day and by night. / And what classes enjoy'd it? The Upper alone – / Upon such they had always exclusively shone; / But when had they ever emitted a spark, / For the people who toil under ground in the dark? /

Anon., *Speech of the Member for Odium*

. . . a Philistine with six fingers on every hand and on every foot six toes, four-and-twenty in number: a Philistine the shaft of whose spear is like a weaver's beam.

Matthew Arnold, *Essays in Criticism*

Had I met him anywhere save in that room and on that occasion, I should have taken him for a gentleman farming his own broad estate. He seemed to have that kind of self-possession and ease about him, together with a certain bantering jollity, which are so natural to fast-handed and well-housed lords of the soil.

Samuel Bamford, *Passages in the Life of a Radical*

The pattern John Bull of his century, strong as the rhinoceros, and with singular humanities and genialities shining through his thick skin.

Thomas Carlyle, *Essay on Scott*

It is especially his bad language that is always good. It is precisely the passages that have always been recognized as good style that would now be regarded as bad form. And it is precisely these violent passages that especially bring out not only the best capacities of Cobbett but also the best capacities of English.

G. K. Chesterton, *William Cobbett*

It is not true that he belonged successively to two parties: it is much truer to say that he never belonged to any. But in so far as there were elements of the Radical in him at the end, there had been traces of them from the beginning. And in so far as he was in one sense a Tory at the beginning, he remained a Tory to the end. The truth is that the confusion was not in Cobbett but in the terms Tory and Radical. They are not exact terms; they are nothing like so exact as Cobbett was.

*Ibid.*

A reviewer likened him to a porcupine. Nothing could have pleased him better. The name had obvious qualities. A porcupine was just what he meant and needed to be, in the hostile environment of Philadelphia. 'Peter Porcupine' he became, eagerly thanking the Democratic reviewer for teaching him that word.

G. D. H. Cole, *Life of William Cobbett*

He was one of the most striking refutations of Lavater I ever witnessed. Never were the looks of any man more completely at variance with his character. There was something so dull and heavy about his whole appearance, that any one, who did not know him, would at once set him down for some country clodpole, to use a favourite expression of his own, who not only never read a book, or had a single idea in his head, but who was a mere man of mortality, without a particle of sensibility of any kind in his composition.

James Grant, *Random Recollections of the House of Commons*

Why will Mr Cobbett persist in getting into Parliament? He will find himself no longer the same man. What member of Parliament, I should like to know, could write his Register? As a popular partisan, he may (for aught I can say) be a match for the whole Honourable House; but, by obtaining a seat in St Stephen's Chapel, he would only be equal to a 576th part of it.

William Hazlitt, *Fugitive Writings*: 'On Personal Identity'

He is not pledged to repeat himself. Every new Register is a kind of new Prospectus. He blesses himself from all ties and shackles on his understanding; he has no mortgage on his brain; his notions are free and unencumbered.

William Hazlitt, *The Spirit of the Age*

He is a kind of fourth estate in the politics of the country.

*Ibid.*

Gnawed by the worm that never dies, his own wretchedness would ever prevent him from making any attempt in favour of human happiness. His usual occupation at home was that of a garrett scribbler, excepting a little *night business* occasionally, to supply unavoidable exigencies. Grub Street did not answer his purpose, and being scented by certain tipstaffs for something more than scribbling, he took *French leave* for France. His evil genius pursued him here [America], and *as his fingers were as long as ever*, he was obliged as suddenly to leave the Republic, which has now drawn forth all his venom, for her attempt to do him *justice*. On his arrival in this country, he figured some time as a pedagogue, but as this employment scarcely furnished him salt to his porridge, he having been literally without bread to eat, and not a second shirt to his back, he resumed his old occupation of scribbling, having little chance of success in the other employments, which drove him to this country. His talent at lies and Billingsgate rhetoric, introduced him to the notice of a certain foreign agent, who was known during the Revolution by the name of *Traitor*.

'Paul Hedgehog', *History of Peter Porcupine*

The pride of purse persecuted him in America, and persecuted him no less in England, as it persecutes us all, and will continue to persecute, until in the fulness of its cup, it shall be laid low. The purseproud Americans were a democracy, and therefore in America, Mr Cobbett was a royalist; the purse-proud English were an aristocracy, and therefore in England, Mr Cobbett was a democrat.

Robert Huish, *Memoirs of the Late Mr Cobbett Esq.*

Somebody said of Cobbett, very truly, that there were two sorts of people he could not endure, those who differed from him and those who agreed with him. These last had always stolen his ideas.

John Stuart Mill, Letter to Robert Harrison, December 1864

He was honest: he never saw more than one side of a subject at a time, and he honestly stated his impression of the side he saw.

Daniel O'Connell, in W. J. O'N. Daunt, *Personal Recollections of the Late Daniel O'Connell M.P.*

*See also* John Cavanagh, Thomas Paine

## COBDEN, RICHARD

1804–65 Statesman

I have a horror of losing my own individuality, which is to me as existence itself.

On himself, refusing Palmerston's offer of cabinet rank, June 1859

Mr Cobden was very anomalous in two respects. He was a sensitive agitator . . . He never spoke ill of anyone. He arraigned principles, but not persons. We fearlessly say that after a career of agitation of thirty years, not one single individual has – we do not say a valid charge, but a producible charge – a charge which he would wish to bring forward against Mr Cobden. You cannot find the man who says, 'Mr Cobden said this of me, and it was not true.'

Walter Bagehot, Obituary notice, 1865, in *Biographical Studies*

The greatest political character the pure middle class of this country has yet produced.

Benjamin Disraeli, Speech in the Commons, 3 April 1865

. . . having sadly mismanaged his own affairs just as he would, if he could, the affairs of the nation.

Lord Palmerston, Letter to Lord John Russell, 4 December 1863

## COCHISE

– d. 1874 Paramount Chief of the Chiricahua Apache

When I was young I walked all over this country, east and west, and saw no other people than the Apaches. After many summers I walked again and found another race of people had come to take it. How is it? Why is it that the Apaches wait to die – that they carry their lives on their fingernails. They roam over the hills and plains and want the heavens to fall on them. The Apaches were once a great nation; they are now but few, and because of this they so carry their lives on their fingernails.

On himself, in Dee Brown, *Bury My Heart at Wounded Knee*

## COCHRAN, SIR CHARLES BLAKE

1872–1951 Showman

It is, I am sure, through his failures that he has made his friends. No other theatrical manager that I have ever known can rally adherents so swiftly in catastrophe. Temperamental stars demand to be allowed to pawn their jewellery for him. Chorus girls, stage managers, members of his office staff eagerly offer him their services indefinitely for nothing. Even hard-boiled backers rush through the flames with their cheque-books over their mouths to aid him, regardless of the fact that the flames are probably consuming many of their own investments.

Noël Coward, *Present Indicative*

When things were good, he resembled a rooster; when bad, a benign bishop.

Vivian Ellis, in *Dictionary of National Biography*

## CODY, WILLIAM FREDERICK, 'BUFFALO BILL'

1846–1917 Showman

Buffalo Bill's
defunct
who used to
ride a watersmooth-silver
stallion
and break onetwothreefourfive pidgeons
just like that Jesus
he was a handsome man
and what i want to know is
how do you like your blueeyed boy
Mister Death.

e.e. cummings, 'Portraits' in *Poems 1923–1954*

*See also* Theodore Roosevelt

## COHAN, GEORGE MICHAEL

1878–1942 Actor, Playwright, Composer, Producer

I can write better plays than any living dancer and dance better than any living playwright.

On himself, quoted in *Show*, March 1962

George M. Cohan always dances interestingly; he has sardonic legs.

Gilbert Seldes, *The Seven Lively Arts*

## COKE, SIR EDWARD

1552–1634 Jurist

He left an estate of eleaven thousand pounds per annum. Sir John Danvers, who knew him, told me he had heard one say to him, reflecting on his great scraping of wealth, that his sonnes would spend his estate faster than he gott it; he replyed, They cannot take more delight in the spending of it than I did in the getting of it.

John Aubrey, *Brief Lives*

You converse with books, not men, and books especially human; and have no excellent choice with men who are the best books: for a man of action and employment you seldom converse with, and then but with your underlings; not freely, but as a schoolmaster with his scholars, ever to teach, never to learn... You will jest at any man in public, without respect of the person's dignity or your own: this disgraceth your gravity more than it can advance the opinion of your wit. You make the law to lean too much to your opinion, whereby you show yourself to be a legal tyrant, striking with that weapon where you please, since you are able to turn the edge any way . . . Having the living of a thousand you relieve few or none.

Francis Bacon, *An Expostulation to The Lord Chief Justice Coke*

The cause of Liberty, I have heard, is much indebted to Coke. If that be synonymous with the cause of Parliament, as for the moment it doubtless was, the debt is probable. In the stretching of precedents, which he has of all sorts and ages, dug up from beyond Pluto and the deepest charnel-houses, and extinct lumber-rooms of Nature, which he produces and can apply and cause to fit by shrinking, or expanding, and on the whole, to suit any foot, – he never had a rival.

Thomas Carlyle, *Historical Sketches*

## COLERIDGE, SAMUEL TAYLOR

1772–1834 Poet, Critic

My instincts are so far dog-like that I love being superior to myself better than my equals.

On himself, *Notebooks*, 1805

Stop, Christian passer-by! – Stop, child of God, / And read with gentle breast. Beneath this sod / A poet lies, or that which once seem'd he. – / O, lift one thought in prayer for S.T.C.; / That he who many a year with toil of breath / Found death in life, may here find life in death! / Mercy for praise – to be forgiven for fame / He ask'd, and hoped, through Christ. / Do thou the same! /

On himself, *Epitaph*

Shall gentle Coleridge pass unnoticed here, / To turgid ode and tumid stanza dear? . . . / Yet none in lofty numbers can surpass / The bard who soars to elegize an ass; / So well the subject suits his noble mind / He brays, the laureat of the long-ear'd kind. /

Lord Byron, *English Bards and Scotch Reviewers*

And Coleridge, too, has lately taken wing, / But like a hawk encumber'd with his hood, – / Explaining metaphysics to the nation – / I wish he would explain his Explanation. /

Lord Byron, *Don Juan*, canto i (fragment)

How great a possibility; how small a realized result.

Thomas Carlyle, Letter to Ralph Waldo Emerson, 12 August 1834

I should very much like to have heard Carlyle's complaint against Coleridge. I keep wavering between admiration of his exceedingly great perceptive and analytical power and other wonderful points, and inclination to turn away altogether from a man who had so great a lack of all reality and actuality.

A. H. Clough, Letter to J. N. Simpkinson, February 1841

. . . Coleridge reminded me of a barrel to which every other man's tongue acted as a spigot, for no sooner did the latter move, than it set his own contents in a flow.

James Fenimore Cooper, *Gleanings in Europe: England*

To take a more common illustration, did he [the reader] ever amuse himself by searching the pockets of a child – three years old, suppose, when buried in slumber . . . ? I have done this . . . Philosophy is puzzled, conjecture and hypothesis are confounded, in the attempt to explain the law of selection which *can* have presided in the child's labours: stones remarkable only for weight, old rusty hinges, nails, crooked skewers, stolen when the cook has turned her back, rags, broken glass, tea-cups having the bottom knocked out, and loads of similar jewels, were the prevailing articles in the *procès verbal.* Yet doubtless, much labour had been incurred, some sense of danger, perhaps, had been faced, and anxieties of a conscious robber endured, in order to amass this splendid treasure. Such in value were the robberies of Coleridge; such their usefulness to himself or anybody else: and such the circumstances of uneasiness under which he had committed them.

Thomas de Quincey (on Coleridge's plagiarisms), *Samuel Taylor Coleridge*

For a few years he had been visited by the Muse (I know of no poet to whom this hackneyed metaphor is better applicable) and thenceforth was a haunted man . . . He was condemned to know that the little poetry he had written was worth more than all he could do with the rest of his life. The author of *Biographia Literaria* was already a ruined man. Sometimes, however, to be a 'ruined man' is itself a vocation.

T. S. Eliot, *The Use of Poetry and the Use of Criticism*

Coleridge's metaphysical interest was quite genuine, and was, like most metaphysical interest, an affair of his emotions. But a literary critic should have no emotions except those immediately provoked by a work of art . . . Coleridge is apt to take leave of the data of criticism, and arouse the suspicion that he has been diverted into a metaphysical hare-and-hounds. His end does not always appear to be the return to the work of art with improved perception and intensified, because more conscious, enjoyment; his centre of interest changes, his feelings are impure.

T. S. Eliot, *The Sacred Wood*

He seemed to breathe in words.

Thomas Colley Grattan, *Beaten Paths and Those Who Trod Them*

He was the first poet I ever knew. His genius at that time had angelic wings and fed on manna. He talked on for ever; and you wished him to talk on for ever. His thoughts did not seem to come with labour and effort; but as if borne on the gusts of genius, and as if the wings of his imagination lifted him from off his feet. His voice rolled on the ear like the pealing organ, and its sound alone was the music of thought. His mind was clothed with wings; and raised on them, he lifted philosophy to heaven.

William Hazlitt, *Lectures on the English Poets*

He is the man of all others to swim on empty bladders in a sea without shore or soundings; to drive an empty stage-coach without passengers or lading, and arrive behind his time; to write marginal notes without a text; to look into a millstone to foster the rising genius of the age; to 'see merit in the chaos of its elements, and discern perfection in the great obscurity of nothing,' as his most favourite author Sir Thomas Browne has it on another occasion.

William Hazlitt, 'Explanations – Conversation on the Drama with Coleridge', in *London Magazine*, December 1820

Negative Capability, that is, when a man is capable of being in uncertainties, mysteries, doubts, without any irritable reaching after fact and reason – Coleridge, for instance, would let go by a fine isolated verisimilitude caught from the Penetralium of mystery, from being incapable of remaining content with half-knowledge.

John Keats, Letter to G. and T. Keats, 21 December 1817

He was a mighty poet and / A subtle-souled psychologist; / All things he seemed to understand, / Of old or new, on sea or land, / Save his own soul, which was a mist. /

Charles Lamb, *Coleridge*

An archangel a little damaged.

Charles Lamb, Letter to William Wordsworth, 1816

Coleridge was a muddle-headed metaphysician who by some strange streak of fortune turned out a few real poems amongst the dreary flood of inanity which was his wont.

William Morris, Letter to F. S. Ellis, 1894 or 1895

Mr Coleridge, to the valuable information acquired from similar sources [old women and sextons], superadds the dreams of crazy theologians, and the mysticism of German Metaphysics, and favours the world with visions in verse, in which the quadruple elements of sexton, old women, Jeremy Taylor, and Emanuel Kant are harmonized into a delicious poetical compound.

Thomas Love Peacock, *The Four Ages of Poetry*

You will see Coleridge – he who sits obscure / In the exceeding lustre and the pure / Intense irradiation of a mind, / Which, through its own internal lightning blind, / Flags wearily through darkness and despair – / A cloud-encircled meteor of the air, / A hooded eagle among blinking owls. /

Percy Bysshe Shelley, *Letter to Maria Gisbourne*

To tell the story of Coleridge without the opium is to tell the story of Hamlet without mentioning the ghost.

Leslie Stephen, *Hours in a Library*

Coleridge the innumerable, the mutable, the atmospheric; Coleridge who is part of Wordsworth, Keats, and Shelley; of his age and of our own; Coleridge whose written words fill hundreds of pages and overflow innumerable margins; whose spoken words still reverberate, so that as we enter his radius he seems not a man, but a swarm, a cloud, a buzz of words, darting this way and that, clustering, quivering, and hanging suspended. So little of this can be caught in any reader's net.

Virginia Woolf, *The Death of the Moth*

A noticeable man with large grey eyes, / And a pale face that seemed undoubtedly / As if a blooming face it ought to be, / Heavy his low-hung lip did oft appear, / Deprest by weight of musing Phantasy; / Profound his forehead was, though not severe. /

William Wordsworth, *Stanzas, Written in My Pocket Copy of Thomson's 'Castle of Indolence'*

*See also* John Cavanagh, Sir Walter Scott, Shakespeare, William Wordsworth

## COLLINS, WILLIAM

1721–59 Poet

I have finished lately eight volumes of Johnson's *Lives of the Poets.* In all that number I observe but one man . . . whose mind seems to have had the slightest tincture of religion. His name was Collins . . . Of him there are some hopes. But from the lives of all the rest there is but one inference to be drawn – that poets are a very worthless wicked set of people.

William Cowper, Letter to John Newton, 19 March 1784

Still alive – happy if insensible of our neglect, not raging at our ingratitude.

Oliver Goldsmith (after visiting him at Chichester), *Polite Literature of Europe*

He is the only one of the minor poets of whom, if he had lived, it cannot be said that he might not have done the greatest things. The germ is there. He is sometimes affected, unmeaning, and obscure; but he also catches rich glimpses of the bowers of Paradise, and has lofty aspirations after the highest seats of the Muses. With a great deal of tinsel and splendid patchwork, he has not been able to hide the solid sterling ore of genius.

William Hazlitt, *Lectures on the English Poets*

He had employed his mind chiefly upon works of fiction and subjects of fancy, and by indulging some peculiar habits of thought was eminently delighted with those flights of imagination which pass the bounds of nature, and to which the mind is reconciled only by a passive acquiescence in popular traditions. He loved fairies, genii, giants and monsters; he delighted to rove through the meanders of inchantment, gaze on the magnificence of golden palaces, to repose by the waterfalls of Elysian gardens.

Samuel Johnson, *Lives of the Poets*

*See also* William Cowper

## COLLINS, (WILLIAM) WILKIE

1824–89 Novelist

I have been writing novels for the last five and thirty years, and I have been regularly in the habit of relieving the weariness which follows on the work of the brain . . . by champagne at one time and old brandy (cognac) at another. If I live until January next, I shall be sixty-six years old, and I am writing another work of fiction. There is my experience.

On himself, Letter to a correspondent enquiring about his use of stimulants, 20 May 1889

The greatest novels have something in them which will ensure their being read, at least by a small number of people, even if the novel, as a literary form, ceases to be written. It is not pretended that the novels of Wilkie Collins have this permanence. They are interesting only if we enjoy 'reading novels'. But novels are still being written; and there is no contemporary novelist who could not learn something from Collins in the art of interesting and exciting the reader. So long as novels are written, the possibilities of melodrama must from time to time be re-explored. The contemporary 'thriller' is in danger of becoming stereotyped . . . The resources of Wilkie Collins are, in comparison, inexhaustible.

T. S. Eliot, *Wilkie Collins and Dickens*

He was soft, plump, and pale, suffered from various ailments, his liver was wrong, his heart weak, his lungs faint, his stomach incompetent, he ate too much and the wrong things. He had a big head, a dingy complexion, was somewhat bald, and his full beard was of a light brown colour. His air was of mild discomfort and fractiousness; he had a queer way of holding his hand, which was small, plump, and unclean, hanging up by the wrist, like a rabbit on its hind legs. He had strong opinions and prejudices, but his nature was obviously kind and lovable, and a humorous vein would occasionally be manifest. One felt he was unfortunate and needed succour.

Julian Hawthorne, *Shapes that Pass*

To Mr Collins belongs the credit of having introduced into fiction those most mysterious of mysteries, the mysteries which are at our own doors. This innovation gave a new impetus to the literature of horrors. It was fatal to the authority of Mrs Radcliffe and her everlasting castle in the Apennines. What are the Apennines to us, or we to the Apennines? . . . Mrs Radcliffe's mysteries were romances pure and simple; while those of Mr Wilkie Collins were stern reality.

Henry James, in *Nation*, 9 November 1865

What brought good Wilkie's genius nigh perdition? / Some demon whispered – 'Wilkie! have a mission.' /

Algernon C. Swinburne, *Essay on Collins*

## COMPTON-BURNETT, DAME IVY

1884–1969 Novelist

I do not see why exposition and description are a necessary part of a novel.

They are not of a play, and both deal with imaginary human beings and their lives. I have been told that I ought to write plays, but cannot see myself making the transition. I read plays with especial pleasure, and in reading novels I am disappointed if a scene is carried through in the voice of the author rather than the voices of the characters. I think that I simply follow my natural bent.

On herself, *Orion*, 1945

There's not much to say. I haven't been at all deedy.

On herself (when asked about her life), in *The Times*, 30 August 1969

To read almost any piece of Compton-Burnett's 'communal dialectics' is to experience a pleasure as intense as most available literary pleasures, and yet page after page . . . is marked by the triviality inseparable from fantasy. There are two things which decisively rescue Miss Compton-Burnett's work from this danger. One is her comic sense; the other a dyad composed of her hatred and her pity.

Kingsley Amis, *What Became of Jane Austen?*

To my sense, Miss Compton-Burnett is not exactly an artist. She is something less valuable but rarer – the inventor of a wholly original species of puzzle. It is probably the first invention of the kind since the crossword, which it far outdoes in imaginative depth . . . Though her novels are not in themselves works of art, the rules of the puzzle are allusions to literary forms and conventions. Reading them is like playing some Monopoly for Intellectuals, in which you can buy, as well as houses and hotels, plaques to set up on them recording that a great writer once lived there.

Brigid Brophy, *Don't Never Forget*

One of the mischievous originalities of Compton-Burnett is to have pursued this insular tendency to the extreme, making it her trademark. She produces Compton-Burnetts, as someone might produce ball-bearings . . . Hence the uniformity of labelling in her titles and the open-stock patterns of her incidents and dialogue. The author, like all reliable old firms, is stressing the *sameness* of the formula; senior service. She has no imitators. The formula is a trade secret.

Mary McCarthy, *The Writing on the Wall*

She was looking formidably severe. I think she was severe. She saw life in the relentless terms of Greek tragedy, its cruelties, ironies – above all its passions – played out against a background of triviality and ennui.

Anthony Powell, in *Spectator*, 6 September 1969

## CONGREVE, WILLIAM

1670–1729 Dramatist

For my part I keep the Commandments, I love my neighbour as my selfe, and to avoid Coveting my neighbour's wife I desire to be coveted by her; which you know is quite another thing.

On himself, Letter to Mrs Edward Porter, Rotterdam, 27 September 1700

When *Congreve* brim full of his Mistresses Charms, / Who had likewise made bold with *Molier* / Came in piping hot from his *Bracegirdle*'s arms / And would have it his title was clear, /

Said *Apollo*, You did most discreetly to take / A part that was easiest and best / Though the rules of Behaviour Distinction should make / And you'd not done amiss to chuse last. /

But never pretend to be modest or Chast / Th'*Old Batchelor* speaks you Obscene, / And *Love for Love* shews, notwithstanding your hast, / That your Thoughts are Impure and Unclean. /

That meaning's lascivious your Dialogues bear / Fit to grace the foul Language of *Stews*, / And tho' you are said to make a Wife of a Play'r / You in those make a Whore of your Muse. /

Anon., *The Tryal of Skill*, 1704

The days of Comedy are gone, alas! / When Congreve's fool could vie with Moliere's *bête*: /Society is smooth'd to that excess, / That manners hardly differ more than dress. /

Lord Byron, *Don Juan*, canto xiii

The charms of his conversation must have been very powerful, since nothing could console Henrietta Dutchess of Marlborough, for the loss of his company, so much as an automaton, or small statue of ivory, made exactly to resemble him, which every day was brought to table. A glass was put in the hand of the statue, which was supposed to bow to her grace and to nod in approbation of what she spoke to it.

Thomas Davies, *Dramatic Miscellanies*, 1784

O that your Brows my Lawrel had sustain'd, / Well had I been Depos'd if You had Reign'd! / The Father had descended for the Son; / For only You are lineal to the Throne. /

John Dryden, Prologue to Congreve's *Double Dealer*

His Double Dealer is much censured by the greater part of the Town: and is defended only by the best Judges, who as you know, are commonly the fewest. Yet it gets ground daily, and has already been acted Eight times. The women thinke he has exposed their Bitchery too much; and the Gentlemen, are offended with him; for the discovery of their follyes: and the way of their Intrigues, under the notion of Friendship to their Ladyes Husbands.

John Dryden, Letter to William Walsh, December 1693

Every page presents a shower of brilliant conceits, is a tissue of epigrams in prose, is a new triumph of wit, a new conquest over dullness. The fire of artificial raillery is nowhere else so well kept up. This style, which he was almost the first to introduce, and which he carried to the utmost pitch of classical refinement, reminds one exactly of Collins' description of wit as opposed to humour,

Whose jewels in his crisped hair / Are placed each other's light to share. /

William Hazlitt, *Lectures on English Comic Writers*

Congreve has merit of the highest kind; he is an original writer who borrowed neither the materials of his plot, nor the manner of his dialogue. Of his plays I cannot speak distinctly; for since I inspected them many years have passed; but what remains upon my memory is, that his characters are commonly fictitious and artificial, with very little of nature, and not much of life. He formed a peculiar idea of comick excellence, which he supposed to consist in gay remarks and unexpected answers; but that which he endeavoured, he seldom failed of performing. His scenes exhibit not much of humour, imagery, or passion, his personages are a kind of intellectual gladiators; every sentence is to ward or strike; the contest of smartness is never intermitted; his wit is a meteor playing to and fro with alternate coruscations. His comedies have therefore, in some degree, the operation of tragedies; they surprise rather than divert, and raise admiration oftener than merriment. But they are the works of a mind replete with images, and quick in combination.

Samuel Johnson, *Lives of the Poets*

No writers have injured the Comedy of England so deeply as Congreve and Sheridan. Both were men of splendid wit and polished taste. Unhappily they made all their characters in their own likeness. Their works bear the same relation to the legitimate drama which a transparency bears to a painting. There are no delicate touches, no hues imperceptibly fading into each other: the whole is lighted up with an universal glare. Outlines and tints are forgotten in the common blaze which illuminates all. The flowers and fruits of the intellect abound, but it is the abundance of a jungle, not of a garden, unwholesome, bewildering, unprofitable from its very plenty, rank from its very fragrance. Every fop, every boor, every valet, is a man of wit.

T. B. Macaulay, *Essays*: 'Machiavelli'

Aye, Mr Tonson, he was Ultimus Romanorum!

Alexander Pope, in conversation with Jacob Tonson, November 1730

The comedies of Congreve must be ranked among the most wonderful and glorious creations of the human mind, although it is quite conceivable that, in certain circumstances, and at a given moment, a whole bench of Bishops might be demoralised by their perusal.

Lytton Strachey, *Portraits in Miniature*

For never did poetick mine before / Produce a richer vein or cleaner ore; / The bullion stamp'd in your refining mind / Serves by retail to furnish half mankind. /

Jonathan Swift, *To Mr Congreve*

Reading in these plays now, is like shutting your ears, and looking at people dancing. What does it mean? The measures, the grimaces, the bowing, shuffling and retreating, the cavaliers seuls advancing upon those ladies – those ladies and men twirling round at the end in a mad galop after which everybody bows, and the quaint rite is celebrated.

W. M. Thackeray, *The English Humourists*

All this pretty morality you have in the comedies of William Congreve, Esquire; they are full of wit, such manners as he observes, he observes with great humour; but ah! it's a weary feast, that banquet of wit where no love is. It palls very soon; sad indigestions follow it, and lonely blank headaches in the mornings.

*Ibid.*

He writes as if he was so accustomed to conquer, that he has a poor opinion of his victims.

*Ibid.*

The language is every where that of Men of Honour, but their Actions are those of Knaves; a proof that he was perfectly well acquainted with human Nature, and frequented what we call polite company.

Voltaire, *Letters Concerning the English Nation*, no. 19, 1733

*See also* Henry Fielding, Alexander Pope

## CONKLING, ROSCOE

1829–88 Politician

He had not only the courage of his convictions, but, that rarer quality among public men, the courage of his contempt.

Anon., in *New York World*, April 1888

. . . could look hyacinthine in just thirty seconds after the appearance of a woman.

Horace Greeley, in *New York Tribune*, May 1871, in David Barr Chidsey, *The Gentleman from New York – A Life of Roscoe Conkling*

No one can approach him. If anybody can approach him, without being conscious that there is something great about Conkling, Conkling himself is conscious of it. He walks in a nimbus of it. If Moses' name had been Conkling when he descended from the Mount, and the Jews had asked him what he saw there, he would have promptly replied, 'Conkling.'

*Ibid.*

## CONNOLLY, CYRIL VERNON

1903–75 Author, Critic

I came to America tourist Third with a cheque for ten pounds and I leave plus five hundred, a wife, a mandarin coat, a set of diamond studs, a state room and bath, a decent box for the ferret. That's what everybody comes to America to do and I don't think I've managed badly for a beginner.

On himself, Letter to Noel Blakiston, 2 April 1930

I have just finished reading *Enemies of Promise* . . . More than [T.S.] Eliot or [Edmund] Wilson you really write about writing in the only way which is interesting to anyone except academics, as a real occupation like banking or fucking with all its attendant egotism, boredom, excitement and terror.

W. H. Auden, Letter to Cyril Connolly, 15 November 1938

He was easily moved to tears, sometimes for deep and genuine reasons, sometimes for trivial ones – the tears of a spoiled child of civilisation. At a restaurant dinner given on some fairly grim PEN Club Conference occasion, he was sitting opposite me and I noticed the tears start in his eyes and then trickle down each cheek. Suddenly he got up from the table, came over to me, and insisted on our changing places. Intense boredom with the conversation of the lady journalist on his left had driven him to this extreme course of action.

Stephen Spender, in *Times Literary Supplement*, 6 December 1974

Not as nice as he looks.

Evelyn Waugh, in *Adam*, no. 385

## CONRAD, JOSEPH (JÒZEF KORZENIOWSKI)

1857–1924 Novelist

My style may be atrocious – but it produces its effect – is as unalterable as . . . the size of my feet – and I will never disguise it in the boots of Wells's (or anybody else's) making . . . I shall make my own boots or perish.

On himself, Letter to Fisher Unwin, 28 May 1896

We could pardon his cheerless themes were it not for the imperturbable solemnity with which he piles the unnecessary on the commonplace.

Anon., in *Literature*, 30 April 1898

I have just read his new book *The Nigger of the 'Narcissus'*, which has moved me to enthusiasm. Where did the man pick up that style, & that *synthetic* way of gathering up a general impression & flinging it at you? Not only his style, but his attitude, affected me deeply. He is so consciously an artist.

Arnold Bennett, Letter to H. G. Wells, 8 December 1897

He was the most consummate, the most engrossed, the most practical, the most common-sensible and the most absolutely passionate man-of-action become conscious man-of-letters that this writer has ever known, read of or conceived of.

Ford Madox Ford, *The March of Literature*

Conrad spent a day finding the *mot juste*; then killed it.

Ford Madox Ford, in Robert Lowell, *Notebook*

What is so elusive about him is that he is always promising to make some general philosophic statement about the universe, and then refraining with a gruff disclaimer . . . He is misty in the middle as well as at the edges . . . the secret casket of his genius contains a vapour rather than a jewel . . . we need not try to write him down philosophically, because there is, in this particular direction, nothing to write. No creed, in fact. Only opinions, and the right to throw them overboard when facts make them look absurd.

E. M. Forster, *Abinger Harvest*

It is agreed by most of the people I know that Conrad is a bad writer, just as it is agreed that T. S. Eliot is a good writer. If I knew that by grinding Mr Eliot into a fine dry powder and sprinkling that powder on Mr Conrad's grave, Mr Conrad would shortly appear, looking very annoyed at the forced return and commence writing, I would leave for London early tomorrow morning with a sausage grinder.

Ernest Hemingway, *Transatlantic Review*, 1924

Why this giving in before you start, that pervades all Conrad and such folks – the Writers among the Ruins. I can't forgive Conrad for being so sad and giving in.

D. H. Lawrence, Letter to Edward Garnett, 30 October 1912

At present Conrad is out of fashion, ostensibly because of his florid style and redundant adjectives (for my part I like a florid style: if your motto is 'Cut out the adjectives', why not go a bit further and revert to a system of grunts and squeals, like the animals?), but actually, I suspect, because he was a gentleman, a type hated by the modern intelligentsia. He is pretty certain to come back into favour. One of the surest signs of his genius is that women dislike his books.

George Orwell, in *New English Weekly*, 23 July 1936

He was very conscious of the various forms of passionate madness to which men are prone, and it was this that gave him such a profound belief in the importance of discipline. His point of view, one might perhaps say, was the antithesis of Rousseau's: 'Man is born in chains, but he can become free.' He becomes free, so I believe Conrad would have said, not by letting loose his impulses, not by being casual and uncontrolled, but by subduing wayward impulse to a dominant purpose.

Bertrand Russell, *Autobiography*

Mr Conrad is wordy; his story is not so much told as seen intermittently through a haze of sentences. His style is like river-mist; for a space things are seen clearly, and then comes a great grey bank of printed matter, page on page, creeping round the reader, swallowing him up. You stumble, you protest, you blunder on, for the drama you saw so cursorily has hold of you; you cannot escape until you have seen it out. You read fast, you run and jump, only to bring yourself to the knees in such mud as will presently be quoted. Then suddenly things loom up again, and in a moment become real, intense, swift.

H. G. Wells, Review of *An Outcast of the Islands*, in *Saturday Review*, 16 May 1896

One could always baffle Conrad by saying 'humour'. It was one of our damned English tricks he had never learned to tackle.

H. G. Wells, in Arthur Mizener, *Ford Madox Ford*

*See also* Ford Madox Ford, James Thurber

## CONSTABLE, JOHN

1776–1837 Painter

I never saw an ugly thing in my life; for let the form of an object be what it may – light, shade, and perspective will always make it beautiful.

On himself, in Charles R. Leslie, *The Life of John Constable*

We have found out Mr Constable's secret, he is a Cornelius Ketel; see Hardung's excellent catalogue of portraits, No. 153: 'Ketel took it into his head to lay aside his brushes and to paint with his fingers only; and at length, finding these tools too easy, undertook to paint with his toes.' We rather suspect that Turner is sometimes a little inclined to this failing, but never so perfectly *in toto* as Mr Constable this year.

Anon., in *Morning Chronicle*, 1831

Where real business is to be done, you are the most energetic and punctual of men. In smaller matters, such as putting on your breeches, you are apt to lose time in deciding which leg shall go in first.

John Fisher, Letter to Constable, 3 July 1823

I like de landscapes of Constable; he is always picturesque, of a fine colour, and de lights always in de right places; but he makes me call for my great coat and umbrella.

Henry Fuseli, in Charles R. Leslie, *The Life of John Constable*

Whether he portray the solemn burst of the approaching tempest – the breezy freshness of morning – or the still deepness of a summer noon – every object represented, from the grandest masses to the smallest plant or spray, seems instinct with, as it were, and breathing the very spirit of the scene. His figures, too, seem naturally called forth by, and form part of, the landscape; we never ask whether they are well placed – there they are, and unless they choose to move on, there they must remain. His quiet lanes and covert nooks serve to introduce a romantic or sentimental episode to divide, not heighten, the interest; all is made subservient to the one object in view, the embodying of a pure apprehension of natural effect.

W. Purton, in Charles R. Leslie, *The Life of John Constable*

Unteachableness seems to have been a main feature of his character, and there is corresponding want of veneration in the way he approaches nature herself. His early education and associations were also against him: they induced in him a morbid preference of subjects of a lower order.

John Ruskin, *Modern Painters*

## COOK, JAMES

1728–79 Navigator, Explorer

. . . a plain, sensible man with an uncommon attention to veracity. Sir John gave me an instance. It was supposed that Cook had said he had seen a nation of men like monkeys and Lord Monboddo had been very happy with this. Sir John happened to tell Cook of this. 'No,' he said, 'I did not say they were like monkeys, I said their faces put me in mind of monkeys.' There was a distinction very fine, but sufficiently perceptible . . . He seemed to have no desire to make people stare, and being a man of steady moral principles, as I thought, did not try to make theories out of what he had seen to confound virtue and vice.

James Boswell, in Alan Moorehead, *The Fatal Impact*

When Cook – lamented, and with tears as just / As ever mingled with heroic dust – / Steer'd Britain's oak into a world unknown, / And in his country's glory sought his own, / Wherever he found man, to nature true, / The rights of man were sacred in his view. / He sooth'd with gifts, and greeted with a smile, / The simple native of the new-found isle; / He spurn'd the wretch that slighted or withstood / The tender argument of kindred blood, / Nor would endure that any should controul / His free-born brethren of the southern pole. /

William Cowper, *Charity*

Had those advent'rous spirits, who explore / Through ocean's trackless wastes, the far-sought shore, / Whether of wealth insatiate, or of power / Conquerors who waste, or ruffians who devour: / Had these possess'd, O Cook! thy gentle mind, / Thy love of arts, thy love of humankind; / Had these pursued thy mild and liberal plan, / Discoveries had not been a curse to man! / Then, bless'd Philanthropy! thy social hands / Had link'd dissever'd worlds in brothers' bands; / Careless, if colour, or if clime divide; / Then lov'd, and loving, man had liv'd, and died. /

Hannah More, in Andrew Kippis, *Cook's Voyages*

## COOK, THOMAS

1808–92 Travel Agent

It seems that some enterprising and unscrupulous man has devised the project of conducting some forty or fifty persons, irrespective of age and sex, from London to Naples and back for a fixed sum.

Charles Lever, Article *circa* 1886, in Edmund Swinglehurst, *The Romantic Journey*

... The excursion monger.

Alfred Munby, Diary, July 1861

## COOLIDGE, (JOHN) CALVIN

1872–1933 Thirtieth United States President

Perhaps one of the most important accomplishments of my administration has been minding my own business.

On himself, at a news conference, 1 March 1929

I think the American people wants a solemn ass as a President. And I think I'll go along with them.

On himself, to Ethel Barrymore, reported in *Time*, 16 May 1955

I have noticed that nothing I never said ever did me any harm.

On himself, *Congressional Record*

[He had] not an international hair on his head.

Anon., in Marcus Cunliffe, *American Presidents and the Presidency*

When an excited man rushed up to Wilson Mizner and said, 'Coolidge is dead,' Mizner asked, 'How do they know?'

Alva Johnston, *The Legendary Mizners*; also attributed to Dorothy Parker

He laughed until you could hear a pin drop.

Ring Lardner, in Robert E. Drennan ed., *Wit's End*

Mr Coolidge's genius for inactivity is developed to a very high point. It is far from being an indolent activity. It is a grim, determined alert inactivity which keeps Mr Coolidge occupied constantly . . . Inactivity is a political philosophy and a party program with Mr Coolidge.

Walter Lippmann, *Men of Destiny*

Though I yield to no one in my admiration for Mr Coolidge, I do wish he did not look as if he had been weaned on a pickle.

Alice Roosevelt Longworth, attributed, in *Crowded Hours* –

*Reminiscences of Alice Roosevelt Longworth*

He slept more than any other President, whether by day or night. Nero fiddled, but Coolidge only snored. When the crash came at last and Hoover began to smoke and bubble, good Cal was safe in Northampton, and still in the hay.

H. L. Mencken, in *American Mercury*, April 1933

There were no thrills while he reigned, but neither were there any headaches. He had no ideas but he was not a nuisance.

H. L. Mencken, in Ishbel Ross, *Grace Coolidge and her Era*

'You must talk to me, Mr Coolidge, I made a bet today that I could get more than two words out of you.'

'You lose,' said the Vice-President with a poker face, and let it go at that.

Ishbel Ross, in *ibid.*

## COOLING, RICHARD

– d. 1697 Civil Servant

Mr Cooling, my Lord Chamberlain's secretary . . . proved very drunk, and did talk, and would have talked all night with us, I not being able to break loose from him, he holding me by the hand . . . Thus he went on, and speaking then of my Lord Sandwich, whom he professed to love exceedingly, says Cooling, 'I know not what, but he is a man methinks that I could love for himself, without other regards; and by your favour,' says he, 'by God there is nothing to be beloved *propter se* but a cunt.' And so he talked very lewdly. And then took notice of my kindness to him on shipboard seven years ago, when the King was coming over, and how much he was obliged to me; but says, 'Pray look upon this acknowledgement of a kindness in me to be a miracle; for,' says he, 'it is against the law at Court for a man that borrows money of me, even to buy his place with, to own it the next Sunday.' And then told us his horse was a Bribe, and his boots a bribe; and told us he was made up of bribes, as an Oxford scholar is set out with men's goods when he goes out of town, and that he makes every sort of tradesman to bribe him; and invited me home to his house, to taste of his bribe-wine. I never heard so much vanity from a man in my life.

Samuel Pepys, Diary, 30 July 1667

## COOPER, ANTHONY ASHLEY,

*see under* SHAFTESBURY, FIRST AND SEVENTH EARLS

## COOPER, GARY (FRANK JAMES)

1901–61 Actor

That fellow is the world's greatest actor. He can do with no effort what the rest of us spent years trying to learn; to be perfectly natural.

John Barrymore, in Jane Mercer, *Great Lovers of the Movies*

Every line in his face spelled honesty. So innate was his integrity he could be cast in phony parts, but never look phony himself.

Tall, gaunt as Lincoln, cast in the frontier mold of Daniel Boone, Sam Houston, Kit Carson, this silent Montana cowpuncher embodied the true-blue virtues that won the West; durability, honesty, and native intelligence.

Frank Capra, *The Name Above the Title*

Gary is an embodiment of the old saying that art consists in concealing its own artfulness. After seeing him on the screen, any young man might say, 'Shucks, I could do that.' The young man would be wrong.

Cecil B. De Mille, *Autobiography*

More people can be found with a knowledge of the likes and dislikes of Mr Gary Cooper than with the simplest idea of the main precepts of, say, Jesus Christ.

Otis Ferguson, *The Film Criticism of Otis Ferguson*

The silent stars move silently, especially Gary Cooper, who came from the Great Open Spaces where men *were* silent.

Adela Rogers St Johns, *The Honeycomb*

*See also* Cecil B. De Mille

## COOPER, JAMES FENIMORE

1789–1851 Author

At the bar of heaven Cooper would have answered: first, I am gentleman, next, I was a sailor, third, I am a patriot, and fourth, and with some derogation, I am a maker of light literature.

Henry Seidel Canby, *Classic Americans*

. . . Cooper is responsible for the fathering of those aboriginal heroes, lovers, and sages, who have long formed a petty nuisance in our literature.

Francis Parkman, in George P. Winston, *John Fiske*

Like all badly educated people he confounded flowery and inflated circumlocution with beauty of style. His taste to the last was sophomoric.

Fred Lewis Pattee, in *American Mercury*, March 1925

In one place in *Deerslayer*, and in the restricted space of two thirds of a page, Cooper has scored 114 offenses against literary art out of a possible 115. It breaks the record.

Mark Twain, *Fenimore Cooper's Literary Offenses*, in Edmund Wilson ed., *The Shock of Recognition*

Everytime a Cooper person is in peril, and absolute silence is worth four dollars a minute, he is sure to step on a dry twig. There may be a hundred handier things to step on, but that wouldn't satisfy Cooper. Cooper requires him to turn out and find a dry twig; and if he can't do it, go and borrow one. In fact, the Leatherstocking series ought to have been called the Broken Twig Series.

*Ibid.*

## COPLEY, JOHN SINGLETON, THE YOUNGER, *see under* LORD LYNDHURST

## COPPE, ABIEZER

1619–72 Ranter

First all my strength my forces were utterly routed, my house I dwelt in fired, my father and mother forsook me, the wife of my bosome loathed me, mine old name was rotted perished; and I was utterly plagued consumed, damned rammed and sunk into nothing, into the bowels of the still eternity (my mother's wombe) out of which I came naked and whereto I returned again naked. And lying a while there, rapt up in silence, at length (the body's outward forme being awake all this while) I heard with my outward ear, (to my apprehension) a most terrible thunderclap, and after that a second. And upon the second thunderclap, which was exceeding terrible, I saw a great body of light, like the light of the sun, and red as fire, in the forme of a drum (as it were) whereupon with exceeding trembling and amazement of the flesh, and with joy unspeakable in the spirit, I clapt my hands and cryed out, Amen halelujah, halelujah amen. And so lay trembling sweating and smoking (for the space of half an howre) at length with a loud voice I (inwardly) cried out, Lord what wilt thou do with me: my most excellent majesty and eternall glory (in me) answered and said, Fear not, I will take thee up into my everlasting kingdom. But thou shalt (first) drink a bitter cup, a bitter cup, a bitter cup; whereupon (being filled with exceeding amazement) I was thrown into the belly of hell (and take what you can of it in these expressions, though the matter is beyond expression), I was among all the devils in hell, even in their most hideous crew. And under all this terror and amazement there was a little spark of transcendent, unspeakable glory, which survived, and sustained itself, triumphing, exulting and exalting itself above the fiends.

On himself, Preface to *The Fiery Flying Roll*

. . . The arrogant and wild deportment of Mr Copp the great Ranter, who made the Fiery Roll, who being brought before the Committee of Examinations, refused to be uncovered, and disguised himself into a madnesse, flinging apples and pears about the room, whereupon the Committee returned him to Newgate whence he came.

*Weekly Intelligencer*, 1–8 October 1649

## CORNWALLIS, CHARLES, MARQUIS

1738–1805 Soldier

Hail, great destroyer (equall'd yet by none) / Of countries not thy master's, nor thine own; / Hatch'd by some demon on a stormy day, / Satan's best substitute to burn and slay . . . / Unnumber'd ghosts, from earth untimely sped, / Can take no rest till you, like them, are dead – / Then die, my Lord; that only chance remains / To wash away dishonourable stains, / For small advantage would your capture bring, / The plundering servant of a bankrupt king. /

Philip Freneau, *To Lord Cornwallis*

His mind was of a character not uncommon. It was entirely passive; the impressions it received from without remained undisturbed by any process from within . . . The mental constitution of the Marquess Cornwallis might be described in few words as being of the highest order of the commonplace.

Edward Thornton, *History of the British Empire in India*, vol. 4

## CORVO, BARON (FREDERICK ROLFE)

1860–1913 Novelist

Rolfe's vice was spiritual more than it was carnal: it might be said that he was a pander and a swindler, because he cared for nothing but his faith. He would be a priest or nothing, so nothing it had to be and he was not ashamed to live on his friends; if he could not have Heaven, he would have Hell, and the last footprints seem to point unmistakably towards the Inferno.

Graham Greene, *The Lost Childhood*

They said of Rolfe that he was certainly possessed of a devil. At least his devil is still alive, it hasn't turned into a sort of golliwog, like the bulk of the nineties' devils . . . He seems to have been a serpent of serpents in the bosom of all the nineties. That in itself endears him to one. The way everyone dropped him with a shudder is almost fascinating.

D. H. Lawrence, in *Adelphi*, December 1925

Rolfe deserves a kinder epitaph than the belated *amende* of the *Aberdeen Free Press*. Who could improve on his own: 'Pray for the repose of his soul. He was so tired.'? Or, as he once wrote to a friend who accused him of selfishness: 'Selfish? Yes, selfish. The selfishness of a square peg in a round hole.'

A. J. A. Symons, *The Quest for Corvo*

Frederick William Rolfe . . . remains one of those writers more read about than read . . . He wrote with great care, and with a sharpness, vivacity, and variety of epithet that give immediate and continuing pleasure, but he was not in any serious sense a novelist or even a writer of fiction. His emotionally injured self is the sole character of his fictions, with everybody else seen through the haze of his paranoia, like figures in a fun-fair mirror . . . The long air-raid siren wail of self-justification precludes sympathy. To read much of Rolfe is to become powerfully aware that we are in the presence of a classic bore. This is not to say that the life is boring, only the work.

Julian Symons, in *Times Literary Supplement*, 3 January 1975

## CORYATE, THOMAS

1577?–1617 Traveller

In Surat being over-kindly used by some of the English, who gave him Sack, which they had brought from *England*, he calling for, as soon as he first heard of it, and crying, *Sack, Sack, is there such a thing as Sack? I pray give me some Sack*, and drinking of it moderately, (for he was very temperate) it increased his flux which he had then upon him: and this caused him within a few days after his very tedious and troublesome travels, (for he went most on foot), at that place to come to his journeys end . . . For if one should go to the extremest part of the world East, another West, another North, and another South, they must all meet at last together in the Field of Bones, wherein our traveller hath now taken up his lodging.

Anthony à Wood, *Athenae Oxonienses*

## COTMAN, JOHN SELL

1782–1842 Painter, Engraver

I think Cotman's a very overrated reputation. Unlike [John] Crome, he was, I think, the slave of his water-colour technique, instead of its master.

Roger Fry, *Reflections on British Painting*

[Roger] Fry could perceive only technical skill and inevitable correctness in Cotman's work. For myself, a Cotman drawing here and there shows the exquisite and final flawlessness of a Sung vase or a Yuan painting, yielding an instant of emotion before its dissolution into purest thought.

Martin Hardie, *Water-Colour Painting in Britain*

With Crome a line was only part of a framework to suggest where light and dark and colour should be placed. With Cotman lines were the very bones on which the life of the work was supported. Even in his watercolours, they are essential to the whole design, used like the leading in a glass window, though not so obtrusively, to enclose the coloured shapes.

*Ibid.*

## COURTAULD, SAMUEL

1876–1947 Industrialist, Art Collector

Art was to him, in his own phrase, 'religion's next-of-kin'.

T. S. R. Boase, in *Dictionary of National Biography 1941–50*

## COWARD, SIR NOËL PIERCE

1899–73 Actor, Dramatist

It was . . . a pleasant game to be discovered sobbing wretchedly in the corners of railway carriages or buses in the hope that someone would take pity on me and perhaps give me tea at Fuller's. This was only rarely successful, the only two responses I can recall being both clergymen. One talked to me for a long time, and told me to trust in God and everything would come right, and the other pinched my knee and gave me sixpence. Of the two, I preferred the latter.

On himself, *Present Indicative*

With *Fallen Angels*, *On with the Dance*, and *The Vortex* all running at once, I was in an enviable position. Everyone but Somerset Maugham said that I was a second Somerset Maugham, with the exception of a few who preferred to describe me as a second Sacha Guitry.

*Ibid.*

My body has certainly wandered a good deal, but I have an uneasy suspicion that my mind has not wandered nearly enough.

*Ibid.*

I've sometimes thought of marrying – and then I've thought again.

On himself, in Ward Morehouse, in *Theatre Arts*, November 1956

*See also* Edna Ferber

## COWLEY, ABRAHAM

1618–67 Poet

He could never forgive any conceit which came in his way; but swept like a drag-net, great and small.

John Dryden, Preface to *Fables Ancient and Modern*

Cowley, like other poets who have written with narrow views, and, instead of tracing intellectual pleasures in the mind of man, paid their court to temporary prejudices, has been at one time too much praised, and too much neglected at another.

Samuel Johnson, *Lives of the Poets*

Who now reads Cowley? if he pleases yet, / His moral pleases, not his pointed wit; / Forgot his Epic, nay Pindaric Art, / But still I love the language of his Heart. /

Alexander Pope, *Imitations of Horace*, book 2, epistle 1

Cowley, I think, would have had grace, for his mind was graceful, if he had had any ear, or if his taste had not been vitiated by the pursuit of wit; for false wit always deviates into tinsel or pertness.

Horace Walpole, Letter to Mr Pinkerton, June 1785

## COWPER, WILLIAM

1731–1800 Poet

I sing the sofa.

On himself, *The Task*

I have no more right to the name of a poet than a maker of mousetraps has to that of an engineer.

On himself, Letter to William Unwin, *circa* 1785

His taste lay in a smiling, colloquial, good-natured humour; his melancholy was a black and diseased melancholy, not a grave and rich contemplativeness.

Sir E. Brydges, *Recollections of Foreign Travel*

They say poets never or rarely go *mad.* Cowper and Collins are instances to the contrary (but Cowper was no poet).

Lord Byron, Letter to Annabella Milbanke, 29 November 1813

With all his boasted simplicity and love of the country, he seldom launches out into general descriptions of nature: he looks at her over his clipped hedges, and from his well-swept garden-walks; or if he makes a bolder experiment now and then, it is with an air of precaution, as if he were afraid of being caught in a shower of rain, or of not being able, in case of any untoward accident, to make good his retreat home. He shakes hands with nature with a pair of fashionable gloves on.

William Hazlitt, *Lectures on the English Poets*

The fairest critic, and the sweetest bard.

James Hurdis, *Address to Criticism*

I could forgive a man for not enjoying Milton; but I would not call that man my friend who should be offended by 'the divine chit-chat of Cowper'.

Charles Lamb, quoting Coleridge's phrase, Letter to Coleridge, 5 December 1796

I say, what a nice clear hand Cowper has got! and how neatly the poor old sod turns a compliment and all the while being able to write the most tragic lines ever writ, about his own damnation and one of the worst – for horrid suffering – of these in the Sapphic metre too. Think of that.

John Cowper Powys, Letter to Nicholas Ross, 27 May 1943

## COZENS, JOHN ROBERT

1752–99 Watercolourist

Cozens was all poetry.

John Constable, Letter to John Fisher, 4 August 1821

## CRABBE, GEORGE

1754–1832 Poet

He exhibits the smallest circumstances of the smallest things. He gives the very costume of meanness; the nonessentials of every trifling incident . . . He describes the interior of a cottage like a person sent there to distrain for rent. He has an eye to the number of arms in an old worm-eaten chair, and takes care to inform himself and the reader whether a joint-stool stands upon three legs or four . . . He takes an inventory of the human heart exactly in the same manner as of the furniture of a sick room: his sentiments have very much the air of fixtures; he gives you the petrifaction of a sigh, and carves a tear, to the life, in stone . . . Crabbe's poetry is like a museum, or curiosity-shop.

William Hazlitt, *Lectures on the English Poets*

Mr Crabbe, it must be confessed, is a repulsive writer. He contrives to 'turn diseases into commodities', and makes a virtue of necessity. He puts us out of conceit with this world, which perhaps a severe divine should do; yet does not, as a charitable divine ought, point to another. His morbid feelings droop and cling to the earth, grovel where they should soar; and throw a dead weight on every aspiration of the soul after the good or beautiful.

William Hazlitt, *The Spirit of the Age*

Comparing the smartnesses of Crabbe with Young's . . . Young moralised at a distance on some external appearances of the human heart; Crabbe entered it *on all fours*, and told the people what an ugly thing it is inside.

Walter Savage Landor, *Imaginary Conversations*

Wordsworth . . . told Anne and I a story the object of which was to show that Crabbe had not imagination. He, Sir George Beaumont and Wordsworth were sitting together in Murray the bookseller's back-room. Sir George after sealing a letter blew out the candle which had enabled him to do so and exchanging a look with Wordsworth began to admire in silence the undulating thread of smoke which slowly arose from the expiring wick when Crabbe put on the extinguisher.

Sir Walter Scott, Journal, 3 January 1827

He had formed an attachment in early life to a young woman who, like himself, was absolutely without fortune; he wrote his poems to obtain patronage and preferment . . . He *pushed* (as the world says) for patronage with these poems, and succeeded; got preferment sufficient, and married. It was not long before his wife became deranged, and when all this was told me by one who knew him well, five years ago, he was still almost confined in his own house, anxiously waiting upon this wife in her long and hopeless malady. A sad history! It is no wonder that he gives so melancholy a picture of human life.

Robert Southey, Letter to J. N. White, 30 September 1808

The sum of all is, that nineteen out of twenty of Crabbe's Pictures are mere matters of fact; with which the Muses have just about as much to do as they have with a Collection of medical reports, or of Law Cases.

William Wordsworth, Letter to Samuel Rogers, 29 September 1805

*See also* Lord Byron, Daniel Defoe, Samuel Johnson

## CRAIG, EDWARD GORDON

1872–1966 Designer

Consider Craig's very odd profession. He has presented himself to the world, and to some extent conquered it, in the capacity of a Thwarted Genius.

George Bernard Shaw, in *Observer*, 8 November 1931

## CRANE, (HAROLD) HART

1899–1932 Poet, Writer

In spite of a robust constitution he suffered from a number of recurring ailments, including acidosis, urethritis, urticaria (or plain hives), constipation, crabs, and rose fever. These he treated with home remedies, chiefly canned tomatoes, larkspur lotion, and an enema bag. He tried to stay away from doctors, possibly because he was afraid of being given the obvious advice: stop drinking.

Malcolm Cowley, *A Second Flowering*

Someone told me that when poor Hart finally met his end by jumping overboard from the Havana boat the last his friends on deck saw of him was a cheerful wave of the hand before he sank and drowned. That last friendly wave was very like Hart Crane.

John Dos Passos, *The Best Times*

He resented the encroachments of rationalism on any part of the poet's province, and, like the natural Platonist he was, consistently maintained that poetry, to remain true to its own nature, must transcend the dictates of scientific logic, and function only according to the laws of its own making.

Philip Horton, *Hart Crane*

Crane was the archetype of the modern American poet whose fundamental mistake lay in thinking that an irrational surrender of the intellect to the will would be the basis of a new mentality.

Allen Tate, in Louis Untermeyer ed., *Modern American Poetry, A Critical Anthology*

## CRANE, STEPHEN

1871–1900 Author

I was a Socialist for two weeks but when a couple of Socialists assured me I had no right to think differently from any other Socialist and then quarrelled with each other about what Socialism meant, I ran away.

On himself, in Jay Martin, *Harvests of Change, American Literature, 1865–1914*

I had thought that there could be only two worse writers than Stephen Crane, namely two Stephen Cranes.

Ambrose Bierce, in Richard O'Connor, *Ambrose Bierce*

This young man has the power to feel. He knows nothing of war, yet he is drenched in blood. Most beginners who deal with this subject splatter themselves merely with ink.

Ambrose Bierce, referring to Crane's *The Red Badge of Courage*, in John Berryman, *Stephen Crane*

Crane was a preternaturally sensitive man; he saw everything, he heard, tasted, felt everything with the exquisite aptitude of a convalescent. The tremor of a butterfly's wing was not too slight to escape him.

Van Wyck Brooks, in Richard M. Weatherford ed., *Stephen Crane, The Critical Heritage*

He drank life to the lees, but at the banquet table where other men took their ease and jested over their wine, he stood a dark and silent figure, sombre as Poe himself, not wishing to be understood; and he took his portion in haste, with his loins girded, and his shoes on his feet, and his staff in his hand, like one who must depart quickly.

Willa Cather, 'When I Knew Stephen Crane', in Maurice Bassan ed., *Stephen Crane, A Collection of Critical Essays*

Tolstoy made the writing of Stephen Crane on the Civil War seem like the brilliant imagining of a sick boy who had never seen war but had only read the battle chronicles and seen the Brady photographs that I had read and seen at my grandparents' house.

Ernest Hemingway, *A Moveable Feast*

Stephen Crane was a vortex of intensity in a generally stagnant sea. He was an artist not as the age understood that word but as the world at large understands it. I do not say that he was a great artist or that he was even of the first tank, but what he had was the real thing and he adulterated it with nothing else.

Edmund Wilson, *The Shores of Light*

## CRANMER, THOMAS

1489–1556 Archbishop of Canterbury, Reformer

I protest before you all, there was never man came more unwillingly to a bishopric than I did to that: insomuch that when King Henry did send for me in post, that I should come over, I prolonged my journey by seven weeks at the least, thinking that he would be forgetful of me in the mean time.

On himself, Statement at his Examination, in John Foxe, *Acts and Monuments*

. . . a name which deserves to be held in everlasting execration; a name which we could not pronounce without almost doubting of the justice of God, were it not for our knowledge of the fact, that the cold-blooded, most perfidious, most impious, most blasphemous caitiff expired at last, amidst those flames which he himself had been the chief cause of kindling.

William Cobbett, *A History of the Protestant Reformation*

And when the wood was kindled, and the fire began to burn near him, stretching out his Arm, he put his right hand into the flame, which he held so stedfast and unmoveable (save that once with the same hand he wiped his face) that all men might see his hand burned before his Body was touched.

John Foxe, *Acts and Monuments*

Cranmer has got the right sow by the ear.

Henry VIII, referring to Cranmer's

part in his divorce from Catherine of Aragon.

*See also* Hugh Latimer, Mary I

## CRASHAW, RICHARD

1613?–49 Poet

What he might eate or weare he took no thought; / His needfull foode he rather found than sought. / He seekes no downes, no sheetes, his bed's still made. / If he can find a chaire or stoole, he's lay'd; / When day peepes in, he quitts his restless rest, / And still, poore soule, before he's up he's dres't. /

Thomas Carre, *Anagram on the Name of Crashaw*

At times . . . his passion for heavenly objects is imperfect because it is partly a substitute for human passion.

T. S. Eliot, *For Lancelot Andrewes*

## CRAZY HORSE (TASHUNCA-UITCO)

*circa* 1849–77 Chief of the Oglala Sioux

We did not ask you white men to come here. The Great Spirit gave us this country as a home. You had yours. We did not interfere with you. The Great Spirit gave us plenty of land to live on, and buffalo, deer, antelope and other game. But you have come here; you are taking my land from me; you are killing off our game, so it is hard for us to live. Now, you tell us to work for a living, but the Great Spirit did not make us to work, but to live by hunting. You white men can work if you want to. We do not interfere with you, and again you say, why do you not become civilized? We do not want your civilization! We would live as our fathers did, and their fathers before them.

On himself, in T. C. McLuhan, *Touch the Earth*

## CRICHTON, JAMES (THE ADMIRABLE)

1560?–82 Prodigy

. . . When Urquhart plunged this charmed figure into the ferment of his fantastic imagination, there emerged a Crichton more admirable than ever, a transcendent Crichton, a unicorn of alchemist's gold. Scot had answered unto Scot; an eccentric had elaborated a prodigy: and there resulted a rhapsody which glorified and fixed the legend in an unrivalled erection of baroque English prose.

Hamish Miles, Introduction to Thomas Urquhart, *The Life and Death of the Admirable Crichtoun*

. . . Matchless Crichtoun, seeing it now high time to put a gallant catastrophe to that so-long-dubious combat, animated with a divinely-inspired fervencie, to fulfil the expectation of the ladyes and crown the Duke's illustrious hopes, changeth his garb, falls to act another part, and, from defender, turns assailant: never did art so grace nature, nor nature second the precepts of art with so much liveliness, and such observancie of time, as when, after he had struck fire out of the steel of his enemie's sword, and gained the feeble thereof, with the fort of his own, by angles of the strongest position, he did, by geometrical flourishes of straight and oblique lines, so practically execute the speculative part, that, as if there had been Remora's and secret charms in the variety of his motion, the fierceness of his foe was in a trice transqualified into the numbness of a pageant. Then it was that, to vindicate the reputation of the Duke's family, and expiate the blood of the three vanquished gentlemen, he alonged a stoccade de pied ferme; then recoyling, he advanced another thrust, and lodged it home; after which, retiring again, his right foot did beat the cadence of

the blow that pierced the belly of this Italian; whose heart and throat being hit with the two former stroaks, these three franch bouts given in upon the back of the other; besides that, if lines were imagined drawn from the hand that livered them to the places which were marked by them, they would represent a perfect Isosceles Triangle, with a perpendicular from the top-angle, cutting the basis in the middle; they likewise give us to understand, that by them he was to be made a sacrifice of atonement for the slaughter of the three aforesaid gentlemen, who were wounded in the very same parts of their bodies by other such three venees as these, each whereof being mortal: and his vital spark exhaling as his blood gushed out, all he spoke was this. That seeing he could not live, his comfort in dying was, that he could not dye by the hand of a braver man, after the uttering of which words he expiring, with the shril clareens of trumpets, bouncing thunder of artillery, bethwacked beating of drums, universal clapping of hands, and loud acclamations of joy for so glorious a victory, the air above them was so rarified by the extremity of the noise and vehement sound, dispelling the thickest and most condensed parts thereof, that . . . the very sparrows and other flying fowls were said to fall to the ground, for want of aire enough to uphold them in their flight.
Sir Thomas Urquhart, *The Life and Death of the Admirable Crichtoun*

He made pedantry romantic. Out of the dry bones of dead philosophies he produced a wonderful effect. We can well believe that neither his mind nor his tongue weighed heavily on abstruse subjects. They touched them and were off. I have likened him to a butterfly, brilliant in colour and light on wing, but he was a butterfly who fed on Cabbages.
Charles Whibley, *The Admirable Crichton*

## CRIPPS, SIR (RICHARD) STAFFORD

1889–1952 Statesman

Our white Gandhi.
Brendan Bracken, Letter to Lord Beaverbrook, 11 November 1947

. . . the modern Savonarola.
Henry Channon, on Cripps's Budget, Diary, 6 April 1948

There but for the grace of God, goes God.
Sir Winston Churchill, on Cripps as Chancellor of the Exchequer, in Louis Kronenberger, *The Cutting Edge*

The trouble is, his chest is a cage in which two squirrels are at war, his conscience and his career.
Winston Churchill, in Lord Moran, Diary

The perfect Octavius.
Michael Foot, *Aneurin Bevan*

It was his supreme and rare merit that he knew the difference between a good argument and a bad one.
Douglas Jay, in W. T. Rodgers ed., *Hugh Gaitskell 1906–63*

. . . the cold ruthlessness of a hanging judge.
Michael Postan, in *ibid.*

## CROCKETT, DAVY

1786–1836 Frontiersman

. . . fame is like a shaved pig with a greased tail, and it is only after it has slipped through the hands of some thousands, that some fellow, by mere chance, holds on to it!
On himself, in Richard M. Dorson ed., *Davy Crockett, American Comic Legend*

I always had the praise o' raisin the tallest and fattest and sassyest gals in all America. They can out-run, out-jump, out-fight, and outscream any crittur in creation; and for scratchin', thar's not a hungry painter, or a patent horse-rake can hold a claw to 'em.

*Ibid.*

'Gentlemen,' says I, 'I'm Davy Crockett, the darling branch o' old Kentuck that can eat up a painter, hold a buffalo out to drink, and put a rifle ball through the moon.'

*Ibid.*

Thar's no human flesh in all creation that's so partial to home and the family circle, square, kitchen, barn, log-hut, pig-pen or fire-place as a Kentuckian. For my own part, I war in the habit, every mornin', of lightin' my pipe, and givin' all my domestic circle – wimmin, colts, wild cats, and kittens – an all-squeezin' hug all round; and the way the brute portion of 'em showed thar sharp ivories, and grinned back double extra satisfaction, war indeed upwards of gratifying to my mortal and sympathetic natur.

*Ibid.*

## CROKER, JOHN WILSON

1780–1857 Essayist, Politician

He was, in short, a man who possessed, in very remarkable degree, a restless instinct for adroit baseness.

Benjamin Disraeli, caricaturing Croker as 'Rigby', in *Coningsby*

. . . that impudent leering Croker . . . I detest him more than cold boiled veal.

T. B. Macaulay, Letter to Hannah M. Macaulay, 1831

Mr Killthedead . . . a great compounder of narcotics, under the denomination of BATTLES, for he never heard of a deadly field, especially if dotage and superstition, to which he was very partial, gained the advantage over generosity and talent, both of which he abhorred, but immediately seizing his goosequill and foolscap,
He fought the Battle o'er again, / And thrice he slew the slain. /

Thomas Love Peacock, *Melincourt*

## CROME, JOHN

1768–1821 Painter

I remember meeting my old friend Mr John Crome, of Norwich (some of whose landscapes are not surpassed even by those of Gainsborough) with several of his pupils, on the banks of the Yare. 'This is our Academy,' he cried out triumphantly, holding up his brush.

John Burnet, *Landscape Painting*

Crome is the quiet man at the party whom chatterers fail to notice. His true subject was not the Norfolk countryside but the stillness at the heart of it.

D. and T. Clifford, *John Crome*

## CROMPTON, SAMUEL

1753–1827 Inventor

In the summer of 1811 he visited the manufacturing districts, and collected information connected with the progress and extent of the cotton manufacture. Encouraged by what he had seen everywhere on his journey, he was assisted, on his return, to present a petition to Parliament for a recompense from the country. The committee, to whom the memorial was referred for examination, reported that Mr Crompton was *entitled* to a *material reward.* Crompton thought his gift should bring him 50,000*l.*; the mechanical public thought he would obtain 25,000*l.*; great, therefore, was the astonishment of every one when Parliament granted him only 5,000*l.* No member engaged in manufacture, or connected with Lancashire, had generosity enough, or respect for justice, to protest against such a mockery of a reward being conferred. At the moment the sorry sum was granted, 360 factories, containing 4,600,000 spindles, were at work, spinning annually 40,000,000 pounds weight of cotton into yarn, and employing 70,000 persons directly in spinning, and 150,000 persons weaving the yarn into cloth, making 660,000 persons depending for their daily bread on the use of the *mule*. Yet Mr Crompton, the ingenious author of all this extraordinary prosperity and wealth, had not, after thirty years toil and bodily labour, been able to raise himself or his family above the condition of common labourers, employing only their own hands in working three of his small muslin-wheels.

Bennet Woodcroft, *Brief Biographies of Inventors of Machines for the Manufacture of Textile Fabrics*

## CROMWELL, OLIVER

1599–1658 Lord Protector

I am neither heir nor executor to Charles Stuart.

On himself, repudiating a royal debt, August 1651

When I went there, I did not think to have done this. But perceiving the spirit of God so strong upon me, I would not consult flesh and blood.

On himself, on his forcible dissolution of Parliament in April 1653, in James Heath, *Flagellum, or the Life and Death, Birth and Burial of Oliver Cromwell*

I was by birth a gentleman, living neither in any considerable height, nor yet in obscurity. I have been called to several employments in the nation, – to serve in parliaments, – and (because I would not be over tedious) I did endeavour to discharge the duty of an honest man in those services, to God, and His people's interest, and of the Commonwealth; having, when time was, a competent acceptation in the hearts of men, and some evidences thereof.

On himself, Speech to the First Parliament of the Protectorate, 12 September 1654

Mr Lely, I desire you would use all your skill to paint my picture truly like me, and not flatter me at all; but remark all these roughnesses, pimples, warts and everything as you see me, otherwise I never will pay a farthing for it.

On himself, in Horace Walpole, *Anecdotes of Painting*

You shall scarce speak to Cromwell about anything, but he will lay his hand on his breast, elevate his eyes, and call God to record; he will weep, howl and repent, even while he doth smite you under the first rib . . . Oh Cromwell! Wither art thou aspiring? . . . He that runs may read and foresee the intent, a new regality.

Anon. Leveller Tract, *The Hunting of the Foxes*

During a great part of the eighteenth century most Tories hated him because he overthrew the monarchy, most Whigs because he overthrew Parliament. Since Carlyle wrote, all liberals have seen in him their champion, and all revolutionists have apotheosized the first great representative of their school; while, on the other side, their opponents have hailed the dictator who put down anarchy. Unless the socialists or the anarchists finally prevail – and perhaps even then – his fame seems as secure as human reputation is likely to be in a changing world.

W. C. Abbott, *Writings and Speeches of Oliver Cromwell*

The commonest charge against Cromwell is hypocrisy – and the commonest basis for that is defective chronology.

*Ibid.*

*Oliver Cromwell* had certainly this afflatus. One that I knew that was at the Battle of *Dunbar*, told me that Oliver was carried on with a Divine impulse; he did Laugh so excessively as if he had been Drunk; his Eyes sparkled with Spirits. He obtain'd a great Victory; but the action was said to be contrary to Human Prudence. The same Fit of Laughter seized *Oliver Cromwell* just before the Battle of *Naseby*; as a Kinsman of mine, and a great favourite of his, Colonel J. P. then present, testified. Cardinal *Mazerine* said, That he was a Lucky Fool.

John Aubrey, *Miscellanies*

. . . he thought Secrecy a Vertue, and Dissimulation no Vice, and Simulation, that is, in plain English, a Lie, or Perfidiousnesse to be a tollerable Fault in case of Necessity.

Richard Baxter, *Reliquiae Baxterianae*

He was of a sanguine complexion, naturally of such a vivacity, hilarity and alacrity as another man is when he hath drunken a cup too much.

*Ibid.*

And as he went on, though he yet resolved not what form the New Commonwealth should be moulded into, yet he thought it but reasonable, that he should be the Chief Person who had been the chief in the Deliverance.

*Ibid.*

He gart kings ken they had a lith in their neck.

Alexander Boswell, Lord Auchinleck, in James Boswell, *Tour of the Hebrides*

. . . A devotee of law, he was forced to be often lawless; a civilian to the core, he had to maintain himself by the sword; with a passion to construct, his task was chiefly to destroy; the most scrupulous of men, he had to ride roughshod over his own scruples and those of others; the tenderest, he had continually to harden his heart; the most English of our greater figures, he spent his life in opposition to the majority of Englishmen; a realist, he was condemned to build that which could not last.

John Buchan, *Oliver Cromwell*

Cromwell was a man in whom ambition had not wholly suppressed, but only suspended, the sentiments of religion.

Edmund Burke, *Letters*, 1791

As close as a Goose / Sat the *Parliament-House* / To hatch the royal Gull; / After much fiddle-faddle, / The Egg proved addle / And *Oliver* came forth *Nol.* /

Samuel Butler, *A Ballad*

Sylla was the first of victors; but our own / The sagest of usurpers, Cromwell; he / Too swept off senates while he hewed the throne / Down to a block – immortal rebel! See / What crimes it costs to be a moment free / And famous through all ages. /

Lord Byron, *Childe Harold*, canto iv

I confess I have an interest in this Mr Cromwell; and indeed, if truth must be said, in him alone. The rest are historical, dead to me; but he is epic, still living. Hail to thee, thou strong one; hail across the long-drawn funeral-aisle and night of Time!

Thomas Carlyle, *Historical Sketches*

In spite of the stupor of Histories, it is beautiful . . . to see how the memory of Cromwell, in its huge inarticulate significance, not able to *speak* a wise word for itself to any one, has nevertheless been growing steadily clearer and clearer in the popular English mind; how from the day when high dignitaries and pamphleteers of the Carrion species did their ever-memorable feat at

Tyburn, onwards to this day the progress does not stop.

Thomas Carlyle, *Letters and Speeches of Oliver Cromwell*

His Grandeur he deriv'd from Heaven alone, / For he was great e'er fortune made him so / And Wars like Mists that rise against the Sun / Made him but greater seem, not greater grow. /

No borrow'd Bays his Temples did adorn, / But to our Crown he did fresh Jewels bring; / Nor was his Vertue poison'd soon as born, / With the too early Thoughts of being King. /

John Dryden, *Heroick Stanzas consecrated to the Memory of His Highness Oliver*

Saw the superb Funerall of the *Protectors*: . . . but it was the joyfullest funerall that ever I saw, for there was none that cried, but dogs, which the souldiers hooted away with a barbarous noise; drinking and taking *tabacco* in the streets as they went. (22 November 1658)

This day (o the stupendious, & inscrutable Judgements of God) were the Carkasses of that arch-rebell *Cromwell*, *Bradshaw* the Judge who condemned his Majestie & *Ireton*, son in law to the Usurper, draged out of their superbe Tombs (in Westminster among the Kings), to *Tyburne* & hanged on the Gallows there from 9 in the morning til 6 at night, & then buried under that fatal and ignominious Monument, in a deepe pitt: Thousands of people (who has seene them in all their pride and pompous insults) being spectators: looke back at November 22, 1658, & be astonish'd – And fear God & honor the King, but meddle not with them who are given to change. (30 January 1661)

John Evelyn, Diary

That slovenly fellow which you see before us, who hath no ornament in his speech; I say that sloven, if we should ever come to have a breach with the King (which God forbid) in such case will be one of the greatest men of England.

John Hampden, speaking to Lord Digby in the House of Commons, overheard by Sir Richard Bulstrode

If you prove not an honest man, I will never trust a fellow with a great nose for your sake.

Sir Arthur Haslerig, *A Word to Generall Cromwell*, 1647

The domestic administration of Cromwell, though it discovers great abilities, was conducted without any plan either of liberty or arbitrary power: perhaps his difficult situation admitted of neither. His foreign enterprises though full of intrepidity were pernicious to national interest and seem more the result of impetuous fury or narrow prejudices, than of cool foresight and deliberation. An eminent personage he was however in many respects, and even a superior genius, but unequal and irregular in his operations. And though not defective in any talent, except that of elocution, the abilities which in him were most admirable and which most contributed to his marvellous success, were the magnanimous resolution of his enterprises, and his peculiar dexterity in discovering the character, and practising on the weaknesses of, mankind . . . his subsequent usurpation was the effect of necessity as well as ambition . . . And upon the whole, his character does not appear more extraordinary and unusual by the mixture of so much absurdity with so much penetration, than by his tempering such violent ambition, and such enraged fanaticism with so much regard to justice and humanity.

David Hume, *History of England*

. . . In a word, as he was guilty of many Crimes against which Damnation is denounced, and for which Hell-fire is prepared, so he had some good qualities which have caused the Memory of some Men in all Ages to be celebrated; and he will be look'd upon by Posterity as a brave badd man.

Edward Hyde, Earl of Clarendon, *History of the Rebellion*

'I am,' said he, 'as much for a government by consent as any man; but where shall we find that consent? Amongst the Prelatical, Presbyterian, Independent, Anabaptist, or Leveling Parties?' . . . Then he fell into the commendation of his own government, boasting of the protection and quiet which the people enjoyed under it, saying, that he was resolved to keep the nation from being imbrued in blood. I said that I was of the opinion too much blood had been already shed, unless there were a better account of it. 'You do well,' said he, 'to charge us with the guilt of blood; but we think there is a good return for what hath been shed.'

Edmund Ludlow, Interview with Cromwell, August 1656

His body was wel compact and strong, his stature under 6 foote (I beleeve about two inches) his head so shaped, as you might see it a storehouse and shop both of a vast treasury of natural parts. His temper exceeding fyery as I have known, but the flame of it kept downe, for the most part, or soon allayed with those moral endowments he had. He was naturally compassionate towards objects in distresse, even to an effeminate measure; though God had made him a heart, wherein was left little roume for any feare, but what was due to himselfe, of which there was a large proportion, yet did he exceed in tenderness towards sufferers. A larger soule, I thinke, hath seldom dwelt in a house of clay than his was.

John Maidston, Letter to John Winthrop, 24 March 1659

So restless *Cromwel* could not cease / In the inglorious Arts of Peace, / But through adventrous War, / Urged his active Star . . . /

And, if we would speak true, / Much to the Man is due. / Who, from his private Gardens, where / He liv'd reserved and austere, / As if his highest plot / To plant the Bergamot, / Could by industrious Valour climbe / To ruine the great Work of Time, / And cast the Kingdome old / Into another Mold . . . /

A *Ceasar* he ere long to *Gaul*, / To Italy an *Hannibal*, / An to all States not free / Shall *Clymacterick* be. /

Andrew Marvell, *An Horation Ode upon Cromwell's Return from Ireland*

*Cromwell*, our chief of men, who through a cloud, / Not of war only, but detractions rude, / Guided by faith and matchless fortitude, / To peace and truth thy glorious way has ploughed / And on the neck of crowned Fortune proud / Has reared God's trophies, and his work pursued, / While Darwen stream with blood of Scots imbrued, / And Dunbar field resounds thy praises loud, / And Worcester's laureate wreath. Yet much remains / To conquer still; peace hath her victories / No less renowned than war: new foes arise, / Threatening to bind our souls with secular chains: / Help us to save free conscience from the paw / Of hireling wolves whose gospel is their maw. /

John Milton, *Sonnet XVI, To the Lord General Cromwell*

At dinner we talked much of Cromwell, all saying he was a brave fellow and did owe his crown he got to himself, as much as any man that ever got one.

Samuel Pepys, Diary, 8 February 1667

There is indeed that necessity which we think there is of saving the vineyard of the Commonwealth if possible by destroying the wild boar that is broke into it.

Edward Sexby, *Killing No Murder*

Whilst he was cautious of his own words, (not putting forth too many lest they should betray his thoughts) he made others talk until he had, as it were, sifted them, and known their most intimate designs.

Sir William Waller, *Recollections*

I . . . had occasion to converse with Mr Cromwell's physician, Dr Simcott, who assured me that for many years his patient was a most splenetick man and had phansies about the cross in that town; and that he had been called up to him at midnight, and such unseasonable hours very many times, upon a strong phansy, which made him believe he was then dying; and there went a story of him, that in the day-time, lying melancholy in his bed, be believed the spirit appeared to him, and told him that he should be the greatest man, (not mentioning the word king) in this Kingdom. Which his uncle, Sir Thomas Steward, who left him all the little estate Cromwell had, told him was traiterous to relate.

Sir Philip Warwick, on Cromwell's early manhood, in *Memoires of the Reigne of King Charles I*

*Cromwell*: 'What if a man should take upon him to be king?'
*Whitelocke*: 'I think that Remedy would be worse than the Disease.'
*Cromwell*: 'Why do you think so?'
*Whitelocke*: 'As to your own Person the Title of King would be of no Advantage, because you have the full Kingly Power in you already . . . I apprehend indeed, less Envy and Danger, and Pomp, but not less Power, and real Opportunities of doing Good in your being General than would be if you had assumed the Title of King.'

Bulstrode Whitelocke, *Memorialls of English Affairs*

In short, every Beast hath some evil Properties; but Cromwel hath the Properties of all evil Beasts.

Archbishop John Williams to King Charles at Oxford, in Hackett, *Life of Archbishop Williams*

. . . the English Monster, the Center of Mischief, a shame to the British Chronicle, a pattern for Tyranny, Murther and Hypocrisie, whose bloody *Caligula, Domitian*, having at last attained the height of his *Ambition*, for Five years space, he wallowed in the blood of many Gallant and *Heroick* Persons.

Gerard Winstanley, *Loyal Martyrology*

*See also* Thomas Jefferson, Theodore Roosevelt

## CROMWELL, RICHARD

1626–1712 Lord Protector

His humanity, ingenuousness, and modesty, the mediocrity of his abilities, and the docility with which he submitted to the guidance of persons wiser than himself, admirably qualified him to be the head of a limited monarchy.

T. B. Macaulay, *History of England*

Richard the fourth just peeping out of squire / (No fault so much as the old one was his sire / For men believed though all went in his name / He'd but be tenant till the landlord came.) / When on a sudden all amazed we found / The seven years Babel tumbled to the ground, / And he, poor heart, thanks to his cunning kin, / Was soon in cuerpo honest Dick again. /
(*in cuerpo* = naked)

Robert Wild, *Iter Boreale*

## CROMWELL, THOMAS, EARL OF ESSEX

1485?–1540 Statesman, Administrator

He was the first chief minister that England had ever had, who was baseborn and yet not a cleric. He stood completely outside the great religious movement of his time, and only made use of it to further his own political ends. He came at a time when things were in an unsettled state and ready for a change: his personality, emotionless, practical, stern, impressed itself on every phase of the national life.

R. B. Merriman, *Life and Letters of Thomas Cromwell*

For Thomas Cromwell was a freak in English history, and that, perhaps, is why he has been so disliked: an iron-fisted bureaucrat who crammed into his brief reign the kind of process which in England, we like to maintain, is carried out insensibly, over centuries. He overhauled the machinery of government as it had never been overhauled since the reign of Henry II; and he overhauled it so drastically that much of it was not radically altered till the reign of Victoria. In six hundred years of history he stands out as the most radical of modernisers. Modern history, if it begins anywhere, begins, in England, with him.

H. R. Trevor-Roper, *England's Moderniser*

## CROSBY, (HARRY LILLIS) 'BING'

1901?–1977 Actor, Singer

If I hadn't found something as easy as singing to earn me a living, I'm afraid the name of Crosby would be adding to the clutter of the stalls that peddle learning to the American public at two fifty a volume. In short, ever since Mother Crosby lent me a hand with my first grammar school composition on why a fly can walk a ceiling, a phenomenon that's always fascinated me, I've cherished a yen to hunt and peck my way into the charmed circle of literati. However the lure of the open road, a topless flivver and a set of second hand drums were my undoing. The gypsy got the best of the bard and the Shakespeare in me has been groaning with frustration ever since.

On himself, Telegram to the radio editor of the Lincoln, Nebraska, *Star*, in Barry Ulanov, *The Incredible Crosby*

I tell you . . . there's just no other gate like that Bing gate; he's the toppest . . . the peerest.

Louis Armstrong, in J. T. H. Mize, *Bing Crosby and the Bing Crosby Style*

I've used an expression – I've been criticised for using it – yet I say it very lovingly . . . once Bing hit success, he placed himself in a little Cellophane bag and he zipped it up and he just will not allow anyone to get inside that bag. He doesn't want to be told that he's good.

Bob Hope, in Charles Thompson, *Bing*

There was once a famous thing that he did while on a television show; he was asked by the interviewer why it was he had this calm about him and a sort of unruffled air? He reached into his pocket and pulled out an enormous wad of dollar bills, and he said 'that helps!'

Stefanie Powers, in *ibid.*

Bing sings like all people think they sing in the shower.

Dinah Shore, in J. T. H. Mize, *Bing Crosby and the Bing Crosby Style*

## CROSSMAN, RICHARD HOWARD STAFFORD

1907–74 Labour Politician, Journalist

I am an old-fashioned Zionist who believes that anti-Semitism and racialism are endemic.

On himself, Diary, 29 September 1964

Minister, you have a very peculiar taste – the kind of peculiar taste which will enable you to enjoy the things that are said about you when your health is proposed.

Dame Evelyn Sharp, in Richard Crossman, Diary, 27 October 1964

## CRUIKSHANK, GEORGE

1792–1878 Cartoonist

A fine rough English diamond.

W. M. Thackeray, *An Essay on the Genius of George Cruikshank*

There must be no smiling with Cruikshank. A man who does not laugh outright is a dullard, and has no heart. Even the old 'Dandy of Sixty' [George IV] must have laughed at his own wondrous grotesque image, as they say Louis Philippe did, who saw all the caricatures that were made of himself. And there are some of Cruikshank's designs which have the blessed faculty of creating laughter as often as you see them.

*Ibid.*

## CUMBERLAND, DUKE OF, ERNEST AUGUSTUS, KING OF HANOVER

1771–1851

Satan next took the army list in hand / Where he found a new 'Field Marshal'; / And when he saw this high command / Conferred on his Highness of Cumberland, / 'Oh were I prone to cavil – or were I not the Devil, / I should say this was somewhat partial; / Since the only wounds that this Warrior gat / Were from God knows whom – and the Devil knows what!' /

Lord Byron, *The Devil's Drive*

. . . what the country cares about is to have a life more, whether male or female, interposed between the succession and the King of Hanover.

Lord Clarendon, Letter to Lord Granville on the birth of Princess Victoria, November 1840

No government can last that has him either for a friend or an enemy.

Lord Grey, in Earl of Stanhope, *Notes of Conversations with the Duke of Wellington 1831–51*

The then Duke of Cumberland (the *foolish* Duke, as he was called), came one night into Foote's green-room at the Haymarket Theatre. 'Well, Foote,' said he, 'Here I am, ready as usual, to swallow all your good things.' – 'Upon my soul,' replied Foote, 'Your Royal Highness must have an excellent digestion, for you never bring any up again.'

Samuel Rogers, *Table Talk*

Go instantly, and take care that *you don't get pelted*!

The Duke of Wellington, advice to Cumberland on William IV's death, June 1837

## CUMMINGS, EDWARD ESTLIN

1894–1962 Poet

He was the most brilliant monologuist I have known. What he poured forth was a mixture of cynical remarks, puns, hyperboles, outrageous metaphors, inconsequence, and tough-guy talk spoken from the corner of his wide expressive mouth: pure Cummings, as if he were rehearsing something that would afterwards appear in print.

Malcolm Cowley, *A Second Flowering*

Of course he was a lyric poet in the bad-boy tradition, broadly speaking, of Catullus and Villon and Verlaine.

*Ibid.*

His mind was essentially extemporaneous. His fits of poetic fury were like the maenadic seizures described in Greek lyrics.
John Dos Passos, *The Best Times*

Cummings's delight in certain things was contagious as a child's. Christmas tree balls, stars, snowflakes. Elephants were his totem. I would never have enjoyed snow so much if I hadn't walked around Washington Square with Cummings in a snowstorm. He loved mice. He had a great eye for sparrows and all pert timid brighteyed creatures.
*Ibid.*

Cummings was one of a continuous line of American artists who have challenged the nation to reassess fundamental aims and values . . . Cummings' poetry is one long letter, pregnant with joy, addressed to most people from an immigrant in nowhere.
Barry A. Marks, *E. E. Cummings*

Cummings, responding to French art, always admiring the French civilization, nonetheless spent most of his life in the United States. He was a goldfinch needing a native tree to sing from.
Eve Triem, *E. E. Cummings*

I think of Cummings as Robinson Crusoe at the moment when he first saw the print of a naked human foot in the sand. That . . . implied a new language – and a readjustment of conscience.
William Carlos Williams, in Roy Harvey Pearce, *The Continuity of American Poetry*

Cummings's style is an eternal adolescent, as fresh and often as winning but as half-baked as boyhood . . . He has apparently no faculty for self-criticism. One imagines him giving off poems as spontaneously as perspiration and with as little application of the intellect.
Edmund Wilson, in S. V. Baum ed., *E. E. Cummings and the Critics*

*See also* W. H. Auden

## CURLL, EDMUND

1675–1747 Bookseller

There is indeed but one bookseller eminent among us for this abomination [sc. printing indecent books], and from him the crime takes the just denomination of *Curlicism.* The fellow is a contemptible wretch in a thousand ways: he is odious in his person, scandalous in his fame; he is marked by nature.
Anon., in *Weekly Journal, or Saturday Post*, 5 April 1718

The caitiff Vaticide.
Alexander Pope, *The Dunciad*, book 2

## CURZON, GEORGE NATHANIEL, MARQUESS CURZON OF KEDLESTON

1859–1925 Statesman

I met Curzon in Downing Street, from whom I got the sort of greeting a corpse would give to an undertaker.
Stanley Baldwin, attributed, 1933, after Baldwin became Prime Minister – a job that Curzon always wanted

Kipling once said to me of Curzon, that his activity was the product of bad health. Ordinary existence was barred to him. So his iron corset may have been responsible for his ill-directed drive and energy which enabled him to destroy the independence of the House of Lords.
Lord Beaverbrook, *Don't Trust to Luck*

Britannia's butler.
Max Beerbohm, in Cecil Beaton, *The Strenuous Years*

Curzon was not perhaps a great man, but he was a supreme Civil Servant.

David Lloyd George, in conversation with Harold Nicolson, 6 July 1936

In parliamentary life, he was to be one who stayed to get his feet wet before deciding that a ship was sinking.

Leonard Mosley, *The Glorious Fault*

Ah, those Curzonian dissertations! . . . As if some stately procession proceeding orderly through Arcs de Triomphe along a straight wide avenue: outriders, escorts, bands; the perfection of accoutrements, the precise marshalling of detail, the sense of conscious continuity, the sense of absolute control. The voice rising at moments in almost histrionic scorn, or dropping at moments into a hush of sudden emotion; and then a flash of March sunshine, a sudden dart of eighteenth-century humour, a pause while his wide shoulders rose and fell in rich amusement. And all this under a cloud of exhaustion, under a cloud of persistent pain.

Harold Nicolson, *Some People*

My name is George Nathaniel Curzon, / I am a most superior person, / My cheek is pink, my hair is sleek, / I dine at Blenheim once a week. /

After lines by Cecil Spring-Rice, in *The Masque of Balliol*

*See also* Lord Kitchener

## CUSTER, GEORGE ARMSTRONG

1839–76 Soldier

Cut off from aid, abandoned in the midst of incredible odds, waving aloft the sabre which had won him victory so often, the pride and glory of his comrades, the noble Custer fell: bequeathing to the nation his sword, to his comrades an example, to his friends a memory, and to his beloved one a hero's name.

Lawrence Barrett, in Frederick Whittaker, *A Complete Life of Gen. George A. Custer*

## CUTHBERT

*circa* 635–87 Saint

In order to make more widely known the height of glory attained after death by God's servant Cuthbert . . . Divine Providence guided the brethren to exhume his bones. After eleven years, they expected to find his flesh reduced to dust and the remains withered, as is usual in dead bodies; and they proposed to place them in a new coffin on the same site but above ground level, so that he might receive the honours due to him. When they informed Bishop Eadbert of their wish, he gave approval and directed that it should be carried out on the anniversary of his burial. This was done, and when they opened the grave, they found the body whole and incorrupt as though still living and the limbs flexible, so that he looked as if he were asleep rather than dead. Furthermore all the vestments in which he was clothed appeared not only spotless but wonderfully fresh and fair.

Bede, *Ecclesiastical History of the English People*, translated by Leo Sherley-Price

## CUTLER, SIR JOHN

1608?–93 Merchant, Miser

Sir John Cutler had a pair of black worsted stockings which his maid darned so often with silk that they became at last a pair of silk stockings.

Dr Arbuthnot, in *Dictionary of National Biography*

Resolve me, Reason, which of these is worse, / Want with a full, or with an empty purse? / Thy life, more wretched, Cutler, was confess'd, / Arise and tell me, was thy death more bless'd? / Cutler saw tenants break, and houses fall, / For very want; he could not build a wall. / His only daughter in a stranger's pow'r, / For very want; he could not pay a dow'r. / A few grey hairs his rev'rend temples crown'd / 'Twas very want that sold them for two pound. / What ev'n deny'd a cordial at his end, / Banish'd the doctor, and expell'd the friend? / What but a want, which you perhaps think mad, / Yet numbers feel the want of what he had. / Cutler and Brutus, dying both exclaim, / 'Virtue! and Wealth! what are ye but a name!' /

Alexander Pope, *Epistle iii, to Allen Lord Bathurst, Of the Use of Riches*

# 'D'

## DALTON, JOHN

1766–1844 Chemist

Mr Dalton's aspect and manner were repulsive. There was no gracefulness belonging to him. His voice was harsh and brawling, his gait stiff and awkward; his style of writing and conversation dry and almost crabbed. In person he was tall, bony, and slender. He never could learn to swim: on investigating this circumstance he found that his specific gravity as a mass was greater than that of water; and he mentioned this in his lectures on natural philosophy in illustration of the capability of different persons for attaining the art of swimming. Independence and simplicity of manner and originality were his best qualities. Though in comparatively humble circumstances he maintained the dignity of the philosophical character. As the first distinct promulgator of the doctrine that the elements of bodies unite in definite proportions to form chemical compounds, he has acquired an undying fame.

Humphry Davy, in W. C. Henry, *Memoirs of the Life and Scientific Researches of John Dalton*

For several years of his life he was in the habit every Thursday afternoon, when the weather permitted, of taking exercise in the open air, and of spending a few hours in company with a few intimate friends, in the enjoyment of his favourite diversion of bowling . . . On these occasions his spirits were buoyant and cheerful, and he entered into the sport with all the keen relish of boyhood. Sometimes, when a fall of snow had taken place, he has been known to request that the snow might be swept from the bowling green that he might not be disappointed of his game. When it came to his turn to bowl, he threw his whole soul into his game, and after he had delivered the bowl from his hand, it was not a little amusing to spectators to see him running after it across the green, stooping down as if talking to the ball, and waving his hands from one side to the other exactly as he wished the bias of the ball to be, and manifesting the most intense interest in its coming near to the point at which he aimed. A small sum, a few pence, was played for each game, in order to pay for the use of the green, and Dalton set down in his pocket-book with the minutest accuracy, the amount of his losses or gains.

Samuel Giles, in *ibid.*

What chemists took from Dalton was not new experimental laws but a new way of practicing chemistry (he himself called it the 'new system of chemical philosophy'), and this proved so rapidly fruitful that only a few of the older chemists in France and Britain were able to resist it.

Thomas S. Kuhn, *The Structure of Scientific Revolutions*

He was not a fluent speaker, and when, as President, he had to make a few remarks when the reader of a paper stopped, he is reported to have sometimes contented himself by saying, 'This paper will no doubt be found interesting by those who take an interest in it'.

J. J. Thomson, *Recollections and Reflections*

## DANA, CHARLES ANDERSON

1819–97 Journalist

I have always felt that whatever the Divine Providence permitted to occur I was not too proud to report.

On himself, in L. Ziff, *The American 1890s*

A master of the half-hidden barb, the deadly understatement, the parody, the pointed doggerel, Dana could skewer a victim in the most gentlemanly language...

W. A. Swanberg, *Pulitzer*

### DANBY, EARL OF (THOMAS OSBORNE)

1631–1712 Statesman

The Cabal had bequeathed to him the art of bribing Parliaments, an art still rude, and giving little promise of the rare perfection to which it was brought in the following century. He improved greatly on the plan of the first inventors. They had merely purchased orators: but every man who had a vote might sell himself to Danby.

T. B. Macaulay, *History of England*

By conserving the national finances he hoped to establish royal independence; by bribing the lesser members of the Commons he obtained the votes of the obscure, even though they cost him the diatribes of the eminent; for he rejoiced more in the votes of ninety-nine silent legislators than the conversion of one notable opponent. He was not the first English statesman to use bribery or influence, but he was the first to realise the value of organised system and personal mediocrity in the methods and material of politics, with which aids he contrived to establish Charles's absolutism on a basis, if not of consent, at least of negotiation and influence.

David Ogg, *England in the Reign of Charles II*

### D'ARBLAY, MADAME, *see under* BURNEY, FANNY

### DARROW, CLARENCE SEWARD

1857–1938 Lawyer, Social Reformer

I don't believe in God because I don't believe in Mother Goose.

On himself, in A. K. Adams, *The Home Book of Humorous Quotations*

We know life is futile. A man who considers that his life is of very wonderful importance is awfully close to a padded cell.

On himself, in a lecture at the University of Chicago, 1929, on 'Facing Life Fearlessly: Omar Khayyam and A. E. Housman'

He advised that Methodists be accepted as jurymen because their religious emotions can be transmuted into love and charity; but warned against taking Presbyterians because they knew right from wrong.

Harry Golden, *For 2¢ Plain*

I had a visit not long ago from Clarence Darrow, the great American barrister for defending murderers. He had only a few days in England, but could not return home without seeing me, because he had so often used my poems to rescue his clients from the electric chair. Loeb and Leopold owe their life sentence partly to me; and he gave me a copy of his speech, in which, sure enough, two of my pieces are misquoted.

A. E. Housman, *Letters*

### DARWIN, CHARLES ROBERT

1809–82 Naturalist

Early in 1856 Lyell advised me to write out my views pretty fully, and I began at once to do so on a scale three or four times as extensive as that which was afterwards followed in my *Origin of Species*; yet it was only an abstract of the materials which I had collected and I got through about half the work on this scale. But my plans were overthrown, for early in the summer of 1858 Mr Wallace, who was then in the Malay archipelago, sent me an essay

*On the Tendency of Varieties to depart indefinitely from the Original Type*; and this essay contained exactly the same theory as mine. Mr Wallace expressed the wish that if I thought well of his essay, I should send it to Lyell for perusal. The circumstances under which I consented at the request of Lyell and Hooker to allow of an abstract from my MS., together with a letter to Asa Gray, dated September 5, 1857, to be published at the same time with Wallace's Essay, are given in the *Journal of the Proceedings of the Linnean Society*, 1858, p. 45. I was at first very unwilling to consent, as I thought Mr Wallace might consider my doing so unjustifiable, for I did not then know how generous and noble was his disposition. The extract from my MS. and the letter to Asa Gray had neither been intended for publication, and were badly written. Mr Wallace's essay, on the other hand, was admirably expressed and quite clear. Nevertheless, our joint productions excited very little attention, and the only published notice of them which I can remember was by Professor Haughton of Dublin, whose verdict was that all that was new in them was false, and what was true was old. This shows how necessary it is that any new view should be explained at considerable length in order to arouse public attention.

On himself, *Autobiography*

I have no patience whatever with these gorilla damnifications of humanity.

Thomas Carlyle, in Edward Latham, *Famous Sayings*

It is no secret that . . . there are many to whom Mr Darwin's death is a wholly irreparable loss. And this not merely because of his wonderfully genial, simple, and generous nature; his cheerful and animated conversation, and the infinite variety and accuracy of his information; but because the more one knew of him, the more he seemed the incorporated ideal of a man of science.

T. H. Huxley, in *Nature*, 1882

Though he cannot be said to have proved the truth of his doctrine, he does seem to have proved that it *may* be true, which I take to be as great a triumph as knowledge and ingenuity could possibly achieve on such a question. Certainly nothing can be at first sight more entirely implausible than his theory, and yet after beginning by thinking it impossible, one arrives at something like an actual belief in it, and one certainly does not relapse into complete disbelief.

John Stuart Mill, Letter to Alexander Bain, April 1860

I do not see that Darwin's supreme service to his fellow men was his demonstration of evolution – man could have lived on quite as happily and perhaps more morally under the old notion that he was specially made in the image of his Maker. Darwin's supreme service was that he won for man absolute freedom in the study of the laws of nature.

H. F. Osborn, *Impressions of Great Naturalists*

I never know whether to be more surprised at Darwin himself for making so much of natural selection, or at his opponents for making so little of it.

Robert Louis Stevenson, '*From his Note Book*'

These two [Darwin and T. H. Huxley] were very great men. They thought boldly, carefully and simply, they spoke and wrote fearlessly and plainly, they lived modestly and decently; they were mighty intellectual liberators.

H. G. Wells, *Experiment in Autobiography*

*See also* Erasmus Darwin, Benjamin Disraeli, T. H. Huxley, John Stuart Mill

## DARWIN, ERASMUS

1731–1802 Poet, Physician

No envy mingles with our praise, / Though could our hearts repine / At any poet's happier lays, / They would, they must, at thine. /

But we, in mutual bondage knit / Of friendship's closest tie, / Can gaze on even Darwin's wit / With an unjaundic'd eye; /

William Cowper, *Lines addressed to Dr Darwin, Author of The Botanic Garden*

A young man once asked him in, as he thought, an offensive manner, whether he did not find stammering very inconvenient. He answered, 'No Sir, it gives me time for reflection, and saves me from asking impertinent questions.'

Ernst Krause, *Erasmus Darwin*

. . . that eager mind, whom fools deride / For laced and periwigged verses on his flowers; / Forgetting how he strode before his age, / And how his grandson caught from his right hand / A fire that lit the world. /

Alfred Noyes, *The Torchbearers*

## D'AVENANT, SIR WILLIAM

1606–68 Dramatist

The King knights *Will* for fighting on his side, / Yet when *Will* comes for fighting to be tried, / There is not one in all the Armies can / Say they ere felt, or saw this fighting man. / Strange that the Knight should not be known i'th Field, / A Face well charg'd, tho nothing in his Shield. / Sure fighting *Will* like *Basilisk* did ride / Among the Troops, and all that saw *Will* dy'd, / Else how could *Will* for fighting be a Knight, / And none alive that ever saw *Will* fight. /

Anon., *Upon Fighting Will, circa* 1644

Such were his virtues that they could command / A general applause from every hand: / His *Exit* then, this on record shall have / A *Clap* did usher *D'Avenant* to his grave. /

Anon., *Epitaph*, in Anthony à Wood, *Athenae Oxonienses*

He gott a terrible clap of a black handsome wench that lay in Axe-yard, Westminster, whom he thought on when he speakes of Dalga in *Gondibert*, which cost him his Nose, with which unlucky mischance many witts were too cruelly bold.

John Aubrey, *Brief Lives*

Mr Shakespear was his God-father & gave him his name. (In all probability he got him). 'Tis further said that one day going from school a grave Doctor in Divinity met him, and ask'd him, *Child wither art thou going in such hast?* to wch the child reply'd *O Sir my Godfather is come to Town, & I am going to ask his blessing.* To wch the Dr said, *Hold Child, you must not take the name of God in vaine.*

Thomas Hearne, Diary, 1709

He is a scholar of Donne's and took his sententiousness and metaphysics from him.

Alexander Pope, *Conversation*

## DAVIDSON, JO

1883–1952 Sculptor

I had brought some photos of my sculpture. Gandhi looked at them intently and said:
'I see you make heroes out of mud.'
And I retorted: 'And sometimes vice-versa.'

On himself, in *Between Sittings*

## DAVIES, JOHN

1565?–1618 Poet

JOHN DAVIES of Hereford (for so he constantly styled himself) was the greatest Master of the Pen that England in his age beheld, for 1. Fast-writing, so incredible his expedition. 2. Fair-writing, some minutes consultation being required to decide, whether his lines were written or printed. 3. Close-writing, A Mysterie indeed, and too Dark for my Dimme Eyes to discover. 4. Various-writing, Secretary, Roman, Court and Text . . . Our Davies had also some pretty excursions into Poetry and could flourish matter as well as Letters, with his Fancy as well as his Pen.

Thomas Fuller, *The History of the Worthies of England*

## DAVIES, SIR JOHN

1569–1626 Poet, Attorney-General

Jo. Davys goes waddling with his arse out behind as though he were about to make everyone that he meets a wall to pisse against.

John Manningham, Diary

## DAVIS, JEFFERSON

1808–89 President of the Confederacy

Oh, the muskets they may rattle / And the cannon they may roar, / But we'll fight for you, Jeff Davis, / Along the Southern shore. /

Anon., in Hudson Strode, *Jefferson Davis: Tragic Hero*

There is no doubt that Jefferson Davis and other leaders of the South have made an army; they are making, it appears, a navy; and they have made what is more than either, they have made a nation.

William Ewart Gladstone, Speech at Newcastle-upon-Tyne, 7 October 1862

. . . ambitious as Lucifer and cold as a lizard.

Sam Houston, in Carl Sandburg, *Abraham Lincoln: The Prairie Years and the War Years*

He is not a cheap Judas. I do not think he would have sold the Saviour for thirty shillings; but for the successorship to Pontius Pilate he would have betrayed Christ and the apostles and the whole Christian Church.

Winfield Scott, in Charles W. Elliott, *Winfield Scott: The Soldier and the Man*

*See also* Theodore Roosevelt

## DAVY, SIR HUMPHRY

1778–1829 Natural Philosopher

Sir H. Davy's greatest discovery was Michael Faraday.

Anon., in the *Oxford Companion to English Literature*

Sir Humphrey Davy / Abominated gravy. / He lived in the odium / Of having discovered Sodium. /

E. C. Bentley, *Biography for Beginners*

Most persons have probably heard of the letter sent to him from Italy, which reached him safely, though it only bore the mysterious superscription:-

SIROMFREDEVI

LONDRA

C. R. Weld, *A History of the Royal Society*

There is an entertaining anecdote illustrative of his popularity, even among the more humble classes. He was passing through the streets one fine night, when he observed a man showing the moon through a telescope. He stopped to look at the earth's satellite and tendered a penny to the exhibitor. But the latter, on learning that his customer was no less a person than the great Davy, exclaimed with an important air, that 'he could not think of taking money from a brother philosopher'.

*Ibid.*

*See also* Michael Faraday

## DAY LEWIS, CECIL

1904–72 Poet

My later work, as far as I may judge, presents a good deal more variety both in subject matter and in verse forms, a more sensuous appeal, and a greater flexibility of line, than my earlier . . . What happens, as far as I can make out, is that I have some deep violent experience which, like an earthquake, throws up layers of my past that were inaccessible to me poetically till then. During the last war, for instance, I found myself able to use in verse for the first time images out of my own childhood. The new material thrown up, the new contours which life presents as a result of the seismic experience, may demand a new kind of poem. It is here that change of technique appears.

On himself, Introduction to *Selected Poems*

DAY LEWIS JOINS UP. Cecil Day Lewis, the poet (a member of the International Association of Writers for the Defence of Culture) has joined the selection Committee of the BOOK SOCIETY . . . On this Committee, Mr Day Lewis no doubt will be Change, Revolution, Youth, the Rising Generation. But this ends his stance as the Poet writing thrillers . . . and establishes him as the Thriller Writer, the Underworld Man, the yesterday's newspaper, the grease in the sink-pipe of letters who has been posed for ten years as spring water . . . Mr Day Lewis and his Legend are now liquidated: the liquid has flowed to its oily shape and low level in the old sardine tin of Respectability. Mr Lewis has drained himself off, a Noyes, a Binyon, a Squire, a dullard. We can get along without him.

Geoffrey Grigson, in *New Verse*, May 1937

Day-Lewis was a handsome man, in dress something of a dandy (in the best sense) and with a similar taste in such things as motor cars. In first coming into a room he might give the impression of austerity, but quite soon the mask would relax into its attractive lines of humour. He was, in fact, no mean anecdotalist, often against himself; at one time he had an hilarious story of catching his own dental plate before it could fly into the stalls after an impassioned end to a poetry reading.

Obituary in *The Times*, 23 May 1972

## DEBS, EUGENE VICTOR

1855–1926 Socialist

While there is a lower class I am in it, while there is a criminal element I am of it, and while there is a soul in prison I am not free.

On himself, during his trial at Canton, Ohio, 16 June 1913

Debs has a face that looks like a death's head . . . as the arch 'Red' talked he was bent at the hips like an old old man, his eerie face peering up and out at the crowd like a necromancer leading a charm.

Anon., in *Los Angeles Times*, 11 September 1908

Away with him! He utters the word 'Love'. / Dark-souled incendiary, madman forlorn, / He dares put humanity above / Discretion. Better never have been born / Than thus to have offended! Learn, good brother, / That Love and Pity are forgotten fables / Told by the drowsy years to one another / With nothing in them to supply our tables. / These are the days of hungry common sense / Millions of men have died to bring these days; / And more must die ere these good days go hence; / For God moves still in most mysterious ways. / And Debs, Debs, Debs, you are out-weighed, out-priced, / These are the days of Caesar, not of Christ – / And yet – suppose – when all was done and said / There *were* a Resurrection from the Dead! /

John Cowper Powys, *To Eugene Debs*

## DEE, JOHN

1527–1608 Mathematician, Astrologer

He used to distill Egge-shells, and 'twas from hence that Ben Johnson had his hint of the *Alkimist*, whom he meant.

John Aubrey, *Brief Lives*

## DEFOE, DANIEL

1661?–1731 Author, Polemicist

As in the case of Goethe, one hesitates to write down that in ninety per cent of his writings outside *Moll Flanders* Defoe is an insufferable bore. Nothing is more dreary than the continual repetition of his accounts of piratical adventures and sneak-thieving in the lives of dull villains . . . With the one exception of his Moll all Defoe's characters are completely invisible and utterly, not so much dead, as unalive in the sense that tailors' dummies are unalive.

Ford Madox Ford, *The March of Literature*

Daniel Defoe, who spent his whole life, and wasted his strength in asserting the right of Dissenters to a toleration (and got no thanks for it but the pillory), was scandalized at the proposal of the general principle, and was equally strenuous in excluding Quakers, Anabaptists, Socinians, Sceptics, and all who did not agree in the *essentials* of Christianity, that is, who did not agree with him, from the benefit of such an indulgence to tender consciences.

William Hazlitt, *Fugitive Writings: On Party Spirit*

The narrative manner of De Foe has a naturalness about it beyond that of any other novel or romance writer. His fictions have all the air of true stories. It is impossible to believe, while you are reading them, that a real person is not narrating to you every where nothing but what really happened to himself. To this, the extreme *homeliness* of their style mainly contributes. We use the word in its best and heartiest sense – that which comes *home* to the reader.

Charles Lamb, *On the Secondary Novels of De Foe*

Few will acknowledge all they owe / To persecuted, brave Defoe. / Achilles, in Homeric song, / May, or he may not, live so long / As Crusoe; few their strength had tried / Without so staunch and safe a guide. / What boy is there who never laid / Under his pillow, half-afraid, / That precious volume, lest the morrow / For unlearnt lesson might bring sorrow? / But nobler lessons he has taught / Wide-awake scholars who fear'd naught: / A Rodney and a Nelson may / Without him not have won the day. /

Walter Savage Landor, *Daniel Defoe*

Earless on high, stood unabash'd De Foe.

Alexander Pope, *The Dunciad*, book 2

That glorious old Non-con, De Foe, sharing with Bunyan the literary honours of the sect, and acknowledging no other chief than Milton.

Henry Crabb Robinson, Letter to Thomas Robinson, 6 May 1848

His great forte is his power of Vraisemblance.

Sir Walter Scott, *Journal*, 8 May 1827

So grave, sententious, dogmatical a Rogue, that there is no enduring him.

Jonathan Swift, *A Letter Concerning the Sacramental Test*

He belongs, indeed, to the school of the great plain writers, whose work is founded upon a knowledge of what is most persistent, though not most seductive, in human nature . . . He is of the school of Crabbe and of Gissing, and not merely a fellow-pupil in the same stern place of learning, but its founder and master.

Virginia Woolf, *The Common Reader*

*See also* Robert Louis Stevenson

## DEKKER, THOMAS

1570?–1641? Dramatist

He clubbed with *Webster* in writing three Plays; and with *Rowley* and *Ford* in another; and I think I may venture to say, that these plays as far exceed those of his own Brain, as a platted Whip-cord exceeds a single Thread in Strength.

Gerard Langbaine, *Account of the English Dramatic Poets*

## DE LA MARE, WALTER JOHN

1873–1956 Poet

One might say that, in every poet, there dwells an Ariel, who sings, and a Prospero, who comprehends . . . Though the role of Prospero in de la Mare's poetry is much greater than one may realize on a first reading, it would not be unfair, I think, to call him an Ariel-dominated poet . . . His most obvious virtues, those which no reader can fail to see immediately, are verbal and formal, the delicacy of his metrical fingering and the graceful architecture of his stanzas.

W. H. Auden, *Forewords and Afterwords*

Walter de la Mare owes much to Christina [Rossetti], and, if there is any labelling to be done, I would put you and de la Mare, that questioning poet, in the same compartment & mark it 'Subtlety and Sensitivity. Perishable. With Care.'

Dylan Thomas, Letter to Pamela Hansford Johnson, 1933

## DE LEON, DANIEL

1852–1914 Socialist

De Leon would have been politically sound if he had not been economically hollow.

William D. Haywood, *Bill Haywood's Book*

## DELIUS, FREDERICK

1862–1934 Composer

The ugliness of some of his music is really masterly.

Anon., in *Sun*, Criticism of Delius's concert on 30 May 1899

His features had that mingled cast of asceticism and shrewdness one mentally associates with high-ranking ecclesiastics. I was also struck by a general air of fastidiousness and sober elegance rarely to be observed in artists of any kind. Unexpectedly contrasting, but not unpleasing, was his style of speech, of which the underlying basis was recognizably provincial. Not for him was the blameless diction so laboriously inculcated and standardized in our leading public schools and ancient universities. He loyally preserved his preference for the Doric dialect of that great northern county of broad acres, which looks down and with compassion upon the miminy-piminy refinements of the softer south. Upon this had been grafted a polyglot mish-mash, acquired during his twenty-four years self-imposed exile from England. Both French and German words interlarded his sentences, and he always spoke of the 'orchester'.

Sir Thomas Beecham, *Frederick Delius*

Delius contrived whenever possible to spend his holidays in Norway . . . Such was his tireless energy that before he took a cottage overlooking the hills he usually walked and climbed above; occasionally Jelka went with him and once the 'then' Mr Beecham also, whom he never forgave for forgetting the sandwiches the day they lunched on a glacier.

Eric Fenby, *Delius*

One feels that all Delius' music is evolved out of the emotions of a past that was never fully realized when it was present, emotions which only became real after they had ceased to be experienced.

Philip Heseltine, *Delius*

Harmony with Delius has always been more of an instinct than an accomplishment.

*Ibid.*

His greatest admirer could hardly describe Delius as a master of form, and even Mr Cecil Gray, in the course of a highly laudatory essay, has admitted that many passages in Delius's music would retain the major element of their charm if all trace of melodic line were removed.

Constant Lambert, *Music Ho!*

It is dangerous to hear Delius's music too often, for its sensuous autumnal beauty induces a profound nostalgia, a passionate and fruitless desire to stop the clocks, to recapture the past. I was once told of a man who on hearing Delius's more sensuous music was seized by an almost uncontrollable urge to remove all his clothing and engage in Pan-like diversions quite unsuited to his profession – which was that of a solicitor's clerk. He was, fortunately, sufficiently controlled to limit his response to the urge to the privacy of his chamber.

Alec Robertson, *More Than Music*

A provincial Debussy.

A. J. P. Taylor, *English History 1914–1945*

## DELMONICO, LORENZO

1813–81 Restaurateur

As Delmonico goes, so goes the dining.

Anon., in Lately Thomas, *Delmonico's*

Men might break or disappear or die – but . . . his cisterns were always open to every falling drop of prosperity.

Sam Ward, *Lyrical Recreations*

## DE MILLE, CECIL BLOUNT

1881–1959 Motion Picture Director

Never have I seen a man with so preeminent a position splash so fondly about in mediocrity, and, like a child building a sand castle, so serenely convinced that he was producing works of art . . . Inspirationally and imaginatively, CB was sterile. His stories, situations, and characters were, almost without exception, unintelligent, unintuitive, and psychologically adolescent. CB was the foreman in a movie factory; he fitted the parts together and demanded that they move as he thought they should. It was an early form of automation.

Norman bel Geddes, *Miracles in the Evening*

Cecil B. de Mille, / Rather against his will, / Was persuaded to leave Moses / Out of 'The Wars of the Roses'. /

Nicolas Bentley, *Clerihew*

A sturdily built, sun-bronzed man came toward me with his hand extended in greeting and although I had never met DeMille, nor seen a picture of him, I knew that this must be he. The pongee sports shirt, well-tailored riding breeches, leather puttees and Napoleonic stride seemed to proclaim the fact that here was the director to end all directors. 'My God', I thought. 'It's an American Benito Mussolini'.

Charles Bickford, *Bulls, Balls, Bicycles and Actors*

Cecil de Mille moved in legends. The first, and one that he struggled very hard to promote, was that he was the world's greatest moving-picture director. He was certainly the best known, more widely hailed than even Griffith or Eisenstein! I heard his name in Russia, years after his death. Albert Speer uses it again and again in his autobiography as a synonym for grandiose, overblown opulence.

Agnes de Mille, *Speak To Me, Dance With Me*

The first motion picture which I remember seeing was *The Sign of the Cross*. Another early film which made an impact on me was Cecil B. DeMille's *King of Kings*. This probably taught me more about the life of Christ than did a great deal of the Sunday school training I had as a boy.

Billy Graham, in *Show*, April 1963

Cecil DeMille's evangelical films are the nearest equivalent today to the glossy German colour prints which sometimes decorated mid-Victorian Bibles. There is the same complete lack of period sense, the same stuffy horse-hair atmosphere of beards and whiskers, and, their best quality, a childlike eye for details which enabled one to spend so many happy minutes spying a new lamb among the rocks, an unobtrusive dove or a mislaid shepherd.

Graham Greene, reviewing *The Crusades* in *Spectator*, 30 August 1935

I had great admiration for him, but I never saw anything that I thought was good. If I tried to tell people to do some of the things he did, I would burst into laughter. Yet he made it work. I learned an awful lot from him by doing exactly the opposite. I once asked Gary Cooper how on earth he could read those goddam lines. 'Well,' he said, 'when DeMille finishes talking to you, they don't seem so bad. But when you see the picture, then you kind of hang your head.'

Howard Hawks, in Kevin Brownlow, *The Parade's Gone By*

Like most great film makers, he began as an artist, and was gradually overwhelmed by the need to prove himself as a businessman.

Charles Higham, *Cecil B. De Mille*

Unabashed by criticism from the erudite, DeMille interlaced fact and fancy into what he publicized as 'historical drama.' Short on fact but long on fancy, his artificially inseminated pictures appealed to the uncritical, who came away from the theatres wagging their heads with satisfaction: they had enjoyed themselves and had had a refresher course in history.

Frances Marion, *Off With Their Heads*

When I saw one of his pictures, I wanted to quit the business.

King Vidor, in Kevin Brownlow, *The Parade's Gone By*

## DEMUTH, CHARLES

1883–1935 Artist

John Marin and I drew our inspiration from the same source, French modernism. He brought his up in buckets and spilt much along the way. I dipped mine out with a teaspoon, but I never spilled a drop.

On himself, in Andrew Carnduff Ritchie, *Charles Demuth*

'What would you most like to do, to know, to be? (In case you are not satisfied.)' Demuth: 'Lay bricks. What it's all about. A brick layer.' 'What do you look forward to?' Demuth: 'The past.'

On himself, 1929, in David Gebhard, *Charles Demuth*

## DENHAM, SIR JOHN

1615–69 Poet

I went to London to visit my Lord of Bristol, having been with Sir John Denham (his Majesty's surveyor) to consult with him about the placing of his palace at Greenwich, which I would have had built between the river and the Queen's house, so as a large square cut should have let in the Thames like a bay, but Sir John was for setting it on piles at the very brink of the water, which I did not assent to, and so came away, knowing Sir John to be a better poet than architect.

John Evelyn, Diary, 19 October 1661

He appears to have had, in common with almost all mankind, the ambition of being upon proper occasions *a merry fellow*, and, in common with most of them, to have been by nature, or by early habits, debarred from it. Nothing is less exhilarating than the ludicrousness of Denham: he does not fail for want of efforts; he is familiar, he is gross, but he is never merry.

Samuel Johnson, *Lives of the Poets*

## DEPEW, CHAUNCEY MITCHELL

1834–1928 Lawyer, Politician

On the 23rd of April Shakespeare, St George and myself were born, and I am the only survivor.

On himself, in John W. Leonard ed., *Best Things By Chauncey M. Depew*

I am reminded of Chauncey Depew, who said to the equally obese William Howard Taft at a dinner before the latter became President, 'I hope, if it is a girl, Mr Taft will name it for his charming wife.' To which Taft responded 'If it is a girl, I shall, of course name it for my lovely helpmate of many years. And if it is a boy, I shall claim the father's prerogative and name it Junior. But, if as I suspect it is only a bag of wind, I shall name it Chauncey Depew.'

Senator Robert Kerr, in Leon A. Harris, *The Fine Art of Political Wit*

## DE QUINCEY, THOMAS

1785–1859 Author

I was necessarily ignorant of the whole art and mystery of opium-taking: and what I took, I took under every disadvantage. But I took it: – and in an hour, oh! heavens! what a revelation! what an upheaving, from its lowest depths, of the inner spirit! what an apocalypse of the world within me! That my pains had vanished, was now a trifle in my eyes: this negative effect was swallowed up in the immensity of those positive effects which had opened before me – in the abyss of divine enjoyment thus suddenly revealed.

On himself, *Confessions of an English Opium-Eater*

He walked with considerable rapidity . . . and with an odd one-sided, and yet straightforward motion, moving his legs only, and neither his arms, head, nor any other part of his body . . . His hat, which had the antediluvian aspect characteristic of the rest of his clothes, was generally stuck on the back of his head, and no one who ever met that antiquated figure, with that strangely dreamy and intellectual face, making its way rapidly, and with an oddly deferential air, through any of the streets of Edinburgh . . . could ever forget it.

J. R. Findley, *Personal Recollections of Thomas De Quincey*

He is a remarkable and very interesting young man; very diminutive in person, which, to strangers, makes him appear insignificant, and so modest, and so very shy that even now I wonder how he ever had the courage to address himself to my Brother by letter. I think of this young man with extraordinary pleasure, as he is a remarkable instance of the power of my Brother's poems, over a lonely and contemplative mind, unwarped by any established laws of taste . . . a pure and innocent mind!

Dorothy Wordsworth, Letter to Lady Beaumont, 6 December 1807

## DERBY, FOURTEENTH EARL OF (EDWARD GEORGE GEOFFREY SMITH STANLEY)

1799–1869 Prime Minister

No generosity, never, to friend or foe; never acknowledged help, a great aristocrat, proud of family and wealth. He only agreed to [the Reform Bill] as he would of old have backed a horse at Newmarket, hated Disraeli, only believed in him as he would have done in an unprincipled trainer. He wins, that is all. He knows the garlic given, etc. He says to those without: 'All fair, gentlemen?'

Lord Clarendon, 1867, in G. W. E. Russell, *Sixty Years of Empire*

It is a strange thing to see Stanley [at Knowsley]; he is certainly the most natural character I ever saw; never seems to think of throwing a veil over any part of himself: it is the straightforward energy which is the cause of this, that makes him so comfortable as he is. In London he is one of the great political Leaders, and the second orator in the House of Commons, and here he is a lively rattling Sportsman, apparently devoted to racing and rabbit-shooting, gay, boisterous, almost clownish in his manners, without a particle of refinement, and if one did not know what his powers are and what his position is, it would be next to impossible to believe that the Stanley of Knowsley could be the Stanley of the House of Commons.

Charles Greville, Diary, 18 July 1837

One after one the Lords of Time advance; / Here Stanley meets – how Stanley scorns! – the glance; / The brilliant chief, irregularly great, / Frank, haughty, rash, the Rupert of Debate; / Nor gout nor toil his freshness can destroy, / And time still leaves all Eton in the boy. / First in the class, and keenest in the ring, / He saps like Gladstone, and he fights like spring! / Yet who not listens, with delighted smile, / To the pure Saxon of that silver style? / In the clear style a heart as clear is seen, / Prompt to the rash, revolting to the mean. /

Lord Lytton, in G. W. E. Russell, *The Queen's Prime Ministers*

To threaten and not to act upon it was too often tried formerly, and was also a maxim of Lord Derby, who was the most difficult and unsatisfactory minister she or indeed anyone had to deal with.

Queen Victoria, Letter to Lord Granville, 30 August 1880

## DERBY, SEVENTEENTH EARL OF (EDWARD STANLEY)

1865–1948 Politician

D. is a very weak-minded fellow I am afraid, and, like the feather pillow, bears the marks of the last person who has sat on him! I hear he is called in London 'genial Judas'!

Douglas Haig, Diary, January 1914

## DEWEY, GEORGE

1837–1917 Sailor

Oh dewy was the morning / Upon the first of May, / And Dewey was the admiral / Down in Manila Bay. / And dewy were the Regent's eyes, / The orbs of royal blue, / And dew we feel discouraged; / I dew not think we dew. /

Eugene Ware, in Topeka *Capital*, 10 May 1898

## DEWEY, JOHN

1859–1952 Philosopher, Pedagogue

In the bedlam of tragedy, melodrama and light opera in which we live, Dewey is still the master of the commonplace.

C. E. Ayres, 'Dewey and His "Studies in Logical Theory"', in Malcolm Cowley and Bernard Smith eds, *Books That Changed Our Minds*

Not only is his own style dull, but his dullness infects everybody who has anything to write about his theories of education.

Max Eastman, *Heroes I Have Known*

## DEWEY, THOMAS EDMUND

1902–71 Lawyer, Politician

. . . snatched defeat from the jaws of victory.

Anon., in R. D. Challener and John Fenton, 'Which Way America? Dulles Always Knew', in *American Heritage*, June 1971

He is just about the nastiest little man I've ever known. He struts sitting down.

Mrs Dykstra, 8 July 1952, in James T. Patterson, *Mr Republican, a biography of Robert A. Taft*

Dewey, cool, cold, low-voiced, was like a softly growling bull terrier willing to take on all comers if he could get in one good bite.

Edwin C. Hill, on Dewey's courtroom manner, in Rupert Hughes, *Thomas E. Dewey, Attorney for the People*

Dewey has thrown his diaper in the ring.

Harold Ickes, in Leon A. Harris, *The Fine Art of Political Wit*

You can't make soufflé rise twice.

Attributed to Alice Roosevelt Longworth, on the 1948 nomination, in James T. Patterson, *Mr Republican, a biography of Robert A. Taft*

You really have to get to know Dewey to dislike him.

James T. Patterson, *Mr Republican, a biography of Robert A. Taft*

Clad each day in a pair of platitudes.

Norman Thomas, in Murray B. Seidler, *Norman Thomas, Respectable Rebel*

Dewey is a ruthless man who considers shooting at sunrise as a cure for inefficiency . . . when a few men get control of the economy of a nation, they find a front man to run the country for them.

Harry S. Truman, in Victor Lasky, *J.F.K. The Man and the Myth*

## DICKENS, CHARLES

1812–70 Novelist

Nothing can be more indefinite than his religion, nor more human. He loves his neighbour for his neighbour's sake, and knows nothing of sin, when it is not crime. Of course this shuts out half of psychology from his sight, and partly explains that he has so few characters and so many caricatures. His humour . . . is only the second cause of his caricaturing and has found its grave in it.

Lord Acton, Letter to Richard Simpson, December 1861

My own experience in reading Dickens, and I doubt whether it is an uncommon one, is to be bounced between violent admiration and violent distaste almost every couple of paragraphs, and this is too uncomfortable a condition to be much alleviated by an inward recital of one's duty not to be fastidious, to gulp down the stuff in gobbets like a man.

Kingsley Amis, *What Became of Jane Austen?*

Dickens's achievement was to create serious literary art out of pop material . . . He also worked in a climate of Christian evangelism that allowed big unqualified moral gestures. Language and morality add dimensions to his cartoons and turn them into literature. We lack enthusiasm and are embarrassed by moral fervour and grandiloquence alike. That is why our attitude to Dickens is ambivalent – nostalgia mixed with distaste, *nausée* in the presence of the spreading chestnut tree.

Anthony Burgess, *Urgent Copy*

At twenty-three Charles Dickens had already made a name for himself as a transcriber of the words of others, being probably the fastest and most accurate reporter ever to take down the inanities of the House of Commons. Politicians have their uses: their dullness may have driven Dickens to original composition.

Clifton Fadiman, *The Selected Writings of Clifton Fadiman: Pickwick & Dickens*

Dickens' people are nearly all flat . . . Nearly every one can be summed up in a sentence, and yet there is this wonderful feeling of human depth . . It is a conjuring trick; at any moment we may look at Mr Pickwick edgeways and find him no thicker than a gramophone record. But we never get the sideways view . . . Those who dislike Dickens have an excellent case. He ought to be bad. He is actually one of our big writers, and his immense success with types suggests that there may be more in flatness than the severer critics admit.

E. M. Forster, *Aspects of the Novel*

And on that grave where English oak and holly / And laurel wreaths entwine, / Deem it not all a too presumptuous folly – / This spray of Western pine! /

Bret Harte, *Dickens in Camp*

One of Dickens's most striking peculiarities is that, whenever in his writing he becomes emotional, he ceases instantly to use his intelligence. The overflowing of his heart drowns his head and even dims his eyes; for, whenever he is in the melting mood, Dickens ceases to be able and probably ceases even to wish to see reality. His one and only desire on these occasions is just to overflow, nothing else. Which he does, with a vengeance and in an atrocious blank verse that is meant to be poetical prose and succeeds only in being the worst kind of fustian.

Aldous Huxley, *Vulgarity in Literature*

An old lady told me once that she had lunched with the Dickens family when she was a child (you must imagine a table full of children) and that Dickens had sat down without a word, leaning his head on his hand in an attitude of profound despondency. One of the Dickens children whispered to her, in commiseration, and explanation, 'Poor Papa is in love again!'

Desmond MacCarthy, *Criticism*

Called on Dickens . . . Asked Dickens to spare the life of Nell in his story, and observed that he was cruel. He blushed.

W. C. Macready, Diary, 21 January 1841

He violated every rule of art / Except the feeling mind and thinking heart. /

John Macy, *Couplets in Criticism*

It may be that it is because this high seriousness is lacking in Dickens's novels that, for all their great merits, they leave us faintly dissatisfied. When we read them now with great French and Russian novels in mind, and not only theirs, but George Eliot's, we are taken aback by their naïveté. In comparison with them, Dickens's are scarcely adult.

W. Somerset Maugham, *Ten Novels and Their Authors*

No one thinks first of Mr Dickens as a writer. He is at once, through his books, a friend. He belongs among the intimates of every pleasant-tempered and large-hearted person. He is not so much the guest as the inmate of our homes. He keeps holidays with us, he helps us to celebrate Christmas with heartier cheer, he shares at every New Year in our good wishes: for, indeed, it is not in his purely literary character that he has done most for us, it is as a man of the largest humanity, who has simply used literature as the means by which to bring himself into relation with his fellow-men.

Charles Eliot Norton, in *North American Review*, April 1868

In its attitude towards Dickens the English public has always been a little like the elephant which feels a blow with a walking-stick as a delightful tickling... Dickens seems to have succeeded in attacking everybody and antagonising nobody.

George Orwell, *Charles Dickens*

Dickens was not the first or the last novelist to find virtue more difficult to portray than the wish for it.

V. S. Pritchett, *Books in General*

The literary loss is infinite – the political one I care less for than you do. Dickens was a pure modernist – a leader of the steam-and-whistle party *par excellence* – and he had no understanding of any power of antiquity except a sort of jackdaw sentiment for cathedral towers. He knew nothing of nobler power of superstition – was essentially a stage manager, and used everything for effect on the pit. His Christmas meant mistletoe and pudding – neither resurrection from dead, nor rising of new stars, nor teaching of wise men, nor shepherds. His hero is essentially the ironmaster.

John Ruskin (on Dickens's death), Letter to Charles Eliot Norton, 19 June 1870

A list of the killed, wounded and missing amongst Mr Dickens's novels would read like an *Extraordinary Gazette*. An interesting child runs as much risk there as any of the troops who stormed the Redan.

James Fitzjames Stephen, *Cambridge Essays*

He was successful beyond any English novelist, probably beyond any novelist that has ever lived, in exactly hitting off the precise tone of thought and feeling that would find favour with the grocers. As Burke said of George Grenville and the House of Commons, Dickens hit the average Englishman of the middle-classes between wind and water.

Leslie Stephen, *The Writings of W. M. Thackeray*

All children ought to love him. I know two that do, and read his books ten times for once that they peruse the dismal preachments of their father. I know one who when she is happy reads *Nicholas Nickleby*; when she is unhappy reads *Nicholas Nickleby*; when she is tired reads *Nicholas Nickleby*; when she is in bed reads *Nicholas Nickleby*; when she has nothing to do reads *Nicholas Nickleby*, and when she has finished the book reads *Nicholas Nickleby* over again. This candid young critic, at ten years of age, said, 'I like Mr Dickens's books much better than your books, Papa;' and frequently expressed her desire that the latter author should write a book like one of Mr Dickens's books. Who can?

W. M. Thackeray, *Charity and Humour* (lecture)

Of all such reformers Mr Sentiment is the most powerful. It is incredible the number of evil practices he has put down: it is to be feared he will soon lack subjects, and that when he has made the working classes comfortable, and got bitter beer put into proper-sized pint bottles, there will be nothing further for him left to do. Mr Sentiment is certainly a very powerful man, and perhaps not the less so that his good poor people are so very good; his hard rich people so very hard; and the genuinely honest so very honest. Namby-pamby in these days is not thrown away if it be introduced in the proper quarters. Divine peeresses are no longer interesting, though possessed of every virtue, but a pattern peasant or an immaculate manufacturing hero may talk as much twaddle as one of Mrs Radcliffe's heroines, and still be listened to.

Anthony Trollope, *The Warden*

We warn Wellington and Peel, we warn Toryism in general, against this young writer. If they had at their disposal the Bastilles and *lettres-de-cachet* of another day, we would advise their prompt application, as soon as he shall set foot in England again ... There is nothing in any of the books he has yet produced of a manifest political character, or of any probable political design. Yet there is that in them all which is calculated to hasten on the great crisis of the English Revolution (speed the hour!) far more effectively than any of the open assaults of Radicalism or Chartism.

*United States Magazine and Democratic Review*, April 1842

He is a very great loss. He had a large loving mind and the strongest sympathy with the poorer classes. He felt sure a better feeling, and much greater union of classes, would take place in time. And I pray earnestly it may.

Queen Victoria, Diary, 11 June 1870

*See also* Rudyard Kipling, D. H. Lawrence, W. Somerset Maugham, Tobias Smollett, H. G. Wells

## DICKINSON, EMILY ELIZABETH

1830–86 Poet

I find ecstasy in living – the mere sense of living is joy enough.

On herself, referring to her seclusion, in Theodora Ward, *The Capsule of the Mind*

I had no portrait, now, but am small, like the Wren, and my Hair is bold, like the chestnut Bur, and my eyes, like the Sherry in the Glass, that the guest leaves.

On herself, Undated letter to Thomas Wentworth Higginson

I had no monarch in my life, and cannot rule myself; and when I try to organize, my little force explodes and leaves me bare and charred.

On herself, Undated letter to Thomas Wentworth Higginson

... an eccentric, dreamy, half-educated recluse in an out-of-the-way New England village (or anywhere else) cannot with impunity set at defiance the laws of gravitation and grammar.

Thomas Bailey Aldrich, 'Re Emily Dickinson', in Caesar R. Blake and Carlton F. Wells eds, *The Recognition of Emily Dickinson*

Emily Dickinson is the perfect flowering of a rare but recognizable variety of the New England Gentlewoman of the past – the lily-of-the-valley variety, virginal, sequestered, to the passing eye most delicate and demure, but ringing all the while spicy bells of derision and delight.

Katherine Bates, in Klaus Lubbers, *Emily Dickinson*

In a life so retired it was inevitable that the main events should be the death of friends, and Emily Dickinson became a prolific writer of notes of condolence.

Northrop Frye, 'Emily Dickinson', in Perry Miller ed., *Major Writers of America*, vol. 2

To this determined little anchoress, so carefully shut up in her provincial cell, nothing was sacred and nothing daunting; she made as free with heaven and hell, life and death, as with the daisies and butterflies outside her window.

Percy Lubbock, 'Determined Little Anchoress', in Caesar R. Blake and Carlton F. Wells eds, *The Recognition of Emily Dickinson*

and in your halfcracked way you chose / silence for entertainment, / chose to have it out at last / on your own premises. /

Adrienne Rich, in Albert J. Gelpi, *Emily Dickinson*

She was inattentive to superficial polish, but at a time when poetry was like furniture put together with putty, gilded, and heavily upholstered, she preserved in her writing the same instinct of sound workmanship that made the Yankee Clipper, the Connecticut clock, and the New England doorway objects of beauty.

George F. Whicher, 'A Centennial Appraisal' in Caesar R. Blake and Carlton F. Wells eds, *The Recognition of Emily Dickinson*

## DILLINGER, JOHN

1902–34 Gangster

A jail is just like a nut with a worm in it. The worm can always get out.

On himself, in Robert Cromie, *Dillinger, A Short and Violent Life*

Stranger, stop and wish me well, / Just say a prayer for my soul in Hell. / I was a good fellow, most people said, / Betrayed by a woman all dressed in red. /

Anon., chalked on an alley wall outside the Biograph Theater just after Dillinger was shot dead, in *ibid:*

Johnnie's just an ordinary fellow. Of course he goes out and holds up banks and things, but he's really just like any other fellow, aside from that.

Mary Kinder (a mistress of Dillinger's), in *ibid.*

He liked people and people liked him – until he was crossed, and then he became dangerous. He wanted what he wanted when he wanted it – and he wanted to come by it easily. He was not driven to crime by his environment or by his associations but sought it out and let it lead him.

Ralph de Toledano, *J. Edgar Hoover*

## DISNEY, WALTER E.

1901–66 Film Producer

I love Mickey Mouse more than any woman I've ever known.

On himself, in Walter Wagner, *You Must Remember This*

[His is] an imagination that can perceive all sorts of fantastic attitudes and action in things so common, so near to anyone's hand, that the sudden contrast of what they might be with what they certainly are not is universally droll, and not to be resisted. Add an uncanny eye for characteristic detail. Add a limitless invention, a happy choice of what seems the best medium for Mr Disney's peculiar talents, its perfection and the combination of it with sound. But his gifts, like a speaker I heard of once, need no introduction, having already endeared themselves to children and associate professors. They are restricted gifts, I suppose; what is astonishing about the man is that he can make an endlessly amusing operetta out of some old razor blades, a needle and a thread, and perhaps a few soft-shell crabs.

Otis Ferguson, *The Film Criticism of Otis Ferguson*

Walt was a rugged individualist. He admired Henry Ford. He thought Ford was the cat's ass. Maybe Ford and

Walt were the last of the great ones, the last of great rugged individualists. Maybe that was why they were impatient with people of lesser talent and impatient with themselves, when they made mistakes.

Ward Kimball, in Walter Wagner, *You Must Remember This*

Walt's virtue is all they want to perpetuate. The great doer of good, the manufacturer of children's entertainment. Sure, he was that. But he said 'shit' and the rest of the words, and as I've said, he'd talk about turds for thirty minutes without pausing for breath.

At the bottom line Walt was a down-to-earth farmer's son who just happened to be a genius.

*Ibid.*

Disney's animal world was one in which violence, conflict, ruthless physical force and utter desperation were normal, accepted elements of experience. It was a world in which kind-heartedness was associated with brutality, in which contempt for the weak prevailed; in which conscience had become a kind of stupidity . . . This was a society in which aggression paid out, inhumanity was practical, and power, being right, was always admirable.

Lloyd Morris, *Not So Long Ago*

*See also* W. H. Auden

## DISRAELI, BENJAMIN, EARL OF BEACONSFIELD

1804–81 Prime Minister, Author

Though I sit down now, the time will come when you will hear me.

On himself, Maiden speech, 7 December 1837

This is the third time that, in the course of six years, during which I have had the lead of the Opposition in the House of Commons, I have stormed the Treasury Benches: twice, fruitlessly, the third time with a tin kettle to my tail which rendered the race hopeless. You cannot, therefore, be surprised, that I am a little wearied of these barren victories, which like Alma, Inkerman, and Balaclava, may be glorious but are certainly nothing more.

On himself, Letter to Lady Londonderry, 2 February 1854

I am myself a gentleman of the Press, and I bear no other scutcheon.

On himself, Speech in the House of Commons, 18 February 1863

My lord, I am on the side of the angels.

On himself, rejecting Darwinianism at the Oxford Diocesan Society, November 1864

Yes, I have climbed to the top of the greasy pole.

On himself, Reminiscence on his being elected Prime Minister

I am dead: dead, but in the Elysian fields.

On himself, on being welcomed to the House of Lords

You have accused me of being a flatterer. It is true. I am a flatterer. I have found it useful. Everyone likes flattery; and when you come to Royalty you should lay it on with a trowel.

On himself, *circa* 1880, in G. W. E. Russell, *Collections and Recollections*

I will not go down to posterity talking bad grammar.

On himself, correcting his last speech for *Hansard*, 31 March 1881

I had rather live but I am not afraid to die.

On himself, last authentically recorded words, April 1881

When I want to read a novel I write one.

On himself, attributed

He was quite remarkable enough to fill a volume of Éloge. Someone wrote to me yesterday that no Jew for 1800 years has played so great a part in the world. That would be no Jew since St Paul; and it is very startling.

Lord Acton, Letter to Mrs Drew, 24 April 1881

[By Bentinck's death] Disraeli was soon left absolutely alone, the only piece upon the board on that side of politics that was above the level of a pawn . . . He was like a subaltern in a great battle where every superior officer was killed or wounded.

Duke of Argyll, *Autobiography and Memoirs*

He is a self-made man, and worships his creator.

John Bright, in A. K. Adams, *The Home Book of Humorous Quotations*

. . . a man who is *never beaten*. Every reverse, every defeat is to him only an admonition to wait and catch his opportunity of retrieving his position.

William Ewart Gladstone, Letter to Malcolm MacColl, 11 August 1877

The downfall of Beaconsfieldism is like the vanishing of some vast magnificent castle in an Italian romance.

William Ewart Gladstone, writing of the Liberal victory of 1880

I think your being the Leader of the Tory party is the greatest triumph that Liberalism has ever achieved.

François Guizot, 1848, in Benjamin Disraeli, *Reminiscences*

The Great Panjandrum.

Alfred Munby, Diary, 16 July 1874

Here's to the man who rode the race, who took the time, who kept the time, and who did the trick.

Sir Mathew Ridley, toast to Disraeli at the Carlton Club, 13 April 1867

. . . the potent wizard himself, with his olive complexion and coal black eyes, and the mighty dome of his forehead (no Christian temple, be sure), is unlike any living creature one has met . . . The face is more like a mask than ever and the division between him and mere mortals more marked. I would as soon have thought of sitting down at table with Hamlet, or Lear, or the Wandering Jew . . . England is the Israel of his imagination, and he will be the Imperial Minister before he dies – if he gets the chance.

Sir John Skelton, *Table Talk of Shirley*

In whatever he has written he has affected something which has been intended to strike his readers as uncommon and therefore grand. Because he has been bright and a man of genius he has carried his object as regards the young. He has struck them with astonishment and aroused in their imagination ideas of a world more glorious, more rich, more witty, more enterprising than their own. But the glory has been the glory of pasteboard and the wealth has been the wealth of tinsel. The wit has been the wit of hairdressers, and the enterprise the enterprise of mountebanks.

Anthony Trollope, *An Autobiography*

The present man will do well, and will be particularly loyal and anxious to please me in every way. He is vy. peculiar, but vy. clever and sensible and vy. conciliatory.

Queen Victoria, Letter to the Crown Princess of Prussia, 29 February 1868

*See also* Earl of Derby, William Ewart Gladstone, Rudyard Kipling, Theodore Roosevelt

## DISRAELI, MRS MARY ANN

1792–1874

She is an excellent creature, but she never can remember which came first, the Greeks or the Romans.

Benjamin Disraeli, attributed

## DODGSON, CHARLES LUTWIDGE, *see under* CARROLL, LEWIS

## DODWELL, HENRY

1641–1711 Jacobite

He has set his heart on being a martyr, and I have set mine on disappointing him.

William III, attributed

## DONNE, JOHN

1573–1631 Poet, Dean of St Paul's

John Donne, Anne Donne, Un-done.

On himself, Letter to his Wife (announcing his dismissal from the service of Sir Thomas Egerton)

Reader! I am to let thee know, / Donne's Body only, lyes below: / For, could the grave his Soul comprize,/ Earth would be richer than the skies. /

Anon. epitaph, written on the wall above Donne's grave the day after his burial

He was the one English love poet who was not afraid to acknowledge that he was composed of body, soul, and mind; and who faithfully recorded all the pitched battles, alarms, treaties, sieges, and fanfares of that extraordinary triangular warfare.

Rupert Brooke, *John Donne*

With Donne, whose muse on dromedary trots, / Wreathe iron pokers into true-love knots; / Rhyme's sturdy cripple, fancy's maze and clue, / Wit's forge and fire-blast, meaning's press and screw. /

Samuel Taylor Coleridge, *On Donne's Poetry*

See lewdness and theology combined, – / A cynic and a sycophantic mind; / A fancy shared party per pale between / Death's heads and skeletons and Aretine! – / Not his peculiar defect or crime, / But the true current mintage of the time. / Such were the establish'd signs and tokens given / To mark a loyal churchman, sound and even, / Free from papistic and fanatic leaven. /

Samuel Taylor Coleridge, from the *Literary Remains*

To read Dryden, Pope, &c., you need only count syllables; but to read Donne you must measure *Time*, and discover the *Time* of each word by the sense of Passion.

Samuel Taylor Coleridge, *Notes, Theological, Political and Miscellaneous*

Few writers have shown a more extraordinary compass of powers than Donne; for he combined what no other man has ever done – the last sublimation of subtlety with the most impassioned majesty.

Thomas De Quincey, in *Blackwood's Magazine*, December 1828

Would not Donne's *Satires*, which abound with so much wit, appear more charming, if he had taken care of his words, and of his numbers? But he followed Horace so very close, that of necessity he must fall with him; and I may safely say it of this present age, that if we are not so great wits as Donne, yet certainly we are better poets.

John Dryden, *A Discourse Concerning the Origine and Progress of Satire*

Were he translated into numbers, and English, he would yet be wanting in the dignity of expression . . . He affects the metaphysics, not only in his satires, but in his amorous verses, where nature only should reign; and perplexes the minds of the fair sex with nice speculations of philosophy, when he should engage their hearts and entertain them with the softnesses of love.

*Ibid.*

About Donne there hangs the shadow of the impure motive; and impure motives lend their aid to a facile success. He is a little of the religious spell-binder, the Reverend Billy Sunday of his time, the flesh-creeper, the sorcerer of emotional orgy. We emphasize this aspect to the point of grotesque. Donne had a trained mind; but without belittling the intensity or the profundity of his experience, we can suggest that this experience was not perfectly controlled, and that he lacked spiritual discipline.

T. S. Eliot, *Lancelot Andrewes*

Donne, I suppose, was such another / Who found no substitute for sense, / To seize and clutch and penetrate; / Expert beyond experience, /

He knew the anguish of the marrow / The ague of the skeleton; / No contact possible to flesh / Allayed the fever of the bone. /

T. S. Eliot, *Whispers of Immortality*

Donne's vocabulary can be very pure and plain; it is close to the natural prose, which is *staccato* and monosyllabic, of love and anger.

Oliver Elton, *The English Muse*

Dr Donne's verses are like the peace of God; they pass all understanding.

King James I, Saying recorded by Archbishop Plume

That Done, for not keeping of accent, deserved hanging.

Ben Jonson, in *Conversations with William Drummond*

That Done himself, for not being understood, would perish.

*Ibid.*

Donne had no imagination, but as much wit, I think, as any writer can possibly have.

Alexander Pope, in Joseph Spence, *Anecdotes*

Verses have Feet given 'em, either to walk graceful and smooth, and sometimes with Majesty and State, like Virgil's, or to run light and easie, like Ovid's, not to stand stock-still, like Dr Donne's, or to hobble like indigested Prose.

Robert Wolseley, Preface to *Valentinian*

I notice that the more precise and learned the thought the greater the beauty, the passion; the intricacy and subtleties of his imagination are the length and depth of the furrow made by his passion. His pedantry and his obscenity – the rock and loam of his Eden – but make me the more certain that one who is but a man like us all has seen God.

W. B. Yeats, Letter to H. J. C. Grierson, 14 November 1912

*See also* William D'Avenant, T. S. Eliot, Hugh Latimer, Andrew Marvell

## DOS PASSOS, JOHN RODRIGO

1896–1970 Novelist, Historian

Sometimes in reading Dos Passos you feel that he is two novelists at war with each other. One of them is a late-Romantic, a tender individualist, an esthete traveling about the world in an ivory tower that is mounted on wheels and coupled to the last car of the Orient Express. The other is a hard-minded realist, a collectivist, a radical historian of the class struggle.

Malcolm Cowley ed., *After the Genteel Tradition*

The picture of the United States which he painted was no trivial or enchanting landscape in pastels of a sweet land of liberty and hope; it was a grim and lugubrious representation, Hogarthian in its cynically penetrating detail of the squalor and misery of a machine-dominated, monopoly-ridden civilization.

John H. Wrenn, *John Dos Passos*

## DOUGLAS, STEPHEN ARNOLD

1813–61 Politician

I could travel from Boston to Chicago by the light of my own effigies.

On himself, in 1854, commenting on the numbers of figures in effigy burned of Douglas across the country in response to his stance on slavery, in James Ford Rhodes, *History of the United States*

. . . between the negro and the crocodile, he took the side of the negro. But between the negro and the white man, he would go for the white man.

On himself, as reported by the *New York Tribune*, 6 December 1858

Douglas never can be president, Sir. No, Sir; Douglas never can be president, Sir. His legs are too short, Sir. His coat, like a cow's tail, hangs too near the ground, Sir.

Thomas Hart Benton, in William Nisbet Chambers, *Old Bullion Benton: Senator from the New West*

As thin as the homoeopathic soup that was made by boiling the shadow of a pigeon that had been starved to death.

Abraham Lincoln, on Douglas's powers of reasoning, in Keith W. Jennison, *The Humorous Mr Lincoln*

He had improvised as States's Attorney and Judge when he knew little law and no jurisprudence. He had improvised as a young Congressman supporting Polk and the Mexican War. He had improvised policies and bills; above all the reckless measure, the worst Pandora's box in our history, for organizing Kansas Territory. As he improvised he battled implacably, for he loved nothing more than political combat. The great weakness of the born improviser is that he over simplifies the problem he faces and forgets that remote results were far more important than the immediate effect.

Allan Nevins, *The Emergence of Lincoln*, vol. 1

He appears to have been called *The Little Giant* more because he was little than because he was a giant.

Irving Stone, *They Also Ran*

. . . the squire of slavery, its very Sancho Panza – ready to do all its humiliating offices.

Charles Sumner, in Gerald M. Capers, *Stephen A. Douglas*

## DOUGLASS, FREDERICK

1817?–95 Abolitionist

Frederick Douglass used to tell me that when he was a Maryland slave, and a good Methodist, he would go into the farthest corner of the tobacco fields and pray to God to bring him liberty; but God never answered his prayers until he prayed with his heels.

Susan B. Anthony, in R. C. Dorr, *Susan B. Anthony*

The life of Frederick Douglass is the history of American slavery epitomized in a single human experience. He saw it all, lived it all, and overcame it all.

Booker T. Washington, *Frederick Douglass*

## DOWLAND, JOHN

1563?–1626? Musician, Composer

He was the *rarest Musician* that his *Age* did behold: Having travailed beyond the Seas, and compounded *English* with *Foreign Skill* in their *faculty* . . . A cheerful *Person* he was, passing his days in lawful merriment, truly answering the *anagram* made of him,

Johannes Doulandus
Annos Ludendo Hausi.
[I passed the years in playing.]

Thomas Fuller, *The History of the Worthies of England*

Here Philomel in silence sits alone, / In depth of winter, on the bared brier, / Whereas the rose had once her beautie shown, / Which lords and ladies did so much desire: / But fruitless now; in winter's frost and snow / It doth despis'd and unregarded grow. /

So since (old friend) thy yeares have made thee white, / And thou for others, hast consum'd thy spring, / How few regard thee, whome thou didst delight, / And farre, and neare came once to heare thee sing: / Ingratefull times, and worthles age of ours, / That lets us pine, when it hath cropt our flowers. /

Henry Peacham, *Minerva Britanna*

He seems to have suffered from too much artistic temperament.

A. L. Rowse, *The Elizabethan Renaissance*

## DOYLE, SIR ARTHUR CONAN

1859–1930 Author

My contention is that Sherlock Holmes *is* literature on a humble but not ignoble level, whereas the mystery writers most in vogue now are not. The old stories are literature, not because of the conjuring tricks and the puzzles, not because of the lively melodrama, which they have in common with many other detective stories, but by virtue of imagination and style. These are fairy-tales, as Conan Doyle intimated in his preface to his last collection, and they are among the most amusing of fairy-tales and not among the least distinguished.

Edmund Wilson, *Classics and Commercials*

Conan Doyle, a few words on the subject of. Don't you find as you age in the wood, as we are both doing, that the tragedy of life is that your early heroes lose their glamour? . . . Now, with Doyle I don't have this feeling. I still revere his work as much as ever. I used to think it swell, and I still think it swell.

P. G. Wodehouse, *Performing Flea*

## DRAKE, SIR FRANCIS

1540?–96 Circumnavigator, Admiral

As for the Expedition of Sir *Francis Drake* in the Year 1587, for the Destroying of the *Spanish* Shipping and Provision upon their own Coast, as I cannot say that there intervened in that Enterprise any sharp Fight or Encounter, so nevertheless it did straightly discover, either that *Spain* is very weak at Home, or very slow to move, when they suffered a small fleet of *English* to make an hostile Invasion or Incursion upon their Havens and Roads from *Cadiz* to Cape *Sacre*, and thence to *Cascous*, and to fire, sink, and carry away at the least ten thousand Ton of their greater Shipping, besides fifty or sixty of their smaller Vessels, and that in the sight and under the favour of their Forts, and almost under the Eye of their great Admiral, the best Commander of *Spain* by Sea, the Marquis de *Santa Cruce*, without ever being disputed with in any Fight of Importance: I remember *Drake*, in the vaunting Stile of a Soldier, would call the Enterprise the Singeing of the King of *Spain*'s Beard.

Francis Bacon, *Considerations Touching a War with Spain*

DRAKE he's in his hammock an' a thousand mile away / (Capten, art tha' sleepin' there below?) / Slung away between the round shot in Nombre Dios Bay / An' dreamin' arl the time o' Plymouth Hoe. /

Henry Newbolt, *Drake's Drum*

He was more skilful in all poyntes of Nauigation, then any that euer was before his time, in his time, or since his death, he was also of a perfect memory, great Observation, Eloquent by Nature, Skilfull in Artillery, Expert and apt to let blood, and giue Physicke unto his people according to the Climate, hee was low of stature, of strong limbs, broad breasted, round headed, browne hayre, full Bearded, his eyes round, large and cleare, well fauoured, fayre, and of a cheerefull countenance.

John Stow, *Annales*

## DREISER, THEODORE

1871–1945 Author

Dreiser was the first American to portray with truth and power our modern world of commerce and mechanization, the first to portray the dismal depersonalization of the individual which results from urbanization and intensifying societal pressure to conform, the first to draw us frankly and grimly as a nation of status-seekers.

Philip L. Gerber, *Theodore Dreiser*

He cannot die – though here's an end to strife – / Who hacked his way through literature to life. /

Kensal Green (Colin Hurry), *Premature Epitaphs*

. . . Dreiser more than any other man, marching alone, usually unappreciated, often hated, has cleared the trail from Victorian and Howellsian timidity and gentility in American fiction to honesty and boldness and passion of life. Without his pioneering, I doubt if any of us could, unless we liked to be sent to jail, seek to express life and beauty and terror.

Sinclair Lewis, in an address on receiving the Nobel Prize for Literature, in Erik Karlfeldt, *Why Sinclair Lewis Won the Nobel Prize*

I spent the better part of forty years trying to induce him to reform and electrify his manner of writing, but so far as I am aware with no more effect than if I had sought to persuade him to take up golf or abandon his belief in non-Euclidian arcana.

H. L. Mencken, in Philip L. Gerber, *Theodore Dreiser*

## DREW, JOHN

1853–1927 Actor

John Drew's acting was so perfectly effortless that it didn't seem to be acting. Some people used to say, without realizing what a tribute they were paying him, that he only played himself, that 'he didn't act but just behaved'.

Ethel Barrymore, *Memories*

Drew not only was a humorist of repute but became noted as an unfailing gentleman, meticulous of dress and elegant of conduct. He did not enjoy off-color stories or smutty remarks. When an acquaintance one day dealt him a salty tale at the bar, Drew said, 'I do not think you know me well enough to tell that kind of story.'

Gene Fowler, *Good Night Sweet Prince*

. . . the Beau Brummel of the American stage.

Margaret Case Harriman, *Blessed Are the Debonair*

The great public seldom complained about the monotony of Drew's roles. It was Drew that they came to see, and not the play in which he was appearing and the more he seemed to be acting himself the better they were pleased. Very early in Drew's starring career his supreme elegance furnished American women with a criterion which they applied to American men. As a result, by the turn of the century he had considerable influence on masculine deportment, attire and social attitude. The 'Drew reformation' made the male residents of Fifth Avenue and Newport seem almost as distinguished as their butlers, and from these exalted precincts a cult of well-bred worldliness spread over the country.

Lloyd Morris, *Curtain Time*

## DRYDEN, LADY ELIZABETH

*circa* 1638–1714 The poet's wife

Here lies my wife. / Here let her lie! / Now she's at rest / And so am I. /

John Dryden, [proposed] *Epitaph for his Wife*

*See also* John Dryden

## DRYDEN, JOHN

1631–1700 Poet

He the black Paths of Sin had travell'd o'er / And found out Vices all unknown before, / To sins once hid in shades of gloomy Night, / He gave new Lustre and reduc'd to Light. / His *Muse* was prostitute upon the Stage, / And's *Wife* was Prostitute to all the age. /

Anon., *The Tory-Poets, A Satyr*

Though they may write in verse, though they may in a certain sense be masters of the art of versification, Dryden and Pope are not classics of our poetry, they are classics of our prose.

Matthew Arnold, *Essays in Criticism*, Second Series

There *Dryden* sits with modest smile, / The master of the middle style. /

W. H. Auden, *New Year Letter*

If Dryden's plays had been as good as their prefaces he would have been a dramatist indeed.

Harley Granville Barker, *On Dramatic Method*

Even John Dryden penned none but mawky plays.

John Bee, *Works of Samuel Foote*

I told him that Voltaire, in a conversation with me, had distinguished Pope and Dryden thus:– 'Pope drives a handsome chariot with a couple of neat trim nags, Dryden a coach, and six stately horses!' JOHNSON: 'Why Sir, the truth is, they both drive coaches and six, but Dryden's horses are either galloping or stumbling; Pope's go at a steady, even trot.'

James Boswell, *Life of Johnson*

Dryden's genius was of that sort which catches fire by its own motion: his chariot-wheels got hot by driving fast.

Samuel Taylor Coleridge, *Table Talk*

Take his Verses, and divest them of their Rhimes, disjoint them in their Numbers, transpose their Expressions, make what Arrangement and Disposition you please of his Words, yet shall there Eternally be Poetry, and something which will be found incapable of being resolv'd into absolute Prose: An incontestable Characteristick of a truly Poetical Genius.

William Congreve, *Epistle Dedicatory to Dryden's Works*

He was certainly a mechanical maker of verses, and in every line he ever wrote, we see indubitable marks of the most indefatigable industry and labour . . . With the unwearied application of a plodding Flemish painter, who draws a shrimp with the most minute exactness, he had all the genius of one of the first masters. Never, I believe, were such talents and such drudgery united.

William Cowper, Letter to Unwin, 5 January 1782

The depreciation or neglect of Dryden is not due to the fact that his work is not poetry, but to a prejudice that the material, the feelings, out of which he built is not poetic. Thus Matthew Arnold observes, in mentioning Dryden and Pope together, that 'their poetry is conceived and composed in their wits, genuine poetry is conceived in the soul'. Arnold was, perhaps, not altogether the detached critic when he wrote this line; he may have been stirred to a defence of his own poetry, conceived and composed in the soul of a mid-century Oxford graduate.

T. S. Eliot, *Essays*: 'John Dryden'

Remember Dryden, & be blind to all his faults.

Thomas Gray, Letter to James Beattie, 2 October 1765

Dryden was a better prose-writer, and a bolder and more varied versifier than Pope. He was a more vigorous thinker, a more correct and logical declaimer, and had more of what may be called strength of mind than Pope, but he had not the same refinement and delicacy of feeling.

William Hazlitt, *Lectures on the English Poets*

He is the most masculine of our poets; his style and his rhythms lay the strongest stress of all our literature on the naked thew and sinew of the English language.

Gerard Manley Hopkins, Letter to Robert Bridges, 6 November 1887

The power that predominated in his intellectual operations was rather strong reason than quick sensibility. Upon all occasions that were presented, he studied rather than felt, and produced sentiments not such as nature enforces, but meditation supplied. With the simple and elemental passions, as they spring separate in the mind, he seems not much acquainted, and seldom describes them but as they are complicated by the various relations of society, and confused in the tumults and agitations of life.

Samuel Johnson, *Lives of the Poets*

The father of English criticism.

*Ibid.*

We feel that he never heartily and sincerely praised any human being, or felt any real enthusiasm for any subject he took up.

John Keble, *Lectures on Poetry*

His mind was of a slovenly character, – fond of splendor, but indifferent to neatness. Hence most of his writings exhibit the sluttish magnificence of a Russian noble, all vermin diamonds, dirty linen and inestimable sables.

T. B. Macaulay, 'John Dryden', in *Edinburgh Review*, January 1828

Ev'n copious Dryden, wanted, or forgot, / The last and greatest Art, the Art to blot. /

Alexander Pope, *Imitations of Horace*, epistle 2, i

I learned versification wholly from Dryden's works; who had improved it much beyond any of our former poets, and would, probably, have brought it to its perfection, had not he been unhappily obliged to write so often in haste.

Alexander Pope, in Joseph Spence, *Anecdotes*

He does not seem to have lived on very amicable terms with his wife, Lady Elizabeth, whom, if we may believe the lampoons of the time, he was compelled by one of her brothers to marry. Thinking herself neglected by the bard, and that he spent too much time in his study, she one day exclaimed, 'Lord, Mr Dryden, how can you be always poring over those musty books? I wish I were a book, and then I should have more of your company.' 'Pray, my dear,' replied old John, 'if you do become a book let it be an almanack, for then I shall change you every year.'

Sir James Prior, *Life of Edmond Malone*

It was King Charles the Second who gave Dryden the hint for writing his poem called 'The Medal'. One day, as the king was walking in the Mall, and talking with Dryden, he said, 'If I was a poet, and I think I am poor enough to be one, I would write a poem on such a subject, in the following manner:' and then gave him the plan for it. – Dryden took the hint, carried the poem as soon as it was finished to the king, and had a present of a hundred broad pieces for it.

Joseph Spence, *Anecdotes*

If Dryden failed to produce plays to match his talent, it is because he was working at a time when the very possibility of serious drama was in doubt. The Athenian and the Elizabethan past threw a lengthening shadow over the future of the dramatic imagination. Dryden was the first of numerous playwrights who found between themselves and the act of theatric invention a psychological barrier. The greatness of past achievement seemed insurmountable.

George Steiner, *The Death of Tragedy*

Read all the prefaces of Dryden, / For these our critics much confide in, / (Tho' merely writ at first for filling / To raise the volume's price, a shilling.) /

Jonathan Swift, *On Poetry*

*See also* John Donne, Henry Fielding, Samuel Johnson, Edmund Kean, Thomas Otway, Alexander Pope

## DULLES, JOHN FOSTER

1888–1959 Lawyer, Government Official

. . . who spent most of his time on aeroplanes and invented Brinkmanship, the most popular game since monopoly.

Richard Armour, *It All Started With Columbus*

I know you're right to this extent – people just don't like that personality of Foster's, while they do like me. The fact remains that he just knows more about foreign affairs than anybody I know. In fact, I'll be immodest and say that there's only one man I know who has seen *more* of the world and talked with more people and *knows* more than he does – and that's me. And I can't take his job and move over there.

Dwight Eisenhower, to Emmet John Hughes, 1960, in Hughes's *The Ordeal of Power: A Political Memoir of the Eisenhower Years*

Dulles was indisputably the conceptual fount, as well as the prime mover of United States foreign policy . . . He was the informing mind, indeed almost the sole keeper of the keys to the ramified web of understandings and relationships that constituted America's posture of categorical anti-Communism and limitless strategic concern.

Townsend Hoopes, *The Devil and John Foster Dulles*

Smooth is an inadequate word for Dulles. His prevarications are so highly polished as to be aesthetically pleasurable.

I. F. Stone, 24 January 1953, in *John Foster Dulles: Portrait of a Liberator*

Dulles is a man of wily and subtle mind. It is difficult to believe that behind his unctuous manner he does not take a cynical amusement in his own monstrous pomposities.

*Ibid.*

*See also* Adlai Stevenson

## DUNBAR, WILLIAM

1465?–1530 Poet

Dunbar writes so scathingly of women that, when he treats of them in a complimentary vein, doubts have been cast upon his authorship.

J. W. Baxter, *Dunbar*

His work lacks Chaucer's comic poise, its smiling abstention (or apparent abstention) from personal involvement. What is worse is that his personal involvement seems at times merely professional. He carries to excess medieval insouciance about inconsistency, so that in his work as a whole the only unity is that of literary zeal. His Muse turns to any subject with whorish readiness; the energy and enthusiasm, the verbal virtuosity, therefore, come at last to seem factitious.

Allan Rodway, *English Comedy*

## DUNCAN, ISADORA

1878–1927 Dancer

Wasn't it Nietzsche who said that he wouldn't believe in a God who could not dance? Neither could I.

On herself, in Lou Tellegen, *Women Have Been Kind*

My Art is just an effort to express the truth of my Being in gesture and movement. It has taken me long years to find even one absolutely true movement. Words have a different meaning. Before the public which has thronged my representations I have had no hesitation. I have given them the most secret impulses of my soul. From the first I have only danced my life. As a child I danced the spontaneous joy of growing things. As an adolescent, I danced with joy turning to apprehension of the first realisation of tragic undercurrents; apprehension of the pitiless brutality and crushing progress of life . . . Later on I danced my struggle with this same life, which the audience had called death, and my wrestling from it its ephemeral joys.

On herself, *My Life*

As she stepped into the machine that was to be her final enemy, Isadora's last spoken words were, by chance, 'Je vois la gloire!'

Janet Flanner, *Paris Was Yesterday*

A Paris *couturier* once said woman's modern freedom in dress is largely due to Isadora. She was the first artist to appear uncinctured, barefooted, and free. She arrived like a glorious bounding Minerva in the midst of a cautious corseted decade. The clergy, hearing of (though supposedly without ever seeing) her bare calf, denounced it as violently as if it had been golden. Despite its longings, for a moment America hesitated, Puritanism rather than poetry coupling lewd and nude in rhyme. But Isadora, originally from California but by then from Berlin, Paris and other points, arrived bearing her gifts as a Greek. She came like a figure from the Elgin marbles. The world over, and in America particularly, Greek sculpture was recognised to be almost notorious for its purity. The overpowering sentiment for Hellenic culture, even in the unschooled United States, silenced the outcries. Isadora had come as antique art and with such backing she became a cult.

*Ibid.*

All her life Isadora had been a practical idealist. She had put into practice certain ideals of art, maternity, and political liberty which people prefer to read as theories on paper. Her ideals of human liberty were not unsimilar to those of Plato, to those of Shelley, to those of Lord Byron, which led him to die dramatically in Greece. All they gained for Isadora were the loss of her passport and the presence of the constabulary on the stage of the Indianapolis Opera House, where the chief of police watched for sedition in the movement of Isadora's knees.

*Ibid.*

. . a woman whose face looked as if it had been made of sugar and someone had licked it.

George Bernard Shaw, in Hesketh Pearson, *Bernard Shaw, a Postscript*

## DUNDAS, HENRY, *see under* MELVILLE, LORD

## DUNSTAN, SAINT

924–88 Archbishop of Canterbury

St Dunstan, as the story goes, / Once pulled the devil by his nose, / With red hot tongs, which made him roar, / That could be heard ten miles or more. /

Nursery rhyme, traditional

*See also* Ethelred

## DUVEEN, JOSEPH, BARON

1869–1939 Art dealer

Early in life, Duveen . . . noticed that Europe had plenty of art and America had plenty of money, and his entire astonishing career was the product of that simple observation.

S. N. Behrman, *Duveen*

## DYER, GEORGE

1755–1841 Author

At length George Dyer's phrenesis has come to a crisis; he is raging and furiously mad. I waited upon the heathen, Thursday was a se'nnight; the first symptom which struck my eye and gave me incontrovertible proof of the fatal truth was a pair of nankeen pantaloons four times too big for him, which the said Heathen did pertinaciously affirm to be new. They were absolutely ingrained with the accumulated dirt of ages; but he affirmed them to be clean.

Charles Lamb, Letter to Thomas Manning, 27 December 1800

I found him busy as a moth over some rotten archive, rummaged out of some seldom-explored press, in a nook at Oriel. With long poring, he is grown almost into a book. He stood as passive as one by the side of the old shelves. I longed to new-coat him in russia, and assign him his place.

Charles Lamb, *Oxford in the Vacation*

# 'E'

## EAKINS, THOMAS

1844–1916 Artist

Tom Eakins was somewhat hipped on nudes.

Mrs Whiteman, in Gordon Hendricks, *The Life and Work of Thomas Eakins*

## EARP, WYATT BERRY STAPP

1848–1929 Lawman

Wyatt's reputation and attainment, such as they were, may have been acclaimed by the Dodge City gang, but elsewhere he was merely another of the flotsam of the frontier.

E. Bartholomew, *Wyatt Earp*

## EDDINGTON, SIR ARTHUR STANLEY

1882–1944 Astrophysicist

On one occasion when Smart found him engrossed with his fundamental theory, he asked Eddington how many people he thought would understand what he was writing – after a pause came the reply, 'Perhaps seven'.

A. V. Douglas, *The Life of Arthur Stanley Eddington*

## EDDY, MARY MORSE BAKER

1821–1910 Founder of the Church of Christ Scientist

What she has really 'discovered' are ways and means of perverting and prostituting the science of healing to her own ecclesiastical aggrandizement, and to the moral and physical depravity of her dupes.

Mrs Josephine Curtis Woodbury, 'Quimbyism, or the Paternity of Christian Science', in *Arena*, 1899

## EDGAR (EADGAR)

944–75

It is a sign of Edgar's competence as a ruler that his reign is singularly devoid of recorded incident.

F. M. Stenton, *Anglo-Saxon History*

## EDGEWORTH, MARIA

1767–1849 Novelist

I have made up my mind to like no Novels really, but Miss Edgeworth's, Yours & my own.

Jane Austen, Letter to her niece Anna Lefroy, 1814

She was a nice little unassuming 'Jeanie Deans-looking body' as we Scotch say – and, if not handsome, certainly not ill-looking. Her conversation was as quiet as herself. One would never have guessed she could write *her name*.

Lord Byron, *Letters and Journals*, 19 January 1821

That is the great clue to bourgeois psychology: the reward business. It is screamingly obvious in Maria Edgeworth's tales, which must have done unspeakable damage to ordinary people. Be good, and you'll have money. Be wicked, and you'll be penniless at last.

D. H. Lawrence, *Introduction to his Paintings*

## EDISON, THOMAS ALVA

1847–1931 Inventor

Since Edison suffered from insomnia, he invented the electric light, so that he could read at night. He had to sweat it out, and this led him to make his famous remark: 'Genius is about 2 per cent inspiration and 98 per cent perspiration.'

Richard Armour, *It All Started With Columbus*

One day while Mr Edison and I were calling on Luther Burbank in California, he asked us to register in his guest book. The book had a column for signature, another for home address, another for occupation and a final one entitled 'Interested in'. Mr Edison signed in a few quick but unhurried motions . . . In the final column he wrote without an instant's hesitation: 'Everything'.

Henry Ford, *My Friend Mr Edison*

Was it true, as legend had it, that Mr Edison, like Napoleon, slept but four hours? Yes, said Mr Ford, but Mr Edison slept twice and sometimes *three times* a day.

Gene Fowler, *Skyline*

He thwarted time and space . . . / . . . But what a bore / It is to hear / The Gramophone next door. /

Kensal Green (Colin Hurry), *Premature Epitaphs*

## EDWARD I

1239–1307

I should not be a better king, however splendidly I was dressed.

On himself, attributed

In a word: As the arm of King Edward I was accounted the measure of a yard, generally in England: so his actions are an excellent model and a praiseworthy platform for succeeding princes to imitate.

Thomas Fuller, *Church History of Britain*

Edward I preferred masterfulness to the arts of political management. In that sense he belonged less to the future than to the past.

K. B. McFarlane, *Edward I*

. . . Edward's posthumous career among scholars has not been as spectacular as that of the Conqueror, but it is not entirely unremarkable. During the last two centuries he has been turned from a strong ruler into a national king; from a national king into an aspiring tyrant; and now from an aspiring tyrant into a conventional, if competent, lord.

G. Templeman, *Edward I and the Historians*

## EDWARD II

1284–1327

No *Prince* ever ascended the *English Throne* with *greater*, or used it with *less* advantage to himself.

Thomas Fuller, *The History of the Worthies of England*

Edward somme tyme kyng was brought from Kenelworthe to the castell of Berkeley, where he was sleyne with a hoote broche putte thro the secrete place posterialle. Wherefore mony peple say that he diede a martir and did mony miracles; neverthelesse kepynge in prison, vilenes and obprobrious dethe cause not a martir, but if the holynesse of lyfe afore be correspondent . . . But women luffynge to goe in pilgremage encrease moche the rumour of suche veneracion, untille that a feble edifienge falle down.

Ranulf Higden, *Polychronicon* (from an old translation)

He is still, as Stubbs truly said, the first king after the Norman Conquest who was not a man of business. Tall, well-built, strong and handsome, he had no serious purpose in life, no better policy than to amuse himself and to save himself worry and trouble. He is one of the best mediaeval examples of the brutal and brainless athlete, established on a throne. He was not, I suspect, exceptionally vicious or depraved. He was just incompetent, idle, frivolous, and incurious. Most of his distractions, for which his nobles severely blamed him, seem to us harmless enough; but contemporary opinion saw something ignoble and unkingly in a monarch who forsook the society of the magnates, his natural associates, and lived with courtiers, favourites, officials on the make, and even men of meaner estate, grooms, watermen, actors, buffoons, ditchers and delvers and other craftsmen.

T. F. Tout, *The Captivity and Death of Edward of Carnarvon*

## EDWARD III

1312–77

In this season the king of Englande toke pleasure to newe reedefy the castell of Wyndsore, the whiche was begonne by kynge Arthure. And there first beganne the table rounde, whereby sprange the fame of so many noble knightes throughout all the worlde. Then Kyng Edwarde determyned to make an order and a brotherhood of a certayne nombre of knyghtes, and to be called knyghtes of the blewe garter: and a feest to be kept yerely at Wynsore on saynt Georges day.

Jean Froissart, *Chronicles*, translated from the French by John Bourchier, Lord Berners

## EDWARD IV

1442–83

This Monarch was famous only for his Beauty and his Courage, of which the Picture we have here given of him, and his undaunted Behaviour in marrying one Woman while engaged to another, are sufficient proofs.

Jane Austen, *The History of England*

He was of visage louelye, of bodye myghtye, stronge, and cleane made: howe bee it in his latter dayes, wyth ouer liberall dyet, sommewhat corpulente and boorelye, and nathelesse not vncomelye; he was of youthe greatlye geuen to fleshlye wantonnesse, from whiche healthe of bodye, in greate prosperitye and fortune, wythoute a specyall grace hardelye refraineth.

Sir Thomas More, *The Historie of Kyng Rycharde the Thirde*

## EDWARD V

1470–83

He is commonly called King Edward the fifth, though his head was ask'd, but never *married* to the English *Crown*; and therefore, in all the Pictures made of him, a distance interposed, *forbiddeth* the *banes* betwixt them.

Thomas Fuller, *The History of the Worthies of England*

## EDWARD VI

1537–53

And here, to use the example of Plutarch, in comparing kings and rulers, the Latins and the Greeks together, if I should seek with whom to match this noble Edward, I find not with whom to make my match more aptly, than with good Josias: for, as the one began his reign at eight years of age, so the other began at nine. Neither were their acts and zealous proceedings in God's cause much discrepant: for as mild Josias plucked down the hill altars, cut down the groves, and destroyed all monuments of idolatry in the temple, the like corruptions, dross, and deformities of popish idolatry (crept into the church of Christ of long time) this evangelical Josias, King Edward, removed and purged out of the true temple of the Lord. Josias restored the true worship and service of God in Jerusalem, and destroyed the idolatrous priests! King Edward likewise, in England abolishing idolatrous masses and false invocation, reduced again religion to a right

sincerity; and more would have brought to perfection, if life and time had answered to his godly purpose. And though he killed not, as Josias did, the idolatrous sacrificers, yet he put them to silence, and removed them out of their places.
John Foxe, *Acts and Monuments*

**EDWARD VII**
1841–1910

Bertie has remarkable social talent. He is lively, quick and sharp when his mind is set on anything, which is seldom . . . But usually his intellect is of no more use than a pistol packed in the bottom of a trunk if one were attacked in the robber-infested Apennines.
Prince Albert, Letter to Princess Frederick William, 1 December 1858

Across the wires the electric message came:/'He is no better, he is much the same.' /
Alfred Austin, attributed

He wasn't clever, but he always did the right thing, which is better than brains.
Lord Fisher, Letter to Reginald McKenna, 14 May 1910

The greatest monarch we've ever had – on a racecourse.
Lord Northcliffe, attributed

Poor Bertie – his is not a nature made to bear sorrow, or a life without amusement and excitement – he gets bitter and irritable.
Queen Victoria, Letter to the Empress Frederick, 12 June 1892

*See also* Lord Fisher

**EDWARD VIII (*subs.* THE DUKE OF WINDSOR)**
1894–1972

What does it matter if I am shot? – I have four brothers.
On himself, Letter to Kitchener, on accompanying his regiment to France, 1914

I have found it impossible to carry the heavy burden of responsibility and to discharge my duties as King as I would wish to do without the help of the woman I love.
On himself, Broadcast, 11 December 1936

Hark! The herald angels sing – / Mrs Simpson pinched our king. /
Anon., in Cleveland Amory, *Who Killed Society?*

The King told [the Duke of Kent] that over two years ago while he knew that he was an excellent Prince of Wales and liked his job, he nevertheless felt that he could never 'stick' being King as he puts it, he was afraid of being a bad one. He could never tolerate the restrictions, the etiquette, the loneliness; so perhaps if this issue had not arisen something else would have.
Henry Channon, Diary, 8 December 1936

From his childhood onward this boy will be surrounded by sycophants and flatterers by the score and will be taught to believe himself as of a superior creation. A line will be drawn between him and the people he is to be called upon some day to reign over. In due course, following the precedent which has already been set he will be sent on a tour round the world, and probably rumours of a morganatic alliance will follow and the end of it all will be the country will be called upon to foot the bill.
James Keir Hardie, to the House of Commons, 28 June 1894, on the motion to congratulate Queen Victoria on the prince's birth

. . . He was born to be a salesman. He would be an admirable representative of Rolls Royce. But an ex-King cannot start selling motor-cars.

Duchess of Windsor, in Harold Nicolson, Diary, 28 May 1947

*See also* Harpo Marx

## EDWARD THE CONFESSOR

– d. 1066

Throughout the whole of his reign people were rushing about all over the country attacking each other . . . And throughout the whole thing, there was Edward, as cool as a cucumber, down on his knees praying from morning till night; what for, no one knows, unless it was that he should be kept out of trouble. If so, it just shows the power of prayer.

Nicolas Bentley, *Golden Sovereigns*

And so, with the Kingdom made safe on all sides . . . the most kindly King Edward passed his life in security and peace, and spent much of his time in the glades and woods in the pleasures of hunting. After divine service, which he gladly and devoutly attended every day, he took much pleasure in hawks and birds of that kind which were brought before him, and was really delighted by the baying and scrambling of the hounds.

*Vita Aedwardi Regis*, translated by F. Barlow

A certain young woman . . . had an infection of the throat and of those parts under the jaw which, from their likeness to an acorn, are called glands. These had so disfigured her face with an evil smelling disease that she could scarcely speak to anyone without great embarrassment. She was informed in a dream that if she were washed in water by King Edward she would be cured of this most troublesome pox . . . And when the king heard of it, he did not disdain to help the weaker sex, for he had the sweetest nature, and was always charming to all suitors. A dish of water was brought; the king dipped in his hands; and with the tips of his fingers he anointed the face of the young woman and the places infected with the disease . . . Those diseased parts that had been treated by the smearing of the king softened and separated from the skin; and, with the pressure of the hand, worms together with pus and blood came out of various holes . . . And hardly had she been at court a week, when all foulness washed away, the grace of God moulded her with beauty.

*Ibid.*

## EDWARD PRINCE OF WALES (THE BLACK PRINCE)

1330–76

Let the boy win his spurs.

Edward III, attributed, at the Battle of Crécy, 1345

## EDWARDS, OLIVER

1711–91? Gentleman

I have tried too in my time to be a philosopher; but, I don't know how, cheerfulness was always breaking in.

On himself, in James Boswell, *Life of Johnson*

## EDWIN (EADWINE), KING OF NORTHUMBRIA

585?–633

So peaceful was it in those parts of Britain under King Edwin's jurisdiction that the proverb still runs that a woman could carry her newborn babe across the island from sea to sea without any fear of harm. Such was the king's concern for the welfare of his people that in a number of places where he had noticed clear springs adjacent to the highway he ordered posts to be erected with brass bowls hanging from them, so that travellers could drink and refresh themselves. And so great was the people's affection for him, and so great was the awe in which he was held, that no one wished or ventured to use these bowls for any other purpose.

Bede, *Ecclesiastical History of the English People*, translated by Leo Sherley-Price

Within his own dominions, Eadwine displayed a genius for civil government which shows how completely the mere age of conquest had passed away. With him began the English proverb so often applied to after kings: 'A woman with her babe might walk scatheless from sea to sea in Eadwine's day.'

J. R. Green, *A Short History of the English People*

## EINSTEIN, ALBERT

1879–1955 Scientist

Three wonderful people called Stein; / There's Gert and there's Ep and there's Ein. / Gert writes in blank verse, / Ep's sculptures are worse / And nobody understands Ein. /

Anon., in Ronald W. Clark, *Einstein: The Life and Times*

Here Einstein lies; / At least, they laid his bier / Just hereabouts – / Or relatively near. /

Kensal Green (Colin Hurry), *Premature Epitaphs*

Even today Einstein's general theory attracts men principally on aesthetic grounds, an appeal that few people outside of mathematics have been able to feel.

Thomas S. Kuhn, *The Structure of Scientific Revolutions*

His public life, as soon as the general theory was published (his fame had already mounted *before* the confirmation), was unlike that which any other scientist is likely to experience again. No one knows quite why, but he sprang into the public consciousness, all over the world, as the symbol of science, the master of the twentieth-century intellect, to a large extent the spokesman for human hope. It seemed that, perhaps as a release from the war, people wanted a human being to revere. It is true that they did not understand what they were revering. Never mind, they believed that here was someone of supreme, if mysterious, excellence.

C. P. Snow, *Variety of Men*

It did not last: the Devil howling *Ho, / Let Einstein be*, restored the status quo. /

J. C. Squire, in *The Faber Book of Comic Verse* (cf. Alexander Pope's couplet on Isaac Newton)

Entering Tom Quad one day, [Gilbert] Murray caught sight of Einstein sitting there with a far-away look on his face. The far-away thought behind that far-away look was evidently a happy one, for, at that moment, the exile's countenance was serene and smiling. 'Dr Einstein, do tell me what you are thinking', Murray said. 'I am thinking,' Einstein answered, 'that after all, this is a very small star'.

Arnold J. Toynbee, *Acquaintances*

When Einstein came to England and was lionized after the war, he was entertained by Haldane. Einstein I know and can converse with very interestingly, in a sort of Ollendorfian French about politics, philosophy and what not, and it is one of the lost good things of my life, that I was never able to participate in the mutual exploration of these two stupendously incongruous minds. Einstein must have been like a gentle bright kitten trying to make friends with a child's balloon, very large and unaccountably unpuncturable.

H. G. Wells, *Experiment in Autobiography*

*See also* Aldous Huxley

## EISENHOWER, DWIGHT DAVID

1890–1969 Thirty-Fourth United States President

Each of us has his portion of ego. At least one night I dreamed that the 22nd amendment [limiting a President to two terms] had been repealed – and it wasn't wholly a nightmare.

On himself, in *New York Times*, 13 May 1962, when asked if he would like to be back in the White House

I feel like bawling on my own shoulder.

On himself, in *New York World-Telegram and Sun*, 5 November 1953, on the anniversary of his election

There is one thing about being President: nobody can tell you when to sit down.

On himself, attributed

Ike is running like a dry creek.

Anon., in Peter F. Drucker, 'The Effective Executive', in *American Heritage Pictorial History of the Presidents*

Golf had long symbolized the Eisenhower years – played by soft, boring men with ample waistlines who went around rich men's country-club courses in the company of wealthy businessmen and were tended by white-haired, dutiful Negroes.

David Halberstam, *The Best and the Brightest*

Eisenhower was a subtle man, and no fool, though in pursuit of his objectives he did not like to be thought of as brilliant; people of brilliance, he thought, were distrusted.

*Ibid.*

As an intellectual, he bestowed upon the games of golf and bridge all the enthusiasm and perseverance that he withheld from books and ideas.

Emmet John Hughes, *The Ordeal of Power: A Political Memoir of the Eisenhower Years*

He was the great tortoise upon whose back the world sat for eight years. We laughed at him; we talked wistfully about moving; and all the while we never knew the cunning beneath the shell.

Murray Kempton, 'The Underestimation of Dwight D. Eisenhower', in *Esquire*, September 1967

What he would have liked said of him is that he achieved the highest objective of his or any other modern Presidency: in a nuclear world, teeming with violence on all sides, he successfully 'waged peace' for the eight years of his incumbency.

Arthur Larson, *Eisenhower: The President Nobody Knew*

I read a very interesting quote by Senator Kerr of Oklahoma. In summing up Ike, he said 'Eisenhower is the only living unknown soldier.' Even this is giving him all the best of it.

Groucho Marx, Letter to Goodman Ace, in *The Groucho Letters*

. . . President Eisenhower's whole life is proof of the stark but simple truth – that no one hates war more than one who has seen a lot of it.

Richard M. Nixon, Radio-Television Address, Moscow, August 1959

Not long ago it was proved that Dwight D. Eisenhower was descended from the royal line of Britain, a proof if one were needed that everyone is descended from everyone.

John Steinbeck, *Travels with Charley*

The General has dedicated himself so many times, he must feel like the cornerstone of a public building.

Adlai Stevenson, in Leon A. Harris, *The Fine Art of Political Wit*

If I talk over the people's head, Ike must be talking under their feet.

*Ibid.*

Senator Taft is the greatest living authority on what General Eisenhower thinks . . . The Republicans have a 'me too' candidate running on a 'yes but' platform, advised by a 'has been' staff . . . General Eisenhower employs the three monkeys standard of campaign morality: see no evil – if it's Republican; hear no evil – unless it is Democratic; and speak no evil – unless Senator Taft says it's all right.

*Ibid.*

*See also* Henry Luce, Adlai Stevenson, Harry S. Truman

## ELDON, LORD (JOHN SCOTT)

1751–1838 Statesman

If I were to begin life again, d--n my eyes, but I would begin as an agitator.

On himself, in Walter Bagehot, *Biographical Studies: Lord Brougham*

Found dead, a rat – no case could sure be harder; / Verdict – Confined a week in Eldon's larder.

Anon., contemporary

He is a thorough-bred Tory . . . but [has] never flinched, never gone back, never missed his way; he is an *out-and-outer* in this respect. His allegiance has been without flaw . . . his implicit understanding is a kind of taffeta-lining to the Crown.

William Hazlitt, *The Spirit of the Age*

A few more drops of Eldonine, and we should have had the People's Charter.

*Quarterly Review*, late 1850s

Next came Fraud, and he had on, / Like Eldon, an ermined gown; / His big tears, for he wept well, / Turned to mill-stones as they fell. /

And the little children, who / Round his feet played to and fro, / Thinking every tear a gem, / Had their brains knocked out by them. /

Percy Bysshe Shelley, *The Mask of Anarchy*

## ELGAR, SIR EDWARD WILLIAM

1857–1934 Composer

If I write a tune you all say it's commonplace – if I don't, you all say it's rot.

On himself, Letter to A. J. Jaeger, 20 October 1898

Lovely day: sun – zephyr – view – window open – liver – pills – proofs – bills – weed-killer – yah!

*Ibid.*, 20 May 1900

I have worked hard for forty years & at last, Providence denies me a decent hearing of my work: so I submit – I always said God was against art and I still believe it. Anything obscene or trivial is blessed in this world and has a reward – I ask for no reward – only to live & to hear my work.

*Ibid.*, 9 October 1900

Oh! Elgar's work's a d---able work, / The warmest work o' the year, / A work to tweak a teetotaller's beak / And make a methody swear. /

*Ibid.*, 14 November 1900

I feel Gibbonsy, Croftish, Byrdlich & foolish all over.

*Ibid.*

I love Elgar's music. It makes me go away feeling I'm a very *bad* man.

Anon. concert-goer, in Atez Orga, *The Proms*

He is furious with me for drastically cutting his A flat symphony – it's a very long work, the musical equivalent of the Towers of St Pancras Station – neo-Gothic you know.

Thomas Beecham, in Neville Cardus, *Sir Thomas Beecham*

Elgar was the last serious composer to be in touch with the great public.

Constant Lambert, *Music Ho!*

... the aggressive Edwardian prosperity that lends so comfortable a background to Elgar's finales is now as strange to us as the England that produced *Greensleeves* and *The Woodes so wilde.* Stranger, in fact, and less sympathetic. In consequence much of Elgar's music, through no fault of its own, has for the present generation an almost intolerable air of smugness, self-assurance and autocratic benevolence.

*Ibid.*

The English public is curious. It can only recognise one composer at a time. Once it was Sullivan. Now it is Elgar.

C. H. H. Parry, attributed, 1918, in Michael Kennedy, *Portrait of Elgar*

He used to bring in hedgehogs from the woods and feed them in the house; he sat in the strawberry bed and wished that someone would bring him champagne in a bedroom jug.

Dora M. Powell, *Edward Elgar: Memories of a Variation*

Edward Elgar, the figurehead of music in England, is a composer whose rank it is neither prudent nor indeed possible to determine. Either it is one so high that only time and posterity can confer it, or else he is one of the Seven Humbugs of Christendom.

George Bernard Shaw, 'Sir Edward Elgar', *Music and Letters*

If I were a king, or a Minister of Fine Arts, I would give Elgar an annuity of a thousand a year on condition that he produced a symphony every eighteen months.

*Ibid.*

*The Apostles* . . . places British music once more definitely in the first place European rank, after two centuries of leather and prunella.

George Bernard Shaw, Letter to *Daily News*, 9 June 1922

He has given us a Land of Hope and Glory; and we have handed him back the glory and kept all the hope for ourselves.

George Bernard Shaw, Letter to *The Times*, 20 December 1932

To the careful observer there is nothing to occasion astonishment or require explanation in the fact that the same Elgar who produced the mystical exaltation of *Gerontius* was an enthusiastic follower of horse-racing.

Sir Jack Westrup, *Sharps and Flats*

## ELIOT, GEORGE (MARY ANN EVANS)

1819–80 Novelist

Whatever may be the success of my stories, I shall be resolute in preserving my incognito, having observed that a *nom de plume* secures all the advantages without the disagreeables of reputation. Perhaps, therefore, it will be well to give you my prospective name, as a tub to throw to the whale in case of curious inquiries, and accordingly I subscribe myself, best and most sympathizing of editors, Yours very truly, George Eliot.

On herself, Letter to John Blackwood, 4 February 1857

My artistic bent is not at all to the presentation of eminently irreproachable characters, but to the presentation of mixed human beings in such a way as to call forth tolerant judgment, pity, and sympathy. And I cannot stir a step aside from what I *feel* to be *true* in character. If anything strikes you as untrue to human nature in my delineations, I shall be very glad if you will point it out to me, that I may reconsider the matter. But alas! inconsistencies and weaknesses are not untrue.

On herself, Letter to John Blackwood, 18 February 1857

In problems of life and thought, which baffled Shakespeare disgracefully, her touch was unfailing. No writer ever lived who had anything like her power of manifold, but disinterested and impartially observant sympathy.

Lord Acton, Letter to Mary Gladstone, 27 December 1880

In her brain-development the Intellect greatly predominates; it is very large, more in length than in its peripheral surface. In the Feelings, the Animal and Moral regions are about equal; the moral being quite sufficient to keep the animal in order and in due subservience, but would not be spontaneously active. The social feelings were very active, particularly the adhesiveness. She was of a most affectionate disposition, always requiring some one to lean upon, preferring what has hitherto been considered the stronger sex, to the other and more impressible. She was not fitted to stand alone.

Charles Bray, Phrenological report, *Autobiography*

I found out in the first two pages that it was a woman's writing – she supposed that in making a door, you last of all put in the *panels*!

Thomas Carlyle (after reading *Adam Bede*), in G. H. Haight, *George Eliot*

I never saw such a woman. There is nothing a bit masculine about her; she is thoroughly feminine and looks and acts as if she were made for nothing but to mother babies. But she has a power of *stating* an argument equal to any man; equal to any man do I say? I have never seen any man, except Herbert Spencer, who could state a case equal to her . . . She didn't talk like a blue-stocking – as if she were aware she had got hold of a big topic – but like a plain woman, who talked of Homer as simply as she would of flat-irons.

John Fiske, Letter to his Wife, 1873

A person whose life and opinions were in notorious antagonism to Christian practice in regard to marriage and Christian theory in regard to dogma. How am I to tell the Dean [Stanley] to do that which, if I were in his place, I should most emphatically refuse to do? . . . One cannot eat one's cake and have it too.

T. H. Huxley, refusing to support a plan to bury her in Poets' Corner in Westminster Abbey

You see, it was really George Eliot who started it all . . . And how wild they all were with her for doing it. It was she who started putting all the action inside. Before, you know, with Fielding and the others, it had been outside. Now I wonder which is right? . . . You know I can't help thinking there ought to be a bit of both.

D. H. Lawrence, in Jessie Chambers, *D. H. Lawrence: A Personal Record*

George Eliot had the heart of Sappho; but the face, with the long proboscis, the protruding teeth of the Apocalyptic horse, betrayed animality.

George Meredith, in *Fortnightly Review*, July 1909

She . . . taking as her text the three words which have been used so often as the inspiring trumpet-calls of men, – the words, *God, Immortality, Duty* – pronounced, with terrible earnestness, how inconceivable was the *first*, how unbelievable the *second*, and yet how peremptory and absolute the *third*. Never, perhaps, have sterner accents affirmed the sovereignty of impersonal and unrecompensing Law. I listened, and night fell; her grave, majestic countenance turned toward me like a sibyll's in the gloom; it was as though she withdrew from my grasp, one by one, the two scrolls of promise, and left me the third scroll only, awful with inevitable fates. And when we stood at length and parted, amid that columnar circuit of the forest-trees, beneath the last twilight of starless skies, I seemed to be gazing, like Titus at Jerusalem, on vacant seats and empty halls, – on a sanctuary with no Presence to hallow it, and heaven left lonely of a God.

F. W. H. Myers, in *Century Magazine*, November 1881

George Sand is often immoral; but she is always beautiful... But in the English Cockney school, which consummates itself in George Eliot, the personages are picked up from behind the counter and out of the gutter; and the landscape, by excursion train to Gravesend, with return ticket for the City-road.

John Ruskin, *Fiction, Fair and Foul*

She was not, she used to say, either an optimist or a pessimist, but a 'meliorist' – a believer that the world could be improved, and was perhaps slowly improving, though with a very strong conviction that the obstacles were enormous and the immediate outlook not especially bright.

Leslie Stephen, *George Eliot*

It is, I think, the defect of George Eliot that she struggles too hard to do work that shall be excellent. She lacks ease. Latterly the signs of this have been conspicuous in her style, which has always been and is singularly correct, but which has become occasionally obscure from her too great desire to be pungent. It is impossible not to feel the struggle, and that feeling begets a flavour of affectation. In *Daniel Deronda*, of which at this moment only a portion has been published, there are sentences which I have found myself compelled to read three times before I have been able to take home to myself all that the writer has intended.

Anthony Trollope, *Autobiography*

*See also* Thomas Hardy

## ELIOT, THOMAS STEARNS

1888–1965 Poet

How unpleasant to meet Mr Eliot! / With his features of clerical cut, / And his brow so grim / And his mouth so prim / And his conversation, so nicely / Restricted to What Precisely / And If and Perhaps and But. /

On himself, *Five Finger Exercises*

Whether one writes a piece of work well or not seems to me a matter of crystallisation – the good sentence, the good word, is only the final stage in the process . . . The words come easily enough, in comparison to the core of it – the *tone* – and nobody can help one in the least with that. Anything *I* have picked up about writing is due to having spent (as I once thought, wasted) a year absorbing the style of F. H. Bradley – the finest philosopher in English.

On himself, Letter to Lytton Strachey, 1 June 1919

The years between fifty and seventy are the hardest. You are always being asked to do things and yet you are not decrepit enough to turn them down.

On himself, in *Time*, 23 October 1950

One can only say that if Mr Eliot had been pleased to write in demotic English *The Waste Land* might not have been, as it just is to all but anthropologists, and literati, so much waste-paper.

Anon., in *Manchester Guardian*, 1922

Mr Eliot does not convince us that his weariness is anything but a habit, an anti-romantic reaction, a new Byronism which he must throw off if he is not to become a recurring decimal in his fear of being a mere vulgar fraction.

Anon., in *Times Literary Supplement* (review of *Ara vus Prec*), 18 March 1920

Eliot started in the enormous confusion of war and post-war England, handicapped in every way. Yet by merit, tact, produce and pertinacity he succeeded in doing what no other American has done – imposing his personality, taste, and even many of his opinions on literary England.

Richard Aldington, in Charles Norman, *Ezra Pound*

When things began to happen to our favourite spot, / A key missing, a library bust defaced, / Then on the tennis-court one morning / Outrageous, the bloody corpse and always, /

Day after day, the unheard-of drought, it was you / Who, not speechless with shock but finding the right / Language for thirst and fear, did most to / Prevent a panic. /

W. H. Auden, *For T. S. Eliot*

As to the influence of this Lloyds Bank clerk / Upon the state of English poetry, I think / It was imperious. By this I mean / He restored to us what had almost gone, / The moral and intellectual porphyrogenitive. / And what had been, before his hegemony, / Expedience and a chaffering of poetic riff raff / Underwent, during his magistracy, the / Imposition of rigorous definitions / And that sense of spiritual onus / Inherent in all Pascalian interpretations. / Also he loved bad jokes. /

George Barker, 'Elegiacs for T. S. Eliot', from *Dreams of a Summer Night*

When the news of Eliot's death came through, commercial television had just presented an abridgement of Middleton's *The Changeling*. Watching it, I thought that this could never have happened if Eliot hadn't opened our eyes to the greatness of the Jacobeans. Spike Milligan, on a comic TV show, could say, 'Not with a banger but a wimpy', and most of the audience caught the reference. Weather forecasters would joke about April being the cruellest month. Demagogues would quote John Donne and novelists make titles out of Donne's poems or religious meditations. The metaphysical poets, still quaint and unreadable in my schooldays, became A-level set-books. And, though not everybody could follow Eliot to the final austerities of Anglicanism, Royalism and Classicism, his affirmation of the importance of tradition was accepted even by the *avant-garde*. For, with Eliot, the past was not a dull and venerable ancestor but a living force which modified the present and was in turn modified by it. Time was not an army of unalterable law; time was a kind of ectoplasm.

Anthony Burgess, *Urgent Copy*

As the years went by, the astringent, sparkling, quality deserted Eliot's prose, which was apt to become arid and sometimes pontifical, bowed down by the honours and ex-cathedra authority which society had bestowed on him. During the war he suddenly found himself accepted as something we were fighting for, like the Four Freedoms or Big Ben. In the Thirties the image had been formed of the cat-addict and cheese-taster, the writer of pawky blurbs, the church-warden, the polite deflater.

Cyril Connolly, *The Evening Colonnade*

Eliot is a great poet because he purified the words of the tribe in novel, beautiful and many-meaninged ways, not because he extended the field of subject-matter available to poetic treatment: he didn't.

Aldous Huxley, *Literature and Science*

That awful boresome man? You can't be serious! Why, he's so *stoopid*! He's such a *bore*, don't you know? I have to tell him all the clues!

Henry Bradshaw Isherwood (on doing crosswords with TSE in their Club), in Christopher Isherwood, *Kathleen and Frank*

Mr T. S. Eliot has even made a virtue of developing himself into an incarnate Echo, as it were (though an *original* Echo, if one can say that). This imitation method, of the *creator-as-scholar* . . . does not appeal to me extremely, I confess.

Percy Wyndham Lewis, Letter to *Spectator*, 2 November 1934

He is very yellow and glum. Perfect manners. He looks like a sacerdotal lawyer – dyspeptic, ascetic, eclectic. Inhibitions. Yet obviously a nice man and a great poet. My admiration for him does not flag. He is without pose and full of poise. He makes one feel that all cleverness is an excuse for thinking hard.

Harold Nicolson, Diary, 2 March 1932

Eliot has remained aloof, but if forced at the pistol's point to choose between Fascism and some more democratic form of Socialism, would probably choose Fascism.

George Orwell, *Inside the Whale*

Sage Homme /

These are the poems of Eliot / By the Uranian Muse begot; / A Man their Mother was, / A Muse their Sire. / How did the printed Infancies result / From Nuptials thus doubly difficult? /

If you must needs enquire / Know diligent Reader / That on each Occasion / Ezra performed the Caesarean Operation. /

Ezra Pound, Letter to T. S. Eliot, 24 December 1921

Mr Eliot . . . is at times an excellent poet and . . . has arrived at the supreme Eminence among English critics largely through disguising himself as a corpse.

Ezra Pound, in *Front*, November 1930

He was a smash of a poet.

Ezra Pound, attributed, in Robert Lowell, *Notebook*

This morning two of my pupils came together to ask me a question about work. One, named Eliot, is very well-dressed & polished, with manners of the finest Etonian type, the other is an unshaven Greek, appropriately named Demos, . . . The two were obviously friends, and had on neither side the slightest consciousness of social difference. I found they were not nearly so well grounded as I had thought; they were absolutely candid, & quite intelligent, but obviously had not been taught with the minute thoroughness that we practise in England. Window-dressing seems irresistible to Americans.

Bertrand Russell, Letter to Lady Ottoline Morrell, March 1914

The secret of Eliot's influence over the young lay in the paradox of his personality. With a gesture of reversing current theories about the self-expressing poet, he dramatized a necessary shift in sensibility, from a subjective concern with the poet's self to an objective one with the values of a civilization endlessly created in men's minds. He wrote a new, a really new poetry, which set up connections with the old, the really old.

Stephen Spender, in Allen Tate, *T. S. Eliot, the Man and his Work*

[Some poets], like Eliot, have become so aware of the huge mechanism of the past that their poems read like scholarly conglomerations of a century's wisdom, and are difficult to follow unless we have an intimate knowledge of Dante, the Golden Bough, and the weather-reports in Sanskrit.

Dylan Thomas, Letter to Pamela Hansford Johnson, 1933

I am made a little tired at hearing Eliot, only in his early forties, present himself as an 'aged eagle' who asks why he should make the effort to stretch his wings.

Edmund Wilson, *Axel's Castle*

I think that Mr Eliot has written some of the loveliest single lines in modern poetry. But how intolerant he is of the old usages and politenesses of society – respect for the weak, consideration for the dull! As I sun myself upon the intense and ravishing beauty of one of his lines, and reflect that I must make a dizzy and dangerous leap to the next, and so on from line to line, like an acrobat flying precariously from bar to bar, I cry out, I confess, for the old decorums, and envy the indolence of my ancestors who, instead of spinning madly through mid-air, dreamt quietly in the shade with a book.

Virginia Woolf, *The Captain's Death Bed*

Pale, marmoreal Eliot was there last week, like a chapped office boy on a high stool, with a cold in his head, until he warms a little, which he did. 'The critics say I am learned and cold,' he said. 'The truth is I am neither.'

Virginia Woolf, Diary, 1921

*See also* Ford Madox Ford, James Joyce

## ELIZABETH I

1533–1603

And to me it shall be a full satisfaction both for the memoriall of my name, and for my glory also, if when I shall let my last breath, it be ingraven upon my Marble Tombe, *Here lyeth ELIZABETH, which raigned a Virgin, and dyed a Virgin.*

On herself, Speech to her first Parliament, 1559

I am more afraid of making a fault in my Latin than of the Kings of Spain, France, Scotland, the whole house of Guise, and all of their confederates.

On herself, in F. Chamberlin, *The Sayings of Queen Elizabeth*

I would rather be a beggar and single than a queen and married.

*Ibid.*

I grieve, yet dare not shew my discontent; / I love, and yet am forced to seem to hate; / I dote, but dare not what I ever meant; / I seem stark mute, yet inwardly doe prate; / I am, and am not – freeze, and yet I burn; / Since from myself my other self I turn. /

*Ibid.*, written when her suitor, the Duke of Alençon, left her for the last time in 1582

I am your anointed Queen. I will never be by violence constrained to do anything. I thank God I am endued with such qualities that if I were turned out of the Realm in my petticoat I were able to live in any place in Christome.

*Ibid.*

I know I have the body of a weak and feeble woman; but I have the heart and stomach of a king, and of a King of England too, and think foul scorn that Parma, or Spain, or any prince of Europe should dare to invade the borders of my realm; to which, rather than any dishonour shall grow by me, I myself will take up arms, I myself will be your general, judge, and rewarder of every one of your virtues in the field.

*Ibid.*, speaking at Tilbury in 1588

The Queen of Scots is lighter of a fair son, and I am but a barren stock.

*Ibid.*, at the time of the birth of the future James I

Though God hath raised me high, yet this I count the glory of my crown: that I have reigned with your loves.

On herself, the 'Golden' Speech, Parliament, 1601

Oh dearest Bess / I like your dress; / Oh sweet Liz / I like your phiz; / Oh dearest Queen / I've never seen / A face more like / A soup-tureen. /

Anon., in Arnold Silcock, *Verse and Worse*

For, which of the kings of this land before her Majesty, had theyr banners ever seene in the Caspian sea? which of them hath ever dealt with the Emperor of Persia, as her Majesty hath done, and obteined for her merchants large & loving privileges? who ever saw before this regiment, an English Ligier in the stately porch of the Grand Signor at Constantinople? who ever found English Consuls & Agents at Tripolis in Syria, at Aleppo, at Babylon, at Balsara, and which is more, who ever heard of Englishmen at Goa before now? what English shippes did heertofore ever anker in the mighty river of Plate? passe and repasse the unpassable (in former opinion) straight of Magellan, range along the coast of Chili, Peru, and all the backside of Nova Hispania, further then any Christian ever passed, travers the mighty bredth of the South sea, land upon the Luzones in despight of the enemy, enter into alliance, amity, and traffike with the princes of the Moluccaes, & the Isle of Java, double the famous Cape of Bona Speranza, arrive at the Isle of Santa Helena, & last of al returne home richly laden with the commodities of China, as the subjects of this now flourishing monarchy have done?

Richard Hakluyt, *The Principall Navigations, Voiages and Discoveries of the English Nation ... The Epistle Dedicatorie*

When she smiled it was pure sunshine, that everyone did choose to bask in, if they could: but anon came a storm from a sudden gathering of clouds, and the thunder fell in wondrous manner on all alike.

Sir John Harrington, *Nugae Antiquae*

Twenty years later, when England and the courts of Europe were agog with the idea that Queen Elizabeth might marry the Earl of Leicester, Lord Leicester told the French Ambassador that he had known Elizabeth since she was a child of eight, and from that very time she had always said: 'I will never marry'. Little notice was paid to the words. It did not occur to anyone, it seems, to look back and recall that when Elizabeth was eight years and five months old, Catherine Howard was beheaded.

Elizabeth Jenkins, *Elizabeth the Great*

Queen Elizabeth never saw her self after she became old in a true glass. They painted her and somytymes would vermilion her nose, she had always about Christmas evens set dice, that threw sixes or five, & she knew not they were other, to make her win & esteame herself fortunate. That she had a membrana on her which made her uncapable of man, though for her delight she tried many, att the coming of Monsieur, ther was a French Chirurgion who took in hand to cut it, yett fear stayed her & his death.

Ben Jonson, in *Conversations with William Drummond of Hawthornden*

An element of lovemaking in diplomacy was always very much to her taste.

Conyers Read, *Mr Secretary Walsingham and the Policy of Queen Elizabeth*

She brought England through a very perilous passage into smooth waters. Unfortunately for her successors the chart by which she steered her erratic course was destroyed with her death.

Conyers Read, *The Tudors*

Of fayre *Eliza* be your siluer song, / That blessed wight: / The flowre of Virgins, may shee florish long, / In princely plight. / For shee is *Syrinx* daughter without spotte, / Which Pan the shepheards God of her begot: / So sprong her grace / Of heauenly race, / No mortall blemishe may her blotte. /

Edmund Spenser, *The Sheepheardes Calendar, April*

*See also* Richard Burton, Sir Martin Frobisher, J. A. Froude, Richard Grenville, Fulke Greville, Henry VII, Charles Kingsley, Sir Walter Raleigh, Christopher Tye, Queen Victoria, John Whitgift

## ELLISTON, ROBERT WILLIAM

1774–1831 Actor

His feelings follow each other like the buckets on a water-wheel, full one instant and empty the next.

Leigh Hunt, in Christopher Murray, *Robert William Elliston, Manager*

'I like Wrench,' a friend was saying to him one day, 'because he is the same natural, easy creature, *on* the stage, that he is *off*.' 'My case exactly,' retorted Elliston – with a charming forgetfulness, that the converse of a proposition does not always lead to the same conclusion – 'I am the same person *off* the stage that I am *on*.' The inference, at first sight, seems identical; but examine it a little, and it confesses only, that the one performer was never, and the other always, *acting*.

Charles Lamb, 'Ellistoniana', in *Englishman's Magazine*, August 1831

Kenný told me that Charles Lamb, sitting down once to play whist with Elliston, whose hands were very dirty, said, after looking at them for some time, 'Well, Elliston, if *dirt* was trumps, what a hand you would have!'

Thomas Moore, *Memoirs, Journal and Correspondence*

When Elliston was in a dying state at his house in Black-friar's road, his friend, Mr Durrant was near him, and being anxious his patient should take some medicine prescribed for him, said, 'Come, come, Elliston, you must indeed swallow this. Take it, and you shall have a wine glass of weak brandy and water!' Elliston raised his eyes, and, with still a comic smile, replied, 'Ah, you rogue – bribery and – *corruption*.'

George Raymond, *Memoirs of R. W. Elliston*

Elliston, who was one of those who consider no behaviour towards the other sex worthy the term civility which falls short of a positive declaration of love – like our forefathers, who fancied their hospitality poor, unless they made their guests dead drunk – used to relate a smart rebuke he once received in one of these moments of stage-coach *innamoramenti*. Addressing himself to a fair fellow-passenger in language somewhat savouring of *Young Wilding*, and perceiving the lady less favourable to his suit than he had expected, concluded by hoping he had not exceeded the bounds of decorum. 'Perhaps not sir', replied she; 'but your limits of decorum are so extremely liberal that you may possibly lose your way in the excursion.'

*Ibid.*

Such, alas, was poor Elliston! – one of those who appeared to regard righteousness as a liberal host does his best wine, using but little of it himself, and reserving his stock for the benefit of his friends.

*Ibid.*

A wretched Tragedian. – his attempts at dignity are ludicrous. He is a fine bustling comedian but he bustles in tragedy also.

Henry Crabb Robinson, Diary, 4 April 1811

If thrown overboard in rags from one side of a ship, he would appear before his tormentors could turn round, upon the other side of the deck, dressed as a gentleman, ready to begin the world again.

Francis Wemyss, *Twenty-six Years of the Life of an Actor and Manager*

## EMERSON, RALPH WALDO

1803–82 Essayist, Poet

Like most poets, preachers, and metaphysicians, he burst into conclusions at a spark of evidence.

Henry Seidel Canby, *Classic Americans*

. . . that everlasting rejecter of all that is, and seeker for he knows not what.

Nathaniel Hawthorne, in Edward Wagenknecht, *Nathaniel Hawthorne: Man and Writer*

He seemed like an exotic transplanted from some angelic nursery.

Oliver Wendell Holmes, in W. L. Schroeder, *Oliver Wendell Holmes, An Appreciation*

Rarely has a man so accurately known the limits of his genius or so unfailingly kept within them.

William James, Address at the Emerson Centenary in Concord, in Milton R. Konvitz and Stephen E. Whicher eds, *Emerson, A Collection of Critical Essays*

There comes Emerson first, whose rich words, every one, / Are like gold nails in temples to hang trophies on; / Whose prose is grand verse, while his verse, the Lord knows, / Is some of it pr – No 'tis not even prose. /

James Russell Lowell, *A Fable for Critics*

I could readily see in Emerson, notwithstanding his merit, a gaping flaw. It was the insinuation, that had he lived in those days when the world was made, he might have offered some valuable suggestions.

Herman Melville, in William Ellery Sedgwick, *Herman Melville, The Tragedy of Mind*

Yet I think Emerson is more than a brilliant fellow. Be his stuff begged, borrowed, or stolen, or of his own domestic manufacture he is an uncommon man. Swear he is a humbug – then he is no common humbug.

Herman Melville, Letter to Evert Duychinck, 3 March 1849

His constant refrain is the omnipotence of imaginative thought; its power first to make the world, then to understand it, and finally to rise above it.

George Santayana, 'Emerson', in Milton R. Konvitz and Stephen E. Whicher eds, *Emerson, A Collection of Critical Essays*

Emerson's writing has a cold, cheerless glitter, like the new furniture in a warehouse, which will come of use by and by.

Alexander Smith, *Dreamthorp*

. . . a gap-toothed and hoary-headed ape, carried at first into notice on the shoulder of Carlyle, and who now in his dotage spits and chatters from a dirtier perch of his own finding and fouling: coryphaeus or choragus of his Bulgarian tribe of autocoprophagous baboons, who make the filth they feed on.

Algernon C. Swinburne, Letter, 30 January 1874

## EPSTEIN, SIR JACOB

1880–1959 Sculptor

From life's grim nightmare he is now released / Who saw in every face the lurking beast. / 'A loss to Art', say friends both proud and loyal, / 'A loss', say others, 'to the Café Royal.' /

Anon., in Arnold Silcock, *Verse and Worse*

Epstein is a great sculptor. I wish he would wash, but I believe Michel Angelo *never* did, so I suppose it is part of the tradition.

Ezra Pound, in Charles Norman, *Ezra Pound*

*See also* Albert Einstein

## ERNEST AUGUSTUS, *see under* CUMBERLAND, DUKE OF

## ERSKINE, THOMAS, LORD

1750–1823 Lord Chancellor

Crazy Lord Erskine is an Ass- / -ortment of all follies: / He was the first to slur the Queen; / But since his trip to Gretna Green, / He's wondrous kind to dollies. /

Theodore Hook, *Ass-Ass-Ination*

The tongue of Cicero and the soul of Hampden.

Lord John Russell, in *Dictionary of National Biography*

## ETHELRED THE UNREADY

968?–1016

Ethelread the Unready . . . was called the Unready because he was never ready when the Danes were. Rather than wait for him the Danes used to fine him large sums called Danegeld, for not being ready. But though they were always ready, the Danes had very bad memories and often used to forget that they had been paid the Danegeld and come back for it almost before they had sailed away. By that time Ethelread was always unready again.

W. C. Sellar and R. J. Yeatman, *1066 and All That*

The evils which give a sinister complexion to the age were the results of conditions which from their very nature were temporary. They were the effects of a state of war under a king of singular incompetence. Their ultimate cause was realized clearly enough by the unknown man or woman who first described him as 'Aethelred unraed' – 'Aethelred No-Counsel'. In the last resort they all arose from the fact that in a series of crises, each of which demanded a concentration of the national energy, the king could neither give direction to his people nor hold his greater subjects firmly to their allegiance.

F. M. Stenton, *Anglo-Saxon History*

The career of his life is said to have been cruel in the beginning, wretched in the middle, and disgraceful in the end.

William of Malmesbury, *History of the Kings of England*, translated by J. Sharpe

Dunstan, indeed, had foretold his worthlessness, having discovered it by a filthy token: for, when quite an infant, the bishops standing round, as he was immersing in the baptismal font, he defiled the sacrament by a natural evacuation: at which Dunstan, being extremely angered, exclaimed, 'By God, and his mother, this will be a sorry fellow.' I have read, that when he was ten years of age, hearing it noised abroad that his brother was killed, he so irritated his furious mother by his weeping, that, not having a whip at hand, she beat the little innocent with some candles she had snatched up . . . On this account he dreaded candles, during the rest of his life, to such a degree, that he would never suffer the light of them to be brought into his presence.

*Ibid.*

## ETHEREGE, SIR GEORGE

1635?–91 Dramatist

How happy should I be cou'd I love the rustling of papers so well as I have done the rustling of Petty coats, cou'd I with as much pleasure harken to the Ministers, when they talk of alliances and changes in affaires of State, as I used to do the women when they tattled of who is well with who, and who is false to such a one.

On himself, Letter to William Jephson, 24 May 1688

You know I am a well-wisher to Laziness.

On himself, Letter to the Earl of Middleton, 13 December 1688

Etherege writes *Airy Songs*, and soft *Lampoons*, / The best of any Man; as for your *Nouns*, / *Grammar*, and *Rules of Art*, he knows 'em not, / Yet writ two Talking *Plays* without one Plot. /

John Wilmot, Earl of Rochester, with the Duke of Buckingham, *Timon*

## EVELYN, JOHN

1620–1706 Diarist, Virtuoso

In fine, a most excellent person he is, and must be allowed a little for a little conceitedness; but he may well be so, being a man so much above others. He read me, though with too much gusto, some little poems of his own, that were not transcendent, yet one or two very pretty epigrams: among others, of a lady looking in at a grate and being pecked at by an eagle that was there.

Samuel Pepys, Diary, 5 November 1665

*See also* Samuel Pepys

# 'F'

## FAIRBANKS, DOUGLAS

1883–1939 Actor

His energy was reserved for the massive action spectaculars with which he enchanted America through the twenties, and when sound ended the fashion he declined to a slightly pathetic ex-idol pursuing beautiful women around Europe. He died at fifty-six in 1939, his tanned body apparently untouched by age but actually so muscle-bound that the blood could barely circulate. He had not so much died, some friends thought, as run down.

John Baxter, *Stunt*

He was by nature very athletic, and enjoyed doing stunts just for the fun of it, off stage. If he saw a gate, rather than go through the gate he'd hop over it. If he saw a desk, he'd rather vault over the desk than walk round it.

Douglas Fairbanks Jr, in John Baxter, *Stunt*

In his early films, made at the time of the First World War, Douglas Fairbanks represented all young democratic Americans, quick-thinking, fast-acting, self reliant and self-made. Ridiculing all fashionable affectations, Fairbanks preached the gospel of pep, the merits of clean living, the obligation to take everything with a smile, the claims of traditional decencies . . . Again and again, in his pictures, Fairbanks demonstrated how ambition, alertness, daring and perpetual hustle would inevitably bring a young American to success, rewarding him both with the fortune he hoped for and the girl of his choice.

Lloyd Morris, *Not So Long Ago*

Douglas had always faced a situation the only way he knew how, by running away from it.

Mary Pickford, *Sunshine and Shadow*

Thomas Edison devoted his life to machines intended to make thinking unnecessary for the masses. Fairbanks is devoting his to pictures calculated to keep their minds off the fact that they do not think.

Terry Ramsaye, in Lloyd Morris, *Not So Long Ago*

## FAIRFAX, THOMAS, LORD

1612–71 Soldier, Statesman

*Fairfax*, whose name in armes through Europe rings / Filling each mouth with envy, or with praise, / And all her jealous monarchs with amaze, / And rumours loud, that daunt remotest kings, / Thy firm unshak'n vertue ever brings / Victory home, though new rebellions raise / Thir Hydra heads, and the fals North displaies / Her brok'n league, to impe their serpent wings, / O yet a nobler task awaites thy hand; / For what can Warr, but endless warr still breed, / Till Truth, and Right from Violence be freed, / And Public Faith cleard from the shamefull brand / Of Public Fraud. In vain doth Valour bleed / While Avarice, and Rapine share the land. /

John Milton, *On the Lord Gen. Fairfax at the siege of Colchester*

Taller as some say when he is in the field than at home.

Joshua Sprigge, *Anglia Rediviva*

## FARADAY, MICHAEL

1791–1867 Scientist

I cannot suppress the remark that the pair Faraday-Maxwell has a most remarkable inner similarity with the pair Galileo-Newton – the former of each pair grasping the relations intuitively, and the second one formulating those relations exactly and applying them quantitatively.

Albert Einstein, *Autobiographical Notes*, translated by P. A. Schlipp

The truth is that Faraday in spite of his many contributions to chemistry was by nature a physicist.

Sir Harold Hartley, *Studies in the History of Chemistry*

Faraday, on the other hand, shews up his unsuccessful as well as his successful experiments, and his crude ideas as well as his developed ones, and the reader, however inferior to him in inductive power, feels sympathy even more than admiration, and is tempted to believe that, if he had the opportunity, he too would be a discoverer.

J. C. Maxwell, *A Treatise on Electricity and Magnetism*

In like manner, Professor Faraday, Sir Humphry Davy's scientific successor, made his first experiments in electricity by means of an old bottle, while he was still a working bookbinder. And it is a curious fact that Faraday was first attracted to the study of chemistry by hearing one of Sir Humphry Davy's lectures on the subject at the Royal Institution. A gentleman, who was a member, calling one day at the shop where Faraday was employed in binding books, found him poring over the article 'Electricity' in an Encyclopaedia placed in his hands to bind. The gentleman, having made inquiries, found he was curious about such subjects, and gave him an order of admission to the Royal Institution, where he attended a course of four lectures delivered by Sir Humphry. He took notes of the lectures, which he showed to the lecturer, who acknowledged their scientific accuracy, and was surprised when informed of the humble position of the reporter. Faraday then expressed his desire to devote himself to the prosecution of chemical studies, from which Sir Humphry at first endeavored to dissuade him; but the young man persisting, he was at length taken into the Royal Institution as an assistant; and eventually the mantle of the brilliant apothecary's boy fell upon the worthy shoulders of the equally brilliant bookbinder's apprentice.

Samuel Smiles, *Self-help*

*See also* Sir Humphry Davy

## FARQUHAR, GEORGE

1678–1707 Dramatist

Our author having received a college exercise from his tutor, upon the miracle of our Saviour's walking upon the water, and coming into the hall for examination the next day, it was found that he had not brought his exercise written as the rest had done; at which the lecturer being displeased, Farquhar offered to make one extempore; and after considering some time, he observed, that he thought it no great miracle, since the man that is born to be hanged, &c. The impiety of this reply quite extinguished all the approbation he expected from its wit.

Baker, Jones and Reed eds, *Biographia Dramatica*

While Mr *Farquhar* was in *Trinity* College *Dublin*, he sent to a Gentleman to borrow Burnet's History of the *Reformation*, but the Gentleman sent him word he never lent any Book out of his Chamber, but if he would come there he should make use of it as long as he pleas'd. A little while later, the Owner of the Book sent to borrow Mr *Farquhar*'s Bellows, he return'd him the Complement, – *I never lend my Bellows out of my own Chamber, but if he be pleas'd to come there, he should make use of them as long as he would.*

W. R. Chetwood, *A General History of the Stage*

He makes us laugh from pleasure, oftener than from malice. He somewhere prides himself in having introduced on the stage the class of comic heroes here spoken of, which has since become a standard character, and which represents the warm-hearted, rattle-brained, thoughtless, high-spirited young fellow, who floats on the back of his misfortunes without repining, who forfeits appearances, but saves his honour, – and he gives us to understand that it was his own.

William Hazlitt, *Lectures on the English Comic Writers*

## FASTOLFE, SIR JOHN

1378?–1459 Knight

Nor is our Comedian [Shakespeare] excusable, by some alteration of his name, writing him *Sir John Falstafe*, (and making him the *property of pleasure* for King *Henry* the fifth to abuse) seeing the *vicinity* of sounds intrench on the memory of *that worthy Knight*, and few do heed the *inconsiderable difference* in spelling of their names.

Thomas Fuller, *The History of the Worthies of England*

## FAULKNER, WILLIAM CUTHBERT

1897–1962 Author

I think I have written a lot and sent it off to print before I actually realized strangers might read it.

On himself, in Malcolm Cowley, *A Second Flowering*

There is no such thing as bad whiskey. Some whiskeys just happen to be better than others. But a man shouldn't fool with booze until he's fifty; then he's a damnfool if he doesn't.

On himself, in J. R. Cofield, 'Many Faces, Many Moods', in James W. Webb and A. Wigfall Green, *William Faulkner of Oxford*

It is as if Mr Faulkner, in a sort of hurried despair, had decided to try to tell us everything, absolutely everything, every last origin or source or quality or qualification, and every possible future or permutation as well, in one terrifically concentrated effort: each sentence to be, as it were, a microcosm. And it must be admitted that the practice is annoying and distracting.

Conrad Aiken, 'William Faulkner: The Novel as Form', in L. W. Wagner ed., *William Faulkner, Four Decades of Criticism*

The truth is that Faulkner unites in his work two of the dominant trends in American literature from the beginning: that of the psychological horror story as developed by Hawthorne, Poe, and Stephen Crane, among others; and that of realistic frontier humor, with Mark Twain as its best example. If you imagine Huckleberry Finn living in the House of Usher and telling uproarious stories while the walls crumble about him, that will give you the double quality of Faulkner's work at its best.

Malcolm Cowley, in Otis E. Wheeler, 'Some Uses of Folk Humor by Faulkner', in *ibid.*

Even those who call Mr Faulkner our greatest literary sadist do not fully appreciate him, for it is not merely his characters who have to run the gauntlet but also his readers.

Clifton Fadiman, in *New Yorker*, 21 April 1934

Mr Faulkner, of course, is interested in making your mind, rather than your flesh creep.

*Ibid.*

Old Corndrinking Mellifluous.
Ernest Hemingway, in Carlos Baker, *Ernest Hemingway, A Life Story*

Poor Faulkner. Does he really think big emotions come from big words?
Ernest Hemingway, in A. E. Hotchner, *Papa Hemingway*

If respect for the human is the central fact of Faulkner's work, what makes that fact significant is that he realizes and dramatizes the difficulty of respecting the human.
Robert Penn Warren, 'William Faulkner', in L. W. Wagner ed., *William Faulkner, Four Decades of Criticism*

Faulkner was shy. Faulkner was arrogant. Faulkner went barefoot on the streets of Oxford [Mississippi]. Faulkner tore up his driveway to discourage visitors.
James W. Webb and A. Wigfall Green, *William Faulkner of Oxford*

## FAWCETT, DAME MILLICENT (MRS HENRY FAWCETT)

1849–1929 Suffragette

It was obvious that to work for political freedom represented only one phase of a many sided movement. The most important departments dealt with 1) education 2) an equal moral standard between men and women 3) professional and industrial liberty and 4) political status. My special experience and training fitted me for work on behalf of the fourth of these; but I recognised that this was only one side of the whole question and I was likewise convinced that whoever worked on any of these branches was, whether he knew it or not, really helping on the other three.
On herself, *What I Remember*

I can never feel that setting fire to houses and churches and letter-boxes and destroying valuable pictures really helps to convince people that women ought to be enfranchised.
On herself, in R. Fulford, *Votes for Women*

## FELL, DR JOHN

1625–86 Dean of Christ Church, Bishop of Oxford

I do not love thee, Doctor Fell, / The reason why I cannot tell, / But this one thing I know full well: / I do not love thee, Doctor Fell. /
Thomas Brown, *Epigrams*, after Martial

Strickt in holding up the college discipline; 4 times in a day at public service in the cathedral, twice at home; loved to have tales brought to him, and be flatterd, and therefore the most obnoxious in his house would choose to please him that way to save themselves. These persons he favoured more; allowed them the chambers that they desired, allowed them pupills, his countenance – while the sober partie that could not or would not tell tales were browbeaten. The college was so much at his beck that he flew further and endeavored to govern the University.
Anthony à Wood, *Life and Times*, 30 November 1660

## FERBER, EDNA

1887–1968 Author

Being an old maid is like death by drowning, a really delightful sensation after you cease to struggle.
On herself, in Robert E. Drennan ed., *Wit's End*

Miss Ferber, who was fond of wearing tailored suits, showed up at the Round Table one afternoon sporting a new suit similar to one Noël Coward was wearing. 'You look almost like a man,'

Coward said as he greeted her. 'So,' Miss Ferber replied, 'do you.'
Robert E. Drennan, *Wit's End*

She squares off at her job in workmanlike fashion and turns out a nationally advertised product that looks as sound as this year's model always does, until next year's model comes along.
T. S. Matthews, in *New Republic*, 6 March 1935

## FIELDING, HENRY
1707–54 Novelist

Charg'd with writing of bawdy, this was F—'s reply: / Tis what DRYDEN and CONGREVE have done as well as I. / Tis true – but they did it with this good pretence, / With an ounce of rank bawdy went a pound of good sense: / But thou hast proportion'd, in thy judgement profound, / Of good sense scarce an ounce, and of bawdy a pound. /
Anon., *The Grub Street Journal*, 3 August 1732

Fielding's essence . . . was a bold spirit of bounding happiness . . . Fielding was a reckless enjoyer. He saw the world – wealth and glory, the best dinner and the worst dinner, the gilded *salon* and the low sponging-house – and he saw that they were good. Down every line of his characteristic writings there runs this elemental energy of keen delight.
Walter Bagehot, in *National Review*, April 1864

A novel, which, like a beggar, should always be kept 'moving on'. Nobody knew this better than Fielding, whose novels, like most good ones, are full of inns.
Augustine Birrell, *Obiter Dicta*

The most singular genius which their island ever produced, whose works it has long been the fashion to abuse in public and to read in secret.
George Borrow, *The Bible in Spain*

Fielding being mentioned, Johnson exclaimed, 'he was a blockhead'; and upon my expressing my astonishment at so strange an assertion, he said, 'What I mean by his being a blockhead is, that he was a barren rascal.'
James Boswell, *Life of Johnson*

There are very different kinds of laughter: you make me laugh with pleasure; but I often laugh, and am angry at the same time with the facetious Mr Fielding.
Lady Dorothy Bradshaigh, Letter to Samuel Richardson, 27 March 1750

The prose Homer of human nature.
Lord Byron, quoted in notes to Anderson's edition of Byron, *Don Juan*

. . . how charming, how wholesome, Fielding always is! To take him up after Richardson is like emerging from a sick room heated by stoves into an open lawn, on a breezy day in May.
Samuel Taylor Coleridge, *Table Talk*, 5 July 1834

I am sorry for Henry Fielding's death, not only as I shall read no more of his writings, but I believe he lost more than others, as no man enjoyed life more than he did . . . His happy constitution (even when he had, with great pains, half demolished it) made him forget everything when he was before a venison pasty or over a flask of champagne, and I am persuaded he has known more happy moments than any prince upon earth. His natural spirits gave him rapture with a cookmaid, and cheerfulness when he was fluxing in a garret.
Lady Mary Wortley Montagu, Letter to Lady Bute, 22 September 1755

I have not been able to read any more than the first volume of Amelia. Poor Fielding! I could not help telling his sister, that I was equally surprised at and concerned for his continued lowness. Had your brother, said I, been born in a stable, or been a runner at a sponging-house, we should have thought him a genius, and wished he had had the advantage of a liberal education, and of being admitted into good company; but it is beyond my conception, that a man of family, and who had some learning, and who really is a writer, should descend so excessively low, in all his pieces.

Samuel Richardson, Letter to Lady Dorothy Bradshaigh, 23 February 1752

Fielding had as much humour perhaps as Addison, but, having no idea of grace, is perpetually disgusting.

Horace Walpole, Letter to Mr Pinkerton, June 1785

*See also* Ring Lardner, Samuel Richardson, Sir Walter Scott, W. M. Thackeray

## FIELDS, W. C. (WILLIAM CLAUDE DUKENFIELD)

1880–1946 Comedian, Actor

I am free of all prejudice. I hate everyone equally.

On himself, in an article by Jerome Beatty Jr, in *Saturday Review*, 28 January 1967

I always keep a supply of stimulant handy in case I see a snake – which I also keep handy.

On himself, in Carey Ford, *The Time of Laughter*

To watch Mr Fields, as Dickensian as anything Dickens ever wrote, is a form of escape for poor human creatures: we who are haunted by pity, by fear, by our sense of right and wrong, who are tongue-tied by conscience, watch with envious love this free spirit robbing the gardener of ten dollars, cheating the country yokels by his own variant of the three-card trick, faking a marriage certificate, and keeping up all the time, in the least worthy and the most embarrassing circumstances, his amazing flow of inflated sentiments.

Graham Greene, reviewing *Poppy* in *Spectator*, 17 July 1936

Nearly everything Bill tried to get into his movies was something that lashed out at the world . . . The peculiar thing is that although he thought he was being pretty mean there wasn't any real sting in it. It was only funny. Bill never really wanted to hurt anybody. He just felt an obligation.

Gregory La Cava, in Robert L. Taylor, *W. C. Fields*

He had read of the keen critical rejection of failures such as Wagner's operas, Lincoln's Gettysburg Address, Walt Whitman's poems and Christ's Sermon on the Mount, and he was sensibly impressed.

Robert Lewis Taylor, *W. C. Fields*

*See also* Florenz Ziegfeld

## FIENNES, WILLIAM, VISCOUNT SAYE AND SELE ('THE GODFATHER')

1582–1662 Puritan Politician

He being ill natur'd, cholerick, severe and rigid, and withal highly conceited of his own worth, did expect great matters at Court; but they failing he sided therefore with the discontented party the Puritan, and took all occasions cunningly to promote a Rebellion. For so it was, that several years before the Civil War began, he being looked upon at that time the *Godfather* of that party, had meetings of them in his house at *Broughton*, where was a room and passage thereunto, which his Servants were prohibited to come near: and when they were of a compleat number, there would be great noises and talkings heard among them, to the admiration of those that lived in the house, yet could they never discern their Lords companions.

Anthony à Wood, *Athenae Oxonienses*

## FIRBANK, (ARTHUR ANNESLEY) RONALD

1886–1926 Novelist

Firbank, whose appearance was as orchidaceous as his fictional fantasies, behaved so strangely that all attempts at ordinary conversation became farcical. His murmured remarks were almost inaudible, and he was too nervous to sit still for more than half a minute at a time. The only coherent information he gave me was when I heavily inquired where his wonderful fruit came from. 'Blenheim', he exclaimed with an hysterical giggle, and then darted away to put a picture-frame straight . . . Watching him through the jungle of orchids, I found it hard to believe that this strange being could have any relationship with the outside world. He was as unreal and anomalous as his writings.

Siegfried Sassoon, *Siegfried's Journey*

His most rational response to my attempts at drawing him out about literature and art was 'I adore italics, don't you?'

*Ibid.*

*See also* Evelyn Waugh

## FISHER, JOHN ARBUTHNOT, LORD FISHER OF KILVERSTONE

1841–1920 Admiral of the Fleet

Fear God and Dread Nought.

Fisher's motto, inscribed on his coat of arms when he was elevated to the peerage

[He] spoke, wrote, and thought in large type and italics, when writing he underlined his argument with two, three, or even four strokes with a broad-nibbed pen, and when talking, with blows of his fist on the palm of the other hand. 'I wish you would stop shaking your fist in my face,' said King Edward [VII] when being subjected to some of Fisher's forcible arguments.

Sir Reginald H. S. Bacon, *The Life of Lord Fisher of Kilverstone*

The lurid imagery and ferocious invective of much of his correspondence (his enemies were all 'skunks', 'pimps', 'sneaks', or worse, often with a harsh modifying adjective like 'pestilent' or 'damnable') give the impression of a man writing at breakneck speed with a pen dipped in molten lava. The expressions with which he closed his letters to intimates, such as 'Yours till Hell freezes' and 'Yours till charcoal sprouts', were characteristic.

Professor A. J. Marder, *From the Dreadnought to Scapa Flow*

## FISKE, MINNIE MADDERN (MARIE AUGUSTA DAVEY)

1865–1932 Actress

As soon as I suspect a fine effect is being achieved by accident, I lose interest. I am not interested in unskilled labor.

On herself, in *Minnie Maddern Fiske. Her Views On Actors, Acting and the Problems of Production, as told to Alexander Woollcott*

## FITZGERALD, EDWARD

1809–83 Poet, Translator

No man's life makes the mumbo-jumbo of psychologists and Freudians more trivial or absurd. Fitzgerald loved men, particularly two men, and knew no sexual attraction to women. Whether or not he could be called homosexual in medico-legal parlance, whether or not anything he did could have laid him open . . . to a charge of gross indecency, is of little consequence. He loved Posh, his big Viking-like fisherman . . . Who cares whether or not they went to bed together?

Rupert Croft-Cooke, *Feasting with Panthers*

These pearls of thought in Persian gulfs were bred, / Each softly lucent as a rounded moon; / The diver Omar plucked them from their bed, / Fitzgerald strung them on an English thread. /

James Russell Lowell, *In a Copy of Omar Khayyam*

Fitzgerald's 'Omar' is worth all the Persian scholarship of a century.

Ezra Pound, *The New Age*, 1917

## FITZGERALD, FRANCIS SCOTT KEY

1896–1940 Author

We're too poor to economize. Economy is a luxury . . . our only salvation is in extravagance.

On himself, in Paul Sann, *The Lawless Decade*

Drink heightens feeling. When I drink, it heightens my emotions and I put it in a story. But then it becomes hard to keep reason and emotion balanced. My stories written when sober are stupid – like the fortune-telling one. It was all reasoned out, not felt.

On himself, in Andrew Turnbull, *Scott Fitzgerald*

Do you know what my own story is? Well, I was always the poorest boy at a rich man's school. Yes, it was that way at prep schools, and at Princeton, too.

On himself, in Morley Callaghan, *That Summer in Paris*

I who knew less of New York than any reporter of six months' standing and less of its society than any hall-room boy in a Ritz stag line, was pushed into the position not only of spokesman for the time but of the typical product of that same moment.

On himself, in Nancy Milford, *Zelda Fitzgerald*

Sometimes I don't know whether Zelda and I are real or whether we are characters in one of my novels.

On himself, in Malcolm Cowley, *A Second Flowering*

Fitzgerald never got rid of anything; the ghosts of his adolescence, the failures of his youth, the doubts of his maturity plagued him to the end. He was supremely a part of the world he described, so much a part that he made himself its king and then, when he saw it begin to crumble, he crumbled with it and led it to death.

John Aldridge, 'Fitzgerald: The Horror and the Vision of Paradise', in Arthur Mizener, *F. Scott Fitzgerald: A Collection of Critical Essays*

One of Scott's troubles was that he had never been able to think clearly. The thing to do with such a 'marvelous talent' as his was to use it. Instead he had made the mistake of loving youth so much that he had jumped straight from there to senility without passing through manhood in between.

Carlos Baker, *Ernest Hemingway, A Life Story*

I often feel about Fitzgerald that he couldn't distinguish between innocence and social climbing.

Saul Bellow, *Paris Review*

It was as if all his novels described a big dance to which he had taken . . . the prettiest girl . . . and as if at the same time he stood outside the ballroom, a little Midwestern boy with his nose to the glass, wondering how much the tickets cost and who paid for the music.

Malcolm Cowley, in Arthur Mizener, *The Far Side of Paradise: A Biography of F. Scott Fitzgerald*

In fact, Mr Fitzgerald – I believe that is how he spells his name – seems to believe that plagiarism begins at home.

Zelda Fitzgerald, in her review of *The Beautiful and Damned*, in Nancy Milford, *Zelda Fitzgerald*

His talent was as natural as the pattern that was made by the dust on a butterfly's wings. At one time he understood it not more than the butterfly did and he did not know when it was brushed or marred. Later he became conscious of his damaged wings and of their construction and he learned to think and could not fly any more because the love of flight was gone and he could only remember it when it had been effortless.

Ernest Hemingway, *A Moveable Feast*

Still, Scott Fitzgerald's life had indeed a legendary quality – for which he himself was in part responsible. It was characteristic that, as a small boy, he should decide he was not the son of his parents. Instead, as he went around earnestly telling the neighbors, he had been wrapped up in a blanket, to which was pinned a piece of paper emblazoned with the name of the royal House of Stuart!

Henry Dan Piper, *F. Scott Fitzgerald, A Critical Portrait*

Fitzgerald was indeed a romantic who wished time to stand still forever at the hour of youth so that an aesthetic paradise might be super-imposed upon life's harsh actuality. This could only be done, it seemed, by the power of money, and accordingly Fitzgerald wrote for money.

D. S. Savage, 'The Significance of F. Scott Fitzgerald', in Arthur Mizener, *F. Scott Fitzgerald: A Collection of Critical Essays*

The first of the last generation.

Gertrude Stein, in John Malcolm Brinnin, *The Third Rose*

Fitzgerald was perhaps the last notable writer to affirm the Romantic fantasy, descended from the Renaissance, of personal ambition and heroism, of life committed to, or thrown away for, some ideal of self.

Lionel Trilling, 'F. Scott Fitzgerald', in Arthur Mizener, *F. Scott Fitzgerald: A Collection of Critical Essays*

It is true that Fitzgerald has been left with a jewel which he doesn't know quite what to do with. For he has been given imagination without intellectual control of it; he has been given the desire for beauty without an aesthetic ideal; and he has been given a gift for expression without very many ideas to express.

Edmund Wilson, *The Shores of Light*

*See also* John O'Hara

## FLAMSTEED, JOHN

1646–1719 First Astronomer Royal

My letters being shown King Charles, he startled at the assertion of the fixed stars' place being false in the catalogue; said, with some vehemence, 'He must have them anew observed, examined and corrected, for the use of his seamen;' and further, (when it was urged to him how necessary it was to have a good stock of observations taken for correcting the motions of the moon and planets), with the same earnestness 'he must have it done'. And when he was asked Who could, or who should, do it? 'The person (says he) that informs you of them'. Whereupon I was appointed to it, with the incompetent allowance aforementioned.

On himself, *History of His Own Life*

## FLAXMAN, JOHN

1755–1826 Sculptor

You, O Dear Flaxman, are a Sublime Archangel, My Friend and Companion from Eternity; in the Divine bosom is our Dwelling place.

William Blake, Letter to Flaxman, 21 September 1800

I mock thee not, tho' I by thee am Mocked. / Thou call'st me Madman, but I call thee Blockhead. /

William Blake, *MS Note-Book 1808–11*

In these designs of Flaxman [on Dante], you have gentlemanly feeling, and fair knowledge of anatomy, and firm setting down of lines, all applied, in the foolishest and worst possible way; you cannot have a more finished example of learned error, amiable want of meaning, and bad drawing with a steady hand.

John Ruskin, *The Elements of Drawing*

## FLECKER, (HERMAN) JAMES ELROY

1884–1915 Poet, Dramatist

Judging from my latest efforts I shall go down to fame (if I go) as a sort of Near East Kipling.

On himself, Letter to Frank Savery, 10 January 1912

His conversation was variegated, amusing, and enriched with booty from the by-ways of knowledge. He was always and restlessly driven by his mind down such paths. He sought beauty everywhere, but preferred, for the most of his life, to find her decoratively clad.

Rupert Brooke, Obituary in *The Times*, 6 January 1915

*See also* W. H. Auden

## FLECKNOE, RICHARD

– d. 1678? Poet

I write chiefly to avoid idleness, and print to avoid the imputation (of idleness), and as others do it to live after they are dead, I do it only not to be thought dead whilst I am alive.

On himself, in Augustine Birrell, *Andrew Marvell*

All human things are subject to decay, / And when fate summons, monarchs must obey. / This Flecknoe found, who, like Augustus, young / Was call'd to empire, and had govern'd long; / In prose and verse, was own'd, without dispute, / Thro' all the realms of *Nonsense*, absolute. /

John Dryden, *MacFlecknoe*

So thin / He stands, as if he only fed had been / With consecrated Wafers: and the *Host* / Hath sure more flesh and blood then he can boast. / This *Basso Relievo* of a Man, / Who as a Camel tall, yet easly can / The Needles Eye thread without any stich, / (His only impossible is to be rich). /

Andrew Marvell, *Fleckno*

*See also* Richard Blackmore

## FLEMING, SIR ALEXANDER

1881–1955 Bacteriologist

Wright, chaffing him, used to say that medical research was just a game to him – and there was some truth in that. On one occasion, when King George and Queen Mary were due to visit the laboratories at St Mary's, Wright wanted Fleming to display some of his bench technique. He did, but suspecting that it might not interest them very much, he also prepared one of his famous bacterial 'rock gardens' from all the available microbes which produced growth of vivid colouring. The story goes that when the Queen saw this she whispered to King George 'What is the use of this?' It was no use – but it amused Fleming.

L. Colebrook, in *Biographical Memoirs of Fellows of the Royal Society*

## FLEMING, IAN LANCASTER

1908–64 Novelist

Probably the fault about my books is that I don't take them seriously enough and meekly accept having my head ragged off about them in the family circle . . . You, after all, write 'novels of suspense' – if not sociological studies – whereas my books are straight pillow fantasies of the bang-bang, kiss-kiss variety.

On himself, Letter to Raymond Chandler

His work combined a passionate interest in the externals of the modern world – its machinery and furniture, in the widest sense of both words – with a strong, simple feeling for the romantic and the strange: the gipsy encampment, the coral grove, the villain's castle, the deadly garden, the mysterious island. Fleming technologized the fairy-tale for us, making marvellous things seem familiar, and familiar things marvellous.

Kingsley Amis, *What Became of Jane Austen?*

Your descriptive passages, as usual, are very good indeed . . . I am willing to accept the centipede, the tarantulas, the land crabs, the giant squid . . . I am even willing to forgive your reckless use of invented verbs – 'I inch, Thou inches, He snakes, I snake, We Palp, They palp', etc, but what I will neither accept nor forgive is the highly inaccurate statement that when it is eleven a.m. in Jamaica, it is six a.m. in dear old England. This, dear boy, to put not too fine a point on it, is a f------ lie. When it is eleven a.m. in Jamaica, it is *four p.m.* in dear old England, and it is carelessness of this kind that makes my eyes steel slits of blue.

Noël Coward, Letter to Fleming on the publication of *Dr No*

As you know I am a confirmed Fleming fan – or should it be addict. The combination of sex, violence, alcohol and – at intervals – good food and nice clothes is, to one who lives such a circumscribed life as I do, irresistible.

Hugh Gaitskell, Letter to Fleming on the publication of *Dr No*

The trouble with Ian is that he gets off with women because he can't get on with them.

Rosamond Lehmann, in John Pearson, *Life of Ian Fleming*

I gave myself a treat, or what I expected to be a treat, by reading Ian Fleming's adventure story about James Bond, called *Goldfinger*. I had been told that it was as good as Simenon. This is nonsense . . . Fleming is so fantastic as to arouse disbelief. This story is too improbable to arouse interest, nor do I like the underlying atmosphere of violence, luxury and lust. I regard it as an obscene book, 'liable to corrupt'.

Harold Nicolson, Diary, 22 November 1959

## FLETCHER, JOHN

1579–1625 Dramatist

The admirable zeal of the Department of Inland Revenue, which a few years earlier had sought to obtain income tax returns from the authors of *The Beggar's Opera*, written over two hundred years before, was now directed to the case of Fletcher, who died in 1625. One day I received a request for his address, which they had been unable to trace, and on the principle of being helpful whenever possible, I replied that to the best of my knowledge it was on the south side of Southwark Cathedral, that he had been there for quite a time and in all probability was not intending an early removal.

Sir Thomas Beecham, *A Mingled Chime*

As we in Humane Bodies see, that lose / An Eye or Limb, the Vertue and the Use / Retreat into the other Eye or Limb, / And make it double. So I say of him: / *Fletcher* was *Beaumont*'s Heir, and did inherit / His searching Judgement, and unbounded Spirit. / His Plays were printed therefore, as they were / Of *Beaumont* too, because his Spirit's there. /

Sir Aston Cockain, *Verse Epistle to his Cosen Charles Cotton*

Though he treated love in perfection, yet Honour, Ambition, Revenge, and generally all the stronger Passions, he either touch'd not, or not masterly. To conclude all; he was a Limb of Shakespeare.

John Dryden, *Preface to Troilus and Cressida, or Truth found too late*

Fletcher was above all an opportunist, in his verse, in his momentary effects, never quite a pastiche; in his structure ready to sacrifice everything to the single scene . . . Fletcher had a cunning guess at feelings, and betrayed them.

T. S. Eliot, *Essays*: 'Philip Massinger'

Mr Fletcher surviving Mr Beaumont, wrote good Comedies of himself . . . Though some think them inferior to the former, and no wonder if a single thread was not so strong as a twisted one.

William Winstanley, *Lives of the Most Famous English Poets*

*See also* Francis Beaumont, Shakespeare

## FLYNN, ERROL LESLIE

1909–59 Actor

My problem lies in reconciling my gross habits with my net income.

On himself, in Jane Mercer, *Great Lovers of the Movies*

A magnificent specimen of the rampant male.

David Niven, *The Moon's A Balloon*

More recent actors in tights just aren't in the running; and, in the Talkie period, no actor swashed so blithe a buckle.

David Shipman, *The Great Movie Stars*

## FOOTE, SAMUEL

1720–77 Actor, Dramatist

If we do not take liberties with our friends, with whom can we take liberties?

On himself, in J. Cradock, *Literary and Miscellaneous Memoirs*

Thou Mimic of *Cibber* – of *Garrick*, thou Ape! / Thou Fop in *Othello*! thou Cypher in Shape! / Thou Trifle in Person! thou Puppet in Voice! / Thou Farce of a Player! thou Rattle for Boys! / Thou Mongrell! thou dirty face Harlequin Thing! / Thou Puff of bad Paste! thou Ginger-bread King! /

Anon., 'On a Pseudo Player', in W. R. Chetwood, *A General History of the Stage*

*Boswell*: Pray, Sir, is not Foote an infidel? *Johnson*: I do not know, Sir, that the fellow is an infidel; but if he be an infidel, he is an infidel as a dog is an infidel; that is to say, he has never thought upon the subject. *Boswell*: I suppose, Sir, he has thought superficially, and seized the first notions which occurred to his mind. *Johnson*: Why, then, Sir, still he is like a dog, that snatches the piece next him. Did you never observe that dogs have not the power of comparing? A dog will take a small bit of meat as readily as a large when both are before him.

James Boswell, *Life of Johnson*

On the 26th of October we dined together at the Mitre tavern. I found fault with Foote for indulging his talent of ridicule at the expense of his visitors, which I colloquially termed making fools of his company. *Johnson*: Why, Sir, when you go to see Foote you do not go to see a saint: you go to see a man who will be entertained at your house, and then bring you on a public stage; who will entertain you at his house, for the very purpose of bringing you on a public stage. Sir, he does not make fools of his company; they whom he exposes are fools already; he only brings them into action.

*Ibid.*

By turns transform'd into all kinds of shapes, / Constant to none, Foote laughs, cries, struts, and scrapes: / Now in the centre, now in van or rear, / The Proteus shifts, bawd, parson, auctioneer. / His strokes of humour, and his bursts of sport / Are all contain'd in this one word, *distort.* /

Charles Churchill, *The Rosciad*

. . . there is no Shakespeare or Roscius upon record who, like Foote, supported a theatre for a series of years by his own acting, in his own writings, and for ten years of the time upon a *wooden leg*! This prop to his person I once saw standing by his bedside, ready dressed in a handsome silk stocking, with a polished shoe and gold buckle, awaiting the owner's getting up. It had a kind of tragi-comical appearance; and I leave to inveterate wags the ingenuity of punning upon a Foote in bed, and a leg out of it.

George Colman, *Random Records*

He had little regard for the feelings of others: if he thought of a witty thing that would create laughter, he said it . . . and of this I can give one notable example. If Foote ever had a serious regard for any one, it was for Holland yet at his death, or rather indeed, after his funeral, he violated all decency concerning him. Holland was the son of a baker at Hampton, and . . . died rather young, and Foote attended as one of the mourners. He was really grieved; and the friend from whom I had the account, declared that his eyes were swollen with tears; yet when the gentleman said to him afterwards, 'So, Foote, you have just attended the funeral of our dear friend Holland;' Foote instantly replied, 'Yes, we have just shoved the little baker into his oven.'

J. Cradock, *Literary and Miscellaneous Memoirs*

Foote is quite impartial, for he tells lies of everybody.

Samuel Johnson, in James Boswell, *Life of Johnson*

There is a witty satirical story of Foote. He had a small bust of Garrick placed upon his bureau. 'You may be surprised (said he), that I allow him to be so near my gold; – but you will observe, he has no hands.'

*Ibid.*

Foote gives a dinner – large company – characters come one by one: – sketches them as they come: – each enters – he glad to see each – At Dinner, his wit, affectation, pride: his expense, his plate, his jokes, his stories; – all laugh; – all go, one by one – all abused, one by one; his toadeaters stay; – he praises himself – in a passion against all the world.

Arthur Murphy, Scheme for projected play, among his papers

*See also* Duke of Cumberland

## FORBES-ROBERTSON, SIR JOHNSTON

1853–1937 Actor

He can present a dramatic hero as a man whose passions are those which have produced the philosophy, the poetry, the art, and the statecraft of the world, and not merely those which have produced its weddings, coroners' inquests, and executions.

George Bernard Shaw, in *Saturday Review*, 2 October 1897

## FORD, FORD MADOX (FORD HERMANN HUEFFER)

1873–1939 Author

I happened to be in a company where a fervent young admirer exclaimed: 'By Jove, the *Good Soldier* is the finest novel in the English language!' whereupon my friend Mr John Rodker, who has always had a properly tempered admiration for my work, remarked in his clear, slow drawl: 'Ah yes. It is, but you have left out a word. It is the finest French novel in the English language!'

On himself, Dedicatory Letter to Stella Ford, 1927, *The Good Soldier*

I learned all I know of Literature from Conrad – and England has learned all it knows of Literature from me.

On himself, in conversation with Herbert Read

. . . His mind was like a Roquefort cheese, so ripe that it was palpably falling to pieces.

Van Wyck Brooks, in Douglas Goldring, *The Last Pre-Raphaelite*

As to Ford he is a sort of lifelong habit.

Joseph Conrad, Letter to H. G. Wells, 1905

You must not mind Hueffer; that is his way. He patronizes me; he patronizes Mr Conrad; he patronizes Mr James. When he goes to Heaven he will patronize God Almighty. But God Almighty will get used to it, for Hueffer is all right!

Stephen Crane, in Ford Madox Ford, *Return to Yesterday*

His forlorn attempts to throw a smokescreen round himself produced through the distorted haze, the apparition of a monster, like a pink elephant, absurd, bizarre, immense.

Edward Crankshaw, in *National Review*, 1948

So fat and Buddhistic and nasal that a dear friend described him as an animated adenoid.

Norman Douglas, in R. A. Cassell, *Ford Madox Ford*

I don't suppose failure disturbed him much: he had never really believed in human happiness, his middle life had been made miserable by passion, and he had come through – with his humour intact, his stock of unreliable anecdotes, the kind of enemies a man ought to have, and a half-belief in a posterity which would care for good writing.

Graham Greene, *The Lost Childhood*

It is not that Ford is difficult to read – in the sense that James is sometimes difficult, or Meredith. But you have to follow him in a mood of alert relaxation; you must not mind being mystified, detained, dragged backward, pulled forward, cheated, hoaxed. You must suspend curiosity and wait patiently until he is ready to explain . . . Ford's approach to his audience is extraordinarily disingenuous, playful and sly. He would have made an ideal Ancient Mariner – accosting you with the air of one who asks only a minute of your time . . . and then enweaving and enwinding you in his great, dazzlingly complicated web.

Christopher Isherwood, *Exhumations*

[Ford] daubs his dove-grey kindliness with a villainous selfish tar, and hops forth a very rook among rooks, but his eyes, after all, remain like the Shulamite's, dove's eyes.

D. H. Lawrence, Letter to Violet Hunt

Hueffer was a flabby lemon and pink giant, who hung his mouth open as though he were an animal at the Zoo inviting buns – especially when ladies were present . . . This ex-collaborator with Joseph Conrad was himself, it always occurred to me, a typical figure out of a Conrad book – a caterer, or corn-factor, coming on board – blowing like a porpoise with the exertion – at some Eastern port.

Percy Wyndham Lewis, *Rude Assignment*

Master, mammoth mumbler.

Robert Lowell, *Life Studies*

He had all his faults, like his moustache, out in front where everyone cd see Yum. au fond a serious character as J.J. the Reverend Eliot and even ole Unc Wim the yeaT were NOT.

Ezra Pound, Letter to Brigit Patmore, 1952

I once told Fordie that if he were placed naked and alone in a room without furniture, I would come back in an hour and find total confusion.

Ezra Pound, in V. S. Pritchett, *The Working Novelist*

Freud Madox Fraud.

Osbert Sitwell, in R. Phelps and P. Deane, *The Literary Life*, 1968

. . . Thank God you / were not delicate, you let the world in / and lied! damn it you lied grossly / sometimes. But it was all, I / see now, a carelessness, the part of a man / that is homeless here on earth. /

William Carlos Williams, *To Ford Madox Ford in Heaven*

## FORD, HENRY

1863–1947 Industrialist

Ford is a 'natural businessman' just as he is a 'natural mechanic', and he is the rarest of all types, in that he is a combination of the two.

Thomas Alva Edison, in John Kenneth Galbraith, *The Liberal Hour*

Machines, he said, were made to free mankind / To live the life of sport and of mind. / Let's hope the end will justify the means / That turned mankind from men into machines. /

Kensal Green (Colin Hurry), *Premature Epitaphs*

He was acquisitive without limit and egotistic without deviation. His mind was astonishingly simple. He could concentrate on a single idea almost as perfectly as the inmate of a State Asylum who can remember the number of every car which passes the gate.

Jonathan Norton Leonard, *The Tragedy of Henry Ford*

This demigod of the machine age had somehow stitched together the incompatibles of the struggle for existence. He was the idol of an American middle class which wants to eat its cake and have it too, the venerated symbol of a system under which people aspire to be neither so self-seeking that they lose caste nor so good that they must spend their days in poverty.

Keith Sward, *The Legend of Henry Ford*

*See also* Walt Disney

## FORD, JOHN

1586?–1639? Dramatist

Deep in a dump John Ford alone was got / With folded arms and melancholy hat. /

Anon., 'On the Time-Poets', in *Choyce Drollery etc.*

He was a well-wisher to the muses . . . and may be known by an anagram instead of his name, generally printed on the title page, viz: FIDE HONOR.
Theophilus Cibber, *Lives of the Poets*

He is a master of the brief mysterious words, so calm in seeming, which well up from the depths of despair. He concentrates the revelation of a soul's agony into a sob or a sigh. The surface seems calm; we scarcely suspect that there is anything beneath; one gasp bubbles up from the drowning heart below, and all is silence.
Havelock Ellis, Introduction to Ford's Plays

He sought for sublimity, not by parcels in metaphors or visible images, but directly where she has her full residence in the heart of man; in the actions and sufferings of the greatest minds. There is a grandeur of the soul above mountains, seas, and the elements. Even in the poor perverted reason of Giovanni and Isabella, we discover traces of that fiery particle, which in the irregular starting from out of the road of beaten action, discovers something of a right line even in obliquity, and shows hints of an improvable greatness in the lowest descents and degradations of our nature.
Charles Lamb, *Specimens of Dramatic Poets*

Ford is rather a sculptor of character than a painter.
Algernon C. Swinburne, *Essays and Studies*

*See also* Thomas Dekker

## FORD, JOHN (SEAN O'FEENEY)

1895–1973 Motion Picture Director

You say someone's called me the greatest poet of the Western saga. I am not a poet, and I don't know what a Western saga is. I would say that is horse-shit. I'm just a hard-nosed, hardworking, run-of-the-mill director.
On himself, in Walter Wagner, *You Must Remember This*

To be quite blunt, I make pictures for money, to pay the rent. There are some great artists in the business. I am not one of them.
*Ibid.*

Whatever John Ford wants, John Ford gets.
Edward G. Robinson, *All My Yesterdays*

I like the old masters, by which I mean John Ford, John Ford . . . and John Ford.
Orson Welles, in Walter Wagner, *You Must Remember This*

## FORDYCE, GEORGE

1736–1802 Physician

Dr Fordyce sometimes drank a good deal at dinner. He was summoned one evening to see a lady patient, when he was more than half-seas-over, and conscious that he was so. Feeling her pulse, and finding himself unable to count its beats, he muttered, 'Drunk by God!' Next morning, recollecting the circumstance, he was greatly vexed: and just as he was thinking what explanation of his behaviour he should offer to the lady, a letter from her was put into his hand. 'She too well knew,' said the letter, 'that he had discovered the unfortunate condition in which she was when he last visited her; and she entreated him to keep the matter secret in consideration of the enclosed (a hundred-pound banknote).'
Samuel Rogers, *Table Talk*

## FORRESTER, CECIL SCOTT

1899–1966 Author

My distaste for my own work lingers on surprisingly. A father looking down at his first-born for the first time may experience a sense of shock, but he generally recovers from it rapidly enough; after a day or two he thinks it is a very wonderful baby indeed. My life would be happier if I reacted in the same way towards my books – the odd thing being that even as it is there are very few people who lead a happier life than mine, despite all the feelings that I have just been describing. I must be like the princess who felt the pea through seven mattresses; each book is a pea.

On himself, *The Hornblower Companion*

## FORSTER, EDWARD MORGAN

1879–1970 Novelist

There is more in him than ever comes out. But he is not dead yet. I hope to see him pregnant with his own soul . . . He sucks his dummy – you know, those child's comforters – long after his age. But there is something very real in him, if he will not cause it to die. He is *much* more than his dummy-sucking, clever little habits allow him to be.

D. H. Lawrence, Letter to Bertrand Russell, 12 February 1915

Forster's world seemed a comedy, neatly layered and staged in a garden whose trim privet hedges were delicate with gossamer conventions. About its lawns he rolled thunderstorms in teacups, most lightly, beautifully.

T. E. Lawrence, in *Spectator*, 6 August 1927

E. M. Forster never gets any further than warming the teapot. He's a rare fine hand at that. Feel this teapot. Is it not beautifully warm? Yes, but there ain't going to be no tea.

Katherine Mansfield, Journal, May 1917

He's a mediocre man – and knows it, or suspects it, which is worse; he will come to no good, and in the meantime he's treated rudely by waiters and is not really admired even by middle-class dowagers.

Lytton Strachey, Letter to James Strachey, 3 February 1914

## FOX, CHARLES JAMES

1749–1806 Statesman

At Almacks' of pigeons I am told there are flocks, / But it's thought the completest is one Mr Fox. / If he touches a card, if he rattles a box, / Away fly the guineas of this Mr Fox. / He has met, I'm afraid, with so many bad knocks, / The cash is not plenty with this Mr Fox, / In gaming 'tis said he's the stoutest of cocks, / No man can play deeper than this Mr Fox, / And he always must lose, for the strongest of locks / Cannot keep any money for this Mr Fox. / No doubt such behaviour exceedingly shocks / The friends and relations of this Mr Fox. /

Anon., in John W. Derry, *Charles James Fox*

Sheridan told us that when Mr Fox went to see the *Gamester*, there appeared, in the next morning's newspapers, paragraphs stating how much the great profligate orator had been affected, and how bitterly he had wept. 'Whereas,' said Mr Sheridan, 'the truth was, Fox listened, as was his custom, attentively; and when Beverley, in the play, said that he would borrow money upon the reversion of his uncle's estate, Fox turned to me and whispered, "Rather odd, hey, that he had not thought of that before."'

Lord Broughton, *Recollections of a Long Life*

His spirit is not owing to his ignorance of the state of men and things; he well knows what snares are spread about his path, from personal animosity, from court intrigues, and possibly from popular delusion. But he has put to hazard his ease, his security, his interest, his power, even his darling popularity, for the benefit of a people whom he has never seen. This is the road that all heroes have trod before him.

Edmund Burke, Speech on 1 December 1783

He seems to have the particular talent of knowing more about what he is saying and with less pains than anybody else – his conversation is like a brilliant player of billiards, the strokes follow one another, piff paff.

Georgiana, Duchess of Devonshire, in E. Lascelles, *Charles James Fox*

What is that fat gentleman in such a passion about?

Lord Eversley, as a child in the gallery of the House of Commons, in G. W. E. Russell, *Collections and Recollections*

About sunset on the 13th September he said: 'I die happy, but I pity you.' Then, as if that were a little sententious, he looked up at his wife, and said: 'It don't signify, my dearest, dearest Liz.'

Christopher Hobhouse, *Fox*

A namesake of Charles James Fox having been hung at Tyburn, the latter enquired of Selwyn whether he had attended the execution? 'No,' was Selwyn's reply, 'I make a point of never frequenting rehearsals.'

G. H. Jesse, *George Selwyn and his Contemporaries*

Fox (in his earlier days I mean), Sheridan, Fitzpatrick, &c led *such* a life! Lord Tankerville assured me that he has played cards at Brookes's from ten o'clock at night till near six o'clock the next afternoon, a waiter standing by to tell them 'whose deal it was,' they being too sleepy to know.

Samuel Rogers, *Table Talk*

With his passion, his power, his courage, his openness, his flashes of imagination, his sympathetic errors, above all his supreme humanity, Fox was a sort of lax Luther, with the splendid faults and qualities of the great reformer.

Lord Rosebery, *Pitt*

If ever from an English heart / O here let prejudice depart, / O partial feeling cast aside, / Record that Fox a Briton died! / When Europe crouched to France's yoke, / When Austria bent and Prussia broke, / And the firm Russian's purpose brave / Was bartered by a timorous slave, / E'en then dishonour's peace he spurned, / The sullen olive-branch returned, / Stood for his country's glory fast, / And nailed her colours to the mast. /

Sir Walter Scott, *Marmion*

He was not a political adventurer, but a knight-errant roaming about in search of a tilt, or, still better, of a mêlée; and not much caring whether his foes were robbers or true men, if only there were enough of them.

Sir George Otto Trevelyan, *The Early History of Charles James Fox*

'There are but forty of them,' said Thurlow of the Opposition of 1793, 'but there is not one of them who would not willingly be hanged for Fox.'

Henry Offley Wakeman, *Life of Charles James Fox*

Charles James Fox was one of those vigorous exuberancies of genius, which this country, where nothing restrains or contracts the mind, pushes forth from time to time . . . He was as agreeable as strong sense divested of graces and wit could make him; and as little disagreeable as such overbearing presumption could allow.

Horace Walpole, *Memoirs*

*See also* Lord North

## FOX, WILLIAM

1879–1952 Motion Picture Producer

What do I need friends for when I am sitting on my money bags?

On himself, in Glendon Allvine, *The Greatest Fox Of Them All*

## FOXE, JOHN

1516?–87 Martyrologist

At length, having farther endeared himself, he then told her, That she would not only grow well of that Consumption, but also live to an exceeding great age. At which words the sick Gentlewoman a little moved, and earnestly beholding Master Fox: As well might you have said (quoth she) that if I should throw this Glass against the Wall, I might believe it would not break to pieces; and holding a Glass in her hand, out of which she had newly drunk, she threw it forth; neither did the Glass, first by chance lighting on a little Chest standing by the Bedside, and afterwards falling upon the ground, either break nor crack in any place about it: And the event fell out accordingly. For the Gentlewoman, being then threescore years of age, lived afterwards for all example of felicity, seldom seen in the off-spring of any Family, being able, before the 90 years of her age (for she lived longer) to reckon three hundred and three score of her Childrens Children and Grand-children.

Anon. memoir of his life, in a Preface to John Foxe, *Acts and Monuments*

## FRANCIS, SIR PHILIP (JUNIUS)

1740–1818 Man of Letters, Editor

Junius has sometimes made his satire felt, but let not injudicious admiration mistake the venom of the shaft for the vigour of the bow. He has sometimes sported with lucky malice; but to him that knows his company, it is not hard to be sarcastick in a mask. While he walks like Jack the Giant-killer in a coat of darkness, he may do much mischief with little strength. Novelty captivates the superficial and thoughtless; vehemence delights the discontented and turbulent. He that contradicts acknowledged truth will always have an audience, he that vilifies established authority will always find abettors.

Samuel Johnson, *Thoughts on the Late Transactions respecting Falkland's Islands*

Junius was clearly a man not destitute of real patriotism and magnanimity, a man whose vices were not of the sordid kind. But he must also have been a man in the highest degree arrogant and insolent, a man prone to malevolence, and prone to the error of mistaking his malevolence for public virtue.

T. B. Maeaulay, *Warren Hastings*

You know as much of [John] Wilkes and [Charles] Townshend as I do . . . The famous *Junius* seems at last to issue from the shop of the former, though the composition is certainly above Wilkes himself. The styles are often blended, and very distinguishable, but nobody knows who it is that deigns to fight in disguise under Wilkes's banner.

Horace Walpole, Letter to Horace Mann, 22 October 1771

## FRANKLIN, BENJAMIN

1706–90 Statesman, Scientist

The body of / Benjamin Franklin, printer, / (Like the cover of an old book, / Its contents worn out, / And stript of its lettering and gilding) / Lies here, food for worms! / Yet the work itself shall not be lost, / For it will, as he believed, appear once more, / In a new / And more beautiful edition, Corrected and amended / By its Author!

On himself, Suggested epitaph, in L. A. Harris, *The Fine Art of Political Wit*

The history of our Revolution will be one continued lie from one end to the other. The essence of the whole will be that Dr Franklin's electrical rod smote the earth and out sprang General Washington. That Franklin electrified him with his rod – and thence forward these two conducted all the policy, negotiations, legislatures, and war.

John Adams, Letter to Dr Benjamin Rush, 4 April 1790

Benjamin Franklin, incarnation of the peddling, tuppenny Yankee.

Jefferson Davis, in Burton Stevenson, *The Home Book of Quotations*

A philosophical Quaker full of mean and thrifty maxims.

John Keats, Letter to George and Georgiana Keats, 14–31 October 1818

And now, I, at least, know why I can't stand Benjamin. He tries to take away my wholeness and my dark forest, my freedom. For how can any man be free, without an illimitable background? And Benjamin tries to shove me into a barbed-wire paddock and make me grow potatoes or Chicagoes.

D. H. Lawrence, *Studies in Classic American Literature*

Prudence is a wooden Juggernaut, before whom Benjamin Franklin walks with the portly air of a high priest.

Robert Louis Stevenson, *Crabbed Age and Youth*

What an adroit old adventurer the subject of this memoir was! In order to get a chance to fly his kite on Sunday he used to hang a key on the string and let on to be fishing for lightning.

Mark Twain, *The Late Benjamin Franklin*

He is our wise prophet of chicanery, the great buffoon, the face on the penny stamp.

William Carlos Williams, *In the American Grain*

*See also* Noah Webster

## FREDERICK AUGUSTUS, *see under* YORK AND ALBANY, DUKE OF

## FREDERICK LOUIS

1707–51 Prince of Wales

I did not think ingrafting my half-witted coxcomb upon a madwoman would mend the breed.

George II, attributed

Here lies Fred, / Who was alive and is dead: / Had it been his father, / I had much rather; / Had it been his brother, / Better than another; / Had it been his sister, / No one would have missed her; / Had it been the whole generation, / Better for the nation: / But since 'tis only Fred, / Who was alive and is dead – / There 's no more to be said. /

Horace Walpole, *Memoirs of George II*

## FRICK, HENRY CLAY

1849–1919 Industrialist, Art Collector

. . . in his palace, seated on a Renaissance throne under a Baldachino and holding in his little hand a copy of the *Saturday Evening Post*.

Anon., in Matthew Josephson, *The Robber Barons*

## FROBISHER, SIR MARTIN

1535?–94 Navigator

Martin, admiral of fifty tons, anchored solemnly in front of the Queen's palace where she was holding her court, and fired a salute. We can imagine Her Majesty, interrupted in a conversation with Walsyngham, discussing, of course, the extraordinary news that the Spanish army in Flanders was not only without a general and without wages, but that the soldiers were going off in companies to loot the villages of Catholic Brabant. The ladies in waiting called Her Majesty's attention to the scene across the river – the diminutive flotilla of – what was the name – Captain Martin Fyrbussher. Bound wither? Ah yes, for Cathay.

William McFee, *Sir Martin Frobisher* (on his salute of the Queen at Greenwich)

## FROST, ROBERT LEE

1874–1963 Poet

I never dared be radical when young / For fear it would make me conservative / when old. /

On himself, *Precaution*

I guess I don't take life very seriously. It's hard to get into this world and hard to get out of it. And what's in between doesn't make much sense. If that sounds pessimistic, let it stand. There's been too much vaporous optimism voiced about life and age.

On himself, in an interview with Robert Peterson in November 1962, in Edward Connery Latham ed., *Interviews with Robert Frost*

I'd just as soon play tennis with the net down.

On himself, commenting on the writing of free verse, in *Newsweek*, 30 January 1956

When Robert Frost was asked to explain one of his poems he replied 'What do you want me to do – say it over again in worser English?'

H. E. F. Donohue, in *New York Herald Tribune Book Weekly*

He is a poet of the minor theme, the casual approach, and the discreetly eccentric attitude.

Yvor Winters, 'Robert Frost: or, the Spiritual Drifter as Poet', in James M. Cox ed., *Robert Frost, A Collection of Critical Essays*

## FROUDE, JAMES ANTHONY

1818–94 Historian

I am going to stick to the History . . . and I believe I shall make something of it. At any rate one has substantial stuff between one's fingers to be moulding at, and not those slime and sea sand ladders to the moon 'opinion'.

On himself, Letter to A. H. Clough, 22 November 1853

Well, when the Liberals are in, Mr Froude is sometimes a Conservative. When the Conservatives are in, Mr Froude is always a Liberal.

His butler's response to a canvassing agent, in Herbert Paul, *Life of Froude*

[Carlyle's] doctrine of heroes . . . comes next in atrocity to the doctrine that the flag covers the goods, that the cause justifies its agents, which is what Froude lives for.

Lord Acton, Letter to Mrs Drew, 10 February 1881

He himself used to say that the interest of life to a thinking man was exhausted at thirty, or thirty-five. After that there remained nothing but the disappointment of earlier visions and hopes. Sometimes there was something almost fearful in the gloom, and utter disbelief, and defiance of his mind.

Sir George Colley, in Herbert Paul, *Life of Froude*

. . . in Froude's case the loss of his faith turned out to be rather like the loss of a heavy port manteau, which one afterwards discovers to have been full of old rags and brickbats.

Lytton Strachey, *Eminent Victorians*

Froude informs the Scottish youth / That parsons do not care for truth. / The Reverend Canon Kingsley cries / History is a pack of lies. / What cause for judgments so malign? / A brief reflection solves the mystery – / Froude believes Kingsley a divine, / And Kingsley goes to Froude for history. /

William Stubbs, Letter to J. R. Green, 17 December 1871

. . . a desultory and theoretical littérateur who wrote more rot on the reign of Elizabeth than Gibbon required for all the Decline and Fall.

Algernon Turnor, Letter to Sir Henry Ponsonby, 13 May 1878

*See also* Charles Kingsley

## FRY, ROGER ELIOT

1866–1934 Art Critic, Painter

His scholarship was impressive, he had studied painting with the thoroughness he brought to all his undertakings, he was at home in galleries all over Europe, he was a formidable art historian; but when he began to paint, he was Mr Facing Both-Ways; a thousand theories assailed him, paralysing every stroke of the brush.

M. Lilly, *Sickert, the Painter and His Circle*

*See also* J. S. Cotman

## FULLER, (SARAH) MARGARET (MARCHIONESS OSSOLI)

1810–50 Transcendentalist, Social Reformer, Critic

She always keeps asking if I don't observé a / Particular likeness 'twixt her and Minerva. /

James Russell Lowell, in James D. Hart, *The Oxford Companion to American Literature*

. . . to whom Venus gave everything except beauty, and Pallas everything except wisdom.

Oscar Wilde, in Arthur W. Brown, *Margaret Fuller*

# ‘G’

## GABLE, (WILLIAM) CLARK

1901–60 Actor

I'm not much of an actor but I'm not bad unless it's one of those things outside my comprehension. I work hard. I'm no Adonis and I'm as American as the telephone poles I used to climb to make a living. So men don't get sore if their womenfolk like me on the screen. I'm one of them, they know it, so it's a compliment to them.

They see me broke, in trouble, scared of things that go bump in the night but coming out fighting, they see me making love to Jean Harlow or Claudette Colbert and they say, If he can do it I can do it, and figure it'll be fun to go home and make love to their wives.

On himself, in Adela Rogers St Johns, *The Honeycomb*

Gable's ruthless realism made him the first great antihero of American movies, a Don Quixote in reverse, who saw the windmill in every giant and the whore in every lady. Before a generation coined the term, he invented *cool.* He was able to wade through the worst of MGM's syrupy sentimentality and shake it off, without a single ruffle to his feathers.

René Jordan, *Clark Gable*

The movies desperately needed someone like Gable and he was in the right place at the right time with the right face. Ears too big, manners too rough, he emerged as the popular thirties Everyman. Men could identify with him as he went about dispensing vicarious thrills such as telling the boss where to get off or bringing the haughty heiress down a peg. For women, he was a promise of powerful earthy sexuality that could hopefully be found at the Woolworth counter.

*Ibid.*

Gable. The King. An exaggeration of A Man.

Adela Rogers St Johns, *The Honeycomb*

## GAINSBOROUGH, THOMAS

1727–88 Painter

He was sure the perplexities of rendering art like a human resemblance, from human blocks, was a trial of patience that would have tempted holy St Anthony to cut his own throat with his palette-knife.

H. Angelo, *Reminiscences*

His subjects are softened and sentimentalised too much, it is not simple unaffected nature that we see, but nature sitting for her picture.

William Hazlitt, ‘On Gainsborough's Pictures’, in *Champion*, 31 July 1814

The charm of Gainsborough is indefinable: there is always something amateurish about him, and one feels like calling him the first (beyond all comparison) of the amateurs. It is not the charm of vigour, but the charm of facility, and of a correctness and softness of style so perfect that they never had occasion to dream of mannerism.

Henry James, ‘The Old Masters at Burlington House’, in *Nation*, 1 February 1877

Gainsborough was a fashionable portrait-painter. He never painted anything or anybody that any Englishman of the day could not have seen and in his turn observed ‘from the life’.

And yet he was as much a fantastic as William Blake in his way. He did not see his sitters, or only saw them in a trance: a very mild, superficial trance, but nevertheless a palpable one. The fancies that hung around them, the flavour of their lives, their illusions about themselves, or about each other, all went to his head as they floated into his studio to be painted, like some enervating bergamot. He was doped with the graceful existence of all these pretty people, and that is how he worked. He saw nothing but pale blue clichés, and never a man or woman. Blake's Jehovah is a far realler person, or at least you can imagine him in the Tottenham Court Road more readily. You would take him for a Hampstead Nature crank, with his long hair, bare feet, and night-shirt.

P. Wyndham Lewis, 'Painting of the Soul', in *Athenaeum*, December 1919

Nothing can be more strongly expressive of Gainsborough's acknowledged goodness of heart, and of his ardent love for the profession, than the exclamation uttered whilst expiring – 'We are all going to Heaven, and Vandyke is of the party.'

James Northcote, *The Life of Sir Joshua Reynolds*

It is certain, that all those odd scratches and marks, which, on a close examination, are so observable in Gainsborough's pictures, and which even to experienced painters appear rather the effect of accident than design: this chaos, this uncouth and shapeless appearance, by a kind of magic, at a certain distance assumes form, and all the parts seem to drop into their proper places.

Joshua Reynolds, *Fourteenth Discourse*, 10 December 1788

The landscape of Gainsborough is soothing, tender, and affecting. The stillness of noon, the depths of twilight, and the dews and pearls of the morning, are all to be found on the canvases of this most benevolent and kind-hearted man. On looking at them we find tears in our eyes, and know not what brings them.

John Ruskin, Lecture at the Royal Institution, 16 June 1836

*See also* John Crome

## GAITSKELL, HUGH TODD NAYLOR

1906–63 Statesman

I became a Socialist . . . not so much because I was a passionate advocate of public ownership but because I came to hate and loathe social injustice, because I disliked the class structure of our society, because I could not tolerate the indefensible difference of status and income which disfigures our society. I hated the insecurity that affected such a large part of our community while others led lives of security and comfort. I became a Socialist because I hated poverty and squalor.

On himself, at the Labour Party Conference, 1955

A desiccated calculating machine.

Aneurin Bevan, in W. T. Rodgers ed., *Hugh Gaitskell 1906–63*

Hugh Gaitskell developed naturally from boyhood to maturity in a singularly straight line.

Maurice Bowra, in *ibid.*

Gaitskell has a Wykehamistical voice and manner and a 13th century face.

Henry Channon, Diary, 10 April 1951

. . . Morally, he was in the bravest of all categories: he flinched, but he always went on.

Roy Jenkins, in W. T. Rodgers ed., *Hugh Gaitskell 1906–63*

He had reasoned himself into international socialism, but his vision of the future was one of England's Jerusalem.
Michael Postan, in *ibid.*

## GALSWORTHY, JOHN

1867–1933 Author

For that is, my dear Jack, what you are – a humanitarian moralist.
Joseph Conrad, Letter to Galsworthy

We had dinner with Galsworthy the night before we left and I was rather disappointed in him. I can't stand pessimism with neither irony nor bitterness.
F. Scott Fitzgerald, Letter to Shane Leslie, 24 May 1921

Galsworthy had not quite enough of the superb courage of his satire. He faltered, and gave in to the Forsytes. It is a thousand pities. He might have been the surgeon the modern soul needs so badly, to cut away the proud flesh of our Forsytes from the living body of men who are fully alive. Instead, he put down the knife and laid on a soft sentimental poultice, and helped to make the corruption worse.
D. H. Lawrence, *Phoenix*

The thing that strikes one about Galsworthy is that though he's trying to be iconoclastic, he has been utterly unable to move his mind outside the wealthy bourgeois society he is attacking . . . All he conceives to be wrong is that human beings are a little too inhumane, a little too fond of money, and aesthetically not quite sensitive enough. When he sets out to depict what he conceives as the desirable type of human being, it turns out to be simply a cultivated, humanitarian version of the upper-middle-class *rentier*, the sort of person who in those days used to haunt picture galleries in Italy and subscribe heavily to the Society for the Prevention of Cruelty to Animals.
George Orwell, *The Rediscovery of Europe*

The fact is that neither Mr Galsworthy nor Mr Kipling has a spark of the woman in him. Thus all their qualities seem to a woman, if one may generalise, crude and immature. They lack suggestive power. And when a book lacks suggestive power, however hard it hits the surface of the mind it cannot penetrate within.
Virginia Woolf, *A Room of One's Own*

## GAMBART, ERNEST

1814–1902 Art Dealer

There is an old he-wolf named Gambart, / Beware of him if thou a lamb art, / Else thy tail and thy toes / And thine innocent nose / Will be ground by the grinders of Gambart. /
Dante Gabriel Rossetti, in Jeremy Maas, *Gambart: Prince of the Victorian Art World*

## GARFIELD, JAMES ABRAM

1831–81 Twentieth United States President

He rushes into a fight with the horns of a bull and the skin of a rabbit.
Jeremiah Black, in John M. Taylor, *Garfield of Ohio: The Available Man*

Garfield has an interest everywhere . . . but in the Kingdom of Heaven.
Oliver P. Brown, in *ibid.*

Garfield has shown that he is not possessed of the backbone of an angle-worm.
Ulysses S. Grant, in *ibid.*

One of the noblest sentences ever uttered was uttered by Mr Garfield before he became President. He was a member of Congress, as I remember it, at the time of Lincoln's assassination. He was at the old Fifth Avenue Hotel and they begged him to go out and say something to the people. He went out and after he had attracted their attention, he said this beautiful thing: 'My fellow citizens, the President is dead, but the Government lives and God Omnipotent reigns.'

Woodrow Wilson, Address, Helena, Montana, 11 September 1919

## GARFIELD, JOHN

1913–52 Actor

Projected on the screens of the world, he was the Eternal Outsider, obliged to glimpse paradise but not to dwell there. John Garfield was the vagabond hood, the urban ne'er do well, the diamond-in-the-rough prodigy, the nervously embattled G.I. In every guise he conveyed an inner turbulence. As a primitive but idealistic sinner, he was as formidable as steel but vulnerably naive, volatile but plaintive. He was a game competitor but a born loser – urgently forceful and forcefully attractive, but never the master of his fate. Because the cards were stacked against him in the script, he was finally pathetic.

Larry Swindell, *Body and Soul: The Story of John Garfield*

## GARLAND, JUDY (FRANCES GUMM)

1922–69 Singer, Actress

If I'm such a legend, then why am I so lonely? If I'm such a legend, then why do I sit at home for hours staring at the damned telephone, hoping it's out of order, even calling the operator asking her if she's *sure* it's not out of order? Let me tell you, legends are all very well if you've got somebody around who loves you, some man who's not afraid to be in love with Judy Garland.

On herself, in John Gruen, *Close-Up*

. . . To watch her pouring out her devotion to 'Dear Mr Gable' and the great, big, wonderful world of the movies was a pleasure almost voyeuristic. One was seeing not the simulated emotions of an accomplished actress, but the real emotions of a real, vulnerable girl passing across her face and coloring her urgent, husky . . . voice with an extraordinary absence of self-consciousness, self-censorship. She gave everything, without reserve – which was to be her triumph and finally, perhaps, her tragedy.

John Russell Taylor and Arthur Jackson, *The Hollywood Musical*

Even with her personal problems, her well-known addiction to 'Wake-me-up-put-me-to-sleep-now-calm-me-down' pills, her unpredictable behavior with concert promoters, showing up hours late and, reportedly, not at all on a few occasions, she was undisputedly a one-of-a-kind human being and artist. No one could deny this. She had played the *enfant terrible* over and over throughout her stormy career. Yet prominent, talented people from virtually every walk of life idolized her, swore by her, defended and protected her, a combined show of fealty unrivaled in the business.

Mel Tormé, *The Other Side of the Rainbow with Judy Garland on the Dawn Patrol*

## GARNER, JOHN NANCE

1868–1967 Politician

Worst damfool mistake I ever made was letting myself be elected Vice-President of the United States. Should have stuck with my old chores as Speaker of the House. I gave up the second most important job in the Government for one that didn't amount to a hill of beans. I spent eight long years as Mr Roosevelt's spare tire.

On himself, in Frank X. Tolbert,

'What is Cactus Jack Up to Now', in *Saturday Evening Post*, 2 November 1963

## GARRICK, DAVID

1717–79 Actor

The painter dead, yet still he charms the eye, / While England lives his fame can never die. / But he who struts his hour upon the stage / Can scarce extend his fame for half an age. / No pen nor pencil can the actor save; / The art and artist share one common grave. /

On himself, in Edgar Pemberton, 'The Marvel of Mary Anderson', *Munsey's Magazine*, vol. 32, 1904–5

That Garrick *ranted* a little, and 'died hard', too *hard*, is upon record.

John Bee, *Works of Samuel Foote*

Dr Burney having remarked that Mr Garrick was beginning to look old, he [Johnson] said, 'Why, Sir, you are not to wonder at that; no man's face has more wear and tear.'

James Boswell, *Life of Johnson*

Sir Joshua Reynolds observed, with great truth, that Johnson considered Garrick to be as it were his *property*. He would allow no man either to blame or to praise Garrick in his presence, without contradicting him.

*Ibid.*

I presume to animadvert on his eulogy on Garrick, in his *Lives of the Poets*, 'You say, Sir, his death eclipsed the gaiety of nations.' *Johnson*: 'I could not have said more or less. It is the truth; *eclipsed*, not *extinguished*; and his death *did* eclipse; it was like a storm.' *Boswell*: But why nations? Did his gaiety extend farther than his own nation? *Johnson*: 'Why, Sir, some exaggeration must be allowed . . .'

*Ibid.*

He took off Dr Johnson most admirably. Indeed I enjoyed it doubly from being in his company; his *see-saw*, his *pawing*, his very *look*, *and* his voice! My *cot*! what an astonishing thing it is that he [Garrick] has not a good ear for music! He took him off in a speech (that has *stuck in his gizzard* ever since some friendly person was so obliging as to repeat it to him). Indeed, I should much wonder if it did not, for it would have been a severe speech if it had been said upon who it would, much more upon Garrick, indeed, I think it must have been exaggerated, or if not, that it was a very severe, ill-natured, unjust thing. 'Yes, yes, Davy has some convivial pleasantries in him, but 'tis a futile Fellow.' A little while after, he took him off in one of his *own convivial pleasantries*, 'No Sir; I'm for the musick of the ancients, it has been corrupted so.'

Fanny Burney, *Journal*, 1777

I have seen you with your magic hammer in your hand, endeavouring to beat your ideas into the heads of creatures who had none of their own. I have seen you, with lamb-like patience, endeavouring to make them comprehend you, and I have seen you when that could not be done – I have seen your lamb turned into a lion; by this your great labour and pains the public was entertained; *they* thought they all acted very fine; they did not see you pull the wires.

Kitty Clive, in W. Clark Russell, *Representative Actors*

Damn him, he could act a gridiron!

Kitty Clive, in William Archer, *Introduction to the Dramatic Essays of Leigh Hunt*

Our Garrick's a salad, for in him we see / Oil, vinegar, sugar, and saltness agree. /

Oliver Goldsmith, in James Boswell, *Life of Johnson*

Here lies David Garrick, describe me who can, / An abridgement of all that was pleasant in man; / As an actor, confest without rival to shine, / As a wit, if not first, in the very first line, / Yet with talents like these, and an excellent heart, / The man had his failings, a dupe to his art; / Like an ill-judging beauty, his colours he spread, / And beplaistered with rouge his own natural red. / On the stage he was natural, simple, affecting, / 'Twas only that, when he was off, he was acting: / With no reason on earth to go out of his way, / He turn'd and he varied full ten times a day. / Tho' secure of our hearts, yet confoundedly sick / If they were not his own by finessing and trick, / He cast off his friends, as a huntsman his pack, / For he knew when he pleas'd he could whistle them back. /

Oliver Goldsmith, *Retaliation*

We have heard it mentioned that once . . . while he was kneeling to repeat the curse, the first row in the pit stood up to see him better; the second row, not willing to lose the precious moments by remonstrating, stood up too; and so, by a tacit movement, the entire pit rose to hear the withering imprecation, while the whole passed in such cautious silence that you might have heard a pin drop.

William Hazlitt, in *London Magazine*, June 1820

But what are the hopes of man! I am disappointed by that stroke of death, which has eclipsed the gaiety of nations and impoverished the public stock of harmless pleasure.

Samuel Johnson, *Lives of the Poets*: 'Edward Smith'

'Garrick,' said Dr Johnson, 'begins to complain of the fatigue of the stage. Sir, a man that bawls turnips all day for his bread does twice as much.'

Samuel Johnson, in J. Cradock, *Literary and Miscellaneous Memoirs*

Garrick's conversation is gay and grotesque. It is a dish of all sorts, but all good things. There is no solid meat in it: there is a want of sentiment in it. Not but that he has sentiment sometimes, and sentiment too, very powerful, and very pleasing; but it has not its full proportion in his conversation.

Samuel Johnson, in James Boswell, *Life of Johnson*

Garrick . . . made himself a slave to his reputation. Amongst the variety of arts observed by his friends to preserve that reputation, one of them was to make himself rare. It was difficult to get him, and when you had him, as difficult to keep him. He never came into company but with a plot how to get out of it. He was for ever receiving messages of his being wanted in another place. It was a rule with him never to leave any company saturated. Being used to exhibit himself at a theatre or a large table, he did not consider an individual as worth powder and shot.

Sir Joshua Reynolds, *Notes on Garrick*

*See also* Thomas Arne, Samuel Foote

## GARRISON, WILLIAM LLOYD

1805–79 Abolitionist, Editor

Confine me as a prisoner – but bind me not as a slave / Punish me as a criminal – but hold me not as a chattel. / Torture me as a man – but drive me not like a beast. / Doubt my sanity – but acknowledge my immortality. /

On himself, on the wall of the jail in Boston where he was confined for the night, 1835

He is the Atlas of abolition. Had not God made *his* forehead strong against the foreheads of the people, the bark of abolition would have been wrecked on the rocks and quicksands of human expediency. So he says. I believe in my soul, we have all overvalued Garrison. And as to himself, pride has driven him mad. I cannot bear to see this ignoble idolatry among abolitionists.

Gamaliel Bailey of New York, 14 October 1837, in G. M. Frederickson ed., *William Lloyd Garrison*

Would find nothing to do in a lonely world, or a world with half-a-dozen inhabitants.

Ralph Waldo Emerson, in Russel B. Nye, *William Lloyd Garrison and the Humanitarian Reformers*

## GASKELL, ELIZABETH CLEGHORN

1810–65 Novelist

A natural unassuming woman whom they have been doing their best to spoil by making a lioness of her.

Jane Welsh Carlyle, Letter, 17 May 1849

The outstanding fact about Mrs Gaskell is her femininity . . . We have only to look at the portrait of Mrs Gaskell, soft-eyed, beneath her charming veil, to see that she was a dove. In an age whose ideal of woman emphasized the feminine qualities at the expense of all others, she was all a woman was expected to be; gentle, domestic, tactful, unintellectual, prone to tears, easily shocked. So far from chafing at the limits imposed on her activities, she accepted them with serene satisfaction.

David Cecil, *Early Victorian Novelists*

Paraclete of the Bartons!

Walter Savage Landor, *To the Author of Mary Barton*

## GAVESTON, PIERS, EARL OF CORNWALL

– d. 1312 Royal Favourite

He himself, confident that he had been confirmed for life in his earldom, albeit he was an alien and had been preferred to so great dignity solely by the king's favour, had now grown so insolent as to despise all the nobles of the land; among whom he called the Earl of Warwick (a man of equal wisdom and integrity) 'the Black Dog of Arden.' When this was reported to the earl, he is said to have replied with calmness: 'If he call me a dog, be sure that I will bite him, so soon as I shall perceive my opportunity.'

*The Chronicle of Lanercost*, translated by Sir Herbert Maxwell

*Gaveston*: I must have wanton Poets, pleasant wits, / Musitians, that with touching of a string / May draw the pliant king which way I please: / Therefore ile have Italian maskes by night, / Sweete speeches, comedies, and pleasing showes, / And in the day when he shall walk abroad, / Like *Sylvian* Nimphes my pages shall be clad, / My men like Satyres grazing on the lawnes, / Shall with their Goate feete daunce an antick hay. / Sometimes a lovelie boy in *Dians* shape, / With haire that gilds the water as it glides, / Crownets of pearl about his naked armes, / And in his sportfull hands an Olive tree, / To hide those parts which men delight to see, / Shall bathe him in a spring. /

Christopher Marlowe, *Edward II*, Act I, Scene i

*See also* Edward II

## GAY, JOHN

1685–1732 Dramatist

The contempt of the world grows upon me, and I now begin to be richer and richer, for I find I could every morning I wake, be content with less than I aimed at the day before. I fancy in time, I shall bring myself into that state which No man ever knew before me, in thinking I have enough. I really am afraid to be content with so little, lest my good friends should censure me for indolence, and the want of laudable ambition, so that it will be absolutely necessary for me to improve my fortune to content them. How solicitous is mankind to please others.

On himself, Letter to Jonathan Swift, 18 February 1727

Life is a Jest, and all Things show it; / I thought so once, but now I know it. /

On himself, Proposed epitaph, in Letter to Alexander Pope, October 1727

For writing in the cause of Virtue, and against the fashionable vices, I am lookt upon at present as the most obnoxious person almost in England... Mr Pope tells me that I am dead and that this obnoxiousness is the reward of my inoffensiveness in my former life.

On himself, Letter to Jonathan Swift, 18 March 1728

Cou'd any man but you think of trusting John Gay with his money; none of his friends wou'd ever trust him with his own whenever they cou'd avoid it.

Lord Bathurst, Letter to Jonathan Swift, 19 April 1731

I have been told of an ingenious observation of Mr Gibbon, that, 'The Beggar's Opera may, perhaps, have sometimes increased the number of highwaymen: but that it has had a beneficial effect in refining that class of men, making them less ferocious, more polite, – in short, more like gentlemen.' Upon this, Mr Courtenay said, that 'Gay was the Orpheus of Highwaymen.'

James Boswell, Note to *Life of Johnson*

Gay is a great eater. 'As the French Philosopher used to prove his existence by *Cogito ergo sum*, the greatest proof of Gay's existence is *Edit, ergo est*.'

William Congreve, as reported by Joseph Spence, *Anecdotes*

He was a satirist without gall. He had a delightful placid vein of invention, fancy, wit, humour, description, ease, and elegance, a happy style, and a versification which seemed to cost him nothing. His *Beggar's Opera* indeed has stings in it, but it appears to have left the writer's mind without any.

William Hazlitt, *A Critical List of Authors*

Much however must be allowed to the author of a new species of composition, though it be not of the highest kind. We owe to Gay the ballad Opera; a mode of comedy which at first was supposed to delight only by its novelty, but has now by the experience of half a century been found so well accommodated to the disposition of a popular audience, that it is likely to keep long possession of the stage. Whether this new drama was the product of judgement or luck, the praise of it must be given to the inventor; and there are many writers read with more reverence, to whom such merit of originality cannot be attributed.

Samuel Johnson, *Lives of the Poets*

Of manners gentle, of Affections mild; / In Wit, a Man; Simplicity, a Child; / With native Humour temp'ring virtuous Rage, / Form'd to delight at once and lash the age; / Above Temptation, in a low Estate, / And uncorrupted ev'n among the Great; / A safe Companion, and an easy Friend, / Unblam'd thro Life, lamented in thy End. / These are Thy Humours! not that here thy Bust / Is mix'd with Heroes, or with Kings thy dust; / But that the worthy and the Good shall say, / Striking their pensive bosoms – *Here* lies *Gay*. /

Alexander Pope, *Epitaph on Mr Gay, in Westminster Abbey*

Good God, how often are we to die before we go quite off this stage? In every friend we lose a part of ourselves, and the best part . . . Would to God the man we have lost had not been so amiable, nor so good!

Alexander Pope, Letter to Jonathan Swift, 5 December 1732

Upon the whole I deliver my judgement; that nothing but servile attachment to a party, affectation of singularity, lamentable dullness, mistaken zeal, or studied hypocrisy, can have any objection against this excellent moral performance of Mr Gay.

Jonathan Swift, on *The Beggar's Opera*, *Intelligencer*, no. 3.

A coach and six horses is the utmost exercise you can bear, and this onely when you can fill it with Such company as is best Suited to your tast, and how glad would you be if it could waft you in the air to avoyd jolting . . . You mortally hate writing onely because it is the thing you chiefly ought to do as well to keep up the vogue you have in the world, as to make you easy in your fortune; you are mercifull to every thing but money, your best friend, whom you treat with inhumanity.

Jonathan Swift, Letter to Gay, May 1732

With . . . kind lordly folks, a real Duke and Duchess, as delightful as those who harboured Don Quixote, and loved that dear old Sancho, Gay lived, and was lapped in cotton, and had his plate of chicken, and his saucer of cream, and frisked, and barked, and wheezed, and grew fat, and so ended.

W. M. Thackeray, *The English Humourists*

*See also* John Fletcher, Jonathan Swift

## GEORGE I

1660–1727

I hate all Boets and Bainters.

On himself, in Lord Campbell, *Life of Mansfield*

When Henry the Eighth left the Pope in the lurch, / The Protestants made him the head of the Church; / But George's good subjects, the Bloomsbury people, / Instead of the Church, made him head of the steeple. /

Anon., in Sir H. M. Imbert Terry, *A Constitutional King*

God in His wrath sent Saul to trouble Jewry, / And George to England in a greater fury; / For George in sin as far exceedeth Saul / As ever Bishop Burnet did Saint Paul. /

Anon., in *ibid.*

No woman came amiss of him, if they were very willing and very fat . . . the standard of His Majesty's taste made all those ladies who aspired to his favour, and who were near the statutable size, strain and swell themselves like the frogs in the fable to rival the bulk and dignity of the ox. Some succeeded, and others burst.

Lord Chesterfield, in A. F. Scott, *Every One A Witness*

George I was lazy and inactive even in his pleasures, which therefore were lowly sensual. He was coolly intrepid and indolently benevolent . . . Importunity alone could make him act, and then only to get rid of it.

Lord Chesterfield, in *ibid.*

George I kept his wife in prison because he believed that she was no better than he was.

Will Cuppy, *The Decline and Fall of Practically Everybody*

George the First knew nothing and desired to know nothing; did nothing and desired to do nothing; and the only good thing that is told of him is that he wished to restore the crown to its hereditary successor.

Samuel Johnson, in James Boswell, *Life of Johnson*

He was passively good-natured, and wished all mankind enjoyed quiet, if they would let him do so.

Lady Mary Wortley Montagu, in Lewis Melville, *The First George*

In private life he would have been called an honest blockhead; and Fortune, that made him a king, added nothing to his happiness, only prejudiced his honesty, and shortened his days. No man was ever more free from ambition; he loved money, but loved to keep his own, without being rapacious of other men's.

*Ibid.*

The king was heard to say in the drawing-room, upon the falling of the South Sea stock: 'We had very good luck; for we sold out last week.'

Joseph Spence, *Anecdotes*

The King, observing with judicious eyes, / The state of both his universities, / To Oxford sent a troop of horse, and why? / That learned body wanted loyalty; / To Cambridge books, as very well discerning / How much that loyal body wanted learning. /

Joseph Trapp, *On George I's Donation to Cambridge*

The King to Oxford sent a troop of horse / For Tories own no argument but force. / With equal skill to Cambridge books he sent, / For Whigs admit no force but argument. /

Sir William Browne, *Riposte to Trapp*

*See also* William III

## GEORGE II

1683–1760

He had no favourites and indeed no friends, having none of that expansion of heart, none of those amiable connecting talents, which are necessary for both. This, together with the sterility of his conversation, made him prefer the company of women, with whom he rather sauntered away than enjoyed his leisure hours. He was addicted to women, but chiefly to such as require little attention and less pay.

Lord Chesterfield, in A. F. Scott, *Every One A Witness*

The best, perhaps, that can be said of him is that on the whole, all things considered, he might have been worse.

Justin McCarthy, *A History of the Four Georges*

O strutting Turkey-cock of Herrenhausen! O naughty little Mahomet! In what Turkish paradise are you now, and where be your painted houris? . . . Friends, he was your fathers' King as well as mine – let us drop a respectful tear over his grave.

W. M. Thackeray, *The Four Georges*

He had the haughtiness of Henry VIII without his spirit; the avarice of Henry VII, without his exactions; the indignities of Charles I, without his bigotry for his prerogative; the vexation of King William, with as little skill in the management of parties; and the gross gallantry of his father, without his goodnature or his honesty: – he might perhaps have been honest, if he had never hated his father, or had ever loved his son.

Horace Walpole, *Memoirs*

Content to bargain for the gratification of his two predominant passions, Hanover and money, he was almost indifferent to the rest of his royal authority, provided exterior observance was not wanting; for he comforted himself if he did not perceive the diminution of Majesty, though it was notorious to all the rest of the world.

*Ibid.*

## GEORGE III

1738–1820

I desire what is good; therefore, everyone who does not agree with me is a traitor.

On himself, in Sir John Fortescue ed., *The Correspondence of George III*

Men of less principle and honesty than I pretend to may look on public measures and opinions as a game; I always act from conviction.

On himself, in Richard Pares, *George III and the Politicians*

Throughout the greater part of his life George III was a kind of consecrated obstruction.

Walter Bagehot, *The English Constitution*

George the Third / Ought never to have occurred. / One can only wonder / At so grotesque a blunder. /

Edmund Clerihew Bentley, *Biography for Beginners*

[Dr Johnson] said to Mr Barnard, 'Sir, they may talk of the king as they will; but he is the finest gentleman I have ever seen.' And he afterwards observed to Mr Langton, 'Sir, his manners are those of as fine a gentleman as we may suppose Louis the Fourteenth or Charles the Second.'

James Boswell, *Life of Johnson*

In the first year of freedom's second dawn / Died George the Third; although no tyrant, one / Who shielded tyrants, till each sense withdrawn / Left him nor mental nor external sun: / A better farmer ne'er brushed dew from lawn, / A worse king never left a realm undone! / He died – but left his subjects still behind, / One half as mad – and 'tother no less blind. /

Lord Byron, *The Vision of Judgement*

He ever warr'd with freedom and the free: / Nations as men, home subjects, foreign foes, / So they utter'd the word 'Liberty!' / Found George the Third their first opponent. Whose / History was ever stain'd as his will be / With national and individual woes? / I grant his household abstinence; I grant / His neutral virtues, which most monarchs want; /

I know he was a constant consort; own / He was a decent sire, and middling lord. / All this is much and most upon a throne; / And temperance, if at Apicius' board, / Is more than at an anchorite's supper shown. / I grant him all the kindest can accord; / And this was well for him, but not for those / Millions who found him what oppression chose. /

*Ibid.*

He came to his sceptre young; he leaves it old: / Look to the state in which he found his realm, / And left it; and his annals too behold, / How to a minion first he gave the helm; / How grew upon his heart a thirst for gold, / The beggar's vice, which can but overwhelm / The meanest hearts; and for the rest, but glance / Thine eye along America and France. /

'Tis true, he was a tool from first to last / (I have the workmen safe); but as a tool / So let him be consumed. From out the past / Of ages, since mankind have known the rule / Of monarchs – from the bloody rolls amass'd / Of sin and slaughter – from the Caesars' school, / Take the worst pupil; and produce a reign / More drench'd with gore, more cumber'd with the slain. /

*Ibid.*

There is a certain continuity in his prejudices, but hardly any in his policy.

F. S. Oliver, *The Endless Adventure*

His madness can best be explained as the breakdown of too costly a struggle to maintain this artificial character –

the reserve and equanimity imposed upon a hot temper and anxious nerves, to say nothing of his resolute fidelity to a hideous queen, and a regimen of violent and exaggerated abstinence designed to counteract strong passions and a tendency to fat.

Richard Pares, *George III and the Politicians*

His maxims, in mid-career, were those of a conscientious bull in a china shop.

*Ibid.*

It is true that George III could only think of one thing at a time, but as that is also one of the most prominent characteristics of the English people, what might have proved a source of weakness served as an additional bond of union between him and them.

Sir Charles Petrie, *The Four Georges*

If he is to be blamed, it must not be for what he did, but for what he was – an unbalanced man of low intelligence. And if he is to be praised, it is because he attempted to discharge honourably tasks that were beyond his powers.

J. H. Plumb, *Men and Places*

When an old lady asked him [John Wolcot, 'Peter Pindar'] if he did not think he was a very bad subject of our most pious King George, he replied, 'I do not know anything about that, Madam, but I *do* know the king has been a devilish good subject for me.'

Cyrus Redding, *Fifty Years Recollections*

By a certain persistent astuteness; by the dexterous utilising of political rivalries; by cajoling some men and betraying others; by a resolute adroitness that turned disaster and even disease into instruments of his aim, the King realised his darling object, of converting the dogeship to which he had succeeded, into a real and to some extent a personal monarchy.

Lord Rosebery, *Pitt*

For the King himself, he seems all good-nature and wishing to satisfy everybody; all his speeches are obliging. I saw him again yesterday, and was surprised to find the levee room had lost so entirely the air of the lion's den. This Sovereign don't stand in one spot, with his eyes fixed royally on the ground, and dropping bits of German news; he walks about and speaks to everybody. I saw him afterwards on the throne, where he is graceful and genteel, sits with dignity, and reads his answers to addresses well.

Horace Walpole, Letter of 1760, in A. F. Scott, *Every One A Witness*

Early one morning he met a boy in the stables at Windsor and said: 'Well, boy! what do you do? What do they pay you?' 'I help in the stable,' said the boy, 'But they only give me victuals and clothes.' 'Be content,' said George, 'I have no more.'

Beckles Willson, *George III*

Ward of the Law! – dread Shadow of a King! / Whose realm had dwindled to one stately room; / Whose universe was gloom immersed in gloom, / Darkness as thick as life o'er life could fling, / Save haply for some feeble glimmering / Of Faith and Hope – if thou, by nature's doom, / Gently hast sunk into the quiet tomb, / Why should we bend in grief, to sorrow cling, / When thankfulness were best? – Fresh-flowing tears, / Or, where tears flow not, sigh succeeding sigh, / Yield to such after-thought the sole reply / Which justly it can claim. The Nation hears / In this deep knell, silent for threescore years / An unexampled voice of awful memory! /

William Wordsworth, *On the Death of His Majesty*

## GEORGE IV

1762–1830

Arthur [Wellington] is king of England, [Daniel] O'Connell is king of Ireland, and I suppose I am Dean of Windsor.

On himself, on the issue of Catholic Emancipation, February 1829, in Lord Colchester, Diary

Alvanley, – who's your fat friend?
Beau Brummell, at the Cyprian's Ball, 1813

But still there is unto a patriot nation, / Which loves so well its country and its king, / A subject of sublimest exultation – / Bear it, ye Muses, on your brightest wing! / Howe'er the mighty locust, Desolation / Strip your green fields, and to your harvest cling, / Gaunt famine never shall approach the throne – / Though Ireland starve, great George weighs twenty stone. /
Lord Byron, *Don Juan*, canto viii

And where is 'Fum' the Fourth, our 'royal bird'? / Gone down, it seems, to Scotland to be fiddled / Unto by Sawney's violin, we have heard: / 'Caw me, caw thee' – for six months hath been hatching / This scene of royal itch and loyal scratching. /
*Ibid.*, canto ix

As a son, as a husband, as a father, and especially as an *adviser of young men*, I deem it my duty to say that, on a review of his whole life, I can find no one good thing to speak of, in either the conduct or the character of this King; and, as an Englishman, I should be ashamed to show my head, if I were not to declare that I deem his reign (including his regency) to have been the most unhappy for the people that England has ever known.
William Cobbett, in *Political Register*, 3 July 1830

King George IV believed that he was at the Battle of Waterloo, and indeed commanded there, and his friends were a little alarmed; but Knighton [his Physician], who was a sensible man, said: 'His Majesty has only to leave off curaçao and rest assured he will gain no more victories.'
Benjamin Disraeli, *Lothair*

The dandy of sixty, who bows with a grace, / And has taste in wigs, collars, cuirasses, and lace; / Who to tricksters and fools leaves the State and its treasure, / And, while Britain's in tears, sails about at his pleasure. /
William Hone, *The Political House that Jack Built*

How Monarchs die is easily explain'd / And thus it might upon the Tomb be chisell'd, / As long as George the Fourth could *reign* he reign'd, / And then he mizzled. /
Thomas Hood, *On a Royal Demise*

A corpulent Adonis of fifty.
Leigh Hunt, in *London Examiner*, 1813

Ye politicians, tell me, pray, / Why thus with woe and care rent? / This is the worst you can say, – / Some wind has blown the Whig away, / And left the *Heir Apparent*. /
Charles Lamb, *Epigram*

A noble, hasty race he ran, / Superbly filthy and fastidious; / He was the world's first gentleman, / And made the appellation hideous. /
W. M. Praed, Proposed epitaph, 1825

An oak tree cannot rise out of macaroons and madeira on the green baize of a card table.
J. B. Priestley, *Prince of Pleasure*

. . . the worst anchoring ground in Europe.
Lord Thurlow, in Christopher Hobhouse, *Fox*

*See also* George Cruikshank

## GEORGES I, II, III AND IV

George the First was always reckoned / Vile, but viler George the Second; /

And what mortal ever heard / Any good of George the Third? / When from earth the Fourth descended / God be praised, the Georges ended. /
Walter Savage Landor, *Epigram*

## GEORGE V
1865–1936

... give yourself more ... rest from the everlasting functions & speeches which get on one's nerves. I warned you what it would be like, these people think one is made of stone & that one can go on for ever.
On himself, Letter to the Prince of Wales, 12 October 1919

The life of the King is moving slowly to its close.
B.B.C. radio news bulletin, in Henry Channon, Diary, 20 January 1936

... The prestige of the monarchy, and the influence of the monarchy, in the prudent and conscientious hands of King George have waxed rather than waned ... No Cabinet, however strong, could afford to disregard the difficulties and doubts put forward by a sovereign who has no interest in party politics, and whose experience is reinforced by continuity and immutability.
Earl of Birkenhead, *America Revisited*

He is all right as a gay young midshipman. He may be all right as a wise old King. But the intervening period when he was Duke of York just shooting at Sandringham, is hard to manage or swallow. For seventeen years he did nothing at all but kill animals and stick in stamps.
Harold Nicolson, Diary, 17 August 1949

*See also* Alexander Fleming

## GEORGE VI
1895–1952

Everything is going nowadays. Before long, I shall also have to go.
On himself, in conversation with Vita Sackville-West, February 1948, in Harold Nicolson, Diary

... looked lonely and wistful as all the males of this family do on State occasions.
Henry Channon, observing the King's first levée, Diary, 6 February 1937

## GERMAIN, LORD GEORGE,
*see under* **SACKVILLE, VISCOUNT**

## GERONIMO
1829–1909 Warrior of the Chiricahua Apache

Forty five years old, erect as a lodgepole pine, every outline of his symmetrical form indicating strength, endurance, arrogance. Abundant black hair draping his shoulders, stern, paint-smeared features, those vindictive eyes, the livid scar, Geronimo, the renegade, strategist, trickster, killer of palefaces – now under arrest, but still defiant.
Joseph Clum (an Indian Agent, recollecting Geronimo upon moment of his capture, in Woodworth Clum, *Apache Agent*

## GERSHWIN, GEORGE
1898–1937 Composer

From Gershwin emanated a new American music not written with the ruthlessness of one who strives to demolish established rules, but based on a new native gusto and wit and awareness. His was a modernity that reflected the civilization we live in as excitingly as the headline in today's newspaper.

Ira Gershwin, in Edward Jablonski and Lawrence D. Stewart, *The Gershwin Years*

We remember a young man / Who remained naive in a sophisticated world / We remember a smile / That was nearly always on his face / A cigar / That was nearly always in his mouth / He was a lucky young man / Lucky to be so in love with the world / And lucky because the world was so in love with him. /

Oscar Hammerstein in Merle Armitage ed., *George Gershwin*

During his start in analysis I said to him 'Does it help your constipation George?' (I used to make fun of analysis.)

He answered, 'No, but now I understand why I have constipation.'

Oscar Levant, *Memoirs of an Amnesiac*

Once when George was speaking about a girl he'd been in love with who'd just married someone else, he said, 'If I wasn't so busy, I'd be upset.'

*Ibid.*

*See also* Oscar Levant

## GIBBON, EDWARD

1737–94 Historian

To the University of Oxford I acknowledge no obligation; and she will as willingly renounce me for a son, as I am willing to disclaim her for a mother. I spent fourteen months at Magdalen College; they proved the fourteen months the most idle and unprofitable of my whole life.

On himself, *Autobiography*

A matrimonial alliance has ever been the object of my terror rather than of my wishes. I was not very strongly pressed by my family or my passions to propagate the name and race of the Gibbons, and if some reasonable temptations occurred in the neighbourhood, the vague idea never proceeded to the length of a serious negotiation.

*Ibid.*

When I contemplate the common lot of mortality, I must acknowledge that I have drawn a high prize in the lottery of life.

*Ibid.*

The time is not far distant, Mr Gibbon, when your most ludicrous self-complacency . . . your affected moral purity perking up every now and then from the corrupt mass like artificial roses shaken off in the dark by some Prostitute on a heap of manure, your heartless scepticism . . . your tumid diction, your monotonous jingle of periods, will be still more exposed and scouted than they have been. Once fairly knocked off from your lofty bedizened stilts, you will be reduced to your just level and true standards.

William Beckford, note in a copy of *The Decline and Fall of the Roman Empire*

Gibbon's style is detestable; but it is not the worst thing about him.

Samuel Taylor Coleridge, *Table Talk*, 15 August 1833

When I read a chapter in Gibbon, I seem to be looking through a luminous haze or fog; figures come and go, I know not how or why, all larger than life, or distorted and discoloured; nothing is real, vivid, true; all is scenical, and, as it were, exhibited by candlelight.

*Ibid.*

Johnson's style was grand and Gibbon's elegant; the stateliness of the former was sometimes pedantic, and the polish of the latter was occasionally finical. Johnson marched to kettle-drums and trumpets; Gibbon moved to flutes and hautboys: Johnson hewed passages through the Alps, while Gibbon levelled walks through parks and gardens.

George Colman, *Random Records*

His person looked as funnily obese / As if a pagod, growing large as man, / Had rashly waddled off its chimney piece, / To visit a Chinese upon a fan. / Such his exterior; curious 'twas to scan! / And oft he rapped his snuffbox, cocked his snout, / And ere his polished periods he began, / Bent forwards, stretching his forefinger out, / And talked in phrases round as he was round about. /

George Colman, *The Luminous Historian*

Another damned, thick, square book! Always scribble, scribble, scribble! Eh! Mr Gibbon?

William Henry, Duke of Gloucester, attributed

There is no Gibbon but Gibbon and Gibbon is his prophet. The solemn march of his cadences, the majestic impropriety of his innuendo are without rivals in the respective annals of British eloquence and British indelicacy.

Philip Guedalla, *Supers and Supermen*

Heard of the death of Mr Gibbon, the calumniator of the despised Nazarene, the derider of Christianity. Awful dispensation! He too was my acquaintence. Lord, I bless thee, considering how much infidel acquaintence I have had, that my soul never came into their secret! How many souls have his writings polluted! Lord preserve others from their contagion.

Hannah More, Diary, 19 January 1774

In some passages he drew the thread of his verbosity finer than the staple of his argument.

Richard Porson, in William Cooke, *Memoirs of Samuel Foote*

Porson thought Gibbon's *Decline and Fall* beyond all comparison the greatest literary production of the eighteenth century, and was in the habit of repeating long passages from it. Yet I have heard him say that 'there could not be a better exercise for a schoolboy than to turn a page of it into English.'

Samuel Rogers, *Table Talk*

Happiness is the word that immediately rises to the mind at the thought of Edward Gibbon . . . His father died at exactly the right moment, and left him exactly the right amount of money.

Lytton Strachey, *Portraits in Miniature*

Gibbon's style is probably the most exclusive in literature. By its very nature it bars out a great multitude of human energies. It makes sympathy impossible, it takes no cognisance of passion, it turns its back upon religion with a withering smile. But that was just what was wanted. Classic beauty came instead. By the penetrating influence of style – automatically, inevitably – lucidity, balance, and precision were everywhere introduced; and the miracle of order was established over the chaos of a thousand years.

*Ibid.*

*See also* J. A. Froude, John Gay, Samuel Johnson

## GIBBONS, ORLANDO

1583–1625 Composer

The purists . . . on account of the confusion arising from all parts singing different words at the same time, pronounce the style, in which his full anthems are composed, to be vicious.

Dr Charles Burney, *A General History of Music*

The best hand in England.
John Chamberlain, Letter to Sir Dudley Carleton, 12 June 1625

The best Finger of the Age.
John Hacket, *Scrinia Reservata*

## GIFFORD, WILLIAM

1756–1826 Journalist, Editor of *Quarterly Review*

Mr Gifford, in short, is possessed of that sort of learning which is likely to result from an over-anxious desire to supply the want of the first rudiments of education; that sort of wit, which is the off-spring of ill-humour or bodily pain; that sort of sense, which arises from a spirit of contradiction and a disposition to cavil at and dispute the opinions of others; and that sort of reputation, which is the consequence of bowing to established authority and ministerial influence.
William Hazlitt, *The Spirit of the Age*

He was a man of rare attainments and many excellent qualities . . . As a commentator he was capital could he have but suppressed his rancour against those who had preceded him in the task but a misconstruction or misinterpretation, nay the misplacing of a comma, was in Gifford's eyes a crime worthy of the most severe animadversions. The same fault of extreme severity went through his critical labours and in general he flagellated with so little pity that people lost their sense for the criminal's guilt in dislike of the savage pleasure which the executioner seemed to take in inflicting the punishment.
Sir Walter Scott, *Journal*, 17 January 1827

## GILBERT, WILLIAM

1540–1603 Natural Philosopher

Gilbert is often thought of solely as an experimenter, and it is true that he was one of the first to design experiments specifically to test theories, but, as has often happened in the history of science, his theoretical ideas have been forgotten, because of a mistaken view that a theory which is later superseded is not interesting, whereas carefully performed experiments are part of the permanent structure of science.
Mary B. Hesse, *Forces and Fields*

Among the honourable Assertors of this Liberty, I must reckon *Gilbert*, who having found an admirable Correspondence between his *Terella*, and the great *Magnet* of the Earth, thought, this Way, to determine this great Question, and spent his Studies and Estate upon this Enquiry; by which *obiter*, he found out many admirable magnetical Experiments: this Man would I have adored, not only as the sole Inventor of Magneticks, a new Science to be added to the Bulk of Learning, but as the Father of the new Philosophy; *Cartesius* [*Descartes*] being but a Builder-upon his Experiments.
Sir Christopher Wren, Inaugural Address, Gresham College, 1657

## GILBERT, SIR WILLIAM SCHWENK

1836–1911 Dramatist, Lyricist

I feel like a lion in a den of Daniels.
On himself, in Hesketh Pearson, *Lives of the Wits*

I am a crumbling man – a magnificent ruin, no doubt, but still a ruin – and like all ruins I look best by moonlight. Give me a sprig of ivy and an owl under my arm and Tintern Abbey would not be in it with me.
On himself, in Leslie Ayre, *The Gilbert and Sullivan Companion*

I found myself politely described in the official list as Mr William Gilbert, *playwright*, suggesting that my work was analogical to that of a wheelwright, or a shipwright, as regards the mechanical character of the process by which our respective results are achieved. There is an excellent word, 'dramatist', which seems to fit the situation, but it is not applied until we are dead, and then we become dramatists, as oxen, sheep and pigs are transfigured into beef, mutton and pork on their demise. You never hear of a novelwright or a picture-wright or a poemwright, and why a playwright?

On himself, in *ibid.*

His foe was folly and his weapon wit.

Anthony Hope (Sir Anthony Hope Hawkins), *Inscription* on the memorial tablet to Gilbert on London's Victoria Embankment, 1915

You say that in serious opera, you must more or less sacrifice yourself. I say that this is just what I have been doing in all our joint pieces.

Sir Arthur Sullivan, Letter to Gilbert, 12 March 1889

Another week's rehearsal with WSG & I should have gone raving mad. I had already ordered some straw for my hair.

Sir Arthur Sullivan, Letter to Frank Burnard, 12 March 1896, about *The Chieftain*

*See also* Henry Irving, Arthur Sullivan

## GILBERT (W.S.) AND SULLIVAN (ARTHUR)

1836–1911 and 1842–1900

Gilbert and Sullivan did not like each other as men; nor did either want to write operettas.

Lord Robert Cecil, Introduction to *The Savoy Operas*

## GILLRAY, JAMES

1757–1815 Caricaturist

Gillray was one of those unaffected wights who accomplish what he undertook without scientific parade, and even without the appearance of rule, or preconcerted plan.

H. Angelo, *Reminiscences*

Poor Gillray was always hipped, and at last sank into that deplorable state of mental aberration, which verifies the couplet, so often quoted, wherein the consanguinity of wit to madness is so eminently proved.

*Ibid.*

Gillray is the man – for the man of the People.

George III, in *ibid.*

Gillray ridicules excess in terms of excess, but his ridicule is fired by a profound distrust, and by fear that sometimes seems to try to control a hostile, superhuman force by giving it a known human face. His hero, often John Bull in one form or another, is usually being imposed upon: a sucker. At other times, his caricatures seem to be statements of pure revulsion against the mendacious uplift of fashionable high art.

David Piper, *The English Face*

## GIRTIN, THOMAS

1775–1802 Watercolourist

Where his predecessors had been calm and dispassionate, Girtin was hot and impulsive. Where their brain had directed and controlled the hand, Girtin's brain, eye and hand were working in unison. Girtin knew that chance must play its part in a successful engagement with watercolour. One has the feeling that whereas the artists before him achieved their results by recognised principles and built up their work to a steady foreseen finish, Girtin never quite knew what had happened, or how the result was achieved, till he saw his drawing as an accomplished thing.

Martin Hardie, *Water-Colour Painting in Britain*

If poor Tom had lived, I should have starved.

J. M. W. Turner, attributed

## GISSING, GEORGE ROBERT

1857–1903 Novelist

Some of his conclusions were conservative, but at heart he was a late-Victorian rebel against the power of convention. His rebellion was muted because he was preoccupied with failure. He had collected as great a store of specialized information about people who failed as Samuel Smiles had collected of people who succeeded.

Asa Briggs, *Victorian Cities*

Gissing's novels are a protest against the form of self-torture that goes by the name of respectability. Gissing was a bookish, over-civilised man, in love with classical antiquity, who found himself trapped in a cold, smoky, Protestant country where it was impossible to be comfortable without a thick padding of money between yourself and the outer world. Behind his rage and querulousness there lay a perception that the horrors of life in late-Victorian England were largely unnecessary. The grime, the stupidity, the ugliness, the sex-starvation, the furtive debauchery, the vulgarity, the bad manners, the censoriousness – these things were unnecessary, since the puritanism of which they were a relic no longer upheld the structure of society.

George Orwell, *George Gissing*

When I admit neglect of Gissing, / They say I don't know what I'm missing. / Until their arguments are subtler, / I think I'll stick to Samuel Butler. /

Dorothy Parker, *Sunset Gun*

*See also* Daniel Defoe

## GLADSTONE, WILLIAM EWART

1809–98 Prime Minister

All the world over, I will back the masses against the classes.

On himself, Speech at Liverpool, June 1886

He talked shop like a tenth muse.

Anon. comment on Gladstone's Budget speeches, in G. W. E. Russell, *Collections and Recollections*

Ah, Oxford on the surface, *but* Liverpool below.

An old Whig's comment in the House of Commons on Gladstone's Budget, February 1860, in Walter Bagehot, *Biographical Studies: Mr Gladstone*

If there were no Tories, I am afraid he would invent them.

Lord Acton, Letter to Mrs Drew, 24 April 1881

An almost spectral kind of phantasm of a man – nothing in him but forms and ceremonies and outside wrappings.

Thomas Carlyle, *Letters*, March 1873

An old man in a hurry.

Lord Randolph Churchill, Speech to the Electors of South Paddington, June 1886

. . . they told me how Mr Gladstone read Homer for fun, which I thought served him right.

Winston Churchill, *My Early Life*

He was generally thought to be very pusillanimous in dealing with foreign affairs. That is not at all the impression I derived. He was wholly ignorant.

Lord Cromer, Letter to Lord Newton, 29 November 1913

A sophisticated rhetorician, inebriated with the exuberance of his own verbosity, and gifted with an egotistical imagination, that can at all times command an interminable and inconsistent series of arguments to malign his opponents, and glorify himself.
Benjamin Disraeli, Speech at Knightsbridge, July 1878

Posterity will do justice to that unprincipled maniac Gladstone – extraordinary mixture of envy, vindictiveness, hypocrisy, and superstition; and with one commanding characteristic – whether Prime Minister, or Leader of Opposition, whether preaching, praying, speechifying or scribbling – never a gentleman!
Benjamin Disraeli, Letter to Lord Derby, 1878

What you say about Gladstone is most just. What restlessness! What vanity! And what unhappiness must be his! Easy to say he is mad. It looks like it. My theory about him is unchanged: a ceaseless Tartuffe from the beginning. That sort of man does not get mad at 70.
Benjamin Disraeli, Letter to Lady Bradford, 3 October 1879

. . . when you have to deal with an earnest man, severely religious and enthusiastic, every attempted arrangement ends in unintelligible correspondence and violated confidence.
Benjamin Disraeli, on being in Opposition, Letter to Montague Corry, 29 January 1881

He has not a single redeeming defect.
Benjamin Disraeli, in A. K. Adams, *The Home Book of Humorous Quotations*

What's the matter with Gladstone? He's all right.
George and Weedon Grossmith, *Diary of a Nobody*

If you were to put that man on a moor with nothing on but his shirt, he would become whatever he pleased.
T. H. Huxley, in Ernest Scott, *Lord Robert Cecil's Goldfield Diary*

I don't object to Gladstone always having the ace of trumps up his sleeve, but merely to his belief that the Almighty put it there.
Henry Labouchere, in Hesketh Pearson, *Lives of the Wits*

'Well,' said Dizzy [being asked to define the distinction between 'misfortune' and 'calamity'], 'if Mr Gladstone fell into the Thames, it would be a misfortune; but, if someone pulled him out, it would be a calamity.'
Hesketh Pearson, *Lives of the Wits*

The defects of his strength grow on him. All black is very black, all white very white.
Lord Rosebery, Diary, 4 August 1887

Oddly enough, about half his compatriots, including a great many of the well-to-do, regarded him as either mad or wicked or both. When I was a child, most of the children I knew were conservatives, and they solemnly assured me, as a well-known fact, that Mr Gladstone ordered twenty top-hats from various hatters every morning, and that Mrs Gladstone had to go round after him and disorder them.
Bertrand Russell, *Unpopular Essays*: 'Eminent Men I Have Known'

Lord Palmerston was quite right when he said to me 'Mr Gladstone is a very dangerous man'. And so vy. arrogant, tyrannical & obstinate with no knowledge of the World or human nature. Papa felt this strongly. Then he was a fanatic in religion – All this & much want of égard towards my feelings (tho' since I was so ill that was better) led him to make him a vy dangerous & unsatisfactory Premier.

Queen Victoria, Letter to her eldest daughter, 24 February 1874

She must say . . . that *she* has felt that Mr Gladstone would have liked to *govern* HER as Bismarck governs the Emperor.

Queen Victoria, Memorandum to her Private Secretary, Gen. Sir Henry Ponsonby, 18 November 1874

He speaks to Me as if I was a public meeting.

Queen Victoria, in George W. E. Russell, *Collections and Recollections*

*See also* Lord Derby, Henry Irving, Queen Victoria

## GLASGOW, ELLEN ANDERSON GHOLSON

1874–1945 Author

Highly individual in American letters is her ability to pass with equal authority from country to city, from rusticity to sophistication, from tobacco field to the drawing room, from irony to tragedy.

Louis Auchincloss, *Ellen Glasgow*

Southern romance is dead. Ellen Glasgow has murdered it.

Carl Van Doren, in E. Stanly Godbold Jr, *Ellen Glasgow and the Woman Within*

## GLENDOWER, OWEN (OWAIN AB GRUFFYDD OF GLYNDWR)

1359?–1416? Welsh Prince

*Hotspur*: . . . sometimes he angers me / With telling me of the mouldwarp and the ant, / Of the dreamer Merlin and his prophecies, / And of a dragon and a finless fish, / A clip-wing'd griffin and a moulten raven, / A couching lion and a ramping cat, / And such a deal of skimble-skamble stuff / As puts me from my faith. I tell you what, – / He held me last night at least ten hours / In reckoning up the several devils' names / That were his lackeys: I cried hum, and well, go to, / But mark'd him not a word. O, he's as tedious / As a tired horse, a railing wife; / Worse than a smoky house: I had rather live /With cheese and garlic in a windmill, far, / Than feed on cates and have him talk to me / In any summer-house in Christendom. /

William Shakespeare, *Henry IV, Part I*, Act III, Scene i

## GLYN, ELINOR

1864–1943 Novelist

Would you like to sin / With Elinor Glyn / On a tiger skin? / Or would you prefer / To err / With her / On some other fur? /

Anon. rhyme

Mrs Glyn achieved the paradox of bringing not only 'good taste' to the colony [Hollywood], but also 'sex appeal'. She coined the word 'It', and taught Rudolph Valentino to kiss the palm of a lady's hand rather than its back.

Cecil Beaton, Introduction to *Three Weeks*

I didn't know. Truly, I didn't know. Mine is a life sheltered to the point of stuffiness. I attend no movies, for any motion-picture theater is as an enlarged and a magnificently decorated lethal chamber to me. I have read but little of Madame Glyn. I did not know that things like *It* were going on. I have misspent my days. When I think of all those hours I flung away in reading Henry James and Santayana, when I might have been reading of life, throbbing, beating, perfumed life, I practically break down. Where, I ask you, have I been, that no true word of Madame Glyn's literary feats has come to me?

Dorothy Parker, in *New Yorker*, 26 November 1927

Copyright cannot exist in a work of a tendency so grossly immoral as this.
Justice Younger, in an action for infringement of copyright brought by Elinor Glyn in 1915, over *Three Weeks*

*See also* Clara Bow

## GLYNN, JOHN

1722–79 Radical

Sir, he was a Wilkite, which I never was.
John Wilkes, attributed, in conversation with George II

## GODDARD, ROBERT HUTCHINGS

1882–1945 Scientist

It has been said that one cannot today design a rocket, construct a rocket, or launch a rocket without infringing one or more of the 214 Goddard patents.
G. Edward Pendray, in Eugene M. Emme, *The History of Rocket Technology*

## GODOLPHIN, SIDNEY, EARL

1645–1712 Statesman

Godolphin had been bred a page at Whitehall, and had early acquired all the flexibility and the self-possession of a veteran courtier ... 'Sidney Godolphin,' said Charles, 'is never in the way, and never out of the way'. This pointed remark goes far to explain Godolphin's extraordinary success.
T. B. Macaulay, *History of England*

## GODWIN, MARY, *see under* WOLLSTONECRAFT, MARY

## GOLDSMITH, OLIVER

1728–74 Poet, Dramatist

Of our friend Goldsmith he said, 'Sir, he is so much afraid of being unnoticed that he often talks merely lest you should forget that he is in the company.' *Boswell*: 'Yes, he stands forward.' *Johnson*: 'True, Sir, but if a man is to stand forward he should wish to do it, not in an awkward posture, not in rags, not so as that he shall only be exposed to ridicule.' *Boswell*: 'For my part I like very well to hear honest Goldsmith talk away carelessly.' *Johnson*: 'Why, yes, Sir; but he should not like to hear himself.'
James Boswell, *Life of Johnson*

I told him what Goldsmith had said to me a few days before, 'As I take my shoes from the shoemaker, and my coat from the tailor, so I take my religion from the priest.' I regretted this loose way of talking. *Johnson*: 'Sir, he knows nothing; he has made up his mind about nothing.'
*Ibid.*

Poor fellow! he hardly knew an ass from a mule, nor a turkey from a goose, but when he saw it on the table.
Richard Cumberland, *Memoirs*

Here, Hermes, says Jove, who with nectar was mellow, / Go fetch me some clay – I will make an odd fellow: / Right and wrong shall be jumbled – much gold and some dross; / Without cause be he pleased, without cause be he cross; / Be sure as I work to throw in contradictions, / A great love of truth; yet a mind turn'd to fictions; / Now mix these ingredients, which warmed in the baking, / Turn to learning, and gaming, religion, and raking. / With the love of a wench, let his writings be chaste; / Tip his tongue with strange matter, his pen with fine taste; / That the rake and the poet o'er all shall prevail, / Set fire to the head, and set fire to the tail: / For the joy of each sex, on the world I'll bestow it: / This Scholar, Rake, Christian, Dupe, Gamester, and Poet, / Thro' a mixture so odd, he shall merit great fame, / And among brother mortals, be *Goldsmith* his name! / When on earth this strange meteor no more shall appear, / You Hermes, shall fetch him, – to make us sport here! /

David Garrick, *Jupiter and Mercury, a Fable*

Here lies Nolly Goldsmith, for shortness called Noll, / Who wrote like an angel, and talk'd like poor Poll. /

David Garrick, *Impromptu Epitaph*

At the breaking up of an evening at a tavern, he entreated the company to sit down, and told them if they would call for another bottle they should hear one of his *bon mots*: – they agreed, and he began thus: – 'I was once told that Sheridan the player, in order to improve himself in stage gestures, had looking glasses, to the number of ten, hung about his room, and that he practised before them; upon which I said, then there were ten ugly fellows together.' – The company were all silent: he asked why they did not laugh, which they not doing, he, without tasting the wine, left the room in anger.

Sir John Hawkins, *Life of Samuel Johnson, LL.D.*

I received one morning a message from poor Goldsmith that he was in great distress, and as it was not in his power to come to me, begging that I would come to him as soon as possible. I sent him a guinea and promised to come to him directly. I accordingly went as soon as I was drest, and found that his landlady had arrested him for his rent, at which he was in a violent passion. I perceived that he had already changed my guinea, and had got a bottle of Madeira and a glass before him. I put the cork into the bottle, desired he would be calm, and began to talk to him of the means by which he might be extricated. He then told me that he had a novel ready for the press, which he produced to me. I looked into it, and saw its merit; told the landlady I should soon return, and, having gone to a bookseller, sold it for sixty pounds. I brought Goldsmith the money, and he discharged his rent, not without rating his landlady in a high tone for having used him so ill.

Samuel Johnson, in James Boswell, *Life of Johnson*

It is amazing how little Goldsmith knows. He seldom comes where he is not more ignorant than anyone else.

*Ibid.*

No man was more foolish when he had not a pen in his hand, or more wise when he had.

*Ibid.*

Goldsmith's mind was entirely unfurnished. When he was engaged in a work, he had all his knowledge to find, which when he found, he knew how to use, but forgot it immediately after he had used it.

Sir Joshua Reynolds, *Notes on Goldsmith*

It is this detached attitude and width of view that give Goldsmith his peculiar flavour as an essayist. Other writers pack their pages fuller and bring us into closer touch with themselves. Goldsmith, on the other hand, keeps just on the edge of the crowd so that we can hear what the common people are saying and note their humours.

Virginia Woolf, *Essays*: 'The Captain's Death Bed'

*See also* Washington Irving

## GOLDWYN, SAMUEL (SAMUEL GOLDFISH)

1882–1974 Motion Picture Producer

For years I have been known for saying 'Include me out.'
On himself, in an address at Balliol College, Oxford, 1 March 1945

A self-made man may prefer a self-made name.
Judge Learned Hand, on granting permission for Samuel Goldfish to change his name to Samuel Goldwyn, in Bosley Crowther, *The Lion's Share*

I think of Samuel Goldwyn as an American Primitive, possessed of a superior instinct for the profession in which he finally found himself. This is not to say that he was not often duped or snowed or conned. Those who retain a part of their innocence are easy prey for those who have lost all theirs.
Garson Kanin, *Hollywood*

## GOMPERS, SAMUEL

1850–1924 Labour Leader

Had Mr Gompers been able to add six inches to his height, he would have been one of our great tragedians.
John Frey, in *Washington Herald*, 5 September 1938

... wholly un-American in appearance: short; with large eyes, dark complexion, heavy-lined face, and hair slightly curly but looking motheaten – he was impressive. As I sat in the audience ... I wrote the name 'Marat' on a slip of paper and handed it to my companion. He nodded.
Walter G. Merrit, *Destination Unknown*

## GORDON, CHARLES GEORGE (GORDON OF KHARTOUM)

1833–85 Soldier

I am not the *rescued lamb*, and I will not be.
On himself, Diary, September 1884

It is quite painful to see men tremble so when they come to see me, that they cannot hold the match to their cigarette.
On himself, Diary, September 1884

In ten or twelve years' time ... some of us will be quite passé; no one will come and court us ... Better a ball in the brain than to flicker out unheeded.
On himself, Diary, November 1884

I like my religious views, they were and are a greatcoat to me.
On himself, in Anthony Nutting, *Gordon: Martyr and Misfit*

A man who habitually consults the Prophet Isaiah when he is in a difficulty is not apt to obey the orders of any one.
Lord Cromer, Letter to Lord Granville, 1884

He has an immense name in Egypt – he is popular at home. He is a strong but sensible opponent of slavery. He has a small bee in his bonnet.
Lord Granville, Letter to W. E. Gladstone, November 1883

Horrible as it is to us I imagine that the manner of his death was not unwelcome to himself. Better wear out than rust out, and better break than wear out.
T. H. Huxley, Letter to S. J. Donnelly, February 1885

The man of England, circled by the sands.
George Meredith, *Epigram*

... One of the very few friends I ever had who came up to my estimate of the Christian hero.
Lord Wolseley, in Julian Symons, *England's Pride*

## GORDON, GEORGE HAMILTON, *see under* ABERDEEN, EARL OF

## GOWER, JOHN

1325?–1408 Poet

O moral Gower, this book I directe / To thee. /

Geoffrey Chaucer, *Troilus and Criseyde*, book v

In order to feel fully how much he [Chaucer] achieved, let any one subject himself to a penitential course of reading in his contemporary Gower . . . Gower has positively raised tediousness to the precision of science, he has made dullness an heirloom for the students of our literary history . . . He is the undertaker of the fair mediaeval legend, and his style has the hateful gloss, that seemingly unnatural length, of a coffin.

James Russell Lowell, *My Study Windows*

## GRABLE, (ELIZABETH RUTH) BETTY

1916–73 Actress

[I'm] strictly an enlisted man's girl.

On herself, in Richard Schickel, *The Stars*

The greatest of all the pin-ups was undoubtedly Betty Grable. She was the 'Gam Girl', on account of her fabulous legs – insured by Twentieth Century Fox for $1,000,000 (more even than Astaire's). Grable's appeal is difficult to understand today. She wasn't a siren; she wasn't even particularly erotic . . . She was a warm-hearted hoyden with an ever-ready shoulder to cry on, a brash, slightly vulgar attraction, and a homeliness, a feeling of being real, that the other pin-ups never had. The guy in his bunk at sea, on watch in some jungle outpost, or waiting on stand-by through long nights to fly the next mission, could look at Grable and those legs and feel that, given the chance, he could find solace with this brand of sympathetic, almost maternal woman. He didn't have a hope in hell of making it with [Ann] Sheridan or the others, but Grable, he felt, could be had.

Clyde Jeavons and Jeremy Pascall, *A Pictorial History of Sex in the Movies*

## GRACE, WILLIAM GILBERT

1848–1915 Cricketer

I puts the ball where I likes, and that beggar, he puts it where he likes.

J. C. Shaw (Nottinghamshire bowler), in Lord Hawke, *Memorial Biography of W. G. Grace*

W. G. Grace was by no conceivable standard a good man. He was in theory a country doctor, took ten years to get qualified, and must have been a much worse one than Doyle, particularly since Grace played cricket six days a week all the summer. At that time cricket was the national game. Grace was the star cricketer and one of the greatest of all Victorian heroes. He played as an amateur, and amateurs were not supposed to be paid. That did not prevent Grace making large sums of money out of the game. He was a cheat, on and off the cricket field. He exhibited almost the exact opposite of Doyle's virtues, including extreme meanness, trickery, and, perhaps oddest of all, physical cowardice.

C. P. Snow, Introduction to A. C. Doyle, *The Case-book of Sherlock Holmes*

## GRANT, ULYSSES SIMPSON

1822–85 Eighteenth United States President

I know only two tunes; one of them is 'Yankee Doodle' and the other isn't.

On himself, in W. E. Woodward, *Meet General Grant*

I had been a light smoker previous to the attack on Donelson . . . In the accounts published in the papers I was represented as smoking a cigar in the midst of the conflict; and many persons, thinking, no doubt, that tobacco was my chief solace, sent me boxes of the choicest brands . . . As many as ten thousand were soon received. I gave away all I could get rid of, but having such a quantity on hand I naturally smoked more than I would have done under ordinary circumstances. I have continued the habit ever since.

On himself, to General Porter, in *ibid.*

The people are tired of a man who has not an idea above a horse or a cigar.

Joseph Brown, 12 December 1871, in William B. Hesseltine, *Ulysses S. Grant*

He is an incurable borrower and when he wants to borrow he knows of only one limit – he wants all you've got. When I was poor he borrowed fifty dollars of me; when I was rich he borrowed fifteen thousand men.

General Bruckner, to Mark Twain, in Bernard DeVoto ed., *Mark Twain in Eruption*

Early in 1869 the cry was for 'no politicians' but the country did not mean 'no brains'.

William Clafin, Letter to W. E. Chandler, 22 August 1870

How is it that Grant, who was behind at Fort Henry, drunk at Donelson, surprised at Shiloh, and driven back from Oxford, Miss., is still in command?

Murat Halstead, Letter to Salmon P. Chase, 19 February 1863

We all thought Richmond, protected as it was by our splendid fortifications and defended by our army of veterans, could not be taken. Yet Grant turned his face to our Capital, and never turned it away until we had surrendered. Now, I have carefully searched the military records of both ancient and modern history, and have never found Grant's superior as a general. I doubt if his superior can be found in all history.

Robert E. Lee, in James Grant Wilson, *General Grant*

When Grant once gets possession of a place, he holds on to it as if he had inherited it.

Abraham Lincoln, Letter to General Benjamin Butler, 22 June 1864

I can't spare this man; he fights.

Abraham Lincoln, in J. F. C. Fuller, *The Generalship of Ulysses S. Grant*

Grant stood by me when I was crazy, and I stood by him when he was drunk, and now we stand by each other.

General William Tecumseh Sherman, attributed, *circa* 1870, in Robert Debs Heinl Jr, *The Dictionary of Military and Naval Quotations*

I always liked the way Grant said that he knew what the other generals would do because after all they had been to school at West Point together and the Mexican war together and the others acted like generals but he acted like one who knew just what the generals opposite him would do because that one had always been like that at West Point and after all what can anybody change to, they have to be what they are and they are so Grant always knew what to do.

Gertrude Stein, *Everybody's Autobiography*

## GRANVILLE, EARL, *see under* CARTERET, JOHN

## GRANVILLE, AUGUSTUS BOZZI

1783–1872 Physician

You know Mrs Carlyle said that Owen's sweetness reminded her of sugar of lead. Granville's was that plus butter of antimony!

Jane Welsh Carlyle, as reported in Leonard Huxley, *Life and Letters of Thomas Henry Huxley*

## GRATTAN, HENRY

1746–1820 Irish Politician

Ever glorious Grattan! the best of the good! / So simple in heart, so sublime in the rest! / With all which Demosthenes wanted endued, / And his rival or victor in all he possess'd. /

Ere Tully arose in the zenith of Rome, / Though unequall'd, preceded, the task was begun – / But Grattan sprung up like a god from the tomb / Of ages, the first, last, the saviour, the *one*! /

With the skill of an Orpheus to soften the brute; / With the fire of Prometheus to kindle mankind; / Even Tyranny listening sate melted or mute, / And Corruption shrunk scorch'd from the glance of his mind. /

Lord Byron, *The Irish Avatar*

I was much struck with the simplicity of Grattan's manners in private life. They were odd, but they were natural. Curran used to take him off, bowing to the very ground, and 'thanking God' he had no peculiarities of gesture or appearance. Rogers used to call him 'a sentimental harlequin,' but Rogers backbites everybody, and Curran, who used to quiz his great friend Godwin to his very face, could hardly respect a fair mark of mimicry in another.

Lord Byron, in Stephen Gwynn, *Henry Grattan and His Times*

Grattan is to be considered rather as the poet of Irish political passion and national ambition, than as the statesman expounding her wants and providing for her necessities.

D. O. Madden, *Speeches of the Rt. Hon. Henry Grattan*

## GRAY, ASA

1810–88 Scientist

At Dubuque I first met a number of men of whom I had often heard but with whom I had not previously come into direct contact. Most prominent among them was Gray. Someone, I remember, looked out of the window and said: 'There goes Asa Gray. If he should say that black was white, I should see it already turning whitish.'

David Starr Jordan, *The Days of a Man*

## GRAY, THOMAS

1716–71 Poet

I shall be but a shrimp of an author.

On himself, Letter to Horace Walpole, 25 February 1768

Gray, a born poet, fell upon an age of reason.

Matthew Arnold, *Essays in Criticism*: 'Gray'

Mr Johnson attacked Mr Gray, and said he was a dull fellow. I said he was reserved and might appear dull in company. But surely he was not dull in his poetry, though he might be extravagant. 'No, Sir,' said Mr Johnson. 'He was dull in company, dull in his closet, dull everywhere. He was dull in a new way; and this made many people think him great. He was a mechanical poet.'

James Boswell, *London Journal*, 28 March 1775

His Letters are inimitably fine. If his poems are sometimes finical and pedantic, his prose is quite free from affectation. He pours his thoughts out upon paper as they arise in his mind; and they arise in his mind without pretence, or constraint, from the pure impulse of learned leisure and contemplative indolence. He is not here on stilts or in buckram; but smiles in his easy chair, as he moralises through the loopholes of retreat, on the bustle and raree-show of the world . . . He had nothing to do but to read and to think, and to tell his friends what he read and thought. His life was a luxurious, thoughtful dream.

William Hazlitt, *Lectures on the English Poets*

I would rather have written that poem [The Elegy], gentlemen, than take Quebec.

James Wolfe, the night before he was killed at Quebec, attributed

He failed as a poet, not because he took too much pains, and so extinguished his animation, but because he had very little of that fiery quality to begin with, and all his pains were of the wrong sort . . . I do not profess to be a person of very various reading; nevertheless, if I were to pluck out of Gray's tail all the feathers which I know belong to other birds, he would be left very bare indeed.

William Wordsworth, in R. P. Gillies, *Memoirs*

*See also* A. E. Housman, Sir Walter Scott

## GREELEY, HORACE

1811–72 Editor, Political Leader

. . . tow-headed, and half-bald at that . . . slouching in dress; goes bent like a hoop, and so rocking in his gait that he walks down both sides of the street at once.

On himself, in William Harlan Hale, *Horace Greeley, Voice of the People*

. . . the repentant male Magdalen of New York journalism.

James Gordon Bennett Sr, in Glyndon G. Van Deusen, *Horace Greeley, Nineteenth-Century Crusader*

## GREENAWAY, (CATHERINE) KATE

1846–1901 Artist, Illustrator

She ruled in a small realm of her own, like the island-valley of Avalon, 'deep-meadowed, happy, fair with orchard lawns', a land of flowers and gardens, of red brick houses with dormer windows, peopled by toddling boys and little girls clad in long, high-waisted gowns, muffs, pelisses and mob-caps. In all her work there is an atmosphere of an earlier peace and simple piety that recalls Izaak Walton and 'fresh sheets that smell of lavender'. The curtains and frocks of dimity and chintz, the houses with the reddest and pinkest of bright bricks, the 'marigolds all in a row' in gardens green as can be, . . . the lads and lasses with rosy cheeks and flaxen curls, all make for what is best in the best of all possible worlds.

Martin Hardie, *Water-Colour Painting in Britain*

## GREENE, ROBERT

1560?–92 Dramatist, Pamphleteer

*Greene*, is the pleasing Object of an eie; / *Greene*, pleasde the eies of all that lookt uppon him. / *Greene*, is the ground of everie Painters die: / *Greene*, gave the ground, to all that wrote upon him. / Nay more the men, that so Eclipst his fame: / Purloynde his Plumes, can they deny the same? /

'R.B., Gent', *Greene's Funeralle*

A rakehell: a makeshift: A scribling foole: / A famous Bayrd in Citty, and Schoole. / Now sicke as a dog: and ever Brainesick: / Where such a raving, and desperate Dick? /

Gabriel Harvey, *Four Letters and Certain Sonnets*

*See also* Thomas Nashe

## GREGORY, ISABELLA AUGUSTA, LADY

1852–1932 Author

She has been to me mother, friend, sister and brother. I cannot realize the world without her – she brought to my wavering thoughts steadfast nobility. All day the thought of losing her is like a conflagration in the rafters. Friendship is all the house I have.

William Butler Yeats (written during an illness of Lady Gregory's), *Journal*, 4 February 1909

Sound of a stick upon the floor, a sound / From somebody that toils from chair to chair; / Beloved books that famous hands have bound, / Old marble heads, old pictures everywhere; / Great rooms where travelled men and children found / Content or joy; a last inheritor / Where none has reigned that lacked a name and fame / Or out of folly into folly came. /

William Butler Yeats, *Coole Park and Ballylee*

## GRENVILLE, GEORGE

1712–70 Prime Minister

Grenville's character was stern, melancholy and pertinacious. Nothing was more remarkable in him than his inclination always to look on the dark side of things. He was the raven of the House of Commons, always croaking defeat in the midst of triumphs, and bankruptcy with an overflowing exchequer.

T. B. Macaulay, *Essays*: 'Chatham'

. . . a fatiguing orator and indefatigable drudge; more likely to disgust than to offend . . . As all his passions were expressed by one livid smile, he never blushed at the variations in his behaviour . . . scarce any man ever wore in his face such outward and visible marks of the hollow, cruel, and rotten heart within.

Horace Walpole, *Memoirs*

## GRENVILLE, SIR RICHARD

1541–91 Naval Commander

Here die I, Richard Grenville, with a joy full and quiet mind, for that I have ended my life as a true soldier ought to do, that hath fought for his countrey, Queene, religion, and honour, whereby my soule most joyfully departeth out of this bodie, and shall alwaies leave behinde it an everlasting fame as a valiant and true soldier that hath done his dutie, as he was bound to do.

On himself, dying words, attributed

## GRESHAM, SIR THOMAS

1519?–79 Merchant, Benefactor

. . . the Wealthiest Citizen in *England* of his age, and the founder of *two* stately Fabricks, the *Old Exchange*, a kind of Colledge for merchants, and *Gresham Colledge*, a kind of Exchange for Scholars.

Thomas Fuller, *The History of the Worthies of England*

. . . the greatest English financier of the century, the government's constant adviser and Royal agent in Antwerp, Sir Thomas Gresham. He was a remarkable man: a sort of combination of a Pierpont Morgan and Keynes of his day.

A. L. Rowse, *The England of Elizabeth*

## GREVILLE, CHARLES CAVENDISH FULKE

1794–1865 Diarist

For fifty years he listened at the door, / He heard some secrets and invented more. / These he wrote down, and

women, statesmen, kings / Became degraded into common things. /
Lord Winchilsea, on the publication of Greville's *Memoirs*

## GREVILLE, FULKE, FIRST BARON BROOKE

1554–1628 Poet

Servant to Queen Elizabeth / Councillor to King James and / Friend to Sir Philip Sidney. /
On himself, *Epitaph*

## GREY, CHARLES, EARL

1764–1845 Prime Minister

Mark my words, within two years you will find that we have become unpopular, for having brought forward the most aristocratic measure that ever was proposed in parliament.
On himself, in conversation with Lord Sidmouth, *á propos* the Reform Bill, April 1832

I have been in the company of no distinguished man in Europe, so much my senior, with whom I have felt myself more at ease, or who has appeared to me better to understand the rights of all in a drawing room.
James Fenimore Cooper, *Gleanings in Europe: England*

## GREY, EDWARD, VISCOUNT GREY OF FALLODON

1862–1933 Statesman

I think he is a man rather to see difficulties than to help people over them.
Arthur Acland, Letter to H. H. Asquith, 1900

. . . he always created difficulties . . . He never came down into the arena and therefore got a false reputation. He was absolutely worthless. By the second year of the war Grey had completely crumpled up. He was pure funk.
David Lloyd George, in conversation with A. J. Sylvester, 5 May 1933

He was a mean man . . . I am glad I trampled upon his carcase. He would have pursued me even from his grave.
David Lloyd George, justifying his criticism of Grey in his *War Memoirs*, in Frances Stevenson, Diary, 29 October 1934

## GREY, LADY JANE (DUDLEY)

1537–54 Pretender to the English Throne

I founde her, in her Chamber, readinge Phaedon Platonis in Greeke, and that with as much delite, as some ientlemen would read a merie tale in Bocase. After salutation, and dewtie done, with some other taulke, I asked hir, whie she would leese soch pastime in the Parke? smiling she answered me: I wisse, all their sporte in the Parke is but a shadoe to that pleasure, that I find in Plato.
Roger Ascham, *The Scholemaster*

Whatever might be the cause, she preserved the same appearance of knowledge, and the contempt of what was generally esteemed pleasure, during the whole of her life, for she declared herself displeased with being appointed Queen, and while conducting to the scaffold, she wrote a sentence in Latin and another in Greek on seeing the dead body of her husband accidentally passing that way.
Jane Austen, *The History of England*

*See also* Mary I

## GREY, ZANE

1872–1939 Author

If Zane went out with a mosquito net to catch minnows, he could make it sound like a Roman Gladiator setting forth to slay whales in the Tiber.

Robert H. Davis, in Jean Karr, *Zane Grey, Man of the West*

## GRIFFITH, DAVID (LEWELYN) WARK

1875–1948 Film Director

I made them *see*, didn't I? . . . I changed everything. Remember how small the world was before I came along. I made them see it both ways in time as well as in space . . .

I brought it all to life. I moved the whole world onto a twenty-foot screen. I was a greater discoverer than Columbus. I condensed history into three hours and made them live it. They still remember Mae Marsh trimming her dress with cotton and putting coal dust on it to look like Ermine when the Colonel, her brother came home. *Griffith touches*, eh? They still talk about Griffith touches.

On himself, in Adela Rogers St Johns, *The Honeycomb*

I never saw [Griffith] dressed in anything but a high, stiff collar, a grey felt hat, high shoes with brass hooks and pulling-loops at the back, and one of a succession of suits none of which could have been less than fifteen years old, and all of which were woefully out of style. He looked like a hard-up, itinerant high-school teacher. His face was grave. When he smiled it was with the benign rigidity of a stone buddha. His nose, like his face, was long and thin, and he had a pronounced under-lip, upon which rested an endless succession of cigarettes.

Norman bel Geddes, *Miracle In the Evening*

Many people who drink heavily – and I think Griffith was one of them – are not reeling drunk, but their senses are dulled. They're too soaked to respond properly. I don't know exactly why Griffith began drinking, whether out of some personal unhappiness or because his world was beginning to float away. He loved the grand world and was very proud of having met people like Winston Churchill. The last years of his life were terribly sad, anyway. I'm afraid that drinkers end by alienating people, and they get terribly lonely. Imagine, dwindling away like that for almost twenty years after having practically invented silent pictures.

George Cukor, in Gavin Lambert, *On Cukor*

. . . Griffith had no rivals. He was the teacher of us all. Not a picture has been made since his time that does not bear some trace of his influence. He did not invent the close-up or some of the other devices with which he has sometimes been credited, but he discovered and he taught everyone how to use them for more beautiful effect and better story-telling on the screen. Above all, he taught us how to photograph thought, not only by bringing the camera close to a player's eyes, but by such devices, novel and daring in their time, as focusing it on a pair of hands clasped in anguish or on some symbolic object that mirrored what was in the player's mind. He did much to teach the motion picture camera its own special language; and for that I, like every other worker in motion pictures, am his debtor.

Cecil B. De Mille, *The Autobiography of Cecil B. De Mille*

With him, we never felt we were working for a salary. He inspired in us his belief that we were involved in a medium that was powerful enough to influence the whole world.

Lillian Gish, *The Movies, Mr Griffith and Me*

His footprints were never asked for, yet no one ever filled his shoes.

Hedda Hopper, *From Under My Hat*

## GUTHRIE, (WOODROW WILSON) 'WOODY'

1912–67 Folk Singer

They called me everything from a rambling honky-tonk hitter to a water-logged harmonica player. One paper down in Kentucky said what us Okies needed next to three good square meals a day was some good music lessons.

On himself, in Howard Taubman, *Music on My Beat: An Intimate Volume of Shop Talk*

## GWYN, NELL (ELEANOUR)

1650–87 Actress, Mistress to Charles II

Hard by the Mall lives a wench call'd Nell, / King Charles the Second he kept her. / She hath got a trick to handle his pr---, / But never lays hands on his sceptre. / All matters of state from her soul she does haste, / And leave to the politic bitches. / The whore's in the right, for 'tis her delight / To be scratching just where it itches. /

Anon., *Nell Gwynne*

She was low in stature, and what the French call *mignonne* and *piquante*, well-formed, handsome, but red-haired, and rather *embonpoint*; of the *enjoué* she was a complete mistress. Airy, fantastic, and sprightly, she sang, danced, and was exactly made for acting light, showy characters, filling them up, as far as they went, most effectually. On the front of Bagnigge Wells, one of her country houses, where she entertained the King with concerts, there was a bust of her, and though it was wretchedly executed, it confirmed the correctness of Lely's pencil. She had remarkably lively eyes, but so small they were almost invisible when she laughed; and a foot, the least of any woman in England.

Anon., *The Manager's Note-Book*

Let not poor Nelly starve!

Charles II, attributed last words

She was, or affected to be very orthodox, and a friend to the clergy and the Church. The story of her paying the debt of a worthy clergyman, whom, as she was going through the city, she saw some bailiffs hurrying to prison, is a known fact; as is also that of her being insulted in her coach at Oxford, by the mob, who mistook her for the Duchess of Portsmouth. Upon which, she looked out of the window, and said, with her usual good humour, *Pray, good people, be civil; I am the protestant whore.* This laconic speech drew on her the blessings of the populace.

James Granger, *Biographical History of England*

The King and Duke of York was at the play; but so great performance of a comical part was never, I believe, in the world before as Nell hath done this, both as mad girle, and then, most and best of all, when she comes in like a young gallant; and hath the motions and carriage of a spark, the most that ever I saw any man have. It makes me, I confess, admire her.

Samuel Pepys, on seeing her play Florimel in Dryden's *Mayden Queene*, Diary, 2 March 1667

This you'd believe, had I but time to tell you, / The pain it costs to poor laborious *Nelly* / While she employs Hands, Fingers, Lips and Thighs, / E're she can raise the Member she enjoys. /

John Wilmot, Earl of Rochester, *On King Charles*

# 'H'

## HAGGARD, SIR HENRY RIDER

1856–1925 Novelist

Only little people are vain. How anybody can be vain, amazes me. I know that in my own small way I grow humbler year by year.

On himself, Journal, 23 March 1915

Sir Rider Haggard / Was completely staggered / When his bride-to-be / Announced 'I AM SHE!'/

W. H. Auden, *Academic Graffiti*

Even your imagination is out of the fifth form.

Andrew Lang, Letter to Rider Haggard

Will there never come a season / Which shall rid us from the curse / Of a prose which knows no reason / And an unmelodious verse: / When the world shall cease to wonder / At the genius of an Ass, / And a boy's eccentric blunder / Shall not bring success to pass: / When mankind shall be delivered / From the clash of magazines, / And the inkstand shall be shivered / Into countless smithereens: / When there stands a muzzled stripling, / Mute, beside a muzzled bore: / When the Rudyards cease from kipling / And the Haggards Ride no more. /

J. K. Stephen, *A Protest in Verse*

## HAIG, DOUGLAS, EARL

1861–1928 Soldier

With the publication of his Private Papers in 1952, he committed suicide 25 years after his death.

Lord Beaverbrook, *Men and Power*

Haig had a first-rate General Staff mind.

Lord Haldane, *An Autobiography*

He was a remote, almost God-like figure, in whom we had complete trust. His personality and his inflexible belief in victory inspired every single man. His was the only army of the great nations at war which did not break.

Sir John Kennedy, in *Scotsman*, 15 August 1959

Haig was devoid of the gift of intelligible and coherent expression.

David Lloyd George, *War Memoirs*

He's quite all right, but he's too —— cautious: he will be so fixed on not giving the Boers a chance, he'll never give himself one.

Colonel Wolls-Sampson, in B. H. Liddel Hart, *History of the First World War*

## HAKLUYT, RICHARD

1552?–1616 Geographer, Chronicler

In a word, many of such useful tracts of sea adventures, which before were scattered as several ships, Mr Hakluyt hath embodied into a fleet, divided into three squadrons, so many several volumes; a work of great honour to England, it being possible that many ports and islands in America, which being base and barren, bear only a bare name for the present, may prove rich places for the future.

Thomas Fuller, *The History of the Worthies of England*

## HALE, SIR MATTHEW

1609–76 Judge

One of his [fencing] masters told him he could teach him no more, for he was now better at his own trade than himself was. This Mr Hale looked on as flattery; so, to make the master discover himself, he promised him the house he lived in, for he was his tenant, if he could hit him a blow on the head; and bade him do his best for he would be as good as his word: so after a little engagement, his master, being really superior to him, hit him on the head, and he performed his promise, for he gave him the house freely; and was not unwilling at that rate to learn to distinguish flattery from plain and simple truth.

Gilbert Burnet, *Life of Sir Mathew Hale*

He became the cushion exceedingly well: his manner of hearing patient, his directions pertinent, and his discourses copious and, although he hesitated often, fluent. His stop for a word, by the produce always paid for the delay; and on some occasions he would utter sentences heroic.

Roger North, *The Life of Right Hon. Francis North, Baron Guildford*

This great man was most unfortunate in his family; for he married his own servant maid, and then for excuse said there was no wisdom below the girdle.

*Ibid.*

## HALE, NATHAN

1755–76 Spy

I only regret that I have but one life to lose for my country.

On himself, at his execution, 22 September 1776

## HALIFAX, MARQUIS OF,

*see under* **SAVILE, GEORGE**

## HALLÉ, SIR CHARLES

1819–95 Musician

I created for myself a singular test by which to know if a piece of music was beautiful or not. There was a spot, a bench under a tree by the side of a very small water-fall, where I loved to sit and 'think music'. Then, going in my mind through a piece of music such as Beethoven's 'Adelaide', or the Cavatina from 'Der Freischutz', I could imagine that I heard it in the air surrounding me, that the whole of nature sang it, and then I knew that it was beautiful. Many pieces would not stand that test, however hard I tried, and these I rejected as indifferent.

On himself, *Autobiography*

I saw one sight in Venice which alone repayed the journey: Charles Hallé in a frock-coat and a white top hat reading the *Daily Telegraph* while seated in a gondola and floating under the Bridge of Sighs.

C. V. Stanford, *Pages from an Unwritten Diary*

## HALLEY, EDMUND

1656–1742 Astronomer

I have no esteem of a man who has lost his reputation both for skill candor & Ingenuity by silly tricks ingratitude & foolish prate. & yt I value not all or any of the shams of him and his Infidel companions being very well satisfied that if Xt and his Appostles were to walk againe upon earth, they should not scape free from ye calumnies of their venomous tongues, but I hate his ill manners not the man, were he either honest or but civil there is none in whose company I could rather desire to be.

John Flamsteed, Letter to Isaac Newton, 24 February 1692

Halley, the astronomer, of whom it was remarked, that 'he could believe any thing but the Scriptures', talking against Christianity as wanting mathematical demonstration, was stopped by Newton, who said, 'Man, you had better hold your tongue; you have never sufficiently considered the matter.'

M. Noble, *A Biographical History of England*

## HAMILTON, ALEXANDER

1757–1804 Statesman

In this dark and insidious manner did this intriguer lay schemes in secret against me, and, like the worm at the root of the peach, did he labor for twelve years, underground and in darkness, to girdle the root, while all the axes of the Anti-Federalists, Democrats, Jacobins, Virginia debtors to English merchants, and French hirelings, chopping as they were for the whole time at the trunk, could not fell the tree.

John Adams, 20 July 1807, in Zoltan Haraszti, *John Adams and the Prophets of Progress*

Hamilton is really a colossus to the anti-republican party. Without numbers, he is a host within himself.

Thomas Jefferson, Letter to James Madison, 21 September 1795

[Hamilton's] touch of the heroic, the touch of the purple, the touch of the gallant, the dashing, the picturesque.

Theodore Roosevelt, Letter to Governor Morris, 28 November 1910

He smote the rock of the natural resources, and abundant streams of revenue gushed forth. He touched the dead corpse of public credit, and it sprang open upon its feet.

Daniel Webster, Speech in the Senate, 10 March 1831

*See also* Aaron Burr, Robert F. Kennedy

## HAMILTON, EMMA, LADY

1761?–1815 Society Lady

Brave Emma! – Good Emma! – If there were more Emmas, there would be more Nelsons.

Lord Nelson, on leaving for his last voyage, in Robert Southey, *Life of Nelson*

*See also* Horatio Nelson

## HAMPDEN, JOHN

1594–1643 Statesman

He was rather of reputation in his own Country, then of publique discourse or fame in the Kingdom, before the businesse of Shippmony, but then he grew the argument of all tounges, evry man enquyringe who and what he was, that durst, at his owne charge supporte the liberty and property of the kingdome, and reskue his Country from being made a prey to the Courte.

Edward Hyde, Earl of Clarendon, *History of the Rebellion*

He had a head to contrive, a tongue to persuade, and a hand to execute, any mischief.

*Ibid.*

Without question, when he first drew the sword, he threw away the scabbard.

*Ibid.*

## HANCOCK, JOHN

1736/7–93 Merchant, Politician

There! John Bull can read my name without spectacles.

On himself, on signing the Declaration of Independence, in Herbert S. Allan, *John Hancock, Patriot in Purple*

## HANDEL, GEORGE FREDERICK

1685–1759 Composer

He was perhaps as great a genius in music as Mr Pope was in poetry; the musical composition of the one being as expressive of the passions, as the happy versification of the other excelled in harmony.

Anon., in *Scots Magazine*, April 1759

Of his peers Beethoven was perhaps the most generous in his appraisal of Handel. 'He was the greatest composer that ever lived. I would uncover my head, and kneel before his tomb.' And again, when forty volumes of Arnold's edition, the gift of A. A. Stumpff . . . came to him in 1826: 'There is the truth.'

Ludwig van Beethoven, in Percy M. Young, *Handel*

To many he remains the greatest dreamer in music the world has ever known. His whole life was a dream; and his every effort was a votive offering to his temple of dreams – that temple which he sought to make beautiful.

Newman Flower, *George Frideric Handel*

If Income Tax collectors ever indulge in community singing, I have no doubt that they sing the choruses from the *Messiah*, for the *Messiah* is the first great anthem of man's enslavement by materialism.

Compton Mackenzie, in G. Hughes and H. van Thal, *The Music Lover's Companion*

Ah, a German and a genius! a prodigy, admit him!

Jonathan Swift, attributed last words

We have heard what Gluck, Mozart, Haydn, and Beethoven said about Handel. What they did in the Potteries may be remembered as a greater tribute. In 1892 the Hanley Glee and Madrigal Society received an invitation to sing Gaul's *Israel in the Wilderness* at the Crystal Palace. The Invitation was declined because the choir preferred to stay at home to practise *Israel in Egypt*.

Percy M. Young, *Handel*

## HARCOURT, LEWIS, FIRST VISCOUNT

1863–1922 Statesman

I have myself a constitutional dislike to limelight, which often disfigures that which it is intended to adorn.

On himself, Speech to the Corona Club, 18 June 1912

Few men have appealed less to the gallery than Mr Harcourt. He does not scan far horizons. He does not declare any vision of a promised land. He has no passionate fervour for humanity and is too honest to pretend any. He is a practical politician, with no dithyrambs. He loves the intricacies of the campaign more than the visionary gleam, the actual more than the potential, present facts more than future fancies. He is the man without a dream.

A. G. Gardiner, *Prophets, Priests and Kings*

## HARCOURT, SIR WILLIAM GEORGE GRANVILLE VENABLES VERNON

1827–1904 Statesman

. . . The big salmon will always be sulking under his stone, and ready for occasional plunges which will not always be free from a sinister intention.

Sir Henry Campbell-Bannerman, Letter to H. H. Asquith, December 1898

## HARDIE, JAMES KEIR

1856–1915 Socialist, Labour Leader

I understand what Christ suffered in Gethsemane as well as any man living.

On himself, speaking to friends after hostility in Aberdare, 6 August 1914

[He] deliberately chooses this policy as the only one he can boss. His only chance of leadership lies in the creation of an organisation 'agin the Government'; he knows little and cares less for any constructive thought or action.

Beatrice Webb, in Kitty Muggeridge and Ruth Adam, *Beatrice Webb: A Life*

## HARDING, WARREN GAMALIEL

1865–1923 Twenty-Ninth United States President

Everybody's second choice.

Anon., in Francis Russell, *President Harding: His Life and Times 1865–1923*

When you get hearts on fire for Harding, you have generated enough heat to set Lake Michigan boiling and turn the Chicago River into a pot roast.

Anon., in *ibid.*

He was an excellent 'mixer', he had the inestimable gift of never forgetting a man's face or his name, and there was always a genuine warmth in his handshake, a real geniality in his smile. He was a regular he-man according to the sign manual of the old days – a great poker player, and not at all averse to putting a foot on the brass rail.

Anon., in *ibid.*

Few deaths are unmingled tragedies. Harding's was not, he died in time.

Samuel Hopkins Adams, in *The American Heritage Pictorial History of the Presidents*, vol. 2

Absolute knowledge have I none. / But my aunt's washerwoman's sister's son / Heard a policeman on his beat / Say to a laborer on the street / That he had a letter just last week – / A letter which he did not seek – / From a Chinese merchant in Timbuctoo, / Who said that his brother in Cuba knew / Of an Indian chief in a Texas town, / Who got the dope from a circus clown, / That a man in Klondike had it straight / From a guy in a South American state, / That a wild man over in Borneo / Was told by a woman who claimed to know, / Of a well-known society rake, / Whose mother-in-law will undertake / To prove that her husband's sister's niece / Has stated plain in a printed piece / That she has a son who never comes home / Who knows all about the Teapot Dome. /

Henry Cabot Lodge, in *The American Heritage Pictorial History of the Presidents*, vol. 2

Harding was not a bad man. He was just a slob.

Alice Roosevelt Longworth, in Ishbel Ross, *Grace Coolidge and her Era*

. . . a tin horn politician with the manner of a rural corn doctor and the mien of a ham actor.

H. L. Mencken, in *Baltimore Evening Sun*, 15 June 1920

He has a bungalow mind.

Woodrow Wilson, in Thomas A. Bailey, *Woodrow Wilson and the Great Betrayal*

## HARDY, THOMAS

1840–1928 Author

People call me a pessimist; and if it is pessimism to think, with Sophocles, that 'not to have been born is best', then I do not reject the designation . . . I do not see that we are likely to improve the world by asseverating, however loudly, that black is white, or at least that black is but a necessary contrast and foil, without which white would be white no longer. That is mere juggling with a metaphor. But my pessimism, if pessimism it be, does not involve the assumption that the world is going to the dogs, and that Ahriman is winning all along the line. On the contrary, my practical philosophy is distinctly meliorist.

On himself, in William Archer, *Real Conversations*

I never cared for life, life cared for me. /
And hence I owe it some fidelity. /
On himself, *Epitaph*

Thomas Hardy / Was never tardy / When summoned to fulfill / The Immanent Will. /
W. H. Auden, *Academic Graffiti*

My first Master was Thomas Hardy, and I think I was very lucky in my choice. He was a good poet, perhaps a great one, but not *too* good. Much as I loved him, even I could see that his diction was often clumsy and forced and that a lot of his poems were plain bad. This gave me hope where a flawless poet might have made me despair. He was modern without being too modern. His world and sensibility were close enough to mine . . . so that, in imitating him, I was being led towards not away from myself, but they were not so close as to obliterate my identity. If I looked through his spectacles, at least I was conscious of a certain eyestrain. Lastly, his metrical variety, his fondness for complicated stanza forms, were an invaluable training in the craft of making.
W. H. Auden, *The Dyer's Hand*

Hardy went down to botanize in the swamps, while Meredith climbed toward the sun. Meredith became, at his best, a sort of daintily dressed Walt Whitman; Hardy became a sort of village atheist brooding and blaspheming over the village idiot.
G. K. Chesterton, *The Victorian Age in Literature*

He seems to me to have written as nearly for the sake of 'self-expression' as a man well can; and the self which he had to express does not strike me as a particularly wholesome or edifying matter of communication. He was indifferent even to the prescripts of good writing: he wrote sometimes overpoweringly well, but always very carelessly; at times his style touches sublimity without ever having passed through the stage of being good.
T. S. Eliot, *After Strange Gods*

A fact about the infancy of Mr Hardy has escaped the interviewers and may be recorded here. On the day of his birth, during a brief absence of his nurse, there slipped into the room an ethereal creature, known as the Spirit of Plastic Beauty. Bending over the cradle she scattered roses on it, and as she strewed them she blessed the babe. 'He shall have an eye to see moral and material loveliness, he shall speak of richly-coloured pastoral places in the accent of Theocritus, he shall write in such a way as to cajole busy men into a sympathy with old, unhappy, far-off things.' She turned and went, but while the nurse still delayed, a withered termagant glided into the room. From her apron she dropped toads among the rose-leaves, and she whispered: 'I am the genius of False Rhetoric, and led by me he shall say things ugly and coarse, not recognizing them to be so, and shall get into a rage about matters that call for philosophic calm, and shall spoil some of his best passages with pedantry and incoherency. He shall not know what things belong to his peace, and he shall plague his most loyal admirers with the barbaric contortions of his dialogue.'
Edmund Gosse, in *Cosmopolis*, January 1896

He complained that they [the critics] accused him of pessimism. One critic singled out as an example of gloom his poem on the woman whose house burned down on her wedding night. 'Of course it's a humorous piece,' said Hardy, 'and the man must have been thick-witted not to see that. On reading his criticism, I went through my last collection of poems with a pencil, marking them S, N, and C according as they were sad, neutral, or cheerful. I found them in pretty equal proportions; which nobody could call pessimism.'

Robert Graves, *Goodbye to All That*

By the side of George Eliot . . . Meredith appears as a shallow exhibitionist . . . and Hardy, decent as he is, as a provincial manufacturer of gauche and heavy fictions that sometimes have corresponding virtues.

F. R. Leavis, *The Great Tradition*

The gloom is not even relieved by a little elegance of diction.

Lytton Strachey, Review of Hardy's poems, *Satires of Circumstance*, *New Statesman*, 19 December 1914

No one has written worse English than Mr Hardy in some of his novels – cumbrous, stilted, ugly, and inexpressive – yes, but at the same time so strangely expressive of something attractive to us in Mr Hardy himself that we would not change it for the perfection of Sterne at his best. It becomes coloured by its surroundings; it becomes literature.

Virginia Woolf, *The Moment*

*See also* John Cowper Powys

## HARIOT, THOMAS

1560–1621 Mathematician, Astronomer

He did not like (or valued not) the old storie of the Creation of the World. He could not beleeve the old position; he would say *ex nihilo nihil fit* nothing comes of nothing. But a *nihilum* killed him at last: for in the top of his Nose came a little red speck (exceeding small) which grew bigger and bigger, and at last killed him. I suppose it was that which the Chirurgians call a *noli me tangere*.

John Aubrey, *Brief Lives*

## HARLEY, ROBERT, EARL OF OXFORD

1661–1724 Statesman

. . . the man himself was of all men the least interesting. There is indeed a whimsical contrast between the very ordinary qualities of his mind and the very extraordinary vicissitudes of his fortune.

T. B. Macaulay, *History of England*

He constantly had, even with his best friends, an air of mystery and reserve which seemed to indicate that he knew some momentous secret, and that his mind was labouring with some vast design. In this way he got and long kept a high reputation for wisdom. It was not till that reputation had made him an Earl, a Knight of the Garter, Lord High Treasurer of England, and master of the fate of Europe, that his admirers began to find out that he was really a dull puzzleheaded man.

*Ibid.*

The Earl of Oxford is a person of as much virtue, as can possibly consist with the love of power; and his love of power is no greater than what is common to men of his superior capacities; neither did any man ever appear to value it less, after he had obtained it, or exert it with more moderation. He is the only instance that ever fell within my memory, or observation, of a person passing from a private life, through the several stages of greatness, without any perceivable impression upon his temper and behaviour.

Jonathan Swift, *An Enquiry Into the Behaviour of the Queen's Last Ministry*

## HARLOW, JEAN (HARLEAN CARPENTER)

1911–37 Actress

Jean Harlow was very soft about her toughness.

George Cukor, in Gavin Lambert, *On Cukor*

There is no sign that her acting would ever have progressed beyond the scope of the restless shoulders and the protuberant breasts; her technique was the gangster's technique – she toted a breast like a man totes a gun.

Graham Greene, reviewing *Saratoga*, in *Night and Day*, 26 August 1937

Harlow's hip-swinging, gum-chewing, slangy, wise-cracking characterisations were a delight. She perfectly understood the roles she invariably played (even to the point of asking her agent, when he phoned with a new part, 'What kinda whore am I this time?') and she brightened every picture she was in. She knew what she was, the audience knew what she was (and revelled in her), even the censor knew what she was, but she got away with it all because she had immense humour, treated sex as fun and could tell the public all they wanted to know about the character she played without ever needing to resort to heavy-handed verbal explanations.

Clyde Jeavons and Jeremy Pascall, *A Pictorial History of Sex in the Movies*

*See also* Marilyn Monroe

## HARMSWORTH, ALFRED, *see under* NORTHCLIFFE, LORD

## HARRINGTON, JAMES

1611–77 Political Theorist

He grew to have a phancy that his Perspiration turned to Flies, and sometimes to Bees; and he had a versatile timber house built in Mr Hart's garden (opposite to St James's parke) to try the experiment. He would turne it to the sun, and sitt towards it; then he had his fox-tayles there to chase away and massacre all the Flies and Bees that were to be found there, and then shut his *Chassees*. Now this Experiment was only to be tried in Warme weather, and some flies would lie so close in the cranies and cloath (with which it was hung) that they would not presently shew themselves. A quarter of an hower after perhaps, a fly or two, or more, might be drawen out of the lurking holes by the warmth; and then he would crye out, Doe you not see it apparently that these come from me? 'Twas the strangest sort of madness that ever I found in any one: talke of any thing els, his discourse would be very ingeniose and pleasant.

John Aubrey, *Brief Lives*

## HARRIS, FRANK

1856–1931 Author, Journalist

In fact Frank Harris has no feelings. It is the secret of his success. Just as the fact that he thinks that other people have none either is the secret of the failure that lies in wait for him somewhere on the way of Life.

Oscar Wilde, Letter to More Adey, 12 May 1897

To survive you one must have a strong brain, an assertive ego, a dynamic character. In your luncheon-parties, in old days, the remains of the guests were taken away with the *débris* of the feast. I have often lunched with you in Park Lane and found myself the only survivor.

Oscar Wilde, Letter to Frank Harris, 13 June 1897

Frank Harris is invited to all the great houses in England – once.

Oscar Wilde, in A. K. Adams, *The Home Book of Humorous Quotations*

## HARRISON, BENJAMIN

1833–1901 Twenty-Third United States President

The President is a good deal like the old camp horse that Dickens described; he is strapped up so he can't fall down.

On himself, Letter to William McKinley, 4 February 1892

... he sweated ice water.

Anon., in Jules Ables, *The Rockefeller Millions*

You may be interested in knowing that we have one of the smallest Presidents the U.S. has ever known. He is narrow, unresponsive and, oh, so cold. The town is full of grumblers. Nobody appears to like H., though, of course, many tolerate him for what he can give out; there is no administration element in town...

... Senators call and say their say to him, and he stands silent ... As one Senator says: 'It's like talking to a hitching post.'

Walter Wellman, Letter to Walter Q. Gresham, 20 March 1889

## HARRISON, WILLIAM HENRY

1773–1841 Ninth United States President

Tippecanoe And Tyler Too!

Anon. campaign slogan

Harrison was the first president to die in office. He had been in his office for thirty days, working on new tariff laws, and probably over-taxed himself.

Richard Armour, *It All Started With Columbus*

General Harrison was sung into the Presidency.

Philip Hone, Diary

The President is the most extraordinary man I ever saw. He does not seem to realize the vast importance of his elevation ... He is as tickled with the Presidency as is a young woman with a new bonnet.

Martin Van Buren, in A. Steinberg, *The First Ten*

## HARTE, (FRANCIS) BRET

1836–1902 Author

Harte's dainty self-complacencies extended to his carriage and gait. His carriage was graceful and easy, his gait was of the mincing sort, but was the right gait for him, for an unaffected one would not have harmonized with the rest of the man and the clothes.

Mark Twain, in Bernard De Voto ed., *Mark Twain in Eruption*

Harte, in a mild and colorless way, was that kind of man – that is to say, he was a man without a country; no, not a man – man is too strong a term; he was an invertebrate without a country.

*Ibid.*

## HARVEY, WILLIAM

1578–1657 Physician

Ah! my old Friend Dr Harvey – I knew him right well. He made me sitt by him 2 or 3 hours together in his meditating apartment discoursing. Why, had he been stiffe, starcht, and retired, as other formall Doctors are, he had known no more than they. From the meanest person, in some way, or other, the learnedst man may learn something. Pride has been one of the greatest stoppers of the Advancement of Learning.

John Aubrey, *Brief Lives*

I remember he kept a pretty young wench to wayte on him, which I guesse he made use of for warmethsake as King David did, and tooke care of her in his Will, as also of his man servant.

*Ibid.*

And I remember that when I asked our famous *Harvey*, in the only Discourse I had with him, (which was but a while before he dyed) What were the things that induc'd him to think of a *Circulation of the Blood*? He answer'd me, that when he took notice that the Valves in the Veins of so many several Parts of the Body, were so Plac'd that they gave free passage to the Blood Towards the Heart, but oppos'd the passage of the Venal Blood the Contrary way: He was invited to imagine, that so Provident a Cause as Nature had not so Plac'd so many Valves without Design: and no Design seem'd more probable, than That, since the Blood could not well, because of the interposing Valves, be sent by the Veins to the Limbs; it should be Sent through the Arteries, and Return through the Veins, whose Valves did not oppose its course that way.

Robert Boyle, *A Disquisition about the Final Causes of Natural Things*

Coy Nature, (which remain'd, though Aged grown, / A Beauteous virgin still, injoyd by none, / Nor seen unveil'd by any one) / When Harvey's violent passion she did see, / Began to tremble and to flee, / Took Sanctuary like *Daphne* in a tree: / There Daphne's lover stop't, and thought it much / The very Leaves of her to touch, / But *Harvey* our *Apollo*, stopt not so, / Into the Bark, and root he after her did goe. /

Abraham Cowley, *Ode upon Dr Harvey*

And truly when ever He hath been pleased to give any of his own Inventions leave to see the light, He hath not deported Himself with Ostentation, or superciliousness, after the custome of many, as if an Oak had spoken, or he had deserved a draught of Hens Milk: but, His Dictates were Oraculous, and Merits above the reach of Elogie, or Reward: but, with exceeding Modesty, as if onely casually, or without any difficultie of inquest, he had fallen upon the Discovery of those Mysteries, which, indeed, he long searched into with profest diligence, and study indefatigable.

George Ent, *Epistle Dedicatory* to Harvey's *Anatomical Exercitations*

*Dr Harvey* was ever afraid of becoming blind: early one morning, for he always rose early, his housekeeper coming into his chamber to call him, opened the window shutters, told him the hour, and asked him if he would not rise. Upon which he asked if she had opened the shutters; she replied yes – then shut them again – she did so – then open them again. But still the effect was the same to him, for he had awakened stone blind. Upon which he told her to fetch him a bottle, (which she herself had observed to stand on a shelf in his chamber for a long time), out of which he drank a large draught, and it being a strong poison, which it is supposed he had long before prepared and set there for this purpose, he expired within three hours after.

Edward Hasted, *The History and Topographical Survey of the County of Kent*

In merit, Harvey's rank must be comparatively low indeed. So much had been discovered by others that little more was left for him to do than to dress it up into a system; and *that*, every judge in such matters will allow, required no extraordinary talents. Yet, easy as it was, it made him *immortal*. But none of his writings shew him to have been a man of uncommon abilities. It were easy to quote many passages, which bring him nearly to a level with the rest of mankind. He lived almost thirty years after Asellius published the Lacteals, yet, to the last, seemed most inclined to think, that no such vessels existed. Thirty hours at any time, should have been sufficient to remove all his doubts.

William Hunter, *Two Introductory Lectures to his Last Course of Anatomical Lectures*

## HASTINGS, LADY ELIZABETH

1682–1739 Philanthropist

Though her mien carries much more invitation than command, to behold her is an immediate check to loose behaviour; to love her was a liberal education.

Sir Richard Steele, in *Tatler*, no. 49

## HASTINGS, WARREN

1732–1818 Colonial Administrator

What age is it permitted me to look back upon, with my bodily and mental faculties, though impaired, not destroyed; and as my memory presents to me the record of times past, to be able to say 'quorum pars non parva fuit', and like a grain of sand in the way of the ball of a billiard table, to have given its excentrick direction to the rolling events of the world, which they would have obtained, if I had never existed.

On himself, Letter to Edward Baber, 6 October 1815

I gave you all, and you have rewarded me with confiscation, disgrace, and a life of impeachment.

On himself, to the House of Commons, in A. M. Davies, *Warren Hastings*, 1935

A mouth extending fierce from ear to ear, / With fangs like those which wolves and tigers wear; / Eyes, whose dark orbs announce, and sullen mood, / A lust of rapine, and a thirst of blood; / Such Hastings was, as by the Commons painted, / (Men shuddered as they look'd, and women fainted –) . . . / Yet he has friends! And they, – nay (strange to tell!) / His very wife, who ought to know him well, / Whose daily sufferings from the worst of men / Should make her wish the wretch impeach'd again, – / Believe him gentle, meek, and true of heart – / O Hastings, what a hypocrite thou art! /

On himself, on his portrait painted by Lemuel Abbott, in *ibid.*

He tried to see India with the eyes of an Indian, his successors saw it with the eyes of Englishmen. He sought to give India the things he knew it needed: they sought to give it the things they thought would benefit it.

A. M. Davies, in *ibid.*

## HATHAWAY, ANNE

1556–1623 Shakespeare's Wife

She hath a way so to control / To rapture the imprisoned soul / And sweetest Heaven on earth display, / That to be Heaven Ann hath a way; / She hath a way / Ann Hathaway – / To be Heaven's self Ann hath a way. /

Charles Dibdin, *A Love Ditty*

## HAWKSMOOR, NICHOLAS

1661–1736 Architect

[Vanbrugh's] approach to architecture was basically simple whereas Hawksmoor's may fairly be called basically complex.

K. Downes, *Hawksmoor*

He was always inclined by his temperament toward that which is sombre and awe-inspiring. Like Michael Angelo's, his architecture was great tragedy.

H. S. Goodhart-Rendel, *Nicholas Hawksmoor*

## HAWTHORNE, NATHANIEL

1804–64 Author

I have another great difficulty in the lack of materials; for I have seen so little of the world that I have nothing but thin air to concoct my stories of, and it is not easy to give a life-like semblance to such shadowy stuff.

On himself, Letter to Henry Wadsworth Longfellow, 1838

I sat down by the wayside of life like a man under enchantment, and a shrubbery sprung up around me, and the bushes grew to be saplings, and the saplings became trees, until no exit appeared possible, through the tangling depths of my obscurity.

On himself, in Malcolm Cowley ed., Introduction to *Nathaniel Hawthorne, The Selected Works*

I am slow to feel – slow, I suppose, to comprehend and, like the anaconda, I need to lubricate any object a great deal before I can swallow it and actually make it my own.

On himself, in Mark Van Doren, *Nathaniel Hawthorne*

I don't want to be a doctor, and live by men's diseases; nor a minister to live by their sins; nor a lawyer to live by their quarrels. So I don't see there's anything left for me but to be an author.

*Ibid.*

He combined in a singular degree the spontaneity of the imagination with a haunting care for moral problems. Man's conscience was his theme but he saw it in the light of a creative fancy which added, out of its own substance, an interest, and, I may almost say, an importance.

Henry James, *Hawthorne*

But Hawthorne, when you have studied him, will be very precious to you. He will have plunged you into melancholy, he will have overshadowed you with black forebodings, he will almost have crushed you with imaginary sorrows; but he will have enabled you to feel yourself an inch taller during the process.

Anthony Trollope, *The Genius of Nathaniel Hawthorne*, in B. Bernard Cohen, *The Recognition of Nathaniel Hawthorne*

. . . he never seemed to be doing anything, and yet he did not like to be disturbed at it.

John Greenleaf Whittier, in Mark Van Doren, *Nathaniel Hawthorne*

*See also* Edgar Allan Poe, Robert Louis Stevenson

## HAY, JOHN MILTON

1838–1905 Politician

I would not do for a Methodist preacher for I am a poor horseman. I would not suit the Baptists for I dislike water. I would fail as an Episcopalian, for I am no ladies' man.

On himself, in A. K. Adams, *The Home Book of Humorous Quotations*

## HAYDON, BENJAMIN ROBERT

1786–1846 Historical Painter

Haydon hardly contemplated a teaspoon without a desire to shout and hurl himself at it.

Edmund Blunden, Introduction to Haydon, *Autobiography*

Painters with poets for the laurels vie: / But should the laureat bands thy claims deny, / Wear thou thy own green palm, Haydon, triumphantly. /

Charles Lamb, *Poem to Haydon*

Haydon believed himself Phidias in the morning, and retired as Michael Angelo at night.

John Ruskin, *Sir Joshua and Holbein* (first draft, 1860)

Haydon! let worthier judges praise the skill / Here by thy pencil shown in truth of lines / And charm of colours; I applaud those signs / Of thought, that give the true poetic skill. /

William Wordsworth, *To B. R. Haydon, On Seeing His Picture of Napoleon Buonaparte on the Island of St Helena*

## HAYES, RUTHERFORD BIRCHARD

1822–93 Nineteenth United States President

Mr Hayes came in by a majority of one, and goes out by unanimous consent.

Anon., in John M. Taylor, *Garfield of Ohio: The Available Man*

He recognized nothing, and neither authorized nor repudiated anybody. According to the newspaper accounts he would hardly go further in political discussion than to accede to the proposition that there was a republican form of government and that this was the hundredth year of the national government.

Anon., in *Nation*, February 1877

It may be asked whether this man of destiny has any marked peculiarities. I answer none whatever. Neither his body nor his mind runs into rickety proportions.

Judge William Johnston, in H. J. Eckenrode, *Rutherford B. Hayes: Statesman of Reunion*

## HAYLEY, WILLIAM

1745–1820 Poet, Biographer

Thy friendship oft has made my heart to ache: / Do be my Enemy for Friendship's sake.

William Blake, *Epigram*

## HAZLITT, WILLIAM

1778–1830 Essayist

Without the aid of prejudice and custom, I should not be able to find my way across the room.

On himself, *Sketches and Essays*: 'On Prejudice'

Hazlitt, the pit-trumpet of Mr Kean at Drury Lane.

Anon., in Philadelphia *National Gazette*, 7 February 1821

If Hazlitt was a godsend to Kean, Kean was scarcely less of a godsend to Hazlitt. The critic made the actor's reputation, but the actor made the critic's immortality *as* a theatrical critic. If Hazlitt had not had Kean to write about, he would certainly have written much less with far inferior life and gusto, and would probably never have collected his articles.

William Archer, Introduction to *Hazlitt on Theatre*, 1895

His manners are 99 in a 100 singularly repulsive.

Samuel Taylor Coleridge, Letter to Thomas Wedgwood, 16 September 1803

Hazlitt possesses considerable Talent; but it is diseased by a morbid hatred of the Beautiful, and killed by the absence of the Imagination, & alas! by a wicked Heart of embruted Appetites. Poor wretch! he is a melancholy instance of the awful Truth – that man cannot be on a Level with the Beasts – he must be above them or below them.

Samuel Taylor Coleridge, Letter to Hugh J. Rose, 25 September 1816

Under this stone does William Hazlitt lie / Thankless of all that God or man could give. / He lived like one who never thought to die, / He died like one who dared not hope to live. /

Samuel Taylor Coleridge, *Epitaph*

Hazlitt . . . had perhaps the most uninteresting mind of all our distinguished critics.

T. S. Eliot, *Essays*: 'John Dryden'

William Hazlitt . . . owned that he could not bear young girls; they drove him mad. So I took him home to my old nurse, where he recovered perfect tranquility.

Charles Lamb, Letter to William Wordsworth, 26 June 1806

*See also* Robert Louis Stevenson

## HEARST, WILLIAM RANDOLPH

1863–1951 Newspaper Proprietor

Please remain. You furnish the pictures and I'll furnish the war.

On himself, Telegram to artist Frederic Remington who desired to return to America from Cuba where he said there was no war in progress, March 1898

He wrote so much about the Yellow Peril that his journalism took its distinctive coloration from the subject.

Richard Armour, *It All Started With Columbus*

## HEMINGWAY, ERNEST MILLER

1899–1961 Author

I'm Ernie Hemorrhoid, the poor man's Pyle.

On himself, when putting on a war correspondent's uniform, in Robert Macerving, *Hemingway in Cuba*

Wearing underwear is as formal as I ever hope to get.

On himself, in A. E. Hotchner, *Papa Hemingway*

But my writing is nothing. My boxing is everything.

On himself, in Morley Callaghan, *That Summer in Paris*

Always remember this. If you have a success, you have it for the wrong reasons. If you become popular it is always because of the worst aspects of your work. They always praise you for the worst aspects. It never fails.

*Ibid.*

When I have an idea, I turn down the flame, as if it were a little alcohol stove, as low as it will go. Then it explodes and that is my idea.

On himself, in James R. Mellow, *Charmed Circle: Gertrude Stein & Co.*

I had learned already never to empty the well of my writing, but always to stop when there was still something there in the deep part of the well, and let it refill at night from the springs that fed it.

On himself, in *A Moveable Feast*

And as for Hemingway himself, why was he always hardening himself up? The answer was obvious. Anyone close to him knew he was really soft and sentimental. It was amusing to remember the Hemingway who had first come to Montparnasse. Ask anybody. Why had he been wearing those three heavy sweaters to make himself look husky and powerful?

Morley Callaghan, *That Summer in Paris*

A literary style . . . of wearing false hair on the chest.

Max Eastman, Review of *Death in the Afternoon*, in Carlos Baker, *Ernest Hemingway, A Life Story*

He is a great writer. If I didn't think so I wouldn't have tried to kill him . . . I was the champ and when I read his stuff I knew he had something. So I dropped a heavy glass skylight on his head at a drinking party. But you can't kill the guy. He's not human.

F. Scott Fitzgerald, in Jed Kiley, *Hemingway, A Title Fight in Ten Rounds*

His inclination is toward megalomania and mine toward melancholy.

F. Scott Fitzgerald, in Carlos Baker, *Ernest Hemingway, A Life Story*

Hemingway's words strike you, each one, as if they were pebbles fetched fresh from a brook. They live and shine, each in its place. So one of his pages has the effect of a brook-bottom into which you look down through the flowing water. The words form a tessellation, each in order beside the other.

Ford Madox Ford, in Edmund Wilson, *The Wound and the Bow*

He comes and sits at my feet and praises me. It makes me nervous.

Ford Madox Ford, in Arthur Mizener, *The Saddest Story, A Biography of Ford Madox Ford*

For Hemingway courage is a permanent element in a tragic formula: life is a trap in which a man is bound to be beaten and at last destroyed, but he emerges triumphant, in his full stature, if he manages to keep his chin up.

W. M. Frohock, *The Novel of Violence in America*

He's the original Limelight Kid, just you watch him for a few months. Wherever the limelight is, you'll find Ernest with his big lovable boyish grin, making hay.

Robert McAlmon, in Malcolm Cowley, *A Second Flowering*

Famous at twenty-five; thirty a master.

Archibald MacLeish, in Carlos Baker, *Hemingway: Writer as Artist*

When I first met Hemingway he had a truly sensitive capacity for emotion, and that was the stuff of the first stories; but he was shy of himself and he began to develop, as a shield, a big Kansas City-boy brutality about it, and so he was 'touchy' because he was really sensitive and ashamed that he was. Then it happened. I saw it happening and tried to save what was fine there, but it was too late. He went the way so many other Americans have gone before, the way they are still going. He became obsessed with sex and violent death.

Gertrude Stein, in John Malcolm Brinnin, *The Third Rose*

Despite Hemingway's preoccupation with physical contests, his heroes are almost always defeated physically, nervously, practically: their victories are moral ones.

Edmund Wilson, *The Wound and the Bow*

## HENDERSON, ARTHUR

1863–1935 Labour Leader, Statesman

We will support Henderson as a rope supports a man who is hanged.

V. I. Lenin, in a message from the Russian Communist Party to the British Labour Party, 1920, in A. J. P. Taylor, *English History 1914–1945*

## HENDRIX, JIMI (JAMES MARSHALL)

1942–70 Musician

A psychedelic hootchie-kootchie man, swathed in red and orange, he was magnificent, at the very edge of the believable and totally real.

Michael Lydon, *Rock Folk*

## HENGIST (d. 488) AND HORSA (d. 455)

Jutish Warlords

What went on between the death of Boadicea and the emergence on the scene of Alfred, nobody seems to have the faintest idea . . . For a time, the land was ruled by squabbling gangs of Nordic nonentities, among whom the names of Hengist and Horsa ring a dim sort of bell. These were the Vikings, who lumbered about in the twilight of the Dark Ages wearing hats tastefully trimmed with cows' horns.

Nicolas Bentley, *Golden Sovereigns*

## HENRY I
1068–1135

The king praises no one whom he has not resolved to ruin.

Bishop Bloet, in Henry of Huntingdon, *History of England*, translated by T. Forester

For, he was very wanton, as appeareth by his numerous natural issue, no fewer than *fourteen*, all by him publicly owned; the males highly advanced, the females richly married, which is justly reported to his praise, it being *lust* to *beget*, but *love* to *bestow* them. His sobriety otherwise was admirable, whose temperance was of proof against any meat objected to his appetite, *Lampreys* alone excepted, on a surfeit whereof he died, *Anno Domini* 1135.

Thomas Fuller, *The History of the Worthies of England*

Henry I was not a creator of institutions; he contributed nothing to the theory of kingship or to the philosophy of government. He created men. It was his contribution to English government and society to insert into the social fabric men with a direct interest in royal government; men who depended on royal government for their rise, and on its continuance for their survival.

R. W. Southern, *The Place of Henry I in English History*

After his death, a monk of Bec saw him in a vision thrust into hell each morning and rescued by the prayers of monks each evening.

*Ibid.*

## HENRY II
1133–89

This King Henry was wise, valiant, and generally fortunate. His faults were such as speak him man, rather than a vicious one. Wisdom enough he had for his work, and work enough for his wisdom, being troubled in all his relations. His wife, Queen Eleanor, brought a great portion, (fair provinces in France), and a great stomach with her; so that it is questionable, whether her froward spirit more drove her husband away from her chaste, or Rosamond's fair face more drew him to her wanton, embraces. His sons (having much of the mother in them) grew up, as in age, in obstinacy against him.

Thomas Fuller, *Church History of Britain*

Henry II, king of England, had a reddish complexion, rather dark, and a large round head. His eyes were grey, bloodshot, and flashed in anger. He had a fiery countenance, his voice was tremulous, and his neck a little bent forward; but his chest was broad, and his arms were muscular. His body was fleshy, and he had an enormous paunch, rather by the fault of nature than from gross feeding. For his diet was temperate, and indeed in all things, considering he was a prince, he was moderate and even parsimonious. In order to reduce and cure, as far as possible, this natural tendency and defect, he waged a continual war, so to speak, with his own belly by taking immoderate exercise . . . At the first dawn of day he would mount a fleet horse, and indefatigably spend the day in riding through the woods, penetrating the depths of forests, and crossing the ridges of hills. On his return home in the evening he was seldom seen to sit down, either before he took his supper or after; for, notwithstanding his own great fatigue, he would weary all his court by being constantly on his legs.

Giraldus Cambrensis, *The Conquest of Ireland*, translated from the Latin by T. Forester

He travelled incessantly, and in stages intolerable, like a public carrier, and, in this matter, he showed scant consideration for his retinue. In dogs and birds he was most expert, and exceeding fond of hunting. He passed nights without sleep and was untiring in his activities. Whenever in his dreams passion mocked him with vain shapes, he used to curse his body, because neither toil nor fasting was able to break or weaken it. I, however, ascribe his activities not to his incontinence but to his fear of becoming too fat.

Walter Map, *De Nugis Curialium*, translated from the Latin by F. Tupper and M. B. Ogle

## HENRY IV

1367–1413

At last, as he was praying before the shrine of St Edward at Westminster Abbey, he was seized with a terrible fit, and was carried into the Abbot's chamber, where he presently died. It had been foretold that he would die at Jerusalem, which certainly is not, and never was, Westminster. But, as the Abbot's room had long been called the Jerusalem chamber, people said it was all the same thing, and were quite satisfied with the prediction.

Charles Dickens, *A Child's History of England*

## HENRY V

1387–1422

Owre kyng went forth to Normandy, / With grace and myyt of chivalry; / The God for hym wrouyt marvelously. /

Anon. ballad in Percy, *Reliques of Ancient English Poetry*

The Kinge daylie and nightlie in his owne person visited and searched the watches, orders and stacions of euerie part of his hoast, and whom he founde dilligent he praised and thanked, and the negligent he corrected and chastised.

Anon., *The First English Life of King Henry the Fifth* (on his conduct during a siege)

And before he was Kyng, what tyme regnyd he Prince of Walyes, he fyll & yntendyd gretly to riot, and drew to wylde company . . . And thanne he beganne to reigne for Kyng, & he rememberyd the gret charge & warrship that he shulde take upon hym; And anon he commaundyd al his peple that were attendaunt to his mysgovernaunce afore tyme, & all his housolde, to come before hym. And when they herde that, they were ful glad, for they subposyd that he wolde a promotyd them into gret offices . . . But for all that, the Prynce kept his countynance ful sadly unto them, And sayde to them: 'Syrys, ye are the peple that I haue cherysyd and mayntyngd in Ryot & wylde governance; and here I geve you all in commaundment, & charge you, that from this day forward that ye forsake all misgovernaunce, lyve aftyr the lawys of Almyghty God, & aftyr the lawys of oure lande. And who that doyth the contrarye, I make feythfull promyse to God, that he shal be trewly ponisyd accordyng to the law, withoute eny favour or grace.'

*The Brut Chronicle*

In the year of our lord 1415, Henry V King of England called together the prelates and lords of his kingdom, and asked their advice, on peril of their souls, whether he had a better grievance against the kingdom of Scotland or against the kingdom of France, to go to war about.

*The Book of Pluscarden*, translated by F. J. H. Skene

Henry V was not the bluff patriot king of Shakespeare's plays; he was a dour and martial fanatic, obsessed by religion and his legal rights.

John Bowle, *England, A Portrait*

*Gloucester*: England ne'er had a king until his time. / Virtue he had, deserving to command: / His brandish'd sword did blind men with his beams; / His arms spread wider than a dragon's wings; / His sparkling eyes, replete with wrathful fire, / More dazzled and drove back his enemies / Than mid-day sun fierce bent against their faces. / What should I say? his deeds exceed all speech, / He ne'er lift up his hand but conquered. /

William Shakespeare, *Henry VI, Part I,* Act I, Scene i

For these Frenchmen, puffed up with pride and lacking in foresight, hurling mocking words at the ambassadors of the King of England, said foolishly to them that as Henry was but a young man, they would send him little balls to play with and soft cushions to rest on until he should have grown to a man's strength. When the king heard these words he was much moved and troubled in spirit; yet he addressed these short, wise and honest words to those standing around him: 'If God wills, and if my life shall be prolonged with health, in a few months I shall play with such balls in the Frenchmen's court-yards that they will lose the game eventually and for their game win but grief. And if they shall sleep too long on their cushions in their chambers, I will awake them, before they wish it, from their slumbers at dawn by beating on their doors.'

John Strecche (on the King's reaction to insults from the ambassadors of the Dauphin), *The Chronicle for the Reign of Henry V,* translated by A. R. Myers

*See also* Sir John Fastolfe

## HENRY VII

1457–1509

He was a Prince, sad, serious, and full of thoughts, and secret observations, and full of notes and memorials of his own hand, especially touching persons. As, who to employ, whom to reward, whom to inquire of, whom to beware of, what were the dependencies, what were the factions, and the like; keeping, as it were, a journal of his thoughts.

Francis Bacon, *History of the Reign of Henry VII*

What the man lacked apparently was any personal charm. They called his son later Bluff King Hal and his granddaughter Good Queen Bess, but none ever gave Henry VII a nickname. He never seems to have caught the popular imagination. What contemporaries chiefly remarked in him was his wisdom, by which they meant his sound common sense. Men feared him, admired him, depended on him, but they did not love him.

Conyers Read, *The Tudors*

. . . Henry Tydder, son of Edmund Tydder, son of Owen Tydder, whiche of his ambitiousness and insociable covetise, encroacheth and usurpid upon hym the name and title of royall estate of this Realme of Englond, where unto he hath no maner interest, right, title, or colour, as every man wel knowoth; for he is discended of bastard blood bothe of ffather side and of mother side, For the said Owen the graunfader was bastard borne, and his moder was daughter un to John, Duke of Somerset, sone unto John, Erle of Somerset, sonne unto Dame Katryne Swynford, and of ther indouble avoutry gotyn, whereby evidently apperith that no title can nor may in him, which fully entendeth to entre this Realme, purposyng a conquest.

Richard III, *The Proclamation against Henry Tudor,* 1485

*See also* George II

## HENRY VIII

1491–1547

Passetyme with good cumpanye / I love, and shall unto I dye, / Gruche so wylle, but none deny, / So God plecyd, so lyf woll I. / For my pastaunce / Hunte, syng, & daunce, / My hert is sett: / All godely sport / To my comfort, / Who shall me lett? /

On himself, in Horace Walpole, *Catalogue of Royal and Noble Authors*

Bluff Henry the Eighth to six spouses was wedded:/One died, one survived, two divorced, two beheaded. /

Anon. nursery rhyme, *circa* 1750

. . . Nothing can be said in his vindication, but that his abolishing Religious Houses and leaving them to the ruinous depredations of time has been of infinite use to the landscape of England in general, which probably was a principal motive for his doing it, since otherwise why should a Man who was of no Religion himself be at so much trouble to abolish one which had for ages been established in the Kingdom?

Jane Austen, *The History of England*

Henry the Eighth / Took a thuctheththion of mateth. / He inthithted that the monkth / Were a lathy lot of thkunkth. /

E. C. Bentley, *More Biography*

I repayring to your Majesty into your prevey Chambre Fynding your grace not as pleasaunte as I trustyd to have done I was so bolde as to aske your grace how ye lykyd the quene Whereunto your grace Sobyrly answeryd saying That I was not all men Surelye my lorde as ye know. I lykyd her beffor not well but now I lyke her moche woorse For quoth your highness I haue Felte her belye and her brestes and therby, as I can Judge She Sholde be noe Mayde which strake me so to the harte when I Felt them that I hadde nother will nor Corage to procede any ferther in other matyrs, saying I have left her as good a mayde as I founde her.

Thomas Cromwell, Letter to Henry VIII, June 1540 (reminding Henry of his words to Cromwell, after his wedding night with Anne of Cleves)

Then, there is a great story belonging to this Field of the Cloth of Gold, showing how the English were distrustful of the French, and the French of the English, until Francis rode alone one morning to Henry's tent; and, going in before he was out of bed, told him in joke that he was his prisoner; and how Henry jumped out of bed and embraced Francis; and how Francis helped Henry to dress, and warmed his linen for him; and how Henry gave Francis a splendid jewelled collar, and how Francis gave Henry, in return, a costly bracelet. All this and a great deal more was so written about, and sung about, and talked about at that time (and indeed since that time too), that the world has had good cause to be sick of it, for ever.

Charles Dickens, *A Child's History of England*

The plain truth is, that he was a most intolerable ruffian, a disgrace to human nature, and a blot of blood and grease upon the History of England.

*Ibid.*

If a lion knew his own strength, hard were it for any man to rule him.

Sir Thomas More, attributed

Could you but see how nobly he is bearing himself, how wise he is, his love for all that is good and right, and specially his love of learning, you would need no wings to fly into the light of this new risen and salutary star. Oh, Erasmus, could you but witness the universal joy, could you but see how proud our people are of their new sovereign, you would weep for pleasure. Heaven smiles, earth triumphs, and flows with milk and honey and nectar. This king of ours is no seeker after gold, or gems, or mines of silver. He desires only the fame of virtue and eternal life.

Lord Mountjoy, Letter to Erasmus, translated by J. A. Froude (on the accession of Henry)

. . . If all the pictures & patterns of a merciless Prince were lost in the World, they might all again be painted to the life, out of the story of this King.

Sir Walter Raleigh, *The Historie of the World*

Possibly he had an Oedipus complex: and possibly from this derived a desire for, yet horror of, incest, which may have shaped some of his sexual life.

Richard Scarisbrick, *Henry VIII*

The Rose both White and Red / In one Rose now doth grow: / Thus thorough every sted / Thereof the fame doth blow. / Grace the seed did sow: / England, now gather floures, / Exclude now all doloures. /

John Skelton, *A Laud and Praise Made for Our Sovereign Lord the King*

The imperial Stature, the colossal stride, / Are yet before me; yet do I behold / The broad full visage, chest of amplest mould, / The vestments 'broidered with barbaric pride: / And lo! a poniard, at the monarch's side, / Hangs ready to be grasped in sympathy / With the keen threatenings of that fulgent eye, / Below the white-rimmed bonnet, far descried. /

William Wordsworth, *Recollection of the Portrait of King Henry Eighth, Trinity Lodge, Cambridge*

*See also* Anne Boleyn, George I, George II, Henry VII, Catherine Howard, Jane Seymour, Thomas Wolsey

## HENRY, PATRICK

1739–99 Statesman, Orator

Is life so dear or peace so sweet, as to be purchased at the price of chains and slavery? Forbid it, Almighty God! I know not what course others may take, but as for me, give me liberty or give me death!

On himself, Speech, Virginia Convention, 23 March 1775

. . . the forest-born Demosthenes.

Lord Byron, in Robert Meade, *Patrick Henry, Practical Revolutionary*

## HEPWORTH, DAME BARBARA

1903–75 Sculptor

It's so natural to work large – it fits one's body. This doesn't mean that I don't like working small because I do. It's refreshing, like painting or drawing, but I've always wanted to go to my arm's length and walk round things, or climb up them. I kept on thinking of large works in a landscape: this has always been a dream in my mind.

On herself, in A. Bowness, *The Complete Sculpture of Barbara Hepworth*

What she does she does admirably. It is rather like the work of a maker of musical instruments. If anyone would know how to make a beautiful belly to a mandolin or a lute it is she. If she were a potter, she would be a potter of distinction and resource. But she comes at a time – as does Mr Moore – when artists are working in a vacuum.

Percy Wyndham Lewis, in *Listener*, October 1946

## HERBERT, EDWARD, LORD HERBERT OF CHERBURY

1583–1648 Courtier, Philosopher

James Ussher, Lord Primate of Ireland, was sent for by him, when in his death-bed, and he would have received the sacrament. He sayd indifferently of it that *if there was good in any-thing 'twas in that*, or *if it did no good 'twould doe no hurt*. The Primate refused it, for which many blamed him. He then turned his head to the other side and expired very serenely.

John Aubrey, *Brief Lives*

## HERBERT, GEORGE

1593–1633 Poet

And HERBERT: he, whose education, / Manners, and parts, by high applauses blown, / Was deeply tainted with Ambition; /

And fitted for a Court, made that his aim: / At last, without regard to Birth or Name, / For a poor Country-Cure, does all disclaim. /

Where, with a soul compos'd of Harmonies, / Like a sweet Swan, he warbles, as he dies / His makers praise, and, his own obsequies. /

Charles Wotton, *To My Old, and Most Worthy Friend, Mr IZAAC WALTON*

## HERBERT, MARY, COUNTESS OF PEMBROKE

1561–1621 Patroness

She was very salacious, and she had a Contrivance that in the Spring of the yeare, when the Stallions were to leape the Mares, they were to be brought before such a part of the house, where she had a *vidette* (a hole to peep out at) to looke on them and please herselfe with their Sport; and then she would act the like sport herselfe with *her* stallions. One of her great Gallants was Crooke-back't Cecill, Earl of Salisbury.

John Aubrey, *Brief Lives*

Underneath this sable hearse / Lies the subject of all verse: / Sidney's sister, Pembroke's mother. / Death, ere thou hast slain another / Fair and learn'd and good as she, / Time shall throw a dart at thee. /

William Browne, *On the Countess Dowager of Pembroke*, 1621 (formerly ascribed to Ben Jonson)

## HEREWARD 'THE WAKE'

*fl.* 1070–1 Saxon Warrior

The next moment the door of the bower was thrown violently open, and in swaggered a noble lad eighteen years old. His face was of extraordinary beauty, save that the lower jaw was too long and heavy, and that his eyes wore a strange and almost sinister expression, from the fact that the one of them was grey and the other blue. He was short, but of immense breadth of chest and strength of limb; while his delicate hands and feet and long locks of golden hair marked him of most noble, and even, as he really was, of ancient royal race.

Charles Kingsley, *Hereward the Wake*

The military drama of the conquest closed with the vast siege operations conducted by William against the Isle of Ely defended by Hereward. Hereward was a man of the Fenland district, with a genius for amphibious guerilla warfare in that difficult country. But his resistance only began after the rest of England had been conquered, and the event was therefore never in doubt. It was but the last and noblest of a series of regional revolts undertaken too late.

G. M. Trevelyan, *History of England*

## HERRICK, ROBERT

1591–1674 Poet

As wearied *Pilgrims*, once possest / Of long'd-for lodging, go to reast: / So I, now having rid my way; / Fix here my Button'd Staffe and stay. / Youth (I confess) hath me mis-led; / But Age hath brought me right to Bed. /

On himself, *His own Epitaph*

The Ariel of poets, sucking 'where the bee sucks' from the rose-heart of nature, and reproducing the fragrance idealized.

Elizabeth Barrett Browning, *The Greek Christian Poets and the English Poets*

Of all our poets this man appears to have had the coarsest mind. Without being intentionally obscene, he is thoroughly filthy, and has not the slightest sense of decency. In an old writer, and especially one of that age, I never saw so large a proportion of what may truly be called either trash or ordure.

Robert Southey, *Commonplace Book* (4th Series)

## HERSCHEL, SIR WILLIAM

1738–1822 Astronomer

In constructing the seven-foot reflector, he finished no fewer than two hundred specula before he produced one that would bear any power that was applied to it, – a striking instance of the persevering laboriousness of the man. While sublimely gauging the heavens with his instruments, he continued patiently to earn his bread by piping to the fashionable frequenters of the Bath Pump-room. So eager was he in his astronomical observations, that he would steal away from the room during an interval of the performance, give a little turn to his telescope, and contentedly return to his oboe.

Samuel Smiles, *Self-help*

Oh, but I have better news for you, Madam, if you have any patriotism as a citizen of this world and wish its longevity. Mr Herschel has found out that our globe is a comely middle-aged personage, and has not so many wrinkles as seven stars, who are evidently our seniors. Nay, he has discovered that the Milky Way is not only a mob of stars, but that there is another dairy of them still farther off, whence I conclude comets are nothing but pails returning from milking, instead of balloons filled with inflammable air.

Horace Walpole, Letter to the Countess of Upper Ossory, 4 July 1785

Oh, I must stop: I shall turn my own brain, which, while it is launching into an ocean of universes, is still admiring pismire Herschel. That he should not have a *wise* look does not surprise me – he may be stupified by his own discoveries.

Horace Walpole, Letter to the Countess of Upper Ossory, 6 September 1787

## HERVEY, JOHN, LORD

1696–1743 Author

*P.* Let *Sporus* tremble – *A.* What? that thing of silk, / *Sporus*, that mere white curd of Ass's milk? / Satire or sense, alas! can *Sporus* feel? / Who breaks a butterfly upon a wheel? / *P.* Yet let me flap this bug with gilded wings, / This painted child of dirt, that stinks and stings; / Whose buzz the witty and the fair annoys, / Yet wit ne'er tastes, and beauty ne'er enjoys: / So well-bred spaniels civilly delight / In mumbling of the game they dare not bite. / Eternal smiles his emptiness betray, / As shallow streams run dimpling all the way. / Whether in florid impotence he speaks, / And, as the prompter breathes, the puppet squeaks; / Or, at the ear of *Eve*, familiar Toad, / Half froth, half venom, spits himself abroad, / In puns, or politics, or tales, or lies, / Or spite, or smut, or rhymes, or blasphemies. /

Alexander Pope, *Epistle to Dr Arbuthnot*

## HEYWOOD, THOMAS

–d. 1650? Dramatist

He was attempting to reach his audience's tears by new means; for no domestic tragedy so far as we know had made the erring wife lovable and the deceived husband dignified. Shakespeare himself is more conservative in tragedy and, infinitely subtler though his treatment of motives may be, he does not essay new problems of conduct or paradoxical situations. Except that it is unformed by any message, is not illustrative of any sociological criticism, and is more humane, *A Woman Killed with Kindness* – a tragedy of a middle class household – anticipates the bloodless tragedies of Ibsen. In another way Heywood may be regarded as the forerunner of Richardson, the school of sensibility, and the *comédie larmoyante* of the eighteenth century.

A. M. Clark, *Thomas Heywood, Playwright and Miscellanist*

In the work of nearly all of his contemporaries who are as well known as he there is at least some inchoate pattern; there is, as it would often be called, personality. Of those of Heywood's plays which are worth reading, each is worth reading for itself, but none throws any illumination upon any other . . . Heywood's is a drama of common life, not, in the highest sense, tragedy at all; there is no supernatural music from behind the wings. He would in any age have been a successful playwright.

T. S. Eliot, *Essays*: 'Thomas Heywood'

'Tis said, that he not only acted himself almost every day, but also wrote each day a Sheet: and that he might loose no time, many of his Plays were composed in the Tavern, on the backside of Tavern Bills, which may be the Occasion that so many of them be lost.

William Winstanley, *Lives of the Most Famous English Poets*

## HICKOK, JAMES BUTLER 'WILD BILL'

1837–76 Soldier, Frontiersman

The Prince of Pistoleers.

Joseph G. Rosa, *They Called Him Wild Bill: The Life and Adventures of James Butler Hickok*

## HILL, JOE (JOEL HÄGGLUND)

1879–1915 Labour Leader

I dreamed I saw Joe Hill last night, / Alive as you and me. / Says I: 'But Joe, you're ten years dead.' / 'I never died,' says he . . ./

And standing there as big as life / And smiling with his eyes, / Joe says, 'What they forgot to kill / Went on to organize.'/

Two verses of five of 'The Ballad of Joe Hill'

## HILL, 'SIR' JOHN

1716?–75 Physician, Playwright

With sleek appearance, and with ambling pace, / And type of vacant head with vacant face, / The Proteus Hill put in his modest plea, – / 'Let favour speak for others, Worth for me.' – / For who, like him, his various powers could call / Into so many shapes, and shine in all? / Who could so nobly grace the motley list, / Actor, Inspector, Doctor, Botanist? / Knows any one so well, – sure no one knows – / At once to play, prescribe, compound, compose? /

Charles Churchill, *The Rosciad*

For Physick & Farces, his equal there scarce is / His Farces are Physick, his Physick a Farce is. /

David Garrick, Letter to Dr John Hawkesworth, *circa* January 1759

## HILLIARD, NICHOLAS

1537–1619 Miniaturist, Goldsmith

A hand, or eye, / By Hilliard drawne, is worth an history, / By a worse painter made. /

John Donne, *The Storme*

## HOARE, SAMUEL JOHN GURNEY, VISCOUNT TEMPLEWOOD

1880–1959 Statesman

He has all the materials that go to the making of a leader of the Conservative party. He is not stupid, but he is very dull. He is not eloquent, but he talks well. He is not honest (politically), but he is most evangelical, a great leader in the Church of England.

He has a little money, but not too much. He always conforms to the party policy. He knows not Ishmael, but he is well acquainted with the life-story of Jacob.

Lord Beaverbrook, Letter to Arthur Brisbane, 20 October 1932

## HOBBES, THOMAS

1588–1679 Philosopher

I am about to take my last voyage, a great leap in the dark.

On himself, attributed last words

Here lies *Tom Hobbes*, the Bug-bear of the Nation, / Whose *Death* hath frighted *Atheism* out of *Fashion*. /

Anon., *An Elegie upon Mr Thomas Hobbes of Malmesbury, Lately Deceased*

In fine, after a thousand shams and fobs / Ninety years eating and immortal jobs, / Here matter lies, and that's an end of Hobbes. /

Anon., in a London broadsheet, 1679

His extraordinary Timorousness Mr Hobs doth very ingeniosely confess and atributes it to the influence of his Mother's Dread of the Spanish Invasion in 88, she being then with child of him.

John Aubrey, *Brief Lives*

He alwayes avoided, as much as he could, to conclude hastily.

*Ibid.*

He desired not the reputation of his wisdome to be taken from the cutt of his beard, but from his reason.

*Ibid.*

He had read much, if one considers his long life; but his contemplation was much more than his reading. He was wont to say that if he had read as much as other men, he should have knowne no more then other men.

*Ibid.*

Mr *Hobbs*, in the Preface to his own bald Translation of the *Ilias*, (studying Poetry as he did Mathematicks, when it was too late) Mr *Hobbs*, I say, begins the praise of *Homer* where he should have ended it.

John Dryden, Preface to *Fables Ancient and Modern*

The contradiction is apparent. Hobbes, the small bourgeois, the clever boy making good at Oxford, is taken into the service of one of the most conservative of the great feudal families, which still ruled large tracts of the economically backward north of England. When Hobbes takes his noble pupils on the grand tour of Europe he meets the most advanced intellects of his time – Galileo, Descartes, Gassendi. He comes home to discuss their ideas with the Duke of Newcastle.

Christopher Hill, *Puritanism and Revolution*

Finally, Hobbes abandoned the old games of text swapping and precedent hunting for logical argument. That is to say, he made reason, not authority, the arbiter of politics. Paradoxically, it is

the absolutist Hobbes who demonstrated that the state exists for man, that it is the product of human reason, and therefore that political theory is a rational science.
*Ibid.*

Hobbes's politics are fitted only to promote tyranny, and his ethics to encourage licentiousness. Though an enemy to religion, he partakes nothing of the spirit of scepticism; but is as positive and dogmatical as if human reason, and his reason in particular, could attain a thorough conviction in these subjects.
David Hume, *History of England*

When God vouchsafed to make man after his own Image, and in his own Likeness, and took so much delight in him, as to give him the command and dominion over all the Inhabitants of the Earth, the Air, and the Sea, it cannot be imagin'd but that at the same time he endued him with Reason, and all the other noble Faculties which were necessary for the administration of that Empire, and the preservation of the several Species which were to succeed the Creation; and therefore to uncreate him to such baseness and villany in his nature, as to make man such a Rascal, and more a Beast in his frame and constitution than those he is appointed to govern, is a power that God never gave to the Devil; nor hath any body assum'd it, till Mr Hobbes took it upon him.
Edward Hyde, Earl of Clarendon, *A Brief View and Survey of the Leviathan*

Where he is wrong, he is wrong from over-simplification, not because the basis of his thought is unreal or fantastic. For this reason, he is still worth refuting.
Bertrand Russell, *History of Western Philosophy*

*Hobbes* clearly proves that ev'ry Creature / Lives in a State of War by Nature. /
Jonathan Swift, *On Poetry: A Rhapsody*

Confirmed also that Thomas Hobs died at Hardwick within 12 miles of Chatsworth, that on his death bed he should say that he was 91 yeares finding out a hole to go out of this world, and at length found it. He died on 4 Dec. Thursday . . . An ill-natured man they say, proud, scornful . . . Hobs his Leviathan hath corrupted the gentry of the nation, hath infused ill principles into them, atheisme . . . Mr Hobs a person of verie acute parts, quick apprehension to the last, ready to answer whatsoever is proposed, and would understand what you meane before you are at the end of half your discourse.
Anthony à Wood, *Life and Times*, 10 December 1679

## HOGARTH, WILLIAM

1697–1764 Painter, Engraver

Oft have I known Thee, HOGARTH, weak and vain, / Thyself the idol of thy awkward strain, / Thro' the dull measure of a summer's day, / In phrase most vile, prate long long hours away, / Whilst Friends with Friends all gaping sit, and gaze / To hear a HOGARTH babble HOGARTH's praise. /
Charles Churchill, *An Epistle to William Hogarth*

He who should call the Ingenious Hogarth a Burlesque Painter, would, in my Opinion, do him very little Honour: for sure it is much easier, much less the Subject of Admiration, to paint a Man with a Nose, or any other Feature of a preposterous Size, or to expose him in some absurd or monstrous Attitude, than to express the Affections of Men on Canvas. It hath been thought a vast Commendation of a Painter, to say his Figures *Seem to breathe*; but surely, it is a much greater and nobler Applause, *that they appear to think*.

Henry Fielding, Preface to *Joseph Andrews*

He was essentially what the French so conveniently call *primaire*, i.e. a man whose limited and reach-me-down culture gives him a ready answer to any problem, who becomes dogmatic, narrow-minded, positive and self-satisfied.

Roger Fry, *Reflections on British Painting*

He does not represent folly or vice in its incipient, or dormant, or *grub* state, but fully grown, with wings, pampered into all sorts of affectation, airy, ostentatious, and extravagant. Folly is there seen at its height – the moon is at the full – at 'the very error of the time.' There is a perpetual collision of eccentricities – a tilt and tournament of absurdities – the prejudices and caprices of mankind are let loose, and set together by the ears, as in a bear-garden.

William Hazlitt, 'On Mr Wilkie's Pictures', in *Champion*, 5 March 1815

Other pictures we look at – his prints we read.

Charles Lamb, *On the Genius and Character of Hogarth in Essays and Sketches*

*See also* Evelyn Waugh

## HOGG, JAMES

1770–1835 Author

The said Hogg is a strange being, but of great, though uncouth, powers. I think very highly of him, as a poet; but he, and half of these Scotch and Lake troubadours, are spoilt by living in little circles and petty societies.

Lord Byron, Letter to Tom Moore, 3 August 1814

The honest grunter.

Sir Walter Scott, *Journal*, 12 December 1825

When supper was half over, James Hogg, the Ettrick Shepherd, appeared. A chair had been designedly left vacant for him between the two aristocrats. His approach was discernible before his person was visible; for he came straight from a cattle fair, and was reeking with the unsavory odours of the sheep and pigs and oxen, in whose company he had been for hours. Nevertheless he soon made himself at home with the fair ladies on each side of him: somewhat too much so, for, supper over, the cloth withdrawn, and the toddy introduced, the song going round, and his next door neighbours being too languid in their manner of joining in the chorus to please him, he turned first to the right hand, then to the left, and slapped both of them on their backs with such good will as to make their blade bones ring again; then, with a yell of an Ojibbaway Indian, he shouted forth 'Noo then, leddies, follow me! Heigh tutti, tutti! Heigh tutti, tutti!'

Julian Charles Young, *Journal*

## HOLMES, OLIVER WENDELL

1809–94 Essayist, Poet, Teacher

I have, in common with yourself, a desire to leave the world a little more human than if I had not lived; for a true humanity is, I believe, our nearest approach to Divinity, while we work out our atmospheric apprenticeships on the surface of this second-class planet.

On himself, Letter to Harriet Beecher Stowe, 1860

To be 70 years young is sometimes far more cheerful than to be forty years old.
On himself, Letter to Julia Ward Howe, 27 May 1879

There was nothing Miltonic about him. There were few stops to his organ.
Grant C. Knight, *American Literature and Culture*

Not since Robert Treat Paine had there been such a master of Yankee small talk . . . But like every talker his discursiveness is inveterate; he wanders far in pursuit of his point and sometimes returns empty-handed. He was always an amateur; life was too agreeable for him to take the trouble to become an artist.
Vernon Louis Parrington, *Main Currents in American Thought*, vol. 2

He kept the windows of his mind open to the winds of scientific inquiry that were blowing briskly to the concern of orthodox souls. Many a barnacled craft was floundering in those gales, and Holmes watched them going-down with visible satisfaction.
Vernon Louis Parrington, in Robert Allen Skotheim, *American Intellectual Histories and Historians*

. . . fat as a baloon – he weighed as much as three hundred, and had double chins all the way down to his stomach.
Mark Twain, in Kenneth S. Lynn, *William Dean Howells, An American Life*

## HOLMES, OLIVER WENDELL JR

1841–1935 Jurist

One of my old formulas is to be an enthusiast in the front part of your heart and ironical at the back.
On himself, in James B. Peabody ed., *The Holmes–Einstein Letters*

## HOLST, GUSTAV THEODORE

1874–1934 Composer

My idea of composition is to spoil as much MS paper as possible.
On himself, Letter to Ralph Vaughan Williams, 15 April 1932

If to have 'lived' it is necessary to have eloped with a *prima donna*, to have played mean tricks on one's friends, to be dirty and drunken – if life means no more than that, then indeed the word has little meaning for a man like Holst. But if to live may be summed up in the words 'Whatsoever thy hand findeth to do, do it with thy might,' then Holst has lived to the full; he has learnt his lesson in the hard school of necessity; he has not run away from the battle but has fought and won.
Ralph Vaughan Williams, 'Gustav Holst', in *Music and Letters*, 1920

## HOMER, WINSLOW

1836–1910 Artist

The life that I have chosen gives me my full hours of enjoyment for the balance of my life. The Sun will not rise, or set, without my notice, and thanks.
On himself, in Lloyd Goodrich, *Winslow Homer*

His style was highly selective. He saw things in a big way: he simplified, he eliminated, he concentrated on the large forms and movements. This bigness of style had been instinctive from the first; as he matured it became a deliberate process. 'Never put more than two waves in a picture; it's fussy,' he once said.
Lloyd Goodrich, *Winslow Homer*

## HONE, WILLIAM

1780–1842 Radical Pamphleteer, Publisher

Hone the publisher's trial you must find very amusing; and as an Englishman very encouraging.

John Keats, Letter to his Brother, 1817

The acquittal of Hone is enough to make one out of love with English Juries.

William Wordsworth, Letter to T. Monkhouse, 1818

## HOOD, THOMAS

1835–74 Poet

Urn a lively Hood.

On himself, shortly before dying

## HOOKE, ROBERT

1635–1703 Physicist

He is but of middling stature, something crooked, pale faced, ànd his face but little belowe, but his head is lardge; his eie full and popping, and not quick; a grey eie. He haz a delicate head of haire, browne, and of an excellent moist curle. He is and ever was very temperate, and moderate in dyet, etc. As he is of prodigious inventive head, so is a person of great vertue and goodness. Now when I have sayd his Inventive faculty is so great, you cannot imagine his Memory to be excellent, for they are like two Bucketts, as one goes up, the other goes downe. He is certainly the greatest Mechanick this day in the World.

John Aubrey, *Brief Lives*

As to his person, he made but a mean appearance, being short of stature, very crooked, pale, lean, and of a megre aspect, with lank brown hair, which he wore till within three years of his death, and his features were not the most regular; but in his younger days he had a sharp, ingenious look, and was very active. And he used to say, he was strait till about sixteen years of age, when being of a thin and weak habit, he first grew awry by frequently using a turner's lathe, and other inclining exercises. His inventive faculty was surprisingly great, which he imployed with indefatigable industry, always contenting himself with little sleep, and that very irregular; for he seldom went to bed till two or three a clock in the morning, and frequently not at all, but pursued his studies the whole night, and took a short nap in the day. This continual expense of spirits, accompanied with a recluse life, may be supposed to have easily produced a melancholy, accompanied with a mistrust and jealousy, which increased with his years. For at first he was communicative with his discoveries and inventions, till, as he was wont to say, some persons improving upon his hints published them for their own, which at last rendered him close and reserved even to a fault; by which means many things are lost, which he affirmed he knew.

J. Ward, *The Lives of the Professors of Gresham College*

## HOOKER, JOSEPH, 'FIGHTING JOE'

1814–79 Soldier

In the 'Fifties', when out in California at the Gold Rush, he became famous for his 'glad eye' for ladies of easy virtue, whence the Californians invented the name 'Hookers' for the type of ladies the debonaire lieutenant liked so well. Likewise he communed with John Barleycorn and was said to be a three bottle man.

George Fort Milton, *Conflict: The American Civil War*

## HOOKER, RICHARD

1554?–1600 Theologian

. . . indeed, my lord, I have received more satisfaction in reading a leaf, or paragraph, in Mr Hooker, though it were but about the fashion of churches, or church-music, or the like, but especially of the Sacraments, than I have had in the reading particular large treatises written but of one of these subjects by others, though very learned men: and I observe there is in Mr Hooker no affected language; but a grave, comprehensive, clear manifestation of reason, and that backed with the authority of the Scripture, the Fathers and Schoolmen.

James I (hearing of Hooker's death), in Izaak Walton, *Life of Hooker*

. . . he designed to write a deliberate, sober treatise of the Church's power to make canons for the use of ceremonies, and by law to impose an obedience to them, as upon her children; and this he proposed to do in eight books of the Laws of Ecclesiastical Polity; intending therein to shew such arguments as should force an assent from all men, if reason, delivered in sweet language, and void of provocation, were able to do it: and, that he might prevent all prejudice, he wrote before it a large preface or epistle to the Dissenting Brethren, wherein there were such bowels of love, and such a commixture of that love with reason, as was never exceeded but in holy writ.

Izaak Walton, *Life of Hooker*

## HOOKER, THOMAS

1586?–1647 Clergyman

. . . the one rich pearl with which Europe more than repaid America for the treasures from her coast.

Ezekiel Rogers, in William Sprague, *Annals of the American Pulpit*

## HOOVER, HERBERT CLARK

1874–1964 Thirty-First United States President

I was in favor of giving former Presidents a seat in the Senate until I passed 75 years. Since then I have less taste for sitting on hardbottomed chairs during long addresses.

On himself, Interview given in retirement

Mellon pulled the whistle, / Hoover rang the bell, / Wall Street gave the signal / And the country went to hell. /

Anon., song of the Bonus Marchers, 1932

Hoover isn't a stuffed shirt. But at times he can give the most convincing impersonation of a stuffed shirt you ever saw.

Anon., in E. Lyons, *Herbert Hoover*

Facts to Hoover's brain are as water to a sponge; they are absorbed into every tiny interstice.

Bernard M. Baruch, in D. Hinshaw, *Herbert Hoover: American Quaker*

If you put a rose in Hoover's hand it would melt.

Gutzon Borghum, in William E. Leuchtenburg, *Franklin D. Roosevelt and the New Deal*

. . . He is not a complicated personality, but rather a personality of monolithic simplicity. With no reflection on anyone, it might be said that whenever and wherever Herbert Hoover has mystified people or has been misunderstood by them, nearly always it has been because he is an extremely plain man living in an extremely fancy age.

James M. Cox, in Springfield, Ohio, *Sun*, 10 August 1949

Such a little man could not have made so big a depression.

Norman Thomas, Letter to Murray B. Seidler, 3 August 1960

## HOOVER, J(OHN) EDGAR

1895–1972 First Director of the Federal Bureau of Investigation

In foreign countries people are forced by their governments to submit to their gestapos. In this country, Hoover has the voluntary support of all those who delight in gangster movies and ten-cent detective magazines.

Anon., in *New Republic*, 19 February 1940

Hoover and the FBI were one – creator and creation. He served eight Presidents as the world's most powerful policeman. With a genius for administration and popular myth, he fashioned his career as an improbable bureaucratic morality play peopled by bad guys and G-men.

Anon., in *Time*, 15 May 1972

As an administrator, he was an erratic, unchallengeable czar, banishing agents to Siberian posts on whimsy, terrorizing them with torrents of implausible rules, insisting on conformity of thought as well as dress.

*Ibid.*, 22 December 1975

A shrewd bureaucratic genius who cared less about crime than about perpetuating his crime-busting image. With his acute public relations sense, he managed to observe his bureau's failings while magnifying its sometime successes. Even his fervent anti-communism has been cast into doubt; some former aides insist that he knew the party was never a genuine internal threat to the nation but a useful popular target to ensure financial and public support for the F.B.I.

*Ibid.*

[Of] medium height, inclined to be chubby, and of dark complexion. His full lips forbid a stern mouth, but he has a piercing glance, which those who have left his service say is the result of practice before a mirror. Hoover walks with a rather mincing step, almost feminine. This gait may be a relic of his valedictorian days, for at all times he appears to be making his way as though the caution of a teacher not to race to the rostrum was ringing in his ears.

Walter Trohan, in *Chicago Tribune*, 21 June 1936

## HOPKINS, GERARD MANLEY

1844–89 Poet

Sprung Rhythm, as he calls it in his sober and sensible preface, is just as easy to write as other forms of verse; and many a humble scribbler of words for music-hall songs has written it well. But he does not: he does not make it audible . . . Also the English language is a thing which I respect very much, and I resent even the violence Keats did to it; and here is a lesser than Keats doing much more . . . His manner strikes me as deliberately adopted to compensate by strangeness for the lack of pure merit, like the manner which Carlyle took up after he was thirty.

A. E. Housman, Letter to Robert Bridges, 30 December 1918

The useful, but monotonous, in their day unduly neglected, as more recently unduly touted, metrical labours of G. Manley Hopkins.

Ezra Pound, *The Nineteenth Century and After*

## HOPKINS, HARRY LLOYD

1890–1946 Politician

Lord Root of the Matter.

Winston Churchill (suggested title should Hopkins ever be awarded a peerage), in Robert E. Sherwood, *Roosevelt and Hopkins, An Intimate History*

He had the purity of St Francis of Assisi combined with the sharp shrewdness of a race track tout.

Joseph E. Davis, in S. F. Charles, *Minister of Relief, Harry L. Hopkins and the Depression*

Harry is the perfect ambassador for my purposes. He doesn't even know the meaning of the word 'protocol'. When he sees a piece of red tape, he just pulls out those old garden shears of his and snips it. And when he's talking to some foreign dignitary, he knows how to slump back in his chair and put his feet up on the conference table and say, 'Oh, *yeah*?'

Franklin Roosevelt, in Robert E. Sherwood, *Roosevelt and Hopkins, An Intimate History*

## HOPPER, HEDDA

1890–1966 Journalist

Being a Hollywood reporter as well as an actress I'm more or less on both sides of the fence.

On herself, in George Eells, *Hedda and Louella*

Timid? As timid as a buzzsaw.

Casey Shawhan, in *ibid.*

## HORSA, *see under* HENGIST

## HOUDINI, HARRY (EHRICH WEISS)

1874–1926 Magician, Escapologist

The man who walked through walls.

Anon., in William Lindsay Gresham, *Houdini*

Ehrich Weiss never doubted his destiny. Crushing defeats, snubs, family pleading for other ambitions did not stop him. Although tireless practice never gave him the polished ease of the star sleight-of-hand performer, he hacked and carved his place on the heights by inventing a whole new form of magic. He hurled at the universe a challenge to bind, fetter, or confine him so that he, in turn, could break free. He triumphed over manacles and prison cells, the wet-sheet packs of insane asylums, webs of fish net, iron boxes bolted shut – anything and everything human ingenuity could provide in an attempt to hold him prisoner. His skill and daring finally fused deeply with the unconscious wish of Everyman; to escape from chains and leg irons, gibbets and coffins . . . by magic.

William Lindsay Gresham, in *ibid.*

He was no master-manipulator of cards and coins, in spite of his ambition to be remembered as a wizard of dexterity. But he did manipulate life and circumstance and the imagination of men.

*Ibid.*

## HOUGHTON, BARON (RICHARD MONCKTON MILNES)

1809–85 Politician, Author

There is only one post fit for you, and that is the office of perpetual president of the Heaven and Hell Amalgamation Society.

Thomas Carlyle, in T. E. Wemyss Reid, *Life of Lord Houghton*

## HOUSMAN, ALFRED EDWARD

1859–1936 Poet

If a line of poetry strays into my memory, my skin bristles so that the razor ceases to act.

On himself, *The Name and Nature of Poetry*

As to your enquiry, I have not published any poem, since the last that you have seen. The other day I had the curiosity to reckon up the complete pieces, printed and unprinted, which I have written since 1896, and they only come to 300 lines . . . In barrenness, at any rate, I hold a high place among English poets, excelling even Gray.

On himself, Letter to Witter Eynner, 28 February 1910

Down to Cambridge with old Gaselee . . . We dress for dinner. Black tie.

We assemble. A. E. Housman and a don disguised as a Shropshire Lad. We have 1789 Madeira and Haut Brion and tripe and oysters and grouse-pie and mushrooms. The firelight flits on the silver of the smaller combination room and there are red shades, highly inflammable, to each candle. Housman is dry, soft, shy, prickly, smooth, conventional, silent, feminine, fussy, pernickety, sensitive, tidy, greedy, and a touch of a toper. 'What is this, my dear Gaselee?' 'This is Estrella 1789.' 'A perfect wine.' Yet not eighteenth-century and still less 1890. A *bon bourgeois* who has seen more sensitive days. He does not talk much except about food. And at 10.30 he rises to take his leave. All his movements are best described in such Trollope expressions.

Harold Nicolson, Diary,
26 September 1931

Housman was Masefield with a dash of Theocritus.

George Orwell, *Inside the Whale*

## HOUSTON, SAMUEL

1793–1863 Soldier, Politician

The President is General Houston of your acquaintance. His career . . . has been strange and wild . . . A domestic tempest of desperate violence, and calamitous consequences; habitual drunkenness; a residence of several years amongst the Cherokee Indians; residing amongst them as a chieftain, and begetting sons and daughters; a sudden reappearance on this stage with better hopes and purposes, and commensurate success, – but still with unreclaimed habits. Finally, however, a new connexion with a young and gentle woman brought up in fear of God, conquered no doubt as women have been from the beginning and will be to the end by a glowing tongue, but in good revenge making conquest of his habits of tremendous cursing and passionate love of drink.

Captain Elliot, Letter to Henry Unwin Addington, 15 November 1842

. . . looked like a prophet inspired by a vision unfolding the events of a thousand years to come.

John Salmon Ford, *Memoirs*

*See also* Gary Cooper

## HOWARD, CATHERINE

– d. 1542 Queen Consort to Henry VIII

Within eighteen months the intrigues in which Catherine had indulged since the age of twelve were uncovered, and she was charged with having committed adultery since her marriage with her cousin Culpepper. During the investigations she escaped from her apartment in Hampton Court and rushed down the gallery towards the chapel where she knew the King was at mass. The guards caught her before she could reach him, and she was dragged back, shrieking: a scene that impressed itself so vividly on the public mind, that the gallery is said to be haunted still.

Elizabeth Jenkins, *Elizabeth the Great*

*See also* Elizabeth I

## HOWARD, HENRIETTA, COUNTESS OF SUFFOLK

1681–1767 Mistress to George II

Nor warp'd by passion, aw'd by rumour, / Not grave thro' pride, or gay through folly, / An equal mixture of good humour, / And sensible soft melancholy. /

Alexander Pope, *To A Certain Lady at Court*

## HOWARD, HENRY, *see under* SURREY, EARL OF

## HOWARTH, HUMPHREY

*fl.* 1800 Physician

Humphrey Howarth, the surgeon, was called out, and made his appearance in the field stark naked, to the astonishment of the challenger, who asked him what he meant. 'I know,' said H., 'that if any part of the clothing is carried into the body by a gunshot wound, festering ensues; and therefore I have met you thus.' His antagonist declared that, fighting with a man in *puris naturalibus* would be quite ridiculous; and accordingly they parted without further discussion.

Samuel Rogers, *Table Talk*

## HOWE, RICHARD, EARL

1726–99 Admiral of the Fleet

His rigid brow seemed to give to every lineament of his countenance the harshness of an Article of War, yet under that unfavourable physiognomy a more humane mind never did honour to nature.

Anon., in Oliver Warner, *A Portrait of Lord Nelson*

'Give us Black Dick and we fear nothing,' echoed from the line at Spithead to the floor of the House of Commons.

Ira D. Grubber, *The Howe Brothers and the American Revolution*

## HOWELLS, WILLIAM DEAN

1837–1920 Author

. . . the lousy cat of our letters.

Ambrose Bierce, in Paul Fatout, *Ambrose Bierce: The Devil's Lexicographer*

You have such a rare faculty of not liking things in a likeable manner. Anyone can be charmingly enthusiastic, but so few can be even tolerably sceptical.

Bret Harte, Undated letter to Howells

Mr Howells was one of the gentlest, sweetest, and most honest of men, but he had the code of a pious old maid whose great delight was to have tea at the vicarage.

Sinclair Lewis, in Jay B. Hubbell, *Who Are the Major American Writers?*

. . . for years Howells was the Dean of American letters, and there was no one else on the faculty.

John Macy, in Alfred Kazin, *On Native Grounds*

Henry James went to France and read Turgenev. W. D. Howells stayed at home and read Henry James.

George Moore, *Confessions of a Young Man*

And so Howells, perforce, became a specialist in women's nerves, an analyst of the tenuous New England conscience, a master of Boston small-talk. It was such materials that shaped his leisurely technique until it falls about his theme with the amplitude of crinoline.

Vernon Louis Parrington, *Main Currents in American Thought*, vol. 3

## HUGHES, HOWARD ROBARD

1905–76 Film Maker, Industrialist, Inventor

I want to be unobtrusive.

On himself, in an interview with United Press International's Aline Mosby

In a nation which increasingly appears to prize social virtues, Howard Hughes remains not merely anti-social but grandly, brilliantly, surpassingly asocial. He is the last private man, the dream we no longer admit.

Joan Didion, *Slouching Towards Bethlehem*

In a sense, Howard Hughes, America's bashful billionaire, epitomizes the dilemma of twentieth century America:

inventive, brilliant, fantastic, overwhelming in technical precocity and accomplishment – suspicious, complex, contradictory, and sometimes downright antediluvian in social outlook.

Albert B. Gerber, *Bashful Billionaire*

Hughes was the only man I ever knew who had to die to prove he had been alive.

Walter Kane, in James Phelan, *Howard Hughes, The Hidden Years*

## HUME, DAVID

1711–76 Philosopher, Historian

I assure you, that without running any of the heights of scepticism, I am apt in a cool hour to suspect, in general, that most of my reasonings will be more useful by furnishing hints and exciting people's curiosity, than as containing any principles that will augment the stock of knowledge, that must pass to future ages.

On himself, Letter to Francis Hutcheson, March 1740

My views of *things* are more conformable to Whig principles; my representation of *persons* to Tory prejudices. Nothing can so much prove that men commonly regard more persons than things, as to find that I am commonly numbered among the Tories.

On himself, Letter to Dr Clephane, 1756

A room in a sober discreet family, who would not be averse to admit a sober, discreet, virtuous, regular, quiet, good-natured man of a bad character – such a room, I say, would suit me extremely.

On himself, Letter to Dr Clephane, September 1757

Never literary attempt was more unfortunate than my Treatise of Human Nature. It fell *dead-born from the press.*

On himself, *My Own Life*

Is it right in you, Sir, to hold up to our view, as 'perfectly wise and virtuous', the *character* and *conduct* of one, who seems to have been possessed with an incurable antipathy to all that is called RELIGION; and who strained every nerve to explode, suppress, and extirpate the spirit of it among men, that its very name, if he could effect it, might no more be had in remembrance?

Anon., *A Letter to Adam Smith*, 1777

Hume is always idiomatic, but his idioms are constantly wrong; many of his best passages are on that account curiously grating and puzzling; you feel they are very like what an Englishman would say, but yet that, after all, somehow or other they are what he never would say; – there is a minute seasoning of imperceptible difference which distracts your attention, and which you are for ever stopping to analyse.

Walter Bagehot, in Alexander Bain, *James Mill*

David Hume ate a swinging great dinner, / And grew every day fatter and fatter; / And yet the huge bulk of a sinner / Said there was neither spirit or matter. /

J. H. Beattie, in *The Faber Book of Comic Verse*

A few weeks before his death, when there were dining with him two or three of his intimate companions, one of them, Dr Smith, happening to complain of the world as spiteful and ill-natured, 'No, no', said Mr Hume, 'here am I, who have written on all sorts of subjects calculated to excite hostility, moral, political and religious, and yet I have no enemies, except indeed, all the Whigs, all the Tories, and all the Christians'.

Henry, Lord Brougham, *Men of Letters and Science in the Time of George III*

Nature, I believe, never formed any man more unlike his real character than David Hume. The powers of phisiognomy were baffled by his countenance; neither could the most skilful, in that science, pretend to discover the smallest traces of the faculties of his mind, in the unmeaning features of his visage. His face was broad and flat, his mouth wide, and without any other expression than that of imbecility. His eyes vacant and spiritless, and the corpusculence of his whole person was far better fitted to communicate the idea of a turtle-eating Alderman, than of a refined philosopher.

James Caulfield, Earl of Charlemont, in Francis Hardy, *Memoirs of The Political and Private Life of James Caulfield Earl of Charlemont*, 1812

A letter from Hume overpaid the labour of ten years.

Edward Gibbon, *Autobiography*

For the sake of this beloved object, DELIBERATE DOUBT, there is no mischief he is not ready to commit, even to the unhinging the national Religion, and unloosing all the hold it has on the minds of the people. And all this for the selfish and unnatural lust of *escaping* from right reason and common sense, *into the calm, though obscure regions of philosophy*. But here we have earthed him; rolled up in the Scoria of a *dogmatist* and *Sceptic*, run down together. He has been long taken for a Philosopher: and so perhaps he may be found – like Aristotle's statue in the block.

Richard Hurd, *Remarks on Mr David Hume's Essay on the Natural History of Religion*

Why, Sir, his style is not English, the structure of his sentences is French. Now the French structure and the English structure may, in the nature of things, be equally good. But if you allow the English language is established, he is wrong. My name might originally have been Nicholson, as well as Johnson; but were you to call me Nicholson now, you would call me very absurdly.

Samuel Johnson, in James Boswell, *Life of Johnson*

The philosophy of Hume was nothing more than the analysis of the word 'cause' into uniform sequence.

Benjamin Jowett, Introduction to Plato, *Parmenides*

Hume, from whose fascinating narrative [i.e. Hume's *History*] the great mass of the reading public are still contented to take their opinions, hated religion so much that he hated liberty for having been allied with religion, and has pleaded the cause of tyranny with the dexterity of an advocate, while affecting the impartiality of a judge.

T. B. Macaulay, *Essays*: 'Milton'

Hume is an accomplished advocate: Without positively asserting much more than he can prove, he gives prominence to all the circumstances which support his case; he glides lightly over those which are unfavourable to it; his own witnesses are applauded and encouraged; the statements which seem to throw discredit on them are controverted; the contradictions into which they fall are explained away; a clear and connected abstract of their evidence is given. Everything that is offered on the other side is scrutinized with the utmost severity; – every suspicious circumstance is a ground for comment and invective; what cannot be denied is extenuated, or passed by without notice; concessions even are sometimes made – but their insidious candour only increases the effect of the vast mass of sophistry.

T. B. Macaulay, in *Edinburgh Quarterly*, vol. 47

David, who there supinely deigns to lie, / The fattest hog in Epicurus' sty, /

Though drunk with Gallic wine and Gallic praise, / David shall bless Old England's halcyon days. /

William Mason, *An Heroic Epistle to Sir William Chambers*

Accordingly, France had Voltaire, and his school of negative thinkers, and England (or rather Scotland) had the profoundest negative thinker on record, David Hume: a man, the peculiarities of whose mind qualified him to detect failures of proof, and want of logical consistency, at a depth which the French Sceptics, with their comparatively feeble powers of analysis and abstraction, stopt far short of, and which German subtlety alone could thoroughly appreciate, or hope to rival.

J. S. Mill, *Dissertations*: 'Bentham'

Hume possessed powers of a very high order; but regard for truth formed no part of his character. He reasoned with surprising acuteness; but the object of his reasonings was not to attain truth, but to show that it was unattainable. His mind, too, was completely enslaved by a taste for literature; not those kinds of literature which teach mankind to know the causes of their happiness and misery, that they may seek the one and avoid the other; but that literature which without regard for truth or utility, seeks only to excite emotion.

J. S. Mill, in *Westminster Review*, October 1824

Hume's philosophy, whether true or false, represents the bankruptcy of eighteenth-century reasonableness. He starts out, like Locke, with the intention of being sensible and empirical, taking nothing on trust, but seeking whatever instruction is to be obtained from experience and observation. But having a better intellect than Locke's, a greater acuteness in analysis, and a smaller capacity for accepting comfortable inconsistencies, he arrives at the disastrous conclusion that from experience and observation nothing is to be learnt.

Bertrand Russell, *History of Western Philosophy*

The growth of unreason throughout the nineteenth century and what has passed of the twentieth is a natural sequel to Hume's destruction of empiricism. It is therefore important to discover whether there is any answer to Hume within the framework of a philosophy that is wholly or mainly empirical. If not, there is no intellectual difference between sanity and insanity. The lunatic who believes that he is a poached egg is to be condemned solely on the ground that he is in a minority, or rather – since we must not assume democracy – on the ground that the government does not agree with him.

*Ibid.*

Upon the whole, I have always considered him, both in his lifetime and since his death, as approaching as nearly to the idea of a perfectly wise and virtuous man, as perhaps the nature of human frailty will permit.

Adam Smith, Letter to William Strachan, November 1776

No mortal being was ever more completely divested of the trammels of the personal and the particular, none ever practised with a more consummate success the divine art of impartiality.

Lytton Strachey, *Portraits in Miniature*, 1931

*See also* Francis Bacon

## HUMPHREY, DUKE OF GLOUCESTER

1391–1447 Statesman

To dine with Duke *Humphrey* . . . For *Humphrey Duke* of Gloucester (commonly called the *good Duke*) was so hospitable, that every man of *Fashion*, otherwise *unprovided*, was welcome to *Dine* with him . . . But after the Death of good Duke Humphrey (when many of his former Almsmen were at a losse for a meals meat) this proverb did *alter its copy*, to Dine with *Duke Humphrey*, importing, to be *Dinnerlesse*.

Thomas Fuller, *The History of the Worthies of England*

## HUNT, (JAMES HENRY) LEIGH

1784–1859 Essayist, Poet

He is perhaps, a little opinionated, as all men who are the *centre* of circles, wide or narrow – the Sir Oracles, in whose name two or three are gathered together – must be, and as even Johnson was; but, withal, a valuable man, and less vain than success, and even the consciousness of preferring 'the right to the expedient' might excuse.

Lord Byron, Journal, 1 December 1813

He improves upon acquaintance. The author translates admirably into the man. Indeed the very faults of his style are virtues in the individual. His natural gaiety and sprightliness of manner, his high animal spirits, and the *vinous* quality of his mind, produce an immediate fascination and intoxication in those who come in contact with him, and carry off in society whatever in his writings may to some seem flat and impertinent. From great sanguineness of temper, from great quickness and unsuspecting simplicity, he runs on to the public as he does at his own fireside, and talks about himself, forgetting that he is not always among friends.

William Hazlitt, *The Spirit of the Age*

What though, for showing truth to flatter'd state, / Kind Hunt was shut in prison, yet has he / In his immortal spirit, been as free / As the sky-searching lark, and as elate. / Minion of grandeur! think you he did wait? / Think you he nought but prison walls did see, / Till, so unwilling, thou unturn'dst the key? / Ah, no! far happier, nobler was his fate! / In Spenser's halls he strayed, and bowers fair, / Culling enchanted flowers; and he flew / With daring Milton through the fields of air: / To regions of his own his genius true / Took happy flights. Who shall his fame impair / When thou art dead, and all thy wretched crew? /

John Keats, *Sonnet written on the day that Mr Leigh Hunt left Prison*

One of those happy souls / Which are the salt of the earth, and without whom / The world would smell like what it is – a tomb. /

P. B. Shelley, Letter to Maria Gladstone, 1 July 1820

L.H. was our spiritual grandfather, a free man . . . A light man, I daresay, but civilised, much more so than my grandfather in the flesh. These free, vigorous spirits advance the world, and when one lights on them in the strange waste of the past one says 'Ah, you're my sort' – a great compliment.

Virginia Woolf, *A Writer's Diary*, 13 August 1921

*See also* John Keats

## HUNTER, JOHN

1728–93 Surgeon

John Hunter once saying to Lord Holland, 'If you wish to see a great man you have one before you. I consider myself a greater man than Sir Isaac Newton.' Explained then why; that discoveries which lengthen life and alleviate sufferings are of infinitely more importance to mankind than any thing relating to the stars, &c. &c.

Thomas Moore, Diary, 4 October 1829

The limitations of John Hunter are obvious. He was hampered by a defective education. He had an almost medieval respect for words as words. He could not express himself clearly, either in writing or by word of mouth, when he dealt with the more difficult problems of surgery, which he knew existed but was unable to solve for want of the ancillary sciences. He was a gross teleologist. His metaphors were often strained and sometimes wholly false. He was confessedly ignorant of the work of his surgical colleagues and foreign contemporaries, and . . . he suffered from frequent and severe attacks of illness which would have incapacitated any one possessed of a less dauntless spirit. But when we have said this we have said all there is to say against him as a man.

Sir D'Arcy Power, *The Hunterian Oration*, 14 February 1925

## HUSKISSON, WILLIAM

1770–1830 Statesman

It's all over with me; bring me my wife, and let me die.

On himself, after being run over by 'The Rocket' at Parkside Station, 15 September 1830

Oh! he is a very good bridge for rats to run over.

Duke of Wellington, on making Huskisson a Cabinet Minister, in Lord Holland, Diary, 8 March 1828

## HUXLEY, ALDOUS LEONARD

1894–1963 Novelist

He is at once the truly clever person and the stupid person's idea of the clever person; he is expected to be relentless, to administer intellectual shocks.

Elizabeth Bowen, in *Spectator*, 11 December 1936

The great Mahatma of all misanthropy . . . this pedant who leeringly gloated over how crayfish copulated (through their third pair of legs) but could never have caught or cooked one; let alone broken in a horse, thrown and branded a steer, flensed a whale, or slaughtered, cut, cured, and cooked anything at all.

Roy Campbell, *Light on a Dark Horse*

People will call Mr Aldous Huxley a pessimist; in the sense of one who makes the worst of it. To me he is that far more gloomy character; the man who makes the best of it.

G. K. Chesterton, *The Common Man*

Mr Aldous Huxley, who is perhaps one of those people who have to perpetrate thirty bad novels before producing a good one, has a certain natural – but little developed – aptitude for seriousness. Unfortunately, this aptitude is hampered by a talent for the rapid assimilation of all that isn't essential and by a gift for chic. Now, the gift for chic, combined with the desire for seriousness, produces a frightful monster: a chic religiosity.

T. S. Eliot, *La Nouvelle Revue Française*, 1 May 1927, translated by Thomas M. Donnan

Aldous Huxley sits there and without looking at you, or at anyone else in particular, emits streams of impersonal sound, like a sort of loudspeaker, about the habits of bees and ants, the excretions of elephants, and sexual intercourse among whales. By a kind of studied fastidiousness avoiding reticent language: For aren't we the unashamed Intelligentsia? And as he speaks a look of anxiety comes on the faces of the women present as though they would be unspeakably shocked if anyone thought they could possibly be shocked by anything.

William Gerhardie, *Memoirs of a Polyglot*

The novelist must be able to get into the skin of the creatures of his invention, see with their eyes and feel with their fingers; but Aldous Huxley sees them like an anatomist. He dissects out their nerves, uncovers their arteries with precision, and peers into the ventricles of their hearts. The process gives rise in the reader to a certain discomfort.

W. Somerset Maugham, Introduction to *Modern English and American Literature*

You were right about Huxley's book [*Ape and Essence*] – it is awful. And do you notice that the more holy he gets, the more his books stink with sex. He cannot get off the subject of flagellating women.

George Orwell, Letter to Richard Rees, 3 March 1949

You could always tell by his conversation which volume of the *Encyclopedia Britannica* he'd been reading. One day it would be Alps, Andes and Apennines, and the next it would be the Himalayas and the Hippocratic Oath.

Bertrand Russell, Letter to R. W. Clark, July 1965

As a young man, though he was always friendly, his silences seemed to stretch for miles, extinguishing life, when they occurred, as a snuffer extinguishes a candle. On the other hand, he was (when uninterrupted) one of the most accomplished talkers I have ever known, and his monologues on every conceivable subject were astonishing floriated variations of an amazing brilliance.

Edith Sitwell, *Taken Care Of*

He was the tallest English author known to me. He was so tall (and thin, so that he seemed to stretch to infinity) that when, long ago, he lived in Hampstead, ribald little boys in that neighbourhood used to call out to him: 'Cole up there, guv'nor?'

Frank Swinnerton, *The Georgian Literary Scene*

Aldous Huxley, as [D. H. Lawrence's] direct protagonist, preaches the sermon of the intellect; his god is cellular, and his heaven a socialist Towards. He would, as someone brighter than myself has said, condense the generative principle into a test-tube; Lawrence, on the other hand, would condense the world into the generative principle, and make his apostles decline not cogitare but copulare.

Dylan Thomas, Letter to Pamela Hansford Johnson, 1933

It used to be fashionable to call him 'intelligent', but he was never particularly intelligent. His habit of reading the *Encyclopaedia Britannica* gives the quality of his appetite for facts and ideas; his interest in the great intellectual movements that were bringing most light in his own time was on exactly the same level as his interest in a twelfth-century heresy, a queer species of carnivorous plant, a special variety of Romanesque architecture or a Greek poet surviving in fragments. Freud, Lenin, Einstein, Joyce – he sometimes expressed about them, in his casual essays, opinions as obtuse and philistine as those of the ordinary Fleet Street journalist.

Edmund Wilson, *Classics and Commercials*

All raw, uncooked, protesting. A descendant, oddly enough, of Mrs H[umphrey] Ward: interest in ideas; makes people into ideas.

Virginia Woolf (on reading *Point Counter Point*), *A Writer's Diary*, 23 January 1935

*See also* D. H. Lawrence

## HUXLEY, THOMAS HENRY

1825–95 Man of Science

Darwin's bull dog.

On himself, attributed

Men differ greatly in their manner of meeting criticism and reacting to it. Huxley found controversy the spice of life. He once testified that a polemic was as little abhorrent to him 'as gin to a reclaimed drunkard'. And a published reply from an opponent evoked the testimony that it 'caused such a flow of bile that I have been the better for it ever since'.

W. B. Cannon, *The Way of an Investigator*

In the sharpest contrast to Darwin stands the figure of T. H. Huxley, inventor and popularizer of the very word biology (Darwin would have called himself a naturalist to the end of his days), and prototype of the non-museum professional biologist. Huxley's efforts were devoted at least as much to establishing the professional status and training of biologists as to purely intellectual propaganda for Darwinism. It was not until students trained in the schools of biology fathered by Huxley began to erupt into systematic work that the influence of Darwin's teachings about species began to make itself felt.

R. A. Crowson, in S. A. Barnett, *A Century of Darwin*

I have sometimes described him as one who is continually taking two irons out of the fire and putting three in; and necessarily, along with the external congestion entailed, there is apt to come internal congestion.

Herbert Spencer, *An Autobiography*

As I knew Huxley he was a yellow-faced, square-faced old man, with bright little brown eyes, lurking as it were in caves under his heavy grey eyebrows, and a mane of grey hair brushed back from his wall of forehead. He lectured in a clear firm voice without hurry and without delay, turning to the black-board behind him to sketch some diagram, and always dusting the chalk from his fingers rather fastidiously before he resumed.

H. G. Wells, *Experiment in Autobiography*

*See also* Charles Darwin, George Lewes

## HYDE, ANNE, DUCHESS OF YORK

1637–71 Court Figure

Paint her with oyster lip and breath of fame / Wide mouth that 'sparagus may well proclaim / With Chanc'llors belly and so large a rump, / There (not behind the coach) her pages jump . . .

Andrew Marvell, *Last Instructions to a Painter*

The Duke of York in all things but his amours was led by the nose by his wife.

Samuel Pepys, Diary, 30 October 1668

March 31, f, died Ann, Duchess of York . . . She died with eating and drinking; died fast and fustie; salacious; lecherous.

Anthony à Wood, *Life and Times*, 31 March 1671

## HYDE, EDWARD, EARL OF CLARENDON

1609–74 Statesman, Historian

He was always pressing the King to mind his affairs, but in vain. He was a good Chancellor, only a little too rough, but very impartial in the administration of justice. He never seemed to understand foreign affairs well: and yet he meddled too much in them. He had too much levity in his wit, and did not always observe the decorum of his post. He was high, and was apt to reject those who addressed themselves to him with too much contempt. He had such a regard to the King, that when places were disposed of, even otherwise than as he advised, yet he would justify what the King did, and disparage the pretensions of others, not without much scorn; which created him many enemies. He was indefatigable in business, tho' the gout did often disable him from waiting on the King: yet, during his Credit, the King came constantly to him when he was laid up by it.

Gilbert Burnet, *History of My Own Time*

No man wrote abler state papers. No man spoke with more weight and dignity in council and in parliament. No man was better acquainted with general maxims of statecraft. No man observed the varieties of character with a more discriminating eye. It must be added that he had a strong sense of moral and religious obligation, a sincere reverence for the laws of his country, and a conscientious regard for the honour and interest of the Crown. But his temper was sour, arrogant and impatient of opposition. Above all, he had been long an exile; and this circumstance alone would have completely disqualified him for the supreme direction of affairs.

T. B. Macaulay, *History of England*

When *Clarindon* had discern'd beforehand, / (As the cause can eas'ly foretell the Effect) / At once three Deluges threat'ning our Land; / 'Twas the season he thought to turn Architect. / Us, *Mars*, and *Apollo*, and *Vulcan* consume; / While he the Betrayer of *England* and *Flander*, / Like the King-fisher chuseth to build in the Broom, / And nestles in flames like the Salamander./

Andrew Marvell, *Clarendon's House-Warming*

Lord, to see how we poor wretches dare not do the King good service for fear of the greatness of these men.

Samuel Pepys, Diary, 14 July 1664

He did say the other day at his table – 'Treachery?' says he, 'I could wish we could prove there was anything of that in it, for that would imply some wit and thoughtfulness; but we are ruined merely by folly and neglect'.

*Ibid.*, 12 July 1667

With what a gorgeous sinuosity, with what a grandiose delicacy, [Clarendon] elaborates through his enormous sentences, the lineaments of a soul.

Lytton Strachey, *Portraits in Miniature*: 'Macaulay'

It has been pointed out that he had little sense of natural scenery or of history's dramatic elements. He did not see the persons of his drama against any background, natural or artificial. His world has not houses, nor courts, nor fields. The personages of his drama seem to move hither and thither, in vast, vacant spaces. He was interested supremely in men, not things, in the conflict of wills and the passions of the mind. History for him was 'Character in Action'.

Charles Whibley, *Edward Hyde*

# 'I'

## INCHBALD, ELIZABETH

1753–1821 Novelist, Dramatist

The impediment in her speech was of that peculiar nature, that it rather imparted an entertaining characteristic to her conversation, than diminished its force . . . One morning waiting on a manager who shall be nameless, with a new play, the gentleman *suddenly* became so violently enamoured, that, dispensing with all preparatory courtesies, he commenced a personal attack, *sans ceremonie*; on which, the lady seizing him by his tail with one hand, with the other rang the bell, till assistance appeared. Ever afterwards, when speaking of this love *rencontre*, she used whimsically to stammer out,

'How f-ortunate for me he did NOT W-EAR a W-IG.'

Frederick Reynolds, *Life and Times of Frederick Reynolds*

## IRETON, HENRY

1611–51 Regicide

A tall black thief, with bushy curled hair, a meagre envious face, sunk hollow eyes, a complection between choler and melancholy, a four square Machiavellian head, and a nose of the fifteens.

Anon., *The Man in the Moon*, 1, 1649

One brave heart, and subtle-working brain . . . a man able with his pen and his sword: 'very stiff in his ways.'

Thomas Carlyle, *Letters and Speeches of Oliver Cromwell*

One line of mine begets many of his, which I doubt makes him sit up too late.

Oliver Cromwell, Letter to his Daughter, Bridget Ireton, 25 October 1646

## IRVING, SIR HENRY

1838–1905 Actor

It is the fate of actors to be judged by echoes which are altogether delusive – when they have passed out of immediate ken, and some fifty years hence some old fool will be saying – there never was an actor like Irving.

On himself, Letter, 1891

Suppose, for instance, Gladstone, who possesses the quality to a wonderful extent, was dramatised. I mean the character. Irving could not play it. Ungoverned rage, sorrow, dread, he can depict, but not pure mental force. He well expresses the emotion of a mind acted on but not of a mind acting on others. He lacks what one may call the muscle and sinew of the brain.

James Albery, Letter to Frank Archer, 1873

Somebody asked Gilbert if he had been to see Irving in *Faust*. 'I go to the pantomime,' said Gilbert, 'only at Christmas.'

Leslie Ayre, *The Gilbert and Sullivan Companion*

He had, in acting, a keen sense of humour – of sardonic, grotesque, fantastic humour. He had an incomparable power for eeriness, for stirring a dim sense of mystery; and not less masterly was he in invoking a dim sense of horror. His dignity was magnificent in purely philosophic or priestly gentleness, or in the gaunt aloofness of philosopher or king. He could be benign with a tinge of malevolence, and arrogant with an undercurrent of sweetness.

Max Beerbohm, in *Saturday Review*, 21 October 1905

One of his stage-tricks is very effective, but quite unworthy of a great artist. He is fond, whenever the scene permits, of shutting down every light – leaving the stage in utter darkness, lit only by the solitary lamp or dull fire which may be in the room; while he has directed from the prompt place or the flies, a closely focussed calcium – which shines only and solely upon *his* face and head; so that you can only see a lot of spectral figures without expression moving about the scene – and one ghostly lighted face shining out of the darkness; an expressive face to be sure – but after all the entirety of the drama disappears, and a conjuror-like exhibition of a sphinx-like wonder takes its place.

Augustin Daly, Letter to his Brother, 18 September 1878

He never 'suffered fools gladly'. I remember an occasion at the Garrick Club, when a new member, anxious to claim familiar acquaintance with him, came up to him, and said: 'Hello, Irving, an extraordinary thing has just happened to me. A total stranger stopped me in the street and said: "God bless me, is that you?"' And Irving replied, in his characteristic staccato: 'And – er – was it?'

Edward Heron-Allen, in Saintsbury and Palmer eds, *We Saw Him Act*

His Hamlet was not Shakespeare's Hamlet, nor his Lear Shakespeare's Lear: they were both avatars of the imaginary Irving in whom he was so absorbingly interested. His huge and enduring success as Shylock was due to his absolutely refusing to allow Shylock to be the discomfited villain of the piece. The Merchant of Venice became the Martyrdom of Irving, which was, it must be confessed, far finer than the tricking of Shylock. His Iachimo, a very fine performance, was better than Shakespeare's Iachimo, and not a bit like him. On the other hand his Lear was an impertinent intrusion of a quite silly conceit of his own into a great play. His Romeo, though a very clever piece of acting, wonderfully stage-managed in the scene where Romeo dragged the body of Paris down a horrible staircase into the tomb of the Capulets, was an absurdity, because it was impossible to accept Irving as Romeo, and he had no power of adapting himself to an author's conception: his creations were his own and they were all Irving.

George Bernard Shaw, *Pen Portraits and Reviews*

He does not merely cut plays, he disembowels them.

George Bernard Shaw, in *Saturday Review*, 26 September 1896

I grant his intellectuality dominates his other powers and gifts, but I have never seen in living man or picture, such distinction of bearing. A splendid figure, and his face very noble. A superb brow; rather small dark eyes which can at moments become immense, and hang like a bowl of dark liquid with light shining through; a most refined curving Roman nose, strong and delicate in line, and *cut clean* (as all his features); a smallish mouth, and full of the most wonderful teeth, even at 55; lips most delicate and refined – firm, firm, firm – and with a rare smile of the most exquisite beauty, and quite-not-to-be-described kind. (He seems always ashamed of his smile, even in very private life, and will withdraw it at once in public.) His chin, and the line from ear to chin, is firm, extremely delicate, and very strong and clean defined. He has an ugly ear! Large, flabby, ill-cut, and pasty looking, pale and lumpy. His hair is superb; beautiful in 1867, when I first met him, when it was blue-black like a raven's wing, it is even more splendid now when it is liberally streaked with white. It is rather long and hangs in lumps on his neck, which is now like the neck of a youth of 20! His skin is very pale, delicate, refined, and stretched tightly over his features. Under the influence of strong emotion, it contracts more, and turning somewhat paler, a grey look comes into his face, and the hollows of his cheeks and eyes show up clearly.

Ellen Terry, *Notes on Irving*

I was at Tewkesbury yesterday, and felt how like he *really* is to the great Abbey there, but his admiration is for something of quite another sort. He tries to be like Milan Cathedral. He never admires the right thing.

*Ibid.*

## IRVING, WASHINGTON

1783–1859 Author, Diplomat

I have no command of my talents, such as they are, and have to watch the varyings of my mind as I would those of a weathercock.

On himself, Undated letter to Sir Walter Scott

It has been a matter of marvel to my European readers, that a man from the wilds of America should express himself in tolerable English. I was looked upon as something new and strange, in literature.

On himself, in his Introduction to *Bracebridge Hall*

He proved that the barbarous American could write as the captains of 1812 had proved that Americans could fight at sea, he tickled John Bull's romantic rib.

Henry Seidel Canby, *Classic Americans*

. . . I don't go upstairs to bed two nights out of seven . . . without taking Washington Irving under my arm; and, when I don't take him, I take his brother Oliver Goldsmith.

Charles Dickens, in Ernest Boll, 'Dickens and Irving', in *Modern Language Quarterly*, December 1944

I never enthused over him: Irving was suckled on the Addisonian-Oxford-Cambridge milk.

Walt Whitman, in Edgar Lee Masters, *Whitman*

# 'J'

## JACKSON, ANDREW

1767–1845 Seventh United States President

Incompetent both by his ignorance and by the fury of his passions. He will be surrounded and governed by incompetent men, whose ascendency over him will be secured by their servility and who will bring to the Government of the nation nothing by their talent for intrigue.

John Quincy Adams, in Meade Minnigerode, *Presidential Years, 1787–1860*

Andrew Jackson was a popular president. He swore he would shake hands with everyone in town and kept his promise. This delayed the business of his administration for several weeks, until they could take off the bandages. One of the first things President Jackson did, after flexing his fingers, was to reward those who had cast more than one ballot for him by appointing them postmasters, judges, generals, and garbage collectors. It was in this last connection that one of his friends made the famous remark, 'To the victors belong the spoils.'

Richard Armour, *It All Started With Columbus*

He was a simple, emotional, and unreflective man with a strong sense of loyalty to personal friends and political supporters; he swung to the democratic camp when the democratic camp swung to him.

Richard Hofstadter, *The American Political Tradition*

Andrew Jackson was eight feet tall / His arm was a hickory limb and a maul. / His sword is so long he dragged it on the ground. / Every friend was an equal. Every foe was a hound. /

Vachel Lindsay, *The Statue of Old Andrew Jackson*

[He] has slain the Indians & flogged the British & . . . therefore is the wisest & greatest man in the nation.

P. H. Magnum of Orange County, North Carolina, 15 April 1824, in Marquis James, *Andrew Jackson – Portrait of a President*

An overwhelming proportion of the material power of the Nation was against him. The great media for the dissemination of information and the molding of public opinion fought him. Haughty and sterile intellectualism opposed him. Musty reaction disapproved him. Hollow and outworn traditionalism shook a trembling finger at him – all but the people of the United States.

Franklin D. Roosevelt, Jackson Day Address, 8 January 1936

. . . that the chief who violated the Constitution, proscribed public virtue and patriotism and introduced high handed corruption into public affairs and debauchery into private circles was the first President who received insult to his person and was an object of assassination.

William Henry Seward, 1835, in G. G. Van Deusen, *William Henry Seward*

*See also* James K. Polk

## JACKSON, THOMAS JONATHAN 'STONEWALL'

1824–63 Soldier

There is Jackson, standing like a stone

wall. Let us determine to die here, and we will conquer.

Brigadier General Barnard E. Bee to his brigade at the first battle of Bull Run, 21 July 1862

Stonewall Jackson, wrapped in his beard and his silence.

Stephen Vincent Benét, *John Brown's Body*

You are better off than I am, for while you have lost your *left*, I have lost my *right* arm.

General Robert E. Lee, in a note to Jackson when the latter was mortally wounded at Chancellorsville, 4 May 1863

Outwardly Jackson was not a stonewall for it was not his nature to be stable and defensive, but vigorously active. He was an avalanche from an unexpected quarter. He was a thunderbolt from a clear sky. And yet he was in character and will more like a stonewall than any man I have known.

James Power Smith, in Elihu S. Riley, *Stonewall Jackson*

## JAMES I (VI OF SCOTLAND)

1566–1625

I will govern according to the common weal, but not according to the common will.

On himself, in a Reply to a demand of the House of Commons, 1621

I am sure ye would not have me renounce my religion for all the world. I am not a Monsieur who can shift his religion as easily as he can shift his shirt when he comes in from tennis.

On himself, attributed

Sound as also his head, which was very full of brains; but his blood was wonderfully tainted with melancholy.

Anon., Post-mortem on the King

Death's Iron Hand hath clos'd those eyes / Which were at once three kingdoms' spies; / Both to foresee and to prevent / Daungers as soon as they were ment: / That head whose working braine alone / Wrought all men's quiet but its owne / Now lyes at rest; o let him have / The peace he lent us, in the grave. /

Anon., in Edmund Howe, *Continuation of Stow's Annales, or Generall Chronicle*

It was one of King James' Maxims, to take no favourite but what was recommended to him by his Queen, that if she afterwards complained of this Dear One, he might answer, It is long of yourself: for you were the party that commended him unto me. Our old master took delight strangely in things of this nature.

Archbishop George Abbot, in *Biographia Britannica*

King James was Bacon's Primum Mobile.

William Blake, *Annotations to Bacon*

This King James, with his large hysterical heart, with his large goggle-eyes, glaring timorously-inquisitive on all persons and objects, as if he would either look through them, or else be fascinated by them, and, so to speak, start forth *into* them, and spend his very soul and eyesight in the frustrate attempt to look through them, – remains to me always a noticeable, not unloveable, man. For every why he has his wherefore ready; prompt as touchwood blazes up, with prismatic radiance, that stonishing lynx-faculty.

Thomas Carlyle, *Historical Sketches*

The loathsome Lackwit, James I.

Samuel Taylor Coleridge, Notebook

Who would not be thy subject, James, t'obey / A Prince, that rules by example, more than sway? / Whose manners draw, more then they powers constraine. /

Ben Jonson, *Epigrammes*

Of James the First, as of John, it may be said that, if his administration had been able and splendid, it would probably have been fatal to our country, and that we owe more to his weakness and meanness than to the wisdom and courage of much better sovereigns. He came to the throne at a critical moment. The time was fast approaching when either the king must become absolute, or the parliament must control the whole executive administration. Had James been like Henry the Fourth, like Maurice of Nassau, or like Gustavus Adolphus, a valiant, active, and politic ruler, had he put himself at the head of the protestants of Europe . . . had he found himself, after great achievements, at the head of fifty thousand troops, brave, well-disciplined, and devotedly attached to his person, the English parliament would soon have been nothing more than a name.

T. B. Macaulay, *History of England*

Old friends are best. King James used to call for his old shoes; they were easiest for his feet.

John Selden, *Table Talk*

An omniscient umpire whom no one consulted.

Hugh Trevor-Roper, *Archbishop Laud*

Hee was naturally of a timourous disposition, which was the reason of his quilted Doublets: His eyes large, ever rowling after any stranger came in his prescence, insomuch, as many for shame have left the roome, as being out of countenance: His beard was very thin: His tongue too large for his mouth, which ever made him speak full in the mouth, and made him drink very uncomely, as if eating his drink, which came out into the cup of each side of his mouth: His skin was as soft as Taffeta Sarsnet, which felt so, because hee never washt his hands, onely rubb'd his fingers ends slightly with the wet end of a napkin: His legs were very weake, having had (as was thought) some foul play in his youth, or rather before he was born, that he was not able to stand at seven years of age, that weaknesse made him ever leaning on other mens shoulders, his walke was ever circular.

Sir Anthony Weldon, *The Court and Character of King James*

Hee was so crafty and cunning in petty things, as the circumventing any great man, the change of a Favourite, &c. insomuch as a very wise man was wont to say, hee beleeved him the wisest foole in Christendome, meaning him wise in small things, but a foole in weighty affaires.

*Ibid.*

James's humour was a tumbling wit that turned things upside down and heaped together incongruous thoughts and images in a hurly-burly jumble, as when he prayed the Pope to permit him the hawking of the stream in purgatory.

D. Harris Willson, *King James VI and I*

*See also* Fulke Greville, Walter Raleigh

## JAMES II

1633–1701

. . . He has even been called dull. He was not dull; but he was cut off. His mind was isolated, and to a whole group of appreciations, impervious . . . Complexity did not bewilder him, rather he missed it altogether . . . He could scheme with things, but not against schemers . . . He thought in straight lines.

Hilaire Belloc, *James II*

That Prince had taken a fancy to Sir Charles' Daughter (though it seems she was not very handsome) and, in consequence of his intrigues with her, he created Miss Sedley Countess of Dorchester. This honour, so far from pleasing, greatly shocked Sir Charles. However libertine himself had been, yet he could not bear the thoughts of his daughter's dishonour; and with regard to this her exaltation, he only considered it as rendering her more conspicuously infamous. He therefore conceived a hatred for the King; and from this, as well as other motives, readily joined to dispossess him of the throne.

A witty saying of Sedley's on this occasion, is recorded. 'I hate ingratitude (said Sir Charles); and therefore, as the King has made my daughter a countess, I will endeavour to make his daughter a queen:' meaning the Princess Mary, married to the Prince of Orange, who dispossessed James of the throne at the ever-glorious Revolution.

David Erskine Baker, Isaac Reed and Stephen Jones eds, *Biographia Dramatica*, 1812

I do affirm that he was the most honest and sincere man I ever knew: a great and good Englishman, and a high protector of trade, and had nothing so much at heart as the glory and strength of the fleet and navy.

Thomas Bruce, Earl of Ailesbury, *Memoirs*

It makes one's flesh creep to think that such a man should have been the ruler of millions . . . A Prince whose malignant cruelties made him loathed by his contemporaries, and whose revolting predilections unless we ascribe them to a diseased brain, are not only a slur on the age which tolerated them, but a disgrace to the higher instincts of our common nature.

H. T. Buckle, *History of Civilization*

He was bred with high notions of the kingly authority, and laid it down for a maxim, that all who opposed the King were rebels in their hearts. He was perpetually in one amour or another, without being very nice in his choice: Upon which the King said once, he believed his Brother had his mistresses given him by his Priests for penance . . . He was naturally eager and revengeful: And was against the taking off any that set up in an opposition to the measures of the Court, and who by that means grew popular in the House of Commons. He was for rougher methods. He continued for many years dissembling his religion, and seemed zealous for the Church of *England*: But it was chiefly on design to hinder all propositions that tended to unite us among our selves.

Gilbert Burnet, *History of My Own Time*

I am weary of travelling and am resolved to go abroad no more. But when I am dead and gone, I know not what my brother will do: I am much afraid that when he comes to wear the Crown he will be obliged to travel again. And yet I will take care to leave my kingdoms to him in peace, wishing he may long keep them so. But this hath all of my fears, little of my hopes, and less of my reason.

Charles II, in Christopher Falkus, *Charles II*

It were almost incredible to tell you, at the latter end of King *James's* Time (though the Rod of Arbitrary Power was always shaking over us) with what Freedom and Contempt the Common People in the open Streets talk'd of his wild Measures to make a whole Protestant Nation Papists; and yet, in the height of our secure and wanton Defiance of him, we of the Vulgar had no farther Notion of any Remedy for this Evil than a satisfy'd Presumption that our Numbers were too great to be mastered by his mere Will and Pleasure; and that though he might be too hard for our Laws, he would never be able to get the better of our Nature; and that to drive all *England* into Popery and Slavery he would find would be teaching an old Lion to dance.

Colley Cibber, *Apology for the Life of Colley Cibber*

Had James ruled in Spain, or even in seventeenth century France, history might now be resounding with his praises, voiced not only by Spaniards or Frenchmen, but by Englishmen. But as he ruled in England, he still waits his apologist.

David Ogg, *England in the Reigns of James II and William III*

My Lord [Sandwich] . . . telling me the story of how the Duke of Yorke hath got my Lord Chancellor's daughter with child, and that she doth lay it to him, and that for certain he did promise her marriage, and had signed it with his blood, but that he by stealth had got the paper out of her Cabinett. And that the King would have him marry her, but that he would not. So that the thing is very bad for the Duke and for them all. But my Lord doth make light of it, as a thing that he believes is not a new thing to the Duke to do abroad. Discoursing concerning what if the Duke should marry her, my Lord told me that among his father's many old sayings that he had writ in a book of his, this is one: that he that doth get a wench with child, and marries her afterward it is as if a man should shit in his hat and then clap it upon his head.

Samuel Pepys, Diary, 7 October 1660

Except he became a protestant, his friends would be obliged to leave him, like a garrison one could no longer defend.

George Savile, Marquis of Halifax, in *Memoirs of Sir John Reresby*

Under the morose face there seemed to be a heart of stone.

Alexander Smellie, *Men of the Covenant*

He would have been an excellent King of Spain.

Charles Whibley, *George Jeffreys*

*See also* Anne Hyde, Barbara Villiers

## JAMES, HENRY

1843–1916 Novelist

I suspect the age of letters is waning, for our time. It is the age of Panama Canals, of Sarah Bernhardt, of Western wheat-raising, of merely material expansion. Art, form, may return, but I doubt that I shall live to see them – I don't believe they are eternal, as the poets say. All the same, I shall try to make them live a little longer!

On himself, Letter to Thomas Perry, February 1881

I have not the least hesitation in saying that I aspire to write in such a way that it would be impossible to an outsider to say whether I am at a given moment an American writing about England or an Englishman writing about America . . . and so far from being ashamed of such an ambiguity I should be exceedingly proud of it, for it would be highly civilised.

On himself, in Pelham Edgar, *Henry James, Man and Author*

Nothing is my *last word* about anything – I am interminably supersubtle and analytic – and with the blessing of heaven, I shall live to make all sorts of representations of all sorts of things. It will take a lot cleverer person than myself to discover my last impression – amongst all these things – of anything.

On himself, Letter to Mrs F. H. Hill, 21 March 1879

In Heaven there'll be no algebra, / No learning dates or names, / But only playing golden harps / And reading Henry James. /

Anon., in Edward Stone, *The Battle and the Books: Some Aspects of Henry James*

It's not that he 'bites off more than he can chaw', as T. G. Appleton said of Nathan, but he chaws more than he bites off.

Mrs Henry Adams, Letter to her Father, December 1881

Henry James / Abhorred the word *Dames*, / And always wrote 'Mommas' / With inverted commas. /

W. H. Auden, *Academic Graffiti*

Few writers have had less journalistic talent than James, and this is his defect, for the supreme masters have one trait in common with the childish scribbling mass, the vulgar curiosity of a police-court reporter. One can easily imagine Stendhal or Tolstoi or Dostoievski becoming involved in a bar-room fight, but James, never. I have read somewhere a story that once, when James was visiting a French friend, the latter's mistress, unobserved, filled his top hat with champagne, but I do not believe it because, try as I will, I simply cannot conceive what James did and said when he put his hat on.

W. H. Auden, *The Dyer's Hand*

He is never in deep gloom or in violent sunshine. But he feels deeply and vividly every delicate shade. We cannot ask for more.

Joseph Conrad, Letter to John Galsworthy, February 1899

Henry James is an author who is difficult for English readers, because he is an American; and who is difficult for Americans, because he is European; and I do not know whether he is possible to other readers at all.

T. S. Eliot, 'A Prediction', in Leon Edel ed., *Henry James, A Collection of Critical Essays*

... the nicest old lady I ever met.

William Faulkner, in Edward Stone, *The Battle and the Books: Some Aspects of Henry James*

Many readers cannot get interested in James, although they can follow what he says (his difficulty has been much exaggerated), and can appreciate his effects. They cannot grant his premise, which is that most of human life has to disappear before he can do us a novel.

E. M. Forster, *Aspects of the Novel*

We sat in a detached room – glimpse of fine study as we passed. H.J. very kind. Laid his hand on my shoulder and said: 'Your name's Moore.'

E. M. Forster, Diary, 1908

The truth is that Mr James's cosmopolitanism is, after all, limited; to be really cosmopolitan, a man must be at home even in his own country.

Thomas Wentworth Higginson, *Short Studies of American Authors*

One of the reasons James found the American scene difficult to deal with was that its brief past had been embodied in so few visible forms.

Harold T. McCarthy, *Henry James, The Creative Process*

Henry James's fictions are like the cobwebs which a spider may spin in the attic of some old house, intricate, delicate and even beautiful, but which at any moment the housemaid's broom with brutal common sense may sweep away.

W. Somerset Maugham, *The Vagrant Mood*

Much of Henry James is what the French, whom he so extravagantly admired, dismiss with a shrug of the shoulders as *littérature*. He did not live, he observed life from a window, and too often was inclined to content himself with no more than what his friends told him they saw when *they* looked out of a window. But what can you know of life unless you have lived it? . . . In the end the point of Henry James is neither his artistry nor his seriousness, but his personality, and this was curious and charming and a trifle absurd.

W. Somerset Maugham, *A Writer's Notebook*

. . . we have Henry James a deserter made by despair; one so depressed by the tacky company at the American first table that he preferred to sit at the second table of the English.

H. L. Mencken, in Edward Stone, *The Battle and the Books: Some Aspects of Henry James*

The interviewer in us would like to ask Henry James why he never married; but it would be in vain to ask, so much does he write like a man to whom all action is repugnant. He confesses himself on every page, as we all do. On every page James is a prude.

George Moore, *Confessions of a Young Man*

PROVINCIALISM... Galdos, Turgenev, Flaubert, Henry James, the whole fight of modern enlightenment is against this . . . Henry James in his unending endeavour to provide a common language, an idiom of manners and meanings for the three nations, England, America, France. Henry James was, despite any literary detachments, the crusader, both in his internationalism, and in his constant propaganda against personal tyranny, against the hundred subtle forms of personal oppressions and coercions. Idiots said he was untouched by emotion.

Ezra Pound, *The New Age*, 1917

When he died one felt there was no one to ask about anything. Up to then one felt someone knew.

Ezra Pound, in *Paris Review*

James felt buried in America; but he came here [England] to be embalmed.

George Bernard Shaw, Letter to Molly Tompkins

It was once irreverently remarked, by a non-Jacobean too-ready with historical analogy, that there were three Henry Jameses – James the First, James the Second, and the Old Pretender.

Frank Swinnerton, *The Georgian Literary Scene*

There has probably been no other major novelist whose work has been so often criticized not so much for what it is but for what certain critics think it should have been. One critic, whose name I do not know, becoming impatient of the carpers, once said that they criticized Henry James as they might criticize a cat for not being a dog.

James Thurber, *The Wings of Henry James*

Leviathan retrieving pebbles . . . a magnificent but painful hippopotamus resolved at any cost, even at the cost of its dignity, upon picking up a pea.

H. G. Wells, *Boon*

James never scuffled with Fact; he treated her as a perfect and unchallenge-able lady; he never questioned a single stitch or flounce of the conventions and interpretations in which she presented herself. He thought that for every social occasion a correct costume could be prescribed and a correct behaviour defined. On the table (an excellent piece) in his hall at Rye lay a number of caps and hats, each with its appropriate gloves and sticks, a tweed cap and a stout stick for the Marsh, a soft comfortable deer-stalker if he were to turn aside to the Golf Club, a light-brown felt hat and a cane for a morning walk down to the Harbour, a grey felt with a black band and a gold-headed cane of greater importance, if afternoon calling in the town was afoot.

H. G. Wells, *Experiment in Autobiography*

James is developing, but he will never arrive at passion, I fear.

Oscar Wilde, Letter to Robert Ross, 12 January 1899

Can you possibly imagine Henry James without an accompaniment of corsets and Prince Alberts with striped trousers.

William Carlos Williams, in Edward Stone, *The Battle and the Books: Some Aspects of Henry James*

We must admit that Henry James has conquered. That courtly, worldly, sentimental old gentleman can still make us afraid of the dark.

Virginia Woolf, 'The Ghost Stories', in Leon Edel ed., *Henry James, A Collection of Critical Essays*

*See also* Ford Madox Ford, Elinor Glyn, William Dean Howells, John Singer Sargent, Hugh Walpole, Edith Wharton

## JAMES, JESSE WOODSON

1847–82 Desperado

Jesse had a wife to mourn all her life. / Two children they were brave. / 'Twas a dirty little coward that shot Mr Howard / And laid Jesse James in his grave. /

It was Bob Ford, the dirty little coward, / I wonder how does he feel, / For he ate of Jesse's bread and slept in Jesse's bed, / Then he laid Jesse James in his grave. /

Jesse was a man, a friend to the poor, / He never would see a man suffer pain; / And with his brother Frank he robbed the Gallatin bank / And stopped the Glendale train. /

*The Ballad of Jesse James*, in Homer Croy, *Jesse James Was My Neighbor*

He never shot a light out in his life, never took a drink at a bar as he watched in the mirror some other man with a view of disposing of him, never rode down a street shooting right and left for the fun of it. He was in the business of train and bank robbery. And he made a success of it as no other man in America has ever done.

Homer Croy, *Jesse James Was My Neighbor*

Jesse James shot children, but only in fact not in folklore.

John Greenway, *The Inevitable Americans*

## JAMES, WILLIAM

1842–1910 Philosopher, Psychologist

James confronted all dogma with skepticism and made skepticism itself a dogma.

Henry Steele Commager, in Robert Allen Skotheim, *American Intellectual Histories and Historians*

It would be incongruous . . . to expect of him that he should build a philosophy like an edifice to go and live in for good. Philosophy to him was rather like a maze in which he happened to find himself wandering, and what he was looking for was the way out.

George Santayana, in Bernard P. Brennan, *William James*

## JAY, JOHN

1745–1829 Jurist, Statesman, Diplomat

One John, surnamed Jay, journeyed into a far country, even unto Great Britain. 2. And the word of Satan came unto him saying, make thou a covenant with this people whereby they may be enabled to bring the *Americans* into bondage, as heretofore. 3. And John answered unto Satan, of a truth . . . Let me find grace in thy sight, that I may secretly betray my country and the place of my nativity.

Anon. parody on the Jay Treaty, in Frank Monaghan, *John Jay*

Damn John Jay! Damn every one that won't damn John Jay! Damn every one that won't put lights in his windows and sit up all night damning John Jay!!!

Anon., 1794, in Herbert Alan Johnson, *John Jay*

## JEFFERSON, THOMAS

1743–1826 Third United States President

Ambition is the subtlest Beast of the Intellectual and Moral Field. It is wonderfully adroit in concealing itself from its owner . . . Jefferson thinks he shall by this step get a Reputation of a humble, modest, meek man, wholly without ambition or vanity. He may even have deceived himself into this Belief. But if a Prospect opens, the World will see and he will feel, that he is as ambitious as Oliver Cromwell though no soldier.

John Adams, Letter to John Quincy Adams, 3 January 1794

I held levees once a week, that all my time might not be wasted by idle visits. Jefferson's whole eight years was a levee . . .

Jefferson and Rush were for liberty and straight hair. I thought curled hair was as republican as straight.

John Adams, Letter to Benjamin Rush, 25 December 1811

Thomas Jefferson still survives.

John Adams, last words. Jefferson in fact was already deceased

His genius is of the old French school. It conceives better than it combines.

John Quincy Adams, Diary, 23 November 1804

Jeffersonian Democracy simply meant the possession of the federal government by the agrarian masses led by an aristocracy of slave-owning planters.

Charles A. Beard, *The Economic Origins of Jeffersonian Democracy*

I think this is the most extraordinary collection of human talent, of human knowledge, that has ever been gathered at the White House – with the possible exception of when Thomas Jefferson dined alone.

John F. Kennedy, Speech at the White House to honour forty-nine Nobel Prize Winners, 1962, in *New York Times*, 30 April 1962

The patriot, fresh from freedom's councils come, / Now pleased retires to lash his slaves at home; / Or woo, perhaps, some black Aspasia's charms, / And dream of Freedom in his bondsmaid's arms. /

Thomas Moore, in Fawn M. Brodie, *Thomas Jefferson, An Intimate History*

A gentleman of thirty two who could calculate an eclipse, survey an estate, tie an artery, plan an edifice, try a cause, break a horse, dance a minuet and play the violin.

James Parton, *Life of Thomas Jefferson*

. . . the moonshine philosopher of Monticello.

Timothy Pickering, in Adrienne Koch ed., *Thomas Jefferson, Great Lives Observed*

I cannot live in this miserable, undone country, where, as the Turks follow their sacred standard, which is a pair of Mahomet's breeches, we are governed by the old red breeches of that prince of projectors, St Thomas of Cantingbury; and surely, Becket himself never had more pilgrims at his shrine than the Saint of Monticello.

John Randolph of Roanoke, in

L. A. Harris, *The Fine Art of Political Wit*

*See also* John Adams, Aaron Burr, Martin Van Buren

## JEFFREY, FRANCIS, LORD

1773–1850 Critic

Never mind his damning the North Pole. *I* have heard him speak disrespectfully of the equator.

Sydney Smith, in Harriet Martineau, *Autobiography*

## JEFFREYS, GEORGE, BARON JEFFREYS OF WEM

1645–89 Judge

He hath in great perfection the three chief qualifications of a lawyer: boldness, boldness, boldness.

Anon., in the *Hatton Correspondence*

He has been so much chased, that I began my critical examination of his history in the hope and belief that I should find that his misdeeds had been exaggerated, and that I might be able to rescue his memory from some portion of the obloquy under which it labours; but I am sorry to say that in my matured opinion, although he appears to have been a man of high talents, of singularly agreeable manners, and entirely free from hypocrisy, his cruelty and his political profligacy have not been sufficiently exposed or reprobated.

Lord Campbell, *Lives of the Chancellors*

The many Hundreds that he hanged in the West, shews he was a stout Man, his Entrails Brass, and his Heart Steel; and this was necessary in the Post where the King had placed him. – Hang, draw and quarter was part of his Loyalty; and yet we may call him a merciful Judge. For he had such Respect for the Souls of Men, that he scarce hanged any but those who were innocent, and of those he sentenced 200 in a forenoon. If he excelled in one thing more than another, 'twas in his haste to send Whiggs to Heaven: for Hang Men first, and try 'em afterwards ... was his peculiar Talent.

John Dunton, *The Merciful Assizes*

There was a fiendish exultation in the way he pronounced sentence on offenders. Their weeping and imploring seemed to titillate him voluptuously; and he loved to scare them into fits by dilating with luxuriant amplification on all the details of what they were to suffer. Thus when he had an opportunity of ordering an unlucky adventuress to be whipped at the cart's tail, 'Hangman,' he would exclaim, 'I charge you to pay particular attention to this lady! Scourge her soundly, man! It is Christmas; a cold time for Madam to strip in! See that you warm her shoulders thoroughly.'

T. B. Macaulay, *History of England*

He took a pleasure in mortifying fraudulent attorneys, and would deal forth his severities with a sort of majesty. He had extraordinary natural abilities, but little acquired beyond what practice in affairs had supplied. He talked fluently, and with spirit; and his weakness was he could not reprehend without scolding; and in such Billingsgate language as should not come out of the mouth of any man. He called it 'giving a lick with the rough side of his tongue'.

Roger North, *Life of Francis North*

## JELLICOE, JOHN RUSHWORTH, EARL

1859–1935 Admiral

Sailor with a flawed cutlass.

Correlli Barnett, *The Swordbearers*

Jellicoe was the only man on either side who could lose the war in an afternoon.

Winston Churchill, *The World Crisis*

He fought to make a German victory impossible rather than a British victory certain.

Cyril Falls, *The First World War*

## JENKINSON, ROBERT BANKS, *see under* LIVERPOOL, LORD

## JENYNS, SOAME

1704–89 Writer, Wit

Here lies a little ugly nauseous elf, / Who judging only from its wretched self, / Feebly attempted, petulant and vain, / The 'Origin of Evil' to explain. /

Anon., *Epitaph on Soame Jenyns* (a reply to Jenyns's attack on Johnson after Johnson's death), in James Boswell, *Life of Johnson*

Though metaphysicks spread the gloom of night, / By reason's star he* guides our aching sight; / The bounds of knowledge marks, and points the way / To pathless wastes, where wilder'd sages stray; / Where, like a farthing link-boy, Jennings stands, / And the dim torch drops from his feeble hands. / (*Johnson)

John Courtenay, *Literary and Moral Character of Dr Johnson*

Soame Jenyns was an old woman and his vocabulary was as trite as could be; and yet, because he wrote in the eighteenth century, he put his poor words and thoughts into shipshape sentences.

A. E. Housman, Review of vols 13–14 of the *Cambridge History of English Literature*

## JEROME, JEROME KLAPKA

1859–1927 Author

I think I may claim to have been, for the first twenty years of my career, the best abused author in England. *Punch* invariably referred to me as ''Arry K'Arry', and would then proceed to solemnly lecture me on the sin of mistaking vulgarity for humour and impertinence for wit . . . Max Beerbohm was always very angry with me. The *Standard* spoke of me as a menace to English letters . . . At the opening dinner of the Krasnapolski restaurant in Oxford Street (now the Frascati), I was placed next to Harold Frederick, just arrived from America. I noticed that he had been looking at me with curiosity. 'Where's your flint hammer?' he asked me suddenly. 'Left it in the cloakroom?' He explained that he had visualized me from reading the English literary journals, and had imagined something prehistoric.

On himself, *My Life and Times*

Costume, dandaical or not, is in the highest degree expressive . . . The bowler of Mr Jerome K. Jerome is a perfect preface to all his works.

Max Beerbohm, *Dandies and Dandies*

## JOHN,

1167?–1216 King of England

Five years did King John lie under this sentence of excommunication; in which time we find him more fortunate in his martial affairs than either before or after. For he made a successful voyage into Ireland, (as greedy a grave for English corpses, as a bottomless bag for their coin), and was very triumphant in a Welsh expedition, and stood on honourable terms in all foreign relations.

Thomas Fuller, *Church History of Britain*

'Foul as it is, hell itself is defiled by the fouler presence of John.' The terrible view of his contemporaries has passed into the sober judgement of history . . . John was the worst outcome of the Plantagenets. He united into one mass of wickedness their insolence, their selfishness, their unbridled lust, their cruelty and tyranny, their shameless-ness, their superstition, their cynical indifference to honour or truth.

J. R. Green, *The History of the English People*

King John was not a good man – / He had his little ways, / And sometimes no one spoke to him / For days and days and days. /

A. A. Milne, *Now We Are Six*

He was the very worst of all our kings: a man whom no oaths could bind, no pressure of conscience, no consideration of policy, restrain from evil; a faithless son, a treacherous brother, an ungrateful master; to his people a hated tyrant. Polluted with every crime that could disgrace a man, false to every obligation that should bind a king, he had lost half his inheritance by sloth, and ruined and desolated the rest. Not devoid of natural ability, craft or energy, with his full share of the personal valour and accomplishments of his house, he yet failed in every design he undertook, and had to bear humiliations which, although not without parallel, never fell on one who deserved them more thoroughly or received less sympathy under them. In the whole view there is no redeeming trait; John seems as incapable of receiving a good impression as of carrying into effect a wise resolution.

Bishop William Stubbs, *The Constitutional History of England*

His death saved the kingdom for his descendants.

*Ibid.*

Unfortunately for his reputation, John was not a great benefactor to monasteries which kept chronicles.

W. C. Warren, *King John*

It is impossible, the evidence being what it is, to pronounce finally upon his character as a man, but it seems clear that he was inadequate for the tasks confronting him as king. Even in his achievements there was always something missing. He subdued nations to his will, but brought only the peace of fear; he was an ingenious administrator, but expedients came before policy; he was a notable judge, but chicanery went along with justice; he was an able ruler, but he did not know when he was squeezing too hard; he was a clever strategist, but his military operations lacked that vital ingredient of success – boldness. He had the mental abilities of a great king, but the inclinations of a petty tyrant.

*Ibid.*

Lo! John self-stripped of his insignia: – crown / Sceptre and mantle, sword and ring laid down / At a proud Legate's feet! The spears that line / Baronial halls, the opprobrious insult feel; / And angry Ocean roars a vain appeal. /

William Wordsworth, *Papal Abuses*

*See also* James I

## JOHN OF GAUNT, DUKE OF LANCASTER

1340–99 Statesman

*King Richard*: Old John of Gaunt, time-honour'd Lancaster.

William Shakespeare, *Richard II*, Act I, Scene i

## JOHN, AUGUSTUS EDWIN

1878–1961 Artist

John! John! / How he's got on! / He owes it, he knows it, to me! / Brass earrings I wear, / And I don't do my hair, / And my feet are as bare as can be; / When I walk down the street, / All the people I meet / They stare at the things I have on! / When Battersea-Parking / You'll hear folks remarking: / 'There goes an Augustus John!'

Song in Revue, in *Monster Matinee*, March 1917

You who revel in the quick / And are Beauty's Bolshevik; / For you know how to undress / And expose her loveliness. /

Oliver St John Gogarty, *Ode 'To Augustus John'*

He had become one of the most popular men in the country. In Soho restaurants 'Entrecôte à la John' was eaten; in theatres any actor impersonating an artist was indistinguishable from him; in several novels he was instantly recognizable as 'the painter'.

Michael Holroyd, *Augustus John*

That standard celebrity.

Percy Wyndham Lewis, *Blasting and Bombardiering*

It was his Rembrandtesque drawings of stumpy brown people, followed by his tribes after tribes of archaic and romantic Gitanos and Gitanas that made him the legitimate successor to Beardsley and Wilde and in exploiting the inveterate exoticism of the educated Englishman and Englishwoman, stamped himself, barbaric chevelure and all, on what might be termed the Augustan decade.

Percy Wyndham Lewis, *History of the Largest Independent Society in England*

John, indeed, is the last of the great improvisers; he was made to throw off his fancies at white heat; and he alone is able to draw nudes in any position, at any angle, as Tiepolo could.

William Rothenstein, *Men and Memories, 1900–22*

When I think of him, I often feel that the only thing to do is to chuck up everything and make a dash for some such safe secluded office-stool as is pressed by dear Maynard [Keynes]'s bottom. The dangers of freedom are appalling! In the meantime it seems to me that one had better buy up every drawing by him that's on the market. For surely he's bound to fizzle out; and then the prices!

Lytton Strachey, Letter to Duncan Grant, 12 April 1907

He exaggerates every little hill and hollow of the face till one looks like a gypsy, grown old in wickedness and hardship. If one looked like any of his pictures the country women would take the clean clothes off the hedges when one passed, as they do at the sight of a tinker.

William Butler Yeats, Letter to John Quinn, 4 October 1907

## JOHNSON, ANDREW

1808–75 Seventeenth United States President

. . . an insolent drunken brute, in comparison with whom Caligula's horse was respectable.

Anon., in *New York World*, 1865

Like a boy whistling down ghosts, the vehemence with which he boasts of his plebian origin shows that it is a sore spot with him, and the pains which he takes to remind us that he was a tailor prove that he is constantly haunted by that unwelcome fact.

Anon., in *Nation*, 6 September 1866

His mind had one compartment for right and one for wrong, but no middle chamber where the two could commingle.

Howard K. Beale, in Michael L. Benedict, *The Impeachment and Trial of Andrew Johnson*

If Andy Johnson was a snake, he would hide in the grass and bite the heels of rich men's children.

Isham G. Harris, in *ibid.*

Like an aching tooth, everyone (sic) is impatient to have the old villain out.

Joseph Medill to John Logan, in

Eric L. McKitrick, *Andrew Johnson: A Profile*

You will remember that in Egypt He sent frogs, locusts, murrain, lice, and finally demanded the first-born of everyone of the oppressors. Almost all of these have been taken from us. We have been oppressed with taxes and debts, and He has sent us worse than lice, and has afflicted us with Andrew Johnson.

Thaddeus Stevens, August 1866, in Fawn M. Brodie, *Thaddeus Stevens*

## JOHNSON, LIONEL PIGOT

1867–1902 Poet

I looked with wonder at the young scholar, who, it proved, was but a year younger than myself, being twenty-three. Not an advanced age, indeed, but not even the knowledge that he was Lionel Johnson could make him look more than fifteen, and he never seemed to look older as long as he lived . . . His little, almost tiny, figure, was so frail that it reminded one of that old Greek philosopher who was so light of weight that he filled his pockets with stones for fear the wind might blow him away.

Richard Le Gallienne, *The Romantic '90s*

Johnson stands out with an austere light behind him like the aureoled head of a little saint.

Katherine Tynan, *Memories*

Lionel Johnson comes the first to mind, / That loved his learning better than mankind, / Though courteous to the worst; much falling he / Brooded upon sanctity / Till all his Greek and Latin learning seemed / A long blast upon the horn that brought / A little nearer to his thought / A measureless consummation that he dreamed. /

William Butler Yeats, *In Memory of Major Robert Gregory*

## JOHNSON, LYNDON BAINES

1908–73 Thirty-Sixth United States President

I have said that I believe in the tight fist and the open mind – a tight fist with money and an open mind to the needs of America.

On himself, Speech at Washington D.C., 4 December 1964

Hey, hey, LBJ! How many kids did you kill today?

Anon., anti-Vietnam war chant

Face-saving, the President observed, was not his major purpose in life. 'While you're trying to save your face,' he declared, 'you're losing your ass.'

Philip L. Geyelin, *Lyndon B. Johnson and the World*

. . . we have many people that have thin skins, Lyndon Johnson is one. His skin is a millionth of an inch thick.

Senator Barry M. Goldwater, in Leon A. Harris, *The Fine Art of Political Wit*

We now have a President who tries to save money by turning off lights in the White House, even as he heads toward a staggering addition to the national debt. 'L.B.J.' should stand for Light Bulb Johnson.

Barry M. Goldwater, Speech in Chicago, 10 April 1964

He was trying to get everyone on board in an office where the best decisions are often the loneliest ones.

David Halberstam, *The Best and the Brightest*

His social vision did not go beyond the classic prescriptions for dealing with injustice: give everybody an equal start, above all education, and meanwhile keep the niggers off your porch.

Christopher Lasch, 'The Presidential Mystique', in H. W. Quint and M. Cantor eds, *Men, Women and Issues in American History*, vol. 2

We've got a wild man in the White House, and we are going to have to treat him as such.

Senator Eugene McCarthy, in Alfred Steinberg, *Sam Johnson's Boy*

He is an incorrigible believer. He believes in everything that works.

James Reston, in *New York Times Magazine*, 17 January 1965

... he was the great legislative prestidigitator of his time. Not since James F. Bynes had Congress seen a man so skilled in modifying a measure to enlist the widest possible support, so adept at the arts of wheedling, trading and arm-twisting, so persistent and so persuasive.

Arthur M. Schlesinger Jr, *A Thousand Days, John F. Kennedy in the White House*

A great, raw man of immense girth, wandering as a stranger in the Pepsi generation. Coarse, earthy – a brutal intrusion into the misty Kennedy renaissance that still clung to the land.

Hugh Sidey, *A Very Personal Presidency*

He is one of the most long-winded men in Washington; a Rabbit, with a remarkably small stock of basic ideas; these consist of a few clichés about freedom, which he translates largely into the freedom of the entrepreneur to make a buck.

I. F. Stone, *In a Time of Torment*

Johnson's instinct for power is as primordial as a salmon's going upstream to spawn.

Theodore H. White, *The Making of the President – 1964*

## JOHNSON, SAMUEL (DOCTOR)

1709–84 Critic, Poet, Lexicographer

I have protracted my work till most of those whom I wished to please have sunk into the grave, and success and miscarriage are empty sounds; I therefore dismiss it with frigid tranquility, having little to fear or hope from censure or from praise.

On himself, Preface to his *Dictionary of the English Language*

If I had no duties, and no reference to futurity, I would spend my life in driving briskly in a post-chaise with a pretty woman.

On himself, in James Boswell, *Life of Johnson*

You must not mind me, madam; I say strange things, but I mean no harm.

On himself, in Fanny Burney, Diary, 23 August 1778

The groans of Learning tell that Johnson dies. / Adieu, rough critic, of Colossal size! / Grateful, ye virtues, round his grave attend, / And boldly guard your energetic friend! / Ye vices keep aloof – a foe to you! / Yet one, the subtlest of your tribe, he knew; / In silence, Envy, to his fame be just, / And, tho' you stain'd his spirit, spare his dust. /

Anon. *Epitaph*, published in several newspapers in February 1796 under the name of Anna Seward (who disavowed it)

That pompous preacher of melancholy moralities.

Jeremy Bentham, *The Book of Fallacies*

'Oho', said Dr Johnson / To Scipio Africanus, / 'If you don't own me a Philosopher, / I'll kick your Roman Anus.'

William Blake, *An Island in the Moon*

He turned to me and said, 'I look upon *myself* as a good-humoured fellow.' The epithet *fellow* applied to the great lexicographer, the stately moralist, the masterly critic, as if he had been *Sam* Johnson, a mere pleasant companion, was highly diverting; and this light notion of himself struck me with wonder. I answered, also smiling, 'No, no, Sir; that will *not* do. You are good-natured, but not good-humoured. You are irascible. You have not patience with folly and absurdity. I believe you would pardon them if there were time to deprecate your vengeance; but punishment follows so quick after sentence that they cannot escape.'

James Boswell, Journal, 14 April 1775

*Johnson*: Well, we had a good talk.
*Boswell*: Yes, Sir, you tossed and gored several persons.

James Boswell, *Life of Johnson*

I compared him . . . to a warm West-Indian climate, where you have a bright sun, quick vegetation, luxuriant foliage, luscious fruits; but where the same heat sometimes produces thunder, lightning, and earthquakes in a terrible degree.

*Ibid.*

That Johnson's stile is obscure, the testimony of all unlearned readers abundantly confirms; and from the same authority the cause may be stated to be his perpetual affectation of expressing his thoughts by the use of polysyllables of Latin derivation: a fault, which confines to men of erudition the most animating enforcements of virtue and the most salutary rules of conduct, by disqualifying all those who have not been made acquainted by a liberal education with the Latin appellations for things, or those, from whose memories the common use of the English names has in the course of time effaced them.

Robert Burrowes, *Essay on the Stile of Doctor Samuel Johnson*

Our English Lexiphanes.

Archibald Campbell, *Lexiphanes, a Dialogue*

Shall we not say, of this great mournful Johnson too, that he guided his difficult confused existence wisely; led it *well*, like a right-valiant man? That waste chaos of Authorship by trade; that waste chaos of Scepticism in religion and politics, in life-theory and life-practice; in his poverty, in his dust and dimness, with the sick body and the rusty coat: he made it do for him, like a brave man. Not wholly without a loadstar in the Eternal; he had still a loadstar, as the brave all need to have: with his eye set on that, he would change his course for nothing in these confused vortices of the lower sea of Time. 'To the Spirit of Lies, bearing death and hunger, he would in no wise strike his flag.' Brave old Samuel: *ultimus Romanorum!*

Thomas Carlyle, *On Heroes and Hero Worship*

POMPOSO (insolent and loud, / Vain idol of a *scribbling* crowd, / Whose very name inspires an awe, / For what his Greatness hath decreed, / Like Laws of PERSIA and of MEDE, / Sacred thro' all the realm of *Wit*, / Must never of Repeal admit.) /

Charles Churchill, *The Ghost*

Who wit with jealous eye surveys, / And sickens at another's praise. /

*Ibid.*

. . . Old dread-death and dread-devil Johnson, that teacher of moping and melancholy . . . If the writings of this time-serving, mean, dastardly old pensioner had got a firm hold of the minds of the people at large, the people would have been bereft of their very souls. These writings, aided by the charm of pompous sound, were fast making their way, till light, reason, and the French revolution came to drive them into oblivion; or, at least, to confine them to the shelves of repentant, married old rakes, and those old stock-jobbers with young wives standing in need of something to keep down the unruly ebullitions which are apt to take place while the 'dearies' are gone hobbling to 'Change.

William Cobbett, *Journal*, November 1821

Dr Dread-Devil . . . said, that there were *no trees* in Scotland. I wonder how they managed to take him round without letting him see trees. I suppose that lick-spittle Boswell, or Mrs Piozzi, tied a bandage over his eyes, when he went over the country which I have been over. I shall sweep away all this bundle of lies.

William Cobbett, *Tour of Scotland*

Dr Johnson seems to have been really more powerful in discoursing *viva voce* in conversation than with his pen in hand. It seems as if the excitement of company called something like reality and consecutiveness into his reasonings, which in his writings I cannot see. His antitheses are almost always verbal only: and sentence after sentence in the *Rambler* may be pointed out to which you cannot attach any definite meaning whatever.

Samuel Taylor Coleridge, *Table Talk*, 1 November 1833

Nor was his energy confin'd alone / To friends around his philosophick throne; / *Its influence wide improv'd our letter'd isle, / And lucid vigour mark'd the general style:* / As Nile's proud waves, swol'n from their oozy bed, / First o'er the neighbouring meads majestick spread; / Till gathering force, they more and more expand, / And with new virtue fertilise the land. /

John Courtenay, *Moral and Literary Character of Dr Johnson*

The Caliban of literature.

Gilbert Cowper, in James Boswell, *Life of Johnson*

Those who demand of poetry a day-dream, or a metamorphosis of their own feeble desires and lusts, or what they believe to be 'intensity' of passion, will not find much in Johnson. He is like Pope and Dryden, Crabbe and Landor, a poet for those who want poetry and not something else, some stay for their own vanity.

T. S. Eliot, *Eighteenth-Century Poetry*

Rabelais and all other wits are nothing compared with him. You may be diverted by them; but Johnson gives you a forcible hug, and shakes laughter out of you whether you will or no.

David Garrick, in James Boswell, *Life of Johnson*

There is no arguing with Johnson; for if his pistol misses fire, he knocks you down with the butt end of it.

Oliver Goldsmith, in *ibid.*

Johnson to be sure has a roughness in his manner; but no man alive has a more tender heart. *He has nothing of the bear but his skin.*

*Ibid.*

If you were to make little fishes talk, they would talk like whales.

*Ibid.*

Johnson wrote a kind of rhyming prose, in which he was as much compelled to finish the different clauses of his sentences, and to balance one period against another, as the writer of heroic verse is to keep to lines of ten syllables with similar terminations. He no sooner acknowledges the merits of his author in one line than the periodical revolution of his style carries the weight of his opinion completely over to the side of objection, thus keeping up a perpetual alternation of perfections and absurdities.

William Hazlitt, *Characters of Shakespeare's Plays*

Here lies poor Johnson; reader have a care; / Tread lightly, lest you rouse a sleeping bear. / Religious, moral, generous and humane / He was; but self-sufficient, rude, and vain; / Ill-bred, and overbearing in dispute, / A scholar and a Christian and a brute. /

Soame Jenyns, *Epitaph on Samuel Johnson*

In this country, to those seriously interested in literature, the cult of Johnson is an exasperation and a challenge . . . Johnson, one finds oneself having again and again to insist, was not only the Great Clubman; he was a great writer and a great highbrow – or would have been, if the word, and the conditions that have produced it, had existed; that is, he assumed a serious interest in things of the mind, and, for all his appeal to 'the common reader', was constantly engaged in the business of bringing home to his public and his associates, whose cult of him was a tribute to the force with which he did it, that there were standards in these things above the ordinary level of the ordinary man.

F. R. Leavis, *The Common Pursuit*

In the foreground is that strange figure which is as familiar to us as the figures of those among whom we have been brought up, the gigantic body, the huge massy face, seamed with the scars of disease, the brown coat, the black worsted stockings, the grey wig with the scorched foretop, the dirty hands, the nails bitten and pared to the quick.

T. B. Macaulay, *Essays*: 'Boswell's Life of Johnson'

What a singular destiny has been that of this remarkable man! To be regarded in his own age as a classic, and in ours as a companion! To receive from his contemporaries that full homage which men of genius have in general received only from posterity! To be more intimately known to posterity than other men are known to their contemporaries! . . . The reputation of those writings, which he probably expected to be immortal, is every day fading; while those peculiarities of manner and that careless table-talk the memory of which, he probably thought, would die with him, are likely to be remembered as long as the English language is spoken in any quarter of the globe.

T. B. Macaulay, *ibid.*

We cannot be in Johnson's company long, without becoming aware that what draws us to him so closely is that he combined a disillusioned estimate of human nature sufficient to launch twenty little cynics, with a craving for love and sympathy urgent enough to turn a weaker nature into a benign sentimentalist.

Desmond MacCarthy, *Criticism*

Gibbon and Dr Johnson . . . were the victims of bad theories. I can read every word that Dr Johnson wrote with delight, for he had good sense, charm and wit . . . He knew good English when he saw it . . . But when he himself sat down to write . . . he mistook the orotund for the dignified. He had not the good breeding to see that simplicity and naturalness are the truest mark of distinction.

W. Somerset Maugham, *The Summing Up*

O rough, pure, stubborn, troubled soul: for whom / A smile of special tenderness men keep – / Who prayed for strength 'to regulate my room', / And 'preservation from immoderate sleep'. /

Christopher Morley, *On a Portrait of Dr Samuel Johnson, LL.D.*

Now that the old lion is dead, every ass thinks he may kick at him.

Samuel Parr, in James Boswell, *Life of Johnson*

Dr Johnson's sayings would not appear so extraordinary, were it not for his *bow-wow way*.

Lord Pembroke, in *ibid.*

The conversation of Johnson is strong and clear, and may be compared to an antique statue, where every vein and muscle is distinct and bold. Ordinary conversation resembles an inferior cast.

Bishop Thomas Percy, in *ibid.*

I own I like not Johnson's turgid style, / That gives an inch th'importance of a mile; / Casts of manure a waggon-load around / To raise a simple daisy from the ground; / Uplifts the club of Hercules – for what? – / To crush a butterfly or brain a gnat; / Creatures a whirlwind from the earth to draw / A goose's feather or exalt a straw; / Sets wheels on wheels in motion – such a clatter: / To force up one poor nipperkin of water; / Bids ocean labour with tremendous roar, / To heave a cockle-shell upon the shore. / Alike in every theme his pompous art, / Heaven's awful thunder, or a rumbling cart! /

Peter Pindar (John Wolcot), *On Dr Samuel Johnson*

Mrs Thrale [Mrs Piozzi] justly and wittily . . . said that Johnson's conversation was by much too strong for a person accustomed to obsequiousness and flattery; it was *mustard in a young child's mouth.*

Mrs Piozzi, in James Boswell, *Life of Johnson*

Terribly afraid of free-thinking, though not hostile to free-eating . . . A great author, notwithstanding his *Dictionary* is imperfect, his *Rambler* pompous, his *Idler* inane, his *Lives* unjust, his poetry inconsiderable, his learning common, his ideas vulgar, his *Irene* a child of mediocrity, his genius and wit moderate, his precepts worldly, his politics narrow, and his religion bigoted.

Robert Potter, *The Art of Criticism as Exemplified by Dr Johnson's Lives of the Most Eminent English Poets*

When we consider the rank which Dr Johnson held, not only in literature, but in society, we cannot help figuring him to ourselves as the benevolent giant of some fairy tale, whose kindnesses and courtesies are still mingled with a part of the rugged ferocity imputed to the fabulous sons of Anak, or rather, perhaps, like a Roman dictator, fetched from his farm, whose wisdom and heroism still relished of his rustic occupation.

Sir Walter Scott, *Lives of the Novelists*

I have not wasted my life trifling with literary fools in taverns as Johnson did when he should have been shaking England with the thunder of his spirit.

George Bernard Shaw, Preface to *Misalliance*

That great Cham of literature.

Tobias Smollett, Letter to John Wilkes, 16 March 1759

Johnson's aesthetic judgements are almost invariably subtle, or solid, or bold; they have always some good quality to recommend them – except one: they are never right.

Lytton Strachey, *Books and Characters*

He is a man of a very clear head, great power of words, and a very gay imagination; but there is no disputing with him. He will not hear you, and having a louder voice than you, must roar you down.

Dr John Taylor, in James Boswell, *Life of Johnson*

His works are the Antipodes of Taste, & he is a Schoolmaster of truth, but never its parent; for his doctrines have no novelty, and are never inculcated with indulgence either to the froward child, or to the Dull one. He has set nothing in a new light, yet is as diffuse as if we had every thing to learn. Modern Writers have improved on the Ancients only by conciseness: Dr Johnstone, like the Chymists of Laputa, endeavours to carry back what has been digested to its pristine & crude principles.

Horace Walpole, *General Criticism of Dr Johnson's Writings*

As an author, Johnson's fame was, to tell the truth, scarcely more than contemporary; for it depended upon *novelty of style*, in an age which loved personal novelties like the clothes of the later Brummell. To them, the not-ungraceful antithetical balancing feats with which he wrote of 'amorous propensities' rather than 'love' were new and strange. As a lexicographer, he was of importance. As a conversationalist, the equivalent of our modern 'brains trust' – who would have been lost without the microphone of Boswell – he was of the first rank.

T. H. White, *The Age of Scandal*

*See also* Henry Adams, James Boswell, David Garrick, Edward Gibbon, Leigh Hunt, Soame Jenyns, Elizabeth Montagu, William Warburton

## JOLSON, AL (ASA YOELSON)

1888–1950 Singer, Actor

It was easy enough to make Jolson happy at home. You just had to cheer him for breakfast, applaud wildly for lunch, and give him a standing ovation for dinner.

George Burns, in Michael Freedland, *Jolson*

Born in Russia, he sang of Dixie and a Sewanee River he never saw until he was forty. He once said 'I've got so much dough that fourteen guys couldn't spend it in their lifetimes. But I'd rather die than quit this business'.

Michael Freedland, *Jolson*

## JONES, INIGO

1573–1652 Architect, Designer

Our only learned architect.

George Chapman, Dedication of *Musaeus* to Jones, 1616

He was more of an artist by education than Wren, had a finer taste in art, had seen more of the best works of the great Italian and ancient Roman masters, had associated more with wits and men of the world than his eminent successor; but he was less of a mathematician, had a less expanded mind, and was less of a philosopher.

J. Elmes, *Sir Christopher Wren*

Dominus Do-all.

Ben Jonson, attributed

He had the painstaking, syntactical temperament of the artist, a gift he shared with Milton. For Milton in returning to the correct traditions of antiquity, tidied up the loose ends of the English language left by the Elizabethan poets and set exacting standards of versification. Inigo Jones did a similar service for architecture and in his own we have a forewarning of the severely grand, minatory and organ note of Milton's poetry.

James Lees-Milne, *The Age of Inigo Jones*

## JONSON, BENJAMIN

1573–1637 Dramatist, Poet

O rare Ben Jonson.

*Epitaph* in Westminster Abbey

Shakespear seeing Ben Johnson in a necessary-house, with a book in his hand reading it very attentively, said he was sorry his memory was so *bad*, that he could not *sh-te without a book*.

Anon., *Shakespeare's Jests, or the Jubilee Jester*, *circa* 1769

He was, (or rather had been) of a cleare & faire skin; his habit was very plaine.

I have heard Mr Lacy the Player say, that he was wont to weare a coat like a coach-mans coate, with slitts under the armepitts. he would many times exceed in drinke: Canarie was his beloved liquour: then he would tumble home to bed; and when he had thoroughly perspired, then to studie.

John Aubrey, *Brief Lives*

Aristotle and the others haunted him... and stiffened a talent and a method already by nature sufficiently stiff.

Harley Granville Barker, *On Dramatic Method*

*Doctor*: The last remedy, like Pigeons to the soles of the feet, must be to apply my dear Friend Mr *Johnson's* Works, but they must be apply'd to his head.
*Codshead*: Oh, have a care Doctor, he hates *Ben. Johnson*, he has an Antipathy to him.
*Crambo*: Oh, I hate *Johnson*, oh, oh, dull, dull, oh oh no Wit.
*Doctor*: 'Tis you are dull... dull! he was the Honour of his Nation, and the Poet of Poets.

William Cavendish, Duke of Newcastle, *The Triumphant Widow, or The Medley of Humours*

Next Jonson sat; in ancient learning train'd / His rigid judgement Fancy's flights restrain'd; / Correctly pruned each wild luxurious thought, / Mark'd out her course, nor spared a glorious fault; / The book of man he read with nicest art, / And ransack'd all the secrets of the heart; / Exerted penetration's utmost force, / And traced each passion to its proper source; / And strongly mark'd in liveliest colours drew, / And brought each foible forth to public view: / The coxcomb felt a lash in every word, / And fools, hung out, their brother fools deterred. / His comic humour kept the world in awe, / And laughter frightened folly more than law. /

Charles Churchill, *The Rosciad*

Whilst Shakespeare gave us wit as salt to our meat, Ben Jonson gave wit as salt instead of meat.

Samuel Taylor Coleridge, *Bristol Lectures*

It was a constant complaint of the old actors who lived in Queen Anne's time, that if Jonson's plays were intermitted for a few years, they could not know how to personate his characters, they were so difficult, and their manners so distant, from those of all other authors. To preserve them required a kind of stage learning, which was traditionally hoarded up.

Thomas Davies, *Dramatic Miscellanies*

in his youth given to Venerie. he thought the use of a maide, nothing in comparison to ye wantoness of a wife & would never have ane other Mistress. he said two accidents strange befell him, one that a man made his owne wyfe to Court him, whom he enjoyed two yeares ere he knew of it, & one day finding them by chance Was passingly delighted with it, one other lay diverse tymes with a woman, who shew him all that he wished except the last act, which she would never agree unto.

William Drummond, in *Conversations with William Drummond of Hawthornden*

He heth consumed a whole night in lying looking to his great toe, about which he hath seen tarters and turks Romans and Carthaginions feight in his imagination.

*Ibid.*

He is a great lover and praiser of himself, a contemner and Scorner of others, given rather to losse a friend, than a Jest, jealous of every word and action of those about him (especially after drink which is one of the Elements in which he liveth), a dissembler of ill parts which raigne in him, a bragger of some good that he wanteth, thinketh nothing well but what either he himself, or some of his friends and Countrymen hath said or done. he is passionately kynde and angry, carelesse either to gaine or keep, Vindictive, but if he be well answered, at himself . . . for any religion as being versed in both, interpreteth best sayings and deeds often to the worst: oppressed with fantasie, which hath ever mastered his reason, a generall disease in many poets. his inventions are smooth and easie but above all he excelleth in a translation.

*Ibid.*

As he did not want imagination, so none ever said he had much to spare.

John Dryden, *An Essay of Dramatic Poesy*

*Johnson* with skill dissected human kind, / And show'd their faults that they their faults might find; / But then, as all anatomists must do, / He to the meanest of mankind did go, / And took from Gibbets such as he would show. /

John Dryden, ascribed, *Covent Garden Drolery*, 1672

The reputation of Jonson has been of the most deadly kind that can be compelled upon the memory of a great poet. To be universally accepted; to be damned by the praise that quenches all desire to read the book; to be afflicted by the imputation of the virtues which excite the least pleasure; and to be read only by historians and antiquaries – this is the most perfect conspiracy of approval. For some generations the name of Jonson has been carried rather as a liability than as an asset in the balance-sheet of English literature . . . Poetry of the surface cannot be understood without study . . . the immediate appeal of Jonson is to the mind; his emotional tone is not in the single verse, but in the design of the whole.

T. S. Eliot, *Essays*: 'Ben Jonson'

His parts were not so *ready* to *run of themselves* as *able to answer the* spur, so that it may be truly said of him, that he had an *Elaborate wit* wrought out by his own industry. He would sit silent in learned company, and suck in (besides wine) their several humours into his observation. What was *ore* in others, he was able to refine to himself.

Thomas Fuller, *The History of the Worthies of England*

He may be said to mine his way into a subject, like a mole, and throws up a prodigious quantity of matter on the surface, so that the richer the soil in which he labours, the less dross and rubbish we have.

William Hazlitt, *On Beaumont and Fletcher*

When I a verse shall make, / Know I have praid thee, / For old *Religions* sake, / Saint *Ben* to aide me. /

Make the way smooth for me, / When I, thy *Herrick*, / Honouring thee, on my knee / Offer my *lyrick*. /

Candles Ile give to thee, / And a new Altar; / And thou Saint Ben, shalt be / Writ in my Psalter. /

Robert Herrick, *His Prayer to Ben Johnson*

You were mad when you writ your *Fox*, and madder when you writ your *Alchymist*; you were mad when you writ *Catilin*, and stark mad when you writ *Sejanus*; but when you writt your *Epigrams* and the *Magnetick Lady* you were not so mad. Excuse me that I am so free with you. The madness I mean is that divine Fury, that heating and heightening Spirit, which *Ovid* speaks of.

James Howell, *Epistolae Ho-Elianae, To My Father Ben Jonson*

Then Jonson came, instructed from the school, / To please in method, and invent by rule. / His studious patience and laborious art, / By regular approach, assail'd the heart. / Cold approbation gave the lingering bayes, / For those who durst not censure, scarce could praise. / A mortal born, he met the general doom, / But left, like Egypt's Kings, a lasting tomb. /

Samuel Johnson, *Prologue at the Opening of the Drury Lane Theatre*

I wonder how you ever durst invay / In Satire, Epigram, or Libell-play / against the manners of the tyme, or men / in full examples of all mischiefs, when / no ill thou could so taske dwells not in thee, / and there the store house of your plotte wee see. / For thou, that hast in thee so many waies / of practizd mischief, hast begott thy bayes / in reading of thy selfe, tickling the age, / stealing all equal glory from the stage, / that I confesse with like forme thou hast writt / of good and badd things, not with equall witt. / The reason is, or may be quickly showne, / the good's translation, butt the ill's thyne owne. /

Inigo Jones, *To His false friend Mr Ben Johnson*, after 1619

In the rest of his Poetry, for he is not wholly Dramatic, as his Underwoods, Epigrams, etc, he is sometimes bold and strenuous, sometimes Magisterial, sometimes Lepid and full enough of conceit, and sometimes a Man, as other Men are.

Edward Phillips, *Theatrum Poetarum*

His lines did relish mirth, but so severe, / That as they tickled, they did wound the ear. / Well then, such virtue cannot die, though stones / Loaded with epitaphs do press his bones: / He lived to me; spite of this martyrdom, / Ben is the self-same poet in the tomb. / You that can aldermen new wits create, / Know, Jonson's skeleton is laureat. /

H. Ramsay, *Upon the Death of Benjamin Jonson*

And everie Comedie / He did intend / An Errata page should be, / To show men faults and teach 'em how to mend. /

Edward Ravenscroft, *Commendatory Verses*, prefixed to Edward Howard, *The Six Days Adventure, or the New Utopia*

I can't read Ben Jonson, especially his comedies. To me he appears to move in a wide sea of glue.

Alfred, Lord Tennyson, in *Alfred Lord Tennyson, A Memoir by His Son*

To know Ben Jonson was in Jonson's eyes a liberal profession.

Charles Whibley, *Edward Hyde*

Every half quarter of an Hour a glass of Sack must be sent of an errand into his Guts, to tell his Brains they must come up quickly, and help out with a line.

Robert Wilde, *The Benefice*

*See also* Francis Beaumont, John Dee, Shakespeare

## JONSON, BENJAMIN

1597–1603 Ben Jonson's son

Rest in soft peace, and, asked, say here doth lie / Ben Jonson his best piece of poetry: / For whose sake, henceforth, all his vows be such / As what he loves may never like too much. /

Ben Jonson, *On My First Son*

## JOWETT, BENJAMIN

1817–93 Scholar

Did you ever hear the story of a man who asked his physician whether he was not dangerously ill? 'No sir, but you are dangerously old.' So I too have come to the creaky places of life.

On himself in old age, Letter to Lady Wemyss

Jowett, in his day, did probably more than any other single man to let some fresh air into the exhausted atmosphere of the [Oxford] common rooms, and to widen the intellectual horizons of the place . . . He never at any time (I should think) had anything definite to teach.

H. H. Asquith, Letter to Lady Horner, 26 October 1891

First come I; my name is Jowett. / There's no knowledge but I know it. / I am Master of this College: / What I don't know isn't knowledge. /

H. C. Beeching, *The Masque of Balliol*

## JOYCE, JAMES AUGUSTINE

1882–1941 Author

My mind rejects the whole social order and Christianity – home, the recognized virtues, classes of life, and religious doctrines . . . I cannot enter the social order except as a vagabond.

On himself, Letter to Nora Barnacle, 1904

It is not my fault that the odor of ashpits and old weeds and offal hangs round my stories. I seriously believe that you will retard the course of civilization in Ireland by preventing the Irish people from having a good look at themselves in my nicely polished looking glass.

On himself, Letter to Grant Richards, who had abandoned plans to publish *Dubliners*, 1906

Mr Joyce has desophisticated language. And it is worth while remarking that no language is so sophisticated as English. It is abstracted to death. Take the word 'doubt': it gives us hardly any sensuous suggestion of hesitancy, of the necessity for choice, of static irresolution. Whereas the German 'Zweifel' does, and, in a lesser degree, the Italian 'dubitare'. Mr Joyce recognizes how inadequate 'doubt' is to express a state of extreme uncertainty, and replaces it by 'in twosome twiminds'.

Samuel Beckett, in Sylvia Beach ed., *Our Exagmination . . . of Work in Progress*

Shakespeare said pretty well everything, and what he left out, James Joyce, with a nudge from meself, put in.

Brendan Behan, in Sean McCann, *The Wit of Brendan Behan*

The key to reading *Ulysses* is to treat it like a comedian would – as a sort of gag book.

*Ibid.*

You must not stink I am attempting to ridicul (de sac!) you or to be smart, but I am so disturd by my inhumility to onthorstand most of the impslocations constrained in your work that (although I am by nominals dump and in fact I consider myself not brilliantly ejewcatered but still of above Averroege men's tality and having maid the most of the oporto unities I kismet) I am writing you, dear mysterre Shame's Voice, to let you no how bed I feeloxerab out it all.

'Vladimir Dixon' (probably Joyce himself), Letter to 'Mister Germ's Choice', in Sylvia Beach ed., *Our Exagmination . . . of Work in Progress*

I am inclined to think that Mr Joyce is riding his method to death.

Ford Madox Ford, *Thus to Revisit*

*Ulysses* is a dogged attempt to cover the universe with mud, an inverted Victorianism, an attempt to make crossness and dirt succeed where sweetness and light failed, a simplification of the human character in the interests of Hell.

E. M. Forster, *Aspects of the Novel*

I never got very much out of *Ulysses*. I think it's an extraordinary book, but so much of it consists of rather lengthy demonstrations of how a novel ought *not* to be written, doesn't it? He does show nearly every conceivable way it should not be written, and then goes on to show how it might be written.

Aldous Huxley, in *Paris Review*

My God, what a clumsy olla putrida James Joyce is! Nothing but old fags and cabbage-stumps of quotations from the Bible and the rest, stewed in the juice of deliberate, journalistic dirty-mindedness.

D. H. Lawrence, Letter to Aldous Huxley, 15 August 1928

The champion Penman.

Percy Wyndham Lewis, *Blasting and Bombardiering*

In retailing the thoughts, half-thoughts, perceptions or inattentions of Bloom and Mrs Bloom, he has sunk a shaft down into the welter of nonsense which lies at the bottom of the mind, and pumping up this stuff (it is an astounding hydraulic feat) presented it as a criticism of life.

Desmond MacCarthy, *Criticism*

Considered as a book . . . *Finnegans Wake* must be pronounced a complete fiasco.

Malcolm Muggeridge, in *Time and Tide*, 20 May 1939

He was very spruce and nervous and chatty. Great rings upon little twitching fingers. Huge concave spectacles which flicked reflections of the lights as he moved his head like a bird, turning it with that definite insistence to the speaker as blind people do who turn to the sound of a voice . . . He told me that a man had taken Oolissays to the Vatican and had hidden it in a prayer-book, and that it had been blessed by the Pope. He was half-amused by this and half-impressed. He saw that I would think it funny, and at the same time he did not think it wholly funny himself. My impression . . . was . . . of a very nervous and refined animal – a gazelle in a drawing-room. His blindness increases that impression. I suppose he is a real person somewhere, but I feel that I have never spent half-an-hour with anyone and been left with an impression of such brittle and vulnerable strangeness.

Harold Nicolson, Letter to Vita Sackville-West, 4 February 1934

*Ulysses* . . . I rather wish I had never read it. It gives me an inferiority complex. When I read a book like that and then come back to my own work, I feel like a eunuch who has taken a course in voice production and can pass himself off fairly well as a bass or a baritone, but if you listen closely you can hear the good old squeak just the same as ever.

George Orwell, Letter to Brenda Salkeld, September 1934

In Ireland they try to make a cat cleanly by rubbing its nose in its own filth. Mr Joyce has tried the same treatment on the human subject. I hope it may prove successful.

George Bernard Shaw, Letter to Sylvia Beach, 11 June 1921

He is a *good* writer. People like him because he is incomprehensible and anybody can understand him. But who came first, Gertrude Stein or James Joyce? Do not forget that my first great book, *Three Lives*, was published in 1908. That was long before *Ulysses*. But Joyce *has* done *something*. His influence, however, is local.

Gertrude Stein (in conversation), in Samuel Putnam, *Paris was our Mistress*

As for Ulysses, I *will not* look at it, *no*, NO.

Lytton Strachey, Letter to James Strachey, 7 May 1922

Experiment? God forbid! Look at the results of experiment in the case of a writer like Joyce. He started off writing very well, then you can watch his going mad with vanity. He ends up a lunatic.

Evelyn Waugh, in *Paris Review*, 1962

Mr Joyce's indecency in *Ulysses* seems to me the conscious and calculated indecency of a desperate man who feels that in order to breathe he must break the windows. At moments, when the window is broken, he is magnificent. But what a waste of energy!

Virginia Woolf, *The Captain's Death Bed*

My own contribution, five and six-pence, is given on condition he [T. S. Eliot] puts publicly to their proper use the first 200 pages of Ulysses. Never have I read such tosh. As for the first 2 Chapters we will let them pass, but the 3rd 4th 5th 6th – merely the scratching of pimples on the body of the bootboy at Claridges. Of course, genius *may* blaze out on page 652 but I have my doubts. And this is what Eliot worships.

Virginia Woolf, Letter to Lytton Strachey (who had written to offer his support for the Eliot Fellowship Fund), 24 August 1922

My considered opinion, after long reflection, is that whilst in many places the effect of *Ulysses* on the reader undoubtedly is somewhat emetic, nowhere does it tend to be an aphrodisiac. *Ulysses* may, therefore, be admitted to the United States.

John M. Woolsey, US District Judge, in his judgment after the prosecution of *Ulysses* for obscenity

A cruel playful mind like a great soft tiger cat.

William Butler Yeats, Letter to Olivia Shakespear, 8 March 1922

*See also* W. H. Auden, Jane Austen, Ford Madox Ford, Aldous Huxley, Leonard Woolf

**'JUNIUS'**, *see under* **SIR PHILIP FRANCIS**; *also*, **EDMUND BURKE**

# 'K'

## KARLOFF, BORIS (WILLIAM HENRY PRATT)

1887–1969 Actor

Like the late Lon Chaney, he reached stardom with thc sole assistance of the make-up man. Any face would have done as well on a big body, and any actor could have produced the short barks and guttural rumbles, the stiff, stuffed sawdust gestures, which was all his parts required of him.

Graham Greene, reviewing *The Black Room* in *Spectator*, 20 September 1935

*See also* Bela Lugosi

## KAUFMAN, GEORGE S.

1889–1961 Playwright, Journalist

Over my dead body.

On himself, Proposed epitaph, in Robert E. Drennan ed., *Wit's End*

When I was born I owed twelve dollars.

*Ibid.*

One day at the Round Table, Aleck Woollcott made a remark which George Kaufman felt derided his Jewish ancestry. After defining his position to Woollcott, G.S.K. got up from his seat and said, 'I am now walking away from this table, out of the dining room, and out of this hotel.' Then surveying the group, he spotted Dorothy Parker – who was of both Jewish and Gentile parentage – and added, 'And I hope that Mrs Parker will walk out with me – half way.'

Robert E. Drennan, *Wit's End*

Kaufman molded me. Kaufman gave me the walk and the talk.

Groucho Marx, in Howard Teichmann, *George S. Kaufman, An Intimate Portrait*

He had great integrity, George did. You never had to watch him when he was dealing.

Harpo Marx, in *ibid.*

## KEAN, CHARLES JOHN

1811–68 Actor

Charles is getting on tonight, he's acting very well. I suppose that is because he is acting with me.

Edmund Kean, attributed, in H. N. Hillebrand, *Edmund Kean*

*See also* W. C. Macready

## KEAN, EDMUND

1787–1833 Actor

Fight for me, I have no resources in myself; mind is gone, and body is hopeless. God knows my heart. I would do, but cannot. Memory, the first of goddesses has forsaken me, and I am left without a hope but from those old resources that the public and myself are tired of. Damn, God damn ambition. The soul leaps, the body falls.

On himself, Letter to the editor of *Star*, March 1830

Mr Kean would seem to apply literally to his art, the lesson of Demosthenes with regard to Oratory – action, action, action. His limbs have no repose or steadiness in scenes of agitated feeling; his hands are kept in unremitting and the most rapid, convulsive, movement; seeking, as it were, a resting place in some part of his upper dress, and occasionally pressed together on the crown of his head. I have marked the process to be the same in his personation of different characters, and I think I may assert that there is no eye which a habit of this kind would not strike as untoward and incongruous. The wild groping of the fingers about the neck and breast reminded me of Dryden's conceit in one of his tragedies, of the fumbling of the tenants of the cemeteries, at the day of resurrection, for their dispersed limbs.

'Betterton', in Philadelphia *National Gazette*, 7 February 1821

He said he always felt his part when acting with a pretty woman, and then only.

Lord Broughton, *Recollections of a Long Life*

Just returned from seeing Kean in Richard. By jove, he is a soul! Life – nature – truth – without exaggeration or diminution. Kemble's Hamlet is perfect; – but Hamlet is not Nature. Richard is a man; and Kean is Richard. Now to my own concerns.

Lord Byron, *Journal*, 19 February 1814

Kean is original; but he copies from himself. His rapid descents from the hyper-tragic to the infra-colloquial though sometimes productive of great effect are often unreasonable. To see him act is like reading Shakespeare by flashes of lightning. I do not think him thorough-bred gentleman enough to play Othello.

Samuel Taylor Coleridge, *Table Talk*

Kean did not simply say the lines but physically performed them, losing himself in a part, and so rediscovering himself; and like the musical virtuosi of the period with their interpolated cadenzas, he opened up spaces between the lines for the silent play of temperament.

Peter Conrad, in *Times Literary Supplement*, 29 August 1975

Novelty will always command notice in London, and Kean's acting, happily, was a novelty on the English stage. His croaking tones – his one-two-three-hop step to the right, and his equally brusque motions to the left – his retching at the back of the stage whenever he wanted to express passion – his dead stops in the middle of sentences – his hirre hurre, hop hop hop! over all passages where sense was to be expressed, took amazingly.

*Edinburgh Magazine*, vol. 16, 1824

We found him, as was usual after the performance of any of his principal parts, stretched on a sofa, retching violently, and throwing up blood. His face was half-washed – one side deadly pale, the other deep copper colour.

Thomas Colley Grattan, *Beaten Paths and Those Who Trod Them*

He presented a mixture of subdued fierceness, unsatisfied triumph, and suppressed dissipation.

*Ibid.*

There is in Mr Kean, an infinite variety of talent, with a certain monotony of genius.

William Hazlitt, 'Mr Kean's Duke Aranza', in *Examiner*, 10 December 1815

He flashed upon the world on the twenty-sixth of January 1814, completely formed and astonishingly new, like a bomb thrown out of the mortar of destiny.

H. N. Hillebrand, *Edmund Kean*

Kean was not only remarkable for the intensity of passionate expression, but for a peculiarity I have never seen so thoroughly realised by another although it is one which belongs to the truth of passion, namely, the expression of *subsiding emotion*. Although fond, far too fond, of abrupt transitions – passing from vehemence to familiarity, and mingling strong lights and shadows with Caravaggio force of unreality – nevertheless his instinct taught him what few actors are taught – that a strong emotion, after discharging itself in one massive current, continues for a time expressing itself in feebler currents.

George Henry Lewes, *On Actors and the Art of Acting*

One of his means of effect – sometimes one of his tricks – was to make long pauses between certain phrases. For instance, on quitting the scene, Sir Edward Mortimer has to say warningly, 'Wilford, remember!' Kean used to pause after 'Wilford,' and during the pause his face underwent a rapid succession of expressions fluently melting into each other, and all tending to one climax or threat; and then the deep tones of 'remember!' came like muttered thunder. Those spectators who were unable to catch these expressions considered the pause a mere trick; and sometimes the pauses were only tricks, but often they were subtle truths.

*Ibid.*

He was a real innovator. But the parts he could play were few. He had no gaiety; he could not laugh; he had no playfulness that was not as the playfulness of a panther showing her claws every moment.

*Ibid.*

Mrs Dimond offers me a place in her box tonight, whence will be seen Massinger's horrible *Sir Giles Overreach*, played by Mr Kean. If he can stretch that hideous character as he does others, quite beyond all the authors meant or wished, it will shock us too much for endurance, though in these days people do require mustard to everything.

Mrs Piozzi (Hester Lynch Thrale), Letter to Sir James Fellowes, 27 December 1816

March 16 . . . Kean about three o'clock in the morning, ordered a hackney coach to his door, took a lighted candle, got in, and rode off. He was not heard of till the Thursday noon when they found him in his room at the theatre fast asleep wrapt up in a large white greatcoat. He then sent for a potence, some ginger etc., and said, 'Send me Lewis or the other woman. I must have a fuck, and then I shall do.' He had it. They let him sleep until about six when they awoke him, dressed him, and he acted but was not very sober. After the play we got him to supper at Sigel's lodgings and got him to a bedroom and locked him up till the morning.

James Winston, Diary, 1825

*See also* William Hazlitt, Sarah Siddons

## KEATON, (JOSEPH FRANK) 'BUSTER'

1895–1966 Actor

Keaton's face ranked almost with Lincoln's as an early American archetype; it was haunting, handsome, almost beautiful, yet it was irreducibly funny; he improved matters by topping it off with a deadly horizontal hat, as flat and thin as a phonograph record. One can never forget Keaton wearing it, standing erect at the prow as his little boat is being launched. The boat goes grandly down the skids and, just as grandly, straight on to the bottom. Keaton never budges. The last you see of him, the water lifts the hat off the stoic head and it floats away.

James Agee, *Agee on Film*, vol. 1

No other comedian could do as much with the deadpan. He used this great, sad, motionless face to suggest various related things: a one-track mind near the track's end of pure insanity: mulish imperturbability under the wildest of circumstances: how dead a human being can get and still be alive: an awe-inspiring sort of patience and power to endure, proper to granite but uncanny in flesh and blood. Everything that he was and did bore out this rigid face and played laughs against it. When he moved his eyes, it was like seeing them move in a statue. His short-legged body was all sudden, machine like angles, governed by a daft aplomb. When he swept a semaphorelike arm to point, you could almost hear the electrical impulse in the signal block. When he ran from a cop his transitions from accelerating walk to easy jog trot to brisk canter to headlong gallop to flogged-piston spring – always floating above this frenzy, the untroubled, untouchable face – were as distinct and as soberly in order as an automatic gearshift.

*Ibid.*

## KEATS, JOHN

1795–1821 Poet

When I have fears that I may cease to be / Before my pen has glean'd my teeming brain, / Before high-piled books, in charactery, / Hold like rich garners the full ripen'd grain; / When I behold, upon the night's starr'd face, / Huge cloudy symbols of a high romance, / And think that I may never live to trace / Their shadows, with the magic hand of chance; / And when I feel, fair creature of an hour, / That I shall never look upon thee more, / Never have relish in the faery power / Of unreflecting love; – then on the shore / Of the wide world I stand alone, and think / Till love and fame to nothingness do sink. /

On himself, *Sonnet*

I never wrote one single Line of Poetry with the least Shadow of public thought.

On himself, Letter to J. H. Reynolds, 9 April 1818

I think I shall be among the English Poets after my death.

On himself, Letter to George and Georgiana Keats, October 1818

I have two luxuries to brood over in my walks, your Loveliness and the hour of my death. O that I could have possession of them both in the same minute.

On himself, Letter to Fanny Brawne, July 1819

Give me books, fruit, french wine and fine weather and a little music out of doors, played by somebody I do not know.

On himself, Letter to Fanny Brawne, 29 August 1819

I feel the flowers growing over me.

On himself, attributed last words

This grave contains all that was mortal of a young English poet, who, on his death bed, in the bitterness of his heart at the malicious power of his enemies, desired these words to be graven on his tombstone, 'Here lies one whose name was writ in water.'

*Epitaph*, on his tombstone in Rome

To exalt into greatness one whose achievement was actually that of an often delightful, if often awkward, decorative poet may have . . . harmful consequences. Any presumption that Keats might in time have become a major artist is cast in doubt by the fact that it is unpromising theories about poetry that derive from defects of character, quite as much as bad influences and the results of illness, which vitiate his existing work.

Kingsley Amis, *What Became of Jane Austen?*

What harm he has done in English Poetry. As Browning is a man with a moderate gift passionately desiring movement and fulness, and obtaining but a confused multitudinousness, so

Keats with a very high gift, is yet also consumed with this desire: and cannot produce the truly living and moving, as his conscience keeps telling him. They will not be patient neither understand that they must begin with an Idea of the world in order not to be prevailed over by the world's multitudinousness: or if they cannot get that, at least with isolated ideas: and all other things shall (perhaps) be added unto them.

Matthew Arnold, Letter to A. H. Clough, 1848–9

And Keats the real / Adonis with the hymeneal / Fresh vernal buds half sunk between / His youthful curls, kissed straight and sheen / In his Rome-grave, by Venus queen. /

Elizabeth Barrett Browning, *A Vision of Poets*

John Keats, who was kill'd off by one critique, / Just as he really promised something great, / If not intelligible, without Greek / Contrived to talk about the Gods of late, / Much as they might have been supposed to speak. / Poor fellow! His was an untoward fate; / 'Tis strange the mind, that very fiery particle, / Should let itself be snuff'd out by an article. /

Lord Byron, *Don Juan*, canto xi

A tadpole of the Lakes.

Lord Byron, Journal, 15 March 1820

Johnny Keats's *piss-a-bed* poetry.

Lord Byron, Letter to John Murray, 12 October 1820

Such writing is a sort of mental masturbation – he is always f--gg--g his *Imagination*. I don't mean he is *indecent*, but viciously soliciting his own ideas into a state, which is neither poetry nor any thing else but a Bedlam vision produced by raw pork and opium.

*Ibid.*, 9 November 1820

'Who killed John Keats?' / 'I', says the Quarterly, / So savage and Tartarly; / ' 'Twas one of my feats.' /

'Who shot the arrow?' / 'The poet-priest Milman / (So ready to kill man), / Or Southey or Barrow.' /

*Ibid.*, 30 July 1821

Almost any young gentleman with a sweet tooth might be expected to write such things. *Isabella* might have been written by a seamstress who had eaten something too rich for supper and slept upon her back.

Jane Welsh Carlyle, to Robert Browning, in William Allingham, Diary

Keats is a miserable creature, hungering after sweets which he can't get; going about saying, 'I am so hungry; I should so like something pleasant!'

Thomas Carlyle, in Wemyss Reid, *Life, Letters, and Friendships of R. M. Milnes*

I began on our friend Keats new Vol – find the same fine flowers spread if I can express myself in the wilderness of poetry – for he launches on the sea without compass – & mounts pegassus without saddle or bridle as usual & if those cursd critics coud be shood out of fashion with their rule & compass & cease from making readers believe a Sonnet cannot be a Sonnet unless it be precisely 14 lines & a long poem as such unless one first sits down to wire-draw out regular argument & then plod after it in a regular manner the same as Taylor cuts out a coat for the carcase – I say then he may push off first rate – but he is a child of nature warm and wild.

John Clare, Letter to James Hessey, 4 July 1820

It is not, we say, that the author has not powers of language, rays of fancy, and gleams of genius – he has all these;

but he is unhappily a disciple of the new school of what has been somewhere called Cockney poetry; which may be defined to consist of the most incongruous ideas in the most uncouth language . . . This author is a copyist of Mr [Leigh] Hunt, but he is more unintelligible, almost as rugged, twice as diffuse, and ten times more tiresome and absurd than his prototype.

J. W. Croker, in *Quarterly Review*, April 1818

Keats has written many beautiful passages, but the general character of his poetry cannot be too much condemned – beyond all other injurious to a taste not yet formed. It is 'sicklied o'er with the very palest cast of thought', & at best resembles one of those beauties who fed upon rose-leaves instead of wholesome flesh, fish, & fowl.

George Darley, Letter to Miss Darley, 9 January 1842

In what other English poet (however superior to him in other respects) are you so *certain* of never opening a page without lighting upon the loveliest imagery and the most eloquent expressions? Name one. Compare any succession of their pages at random, and see if the young poet is not sure to present his stock of beauty; crude it may be, in many instances; too indiscriminate in general; never, perhaps, thoroughly perfect in cultivation; but there it is, exquisite of its kind, and filling envy with despair.

Leigh Hunt, *Imagination and Fancy*

Keats, at a time when the phrase had not yet been invented, practised the theory of art for art's sake. He is the type, not of the poet, but of the artist. He was not a great personality, his work comes to us as a greater thing than his personality. When we read his verse, we think of the verse, not of John Keats.

F. R. Leavis, *Revaluation*

Keats caught cold in training for a genius, and, after a lingering illness, died . . . But death, even the death of the radically presumptuous profligate, is a serious thing; and as we believe that Keats was made presumptuous chiefly by the treacherous puffing of his cockney fellow gossips, and profligate in his poems merely to make them saleable, we regret that he did not live long enough to acquire common sense, and abjure the pestilent and perfidious gang who betrayed his weakness to the grave, and are now panegyrising his memory into contempt.

*Literary Gazette and Journal of Belles Lettres*, Review of Shelley's *Adonais*, 8 December 1821

We venture to make one small prophecy, that his bookseller will not a second time venture £50 upon any thing he can write. It is a better and a wiser thing to be a starved apothecary than a starved poet; so back to the shop Mr John, back to 'plasters, pills, and ointment boxes', &c. But, for Heaven's sake, young Sangrado, be a little more sparing of extenuatives and soporifics in your practice than you have been in your poetry.

J. G. Lockhart, in *Blackwood's Magazine*, August 1818

The genius of the lamented person to whose memory I have dedicated these unworthy verses, was not less delicate and fragile than it was beautiful; and where canker-worms abound, what wonder, if its young flower was blighted in the bud? The savage criticism on his *Endymion*, which appeared in the *Quarterly Review*, produced the most violent effect on his susceptible mind; the agitation thus originated ended in the rupture of a blood-vessel in the lungs; a rapid consumption ensued, and the succeeding acknowledgements from more candid critics, of the true greatness of his powers, were ineffectual to heal the wound thus wantonly inflicted.

Percy Bysshe Shelley, Preface to *Adonais*

I weep for Adonais – he is dead! / O, weep for Adonais! though our tears / Thaw not the frost which binds so dear a head! / And thou, sad Hour, selected from all years / To mourn our loss, rouse thy obscure compeers, / And teach them thine own sorrow, say: 'With me / Died Adonais; till the Future dares / Forget the Past, his fate and fame shall be / An echo and a light unto eternity!' /

P. B. Shelley, *Adonais*

It is in Keats that one observes the beginning of the artistic renaissance of England. Byron was a rebel, and Shelley a dreamer; but in the calmness and clearness of his vision, his self-control, his unerring sense of beauty, and his recognition of a separate realm for the imagination, Keats was the pure and serene artist, the forerunner of the Pre-Raphaelite school.

Oscar Wilde, reported in *New York World*, 1882

His art is happy, but who knows his mind? / I see a schoolboy when I think of him, / With face and nose pressed to a sweet-shop window, / For certainly he sank into his grave / His senses and his heart unsatisfied, / And made – being poor, ailing and ignorant, / Shut out from all the luxury of the world, / The coarse-bred son of a livery-stable keeper – / Luxuriant song. /

William Butler Yeats, *Ego Dominus Tuus*

*See also* Rupert Brooke, Samuel Taylor Coleridge, Gerard Manley Hopkins, Rudyard Kipling, James Wolfe, William Butler Yeats

## KELVIN, LORD, *see under* THOMSON, WILLIAM

## KEMBLE, JOHN PHILIP

1757–1823 Actor

Lo, Kemble comes, the Euclid of the stage; / Who moves in given angles, squares a start, / And blows his Roman beak by rules of art; / Writhes with a grace to agony unknown, / And gallops half an octave in a groan. /

Anon., *The Thespiad*, 1809

The Garrick school was all *rapidity* and *Passion*, while the Kemble school was so full of *paw* and *pause*, that, at first, the performers, thinking their new competitors had either lost their cues, or forgotten their parts, used frequently to prompt them.

Ann Crawford, *circa* 1785, in Frederick Reynolds, *Life and Times of Frederick Reynolds*

Mr Kemble's pauses are I believe, very judicious, though to many they appeared long. The actor must take into the account the tone of the audience; for the rule of acting, in conformity to the rule of speaking, must not contradict the general sense. A player cannot, with safety to himself, affect to appear wiser than his judges.

Thomas Davies, *Dramatic Miscellanies*

The very tone of Mr Kemble's voice has something retrospective in it – it is an echo of the past.

William Hazlitt, 'Mr Kean's Macbeth', in *Champion*, 13 November 1814

He is the very still-life and statuary of the stage; a perfect figure of a man; a petrification of sentiment, that heaves no sigh and sheds no tear; an icicle upon the bust of Tragedy.

William Hazlitt, 'Mr Kemble's Sir Giles Overreach', in *Examiner*, 5 May 1816

In that prodigious prosing paper, the *Times*, which seems to be written as well as printed by a steam engine, Mr

Kemble is compared to the ruin of a magnificent temple, in which the divinity still resides. This is not the case. The temple is unimpaired; but the divinity is sometimes from home.

William Hazlitt, on Kemble as Macbeth, 'Mrs Siddons', in *Examiner*, 16 June 1816

We feel more respect for John Kemble in a plain coat than for Lord Chancellor on the woolsack.

William Hazlitt, 'On Actors and Acting', in *Examiner*, 5 January 1817

I have known him make an eternal groan upon the interjection *Oh*! as if he were determined to show that his misery had not affected his lungs; and to represent an energetical address he has kept so continual a jerking and nodding of the head, that at last, if he represented anything at all, it could be nothing but St Vitus' Dance.

Leigh Hunt, *Critical Essays on the Performers of the London Theatres*, 1807

One night, when John Kemble was performing at some country theatre one of his most favourite parts, he was much interrupted from time to time, by the squalling of a young child in one of the galleries. At length, angered by this rival performance, Kemble walked with solemn step to the front of the stage, and addressing the audience in his most tragic tones, said, 'Ladies and Gentlemen, unless the play is stopped, the child cannot possibly go on.'

Thomas Moore, *Memoirs, Journal and Correspondence*

When Kemble was living at Lausanne, he used to feel rather jealous of Mont Blanc; he disliked to hear people always asking, 'How does Mont Blanc look this morning?'

Samuel Rogers, *Table Talk*

*See also* Edmund Kean

## KEMPENFELT, RICHARD

1718–82 Naval Commander

Toll for the brave! / Brave Kempenfelt is gone; / His last sea-fight is fought, / His work of glory done. /

William Cowper, *Loss of the Royal George*

His sword was in its sheath, / His fingers held the pen, / When Kempenfelt went down / With twice four hundred men. /

*Ibid.*

## KENNEDY, JOHN FITZGERALD

1917–63 Thirty-Fifth United States President

I guess he [Harry S. Truman] will apologize for calling me an S.O.B. and I will apologize for being one.

On himself, in Victor Lasky, *J.F.K.: The Man and the Myth*

It has recently been observed that whether I serve one or two terms in the Presidency, I will find myself at the end of that period at what might be called an awkward age – too old to begin a new career and too young to write my memoirs.

On himself, in Leon A. Harris, *The Fine Art of Political Wit*

An idealist without illusions.

On himself, in Arthur M. Schlesinger Jr, *A Thousand Days, John F. Kennedy in the White House*

It's really quite a Roman administration – great dinners, great tours, great redecoration. Kennedy is undoubtedly talented, but ever since he was a tiny boy he's had one idea – succeeding. His speaking style is pseudo-Roman: 'Ask not what your country can do for you...' Why not say, 'Don't ask . . .'? 'Ask not . . .' is the style of a man playing the role of being President, not of a man being President.

Herb Gold, in *New York Post*, 1 June 1962

There is something very eighteenth century about this young man. He is always on his toes during our discussion. But in the evening there will be music and wine and pretty women.

Harold Macmillan, in *New York Journal-American*, 21 January 1962

[Kennedy had] the wisdom of a man who senses death within him and gambles that he can cure it by risking his life.

Norman Mailer, in Arthur M. Schlesinger Jr, *A Thousand Days, John F. Kennedy in the White House*

There is a lot of he-coon ingrained in the hide of the new President. He strikes me as practically cold all the way, with a hard blue eye on Valhalla.

Robert Ruark, *New York World Telegram and Sun*, 21 December 1960

It is said the President is willing to laugh at himself. That is fine. But when is he going to extend that privilege to us?

Mort Sahl, in Victor Lasky, *J.F.K.: The Man and the Myth*

. . . a skeptical mind, a laconic tongue, enormous personal charm, an agreeable disdain for the rituals of Massachusetts politics and a detachment from the niceties of American liberalism.

Arthur M. Schlesinger Jr, *A Thousand Days, John F. Kennedy in the White House*

. . . perhaps the truth is that in some ways John Fitzgerald Kennedy died just in time. He died in time to be remembered as he would like to be remembered, as ever-young, still victorious, struck down undefeated, with almost all the potentates and rulers of mankind, friend and foe, come to mourn at his bier. For somehow one has the feeling that in the tangled dramaturgy of events, this sudden assassination was for the author the only satisfactory way out. The Kennedy Administration was approaching an impasse, certainly at home, quite possibly abroad, from which there seemed no escape.

I. F. Stone, 'We All Had A Finger On That Trigger', in Neil Middleton ed., *The Best of I. F. Stone*

The liberals like his rhetoric and the conservatives like his inaction.

Norman Thomas, in Murray B. Seidler, *Norman Thomas, Respectable Rebel*

*See also* Robert F. Kennedy, Adlai Stevenson

## KENNEDY, ROBERT FRANCIS

1925–68 Politician

I was the seventh of nine children. And when you come from that far down, you have to struggle to survive.

On himself, in B. G. Clinch, *The Kennedy Neurosis*

It was impossible to watch Robert Kennedy among the mobs in the streets in 1968, without realising that most of the people who surged around him would not have been in the least surprised if he had walked upon the waters.

Henry Fairlie, *The Kennedy Promise, The Politics of Expectation*

That was the Kennedy way. You bit off more than you could chew, and then you chewed it.

Gerald Gardner, *Robert Kennedy in New York*

There were several qualities which set him apart from others in office. The first was total confidence in his relationship with the President. The second was an almost absolute insistence on being well and honestly briefed. The third was a capacity, indeed an instinct, to see world events not so much in terms of a great global chess game, but in human terms. As such he retained his commonsense, it was at least as strong as his ideology (when others were talking about a surgical air strike against Cuba during the missile crisis, he said very simply he did not want his brother to be Tojo of the 1960's). Out of all of this came the final characteristic, the capacity to grow, change and to admit error.

David Halberstam, *The Best and the Brightest*

. . . the highest-ranking withdrawn adolescent since Alexander Hamilton in 1794.

Murray Kempton, in 'Bobby: To Be or Not to Be', in *Newsweek*, 29 January 1968

I see Jack in older years as the nice rosy-faced old Irishman with the clay pipe in his mouth, a rather nice broth of a boy. Not Bobby. Bobby could have been a revolutionary priest.

Alice Roosevelt Longworth, in George Plimpton ed., *Interviews by Jean Stein, American Journey: The Life and Times of Robert Kennedy*

His death seemed like the death of one's own adolescence. It's partly his character and something athletic about him, which is typical of school boys; he's very much sort of Massachusetts Eastern shore, he's almost the Eastern Seaboard boy.

Robert Lowell, in *ibid.*

. . . he was fundamentally a hack, but he could be awed by the radicals.

Robert Scheer, in *ibid.*

His obvious characteristics are energy, vindictiveness, and simple mindedness about human motives which may yet bring him down. To Bobby the world is black or white. Them and Us. He has none of his brother's human ease or charity.

Gore Vidal, March 1963, in Margaret Laing, *Robert Kennedy*

## KENT, WILLIAM

1686–1748 Architect

William Kent was one of those generally accomplished persons who can do everything up to a certain point, and nothing well.

Sir Reginald Blomfield, *A History of Renaissance Architecture in England 1500–1800*

He was not a thinker; he was only a second-rate artist with a well-developed sense of decoration.

J. Summerson, *Architecture in Britain 1530–1830*

Mahomet imagined an Elysium, but Kent created many.

Horace Walpole, *Anecdotes of Painters in England*

Kent leaped the fence, and saw that all Nature was a garden.

Horace Walpole, *On Modern Gardening*

Mr Kent's passion, clumps – that is, sticking a dozen trees here and there till a lawn looks like a ten of spades.

Horace Walpole, Letter to Sir Horace Mann, 20 June 1743

*See also* Robert Adam, John Vanbrugh

## KERN, JEROME DAVID

1885–1945 Composer

I am trying to do something for the future of American music, which today has no class whatsoever and is mere barbaric mouthing.

On himself, Letter to *New York Times*, 1920

Who is this Jerome Kern whose music towers in an Eiffel way above the average primitive hurdy-gurdy accompaniment of the present-day musical comedy?

Alan Dale, in David Ewen, *Great Men of America's Popular Song*

A small, amicable, quiet man, with tremendous stores of nervous energy, Kern wore horn-rimmed glasses, smoked constantly, poured forth hundreds of facile tunes with a radio blaring in his ears, and modestly called himself a dull fellow with little talent and lots of luck.

Wesley Towner, in Max Wilk, *They're Playing Our Song*

## KEROUAC, (JEAN LOUIS) JACK

1922–69 Author

My work comprises one vast book like Proust's *Remembrance of Things Past*, except that my remembrances are written on the run instead of afterwards in a sickbed.

On himself, in Bernard Duffey, 'Jack Kerouac', in Joseph J. Waldemeir ed., *Recent American Fiction*

As the man who'd thought up the term 'beat generation', Kerouac insisted that he alone understood it. It meant 'beatific', trying to be in a state of beatitude, like St Francis, trying to love all life, being utterly sincere and kind and cultivating 'joy of heart'.

Ann Charters, *Kerouac*

Kerouac . . . tried LSD only once. This was with Timothy Leary at Harvard in January 1961. After this experience with LSD Kerouac was sure it had been introduced into America by the Russians as part of a plot to weaken the country.

*Ibid.*

. . . American lonely Prose Trumpeter of drunken Buddha Sacred Heart. /

Allen Ginsberg, in *ibid.*

*See also* Joseph McCarthy

## KEROUAILLE, LOUISE RENÉE DE, DUCHESS OF PORTSMOUTH AND AUBIGNY

1649–1734 Mistress to Charles II

Portsmouth, that pocky bitch / A damn'd Papistical drab / An ugly deform'd witch / Eaten up with the mange and scab /

This French hag's pocky bum / So powerful is of late / Although its both blind and dumb / It rules both Church and State. /

Anon., *A Satire*, 1680

Following his Majestie this morning through the Gallerie, I went (with the few who attended him) into the Dutchesse of Portsmouth's dressing roome, within her bed-chamber, where she was in her morning loose garment, her maides combing her, newly out of her bed: His Majestie and the Gallants standing about her: but that which ingag'd my curiositie, was the rich and splendid furniture of this woman's Appartment, now twice or thrice, puld down and rebuilt, to satisfie her prodigal & expensive pleasures, whilst her Majestie dos not exceede, some gentlemens ladies furniture and accomodation . . . Lord what contentment can there be in the riches and splendor of this world, purchas'd with vice and dishonor.

John Evelyn, Diary, 4 October 1683

The last especially was quite out of the Definition of an ordinary Mistress: the Causes and the Manner of her first being introduced were very different. A very peculiar Distinction was spoken of, some extraordinary Solemnities that might Dignify, though not sanctify, her function. Her Chamber was the true Cabinet Council. The King did always by his Councils, as he did sometimes by his Meals; he sat down out of form, with the *Queen*, but he supped *below stairs.*

George Savile, Marquis of Halifax, *A Character of King Charles the Second*

*See also* Nell Gwyn, Barbara Villiers

## KEYNES, JOHN MAYNARD, BARON

1883–1946 Economist

I work for a Government I despise for ends I think criminal.

On himself at the Treasury, Letter to Duncan Grant, December 1917

I was a voice crying in the wilderness and had, therefore, to cry loudly.

On himself, on Reparations, Letter to Professor Calvin Hoover, 6 December 1945

Keynes is the Treasury man in Paris – clear headed, self confident, with an unerring memory and unsurpassable digestion. But while he is one of the most influential men behind the scenes . . . he looks at large political problems too much from the aspect of currency and exchange; . . . in large affairs his advice is often based upon premises which may be correct in technique, but utterly misleading in practice . . . He is a wonderful fellow, but has passed his life in cloister and has had no experience in handling men or in assessing their temperaments.

Lord Crawford and Balcarres, Diary, 9 April 1919

He went about the world carrying with him everywhere a feeling of the bishop *in partibus.* True salvation was elsewhere, among the faithful at Cambridge. When he concerned himself with politics and economics he left his soul at home. This is the reason for a certain hard, glittering, inhuman quality in most of his writing.

Bertrand Russell, *Autobiography*

Keynes's intellect was the sharpest and clearest that I have ever known. When I argued with him, I felt that I took my life in my hands, and I seldom emerged without feeling something of a fool. I was sometimes inclined to feel that so much cleverness must be incompatible with depth, but I do not think this feeling was justified.

*Ibid.*

. . . it is one of his queer characteristics that one often wants, one cannot tell why, to make a malicious attack on him, and that, when the time comes, one refrains, one cannot tell why. His sense of values, and indeed all his feelings, offer the spectacle of a complete paradox. He is a hedonist and a follower of [G. E.] Moore; he is lascivious without lust; he is an Apostle without tears.

Lytton Strachey, in Milo Keynes ed., *Essays on John Maynard Keynes*

*See also* Sir Thomas Gresham, Augustus John

## KIDD, WILLIAM

*circa* 1645–1701 Pirate

This person in the gaudy clothes / Is worthy Captain Kidd / They say he never buried gold / *I think, perhaps, he did.* / They say it's all a story that / His favorite little song / Was 'Make these lubbers walk the plank!' / *I think, perhaps, they're wrong.* /

Stephen Vincent Benét, *Captain Kidd*

## KING, EDWARD

1612–37 Poet

For Lycidas is dead, dead ere his prime, / Young Lycidas, and hath not left his peer: / Who would not sing for Lycidas? he well knew / Himself to sing, and build the lofty rhyme. / He must not flote upon his wat'ry bier / Unwept, and welter to the parching wind, / Without the meed of some melodious tear. /

John Milton, *Lycidas*

## KING, MARTIN LUTHER, JR

1929–68 Civil Rights Advocate, Clergyman

I want to be the white man's brother, not his brother-in-law.

On himself, in *New York Journal-American*, 10 September 1962

Yes, if you want to say that I was a drum major, say that I was a drum major for justice; say that I was a drum major for peace; I was a drum major for righteousness. And all of the other shallow things will not matter.

On himself, suggesting his own eulogy in a sermon delivered 4 February 1968, in Coretta Scott King, *My Life with Martin Luther King, Jr*

Conventional commentators these days like to speak of King's nobility, and the purity of his humanism, and they sigh that the world is not ready for him. But it is more accurate to say that King is not ready for the world.

Andrew Kopkind, in David L. Lewis, *Martin Luther King*

He got the [Nobel] peace prize, we got the problem. I don't want the white man giving me medals. If I'm following a general, and he's leading me into battle, and the enemy tends to give him rewards, or awards, I get suspicious of him. Especially if he gets a peace award before the war is over.

Malcolm X, in Peter Goldman, *The Death and Life of Malcolm X*

In a movement in which respect is accorded in direct proportion to the number of times one has been arrested, King appears to keep the number of times he goes to jail to a minimum. In a movement in which successful leaders are those who share in the hardships of their followers, in the risks they take, in the beatings they receive, in the length of time they spend in jail, King tends to leave prison for other important engagements.

August Meier, 'The Conservative Militant', in C. Eric Lincoln ed., *Martin Luther King, Jr: A Profile*

He stood in that line of saints which goes back from Gandhi to Jesus; his violent end, like theirs, reflects the hostility of mankind to those who annoy it by trying hard to pull it one more painful step farther up the ladder from ape to angel.

I. F. Stone, 'The Fire Has Only Just Begun', in Neil Middleton ed., *The Best of I. F. Stone*

He was a Negro, but with / a soul as pure as the white snow. / He was killed by whites / with black souls. / When I received this news / that same bullet entered me. / That bullet killed him, / but by that bullet I was reborn, / and I was reborn a Negro. /

Yevgeny Yevtushenko, upon hearing of King's assassination, translated in William Robert Miller, *Martin Luther King, Jr*

## KINGSLEY, CHARLES

1819–75 Author, Cleric

Hast thou read Kingsley's 'Westward-ho!'? . . . a fine foe-exterminating book of Elizabeth's time, done and written in the religious spirit of Joshua and David. For Spaniards read Russians, and it is truly a tract for the times, *selon toi*.

Caroline Fox, Letter to Elizabeth Carne, June 1855

He has attempted (as I may call it) to *poison the wells*.

Cardinal Newman, *Apologia Pro Vita Sua*

Froude informs the Scottish youth / That parsons do not care for truth. / The Reverend Canon Kingsley cries / History is a pack of lies. / What cause for judgements so malign? / A brief reflection solves the mystery – / Froude believes Kingsley a divine, / And Kingsley goes to Froude for history. /

Bishop William Stubbs, Letter to J. R. Green, 17 December 1871

*See also* J. A. Froude, Shakespeare

## KIPLING, (JOSEPH) RUDYARD

1865–1936 Author

K is for Kipling / A builder of rhymes, / Who 'lest we forget' / All our national crimes / Sets them forth at great length / In large type in *The Times*. /

Anon., Alphabet of Authors, *circa* 1902

There are some poets, Kipling for example, whose relation to language reminds one of a drill sergeant: the words are taught to wash behind their ears, stand properly at attention and execute complicated maneuvers, but at the cost of never being allowed to think for themselves. There are others, Swinburne for example, who remind one more of Svengali: under their hypnotic suggestion, an extraordinary performance is put on, not by raw recruits, but by feeble-minded schoolchildren.

W. H. Auden, *The Dyer's Hand*

What is it then, that makes Kipling so extraordinary? Is it not that while virtually every other European writer since the fall of the Roman Empire has felt that the dangers threatening civilization came from *inside* that civilization (or from inside the individual consciousness), Kipling is obsessed by a sense of dangers threatening from *outside*?

W. H. Auden, *Forewords and Afterwords*

Wot! haven't you heard of Kiplingson? whose name and fame have spread / As far as the Flag of England waves, and the Tory prints are read? /

I was raised in the lap of Jingo, sir, till I grew to the height of a man, / And a wonderful Literary Gent, I emerged upon Hindostan! /

I sounded the praise of the Empire, sir, I pitch'd out piping hot / The new old stories of British bounce (see Lever and Michael Scott); /

And rapid as light my glory spread, till thro' Cockaigne it flew, / And I grew the joy of the Cockney cliques, and the pet of the Jingo Jew! /

Robert Buchanan, *The Ballad of Kiplingson*

Mr Rudyard Kipling has asked in a celebrated epigram what they can know of England who only England know. It is a far deeper and sharper question to ask: 'What can they know of England who know only the world?' . . . Mr Kipling does certainly know the world; he is a man of the world, with all the narrowness that belongs to those imprisoned in that planet. He knows England as an intelligent English gentleman knows Venice.

G. K. Chesterton, *Heretics*

Some of his work is of impeccable form and because of that little thing he shall sojourn in Hell only a very short while.

Joseph Conrad, Letter to R. B. Cunningham Graham, 1897

We, the mere novelists of nowadays, are nearly all of us woman-ridden . . . But Kipling's women are – just women

. . . Kipling puts women in their place, whether the kitchen or the drawing-room. And because he does so, the woman who appreciates any but his stories of children is a rarity, to be either married or made a pal of, according to your temperament, as soon as found.

Gilbert Frankau, in *London Magazine*, August 1928

KIPLING, RUDYARD, Poet Laureate and Recruiting Sergeant, was born all over the world, some eighteen years ago. After a lurid infancy at Westward Ho! in the company of Stalky & Co., he emigrated to India at the age of six and swallowed it whole. In the following year the British Empire was placed in his charge, and it is still there. A misgiving that England may have gone too far struck him in 1897, he wrote 'The Recessional', but there are signs that he has since forgotten it.

C. L. Graves and E. V. Lucas, *Lives of the 'Lustrious*

I commented on the fact that he had wide fame and was known as 'the great Mr Kipling', which should be a consolation to him. He thrust the idea aside with a gesture of disgust. 'What is it worth – what *is* it all worth?' he answered. Moreover he went on to show that anything which any of us did *well* was no credit to us: that it came from somewhere else: 'We are only telephone wires.'

Rider Haggard, Journal, 22 May 1918

In his earliest time I thought he perhaps contained the seeds of an English Balzac; but I have given that up in proportion as he has come down steadily from the simple in subject to the more simple – from the Anglo-Indians to the natives, from the natives to the Tommies, from the Tommies to the quadrupeds, from the quadrupeds to the fish, and from the fish to the engines and screws.

Henry James, Letter to Grace Norton, 25 December 1897

To put the thing in its shortest possible way, Kipling is first and foremost the poet of work. It is really remarkable how poetry and fiction before his time had avoided this subject. They had dealt almost exclusively with men in their 'private hours' – with love-affairs, crimes, sport, illness and changes of fortune . . . A whole range of strong sentiments and emotions – for many men, the strongest of all – went with them. For, as Pepys once noted with surprise, there is a great pleasure in talking of business. It was Kipling who first reclaimed for literature this enormous territory.

C. S. Lewis, *Literature and Life*

This pickle has a peculiar mordant quality which distinguishes it from all others. The chief ingredient is unwashed English, chopped, broken, and bruised with a brazen instrument. Then work in chips and fragments of cynicism, 'B.V.' [James Thomson]'s poems, the seven cardinal sins, the *Soldier's Pocket Book*, the *Civil Service Regulations*, Simla manners, profanity, an Ekka pony, the Southern Cross, and genius. Spice with a Tipperary brogue.

E. V. Lucas, 'Literary Recipe for Kipling Chutnee', in *Privateer*, 1892

Mr Kipling's world is a barrack full of oaths and clatter of sabres; but his language is copious, rich, sonorous. One is tempted to say that none since the Elizabethans has written so copiously. Others have written more beautifully, but no one that I can call to mind at this moment has written so copiously. Shelley and Wordsworth, Landor and Pater, wrote with part of the language; but who else, except

Whitman, has written with the whole language since the Elizabethans?

George Moore, *Avowals*

The huge paradox of Kipling is never more apparent than when you read the reviews of a new book of his. This extraordinary writer, whom we are accustomed to see billed as speaking to the world's hugest fiction audience, is really the subtlest of highbrows. His finest things would bore the slackwit reader just as Shakespeare does . . . He writes a story ostensibly about big howitzers, and it is really a lover's tribute to Jane Austen. He writes a story apparently about wireless, and it means nothing save to a student of Keats.

Christopher Morley, in *Saturday Review of Literature*, 2 October 1926

Rudyard the dud yard, / Rudyard the false measure, / Told 'em that glory / Ain't always a pleasure, / But said it wuz glorious nevertheless / To lick the boots of the bloke / That makes the worst mess. /

Ezra Pound, *Poems of Alfred Venison* (*Alf's Fourth Bit*)

Kipling has done more than any other since Disraeli to show the world that the British race is sound at core and that rust or dry-rot are strangers to it.

Cecil Rhodes, in J. G. McDonald, *Rhodes: A Life*

He is a stranger to me but he is a most remarkable man – and I am the other one. Between us we cover all knowledge; he knows all that can be known and I know the rest.

Mark Twain, *Autobiography*

. . . You're *our* partic'lar author, you're our patron an' our friend, / You're the poet of the cuss-word and the swear, / You're the poet of the people where the red-mapped lands extend. /

Edgar Wallace, welcoming Kipling to Cape Town, January 1898

As one turns over the pages of his *Plain Tales from the Hills*, one feels as if one were seated under a palm-tree reading life by superb flashes of vulgarity. The bright colours of the bazaars dazzle one's eyes. The jaded commonplace Anglo-Indians are in exquisite incongruity with their surroundings. The mere lack of style in the storyteller gives an odd journalistic realism to what he tells us. From the point of view of literature Mr Kipling is a man of talent who drops his aspirates. From the point of view of life he is a reporter who knows vulgarity better than anyone has ever known it. Dickens knew its clothes. Mr Kipling knows its essence. He is our best authority on the second-rate. He terrifies us by his truth, and makes his sordid subject matter marvellous by the brilliancy of its setting.

Oscar Wilde, 'The Critic as Artist', in *Nineteenth Century*, 1890

*See also* John Galsworthy, Rider Haggard, H. G. Wells

## KITCHENER, HORATIO HERBERT, EARL OF KHARTOUM AND BROOME

1850–1916 Soldier

He is to Lord Curzon what the broadsword is to the rapier.

Anon. comment in a Simla newspaper, 1908

The great armies that he called into being are his living monument, and no nobler monument has been raised to man.

Obituary in *The Times*, 1916

The great poster.

Margot, Lady Asquith, in A. J. P. Taylor, *English History 1914–1945*

I don't think Ld Kitchener is a model of good taste.

Alice Balfour, Diary, 6 June 1899

Lord K. is playing hell with its lid off at the War Office – What the papers call 'standing no nonsense' but which often means 'listening to no sense'.
Lady Jean Hamilton, Diary, 12 August 1914

He is fearfully wrong-headed sometimes, but he is always *homme sérieux* practising himself, and enforcing upon others, the highest standard of *workmanlike* strenuousness, indefatigable industry and iron perseverance. Great qualities these in a wishy-washy world.
Lord Milner, Letter to Lady Edward Cecil, January 1902

On 5 June the *Hampshire*, with Kitchener on board, struck a mine within two hours of leaving Scapa Flow. Kitchener and most of the crew were drowned. So perished the only British military idol of the first World war. The next morning [Lord] Northcliffe burst into his sister's drawing-room with the words: 'Providence is on the side of the British Empire after all.'
A. J. P. Taylor, *English History 1914–1945*

*See also* Theodore Roosevelt

## KNELLER, SIR GODFREY (GOTTFRIED KNILLER)

1646–1723 Painter

. . . where true Design, / Postures unforc'd, and lively Colours joyn, / Likeness is ever there; but still the best, / Like proper Thoughts in lofty Language drest, / Where Light, to shades descending, plays, not strives, / Dyes by degrees, and by degrees revives. / Of various Parts a perfect whole is wrought; / Thy Pictures think, and we Divine their Thought. /
John Dryden, *To Sir Godfrey Kneller*

That man of wigs and drapery.
John Fisher, Letter to John Constable, 9 May 1823

Kneller, by Heav'n and not a Master taught, / Whose Art was Nature, and whose Pictures thought; / Now for two ages having snatch'd from fate / Whate'er was Beauteous, or Whate'er was Great, / Lies crown'd with Princes Honours, Poets Lays, / Due to his Merit, and brave Thirst of Praise. / Living, great Nature fear'd he might outvie / Her works; and dying, fears herself may die. /
Alexander Pope, *Epitaph on Sir Godfrey Kneller*, in Westminster Abbey

As I was sitting by Sir Godfrey Kneller one day, whilst he was drawing a picture, he stopped and said, 'I can't do so well as I should do, unless you flatter me a little, pray flatter me, Mr Pope! you know I love to be flattered.'
Alexander Pope, in Joseph Spence, *Anecdotes*

The fool has got a country house near Hampton Court, and is so busy about fitting it up (to receive nobody), that there is no getting him to work.
Sir John Vanbrugh, Letter to J. Tonson, 15 June 1703

When Kneller in his last hours was dreading the approach of death Pope tried to comfort him by saying that as he had been a good man in this world the Almighty would be sure to look after him in the next, but the painter was too much attached to his country house and its material comforts to be interested in the possible joys of Heaven. 'Ah, my good friend, Mr Pope,' he cried, 'I wish God would allow me to stay at Whitton.'
William T. Whitley, *Artists and their Friends in England*

*See also* Alexander Pope

## KNOX, JOHN

1505–72 Scottish Reformer

One is tempted almost to say that there was more of Jesus in St Theresa's little finger than in John Knox's whole body.

Matthew Arnold, *Literature and Dogma*

I saw him everie day of his doctrine go hulie and fear, with a furring of martriks about his neck, a staff in an hand, and guid godlie Robert Ballanden, his servand, halding upe the uther oxtar, from the Abbay to the paroche kirk; and be the said Richart and another servant, lifted upe to the pulpit, whar he behivit to lean at his first entrie; bot or he haid done with his sermont, he was sa active and vigorous that he was lyk to ding that pulpit in blads, and fly out of it.

James Melvill, *The Lyff of John Knox*

Whose love is given over-well / Shall look on Helen's face in hell, / Whilst they whose love is thin and wise / May view John Knox in Paradise. /

Dorothy Parker, in *The Faber Book of Comic Verse*

A man of a fearless heart and a fluent eloquence; violent, indeed, and sometimes coarse, but the better fitted to obtain influence in a coarse and turbulent age, – capable at once of reasoning with the wiser nobility, and inspiring with his own spirit and zeal the fierce populace. Toleration, and that species of candour which makes allowance for the prejudices of birth or situation, were unknown to his uncompromising mind; and this deficiency made him the more fit to play the distinguished part to which he was called.

Sir Walter Scott, *History of Scotland*

The lantern of his analysis did not always shine with a very serviceable light; but he had the virtue, at least, to carry it into many places of fictitious holiness, and was not abashed by the tinsel divinity that hedged kings and queens from his contemporaries.

Robert Louis Stevenson, *John Knox*

## KYD, THOMAS

1558–94 Dramatist

Sporting Kyd, or Marlowe's mighty line.

Ben Jonson, *To the Memory of Shakespeare*

Murderous topics were always congenial to the dramatist.

Sir Sidney Lee, in *Dictionary of National Biography*

# 'L'

## LADD, ALAN WALBRIDGE

1913–64 Actor

Hard, bitter and occasionally charming, he is after all a small boy's idea of a tough.

Raymond Chandler, *Raymond Chandler Speaking*

In the hierarchy of tough-guy stars, Alan Ladd holds an honoured name: through 50 or so formula pictures he strolled, stone-faced, in roles which fitted him as snugly as the iron strapped to his side. No one ever pretended that he could act.

David Shipman, *The Great Movie Stars*

## LA GUARDIA, FIORELLO HENRY

1882–1947 Politician

I invented the low blow.

On himself, in Arthur Mann, *La Guardia Comes to Power*

Seven times he's won elections, / Seven times he's reached the top. / He is proud he's an American / And he's proud he is a wop! / Just remember Chris Columbus . . . / Now join in the chorus all . . . / We are following La Guardia / To his chair in City Hall. /

Anon. campaign song

They have counted nine over Fiorello upon occasion but never ten.

Heywood Broun, in Arthur Mann, *La Guardia: A Fighter Against His Times*

. . . come up and see me sometime, and bring La Guardia.

Mae West, after La Guardia had described a show of hers as indecent, in *ibid.*

## LAMB, LADY CAROLINE

1785–1828 Novelist

. . . Lady Caroline Lamb defined truth to be what one thinks at the moment.

Lord Broughton, *Recollections of a Long Life*, December 1815

I have much to do & little time to do it in – certainly not an instant to spare to a person for whom the iron (to use her metaphor) retains all the *heat* but none of the flexibility . . . I know not whom I may love but to the latest hour of my life I shall hate that woman. – *Now* you know my sentiments – they will be the same on my death-bed. – To her I do not express this because I have no desire to make her uncomfortable – but such is the state of my mind towards her for reasons I shall not refer to & I beg to be spared from meeting her until we may be chained together in Dante's Inferno.

Lord Byron, Letter to Lady Melbourne, 5 April 1813

A word to you of Lady Caroline Lamb – I speak from experience – *keep clear of her* – (I do not mean as a woman – that is all fair) she is a villainous intriguante – in every sense of the word – mad & malignant – capable of all & every mischief – above all – guard your *connections* from her society – with all her apparent absurdity there is an indefatigable & active spirit of meanness & destruction about her – which delights & often succeeds in inflicting misery.

Lord Byron, Letter to James Wedderburn Webster, 4 September 1815

I was more sinned against than sinning.

Lord Byron, in Lady Blessington, *Conversations of Lord Byron*

## LAMB, CHARLES

1775–1834 Essayist

I love to lose myself in other men's minds. When I am not walking, I am reading; I cannot sit and think. Books think for me.

On himself, *Last Essays of Elia, Detached Thoughts on Books and Reading*

My attachments are all local, purely local. I have no passion . . . to groves and vallies. The rooms where I was born, the furniture which has been before my eyes all my life, a book case which has followed me about . . . wherever I have moved – old chairs, old tables, streets, squares, where I have sunned myself, my old school, – these are my mistresses. Have I not enough, without your mountains?

On himself, Letter to William Wordsworth, 30 January 1801

Anything awful makes me laugh. I misbehaved once at a funeral.

On himself, Letter to Robert Southey, 1815

How I like to be liked, and what I do to be liked!

On himself, Letter to Dorothy Wordsworth, 8 January 1821

Charles Lamb . . . now a Gentleman at large, can remember few specialities in his life worth noting except that he once caught a swallow flying (*teste sua manu*); below the middle stature, cast of face slightly Jewish, with no Judaic tinge in his complexional religion; stammers abominably and is therefore more apt to discharge his occasional conversation in a quaint aphorism or a poor quibble than in set and edifying speeches; has consequently been libelled as a person always aiming at wit, which, as he told a dull fellow that charged him with it, is at least as good as aiming at dulness; a small eater but not drinker; confesses a partiality for the production of the juniper berry, was a fierce smoker of Tobacco, but may be resembled to a volcano burnt out, emitting only now and then a casual puff.

On himself, *Autobiographical Sketch*, 10 April 1827

May my last breath be drawn through a pipe and exhaled in a pun.

On himself, in A. K. Adams, *The Home Book of Humorous Quotations*

In everything that relates to science, I am a whole encyclopedia behind the rest of the world.

On himself, in *ibid.*

His sayings are generally like women's letters; all the pith is in the postscript.

William Hazlitt, *Boswell Redivivus*

There is a spirit in Mr Lamb's productions, which is in itself so *anti-critical*, and tends so much to reconcile us to all that is in the world, that the effect is almost neutralizing to everything but complacency and a queer admiration – his very criticisms chiefly tend to overthrow the critical spirit.

Leigh Hunt, in *Examiner*, March 1819

And Lamb, the frolic and the gentle, / Has vanished from his lonely hearth. /

William Wordsworth, *Extempore Effusion upon the Death of James Hogg*

*See also* R. W. Elliston, Robert Louis Stevenson

## LAMB, WILLIAM, *see under* MELBOURNE, VISCOUNT

## LAMBERT, JOHN

1619–83 Soldier

My Lord did seem to wonder much why Lambert was so willing to be put into the Toure, and thinks he hath some design in it; but I think that he is so poor that he cannot use his liberty for debts if he were at liberty – and so it is as good and better for him to be there then anywhere else.

Samuel Pepys, Diary, 7 March 1660

## LANDOR, WALTER SAVAGE

1775–1864 Poet

What is it that Mr Landor wants, to make him a poet? His powers are certainly very considerable, but he seems to be totally deficient in that modifying faculty, which compresses several units into one whole . . . Hence his poems, taken as wholes, are unintelligible; you have eminences excessively bright, and all the ground around and in between them in darkness. Besides which, he has never learned, with all his energy, how to write simple and lucid English.

Samuel Taylor Coleridge, *Table Talk*, 1 January 1834

Landor . . . is very eighteenth century. He differs from Wordsworth in having no new life to offer. What he offers, in prose as well as in verse, is literature. If his phrasing is 'clean-cut', it is not because it defines and conveys sharply any strongly felt significance; to say 'clean cut' is merely to intimate that he affects a 'lapidary' manner. He cultivates this for its own sake, choosing his themes as occasions for exercising it.

F. R. Leavis, *Revaluation*

Landor has not been a popular author. His collected works are nevertheless the best substitute for a University education that can be offered to any young man in a hurry.

Ezra Pound, in *Future*, November 1917

*See also* Samuel Johnson, Rudyard Kipling

## LANSBURY, GEORGE

1859–1940 Newspaperman, Labour Politician

. . . not a very clear head, but with a heart that reaches beyond the stars.

Harold Laski, Letter to Maurice Firuski, August 1920

The most lovable figure in modern politics.

A. J. P. Taylor, *English History 1914–1945*

## LANSDOWNE, MARQUIS OF, *see under* SHELBURNE, LORD

## LARDNER, RINGGOLD WILMER

1885–1933 Author, Journalist

He [William Howard Taft] looked at me as if I was a side dish he hadn't ordered.

On himself, in A. K. Adams, *The Home Book of Humorous Quotations*

Jupiter on tiptoes.

Ernest Hemingway, in Carlos Baker, *Ernest Hemingway, A Life Story*

Mr Lardner does not waste a moment when he writes in thinking whether he is using American slang or Shakespeare's English; whether he is remembering Fielding or forgetting Fielding; whether he is proud of being American or ashamed of not being Japanese; all his mind is on his story. Hence, incidentally, he writes the best prose that has come our way.

Virginia Woolf, in Walton R. Patrick, *Ring Lardner*

## LASKI, HAROLD JOSEPH

1893–1950 Political Author

Yes, my friend, we are both Marxists, you in your way, I in Marx's.

On himself, reply to an interrupter

at a public meeting, in Kingsley Martin, *Harold Laski*

I have the feeling that I am already a ghost in a play that is over.

On himself, Letter to Felix Frankfurter, September 1947

Your chairman today is an example of that dangerous species who, so far as my knowledge goes, is in our movement rarely trusted and never praised – the species whose professional work is criticism and thought . . . I represent something a little different from the past, British by birth, middle class by origin, Jewish by inheritance – symbolic of the vital fact that the Labour party knows no boundaries save those which are defined by faith in its principles and policies.

On himself, as acting chairman of the 1944 Labour Party Conference, in Kingsley Martin, *Harold Laski*

[Laski has] had a backdoor key to the White House. A surprising number of us, Professor, have begun to think it is time to change the lock.

Mr Woodruff of Michigan, on Roosevelt's friendship with Laski, in *Congressional Record*, 6 February 1946

## LATIMER, HUGH, BISHOP OF WORCESTER

1485–1555 Martyr

Then they brought a Faggot, kindled with fire, and laid the same down at D. *Ridleys* feet. To whom Mr *Latimer* spake in this manner; Be of good comfort, Mr *Ridley*, and play the man, we shall this day light such a candle by Gods grace in *England*, as I trust shall never be put out.

John Foxe, *Acts and Monuments*

He was no great scholar: he knew no Greek: he took his doctrinal position from Cranmer and left disputation to Ridley. He was a preacher, and a court preacher, too. Not a fashionable court preacher, like John Donne or the great Jesuit preachers of the next century, exploring and illuminating the intimate spiritual recesses of rich patrons and great ladies, but a tribune of the people who preached his message menacingly, like Hosea or Amos, to the face of Kings.

H. R. Trevor-Roper, *Hugh Latimer and the English Commonwealth*

*See also* Mary I

## LAUD, WILLIAM

1573–1645 Archbishop of Canterbury

He is half a precisian in the outward man; he loveth little bands, short hair, grave looks; but had rather be slain at Tyburn than preach in a cloak.

Anon., *The Character of an Untrue Bishop*

Although he came with confidence to the scaffold, and the blood wrought lively in his cheeks, yet when he did lye down upon the block he trembled every joint of him; the sense of something after death, and the undiscovered country unto which his soul was wandering startling his resolution, and possessing every joint of him with an universal palsey of fear.

Anon., in *Post* (London), January 1644

This little man with his horseshoe brows, and prim mouth, and sharp restless eyes is too subtle a figure for an easy verdict. It is clear that he had great natural gifts of head and heart . . . [But] . . . there was a cold donnish insensitiveness about him . . . he applied the brain of a college pedant to the spacious life of England.

John Buchan, *Oliver Cromwell*

He pluckt down Puritans and Property, to build up Paul's and Prerogative.

Lord Falkland, as paraphrased by Sir Philip Warwick, *Memoirs of the Reign of Charles I*

The one second-rate Englishman who had exercised a wide influence upon the history of the world.

H. A. L. Fisher, *History of Europe*

Laud hath a restless spirit, and cannot see when things are well, but loves to bring matters to a pitch of reformation floating in his own brain.

James I, attributed

Nor deem, when Learning her last prize bestows / The glitt'ring eminence exempt from foes; / See, when the vulgar 'scapes, despis'd or aw'd, / Rebellions vengeful talons seize on Laud. / From meaner minds though smaller fines content / The plunder'd palace, or sequester'd rent, / Mark'd out by dangerous parts, he meets the shock, / And fatal Learning leads him to the block. /

Samuel Johnson, *The Vanity of Human Wishes*

You would be ruled by nobody, nor communicate yourself to any that I know, nor make yourself any party at Court, but stood upon yourself: it may be that was your fault.

Sir John Lamb, Letter to Laud, 1641

His understanding was narrow; and his commerce with the world had been small. He was by nature rash, irritable, quick to feel for his own dignity, slow to sympathise with the sufferings of others, and prone to the error, common in superstitious men, of mistaking his own peevish and malignant moods for emotions of pious zeal.

T. B. Macaulay, *History of England*

Many writers have been tempted to digress from their immediate topic in order to dismiss Laud in an epigram: but between his grandiose design and its calamitous event the gulf is too vast for so delicate a bridge. What single definition can embrace his comprehensive social ideal, and his narrow-minded application of it: his tolerant theology and his intolerant methods: his huge efforts and their tenuous results: the social justice which he advocated, and the savage punishments which he inflicted? Yet the ideal, and the practical, in Laud's policy cannot be treated apart, for his ideal was only expressed in his practice – 'Thorough' is not the motto of a doctrinaire – and his practice, though shaped by an ideal, was plainly inspired by his acute appreciation of actual conditions.

Hugh Trevor-Roper, *Archbishop Laud*

## LAUDERDALE, DUKE OF (JOHN MAITLAND)

1616–82 Statesman

This haughty monster with his ugly claws, / First temper'd poison to destroy our laws; / Declares the Council edicts are beyond / The most authentic statutes of the land; / Sets up in Scotland, *à la mode de France*, / Taxes, excise, and army does advance. / This saracen his country's freedom broke / To bring upon our necks the heavier yoke. / This is the savage pimp without dispute / First brought his mother for a prostitute; / Of all the miscreants ever went to hell / This villain rampant bears away the bell. /

Anon., *An Historical Poem*, 1680

He made a very ill appearance: He was very big: His hair red, hanging odly about him: His tongue was too big for his mouth, which made him bedew all that he talked to: And his whole manner was rough and boisterous, and very unfit for a Court. He was very learned, not only in *Latin*, in which he was a master, but in *Greek* and *Hebrew*. He had read a great deal of divinity, and almost all the historians ancient and modern: So that he had great materials. He had with these an extraordinary memory, and copious but unpolished expression. He was a man, as the Duke of *Buckingham* called him to me, of a blundering understanding. He was haughty beyond expression, abject to those he saw he must stoop to, but imperious to all others. He had a violence of passion that carried him often to fits like madness, in which he had no temper. If he took a thing wrong, it was a vain thing to study to convince him: That would rather provoke him to swear, he would never be of another mind: He was to be let alone: And perhaps he would have forgot what he had said, and come about of his own accord. He was the coldest friend and the violentest enemy I ever knew: I felt it too much not to know it.

Gilbert Burnet, *History of My Own Time*

## LAUGHTON, CHARLES

1899–1962 Actor

We got on very well – in spite of his strange habits, such as a terrific prejudice concerning Jews and needing strange off-stage noises to get himself in the mood for acting. He was the first actor I encountered who prepared to make a laughing entrance by going around doing *ha-ha!* sounds for hours.

George Cukor, in Gavin Lambert, *On Cukor*

I always admired his courage in revealing the sensual side of his nature with such honesty and power. In the part of Angelo he trod the stage like an evil bat, with the billowing silk sleeves of his black gown flapping round him as he prowled up and down the stage, and he had immense drive, with a strong vein of poetic imagination which gave his performance colour and excitement. One might say, perhaps, that whereas [Leslie] Faber and [Cedric] Hardwicke were highly skilled dyed-in-the-wool professionals, Laughton was an inspired amateur. The first two men were perfectionists, calculating their acting to a nicety, and both struck me as being basically modest men, dry, witty, cynical. Laughton was more of an exhibitionist. His monsters were vicious with a kind of childlike naiveté fascinating in its contradictions. In *Macbeth* he made a sensation only in the Banquet Scene when confronted with the Ghost of Banquo, while in *King Lear* his scene on Dover Cliff made the greatest impression. He could not find and sustain the progression necessary to achieve either of these great parts to the full. How often stage and screen, dividing the loyalties of talented actors, have played havoc with their sense of direction and crippled their potentialities in consequence.

Sir John Gielgud, *Distinguished Company*

## LAUREL, STAN (ARTHUR STANLEY JEFFERSON) AND HARDY, OLIVER

1890–1965 and 1892–1957 Comedians

As a team, they complemented each other perfectly, not only physically, but also in terms of personality. Laurel was the eternal innocent – trusting, babyish, so stupid that when a good idea comes to him it is gone before he can grasp it and make use of it, and with a streak of childish maliciousness in him which comes to the surface when pressed a little too far. Hardy on the other hand, was completely adult – the bon vivant and gallant of the old school, with flowery gestures and eloquent speech, pompous and opinionated, and only temporarily deflated when his ego is punctured – as it always was, without fail!

Joe Franklin, *Classics of the Silent Screen*

Of all the silent comedians, Laurel and Hardy are perhaps most threatening to women, as they combine the physical ruination with misogyny. One epicene and gross, the other emaciated, they are an aesthetic offense. With their disaster-prone bodies and their exclusive relationship that not only shuts out women but questions their very necessity, they constitute a two-man wrecking team of female – that is, civilized and bourgeois – society.

Molly Haskell, *From Reverence to Rape*

## LAW, ANDREW BONAR

1858–1923 Prime Minister

Has not the brains of a Glasgow baillie.

H. H. Asquith, speaking to David Lloyd George, in Frances Stevenson, Diary, 27 November 1916

It is fitting that we should have buried the Unknown Prime Minister by the side of the Unknown Soldier.

H. H. Asquith, on the interment of Law's ashes in Westminster Abbey, 1923

Of course the most characteristic thing to those who knew him would be a ginger cake and a glass of milk, to which I brought him home pretty nearly every night for about four years!

Stanley Baldwin, Letter to Lord Beaverbrook, 18 December 1928

He was almost devoid of Conservative principles. This Presbyterian from Canada had no imaginative reverence for the traditions and symbols of the past, no special care for vested interests, no attachment whatever to the Upper Classes, the City, the Army, or the Church . . . [His] Conservatism . . . proceeded from caution, scepticism, lack of faith, a distrust of any intellectual process which proceeded more than one or two steps ahead or any emotional enthusiasm which grasped at an intangible object, and an extreme respect for all kinds of *Success*.

John Maynard Keynes, *Essays in Biography*

Bonar would never make up his mind on anything. Once a question had been decided, Bonar would stick to it and fight for it to a finish, but he would never help in the taking of a decision.

David Lloyd George, in A. J. Sylvester, *Life with Lloyd George*

I told Bonar that . . . I had been to a Mozart concert and the music was wonderful. Bonar casually and languidly remarked: 'I don't care for music.' As we motored along, there was the Mediterranean blue sea on one side and the rolling snow-capped Alpes Maritimes on the other. This inspired me to exclaim: 'Look, Bonar, what a wonderful scene that is.' 'I don't care for scenery,' remarked Bonar. Presently we came to a bridge . . . I said to Bonar: 'Look, Bonar, aren't those handsome women?' 'I don't care for women,' remarked Bonar very drily. 'Then what the hell do you care for?' I asked. Then in his very soft voice, and quieter still, Bonar replied: 'I like bridge.'

*Ibid.*

Bonar always jibs a good deal before taking a long jump.

Frances Stevenson, Diary, 16 March 1920

## LAWRENCE, DAVID HERBERT

1885–1930 Novelist, Poet, Painter, Playwright

I always say, my motto is 'Art for my sake'.

On himself, Letter to Ernest Collings, 24 December 1912

I'll do my life work, sticking up for the love between man and woman.

On himself, Letter to Sally Hopkin, 25 December 1912

I'm like Carlyle, who, they say, wrote 50 volumes on the value of silence.

On himself, Letter to Ernest Collings, 17 January 1913

A book should either be a bandit or a rebel or a man in a crowd. People should either run for their lives, or come under the colours, or say *how do you do?* I hate the actor-and-the audience business. An author should be in among the crowd, kicking their shins or cheering on to some mischief or merriment. That rather cheap seat in the gods where one sits with fellows like Anatole France and benignly looks down on the foibles, follies and frenzies of so-called fellow-men just annoys me. After all the world is not a stage – not to me: nor a theatre: nor a show-house of any sort . . . Whoever reads me will be in the thick of the scrimmage, and if he doesn't like it – if he wants a safe seat in the audience – let him read somebody else.

On himself, Letter to Carlo Linati, 22 January 1925

About *Lady C.* – you mustn't think I advocate perpetual sex. Far from it. Nothing nauseates me more than promiscuous sex in and out of season. But I want, with *Lady C.*, to make an *adjustment in consciousness* to the basic physical realities. I realize that one of the reasons why the common people often keep – or kept – the good *natural glow* of life, just warm life, longer than educated people, was because it was still possible for them to say fuck! or shit without either a shudder or a sensation. If a man had been able to say to you when you were young and in love: an' if tha shits, an' if tha pisses, I'm glad, I shouldna want a woman who couldna shit nor piss – surely it would have been a liberation to you, and it would have helped to keep your hear warm.

On himself, Letter to Lady Ottoline Morrell, 28 December 1928

One of the great denouncers, the great missionaries the English send to themselves to tell them they are crass, gross, lost, dead, mad and addicted to unnatural vice. I suppose it is a good thing that these chaps continue to roll up, though in this case I wonder whether as much silly conduct has not been encouraged as heartless conduct deterred. However that may be, it is a chilling disappointment to take an actual look at the denunciations and be confronted not only by egomania, fatuity and gimcrack theorizing, but bitterness and censoriousness as well. It might even be more intelligent to leave Lawrence on his pinnacle, inspiring, unapproachable and unread.

Kingsley Amis, *What Became of Jane Austen?*

Lawrence seemed to me sometimes to suffer from a delusion similar to the delusion of the sick man who thinks that if a given quantity of medicine will do him good, twice the quantity will do him twice the good.

Arnold Bennett, in *Evening Standard*, 12 April 1930

Since he had dismissed the brain for the belly-worship of his creed, the vision of a peaceful and rational society could have no attractions for him. He was an enemy of the mind; and though somehow he might have repudiated this as shrilly as he repudiated all accepted standards, he remained a mouthpiece of reaction in contemporary letters. The 'mindless, eyeless, hysterical mass-consciousness' with which his work is identified has become the bane of modern Europe.

Roger Dataller, *The Plain Man and the Novel*

In the work of D. H. Lawrence . . . is found the profoundest research into human nature, as well as the most erratic and uneven writing, by any writer of our generation.

T. S. Eliot, in *Vanity Fair*, July 1923

He kept his trivialities for poetry in the way most writers of both keep them for prose.

D. J. Enright, in *New Statesman*, 30 October 1964

This pictorial account of the day-to-day life of an English gamekeeper is full of considerable interest to outdoor minded readers, as it contains many passages on pheasant-raising, the apprehending of poachers, ways to control vermin, and other chores and duties of the professional gamekeeper. Unfortunately, one is obliged to wade through many pages of extraneous material in order to discover and savour those sidelights on the management of a midland shooting estate, and in this reviewer's opinion the book cannot take the place of J. R. Miller's *Practical Gamekeeping*.

*Field and Stream* review of *Lady Chatterley's Lover*

I cannot say that I liked Lawrence much. He remained too disturbing even when I got to know him well. He had so much need of moral support to take the place of his mother's influence that he kept one – everyone who at all came into contact with him – in a constant state of solicitude. He claimed moral support imperiously – and physical care too.

Ford Madox Ford, *Mightier than the Sword*

Lawrence himself is, as far as I know, the only prophetic novelist writing to-day – all the rest are fantasists or preachers: the only living novelist in whom the song predominates, who has the rapt bardic quality, and whom it is idle to criticize. He invites criticism because he is a preacher also – it is this minor aspect of him which makes him so difficult and misleading – an excessively clever preacher who knows how to play on the nerves of his congregation. Nothing is more disconcerting than to sit down, so to speak, before your prophet, and then suddenly to receive his boot in the pit of your stomach.

E. M. Forster, *Aspects of the Novel*

I'll tell you a poet with a method that is a method: Lawrence. I came across a poem of his in a new *Imagiste* Anthology just published here, and it was such a poem that I wanted to go right to the man that wrote it and say something.

Robert Frost, Letter to Edward Garnett, 12 June 1915

*Lawrence* thought every woman should / Be shown that her desires are good, / That *amor naturale*'s error / Lies in obeying Ego's terror. / *Lawrence*, too, contrived to train us / In the importance of the anus, / Not *Sade*-like as a matter of course, / But to return us to a Source / Which, with some conscientious plumbing / Could liberate the Second Coming. /

John Fuller, *The Art of Love*

It's not good enough to spend time and ink in describing the penultimate sensations and physical movements of people getting into a state of rut . . . The body's never worthwhile, and the sooner Lawrence recognizes that, the better – the men we swear by – Tolstoy, Turgenev, Chekov, Maupassant, Flaubert, France – knew that great truth, they only use the body, and that sparingly, to reveal the soul.

John Galsworthy, Letter to Edward Garnett, 13 April 1914

For Lawrence, existence was one continuous convalescence; it was as though he were newly re-born from a mortal illness every day of his life.

Aldous Huxley, Introduction to *The Letters of D. H. Lawrence*

Though without any of Nietzsche's nobility of character and capacity to endure neglect and solitude, Lawrence in his slight way, often recalls Nietzsche, another poet enmeshed in the will, and solacing his impotence with dreams of new forms of life in which he would be the master.

Hugh Kingsmill, *D. H. Lawrence*

Lawrence was so direct, such a real puritan! He hated any *haut-goût* or lewdness. Fine underclothing and all the apparatus of the seducing sort were just stupid to him. All tricks; why tricks? Passionate people don't need tricks.

Frieda Lawrence, *Not I, But the Wind...*

I have heard so much about 'form'... why are you English so keen on it? Their own form wants smashing in almost any direction, but they can't come out of their snail house. I know it is so much safer. That's what I love Lawrence for, that he is so plucky and honest in his work, he dares to come out in the open and plants his stuff down bald and naked; really he is the only revolutionary worthy of the name, that I know; any new thing must find a new shape, then afterwards one can call it 'art'.

Frieda Lawrence, Letter to Edward Garnett, 1912

Then there is his sanity, his poise. There is a tendency among certain critics, especially in Germany, to regard D. H. Lawrence as a neurotic. That foolish legend will, we trust, be killed by this publication. The whole correspondence of D. H. Lawrence pulsates with sanity, even in little things. 'Don't you,' he writes, 'think it's nonsense when M. says that my world is not the ordinary man's world, and that I am a sort of animal with a sixth sense? ... They all seem determined to make a freak of me – to save their own short-failings, and make them "normal".' Lawrence was obviously exceptional, even eccentric, but he was not a neurotic.

F. R. Leavis, Review of Lawrence's *Letters*, in *New Statesman*, 1 October 1932

He sees more than a human being ought to see. Perhaps that's why he hates humanity so much.

Vernon Lee, in Aldous Huxley, Introduction to *Letters of D. H. Lawrence*

We know what sort of picture D. H. Lawrence would paint if he took to the brush instead of the pen. For he did so, luckily, and even held exhibitions. As one might have expected, it turned out to be incompetent Gauguin.

Percy Wyndham Lewis, *Men Without Art*

Lawrence's animal natures, just because of their irreducible obscenity, are the purest bodies in our current literature. Animated by a metaphysical conception they act through obedience to fundamental laws of nature. Of these laws Lawrence admits his complete ignorance. He created his metaphysical world by faith; he proceeds only by intuition. He may have been utterly wrong, but he is absolutely consistent.

Henry Miller, *The Cosmological Eye*

Lawrentian sexuality seems to be guided by somewhat the same principle one finds expressed in Rainwater's study of the working class (also the doctrine of the nineteenth-century middle classes) – 'sex is for the man'. Lawrence's knowledge of Freud was sketchy and secondhand, but he appears to be well acquainted with the theories of female passivity and male activity and doubtless found them very convenient. Ladies – even when they are 'cunt' – don't move.

Kate Millett, *Sexual Politics*

Lawrence at first sight does not seem to be a pessimistic writer, because, like Dickens, he is a 'change-of-heart' man and constantly insisting that life here and now would be all right if only you looked at it a little differently. But what he is demanding is a movement away from our mechanised civilisation, which is not going to happen, and which he knows is not going to happen . . . The kind of life that he is always pointing to, a life centring round the simple mysteries – sex, earth, fire, water, blood – is merely a lost cause.

George Orwell, *Inside the Whale*

Detestable person but needs watching. I think he learned the proper treatment of modern subjects before I did.

Ezra Pound, Letter to Harriet Monroe, March 1913

Lawrence is very like Shelley – just as fine, but with a similar impatience of fact. The revolution he hopes for is just like Shelley's prophecy of banded anarchs fleeing while the people celebrate a feast of love. His psychology of people is amazingly good up to a point, but at a certain point he gets misled by love of violent colouring.

Bertrand Russell, Letter to Lady Ottoline Morrell, July 1915

Lawrence is in a long line of people, beginning with Heraclitus & ending with Hitler, whose ruling motive is hatred derived from megalomania, & I am sorry to see that I was once so far out in estimating him.

*Ibid.*, February 1937

Mr Lawrence looked like a plaster gnome on a stone toadstool in some suburban garden. At the same time he bore some resemblance to a bad self-portrait by Van Gogh. He had a rather matted, dank appearance. He looked as if he had just returned from spending an uncomfortable night in a very dark cave, hiding, perhaps, in the darkness, from something which, at the same time, he on his side was hunting.

Edith Sitwell, *Taken Care Of*

[Aldous Huxley] would, as someone brighter than myself has said, condense the generative principle into a test-tube; Lawrence, on the other hand, would condense the world into the generative principle, and make his apostles decline not cogitare but copulare.

Dylan Thomas, Letter to Pamela Hansford Johnson, 1933

Like Hitler, Lawrence gives an impression of proceeding somnambulistically – arms outstretched, vision confident but unseeing, footfall certain because unconscious. Many of his ideas, indeed, particularly in his last years, were decidedly Hitlerian; much in *Apocalypse* could have gone straight into *Mein Kampf.*

*Times Literary Supplement*, Review of Richard Aldington's *Portrait of a Genius, But . . .*, 1950

*See also* W. H. Auden, Aldous Huxley, Wilfred Owen, Bertrand Russell, Dylan Thomas

## LAWRENCE, GERTRUDE

1898–1952 Singer, Actress

Gertie has an astounding sense of the complete reality of the moment, and her moments, dictated by the extreme variability of her moods, change so swiftly that it is frequently difficult to discover what, apart from eating, sleeping, and acting, is true of her at all.

Noël Coward, *Present Indicative*

## LAWRENCE, SIR THOMAS

1769–1830 Painter

He was sensible that his own pictures 'had too much of a metallic appearance, – too many shining lights.'

Joseph Farington, Diary, 22 July 1798

Lawrence ... made his art into a trade.

Lord Gower, *Romney and Lawrence*

His manner was elegant, but not high bred. He had too much that air of always submitting. He had smiled so often & so long, that at last his smile wore the appearance of being set in enamel.

Benjamin R. Haydon, Diary, 9 January 1830

He is, from habit of coaxing his subjects I suppose, a little too fairspoken, otherwise very pleasant.

Sir Walter Scott, Diary, 3 October 1827

## LAWRENCE, THOMAS EDWARD (OF ARABIA)

1888–1935 Author, Soldier

All the subject provinces of the Empire, to me were not worth one English boy.

On himself, Introduction to *Seven Pillars of Wisdom*

I drew these tides of men into my hands / And wrote my will across the sky in stars. /

*Ibid.*

I was an Irish nobody. I did something. It was a failure. And I became an Irish nobody again.

On himself, as reported by William Butler Yeats, in Percy Wyndham Lewis, *Blasting and Bombadiering*

Arabian Lawrence, who, whatever his claims as a man, was surely a sonorous fake as a writer.

Kingsley Amis, *What Became of Jane Austen?*

... a bore and a bounder and a prig. He was intoxicated with his own youth, and loathed any milieu which he couldn't dominate. Certainly he had none of a gentleman's instincts, strutting about Peace Conferences in Arab dress.

Henry Channon, Diary, 25 May 1935

He had ... a self-will of heroic, even of Titanic, proportions; and one has the impression that he lived for the most part in one of the more painful corners of the inferno. He is one of those great men for whom one feels intensely sorry, because he was nothing but a great man.

Aldous Huxley, Letter to Victoria Ocampo, 1946

There are those who have tried to dismiss his story with a flourish of the Union Jack, a psychoanalytical catchword or a sneer; it should move our deepest admiration and pity. Like Shelley and like Baudelaire, it may be said of him that he suffered, in his own person, the neurotic ills of an entire generation.

Christopher Isherwood, *Exhumations*

It should be noted that there is now no intelligentsia that is not in some sense 'left'. Perhaps the last right-wing intellectual was T. E. Lawrence.

George Orwell, *The Lion and the Unicorn*

A callow and terrified Marbot, placed in command of a sardonic Napoleon at Austerlitz and Jena, would have felt much as your superiors must in command of Lawrence the great.

George Bernard Shaw, Letter to Lawrence, 17 December 1922

Lawrence licentiate to dream and to dare.

Sir Ronald Storrs, *Orientations*

## LEACOCK, STEPHEN BUTLER
1869–1944 Author

Presently I shall be introduced as 'this venerable old gentleman' and the axe will fall when they raise me to the degree of 'grand old man'. That means on our continent any one with snow-white hair who has kept out of jail till eighty.

On himself, *Three Score and Ten*

## LEAR, EDWARD
1812–88 Author, Artist

'How pleasant to know Mr Lear!' / Who has written such volumes of stuff! / Some think him ill-tempered and queer, / But a few think him pleasant enough. /

On himself, Preface to *Nonsense Songs*

I went to the city today, to put the £125 I got for the 'Book of Nonsense' into the funds. It is doubtless a very unusual thing for an artist to put by money, for the whole way from Temple Bar to the Bank was *crowded* with carriages and people – so immense a sensation did this occurrence make. And all the way back it was the same, which was very gratifying.

On himself, Letter to Lady Waldegrave, 4 November 1862

Considering that I myself in 1833 had every sort of syphilitic disease, who am I to blame others, who have had less education and more temptation.

On himself, Diary, 20 February 1885

His non-sense is not vacuity of sense: it is a parody of sense, and that is the sense of it. 'The Jumblies' is a poem of adventure, and of nostalgia for the romance of foreign voyage and exploration; 'The Yongy-Bongy-Bo' and 'The Dong with a Luminous Nose' are poems of unrequited passion – 'blues' in fact.

T. S. Eliot, *The Music of Poetry*

Even today, epilepsy is a lonely disease, and although the idea of 'demoniac possession' can now be laughed at, there are still irrational lingerings of shame. In the early nineteenth century it was obscured by ignorance and old wives tales, and one of these was that attacks could be brought on by masturbation. Lear certainly believed that there could be a connection between the two, and as an adult he constantly blamed the attacks on his lack of will power. The usual threat offered to a little boy was that his penis would drop off and, like the Pobble whose toes disappeared when the scarlet flannel wrapper was taken away, Edward must sometimes have thought that he would be happier without it; the Pobble was given a feminine concoction of 'Lavender water tinged with pink', and perhaps this was the best solution.

Vivien Noakes, *Edward Lear, the Life of a Wanderer*

Illyrian woodlands, echoing falls / Of water, sheets of summer glass, / The long divine Peneian pass, / The vast Akrokeraunian walls, /

Tomohrit, Athos, all things fair, / With such a pencil, such a pen, / You shadow forth to distant men, / I read, and felt that I was there. /

Alfred, Lord Tennyson, *To E.L. on his Travels in Greece*

## LEE, NATHANIEL
1653?–92 Dramatist

There in a Den remov'd from human Eyes, / Possest with Muse, the Brain-sick Poet lyes, / Too miserably wretched to be nam'd; / For Plays, for Heroes, and for Passion fam'd / Thoughtless he raves his sleepless Hours away, / In Chains all nights, in Darkness al the Day. / And if he gets some Intervals from Pain, / The Fit returns; he foams, and bites his Chain, / His Eye-balls rowl, and he grows mad again. /

Anon., *A Satyr on the Poets*

The truth is, the poet's imagination ran away with his reason. While in Bedlam, he made that famous witty reply to a coxcomb scribbler, who had the cruelty to jeer him with his misfortune, by observing that it was an easy thing to write like a madman: '*No* (said Lee) *it is* not *an easy thing to write like a madman; but it is very easy to write like a fool.*'

Baker, Reed and Jones eds, *Biographica Dramatica*

## LEE, ROBERT EDWARD

1807–70 Confederate General

What General Lee's feelings were I do not know, as he was a man of much dignity, with an impassable face, it was impossible to say whether he felt inwardly glad that the end had finally come, or felt sad over the result, and was too manly to show it. Whatever his feelings, they were entirely concealed from my observation; but my own feelings . . . were sad and depressed. I felt like anything rather than rejoicing at the downfall of a foe who had fought so long and valiantly, and had suffered so much for a cause.

Ulysses S. Grant, in Margaret Sanborn, *Robert E. Lee: The Complete Man 1861–1870*

He was a foe without hate, a friend without treachery, a soldier without cruelty, and a victim without murmuring. He was a public officer without vices, a private citizen without wrong, a neighbor without hypocrisy, and a man without guilt. He was Caesar without his ambition, Frederick without his tyranny, Napoleon without his selfishness and Washington without his reward.

Benjamin H. Hill, in Robert Debs Heinl Jr, *The Dictionary of Military and Naval Quotations*

If I were on my death bed, and the President should tell me that a great battle was to be fought for the liberty or slavery of the country, and asked my judgment as to the ability of a commander, I would say with my dying breath, let it be Robert E. Lee.

General Winfield Scott, in Burke Davis, *They Called Him Stonewall*

An angel's heart, an angel's mouth, / Not Homer's could alone for me / Hymn well the great Confederate South, / Virginia first and *Lee*! /

Philip Stanhope Worsley, inscribed in a presentation copy of his translation of the *Iliad* to General Lee, January 1866

## LELY, SIR PETER (PIETER VAN DER FAES)

1618–80 Portrait Painter

Sir Peter, in his faces, preserves a languishing air, and a drowsy sweetness peculiar to himself.

*The Biographical Magazine*, 1794

Th'amazed world shall henceforth find / None but my *Lilly* ever drew a *Mind*. /

Richard Lovelace, *To my Worthy Friend Mr Peter Lilly*

Cheat *hocus-pocus*-Nature an Essay / O' th' Spring affords us, *Presto* and away; / You all the year do chain her, and her fruits, / Roots to their Beds, and flowers to their Roots. / Have not mine eyes feasted i' th' frozen *Zone*, / Upon a fresh new-grown Collation / Of Apples, unknown sweets, that seem'd to me / Hanging to tempt as on the fatal Tree; / So delicately limn'd I vow'd to try / My appetite impos'd upon my Eye. / You Sir alone, Fame and all conqu'ring Rime, / Files the set teeth of all devouring time. /

Richard Lovelace, *Peinture*

Lely supplied the want of taste with *clinquant*; his nymphs trail fringes and embroidery through purling streams. Add, that Vandyck's habits are those of the times; Lely's a sort of fantastic nightgowns, fastened with a single pin. The latter was in truth the ladies'-painter.

Horace Walpole, *Anecdotes of Painters in England*

*See also* Oliver Cromwell, Nell Gwyn

## LETTSOM, JOHN COAKLEY

1744–1815 Physician

When people's ill, they comes to I, / I physics, bleeds, and sweats 'em; / Sometimes they live, sometimes they die. / What's that to I? I lets 'em. /

On himself, *Epigram*

## LEVANT, OSCAR

1906–72 Author, Actor, Musician

My behavior has been impeccable; I've been unconscious for the past six months.

On himself, *The Memoirs of an Amnesiac*

Underneath this flabby exterior is an enormous lack of character.

*Ibid.*

I don't drink. I don't like it. It makes me feel good.

On himself, in *Time*, 5 May 1950

For one year and one month he declared my house his house. For one year and one month he ate my food, played my piano, ran up my phone bill, burned cigarette holes in my landlady's furniture, monopolized my record player and my coffeepot, gave his guests the run of the joint, insulted my guests, and never stopped complaining. He was an insomniac. He was an egomaniac. He was a leech and a lunatic . . . But I loved the guy.

He honestly believed he was taking what was coming to him and nothing more. This was not to be confused with generosity, which Oscar didn't know how to accept. If anybody offered to help him out, his favorite reply was, 'Do me a favor – don't do me a favor'. But if it was he who asked the favor it was all right. Oscar was utterly unable to enjoy an equal relationship with anybody. It had to be one-sided, on his side, with the single exception of George Gershwin. Once I understood this and accepted it, I found Oscar to be one of the most rewarding men I had ever known. I lost a house, but I gained a friend.

Harpo Marx, *Harpo Speaks*

There is absolutely nothing wrong with Oscar Levant that a miracle cannot fix.

Alexander Woollcott, in Margaret Case Harriman, *The Vicious Circle*

*See also* Harpo Marx

## LEVET(T), ROBERT

1701?–82 Physician

Officious, innocent, sincere, / Of every friendless name the friend. /

Samuel Johnson, *On the Death of Mr Levet*

## LEWES, GEORGE HENRY

1817–78 Author, Journalist

He was the son of a clown. He had the legs of his father in his brain.

George Meredith, in *Fortnightly Review*, July 1909

George Lewes, who was present, looked surprised and then cried out –

'Oh, I'm not like that, I commence to write at once, directly the pen is in my hand! In fact, I boil at a low temperature!'

'Indeed,' cut in Mr Huxley, 'That is very interesting, for, as you know, to boil at a low temperature implies a vacuum in the upper region.'

'Two', *Home Life with Herbert Spencer*

## LEWIS, MERIWETHER

1774–1809 Explorer

I am no coward; but I am *so* strong, *so hard to die* . . . If I had not done it, someone else would.

On himself, dying words, having committed suicide, in John Bakeless, *Lewis and Clark*

## LEWIS, PERCY WYNDHAM

1884–1957 Novelist, Painter

I am a portmanteau-man.

On himself, *Blasting and Bombardiering*

I have been called a Rogue Elephant, a Cannibal Shark, and a crocodile. I am none the worse. I remain a caged, and rather sardonic, Lion in a particularly contemptible and ill-run Zoo.

*Ibid.*

That lonely old volcano of the Right.

W. H. Auden, in Roy Campbell, in *Time and Tide*, 7 July 1951

We leave the Martyr's Stake at Abergwilly / To Wyndham Lewis with a box of soldiers (blonde) / Regretting one so bright should be so silly. /

W. H. Auden and Louis MacNeice, *Letters from Iceland*

One of his minor purposes is to disembowel his enemies, who are numerous, for the simple reason that he wants them to be numerous. He would be less tiresome if he were more urbane.

Arnold Bennett, in *Evening Standard*, 28 April 1927

In the work of Mr Lewis we recognize the thought of the modern and the energy of the cave-man.

T. S. Eliot, reviewing Lewis's *Tarr*

I do not think I have ever seen a nastier-looking man . . . Under the black hat, when I had first seen them, the eyes had been those of an unsuccessful rapist.

Ernest Hemingway, *A Moveable Feast*

Enough talent to set up dozens of ordinary writers has been poured into Wyndham Lewis's so-called novels, such as *Tarr* or *Snooty Baronet*. Yet it would be a very heavy labour to read one of these books right through. Some indefinable quality, a sort of literary vitamin . . . is absent from them.

George Orwell, in *Tribune*, 2 November 1945

The whole public and even those of us who then knew him best, have been so befuddled with the concept of Lewis as EXPLOSIVE that scarcely anyone has had the sense or the patience to look calmly at his perfectly suave and equipoised observations of letters. The difference between a gun and a tree is a difference of tempo. The tree explodes every spring.

Ezra Pound, in *Criterion*, July 1937

A buffalo in wolf's clothing.

Robert Ross, in Percy Wyndham Lewis, *Blasting and Bombardiering*

Mr Lewis's pictures appeared, as a very great painter said to me, to have been painted by a mailed fist in a cotton glove.

Edith Sitwell, *Taken Care Of*

## LEWIS, SINCLAIR

1885–1951 Author

He was a writer who drank, not, as so many have believed, a drunk who wrote.

James Lundquist, *Sinclair Lewis*

In any imaginable society he would be as noticeable as a bashful cyclone. He enters a room with a diffident insolence, bracing himself against what lies in wait for him. After all his harsh campaigns, he has still an eager, shy desire to please.

Carl Van Doren, *Sinclair Lewis*

He is a master of that species of art to which belong glass flowers, imitation fruit, Mme Tussaud's waxworks, and barnyard symphonies, which aims at deceiving the spectator into thinking that the work in question is not an artificial product but the real thing.

T. K. Whipple, *Spokesmen*

Lewis is the most successful critic of American society because he is himself the best proof that his charges are just.

*Ibid.*

## LILBURNE, JOHN

1614?–57 Leveller

Is *John* departed, and is *Lilburn* gone? / Farewell to both, to *Lilburn* and to *John*. / Yet, being dead, take this Advice from me, / Let them not both in one Grave buried be: / Lay *John* here, and *Lilburn* thereabout, / For, if they both should meet, they would fall out. /

Anon. near contemporary

So suddenly addicted still / To's only Principle, his *will*, / That whatso'er it chanc'd to prove, / Nor force of Argument could move: / Nor *Law*, nor *Cavalcade* of *Ho'burn* / Could render half a Grain less stubborn, / For he at any Time would hang / For th'opportunity t'*harangue*: / And rather on a Gibbet dangle, / Than miss his dear Delight, to wrangle. /

Samuel Butler, *Hudibras*, part iii

## LILLY, WILLIAM

1602–81 Astrologer

I home by coach, taking Mr Booker [the astrologer] with me, who did tell me a great many fooleries, which may be done by nativities, and blaming Mr Lilly for writing to please his friends and to keep in with the times (as he did formerly to his own dishonour), and not according to the rules of art, by which he could not well err, as he had done.

Samuel Pepys, Diary, 24 October 1660

## LINCOLN, ABRAHAM

1809–65 Sixteenth United States President

Abraham Lincoln his hand and pen / He will be good but god knows when. /

On himself, childhood couplet

As President, I have no eyes but constitutional eyes; I cannot see you.

On himself, in a reply to South Carolina commissioners on the secession question

Fox populi.

Anon., in *Vanity Fair*, 1863

His mind works in the right directions but seldom works clearly and cleanly. His bread is of unbolted flour, and much straw, too, mixes in the bran, and sometimes gravel stones.

Henry Ward Beecher, Letter to Salmon Chase

. . . This man's appearance, his pedigree, his coarse low jokes and anecdotes, his vulgar similes and his frivolity, are a disgrace to the seat he holds.

John Wilkes Booth, in Lord Longford, *Abraham Lincoln*

Mr Lincoln is like a waiter in a large eating house where all the bells are ringing at once; he cannot serve them all at once and so some grumblers are to be expected.

John Bright, *Cincinnati Gazette*, 1864

We must be ready for, and let the clown appear, and hug ourselves that we are well off, if we have got good nature, honest meaning, and fidelity to public interest, with bad manners, – instead of an elegant roué and malignant self seeker.

Ralph Waldo Emerson, in Denis Tilden Lynch, *'Boss Tweed' – The Story of a Grim Generation*

His heart was as great as the world, but there was no room in it to hold a memory of a wrong.

Ralph Waldo Emerson, *Letters and Social Aims: Greatness*

Lincoln had faith in time, and time has justified his faith.

Benjamin Harrison, *Lincoln Day Address*, Chicago, 1898

A bronzed lank man! His suit of ancient black / A famous high-top hat and plain worn shawl / Make him the quaint great figure that men love, / The prairie lawyer, master of us all. /

Vachel Lindsay, *Abraham Lincoln Walks at Midnight*

The catastrophe of Lincoln, though it was a great shock, does not cloud the prospect. How could one have wished him a happier death? He died almost unconsciously in the fulness of success, and martyrdom in so great a cause consecrates his name through all history. Such a death is the crown of a noble life.

John Stuart Mill, Letter to Max Kyllman, May 1865

Lincoln? / He was a mystery in smoke and flags / Saying yes to the smoke, yes to the flags, / Yes to the paradoxes of democracy, / Yes to the hopes of government / Of the people by the people for the people, / No to debauchery of the public mind, / No to personal malice nursed and fed, / Yes to the Constitution when a help, / No to the Constitution when a hindrance, / Yes to man as a struggler amid illusions, / Each man fated to answer for himself: / Which of the faiths and illusions of mankind / Must I choose for my own sustaining light / To bring me beyond the present wilderness? /

Carl Sandburg, *The People, Yes*

Indeed it may be said that if it was Lincoln's destiny to go down in history as the Great Emancipator, rarely has a man embraced his destiny with greater reluctance than he.

Kenneth Stampp, in Lerone Bennett Jr, 'Was Abe Lincoln a White Supremacist?', in D. E. Fehrenbacher ed., *The Leadership of Abraham Lincoln*

The Union with him in sentiment rose to the sublimity of religious mysticism; while his ideas of its structure and formation in logic rested upon nothing but the subtleties of sophism.

Alexander H. Stephens, 1870, in *ibid.*

He is a barbarian, Scythian, Yahoo, a gorilla in respect of outward polish, but a most sensible, straightforward old codger.

George Templeton Strong, in Allen Nevins ed., *The Diary of George Templeton Strong*

O Captain! My Captain! our fearful trip is done, / The ship has weather'd every rock, the prize we sought is won. / The port is near, the bells I hear, the people all exulting, / While follow eyes the steady keel, the vessel grim and daring; / But o heart! heart! heart! / O the bleeding drops of red, / Where on the deck my captain lies, / Fallen cold and dead. /

Walt Whitman, *O Captain! My Captain!*

This dust was once a man, / Gentle, plain, just and resolute, under whose cautious hand, / Against the foulest crime in history known in any land or age, / Was saved the Union of these States. /

Walt Whitman, *This Dust was Once the Man*

. . . the grandest figure on the crowded canvas of the drama of the nineteenth century.

Walt Whitman, in Carl Sandburg, *Abraham Lincoln: The Prairie Years and the War Years*

*See also* Matthew Arnold, Gary Cooper, Charles A. Lindbergh, James K. Polk, Theodore Roosevelt, Carl Sandburg, Adlai Stevenson

## LINDBERGH, CHARLES AUGUSTUS

1902–74 Aviator

How Lincoln would have held him / As gently as a babe – / And, come to think, by Jonathan! / The youngster looks like Abe. /

Anon., from popular American song of the late 1920s

Alone, yet never lonely, / Serene, beyond mischance, / The world was his, his only, / When Lindbergh flew to France! /

Aline Michaelis, *Lindbergh*

## LINDSAY, (NICHOLAS) VACHEL

1879–1931 Poet

I am not only sophisticated, but all my ancestors were sophisticated.

On himself, in T. K. Whipple, *Spokesmen*

Fundamentally, Mr Lindsay was a remarkable poet; altogether he never comes to as much as he should. Probably he never had much of a chance. He grew up in the Babbitt country. He was, when young, a Babbitt himself, and to this day he has not ceased trying to transmute the activities of Babbitry into the stuff of dreams and fantasy.

Heywood Broun, in *ibid.*

Much of Lindsay will die; he will not live as either a prophet or a politician. But the vitality which impels the best of his galloping meters will persist; his innocent wildness of imagination, outlasting his naive programs, will charm even those to whom his declamations are no longer a novelty. His gospel is no less original for being preached through a saxophone.

Louis Untermeyer ed., *Modern American Poetry, A Critical Anthology*

## LIPPMANN, WALTER

1889–1974 Editor, Author

He is a great man because he agrees with me.

Lyndon B. Johnson, in Philip Geyelin, *Lyndon B. Johnson and the World*

Walter. Look, don't think.

Helen Lippmann, shouting to her husband at Seal Harbor, Maine, while he was climbing on some rocks

## LIVERPOOL, EARL OF (ROBERT BANKS JENKINSON)

1770–1828 Prime Minister

. . . the Arch-Mediocrity.

Benjamin Disraeli, *Coningsby*

His test of priestly celebrity was the decent editorship of a Greek play. He sought for the successors of the apostles, for the stewards of the mysteries of Sinai and Calvary, among third rate hunters after syllables.

Benjamin Disraeli, of Lord Liverpool's selection of bishops, in *Tancred*

The Earl of Liverpool, whom Madame de Stael is said to have described as having 'a talent for silence'.

Leigh Hunt, *Autobiography*

Liverpool has acted as he always does to a friend in personal questions – shabbily, timidly and ill.

Lord Palmerston, Letter to William Temple, June 1826

## LIVINGSTONE, DAVID

1813–73 Missionary

I never met a man who fulfilled more completely my idea of a perfect Christian gentleman.

Sir Bartle Frere, *Proceedings of the Royal Geographical Society*, 1874

There is a group of respectable Arabs, and as I come nearer I see the white face of an old man among them. He has a cap with a gold band round it; his dress is a short jacket of red blanket cloth; and his pants – well, I didn't observe. I am shaking hands with him. We raise our hats, and I say, 'Doctor Livingstone, I presume?' and he says, 'Yes'.

H. M. Stanley, *How I Found Livingstone*

## LLOYD GEORGE, DAVID, EARL LLOYD GEORGE OF DWYFOR

1863–1945 Prime Minister

I hate fences, I always feel like knocking down every fence I come across!

On himself, in Frances Stevenson, Diary, 30 November 1915

Lloyd George knew my father. / My father knew Lloyd George. /

Anon., Popular catch of the First World War

Lloyd George has a bigger sound in American than 'Prime Minister' . . . For Lloyd George is the man who does things, and that means everything to America.

Member of the American Luncheon Club speaking to Lloyd George, in Frances Stevenson, Diary, 9 April 1917

He couldn't see a belt without hitting below it.

Margot, Lady Asquith, *Autobiography*

He did not seem to care which way he travelled providing he was in the driver's seat.

Lord Beaverbrook, *Decline and Fall of Lloyd George*

You know you are an acquired flavour, but, once acquired, people like you very much.

John Burns, in conversation with Lloyd George, in A. J. Sylvester, Diary, 5 January 1937

With so much dishonour, you might have bought us a little peace.

Lord Hugh Cecil, on his Irish policy, 1916, in Lord David Cecil, *The Cecils of Hatfield House*

Count not his broken pledges as a crime. / He *meant* them, HOW he meant them – at the time. /

Kensal Green (Colin Hurry), *Premature Epitaphs*

The trouble with Lloyd George is that he thinks in images, not in concepts.

Lord Haldane, 1919, in Dudley Sommer, *Haldane of Cloan*

. . . He could charm a bird off a branch but was himself always unmoved.

Tom Jones, in *Observer*, 25 January 1976

. . . this extraordinary figure of our time, this siren, this goat-footed bard, this half-human visitor to our age from the hag-ridden magic and enchanted woods of Celtic antiquity. One catches in his company that flavour of final purposelessness, inner irresponsibility, existence outside or away from our Saxon good and evil, mixed with cunning, remorselessness, love of power, that lend fascination, enthralment, and terror to the fair-seeming magicians of North-European folklore . . . Lloyd George is rooted in nothing; he is void and without content; he lives and feeds in his immediate surroundings; he is an instrument and a player at the same time which plays on the company and is played on by them too; he is a prism, as I have heard him described, which collects light and distorts it and is most brilliant if the light comes from many quarters at once; a vampire and a medium in one.

John Maynard Keynes, *Essays in Biography*

The little Welshman is peppery, but he means to win – which is what matters!

Lord Kitchener, in Sir George Arthur, *Life of Lord Kitchener*

L.G. said to me that once one had assured oneself of food and shelter, which meant security, the next thing that mattered was advertisement.

A. J. Sylvester, Diary, 27 April 1933

A master of improvised speech and improvised policies.

A. J. P. Taylor, *English History, 1914–1945*

*See also* Nancy Astor, Woodrow Wilson

## LOCKE, JOHN

1632–1704 Philosopher

. . . Locke, we feel, is not so much cleverer than ourselves as to be capable of playing tricks with us even if he wanted to do so. He is the Mr Baldwin of philosophy, and he derives from his literary style some of the advantages which that statesman owed to his pipe and his pigs.

C. D. Broad, *Ethics and the History of Philosophy*

Against Locke's philosophy I think it an unanswerable objection that, although he carried his throat about with him in this world for seventy-two years, no man ever condescended to cut it.

Thomas De Quincey, *On Murder Considered As One of the Fine Arts*

So religion and science were reconciled by limiting the sphere of each. Locke's synthesis performed a social function invaluable for his class. But it was woefully incomplete, for it left out the dialectical element of thought which the Puritan revolutionaries and the early scientists had grasped. It was the dogma of a static civilization.

Christopher Hill, *Puritanism and Revolution*

Perhaps I rather restore the word, idea, to its original sense, from which Mr *Locke* had perverted it, in making it stand for all our perceptions.

David Hume, *A Treatise on Human Nature*, part 1, footnote

No one has yet succeeded in inventing a philosophy at once credible and self-consistent. Locke aimed at credibility, and achieved it at the expense of consistency. Most of the great philosophers have done the opposite. A philosophy which is not self-consistent cannot be wholly true, but a philosophy which is self-consistent can very well be wholly false.

Bertrand Russell, *History of Western Philosophy*

Some of Locke's opinions are so odd that I cannot see how to make them sound sensible. He says that a man must not have so many plums that they are bound to go bad before he and his family can eat them; but he may have as much gold and as many diamonds as he can lawfully get, because gold and diamonds do not go bad. It does not occur to him that the man who has the plums might sell them before they go bad.

*Ibid.*

. . . Mr Locke never loved the trade of disputing in public in the schools but was always wont to declaim against it as being rather invented for wrangling or ostentation than to discover truth.

James Tyrrell, according to Lady Masham, in Maurice Cranston, *John Locke*

This great Man could never subject himself to the tedious Fatigue of Calculations, nor to the Dry Pursuit of Mathematical Truths, which do not at first present any sensible Objects to the Mind; and no one has given better Proofs than he, that 'tis possible for a Man to have a Geometrical Head, without the Assistance of Geometry.

Voltaire, *Letters Concerning the English Nation*

This John Locke was a man of turbulent spirit, clamorous and never contented. The club wrote and took notes from the mouth of their master [Peter Stahl], who sat at the upper end of the table, but the said John Locke scorned to do it, so that while every man besides of the club were writing, he would be prating and troublesome.

Anthony à Wood, *Athenae Oxonienses*

*See also* David Hume

## LODGE, HENRY CABOT

1850–1924 Politician, Author

Some men can engage in the fiercest political controversies without arousing personal animosity. Lodge was not one of them . . . [He] could enrage his antagonists by making them feel their own impotence to enrage him.

Anon., in *Outlook*, 19 November 1924

In discussion he was one of those who care more for drowning his adversary than for discovering some common ground for possible agreement.

Margaret Chanler, in John A. Garraty, *Henry Cabot Lodge*

. . . [his mind was like the soil of New England] naturally barren, but highly cultivated.

Chauncey M. Depew, in Thomas A. Bailey, *Woodrow Wilson and the Lost Peace*

He was as cool as an undertaker at a hanging.

H. L. Mencken, in *Baltimore Evening Sun*, 15 June 1920

## LODGE, THOMAS

1558–1625 Author

In witt, simple; in learning, ignorant; in attempt, rash; in name, Lodge.

Stephen Gosson, *Playes Confuted in Five Actions*

## LONDON, JACK

1876–1916 Writer

I tramped all through the United States, from California to Boston, and up and down, returning to the Pacific Coast by way of Canada, where I got into jail and served a term for vagrancy, and the whole tramping experience made me become a Socialist.

On himself, *Star Rover*

I dream of beautiful horses and fine soil. I dream of the beautiful things I own . . . And I write for no other purpose than to add to the beauty that now belongs to me. I write a book for no other reason than to add three or four hundred acres to my magnificent estate.

On himself, in Charles Child Walcutt, *Jack London*

. . . small, dark, full of movement, with eyes that could glow like topazes when something exciting was happening . . . I shall always think of him as the most lovable child I ever met . . . Like Peter Pan, he never grew up, and he lived his own stories with such intensity that he ended by believing them himself.

Ford Madox Ford, in Richard O'Connor, *Jack London*

Like his country, London was corporally mature, innerly a child. He mastered the outward circumstance of life, and then played with toys. The world was his by physical and intellectual possession: but he preferred to live in a nursery and blamed his excess drinking on the fact that no nurse was there to keep the liquor from his lips.

Waldo Frank, in Joan London, *Jack London*

Grandiloquent without being a fraud, he was the period's greatest crusader and the period's most unashamed hack.

Alfred Kazin, *On Native Grounds*

All his life he grasped whatever straw of salvation lay nearest at hand, and if he joined Karl Marx to the Superman with a boyish glee that has shocked American Marxists ever since, it is interesting to remember that he joined Herbert Spencer to Shelley, and astrology to philosophy, with as carefree a will.

*Ibid.*

## LONG, HUEY PIERCE

1893–1935 Politician

Oh, hell, say that I'm *sui generis* and let it go at that.

On himself, in T. Harry Williams, 'The Gentleman from Louisiana: Demagogue or Democrat', *Journal of Southern History*, vol. 26, February 1960

The Prince of Piffle.

Anon., New Orleans newspaper item, 1923

[A] sartorial aurora borealis.

Anon., in *New York Times*, in G. Wolfskill and J. A. Hudson, *All but the People: Franklin D. Roosevelt and his Critics, 1933–39*

The trouble with Senator Long is that he is suffering from halitosis of the intellect. That's presuming Emperor Long has an intellect.

Harold Ickes, in *ibid.*

When it comes to arousing prejudice and passion, when it comes to ranting and raving, when it comes to vituperation and vilification, when it comes to denunciation and demagoguery, there is one who stands out by himself alone. He has many imitators but no equals.

Jared Y. Sanders, *Tangpahoa Parish News*, 2 December 1926

At bottom, Huey Long resembled . . . a Latin American dictator . . . like Vargas and Peron, Long was in revolt against economic colonialism, against the oligarchy, against the smug and antiquated past; like them, he stood in a muddled way for economic modernization and social justice; like them, he was most threatened by his own arrogance and cupidity, his weakness for soft living and his rage for personal power.

Arthur M. Schlesinger Jr, *The Politics of Upheaval*

He was a liar, and he was nothing but a damn demagogue.

It didn't surprise me when they shot him. These demagogues, the ones that live by demagoguery. They all end up the same way.

Harry S. Truman, in Merle Miller, *Plain Speaking – An Oral Biography of Harry S. Truman*

. . . a Winston Churchill who has never been at Harrow.

H. G. Wells, in Arthur M. Schlesinger Jr, *The Politics of Upheaval*

He is the most formidable kind of brer fox, the self-abnegating kind that will profess ignorance, who will check his dignity with his hat if he can serve his plans by buffoonery.

Rebecca West, in *ibid.*

## LONGCHAMP, WILLIAM, BISHOP OF ELY

– d. 1197 Statesman

The Chancellor in name only, disturbed by the thought of his lost power and his present condition, tried in every way to get round the prohibition against his crossing the Channel, and in a variety of ways and more than once he made a laughing stock of himself. I shall not mention that he was caught and held both in a monk's habit and in woman's clothing, but it is well remembered what vast stores of goods and what enormous treasures the Flemings took from him when he landed at last in Flanders.

Richard of Devizes, *Chronicle*, translated from the Latin by J. T. Appleby

## LONGFELLOW, HENRY WADSWORTH

1807–82 Poet

Most of the time am alone; smoke a great deal; wear a broad-brimmed black hat, black frock-coat, a black cane. Molest no one. Dine out frequently. In winter go much into Boston society.

On himself, in Thomas Wentworth Higginson, *Old Cambridge*

Longfellow is to poetry what the barrel-organ is to music.

Van Wyck Brooks, in Newton Arvin, *Longfellow, His Life and Work*

Longfellow's soul was not an ocean. It was a lake, clear, calm and cool. The great storms of the sea never reached it. And yet this lake had its depths. Buried cities lay under its surface.

Van Wyck Brooks, *The Flowering of New England 1815–1865*

A dandy Pindar.

Margaret Fuller, in Thomas Wentworth Higginson, *Old Cambridge*

. . . you reach and touch me always with the simple directness of a summer landscape, an evening sky, or a skylark's song. You rest me as Nature rests me always – on a lighter plane than my ordinary level . . .

Bret Harte, Letter to Longfellow, 9 November 1875

Decorum, excessive moderation, and a bold didacticism that sometimes descends into downright foolish bathos; a lack of imaginative passion or the instinct of rebellion: all these have reduced him, in much of his writing, from a true poet to a cultural influence.

Stanley J. Kunitz and Howard Haycraft eds, *American Authors, 1600–1900*

Longfellow, reminiscent, polished, elegant, with the air of finest conventional library, picture-gallery or parlor, with ladies and gentlemen in them, and plush and rosewood, and ground-glass lamps, and mahogany and ebony furniture, and a silver inkstand and scented satin paper to write on.

Walt Whitman, in Edgar Lee Masters, *Whitman*

*See also* Ezra Pound

## LORRE, PETER

1904–64 Actor

Lorre, with every physical handicap, can convince you of the goodness, the starved tenderness of his vice-entangled soul. Those marbly pupils in the pasty spherical face are like the eye pieces of a microscope through which you can see laid flat on the slide the entangled mind of a man: love and lust, nobility and perversity, hatred of itself and despair jumping out at you from the jelly.

Graham Greene, *Graham Greene On Film*

## LOVELACE, RICHARD

1618–58 Cavalier Poet

But when the beauteous Ladies came to know / That their deare *Lovelace* was endanger'd so: / *Lovelace* that thaw'd the most congealed brest, / He who lov'd best and them defended best. / Whose hand so rudely grasps the steely brand, / Whose hand so gently melts the Ladies hand / They all in mutiny though yet undrest / Sally'd and would in his defence contest. /

Andrew Marvell, *To his Noble Friend Mr Richard Lovelace Upon His Poems*

Richard Lovelace . . . became a Gent. Commoner of *Glocester Hall* in the beginning of the Year 1634, and in that of his age 16, being then accounted the most amiable and beautiful Person that every Eye beheld, a Person also of innate modesty, virtue and courtly deportment, which made him then, but especially after, when he retired to the great City, much admired and adored by the Female Sex. In 1636, when the King and Queen were for some days entertained at *Oxon.*, he was, at the request of a great Lady belonging to the Queen, made to the Archb. of *Cant.* then Chancellor of the University, actually created, among other Persons of Quality, Master of Arts, tho' but of two Years standing; at which time his Conversation being made public, and consequently his ingenuity and generous Soul discovered, he became as much admired by the Male, as before by the Female, Sex.

Anthony à Wood, *Athenae Oxonienses*

## LOWELL, AMY

1874–1925 Poet, Critic

The future's her goose and I dare say she'll wing it, / Though the triumph will need her own power to sing it. / Although I'm no prophet, I'll hazard a guess / She'll be rated by time as more rather than less. /

On herself, *A Critical Fable*

When I get through with that girl she'll think she was born in free verse.

Ezra Pound, in Horace Gregory, *Amy Lowell*

. . . our only hippo-poetess.

Ezra Pound, in Charles Norman, *Ezra Pound*

When she reached her accustomed suite at the Belmont Hotel, in New York City, where she stopped several times a year, every large mirror had to be swathed in black, every clock stopped, and the sixteen pillows produced.

Clement Wood, *Amy Lowell*

Amy Lowell, neither distinguished poet nor great critic, was still Amy Lowell and played her part well. The rest may ultimately be largely silence.

*Ibid.*

## LOWELL, JAMES RUSSELL

1819–91 Poet, Diplomat

There is Lowell, who's striving Parnassus to climb / With a whole bale of isms tied together with rhyme, / He might get on alone, spite of brambles and boulders, / But he can't with the bundle he has on his shoulders. /

On himself, *A Fable for Critics*

Lowell was a bookman, pure and simple, born and bred in an alcove; and he basked and ripened in the sun of books till he grew as mellow as a meerschaum.

Van Wyck Brooks, *The Flowering of New England 1815–1865*

He was strong without narrowness, he was wide without bitterness and glad without fatuity.

Henry James, in Arthur Hobson Quinn, 'The Establishment of National Literature', in Quinn ed., *The Literature of the American People*

Lowell was not a grower – he was a builder. He *built* poems: he didn't put in the seed, and water the seed, and send down his sun – letting the rest take care of itself: he measured his poems – kept them within the formula.

Walt Whitman, in Edgar Lee Masters, *Whitman*

A poet, statesman, and an American in one! A sort of three-headed Cerberus of Civilisation, who barks when he is baited, and is often mistaken for a lion, at a distance.

Oscar Wilde, Letter to Mrs Alfred Hunt, 17 February 1881

## LUCE, HENRY ROBINSON

1898–1967 Publisher

I am a Protestant, a Republican and a free-enterpriser, which means I am biased in favor of God, Eisenhower and the stockholders of Time Inc. – and if anybody who objects doesn't know this by now, why the hell are they still spending 35 cents for the magazine?

On himself, in W. A. Swanberg, *Luce and His Empire*

I'm a Jesuit of journalism – a persuader.

On himself, in John Kobler, *Luce, His Time, Life, and Fortune*

I think it is Mr Luce's unique contribution to American journalism that he placed into the hands of the people yesterday's newspaper and today's garbage homogenized into one neat package.

Herbert Lawrence Block (Herblock), in W. A. Swanberg, *Luce and His Empire*

He really thought there was nothing he could not do, so he often did it.

Archibald MacLeish, in *ibid.*

## LUGOSI, BELA

1882–1956 Actor

Poor old Bela. It was a strange thing. He really was a shy, sensitive and talented man. But he made a fatal mistake. He never took the trouble to learn our language and consequently he was very suspicious of tricks, fearful of what he regarded as scene-stealing. Later, when he realized I didn't go in for such nonsense we became friends. But we never really socialised. Our lives, our tastes, were quite different. Ours was simply a professional relationship.

Boris Karloff, in John Brosnan, *The Horror People*

For some people, he was the embodiment of dark, mysterious forces, a harbinger of evil from the world of shadow. For others he was merely a ham actor appearing in a type of film unsuitable for children and often unfit for adults.

Arthur Lennig, *The Count*

If Lugosi chews the scenery at times, he chews with grandiose vigor, and often that chewing provides our only nourishment. This much can be said; he is never dull. When he is on the screen, the film moves, and when he is not, the film is generally a species of the 'undead'.

*Ibid.*

## LUTYENS, SIR EDWIN LANDSEER

1869–1944 Architect

I had proposed that we should lunch together at the Garrick Club, because I had obviously to ask father if he had any serious objection to the writing or the writer of this essay. But, when I broached the matter, he merely mumbled in obvious embarrassment: 'Oh, my!' – just as his father used to do. Then, as the fish was served, he looked at me seriously over the rims of his two pairs of spectacles and remarked: 'The piece of cod passeth all understanding.'

Robert Lutyens, *Sir Edwin Lutyens*

That most delightful, good-natured, irresponsible, imaginative jester of genius.

Vita Sackville-West, *Pepita*

## LYLY, JOHN

1554–1606 Dramatist, Author

The noble Sydney . . . / . . . did first reduce / Our tongue from Lillies writing then in use; / Talking of stones, stars, plants, of fishes, flyes, / Playing with words, and idle similies, / As th'English, apes and very zanies be / Of every thing, that they doe heare and see, / So imitating his ridiculous tricks, / They spake and writ, all like meere lunatiques. /

Michael Drayton, *To My Most Dearely Loved Friend Henery Reynolds Esquire*

Himself a mad lad, as ever twanged, never troubled with any substance of wit or circumstance of honesty, sometime the fiddlestick of Oxford, now the very babble of London.

Gabriel Harvey, *Advertisement for Papp-hatchett and Martin Marprelate*, 1590

## LYNDHURST, LORD (JOHN SINGLETON COPLEY THE YOUNGER)

1772–1863 Jurist

He wanted to serve a temporary purpose, and he did so always. He regarded politics as a game; to be played first for himself, and then for his party. He did not act contrary to his opinion, but he did not care to form a true opinion.

Walter Bagehot, *Biographical Studies*: 'What Lord Lyndhurst really was'

Lady Tankerville asked Lord Lyndhurst, whether he believed in Platonic Friendship?

'After but not before,' was the reply.

Benjamin Disraeli, *Reminiscences*

## LYTTELTON, GEORGE, BARON

1709–73 Politician

Wrapped up like a Laputan in intense thought . . . he leaves his hat in one room, his sword in another, and would leave his shoes in a third if his buckles, though awry, did not save them; his legs and arms . . . seem to have undergone the *question extraordinaire*; and his head, always hanging upon one or other of his shoulders, seems to have received the first stroke of the block.

Philip Dormer Stanhope, Earl of Chesterfield, *Letters*

That man sat down to write a book, to tell the world what the world had all his life been telling him.

Samuel Johnson, in James Boswell, *Life of Johnson*

From these abstracted of, / You wander through the philosophic world; / Where in bright train continual wonders rise / Or to the curious or the pious eye. / And oft, conducted by historic truth, / You tread the long extent of backward time, / Planning with warm benevolence of mind / And honest zeal, unwarped by party rage, / Britannia's weal – how from the venal gulf / To raise her virtue and her arts revive. /

James Thomson, *The Seasons: Spring*

Absurdity was predominant in Lyttelton's composition: it entered equally into his politics, his apologies, his public pretences, his private conversations. With the figure of a spectre, and the gesticulations of a puppet, he talked heroics through his nose, made declamations at a visit, and played cards with scraps of history or sentences of Pindar.

Horace Walpole, *Memoirs*

## LYTTON (BULWER-LYTTON), EDWARD GEORGE EARLE, LORD

1803–73 Author, Statesman

'Ada' used to shock Lytton by her barefaced atheism. He maintained a correspondence with her on the Immortality of the Soul, which will probably some day be published for he never wrote an invitation to dinner without an eye to posterity.

At one time, he flattered himself, that he had a little shaken her; she had hinted at some sort of Pantheistic compromise. 'Never,' said Lytton, 'I *must* have *identity*.'

He exceeded Cicero.

Benjamin Disraeli, *Reminiscences*

Lytton cashed his cheque on fame for ready money.

Desmond MacCarthy, *Experience*

If he would but leave off scents for his handkerchief, and oil for his hair: if he would but confine himself to three clean shirts in a week, a couple of coats in a year, a beef-steak and onions for dinner, his beaker a pewter pot, his carpet a sanded floor, how much might be made of him even yet.

W. M. Thackeray, Review of Lytton's *Ernest Maltravers*

*See also* Thomas Beecham, W. Somerset Maugham, Lord Palmerston, H. G. Wells

# 'M'

## MACARTHUR, DOUGLAS

1880–1964 Soldier

I came through and I shall return.
On himself, Statement to reporters in Australia in 1943 having been evacuated from the Philippines during the Second World War

Old soldiers never die; they just fade away.
On himself, Address to a joint session of the United States Congress, 19 April 1951

The shadows are lengthening for me. The twilight is here. My days of old have vanished tone and tint; they have gone glimmering through the dreams of things that were. Their memory is one of wondrous beauty, watered by tears and coaxed and caressed by the smiles of yesterday. I listen vainly, but with thirsty ear, for the witching melody of faint bugles blowing reveille, of far drums beating the long roll. In my dreams I hear again the crash of guns, the rattle of musketry, the strange mournful mutter of the battlefield. But in the evening of my memory, always I come back to West Point. Always there echoes and re-echoes in my ears – Duty – Honor – Country.
On himself, Farewell address to the cadets of West Point, 12 May 1962

Oh yes, I studied dramatics under him for twelve years.
Dwight D. Eisenhower, in Quentin Reynolds, *By Quentin Reynolds*

Let him go, let him go, we are the braver, / Stain his hands with our blood, dye them forever. / Recall, oh ye kinsmen, how he left us to die, / Starved and insulted by his infamous lie; / How he seduced us with boasts of defense; / How he traduced us with plans of offense. / When his publicity chairman presides, / Vaunts his fame as high as the Bay of Fundy tides – / Recollect bonus boys gassed out by him / Remember Bataan boys sacrificed for him. / Try him, Tribunal of Public Opinion / Brothers, condemn him through our dominion / Then when he stands before Judges Olympian, / Quakes at his final court-martial: oblivion. /
Aquill Penn (pseud.), *The Lost Leader*, written in a Japanese prisoner of war camp in June 1943

I fired him because he wouldn't respect the authority of the President. That's the answer to that. I didn't fire him because he was a dumb son of a bitch, although he was, but that's not against the law for generals. If it was half to three quarters of them would be in jail.
Harry S. Truman, commenting on his removal of MacArthur from command of U.S. and U.N. troops in Korea, in Merle Miller, *Plain Speaking: An Oral Biography of Harry S. Truman*

## MACAULAY, THOMAS BABINGTON, LORD

1800–59 Historian, Essayist, Politician

I am far from insensible to the pleasure of having fame, rank, and this opulence which has come so late.
On himself, Journal, 1 January 1858

He never starts except for the end in view. His hook and bait will only catch a particular fish, – there is no vague cast of the net.
Lord Acton, Letter to William Ewart Gladstone, 21 June 1876

The great apostle of the Philistines.
Matthew Arnold, *Essays in Criticism*: 'Joubert'

Macaulay is well for a while, but one wouldn't *live* under Niagara.
Thomas Carlyle, in R. A. Milnes, *Notebook*

. . . vague generalities handled with that brilliant imagination which tickles the ear and amuses the fancy without satisfying the reason.
John Wilson Croker, to the House of Commons, 22 September 1831

The worst of it is that Macaulay, like Rousseau, talked his nonsense so well that it still passes for gospel with all those who have advanced as far as reading, but have not as yet attained to thinking.
George Birkbeck Hill, *Footsteps of Dr Johnson*

He has written some very brilliant essays – very transparent in artifice, and I suspect not over honest in scope and management, but he has written *no history*.
John G. Lockhart, Letter to John Wilson Croker, 12 January 1849

His object is to strike, and he attains it; but it is by scene-painting – he aims at stronger effects than truth warrants, and so caricatures many of his personages as to leave it unaccountable how they have done what they did.
John Stuart Mill, commenting on Macaulay's *Essays*, Letter to Arthur Hardy, September 1856

Then the favourite comes with his trumpets and drums, / And his arms and his metaphors crossed. /
W. M. Praed, undergraduate squib, 1820

A sentence of Macaulay's . . . may have no more sense in it than a blot pinched between doubled paper.
John Ruskin, *Praeterita*

He has occasional flashes of silence, that make his conversation perfectly delightful.
Sydney Smith, in Lady Holland, *Memoirs of Sydney Smith*

Macaulay is like a book in breeches.
*Ibid.*

. . . that style which, with its metallic exactness and its fatal efficiency, was certainly one of the most remarkable products of the industrial revolution.
Lytton Strachey, *Portraits in Miniature*

He seems to have been created *en bloc.* His manner never changed; as soon as he could write at all – at the age of eight – he wrote in the style of his History. The three main factors in his intellectual growth, – the Clapham sect, Cambridge, Holland House – were not so much influences as suitable environments for the development of a predetermined personality. Whatever had happened to him he would always have been a middle class intellectual with whig views . . . And there he is – squat, square and perpetually talking – on Parnassus.
*Ibid.*

## MCCARTHY, JOSEPH

1908–57 Politician

McCarthyism is Americanism with its sleeves rolled.
On himself, in a 1952 speech, in Richard H. Rovere, *Senator Joe McCarthy*

McCarthy is the only major politician in the country who can be labelled 'liar' without fear of libel.
Joseph and Stewart Alsop, syndicated column, 3 December 1953

The late Joseph R. McCarthy, a United States Senator from Wisconsin, was in many ways the most gifted demagogue ever bred on these shores.

No bolder seditionist ever moved among us – nor any politician with a surer, swifter access to the dark places of the American mind.

Richard H. Rovere, *Senator Joe McCarthy*

This sovereign of the assemblies was 'foul mouthed' all right, and 'a low mean fellow', and he wanted no one to think otherwise of him. He was a master of the scabrous and the scatological; his talk was laced with obscenity. He was a vulgarian by method as well as, probably, by instinct. He belched and burped in public. If he did not dissemble much, if he did little to hide from the world the sort of human being he was, it was because he had the shrewdness to see that this was not in his case necessary. He seemed to understand, as no other politician of this stature ever has, the perverse appeal of the bum, the mucker, the Dead End kid, the James Jones-Nelson Algren-Jack Kerouac hero of a nation uneasy in its growing order and stability.

*Ibid.*

... this Typhoid Mary of conformity.

*Ibid.*

## MCCLELLAN, GEORGE BRINTON

1826–85 Soldier

[McClellan] is an admirable Engineer, but he seems to have a special talent for the stationary engine.

Abraham Lincoln, in Robert Debs Heinl Jr, *The Dictionary of Military and Naval Quotations*

My dear McClellan:

If you don't want to use the army, I should like to borrow it for a while.

Yours respectfully,
A. Lincoln.

Abraham Lincoln, Letter to McClellan, complaining that the general was failing in his duties as commander in chief of the Army of the Potomac, in Carl Sandburg, *Abraham Lincoln, The Prairie Years and the War Years*

So McClellan sent a telegram to Lincoln one day: 'Have captured two cows. What disposition should I make of them?' And Lincoln:' Milk'em, George.'

Carl Sandburg, *ibid.*

## MACDONALD, (JAMES) RAMSAY

1866–1937 Prime Minister

If God were to come to me and say, 'Ramsay, would you rather be a country gentleman than a Prime Minister?', I should reply, 'Please God, a country gentleman.'

On himself, in Harold Nicolson, Diary, 5 October 1930

Ramsay MacDonald is trying to ride two horses. He is trying to appear a strong, virile fellow, who is justified in the eyes of the public, in running after the great ladies in society. In short, a reincarnation of Palmerston.

The other horse is the ailing, sick, weary Titan, carrying the world on his shoulders. A brave, courageous creature, indomitable in his will-power in the face of all the afflictions God has visited on him – somewhat in spite of God.

The truth is, he is an old humbug.

Lord Beaverbrook, Letter to Sir Robert Borden, 14 August 1932

... the boneless wonder...

Winston Churchill, Comment on MacDonald's conciliation of his Roman Catholic supporters, 1931

We know that he has, more than any other man, the gift of compressing the largest amount of words into the smallest amount of thought.

Winston Churchill, Speech in the Commons, March 1933

Ramsay was like the fellow who said: 'I'ze eating very well indeed. I'ze drinking very well indeed. But it's when I'ze asked to do anything in the way of work that I feels all wrong.'

Winston Churchill, 1933, in A. J. Sylvester, *Life with Lloyd George*

. . . MacDonald was conscientious almost to a fault, and he never acquired the art of delegating responsibility; it was said of him that he had been known, when prime minister, to look up trains for one of his secretaries.

Lord Elton, in *Dictionary of National Biography 1931–1940*

He is leading the gentlemen of England, and there is no price he would not pay for that.

Harold Laski, Letter to Felix Frankfurter, 1931

He had sufficient conscience to bother him, but not sufficient to keep him straight.

David Lloyd George, in A. J. Sylvester, Diary, 29 August 1938

MacDonald owes his pre-eminence largely to the fact that he is the only artist, the only aristocrat by temperament and talent in a Party of plebeians and plain men.

Beatrice Webb, Diary, May 1930

## MCKINLEY, WILLIAM

1843–1901 Twenty-Fifth United States President

I would rather have my political economy founded upon the everyday experience of the puddler or the potter than the learning of the professor.

On himself, in Paul W. Glad, *McKinley, Bryan and the People*

Looking for all the world like a benign undertaker, he embalmed himself for posterity. Never permitting himself to be photographed in disarray, he would change his white vests, when wrinkled, several times a day.

Thomas A. Bailey, *Presidential Greatness*

The bullet that pierced Goebel's breast / Can not be found in all the West; / Good reason, it is speeding here / To stretch McKinley on his bier. /

Ambrose Bierce, in A. W. Johns, *The Man Who Shot McKinley*

McKinley keeps his ear to the ground so close that he gets it full of grasshoppers much of the time.

'Uncle' Joe Cannon, in H. J. Sievers, *Benjamin Harrison: Hoosier President*

I was more surprised to learn from the autopsy of the President that he was dying of old age at 58, if he had not been shot.

John Hay, Letter to Henry Adams, 21 October 1901

Where is McKinley, Mark Hanna's McKinley, / His slave, his echo, his suit of clothes? / Gone to join the shadows, with the pomps of that time, / And the flame of that summer's prairie rose. /

Vachel Lindsay, *Bryan, Bryan, Bryan, Bryan*

. . . had about as much backbone as a chocolate éclair.

Theodore Roosevelt, as reported by Secretary Long, in D. H. Elletson, *Roosevelt and Wilson: A Comparative Study*

Not long ago we had two men running for the President. There was Mr McKinley on the one hand and Mr Bryan on the other. If we'd have had an 'Anti-Doughnut Party' neither would have been elected.

Mark Twain, in Philip S. Foner, *Mark Twain Social Critic*

He weighed out his saccharine on apothecary scales, just enough and no more for the dose that cheers but does not inebriate.

William Allen White, in Paul W. Glad, *McKinley, Bryan and the People*

He shook hands with exactly the amount of cordiality and with precisely the lack of intimacy that deceived men into thinking well of him, too well of him.

*Ibid.*

He walked among men a bronze statue, for thirty years determinedly looking for his pedestal.

William Allen White, in Ralph G. Martin, *Ballots and Bandwagons*

## MACKINTOSH, SIR JAMES

1765–1832 Philosopher

Sir Jammy (the humane *code-softener*).

William Cobbett, *Journal*, 31 October 1825

Mr Mackintosh's Lectures were after all but a kind of philosophical centos. They were profound, brilliant, new to his hearers; but the profundity, the brilliancy, the novelty were not his own. He was like Dr Pangloss (not Voltaire's, but Coleman's) who speaks only in quotations; and the pith, the marrow of Sir James's reasoning and rhetoric at that memorable period might be put within inverted commas.

William Hazlitt, *The Spirit of the Age*

Though thou'rt like Judas, an apostate black, / In the resemblance thou dost one thing lack; / When he had gotten his ill-purchas'd pelf, / He went away, and wisely hang'd himself: / This thou may do at last, yet much I doubt / If thou hast any bowels to gush out! /

Charles Lamb, *Epigram*

## MCPHERSON, AIMEE SEMPLE

1890–1944 Evangelist

Your sister in the King's glad service.

On herself, in William G. McLoughlin, 'Aimee Semple McPherson', *Journal of Popular Culture*, Winter 1967

The Barnum of religion.

Anon., in *Notable American Women*, vol. 2

Mrs McPherson has the nerve of a brass monkey and the philosophy of the Midway – 'Never give a sucker an even break' – is grounded in her.

Morrow Mayo ,'Aimee Rises from the Sea', in *New Republic*, 25 December 1929

## MACREADY, WILLIAM CHARLES

1793–1873 Actor

Mr Macready sometimes, to express uneasiness and agitation, composes his cravat as he would in a drawing-room.

William Hazlitt, in *Examiner*, 6 October 1816

We do not always see the reason for his *fortes* and *pianos*: his grace looks more the effect of study than habit: his personal character does not seem so concerned in what he does. You are not sure what sort of person he will be when he leaves the stage.

Leigh Hunt, 'Macready as Virginius', in *Tatler*, 19 October 1830

His declamation was mannered and unmusical; yet his intelligence always made him follow the winding meanings through the involutions of the verse, and never allowed you to feel, as you feel in the declamation of Charles Kean, and many other actors, that he was speaking words which he did not thoroughly understand. The trick of a broken and spasmodic rhythm might destroy the music proper to the verse, but it did not perplex you with false emphasis or intonations wandering at hazard.

George Henry Lewes, *On Actors and the Art of Acting*

Macready it is said, used to spend some minutes behind the scenes, lashing himself into an imaginative rage by cursing *sotto voce*, and shaking violently a ladder fixed against the wall.
*Ibid.*

## MCTAGGART, JOHN MCTAGGART ELLIS

1866–1925 Philosopher

If Hegel be the inspired, and too often incoherent, prophet of the Absolute; and if Bradley be its chivalrous knight, ready to challenge anyone who dares to question its pre-eminence; McTaggart is its devoted and extremely astute family solicitor.
C. D. Broad, *Ethics and the History of Philosophy*

## MADISON, JAMES

1750/1–1836 Fourth United States President

Mr Madison is, as I always knew him, slow in taking his ground, but firm when the storm rises.
Albert Gallatin, in Irving Brant, *The Fourth President, A Life of James Madison*

*See also* Martin Van Buren

## MAHAN, ALFRED THAYER

1840–1914 Sailor, Historian

It was inevitable that the English-German imperialistic rivalry should have ended in struggle: it was this American's unenviable distinction however to have armed both foes, ideologically and physically, for the contest.
Louis M. Hacker, 'The Incendiary Mahan', in *Scribner's Magazine*, April 1934

. . . Mahan, the maritime Clausewitz, the Schlieffen of the sea.
Barbara W. Tuchman, *The Guns of August*

## MAITLAND, JOHN, *see under* LAUDERDALE, DUKE OF

## MALCOLM X (MALCOLM LITTLE)

1925–65 Civil Rights Activist, Religious Leader

Black history began with Malcolm X.
Eldridge Cleaver, in Peter Goldman, *The Death and Life of Malcolm X*

He meant to haunt us – to play on our fears and quicken our guilts and deflate our dreams that everything was getting better – and he did.
Peter Goldman, *ibid.*

Malcolm was a destroyer of myths and the webs of mystification . . . He was a black son and brother who had audaciously returned to us from a very long trip through lands ruled by god-kings and magician-tricksters. He brought back the truth about the racket of racism, oppression and imperialism.
Patricia Robinson, 'Malcolm X, Our Revolutionary Son and Brother', in John Henry Clarke ed., *Malcolm X: The man and his time*

## MALORY, SIR THOMAS

1400?–70? Author

In our forefathers tyme, when papistrie, as a standyng pool, covered and overflowed all England, fewe bookes were read in our tong, savyng certaine bookes Chevalrie, as they sayd, for pastime and pleasure, which, as some say, were made in Monasteries, by idle Monkes, or wanton Chanons: as for example, *Morte Arthure*: the whole pleasure of which booke standeth in two speciall poyntes, in open mans slaughter, and bold bawdrie: In which book those be counted the noblest Knightes, that do kill most men without any quarrell, and commit fowlest aduoulteries by subtlest shifts . . . This is good stuffe, or wise men to laughe at, or honest men to take pleasure at.

Roger Ascham, *The Schoolmaster*

Malory's description of himself as 'the servant of Jesu both day and night' has been assumed to imply that he was a priest, but his description of himself as a 'knight' confutes the suggestion. Pious ejaculation at the conclusion of their labours is characteristic of medieval authors.

Sidney Lee, in *Dictionary of National Biography*

## MALTHUS, THOMAS ROBERT

1766–1834 Political Economist, Clergyman

Had Adeline read Malthus? I can't tell; / I wish she had: his book's the eleventh commandment, / Which says, 'Thou shalt not marry,' unless *well*: / This he (as far as I can understand) meant: / 'Tis not my purpose on his views to dwell, / Nor canvass what 'so eminent a hand' meant; / But certes it conducts to lives ascetic, / Or turning marriage into arithmetic. /

Lord Byron, *Don Juan*, canto xv

Mr Malthus's system is one, 'in which the wicked cease from troubling, and in which the weary are at rest.' To persons of an irritable and nervous disposition, who are fond of kicking against the pricks, who have tasted of the bitterness of the knowledge of good and evil, and to whom whatever is amiss in others sticks not merely like a burr, but like a pitch-plaister, the advantage of such a system is incalculable.

William Hazlitt, *Reply to the Essay on Population by the Rev. T. R. Malthus*

Malthus is a real moral philosopher, and I would almost consent to speak as inarticulately, if I could think and act as wisely.

Sydney Smith, Letter to a friend, July 1821

Philosopher Malthus came here last week. I got an agreeable party for him of unmarried people. There was only one lady who had had a child; but he is a good-natured man, and, if there are no appearances of approaching fertility, is civil to every lady.

*Ibid.*, 1831

## MANNING, HENRY EDWARD, CARDINAL

1808–92 Theologian

I am conscious of a desire to be in such a position (1) as I had in times past, (2) as my present circumstances imply, (3) as my friends think me fit for, (4) as I feel my own faculties tend to. But, God being my helper, I will not seek it by the lifting of a finger or the speaking of a word.

On himself, Diary, *circa* 1851

I am a Mosaic Radical.

On himself, in old age, in Lytton Strachey, *Eminent Victorians*

I do not know whether I am on my head or my heels when I have active relations with you. In spite of my friendly feelings, this is the judgment of my intellect.

Cardinal Newman, Letter to Manning, 1866

. . . As he entered the ante-room where one awaited his approach, the most Protestant knee instinctively bent.

G. W. E. Russell, *Collections and Recollections*

## MANSFIELD, KATHERINE (KATHLEEN MANSFIELD BEAUCHAMP)

1888–1923 Author

Trying to read her after Chekhov was like hearing the carefully artificial tales of a young old-maid compared to those of an articulate and knowing physician who was a good and simple writer.

Ernest Hemingway, *A Moveable Feast*

I think that in some abstruse way [John Middleton] Murry corrupted and perverted and destroyed Katherine both as a person and a writer. She was a very serious writer, but her gifts were those of an intense realist, with a superb sense of ironic humour and fundamental cynicism. She got enmeshed in the sticky sentimentality of Murry and wrote against the grain of her own nature. At the bottom of her mind she knew this, I think, and it enraged her.

Leonard Woolf, *Beginning Again*

We could both wish that our first impression of K.M. was not that she stinks like a – well, civet cat that had taken to street walking. In truth, I'm a little shocked by her commonness at first sight; lines so hard and cheap. However, when this diminishes, she is so intelligent and inscrutable that she repays friendship.

Virginia Woolf, *A Writer's Diary*, 11 October 1917

## MANSFIELD, EARL OF (WILLIAM MURRAY)

1705–93 Judge

My desire to disturb no man for conscience sake is pretty well known and, I hope, will be had in remembrance.

On himself, in Bonamy Dobrée ed., *Anne to Victoria*

He [Johnson] would not allow Scotland to derive any credit from Lord Mansfield; for he was educated in England. 'Much,' said he, 'may be made of a Scotchman, if he be *caught* young.'

James Boswell, *Life of Johnson*

Sir, you may as well maintain that a carrier, who has driven a pack-horse between Edinburgh and Berwick for thirty years, does not know the road, as that Lord Mansfield does not know the law of England.

James Boswell, *Journal of A Tour of the Hebrides*

So then – the Vandals of our isle, / Sworn foes to sense and law, / Have burnt to dust a nobler pile / Than ever Roman saw! /

And MURRAY sighs o'er Pope and Swift, / And many a treasure more, / The well-judg'd purchase and the gift / That grac'd his letter'd store. /

*Their* pages mangled, burnt, and torn, / The loss was *his alone*; / But ages yet to come shall mourn / The burning of *his own*. /

William Cowper, *On the Burning of Lord Mansfield's Library Together with his MSS by the Mob in the Month of June 1780*

## MARLBOROUGH, DUKE OF (JOHN CHURCHILL)

1650–1722 Soldier

'Twas then great Marlbro's mighty soul was prov'd, / That in the shock of charging hosts unmov'd, / Amidst confusion, horror and despair, / Examin'd all the dreadful scenes of war; / In peaceful thought the field of death survey'd, / To fainting squadrons sent the timely aid, / Inspir'd repuls'd battalions to engage, / And taught the doubtful battle where to rage. /

Joseph Addison, *The Campaign*

And glory long has made the sages smile; / 'Tis something, nothing, words, illusion, wind – / Depending more upon the historian's style / Than on the name a person leaves behind: / Troy owes to Homer what whist owes to Hoyle: / The present century was growing blind / To the great Marlborough's skill in giving knocks, / Until his late Life by Archdeacon Coxe. /

Lord Byron, *Don Juan*, canto iii

A note of what is to bee got to the Duke of Marl.'s History. Vigilance, Sobriety, Regularity, Humility, Presence of Mind, Voyd of Capriciousness, execution of orders well given, Health proceeding from temperance, Early up, Never taken at a Why Not.

Sarah Churchill, Duchess of Marlborough, in Iris Butler, *Rule of Three*

By his invincible genius in war and his scarcely less admirable qualities of wisdom and management he had completed that glorious process that carried England from her dependency upon France . . . to ten years' leadership of Europe. Although this proud task was for a space cast aside by faction . . . the greatness of Britain and her claims to empire were established upon foundations that have lasted to this day. He had proved himself the 'good Englishman' he aspired to be, and History may declare that if he had had more power his country would have had more strength and happiness, and Europe a surer progress.

Winston Churchill, *Marlborough*, vol. 1

Of honour or the finer sentiments of mankind he knew nothing; and he turned without a shock from guiding Europe and winning great victories to heap up a matchless fortune by peculation and greed. He is perhaps the only instance of a man of real greatness who loved money for money's sake.

John Richard Green, *A Short History of the English People*

In life's last scene what prodigies surprise, / Fears of the brave, and follies of the wise! / From Marlborough's eyes the streams of dotage flow, / And Swift expires a driv'ller and a show. /

Samuel Johnson, *The Vanity of Human Wishes*

Threescore, I think, is pretty high; / 'Twas time in conscience he should die. / This world he cumber'd long enough; / He burnt his candle to the snuff; / And that's the reason, some folks think, / He left behind so great a stink. / Behold his funeral appears, / Nor widow's sighs, nor orphan's tears, / Wont at such times each heart to pierce, / Attend the progress of his hearse. / But what of that, his friends may say, / He had those honours in his day. / True to his profit and his pride, / He made them weep before he dy'd. /

Nathaniel Mist (also attributed to Jonathan Swift), in Michael Foot, *The Pen and the Sword*

'Great praise the Duke of Marlbro' won, / And our good Prince Eugene.' / 'Why 't was a very wicked thing!' / Said little Wilhelmine. / 'Nay . . nay . . my little girl', quoth he, / 'It was a famous victory. /

'And everybody praised the Duke / Who this great fight did win.' / 'But what good came of it at last?' / Quoth little Peterkin. / 'Why that I cannot tell,' said he, / 'But 't was a famous victory.'

Robert Southey, *The Battle of Blenheim*

It was Marlborough who first taught us to be proud of our standing army as a national institution, and the spirit of confidence which pervaded Wellington's army in the Peninsula, and to a still more remarkable degree shows itself now in Queen Victoria's army, may be said to have been born at Blenheim, baptized at Ramillies, and confirmed at Oudenarde.

Lord Wolseley, *Life of Marlborough*

*See also* Lord Peterborough, Jonathan Swift

## MARLOWE, CHRISTOPHER

1564–93 Dramatist

Marlowe was happy in his buskin Muse – / Alas, unhappy in his life and end; / Pity it is that wit so ill should dwell, / Wit lent from heaven, but vices sent from hell. / Our theatre hath lost, Pluto hath got, / A tragic penman for a dreary plot. /

Anon., in *The Return from Parnassus*

Hee saieth & verely beleveth that one Marlowe is able to shewe more sounde reasons for Atheisme than any devine in Englande is able to geve to prove devinitie that Marloe tolde him that hee hath read the Atheist lecture to Sr Walter Raliegh & others.

Anon., in *Remembraunces of Words and Matter againste Ric Cholmeley*

Next Marlowe, bathed in the Thespian Springs, / Had in him those brave translunary things / That your first poets had: his raptures were / All air and fire, which made his verses clear, / For that fine madness still he did retain, / Which rightly should possess a poet's brain. /

Michael Drayton, *Of Poets and Poetry*

There is a lust of power in his writings, a hunger and thirst after unrighteousness, a glow of the imagination unhallowed by any thing except its own energies. His thoughts burn within him like a furnace with bickering flames; or throwing out black smoke and mists, that hide the dawn of genius, or like a poisonous mineral, corrode the heart.

William Hazlitt, *Lectures on the Dramatic Literature of the Age of Elizabeth*

Marlowe, the moment the exhaustion of the imaginative fit deprives him of the power of raving, becomes childish in thought, vulgar and wooden in humour, and stupid in his attempts at invention. He is the true Elizabethan blank-verse beast, itching to frighten other people with the superstitious terrors and cruelties in which he does not himself believe, and wallowing in blood, violence, muscularity of expression and strenuous animal passion as only literary men do when they are thoroughly depraved by solitary work, sedentary cowardice, and starvation of the sympathetic centres. It is not surprising to learn that Marlowe was stabbed in a tavern brawl; what would be utterly unbelievable would be his having succeeded in stabbing anyone else.

George Bernard Shaw, in *Saturday Review*, 11 July 1896

The first English poet whose powers can be called sublime was Christopher Marlowe.

Algernon C. Swinburne, *The Age of Shakespeare*

Nor was any great writer's influence on his fellows more utterly and unmixedly an influence for good. He first, and he alone, guided Shakespeare into the right way of work; his music, in which there is no echo of any man's before him, found its own echo in the more prolonged but hardly more exalted harmony of Milton's. He is the greatest discoverer, the most daring and intrepid pioneer, in all our poetic literature. Before him was neither genuine blank verse nor genuine tragedy in our language. After his arrival the way was prepared, the paths were made straight, for Shakespeare.

*Ibid.*

It so hapned that at Detford, a little village about three miles distant from London, as he went to stab with his ponyard one named Ingram, that had invited him thither to a feast, and was then playing at tables, he quickly perceyving it, so avoyded the thrust, that withal drawing out his dagger for his defence hee stabd this Marlowe into the eye, in such sort, that his braines comming out at the daggers point, hee shortly after dyed.

William Vaughan, *Golden Grove*, 1600

*See also* Thomas Kyd, Thomas Nashe

## MARSTON, JOHN

1575?–1634 Dramatist

Marston is a writer of great merit, who rose to tragedy from the ground of comedy, and whose *forte* was not sympathy, either with the stronger or softer emotions, but an impatient scorn and bitter indignation against the vices and follies of men, which vented itself either in comic irony or in lofty invective. He was properly a satirist.

William Hazlitt, *Lectures on the Age of Elizabeth*

Jo. MARSTONE the last Christmas, when he daunced with Alderman Mores wives daughter, a Spaniard borne, fell into a strange commendation of her wit and beauty. When he had done, she thought to pay him home, and told him she *thought* he was a poet. ' 'Tis true,' said he, 'for poets feigne and lye, and soe did I, when I commended your beauty, for you are exceedingly foule.'

John Manningham, Diary, 21 November 1602

## MARTINEAU, HARRIET

1802–76 Author

I see no reason why the existence of Harriet Martineau should be perpetuated.

On herself, attributed last words

I cannot but praise a person whose one effort seems to have been to deal perfectly honestly and sincerely with herself, although for the speculations into which this effort has led her I have not the slightest sympathy.

Matthew Arnold, Letter to his Mother, May 1855

I fancied you would be struck by Miss Martineau's lucid and able style. She is a very admirable woman – and the most logical intellect of the age, for a woman. On this account it is that the men throw stones at her, and that many of her own sex throw dirt; but if I begin of this subject I shall end by gnashing my teeth.

Elizabeth Barrett Browning, Letter to H. S. Boyd, 24 December 1844

## MARVELL, ANDREW

1621–78 Poet

He was a great master of the Latin tongue; an excellent poet in Latin or English: for Latin verses there was no man could come into competition with him . . . He kept bottles of wine at his lodgeing, and many times he would drinke liberally by himselfe to refresh his spirits, and exalt his Muse.

John Aubrey, *Brief Lives*

Politically he was a Parliamentarian, intellectually he was a rationalist, temperamentally he was a satirist . . . He retained the mystical individualism of the Renaissance while recognizing its inadequacy, and as a consequence a tension is generated in his poetry comparable to that in the later poems of Yeats, who also had a foot in two cultural camps.

F. W. Bateson, *English Poetry: A Critical Introduction*

This is one of the great differences between Donne and Marvell: while Donne, one might almost say, devised entirely new ways of saying entirely new things, Marvell assimilated, recombined, and perfected from his contemporaries various new ways of saying old ones.

J. B. Leishman, *Proceedings of the British Academy*, 1961

## MARX, (JULIUS HENRY) 'GROUCHO'

1890–1977 Comedian

They say a man is as old as the woman he feels. In that case I'm eighty-five . . . I want it known here and now that this is what I want on my tombstone. Here lies Groucho Marx, and Lies and Lies and Lies. P.S. He never kissed an ugly girl.

On himself, in *The Secret Word is Groucho*

Please accept my resignation. I don't want to belong to any club that will accept me as a member.

On himself, Telegram to the Friar's Club, Hollywood. (There are various versions of this famous one-liner, all ostensibly authentic.)

My sex life is now reduced to fan letters from an elderly lesbian who would like to borrow $800; phone calls from a flagrant fairy with chronic low blood pressure (he'd like to get in pictures); and Pincus' dog who howls mournfully under my window every night.

On himself, Letter to Harry Kurnitz, 3 October 1950

What put him in a better mood was being mistaken for someone else – like the day a Beverly Hills dowager, obviously on the lookout for a non-Japanese gardener to work her own place, drove by in a Cadillac and stopped in front of father's house. Father was dressed in old pants and a sweat-shirt, and he was down on his hands and knees in a flower bed, working with a trowel.

'Oh gardener,' the dowager called out the window to the crouched figure in the garden, 'how much does the lady of the house pay you a month?'

'Oh I don't get paid in dollars,' answered Father. 'The lady of the house just lets me sleep with her.'

Arthur Marx, *Son of Groucho*

On his climb up the ladder he has enjoyed life to the utmost. He has shaken hands with Presidents, danced cheek to cheek with Marlene Dietrich, played baseball with Lou Gehrig, traded backhands with Jack Kramer, strummed guitar duets with the great Segovia, and he's insulted nearly everyone worth insulting.

Arthur Marx, *Life with Groucho*

## MARX, (ADOLPH) 'HARPO'

1893–1964 Comedian, Musician

I was the same kind of father as I was a harpist – I played by ear.

On himself, in Harpo Marx, *Harpo Speaks*

I've played piano in a whorehouse. I've smuggled secret papers out of Russia. I've spent an evening on the divan with Peggy Hopkins Joyce. I've taught a gangster mob how to play Pinchie Winchie. I've played croquet with Herbert Bayard Swope while he kept Governor Al Smith waiting on the phone. I've gambled with Nick the Greek, sat on the floor with Greta Garbo, sparred with Benny Leonard, horsed around with the Prince of Wales, played Ping-pong with George Gershwin. George Bernard Shaw has asked me for advice. Oscar Levant has played private concerts for me at a buck a throw. I have golfed with Ben Hogan and Sam Snead. I've basked on the Riviera with Somerset Maugham and Elsa Maxwell. I've been thrown out of the casino at Monte Carlo. Flush with triumph at the poker table, I've challenged Alexander Woollcott to anagrams and Alice Duer Miller to a spelling match. I've given lessons to some of the world's greatest musicians. I've been a member of the two most famous Round Tables since the days of King Arthur – sitting with the finest creative minds of the 1920's at the Algonquin in New York, and with Hollywood's sharpest professional wits at the Hillcrest . . .

The truth is, I had no business doing any of these things. I couldn't read a note of music. I never finished the second grade. But I was having too much fun to recognize myself as an ignorant upstart.

On himself, in *ibid.*

One of Harpo's more disconcerting penchants was for running around in the nude. He would invite a group of friends to his house and greet them in the drawing room stark naked and smiling.

Norman bel Geddes, *Miracle In the Evening*

In his private world all was pleasant. If he felt displeased by anything going on in front of him, he smiled, closed his eyes and fell asleep. He was able to fall asleep in a dentist's chair and remain asleep while having a tooth filled.

Ben Hecht, *A Child of the Century*

## MARY I
1516–58

'When I am dead and my body is opened,' she said to those around her, 'ye shall find CALAIS written on my heart'. I should have thought, if anything were written on it, they would have found the words – JANE GREY, HOOPER, ROGERS, RIDLEY, LATIMER, CRANMER, AND THREE HUNDRED PEOPLE BURNT ALIVE WITHIN FOUR YEARS OF MY WICKED REIGN, INCLUDING SIXTY WOMEN AND FORTY LITTLE CHILDREN.

Charles Dickens, *A Child's History of England*

The lady Mary my sister came to me to Whestminster, wheare after salutacions she was called with my counsel into a chambre, where was declared how long I had suffered her masse against my will in hope of her reconciliation, and how now, being no hope, which I perceived by her lettres, except I saw some short amendment, I could not beare it. She answerid that her soul was God's, and by her faith she wold not chaung, nor dissemble her opinion with contrary doinges. It was said I constrained not her faith, but willed her not as a king to rule but as a subject to obey. And that her exaumple might breed to much inconvenience.

Edward VI, *Chronicle*

It was her particular misfortune that the two things in the world to which she was devoted, her husband and her religion, were the two things which most estranged her from her people.

Conyers Read, *The Tudors*

## MARY II
1662–94 Queen Consort to William III

Oft have we heard of impious sons before / Rebelled for crowns their royal parents wore; / But of unnatural daughters rarely hear / 'Till those of hapless James and old king Lear. / But worse than cruel lustful Goneril thou! / She took but what her father did allow; / But thou, more impious, robb'st thy father's brow. / Him both of power and glory you disarm, / Make him by lies the people's hate and scorn, / Then turn him forth to perish in a storm. /

Anon., *The Female Parricide*, 1689

Her understanding, though very imperfectly cultivated, was quick. There was no want of feminine wit and shrewdness in her conversation; and her letters were so well expressed that they deserved to be well spelt.

T. B. Macaulay, *History of England*

*See also* William III

## MARY STUART, QUEEN OF SCOTS

1542–87

Mary, Mary, quite contrary, / How does your garden grow? / With silver bells, and cockle shells, / And pretty maids all in a row. /

Nursery rhyme, traditionally taken to refer to Mary

The meanest hind in fair Scotland / May rove their sweets amang; / But I, the Queen of a' Scotland, / Maun lie in prison strang. / I was the Queen o' bonie France / Where happy I hae been; / Fu' lightly rase I in the morn, / As blythe lay down at e'en; / And I'm the Sovereign of Scotland, / And mony a traitor there; / Yet here I lie in foreign hands / And never-ending care. /

Robert Burns, *Lament of Mary Queen of Scots*

Let men patiently abide, and turn unto their God, and then shall he either destroy that whore in her whoredom, or else he shall put it in the hearts of a multitude to take the same vengeance upon her that has been taken of Jezebel and Athaliah, yea, and of others of whom profane histories make mention; for greater abomination was never in the nature of any woman than is in her, whereof we have but seen only the buds.

John Knox, *History of the Reformation in Scotland*

There was one more ceremony to accomplish. The executioner must exhibit the head and speak the customary words. The masked black figure stooped and rose, crying in a loud voice: 'Long live the Queen!' But all he held in his hand that had belonged to the rival queen of hearts was a kerchief, and pinned to it an elaborate auburn wig. Rolled nearer the edge of the platform, shrunken and withered and grey, with a spare silver stubble on the small shiny skull was the head of the martyr. Mary Stuart had always known how to embarrass her enemies.

Garrett Mattingly, *The Defeat of the Spanish Armada*

Fresch, fulgent, flurist, fragrant flour, formois / Lantern to lufe, of ladeis lamp and lot, / Cherie maist chaist, chief charbucle and chois; / Smaill sweit smaragde, smelling but smit of smot. /

Alexander Scot, *Ane New Zeir Gift To the Quene Mary Quhen scho come first hame*

It would be idle to dwell on the story of this princess, too well known for having the misfortune to be born in the same age, in the same island with, and to be handsomer than Elizabeth. Mary had the weakness to set up a claim to a greater kingdom than her own, without any army; and was at last reduced by her crimes to be a saint in a religion which was opposite to what her rival professed out of policy.

Horace Walpole, *Catalogue of the Royal and Noble Authors*

The most notorious whore in all the world.

Peter Wentworth, in J. E. Neale, *Peter Wentworth*

*See also* Elizabeth I

## MARY, VICTORIA MARY AUGUSTA LOUISE OLGA PAULINE CLAUDINE AGNES

1867–1953 Queen Consort to George V

Queen Mary looking like the Jungfrau, white and sparkling in the sun.

Henry Channon, Diary, 22 June 1937

## MASEFIELD, JOHN

1878–1967 Poet

Masefield gloomyish, and very precise in diction. Fine voice. Diction of a public speaker.

Arnold Bennett, Journal, 14 December 1918

A nervous, generous, correct man, very sensitive to criticism . . . He wrote in a hut in his garden, surrounded by tall gorse-bushes, and only appeared at meal-times. In the evening he used to read his day's work over to Mrs Masefield, and they corrected it together.

Robert Graves, *Goodbye to All That*

He's a horrible sentimentalist – the cheap Byron of the day – his stuff is Lara 1913.

D. H. Lawrence, Letter to Edward Garnett, 3 March 1913

Masefield was the first Georgian poet to arouse excitement in more than a clique. Since that time, which was in 1911, he has been subjected to so much condemnation on the part of successive schools of poets that he is rather in the position of Nanki Poo in 'The Mikado', when Ko-Ko explains that he is 'as good as dead – practically he *is* dead.' Nanki Poo, of course, is not at all dead, and in fact is upon the stage at the time.

Frank Swinnerton, *The Georgian Litarary Scene*

*See also* A. E. Housman

## MASSINGER, PHILIP

1583–1640 Dramatist

The comic Scenes in Massinger not only do not harmonize with the tragic, not only interrupt the feeling, but degrade the characters that are to form any Part in the action of the Piece so as to render them unfit for any *tragic interest* – as when a gentleman is insulted by a mere Blackguard – it is the same as if any other action of nature had occurred, as if a Pig had run under his legs, or his horse threw him.

Samuel Taylor Coleridge, *Notes for a Lecture*

His ways of thinking and feeling isolated him from both the Elizabethan and the later Caroline mind. He might almost have been a great realist; he is killed by conventions which were suitable for the preceding literary generation, but not for his. Had Massinger been a greater man, a man of more intellectual courage, the current of English literature immediately after him might have taken a different course. The defect is precisely a defect of personality. He is not, however, the only man of letters who, at the moment when a new view of life is wanted, has looked at life through the eyes of his predecessors, and only at manners through his own.

T. S. Eliot, *Essays*: 'Philip Massinger'

## MATHER, COTTON

1662/3–1727/8 Clergyman, Author, Politician

Grim Cotton Mather / Was always seeing witches. / Daylight, moonlight, / They buzzed about his head, / Pinching him and plaguing him / With aches and pains and stitches, / Witches in his pulpit, / Witches by his bed. /

Stephen Vincent Benét, *Cotton Mather*

## MAUGHAM, (WILLIAM) SOMERSET

1874–1965 Novelist

My first book, published in 1897, was something of a success. Edmund Gosse admired and praised it. After that

I published other books and became a popular dramatist . . . I used to meet Gosse once or twice a year and continued to do so for twenty years, but I never met him without his saying to me in his unctuous way: 'Oh, my dear Maugham, I liked your *Liza of Lambeth* so much. How wise you are never to have written anything else.'

On himself, *A Writer's Notebook*

I discovered my limitations and it seemed to me that the only sensible thing was to aim at what excellence I could within them. I knew that I had no lyrical quality, I had a small vocabulary and no efforts that I could make to enlarge it much availed me. I had little gift of metaphors; the original and striking simile seldom occurred to me. Poetic flights and the great imaginative sweep were beyond my powers . . . I knew that I should never write as well as I could wish, but I thought with pains I could arrive at writing as well as my natural defects allowed. On taking thought it seemed to me that I must aim at lucidity, simplicity and euphony. I have put these three qualities in the order of the importance I assigned to them.

On himself, *The Summing Up*

I always reserve to myself the privilege of changing my mind. It's the only one elderly gentlemen share with pretty women.

On himself, *The Aide*

Most writers discipline themselves to working certain hours, then knock off for relaxation until the morrow. Charles Morgan writes for a limited time each day, after which he goes out to cut wood; Willie Maugham has a stopwatch by his side and, on completion of the day's quota, goes to the terrace and prepares for the elaborate ritual of the dry martini.

Cecil Beaton, *The Strenuous Years*

Willie can be extremely capricious. He can turn violently against an old friend for some quite small reason: a guest who has upheld unpopular views, who has been argumentative or shown bad manners at the card table, has been told to pack his bags and leave forthwith. Willie admitted that his temper was so violent that he could quite well imagine, in a moment of rage, killing someone . . . One day recently Willie was walking in the garden with his companion, Alan Searle, when they stopped in their tracks to watch the progress of a snail. Alan picked up a small bit of gravel and tossed it at the snail. Willie shouted: 'Don't do that!' Alan threw another little pebble. The next thing Alan knew he was lying with an unrecognizable face in a nearby hospital.

*Ibid.*

W. Somerset Maugham prefers small parties, / 'Four is a wonderful number,' he decrees. / 'Six is all right, and eight will do in a pinch. / After that, it's not a party: it's a rabble.'

Bennett Cerf, *The Laugh's On Me*

Somerset Maugham I met only once, on the steps of the Opera. He looked exceedingly wicked . . . Two fundamental failings rob him of greatness. His works do not suggest those 'mysteries' which, as Proust puts it, 'have their explanation probably only in other worlds and a presentiment of which is precisely what moves us most in life and in art'. His other fault is the fear of appearing old-fashioned.

William Gerhardie, *Memoirs of a Polyglot*

He is for our day, I suppose, what Bulwer-Lytton was for Dickens's: a half-trashy novelist, who writes badly, but is patronized by half-serious readers, who do not care much about writing.

Edmund Wilson, *Classics and Commercials*

*See also* Harpo Marx

## MAXWELL, JAMES CLERK

1831–79 Physicist

Before Maxwell, Physical Reality, in so far as it was to represent the processes of nature, was thought of as consisting in material particles, whose variations consist only in movements governed by partial differential equations. Since Maxwell's time, Physical Reality has been thought of as represented by continuous fields, governed by partial differential equations, and not capable of any mechanical interpretation. This change in the conception of Reality is the most profound and the most fruitful that physics has experienced since the time of Newton.

Albert Einstein, in J. J. Thomson *et al., James Clerk Maxwell. A Commemoration Volume*

*See also* Michael Faraday

## MAYER, LOUIS BURT

1885–1957 Motion Picture Producer

I remembered him as a hard-faced, badly-spoken and crass little man . . . [He] wore a two-hundred-and-fifty-dollar suit, had the glibness of a self-taught evangelist and was mantled in the arrogance of success.

Charles Bickford, *Bulls, Balls, Bicycles and Actors*

The reason so many people showed up at his funeral was because they wanted to make sure he was dead.

Samuel Goldwyn, in Bosley Crowther, *Hollywood Rajah*

I will say that it was clear that behind his gutta-percha face and roly-poly figure (contained in some of the best tailoring I've ever seen) it was evident there was a man of steel – but well-mannered steel, the very best quality steel, which meant the hardest and most impenetrable steel.

Edward G. Robinson, *All My Yesterdays*

## MELBOURNE, VISCOUNT (WILLIAM LAMB)

1779–1848 Statesman, Prime Minister

I hate to be considered ill-used; I have always thought complaints of ill-usage contemptible, whether from a seduced disappointed girl, or a turned-out Prime Minister.

On himself, in Emily Eden, Letter to Mrs Lister, 23 November 1834

Lord Melbourne sees [the Queen] every day for a couple of hours, and his situation is certainly the most dictatorial, the most despotic, that the world has ever seen. Wolsey and Walpole were in strait waistcoats compared to him.

John Wilson Croker, Letter to Sir Robert Peel, 15 August 1837

I have no doubt [Melbourne] is passionately fond of [the Queen], as he might be of his daughter if he had one; and the more because he is a man with a capacity for loving without anything to love. It is become his province to educate, instruct and form the most interesting mind and character in the world.

Charles Greville, *The Greville Memoirs*

. . . the person who makes me feel safe and comfortable.

Queen Victoria, Diary, 4 July 1838

## MELVILLE, HERMAN

1819–91 Author

Though I wrote the Gospels in this century, I should die in the gutter.

On himself, Letter to Nathaniel Hawthorne, 29 June 1851

A rover, whose imagination had been disciplined neither by Puritanism nor by a formal education, he lashed, like his own whales, into bloody foam when the lance of doubt finally struck him through.

Henry Seidel Canby, *Classic Americans*

Melville's idea of art is much more Promethean; he thought of a work of art as something never finished, something that remained living, organic, and emergent.

Richard Chase, 'Herman Melville', in Perry Miller ed., *Major Writers of America*, vol. 1

Normally he was not a man of noticeable appearance; but when the narrative inspiration was on him, he looked like all the things he was describing – savages, sea-captains, the lovely Fayaway in her canoe, or the terrible Moby Dick himself.

Julian Hawthorne, in Eleanor Melville Metcalf, *Herman Melville*

We have had writers of rhetoric who had the good fortune to find a little in a chronicle of another man and from voyaging, of how things, actual things can be, whales for instance, and this knowledge is wrapped in the rhetoric like plums in a pudding. Occasionally it is there, alone, unwrapped in pudding, and it is good. This is Melville.

Ernest Hemingway, in Carlos Baker, *Hemingway: Writer as Artist*

Melville has the strange, uncanny magic of sea-creatures, and some of their repulsiveness. He isn't quite a land animal. There is something slithery about him. Something always half-seas-over. In his life they said he was mad – or crazy. But he was over the border.

D. H. Lawrence, *Studies in Classical American Literature*

## MELVILLE, VISCOUNT (HENRY DUNDAS)

1742–1811 Statesman

Now thou art off, I long to see, / In thine own language, 'Who wants me?' / It will not be at all surprising / To catch thee, HARRY, advertising. / If mad to face a second storm, / Take an Advertisement in form. / 'A steady Man, near sixty years of age, / Would very willingly engage / As Butler to a Minister of State, / And overlook the Plate. / But should the Plate by chance be carried off, / And not a hogshead or a bottle left; / He begs to say, he won't be fool enough / To answer for the leakage or the theft. / If wanted he can have, by God's good grace, / An excellent character from his last place. / Please to direct to Mr H. Dundas, / At the old sign – the Bottle and the Glass.' /

Peter Pindar (John Wolcot), *Odes to the Ins and Outs*

The Right Honourable Gentleman is indebted to his memory for his jests, and to his imagination for his facts.

Richard Brinsley Sheridan, Reply to Dundas in the House of Commons

Never did any man conceal deeper views of every kind under the appearance of careless inattention to self-interest. In him was exemplified the remark that 'Ars est celare Artem', and the seeming want of caution or artifice in his ordinary intercourse, capacitated him for contending successfully with men of more habitual self-command.

Nathaniel Wraxall, *Memoirs*

## MENCKEN, HENRY LOUIS

1880–1956 Author, Editor, Critic

The older I grow the more I distrust the familiar doctrine that age brings wisdom.

On himself, in *Prejudices*, series 3

If after I depart this vale, you remember me and have thought to please my ghost, forgive some sinner and wink your eye at a homely girl.

On himself, December 1921, in H. L. Mencken ed., *The Smart Set*

I've made it a rule never to drink by daylight and never to refuse a drink after dark.

On himself, in A. K. Adams, *The Home Book of Humorous Quotations*

I get little enjoyment out of women, more out of alcohol, most out of ideas.

On himself, in Edgar Kemler, *The Irreverent Mr Mencken*

I never listen to debates. They are dreadful things indeed. The plain truth is that I am not a fair man, and don't want to hear both sides. On all known subjects, ranging from aviation to xylophone-playing, I have fixed and invariable ideas. They have not changed since I was four or five.

On himself, Letter to Jim Tully, 1940

To him Pegasus was just a runaway horse.

Benjamin de Casseres, *Mencken and Shaw*

My regret is that Mencken does not contradict himself more. Logic is his sin.

*Ibid.*

He edited a magazine called 'The Smart Set' which is like calling Cape Kennedy 'Lovers' Lane'.

Ben Hecht, *Letters from Bohemia*

What he believed in and what his readers wanted to be told were soon indistinguishable; his work became a series of circus tricks, a perpetual search for some new object of middle-class culture to belabor and some new habit or caprice of *Homo Americanus* to ridicule.

Alfred Kazin, *On Native Grounds*

The more he reflected upon the Fascist experiment, the more he believed that Fascism, for better or for worse, had a promising future in the Western world, and that an 'intelligent Fascism' operated by incorruptible naval officers might be just the thing for America.

Edgar Kemler, *The Irreverent Mr Mencken*

He launched a massive attack on everything this country held inviolate, on most of what it held self evident. He showed how our politics was dominated by time-servers and demagogues, our religion by bigots, our culture by puritans. He showed how the average citizen, both in himself and in the way he let himself be pulled round by the nose, was a boob.

Louis Kronenberger, 'H. L. Mencken', in Malcolm Cowley ed., *After the Genteel Tradition*

## MEREDITH, GEORGE

1828–1909 Novelist, Poet

Mr Meredith, the only living novelist in England who rivals Ouida in sheer vitality, packs tight all his pages with wit, philosophy, poetry, and psychological analysis. His obscurity, like that of Carlyle and Browning, is due less to extreme subtlety than to the plethoric abundance of his ideas. He cannot stop to express himself. If he could, he might be more popular.

Max Beerbohm, *Ouida*

At his best, a sort of daintily dressed Walt Whitman.

G. K. Chesterton, *The Victorian Age in Literature*

What with the faking, what with the preaching, which was never agreeable and is now said to be hollow, and what with the home counties posing as the universe, it is no wonder Meredith now lies in the trough.

E. M. Forster, *Aspects of the Novel*

He spoke as one afoot will wind / A morning horn ere men awake; / His note was trenchant, turning kind. / He was of those whose wit can shake / And riddle to the very core / The counterfeits that Time will break. /

Thomas Hardy, *George Meredith*

Meredith is, to me, chiefly a stink. I should never write on him as I detest him too much ever to trust myself as critic of him.

Ezra Pound, Letter to John Quinn, 4 June 1918

Ah! Meredith! Who can define him? His style is chaos illumined by flashes of lightning. As a writer he has mastered everything except language: as a novelist he can do everything except tell a story: as an artist he is everything except articulate.

Oscar Wilde, *The Decay of Lying*

Meredith deserves our gratitude and excites our interest as a great innovator. Many of our doubts about him and much of our inability to frame any definite opinion of his work comes from the fact that it is experimental and thus contains elements that do not fuse harmoniously – the qualities are at odds: the one quality that binds and concentrates has been omitted. To read Meredith, then, to our greatest advantage we must make certain allowances and relax certain standards. We must not expect the perfect quietude of a traditional style nor the triumphs of a patient and pedestrian psychology.

Virginia Woolf, *The Second Common Reader*

*See also* Robert Browning, Samuel Butler, Ford Madox Ford, Thomas Hardy

## MIDDLETON, THOMAS

1570?–1627 Dramatist

Facetious Middleton, thy witty Muse / Hath pleased all that books or men peruse. / If any thee despise, he doth but show, / Antipathy to wit in doing so: / Thy fame's above his malice, and 'twill be / Dispraise enough for him to censure thee. /

Anon., *Wit's Recreations*

Squibbling Middleton.

Anon., from a poem in Gerard Langbaine, *Account of the English Dramatic Poets*

He remains merely a name, a voice, the author of certain plays, which are all of them great plays. He has no point of view, is neither sentimental nor cynical; he is neither resigned, nor disillusioned, nor romantic; he has no message. He is merely the name which associates six or seven great plays . . . [The] mixture of tedious discourse and sudden reality is everywhere in the work of Middleton, in his comedy also. In *The Roaring Girl* we read with toil through a mass of conventional intrigue, and suddenly realise that we are, and have been for some time without knowing it, observing a real and unique human being. In reading the *Changeling*, we may think, till almost the end of the play, that we have been concerned merely with a fantastic Elizabethan morality, and then discover that we are looking on at a dispassionate exposure of fundamental passions of any time and any place.

T. S. Eliot, *Essays*: 'Thomas Middleton'

He is lamentably deficient in the plot and dénouement of the story. It is like the rough draught of a tragedy, with a number of fine things thrown in, and the best made use of first; but it tends to no fixed goal, and the interest decreases, instead of increasing, as we read on, for want of previous arrangement and an eye to the whole . . . The author's power is *in* the subject, not *over* it; or he is in possession of excellent materials which he husbands very ill. This character, though it applies more particularly to Middleton, might be applied generally to the age.

William Hazlitt, *Lectures on the Age of Elizabeth*

*See also* T. S. Eliot

## MILBANKE, ANNABELLA, LADY BYRON

1792–1860

The Princess of Parallelograms.

Lord Byron, in conversation with Lady Melbourne

## MILL, JAMES

1773–1836 Philosopher

He argues against oppression less because he loves the oppressed many, than because he hates the oppressing few.

Jeremy Bentham, according to John Bowring, *Memoirs of Bentham*

He is an Aristotelian of the fifteenth century, born out of due season.

T. B. Macaulay, 'Mill's Essay on Government', in *Edinburgh Review*, March 1829

Our objection to the essay of Mr Mill is fundamental. We believe that it is utterly impossible to deduce the science of government from the principles of human nature.

*Ibid.*

In his views of life he partook of the character of the Stoic, the Epicurean, and the Cynic, not in the modern but the ancient sense of the word. In his personal qualities the Stoic predominated. His standard of morals was Epicurean, inasmuch as it was utilitarian, taking as the exclusive test of right and wrong the tendency of actions to produce pleasure or pain. But he had (and this was the Cynic element) scarcely any belief in pleasure; at least in his later years, of which alone, on this point, I can speak confidently. He was not insensible to pleasures; but he deemed very few of them worth the price which, at least in the present state of society, must be paid for them.

John Stuart Mill, *Autobiography*

## MILL, JOHN STUART

1806–73 Philosopher

I have never, at least since I had any convictions of my own, belonged to the benevolentiary, soup-kitchen school. Though I hold the good of the species (or rather of its separate units) to be the ultimate end (which is the alpha and omega of my utilitarianism), I believe with the fullest belief that this end can in no other way be forwarded but by the means you speak of, namely, by each taking for his exclusive aim the development of what is best in *himself*.

On himself, Letter to Thomas Carlyle, January 1834

You may think it presumptuous in a man to be finishing a treatise on logic and not to have made up his mind finally on these great matters. But mine professes to be a logic of experience only, and to throw no further light upon the existence of truths not experimental, than is thrown by showing to what extent reasoning from experience will carry us. Above all mine is a logic of the indicative mood alone – the logic of the imperative, in which the major premiss says not *is* but *ought*, I do not meddle with.

On himself, Letter to John Sterling, November 1839

I did not invent the word, but found it in one of [John] Galt's novels, the *Annals of the Parish*, in which the Scotch clergyman, of whom the book is a supposed autobiography, is represented as warning his parishioners not to leave the Gospel and become utilitarians. With a boy's fondness for a name and a banner I seized on the word, and for some years called myself and others by it as a sectarian appellation, and it came to be occasionally used by some others holding the opinions which it was intended to designate.

On himself and the origin of the term Utilitarianism, in *Autobiography of John Stuart Mill*

I am thus one of the very few examples, in this country, of one who has not thrown off religious belief, but never had it: I grew up in a negative state with regard to it. I looked upon the modern exactly as I did upon the ancient religion, as something which in no way concerned me.

*Ibid.*

In his mind, philosophy seemed to mean chiefly advanced views in politics and in ethics; which, of course, came into collision with religious orthodoxy and the received commonplaces of society. Such a view of the functions of a University would not be put forth by any man that had ever resided in a University; and this is not the only occasion when Mill dogmatized on Universities in total ignorance of their working.

Alexander Bain, commenting on Mill's critique of Sedgwick, in *John Stuart Mill*

He was all his life possessed of the idea that differences of character, individual and national, were due to accidents and circumstances that might possibly be, in part, controlled; on this doctrine rested his chief hope in the future. He would not allow that human beings at birth are so very different as they afterwards turn out.

*Ibid.*

He grants that women are physically inferior, but seems to think that this does not affect their mental powers. He never takes account of the fact, that the large diversion of force for the procreative function must give some general inferiority in all things where that does not come in, unless women are made on the whole much stronger than men. In an allusion to his experience of the Independent States of India, he tells us that in three cases out of four, if a superior instance of good government occurs, it is in a woman's reign; which looks like the fallacy of proving too much.

*Ibid.*

Ah poor fellow! he had to get himself out of Benthamism; and all the emotions and sufferings he has endured have helped him to thoughts that never entered Bentham's head. However, he is still too fond of demonstrating everything. If John Mill were to get up to heaven, he would be hardly content till he had made out how it all was. For my part I don't much trouble myself about the machinery of the place; whether there is an operative of angels or an industrial class, I'm willing to leave all that.

Thomas Carlyle, in Caroline Fox, *Journal*

This method of early, intense application he would not recommend to others; in most cases it would not answer, and where it does, the buoyancy of youth is entirely superseded by the maturity of manhood, and action is very likely to be merged in reflection. 'I never was a boy,' he said, 'never played at cricket; it is better to let Nature have her own way.'

Caroline Fox, *ibid.*

We well knew Mr Mill's intellectual eminence before he entered Parliament. What his conduct there principally disclosed, at least to me, was his singular moral elevation. I remember now that at the time, more than twenty years back, I used familiarly to call him the Saint of Rationalism, a phrase roughly and partially what I now mean. Of all the motives, stings and stimulants that reach men through their egoism in Parliament, no part could move or even touch him. His conduct and his language were, in this respect a sermon. Again, though he was a philosopher, he was not, I think, a man of crotchets.

William Ewart Gladstone, in W. L. Courtney, *Life of John Stuart Mill*

As for Mill as a thinker – a man who knew nothing of Plato and Darwin gives me very little. His reputation is curious to me. I gain nothing, I have gained nothing from him – an arid, dry man with moods of sentiment – a type that is poor, and, I fancy, common. But Darwinism has of course shattered many reputations besides his, and I hope that individual liberty has had its day, for a time. His later religious views show an outstanding silliness and sentimentality.

Oscar Wilde, Letter to W. L. Courtney, 1889

## MILLAIS, SIR JOHN EVERETT

1829–96 Artist

This strangely unequal painter – a painter whose imperfectly great powers always suggest to me the legend of the spiteful fairy at the christening feast. The name of Mr Millais's spiteful fairy is vulgarity.

Henry James, 'The Grosvenor Gallery', in *Nation*, 23 May 1878

He at last the champion great Millais / Attaining Academic opulence, / Wind up his signature with A.R.A. / So rivers merge in the perpetual sea; / So luscious fruit must fall when over-ripe / And so the consummated P.R.B. /

Christina Rossetti, in William Rossetti, *Dante Gabriel Rossetti*

He was an angelic and blustering personification of John Bull, what the Germans call *der Stock-Engländer*. He answered to the *stage* idea of the superior officer, although the superior officer is characterised rather by the gentleness, the tact and the scrupulous sympathy which command by persuasion. Millais was a man who . . . *ne se doutait de rien.*

Walter Richard Sickert, in *Fortnightly Review*, June 1929

When Millais said 'Art', he meant British Art. And when he said 'British Art', he meant the painting of John Everett Millais.

*Ibid.*

## MILTON, JOHN

1608–74 Poet, Polemicist

. . . Sad task, yet argument / Not less but more Heroic than the wrath / Of stern *Achilles* on his Foe pursu'd / Thrice Fugitive about Troy Wall; or Rage / Of *Turnus* for Lavinia disespous'd, / Or *Neptune's* ire or *Juno's*, that so long / Perplex'd the *Greek* and *Cytherea's* Son; / If answerable style I can obtain / Of my Celestial Patroness, who deigns / Her nightly visitation unimplor'd, / And dictates to me slumb'ring, or inspires / Easy my unpremeditated Verse; / Since first this Subject for Heroic Song / Pleas'd me long choosing, and beginning late; / Not sedulous by Nature to indite / Wars, hitherto the only Argument / Heroic deem'd, chief maistry to dissect / With long and tedious havoc fabl'd Knights / In Battles feign'd; the better fortitude / Of Patience and Heroic Martyrdom / Unsung; or to describe Races and Games, / Or tilting Furniture, emblazon'd Shields, / Impresses quaint, Caparisons and Steeds; / Bases and tinsel Trappings, gorgeous Knights / At Joust and Tournament; then marshall'd Feast / Serv'd up in Hall with Sewers, and Seneschals; / The skill of Artifice or Office mean, / Not that which justly gives Heroic name / To Person or to Poem. Mee of these / Nor skill'd nor studious, higher Argument / Remains, sufficient of itself to raise / That name, unless an age too late, or cold / Climate, or Years damp my intended wing / Deprest; and much they may, if all be mine, / Not Hers who brings it nightly to my Ear. /

On himself, *Paradise Lost*, book ix

Our Language sunk under him, and was unequal to that greatness of soul which furnished him with such glorious conceptions.

Joseph Addison, in *Spectator*, no. 297

He had abroun hayre. His complexion exceeding faire – he was so faire that they called him *the Lady of Christ's College*.

John Aubrey, *Brief Lives*

But in Milton, the Father is Destiny, the Son a Ratio of the five senses, & the Holy-ghost a Vacuum!

Note: the reason Milton wrote in fetters when he wrote of Angels & God, and at liberty when of Devils & Hell, is because he was a true Poet and of the Devil's party without knowing it.

William Blake, *The Marriage of Heaven and Hell*

If fallen in evil days on evil tongues, / Milton appealed to the Avenger, Time, / If Time, the Avenger, execrates his wrongs, / And makes the word 'Miltonic' mean '*sublime*', / *He* deign'd not to belie his soul in songs, / Nor turn his very talent to a crime; / *He* did not loathe the Sire to laud the Son, / But closed the tyrant-hater he begun. /

Lord Byron, *Don Juan*, canto i (fragment)

Milton's the prince of poets – so we say; / A little heavy, but no less divine. /

*Ibid.*, canto iii

Indeed, the whole of Milton's poem [*Paradise Lost*] is such barbarous trash, so outrageously offensive to reason and to common sense that one is naturally led to wonder how it can have been tolerated by a people, amongst whom astronomy, navigation, and chemistry are understood.

William Cobbett, *Year's Residence in the United States*

Shakespeare is the Spinozistic deity – an omnipresent creativeness. Milton is the deity of prescience; he stands *ab extra*, and drives a fiery chariot and four, making the horses feel the iron curb which holds them in.

Samuel Taylor Coleridge, *Table Talk*

Milton has carefully marked in his Satan the intense selfishness, the alcohol of egotism, which would rather reign in hell than serve in heaven. To place this lust of self in opposition to denial of self or duty, and to show what exertions it would make, and what pains endure to accomplish its ends, is Milton's particular object in the character of Satan. But around this character he throws a singularity of daring, a grandeur of sufferance and a ruined splendour, which constitute the very height of poetic sublimity.

Samuel Taylor Coleridge, *Lecture on Milton*, March 1819

Greece, sound thy Homer's, Rome thy Virgil's name, / But England's Milton equals both in fame. /

William Cowper, *To John Milton*

Ages elaps'd ere Homer's lamp appear'd, / And ages ere the Mantuan swan was heard: / To carry nature lengths unknown before, / To give a Milton birth, ask'd ages more. / Thus genius rose and set at order'd times, / And shot a day-spring into distant climes, / Ennobling e'vry region that he chose; / He sunk in Greece, in Italy he rose; / And, tedious years of

Gothic darkness pass'd, / Emerg'd all splendour in our isle at last. /

William Cowper, *Table Talk*

It is only in the period that the wave-length of Milton's verse is to be found: it is his ability to give a perfect and unique pattern to every paragraph, such that the full beauty of the line is found in its context, and his ability to work in larger musical units than any other poet – that is to me the most conclusive evidence of Milton's supreme mastery. The peculiar feeling, almost a physical sensation of a breathless leap, communicated by Milton's long periods, and by his alone, is impossible to procure from rhymed verse.

T. S. Eliot, *Essays*: 'Milton II'

I suppose that in Satan determining to destroy the innocent happiness of Eden, for the highest political motives, without hatred, not without tears, we may find some echo of the Elizabethan fulness of life that Milton as a poet abandoned, and as a Puritan helped to destroy.

William Empson, *Some Versions of Pastoral*

I should say that Milton's experience of propaganda is what makes his later poetry so very dramatic; that is, though he is a furious partisan, he can always imagine with all its force exactly what the reply of the opponent would be. As to his integrity, he was such an inconvenient propagandist that the Government deserve credit for having the nerve to appoint and retain him.

William Empson, *Milton's God*

Malt does more than Milton can, / To justify God's ways to man. /

A. E. Housman, *A Shropshire Lad*, lxii

It is not strange that Milton received no encouragement after the restoration: it is more to be admired that he escaped with his life. Many of the cavaliers blamed extremely that lenity towards him, which was so honourable in the king, and advantageous to posterity.

David Hume, *The History of England*

He thought woman made only for obedience, and man only for rebellion.

Samuel Johnson, *Lives of the Poets*

Milton never learned the art of doing little things with grace; he overlooked the milder excellence of suavity and softness; he was a *Lion* that had no skill in *dandling the Kid.*

*Ibid.*

The characteristick quality of his poem is sublimity. He sometimes descends to the elegant, but his element is the great. He can occasionally invest himself with grace; but his natural port is gigantick loftiness. He can please when pleasure is required; but it is his peculiar power to astonish.

*Ibid.*

The plan of *Paradise Lost* has this inconvenience, that it comprises neither human actions nor human manners. The man and woman who act and suffer, are in a state which no other man or woman can ever know. The reader finds no transaction in which he can be engaged; beholds no condition in which he can by any effort of imagination place himself; he has, therefore, little natural curiosity or sympathy.

*Ibid.*

We read Milton for instruction, retire harassed and overburdened, and look elsewhere for recreation; we desert our master, and seek for companions.

*Ibid.*

Milton, Madam, was a genius that could cut a Colossus from a rock; but could not carve heads upon cherry-stones.

Samuel Johnson, in James Boswell, *Life of Johnson*

I have but lately been on my guard against Milton. Life to him would be death to me. Miltonic verse cannot be written but in the vein of art – I wish to devote myself to another sensation.

John Keats, Letter to George and Georgiana Keats, 17 September 1819

Milton almost requires a solemn service of music to be played before you enter upon him.

Charles Lamb, *Last Essays of Elia*: 'Detached Thoughts on Books and Reading'

Milton seems to the colleges profound because he wrote of hell, a great place, and is dead.

Stephen Leacock, *Charles Dickens*

Even in the first two books of *Paradise Lost* . . . we feel, after a few hundred lines, our sense of dissatisfaction growing into something stronger. In the end we find ourselves protesting – protesting against the routine gesture, the heavy fall, of the verse, flinching from the foreseen thud that comes so inevitably, and, at last, irresistibly: for reading *Paradise Lost* is a matter of resisting, of standing up against, the verse-movement, of subduing it into something tolerably like sensitiveness, and in the end our resistance is worn down; we surrender at last to the monotony of ritual.

F. R. Leavis, *Revaluation*

Nearly every sentence in Milton has that power which physicists sometimes think we shall have to attribute to matter – the power of action at a distance.

C. S. Lewis, *A Preface to Paradise Lost*

The spirits of Milton are unlike those of almost all other writers. His fiends, in particular, are wonderful creations. They are not metaphysical abstractions. They are not wicked men. They are not ugly beasts. They have no horns, no tails, none of the fee-faw-fum of Tasso and Klopstock. They have just enough in common with human nature to be intelligible to human beings. Their characters are, like their forms, marked by a certain dim resemblance to those of men, but exaggerated to gigantic dimensions, and veiled in mysterious gloom.

T. B. Macaulay, *Essays*: 'Milton'

If ever despondency and asperity could be excused in any man, they might have been excused in Milton. But the strength of his mind overcame every calamity. Neither blindness, nor gout, nor age, nor penury, nor domestic afflictions, nor political disappointments, nor abuse, nor proscription, nor neglect, had power to disturb his sedate and majestic patience. His spirits do not seem to have been high, but they were singularly equable.

*Ibid.*

Poetry is what Milton saw when he went blind.

Don Marquis, in Edward Anthony, *O Rare Don Marquis*

When I beheld the Poet blind, yet bold, / In slender Book his vast Design unfold, / *Messiah* Crown'd, *God's* reconciled Decree, / Rebelling *Angels*, the Forbidden Tree, / Heav'n, Hell, Earth, Chaos, All; the Argument / Held me a while misdoubting his Intent, / That he would ruine (for I saw him strong) / The sacred Truths to Fable and old Song, / (So *Sampson* groap'd the Temples Posts in spight) / The World o'erwhelming to revenge his Sight. /

Andrew Marvell, *On Mr Milton's Paradise Lost*

To pass under the spell of Milton is to be condemned to imitate him. It is quite different with Shakespeare. Shakespeare baffles and liberates; Milton is perspicuous and constricts.

John Middleton Murry, *Heaven and Earth*

Milton's style, in his Paradise Lost, is not natural; 'tis an exotic style. – As his subject lies a good deal out of our world, it has a particular propriety in those parts of the poem: and, when he is on earth, wherever he is describing our parents in Paradise, you see he uses a more easy and natural way of writing. – Though his formal style may fit the higher parts of his own poem, it does very ill for others who write on natural and pastoral subjects.

Alexander Pope, in Joseph Spence, *Anecdotes*

Milton's Devil as a moral being is far superior to his God, as one who perseveres in some purpose which he has conceived to be excellent, in spite of adversity and torture, is to one who in the cold security of undoubted triumph inflicts the most horrible revenge upon his enemy, not from mistaken notions of inducing him to repent of a perseverance in enmity, but with the alleged design of exasperating him to new torments. Milton has so far violated the popular creed (if this shall be judged a violation), as to have alleged no superiority of moral virtue to his God over his Devil. And this bold neglect of direct moral purpose is the most decisive proof of Milton's genius.

Percy Bysshe Shelley, *Defence of Poetry*

O mighty-mouth'd inventor of harmonies, / O skill'd to sing of Time or Eternity, / God-gifted organ-voice of England, / Milton, a name to resound for ages. /

Alfred, Lord Tennyson, *Milton*

That mighty orb of song, The divine Milton.

William Wordsworth, *The Excursion*

Milton! thou shouldst be living at this hour: / England hath need of thee: she is a fen / Of stagnant waters. /

William Wordsworth, *National Independence and Liberty*

Thy soul was like a Star, and dwelt apart; / Thou hadst a voice whose sound was like the sea: / Pure as the naked heavens, majestic, free, / So didst thou travel on life's common way, / In cheerful godliness; and yet thy heart / The lowliest duties on herself did lay. /

*Ibid.*

*See also* William Cowper, Daniel Defoe, Oliver Wendell Holmes Sr, Leigh Hunt, Inigo Jones, Bertrand Russell, Carl Sandburg, Edmund Spenser, Alfred, Lord Tennyson, William Wordsworth

## MITFORD, NANCY

1905–73 Novelist

Evelyn Waugh liked the company of young women and took them to nightclubs, though he never danced. His terms of praise were unusual. Very high was 'Nice short girl' – Evelyn was very conscious of being himself on the short side – or of Nancy Mitford, 'Nice cheap girl to take out for the evening. Costs you only eighteen and six for an orangeade in a nightclub.'

Maurice Bowra, *Memories*

Nancy had been named after the Nancies of seafaring ballads, and her thick, dark, curly hair, worn (after the ill-fated shingling) in a very short upsweep, her tall, fashionably boyish figure and her penchant for the exotic did give her something of the aspect of an elegant pirate's moll.

Jessica Mitford, *Hons and Rebels*

I have long revered you as an agitator – agitatrix, *agitateuse*? – of genius. You have only to publish a few cool reflections on 18th-century furniture to set gangs on the prowl through the Faubourg St Germain splashing the walls with 'Nancy, go home'.

Evelyn Waugh, *Open Letter to the*

*Hon Mrs Peter Rodd (Nancy Mitford) on a Very Serious Subject*

## MIX, (THOMAS HEZEKIAH) TOM

1880–1940 Actor

As gaudy in dress as [William S.] Hart had been simple, he was prone to wear white evening suits, purple tuxedos, cowboy outfits decorated with diamonds. Over the gate of his Beverly Hills mansion, his monogram shone in electric lights. When he supplanted Hart in the nation's affections, he brought with him an idealized conception of the cowboy as a clean-living, sportsmanlike fellow that was to linger on the screen for years.

Donald W. La Badie, 'The Last Round-up', in *Show*, September 1962

They say he rides like part of the horse, but they don't say what part.

Robert E. Sherwood, in Robert E. Drennan ed., *Wit's End*

## MONCK, GEORGE, DUKE OF ALBEMARLE

1608–70 Soldier, Statesman

Little General Monk / Sat upon a trunk, / Eating a crust of bread; / There fell a hot coal / And burnt in his clothes a hole, / Now little General Monk is dead. /

Nursery rhyme, traditional

His nature was cautious and somewhat sluggish; nor was he at all disposed to hazard sure and moderate advantages for the chance of obtaining even the most splendid success. He seems to have been impelled to attack the new rulers of the commonwealth less by the hope that, if he overthrew them, he should become great, than by the fear that, if he submitted to them, he should not even be secure.

T. B. Macaulay, *History of England*

## MONMOUTH, DUKE OF (JAMES FITZROY SCOTT)

1649–85 Soldier

Disgrac'd, undone, forlorn, made Fortune's sport / Banish'd the Kingdom first, and then the Court; / Out of my places turn'd, and out of doors / And made the meanest of your sons of whores, / The scene of laughter, and the common chats / Of your salt bitches and your other brats; / Forc'd to a private life, to whore and drink / On my past grandeur and my folly think. / Would I had been the brat of some mean drab / Whom fear or shame had caus'd to choke or stab / Rather than be the issue of a King / And by him made so wretched scorn'd a thing. /

Anon., *Letter of the Duke of Monmouth to the King*

Have I done all that royal dad could do / And do you threaten now to be untrue? / Oh! that my pr--- when I thy dam did f--- / Had in some turkey's a---, or cow's been stuck! / Then I had been when the base deed was done / Sure to have got no rebel to my son. /

Anon., *The King's Answer*

To lure, like Monmouth, associates, and humble followers on fools' errands to their doom can find no defenders.

Winston Churchill, *Marlborough, His Life and Times*

Of all this Numerous Progeny was none / So Beautiful so Brave as *Absalom*: / Whether inspir'd by some diviner Lust / His father got him with a greater Gust, / Or that his Conscious Destiny made way / By manly Beauty to Imperial Sway. /

John Dryden, *Absalom and Achitophel*

## MONROE, JAMES

1758–1831 Fifth United States President

James Monroe came from Virginia, the mother of presidents. Little is known of his father, except that he was devoted to Virginia.

Richard Armour, *It All Started With Columbus*

I have known many much more rapid in reaching a conclusion, but few with a certainty so unerring.

John C. Calhoun, Letter to S. L. Gouverneur, 8 August 1818

His services as President might be summed up in four words – he personified an interim. The War of 1812... was merely the symptom of a profound change in domestic and international relations. After the shock of such a change, an interim was necessary; and if the interim was necessary, the personification was honorable.

George Dangerfield, *The Era of Good Feelings*

He was a man whose soul might be turned wrong side outwards without discovering a blemish to the world.

Thomas Jefferson, in Daniel C. Gilman, *James Monroe*

## MONROE, MARILYN (NORMA JEAN BAKER)

1926–62 Actress

When I just wrote 'this is the end of Norma Jean' I blushed as if I had been caught in a lie. Because this sad, bitter child who grew up too fast is hardly ever out of my heart. With success all around me, I can still feel her frightened eyes looking out of mine. She keeps saying 'I never lived, I was never loved', and often I get confused and think it's I who am saying it.

On herself, in *My Story*

A sex symbol becomes a thing. I hate being a thing.

On herself, in Jeremy Pascall and Clive Jeavons, *A Pictorial History of Sex in the Movies*

She had this absolute, unerring touch with comedy. In real life she didn't seem funny, but she had this touch. She acted as if she didn't quite understand why it was funny, which is what made it so funny. She could also do low comedy – pratfalls and things like that – but I think her friends told her it wasn't worthy of her. As a director, I really had very little influence on her. All I could do was make a climate that was agreeable to her. Every day was an agony of struggle for her, just to get there. It wasn't just willfulness, it was . . . like the comedy, something she didn't seem to understand.

George Cukor, in Gavin Lambert, *On Cukor*

If she was a victim of any kind, she was a victim of friends.

*Ibid.*

A phenomenon of nature, like Niagara Falls and the Grand Canyon.

Nunnally Johnson, in William Manchester, *The Glory and the Dream*

So we think of Marilyn who was every man's love affair with America. Marilyn Monroe who was blonde and beautiful and had a sweet little rinky-dink of a voice and all the cleanliness of all the clean American backyards. She was our angel, the sweet angel of sex, and the sugar of sex came up from her like a resonance of sound in the clearest grain of a violin. Across five continents the men who knew the most about love would covet her, and the classical pimples of the adolescent working his first gas pump would also pump for her, since Marilyn was deliverance, a very Stradivarius of sex, so gorgeous, forgiving, humorous, compliant and tender that even the most mediocre musician would relax his lack of art in the dissolving magic of her violin.

Norman Mailer, *Marilyn*

After *Yank* ran a picture of her in an article on women in war work she was given a screen test . . . The first man to see the rushes said: 'I got a cold chill. This girl had something I hadn't seen since silent pictures. This is the first girl who looked like one of those lush stars of the silent era. Every frame of the test radiated sex.' Billy Wilder, who later directed her in *Some Like It Hot*, called it 'flesh impact' and said the only other stars who had it were Clara Bow, Jean Harlow, and Rita Hayworth.

William Manchester, *The Glory and the Dream*

She was the bastard daughter of a paranoid schizophrenic . . . a girl with a desperate, insatiable yearning to be wanted . . . Her first husband taught her sexual ecstasy on a Murphy bed. She gloried in it and would pursue it for the rest of her life, but it wasn't enough; she craved the adoration of millions.

*Ibid.*

It's Mae West, Theda Bara, and Bo Peep all rolled into one.

Groucho Marx, in Marilyn Monroe, *My Story*

It was like going to the dentist, making a picture with her. It was hell at the time, but after it was all over, it was wonderful.

Billy Wilder, in Earl Wilson, *The Show Business Nobody Knows*

## MONTAGU, ELIZABETH

1720–1800 Author, Hostess

He told us, 'I dined yesterday at Mrs Garrick's with Mrs Carter, Miss Hannah More, and Miss Fanny Burney. Three such women are not to be found . . .' *Boswell*: 'Might not Mrs Montagu have been a fourth?' *Johnson*: 'Sir, Mrs Montagu does not make a trade of her wit; but Mrs Montagu is a very extraordinary woman; she has a constant stream of conversation, and it is always impregnated; it has always meaning.'

James Boswell, *Life of Johnson*

To the same Patroness resort, / (Secure of favour at her court) / Strong Genius, from whose forge of thought / Forms rise, to quick perfection wrought, / Which, though new-born, with vigour move, / Like Pallas springing arm'd from Jove – / Imagination, scatt'ring round / Wild roses over furrow'd ground, / Which Labour of his frowns beguile, / And teach Philosophy a smile – / All these to MONTAGU's repair, / Ambitious of a shelter there. /

William Cowper, *On Mrs Montagu's Feather Hangings*

She is not only the finest genius, but the finest lady I ever saw; she lives in the highest style of magnificence; her apartments are in the most splendid taste; but what baubles are these when speaking of a Montagu!

Hannah More, in Rebecca West, *Elizabeth Montagu*

It is a life that knew only once the touch of defeat, yet it radiates a low degree of light and heat. It dispenses through the ages hardly more warmth than chandeliers blazing away behind the closed windows of a great house; and even in its own day it could not relieve Mrs Montagu herself from a sensation of debilitating chill. For what saves her record from being intolerable is that she was the first to think it so.

Rebecca West, *ibid.*

## MONTAGU, LADY MARY WORTLEY

1689–1762 Bellettriste

Lady Mary lived before the age in which people waste half their lives in washing the whole of their persons.

Walter Bagehot, *Estimations in Criticism*

. . . Bye the bye, her Ladyship, as far as I can judge, has lied, but not half so much as any other woman would have done in the same situation.

Lord Byron, Letter to Mrs Catherine Gordon Byron, 28 June 1810

Rufa, whose eye quick-glancing o'er the Park / Attracts each light gay meteor of a Spark, / Agrees as ill with Rufa studying Locke, / As Sappho's diamonds with her dirty smock, / Or Sappho at her toilet's greazy task, /With Sappho fragrant at an evening Mask: / So morning Insects that in Muck begun, / Shine, buzz, and fly-blow in the setting sun. /

Alexander Pope, *Moral Essays*, epistle ii

Lady Mary is arrived; I have seen her; I think her avarice, her art, and her vivacity are all increased. Her dress, like her language, is a *galimatias* of several countries; the groundwork rags and the embroidery nastiness. She needs no cap, no handkerchief, no gown, no petticoat, and no shoes.

Horace Walpole, Letter to Sir Horace Mann, 2 February 1762

## MONTAGU, JOHN, *see under* SANDWICH, EARL OF

## MONTGOMERY OF ALAMEIN, VISCOUNT

1887–1979 Soldier

In defeat unbeatable; in victory unbearable.

Sir Winston Churchill, in Edward Marsh, *Ambrosia and Small Beer*

## MONTGOMERY, ROBERT

1807–55 Poet

His writings bear the same relation to poetry as a Turkey-carpet bears to a picture. There are colours in the Turkey-carpet out of which a picture might be made. There are words in Mr Montgomery's verses which, when disposed in certain orders and combinations, have made, and will again make good poetry. But, as they now stand, they seem to be put together on principle, in such a manner as to give no image of anything in the 'heavens above, or in the earth beneath, or in the waters under the earth.'

T. B. Macaulay, *Essays*: 'Robert Montgomery's Poems'

He is a fine young man, who has been wickedly puffed and wickedly abused, and who is in no little danger of being spoiled by forcing . . . He has rushed in where angels fear to tread. He has attempted subjects which ought never to be attempted, and in which it is impossible not to fail; yet these very subjects have obtained for him popularity, and the profit without which he could not have obtained the education of which he was worthy, as well as ambitious. When he lowers his flight, I wish he may not find that he has weakened his wings by straining them.

Robert Southey, Letter to Caroline Bowles, 26 August 1832

## MOODY, DWIGHT LYMAN

1837–99 Evangelist

Having heard Moody I am satisfied / But I shall not come to him to be saved. / He is not my idea of a Saviour. / I do not believe in him / Nor his God / Nor his method of swaying sinners nor his stories which sound like lies. / I Walt tell him he is an ignorant charlatan, a mistaken enthusiast, / and that Boston will ere long desire him to *git*. /

Walt Whitman, from a parody of his *Passage to India*

## MOORE, GEORGE AUGUSTUS

1852–1933 Author

I came into the world apparently with a nature like a smooth sheet of wax, bearing no impress, but capable of receiving any; of being moulded into all shapes. Nor am I exaggerating when I say I think that I might equally have been a Pharaoh, an ostler, a pimp, an archbishop, and that in the fulfilment of the duties of each a certain measure of success would have been mine.

On himself, *Confessions of a Young Man*

It would be an understatement to say that his face was as a mask which revealed nothing. His face was as a mask of gauze through which Nothing was quite clearly visible. And then, all of a sudden, there would appear – Something. There came a gleam from within the pale-blue eyes, and a sort of ripple passed up over the modelling of the flaccid cheeks; the chin suddenly receded a little further, – and *Voilà Moore qui parle! Silence, la compagnie! Moore parle.*

Max Beerbohm, *George Moore*

... that old pink petulant walrus.

Henry Channon, Diary, 20 May 1941

We should really be much more interested in Mr Moore if he were not quite so interested in himself. We feel as if we were being shown through a gallery of really fine pictures, into each of which, by some useless and discordant convention, the artist had represented the same figure in the same attitude. 'The Grand Canal with a distant view of Mr Moore', 'Effect of Mr Moore through a Scotch Mist', 'Mr Moore by Firelight', 'Ruins of Mr Moore by Moonlight'.

G. K. Chesterton, *Heretics*

Susan Mitchell sensed something lacking. Women are like that. She wrote, 'Some men kiss and do not tell, some kiss and tell; but George Moore told and did not kiss.'

Oliver St John Gogarty, *As I Was Walking down Sackville Street*

The technical perfection of the novels of Mr George Moore does not prevent them from being faultlessly dead.

Q. D. Leavis, *Fiction and the Reading Public*

'Do you know George Moore?' I asked him [Oscar Wilde] one day when he had been rolling the British Zola's novels round the ring. 'Know him? I know him so well that I haven't spoken to him in ten years.'

Vincent O'Sullivan, *Aspects of Wilde*

George Moore . . . looked like a very prosperous Mellon's Food baby.

Gertrude Stein, *The Autobiography of Alice B. Toklas*

George Moore is always conducting his education in public.

Oscar Wilde, in conversation with Max Beerbohm

That vague formless obscene face.

Oscar Wilde, Letter to Reginald Turner, February 1899

He leads his readers to the latrine and locks them in.

Oscar Wilde, in Hesketh Pearson, *The Life of Oscar Wilde*

Moore once had visits from the Muse / But fearing that she would refuse / An ancient lecher took to geese / He now gets novels at his ease. /

William Butler Yeats, Journal, 9 March 1909

Moore dismissed his sixth cook the day I left – six in three weeks. One brought in a policeman, Moore made so much noise. Moore brought the policeman into the dining room and said 'Is there a law in this country to compel me to eat that abominable omelette?'

William Butler Yeats, Letter to Lady Gregory, May 1901

*See also* Lytton Strachey, William Wordsworth

## MOORE, GEORGE EDWARD

1873–1958 Philosopher

I have never but once succeeded in making him tell a lie, and that was by a subterfuge. 'Moore,' I said, 'do you *always* speak the truth?' 'No,' he replied. I believe this to be the only lie he ever told.

Bertrand Russell, *Autobiography*, vol. 1

One of the pet amusements of all Moore's friends was to watch him trying to light a pipe. He would light a match, and then begin to argue, and continue until the match burnt his fingers. Then he would light another, and so on, until the box was finished. This was no doubt fortunate for his health, as it provided moments during which he was not smoking.

*Ibid.*

. . . G. E. Moore was a perfect March Hare. His gown was always covered with chalk, his cap was in rags or missing, and his hair was a tangle which had never known the brush within man's memory. Its order and repose were not improved by an irascible habit of running his hands through it. He would go across town to his class, with no more formal footwear than his bedroom slippers, and the space between these and his trousers (which were several inches too short) was filled with wrinkled white socks.

Norbert Wiener, *Ex-Prodigy*

*See also* Lord Keynes, Ludwig Wittgenstein

## MOORE, SIR JOHN

1761–1809 Soldier

When you are a man, come to me, and I will give you a real sword, for your dear Uncle's sake.

Lady Hester Stanhope, in a note accompanying a gift of toys to Moore's nephew John, 1809

Not a drum was heard, not a funeral note, / As his corpse to the rampart we hurried; / Not a soldier discharged his farewell shot / O'er the grave where our hero we buried. /

We buried him darkly at dead of night, / The sods with our bayonets turning; / By the struggling moonbeam's misty light / And the lantern dimly burning. /

No useless coffin enclosed his breast, / Not in sheet or in shroud we wound him; / But he lay like a warrior taking his rest, / With his martial cloak around him. /

Few and short were the prayers we said, / And we spoke not a word of sorrow; / But we steadfastly gazed on the face that was dead, / And we bitterly thought of the morrow. /

We thought, as we hollow'd his narrow bed / And smoothed down his lonely pillow, / That the foe and the stranger would tread o'er his head, / And we far away on the billow! /

Lightly they'll talk of the spirit that's gone / And o'er his cold ashes upbraid him, – / But little he'll rock, if they let him sleep on / In the grave where a Briton has laid him. /

But half of our heavy task was done / When the clock struck the hour for retiring: / And we heard the distant and random gun / That the foe was sullenly firing. /

Slowly and sadly we laid him down, / From the field of his fame fresh and gory; / We carved not a line, and we raised not a stone – / But we left him alone with his glory. /

Charles Wolfe, *The Burial of Sir John Moore at Corunna*

## MOORE, MARIANNE CRAIG

1887–1972 Poet

Anything that is a stumbling block to my reader is a matter of regret to me and punctuation ought to be exact. Under ordinary circumstances, it is as great a hardship to me to be obliged to alter punctuation as to alter words, though I will admit that at times I am heady and irresponsible.

On herself, Letter to Ezra Pound, 19 January 1919

She takes the museum piece out of its glass case, and sets it against the living flower. She produces living plants out of the herbarium and living animals from the bestiary.

Louise Boyan, 'American Timeless', in *Quarterly Review of Literature*, vol. 4, no. 2

And there is one final, and 'magnificent' compliment: Miss Moore's poetry is as 'feminine' as Christina Rossetti's, one never forgets that it is written by a woman; but with both one never thinks of this as anything but a positive virtue.

T. S. Eliot, *Essays*: 'Marianne Moore'

Miss Moore's relation to the soil is not a simple one, or rather it is to various soils – to that of Latium and to that of Attica I believe (or at least to that of the Aegean littoral) as well as most positively to soil (well top-dressed) of America.

*Ibid.*

Miss Moore leaves the stones she picks up carefully uncut, but places them in an unimaginably complicated and difficult setting, to sparkle under the Northern Light of her continual irony.

Randall Jarrell, 'Her Shield', in Donald Hall ed., *Marianne Moore, A Collection of Critical Essays*

It is a talent which diminishes the tom-toming on the hollow men of a waste-land to an irrelevant pitter-patter.

William Carlos Williams, 'Marianne Moore', in *ibid.*

## MOORE, THOMAS

1779–1852 Poet, Author

Lalla Rookh / Is a naughty book / By Tommy Moore, / Who has written four; / Each warmer / Than the former, / So the most recent / Is the least decent. /

Anon., *On T. Moore's Poems*

Moore always smiles whenever he recites; / He smiles, you think, approving what he writes? / And yet in this no vanity is shown: / A modest man may like what's not his own. /

Anon., in *Elegant Extracts*

Mr Moore *is* a *poet*, and therefore is *not* a reasoner.

Peregrine Bingham, in *Westminster Review*, January 1824

Young Catullus of his day / As sweet, but as immoral, in his lay! /

Lord Byron, *English Bards and Scotch Reviewers*

The poet of all circles, and the idol of his own.

Lord Byron, Dedication to *The Corsair*

In society, he is gentlemanly, gentle, and altogether more pleasing than any individual with whom I am acquainted ... He has but one fault – and that one I daily regret – he is not *here*.

Lord Byron, Journal, 22 November 1813

Highly gifted, yet meanly endowed; he had too much genius for so little independence of spirit. He rose above the depressing influences of low birth to sink under the caresses of the high-born.

Thomas Colley Grattan, *Beaten Paths and Those Who Trod Them*

He looked as if begotten between a toad and cupid.

Theodore Hook, in *ibid.*

When Moore is merry he ceases to be a poet so utterly that we are tempted to ask when did he begin.

George Bernard Shaw, *Pen Portraits and Reviews*

*See also* Lord Byron, Alexander Pope, William Butler Yeats

## MORDAUNT, CHARLES, *see under* PETERBOROUGH, EARL OF

## MORE, HANNAH

1745–1833 Writer

Mrs Hannah More is another celebrated modern poetess, and I believe still living. She has written a great deal which I have never read.

William Hazlitt, *Lectures on the English Poets*

Much as I love your writings, I respect yet more your heart and your goodness. You are so good, that I believe you would go to heaven, even though there were no Sunday, and only six *working* days in the week.

Horace Walpole, Letter to Mrs H. More, 1788

## MORE, SIR THOMAS

1478–1535 Statesman, Author, Saint

I pray Sir give me aid in my going up; as for my coming down I can make shift for myself.

On himself, attributed, as he ascended the scaffold for his execution

You will never get credit for beheading me, my neck is so short.

On himself, attributed, remark made to his executioners

Memorandum that in his Utopia his lawe is that the young people are to see each other stark naked before marriage. Sir [William] Roper, of Eltham in Kent, came one morning, pretty early, to my lord, with a proposall to marry one of his daughters. My lord's daughters were then both together a bed in a truckle-bed in their father's chamber asleep. He carries Sir [William] into the chamber and takes the sheet by the corner and suddenly whippes it off. They lay on their Backs, and their smocks up as high as their armpitts. This awakened them, and immediately they turned on their Bellies. Quoth Roper, I have seen both sides, and so gave a patt on her Buttock he made choice of, sayeing, Thou art mine. Here was all the trouble of the wooing.

John Aubrey, *Brief Lives*

When *More* some time had Chancellor been / No more suits did remain, / The same shall never more be seen / Till *More* be there again. /

Thomas Fuller, *The History of the Worthies of England*

When we reflect that Sir Thomas More was ready to die for the doctrine of transubstantiation, we cannot but feel some doubt whether the doctrine of transubstantiation may not triumph over all opposition. More was a man of eminent talents. He had all the information on the subject that we have, or that, while the world lasts, any human being will have.

T. B. Macaulay, *Essays*: 'Ranke's History of the Popes'

. . . No such culprit stood at any European bar for a thousand years. It is rather from caution than from necessity that the ages of Roman domination are excluded from the comparison. It does not seem that in any moral respect Socrates himself could claim a superiority.

Sir James Mackintosh, *Life of Sir Thomas More*

So on a tyme, walking with me alonge the teames side at Chelsey, in talking of other things he said vnto me: 'Nowe wold to our Lord, sonne Roper, vppon condicion that three things were well established in Christendome, I were put in a sack, and here presently caste into the Thames.'

'What greate things be those, Sir,' quoth I, 'that should moue you so to wish?'

'In faith, sonne, they be these,' said he. 'The first is, that where the moste part of Christen princes be at mortall warre, they were all at an uniuersall peace. The second, that wheare the Church of Christe is at this presente sore afflicted with many errors and heresees, it were setled in a perfect vniformity of religion. The third, that where the kings matter of his mariage is nowe come question, it were to the glory of god and quietnes of al partes brought to a good conclusion.'

William Roper, *The Lyfe of Sir Thomas Moore*

And albeit his mynde served him to the second daughter, for that he thought her the fairest and best favoured, yeat when he considered that it wold be both greate greif and some shame also to the eldest to see your yonger sister in mariage preferred before her, he then of a certayne pity framed his fancy towardes her, and soon after maryed her.

*Ibid.*, on More's choice of a wife among the three daughters of Master Colte

. . . More and his fellow-martyr Fisher were not canonised for four centuries; and some explanation is required of this surprising delay. Partly, no doubt, it was due to the view held of More in Rome. Like Newman long afterwards, More was suspect as a Liberal Catholic, a Catholic who appealed (as he still appeals) to Protestants, who was indeed himself half-Protestant. Belonging to the age and sharing the views of his friend Erasmus, he had doubted the value of monasticism, wished to reduce the externals of worship, to admit lay reason into dogmatic studies, to meet reform half-way and salvage thereby a purified religion. But in fact, when Rome was saved it was not by such measures: the Counter-Reformation was not a compliance with Reform but a defiance of it.

H. R. Trevor-Roper, *Sir Thomas More and the English Lay Recusants*

*See also* George Orwell

## MORGAN, JOHN PIERPONT

1837–1913 Banker, Financier, Art Collector

I owe the public nothing.

On himself, in Matthew Josephson, *The Robber Barons*

It's Morgan's, it's Morgan's, / The great financial Gorgon's. /

Anon. song

Mr Morgan buys his partners; I grow my own.

Andrew Carnegie, attributed

Morgan's ruby nose added to his personal fame and with some humor he once said it 'would be impossible for me to appear on the streets without it.' His nose, he remarked on another occasion, 'was part of the American business structure.'

Stewart Holbrook, *The Age of the Moguls*

*See also* Al Capone, Thomas Gresham

## MORLEY, THOMAS

1557–1604? Musician

Master Morley supposing, perhaps, that the harmony which was to be heard through the clattering of knives, forks, spoons, and plates, with the gingling of glasses, and clamorous conversation of a city-feast, need not be very accurate or refined, was not very nice in setting parts to these tunes, which are so far from correct, that almost any one of the city waits would, in musical cant, have *vamped* as good an accompaniment.

Dr Charles Burney, *A General History of Music*

Such was old Orpheus cunning / That senseless things drew near him / And herds of beasts to hear him / The stock, the stone, the Ox, the Ass came running. / MORLEY! but this enchanting / To thee, to be the Musick-God is wanting. / And yet thou needst not fear him; / Draw thou the Shepherd still and Bonny-lasses, / And envy him not stocks, stones, Oxen, Asses. /

Michael Drayton, attributed, *Mr M.D. to the Author*, in *The First Book of Balletts to Five Voyces*

Death hath deprived me of my dearest friend, / My dearest friend is dead and laid in grave, / In grave he rests until the world shall end, / The world shall end, as end must all things have. / All things must have an end that nature wrought, / That nature wrought, must unto dust be brought. /

Thomas Weelkes, *A Remembrance of My Friend Mr Thomas Morley, Airs or Fantastic Spirits*

## MORRELL, LADY OTTOLINE VIOLET ANNE

1873–1938 Hostess

I did not know I loved you till I heard myself telling you so – for one instant I thought 'Good God, what have I said?' and then I knew it was the truth.

Bertrand Russell, Letter to Ottoline Morrell, March 1911

. . . Loving you is like loving a red-hot poker, which is a worse bedfellow than even Lytton's umbrella: every caress brings on agony.

Bertrand Russell, Letter to Ottoline Morrell, June 1912

## MORRIS, WILLIAM

1834–96 Poet, Painter, Designer

His method, his mingling of the couplet measure and the old stanza in his tales . . . looks somehow like writing in ruins.

R. W. Dixon, Letter to Gerard Manley Hopkins, 4 November 1881

Morris . . . had just been talking to some members of a ship's crew whom he had met in Fenchurch Street. They had remained for some time under the impression that he was a ship's captain. This had pleased him very much, for it was his ambition to be taken for such a man . . . With a grey beard like the foam of the sea, with grey hair through which he continually ran his hands, erect and curly on his forehead, with a hooked nose, a florid complexion and clean, clear eyes, dressed in a blue serge coat, and carrying, as a rule, a satchel, to meet him was always, as it were, to meet a sailor ashore.

Ford Madox Ford, *Ancient Lights*

He's an extraordinary example, in short, of a delicate sensitive genius and taste, served by a perfectly healthy body and temper.

Henry James, Letter to Alice James, 12 March 1869

I can't understand how a man who, on the whole, enjoys dinner – and breakfast – and supper – to that extent of fat – can write such lovely poems about Misery.

John Ruskin, Letter to Joan Agnew, 21 January 1870

I feel nothing but elation when I think of Morris. My intercourse with him was so satisfying that I should be the most ungrateful of men if I asked for more. You can lose a man like that by your own death, but not by his. And so, until then, let us rejoice in him.

George Bernard Shaw (on Morris's death), in *Saturday Review*, 10 October 1896

The dream-world of Morris was as much the antithesis of daily life as with other men of genius, but he was never conscious of the antithesis and so knew nothing of intellectual suffering.

William Butler Yeats, *Autobiographies*

The one perfectly happy and fortunate poet of modern times.

William Butler Yeats, *Ideas of Good and Evil*

*See also* Alfred, Lord Tennyson, Virginia Woolf, William Butler Yeats

## MORSE, SAMUEL FINLEY BREESE

1791–1872 Artist, Inventor

Communication was improved by S. O. S. Morse, who invented the telegraph and organized the first union of telegraph operators in the West, known as the Western Union. He also developed the secret code that bears his name. Morse's first message on the telegraph was the reverent question, 'What hath God wrought?' which is Morse code for 'don't write, telegraph.'

Richard Armour, *It All Started With Columbus*

Even the telegraph was seen as an extraneous enterprise which Morse expected would free him to paint all the harder. Although his soaring imagination informed him at once that his invention was to be of vast importance to mankind, although his religious idealism assured him that he was divinely and wondrously appointed to this task, he nevertheless continued to think of himself as a painter. He could not know the decades of labor and contention in which his telegraph was to involve him, nor could he foresee what a cruel and ungrateful mistress art was to prove.

Harry B. Wehle, *Samuel F. B. Morse*

## MORTON, JOHN, CARDINAL

1420?–1500 Statesman

He was a great instrument in advancing a voluntary contribution to the king through the land; persuading prodigals to part with their money, because they did spend it most, and the covetous, because they might spare it best; so making both extremes to meet in one medium, to supply the king's necessities.

Thomas Fuller, on 'Morton's Fork', *The History of the Worthies of England*

## MUIR, JOHN

1838–1914 Naturalist, Explorer

I am very, very blessed. The Valley is full of people, but they do not annoy me. I revolved in pathless places and in higher rocks than *the world* and his ribbony wife can reach.

On himself, Letter to Mrs Ezra S. Carr, 29 July 1870

I was once free as any pine-playing wind, and feel that I have still a good length of line, but alack! there seems to be a hook or two of civilization in me that I would fain pull out, yet *would not pull out* – O, O, O!!!

On himself, in William Bade ed., *The Life and Letters of John Muir*, vol. 2

## MUNI, PAUL (MUNI WEISENFREUND)

1895–1967 Actor

Paul was a most attractive man, I thought. Evidently he did not think so and usually retreated behind a beard. Transference is one thing, but I sincerely believe the audience wants to become familiar with certain physical attributes that are ever present in each performance. Mr Muni seemed intent on submerging himself so completely that he disappeared. His wife used to say 'I've lived with more men than any other woman'. There is no question that his technique as an actor was superb. But for me, beneath the exquisite petit point of details, the loss of his own sovereignty worked conversely to rob some of his characterisations of blood. It is a criticism that I aim at the naturalist actors. Paul's intellect was always at work. He fought the good fight and added greatly to the dignity and respectability of Hollywood.

Bette Davis, *The Lonely Life*

## MURRAY, GEORGE GILBERT AIMÉ

1866–1957 Classical Scholar, Translator

We need a number of educated poets who shall at least have opinions about Greek drama, and whether it is or is not of any use to us. And it must be said that Professor Gilbert Murray is not the man for this. Greek poetry will never have the slightest vitalizing effect upon English poetry if it can only appear masquerading as a vulgar debasement of the eminently personal idiom of Swinburne. These are strong words to use against the most popular Hellenist of his time; but we must witness of Professor Murray ere we die that these things are not otherwise but thus.

T. S. Eliot, *The Sacred Wood*

Gentle-voiced and with the spiritual look of the strict vegetarian, [he was] doing preliminary propaganda work for the League of Nations. Once, as I sat talking to him in his study about Aristotle's *Poetics*, while he walked up and down, I suddenly asked: 'Exactly what is the principle of that walk of yours? Are you trying to avoid the flowers on the rug, or are you trying to keep to the squares?' My own compulsion-neuroses made it easy for me to notice them in others. He wheeled around sharply: 'You're the first person who has caught me out,' he said. 'No, it's not the flowers or the squares; it's a habit that I have got into of doing things in sevens. I take seven steps, you see, then I change direction and go another seven steps, then I turn around. I consulted Browne, the Professor of Psychology, about it the other day, but he assured me it isn't a dangerous habit. He said: "When you find yourself getting into multiples of seven, come to me again." '

Robert Graves, *Goodbye to All That*

## MURRAY, JOHN

1778–1843 Publisher

He is a rogue of course, but a civil one.

Jane Austen, Letter to Cassandra Austen, 17 October 1815

I believe M. to be a good man, with a personal regard for me. But a bargain is in its very essence a *hostile* transaction . . . even between brethren, [it] is a declaration of war.

Lord Byron, Letter to Douglas Kinnaird, 14 July 1821

The most timid of God's booksellers.

Lord Byron, in Thomas Medwin, *Conversations of Lord Byron*

Southey says, in alteration of Byron's phrase, that M. is the most timorous not of God's but of the Devil's booksellers.

Sir Walter Scott, Journal, 7 December 1825

*See also* Sir Walter Scott

## MURRAY, WILLIAM, *see under* MANSFIELD, LORD

# 'N'

## NAPIER, SIR CHARLES JAMES

1782–1853 Soldier, Administrator

The hundred-gun ship has taken the little cock-boat in tow, and it will follow for ever over the ocean of time.

On himself, when praised by the Duke of Wellington, 1843

*Peccavi* – I have Scinde.

On himself, after taking Scinde, 1843

When he went into a campaign he took with him but a piece of soap and a pair of towels; he dined off a hunch of bread and a cup of water. 'A warrior', said he, 'should not care for wine or luxury, for fine turbans or embroidered shulwars; his talwar should be bright, and never mind whether his papooshes are shiny.' Napeer Singh was a lion indeed . . . But this lion, though the bravest of animals, was the most quarrelsome that ever lashed a tail and roared in a jungle.

W. M. Thackeray, *The Tale of Koompanee Jehan*

## NASH, JOHN

1752–1835 Architect

Augustus at Rome was for building renown'd, / And of marble he left what of brick he had found; / But is not our Nash, too, a very great master? – / He finds us all brick and leaves us all plaster. /

Anon., in *Quarterly Review*, vol. 34, 1826

Nash embodied everything which the nineteenth century hated about the eighteenth.

John Summerson, *Architecture in Britain 1530–1830*

## NASH, OGDEN

1902–71 Poet

Being both viable and friable I wish to prolong my existence.

On himself, in *Saturday Evening Post*

As a poet Nash works under two disadvantages: he is a humorist, and he is easy to understand.

Clifton Fadiman, *Party of One*

Hurrah, Mr Nash, for your writings laughable! / We liked you surly, we love you affable, / And think your poems designed for the nursery / Almost the best in your bulging versery. /

Phyllis McGinley, in *Saturday Review of Literature*, 10 October 1936

Nash is the laureate of a generation which had to develop its own wry, none-too-joyful humor as the alternative to simply lying down on the floor and screaming.

Russell Maloney, in *New York Times Book Review*, 14 October 1945

## NASHE, THOMAS

1567–1601 Author

He can raile (what mad Bedlam cannot raile?) but the favour of his railing, is grosely fell, and smelleth noysomly of the pumps, or a nastier thing. His gayest floorishes, are but Gascoignes weedes, or Tarletons trickes, or Greenes crankes, or Marlowes bravados: his jestes, but the dregges of common scurrilitie, the shreds of the theater, or the ofscouring of new Pamflets: his freshest nippitatie, but the froth of stale inventions, long since lothsome to quick tastes: his shroving ware, but lenten stuffe, like the old pickle herring: his lustiest verdure, but rank ordure, not to be named in Civilitie, or Rhetorique.

Gabriel Harvey, *Pierces Supererogation*

## NATION, CARRY AMELIA MOORE

1846–1911 Temperance Agitator

. . . a bulldog running along at the feet of Jesus, barking at what He doesn't like.

On herself, in Herbert Asbury, *Carry Nation*

Sing a song of six joints, / With bottles full of rye; / Four and twenty beer kegs, / Stacked up on the sly. / When the kegs were opened, / The beer began to sing, / 'Hurrah for Carry Nation, / Her work beats anything.'

Anon., Satire in *ibid.*

. . . Carrie Nation was responsible for legislation that required printing the alcoholic content on the label so that sick people would know whether they were getting enough alcohol to do them any good.

Richard Armour, *It All Started With Columbus*

There came to our town an old pelican / Whose manner was scarcely angelican: / To a man who sold beer / She said, 'Say, look here! / If you want me to save you from helican.' /

Ironquill (pseud.), in *The Capital* (Topeka)

## NELSON, HORATIO, VISCOUNT

1758–1805 Admiral

Before this time tomorrow I shall have gained a peerage, or Westminster Abbey.

On himself, shortly before the Battle of the Nile, August 1798, in Robert Southey, *Life of Nelson*

Nelson for ever – any time / Am I his to command in prose or rhyme! / Give me of Nelson only a touch, / And I save it, be it little or much: / Here's one our Captain gives, and so / Down at the word, by George, shall it go! / They say that at Greenwich they point the beholder / To Nelson's coat, 'still with tar on the shoulder: / 'For he used to lean with one shoulder digging, / 'Jigging, as it were, and zig-zag-zigging / 'Up against the mizzen-rigging!' /

Robert Browning, *Nationality in Drinks*

He brought heroism into the line of duty.

Joseph Conrad, in Robert Debs Heinl Jr, *The Dictionary of Military and Naval Quotations*

Rarely has a man been more favored in the hour of his appearing, never one so fortunate in the moment of his death.

Alfred Thayer Mahan, *The Life of Nelson*

He leads: we hear our Seaman's call / In the roll of battles won; / For he is Britain's Admiral / Till the setting of her sun. /

George Meredith, *Trafalgar Day*

The love she [Lady Hamilton] makes to Nelson is not only ridiculous, but disgusting: not only the rooms, but the whole house, staircase and all, are covered with nothing but pictures of her and him, of all sizes and sorts, and representations of his naval actions, coats-of-arms, pieces of plate in his honour, the flag-staff of L'Orient, &c. – an excess of vanity which counteracts its purpose. If it was Lady Hamilton's house there might be a pretence for it; to make his own house a meer looking-glass to view himself all day is bad taste.

Lord Minto, Letter to Lady Minto, March 1802

'Do you know,' said he to Mr Ferguson, 'what is shown on board the commander-in-chief? No. 39!' Mr Ferguson asked what that meant? – 'Why, to leave off action! Now damn me if I do! You know, Foley', turning to the captain, 'I have only one eye, – I have a right to be blind sometimes,' – and then putting the glass to his blind eye, in that mood of mind which sports with bitterness, he exclaimed, 'I really do not see the signal!' Presently he exclaimed, 'Damn the signal! Keep mine for closer battle flying! That's the way I answer such signals. Nail mine to the mast!'

Robert Southey, on the Battle of Copenhagen, *Life of Nelson*

It was Nelson's maxim, that, to negotiate with effect, force should be at hand, and in a situation to act.

*Ibid.*

Presently, calling [Captain] Hardy back, he said to him, in a low voice, 'Don't throw me overboard'; and he desired that he might be buried by his parents, unless it should please the king to order otherwise. Then, reverting to his private feelings: 'Take care of my dear Lady Hamilton, Hardy; take care of poor Lady Hamilton. – Kiss me, Hardy,' said he. Hardy knelt down and kissed his cheek: and Nelson said, 'Now I am satisfied. Thank God, I have done my duty.'

*Ibid.*, describing Nelson's death at Trafalgar

Always in his element and always on his element.

G. M. Trevelyan, *History of England*

*See also* Daniel Defoe

## NEWCASTLE, DUKE OF (THOMAS PELHAM-HOLLES)

1693–1768 Statesman

. . . the Duke of Newcastle . . . made his entry with as much alacrity and noise as usual, mightily out of breath though mightily in words, and in his hand a bundle of papers as big as his head and with little more in them.

Lord Hervey, in Lewis Namier, *Crossroads of Power*

No man was so unmercifully satirised. But in truth he was himself a satire ready made. All that the art of a satirist does for other men, nature had done for him.

T. B. Macaulay, *Essays*: 'Horace Walpole's Letters'

He was a living, moving, talking caricature. His gait was a shuffling trot, his utterance a rapid stutter; he was always in a hurry; he was never in time; he abounded in fulsome caresses and hysterical tears. His oratory resembled that of Justice Shallow. It was nonsense, effervescent in animal spirits and impertinence.

*Ibid.*

## NEWMAN, JOHN HENRY, CARDINAL

1801–90 Theologian

Point 4. I shall come back from Rome with a prestige, as if I had a blunderbuss in my pocket.

On himself, Personal memorandum, 15 January 1854

From the age of fifteen, dogma has been the fundamental principle of my religion: I know no other religion; I cannot enter into the idea of any other sort of religion; religion, as a mere sentiment, is to me a dream and a mockery.

On himself, *History of my Religious Opinions*

It's true these have been years of strife, but after all there's the Cardinal's Hat.

On himself, dying words, August 1890

To me he seems to have been the most artificial man of our generation, full of ecclesiastical loves and hatred. Considering what he really was, it is wonderful what a space he has filled in the eyes of mankind. In speculation he was habitually untruthful and not much better in practice. His conscience had been taken out and the Church put in its place. Yet he was a man of genius, and a good man in the sense of being disinterested.

Benjamin Jowett, Letter to Margot Tennant, 22 May 1891

It is remarkably interesting, it is like listening to the voice of one from the dead.

Cardinal Manning, Comment on Newman's *Apologia pro Vita Sua*, 1864

Poor Newman! He was a great hater!

Cardinal Manning, *circa* 1891, in Lytton Strachey, *Eminent Victorians*

When Newman was a child he 'wished that he could believe the Arabian Nights were true.' When he came to be a man, his wish seems to have been granted.

Lytton Strachey, in *ibid.*

*See also* Sir Thomas More

## NEWTON, SIR ISAAC

1642–1727 Natural Philosopher, Mathematician

I don't know what I may seem to the world, but, as to myself, I seem to have been only like a boy playing on the sea shore, and diverting myself in now and then finding a smoother pebble or prettier shell than ordinary, whilst the great ocean of truth lay all undiscovered before me.

On himself, in Joseph Spence, *Anecdotes*

Reason and Newton, they are quite two things: / For so the swallow and the sparrow sings, / Reason says Miracle, Newton says Doubt. /

William Blake, *You Don't Believe*

When Newton saw an apple fall, he found / In that slight startle from his contemplation – / 'Tis *said* (for I'll not answer above ground / For any sage's creed or calculation) – / A mode of proving that the earth turned round / In a most natural whirl, called 'gravitation'; / And this is the sole mortal who could grapple, / Since Adam, with a fall, or with an apple. /

Lord Byron, *Don Juan*, canto x

Enough of this. Newton forgive me. You found the only way that, in your day, was at all possible for a man of the highest powers of intellect and creativity. The concepts that you created still dominate the way we think in physics, although we now know that they must be replaced by others farther removed from the sphere of immediate experience if we want to try for a more profound understanding of the way things are interrelated.

Albert Einstein, *Autobiographical Notes*

One trait of his early disposition is told of him: he had then a rude method of measuring the force of the wind blowing against him, by observing how much further he could leap in the direction of the wind, or blowing on his back, than he could leap the contrary way, or opposed to the wind; an early mark of his original infantine genius.

William Hutton, *Philosophical and Mathematical Dictionary*

Must a theory of motion explain the cause of the attractive forces between particles of matter or may it simply note the existence of such forces? Newton's dynamics was widely rejected because, unlike both Aristotle's and Descartes's theories, it implied the latter answer to the question. When

Newton's theory had been accepted, a question was therefore banished from science. That question, however, was one that general relativity may proudly claim to have solved.

Thomas Kuhn, *The Structure of Scientific Revolutions*

Anecdote of Newton, showing his extreme absence; inviting a friend to dinner and forgetting it: the friend arriving, and finding the philosopher in a fit of abstraction. Dinner brought up for *one*: the friend (without disturbing Newton) sitting down and dispatching it, and Newton, after recovering from his reverie, looking at the empty dishes and saying, 'Well really, if it wasn't for the proof before my eyes, I could have sworn that I had not yet dined'.

Thomas Moore, Diary, 18 January 1828

At some seldom times when he designed to dine in hall, would turn to the left hand and go out into the street, when making a stop he found his mistake, would hastily turn back, and then sometimes instead of going into hall, return to his chamber again.

Humphrey Newton, Letter to John Conduit, 1728

Nature and Nature's laws lay hid in Night: / God said, Let Newton be! and all was light. /

Alexander Pope, *Epitaph for Sir Isaac Newton*

Sir Isaac Newton, though so deep in Algebra and Fluxions, could not readily make up a common account: and, when he was Master of the Mint, used to get somebody to make up his accounts for him.

Alexander Pope, in Joseph Spence, *Anecdotes*

He was thus able to enunciate his law of universal gravitation: 'Every body attracts every other with a force directly proportional to the product of their masses and inversely proportional to the square of the distance between them'. From this formula he was able to deduce everything in planetary theory: the motions of the planets and their satellites, the orbits of comets, the tides. It appeared later that even the minute departures from elliptical orbits on the part of the planets were deducible from Newton's law. The triumph was so complete that Newton was in danger of becoming another Aristotle, and imposing an insuperable barrier to progress. In England, it was not till a century after his death that men freed themselves from his authority sufficiently to do important original work in the subjects of which he had treated.

Bertrand Russell, *History of Western Philosophy*

Newton, when at school, stood at the bottom of the lowermost form but one. The boy above Newton having kicked him, the dunce showed his pluck by challenging him to a fight, and beat him. Then he set to work with a will, and determined also to vanquish his antagonist as a scholar, which he did, rising to the top of his class.

Samuel Smiles, *Self-help*

Pray, Sir Isaac, may I ask you what is your opinion of the immortality of the soul? – [asked Signora Antonio Cocchi].

– Madam, I'm an experimental Philosopher.

Joseph Spence, *Anecdotes*

Have ye not listened while he bound the Suns / And planets to their spheres? th'unequal task / Of human-kind till then. Oft had they roll'd / O'er erring man the year, and oft disgraced / The pride of Schools, before their course was known / Full in its causes and effects to him, / All piercing sage! who sat not down and dream'd / Romantic schemes, defended by the din / Of specious words, and tyranny of names;

/ But, bidding his amazing mind attend, / And with heroic patience years on years / Deep-searching, saw at last the System dawn, / And shine, of all his race, on him alone. /

James Thomson, *To the Memory of Sir Isaac Newton*

I do not dislike the French from the vulgar antipathy between neighbouring nations, but for their insolent and unfounded airs of superiority. In arms we have almost always outshone them: and till they have excelled Newton, and come near to Shakespeare, pre-eminence in genius must remain with us.

Horace Walpole, Letter to Hannah More, 14 October 1787

One of Sir I. Newton's philosophical friends abroad had sent him a curious prism, which was taken to the Custom-house, and was at that time a scarce commodity in this kingdom. Sir Isaac, laying claim to it, was asked by the officers what the value of the glass was, that they might accordingly regulate the duty. The great Newton, whose business was more with the universe than with duties and drawbacks, and who rated the prism according to his own idea of its use and excellence, answered, 'That the value was so great that he could not ascertain it'. Being again pressed to set some fixed estimate upon it, he persisted in his reply, 'That he could not say what it was worth, for that the value was inestimable'. The honest Custom-house officers accordingly took him at his word, and made him pay a most exorbitant duty for the prism, which he might have taken away upon only paying a rate according to the weight of the glass!

C. R. Weld, *A History of the Royal Society*

The pathetic desire of mankind to find themselves starting from an intellectual basis which is clear, distinct, and certain, is illustrated by Newton's boast, *hypotheses non fingo* [I do not frame hypotheses], at the same time when he enunciated his law of universal gravitation. This law states that every particle of matter attracts every other particle of matter; though at the moment of enunciation only planets and heavenly bodies had been observed to attract 'particles of matter'.

Alfred North Whitehead, *The Function of Reason*

The antechapel where the statue stood / Of Newton with his prism and silent face, / The marble index of a mind forever / Voyaging through strange seas of thought alone. /

William Wordsworth, *The Prelude*, book 30

*See also* Michael Faraday, Edmund Halley, John Hunter, J. M. W. Turner

## NIGHTINGALE, FLORENCE

1820–1910 Hospital Reformer

What a comfort it was to see her pass. She would speak to one, and nod and smile to as many more; but she could not do it to all you know. We lay there by the hundreds; but we could kiss her shadow as it fell and lay our heads on the pillow again content.

A patient in the Crimean War, in Cecil Woodham-Smith, *Florence Nightingale*

She began to think, as well as to live, her time, and she discovered the new formula for the electronic age: Medicare.

Marshall McLuhan, *Understanding Media*

If you prefer to do your work rather by moving the hidden springs than by allowing yourself to be known to the world as doing what you really do, it is not for me to make any observations on this preference (inasmuch as I am bound to presume you have good reasons for it) other than to say that I much regret that this preference is so very general among women.

John Stuart Mill, Letter to Florence Nightingale, December 1867

Yet her conception of God was certainly not orthodox. She felt towards Him as she might have felt towards a glorified sanitary engineer; and in some of her speculations she seems hardly to distinguish between the Deity and the Drains.

Lytton Strachey, *Eminent Victorians*

You are, I know, well aware of the high sense I entertain of the Christian devotion which you have displayed during this great and bloody war, and I need hardly repeat to you how warm my admiration is for your services, which are fully equal to those of my dear and brave soldiers, whose sufferings you have had the *privilege* of alleviating in so merciful a manner. I am, however, anxious of marking my feelings in a manner which I trust will be agreeable to you, and therefore send you with this letter a brooch, the form and emblems of which commemorate your great and blessed work, and which, I hope, you will wear as a mark of the high approbation of your Sovereign!

Queen Victoria, Letter to Florence Nightingale, January 1856

## NOLLEKENS, JOSEPH

1737–1823 Sculptor

Nollekens was much superior to any other, in knowledge of the figure & in execution. He had not much mind, but great experience.

N. Marchant, in Joseph Farington, Diary, April 1806

To the beauties of the immortal Shakespeare he was absolutely insensible, nor did he ever visit the theatre when his plays were performed; though he was actively alive to a pantomime, and frequently spoke of the capital and curious tricks in Harlequin Sorcerer. He also recollected with pleasure Mr Rich's wonderful and singular power of scratching his ear with his foot like a dog; and the street-exhibition of Punch and his wife delighted him beyond expression.

J. T. Smith, *Nollekens and His Times*

## NORTH, FREDERICK, EARL OF GUILFORD

1732–92 Prime Minister

Heber told me a capital jest of Frederick North at Algiers. North asked the Dey permission to see his women. After some parley the Dey said, 'He is so ugly, let him see them all'.

Lord Broughton, *Recollections of a Long Life*

When Barré stern, with accents deep, / Calls up Lord North and murders sleep, / And if his Lordship rise to speak, / Then wit and argument awake. /

David Garrick, in Alan Valentine, *Lord North*

He fills a chair.

Samuel Johnson, in James Boswell, *Life of Johnson*

The noble lord in the blue ribbon is actuated in all his measures by the most disinterested zeal for his country. He wants only one quality to make him a great and distinguished statesman; I mean a more despotic and commanding temper.

Lord Melville, in Nathaniel Wraxall, *Memoirs*

LORD NORTH told Charles Fox, as they both sipp'd their broth, / I know by Britannia's queer looks, / That the wench is offended such foes should unite, / And will scratch us both *out of her books.* / Thus Fox, in reply, damn it, North, never mind, / Should she curse our new creed of belief, / She may black that page where our names have long stood, / For we both must *turn o'er a new leaf.* /

Anthony Pasquin (John Williams), *An Epigram Written at the time of the Coalition between Lord North and Charles Fox*

Lord North was a coarse and heavy man, with a wide mouth, thick lips, and puffy cheeks, which seemed typical of his policy.

J. H. Rose, in Sir Charles Petrie, *The Four Georges*

Two large prominent eyes that rolled about to no purpose (for he was utterly short-sighted), a wide mouth, thick lips and inflated visage, gave him the air of a blind trumpeter. A deep untuneable voice, which, instead of modulating, he enforced with unnecessary pomp, a total neglect of his person, and ignorance of every civil attention, disgusted all who judge by appearance, or withhold their approbation till it is courted. But within that rude casket were enclosed many useful talents . . . What he did, he did without a mask, and was not delicate in choosing his means.

Horace Walpole, *Memoirs*

He had neither system nor principles nor shame; sought neither the favour of the Crown or of the people, but enjoyed the good luck of fortune with a gluttonous Epicurism that was equally careless of glory or disgrace.

*Ibid.*

## NORTHCLIFFE, VISCOUNT (ALFRED CHARLES WILLIAM HARMSWORTH)

1865–1922 Journalist, Newspaper Proprietor

Have you heard? The Prime Minister has resigned and Northcliffe has sent for the King.

Anon., popular saying, 1919, in Hamilton Fyfe, *Northcliffe*

. . . the greatest figure who ever strode down Fleet St.

Lord Beaverbrook, *Politicians and the War*

The late Lord Northcliffe would not print anything in criticism of himself. He would always print the words of praise. Even from the publicity point of view, he was wrong.

Lord Beaverbrook, Letter to Tom Driberg, 3 December 1952

The democracy knows you as the poisoner of the streams of human intercourse, the fermenter of war, the preacher of hate, the unscrupulous enemy of human society.

A. G. Gardner, *Open Letter to Northcliffe*, December 1914

*Northcliffe:* The trouble with you, Shaw, is that you look as if there were a famine in the land. *Shaw:* The trouble with you, Northcliffe, is that you look as if you were the cause of it.

George Bernard Shaw, attributed, in *The Penguin Dictionary of Modern Quotations*

He is an extraordinarily commonplace man, with a very good brain for business. He is rather dull to talk to, very vain, but kind-hearted I should say. Nothing original. Those are the men that get on.

Frances Stevenson, Diary, 19 May 1917

He aspired to power instead of influence, and as a result forfeited both.

A. J. P. Taylor, *English History, 1914–1945*

*See also* Lord Kitchener

## NOVELLO, IVOR (DAVID IVOR DAVIES)

1893–1951 Actor, Composer

It is time that some official recognition were shown of his achievement in keeping the British flag flying over Ruritania.

Anon., in *Evening Standard*, 1951

It was a shock to discover that Ivor Novello was addicted to Nescafé.

Gabriele Annan, Review of Sandy Wilson's *Ivor* in *The Times Literary Supplement*, 19 December 1975

I lift my hat to Mr Novello. He can wade through tosh with the straightest face: the tongue never visibly approaches the cheek. Both as actor and as author he can pursue adventures too preposterous even for the films and do it with that solemn fixity of purpose which romantic melodrama inexorably demands.

Ivor Brown, in *Observer*, 1935

My image of this romantic handsome youth who had composed 'Keep the home fires burning' drooped and died and lay in the gutter between the tramlines and the kerb. The reason for this was that I had caught him in a completely 'off' moment. He was not sitting at a grand piano. He was not in naval uniform. The eager Galahad expression which distinguished every photograph of him was lacking. His face was yellow, and he had omitted to shave owing to a morning rehearsal. He was wearing an odd overcoat with an Astrakhan collar, and a degraded brown hat, and if he had suddenly produced a violin from somewhere and played the 'Barcarole' from *The Tales of Hoffman*, I should have given him threepence from sheer pity.

Noël Coward, *Present Indicative*

Mr Novello plays the King with all the assurance of a man who has gauged public taste down to the last emotional millimetre.

Milton Shulman, in *Evening Standard*, reviewing *King's Rhapsody*, 1949

## NOVELLO, VINCENT

1781–1861 Editor, Composer, Organist

But when this master of the spell, not content to have laid a soul prostrate, goes on, in his power, to inflict more bliss than lies in her capacity to receive, – impatient to overcome her 'earthly' with his 'heavenly,' – still pouring in, for protracted hours, fresh waves and fresh from the sea of sound, or from that inexhausted *German* ocean, above which, in triumphant progress, dolphin-seated, ride those Arions *Haydn* and *Mozart*, with their attendant Tritons, *Bach*, *Beethoven*, and a countless tribe, whom to attempt to reckon up would but plunge me again in the deeps, – I stagger under the weight of harmony, reeling to and fro at my wits' end; – clouds, as of frankincense, oppress me – priests, altars, censers, dazzle before me – the genius of *his* religion hath me in her toils – a shadowy triple tiara invests the brow of my friend, late so naked, so ingenuous – he is Pope, – and by him sits, like as in the anomaly of dreams, a she-Pope, too – tri-coroneted like himself! – I am converted, and yet a Protestant; – at once *malleus hereticorum*, and myself grand heresiarch: or three heresies centre in my person: – I am Marcion, Elbion, and Cerinthus – Gog and Magog – what not? – till the coming in of the friendly supper-tray dissipates the figment, and a draught of true Lutheran beer (in which chiefly my friend shows himself no bigot) at once reconciles me to the rationalities of a purer faith; and restores to me the genuine unterrifying aspects of my pleasant-countenanced host and hostess.

Charles Lamb, *Essays of Elia*: 'A Chapter on Ears'

# 'O'

## OAKLEY, ANNIE (PHOEBE MOZEE)

1860–1926 Sharp shooter

Little Sure-Shot.
  Sitting Bull's nickname for Oakley

## OATES, LAWRENCE EDWARD GRACE

1880–1912 Antarctic Explorer

I am just going outside, and may be some time.
  On himself, Last Message, in R. F. Scott, Antarctic Diary, 16 March 1912

## OATES, TITUS

1649–1705 Perjurer

As I'm informed on Monday last you sat / As dismal as a melancholy cat, / Folding your arms, and pulling down your hat / Over your eyes and groaning in a chair, / As if you did for God knows what despair. / Fye, Doctor, fye! You know it is a folly, / Thus to submit and yield to melancholy. /
  Thomas Brown, *Advice to Dr Oates . . . When a Prisoner in the King's Bench*

What need you care whose dunghill, Sir, you shit on! / Those who take up the sword for G--- must fight on. /
  *Ibid.*

A comical passage happen'd at the *Commons*, which I think very well worth sending you: the Doctor going thither for a licence, two scurvy questions were asked him: The first was, Whether he would have a licence to marry a boy or a girl? The second, whether he would have a licence for *behind*, or *before*?
  Thomas Brown, *The Widow's Wedding, or a True Account of Doctor Oates's Marriage*

*The Articles of Marriage were as follows*: *Imprimis*, the Doctor promises, *in verba Sacerdotis*, never to keep a male-servant in his house under sixty, and to hang up a picture of the destruction of *Sodom* in his bedchamber; . . . *Item* The Doctor promises that he will never offer to attack, either in bed or couch, joint-stool or table, the body of the aforesaid *Mrs Margaret Wells*, *a parte post*, but to comfort, refresh, and relieve her *a parte ante*, giving the aforesaid *Mrs Margaret Wells*, in case he offend after that manner, full leave to make herself amends *before*, as she pleases. As also on a second trespass, to burn his peace-maker: However with this proviso, that whenever the aforesaid *Mrs Margaret Wells* happens to be under the dominion of the moon, that is to say, whenever it is term-time with the aforesaid *Mrs Margaret Wells*, then the above-mentioned Doctor shall have full power, liberty and authority, to enter the *Westminster-Hall* of her body at which door he pleases.
  *Ibid.*

Sunk were his Eyes, his Voice was harsh and loud, / Sure signe he neither Cholerick was, nor Proud: / His long Chin prov'd his Wit; his Saint-like Grace / A Church Vermilion, and a *Moses*'s Face. / His Memory miraculously great, / Could Plots, exceeding man's belief, repeat; / Which therefore cannot be accounted Lies, / For humane Wit could never such devise. / Some future Truths are mingled in his Book; / But where the Witness fail'd, the Prophet spoke. /

John Dryden, *Absalom and Achitophel*

For my part, I do looke on *Oates* as a vaine, insolent man, puff'd up, with the favour of the Commons, for having discovered something realy true; as more especialy detecting the dangerous intrigue of Coleman, proved out of his owne letters; & of a general designe, which the Jesuiticall party of the Papists ever had, & still have to ruine the Church of England; but that he was trusted with those great secrets he pretended, or had any solid ground for what he accused divers noble men of, I have many reasons to induce my contrary beliefs.

John Evelyn, Diary, 18 July 1679

*Oates*, who had but two days before ben pilloried at severall places, & whip't at the Carts tails from Newgate to Algate; was this day placed in a sledge (being not able to go by reason of his so late scourging) & dragd from Prison to Tyburn, & whip'd againe all the way, which some thought to be very severe and extraordinary; but in case he were gilty of the perjuries, & so of the death of many innocents, as I feare he was; his punishment was but what he well deserv'd: I chanc'd to pass in my Coach just as Execution was doing on him: *A strange revolution.*

*Ibid.*, 22 May 1685

Such a mans Testimonie should not be taken against the life of a Dog.

At the trial of Lord Stafford, in *ibid.*, 6 December 1680

Whene'er it swore, to prove the oaths were true / Out of its mouth at random halters flew. / Round some unwary neck, by magic thrown / Though still the cunning Devil sav'd its own. /

Thomas Otway, Prologue to Aphra Behn, *City Heiress*

## OCCAM, WILLIAM

– d. 1349? Philosopher

Occam is best known for a maxim which is not to be found in his works, but has acquired the name of 'Occam's razor'. This maxim says: 'Entities are not to be multiplied without necessity.' Although he did not say this, he said something which has much the same effect, namely: 'It is vain to do with more what can be done with fewer.' That is to say, if everything in some science can be interpreted without assuming this or that hypothetical entity, there is no ground for assuming it. I have myself found this is a most fruitful principle in logical analysis.

Bertrand Russell, *History of Western Philosophy*

## O'CONNELL, DANIEL

1775–1847 Politician

I can drive a coach and six through any act of Parliament.

On himself, in Edward Latham, *Famous Sayings*

Generally, an agitator is a rough man of the O'Connell type, who says anything himself, and lets others say anything. You 'peg into me and I will peg into you, and let us see which will win,' is his motto.

Walter Bagehot, 1865, *Biographical Studies*

His fame blazed like a straw bonfire, and has left behind it scarce a shovelful of ashes. Never any public man had it in his power to do so much good for his country, nor was there ever one who accomplished so little.

J. A. Froude, *Short Studies*

Once to my sight the giant thus was given: / Walled by wide air, and roofed by boundless heaven, / Beneath his feet the human ocean lay, / And wave on wave flowed into space away. / Methought no clarion could have sent its sound / Even to the centre of the hosts around; / But, as I thought, rose the sonorous swell / As from some church tower swings the silvery bell. / Aloft and clear, from airy tide to tide / It glided, easy as a bird may glide; / To the last verge of that vast audience sent, / It played with each wild passion as it went; / Now stirred the uproar, now the murmur stilled, / With sobs or laughter answered as it willed. / Then did I know what spells of infinite choice, / To rouse or lull hath the sweet human voice; / Then did I seem to seize the sudden clue / To that grand troublous Life Antique – to view, / Under the rockstand of Demosthenes, / Mutable Athens heave her noisy seas. /

Lord Lytton, on O'Connell's oratory in the House of Commons, in G. W. E. Russell, *Collections and Recollections*

He was a lawyer; and never could come to the point of denying and defying all British law. He was a Catholic . . . and would not see that the Church had ever been the enemy of Irish Freedom. He was an aristocrat . . . and the name of a Republic was odious to him . . . his success as a Catholic Agitator ruined both him and his country . . . by eternally half-unsheathing a visionary sword, which friends and foes alike knew to be a phantom.

John Mitchel, *Jail Journal*

The only way to deal with such a man as O'Connell is to hang him up and erect a statue to him under the gallows.

Sydney Smith, *Table Talk*

*See also* George IV

## ODETS, CLIFFORD

1906–63 Playwright

If you have acquired by now the distressing sense that I am situating myself historically, correct! Talent should be respected.

On himself, Preface to *Six Plays by Clifford Odets*

I believe in the vast potentialities of mankind . . . I want to find out how mankind can be helped out of the animal kingdom into the clear sweet air.

On himself, Letter to John Mason Brown, 1935

## OGLETHORPE, JAMES EDWARD

1696–1785 Founder of Georgia

The Last Leaf on the Tree / My grandmamma has said – / Poor old lady, she is dead / Long ago – / That he had a Roman nose, / And his cheek was like a rose / In the snow. / But now his nose is thin / And it rests upon his chin / Like a staff. / And a crook is in his back / And a melancholy crack / In his laugh. / I know it is a sin / For me to sit and grin / At him here; / But the old three-cornered hat, / And the breeches, and all that / Are so queer. /

Oliver Wendell Holmes, in *The Oxford Book of American Verse*

## O'HARA, JOHN HENRY

1905–70 Author

To put the matter in the simplest possible terms, the middle brows like O'Hara because his books remind them of the life they imagine themselves to be leading.

John W. Aldridge, *Time to Murder and Create*

O'Hara's men and women dance around the Victorian traditions of class distinction and sexual restraint like savages around a cross left by murdered missionaries and now adorned with shrunken heads.

Louis Auchincloss, *Reflections of a Jacobite*

I had to admit that in his old-fashioned way O'Hara was still romantic about sex; like Scott Fitzgerald he thought of it as an upper-class prerogative.

Alfred Kazin, *Contemporaries*: 'Lady Chatterley in America'

## O. HENRY (WILLIAM SYDNEY PORTER)

1862–1910 Author

This is that dubious hero of the press / Whose slangy tongue and insolent address / Were spiced to rouse on Sunday afternoon / The man with yellow journals round him strewn. / We laughed and dozed, then roused and read again, / And vowed O. Henry funniest of men. / He always worked a triple-hinged surprise / To end the scene and make one rub his eyes. /

Vachel Lindsay, *The Knight in Disguise*

## OLDFIELD, ANNE

1683–1730 Actress

I was too young to view her first Dawn on the Stage, but yet had the infinite Satisfaction of her Meridian Lustre, a Glow of Charms not to be beheld but with a trembling Eye, which held her Influence till set in Night.

W. R. Chetwood, *A General History of the Stage*

The Part of *Sophonisba* . . . was reputed the Cause of her Death; for in her Execution she went beyond Wonder, to Astonishment! From that Time, her Decay came slowly on, and never left her till it conducted her to eternal Rest . . .

*Ibid.*

Mrs Oldfield happened to be in some danger in a Gravesend Boat, and when the rest of the passengers lamented their imagined approaching fate, she, with a conscious dignity, told them their deaths would be only a private loss; – 'But I am a public concern'.

Thomas Davies, *Dramatic Miscellanies*

Odious! in woollen! 'twould a saint provoke! – / Were the last words which poor Narcissus spoke. – / No! Let a charming chintz and brussels lace / Wrap my cold limbs and shade my lifeless face. / One would not, sure, be frightful when one's dead; / And Betty, give this cheek a little red. /

Alexander Pope, characterizing Mrs Oldfield as a coquette, in *Epistle to Richard Temple, Viscount Cobham*

## O'NEILL, EUGENE GLADSTONE

1888–1953 Playwright

Most modern plays are concerned with the relation between man and man, but that does not interest me at all. I am interested only in the relation between man and God.

On himself, in Jordan Y. Miller, *Eugene O'Neill*, in Warren G. French and Walter E. Kidd eds, *American Winners of the Nobel Literary Prize*

If one does not like O'Neill, it is not really him that one dislikes; it is our age – of which like the rest of us he is more the victim than the master.

Eric Bentley, 'Trying to Like O'Neill', in John Gassner ed., *O'Neill: A Collection of Critical Essays*

Though he possesses the tragic vision, he cannot claim the tragic tongue.

John Mason Brown, in Frederic I. Carpenter, *Eugene O'Neill*

Strindberg is in his grave, and the German expressionists are already on their way to the cemetery. O'Neill should give up buying tin wreaths and following funeral processions. His path lies in the other direction.

George Jean Nathan, 'Eugene O'Neill', in Alan S. Downer ed., *American Drama and Its Critics*

He'll probably never write a good play again.

George Bernard Shaw, upon hearing that O'Neill had sworn off drinking, in Arthur and Barbara Gelb, *O'Neill*

Life and death, good and evil, spirit and flesh, male and female, the all and the one, Anthony and Dionysius – O'Neill's is a world of these antithetical absolutes such as religion rather than philosophy conceives, a world of pluses and minuses; and his literary effort is an algebraic attempt to solve these equations.

Lionel Trilling, 'Eugene O'Neill', in Malcolm Cowley ed., *After the Genteel Tradition*

O'Neill gave birth to the American theatre and died for it.

Tennessee Williams, in Arthur and Barbara Gelb, *O'Neill*

## OPIE, JOHN

1761–1807 Painter

I mix them with my brains, sir.

On himself, being asked how he mixed his colours

## ORWELL, GEORGE (ERIC ARTHUR BLAIR)

1903–50 Author

Every line of serious work that I have written since 1936 has been written, directly or indirectly, *against* totalitarianism and *for* democratic Socialism, as I understand it. It seems to me nonsense, in a period like our own, to think that one can avoid writing of such subjects. Everyone writes of them in one guise or another. It is simply a question of which side one takes and what approach one follows.

On himself, *Why I Write*

I often feel that I will never pick up a book by Orwell again until I have read a frank discussion of the dishonesty and hysteria that mar some of his best work.

Kingsley Amis, *What Became of Jane Austen?*

Some of your American readers may not realise Mr Orwell's status in this country and take his commentary seriously. We all like him here, though the standard of his pamphleteering is going down of late, and we know him as the preacher of a doctrine of Physical Courage as an Asset to the left-wing intellectual, and so forth. I think we all agree that he is pretty thoroughly out of touch with any writing under thirty years of age.

Alex Comfort, in *Partisan Review*, 1942

He would not blow his nose without moralising on conditions in the handkerchief industry.

Cyril Connolly, *The Evening Colonnade*

Mr Orwell . . . is a silly billy. He's full of political tittletattle – but he gets it all wrong. He thinks people are always falling in love with political Stars. I am so glad that emotional public schoolboy has transferred his excitable loyalties to the Partisans.

Percy Wyndham Lewis, Letter to Dwight Macdonald, 26 January 1947

Orwell's mania to identify himself with the poor and outcast in England . . . They had been wronged by his class, and he must somehow make it up. So he stayed in workhouses, consorted with down-and-outs, and in *The Road to*

*Wigan Pier* gave what he considered to be an authentic picture of working-class life. Actually, as I occasionally ventured to remark to him, I think his data was derived much more from the *News of the World* and seaside picture postcards – two of his ruling passions – and even from Dickens, than from direct observation.

Malcolm Muggeridge, in M. Gross, *The World of George Orwell*

Orwell . . . could recognize the putrescence seeping out of the pores of the time, and was unable to lift his nostrils clear . . . Orwell's strength and significance is that . . . he never looked for the familiar deodorant of self-deception or sought out the sweetened balms of elegant literary evasion. He sniffed and wrote on the same quivering reflex.

Dennis Potter, in *The Times*, 5 October 1968

There was something about him, the proud man apart, the Don Quixote on a bicycle (and if Saint Thomas More was the first Englishman, as one historian called him, then Orwell was perhaps the last) that caught one's imagination right away. That made one think of a knight errant and of social justice as the Holy Grail. One felt safe with him; he was so intellectually honest. His mind was a court where the judge was the lawyer for the defence.

Paul Potts, in *London Magazine*, March 1957

Thoroughgoing, Orwell changed his identity with his name. Curiously though, the change is not *so* radical: he exchanged ordinarinesses. On to the terrifying *tabula rasa* that was Eric Blair he etched the familiar features – the spiv's moustache, the centre parting, the short back and sides – the persona of the ordinary bloke, someone whose name might have been George Hair-oil . . . [In] Miss Buddicom's account of their first meeting . . . Orwell was standing on his head. Asked why, he replied, 'You are noticed more if you stand on your head than if you are the right way up.' It is irresistibly symbolic. He continued to get the same effect by turning the world upside down.

Craig Raine, in *New Statesman*, 17 May 1974

## OSBORNE, THOMAS, *see under* DANBY, EARL OF

## OTIS, JAMES

1725–83 Politician, Publicist

He talks so much and takes up so much of our time, and fills it with trash, obsceneness, profaneness, nonsense and distraction, that we have no[ne] left for rational amusements or inquiries . . . I never saw such an object of admiration, reverence, contempt, and compassion, all at once . . . I fear, I tremble, I mourn for the man and for his country; many others mourn over him, with tears in their eyes.

John Adams, *Papers*, 1

## OTWAY, THOMAS

1652–85 Dramatist

But Wine does now the Poet's breast inspire, / Wine, that doth kindle all our youthful fire, / Wine that makes *Ot--y* write and fools admire; / His verse of wine stinks worse than bawdy Punk / For he never writes a verse but when he is drunk. /

Anon., *The Tory Poets*

His person was of the middle size, inclinable to fatness. He had a thoughtful, speaking eye, and that was all.

Anon., in *Gentleman's Magazine*, 1745

But everyone knows Mr Otway's good Nature, which will not permit him to shock any one of our Sex to their Faces.

Aphra Behn, *Familiar Letters of Love, Gallantry and Several Occasions*

To Thomas Otway was reserved the honour of giving tragedy its true and genuine tone of language, divested of unnatural flight and unnecessary pomp.

Thomas Davies, *Dramatic Miscellanies*

There is . . . extant a joke which Otway is said to have played off on Dryden, when their relations were strained . . . It is said that they lived in houses facing each other, and Otway wrote sarcastically on Dryden's door one night

Here Dryden lives, a poet and a wit.

to which Dryden replied the next night by writing on Otway's door:

Here Otway lives – exactly opposite.

J. C. Ghosh, *Works of Thomas Otway*

He had susceptibility of feeling, and warmth of genius; but he had not equal depth of thought or loftiness of imagination, and indulged his mere sensibility too much, yielding to the immediate impression or emotion excited in his own mind, and not placing himself enough in the minds and situations of others, or following the workings of nature sufficiently with keenness of eye and strength of will into its heights and depths, its strongholds as well as its weak sides.

William Hazlitt, *On Ancient and Modern Literature*

Otway's comedies do no sort of credit to him: on the contrary, they are as desperate as his fortunes.

William Hazlitt, *Lectures on English Comic Writers*

'Tis a talent of nature rather than an effect of judgement to write so movingly.

Alexander Pope, in Joseph Spence, *Anecdotes*

Tom O(tway) came next, Tom S(hadwell's) dear *Zany*; / And swear for *Heroicks*, he writes best of any; / *Don Carlos* his Pockets so amply had fill'd, / That his *Mange* was quite cur'd, and his *Lice*, were all kill'd. / But *Apollo*, had seen his Face on the *Stage*, / And prudently did not think fit to engage, / The scum of a *Play-house*, for the Prop of an *Age*. /

John Wilmot, Earl of Rochester, *A Session of the Poets*

## OWEN, SIR RICHARD

1804–92 Naturalist

Owen believes that no animal has sensation unless furnished with a brain, therefore the cuttlefish is the lowest creature which can effectively be treated with cruelty. Examined a long series of skulls: those of babies so much phrenologically better than grown persons – which Owen thinks quite natural, as they came uncontaminated from the Author of all Goodness, and degenerate after contact with the world.

Caroline Fox, Journals, May 1842

*See also* Augustus Granville

## OWEN, ROBERT

1771–1858 Socialist

The mission of my life appears to be, to prepare the population of the world to understand the vast importance of the second creation of Humanity, from the birth of each individual, through the agency of man, by creating entirely new surroundings in which to place all through life, and by which a new human nature would appear to arise from the new surrounding.

On himself, *The Life of Robert Owen by Himself*

This gentleman is for establishing innumerable *communities* of paupers! Each is to be resident in an *inclosure*, somewhat resembling a barrack establishment, only more extensive. I do not clearly understand whether the sisterhoods and brotherhoods are to form distinct communities, or whether they are to mix promiscuously; but I perceive they are to be under a very *regular discipline*; and that wonderful peace, happiness and national benefit are to be the result!

William Cobbett, *Political Register*, 2 August 1817

English Socialism arose with Owen, a manufacturer, and proceeds therefore with great consideration towards the bourgeoisie and great injustice toward the proletariat in its methods, although it culminates in demanding the abolition of the class antagonism between bourgeoisie and proletariat.

Friedrich Engels, *Condition of the Working Class*

The doctrine of Universal Benevolence, the belief in the Omnipotence of Truth, and in the Perfectibility of Human Nature, are not new, but 'Old, old' Master Robert Owen; – why then do you say that they are new? They are not only old, but superannuated, they are dead and buried, they are reduced to mummy, they are put in the catacombs at Paris, they are sealed up in patent coffins, they have been dug up again and anatomised, they have been drawn, quartered and gibbeted, they have become black, dry, parched in the sun, loose, and rotten, and are dispersed to all the winds of Heaven!

William Hazlitt, *Political Essays*

He was the first publicist among us who looked with royal eyes upon children. He regarded grown persons as being proprietors of the world – bound to extend the rites of hospitality to all arrivals in it.

George Holyoake, *History of Co-operation*

I must confess, also, that I was one of those who, at one time, was favourably impressed with many of Mr Owen's views, and, more especially, with those of a community of property. This notion has a peculiar attraction for the plodding, toiling, ill-remunerated sons and daughters of labour.

William Lovett, *Life and Struggles*

My father made another still greater mistake. A believer in the force of circumstances and of the instinct of self interest to reform all men, however ignorant or vicious, he admitted into his village all comers, without recommendatory introduction or any examination whatever. This error was the more fatal, because it is in the nature of any novel experiment, or any putting forth of new views which may tend to revolutionize the opinions or habits of society, to attract to itself . . . waifs and strays from the surrounding society; men and women of crude, ill-considered, extravagant notions; nay, worse, vagrants who regard the latest heresy but as a stalking horse for pecuniary gain, or a convenient cloak for immoral demeanour.

Robert Dale Owen, on the failure of New Harmony, *Threading My Way*

Mr Owen then was, and is still, persuaded that he was the first who ever observed that man was the creature of his circumstances. On this supposed discovery he founded his system. Never having read a metaphysical book, nor held a metaphysical conversation, nor having even heard of the disputes concerning free-will and necessity, he had no clear conception of his subject, and his views were obscure. Yet he had all along been preaching and publishing and projecting and predicting in the fullest conviction that he could command circumstances or create them, and place men above their control when necessary.

Francis Place, in Graham Wallace, *Life of Francis Place*

## OWEN, WILFRED

1893–1918 Poet

My subject is War, and the pity of War. The poetry is in the pity.

On himself, Preface to *Poems*

I am held peer by the Georgians; I am a poet's poet.

On himself, Letter to his Mother, January 1918

It is now quite clear that the fundamental biographic fact about Owen is that he was his mother's boy: his family situation was sufficiently like that of D. H. Lawrence for the comparison to be made . . . What the *Letters* cry out on nearly every page is that it was she, Owen's mother, who magnetised his love, his intimacy, his tenderness . . . Of the 673 Owen letters that survive, 631 are to her . . . It is their frequency, their atmosphere of being written to someone who understands and appreciates everything, and above all their explicit declarations that drive the point home.

Philip Larkin, in *Encounter*, March 1975

When I excluded Wilfred Owen [from *The Oxford Book of Modern Verse*], whom I consider unworthy of the poets' corner of a country newspaper, I did not know I was excluding a revered sandwich-board Man of the revolution & that some body has put his worst & most famous poem in a glass-case in the British Museum – however if I had known it I would have excluded him just the same. He is all blood, dirt & sucked sugar stick.

William Butler Yeats, Letter to Dorothy Wellesley, 21 December 1936

# 'P'

## PAGE, WALTER HINES

1855–1918 Journalist, Diplomat

Page could reject a story with a letter that was so complimentary and made everybody feel so happy that you could take it to a bank and borrow money on it.

O. Henry, in Burton J. Hendrick, *The Life and Letters of Walter H. Page*

## PAINE, THOMAS

1737–1809 Revolutionary, Author

My country is the world, and my religion is to do good.

On himself, *The Rights of Man*

I know not whether any man in the world has had more influence on its inhabitants or affairs for the last thirty years than Tom Paine. There can be no severer satyr on the age. For such a mongrel between pig and puppy, begotten by a wild boar on a bitch wolf, never before in any age of the world was suffered by the poltroonery of mankind, to run through such a career of mischief. Call it then the Age of Paine.

John Adams, Letter to Benjamin Waterhouse, 29 October 1805

What a poor ignorant, malicious, short-sighted, crapulous mass, is Tom Paine's *Common Sense.*

John Adams, Letter to Thomas Jefferson, 22 June 1819

. . . has no country, no affections that constitute the pillars of patriotism.

John Quincy Adams, Letter to John Adams, 3 April 1797

There never was a man less beloved in a place than Paine in this, having at different times disputed with everybody. The most rational thing he could have done would have been to have died the instant he had finished his *Common Sense,* for he never again will have it in his power to leave the world with so much credit.

Sarah Franklin Bache, Letter to Benjamin Franklin, 14 January 1781

In digging up your bones, Tom Paine, / Will. Cobbett has done well: / You visit him on earth again, / He'll visit you in hell. /

Lord Byron, *Epigram*

Nor is our England without her missionaries . . . Her Paine: rebellious Staymaker; unkempt; who feels that he, a single Needleman, did, by his *Common Sense* Pamphlet, free America; – that he can will free all this World, perhaps even the other.

Thomas Carlyle, *The French Revolution*

Thomas Paine invented the name of the Age of Reason; and he was one of those sincere but curiously simple men who really did think that the age of reason was beginning, at about the time when it was really ending.

G. K. Chesterton, *William Cobbett*

At his expiring flambeau I lighted my taper.

William Cobbett, in Audrey Williamson, *Thomas Paine: His Life, Work and Times*

Sturdy Tom Paine, biographers relate, / Once with his friends engaged in warm debate. / Said they, 'Minorities are always right'; / Said he, 'The truth is just the opposite'. / Finding them stubborn, 'Frankly now,' asked he, / 'In this opinion do ye all agree; / All, every one, without exception?' When / They thus affirmed unanimously, – 'Then / Correct,' said he, 'My sentiment must be, / For I myself am the minority.' /

Richard Garnett, *Tom Paine*

A mouse nibbling at the wing of an archangel.

Robert Hall, in Gregory's *Life of Paine*

Paine thought more than he read.

Thomas Jefferson, Letter to J. Cartwright, 1824

*Janius* is our own, / Who props a bank, altho' he scorn'd a throne; / And, should his heart with just resentments burn, / Would scorn a bank and prop a throne in turn; / But should both bank and throne reject the job, / Would damn them both and idolize the mob; / And if all three should scorn the honest fellow, / For *Daniel Shays* and *Liberty* would bellow. /

Peter Markoe, in David Freeman Hawke, *Paine*

What he gave to English people was a new rhetoric of radical egalitarianism, which touched the deepest responses of the 'free-born Englishman' and then penetrated the sub-political attitudes of the urban working people.

E. P. Thompson, *The Making of the English Working Class*

Can nothing be done in our Assembly for poor Paine? Must the merits of *Common Sense* continue to glide down the stream of time unrewarded by this country? His writings certainly have had a powerful effect upon the public mind. Ought they not, then, to meet an adequate reward?

George Washington, Letter to James Madison, 12 June 1784

It was pre-eminently from him that the working classes and working class movements of the nineteenth century first learnt to think, and what they learnt was common sense, toleration, reason, humanity, a hatred of privilege and the abuse of power, a love of liberty in life, speech, and thought. It was in fact from Tom Paine that they learnt to lisp the language of democracy.

Leonard Woolf, *Tom Paine*

## PALMER, SAMUEL

1805–81 Painter

I have beheld as in the spirit, such nooks, caught such glimpses of the perfumed and enchanted twilight – of natural midsummer, as well as, at other times of day, other scenes, as passed thro' the intense purifying separating transmuting heat of the soul's infabulous alchymy, would divinely consist with the severe and stately port of the human, as with the moon thron'd among constellations, and varieties of lesser glories, the regal pomp and glistening brilliance and solemn attendance of her starry train.

On himself, Letter to George Richmond, November 1827

If you've a mangy cat to draw, christen it Palmer.

On himself, Letter to George Richmond, 19 August 1836

There are two pictures by a Mr Palmer so amazing that we felt the most intense curiosity to see what manner of man it was who produced such performances. We think if he would show himself with a label round his neck, *The Painter of A View in Kent*, he would make something of it at a shilling a head. What a Hanging Committee means by hanging these pictures without the painter to explain them is past conjecture.

Anon., in *European Magazine*, 1825

You feel . . . that Palmer is telling you not what he has seen but of his thoughts

– his thoughts of the glory of the sun, the magic of moonlight, the mystery of the stars, thatched cottages couched under immemorial trees; the enigmatic beauty of lanterns swinging in the night; lamp-light giving gold to a window-blind; the goodness of harvest and ripe fruitage; men that drive the plough and scatter the grain; all the bounty and beauty that make the history and happiness of rural England.

M. Hardie, *Water-Colour Painting in Britain*

## PALMERSTON, VISCOUNT (HENRY JOHN TEMPLE)

1784–1865 Prime Minister

I have . . . been acting the part of a very distinguished tightrope dancer and much astonishing the public by my individual performances and feats . . . So far, so well; but even Madame Sacqui, when she had mounted her rope and flourished among her rockets, never thought of making the rope her perch, but providently came down to avoid a dangerous fall.

On himself, Letter to Stephen Sulivan, December 1852

Die, my dear doctor! That's the *last* thing I shall do.

On himself, attributed last words

If the Devil has a son / It is surely Palmerston. /

Anon., popular catch

[He] is tolerated because he is cheerful and wounds no pride, and because he is old and excites no envy.

Lord Acton, Letter to Richard Simpson, 1862

Do the exact opposite of what [Palmerston] did. His administration at the Foreign Office was one long crime.

John Bright, Advice to Lord Rosebery, in latter's Diary, 17 March 1886

. . . a Conservative Minister working with Radical tools and keeping up a show of Liberalism in his foreign policy.

Lord Derby, 1856, in Robert Blake, *Disraeli*

Lytton who was always mourning over his lost youth, & was ridiculously made up, delighted in Palmerston, leading the House of Commons at 76! He sat opposite him with an expression of contemplative admiration. It was not however his wit, or his eloquence, or his dexterity that excited this sentiment. It was his age. 'That man,' he said to me one day 'is a future.'

Benjamin Disraeli, *Reminiscences*

'The Prime Minister . . . was upwards of 80 years of age. He ate for dinner two plates of turtle-soup; he was then served very amply to a plate of cod and oyster sauce, he then took a paté, afterwards he was helped to two very greasy-looking entrees; he then despatched a plate of roast mutton; there then appeared before him the largest, & to my mind the hardest, slice of ham that ever figured on the table of a nobleman, yet it disappeared, just in time for him to answer the enquiry of his butler "Snipe, my lord, or pheasant?" He instantly replied pheasant: thus completing the ninth dish of meat at that meal. I need not now tell you what is the state of his health.' This is a literal report of an anecdote told by the Speaker with much grave humor.

*Ibid.*

Your dexterity seems a happy compound of the smartness of an attorney's clerk and the intrigue of a Greek of the lower empire.

Benjamin Disraeli, attributed

It was easy to settle affairs with Palmerston because he was a man of the world, and was therefore governed by the principle of honor.

Benjamin Disraeli, Letter to Montague Corry, 29 January 1881

In the march of his epoch he was behind the eager but before the slow.
Sir Henry Bulwer Lytton, *The Life of Henry John Temple, Viscount Palmerston*

Of all kinds of ability, ingenuity is perhaps the least likely to expand into genius, or to exhaust itself with years.
Harriet Martineau, *History of England 1800–1815*

His style was not only devoid of ornament and rhetorical device, but it was slipshod and untidy . . . He eked out his sentences with 'hum' and 'hah'; cleared his throat, and flourished his pocket-handkerchief, and sucked his orange; he rounded his periods with 'You know what I mean,' and 'all that sort of thing'; and seemed actually to revel in an anticlimax. It taxed the skill of the reporters' gallery to trim his speeches into decent form; and yet no one was listened to with keener interest, no one was so much dreaded as an opponent, and no one ever approached him in the art of putting a plausible face upon a doubtful policy, and making the worse appear the better cause. Palmerston's Parliamentary success is a perfect illustration of the doctrine laid down by Demosthenes. If what really matters is that the speaker should have the same predilections as the majority, and should entertain the same likes and dislikes as his country, Palmerston was unsurpassed.
G. W. E. Russell, *Sixty Years of Empire*

*See also* W. E. Gladstone, Ramsay MacDonald, Theodore Roosevelt

## PANKHURST, DAME CHRISTABEL HENRIETTE

1880–1958 Suffragette

She knows everything and can see through everything.
Mrs Drummond, Speech, as reported in *Suffragette*, 12 December 1913

Christabel cared less for the political vote itself than for the dignity of her sex, and she denounced the false dignity earned by submission and extolled the true dignity accorded by revolt. She never made any secret of the fact that to her the means were even more important than the end. Militancy to her meant the putting off of the slave *spirit*.
Emmeline Pethwick-Lawrence, *My Part in a Changing World*

Christabel may well have been a lesbian, but the evidence is circumstantial rather than explicit; she never married and the copious documents relating to her life do not allude to any heterosexual involvements. All the available evidence indicates that she had stronger emotional attachments to women than to men. As far as the history of the WSPU is concerned the exact nature of Christabel's sex-life is less significant than the fact that by 1913 she had grown into a state of mind in which she was completely adverse to any form of co-operation with men.
Andrew Rosen, *Rise up Women*

## PANKHURST, EMMELINE

1858–1928 Suffragette

When I began this Militant Campaign I was a Poor Law Guardian, and it was my duty to go through a workhouse infirmary, and I shall never forget seeing a little girl of thirteen lying on a bed playing with a doll. I was told she was on the eve of becoming a mother, and she was infected with a loathsome disease, and on the point of bringing, no doubt, a diseased child into the world. Was that not enough to make me a militant Suffragette? We women suffragists have a great mission – the greatest mission the world has ever known. It is to free half the human race, and through that freedom to save the rest.

On herself, Speech, in *Votes for Women*, 25 October 1912

What an extraordinary mixture of idealism and lunacy! Hasn't she the sense to see that the very worst method of campaigning for the franchise is to try and intimidate or blackmail a man into giving her what he would gladly give her otherwise.

David Lloyd George, in Richard Lloyd George, *Lloyd George*

She was as she instinctively knew, cast for a great role. She had a temperament akin to genius. She could have been a queen on the Stage or in the Salon. Circumstances had baulked her in the fulfilment of her destiny. But the smouldering spark leapt into flame when her daughter Christabel initiated militancy. It was fed by a passion for her first born. She dwelt on the name of her daughter 'Christabel the Anointed One', the young deliverer who was to emancipate the new generation of women. Mrs Pankhurst was driven on by her 'daemon' to fulfil her destiny and to provide herself, as she said, with a 'niche in history'.

Emmeline Pethwick-Lawrence, *My Part in a Changing World*

## PARKER, DOROTHY ROTHSCHILD

1893–1967 Writer, Essayist

Four be the things I'd been better without: / Love, curiosity, freckles and doubt. /

On herself, *Inventory*

I require only three things of a man. He must be handsome, ruthless, and stupid.

On herself, in John Keats, *You Might As Well Live*

But I, despite expert advice / Keep doing things I think are nice, / And though to good I never come – / Inseparable my nose and thumb. /

On herself, in Robert E. Drennan ed., *Wit's End*

Mrs Parker remarked, at the reception following her remarriage to Alan Campbell: 'People who haven't talked to each other in years are on speaking terms again today – including the bride and groom.'

*Ibid.*

Discussing a job with a prospective employer, Mrs Parker explained, 'Salary is no object; I want only enough to keep body and soul apart.'

*Ibid.*

If I had any decency, I'd be dead. Most of my friends are.

*Ibid.* (on her seventieth birthday)

This is on me.

*Ibid.* (proposed epitaph)

Excuse my dust.

On herself, *Her Own Epitaph*

Mrs Parker once collided with Clare Boothe Luce in a doorway. 'Age before beauty,' cracked Mrs Luce. 'Pearls before swine,' said Mrs Parker, gliding through the door.

Robert E. Drennan ed., *Wit's End*

. . . a combination of Little Nell and Lady Macbeth.

Alexander Woollcott, in *ibid.*

I found her in hospital typing away lugubriously. She had given her address as Bedpan Alley and represented herself as writing her way out. There was a hospital bill to pay before she dared to get well . . .

Alexander Woollcott, *While Rome Burns*

*See also* Calvin Coolidge, George S. Kaufman

## PARNELL, CHARLES STEWART

1846–91 Irish Leader

The impression made by one of his more elaborate speeches might be compared to that which one receives from a grey sunless day with an east wind, a day in which everything shows clear, but also hard and cold.

James Bryce, *Studies in Contemporary Biography*

It is a very dangerous thing to approach an expiring cat.

Sir William Harcourt, Letter to William Ewart Gladstone, 22 November 1890

That man suspected his own shadow. He was unhappy and saw little good in the world, but I do think he meant well by Ireland.

Cecil J. Rhodes, in J. G. McDonald, *Rhodes: A Life*

The Bishops and the Party / That tragic story made, / A husband that had sold his wife / And after that betrayed; / But stories that live longest / Are sung above the glass, / And Parnell loved his country, / And Parnell loved his lass. /

William Butler Yeats, *Come Gather Round Me, Parnellites*

The fall of Parnell left Ireland with a dead god instead of a leader.

G. M. Young, *Victorian England: Portrait of an Age*

## PARRY, SIR CHARLES HUBERT HASTINGS

1848–1918 Composer

It is a good thing Parry died when he did; otherwise he might have set the whole Bible to music.

Frederick Delius, in Philip Heseltine, *Delius*

I cannot stand Parry's orchestra: it's dead and never more than an *organ part arranged.*

Edward Elgar, Letter to A. J. Jaeger, March 1898

That healthy vigorous beefsteak optimism of Parry.

Gustav Holst, Letter to Ralph Vaughan Williams, 1903

With many composers you gradually become aware that they have the defects of their qualities. With Parry the process is reversed; it is only by degrees that you discover him to possess the qualities of his defects.

R. O. Morris, *Music and Letters,* March 1920

As a composer he has ceased to be for the simple reason that as a composer he never was.

Parry's music is not an artist's picture of the emotions with which it deals; it is only a guide book to the emotions, a conscientiously constructed chart of them, done by a plodding cartographer without the visionary inner eye.

Ernest Newman, in *Musical Courier,* 1919

Parry never tried to divorce art from life: he once said to me 'Write choral music, as befits an Englishman and a democrat.'

Ralph Vaughan Williams, talking at the Composers' Concourse, 1957

## PASSFIELD, LORD, *see under* WEBB, SIDNEY

## PATER, WALTER HORATIO

1839–94 Critic, Essayist

Mr Walter Pater's style is, to me, like the face of some old woman who has been to Madame Rachel and had herself enamelled. The bloom is nothing but powder and paint and the odour is cherry-blossom.

Samuel Butler, *Notebooks*

Faint, pale, embarrassed, exquisite Pater! He reminds me, in the disturbed midnight of our actual literature, of one of those lucent match boxes which you place, on going to bed, near the candle, to show you, in the darkness, where you can strike a light: he shines in the uneasy gloom – vaguely, and has a phosphorescence, not a flame.

Henry James, Letter to Edmund Gosse, 13 December 1894

Alma Pater.

Osbert Lancaster, written on a photograph of Pater when Lancaster was at Oxford, in John Betjeman, *Summoned by Bells*

So you are going to see Pater! That will be delightful. But I must tell you one thing about him, to save you from disappointment. You must not expect him to talk like his prose. Of course, no true artist ever does that. But, besides that, he never talks about anything that interests him. He will not breathe one golden word about the Renaissance. No! he will probably say something like this: 'So you wear cork soles in your shoes? Is that really true? And do you find them comfortable? . . . How extremely interesting!'

Oscar Wilde, in Richard Le Gallienne, *The Romantic '90s*

*See also* Rudyard Kipling, William Wordsworth

## PATTON, GEORGE SMITH

1885–1945 Soldier

I know that my ambition is selfish and cold yet it is not a selfish selfishness for instead of sparing me, it makes me exert myself to the uttermost to attain an end which will do neither me nor anyone else any good . . . I will do my best to attain what I consider – wrongly perhaps – my destiny.

On himself, in Martin Blumenson, *The Patton Papers*

Old Blood and Guts.

Anon., in *ibid.*

Patton was an acolyte to Mars.

Colonel J. J. Farley, 17 November 1964, in Robert Hebs Heinl Jr, *The Dictionary of Military and Naval Quotations*

## PAXTON, SIR JOSEPH

1801–65 Architect, Landscape Designer

His life was simple, his ingenuity unfailing, his energy unbounded, his health robust, his taste dubious.

R. Furneaux-Jordan, *Sir Joseph Paxton*

From his earliest days at Chatsworth, Paxton displayed, as fully as any man of his time, that thoroughly Victorian blend of romanticism and realism. If the Chatsworth cascades and fountains were conceived as a faerie fantasy, the pumps and pipes and jets, designed in the Estate Office, were efficient and durable. It was the marriage of these two opposed ways of thought which lifted Paxton's talents to the level of genius.

*Ibid.*

The quantity of bodily industry which that Crystal Palace expresses is very great. So far it is good.

The quantity of thought it expresses is, I suppose, a single and very admirable thought of Sir Joseph Paxton's, probably not a bit brighter than thousands of thoughts which pass through his active and intelligent brain every hour – that it might be possible to build a greenhouse larger than ever greenhouse was built before. This thought, and some very ordinary algebra, are as much as all that glass can represent of human intellect.

John Ruskin, *The Stones of Venice*, Appendix 7

## PEABODY, GEORGE

1795–1869 Financier, Philanthropist

Let all the rich, who mean, when they shall die / To do great things by legacy, / How to make sure a worthy end, and see / And taste the pleasure, learn of Peabody. /

George T. Dole, Poem delivered before the Phi Beta Kappa Society of Yale University, 1868

## PEACOCK, THOMAS LOVE

1785–1866 Novelist

A minor master . . . far more energetically original than the chorus of drowsy Victorian and Edwardian eulogy would imply. That enchanting urbanity, which gave him command of a whole range between witty seriousness and demented knockabout, was something which disappeared from the English novel almost before it had properly arrived.

Kingsley Amis, *What Became of Jane Austen?*

The art of satire, in his hands, resolved itself into a kind of cookery; almost, indeed, into the concoction of a simple dish, with much the same ingredients, which the *chef* spends fifteen years in garnishing and making perfect; which is named after him, and copied by others, but of which the open secret dies with him.

Oliver Elton, *A Survey of English Literature*

When one reads Peacock aloud one soon notices that the style is tuned to the cadence of the human voice rather than to the sweep of the eye, which accounts for so much of its balance and variations of rhythm and tone. Wilson thought of flute music in connection with the qualities of clarity and purity of tone in Peacock's style, but the roundness and fullness of the style evoke the sound of the French horn as well.

George Bernard Shaw, Preface to *Man and Superman*

His fine wit / Makes such a wound, the knife is lost in it; / A strain too learned for a shallow age, / Too wise for selfish bigots; let his page / Which charms the chosen spirits of the time, / Fold itself up for the serener clime / Of years to come, and find its recompense / In that just expectation. /

Percy Bysshe Shelley, *Letter to Maria Gisborne*

## PEAKE, MERVYN LAURENCE

1911–68 Novelist

To canalize my chaos. To pour it out through the gutters of Gormenghast. To make not only tremendous stories in paint that approximate to the visual images in Gormenghast, but to create arabesques, abstracts, of thrilling colour, worlds on their own, landscapes and roofscapes and skyscapes peopled with hierophants and lords – the fantastic and the grotesque, and to use paint as though it were meat and drink.

On himself, Letter to Maeve Gilmore

His inglorious war was spent first as a gunner on the Isle of Sheppey, then as a sapper in Blackpool, where – his mechanical incompetence being exposed – he employed his artistic gifts printing beautiful cards saying 'Only officers may use this lavatory.'

Anon., in *Times Literary Supplement*, 25 June 1970

Peake has been praised, but he has also been mistrusted. His prose works are not easily classifiable: they are unique as, say, the books of Peacock or Lovecraft are unique . . . It is difficult, in post-war English writing, to get away with big rhetorical gestures. Peake manages it because, with him, grandiloquence never means diffuseness; there is no musical emptiness in the most romantic of his descriptions; he is always exact.

Anthony Burgess, Introduction to *Titus Groan*

For Mervyn, going down into the underground was not a straightforward, upright, and still journey down an escalator, but a sliding descent down the rail. I could never summon up courage to follow, so that sometimes he would reach the bottom, go up the other escalator, and pass me by once more at, it seemed, even greater speed, in time to take my hand as I staidly tripped off the bottom step. We often went to Lyons for meals, and I suppose we were neither of us the most regular looking customers . . . Mervyn sometimes ordered stewed camel. It probably wasn't very funny, and the waitresses obviously thought not.

Maeve Gilmore, *A World Away*

## PEARSON, DREW (ANDREW RUSSELL)

1897–1969 Journalist

I operate by sense of smell. If something smells wrong, I go to work.

On himself, in Oliver Pilat, *Drew Pearson*

He is not a sunnavabitch. He is only a filthy brain child, conceived in ruthlessness and dedicated to the proposition that Judas Iscariot was a piker.

Senator William Jenner of Indiana, in Morris A. Bealle, *All American Louse*

## PEEL, JOHN

1776–1857 Huntsman

D'ye ken John Peel with his coat so gay? / D'ye ken John Peel at the break of the day? / D'ye ken John Peel when he's far far away / With his hounds and his horn in the morning? /

'Twas the sound of his horn called me from my bed, / And the cry of his hounds has me oft-times led; / For Peel's view halloo would waken the dead, / Or a fox from his lair in the morning.

John Woodcock Graves, *John Peel*

## PEEL, SIR ROBERT

1788–1850 Prime Minister

I shall leave a name execrated by every monopolist, but it may be . . . sometimes remembered with expressions of goodwill in the abodes of those whose lot it is to labour and to earn their daily bread in the sweat of their brow, when they shall recruit their exhausted strength with abundant and untaxed food, the sweeter because it is no longer unleavened with a sense of injustice.

On himself, repealing the Corn Laws in the Commons

His offence is not merely an offence against party, but against morals.

Anon., in *Morning Herald*, 30 June 1846, after the fall of the Tory government

[Disraeli] attributed Peel's great power and effect in the House to having always had Blue Books by heart, and having thereby the appearance of a fund of greater knowledge than he really possessed.

William Beresford, Letter to Lord Stanley, September 1849

Sir Robert Peel was a man who had stupidity in the soul. It went, as it often does, along with all the talents of a man of business and a man of the world. He was the kind of man who only knows things by their labels, and has not only no comprehension but no curiosity touching their substance or what they are made of.

G. K. Chesterton, *William Cobbett*

If there is a word between persuasive and coaxing, I should select it as the one that best describes the manner of Mr Peel. The latter would do him great injustice, as it wants his dignity, and argument, and force; and the former would . . . do injustice to the truth.

James Fenimore Cooper, *Gleanings in Europe: England*

The right honourable gentleman caught the Whigs bathing, and walked away with their clothes.

Benjamin Disraeli, Speech, February 1845, referring to the opening of letters by governments

His life has been a great appropriation clause. He is a burglar of other's intellect . . . there is no statesman who has committed political petty larceny on so great a scale.

Benjamin Disraeli, to the House of Commons, 15 May 1847

Peel died at peace with all mankind; even with Disraeli. The last thing he did was to cheer Disraeli. It was not a very loud cheer, but it *was* a cheer; it was distinct. I sat next to him.

William Ewart Gladstone, in Benjamin Disraeli, *Reminiscences*

Peel! what is Peel to me? Damn Peel!

Lord Lyndhurst, speaking to his fellow peers about amending the Municipal Reform Bill, 1835

In the administration of public affairs, as surely as a great act or measure is impracticable, you forthwith achieve it.

Harriet Martineau, Letter to Peel, 22 February 1846

His smile was like the silver plate on a coffin.

Daniel O'Connell, in G. M. Trevelyan, *British History in the Nineteenth Century*

He has abundance of human honesty and not much of Divine faith; he will never do a dishonourable thing, he will be ashamed of doing a religious one.

Lord Shaftesbury, Diary, 24 July 1841

The truth is that Peel is afraid of the Opposition, his colleagues and his supporters. He is afraid to place himself on high ground. He never fixes his mind on any good principle to be held in discussion; nor on any principle at all till he gets into the House of Commons; and then he seeks for one which he thinks will be safe.

Duke of Wellington, Letter to Mrs Arbuthnot, April 1828

I have no small talk and Peel has no manners.

Duke of Wellington, in G. W. E. Russell, *Collections and Recollections*

That is a gentleman, who never sees the end of a campaign.

Duke of Wellington, in Benjamin Disraeli, *Reminiscences*

*See also* Charles Dickens

## PEELE, GEORGE

1556–96 Poet

This person was living, in his middle age, in the latter end of Q. *Elizabeth*, but when, or where he dyed, I cannot tell; for so it is, and always hath been, that most Poets dye poor, and consequently obscurely, and a hard matter it is to trace them to their graves.

Anthony à Wood, *Athenae Oxonienses*

## PELHAM-HOLLES, THOMAS, *see under* NEWCASTLE, DUKE OF

## PENN, WILLIAM

1644–1718 Founder of Pennsylvania

Quoth Martyr Charles to William Penn, / 'Tis best to let things be: / They're used to looking up at you, / And they can see through me. /

Anon., *Notes and Queries*, tenth series, vol. 10: 227

The first Sense he had of God was when he was 11 years old at Chigwell, being retired into a chamber alone; he was so suddenly surprized with an inward comfort and (as he thought) an externall glory in the roome that he has many times sayd that from thence he had the Seale of Divinity, and Immortality, that there was a God and that the Soule of man was capable of enjoying his divine communications. His schoolmaster was not of his Perswasion.

John Aubrey, *Brief Lives*

. . . in a century when theological argument was regarded as the chief end of man, Penn yielded to the prevalent fashion of striving to unscrew the inscrutable and indulged in the futile custom of dogmatizing about the unknowable.

William Bull, *William Penn: A Topical Biography*

He had such an opinion of his own faculty of persuading, that he thought none could stand before it: 'Tho he was singular in that opinion: For he had a tedious luscious way, that was not apt to overcome a man's reason, tho' it might tire his patience.

Gilbert Burnet, *History of His Own Time*

He will always be mentioned with honour as a founder of a colony, who did not in his dealings with a savage people, abuse the strength derived from civilization, and as a lawgiver who, in the age of persecution, made religious liberty the corner stone of a polity. But his writings and his life furnish abundant proofs that he was not a man of strong sense. He had no skill in reading the characters of others. His confidence in persons less virtuous than himself led him into great errors and misfortunes. His enthusiasm for one great principle sometimes impelled him to violate other great principles which he ought to have held sacred.

T. B. Macaulay, *History of England*

Mrs Turner tells me that Mr Will Pen, who is lately come over from Ireland, is a Quaker again, or some very melancholy thing; that he cares for no company, nor comes into any – which is a pleasant thing, after his being abroad so long – and his father such a hypocritical rogue, and at this time an atheist.

Samuel Pepys, Diary, 29 December 1667

He was learned without vanity, apt without forwardness, facetious in conversation yet weighty and serious, of an extraordinary greatness of mind, yet void of the strain of ambition, as free from rigid gravity as he was clear of unseemly levity. A man, a scholar, a Friend, a minister surpassing in superlative endowments whose memorial will be valued by the wise and blessed with the just.

Testimony of Reading Quarterly Meeting, in C. O. Peare, *William Penn, A Biography*

## PEPYS, SAMUEL

1633–1703 Diarist, Naval Administrator

. . . among the rest Mr Christmas my old schoolfellow, with whom I had much talk. He did remember that I was a great roundhead when I was a boy, and I was much afeard that he would have remembered the words that I said the day that the King was beheaded (that were I to preach upon him my text should be: 'The memory of the wicked shall rot'); but that I found afterward that he did go away from schoole before that time.

On himself, Diary, 1 November 1660

. . . So by coach with my wife and Mercer to the park; but the King being there, and I nowadays being doubtful of being seen in any pleasure, did part from the Tour, and away out of the Park to Knightsbridge and there eat and drank in the coach, and so home, and I, after a while at my office, home to supper and to bed – having got a great Cold, I think by pulling off my periwigg so often.

*Ibid.*, 24 April 1665

Music and women I cannot but give way to, whatever my business is.

*Ibid.*, 9 March 1666

And so to Mrs Martin and there did what je voudrais avec her, both devante and backward, which is also muy bon plazer.

*Ibid.*, 3 June 1666

The truth is, I do indulge myself a little more the pleasure, knowing that this is the proper age of my life to do it, and out of my observation that most men do thrive in the world do forget to take pleasure during the time that they are getting their estate but reserve that till they have got one, and then it is too late for them to enjoy it with any pleasure.

*Ibid.*, 10 March 1666

To church; and with my mourning, very handsome, and new periweg, make a great show.

*Ibid.*, 31 March 1667

And so I betake myself to that course, which is almost as much as to see myself go into the grave; for which, and all the discomforts that will accompany me being blind, the good God prepare me!

*Ibid.*, last entry, 31 May 1669

In S. Pepys, the *Understanding* is *hypertrophied* to the necrosis or marasmus of the Reason and Imagination, while far-sighted (yet Oh! how short-sighted) Self-interest fills the place of Conscience.

Samuel Taylor Coleridge, Annotation to copy of Pepys's Diary, ed. Lord Braybrooke, 1825

The Paul Pry of his day.

David Masson, in *Quarterly Review*, July and October 1856

Matter-of-factly, like the screech of a sash-window being thrown open, begins one of the greatest texts in our history and in our literature. The subject of this biography turns his head to us across the centuries and addresses us as though we were across the room. Not to be moved is to be deficient in humanity.

Richard Ollard, *Pepys*

Conviviality . . . was not second but first nature to Pepys.

*Ibid.*

Pepys's animating principle bureaucratised his surroundings just as culture put into a glass of milk transforms it into yoghurt.

*Ibid.*

Among the famous characters of the period were Samuel Pepys, who is memorable for keeping a Diary and going to bed a great deal, and his wife Evelyn, who kept another memorable Diary, but did not go to bed in it.

W. C. Sellar and R. J. Yeatman, *1066 and All That*

Here we have a mouth pouting, moist with desires; eyes greedy, protuberant, and yet apt for weeping too, a nose great alike in character and dimensions; and altogether a most fleshly, melting countenance. The face is attractive by its promise of reciprocity. I have used the word *greedy*, but the reader must not suppose that he can change it for that closely kindred one of *hungry*, for there is here no aspiration, no waiting for better things, but an animal joy in all that comes. It could never be the face of an artist; it is the face of a *viveur* – kindly, pleased and pleasing, protected from excess and upheld in contentment by the shifting versatility of his desires.

Robert Louis Stevenson, *Samuel Pepys*, on Pepys's portrait

He had a kind of idealism in pleasure; like the princess in the fairy story, he was conscious of a rose-leaf out of place.

*Ibid.*

'Tis never any drudgery to wait on Mr Pepys, whose conversation, I think, is more nearly akin to what we are taught to hope for in Heaven, than that of anybody else I know.

Humphrey Wanley, in Richard Ollard, *Pepys*

*See also* Rudyard Kipling

## PERCEVAL, SPENCER

1762–1812 Prime Minister

It is a great misfortune to Mr Perceval to write in a style that would disgrace a washerwoman.

George IV, *Letters*, 1812

## PERRY, OLIVER HAZARD

1785–1819 Sailor

We have met the enemy and they are ours.

On himself, in announcing American victory over the British at the naval battle of Lake Erie, 10 September 1813

## PERSHING, JOHN JOSEPH

1860–1948 Soldier

Oh to be in Paris now that Pershing's there! / To hear the waves of welcome that greet him everywhere; / To see the children and the girls a-pelting him with flowers, / And feel that every petal is meant for us and ours. /

Anon., on Pershing's arrival in France as the head of the United States Expeditionary Force in World War I

He was no tin soldier and certainly no figurine saint.

Donald Smythe, *Guerrilla Warrior: The Early Life of John J. Pershing*

## PETERBOROUGH, EARL OF (CHARLES MORDAUNT)

1658–1735 Soldier, Admiral, Diplomat

A bitter woman summed him up as a man who to vileness of soul had joined a sort of knight errantry. An enthusiastic admirer fondly pictured him as a hangdog he dearly loved, and the ramblingest lying rogue on earth.

William Stebbing, *Peterborough*

Everybody has read how a London mob, mistaking, which must have been difficult for the blindest mob, the restless wiry earl for the stately and serene Duke of Marlborough, was threatening violence, when Peterborough disabused it . . . 'In the first place, I have only five guineas in my pocket, and secondly, here they are entirely at your service.'

*Ibid.*

. . . a player at the game of life, for whom thrones, armies, senates, hearts, honour, were pawns to be moved hither and thither for sport; a streak of phosphoric light, trailing, full of illusions and full of charm, across fifty years of English annals; one of the most fantastically bright spirits that ever gaily dug holes for history to fill up.

*Ibid.*

His career was a series of unconnected actions. His motives were mere impulses. He sailed with all canvas spread, but without a rudder; he admitted of no rule of duty, and his sole, but unacknowledged end, was the gratification of his inordinate self-esteem.

E. B. G. Warburton, *Life of Peterborough*

*See also* Alexander Pope

## PETTY, SIR WILLIAM

1623–87 Political Economist

I remember about 1660 there was a great difference between him and Sir Hierome Sanchy, one of Oliver's knights. They printed one against the other: This knight was wont to preach at Dublin. The Knight had been a soldier, and challenged Sir William to fight with him. Sir William is extremely short-sighted, and being the challengee it belonged to him to nominate place and weapon. He nominated for the place, a darke Cellar, and the weapon to be a great Carpenter's Axe. This turned the Knight's challenge into ridicule, and so it came to nought.

John Aubrey, *Brief Lives*

Thence to White-hall, where in the Duke's chamber the King came and stayed an hour or two, laughing at Sir W Petty, who was there about his boat, and at Gresham College in general. At which poor Petty was I perceive at some loss, but did argue discreetly and bear the unreasonable follies of the King's objections and other bystanders with great discretion – and offered to take odds against the King's best boats; but the King would not lay, but cried him down with words only. Gresham College he mightily laughed at for spending time only in weighing of ayre, and doing nothing else since they sat.

Samuel Pepys, Diary, 1 February 1664

In *Dec.* 1650 his name was wonderfully cried up for being the chief person in the recovery to life of one *Ann Green*, who was hang'd in *Oxford Castle* on the 14 of the same month, for making away her bastard child; at which time, instead of recovering her, he intended to have her made an anatomy.

Anthony à Wood, *Athenae Oxonienses*

## PETTY, WILLIAM, MARQUIS OF LANSDOWNE, *see under* SHELBURNE, LORD

## PHILIPS, AMBROSE

1674–1749 Poet

Namby Pamby.

Henry Carey, *Namby Pamby: or a Panegyric on the New Versification*

Men sometimes suffer by injudicious kindness; Philips became ridiculous, without his own fault, by the absurd admiration of his friends, who decorated him with honorary garlands which the first breath of contradiction blasted.

Samuel Johnson, *Lives of the Poets*

. . . a good Whig and a middling poet.

T. B. Macaulay, *Essays*: 'Addison'

If Justice Philips' costive head / Some frigid rhymes disburses; / They shall like Persian tales be read / And glad both babes and nurses. /

Jonathan Swift, *Sandys's Ghost*

## PHILLIPS, WENDELL

1811–84 Abolitionist

He was about the only Bostonian of his time who wore no middle name and he was therefore considered half naked.

Frank Sullivan, *A Garland of Ibids*

## PIERCE, FRANKLIN

1804–69 Fourteenth United States President

We Polked you in 1844 and we shall Pierce you in 1852.

Anon. Democratic Party election slogan referring to the comparative anonymity of two presidential candidates who were elected

Many persons have difficulty remembering what President Franklin Pierce is best remembered for, and he is therefore probably best forgotten.

Richard Armour, *It All Started With Columbus*

. . . a man who cannot be befriended; whose miserable administration admits but of one excuse, imbecility. Pierce was either the worst, or he was the weakest, of all our Presidents.

Ralph Waldo Emerson, in Mark Van Doren, *Nathaniel Hawthorne*

It was said that the delicate matter of his excessive conviviality was talked over with him and he promised to walk circumspectly should he become President.

James Ford Rhodes, in Meade Minnigerode, *Presidential Years 1787–1860*

He's got the best picture in the White House, Franklin Pierce, but being President involves a little bit more than just winning a beauty contest, and he was another one that was a complete fizzle . . . Pierce didn't know what was going on, and even if he had, he wouldn't of known what to do about it.

Harry S. Truman, in Merle Miller, *Plain Speaking: An Oral Biography of Harry S. Truman*

## PINKERTON, ALLAN

1819–84 Detective

From cooper to copper.

Anon., popular expression referring to Pinkerton's early career as a barrel maker

## PITT, WILLIAM, THE ELDER,

*see under* **CHATHAM, FIRST EARL OF**

## PITT, WILLIAM (THE YOUNGER)

1759–1806 Prime Minister

He was the parent of more practical reforms in administration and political economy than almost any other English statesman . . . But he approached them with his eye, not on the horizon like a man of the study, but always on the treacherous and broken ground at his feet.

Arthur Bryant, *The Years of Endurance*

He was not merely a chip of the old block, but the old block itself.

Edmund Burke, commenting upon Pitt's maiden speech, February 1781

With death doom'd to grapple, / Beneath this cold slab, he / Who lied in the Chapel / Now lies in the Abbey. /

Lord Byron, *Epitaph for William Pitt*

Pitt too had his pride, / And as a high-soul'd minister of state is / Renown'd for ruining Great Britain gratis. /

Lord Byron, *Don Juan*, canto ix

And oh! if again the rude whirlwind should rise, / The dawnings of peace should fresh darkness deform, / The regrets of the good and the fears of the wise / Shall turn to the Pilot that weathered the Storm. /

George Canning, *Song*, 1802

Pitt is to Addington / As London is to Paddington. /

George Canning, *The Oracle*

If I should smoke . . . William would instantly call for a pipe.

William Pitt the Elder (Earl of Chatham), in John Ehrmann, *The Younger Pitt*

The great snorting bawler.
William Cobbett, *Rural Rides*

Pitt deem'd himself an Eagle – what a flat! / What was he? A poor wheeling, fluttering Bat – / An Imp of Darkness – busy catching flies! / Here, there, up, down, off, on – shriek, shriek – snap, snap – / His gaping mouth a very lucky trap, / Quick seizing for his hungry maw – Supplies. /
Peter Pindar (John Wolcot), *Odes to the Ins and Outs*, II

Pitt was endowed with mental powers of the first order; his readiness, his apprehension, his resource were extraordinary; the daily parliamentary demand on his brain and nerve power he met with serene and inexhaustible affluence; his industry, administrative activity, and public spirit were unrivalled; it was perhaps impossible to carry the force of sheer ability further; he was a portent.
Earl of Rosebery, *Pitt*

*See also* James Wolfe

## POCAHANTAS

*circa* 1595–1617 Princess of the Tidewater Confederacy

Our Mother, Pocahontas / Her skin was rosy copper-red. / And high she held her beauteous head. / Her step was like a rustling leaf: / Her heart a nest, untouched of grief. / She dreamed of sons like Powhatan, / And through her blood the lightning ran. / Love-cries with the birds she sung, / Bird like / In the grape-vine swung. / The Forest, arching low and wide / Gloried in its Indian bride. /
Vachel Lindsay, *Our Mother Pocahontas*

## POE, EDGAR ALLAN

1809–49 Poet, Critic, Author

I never was in the *habit* of intoxication . . . But, for a brief period, while I resided in Richmond, and edited the *Messenger* I certainly did give way, at long intervals, to the temptation held out on all sides by the spirit of Southern conviviality.
On himself, Letter to Dr J. E. Snodgrass, 1 April 1841

. . . an unmanly sort of man whose love-life seems to have been largely confined to crying in laps and playing house.
W. H. Auden, in Richard Wilbur, 'Edgar Allan Poe', in Perry Miller ed., *Major Writers of America*, vol. 1

Edgar Allan Poe / Was passionately fond of roe. / He always liked to chew some / When writing anything gruesome. /
Edmund Clerihew Bentley, *More Biography*

It is high irony that Poe should have invented the detective story, that stand-by for breadwinning of the hack writer, and yet half starved himself.
Henry Seidel Canby, *Classic Americans*

That Poe had a powerful intellect is undeniable: but it seems to me the intellect of a highly gifted young person before puberty. The forms which his lively curiosity takes are those in which a pre-adolescent mentality delights: wonders of nature and of mechanics and of the supernatural, cryptograms and cyphers, puzzles and labyrinths, mechanical chess-players and wild flights of speculation.
T. S. Eliot, *Essays*

The jingle man.
Ralph Waldo Emerson, in *ibid.*

The substance of Poe is refined; it is his form that is vulgar. He is, as it were, one of Nature's gentlemen, unhappily cursed with incorrigible bad taste.

Aldous Huxley, 'Vulgarity in Literature', in Robert Regan ed., *Poe, A Collection of Critical Essays*

With all due respects to the very original genius of the author of the 'Tales of Mystery', it seems to us that to take him with more than a certain degree of seriousness is to lack seriousness one's self.

Henry James, *Comments*

Poe had a pretty bitter doom. Doomed to seethe down his soul in a great continuous convulsion of disintegration, and doomed to register the process. And then doomed to be abused for it, when he had performed some of the bitterest tasks of human experience that can be asked of a man. Necessary tasks too. For the human soul must suffer its own disintegration, consciously, if ever it is to survive.

D. H. Lawrence, *Studies in Classic American Literature*

The hurrying great ones scorn his Raven's croak, / And well may mock his mystifying cloak / Inscribed with runes from tongues he has not read, / To make the ignoramus turn his head. / The artificial glitter of his eyes / Has captured half-grown boys. They think him wise / Some shallow player-folk esteem him deep, / Soothed by his steady wand's mesmeric sweep. /

Vachel Lindsay, *The Wizard in the Street*

. . . three-fifths of him genius and two-fifths sheer fudge.

James Russell Lowell, *A Fable for Critics*

Poe is a kind of Hawthorne with delirium tremens.

Leslie Stephen, *Hours in a Library*

. . . Poe's verses illustrate an intense faculty for technical and abstract beauty, with the rhyming art to excess, an incorrigible propensity toward nocturnal themes, a demoniac undertone behind every page – and, by final judgment, probably belong among the electric lights of imaginative literature, brilliant and dazzling, but with no heat.

Walt Whitman, *Edgar Poe's Significance*

*See also* J. C. Powys, Alfred, Lord Tennyson

## POLK, JAMES KNOX

1795–1849 Eleventh United States President

. . . he is sold soul and body to that grim idiot, half albino, half negro, the compound of democracy and of slavery, which, by the slave representation in Congress, rules and ruins the Union.

John Quincy Adams, in *New York Herald*

Polk's mind was rigid, narrow, obstinate, far from first-rate . . . But if his mind was narrow it was powerful and he had guts. If he was orthodox, his integrity was absolute and he could not be scared, manipulated, or brought to heel. No one bluffed him, no one moved him with direct or oblique pressure. Furthermore, he knew how to get things done, which is the first necessity of government, and he knew what he wanted done, which is the second . . . He was to be the only 'strong' President between Jackson and Lincoln. He was to fix the mold of the future in America down to 1860, and therefore for a long time afterward. That is who James Polk was.

Bernard De Voto, in Saul Braun, in *The American Heritage History of the Presidents of the United States*

. . . a victim of the use of water as a beverage.

Samuel Houston, in Llerena Friend, *Sam Houston, The Great Designer*

Polk's appointments all in all are the most damnable set that was ever made by any President since the government was organized . . . He has a set of interested *parasites* about him, who flatter him until he does not know himself. He seems to be acting upon the principle of hanging an old friend for the purpose of making two new ones.

Andrew Johnson, in Eric L. McKitrick, *Andrew Johnson: A Profile*

Had it not been for the press, James K. Polk might as well have retired to a monastery instead of occupying the White House as far as his Presidential contacts with the public were concerned.

James E. Pollard, *The Presidents and the Press*

. . . He was not fastidious; he was not thoughtful of the rights of other peoples, other races, other political parties than his own . . . His motto for Americans and white men was to keep what they had and catch what they could.

James Schouler, *History of the United States*

*See also* Franklin Pierce

## POLLOCK, JACKSON

1912–56 Artist

Abstract painting is abstract. It confronts you. There was a reviewer a while back who wrote that my pictures didn't have any beginning or any end. He didn't mean it as a compliment, but it was. It was a fine compliment.

On himself, in Francis V. O'Connor, *Jackson Pollock*

Before I get started on my own stuff and forget everything else I want to tell you I think the little sketches you left around here are magnificent. Your color is rich and beautiful. You've the stuff old kid – all you have to do is keep it up. You ought to give some time to drawing – but I do not somehow or other feel the lack of drawing in the stuff left here. It seems to *go* without it.

Thomas Hart Benton, Letter to Pollock, 1935

What is thought to be Pollock's bad taste is in reality simply his willingness to be ugly in terms of contemporary taste. In the course of time this ugliness will become a new standard of beauty. Besides, Pollock submits to a habit of discipline derived from cubism; and even as he goes away from cubism he carries with him the unity of style with which it endowed him when in the beginning he put himself under its influence. Thus Pollock's superiority to his contemporaries in his country lies in his ability to create a genuinely violent and extravagant art without losing stylistic control. His emotion starts out pictorially; it does not have to be castrated and translated in order to be put into a picture.

Clement Greenberg, in *Nation*, 13 April 1946

The nervous, if rough, calligraphy of Pollock's work may hide a protest against the cool architectural objectivity of the abstractionist mode as it makes its subjective statement. Pollock does not seem to be especially talented, there being too much of an air of baked-macaroni about some of his patterns, as though they were scrambled baroque designs.

Parker Tyler, in *View*, May 1945

## PONSONBY, HENRIETTA, *see under* BESSBOROUGH, LADY

## POPE, ALEXANDER

1688–1744 Poet

I left no calling for this idle trade, / No duty broke, no father disobey'd. / The Muse but serv'd to ease some

friend, not Wife, / To help me thro' this long disease, my Life. /
On himself, *Epistle to Dr Arbuthnot*

Yes I am proud; I must be proud to see / Men, not afraid of God, afraid of me. /
On himself, *Epilogue to the Satires*

Heroes and Kings! your distance keep; / In peace let one poor Poet sleep, / Who never flatter'd folks like you: / Let Horace blush, and Virgil too. /
On himself, *For One Who Would Not be Buried in Westminster Abbey*

Wordsworth says somewhere that wherever Virgil seems to have composed 'with his eye on the object', Dryden fails to render him. Homer invariably composes 'with his eye on the object', whether the object be a moral or a material one: Pope composes with his eye on his style, into which he translates his object, whatever it is.
Matthew Arnold, *On Translating Homer*

If Wordsworth had Pope in mind when he advised Poets to write 'in the language really used by men' he was singularly in error. Should one compare Pope at his best with any of the Romantics, including Wordsworth, at their best, it is Pope who writes as men normally speak to each other and the latter who go in for 'poetic' language.
W. H. Auden, *Forewords and Afterwords*

It is a pretty poem, Mr Pope, but you must not call it Homer.
Richard Bentley, on Pope's translation, in Samuel Johnson, *Lives of the Poets*

I spoke against his Homer, and the portentuous cub never forgives.
Richard Bentley, in Francis Wrangham, *British Plutarch*

One whom it was easy to hate, but still easier to quote.
Augustine Birrell, *Obiter Dicta*

I told him that Voltaire, in a conversation with me, had distinguished Pope and Dryden thus: – 'Pope drives a handsome chariot, with a couple of neat trim nags; Dryden, a coach and six stately horses.' *Johnson*: 'Why, Sir, the truth is, they both drive coaches and six; but Dryden's horses are either galloping or stumbling: Pope's go at a steady even trot.'
James Boswell, *Life of Johnson*

I wonder he is not thrashed; but his littleness is his protection; no man shoots a wren.
William Broome, Letter to Elijah Fenton, 3 May 1728

Better to err with Pope, than shine with Pye.
Lord Byron, *English Bards and Scotch Reviewers*

I took Moore's poems and my own and some others, and went over them side by side with Pope's, and I was really astonished (I ought not to have been so) and mortified at the ineffable distance in point of sense, harmony, effect, and even *imagination*, passion, and *invention*, between the little Queen Anne's man, and us of the Lower Empire.
Lord Byron, Letter to John Murray, 1817

I have a dark suspicion that a modern poet might manufacture an admirable lyric out of almost every line of Pope.
G. K. Chesterton, *Twelve Types*

O for another Dunciad – a POPE / To purge this dump with his gigantic boot – / Drive fools to water, aspirin or rope – / Make idle lamp-posts bear their fitting fruit: / Private invective's far too long been mute. /

Alex Comfort, 'Letter to an American Visitor', in *Tribune*, 4 June 1943

Then Pope, as harmony itself exact, / In verse well disciplin'd, complete, compact, / Gave virtue and morality a grace, / That, quite eclipsing Pleasure's painted face, / Levied a tax of wonder and applause, / Ev'n on the fools that trampled on their laws. / But he (his musical finesse was such, / So nice his ear, so delicate his touch) / Made poetry a mere mechanic art; / And ev'ry warbler has his tune by heart. /

William Cowper, *Table Talk*

Let us take the initial and final letters of his Surname, *viz.*, *A. P--E*, and they give you the Idea of an *Ape*. – *Pope* comes from the Latin word *Popa*, which signifies a little Wart; or from *Poppysma*, because he was continually *popping* out squibs of wit, or rather *Po-pysmata*, or *Po-piams*.

John Dennis, *Daily Journal*, 11 June 1728

. . . Pope's translation [of Homer] is a portrait endowed with every merit except that of likeness to the original.

Edward Gibbon, *Autobiography*

Europe has not as yet recovered from the Renaissance, nor has English poetry recovered from Alexander Pope.

Oliver St J. Gogarty, *As I Was Going Down Sackville Street*

It cannot be denied, that his chief excellence lay more in diminishing, than in aggrandizing objects; in checking, not in encouraging our enthusiasm; in sneering at the extravagances of fancy or passion, instead of giving a loose to them; in describing a row of pins and needles, rather than the embattled spears of Greeks and Trojans; in penning a lampoon or a compliment, and in praising Martha Blount.

William Hazlitt, *Lectures on the English Poets*

When I hear anyone say, with definite emphasis, that Pope was a poet, I suspect him of calling in ambiguity of language to promote confusion of thought. That Pope was a poet is true; but it is one of those truths which are beloved of liars, because they serve so well the cause of falsehood. That Pope was not a poet is false; but a righteous man, standing in awe of the last judgement and the lake which burneth with fire and brimstone, might well prefer to say it.

A. E. Housman, *The Name and Nature of Poetry*

His more ambitious works may be defined as careless thinking carefully versified.

James Russell Lowell, *My Study Windows*

No poet? Calculated commonplace? / Ten razor blades in one neat couplet case! /

John Macy, *Couplets in Criticism*

Pope courted with the utmost assiduity all the old men from whom he could hope a legacy: the Duke of Buckingham, Lord Peterborough, Sir Godfrey Kneller, Mr Wycherley, Mr Congreve, Lord Harcourt etc., and I do not doubt projected to sweep the Dean's [Jonathan Swift's] whole inheritance if he could have persuaded him to throw up his Deanery and come die in his house; and his general preaching against money was meant to induce people to throw it away that he might pick it up.

Lady Mary Wortley Montagu, Letter to Lady Bute

Mr Addison wrote a letter to Mr Pope, when young, in which he desired him not to list himself under either party: 'You,' says he, 'who will deserve the praise of the whole nation, should not content yourself with the half of it.'

Joseph Spence, *Anecdotes*

You . . . are a kind of Hermit, how great a noise you make soever by your Ill nature in not letting the honest Villains of the Times enjoy themselves in this world, which is their only happiness, and terrifying them with another. I should have added in my libel that of all men living you are most happy in your Enemies and your Friends: and I will swear you have fifty times more Charity for mankind than I could ever pretend to.

Jonathan Swift, Letter to Alexander Pope, 1 May 1733

The sublime and the pathetic are the two chief nerves of all genuine poetry. What is there transcendently sublime or pathetic in Pope?

Joseph Warton, *Essay on the Writings and Genius of Pope*

*See also* William Blackstone, John Donne, John Dryden, John Gay, G. F. Handel, Samuel Johnson, Godfrey Kneller, Lord Mansfield, Walter Raleigh, Jonathan Swift

## PORSON, RICHARD

1759–1808 Greek Scholar

I went to Frankfurt, and got drunk / With that most learned professor, Brunck; / I went to Worts, and got more drunken / With that more learn'd professor, Ruhnken. /

On himself, *Facetiae Cantabrigiensis*

I doubt if I could produce any original work which would command the attention of posterity. I can be known only by my notes: and I am quite satisfied if, three hundred years hence, it shall be said that 'one Porson lived towards the close of the eighteenth century, who did a great deal for the text of Euripedes.'

On himself, in William Maltby, *Porsoniana*

Porson was walking with a Trinitarian friend; they had been speaking of the Trinity. A buggy came by with three men in it: 'There,' says he, 'is an illustration of the Trinity.' 'No,' said his friend Porson, 'you must show me one man in *three* buggies, if you can.'

E. H. Barker, *Literary Recollections and Contemporary Reminiscences*

Tooke used to say that 'Porson would drink ink rather than not drink at all.' Indeed, he would drink anything. He was sitting with a gentleman, after dinner, in the chambers of a mutual friend, a Templar, who was then ill, confined to bed. A servant came into the room, sent thither by his master for a bottle of embrocation which was on the chimney-piece. 'I drank it an hour ago,' said Porson.

William Maltby, *Porsoniana*

*See also* Robert Southey

## PORTER, COLE

1893–1964 Composer, Lyricist

The Adlai Stevenson of songwriters.

Richard Adler, in George Eells, *The Life that Late He Led; A biography of Cole Porter*

Porter deliberately chose to be a snob, at least to all appearances. He inherited money and loved it; but he made much more by himself and loved it as well. He spent freely and gained it freely; he even complained about taxes in a lighthearted vein. 'My ninety-two percent, I suppose, supports some unknown government bureau,' he said. He was determined to be a gay divorcé from life and never abandoned the pose.

Richard G. Hubler, *The Cole Porter Story*

Of all the theatre men only Cole Porter truly seemed to have been born into café society, to be the perfect smart cracker gentleman. He had a million dollars and a beautiful wife (so sophisticated that she didn't know how to open a door) . . . He wore gold garters and had visited India, China, Japan, Cambodia but he liked the music of Bali best. As he floated down the Rhine in a boat he composed 'You're the Top'.

Ian Whitcomb, *After the Ball: Pop Music from Rag to Rock*

## PORTLAND, EARL OF, *see under* BENTINCK, WILLIAM

## PORTSMOUTH, DUCHESS OF, *see under* KEROUAILLE, LOUISE DE

## POUND, EZRA WESTON LOOMIS

1885–1972 Poet

I am also at work on a cryselephantine poem of immeasurable length which will occupy me for the next four decades unless it becomes a bore.

On himself, referring to initial work on the Cantos, in a letter to Milton Bronner, 21 September 1915

How did it go in the madhouse? Rather badly. But what other place could one live in America?

On himself, on his imprisonment in St Elizabeth's Hospital, Washington, D.C., in Charles Norman, *Ezra Pound*

I see they call me Mussolini's boy. I only saw the bastard once. No German or Italian was ever in position to give me an order. So I took none. But a German near my home at Rapallo told me they were paying good money for broadcasts. That was a fatal mistake.

On himself, referring to the start of his Italian broadcasts, in *ibid.*

The bays that formerly old Dante crowned / Are worn today by Ezra Loomis Pound. /

Anon., in *Punch*, 22 January 1913

His costume – the velvet jacket and the open-road shirt – was that of the English aesthete of the period. There was a touch of Whistler about him; his language, on the other hand, was Huckleberry Finn's.

Sylvia Beach, *Shakespeare and Company*

Pound did not create the poets: but he created a situation in which for the first time, there was a 'modern movement in poetry' in which English and American poets collaborated, knew each other's works and influenced each other . . . If it had not been for the work that Pound did in the years of which I have been talking, the isolation of American poets might have continued for a long time.

T. S. Eliot, 'Ezra Pound', in *Poetry: A Magazine of Verse*, 1946

I have never known a man, of any nationality, to live so long out of his native country without seeming to settle anywhere else.

T. S. Eliot, 'Ezra Pound', in Walter Sutton ed., *Ezra Pound, A Collection of Critical Essays*

A minister of the arts without portfolio.

Horace Gregory, *Ezra Pound*

In fact my complaint against Ezra is that, having attracted one time and again with the promise of delightful cerebral embraces, he is forever bidding me adieu with no more than a languid handshake – a suave, a fastidious, an irreproachable, but still a handshake . . . he has always about him the air of a mimic . . . He does not present to me a style – but a series of portrayals . . . To me Pound remains the exquisite showman minus the show.

Ben Hecht, *Pounding Ezra*

Any poet born in this century or in the last ten years of the preceding century who can honestly say that he has not been influenced by or learned greatly from the work of Ezra Pound deserves to be pitied rather than rebuked.

Ernest Hemingway, in Carlos Baker, *Ernest Hemingway, A Life Story*

Pound has spent his life trying to live down a family scandal: – he's Longfellow's grand-nephew.

D. H. Lawrence, Letter to Robert Graves

He has no real creative theme. His versification and his *Procédés* are servants to wilful ideas and platform vehemences. His moral attitudes and absolutisms are bullying assertions, and have the uncreative blatancy of one whose Social Credit consorts naturally with Fascism and anti-Semitism.

F. R. Leavis, 'Ezra Pound', in Walter Sutton ed., *Ezra Pound, A Collection of Critical Essays*

Ezra Pound, I feel, is probably a poet of a higher and rarer order than it is easy at times to realize, because of much irrelevant dust kicked up by his personality as it rushes, strides or charges across the temporal scene.

Percy Wyndham Lewis, in William Van O'Connor, *Ezra Pound*

The United States, for all that it lay over the ocean, presented a broad target, and he fired away. His preoccupation with it, which never left him, was that of a lover who abuses his mistress through the mails and then wonders why she doesn't love him.

Charles Norman, *Ezra Pound*

A village explainer, excellent if you were a village, but if you were not, not.

Gertrude Stein, in Malcolm Cowley, *Exile's Return*

To talk over a poem with him is like getting you to put a sentence into dialect. All becomes clear and natural. Yet in his own work he is very uncertain, often very bad though very interesting sometimes. He spoils himself by too many experiments and has more sound principles than taste.

William Butler Yeats, Letter to Lady Gregory

Ezra Pound has made flux his theme; plot, characterization, logical discourse, seem to him abstractions unsuitable to a man of his generation.

William Butler Yeats, 'Ezra Pound', in Walter Sutton ed., *Ezra Pound, A Collection of Critical Essays*

## POWER, TYRONE EDMUND

1914–58 Actor

I've done an awful lot of stuff that's a monument to public patience.

On himself, in David Shipman, *The Great Movie Stars*

## POWYS, JOHN COWPER

1872–1963 Novelist

Yes, I am a born Clown and therefore just suited to write fairy stories as I have done since I was ten years old when at Dorchester, Dorset, Thomas Hardy taught me to like Edgar Allan Poe, and Poe taught me about those 'Mimes in the form of God on high, blind puppets that come and go at bidding of vast formless things that move the scenery to and fro and flap from out their condor wings invisible woe.'

On himself, Letter to Nicholas Ross, 9 February 1960

My 'lecturing' really was . . . a sort of focussing, through one single twisting, leaping, shuffling, skipping, bowing and scraping human figure, of some special comic-tragic vein in the planetary consciousness . . . I often found it *impossible to stop*. That was my worst fault as a lecturer. I used to *try* to stop; and even begin my peroration; but something, some delicate nuance, some metaphysical nicety, would come sliding into my brain, and I would go whirling on again in my spiral dance, like that mad storm god in Hiawatha. There were even times when I would lecture without a pause and in a constant mounting crescendo for no less than two hours!

On himself, *Autobiography*

He seemed like one of the Gods returned to earth from Olympus or Valhalla, or a flaming Montezuma, not in spangled loin cloths and beaten discs of thin gold, but in modern dress.

Nicholas Ross, *J.C.P. and J.R.N.R.* (an introduction to Powys's letters to Ross)

## PRESLEY, ELVIS ARON

1935–77 Singer

I was on the show (at Overton Park, Memphis) as an extra added single . . . and I came out on stage and uh, uh, I was scared stiff. My first big appearance, in front of an audience. And I came out and I was doin' a fast-type tune, uh, one of my first records, and ever'body was hollerin' and I didn't know what they was hollerin' at. Ever'body was screamin' and ever'thing, and, uh, I came off stage and my manager told me they were hollerin' because I was wigglin'. Well, I went back out for an encore and, I, I, I kind-a did a little more and the more I did, the wilder they went.

On himself, Interview with *TV Guide*, 1956

Elvis Presley, the Hillbilly Cat, Swivel-Hips, the King of Rock and Roll, the King of Bebop, the King of Country Music, simply, the King.

Michael Bane, *Country Music*, December 1977

So Elvis Presley came, strumming a weird guitar and wagging his tail across the continent, ripping off fame and fortune as he scrunched his way, and, like a latter-day Johnny Appleseed, sowing seeds of a new rhythm and style in the white souls of the new white youth of America, whose inner hunger and need was no longer satisfied with the antiseptic white shoes and whiter songs of Pat Boone. 'You can do anything,' sang Elvis to Pat Boone's white shoes, 'but don't you step on my Blue Suede Shoes!'

Eldridge Cleaver, *Soul On Ice*

The hair was a Vaseline cathedral, the mouth a touchingly uncertain sneer of allure. One, two-wham! Like a berserk blender the lusty young pelvis whirred and the notorious git-tar slammed forward with a jolt that symbolically deflowered a generation of teenagers and knocked chips off 90 million older shoulders. Then out of the half-melted vanilla face a wild black baritone came bawling in orgasmic lurches. *Whu-huh-huh-huh f'the money! Two f'the show! Three t'git riddy naa GO CAAT GO!*

Brad Darrach, *Life*, Winter 1977

Mr Presley made another television appearance last night on the Milton Berle show over Channel 4 . . . he might possibly be classified as an entertainer. Or, perhaps quite as easily as an assignment for a sociologist.

Jack Gould, *New York Times*, 7 June 1956

For Elvis there was no escape in art, since his original triumph was his very artlessness. He didn't write songs, nor did he aspire to anything more than success. Even his films were no more than a magnification of his image, a further reinforcement of the impossible perfection which transformed him, like all our public figures, from a living presence into an all-purpose, economy-rate icon.

Peter Gurnalnick, *Country Music*, December 1977

The key phrases are pressure from other people, investments mushrooming and dying strangely.

Antonia Lamb, Horoscope forecast prepared for Elvis in 1970

## PRIESTLEY, JOSEPH

1733–1804 Theologian, Man of Science

Of Dr Priestley's theological works, he [Samuel Johnson] remarked, that they tended to unsettle every thing, and yet settled nothing.

James Boswell, *Life of Johnson*

The attention of Dr Priestley, the founder of a new department of science, and the discoverer of many gases, was accidentally drawn to the subject by the circumstance of his residing in the neighbourhood of a large brewery. Being an attentive observer, he noted, in visiting the brewery, the peculiar appearances attending the extinction of lighted chips in the gas floating over the fermented liquor. He was forty years old at the time, and knew nothing of chemistry; he obtained access, however, to books, which taught him little, for as yet nothing was known on the subject. Then he commenced experimenting, devising his own apparatus, which was of the rudest description. The curious results of his first experiments led to others, which in his hands shortly became the science of pneumatic chemistry.

Samuel Smiles, *Self-help*

The most seditious hand-bills were stuck up in London and Birmingham, and Dr Priestley is said to have boasted that at the latter he could raise 20,000 men; and so indeed he has, but against himself.

Horace Walpole, Letter to Mary Berry, 20 July 1791

## PRIMROSE, ARCHIBALD PHILIP, *see under* ROSEBERY, EARL OF

## PRIOR, MATTHEW

1664–1721 Poet

Nobles and heralds, by your leave, / Here lies what once was Matthew Prior; / The son of Adam and of Eve, / Can Bourbon or Nassau go higher? /

On himself, *Epitaph*

Mrs Thrale disputed with him (*sc.* Johnson) on the merit of Prior. He attacked him powerfully; said, he wrote of love like a man who had never felt it: his love verses were college verses . . Mrs Thrale stood to her gun with great courage . . . till he at last silenced her by saying, 'My dear Lady, talk no more of this. Nonsense can be defended but by nonsense.'

James Boswell, *Life of Johnson*

No one has exceeded him in the laughing grace with which he glances at a subject that will not bear examining, with which he gently hints at what cannot be directly insisted on, with which he half conceals, and half draws aside the veil from some of the Muses' nicest mysteries. His Muse is, in fact, a giddy wanton flirt, who spends her time in playing at snap-dragon and blind-man's buff, who tells what she should not, and knows more than she tells.

William Hazlitt, *Lectures on the English Poets*

Is not Prior the most indecent of tale-tellers, not even excepting La Fontaine; and how often do we see his works in female hands!

Sir Walter Scott, in J. G. Lockhart, *Life of Scott*

## PRITCHARD, HANNAH

1711–68 Actress

This lady was so very natural an actress, and was so powerfully affected by her feelings, that she seldom retired from any great tragic part without being in some degree affected by a stomachic complaint.

William Cooke, *Memoirs of Samuel Foot*

## PRYNNE, WILLIAM

1600–69 Pamphleteer, Politician

The more I am beat down, the more I am lift up.

On himself, in William M. Lamont, *Marginal Prynne*

Here earless William Pryn doth lye / And so will eternally / For when the last trump sounds to appeare / He that hath eares then let him heare. /

Anon., in Anthony à Wood, *Life and Times*

His manner of studie was thus: he wore a long quilt cap, which came 2 or 3, at lest, inches over his eies, which served him as an Umbrella to defend his Eies from the light. About every three houres his man was to bring him a roll and a pot of Ale to refocillate his wasted spirits; so he studied and dranke, and munched some bread; and this maintained him till night, and then, he made a good Supper: now he did well not to dine, which breaks off one's fancy, which will not presently be regained: and 'tis with Invention as a flux, when once it is flowing, it runs amaine: if it is checked, flows but *guttim:* and the like for perspiration, check it and 'tis spoyled.

John Aubrey, *Brief Lives*

He delivers the words as a Parrat, that pronounceth the Syllables, but not as a man that understands the meaning.

Sir Richard Baker, *Theatrum Triumphans*

. . . one of your friends not long since told me, *there was as great disproportion betwixt you and me, to write upon controverting the things of God, as there is betwixt a tall cedar and a little shrub:* unto which I replyed, *goe you, and tell the tall Cedar, the little shrub will have a bout with him.*

John Lilburne, *A Copie of a Letter to Mr William Prynne Esq.*

Mr Prinn . . . did discourse with me a good while alone in the garden about the laws of England, telling me the many faults in them; and among others, their obscurity through multitude of long statutes, which he is about to abstract out of all of a sort, and as he lives, and parliaments come, get them put into laws and the other statutes repealed; and then it will be a short work to know the law – which appears a very noble good thing.

Samuel Pepys, Diary, 25 April 1666

*Looke here* Thou *that hast* malice *to the Stage, / And* Impudence *enough for the whole Age*; / Voluminously-Ignorant! *be vext / To read this Tragedy, and thy owne be next.* /

James Shirley, 'Commendatory Verses' to John Ford's *Love's Sacrifice*

*M. Nedham* the Weather-cock tells us, that *he was one of the greatest paper worms that ever crept into a closet of a library, &c.* and others that *he never intended an end in writing books*, and that his study or reading *was not only a wearisomeness to the flesh, but to the ears.*

Anthony à Wood, *Athenae Oxonienses*

## PUGIN, AUGUSTUS WELBY NORTHMORE

1812–52 Architect

I have passed my life in thinking of fine things, studying fine things, designing fine things and realising very poor ones.

On himself, *Remarks on Articles in The Rambler*

Pugin is the Janus of the Gothic Revival; his buildings look back to the picturesque past, his writings look forward to the ethical future.

Kenneth Clark, *The Gothic Revival*

He had a most sincere love for his profession, a hearty honest enthusiasm for pixes and piscinas; and though he will never design so much as a pix or a piscina thoroughly well, yet better than most of the experimental architects of the day. Employ him by all means, but on small work. Expect no cathedrals of him: but no one at present, can design a better finial.

John Ruskin, *The Stones of Venice*, Appendix xii

*See also* Sir Gilbert Scott

## PULITZER, JOSEPH

1847–1911 Journalist

He was the damnedest best man in the world to have in a newspaper office for one hour in the morning. For the remainder of the day he was a damned nuisance.

John A. Cockerill, in W. A. Swanberg, *Pulitzer*

... this Dick Turpin of journalism.

Charles Anderson Dana, in James Wyman Barrett, *Joseph Pulitzer and His World*

He came to this country, not to promote the cause of his race or his native land, but to push the fortunes of that part of Jewry which is situated over the soles of his boots and under the hat that covers his head.

Charles Anderson Dana, in W. A. Swanberg, *Pulitzer*

The only consideration which guides this fellow in the control of his precious paper is to keep out of the reach of criminal prosecution.

Leander Richardson, in George Juergens, *Joseph Pulitzer and The New York World*

It was by this appeal to the basest passions of the crowd that Mr Pulitzer succeeded; like many another he deliberately stooped for success, and then, having achieved it, slowly put on garments of righteousness.

Oswald Garrison Villard, *Some Newspapers and Newspaper-Men*

## PURCELL, HENRY

1658?–95 Composer

Musick is yet but in its Nonage, a forward Child, which gives hope of what it may be hereafter in *England*, when the Masters of it shall find more Encouragement. 'Tis now learning *Italian*, which is its best Master, and studying a little of the *French* Air, to give it somewhat more of Gayety and Fashion. Thus being farther from the Sun, we are of later Growth than our Neighbor Countries, and must be content to shake off our Barbarity by degrees.

On himself, Preface to *Dioclesian*

He was so superior to all his predecessors, that his compositions seemed to speak a new language; yet, however different from that to which the public had been long accustomed, it was universally understood. His songs seem to contain whatever the ear could then wish, or heart could feel.

Dr Charles Burney, *A General History of Music*

Purcell . . . had always an inferior band to the Italian opera composers, as well as inferior fingers, and an inferior audience, to write for.

*Ibid.*

Mark how the lark and linnet sing, / With rival notes / They strain their warbling throats, / To welcome in the spring. / But in the close of night / When Philomel begins her heav'nly lay, / They cease their mutual spight, / Drink in her Music with delight, / And list'ning and silent, and silent and list'ning, / And list'ning and silent obey. /

So ceas'd the rival crew when Purcell came, / They sung no more, or only sung his fame. / Struck dumb they all admir'd the godlike man: / The godlike man / Alas! too soon retir'd / As he too late began. / We beg not hell our Orpheus to restore: / Had he been there, / Their sovereign's fear / Had sent him back before. / The pow'r of harmony too well they know / Would long ere this have tun'd their jarring sphere, / And left no hell below. /

The heav'nly choir, who heard his notes from high, / Let down the scale of Music from the sky: / They handed him along, / And all the way he taught, and all the way they sung. / Ye brethren of the lyre, and tuneful voice, / Lament his lot, but at your own rejoice. / Now live secure and linger out your days, / The gods are pleas'd alone with Purcell's lays, / Nor know to mend their choice. /

John Dryden, *Ode on the Death of Mr Henry Purcell*

A mate to a cock, and corn tall as wheat, / Is his Christian name who in musick's compleat: / His surname begins with the grace of a cat, / And concludes with the house of a hermit; note that. / His skill and performance each auditor wins, / But the poet deserves a good kick on the shins. /

Mr Tomlinson, *The Pleasant Musical Companion*, 1701, translated from the original Latin by Sir John Hawkins

*See also* John Blow

## PYM, JOHN

1584–1643 Parliamentarian

The most popular man, and the most able to do hurte, that hath lived in any tyme.

Edward Hyde, Earl of Clarendon, *History of the Rebellion*

# 'Q'

## QUANTRILL, WILLIAM CLARKE

1837–65 Bandit

Because of Quantrill, widows wailed, orphans cried, maidens wept.

William E. Connelley, *Quantrill and the Border Wars*

## QUILLER-COUCH, SIR ARTHUR THOMAS

1863–1944 Author, Academic

Judged by subsequent Cambridge standards, he often seems impossibly florid, and on the whole his critical methods are what can only be described as under-ingenious. But in 1912 the world was younger, and professors could still talk about criticism in terms of an adventure.

John Gross, on Quiller-Couch's tenure as King Edward VII Professor at Cambridge, *The Rise and Fall of the Man of Letters*

In Cambridge memories, there must linger many and varied pictures of Q: there was the professorial figure clad, literally, in a wedding-garment in preparation for the lecture-room; there was the figure of the countryman, in tweeds, strolling into the Pitt Club for lunch; there was the Commodore's figure, ready to spend an afternoon with the Cruising Club; there was the post-prandial figure in his rooms in Jesus, dispensing good talk, good liquor and good fellowship to his guests. And at the back of it all was the sense of style, a sense which governed his dress and his manners as surely as his writing.

S. C. Roberts, Introduction to Quiller-Couch's *Memories and Opinions*

# 'R'

## RADCLIFFE, ANN

1764–1823 Novelist

Charming as were all Mrs Radcliffe's works, charming even as were the works of all her imitators, it was not in them, perhaps, that human nature, at least in the midland counties of England, was to be looked for.

Jane Austen, *Northanger Abbey*

Her descriptions of scenery, indeed, are vague and wordy to the last degree . . . her characters are insipid, the shadows of a shade, continued on, under different names, through all her novels: her story comes to nothing. But in harrowing up the soul with imaginary horrors, and making the flesh creep, and the nerves thrill, she is unrivalled among her fair country-women . . . She makes her readers twice children.

William Hazlitt, *Lectures on the English Comic Writers*

I am going into scenery whence I intend to tip you a Damosel Radcliffe – I'll cavern you, and grotto you, and waterfall you, and wood you, and immense-rock you, and tremendous sound you, and solitude you.

John Keats, Letter to J. H. Reynolds, 14 March 1818

Mrs Radcliffe makes an appeal less to the nerves than to the imagination, using as we have seen the desiccated idiom of the age, like Scott, and she does achieve a total effect.

Q. D. Leavis, *Fiction and the Reading Public*

## RAGLAN, LORD (FITZROY JAMES HENRY SOMERSET)

1788–1855 Soldier

Hallo! don't carry away that arm till I have taken off my ring.

On himself, during his operation after Waterloo, 1815

Not since we landed has Raglan shown one particle of military knowledge . . . I wish they would reinforce us with a new Commander-in-Chief, and put this one in petticoats and send him home.

Robert Portal, Letter to his Mother from the Crimea, October 1854

## RALEIGH, SIR WALTER

1552?–1618 Adventurer, Author, Statesman

If any man accuseth me to my face, I will answer him with my mouth; but my tail is good enough to return an answer to such who traduceth me behind my back.

On himself, in Thomas Fuller, *The History of the Worthies of England*

Old Sir Thomas Malette, one of the Judges of the Kings Bench, knew Sir Walter Ralegh and sayd that notwith-standing his great Travells, Conver-sation, Learning, etc., yet he spake broad Devonshire to his dyeing day.

John Aubrey, *Brief Lives*

He loved a wench well; and one time getting up one of the Mayds of Honour up against a tree in a Wood ('twas his first Lady) who seemed at first boarding to be somewhat fearfull of her Honour, and modest, she cryed, sweet Sir Walter, what doe you me ask? Will you undoe me? Nay, sweet Sir Walter! Sweet Sir Walter! Sir Walter! At last, as the danger and the pleasure at the same time grew higher, she cryed in the extasey, Swisser Swatter Swisser Swatter.

*Ibid.*

Mr Walt humbled himselfe to his Father, and promised he would behave himself mightily mannerly. So away they went . . . He sate nexte to his Father and was very demure at least half dinner time. Then sayd he, I this morning, not having the feare of God before my eies, but by the instigation of the devill, went to a Whore. I was very eager of her, kissed and embraced her, and went to enjoy her, but she thrust me from her, and vowed I should not *For your father lay with me but an hower ago*. Sir Walt, being so strangely supprized and putt out of his countenance at so great a Table, gives his son a damned blow over the face; his son, as rude as he was, would not strike his father, but strikes over the face of the Gentleman that sate next to him, and sayed *Box about, 'twill come to my Father anon.* 'Tis now a common used Proverb.

*Ibid.*

He tooke a pipe of Tobacco a little before he went to the scaffold, which some formall persons were scandalised at, but I thinke twas well and properly donne, to settle his spirits.

*Ibid.*

I will prove you the notoriousest traitor that ever came to the bar . . . Nay, I will prove all; thou art a monster; thou has an English face but a Spanish heart.

Edward Coke, at Raleigh's trial, 17 November 1603

I have known many persons who turned their gold into smoke, but you are the first to turn smoke into gold.

Queen Elizabeth I (on his introduction of tobacco into England), in F. Chamberlin, *The Sayings of Queen Elizabeth*

This Captain Raleigh coming out of Ireland to the English Court in good habit (his clothes being then a considerable part of his estate) found the Queen walking, till, meeting with a plashy place, she seemed to scruple going thereon. Presently Raleigh cast and spread his new plush cloak on the ground; whereon the Queen trod gently, rewarding him afterwards with many suits, for his free and seasonable tender of so fair a foot-cloth. Thus an advantageous admission into the first notice of a Prince is more than half a degree to preferment.

Thomas Fuller, *The History of the Worthies of England*

Only my father would keep such a bird in a cage.

Prince Henry, attributed, son to James I, on Raleigh's continuing imprisonment in the Tower

In talking over the design for a dictionary that might be authoritative for our English writers, Mr Pope rejected Sir Walter Ralegh twice, as too affected.

Joseph Spence, *Anecdotes*

He was one that fortune had pickt up out of purpose, of whom to make an example, or to use as her Tennis-Ball, thereby to show what she could do; for she tost him up of nothing, and to and fro to greatness, and from thence down to little more than to that wherein she found him (a bare Gentleman).

Anthony à Wood, *Athenae Oxonienses*

*See also* Christopher Marlowe

## RAMSAY, ALLAN

1713–84 Portrait Painter

His marriage to his art implied no fervent devotion: it was fundamentally a *mariage de convenance*, promising serenity and harmony rather than the fulfilment of a grand passion; and one feels that he achieved these qualities in his paintings out of the clear knowledge that they represented the limits beyond which his genius could not carry him.

A. Smart, *The Life and Art of Allan Ramsay*

His pictures are much superior in merrit than other portrait painters – his mens pictures strong likeness firm in drawing – and true flesh colouring natural tinctures. his Lady delicate and Genteel – easy free likeness. their habits and dresses well disposed and airy. his flesh tender his silks & satins &c shineing beautiful & clean – with great Variety.

George Vertue, *Notebooks*

## RANK, JOSEPH ARTHUR, LORD

1888–1972 Industrialist, Film Magnate

A deeply and sincerely religious man, he was strongly motivated by the belief that he was selected by Divine Providence to provide the people of this country with the best quality flour and bread, the stuff of life as he liked to call it, at the cheapest price.

Sir Ernest Chain, in *The Times*, 5 April 1972

## RANSOM, JOHN CROWE

1882–1974 Poet

Ransom seems in his poems, as most modern poets do not, sympathetic and charming, full of tenderness and affection, wanting the light and sorry for the dark – moral and condemning only when he has to be, not because he wants to be; loving neither the sterner vices nor the sterner virtues.

Randall Jarrell, 'John Ransom's Poetry', in Thomas Daniel Young ed., *John Crowe Ransom*

He is an academic poet, always seeking his most potent effect from the built-in paradox of his poetics: the intensification of feeling that comes from ascetic techniques.

Thornton H. Parsons, *John Crowe Ransom*

Reading him we are at once delighted and made profoundly aware of what it is to be men with all the burden and glory of our contradictions. This, I believe, is how Ransom, that genial pluralist, would like to have it.

John C. Stewart, *John Crowe Ransom*

A Water-Colorist.

Edmund Wilson, in Thornton H. Parsons, *John Crowe Ransom*

## READE, CHARLES

1814–84 Novelist

If you have the sort of mind that takes pleasure in dates, lists, catalogues, concrete details, descriptions of processes, junk-shop windows and back numbers of *Exchange and Mart*, the sort of mind that likes knowing exactly how a mediaeval catapult worked or just what objects a prison-cell of the eighteen-forties contained, then you can hardly help enjoying Reade. He himself, of course, did not see his work in quite this light.

George Orwell, in *New Statesman and Nation*, 17 August 1940

## REITH, JOHN CHARLES WALSHAM, LORD

1889–1971 Communications Pioneer

A figure of Ariel sculpted by Eric Gill in the late 1920's for the façade of the British Broadcasting Corporation building, has had a peculiar and almost embarrassing history. Lord Reith, then head of the BBC, complained that the sculptor had emphasized Ariel's reproductive organ beyond necessity. Gill refused to make any changes. It was decided to submit the matter to arbitration; Sir Israel Gollancz, the noted Shakespearian scholar and editor, and Israel Zangwill the novelist were among the Shakespearians deputized to investigate. After concluding that Ariel's approximate age should be thirteen, they called in a Doctor, who agreed with Lord Reith that for such a boy the genitals were overemphasized. The necessary surgery was performed and the statue of Ariel put into the place it still occupies on the building.

Louis Marder, *His Exits and His Entrances*

## REMINGTON, FREDERIC

1861–1909 Artist, Author

Evening overtook me one night in Montana and by good luck I made the camp-fire of an old wagon freighter who shared his coffee and bacon with me. I was nineteen years of age and he was a very old man . . . During his long life he had followed the receding frontiers . . . 'And now' he said, 'there is no more West. In a few years the railroad will come along the Yellowstone . . .' He had his point of view and he made a new one for me . . . I saw men all ready swarming into the land. I knew the derby hat, the smoking chimneys, the cord-binders, and the thirty-day notes were upon us in a restless surge. I knew the wild riders and the vacant land were about to vanish forever . . . and the more I considered the subject, the bigger the forever loomed. Without knowing exactly how to do it, I began to try to record some facts around me, and the more I looked the more the panorama unfolded.

On himself, in *Collier's*, 18 May 1905

His whole life as a documentary artist was dedicated to the singular thesis of being the pictorial historian of our Old West. His horizon was broad both historically and geographically. Most of what he recorded was from firsthand intimate association, at a time when the Western frontier was in its most exciting full bloom . . . Remington's artistic credo was truthful realism and the 'little people' who are always the human grist for the mill of history, rather than the organized campaigns, spectacular events, and the big names that are the meat of most historians.

Harold McCracken, *The Frederic Remington Book*

## REVERE, PAUL

1735–1818 Silversmith, Revolutionary

Although hardly a man is now alive who remembers the entire poem that was written about his exploits, Paul Revere got up at midnight and awakened everyone with his cries. He had seen a light in the steeple of Old North Church, and knew at once that the British were coming by land or sea. Accompanied by William Dawes, he carried the news from Boston to Concord and from Ghent to Aix. When dawn broke, the countryside swarmed with countrymen.

Richard Armour, *It All Started With Columbus*

For, borne on the night-wind of the Past, / Through all our history, to the last, / In the hour of darkness and peril and need, / The people will wake and listen to hear / The hurrying hoof-beats of that steed, / And the midnight message of Paul Revere. /

Henry Wadsworth Longfellow, *Paul Revere's Ride*

## REYNOLDS, SIR JOSHUA

1723–92 Painter

When S$^{r}$ J— R— died / All Nature was degraded; / The King drop'd a tear into the Queen's Ear, / And all his Pictures faded. /

William Blake, *Annotations to Reynolds's Discourses*

I consider Reynolds's Discourses to the Royal Academy as the Simulations of the Hypocrite who smiles particularly where he means to Betray. His Praises of Rafael is like the Hysteric Smile of Revenge. His Softness & Candour, the hidden trap & the poisoned feast. He praises Michel Angelo for Qualities which Michel Angelo abhorr'd, & he blames Rafael for the only Qualities which Rafael valued. Whether Reynolds knew what he was doing is nothing to me: the Mischief is just the same whether a Man does it Ignorantly or Knowingly. I always consider'd True Art & True Artists to be particularly Insulted & Degraded by the Reputation of these Discourses, As much as they were Degraded by the Reputation of Reynolds's Paintings, & that such Artists as Reynolds are at all times Hired by the Satans for the Depression of Art – A Pretence of Art, to destroy Art.

*Ibid.*

O reader behold the philosopher's grave! / He was born quite a fool but he died quite a knave. /

William Blake, *Epitaph*

It is . . . to Reynolds that the honour of establishing the English school belongs.

John Constable, Lecture at the Royal Institution, June 1836

Damn him, how various he is!

Thomas Gainsborough, in E. Waterhouse, *Painting in Britain 1530–1790*

Here Reynolds is laid, and to tell you my mind, / He has not left a better or wiser behind; / His pencil was striking, resistless and grand, / His manners were gentle, complying and bland; / Still born to improve us in every part, / His pencil our faces, his manners our heart: / To coxcombs averse, yet most civilly staring, / When they judged without skill he was still hard of hearing: / When they talk'd of their Raphaels, Correggios and stuff, / He shifted his trumpet, and only took snuff. /

Oliver Goldsmith, *Retaliation*

He became rich by the accumulation of borrowed wealth, and his genius was the offspring of taste. He combined and applied the materials of others to his own purposes, with admirable success; he was an industrious compiler, or skilful translator, not an original inventor in art.

William Hazlitt, 'Character of Sir Joshua Reynolds', in *Champion*, 30 October 1814

I know of no man who has passed through life with more observation than Reynolds.

Samuel Johnson, in James Boswell, *Life of Johnson*

The link that united him to Michel Angelo was the sense of ideal greatness; the noblest of all perceptions. It is this sublimity of thought that marks the first-rate genius; this impelling fancy which has nowhere its defined form, yet every-where its image; and while pursuing excellence too perfect to be attained, creates new beauty that cannot be surpassed!

Sir Thomas Lawrence, Address to the Students of the Royal Academy, 1823

His theory and his practice are evidently at variance; he speaks of the cold painters of portraits, and ranks them on a level with the epigrammatist and the sonnetteer, yet devoted his life to portraits. How to account for this dereliction of his theory may be difficult; the reason given by himself was, that he adapted his style to the taste of the age in which he lived; and again, that a man does not always do what he would, but what he can.

James Northcote, *The Life of Sir Joshua Reynolds*

Compar'd, to other painting-men, / Thou art an eagle to a wren! /

Peter Pindar (John Wolcot), *Lyric Odes to the Royal Academicians*, 1782, Ode I

He rejoices in showing you his skill; and those of you who succeed in learning what painter's work really is, will one day rejoice also, even to laughter – the highest laughter which springs of pure delight, in watching the fortitude and fire of a hand which strikes forth its will upon the canvas as easily as the wind strikes it on the sea. He rejoices in all abstract beauty and rhythm and melody of design; he will never give you a colour that is not lovely, nor a shade that is unnecessary, nor a line that is ungraceful. But all his power and all his invention are held by him subordinate – and the more obediently because of their nobleness, – to his true leading purpose of setting before you such likeness of the living presence of an English gentleman or an English lady, as shall be worthy of being looked upon for ever.

John Ruskin, *Lectures on Art*, IV

Sir Joshua is the ablest man I know on a canvas.

George Selwyn, attributed, on hearing that Reynolds intended standing for Parliament

Sir Joshua Reynolds used great quantities of snuff, and he would take it so freely when he was painting, that it frequently inconvenienced those sitters who were not addicted to it: so that by sneezing they much deranged their positions, and often totally destroyed expressions which might never return.

J. T. Smith, *Nollekens and His Times*

All his own geese are swans, as the swans of others are geese.

Horace Walpole, Letter to the Countess of Upper Ossory, December 1786

*See also* David Garrick, George Romney

## RHODES, CECIL JOHN

1853–1902 Imperialist

Some people like to have cows in their parks. I like to have people.

On himself, opening Groote Schuur to the public, in Cecil Headlam, *Milner Papers*

So little done, so much to do.

On himself, dying words, in J. G. McDonald, *Rhodes: A Life*

Africa possessed my bones.

On himself, in *ibid.*

He has grey curly hair and a face like a jubilee bonfire.

Lionel Curtis, *With Milner in South Africa*

Dreamer devout, by vision led / Beyond our guess or reach, / The travail of his spirit bred / Cities in place of speech. / So huge the all-mastering thought that drove – / So brief the term allowed – / Nations, not words he linked to prove / His faith before the crowd. /

Rudyard Kipling, *The Burial*

Too big to get through the gates of hell.

Olive Schreiner, in Elizabeth Pakenham, *Jameson's Raid*

I admire him, I frankly confess it; and when his time comes I shall buy a piece of the rope for a keepsake.

Mark Twain, *Following the Equator*

## RICE, SIR STEPHEN

1637–1715 Politician

'I will drive', he used to say, 'a coach and six through the Act of Settlement.'

T. B. Macaulay, *History of England*

## RICHARD I, COEUR DE LION

1157–99

Coeur-de-Lion was not a theatrical popinjay with greaves and steel-cap on it but a man living upon victuals.

Thomas Carlyle, *Past and Present*

The inadequacy of our insular method in popular history is perfectly shown in the treatment of Richard Coeur de Lion. His tale is told with the implication that his departure for the crusade was something like the escapade of a schoolboy running away to sea. It was, in this view, a pardonable or lovable prank; whereas in truth it was more like a responsible Englishman now going to the Front. Christendom was nearly one nation, and the Front was the Holy Land.

G. K. Chesterton, *A Short History of England*

Richard I was rather a knight-errant than a king. His history is more that of a Crusade than of a reign.

Sir James Mackintosh, *History of England*

He was the least English of all the kings of England; and the fact that he was and continued to be almost a stranger to the country which he was called upon to govern accounts for his initial mistakes. He came to England on 13 August 1189, and left it, after four months, on 12 December. He revisited it, when he was released from captivity, on 13 March 1194, and after a stay of two months returned to France where he spent the remainder of his life. These six months were all that he devoted to his kingdom in his ten years' reign. He used England as a bank on which to draw and overdraw in order to finance his ambitious exploits abroad . . . Twice in the course of four years England was called upon to furnish money on a wholly unprecedented scale: first for the crusade, and secondly for the king's ransom when he fell into the hands of the emperor on his return.

A. L. Poole, *From Domesday Book to Magna Carta*

## RICHARD II

1367–1400

On Saint Matthew's day [21 September], just two years after the beheading of the earl of Arundel, I, the writer of this history, was in the Tower, wherein King Richard was a prisoner, and I was present while he dined, and I marked his mood and bearing, having been taken thither for that very purpose by Sir William Beauchamp. And there and then the king discoursed sorrowfully in these words: 'My God! a wonderful land is this, and a fickle; which has exiled, slain, destroyed, or ruined so many kings, rulers, and great men, and is ever tainted and toileth with strife and variance and envy'; and then he recounted the histories and names of sufferers from the earliest habitation of the kingdom.

Adam of Usk, *Chronicle*, translated by A. R. Myers

The gallant boy of Smithfield became an early modern tyrant; neurotic, introspective and revengeful – so 'treacherous' said his enemies, that he was 'a disgrace to the whole realm.' Nor was he interested in campaigns in France. Artistic and extravagant – 'he kept the greatest port and maintained the most plentiful house that ever any King of England did'. He was also far too sensitive: brought back the body of his favourite, Robert de Vere, Earl of Oxford, who had been exiled in the

Low Countries; opened his coffin, contemplated his friend's face, stroked the fingers and adorned them with jewels before a splendid reburial.

John Bowle, *England, A Portrait*

. . . his reign is the first attempt of an English king to rule as an autocrat *on principle*, and as such it is a tragedy complete in itself. It has an artistic unity independent alike of earlier and later events, just because Richard II suddenly and violently tried to break with the *modus vivendi* of centuries. The modern notion of Divine Right can be traced back to Richard II and no further.

V. H. Galbraith, *A New Life of Richard II*

*Gaunt*: His rash fierce blaze of riot cannot last, / For violent fires soon burn out themselves. /

Shakespeare, *Richard II*, Act II, Scene i

A weak, vain, frivolous, and inconstant prince; without weight to balance the scales of government; without discernement to chuse a good ministry; without virtue to oppose the measures and advice of evil counsellors, even when they happened to clash with his own principles and opinion. He was a dupe to flattery, a slave to ostentation, and not more apt to give up his reason to the suggestion of sycophants and vitious ministers, than to sacrifice those ministers to his safety. He was idle, profuse, and profligate, and, though brave by starts, naturally pusillanimous and irresolute. His pride and resentment prompted him to cruelty and breach of faith: while his necessities obliged him to fleece his people, and degrade the dignity of his character and station.

Tobias Smollett, *The History of England from the Descent of Julius Caesar to the Treaty of Aix-la-Chapelle*

## RICHARD III

1452–85

Robespierre vindicating, in the midst of massacre, the existence of a God of mercy, is like our own Richard III issuing his Proclamation against Vice after the murder of his nephews. The sentiments professed by either may be admirable in themselves, but they only serve to deepen the general abhorrence of the character they contrast.

Lord Lytton, *The Reign of Terror*

Richarde the thirde sonne, of whom we nowe entreate, was in witte and courage egall with either of them, in bodye and prowesse farre vnder them bothe, little of stature, ill fetured of limmes, croke backed, his left shoulder much higher then his right, hard fauored of visage, and suche as in states called warlye, in other menne otherwise, he was malicious, wrathfull, enuious and, from afore his birth, euer frowarde . . . None euill captaine was hee in the warre, as to whiche his disposicion was more metely then for peace . . . He was close and secrete, a deepe dissimuler, lowlye of countenaunce, arrogant of heart, outwardly coumpinable where he inwardely hated, not letting to kisse whom he thoughte to kyll; dispitious and cruell, not for evill will alway, but ofter for ambicion, and either for the suretie or encrease of his estate. Frende and foo was muche what indifferent, where his aduantage grew, he spared no man's deathe, whose life withstode his purpose.

Sir Thomas More, *The Historie of Kyng Rycharde the Thirde*

The truth I take to have been this. Richard, who was slender and not tall, had one shoulder a little higher than the other: a defect, by the magnifying glasses of party, by distance of time and by the amplification of tradition, easily swelled to shocking deformity;

for falsehood itself generally pays so much respect to truth as to make it the basis of its superstructure.

Horace Walpole, *Historic Doubts on the Life and Reign of King Richard the Third*

## RICHARD, EARL OF CORNWALL

1209–72 King of the Romans

The archbishop of Cologne advised his brethren to choose some one rich enough to support the dignity, not strong enough to be feared by the electors: both requisites met in the Plantagenet Richard, earl of Cornwall, brother of the English Henry III. He received three, eventually four votes, came to Germany and was crowned at Aachen. But three of the electors, finding that the sums he had paid to them were smaller than those received by others, seceded in disgust, and chose Alfonso X of Castile, who, shrewder than his competitor, continued to watch the stars at Toledo, enjoying the splendours of his title while troubling himself about it no further than to issue now and then a proclamation.

James Bryce, *The Holy Roman Empire*

## RICHARDSON, SAMUEL

1689–1761 Novelist

*Erskine*: Surely, Sir, Richardson is very tedious.
*Johnson*: Why, Sir, if you were to read Richardson for the story, your impatience would be so much fretted, that you would hang yourself. But you must read him for the sentiment, and consider the story as only giving occasion to the sentiment.

James Boswell, *Life of Johnson*

I confess that it has cost, and still costs, my philosophy some exertion not to be vexed that I must admire, aye, greatly admire, Richardson. His mind is so very vile a mind, so cozy, hypocritical, praise-mad, canting, envious, concupiscent.

Samuel Taylor Coleridge, *Animae Poetae*

There is more knowledge of the heart in one letter of Richardson's than in all *Tom Jones*.

Samuel Johnson, in James Boswell, *Life of Johnson*

You think I love flattery, and so I do; but a little too much always disgusts me. That fellow Richardson, on the contrary, could not be contented to sail quietly down the stream of his reputation, without longing to taste the froth from every stroke of the oar.

Samuel Johnson, *Miscellanies*

I was such an old fool as to weep over *Clarissa Harlowe* like any milkmaid of sixteen over the *Ballad of the Ladies Fall*. To say truth, the first volume softened me by a near resemblance of my maiden days, but on the whole 'tis most miserable stuff... Yet the circumstances are so laid as to inspire tenderness, and I look upon this and *Pamela* to be two books that will do more general mischief than the works of Lord Rochester.

Lady Mary Wortley Montagu, Letter to Lady Bute, 1 March 1752

The follies of modern novel writing render it impossible for young people to understand the perfection of the human nature in his conception, and delicacy of finish in his dialogue, rendering all his greater scenes unsurpassable in their own manner of art. They belong to a time of the English language in which it could express with precision the most delicate phases of sentiment, necessarily now lost under American, Cockney, or scholastic slang.

John Ruskin, *Praeterita*

The works of Richardson . . . are pictures of high life as conceived by a bookseller, and romances as they would be spiritualized by a Methodist preacher.

Horace Walpole, Letter to Sir Horace Mann, 20 December 1764

*See also* Thomas Heywood

## RIDLEY, NICHOLAS

1500?–55 Bishop of London, Martyr

But Master Ridley by reason of the evil making of the fire unto him, because the wooden faggits were laid about the goss, and over high built, the fire burned first beneath, being kept down by the wood. Which when he felt, he desired them for Christs sake to let the fire come unto him, Which when his Brother in law heard, but he had not understood, intending to rid him out of his pain (for the which cause he gave attendance) as one in such sorrow, not well advised what he did, heaped faggots upon him, so that he clean covered him, which made the fire more vehement beneath, that it burned clean all his nether parts, before it once touched the upper, and that made him leap up and down under the faggots and often desire them to let the fire come unto him, saying: I cannot burn. Which indeed appeared well: for after his legs were consumed by reason of his struggling through the pain (whereof he had no release, but only his contentation in God) he showed that side toward us clean, shirt and all untouched with flame. Yet in all this torment he forgot not to call unto God still, having in his mouth, Lord have mercy upon me, intermingling his cry, let the fire come unto me, I cannot burn. In which pains he laboured till one of the standers by with his bill pulled off the Faggots above, and where he saw the fire flame up, he wrested himself unto that side. And when the flame touched the Gunpowder, he was seen stirr no more, but burned on the other side, falling down at Master *Latimers* feet.

John Foxe, *Acts and Monuments*

*See also* Hugh Latimer, Mary I

## RILEY, JAMES WHITCOMB

1849–1916 Poet

My work did itself. I'm only the willer bark through which the whistle comes.

On himself, in Stanley J. Kunitz and Howard Haycraft eds, *American Authors, 1600–1900*

His pathos is bathos, his sentiment sediment, his 'homely philosophy' brute platitudes – beasts of the field of thought.

Ambrose Bierce, in Paul Fatout, *Ambrose Bierce: The Devil's Lexicographer*

. . . the unctuous, over-cheerful, word-mouthing, flabby-faced citizen who condescendingly tells Providence, in flowery and well-rounded periods, where to get off.

Hewitt Howland, in Richard Crowder, *Those Innocent Years*

## ROBERTS, FREDERICK SLEIGH, FIRST EARL OF KANDAHAR, PRETORIA AND WATERFORD

1832–1914 Soldier

He says his prayers every night, and leaves the rest to God.

Lady Roberts, in J. L. Garvin, *Life of Joseph Chamberlain*

## ROBERTSON, PATRICK, LORD

1794–1855 Author

Here lies that peerless paper peer Lord Peter, / Who broke the laws of God and man and metre. /

Sir Walter Scott, *Epitaph*

## ROBINSON, EDWIN ARLINGTON

1869–1935 Poet

Always defeat – always failure: surely the theme of human failure, with all its variations and nuances, has been treated so exhaustively by no other poet as by Robinson. One would not have believed there were so many ways to fail.

T. K. Whipple, *Spokesmen*

## ROBINSON, SIR THOMAS

1700?–77 Civil Servant

Unlike my subject will I frame my song, / It shall be witty and it shan't be long. /

Lord Chesterfield, *Epigram*

## ROCHE, SIR BOYLE

1743–1807 Irish Politician

Every time he opens his mouth he puts his foot in it.

Anon., *circa* 1770

## ROCHESTER, EARL OF, *see under* WILMOT, JOHN

## ROCKEFELLER, JOHN DAVISON

1839–1937 Industrialist, Philanthropist

I believe the power to make money is a gift of God . . . to be developed and used to the best of our ability for the good of mankind. Having been endowed with the gift I possess, I believe it is my duty to make money and still more money, and to use the money I make for the good of my fellow man according to the dictates of my conscience.

On himself, in Matthew Josephson, *The Robber Barons*

I'm bound to be rich! *Bound to be rich!*

*Ibid.*

I had no ambition to make a fortune. Mere money-making has never been my goal. I had an ambition to build.

On himself, in Allan Nevins, *Study in Power: John D. Rockefeller*, vol. 1

I have ways of making money you know nothing of.

On himself, 1872, in Jules Abels, *The Rockefeller Millions*

Rockefeller's voice may not be the voice of God, but nevertheless it speaks the final word, for whoever opposes Rockefeller has lost before the battle starts.

Anon., in William H. Allen, *Rockefeller*

St John of the Rocks.

Anon., popular nickname, in *Life*, 6 July 1911

He is the father of trusts, the world's foremost pioneer centralizer of business machinery and power, the vaulting apostle and exemplar of business efficiency, the demonstrator-in-chief of cooperation's superiority over competition, – always for cooperators and frequently for consumers.

William H. Allen, *Rockefeller*

Rockefeller made his money in oil, which he discovered at the bottom of wells. Oil was crude in those days, but so was Rockefeller. Now both are considered quite refined.

Richard Armour, *It All Started With Columbus*

John D. Rockefeller can be fully described as a man made in the image of the ideal money maker . . . An ideal money-maker is a machine the details of which are diagrammed on the asbestos blueprints which paper the walls of hell.

Thomas Lawson, in Jules Abels, *The Rockefeller Millions*

While his subtle, ruminative, daring mind solved large problems by an acid process of thought, he presented to the world a front of silence which was like smooth steel.

Allen Nevins, *Study in Power: John D. Rockefeller*, vol. 1

## ROCKINGHAM, MARQUIS OF (CHARLES WATSON-WENTWORTH)

1730–82 Prime Minister

His virtues were his arts. In opposition he respected the principles of government; in administration he provided for the liberties of the people. He employed his moment of power in realizing everything which he had proposed in a popular situation – the distinguishing mark of his public conduct. Reserved in profession, sure in performance, he laid the foundation of a solid confidence.

Edmund Burke, *Epitaph on Rockingham*, carved on a monument at Wentworth Woodhouse

He could neither speak nor write with ease, and was handicapped by inexperience, boils, and a passion for Newmarket.

O. A. Sherard, *A Life of John Wilkes*

Rockingham himself was a high-minded man with that type of negative virtue which wealth and position make easy. In the midst of a corrupt generation he was too rich to accept a bribe and too unimaginative to offer one. In the midst of a loose people he preserved an admirably starchy disposition.

*Ibid.*

## ROGERS, SAMUEL

1763–1855 Poet

'They tell me I say ill-natured things,' he observed in his slow, quiet, deliberate way: 'I have a weak voice; if I did not say ill-natured things, no one would hear what I said.'

Henry Taylor, *Autobiography*

*See also* Lord Byron, Sir Walter Scott

## ROGERS, WILL (WILLIAM PENN ADAIR ROGERS)

1879–1935 Comedian

I don't make jokes; I just watch the government and report the facts.

On himself, in a syndicated column

My folks didn't come over on the *Mayflower*, but they were there to meet the boat.

*Ibid.*

Well, there was a move on foot for making fewer and worse pictures so they hired me.

On himself, in William Cahn, *A Pictorial History of the Great Comedians*

He is practically the only public figure I know who has kept his hair, his wife, and his sense of humor twenty-five years.

Marie Dressler, *My Own Story*

The bosom friend of senators and congressmen was about as daring as an early Shirley Temple movie.

James Thurber, in Joe McCarthy ed., *Fred Allen's Letters*

## ROLFE, FREDERICK, *see under* CORVO, BARON

## ROMNEY, GEORGE

1734–1802 Painter

Romney in the mean time shy, private, studious and contemplative; conscious of all the disadvantages and privations of a very stinted education; of a habit naturally hypochondriac, with aspen nerves, that every breath could ruffle, was at once in art the rival, and in nature the very contrast of Sir Joshua [Reynolds].

Richard Cumberland, *Memoirs*

Sir Joshua [Reynolds] disliked Romney so much that he would not even allude to him by name, but in after-years, when he had to refer to him, spoke of him as 'the man in Cavendish Square'.

Lord Ronald Gower, *Romney and Lawrence*

My more than father.

Lady Hamilton, 1791, in H. Gambin, *George Romney and His Art*

He is *par excellence*, a painter of handsome men and women, and the interpreter of a certain high-bred, aquiline sensibility of repression.

David Piper, *The English Face*

Romney, as a portrait painter, had the dispassionate eye of the camera in expert professional hands, who know that the instrument cannot lie but are not concerned in making it tell the truth.

E. Waterhouse, *Painting in Britain 1530–1790*

## ROOSEVELT, (ANNA) ELEANOR

1884–1962 Humanitarian

She ain't stuck up, she ain't dressed up, and she ain't afeared to talk.

Anon., 1933, in *Anna Eleanor Roosevelt: Memorial Addresses in the House of Representatives, Joint Committee on Printing*

A symbol of compassion in a world of increasing righteousness.

Henry Kissinger, in Joseph Lash, *Eleanor: the Years Alone*

Eleanor is a Trojan mare.

Alice Roosevelt Longworth, in James Brough, *Princess Alice*

No woman has ever so comforted the distressed or so distressed the comfortable.

Claire Booth Luce, in *Anna Eleanor Roosevelt: Memorial Addresses in the House of Representatives, Joint Committee on Printing*

There have been famous women known the world over for their profiles on coins or their images in light but the world knows Eleanor Roosevelt by heart.

Archibald MacLeish, in *ibid.*

Falsity withered in her presence Hypocrisy left the room.

Adlai Stevenson, Address at the Democratic National Convention, 1962

She would rather light a candle than curse the darkness, and her glow has warmed the world.

Adlai Stevenson, Address to the United Nations General Assembly, 9 November 1962

*See also* Franklin D. Roosevelt

## ROOSEVELT, FRANKLIN DELANO

1882–1945 Thirty-Second United States President

God has led the President by the hand for a long while, but even God gets tired sometimes.

Anon. clergyman, in *Spectator*, 5 February 1943

Roosevelt is my shepherd, I am in want. / He maketh me to lie down on park benches; / He leadeth me beside the still factories. / He disturbeth my soul: / He leadeth me in the Paths of destruction for his Party's sake. / Yea, though I walk through the valley of recession, / I anticipate no recovery / For he is with me; / His promises and pipe dreams they no longer fool me. /

He prepareth a reduction in my salary in the presence of my creditors; / He anointeth my small income with taxes; / Surely unemployment and poverty shall follow me all the days of the New Deal, / And I will dwell in a mortgaged house forever. /

Anon., in G. Wolfskill and J. A. Hudson, *All But the People: Franklin D. Roosevelt and his Critics, 1933–39*

It is a mystery to me how each morning he selects the few things he *can* do from the thousands he *should* do.

Anon., in W. E. Binkley, *The Man in the White House*

I'd rather be right than Roosevelt.

Heywood Broun, in Robert E. Drennan ed., *Wit's End*

Roosevelt had exploded one of the most popular myths in America . . . He had dissociated the concept of wealth from the concept of virtue.

James MacGregor Burns, *Roosevelt: The Lion and the Fox*

[A] chameleon on plaid.

Herbert Hoover, in James MacGregor Burns, *Roosevelt: The Lion and the Fox*

. . . the man who started more creations than were ever begun since Genesis – and finished none.

Hugh Johnson, 1937, in G. Wolfskill and J. A. Hudson, *All But the People: Franklin D. Roosevelt and his Critics, 1933–39*

He was the only person I ever knew – anywhere – who was never afraid. God, how he could take it for us all.

Lyndon Baines Johnson, in James MacGregor Burns, *Roosevelt: The Lion and the Fox*

. . . make no mistake, he is a force – a man of superior but impenetrable mind, but perfectly ruthless, a highly versatile mind which you cannot foresee.

Carl G. Jung, 1936, in Arthur M. Schlesinger Jr, 'Behind the Mask', in W. E. Leuchtenburg ed., *Franklin D. Roosevelt, A Profile*

I have always found Roosevelt an amusing fellow, but I would not employ him, except for reasons of personal friendship, as a geek in a common carnival.

Murray Kempton, in Victor Lasky, *J. F. K., The Man and the Myth*

Roosevelt is a Jeffersonian democrat, projected into the industrial age. Deeply religious, profoundly American, an aristocrat with that magnanimity of spirit which loathes cruelty and special privileges, he is less concerned with inferences from a system than with adaptation of intuitions.

Harold J. Laski, in *New Statesman and Nation*, 14 March 1942

He's so doggone smart that fust thing I know I'll be working fer him – and I ain't goin' to.

Huey Long, in Arthur Schlesinger, *The Politics of Upheaval*

. . . two-thirds mush and one-third Eleanor.

Alice Roosevelt Longworth, in G. Wolfskill and J. A. Hudson, *All But the People: Franklin D. Roosevelt and his Critics, 1933–39*

If he became convinced tomorrow that coming out for cannibalism would get him the votes he so sorely needs, he would begin fattening a missionary in the White House backyard come Wednesday.

H. L. Mencken, in W. E. Leuchtenburg ed., *Franklin D. Roosevelt, A Profile*

To look on his policies as the result of a unified plan . . . was to believe that the accumulation of stuffed snakes, baseball pictures, school flags, old tennis shoes, and the like in a boy's bedroom were the design of an interior decorator.

Raymond Morley, in James MacGregor Burns, *Roosevelt: The Lion and the Fox*

Mr Roosevelt did not carry out the Socialist platform, unless he carried it out on a stretcher.

Norman Thomas, in G. Wolfskill and J. A. Hudson, *All But the People: Franklin D. Roosevelt and his Critics, 1933–39*

He demonstrates that comprehensive new ideas can be taken up, tried out and made operative in general affairs without rigidity or dogma. He is continuously revolutionary in a new way without ever provoking a stark revolutionary crisis.

H. G. Wells, in Arthur M. Schlesinger Jr, 'Behind the Mask', in W. E. Leuchtenburg ed., *Franklin D. Roosevelt, A Profile*

Poetry, religion, and Franklin D. / The three abominations be. / Why mince words? I do not feel / Kindly toward the Nouveau Deal / Hopkins peddles quack elixir / Tugwell is a phony fixer / Another lapse / For Homo saps / Yahweh! /

E. B. White, in 'H. L. Mencken meets a Poet in the West Side YMCA', from *The Fox of Peapack and other Poems*

Roosevelt and I took office at the same time, only my company is running at a profit while his company is running at a loss.

Wendell Willkie, in Irving Stone, *They Also Ran*, referring to Willkie's becoming head of Commonwealth and Southern at the time Roosevelt was elected President

In the beginning, Franklin created the AAA and the NRA. And the NRA was without form, and void; and the Astor yacht was upon the face of the deep.

Howard Wolf, 'Greener Pastures', in G. Wolfskill and J. A. Hudson, *All But the People: Franklin D. Roosevelt and his Critics, 1933–39*

*See also* Norman Thomas, Harry S. Truman, Wendell Willkie

## ROOSEVELT, THEODORE

1858–1919 Twenty-Sixth United States President

The great virtue of my radicalism lies in the fact that I am perfectly ready, if necessary, to be radical on the conservative side.

On himself, to William Howard Taft, 4 September 1906

I am as strong as a bull moose and you can use me to the limit.

On himself, in a speech, 14 October 1912

I wish to preach, not the doctrine of ignoble ease, but the doctrine of the strenuous life.

On himself, Speech before the Hamilton Club of Chicago, 10 April 1899

There is a homely adage which runs, 'Speak softly and carry a big stick; you will go far'.

On himself, Speech at Minnesota State Fair, 2 September 1901

How I wish I wasn't a reformer, Oh Senator! But I suppose I must live up to my part, like the Negro minstrel who blacked himself all over!

On himself, Letter to Chauncey Depew, in Richard Hofstadter, *The American Political Tradition*

A smack of Lord Cromer, Jeff Davis a touch of him; / A little of Lincoln, but not very much of him; / Kitchener,

Bismarck and Germany's Will, / Jupiter, Chamberlain, Buffalo Bill. /
Anon., *Roosevelt!*

Nobody likes him now but the people.
Lord Bryce, in Lawrence F. Abbott ed., *The Letters of Archie Butt, Personal Aide to President Roosevelt*

Now look, that damned cowboy is President of the United States.
Mark Hanna, in a conversation with H. H. Kohlsaat, 16 September 1901

. . . he raises intelligence to the quick flash of intuition.
John Hay, in E. E. Morison, Introduction, *The Letters of Theodore Roosevelt*, vol. 5

Workingmen believed / He busted trusts, / And put his picture in their windows. / 'What he'd have done in France!' / They said. / Perhaps he would – / He could have died / Perhaps, / Though generals rarely die except in bed, / As he did finally. / And all the legends that he started in his life / Live on and prosper / Unhampered now by his existence. /
Ernest Hemingway, *T. Roosevelt*

. . . he was the master therapist of the middle classes.
Richard Hofstadter, *The American Political Tradition*

The Constitution rides behind / And Big Stick rides before, / Which is the rule of precedent / In the reign of Theodore. /
Wallace Irwin, *The Ballad of Grizzly Gulch*

When the stuffed prophets quarrel, when the sawdust / comes out, I think of Roosevelt's genuine sins. / Once more my rash love for that cinnamon bear, / *Begins!*
Vachel Lindsay, *Roosevelt*

Where is Roosevelt, the young dude cowboy, / Who hated Bryan, then aped his way? / Gone to join the shadows with mighty Cromwell / And tall King Saul, till the judgement day. /
Vachel Lindsay, *Bryan, Bryan, Bryan, Bryan*

The talk begins. / He's dressed in canvas khaki, flannel shirt, / Laced boots for farming, chopping trees, perhaps; / A stocky frame, curtains of skin on cheeks / Drained slightly of their fat; gash in the neck / Where pus was emptied lately; one eye dim, / And growing dimmer; almost blind in that. / And when he walks he rolls a little like / A man whose youth is fading, like a cart / That rolls when springs are old. He is a moose, / Scarred, battered from the hunters, thickets, stones; / Some finest tips of antlers broken off, / And eyes where images of ancient things / Flit back and forth across them, keeping still / A certain slumberous indifference / Or wisdom, it may be. /
Edgar Lee Masters, *At Sagamore Hill*

He hated all pretension save his own pretension.
H. L. Mencken, *Prejudices, Second Series*

No man, facing him in the heat of controversy, ever actually got a square deal. He took extravagant advantages; he played to the worst idiocies of the mob; he hit below the belt almost habitually. One never thinks of him as a duelist, say of the school of Disraeli, Palmerston and, to drop a bit, Blaine. One always thinks of him as a glorified bouncer engaged eternally in cleaning out barrooms – and not too proud to gouge when the inspiration came to him, or to bite in the clinches, or to oppose the relatively fragile brass knuckles of the code with chair legs, bung-starters, cuspidors, demijohns and ice picks.
*Ibid.*

Tempted sufficiently, he would sacrifice anything and everything to get applause. Thus the statesman was debauched by the politician and the philosopher was elbowed out of sight by the popinjay.

*Ibid.*

Theodore Roosevelt thought with his hips.

Lincoln Steffens, in James MacGregor Burns, *Roosevelt: The Lion and the Fox*

Roosevelt bit me and I went mad.

William Allen White, in Richard Hofstadter, *The American Political Tradition*

Teddy was reform in a derby, the gayest, cockiest, most fashionable derby you ever saw.

William Allen White, in Eric Goldman, *Rendezvous With Destiny*

Our hero is a man of peace, / Preparedness he implores; / His sword within his scabbard sleeps, / But mercy, how it snores. /

McLandburgh Wilson, in A. K. Adams, *The Home Book of Humorous Quotations*

*See also* William Howard Taft, Woodrow Wilson

## ROSEBERY, EARL OF (ARCHIBALD PHILIP PRIMROSE)

1847–1929 Prime Minister

I must plough my furrow alone. That is my fate, agreeable or the reverse; but before I get to the end of that furrow it is possible that I may find myself not alone.

On himself, Speech to the City Liberal Club, 19 July 1901

He failed to separate the awkward incidents of the hour from the long swing of events, which he so clearly understood. Toughness when nothing particular was happening was not the form of fortitude in which he excelled. He was unduly attracted by the dramatic, and by the pleasure of making a fine gesture.

Winston Churchill, *Great Contemporaries*

[He was] sometimes called 'Nature's Welfare State'. This is in reference to the fact that by marrying a Rothschild, being Prime Minister and winning the Derby, he demonstrated that it was possible to improve one's financial status and run the Empire without neglecting the study of form.

Claud Cockburn, *Aspects of English History*

He is subjective, personal, a harp responsive to every breeze that blows ... He passes quickly through the whole gamut of emotion ... He is a creature of moods and moments, and spiritually he often dies young.

A. G. Gardiner, *Prophets, Priests and Kings*

Without you the new Government would be ridiculous, with you it is only impossible.

Sir William Harcourt, Letter to Rosebery, August 1892

He is a one-eyed fellow in blinkers.

David Lloyd George, September 1932, in A. J. Sylvester, *Life with Lloyd George*

A dark horse in a loose box.

John Morley, in A. G. Gardiner, *Life of Sir William Harcourt*

[Gladstone's] successor is a poor creature who would be, if he could, like him & who, like him, would willingly sell England for power. But when he tries to roar like a lion, he only brays like an ass.

Sir Garnett Wolseley, Letter to the Duke of Cambridge, June 1896

## ROSSETTI, CHRISTINA GEORGINA

1830–94 Poet

Miss Christina was exactly the pure and docile-hearted damsel that her brother portrayed God's Virgin pre-elect to be.

William Holman-Hunt, *Pre-Raphaelitism and the Pre-Raphaelite Brotherhood*

I think she is the best poet alive . . . The worst of it is you cannot lecture on really pure poetry any more than you can talk about the ingredients of pure water – it is adulterated, methylated, sanded poetry that makes the best lectures. The only thing that Christina makes me want to do, is cry, not lecture.

Sir Walter Raleigh, in Virginia Woolf, *Second Common Reader*

Christina Rossetti is too little known, except by some of her moralistic verses; she had a most delicate command of rhythm, . . . a delicate sense of the sound of words, and a highly competent technical ability which never appeared laboured because of its simplicity . . . But it is her perspective of life that interests me most: sweet, small & narrow, delicate to the point of elusion.

Dylan Thomas, Letter to Pamela Hansford Johnson, 1933

*See also* Walter de la Mare, Marianne Moore

## ROSSETTI, DANTE GABRIEL

1828–82 Poet, Painter

*The Rossetti Exhibition.* I have been to see it and am pleased to find it more odious than I had even dared to hope.

Samuel Butler, *Notebooks*

I should say that Rossetti was a man without any principles at all, who earnestly desired to find some means of salvation along the lines of least resistance.

Ford Madox Ford, *Ancient Lights*

The writer's father once declared that D. G. Rossetti wrote the thoughts of Dante in the language of Shakespeare – to which this writer replied that Rossetti would have been better employed if he had written the thoughts of Rossetti in the language of Victoria.

Ford Madox Ford, *The March of Literature*

I do not want to overrate Rossetti. I can see plainly enough that his technical power as a poet was far superior to his skill of hand as a painter; his draughtsmanship sometimes leaves a good deal to be desired, and even his palette was not as rich as that of the great masters. But there was what one critic has well called the 're-birth of wonder' in all his work; to him the world was an enchanted place and his women were all heroines of the spirit.

Frank Harris, *My Life and Loves*

Rossetti, dear Rossetti / I love your work, / but you were really / a bit of a jerk. /

George MacBeth, *Pictures from an Exhibition*

He was the only one of our modern painters who taught disciples for love of them. He was not really an Englishman, but a great Italian tormented in the Inferno of London; doing the best he could, and teaching the best he could; but the 'could' shortened by the strength of his animal passions, without any trained control, or guiding faith.

John Ruskin, *Praeterita*

Mr Rossetti threw more than half his strength into literature, and in that precise measure, left himself unequal to his appointed task in painting.

John Ruskin, *On the Old Road*

A prince among parasites.
James McNeill Whistler, in Joseph and Elizabeth Robins Pennell, *The Whistler Journal*

## ROTHSCHILD, SIR NATHAN MEYER, BARON ROTHSCHILD OF TRING

1840–1915 Banker, Philanthropist

I've got to keep breathing: it'll be my worst business mistake if I don't.
On himself, comment on the financial disruptions of war, 1915, in Frederic Morton, *The Rothschilds*

I go to the bank every morning and when I say 'no' I return home at night without a worry. But when I say 'yes' it's like putting your finger into a machine – the whirring wheels may drag your whole body in after the finger.
On himself, in Virginia Cowles, *The Rothschilds: A Family of Fortune*

Is Lord Rothschild the dictator of this country? Are we really to have all the ways of reform, financial and social, blocked simply by a notice board: 'No thoroughfare. By order of Nathaniel Rothschild'.
David Lloyd George, defending his Budget taxation plans against opposition, 1909

## ROWE, NICHOLAS

1674–1718 Poet Laureate, Dramatist

A Gentleman, who lov'd to lie in Bed all Day for his Ease, and to sit up all Night for his Pleasure.
John Dennis, *Original Letters*

The genius of Rowe was slow and timid, and loved the ground.
William Hazlitt, 'The Fair Penitent', in *Examiner*, 10 March 1816

## ROWLANDSON, THOMAS

1756–1827 Painter, Caricaturist

He burlesqued even the burlesque.
H. Angelo, *Reminiscences*

The latter once gave offence, by carrying a pea-shooter into the life-academy, and, whilst old Moser was adjusting the female model, and had just directed her contour, Rowlandson let fly a pea, which making her start, she threw herself entirely out of position, and interrupted the gravity of the study for the whole evening. For this offence, Master Rowlandson went near to getting himself expelled.
*Ibid.*

To think of Regency England is to think in terms of Rowlandson.
M. Hardie, *Water-Colour Painting in Britain*

Rowlandson had more feeling for individual comic incident than for an artistic or intellectual whole; his larger compositions, complex and skilful though they often are, seem very often to be imposed upon the material rather than a truly organic growth from the nature of the subject-matter.
John Hayes, *Rowlandson: Watercolours and Drawings*

## RUNYON, (ALFRED) DAMON

1884–1946 Author

. . . hired Hessian at the Typewriter.
On himself, in Edwin P. Hoyt, *A Gentleman of Broadway*

He lived, by preference, amid the tinsel and the glaring lights of midnight, the sheen of asphalt in the rainy blackness, and the wistful crackling of discarded want-ads that curled around his legs in the biting winds of January.
Edwin P. Hoyt, *ibid.*

## RUPERT, PRINCE, COUNT PALATINE OF THE RHINE

1619–82 Soldier

. . . the last Elizabethan, and the firs Whig.

John Buchan, Lord Tweedsmuir, Preface to George Edinger, *Rupert of the Rhine*

A man who hath had his hand very deep in the blood of many innocent men.

Oliver Cromwell, Letter to David Lesley, 14 August 1650

He was the last knight errant; he was the first liberal politician.

George Edinger, *Rupert of the Rhine*

The Prince was rough, and passionate, and loved not debate, liked what was proposed, as he liked the persons who proposed it.

Edward Hyde, Earl of Clarendon, *History of the Rebellion*

Rupert that knew not fear, but health did want, / Kept state, suspended in a *chaise-volante*; / All save his head shut in that wooden case, / He show'd but like a broken weatherglass; / But arm'd in a whole lion cap-a-chin / Did represent the Hercules within. / Dear shall the Dutch his twinging anguish know / And feel what valour whet with pain can do. /

Andrew Marvell, *Second Advice to a Painter*

## RUSH, BENJAMIN

1745–1813 Physician, Revolutionary

*Bleeding Puff. – From the New-York Paper.* – 'This day there is to be a meeting of the trustees of Columbia College. The object of their meeting is to invite Dr Benjamin Rush to a professorship of the practice of physic in Columbia College. A correspondent is happy in remarking, that there are few obstacles in a choice which must result in so many advantages to Columbia College. *He is a man born to be useful to society*'.

And so is a *musquito*, a *horse-leech*, a *ferret*, a *pole cat*, a *weazel*: for these are all bleeders, and understand their business full as well as Doctor Rush does his.

William Cobbett, *Peter Porcupine's Works*

## RUSKIN, JOHN

1819–1900 Author

Yesterday, I came on a poor little child lying flat on the pavement in Bologna – sleeping like a corpse – possibly from too little food. I pulled up immediately – not in pity, but in *delight* at the folds of its poor little ragged chemise over the thin bosom – and gave the mother money – not in charity, but to keep the flies off it while I made a sketch. I don't see how this is to be avoided, but it is very hardening.

On himself, Letter to his Parents, 1845

For myself, I am never satisfied that I have handled a subject properly till I have contradicted myself at least three times.

On himself, Inaugural Address at the Cambridge School of Art, 1858

The Doctors say it was overwork and worry, which is partly true, and partly not. *Mere* overwork or worry might have soon ended me, but it would not have driven me crazy. I went crazy about St Ursula and the other saints, – chiefly young-lady saints.

On himself, Letter to Charles Eliot Norton, July 1878

I takes and paints, / Hears no complaints, / And sells before I'm dry; / Till savage Ruskin / He sticks his tusk in, / Then nobody will buy. /

Anon., 'Poem by a Perfectly Furious Academician', in *Punch*

A bottle of beautiful soda-water.

Thomas Carlyle, Letter to John Carlyle, 27 November 1855

He is a chartered libertine – he has possessed himself by prescription of the function of a general scold.

Henry James, 'On Whistler and Ruskin', in *Nation*, 19 December 1878

Leave to squeamish Ruskin / Popish Apennines, / Dirty stones of Venice / And his gas-lamps seven; / We've the stones of Snowdon / And the lamps of heaven. /

Charles Kingsley, *Letter to Thomas Hughes*

. . . rising up & down on his toes, after his manner, with his hands in his tail-pockets, and finally jaunting downstairs in the same springy fashion, with the prim smile of Sir Oracle upon his dry lips.

Alfred Munby, Diary, 8 November 1860

The bulk of Ruskin's writing is not invalidated because of his attack on Whistler. A certain girlish petulance of style that distinguished Ruskin was not altogether a defect. It served to irritate and fix attention, where a more evenly judicial writer might have remained unread.

W. R. Sickert, 'The Spirit of the Hive', in *New Age*, 26 May 1910

What greater sarcasm can Mr Ruskin pass upon than that he preaches to young men what he cannot perform! Why, unsatisfied with his own conscious power, should he choose to become the type of incompetence by talking for forty years of what he has never done!

James McNeill Whistler, *Whistler v Ruskin: Art and Art Critics*

We are told that Mr Ruskin has devoted his long life to art, and as a result is 'Slade Professor' at Oxford. In the same sentence we have thus his position and its worth. It suffices not, Messieurs! A life passed among pictures does not make a painter – else the policeman in the National Gallery might assert himself. As well allege that he who lives in a library must needs die a poet. Let not Mr Ruskin flatter himself that more education makes the difference between himself and the policeman both standing gazing in the gallery.

James McNeill Whistler, *The Gentle Art of Making Enemies*

There is hardly a page of his writings which can be properly apprehended until it is collated with the condition of his mind and the circumstances of his life not only at the general period within which the book falls, but on the actual day on which that particular page was written.

R. H. Wilenski, *John Ruskin*

The mind of Ruskin, endowed with every gift except the gift to organize the others, was more tumultuous than the tumult in which it was involved. The deceptive lucidity of his intoxicating style displayed, or concealed, an intellect as profound, penetrating, and subtle as any that England has seen; and as fanciful, as glancing, and as wayward as the mind of a child.

G. M. Young, *Victorian England*

## RUSSELL, BERTRAND ARTHUR WILLIAM, THIRD EARL

1872–1970 Philosopher

I can only say that, while my own opinions as to ethics do not satisfy me, other people's satisfy me still less.

On himself, *Reply to My Critics*

I like mathematics because it is *not* human & has nothing particular to do with this planet or with the whole accidental universe – because, like

Spinoza's God, it won't love us in return.

On himself, Letter to Lady Ottoline Morrell, March 1912

Here I have not a care in the world: the rest to nerves and will is heavenly. One is free from the torturing question: What more might I be doing? Is there any effective action that I haven't thought of? Have I a right to let the whole thing go and return to philosophy? Here I have to let the whole thing go, which is far more restful than choosing to let it go and doubting if one's choice is justified. Prison has some of the advantages of the Catholic Church.

On himself, Letter from prison to Frank Russell, May 1918

I'm as drunk as a Lord, but then I am one, so what does it matter?

On himself, in Ralph Schoenmann ed., *Bertrand Russell, Philosopher of the Century*

I have a certain hesitation in starting my biography too soon for fear of something important having not yet happened. Suppose I should end my days as President of Mexico; the biography would seem incomplete if it did not mention this fact.

On himself, Letter to Stanley Unwin, November 1930

At the age of eleven, I began Euclid, with my brother as my tutor. This was one of the great events of my life, as dazzling as first love. I had not imagined that there was anything so delicious in the world. After I had learned the fifth proposition, my brother told me that it was generally considered difficult, but I found no difficulty whatever. This was the first time it had dawned upon me that I might have some intelligence.

On himself, *Autobiography*

I have always thought respectable people scoundrels and I look anxiously at my face every morning for signs of my becoming a scoundrel.

On himself, in Alan Wood, *The Passionate Sceptic*

Although we may oppose the plan / Of giving womenfolk a vote, / Still to the ordinary man / Few things are more engaging than / The Russell of the Petticoat. /

Anon., *circa* 1907, during Russell's campaign for Women's Suffrage

Said Lord Russell to Lady Cecilia, / I certainly wish I could feel ya, / Your data excite me, / It would surely delight me / To sense your unsensed sensibilia. /

Anon., contemporary, in Ronald W. Clark, *Life of Bertrand Russell*

The Ass in the Lion's Skin and the Wolf in Sheep's Clothing represent familiar human types, but we have no image for the traitor who pretends to be a Mugwump.

Undated War Office article of Summer 1916

I believe that it can be shown that all Russell's philosophy has been based on this quest for reassurance. It is sceptical in the sense that it questions all claims, but it also tries to find a solid base for them. The reason why Russell was always attempting to reduce things was to give fewer hostages to fortune.

A. J. Ayer, in Bryan Magee, *Modern British Philosophy*

Hither flock all the crowd whom love has wrecked / Of intellectuals without intellect / And sexless folk whose sexes intersect: / All who in Russell's burly frame admire / The 'lineaments of gratified desire', / And of despair have baulked the yawning precipice / By swotting up his melancholy recipes / For 'happiness' – of which he is the cook / And knows the weight, the flavour, and the look, / Just how much self-control you have to spice it with: / How to 'rechauffe' the stock-pot of desire / Although the devil pisses on the fire: / How much long-suffering and how much bonhomie / You must stir up, with patience and economy, / To get it right . . . /

Roy Campbell, *The Georgiad*

Meeting [D. H.] Lawrence, I told him how enchanted I had been by the lucidity, the suppleness and pliability of Bertrand Russell's mind. He sniffed. 'Have you seen him in a bathing-dress?' he asked. 'Poor Bertie Russell! He is all Disembodied Mind.'

William Gerhardie, *Memoirs of a Polyglot*

He is not a philosopher in the accepted meaning of the word; not a lover of wisdom; not a searcher after wisdom; not an explorer of that universal science which aims at the explanation of all phenomena of the universe by ultimate causes; that in the opinion of your deponent and multitudes of other persons he is a sophist; practices sophism; that by cunning contrivances, tricks and devices and by mere quibbling, he puts forth fallacious arguments and arguments that are not supported by sound reasoning; and he draws inferences which are not justly deduced from a sound premise; that all his alleged doctrines which he calls philosophy are just cheap, tawdry, worn out, patched up fetishes and propositions, devised for the purpose of misleading the people.

Joseph Goldstein, prosecuting counsel, in the New York court case against Russell, 1940

If I were the Prince of Peace, I would choose a less provocative Ambassador.

A. E. Housman, in Alan Wood, *Bertrand Russell, The Passionate Sceptic*

The enemy of all mankind, you are, full of the lust of enmity. It is *not* the hatred of falsehood which inspires you. It is the hatred of people, of flesh and blood. It is a perverted, mental blood-lust. Why don't you own it?

D. H. Lawrence, Letter to Bertrand Russell, September 1915

What ails Russell is, in matters of life and emotion, the inexperience of youth. He is, vitally, emotionally, much too inexperienced in personal contact and conflict, for a man of his age and calibre. It isn't that life has been too much for him, but too little.

D. H. Lawrence, Letter to Lady Ottoline Morrell, 1915

Lord Russell explained that he had two models for his own style – Milton's prose and Baedeker's guide-books. The Puritan never wrote without passion, he said, and the cicerone used only a few words in recommending sights, hotels, and restaurants. Passion was the voice of reason, economy the signature of brilliance.

Ved Mehta, *Fly and the Fly-Bottle*

He only feels life through his brain, or through sex, and there is a gulf between these two separate departments.

Lady Ottoline Morrell, in Robert Gathorne-Hardy, *Ottoline at Garsington*

It's not just a question of clarity, it's a question of professional ethics.

Karl Popper, commending Russell's style, in Bryan Magee ed., *Modern British Philosophy*

Russell thought one ought to know a lot about, say, the rods and cones in the eye, and I don't pretend to know anything about them, and, if I may speak a bit rudely, I don't want to.

Gilbert Ryle, in *ibid.*

His writings were most pessimistic, but he himself always appeared in the best of spirits – a feature which I had also noticed in pessimists on frontier expeditions. Apparently the way to really enjoy oneself is to be full of dark forebodings and expect the worst; then if the worst actually happens it is only what one had expected, and if anything less than the worst occurs one can be in uproarious good-humour.

Sir Francis Younghusband, *The Light of Experience*

*See also* Ludwig Wittgenstein

## RUSSELL, JOHN, FIRST EARL

1792–1878 Prime Minister

Finality Jack.

Nickname, derived from his view that the 1832 Reform Bill represented the fullest extent of the Franchise

The foreign policy of the Noble Earl... may be summed up in two truly expressive words, 'meddle' and 'muddle'.

Lord Derby, Speech in the House of Lords, February 1864

If a traveller were informed that such a man was leader of the House of Commons, he may well begin to comprehend how the Egyptians worshipped an insect.

Benjamin Disraeli, attributed

He has risen with adversity. He seemed below par as a leader in 1835, when he had a clear majority, and the ball nearly at his feet: in each successive year the strength of his Government has fallen and his own has risen.

William Ewart Gladstone, 1841, in A. Wyatt Tilby, *Lord John Russell*

How formed to lead, if not too proud to please! / His fame would fire you, but his manners freeze. / Like or dislike, he does not care a jot; / He wants your vote, but your affections not; / Yet human hearts need sun as well as oats – / So cold a climate plays the deuce with votes. /

Lord Lytton, in G. W. E. Russell, *Collections and Recollections*

So much for these statesmen of ours – they always remind me of what Southey said to me at Keswick; pointing in a little Bible-book for children, in size and shape an inch cube, to a woodcut of Samson with a gate on his back about twenty times his own size, he said, 'That is Lord John Russell carrying away the British Constitution'; and sure enough that is about the proportion between the men and the work they have in hand.

John Stuart Mill, Letter to John Sterling, July 1833

The people along the [Devonshire] road were very much disappointed by his smallness. I told them he was much larger before the [Reform] bill was thrown out, but was reduced by excessive anxiety about the people. This brought tears into their eyes.

Sydney Smith, in Lady Holland, *Memoirs of Sydney Smith*

Johnny has upset the coach.

Lord Stanley, Note passed to Sir James Graham in the House of Commons on Russell's speech to the House on Irish Disestablishment, 1834

*See also* Queen Victoria

## RUTHERFORD, ERNEST, BARON RUTHERFORD OF NELSON AND CAMBRIDGE

1871–1937 Physicist

As I was standing in the drawing-room at Trinity, a *clergyman* came in. And I said to him: 'I'm Lord Rutherford'. And he said to me, 'I'm the Archbishop of York'. And I don't suppose either of us believed the other.

On himself, in C. P. Snow, *Variety of Men*

I went to no more lectures, except to Rutherford, whom I could not resist. He would boom on, talking about all kinds of interesting things, occasionally producing gems like 'integral *y. dx*; *dx* is small, we will neglect this'. He talked so easily and informally, he knew it all in an instinctive, relaxed way and the answer always somehow came out right. As someone said: 'The $\alpha$ particles were his friends, he knew what they would do' (there was a story, which I have not verified, that in one of his early papers the mass of an $\alpha$ particle came out as 3.3 on which he commented: 'we take four as the nearest integer').

Sir Edward Bullard, in *Nature*, 30 August 1974

On the occasion of one of his discoveries, the writer said to him: 'You are a lucky man, Rutherford, always on the crest of the wave!' To which he laughingly replied, 'Well! I made the wave, didn't I?' and he added soberly, 'At least to some extent.'

A. S. Eve and J. Chadwick, in *Obituary Notices of Fellows of the Royal Society*

The difficulty is to separate the inner man from the Rutherfordiana, much of which is quite genuine. From behind a screen in a Cambridge tailor's, a friend and I heard a reverberating voice; 'That shirt's too tight round the neck. Every day I grow in girth. *And* in mentality.'

C. P. Snow, *Variety of Men*

His estimate of his own powers was realistic, but if it erred at all, it did not err on the modest side. 'There is no room for this particle in the atom as designed by *me*,' I once heard him assure a large audience. It was part of his nature that, stupendous as his work was, he should consider it ten per cent more so.

*Ibid.*

# 'S'

## SACCO, NICOLA, *and* VANZETTI, BARTOLOMEO

1891–1927 and 1888–1927 Anarchists

Never in our full life could we hope to do such work for tolerance, for justice, for man's understanding of men as now we do by accident . . . The last moment belongs to us – that agony is our triumph.

Bartolomeo Vanzetti, Statement to judge preparing to deliver death sentence, in Eugene Lyons, *The Life and Death of Sacco and Vanzetti*

## SACKVILLE, VISCOUNT (LORD GEORGE GERMAIN)

1716–85 Soldier, Statesman

Sackvilles alone anticipate defeat, / And ere they dare the battle, sound retreat. /

Charles Churchill, *The Candidate*

As those rare acts which Honour taught / Our daring sons where Granby fought, / Or those which, with superior skill, / SACKVILLE achiev'd by standing still. /

Charles Churchill, *The Ghost*

Fear and self-interest were the motives that led men to acquiesce to his political power. He had long since demonstrated that those who opposed him were likely to suffer for it; that he could be unforgiving to men who stood in his way, and revengeful to those who openly opposed him. If he could not break a man, he could damage his reputation by the subtle arts of organized insinuation.

Alan Valentine, *Lord George Germain*

## SACKVILLE-WEST, VICTORIA MARY (VITA)

1892–1962 Novelist, Poet

Viti is not a person one can take for granted. She is a dark river moving deeply in shadows. She really does not care for the domestic affections. She would wish life to be conducted on a series of *grandes passions*. Or she thinks she would. In practice, had I been a passionate man, I should have suffered tortures of jealousy on her behalf, have made endless scenes, and we should now have separated, I living in Montevideo as H.M. Minister and she breeding Samoyeds in the Gobi desert.

Harold Nicolson, Diary, 24 December 1933

## ST JOHN, HENRY, *see under* BOLINGBROKE, VISCOUNT

## SALISBURY, THIRD MARQUIS OF (ROBERT ARTHUR TALBOT GASCOYNE CECIL)

1830–1903 Prime Minister

. . . If the Conservatives abandoned the principles for which I joined them, I should walk for the last time down the steps of the Carlton Club without casting a glance of regret behind me.

On himself, in Lord David Cecil, *The Cecils of Hatfield House*

. . . when he came . . . to explain in dulcet tones the entire fulfilment of the treaty of Berlin, he shone like the peaceful evening star. But sometimes he is like the red planet Mars, and occasionally he flames in the midnight sky, not only perplexing nations but perplexing his own nearest friends and followers.

The Duke of Argyll, speaking in the House of Lords, May 1879

. . . that strange powerful inscrutable and brilliant obstructive deadweight at the top.

Lord Curzon, in Lord David Cecil, *The Cecils of Hatfield House*

He is a great master of gibes and flouts and jeers.

Benjamin Disraeli, to the House of Commons, 5 August 1874

Sal. seems most prejudiced and not to be aware that his principal object in being sent to Const[antinople] is to keep the Russians out of Turkey, not to create an ideal existence for Turkish Xtians. He is more Russian than Ignatyev: *plus Arabe que l'Arabie*!

Benjamin Disraeli, Letter to Lord Derby, 28 December 1876

I am always very glad when Lord Salisbury makes a great speech . . . It is sure to contain at least one blazing indiscretion which it is a delight to remember.

A. E. Parker, Earl of Morley, Speech at Hull, 25 November 1887

I have a few glass cases in which I put those people who by their excellence deserve them. Now take Lord Salisbury. I have a fine glass case for him. As a statesman he stands alone. There is no-one who can fairly be compared with him. He is always reliable, always good; and therefore I have made a glass case for him.

Cecil Rhodes, in Philip Jourdan, *Cecil Rhodes: His Private Life*

My greatest Prime Minister.

Queen Victoria, in Lord David Cecil, *The Cecils of Hatfield House*

## SANDBURG, CARL

1878–1967 Author

Here is the difference between Dante, Milton, and me. They wrote about hell and never saw the place. I wrote about Chicago after looking the town over for years and years.

On himself, in Harry Golden, *Carl Sandburg*

. . . a pacifist between wars.

Robert Frost, in *ibid.*

On the day that God made Carl He didn't do anything else that day but sit around and feel good.

Edward Steichen, in *ibid.*

Under close scrutiny Sandburg's verse reminds us of the blobs of living jelly or plankton brought up by deep-sea dredging; it is a kind of protoplasmic poetry, lacking higher organization.

George F. Whicher, 'The Twentieth Century', in Arthur Hobson Quinn ed., *The Literature of the American People*

. . . there are moments when one is tempted to feel that the cruellest thing that has happened to Lincoln since he was shot by Booth has been to fall into the hands of Carl Sandburg.

Edmund Wilson, in Gay Wilson Allen, *Carl Sandburg*

## SANDWICH, EARL OF (JOHN MONTAGU)

1718–92 Statesman

Consult his person, dress, and air, / He seems, which strangers well might swear, / The master, or, by courtesy, / The captain of a colliery. / Look at his visage, and agree / Half-hang'd he seems, just from the tree / Escaped; a rope may sometimes break, / Or men be cut down by mistake. /

Charles Churchill, *The Duellist*

To run a horse, to make a match, / To revel deep, to roar a catch, / To knock a tottering watchman down, / To sweat a woman of the town; / By fits to keep the peace, or break it, / In turn to give a pox, or take it; / He is, in faith, most excellent, / And, in the world's most full intent, / A true choice spirit, we admit; / With wits a fool, with fools a wit. /

*Ibid.*

Sandwich had a predilection to guilt, if he could couple it with artifice and treachery.

Horace Walpole, *Memoirs*

## SARGENT, JOHN SINGER

1856–1925 Artist

Every time I paint a portrait I lose a friend.

On himself, attributed

It is positively dangerous to sit to Sargent. It is taking your face in your hands.

Anon., to W. Graham Robertson, in Richard Ormond, *John Singer Sargent*

His advice to a fellow-painter was: 'Begin with Frans Hals, copy and study Frans Hals, after that go to Madrid and copy Velasquez, leave Velasquez, till you have got all you can out of Frans Hals'.

Harold Acton, *The Memoirs of an Aesthete*

Sargent's portrait of Henry James is nearly finished, and I hear is a masterpiece. There is a plaid waistcoat in it, heaving like a sea in storm, which is said to be prodigious.

Edmund Gosse, Letter to Thomas Hardy, 1913

John is very stiff, a sort of completely accentless mongrel, not at all like Curtis or Newman; rather French, faubourg sort of manners. Ugly, not at all changed in feature, except for a beard. He was very shy, having I suppose a vague sense that there were poets about.

Vernon Lee (Violet Paget), in Richard Ormond, *John Singer Sargent*

Sargent used frequently to halt his painting to rest his sitters by playing to them. Dr Playfair's maid once commented of his practice: 'Isn't it nice that Mr Sargent feels like painting when he tires of playing the piano.'

David McKibbin, *Sargent's Boston*

While painting, he rushed bull-like at his canvas, spluttering and gasping, and muttering imprecations and incantations to himself in the throes of creation. 'Demons!', repeated several times, was his favourite expression.

Richard Ormond, *John Singer Sargent*

An American, born in Italy, educated in France, who looks like a German, speaks like an Englishman, and paints like a Spaniard.

William Starkweather, 'The Art of John S. Sargent', in *Mentor*, October 1924

A sepulchre of dulness and propriety.

James McNeill Whistler, in Richard Ormond, *John Singer Sargent*

*See also* William Butler Yeats

## SARGENT, SIR MALCOLM

1895–1967 Conductor

I spend up to six hours a day waving my arms about and if everyone else did the same they would stay much healthier.

On himself, in Leslie Ayre, *The Wit of Music*

After one of my concerts, a critic wrote that I had given a 'perfunctory' performance of a certain work . . . I was annoyed about it and pointed out that, whereas he was entitled to give an opinion about my performance, to say that it was 'perfunctory' was to suggest that I had not given proper attention to the job I was paid to do.

Some time later the same critic wrote

a notice of another of my concerts. He began, 'If one did not know that Malcolm Sargent takes meticulous care over the preparation of his concerts, one might have thought that this was a perfunctory performance –'

There was nothing else for it. We became friends and remained so through the years.

On himself, in Leslie Ayre, *The Proms*

'What do you have to know to play the cymbals?' someone asked Sir Malcolm Sargent. 'Nothing,' was the reply. 'Just when.'

Leslie Ayre, *The Wit of Music*

You have only to see the eyes of a choral society screwing into him like a thousand gimlets to know what he means to them . . . He plays upon their imaginations and minds like a mesmerist.

Bernard Shore, *The Orchestra Speaks*

## SASSOON, SIEGFRIED LORRAINE

1886–1967 Author

A booby-trapped idealist.

On himself, *Siegfried's Journey*

## SAVAGE, RICHARD

– d. 1743 Poet

Hack, spendthrift, starveling, duellist in turn; / Too cross to cherish yet too fierce to spurn; / Begrimed with ink or brave with wine and blood; / Spirit of fire and manikin of mud; / Now shining clear, now fain to starve and skulk; / Star of the cellar, pensioner of the bulk; / At once the child of passion and the slave; / Brawling his way to an unhonoured grave – / That was DICK SAVAGE. /

W. E. Henley, *Hawthorn and Lavender*

There are no proper judges of his conduct who have slumbered away their time on the down of plenty, nor will any wise man presume to say, 'Had I been in Savage's condition, I should have lived or written better than Savage.'

Samuel Johnson, *Lives of the Poets*

## SAVILE, GEORGE, MARQUIS OF HALIFAX

1633–95 Author, Politician

When he talked to me as a philosopher of his contempt for the world, I asked him, what he meant by getting so many new titles, which I call'd the hanging himself about with bells and tinsel. He had no other excuse for it, but this, that, since the world were such fools as to value those matters, a man must be a fool for company: He considered them but as rattles: Yet rattles please children: So these might be of use to his family.

Gilbert Burnet, *History of My Own Times*

Jotham of pregnant wit and piercing thought, / Endowed by nature, and by learning taught /To move Assemblies, but who only tried / The worse awhile, then chose the better side; / Nor chose alone, but turned the balance too; / So much the weight of one brave man can do. /

John Dryden, *Absalom and Achitophel*

This man, who possessed the finest genius and most extensive capacity of all employed in public affairs during the present reign, affected a species of neutrality between the parties, and was esteemed the head of that small body known as Trimmers. This conduct, which is more natural to men of integrity than of ambition, could not, however, procure him the former character, and he was always, with reason, regarded as an intriguer rather than a patriot.

David Hume, *History of England*

He passed from faction to faction. But instead of adopting and inflaming the passions of those whom he joined, he tried to diffuse amongst them something of the spirit of those whom he had just left.

T. B. Macaulay, *Essays*: 'Sir William Temple'

The party to which he at any moment belonged was the party which, at that moment, he liked least, because it was the party of which, at that moment, he had the nearest view. He was therefore always severe upon his violent associates, and was always in friendly relations with his moderate opponents.

T. B. Macaulay, *History of England*

## SCOTT, CHARLES PRESTWICH

1846–1932 Editor of *Guardian*

He makes righteousness readable.

James Bone, attributed

## SCOTT, SIR GEORGE GILBERT

1811–78 Architect

Gilbert Scott was the supreme model of a Samuel Smiles self-made man . . . with all the vigour and all the lack of subtlety that one would expect.

R. Furneaux-Jordan, *Victorian Architecture*

It must have seemed so easy in his day to be a Gothic architect, and he should have proved to us that it was impossible. In this way he was a teacher if we would learn.

W. R. Lethaby, *Philip Webb and His Work*

It is always tempting to choose an individual or two in order to epitomise a movement or an age, and in the case of Sir George Scott the temptation is irresistible. For not only was he the leading architect of the Gothic Revival in its respectable phase, but also he seems completely representative of what we have come to consider the Victorian character. His religion was not romantic in the Pugin manner; his self-assurance was, on the surface at least, colossal; his instinct for combining financial success with a rather smug morality seems to be the very essence of his time; and his enormous output of bad and indifferent architecture reflects that Victorian philistinism that sprang from the moralisation of art.

R. Turnor, *Nineteenth Century Architecture in Britain*

## SCOTT, JAMES FITZROY, *see under* MONMOUTH, DUKE OF

## SCOTT, JOHN, *see under* ELDON, EARL OF

## SCOTT, ROBERT FALCON

1868–1912 Antarctic Explorer

. . . For my own sake I do not regret this journey, which has shewn that Englishmen can endure hardships, help one another, and meet death with as great a fortitude as ever in the past. We took risks, we knew we took them; things have come out against us, and therefore we have no cause for complaint, but bow to the will of Providence, determined still to do our best to the last.

On himself, 'Message to the Public', written shortly before his death, March 1912

## SCOTT, SIR WALTER

1771–1832 Author

Scott became the historiographer-royal of feudalisms.

Matthew Arnold, *Essays in Criticism*: 'Heinrich Heine'

Walter Scott has no business to write novels, especially good ones. – It is not fair. – He has Fame and Profit enough as a Poet, and should not be taking the bread out of other people's mouths. – I do not like him, & do not mean to like *Waverley* if I can help it – but fear I must.

Jane Austen, Letter to Anna Austen, 28 September 1814

And think'st thou, Scott! by vain conceit perchance, / On public taste to foist thy stale romance / Though Murray with his Miller may combine / To yield thy muse just half-a-crown per line? / No! when the sons of song descend to trade, / Their bays are sear, their former laurels fade. / Let such forgo the poet's sacred name / Who rack their brains for lucre, not for fame. /

Lord Byron, *English Bards and Scotch Reviewers*

He is undoubtedly the Monarch of Parnassus, and the most *English* of bards. I should place Rogers next in the living list . . . Moore and Campbell both *third* – Southey and Wordsworth and Coleridge – the rest οἱ πολλοί – thus: –

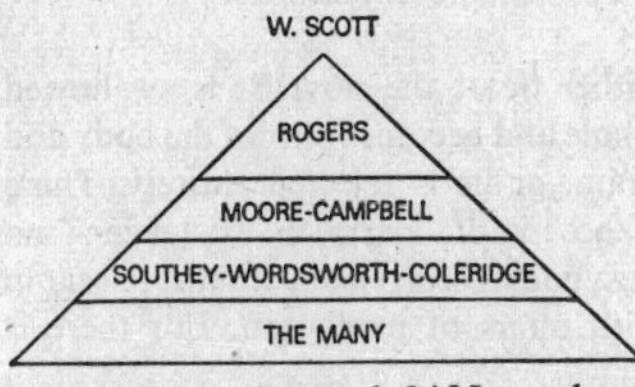


Lord Byron, Journal, 24 November 1813

. . . Grand work, Scotch Fielding, as well as great English Poet – wonderful man! I long to get drunk with him.

*Ibid.*, 5 January 1821

The Waverley Novels . . . spread Gothic sentiment to every class of reader . . . They described real historical events and associated them with clear description of Gothic architecture . . . Scott was a more reliable guide to the Middle Ages than previous Gothic poets and novelists; for, like Gray and Warton, he combined literature with archaeology. It was the wealth of archaeological detail in Scott's novels which made his picture of the Middle Ages so satisfying, and so much more influential than the mere melancholy of the poets.

Kenneth Clark, *The Gothic Revival*

On Waterloo's ensanguined plain / Lie tens of thousands of the slain; / But none, by sabre or by shot, / Fell half so flat as Walter Scott. /

Thomas, Lord Erskine, *On Scott's 'The Field of Waterloo'*

The public has done for good with the slipshod methods of amateur literary hacks like Scott. That Scott will live as an historical figure we need neither doubt nor regret. He was, like Chateaubriand and like Goethe, a good man . . . His very last words – spoken to his son-in-law – were: 'Be a good man, my dear, be a *good* man.' A good *man*, you observe, not a good biographer or a good writer to the signet. And the proudest boast of Scott was that he had never in all the immense array of his hack scrapbag written one word that the purest maiden seated in the privacy of her bedchamber could not read without a blush. That too is historic.

Ford Madox Ford, *The March of Literature*

For my own part I do not care for him, and find it difficult to understand his continued reputation . . . When we fish him out of the river of time . . . he is seen to have a trivial mind and a heavy style. He cannot construct. He has neither artistic detachment nor passion, and how can a writer who is devoid of both, create characters who will move us deeply? . . . He only has a temperate heart and gentlemanly feelings, and an intelligent affection for the countryside: and this is not basis enough for great novels.

E. M. Forster, *Aspects of the Novel*

Sir Walter Scott is undoubtedly the most popular writer of the age – the 'lord of the ascendant' for the time being. He is just half what the human intellect is capable of being: if you take the universe, and divide it into two parts, he knows all that it *has been*; all that it *is to be* is nothing to him . . . He is 'laudator temporis acti' – a '*prophesier* of things past'. The old world is to him a crowded map; the new one a dull, hateful blank. He dotes on all well-authenticated superstitions; he shudders at the shadow of innovation . . . Sir Walter would make a bad hand of a description of the *Millennium*, unless he could lay the scene in Scotland five hundred years ago.

William Hazlitt, *The Spirit of the Age*

His works (taken together) are almost like a new edition of human nature. This is indeed to be an author!

William Hazlitt, *English Literature*

Scott was a born story-teller: we can give him no higher praise. Surveying his works, his character, his method, as a whole, we can liken him to nothing better than to a strong and kindly elder brother, who gathers his juvenile public about him at eventide, and pours out a stream of wondrous improvisation . . . And thoroughly to enjoy him, we must again become as credulous as children at twilight.

Henry James, in *North American Review*, October 1864

These, then, are the moral services, – many and great, – which Scott has rendered, positively and negatively, consciously and unconsciously, to society. He has softened national prejudices; he has encouraged innocent tastes in every region of the world; he has imparted to certain influential classes the conviction that human nature works alike in all; he has exposed priestcraft and fanaticism; he has effectively satirized eccentricities, unamiablenesses, and follies; he has irresistibly recommended benignity in the survey of life, and indicated the glory of a higher kind of benevolence; and finally, he has advocated the rights of women.

Harriet Martineau, in *Tait's Edinburgh Magazine*, January 1833

He has the rare talent of pleasing all ranks and classes of men, from the peer to the peasant, and all orders and degrees of mind, from the philosopher to the man-milliner 'of whom nine make a taylor'. On the arrival of *Rob Roy*, as formerly on that of *Marmion*, the scholar lays aside his Plato, the statesman suspends his calculations, the young lady deserts her hoop, the critic smiles as he trims his lamp, thanking God for his good fortune, and the weary artisan resigns his sleep for the refreshment of the magic page.

Thomas Love Peacock, *An Essay on Fashionable Literature*

Either Scott the novelist is swallowed whole and becomes part of the body and brain, or he is rejected entirely. There is no middle party in existence – no busybodies run from camp to camp with offers of mediation. For there is no war.

Virginia Woolf, *The Moment*

I don't like to say all this, or to take to pieces some of the best reputed passages of Scott's verse, especially in the presence of my wife, because she thinks me too fastidious; but as a poet Scott *cannot* live, for he has never in verse written anything addressed to the immortal part of man. In making amusing stories in verse, he will be superseded by some newer versifier; what he writes in the way of natural description is merely rhyming nonsense.

William Wordsworth, in conversation (reported by Mrs Davy), 11 July 1844

*See also* Lord Byron, Ann Radcliffe, Shakespeare

## SCROGGS, SIR WILLIAM

1623?–83 Lord Chief Justice

The Chief was Arod, whose corrupted youth / Has made his soul an enemy to truth. / But nature furnished him with parts and wit / For bold attempts and deep intriguing fit; / Small was his learning and his eloquence / Did please the rabble, nauseate men of sense. / Bold was his spirit, nimble and loud his tongue, / Which more than law, or reason takes the throng. / Him, part by money, partly by her grace / The cov'tous Queen rais'd to a Judge's place, / And as he bought his place, he justice sold / Weighing his causes not by law but gold. / He made the Justice seat a common mart: / Well skill'd he was in the mysterious art / Of finding varnish for an unsound cause, / And for the sound, imaginary flaws. /

John Caryll, *Naboth's Vineyard*

## SELWYN, GEORGE AUGUSTUS

1719–91 Wit, Politician

If I am alive I shall be glad to see him; if I am dead, he'll be glad to see me.

Lord Holland, expecting Selwyn on his death-bed

The beautiful Lady Coventry was one day exhibiting to him a splendid new dress, covered with large silver spangles the size of a shilling, and enquired of him whether he admired her taste. – 'Why,' he said, 'you will be change for a guinea.'

G. H. Jesse, *George Selwyn and his Contemporaries*

If, this gay fav'rite lost, they yet can live, / A tear to Selwyn let the Graces give! / With rapid kindness teach Oblivion's pall / O'er the sunk foibles of the man to fall; / And fondly dictate to a faithful Muse / The prime distinction of the friend they lose. / 'Twas social wit, which, never kindling strife,/ Blazed in the small sweet courtesies of life; / Those little sapphires round the diamond shone, / Lending soft radiance to the richer stone. /

Dr John Warner, *Epitaph on George Selwyn*

*See also* Charles James Fox

## SELZNICK, DAVID O.

1902–65 Motion Picture Producer

Selznick has been described as overbearing, egocentric, aggressive, exhausting and impossible. Correspondent Lloyd Shearer once wrote that Selznick gave the impression that he stormed through life demanding to see the manager – and that, when the manager appeared, Selznick would hand him a twenty-page memo announcing his instant banishment to Elba.

Rudy Behlmer, *Memo from David O. Selznick*

He was a dynamic, flamboyant, spoiled, utterly egotistical man. Compared with Orson [Welles] he was semi-educated and uninspired, but he had an infallible, instinctive sense of the motion picture business with its strange blend of blatant romanticism and commercial preoccupation . . . For all his arrogance and exasperating self-indulgence, he was a man of intelligence and considerable charm – a typically Hollywood combination of oafishness and sophistication.

John Houseman, *Runthrough*

## SENNETT, MACK (MICHAEL SINNOTT)

1884–1960 Motion Picture Director

It wasn't me, the Old Man, who was so funny; it was the comical people I had around me. I called myself 'King of Comedy', a solemn and foolish title if there ever was one, but I was a harassed monarch. I worked most of the time. It was only in the evenings that I laughed.

On himself, in *King of Comedy*

A big, rough, tough plumber named Mack Sennett knew about gadgets such as movie cameras and klieg lights and about laughter from his mother, who, before he left Ireland, was buddies with the leprechauns. He put these together as Clowns and Keystone Cops, Chases, the original Sennett Comedies and Bathing Beauties, and made them a stone of the corner on which the Movies were built.

Adela Rogers St Johns, *The Honeycomb*

## SETTLE, ELKANAH

1648–1724 Poet

*Doeg*, though without knowing how or why / Made still a blund'ring kind of Melody; / Spur'd boldly on, and Dash'd through Thick and Thin, / Through Sense and Non-sense, never out nor in; / Free from all meaning, whether good or bad, / And in one Word, Heroically mad, / He was too warm on Picking-work to dwell, / But Faggoted his Notions as they Fell, / And, if they Rhim'd and Rattled, all was well. / Spightfull he is not, though he wrote a Satyr, / For still there goes some *Thinking* to ill-Nature: / He needs no more than Birds and Beasts to think, / All his Occasions are to eat and Drink. / If he call Rogue and Rascal from a Garrat / He means you no more mischief than a Parat. /

John Dryden, *The Second Part of Absalom and Achitophel*

There is something in *names* which one cannot help feeling. Now *Elkanah Settle* sounds so *queer*, who can expect much from that name?

John Wilkes, in James Boswell, *Life of Johnson*

## SEWARD, ANNA, 'THE SWAN OF LITCHFIELD'

1747–1809 Author

. . . here is Miss Seward with 6 tomes of the most disgusting trash, sailing over Styx with a Foolscap over her periwig as complacent as can be. – Of all Bitches dead or alive a scribbling woman is the most canine. – Scott is her Editor, I suppose because she lards him in every page.

Lord Byron, Letter to John Cam Hobhouse, 17 November 1811

## SEYMOUR, JANE

1509–37 Queen Consort to Henry VIII

Of all the wives of King *Henry* she only had the happiness to die in his full favour, the 14th of *Octob.* 1537, and is buried in the quire of *Windsor* Chappell, the King continuing in *real mourning* for her even all the *Festival* of *Christmas*.

Thomas Fuller, *The History of the Worthies of England*

## SHADWELL, THOMAS

1642–92 Dramatist

*Tom* writ, his readers still slept o'er his book; / For *Tom took opium*, and they opiates took. /

Thomas Brown, *In Obitum T. Shadwell, pinguis memoriae 1693*

Now stop your Noses, Readers all and some, / For here's a tun of Midnight work to come, / *Og* from a Treason

Tavern rowling home. / Round as a Globe, and Liquored every chink, / Goodly and Great he Sayls behind his Link; / With all this Bulk there's nothing lost in *Og* / For ev'ry inch that is not Fool is Rogue: / A Monstrous Mass of foul corrupted matter, / As all the Devils had spew'd to make the Batter. / When wine has given him Courage to Blaspheme, / He curses God, but God before curst him; / And if Man could have reason, none has more, / That made his Paunch so rich, and him so Poor. /

John Dryden, *The Second Part of Absalom and Achitophel*

Shadwell alone my perfect image bears, / Mature in dulness from his tender years; / Shadwell alone of all my Sons is he / Who stands confirmed in full stupidity. / The rest to some faint meaning make pretence, / But Shadwell never deviates into sense. /

John Dryden, *Mac Flecknoe*

Thou last great Prophet of Tautology.

*Ibid.*

He has often call'd me an Atheist in print; I would believe more charitably of him, and that he only goes the *broad way*, because the other is too *narrow* for him. He may see, by this, that I do not delight to meddle with his course of life, and his immoralities, though I have a bead-roll of them. I have hitherto contented myself with the ridiculous part of him, which is enough, in all conscience, to employ one man; even without the story of his late fall at the Old Devil, where he broke no ribs, because the hardness of the stairs could reach no bones; and, for my part, I do not wonder how he came to fall, for I have always known him heavy; the miracle is, how he got up again.

John Dryden, *Vindication of 'The Duke of Guise'*

The *Virtuoso* of Shadwell does not maintain his character with equal strength to the end, and this was that writer's general fault. Wycherley used to say of him that 'he knew how to start a fool very well, but that he was never able to run him down'.

Alexander Pope, in Joseph Spence, *Anecdotes*

*See also* Thomas Otway

## SHAFTESBURY, FIRST EARL OF (ANTHONY ASHLEY COOPER)

1621–83 Statesman

A little limping peer – though crazy yet in action nimble and as busy as a body-louse.

Anon., Letter to the Bishop of Meath, June 1680

Greatest of men, yet man's least friend, farewell, / Wit's mightiest, but most useless miracle; / Where nature all her richest treasures stor'd / To make one vast unprofitable hoard. / So high as thine no orb of fire could roll, / The brightest yet the most eccentric soul; / Whom 'midst wealth, honours, fame, yet want of ease, / No pow'r could e'er oblige, no state could please, / Be in thy grave with peaceful slumbers bless'd / And find thy whole life's only stranger, rest. /

Anon., *Shaftesbury's Farewell*, February 1683

Nature made him a perverse wight, whose nose / Extracts the essence of his gouty toes; / Double with head to tail he crawls apart: / His body's th'emblem of his double heart. /

Anon., *The Cabal*, contemporary

His morals were of a piece with his religion, that is, he had very little of either morality or Christianity.

Gilbert Burnet, *History of My Own Time*

'Mong these there was a *Politician* / With more heads than a *Beast in Vision*, / And more Intrigues in ev'ry one / Than all the Whores of Babylon: / So politic, as if one Eye / Upon the other were a Spy, / That, to trepan the one to think / The other blind, both strove to blink: / And in his dark pragmatic Way / As busy as a Child at Play. /

Samuel Butler, *Hudibras*, part 3

His body thus, and soul together vie / In vice's empire for the sov'reignty; / In ulcers that, this does abound in sin, / Lazar without, and Lucifer within. / The silver pipe is no sufficient drain / For the corruption of this little man, / Who, though he ulcers has in ev'ry part / Is nowhere so corrupt as in his heart. /

John Caryll, *The Hypocrite*

A Name to all succeeding Ages curst, / For close Designs and crooked Counsels fit, / Sagacious, Bold and Turbulent of wit, / Restless, unfit in Principles and Place, / In Pow'r unpleased, impatient of Disgrace; / A fiery Soul, which working out its way, / Fretted the Pigmy Body to decay: / And o'r informed the Tenement of Clay. / A daring Pilot in extremity; / Pleas'd with the Danger, when the Waves went high / He sought the Storms; but, for a Calm unfit, / Would Steer too nigh the Sands to boast his Wit. / Great Wits are sure to Madness near alli'd / And thin Partitions do their Bounds divide; / Else, why should he, with Wealth and Honour blest, / Refuse his Age the needful Hours of Rest? / Punish a Body which he could not please, / Bankrupt of Life, yet prodigal of Ease? /

And all to leave what with his Toil he won / To that unfeather'd two-legged thing, a Son; / Got, while his Soul did huddled notions trie; / And born a shapeless lump, like Anarchy. / In Friendship false, implacable in hate, / Resolved to Ruin or to Rule the State. /

John Dryden, *Absalom and Achitophel*

A Martial Heroe first, with early Care, / Blown, like a Pigmee by the Winds, to war. / A beardless Chief, a Rebel e'er a Man, / (So young his Hatred to his Prince began). / Next this, (how wildly will Ambition steer!) / A Vermin wriggling in th'usurper's ear, / Bartring his venal wit for sums of Gold, / He cast himself into the Saint-like mould, / Groan'd sigh'd and pray'd, while Godliness was Gain, / The lowdest bag-pipe of the Sqeaking Train. / But as 'tis hard to cheat a juggler's eyes, / His open lewdness he cou'd ne'er disguise. / There split the Saint: for Hypocritique Zeal / Allows no Sins but those it can conceal . . . / Pow'r was his aym; but, thrown from that pretence, / The Wretch turned loyal in his own defence, / And Malice reconcil'd him to his Prince. /

John Dryden, *The Medall*

The King and the Duke of York used to call him *Little Sincerity*, while with others at court, he went under the title of *Lord Shiftesbury*.

Augustus Jessop, *Note to Roger North's Life of . . . Lord Keeper Guildford*

I have heard him also say that he desired no more of any man but that he would talk; if he would but talk said he, let him talk as he pleases. And, indeed, I never knew anyone to penetrate so quick into men's hearts, and from a small opening survey that dark cabinet, as he would. He would understand men's true errand as soon as they had opened their mouths, and began their story in appearance to another purpose.

John Locke, *Fragment of Memoir of Shaftesbury*

It is certain that, just before the Restoration, he declared to the Regicides that he would be damned, body and soul, rather than suffer a hair of their heads to be hurt, and that, just after the Restoration, he was one of the judges who sentenced them to death. It is certain that he was a principal member of the most profligate Administration ever known, and that he was afterwards a principal member of the most profligate Opposition ever known. It is certain that, in power, he did not scruple to violate the great fundamental principle of the Constitution, in order to exalt the Catholics, and that, out of power, he did not scruple to violate every principle of justice, in order to destroy them . . . From the misguided friends of Toleration, he borrowed their contempt for the Constitution, and from the misguided friends of civil Liberty their contempt for the rights of conscience . . . his life was such that every part of it, as if by a skilful contrivance reflects infamy on every other. We should never have known how abandoned a prostitute he was in place, if we had not known how desperate an incendiary he was out of it . . . As often as he is charged with one treason, his advocates vindicate him by confessing two.

T. B. Macaulay, *Essay*: 'Sir William Temple'

## SHAFTESBURY, SEVENTH EARL OF (ANTHONY ASHLEY COOPER)

1801–85 Philanthropist, Statesman

The League hate me as an aristocrat; the landowners, as a Radical; the wealthy of all opinions, as a mover of inconvenient principles. The Tractarians loathe me as an ultra-Protestant; the Dissenters, as a Churchman; the High Church think me abominably low, the Low Church some degrees too high. I have no political party; the Whigs, I know, regard me as leaning very decidedly to the Conservatives; the Conservatives declare that I have greatly injured the Government of Sir R. Peel. I have thus the approval and support of neither; the floating men of all sides, opinions, ranks, and professions, who dislike what they call a 'saint', join in the hatred, and rejoice in it. Every class is against me, and a host of partisans in every grade. The working people, catching the infection, will go next, and then, 'farewell, King'; farewell any hopes of further usefulness.

On himself, Diary, October 1845

I cannot bear to leave the world with all the misery in it.

On himself, aged eighty-four, in G. W. E. Russell, *Collections and Recollections*

Lord Shaftesbury would have been in a lunatic asylum if he had not devoted himself to reforming lunatic asylums.

Florence Nightingale, quoted in *Times Literary Supplement*, 8 November 1974

## SHAKESPEARE, WILLIAM

1564–1616 Dramatist

There is something so wild, and yet so solemn in his speeches of his ghosts, fairies, witches and the like imaginary persons, that we cannot forbear thinking them natural, though we have no rule by which to judge of them, and must confess, if there are such beings in the world, it looks highly probable as if they should talk and act as he has represented them.

Joseph Addison, in *Spectator*, 1 July 1712

Others abide our question. Thou art free. / We ask and ask – thou smilest and art still / Out-topping knowledge. For the loftiest hill, / Who to the stars uncrowns his majesty, /

Planting his stedfast footsteps in the sea, / Making the heaven of heavens his dwelling-place, / Spares but the cloudy border of his base, / To the foil'd searching of mortality; /

And thou, who didst the stars and sunbeams know, / Self-school'd, self-scann'd, self-honour'd, self-secure, / Didst tread on earth unguess'd at. – Better so! /

All pains the immortal spirit must endure, / All weakness which impairs, all griefs which bow, / Find their sole speech in that victorious brow. /
Matthew Arnold, *Shakespeare*

I keep saying, Shakespeare, Shakespeare, you are as obscure as life is.
Matthew Arnold, Letter to A. H. Clough, December 1847

Shakespeare is in the singularly fortunate position of being, to all intents and purposes, anonymous.
W. H. Auden, *Forewords and Afterwords*

Shakespeare's form is apparent mainly in terms of power. He works by means of contrast between character and character, by tension and relaxation, climax and anti-climax, by changes of tone and pace, by every sort of variation between scene and scene. We could illustrate the form of *King Lear* by a chart, a sort of temperature chart, with plot, and sub-plot and characters marked by ink lines of different colours, zigzagging up and down and crossing and recrossing; the rise and fall to show volume of emotion, while a separate line could mark increase and decrease of pace. We can rightly call this form I think, for all that it is form in motion.
Harley Granville Barker, *On Dramatic Method*

Shakespeare's name, you may depend on it, stands absurdly too high and will go down. He had no invention as to stories, none whatever. He took all his plots from old novels, and threw their stories into a dramatic shape, at as little expense of thought as you or I could turn his plays back again into prose tales. That he threw over whatever he did write some flashes of genius, nobody can deny: but this was all. Suppose anyone to have had the *dramatic* handling for the first time of such ready-made stories as Lear, Macbeth, &c. and he would be a sad fellow indeed, if he did not make something very grand of them.
Lord Byron, Letter to James Hogg, 24 March 1814

Like a miraculous celestial Light-ship, woven all of sheet-lightning and sunbeams.
Thomas Carlyle, *Historical Sketches of Notable Persons and Events in the Reigns of James I and Charles I*

Shakespere's intellectual action is wholly unlike that of Ben Jonson or Beaumont and Fletcher. The latter see the totality of a sentence or passage, and then project it entire. Shakespere goes on creating, and evolving B. out of A., and C. out of B., and so on, just as a serpent moves, which makes a fulcrum of its own body, and seems forever twisting and untwisting its own strength.
Samuel Taylor Coleridge, *Table Talk*, 5 March 1834

Our myriad-minded Shakespeare.
Samuel Taylor Coleridge, *Biographia Literaria*

As for *Shakespeare*, he is too guilty (of immodesty) to make an Evidence: but I think he gains not much by his Misbehaviour; he has commonly *Plautus's Fate*, where there is most smut there is least Sense.
Jeremy Collier, *A Short View of the Immorality and Profaneness of the English Stage*

Some say (good *Will*) which I, in sport do sing, / Hadst thou not plaid some Kingly parts in sport, / Thou hadst been a companion for a King; / And, beene a King among the meaner sort. / Some others raile; but, raile as they thinke fit, / Thou hast no rayling, but, a raigning Wit: / *And* honesty *thou sow'st, which they do reape, / So, to increase their* Stocke *which they do keepe.* /

John Davies of Hereford, *The Scourge of Folly*, *circa* 1611

*Shakespear* having neither had Time to correct, nor friends to consult must necessarily have frequently left such faults in his Writings, for the Correction of which either a great deal of Time or a judicious and well-natur'd Friend is indispensably necessary.

John Dennis, *On the Genius and Writings of Shakespeare*

To begin with *Shakespeare*: he was the man who of all Modern, and perhaps Ancient Poets, had the largest and most comprehensive soul. All the Images of Nature were still present to him, and he drew them not laboriously but luckily: when he describes any thing, you more than see it, you feel it too. Those who accuse him to have wanted learning, give him the greater commendation: he was naturally learn'd; he needed not the spectacles of Books to read Nature; he look'd inwards, and found her there. I cannot say he is everywhere alike; were he so, I should do him injury to compare him with the greatest of Mankind. He is many times flat, insipid; his Comick wit degenerating into clenches, his serious swelling into Bombast. But he is alwayes great, when some great occasion is presented to him; no man can say he ever had a fit subject for his wit, and did not then raise himself as high above the rest of Poets.

John Dryden, *Essay on Dramatic Poesy*

*Shakspear* (who with some errors not to be avoided in that age, had, undoubtedly a larger Soul of Poesie than ever any of our Nation) was the first, who to shun the pains of continuall rhyming, invented that kind of writing, which we call blanck verse, but the French, more properly, *Prose Mesuree*, into which the *English* Tongue so naturally Slides, that in writing Prose 'tis hardly to be avoyded.

John Dryden, Dedication to *The Rival Ladies*

Never did any author precipitate himself from such heights of thought to so low expressions, as he often does. He is the very *Janus* of poets; he wears, almost everywhere two faces: and you have scarce begun to admire the one, e're you despise the other.

John Dryden, *The Conquest of Granada: Defence of the Epilogue*

His excellencies came and were not sought, / His words like casual Atoms made a thought: / Drew up themselves in rank and file, and writ, / He wondring how the devil it were such wit. / Thus like the drunken Tinker in his Play, / He grew a Prince and never knew which way. /

John Dryden, *Covent Garden Drolery*

If Shakespeare were stripped of all the bombasts in his passions, and dressed in the most vulgar words, we should still find the beauties of his thoughts remaining: if his embroideries were burnt down, there would still be silver at the bottom of the melting-pot.

John Dryden, Preface to *Troilus and Cressida*

If the only way to prove that Shakespeare did not feel and think exactly as people felt and thought in 1815, or in 1860, or in 1880, is to show that he felt and thought as we felt and thought in 1927, then we must accept gratefully that alternative.

T. S. Eliot, *Shakespeare and the Stoicism of Seneca*

I do not believe that any writer has ever exposed this *bovaryisme*, the human will to see things as they are not, more clearly than Shakespeare.

*Ibid.*

Shakespeare is the only biographer of Shakespeare.

Ralph Waldo Emerson, *Representative Men*

'Shakespeare', says a Brother of the *Craft*, 'is a vast garden of criticism:' and certainly no one can be favoured with more weeders gratis.

Richard Farmer, *An Essay on The Learning of Shakespeare*

Once when visiting Stratford-on-Avon with Toole, [Henry Irving] saw a rustic sitting on a fence, whom they submitted to an interrogatory. 'That's Shakespeare's house, isn't it?' it was asked innocently. 'Yes.' 'Ever been there?' 'Noa.' 'How long has he been dead?' 'Dunno.' 'What did he do?' 'Dunno.' 'Did he not write?' 'Oh yes, he did summat.' 'What was it?' 'Well, I think he writ *Boible*.'

Percy Fitzgerald, *Henry Irving*

A sycophant, a flatterer, a breaker of marriage vows, a whining and inconstant person.

Ebenezer Forsyth, *Shakespeare: Some Notes on his Character and Writings*

The name 'William Shakespeare' is very probably a pseudonym behind which a great unknown lies concealed. Edward de Vere, Earl of Oxford, a man who has been thought to be identifiable with the author of Shakespeare's works, lost a beloved and admired father while he was still a boy and completely repudiated his mother, who contracted a new marriage very soon after her husband's death.

Sigmund Freud, *An Outline of Psychoanalysis*, translated by James Strachey

He was an eminent instance of the truth of that Rule, *Poeta non fit sed nascitur*, one is not made, but born a Poet. Indeed his learning was very little, so that as Cornish *diamonds* are not polished by any Lapidary, but are pointed and smoothed even as they are taken out of the Earth, so *nature* it self was all the *art* which was used upon him.

Thomas Fuller, *The History of the Worthies of England*

I cannot read him, he is such a bombast fellow.

George II, attributed

As to the Soul, perhaps they may have none on the Continent; but I do think we have such things in England. Shakespear, for example, I believe had several to his own share.

Thomas Gray, Letter to Horace Walpole, March 1771

There is an upstart Crow, beautified with our feathers, that with his *Tygers heart wrapped in a Players hide*, supposes he is as well able to bumbast out a blanke verse as the best of you: and being an absolute Johannes fac totum, is in his owne conceit the onely Shake-scene in a countrie.

Robert Greene, *Green's Groats-worth of Wit; bought with a Million of Repentaunce*

The victim of spiritual emotions that involve criminatory reflections does not usually protrude them voluntarily on the consideration of society; and, if the personal theory be accepted, we must concede the possibility of our national dramatist gratuitously confessing his sins and revealing those of others, proclaiming his disgrace and avowing his repentance in poetical circulars distributed by the delinquent himself amongst his most intimate friends.

J. D. Halliwell-Phillipps, on the Sonnets, *Outlines of the Life of Shakespeare*

Homosexuality? No, I know nothing of the joys of homosexuality. My friend Oscar can no doubt tell you all about that. But I must say that if *Shakespeare* asked me, I would have to submit.

Frank Harris, attributed, remark over luncheon in the Café Royal

The plays he purchased or obtained surreptitiously, which became his 'property', and which are now called his, were never set upon the stage in their original state. They were first spiced with obscenity, blackguardism and impurities, before they were produced; and this business he voluntarily assumed, and faithfully did he perform his share of the management in that respect. It brought *money* to the house.

Colonel Joseph C. Hart, *The Romance of Yachting*

The striking feature of Shakespeare's mind was its generic quality, its power of communication with all other minds, – so that it contained a universe of thought and feeling within itself, and had no one particular bias, or exclusive excellence more than another. He was just like any other man, but that he was like all other men. He was the least of an egotist that it was possible to be. He was nothing in himself, but he was all that others were, or that they could become.

William Hazlitt, *On Shakespeare and Milton*

His language is hieroglyphical. It translates thoughts into visible images. It abounds in sudden transitions and elliptical expressions. This is the source of his mixed metaphors, which are only abbreviated forms of speech. These, however, give no pain from long custom. They have, in fact, become idioms in the language. They are the building and not the scaffolding, to thought.

*Ibid.*

Shakespeare was the least of a coxcomb of any one that ever lived, and much of a gentleman.

*Ibid.*

Who shall say that he never proved a Tarquin to some unchronicled Lucrece?

W. Carew Hazlitt, *Shakespeare, Himself and His Work*

There was also *Shakespeere*, who (as *Cupid* informed me) creepes into the women's closets about bed time, and if it were not for some of the old out-of-date Grandames (who are set over the rest as their tutoresses) the young sparkish Girles would read in *Shakespeere* day and night, so that they would open the Booke or Tome, and the Men with a Fescue in their hands should point to the Verse.

John Johnson, *The Academy of Love, Describing ye folly of young men and ye fallacy of women*

The dialogue of this author is often so evidently determined by the incident which produces it, and is pursued with so much ease and simplicity, that it seems scarcely to claim the merit of fiction, but to have been gleaned by diligent selection out of common conversation, and common occurrencies.

Samuel Johnson, Preface to *The Plays of William Shakespeare*

His tragedy seems to be skill, his comedy to be instinct.

*Ibid.*

The stream of Time, which is continually washing the dissoluble fabricks of other poets, passes without injury by the adamant of *Shakespeare*.

*Ibid.*

It is incident to him to be now and then entangled with an unwieldy sentiment, which he cannot well express, and will not reject; he struggles with it a while, and if it continues stubborn, comprises it in words such as occur, and leaves it to be disentangled and evolved by those who have more leisure to bestow upon it.

*Ibid.*

A quibble is to *Shakespeare*, what luminous vapours are to the traveller; he follows it at all adventures, it is sure to lead him out of his way, and sure to engulf him in the mire. It has some malignant power over his mind, and its fascinations are irresistible. Whatever be the dignity or profundity of his disquisition, whether he be enlarging knowledge or exalting affection, whether he be amusing attention with incidents, or enchaining it in suspense, let but a quibble spring up before him, and he leaves his work unfinished. A quibble is the golden apple for which he will always turn aside from his career, or stoop from his elevation. A quibble, poor and barren as it is, gave him such delight, that he was content to purchase it, by the sacrifice of reason, propriety and truth. A quibble was to him the fatal *Cleopatra* for which he lost the world and was content to lose it.

*Ibid.*

Soule of the Age! / The applause! delight! the wonder of our Stage! / My *Shakespeare*, rise; I will not lodge thee by / *Chaucer* or *Spencer*, or bid *Beaumont* lye / A little further, to make thee a roome: / Thou art a Moniment, without a Tombe, / And art alive still, while thy booke doth live, / And we have wits to read, and praise to give. /

Ben Jonson, *To the Memory of my beloved, the Author Mr William Shakespeare*

He was not of an age, but for all time! / And all the *Muses* still were in their prime, / When like *Apollo* he came forth to warme / Our eares, or like a *Mercury* to charme! /

*Ibid.*

Yet must I not give Nature all; Thy Art, / My gentle Shakespeare, must enjoy a part. / For though the Poets matter, Nature be, / His Art doth give the fashion. And, that he, / Who casts to write a living line, must sweat, / (Such as thine are) and strike the second heat / Upon the *Muses* anvile: turne the same, / (And himselfe with it) that he thinks to frame; / Or for the lawrell, he may gaine a scorne, / For a good *Poet's* made, as well as borne, / And such wert thou. /

*Ibid.*

Shaksperr wanted Arte.

Ben Jonson, in his *Conversations with William Drummond of Hawthornden*

I *remember*, the Players have often mentioned it as an honour to *Shakespeare*, that in his writing, (whatsoever he penned) hee never blotted out a line. My answer hath been, would he had blotted a thousand.

Ben Jonson, *Timber, or Discoverie made upon man and matter*

Several things dove-tailed in my mind, and at once it struck me what quality went to form a man of achievement, especially in literature, and which Shakespeare possessed so enormously – I mean *Negative Capability*, that is, when a man is capable of being in uncertainties, mysteries, doubts, without any irritable reaching after fact and reason. Coleridge, for instance, would let go by a fine isolated verisimilitude caught from the Penetralium of mystery, from being incapable of remaining content with half-knowledge. This pursued through volumes would perhaps take us no further than this, that with a great poet the sense of Beauty overcomes every other consideration, or rather obliterates all consideration.

John Keats, Letter to George and Thomas Keats, 28 December 1817

A Man's life of any worth is a continual allegory, and very few eyes can see the Mystery of his life – a life, like the scriptures, figurative – which such people can no more make out than they can the Hebrew Bible. Lord Byron cuts a figure, but he is not figurative – Shakespeare led a life of Allegory: his works are the comments on it.

John Keats, Letter to George and Georgiana Keats, 24 February 1819

Not a single one is very admirable . . . They are hot and pothery: there is much condensation, little delicacy; like raspberry jam without cream, without crust, without bread; to break its viscidity.

Walter Savage Landor, on Shakespeare's sonnets, *Imaginary Conversations – Southey and Landor*

When I read Shakespeare I am struck with wonder / That such trivial people should muse and thunder / In such lovely language. /

D. H. Lawrence, *When I read Shakespeare*

Shakespeare is a good raft whereon to float securely down the stream of time; fasten yourself to that and your immortality is safe.

George Henry Lewes, *On Actors and the Art of Acting*

Wee wondred (*Shake-speare*) that thou went'st so soone / From the Worlds-Stage, to the Graves-Tyring-roome. / Wee thought thee dead, but this thy printed worth, / Tels thy Spectators, that thou wentst but forth / To enter with applause. An Actors Art, / Can dye, and live, to acte a second part. / That's but an *Exit* of Mortalitie; / This, a Re-entrance to a Plaudite.

'I.M.', *To the Memorie of M. W. Shake-speare*, 1623

Desmond MacCarthy . . . said somewhere that trying to work out Shakespeare's personality was like looking at a very dark glazed picture in the National Portrait Gallery: at first you see nothing, then you begin to recognise features, and then you realise that they are your own.

Desmond MacCarthy, in Samuel Schoenbaum, *Shakespeare's Lives*

Upon a tyme when Burbidge played Rich 3. there was a citizen greue soe farr in liking with him, that before shee went from the play shee appointed him to come that night unto her by the name of Ri: the 3. Shakespeare overhearing their conclusion went before, was intertained, and at his game ere Burbidge came. Then message being brought that Rich. the 3rd was at the dore, Shakespeare caused returne to be made that William the Conquerour was before Rich. the 3.

John Manningham, Diary, 13 March 1602

On this planet, the reputation of Shakespeare is secure.

Louis Marder, *His Exits and His Entrances*

What needs my Shakespeare for his honoured bones, / The labour of an age in piled stones? / Or that his hallowed reliques should be hid / Under a starry-pointing pyramid? / Dear Son of Memory, great heir of Fame, / What need'st thou such weak witness of thy name? / Thou in our wonder and astonishment / Hast built thyself a live-long monument. / For whilst to the shame of slow-endeavouring art / Thy easy numbers flow, and that each heart / Hath from the leaves of thy unvalued book / Those delphic lines with deep impression took, / Then thou our fancy of itself bereaving, / Dost make us marble with too much conceiving; / And so sepulchered in such pomp dost lie, / That kings for such a tomb would wish to die. /

John Milton, *An Epitaph on the Admirable Dramatic Poet, W. Shakespeare*

If Dr Gall the craniologist's assertion is to be believed, the organ of robbery (covetiveness) and the organ for forming good dramatic plots, are one and the same; he certainly proved himself a great adept in the latter, and no doubt was so in the former.

W. T. Moncrieff, *New Guide to the Spa of Leamington Priors*

Him we may profess rather to feel than to understand; and it is safer to say, on many occasions, that we are possessed by him, than that we possess him.

Maurice Morgann, *An Essay on the Dramatick Character of Sir John Falstaff*

The Poetry of *Shakespeare* was Inspiration indeed: he is not so much an Imitator as an Instrument, of Nature; and 'tis not so just to say that he speaks from her, as that she speaks thro' him.

Alexander Pope, Preface to *The Works of Shakespeare*

His poetry has been cut into minute indigestible fragments, and used like wedding cake, not to eat, but to dream upon.

Walter Raleigh, *Shakespeare*

Shakespeare is like a picture full of anachronisms – geographical blunders, forgetfulness of his plot, and even sometimes of character – but he produces a high value picture because his mind is intent upon the general effect . . . he does not stoop to a cold explanation of his intention in the character, though perhaps a single line would be enough, but concluding that you are possessed with the character as much as he was himself.

Sir Joshua Reynolds, *Notes on Shakespeare*

The top of his performance was the ghost in his own *Hamlet*.

Nicholas Rowe, *Some Account of the Life, etc, of Mr William Shakespeare*, 1709

From the quantitative data a portrait of the dramatist emerges. A bi-sexual personality, predominantly masculine, aggressive, prone to wide fluctuations of mood, this Shakespeare tried to suppress his feminine traits and justify his existence by vigorous, even ruthless action. The homosexual tendency helps to explain the poet's paranoic suspiciousness, his jealous imagining that other men have been coming between him and the woman or women he loves. Over the years sensuality and self-indulgence grew more and more repugnant to Shakespeare, but he did not easily accept spiritualised emotions – 'he could not admit the loving kindness of Christian charity without feeling threatened with overwhelming weakness.'

Samuel Schoenbaum, *Shakespeare's Lives*, summarizing the conclusions of Harold Grier McCurdy, *The Personality of Shakespeare*

In playing Shakespeare, play *to* the lines, *through* the lines, *on* the lines, but never *between* the lines. There simply isn't time for it. You would not stick five bars rest into a Beethoven symphony to pick up your drumsticks; and similarly you must not stop the Shakespeare orchestra for business. Nothing short of a procession or a fight should make anything so extraordinary as a silence during a Shakespearian performance.

George Bernard Shaw, Letter to Ellen Terry, 23 September 1896

With the single exception of Homer, there is no eminent writer, not even Sir Walter Scott, whom I can despise so entirely as I despise Shakespeare when I measure my mind against his.

George Bernard Shaw, in *Saturday Review*, 26 September 1896

Even when Shakespeare, in his efforts to be a social philosopher, does rise for an instant to the level of a sixth-rate Kingsley, his solemn self-complacency infuriates me. And yet, so wonderful is his art, that it is not easy to disentangle what is unbearable from what is irresistible.

George Bernard Shaw, in *Saturday Review*, 5 December 1896

My capers are part of a bigger design than you think: Shakespeare, for instance, is to me one of the Towers of the Bastille, and down he must come.

George Bernard Shaw, Letter to Ellen Terry, 27 January 1897

Meanwhile / Immortal William dead and turned to Clay / May stop a hole to keep the wind away. / Oh that the earth which kept the world in awe / Should patch a wall t'expel the winter's flaw! /

George Bernard Shaw, *Shakes Versus Shav*

Hope to mend Shakespear! or to match his Style! / 'Tis such a Jest, would make a *Stoick* smile. /

John Sheffield, Earl of Mulgrave, Prologue to his alteration of *Julius Caesar*, 1692

It is difficult to resist the conclusion that he was getting bored himself. Bored with people, bored with real life, bored with drama, bored, in fact, with everything except poetry and poetical dreams. He is no longer interested, one often feels, in what happens, or who says what, so long as he can find place for a faultless lyric, or a new unimagined rhythmical effect, or a grand and mystic speech . . . Half enchanted by visions of loveliness, and half bored to death; on the one side inspired by a soaring fancy to the singing of ethereal songs, and on the other urged by a general disgust to burst occasionally through his torpor into bitter and violent speech. If we are to learn anything of his mind from his last works, it is surely this.

Lytton Strachey, *Books and Characters*: 'Shakespeare's Final Period'

He is fair game, like the Bible, and may be made use of nowadays even for advertisements of soap and razors.

Ralph Vaughan Williams, Preface to *Sir John In Love*

This enormous dunghill ['son énorme fumier'].

Voltaire, Letter to d'Argental, 19 July 1776

We must be free or die, who speak the tongue / That Shakespeare spake . . . /

William Wordsworth, *National Independence and Liberty*

Scorn not the Sonnet; Critic, you have frowned, / Mindless of its just honours; with this key / Shakespeare unlocked his heart. /

William Wordsworth, *Miscellaneous Sonnets*

Do you suppose for one moment that Shakespeare educated Hamlet and King Lear by telling them what he thought and believed? As I see it, Hamlet and Lear educated Shakespeare, and I have no doubt that in the process of that education he found out that he was an altogether different man to what he thought himself, and had altogether different beliefs.

William Butler Yeats, Letter to Sean O'Casey, 20 April 1928

Shakespeare, – what *trash* are his works in the gross.

Edward Young, in Joseph Spence, *Anecdotes*

*See also* Edward Alleyn, Francis Beaumont, William Blake, John Bunyan, William D'Avenant, Chauncey Depew, George Eliot, Sir John Fastolfe, John Fletcher, Samuel Foote, Anne Hathaway, Thomas Heywood, Henry Irving, Ben Jonson, James Joyce, Edmund Kean, Rudyard Kipling, Ring Lardner, Christopher Marlowe, John Milton, Sir Isaac Newton, Joseph Nollekens, D. G. Rossetti, George Bernard Shaw, Herbert Beerbohm Tree, John Webster, William Wordsworth, William Butler Yeats

## SHAW, GEORGE BERNARD

1856–1950 Dramatist

The first moral lesson I can remember as a tiny child was the lesson of teetotalism, instilled by my father, a futile person you would have thought him. One night, when I was about as tall as his boots, he took me out for a walk. In the course of it I conceived a monstrous, incredible suspicion. When I got home I stole to my mother and in an awestruck whisper said to her, 'Mamma, I think Papa's drunk.' She turned away with impatient disgust, and said 'When is he ever anything else?' I have never believed anything since: then the scoffer began . . . Oh, a devil of a childhood, Ellen, rich only in dreams, frightful in realities.

On himself, Letter to Ellen Terry, 11 June 1897

It is significant of the difference between my temperament and Mr Pinero's that when he, as a little boy, first heard Ever of Thee I'm Fondly Dreaming, he wept; whereas, at the same tender age, I simply noted with scorn the obvious plagiarism from Cheer Boys, Cheer.

On himself, in *Saturday Review*, 5 February 1898

He will fill his fountain pen with your heart's blood, and sell your most sacred emotions on the stage. He is a mass of imagination with no heart. He is a writing and talking machine that has worked for nearly forty years until its skill is devilish . . . All his goods are in the shop window, and he'll steal *your* goods and put them there too.

On himself, Letter to Mrs Patrick Campbell, 8 November 1912

I am like a dentist, there is so much that is wounding about my work.

On himself, Letter to Mrs Patrick Campbell, 8 December 1912

I am of the true Shakespearian type: I understand everything and everyone and am nobody and nothing.

On himself, Letter to Frank Harris, 20 June 1930

I am not a professional liar. I am even ashamed of the extent to which in my human infirmity I have been an amateur one.

On himself, *Love Among the Artists*

I am as much a woman, as Lady So-and-So is a man: say ninety five per cent.

On himself, in Blanche Patch, *Thirty Years with GBS*

You are talking to a man who is three-quarters of a ghost.

On himself, in his nineties, to a spiritualist, in *ibid.*

My only policy is to profess evil and do good.

On himself, in Stephen Winsten, *Bernard Shaw*

The Mozart of English letters he is not – the music of the Marble statue is beyond him – the Rossini, yes. He has all the brio, humour, cruel clarity and virtuosity of that Master of *Opera Buffa.*

W. H. Auden, Footnote to 'The Globe', in *The Dyer's Hand*

It is all very well to believe, as Shaw did, that all criticism is prejudiced, but, with Shaw's dramatic criticism, the prejudice is more important than anything else.

Eric Bentley, Introduction to *Shaw on Music*

– Oh dear me – its too late to do anything but *accept* you and *love* you – but when you were quite a little boy somebody ought to have said 'hush' just once.

Mrs Patrick Campbell, Letter to GBS, 1 November 1912

I believe you have eaten your own heart.

*Ibid.*, 1 February 1939

Yes: I am glad I invented you, and that it is the cleverest thing I ever did.

*Ibid.*

God help us if he would ever eat a beef-steak.

Mrs Patrick Campbell, in Bertrand Russell, *Autobiography*, vol. 2

He is a daring pilgrim who has set out from the grave to find the cradle. He started from points of view which no one else was clever enough to discover, and he is at last discovering points of view which no one else was ever stupid enough to ignore.

G. K. Chesterton, *Essays*: 'Shaw the Puritan'

His brain is a half-inch layer of champagne poured over a bucket of Methodist near-beer.

Benjamin de Casseres, *Mencken and Shaw*

Shaw is a Puritan who missed the Mayflower by five minutes.

*Ibid.*

Shaw's relations with women have always been gallant, coy even. The number he has surrendered to physically have been few – perhaps not half a dozen in all – the first man to have cut a swathe through the theatre and left it strewn with virgins.

Frank Harris, *Bernard Shaw*

Mr Shaw, I don't know what we are going to talk about, because I agree with everything you have ever written or said.

Leslie Henson, in Blanche Patch, *Thirty Years with GBS*

Any sexual relationship which could not provide an alternative world, made largely out of words, tended to disgust him.

Michael Holyroyd, *GBS, Sex, and Second Childhood*

He believed in art for action's sake.

*Ibid.*

I'm afraid *The Intelligent Woman's Guide* I shall have to leave to the intelligent woman: it is too boring for the intelligent man, if I'm any sample. Too much gas-bag.

D. H. Lawrence, Letter to Martin Secker, 24 July 1928

He has a curious blank in his make-up. To him all sex is infidelity and only infidelity is sex. Marriage is sexless, null. Sex is only manifested in infidelity, and the queen of sex is the chief prostitute. If sex crops up in marriage, it is because one party falls in love with somebody else, and wants to be unfaithful. Infidelity is sex and prostitutes know all about it. Wives know nothing and are nothing, in that respect.

D. H. Lawrence, *A Propos of Lady Chatterley's Lover*

He said he was a finer fellow than Shakespeare. I merely preferred myself to Mr Shaw.

Percy Wyndham Lewis, *Blasting and Bombardiering*

That noisiest of all old cocks.

*Ibid.*

Have you seen any more of your friends who worship Bernard Shaw? Tell them that Shaw is Carlyle & water, that he ought to have been a Quaker (cocoa and commercial dishonesty), that he has squandered what talents he may have had back in the '80's in inventing metaphysical reasons for behaving like a scoundrel, that he suffers from an inferiority complex towards Shakespeare, & that he is the critic, cultured critic (not very cultured but it is what B meant) that Samuel Butler prayed to be delivered from.

George Orwell, Letter to Brenda Salkeld, March 1933

A strange lady giving an address in Zurich wrote him a proposal thus: 'You have the greatest brain in the world, and I have the most beautiful body; so we ought to produce the most perfect child.' Shaw asked: 'What if the child inherits my body and your brains?'

Hesketh Pearson, *Bernard Shaw, His Life and Personality*

Knowing he hated bloodsports and would agree with the sentiment, Lady Astor remarked, 'I hate killing for pleasure.' As he said nothing, one of her children probed: 'Do you hate killing for pleasure?' 'It depends upon whom you kill', he answered.

Hesketh Pearson, *Lives of the Wits*

1908 saw a stirring. By 1912 it was established, at least in Ormond St, that the cardboard Shaw and the suety Wells were NOT the voice.

Ezra Pound, in *Criterion*, 1937

He went through the fiery furnace, but never a hair was missed / From the heels of our most Colossal Arch-Super-Egotist. /

*Punch*, March 1917

I think envy plays a part in his philosophy in this sense, that if he allowed himself to admit that goodness of things he lacks and others possess, he would feel such intolerable envy that he would find life unbearable. Also he hates self-control, and makes up theories with a view to proving that self-control is pernicious. I couldn't get on with *Man and Superman*: it disgusted me. I don't think he is a soul in Hell dancing on red-hot iron. I think his Hell is merely diseased vanity and a morbid fear of being laughed at.

Bertrand Russell, Letter to Lowes Dickinson, July 1904

George Too Shaw To Be Good.

Dylan Thomas, Letter to Pamela Hansford Johnson, October 1933

For one thing, it [*Heartbreak House*] is improvised work. Shaw admitted he made it up as he went along, not knowing from day to day what his characters would do or say or become. He always tended to work this way, regarding a play essentially as an organism with a life of its own; one need only nurture it and let it assume its own shape. He even used to keep a checkerboard at hand to remind himself who was onstage and who was off at any given moment in the writing. There is no doubt this method served him as well as any other; his night mind was not, to say the least, fantastic. I am sure deep in his unconscious there lurked not the usual nightmare monsters of the rest of us, but yards of thesis, antithesis, and synthesis, all neatly labelled and filed. Yet in *Heartbreak House* Shaw's improvisatory genius breaks down; he keeps marching into conversational culs-de-sac.

Gore Vidal, *Essays*: 'Love love love'

He hasn't an enemy in the world, and none of his friends like him.

Oscar Wilde, in G. B. Shaw, *Sixteen Self Sketches*

Mr Bernard Shaw has no enemies but is intensely disliked by all his friends.

Oscar Wilde, in William Butler Yeats, *Autobiographies*

This is the first generation in which the spirit of literature has been conquered by the spirit of the press, of hurry, of immediate interests, and Bernard Shaw is the Joseph whose prosperity has brought his brethren into captivity.

William Butler Yeats, Letter to Edmund Gosse, 12 April 1910

I agree about Shaw – he is haunted by the mystery he flouts. He is an atheist who trembles in the haunted corridor.

William Butler Yeats, Letter to George Russell ('AE'), 1 July 1921

Presently I had a nightmare that I was haunted by a sewing-machine that clicked and shone, but the incredible thing was that the machine smiled, smiled perpetually. Yet I delighted in Shaw, the formidable man. He could hit my enemies, and the enemies of those I loved, as I could never hit, as no living author that was dear to me could ever hit.

William Butler Yeats, *Autobiographies*

## SHAW, T. E., *see under* LAWRENCE, T. E.

## SHEFFIELD, JOHN, EARL OF MULGRAVE AND NORMANBY

1648–1721 Poet

I am not so young now but that I can chew the cud of lechery with some satisfaction. You who are so amorous and vigorous may have your mind wholly taken up with the present, but we grave decay'd people, alas, are glad to steal a thought some times towards the past, and then are to ask God forgiveness for it too.

On himself, Letter to George Etherege, 7 March 1687

## SHELBURNE, EARL OF (WILLIAM PETTY, MARQUIS OF LANSDOWNE)

1737–1805 Politician

D--- it! I never could see through varnish, and there's an end.

Thomas Gainsborough, finding it impossible to paint Shelburne's portrait, in *The Autobiography of Mrs Piozzi*

The jesuit of Berkeley Square.

George III, in *The Correspondence of George III with Lord North*

His falsehood was so constant and notorious, that it was rather his profession than his instrument. It was like a fictitious violin, which is hung out of a music shop to indicate in what goods the tradesman deals; not to be of service, nor to be depended on for playing a true note. He was so well known that he could only deceive by speaking truth. His plausibility was less an artifice than a habit; and his smiles were so excited that, like the rattle of the snake, they warned before he had time to bite. Both his heart and his face were brave; he feared neither danger nor detection. He was as fond of insincerity as if he had been the inventor, and practised it with as little caution as if he thought nobody else had discovered the secret.

Horace Walpole, *Journal of the Reign of George III*

## SHELLEY, MARY WOLLSTONECRAFT

1797–1851 Authoress

Mrs Shelley is very clever, indeed it would be difficult for her not to be so; the daughter of Mary Wollstonecraft and Godwin, and the wife of Shelley, could be no common person.

Lord Byron, in Lady Blessington, *Conversations with Lord Byron*

The author seems to us to disclose uncommon powers of poetic imagination. The feeling with which we perused the unexpected and fearful, yet, allowing the possibility of the event, very natural conclusion of Frankenstein's experiment, shook a little even our firm nerves.

Sir Walter Scott, Review of *Frankenstein*, in *Blackwood's Magazine*, March 1818

## SHELLEY, PERCY BYSSHE

1792–1822 Poet

Less oft is peace in Shelley's mind, / Than calm in waters, seen. /

On himself, *To Jane: The Recollection*

In this have I long believed, that my power consists in sympathy and that part of imagination which relates to sentiment and contemplation. I am formed, if for anything not in common with the herd of mankind, to apprehend the minute and remote distinctions of feeling, whether relative to external nature or the living things which surround us, and to communicate the conceptions which result from considering either the moral or the material universe as a whole.

On himself, Letter to William Godwin, 1817

I have an unpurchasable mind.

On himself, in conversation with Henry Addington, 1802

A beautiful and ineffectual angel, beating in the void his luminous wings in vain.

Matthew Arnold, *Essays in Criticism*: 'Byron'

Ah, did you once see Shelley plain, / And did he stop and speak to you? / And did you speak to him again, / How strange it seems, and new! /

Robert Browning, *Memorabilia*

Meantime, as I call Shelley a moral man, because he was true, simple-hearted, and brave, and because what he acted corresponded to what he knew, so I call him a man of religious mind, because every audacious negative cast up by him against the Divine was interpenetrated with a mood of reverence and adoration – and because I find him everywhere taking for granted some of the capital dogmas of Christianity, while most vehemently denying their historical basement.

Robert Browning, *Shelley*

As to poor Shelley, who is another bugbear to you and the world, he is, to my knowledge, the *least* selfish and the mildest of men – a man who has made more sacrifice of his fortune and feelings for others than any I ever heard of. With his speculative opinions I have nothing in common, nor desire to have.

Lord Byron, Letter to Thomas Moore, 4 March 1822

He is one of the many whom we cannot read without wonder, or without pain: when I consider his powers of mind, I am proud that he was an Etonian: when I remember their perversion, I wish he had never been one. However, he has made his election; and where Justice cannot approve, Charity can at least be silent!

*Etonian*, 1821

The splendours, the almost supernatural beauty of the active mind of Shelley will obviously forever gild his poems and blind one to the mediocrity of thousands of his inferior lines. But the gold is an exterior gold; we bring it ourselves to his shrine, and his shining soul only very seldom illuminates his poems from within. He is almost never natural; he is almost never not intent on showing himself the champion of freedom, the Satan of a Hanoverian Heaven.

Ford Madox Ford, *The March of Literature*

Mr Shelley's style is to poetry what astrology is to natural science – a passionate dream, a straining after impossibilities, a record of fond conjectures, a confused embodying of vague abstractions – a fever of the soul, thirsting and craving after what it cannot have, indulging its love of power and novelty at the expense of truth and nature, associating ideas by contraries, and wasting great powers by their application to unattainable objects.

William Hazlitt, in *Edinburgh Review*

He had a fire in his eye, a fever in his blood, a maggot in his brain, a hectic flutter in his speech, which mark out the philosophic fanatic.

William Hazlitt, *Table Talk*

You, I am sure, will forgive me for sincerely remarking that you might curb your magnanimity, and be more of an artist, and load every rift of your subject with ore.

John Keats, Letter to Shelley, August 1820

'Follow your instincts' is his one moral rule, confounding the very lowest animal instincts with those lofty ideas of right, which it was the will of Heaven that he should retain, ay, and love, to the very last, and so reducing them all to the level of sentiments. 'Follow your instincts' – But what if our instincts lead us to eat animal food? 'Then you must follow the instincts of me, Percy Bysshe Shelley. I think it horrible, cruel, it offends my taste.' What if our instincts lead us to tyrannise over our fellow-men? 'Then you must repress those instincts. I, Shelley, think that, too, horrible and cruel.' Whether it be vegetarianism or liberty, the rule is practically the same – sentiment: which, in his case, as in the case of all sentimentalists, turns out to mean at last, not the sentiments of mankind in general, but the private sentiments of the writer. This is Shelley; a sentimentalist pure and simple; incapable of anything like inductive reasoning.

Charles Kingsley, *Thoughts on Shelley and Byron*

That 'quivering intensity', offered in itself apart from any substance, offered instead of any object, is what, though it may make Shelley intoxicating at fifteen, makes him almost unreadable, except in very small quantities of his best, to the mature. Even when he is in his own way unmistakably a distinguished poet . . . it is impossible to go on reading him at any length with pleasure; the elusive imagery, the high-pitched emotions, the tone and movement, the ardours, ecstasies, and despairs, are too much the same all through. The effect is of vanity and emptiness (Arnold was right) as well as monotony.

F. R. Leavis, *Revaluation*

But Shelley had a hyper-thyroid face.

Sir John Squire, *Ballade of the Glandular Hypothesis*

Mr Shelley and his disciples – the followers (if I may so call them) of the PHANTASTIC SCHOOL, labour to effect a revolution . . . They would transfer the domicile of poetry to regions where reason, far from having any supremacy or rule, is all but unknown, an alien and an outcast; to seats of anarchy and abstraction, where imagination exercises the shadow of an authority, over a people of phantoms, in a land of dreams.

Henry Taylor, Preface to *Philip van Artevelde*

Shelley should not be read, but inhaled through a gas pipe.

Lionel Trilling, in Clifton Fadiman, *Enter Conversing*

*See also* Robert Browning, Lord Byron, Samuel Taylor Coleridge, Isadora Duncan, John Keats, Rudyard Kipling, D. H. Lawrence, T. E. Lawrence, Jack London, William Wordsworth, William Butler Yeats

## SHERIDAN, RICHARD BRINSLEY

1751–1816 Statesman, Dramatist

What I write in a Hurry I always feel to be not worth reading, and what I try to take Pains with, I am sure never to finish.

On himself, Letter to David Garrick, 10 January 1778

How unceasingly do I meditate on Death, and how continually do I act as if the thought of it had never crossed my mind.

On himself, Letter to his Wife, November 1804

Sure I am, that there is no Person who has been near to me and confidentially acquainted with my private affairs and personal difficulties and who has witness'd my conduct under them that has not been confirmed or improved in principle and integrity in his views and transactions in this Life. You will forgive my having said thus much of myself – it may be egotism, but it is Fact.

*Ibid.*, 20 April 1810

You told me lately in one of your Letters that I was too apt to eat the calf in the Cow's belly, apologizing for the homeliness of the Phraze, and dared me to deny it. I do not wholly deny it, but I do assert that in most of the great cases in which I have suffered by eagerness of anticipation the cause has been more infinitely in the roguery and insincerity of others than even in my own credulity and indolence.

*Ibid.*, November 1814

Good at a fight, but better at a play;
Godlike in giving, but the devil to pay.

Lord Byron, *On a Cast of Sheridan's Hand*

Every man has his element: Sheridan's is hot water.

Lord Eldon, in Lord Broughton, *Recollections of a Long Life*

We cannot help thinking that there are marks of an uneasy turn of mind in all Sheridan's productions. There is almost always some real pain going on amongst his characters. They are always perplexing, mortifying, or distressing one another; snatching their jokes out of some misery, as if they were playing at snap-dragon . . . Sheridan's comedy is all-stinging satire. His bees want honey.

Leigh Hunt, on *The School for Scandal*, in *Tatler*, 27 October 1830

It is said that, as he sat at the Piazza Coffee-house, during the fire [in Drury Lane], taking some refreshment, a friend of his having remarked on the philosophic calmness with which he bore his misfortune, Sheridan answered, 'A man may surely be allowed to take a glass of wine *by his own fireside.*'

Thomas Moore, *Memoirs of the Life of R. B. Sheridan*

To such minutiae of effect did he attend, that I have found in more than one instance, a memorandum made of the precise place in which the words

'Good God, Mr Speaker,' were to be introduced.
*Ibid.*

His hours of composition, as long as he continued to be an author, were at night, and . . . he required a profusion of lights around him, while he wrote. Wine too, was one of his favourite helps to inspiration; – 'If the thought (he would say) is slow to come, a glass of good wine encourages it, and when it *does* come, a glass of good wine rewards it.'
*Ibid.*

Never examining accounts, nor referring to receipts, he seemed as if . . . he wished to make *paying* as like as possible to *giving*.
*Ibid.*

Somebody told me, (but not your Father) that the Opera Singers would not be likely to get any money out of Sheridan this year. 'Why, that fellow grows fat,' says I, 'like Heliogabalus, upon the tongues of nightingales.'
Mrs Piozzi (Hester Lynch Thrale), Letter to Fanny Burney, 22 November 1781

Sheridan was listened to with such attention that you might have heard a pin drop.
Samuel Rogers, *Table Talk*

Sheridan had very fine eyes, and he was not a little vain of them. He said to me on his death-bed, 'Tell Lady Besborough that my eyes will look up on the coffin-lid as brightly as ever.'
*Ibid.*

The work of Sheridan begins to be taken at its true value – as a clever but emasculated *rifacimento* [*remoulding*].
Lytton Strachey, *Portraits in Miniature*

Fox outlived his vices; those of Sheridan accompanied him to the tomb.
Sir Nathaniel Wraxall, *Historica and Posthumous Memoirs*

*See also* Robert Burns, Charles James Fox, Sarah Siddons

## SHERIDAN, THOMAS

1719–88 Actor

Why, Sir, Sherry is dull, naturally dull; but it must have taken a great deal of pains to become what we now see him. Such an excess of stupidity, Sir, is not in Nature.
Samuel Johnson, in James Boswell, *Life of Johnson*

Sir, it is burning a farthing candle at Dover, to shew a light at Calais.
*Ibid.*, on Sheridan's style

*See also* Oliver Goldsmith

## SHERMAN, WILLIAM TECUMSEH

1820–91 General

I will not accept if nominated, and will not serve if elected.
On himself, telegram to John B. Henderson, Chairman of the Republican National Convention at Chicago, declining the presidential nomination, 5 June 1884

Sherman, hurrah, we'll go with him / Wherever it may be / Through Carolina's cotton fields / Or Georgia to the sea. /
Anon., Soldiers' marching song

It would seem as if in him, all the attributes of man were merged into the enormities of the demon, as if Heaven intended in him to manifest depths of depravity yet untouched by a fallen race . . . unsated still in his demoniac vengeance he sweeps over the

country like a simoom of destruction.
Anon., Editorial in *Macon Telegraph* (Georgia), 5 December 1864

No living American was so loved and venerated as he. To look upon his face, to hear his name, was to have one's love of country intensified. He served his country, not for fame, not out of a sense of professional duty, but for love of the flag and of the beneficent civil institutions of which it was the emblem. He was an ideal soldier, and shared to the fullest the *esprit de corps* of the army; but he cherished the civil institutions organized under the constitution, and was a soldier only that these might be perpetuated in undiminished usefulness and honor.
President Benjamin Harrison, in *Congressional Record*

## SHERRINGTON, SIR CHARLES SCOTT

1857–1952 Physiologist

In the summer of 1915 he disappeared on a bicycle, presumably for a holiday, leaving no address: a collar stud, which was lost and could not be replaced, disclosed his whereabouts. He was a bench-worker 'incognito' at a munitions plant in Birmingham. His shift time, 7 a.m.–6 p.m., did not permit any visit to a shop to obtain a collar stud. His great interest in industrial fatigue – he was Chairman of the Industrial Fatigue Board in 1918 – had determined him to study fatigue 'in situ'... He was then nearly 60.
C. E. R. Sherrington, *Charles Scott Sherrington, 1857–1952*

## SHIRLEY, JAMES

1596–1666 Poet

James, thou and I did spend some precious yeares / At Katherine-Hall; since when, we sometimes feele / In our poetick braines, (as plaine appeares) / A whirling tricke, then caught from Katherine's wheele. /
Thomas Bancroft, *To James Shirley*

## SHORT, REV. THOMAS

1789–1879 Oxford Academic

Match me such marvel, save in college port, / That rose-red liquor, half as old as Short. /
Anon. epigram, after J. W. Burgon

## SICKERT, WALTER RICHARD

1860–1942 Painter

As Sickert wrote to Miss Sands, he could not 'conceive heaven' without
'1. painting in a sunny room an iron bedstead in the morning
2. painting in a North light studio from drawings till tea-time
3. giving a few lessons to eager students of both sexes at night.'
W. Baron, *Sickert*

Although he left the footlights for the studio so early, Sickert has been an actor all his life, the world his theatre, the gallery his stage, and the whole picture-going public his audience.
R. Emmons, *The Life and Opinions of Walter Richard Sickert*

Sickert shows us a world which is drab, dirty, disillusioned, a world whose pleasures are mirthless and whose devil is boredom. A world, in fact, such as we know.
John Rothenstein, *The Artists of the 1890s*

Sickert's genius for discovering the dreariest house and most forbidding rooms in which to work was a source of wonder and amusement to me. He himself was so fastidious in his person, in his manners, in the choice of his clothes; was he affecting a kind of dandyism *à rebours*?
William Rothenstein, *Men and Memories*

## SIDDONS, SARAH

1755–1831 Actress

When Mrs Siddons came into the room, there happened to be no chair ready for her, which he [Dr Johnson] observing, said with a smile, 'Madam, you who so often occasion a want of seats to other people, will the more easily excuse the want of one yourself.'

James Boswell, *Life of Johnson*

My friend Douglas Kinnaird told a story, rather too long, about Mrs Siddons and Kean acting together at some Irish Theatre. Kean got drunk and Mrs Siddons got all the applause. The next night Kean acted Jaffier, and Mrs Siddons Belvidera, and then 'he got all the applause', and, said Sheridan, 'she got drunk I suppose.'

Lord Broughton, *Recollections of a Long Life*

She was the stateliest ornament of the public mind.

William Hazlitt, 'Mrs Siddons', in *Examiner*, 16 June 1816

She is out of the pale of all theories and annihilates all rules. Wherever she sits there is grace and grandeur, there is tragedy personified. Her seat is the undivided throne of the Tragic Muse. She had no need of the robes, the sweeping train, the ornaments of the stage; in herself she is as great as any being she ever represented in the ripeness and plenitude of her power.

William Hazlitt, *Table Talk: Whether Actors ought to Sit in the Boxes*

She can overpower, astonish, afflict, but she cannot win: her majestic presence and commanding features seem to disregard love, as a trifle to which they cannot descend.

Leigh Hunt, *Critical Essays on the Performers of the London Theatres*

Her voice appeared to have lost its brilliancy (like a beautiful face through a veil).

Henry Crabb Robinson, Diary, 21 April 1812

When without motion her arms are not genteel.

Horace Walpole, Letter to the Countess of Upper Ossory, 3 November 1782

## SIDMOUTH, LORD, *see under* ADDINGTON, HENRY

## SIDNEY, SIR PHILIP

1554–86 Statesman, Soldier, Poet

Sidney did not keep a decorum in making every one speak as well as himself.

Ben Jonson, in *Conversations with William Drummond of Hawthornden*

So that whereas (through the fame of his high deserts) he was then, or rather before, in election for the Crown of *Poland*, the Queen of England refused to further his advancement, not out of emulation, but out of fear to lose the jewel of her times.

Anthony à Wood, *Athenae Oxonienses*

*See also* Fulke Greville, John Lyly

## SIMON, JOHN ALLESBROOK, VISCOUNT

1873–1954 Politician

Simon has sat on the fence so long that the iron has entered his soul.

David Lloyd George, in A. J. P. Taylor, *English History 1914–1945*

## SINCLAIR, UPTON BEALL

1878–1968 Author, Socialist

Few American public figures, let alone American inspirational novelists, have written so many books, delivered so many lectures, covered as much territory, advocated so many causes or composed so many letters to the editor, got mixed up in so many scandals, been so insulted, ridiculed, spied on, tricked and left holding the bag – few, in short, have jumped so nimbly from so many frying pans into so many fires, and none has ever managed to keep so sunny and buoyant while the flames were leaping around him.

Robert Cantwell, 'Upton Sinclair', in Malcoln Cowley ed., *After the Genteel Tradition*

He was intense, nervous, chaste, easily influenced, perplexed about religious problems and worried about sex; an amateur violinist who lectured his sweet-hearts about venereal diseases, went on fantastic bicycle rides of a hundred miles a day and suffered from blinding surges of unfocused emotion that he interpreted as symptoms of genius.

*Ibid.*

. . . propaganda for the sake of political action can and does in Sinclair's fiction become tedious. One gets tired of watching Mr Sinclair spy a capitalist behind every woodpile.

Grant C. Knight, *American Literature and Culture*

It is alive and warm. It is brutal with life. It is written of sweat and blood, and groans with tears. It depicts not what man ought to be, but what man is compelled to be in our world, in the Twentieth Century.

Jack London, referring to Sinclair's *The Jungle*, in Jay Martin, *Harvests of Change, American Literature, 1865–1914*

No man in American history has denounced more different people than you have, or in more violent terms, and yet no man that I can recall complains more bitterly when he happens to be hit. Why not stop caterwauling for a while, and try to play the game according to the rules?

H. L. Mencken, Letter to Sinclair, 2 May 1936

You are now in class with Masters and Frost, loafers, hiders. Which is a damn pity, as you have been some good at alternating intervals.

Ezra Pound, Letter to Sinclair, 26 September 1936

## SITTING BULL

*circa* 1831–90 Sachem of the Hunkpapa Sioux Nation

When I was a boy the Sioux owned the world; the sun rose and set on their land; they sent ten thousand men to battle. Where are the warriors today? Who slew them? Where are our lands? Who owns them? What white man can say I ever stole his land or a penny of his money? Yet, they say I am a thief. What white woman, however lonely, was ever captive or insulted by me? Yet they say I am a bad Indian. What white man has ever seen me drunk? Who has ever come to me hungry and unfed? Who has ever seen me beat my wives or abuse my children? What law have I broken? Is it wrong for me to love my own? Is it wicked for me because my skin is red? Because I am a Sioux; because I was born where my father lived; because I would die for my people and my country?

On himself, in T. C. McLuhan, *Touch the Earth*

## SITWELL, DAME EDITH

1887–1964 Authoress

The most trying attitude of all that the public has adopted is that of accusing me of trying to '*épater le bourgeois*' – (such bad manners. One assumes intelligence in one's audience) and of doing this in order to get publicity . . . That is the reason why I live here in France, now, instead of in London; for it is no use people trying to get at me and behave as the crowds behave to the wretched lions and tigers at the Zoo.

On herself, Letter to R. G. Howarth, 24 February 1937

It is a dangerous thing to say, but I can say it to you. Sometimes, when I begin a poem, it is almost like automatic writing. Then I use my mind on it afterwards.

On herself, Letter to Maurice Bowra, 24 January 1944

Nobody has ever been more alive than I! I am like an unpopular electric eel in a pond full of flatfish.

On herself, in John Lehmann, *A Nest of Tigers*

When we come to compare the collected poems of Dame Edith Sitwell with those of Yeats, or Mr Eliot or Professor Auden, it will be found that hers have the purest poetical content of them all.

Cyril Connolly, in *Sunday Times*, 29 July 1957

Writers who detach tragedy from the persons who suffer it are generally to be seen soon after wearing someone else's bleeding heart on their own safe sleeves – an odious transaction, and an odious transaction is what Dame Edith Sitwell's atomic poetry seems to me to be.

D. J. Enright, in *New Statesman*

The Sitwells belong to the history of publicity rather than of poetry.

F. R. Leavis, *New Bearings in English Poetry*

Edith – she is a poetess by the way – is a bad loser. When worsted in argument, she throws Queensberry Rules to the winds. She once called me Percy.

Percy Wyndham Lewis, *Blasting and Bombardiering*

Then Edith Sitwell appeared, her nose longer than an ant-eater's, and read some of her absurd stuff.

Lytton Strachey, recalling an evening at Arnold Bennett's house, Letter to Dora Carrington, 28 June 1921

So you've been reviewing Edith Sitwell's latest piece of virgin dung, have you? Isn't she a poisonous thing of a woman, lying, concealing, flipping, plagiarising, misquoting, and being as clever a crooked literary publicist as ever.

Dylan Thomas, Letter to Glyn Jones, 1934

With the Sitwells, at Renishaw . . . Sachie likes talking about sex. Osbert very shy. Edith wholly ignorant. We talked of slums. She said the poor streets of Scarborough were terrible but that she did not think that the fishermen took drugs very much. She also said that port was made with methylated spirit: she knew this for a fact because her charwoman told her.

Evelyn Waugh, Diary, 23 August 1930

My wife . . . liked delicate fantasy after the manner of Edith Sitwell, to whom I am as appreciatively indifferent as I am to the quaint patterns of old chintzes, the designs on dinner plates or the charm of nursery rhymes.

H. G. Wells, *Experiment in Autobiography*

## SMART, CHRISTOPHER

1722–71 Poet

*Johnson*: 'It seems as if his mind has ceased to struggle with the disease; for he grows fat upon it.' *Burney*: 'Perhaps, Sir, that may be from want of exercise.' *Johnson*: 'No, Sir; he has partly as much exercise as he used to have, for he digs in the garden. Indeed, before his confinement, he used for exercise to walk to the ale-house; but he was *carried* back again. I did not think he ought to be shut up. His infirmities were not noxious to society. He insisted on people praying with him; and I'd as lief pray with Kit Smart as any one else. Another charge was, that he did not love clean linen; and I have no passion for it.'

James Boswell, *Life of Johnson*

Mr Morgan argued with him . . . in vain . . . 'Pray, Sir, (said he) whether do you reckon Derrick or Smart the best poet'; Johnson at once felt himself roused; and answered, 'Sir, there is no settling the point of precedency between a louse and a flea.'

*Ibid.*

Smart's melancholy shewed itself only in a preternatural excitement to prayer – taking *au pied de la lettre* our blessed Saviour's injunction to *pray without ceasing*. – So that beginning by regular addresses to the Almighty, he went on to call his friends from their dinners, or beds, or places of recreation, whenever that impulse towards prayer pressed upon his mind. In every other transaction of life no man's wits could be more regular than those of Smart.

Mrs Piozzi (Hester Lynch Thrale), *The British Synonymy*

## SMILES, SAMUEL

1812–1904 Author, Social Reformer

My object in writing out *Self-Help*, and delivering it at first in the form of lectures, and afterwards rewriting and publishing it in the form of a book, was principally to illustrate and enforce the power of George Stephenson's great word – PERSEVERANCE.

On himself, *Autobiography*

He was 'fonder of frolic than of learning' when a young man and was not even thrifty. 'I thought,' he said, 'that the principal use of money was to be spent.' He even forced open his money box with a table knife in order to collect the few pennies he had bothered to save. His later life was an exercise in self-discipline; before he moulded others, he set out to mould himself. This is perhaps the most important thing about him as a person.

Asa Briggs, *Victorian People*

I remember Dr Smiles as the kindest old man, with a white head and beard, full of sympathy for children and love for animals. He even took an interest in my doll, and was particularly keen about my money-box, frequently asking how it was getting on. Sometimes he dropped in a penny by way of encouragement. I see it all now. He knew that if a child be taught to save and take care of its pennies that child will generally grow up thrifty, whereas money easily gained is readily lost, while he who buys what he does not want frequently ends up by wanting what he cannot buy.

Mrs Alec Tweedie, in Thomas Bowen, *Life and Works of Smiles*

*See also* Gilbert Scott

## SMITH, ADAM

1723–90 Political Economist

He was the most absent man in company that I ever saw – moving his lips and talking to himself, and smiling in the midst of large companies. If you awakened him from his reverie, and made him attend to the subject of the conversation, he immediately began a harangue, and never stopped till he told you all he knew about it, and with the utmost philosophical ingenuity.

Alexander Carlyle, in R. B. Haldane, *Adam Smith*

'Be seated, gentlemen,' said Smith on one occasion. 'No,' replied Pitt, 'we will stand till you are first seated; for we are all your scholars.'

C. R. Fay, *Adam Smith and the Scotland of His Day*

His achievements are not accidents. If the architects' plans are compared with history, they will be found to have been executed in large part by the builders of the nineteenth century.

Francis W. Hirst, *Adam Smith*

Smith has issued from the seclusion of a professorship of morals, from the drudgery of a commissionership of customs, to sit in the council-chamber of princes. His word has rung through the study to the platform. It has been proclaimed by the agitator, conned by the statesman, and printed in a thousand statutes.

*Ibid.*

*See also* David Hume

## SMITH, ALFRED EMANUEL

1873–1944 Politician

[He] could make statistics sit up, beg, roll over and bark.

Anon., in Oscar Handlin, *Al Smith and His America*

. . . ruined by associating with rich men – a thing far more dangerous to politicians than even booze or the sound of their own voices.

H. L. Mencken, in Richard O'Connor, *The First Hurrah*

The plain fact is that Al, as a good New Yorker, is as provincial as a Kansas farmer. He is not only not interested in the great problems that heave and lather the country: he has never heard of them.

H. L. Mencken, July 1927, in *A Carnival of Buncombe*

He exchanged the old blue serge suit for a white tie and tails, the brown derby for a top hat. He took off the square-toe brogans with which he had climbed from the sidewalks of New York to dizzy heights and put on a pair of pumps. It takes a damn good acrobat to do that while at the top of the ladder.

Mayor Jimmy Walker of New York, in Richard O'Connor, *The First Hurrah*

## SMITH, BESSIE

*circa* 1898–1937 Singer

'It's a long, old road' as Bessie Smith puts it, 'but it's got to find an end.' And so, she wearily, doggedly informs us, 'I picked up my bag, baby, and I tried it again'. Her song ends on a very bitter and revealing note. 'You can't trust nobody, you might as well be alone/Found my long-lost friend, and I might as well stayed at home!' Still, she was driven to find that long-lost friend, to grasp again, with fearful hope, the unwilling, unloving, human hand.

James Baldwin, 'Four AM', in *Show*, October 1964

## SMITH, FREDERICK EDWIN, *see under* BIRKENHEAD, EARL OF

## SMITH, JOSEPH

1805–44 Mormon Prophet

No man knows my history . . . If I had not experienced what I have, I could not have believed it myself.

On himself, Funeral sermon, 4 April 1844, in Fawn Brodie, *No Man Knows My History*

The Saints, the Saints, his only pride, / For them he lived, for them he died. / Their joys were his, their sorrows too; / He loved the Saints, he loved Nauvoo. /

John Taylor, *The Seer*

Whenever he found his speech growing too modern – which was about every sentence or two – he ladled in a few such scriptural phrases as 'exceeding sore', 'and it came to pass', etc., and made things satisfactory again. 'And it came to pass' was his pet. If he had left that out, his Bible would have been only a pamphlet.

Mark Twain, in M. H. Werner, *Brigham Young*

## SMITH, (LLOYD) LOGAN PEARSALL

1865–1946 Author

I love money; just to be in the room with a millionaire makes me less forlorn.

On himself, *Trivia*

People say that life is the thing, but I prefer reading.

*Ibid.*

How can you say that my life is not a success? Have I not for more than sixty years got enough to eat and escaped being eaten.

*Ibid.*

## SMITH, SYDNEY

1771–1845 Wit

The Smiths never had any arms, and have invariably sealed their letters with their thumbs.

On himself, in Earl of Ilchester ed., *The Journal of Elizabeth Lady Holland, 1791–1811*

When I am in the pulpit, I have the pleasure of seeing my audience nod approbation while they sleep.

On himself, attributed

The whole of my life has passed like a razor – in hot water or a scrape.

*Ibid.*

My idea of heaven is eating *pâtés de foie gras* to the sound of trumpets.

*Ibid.*

You and I are the exceptions to the laws of nature; you have risen by your gravity, and I have sunk by my levity.

On himself, remark to his brother

I cannot cure myself of punctuality.

On himself, in Douglas Jerrold ed., *Bon-Mots of Sydney Smith*

## SMITHERS, LEONARD

1861–1909 Publisher

He loves first editions, especially of women.

Oscar Wilde, Letter to Reginald Turner, 10 August 1897

## SMOLLETT, TOBIAS GEORGE

1721–71 Novelist

Smollett's 'Travels in France and Italy' . . . gives the impression of a sound, sincere personality, not very cultured in the arts, but immensely well informed, and breathing a hard, comfortable common sense at every pore. A doctor's personality, and yet still more the personality of a police magistrate; slightly less *doux*, and more downright, than that of Fielding.

Arnold Bennett, Journal, 25 September 1907

It is extremely strange that both Mr Dickens and Mr Thackeray, two men whose writings were so singularly pure, should have quoted Smollett as such a witty writer, and have considered him, or affected to consider him, their master; it would puzzle any one to find a witty passage in Dickens or Thackeray with a *double entendre* in it; it would puzzle any man to find a funny passage in Smollett without one.

Henry Kingsley, *Fireside Studies*

For a short period during the interregnum between Pope and Johnson he was a kind of literary Protector.

Thomas Seccombe, *The Age of Johnson*

Next Sm-ll-t came. What author dare resist / Historian, critic, bard, and novellist? / 'To reach thy temple, honour'd Fame,' he cry'd / 'Where's, where's an avenue I have not try'd?' /
Cuthbert Shaw, *The Race*

## SOMERSET, FITZROY JAMES HENRY, *see under* RAGLAN, LORD

## SOUTHEY, ROBERT
1774–1843 Poet

Robert the Rhymer who lived at the Lakes / Describes himself thus, to prevent mistakes; / Or rather, perhaps, be it said, to correct them, / There being plenty about for those who collect them . . . / A man he is by nature merry, / Somewhat Tom-foolish, and comical, very; / Who has gone through the world, not mindful of pelf, / Upon easy terms, thank Heaven, with himself . . . / Having some friends whom he loves dearly / And no lack of foes, whom he laughs at sincerely; / And never for great, nor for little things, / Has he fretted his guts to fiddle-strings. /
On himself, *Robert the Rhymer*

My ways are as broad as the king's high-road, and my means lie in an ink-stand.
On himself, in Edward Latham, *Famous Sayings*

He had written praises of a Regicide; / He had written praises of all kings whatever; / He had written for republics far and wide, / And then against them bitterer than ever; / For pantisocracy he once had cried / Aloud, a scheme less moral than 'twas clever; / Then grew a hearty anti-jacobin – / Had turned his coat – and would have turned his skin. /
Lord Byron, *The Vision of Judgment*

Bob Southey! You're a poet – Poet laureate, / And representative of all the race, / Although 'tis true that you've turned out a Tory at / Last – yours has lately been a common case. /
Lord Byron, Dedication to *Don Juan*

Yesterday, at Holland-house, I was introduced to Southey – the best looking bard I have seen for some time. To have that poet's head and shoulders, I would almost have written his Sapphics.
Lord Byron, Letter to Thomas Moore, 27 September 1813

The living undertaker of epics.
William Hazlitt, *Lectures on the English Poets*

Beneath these poppies buried deep, / The bones of Bob the bard lie hid; / Peace to his manes; and may he sleep / As soundly as his readers did! . . . /

Death, weary of so dull a writer, / Put to his books a *finis* thus. / Oh! may the earth on him lie lighter / Than did his quartos upon us! /
Thomas Moore, *Epitaph on Robert Southey*

A celebrated poet, Mr Feathernest, to whom the Marquis had recently given a place in exchange for his conscience. It was thought by Mr Feathernest's friends, that he had made a very good bargain. The poet had, in consequence, burned his Odes to Truth and Liberty, and had published a volume of Panegyrical Addresses 'to all the crowned heads in Europe', with the motto, 'Whatever is at court, is right.'
Thomas Love Peacock, *Melincourt*

. . . I told Porson that Southey had said to me, 'My *Madoc* has brought me in a mere trifle; but that poem will be a valuable possession to my family.' Porson answered, '*Madoc* will be read – when Homer and Virgil are forgotten.'
Samuel Rogers, *Table Talk*

*See also* John Keats, John Murray, Lord Russell, Sir Walter Scott

## SPENCER, HERBERT

1820–1903 Philosopher, Psychologist

My *Principles of Psychology* is not 'caviare to the public', but cod-liver oil, for although it is nasty to take at the time, it does good afterwards.

On himself, in 'Two', *Home Life with Herbert Spencer*

You see, I am like an elephant's trunk, which roots up trees and picks up sixpences.

*Ibid.*

The expression often used by Mr Herbert Spencer of the Survival of the Fittest is more accurate, and is sometimes equally convenient.

Charles Darwin, *The Origin of Species*

Mr Spencer is a very considerable writer, and I set great store by his works. But we are very old friends, and he has endured me as a sort of 'devil's-advocate' for thirty-odd years. He thinks that if I can pick no holes in what he says he is safe. But I pick a great many holes, and we agree to differ.

T. H. Huxley, Letter to Lady Welby, April 1884

Oh! you know, Spencer's idea of a tragedy is a deduction killed by a fact.

T. H. Huxley, in Herbert Spencer, *An Autobiography*

He is a considerable thinker, though anything but safe – and is on the whole an ally, in spite of his Universal Postulate ... His notion that we cannot think the annihilation or diminution of force I remember well – and I thought it out-Whewelled Whewell. The conservation of thought has hardly yet got to be believed, and already its negation is declared inconceivable. But this is Spencer all over; he throws himself with a certain deliberate impetuosity into the last new theory that chimes with his general way of thinking, and treats it as proved as soon as he is able to found a connected exposition of phenomena upon it.

John Stuart Mill, Letter to Alexander Bain, March 1864

*See also* George Eliot, Jack London

## SPENSER, EDMUND

1552?–99 Poet

Old *Spencer* next, warm'd with Poetick Rage, / In Antick Tales amus'd a Barb'rous Age; / An Age that yet uncultivate and Rude, / Where-e'er the Poet's Fancy led, pursu'd / Through pathless Fields, and unfrequented Floods, / To Dens of Dragons, and Enchanted Woods. /

Joseph Addison, in *Annual Miscellany*, 1694

*Spencer ...*
*... lost a Noble* Muse in *Fairy-land.*

Knightly Chetwood, *Commendatory Verses prefixed to An Essay on Translated Verse, by the Earl of Roscommon*

Our ancient verse, (as homely as the Times), / Was rude, unmeasur'd, only lagg'd with Rhymes: / Number and Cadence, that have since been Shown, / To those unpolish'd Writers were unknown. / Fairfax was He, who, in that Darker Age, / By his just Rules restrain'd Poetic Rage; / Spencer did next in Pastorals excel, / And taught the Noble Art of Writing well: / To stricter Rules the Stanza did restrain, / And found for Poetry a richer Veine. /

John Dryden, *The Art of Poetry*

*Spenser* more than once insinuates, that the Soul of *Chaucer* was transfus'd into his Body; and that he was begotten by him Two hundred years after his Decease. *Milton* has acknow-

ledg'd to me, that *Spenser* was his Original.
John Dryden, Preface to *The Fables*

Discouraged, scorn'd, his writings vilified, / Poorly – poor man – he liv'd; poorly – poor man – he died. /
Phineas Fletcher, *The Purple Island*, canto 4

The poet of imaginative Protestantism.
S. R. Gardiner, *Cromwell's Place in History*, 1897

The Nobility of the Spensers has been illustrated and enriched by the trophies of Marlborough, but I exhort them to consider the Faerie Queene as the most precious jewel of their coronet.
Edward Gibbon, *Memoirs*

That virtue therefore which is but a youngling in the contemplation of evil, and knows not the utmost that vice promises to her followers, and rejects it, is but a blank virtue, not a pure; her whiteness is but an excremental whiteness; Which was the reason why our sage and serious Poet Spenser, whom I dare be known to think a better teacher than Scotus or Aquinas, describing true temperance under the person of Guion, brings him in with his palmer through the cave of Mammon, and the bower of earthly bliss that he might see and know, and yet abstain.
John Milton, *Areopagitica*

*See also* Leigh Hunt, Shakespeare, William Butler Yeats

## STANFORD, SIR CHARLES VILLIERS

1852–1924 Composer

The stuff I hate and which I know is ruining any chance for good music in England is stuff like Stanford's which is neither fish, flesh, fowl nor good red-herring.
Edward Elgar, Letter to A. J. Jaeger, 11 December 1898

His very facility prevented him from knowing when he was genuinely inspired and when his work was routine stuff.
Ralph Vaughan Williams, at the Composers' Concourse, 1957

*See also* Ralph Vaughan Williams

## STANHOPE, LADY HESTER LUCY

1776–1839 Eccentric

Lady Hester's was a nose of wild ambitions, of pride grown fantastical, a nose that scorned the earth, shooting off, one fancies, towards some eternally eccentric heaven. It was a nose, in fact, altogether in the air.
Lytton Strachey, *Books and Characters*: 'Lady Hester Stanhope'

## STANHOPE, PHILIP DORMER, *see under* CHESTERFIELD, LORD

## STANLEY, EDWARD GEORGE GEOFFREY SMITH, *see under* DERBY, EARL OF

## STANLEY, SIR HENRY MORTON

1841–1904 Explorer

I am partial to adventures, but I never attempt the impossible.
On himself, to King Leopold II, April 1890, in Frank Hird, *H. M. Stanley: The Authoritative Life*

He represented both the old romance of adventurous travel and the new romance of mechanical efficiency. It was his luck to do considerable things exactly at the time when exploration had become scientific, but had not ceased to be picturesque. A generation before, there was glamour, but little good business in the conquest of the wild; on the whole, the betting was decidedly on the wild. A generation later the glamour had largely departed, though the business was very good business indeed. But in the high and palmy days of Stanley, the explorer had the best of both worlds. He was admired as a disinterested knight errant, and rewarded handsomely for not being one.

E. T. Raymond, *Portraits of the Nineties*

The nineteenth century had a pathetic faith in its Press, and even in the American Press; and it revelled in the vision of one strong, silent man, by the power of a mighty banking account, hurling a second strong, silent man across a dark continent to the succour of a third strong, silent man.

*Ibid.*, also referring to J. C. Bennett of the *New York Herald*

In the mixture of the absurd and the serious . . . Mark Twain compared Stanley favorably with Columbus: Columbus started out to discover America, but all he had to do was to sit in his cabin and hold his grip and sail straight on, and America would discover itself. Here it was, barring his passage the whole length and breadth of the South American continent, and he couldn't get by it. He'd got to discover it. But Stanley started out to find Dr Livingstone, who was scattered abroad, as you may say, length and breadth of a vast slab of Africa as big as the United States. It was a blind kind of search.

Mark Twain, reported in Arthur Montefiore, *The Life of Henry M. Stanley*

## STANTON, EDWIN MCMASTERS

1814–69 Politician

. . . the man's public character is a public mistake.

Abraham Lincoln, comment to T. S. Barnett

[Stanton] is the most unmitigated scoundrel I ever knew, heard or read of; if Stanton had lived during Jesus' lifetime, Judas Iscariot would have remained a respected member of the fraternity of apostles.

George Brinton McClellan, in Benjamin P. Thomas and Harold M. Hyman, *Stanton: The Life and Times of Lincoln's Secretary of War*

## STANTON, ELIZABETH CADY

1815–1902 Suffragette

If Mrs Stanton would attend a little more to her domestic duties and a little less to those of the great public, perhaps she would exalt her sex quite as much as she does by quixotically fighting windmills in their gratuitous behalf, and might possibly set a notable example of domestic felicity. No married woman can convert herself into a feminine Knight of the Rueful Visage and ride about the country attempting to redress imaginary wrongs without leaving her own household in a neglected condition that must be an eloquent witness against her.

Anon., in *New York Sunday Times*, January 1868

As usual when she had fired her gun she went home and left me to finish the battle.

Susan B. Anthony, after Mrs Stanton had addressed a convention on the subject of divorce, June 1860

## STEELE, SIR RICHARD

1672–1729 Essayist, Dramatist, Politician

He maintained a perpetual struggle between reason and appetite.

Theophilus Cibber, *Lives of the Poets*

It is our belief that no man so much as Steele has suffered from *compassion*.

It was out of his own bitter experience that he shrewdly called it, himself, the best disguise of malice, and said that the most apposite course to cry a man down was to lament him.

John Forster, *Biographical Essays*

A scholar among rakes, and a rake among scholars.

T. B. Macaulay, *Essays*: 'The Life and Writings of Addison'

I am recreating my mind with the brisk sallies and quick turns of wit, which Mr Steele in his liveliest and freest humours darts about him.

Alexander Pope, Letter to Caryll, 14 August 1713

But if I may with freedom talk, / All this is foreign to thy walk: / Thy genius has perhaps a knack / At trudging in a beaten track, / But is for state-affairs as fit / As mine for politicks or wit. / Then let us both in time grow wise, / Nor higher than our talents rise; / To some snug cellar we'll repair / From duns and debts, and drown our care. /

Jonathan Swift, *Imitations of Horace*, ode 1, book 2

## STEIN, GERTRUDE

1874–1946 Poet, Author

Think of the Bible and Homer, think of Shakespeare and think of me.

On herself, in B. L. Reid, *Art by Subtraction*

Now listen! I'm no fool. I know that in daily life we don't go around saying 'is a . . . is . . . is . . .' Yes, I'm no fool; but I think that in that line the rose is red for the first time in English poetry for a hundred years.

On herself, in John Malcolm Brinnin, *The Third Rose*

Reading Gertrude Stein at length is not unlike making one's way through an interminable and badly printed game book.

Richard Bridgeman, *Gertrude Stein in Pieces*

While she believed that most writers failed to allow writing to express all that it could, in her own practice she scrupulously saw to it that writing expressed less than it would.

John Malcolm Brinnin, *The Third Rose*

To produce pure proletarian art the artist must be at one with the worker; this is impossible, not for political reasons, but because the artist never is at one with any public. The grandest attempt to escape from this is provided by Gertrude Stein, who claims to be a direct expression of the Zeitgeist (the present stage of the dialectic process) and therefore to need no other relation to a public of any kind. She has in fact a very definite relation to her public, and I should call her work a version of child-cult.

William Empson, *Some Versions of Pastoral*

My notion is that Miss Stein has set herself to solve, and has succeeded in solving, the most difficult problem in prose composition – to write something that will not arrest the attention in any way, manner, shape, or form. If you think this is easy, try it. I know of no one except Miss Stein who can roll out this completely non-resistant prose, prose that puts you at once in a condition resembling the early stages of grippe – the eyes and legs heavy, the top of the skull wandering around in an uncertain and independent manner, the heart ponderously, tiredly beating.

Clifton Fadiman, in B. L. Reid, *Art by Subtraction*

Miss Stein was a past master in making nothing happen very slowly.

Clifton Fadiman, *The Selected*

*Writings of Clifton Fadiman*: 'Puzzlements'

What an old covered-wagon she is!
F. Scott Fitzgerald, in John Malcolm Brinnin, *The Third Rose*

Gertrude Stein and me are just like brothers...
Ernest Hemingway, in *ibid.*

Gertrude Stein's prose-song is a cold, black suet-pudding. We can represent it as a cold suet-roll of fabulously reptilian length. Cut it at any point, it is the same thing; the same heavy, sticky, opaque mass all through, and all along . . . it is mournful and monstrous, composed of dead and inanimate material. It is all fat, without nerve.
Percy Wyndham Lewis, in *ibid.*

She has outdistanced any of the symbolists in using words for pure purposes of suggestion – she has gone so far that she no longer even suggests.
Edmund Wilson, in B. L. Reid, *Art by Subtraction*

*See also* Albert Einstein, Alice B. Toklas

## STEINBECK, JOHN ERNST

1902–68 Author

His remarkable, almost uncanny ability to meet the intellectual and emotional needs of a depression-trained reading public contrasts vividly with the work of those novelists who, with almost missionary zeal, were trying to influence the public mind.
Frederick J. Hoffman, *The Modern Novel in America*

Nothing in his books is so dim, insignificantly enough, as the human beings who live in them, and few of them are intensely imagined as human beings at all.
Alfred Kazin, *On Native Grounds*

The world of John Steinbeck's novels is a beautiful warm valley with disaster hanging over it. This is the essential feature story after story. Steinbeck may change his outlook, as he has from the lyric to the sociological, or he may change his technical approach, as he has from romantic to dramatic narrative, but the valley microcosm remains as the setting of his work, and his people continue to be foredoomed with an almost calvinistic regularity.
Harry Thornton Moore, *The Novels of John Steinbeck*

## STEPHEN

*circa* 1097–1154 King of England

Stephen was no hero. Although he was an excellent warrior and showed enterprise and speed in the beginning of campaigns and sieges, he too often failed to complete them; and though he seemed cheerful and gay, beneath the surface he was mistrustful and sly. He was basically smallminded, and as a result he did not inspire the devotion which his grandfather or uncle had inspired; even his panegyrist, the author of the *Gesta Stephani*, found him colourless.
R. H. C. Davis, *King Stephen*

He was a man of great renown in the practice of arms, but for the rest almost an incompetent, except that he was rather inclined to evil.
Walter Map, *De Nugis Curialium*, translated from the Latin by F. Tupper and M. B. Ogle

## STEPHENS, ALEXANDER HAMILTON

1812–83 Politician

I could swallow him whole and never know the difference.
Judge Walter T. Colquitt, in E. Ramsay Richardson, *Little Aleck*

Never have I seen so small a nubbin come out of so much husk.

Abraham Lincoln, on meeting Stephens, in R. R. Von Abele, *Alexander H. Stephens*

## STEPHENSON, GEORGE

1781–1848 Inventor

Stephenson, the great Engineer, told Lichfield that he had travelled on the Manchester and Liverpool railroad for many miles at the rate of a mile a minute, but his doubt was not how fast his Engines could be made to go, but at what pace it would be proper to stop, that he could make them travel with greater speed than any bird can cleave the air, and he had ascertained that 400 miles an hour was the extreme velocity which the human frame could endure.

Charles Greville, Diary, 28 January 1834

The whole secret of Mr Stephenson's success in life was his careful improvement of time, which is the rock out of which fortunes are carved and great characters formed. He believed in genius to the extent that Buffon did when he said that 'patience is genius'; or as some other thinker put it, when he defined genius to be the power of making efforts. But he never would have it that he was a genius, or that he had done anything which other men, equally laborious and persevering as himself, could not have accomplished. He repeatedly said to the young men about him: 'Do as I have done – persevere!'

Samuel Smiles, *Lives of the Engineers*

*See also* Samuel Smiles

## STERNE, LAURENCE

1713–68 Author

Ah, I am as bad as that dog Sterne, who preferred whining over 'a dead ass to relieving a living mother' – villain – hypocrite – slave – sycophant! but *I* am no better.

Lord Byron, Journal, 1 December 1813

His works consist only of *morceaux* – of brilliant passages.

William Hazlitt, *Lectures on the English Comic Writers*

*Tristram Shandy* may perhaps go on a little longer; but we will not follow him. With all his drollery there is a sameness of extravagance which tires us. We have just a succession of Surprise, surprise, surprise.

David Hume, in James Boswell, *Private Papers from Malahide Castle*

That great spunky unflincher.

B. S. Johnson, *See the Old Lady Decently*

Nothing odd will do long, *Tristram Shandy* did not last.

Samuel Johnson, in James Boswell, Journal, 26 March 1776

Soon after *Tristram* appeared, Sterne asked a Yorkshire lady of fortune and condition whether she had read his book. 'I have not, Mr Sterne,' was the answer; 'and, to be plain with you, I am informed it is not proper for female perusal.' – 'My dear good lady,' replied the author, 'do not be gulled by such stories; the book is like your young heir there,' (pointing to a child of three years old, who was rolling on the carpet in his white tunic) 'he shows at times a good deal that is usually concealed, but it is all in perfect innocence!'

Sir Walter Scott, *Laurence Sterne*

*See also* Thomas Hardy

## STEVENS, THADDEUS

1792–1868 Politician, Lawyer

Whoever cracked Thaddeus Stevens'

skull would let out the brains of the Republican Party.

Anon. saying in Fawn M. Brodie, *Thaddeus Stevens, Scourge of the South*

[Stevens'] mind, so far as his sense of obligation to God was concerned, was a howling wilderness.

Jeremiah Black, in Alphonse B. Miller, *Thaddeus Stevens*

To the Memory of
Thaddeus Stevens
Ah, Alas, Alas,
the
Great unchained
is
Chained at last.

John H. McClellan, in Fawn M. Brodie, *Thaddeus Stevens, Scourge of the South*

## STEVENS, WALLACE

1879–1955 Poet, Businessman

Life is an affair of people not of places. But for me life is an affair of places and that is the trouble.

On himself, in William Burney, *Wallace Stevens*

Stevens' place is therefore clearly in the tradition of existentialist romanticism. The fertile fact or sensation is primary; everything including the existence or non-existence of God, follows from that. The only order worth looking for is the order of chaos itself.

William Burney, in *ibid.*

Wallace Stevens was really very much annoyed at being catalogued, categorized, and compelled to be scientific about what he was doing – to give satisfaction, to answer the teachers. He wouldn't do that. He was independent.

Marianne Moore, in Charles Tomlinson ed., *Marianne Moore, A Collection of Critical Essays*

The merging of the abstract and the mental with the concrete and the sensual is perhaps the most characteristic quality of Stevens' style. If a poem begins with a generalization, he will proceed to illustrate it, or, if a poem commences with a series of illustrative particulars, it will end with a generalization.

Robert Pack, *Wallace Stevens*

Something of the talent of a Sherlock Holmes is needed to penetrate Stevens' oblique implications. His poetry is keyed to readers who delight in solving puzzles.

George F. Whicher, 'The Twentieth Century', in Arthur Hobson Quinn ed., *The Literature of the American People*

His gift for combining words is baffling and fantastic but sure: even when you do not know what he is saying, you know that he is saying it well.

Edmund Wilson, 'Wallace Stevens and E. E. Cummings', in S. U. Baum ed., *e. e. cummings and the Critics*

## STEVENSON, ADLAI EWING

1900–65 Statesman, Diplomat, Lawyer

Someone asked . . . how I felt [on being defeated for the Presidency by Dwight Eisenhower] and I was reminded of a story that a fellow townsman of ours used to tell – Abraham Lincoln. They asked him how he felt once after an unsuccessful election. He said he felt like a little boy who has stubbed his toe in the dark. He said that he was too old to cry, but it hurt too much to laugh.

On himself, Speech of 5 November 1952

I regret that I have but one law firm to give to my country.

On himself, referring to the Kennedy administration's use of lawyers from his Chicago office

It's an odd thing to say, but everybody who has served at the United Nations has known me personally or by my writings or travel. And they were about 98 percent pro-Democratic during my campaigns. I've often said it was a damn shame I ran for President of the wrong country.

On himself, in Alden Whitman, *Portrait, Adlai E. Stevenson, Politician, Diplomat, Friend*

Through all the placid confidence of the Eisenhower era and the clumsy crusades of Dulles, he reminded the world that there was another America – sensitive, self critical, thoughtful and visionary. At home he kept the light of intellect burning through a period when it was not fashionable to think.

Anon., in *The Times*, 14 July 1965

... unexceptional as a glass of decent Beaujolais.

Anon., in *Newsweek*, 26 July 1965

The verdict may be that it was not only his wit but his psyche that was out of phase with the times. He remained a gentleman in the face of a declining political market for civility.

Henry S. Ashmore, in Edward P. Doyle ed., *As We Knew Adlai, The Stevenson Story by Twenty-Two Friends*

You would be as likely, in fact, to find Adlai Stevenson in public without his pants as without the protective armor of his calm, urbane self-assurance.

Cabell Phillips, in *New York Times Magazine*, September 1965

... Stevenson had made Kennedy's rise possible . . . His lofty conception of politics, his conviction that affluence was not enough for the good life, his impatience with liberal clichés, his contempt for conservative complacency, his summons to the young, his demand for new ideas, his respect for people who had them, his belief that history afforded no easy answers, his call for strong public leadership – all this set the tone for a new era of Democratic politics.

Arthur M. Schlesinger Jr, *A Thousand Days, John Kennedy in the White House*

The real trouble with Stevenson is that he's no better than a regular sissy.

Harry S. Truman, in Merle Miller, *Plain Speaking, An Oral Biography of Harry S. Truman*

He was called an egg-head, and he tossed back a Latinism of his own devising: 'Via ovum cranium difficilis est' ('The way of the egghead is hard').

Alden Whitman, *Portrait, Adlai E. Stevenson, Politician, Diplomat, Friend*

*See also* Cole Porter

## STEVENSON, ROBERT LOUIS (BALFOUR)

1850–94 Author

I am a rogue at egotism myself: and, to be plain, I have rarely or never liked a man who was not.

On himself, Letter to an Australian admirer, *circa* 1877

I have played the sedulous ape to Hazlitt, to Lamb, to Wordsworth, to Sir Thomas Browne, to Defoe, to Hawthorne, to Montaigne, to Baudelaire and to Obermann.

On himself, *Memories and Portraits*

I am an Epick writer with a k to it, but without the necessary genius.

On himself, Letter to Henry James, December 1892

There is always in his work a certain clean-cut angularity which makes us remember that he was fond of cutting wood with an axe.

G. K. Chesterton, *Twelve Types*

Stevenson seemed to pick the right word up on the point of his pen, like a man playing spillikins.

G. K. Chesterton, *The Victorian Age in Literature*

Valiant in velvet, light in ragged luck, / Most vain, most generous, sternly critical, / Buffoon and poet, lover and sensualist; / A deal of Ariel, just a streak of Puck, / Much Antony, of Hamlet most of all, / And something of the Shorter-Catechist.

W. E. Henley, *In Hospital*

I think of Mr Stevenson as a consumptive youth weaving garlands of sad flowers with pale, weak hands, or leaning to a large plate-glass window and scratching thereon exquisite profiles with a diamond pencil.

George Moore, *Confessions of a Young Man*

Stevenson's letters most disappointing also. I see that romantic surroundings are the worst surroundings possible for a romantic writer. In Gower Street, Stevenson could have written a new *Trois Mousquetaires*. In Samoa he wrote letters to the *Times* about Germans. I see also the traces of a terrible *strain* to lead a natural life. To chop wood with any advantage to oneself or profit to others, one should not be able to describe the process. In point of fact the natural life is the unconscious life. Stevenson merely extended the sphere of the artificial by taking to digging.

Oscar Wilde, Letter to Robert Ross, 6 April 1897

*See also* Samuel Butler

## STEWART, ROBERT, *see under* CASTLEREAGH, VISCOUNT

## STIEGLITZ, ALFRED

1864–1946 Photographer

There is something in me which seeks a balance, a relationship which can be put in a formula. But there is also something in me which, as soon as I have found the formula, insists upon kicking the stuffing out of it.

On himself, in Herbert J. Seligmann, *Alfred Stieglitz Talking*

I remember him dark and I felt him having white hair. He can do both of these things or anything. Now that sounds as if it were the same thing or not a difficult thing but it is just is, it is a difficult thing to do two things as one, but he just can that is what Stieglitz is and he is important to every one oh yes he is whether they know it or not oh yes he is. There are some who are important to every one whether any one knows anything of that one or not and Stieglitz is such a one, he is that one, he is indeed, there is no question but that he is such a one, he is that one, he is indeed, there is no question but that he is such a one no question indeed, but that he is one, who is an important one for every one, no matter whether they do or whether they do not know anything about any such thing about any such one about him

That is what Stieglitz is. / Any one can recognize him. / Any one does know that there are such ones, all of us do know that / Stieglitz is such a one. / That he is one. / 291 /

Gertrude Stein, *Stieglitz*

## STOPES, MARIE CHARLOTTE CARMICHAEL

1880–1958 Advocate of Birth Control

Dr Marie Stopes / After reading the Lives of the Popes, / Remarked: 'What a difference it would have made to these Pages / If I had been born in the Middle Ages.' /

Hon. Mrs Geoffrey Edwards, in
Arnold Silcock, *Verse and Worse*

I think you should insist on the separation in the public mind of your incidental work as a scientific critic of methods of contraception with your main profession as a teacher of matrimonial technique.

George Bernard Shaw, Letter to
Marie Stopes, October 1928

## STOWE, HARRIET ELIZABETH BEECHER

1811–96 Author, Humanitarian

[I] no more thought of style or literary excellence than the mother who rushes into the street and cries for help to save her children from a burning house, thinks of the teachings of the rhetorician or the elocutionist.

On herself, referring to *Uncle Tom's Cabin*, in Forrest Wilson, *Crusader in Crinoline, The Life of Harriet Beecher Stowe*

I am a little bit of a woman, – somewhat more than forty, about as thin and dry as a pinch of snuff; never very much to look at in my best of days, and looking like a used-up article now.

On herself, Letter to Mrs Fallen, 1853

I make no mental effort of any sort; my brain is tired out. It was a woman's brain and not a man's, and finally from sheer fatigue and exhaustion in the march and strife of life it gave out before the end was reached. And now I rest me, like a moored boat, rising and falling on the water, with loosened cordage and flapping sail.

On herself, Letter to Oliver Wendell Holmes, 5 February 1893

... Harriet Beecher Stowe, whose *Uncle Tom's Cabin* was the first evidence to America that no hurricane can be so disastrous to a country as a ruthlessly humanitarian woman.

Sinclair Lewis, Introduction to Paxton Hibben, *Henry Ward Beecher: An American Portrait*

## STRACHEY, (GILES) LYTTON

1880–1932 Author, Historian

To preserve, for instance, a becoming brevity – a brevity which excludes everything that is redundant and nothing that is significant – that, surely, is the first duty of the biographer. The second, no less surely, is to maintain his own freedom of spirit.

On himself, Preface to *Eminent Victorians*

Incapable of creation in life or in literature, his writings were a substitute for both.

T. R. Barnes, *Scrutiny*

Lytton Strachey peered at everyone through thick glasses, looking like an owl in daylight. He is immensely tall, and could be even twice his height if he were not as bent as sloppy asparagus.

Cecil Beaton, Diary, 1923

An emaciated face of ivory whiteness above a long square-cut auburn beard, and below a head of very long sleek dark brown hair. The nose was nothing if not aquiline, and Nature had chiselled it with great delicacy. The eyes, behind a pair of gold-rimmed spectacles, eyes of an inquirer and cogitator, were large and brown and luminous. The man to whom they belonged must, I judged, though he sat stooping low down over his table, be extremely tall. He wore a jacket of brown velveteen, a soft shirt, and a dark red tie. I greatly wondered who he was. He looked rather like one of the Twelve Apostles, and I decided that he resembled especially the doubting one, Thomas, who was also called Didymus.

Max Beerbohm, on seeing Strachey

for the first time in the Savile Club, in May 1912, *Mainly on the Air*

One observed a number of discordant features – a feminine sensibility, a delight in the absurd, a taste for exaggeration and melodrama, a very mature judgement, and then some lack of human substance, some hereditary thinness in the blood that at times gave people who met him an odd feeling in the spine. He seemed almost indecently lacking in ordinariness.

Gerald Brenan, *South from Granada*

*Eminent Victorians* is the work of a great anarch, a revolutionary textbook on bourgeois society written in the language through which the bourgeois ear could be lulled and beguiled, the Mandarin style. And the bourgeois responded with fascination to the music, like seals to the Eriskay love-lilt.

Cyril Connolly, *Enemies of Promise*

Lytton Strachey was unfit [for war service], but instead of allowing himself to be rejected by the doctors preferred to appear before a military tribunal as a conscientious objector. He told us of the extraordinary impression caused by an air-cushion which he inflated in court as a protest against the hardness of the benches. Asked by the chairman the usual question: 'I understand, Mr Strachey, that you have a conscientious objection to war?', he replied (in his curious falsetto voice): 'Oh, no, not at all, only to *this* war.' And to the chairman's other stock question, which had previously never failed to embarrass the claimant: 'Tell me, Mr Strachey, what would you do if you saw a German soldier trying to violate your sister?' he replied with an air of noble virtue: 'I would try to get between them.'

Robert Graves, *Goodbye to All That*

At another party, the conversation turned to the question of which great historical character the people there would most have liked to go to bed with. The men voted for Cleopatra, Kitty Fisher and so on, but when it came to Lytton's turn he declared shrilly: 'Julius Caesar!'

Michael Holroyd, *Lytton Strachey*

On one occasion, some friends were discussing George Moore's extensive revisions to his novels, and one of them asked Lytton about his own amendments. 'I write very slowly, and in faultless sentences,' he replied.

*Ibid.*

Strachey is never direct: and not, I think, in himself wholesome. But I don't know him, and my memory of his books tangles itself with my memory of Henry Lamb's marvellous portrait of an outraged wet mackerel of a man, dropped like an old cloak into a basket-chair. If the portrait meant anything it meant that Lytton Strachey was no good.

T. E. Lawrence, Letter to Robert Graves, 1 October 1927

Pass a person through your mind, with all the documents, and see what comes out. That seems to be your method. Also choose them, in the first place, because you dislike them.

Walter Raleigh, commenting on *Eminent Victorians*, Letter to Strachey, May 1918

The man who brilliantly ruined the art of biography.

George Sherburn, Introduction to *Selections from Pope*

Lytton Strachey was a major Bloomsbury idol of this time. I knew him but slightly, and don't like his work. Also his letters to Virginia Woolf, now published, make me blush from head to foot, with the exclamations of 'oh deary Mary me!' and the enumeration of Countesses known and dimly related to them . . . He seemed to have been cut out of very thin cardboard.

Edith Sitwell, *Taken Care Of*

He has fabricated, chiefly from eighteenth-century material, a very discreet code of manners of his own, which allows him to sit at the table with the highest in the land and to say a great many things under cover of that exquisite apparel which, had they gone naked, would have been chased by the men-servants from the room.

Virginia Woolf, *The Captain's Death Bed*

*See also* Lady Ottoline Morrell

## STRAFFORD, EARL OF (THOMAS WENTWORTH)

1593–1641 Statesman

And so, thorough let us go, and spare not.

On himself, Letter to William Laud, 15 May 1634

He was a simple man of strong affections, and he wrote the most endearing letters to his children.

John Buchan, *Oliver Cromwell*

Wentworth is a man of dark countenance, a stern down-looking man, full of thoughts, energies, – of tender affections gone mostly to the shape of pride and sorrow, of rage sleeping in stern composure, kept strictly under lock and key; cross him not abruptly, he is a choleric man, and from under his dark brows flashes a look not pleasant to me. Poor Wentworth, his very nerves are all shattered, he lives in perpetual pain of body, such a force of soul has he to exert. He must bear an Atlas burden of Irish and other unreasons: from a whole chaos of angry babble he has to extract the word or two of meaning, and compress the rest into silence. A withered figure, scathed and parched as by internal, and external fire. Noble enough; yes, and even beautiful and tragical; at all events, terrible enough. He reverences King Charles, which is extremely miraculous, yet partially to be comprehended; King Charles, and I think, no other creature under this sky. Nay, at bottom, King Charles is but his Talismanic Figure, his conjuration Formula, with which he will conjure the world; he must not break or scratch that figure, or where were he? At bottom does not even reverence King Charles; he looks into the grim sea of fate stretching dark into the Infinite and the Eternal, and himself alone there; and reverences in strange ways only that, and what holds of that. A proud, mournful, scathed and withered man, with a prouder magazine of rage lying in him.

Thomas Carlyle, *Historical Sketches*

My Lord of Strafford's condition is happier than mine.

Charles I, attributed, on agreeing to Strafford's execution, May 1641

He was no doubte of greate observation, and a piercing judgement both into things and persons, but his too good skill in persons made him judge the worse of things, for it was his misfortune to be of a tyme wherin very few wise men were aequally imployed with him . . . and decerning many defects in most men, he too much neglected what they sayd or did. Of all his passyons his pryde was most predominant, which a moderate exercise of ill fortune might have corrected and reformed, and which was by the hande of heaven strangely punished, by bringing his destruction upon him, by two thinges, that he most despised, the people, and Sr Harry Vane.

Edward Hyde, Earl of Clarendon, *History of the Rebellion*

He is dead with more honour than any of them will gain which hunted after his life.

William Laud, attributed, 1644

Sure I am, that his station was like those turfs of earth or sea-banks, which by the storm swept away, left all the in-land to be drown'd by popular tumult.

Sir Philip Warwick, *Memoires of the Reigne of King Charles I*

## STUART, CHARLES EDWARD LOUIS PHILIP CASIMIR

1720–88 The Young Pretender

Over the water and over the lea, / And over the water to Charley. / Charley loves good ale and wine, / And Charley loves good brandy, / And Charley loves a pretty girl, / As sweet as sugar candy. /

Over the water and over the lea, / And over the water to Charley. / I'll have none of your nasty beef, / Nor I'll have none of your barley; / But I'll have some of your very best flour / To make a white cake for my Charley. /

Nursery rhyme, traditional

An' Charlie he's my darling, my darling, my darling, / Charlie he's my darling, the young Chevalier.

Robert Burns, *Charlie he's my darling*, refrain

God bless the King, I mean the Faith's Defender; / God bless – no harm in blessing – the Pretender; / But who Pretender is, or who is King, / God bless us all – that's quite another thing. /

John Byrom, *To an Officer in the Army*

Only ladies in Highland industry shops speak of him with any affection, which seems appropriate since all Charles bequeathed to Scotland that was of any benefit was a tourist industry.

Margaret Forster, *The Rash Adventurer*

## STUART, FRANCES TERESA, DUCHESS OF RICHMOND AND LENNOX

1647–1702 Mistress to Charles II

At my Goldsmith's did observe the King's new Medall, where in little there is Mrs Stewards face, as well done as ever I saw anything in my whole life, I think – and a pretty thing it is that he should choose her face to represent Britannia by.

Samuel Pepys, Diary, 25 February 1667

The King begins to be mightily reclaimed, and sups every night with great pleasure with the Queene: and yet, it seems, he is mighty hot upon the Duchess of Richmond; insomuch that, upon Sunday was se'ennight at night, after he had ordered his Guards and Coach to be ready to carry him to the park, he did on a sudden take a pair of oars or sculler, and all alone, or but one with him, go to Somerset House, and there, the garden door not being open, himself clamber over the wall to make a visit to her; which is a horrid shame.

*Ibid.*, 19 May 1668

## STUART, GILBERT

1755–1828 Artist

No man ever painted history if he could obtain employment in portraits.

On himself, in E. P. Richardson, *Gilbert Stuart*

When Stuart the painter died, a eulogium on his character appeared in one of the American papers, in which it was said that he left the brightest prospects in England, and returned to his own country, from his admiration of her new institutions, and a desire to paint the portrait of Washington. On hearing this, Sir Thomas Lawrence said: 'I knew Stuart well; and I believe the real cause of his leaving England was his having become tired of the inside of some of our prisons.' 'Well, then', said Lord Holland, 'after all, it was his love of freedom that took him to America.'

Charles Robert Leslie, *Autobiography*

He nails the face to the canvas.

Benjamin West, attributed, in William Temple Franklin, Letter to Benjamin Franklin, 9 November 1784

## STUART, JAMES FRANCIS EDWARD

1688–1766 The Old Pretender

Modern psychologists would hint at traumas set up by the circumstances of his birth, his abrupt departure from England, the uncertainty of life at Saint Germain, his father's doctrine of the divine right of kings conflicting so obviously against the will of the people. And they would no doubt be correct. James Francis Edward was a born loser.

Christopher Sinclair-Stevenson, *Inglorious Rebellion*

## STUART, JOHN *see under* BUTE, EARL OF

## STUART, MARY, *see under* MARY QUEEN OF SCOTS

## STUBBS, GEORGE

1724–1806 Painter, Anatomist

The wide Creation waits upon his call, / He paints each species and excels in all, / Whilst wondering Nature asks with jealous tone, / Which Stubbs's labours are and which her own? /

Anon., Pamphlet by 'An Impartial Hand', in *Exhibition*, 1766

Stubbs is useful, but his Horses are not broad enough in light & shadow for a Painter. They may be just as correct without violating the principles of effect. They are delicate, minute, & sweetly drawn, with great character, but they want substance, for they have hardly any light & shadow.

Benjamin Robert Haydon, Diary, 25 April 1826

'Tis said that nought so much the temper rubs / Of that ingenious artist, Mister Stubbs, / As calling him a horse-painter – how strange / That Stubbs the title should desire to change! /

Peter Pindar (John Wolcot), *Lyric Odes to the Royal Academicians*, 1782, ode 7

Well pleas'd thy horses, Stubbs, I view, / And eke thy dogs, to *homely* nature true: / Let modern artist match thee, if they can – / Such animals thy genius suit: / Then stick, I beg thee, to the brute. / And meddle not with woman, nor with man. /

*Ibid.*, ode 15

He certainly stands in that company of artists – Dürer being one of its representatives – who, from the centre of their nature, have enjoyed a wide-ranging and unassailable capacity and whose works have the characteristic named by Sir Henry Wotton in his definition of good architecture, 'firmness', a principle implying the most comprehensive definition of craftsmanship and requiring mental discipline as well as skill of hand. Unlike Hogarth, who said that he had to get things wrong before he got them right, Stubbs possessed a natural virtuosity, which he never forfeited or lost but which was always unpretentious in its effect.

Basil Taylor, *Stubbs*

## SULLIVAN, SIR ARTHUR SEYMOUR

1842–1900 Composer

We all have the same eight notes to work with.

On himself, attributed, when accused of plagiarizing

He is like a man who sits on a stove and then complains that his backside is burning.

W. S. Gilbert, in Leslie Ayre, *The Gilbert and Sullivan Companion*

It has been said that he was lucky in his chief collaborator: it should be added that no man ever more thoroughly deserved his luck.

Sir Henry Hadow, *English Music*

They trained him to make Europe yawn; and he took advantage of their teaching to make London and New York laugh and whistle.

George Bernard Shaw, in *Scots Observer*, 6 September 1890

Sullivan's genius was in making it impossible for opera-goers subsequently to tell whether the words or the tunes came first.

Percy M. Young, *A Critical Dictionary of Composers and Their Music*

*See also* W. S. Gilbert, Gilbert and Sullivan

## SULLIVAN, JOHN LAWRENCE

1858–1918 Boxer

'*East side, west side, all around the town / The tots sang: "Ring a rosie –" / "London Bridge is falling down."*' / And . . . / John L. Sullivan / The strong boy / Of Boston / Broke every single rib of Jake Kilrain. /

Vachel Lindsay, *John L. Sullivan, The Strong Boy of Boston*

## SUMNER, CHARLES

1811–74 Politician, Abolitionist

A foul-mouthed poltroon, [who] when caned for cowardly vituperation falls to the floor in an inanimate lump of incarnate cowardice.

Anon., in *Richmond Examiner*, 1856

. . . the great orb of the State Department who rises periodically in his effulgence and sends his rays down the steep places here to cast a good many dollars into the sea.

Roscoe Conkling, in David Donald, *Charles Sumner and the Rights of Man*

It characterizes the man for me that he hates Charles Sumner, for it shows that he cannot discriminate between a foible and a vice.

Ralph Waldo Emerson, in *ibid.*

He works his adjectives so hard that if they ever catch him alone, they will murder him.

E. L. Godkin, in *ibid.*

## SUNDAY, WILLIAM ASHLEY, 'BILLY'

1862–1935 Evangelist

A rube of the rubes.

On himself, in Sydney Ahlstrom, *A Religious History of the American People*

The acrobat dervish of evangelism.

Anon., in *New York Times*, 7 November 1935

## SURREY, EARL OF (HENRY HOWARD)

1517?–47 Poet

Sir Thomas Wyatt / Never went on a diet, / Unlike the Earl of Surrey, / Who ate nothing but curry. /

W. H. Auden, *Academic Graffiti*

*Surrey*, the *Granville* of a former Age: / Matchless his Pen, victorious was his Lance; / Bold in the Lists, and graceful in the Dance. /

Alexander Pope, *Windsor-Forest*

## SWIFT, JONATHAN

1667–1745 Author

Yet malice never was his aim; / He lash'd the vice, but spared the name; /

No individual could resent, / Where thousands equally were meant. /
On himself, *On the Death of Dr Swift*

Poor Pope will grieve a month, and Gay / A week, and Arbuthnot a day. / St John himself will scarce forbear / To bite his pen, and drop a tear. / The rest will give a shrug, and cry, / 'I'm sorry – but we all must die!'
*Ibid.*

I shall be like that tree, I shall die at the top.
On himself, attributed

When people ask me how I governed Ireland, I say that I pleased Dr Swift.
Lord Carteret, Letter to Swift, March 1737

Swift was *anima Rabelaisii habitans in sicco* – the soul of Rabelais dwelling in a dry place.
Samuel Taylor Coleridge, *Table Talk*

Cousin Swift, you will never be a poet.
John Dryden, in Samuel Johnson, *Lives of the Poets*

Dr Tyrrell asked Carlyle whom he considered the greatest writer of English Prose. 'Swaft! for his parfaict lucidity.'
Oliver St J. Gogarty, *As I Was Going Down Sackville Street*

In life's last scene what prodigies surprise, / Fears of the brave, and follies of the wise! / From Marlb'rough's eyes the streams of dotage flow, / And Swift expires a driv'ler and a show. /
Samuel Johnson, *The Vanity of Human Wishes*

Nobody can deny but religion is a comfort to the distressed, a cordial to the sick, . . . therefore whoever would argue or laugh it out of the world without giving some equivalent for it ought to be treated as a common enemy. But when this language comes from a churchman who enjoys large benefices and dignities from that very church he openly despises it is an object of horror for which I want a name, and can only be excused by madness, which I think the Dean was always strongly touched with. His character seems to me a parallel with that of Caligula, and had he had the same power, would have made the same use of it.
Lady Mary Wortley Montagu, Letter to Lady Bute, 23 June 1754

We are right to think of Swift as a rebel and iconoclast, but except in certain secondary matters, such as his insistence that women should receive the same education as men, he cannot be labelled 'left'. He is a Tory anarchist, despising authority while disbelieving in liberty, and preserving the aristocratic outlook while seeing clearly that the existing aristocracy is degenerate and contemptible.
George Orwell, *Politics vs Literature*

Jonathan Swift / Had the gift, / By fatherige, motherige, / And by brotherige, / To come from Gutherige, / But now is spoil'd clean, / And an Irish Dean. /
Alexander Pope, *Lines on Swift's Ancestors*

I'll send you my bill of fare said Lord B[olingbroke] when trying to persuade Dr Swift to dine with him. – 'Send me your bill of company,' was Swift's answer to him.
Joseph Spence, *Anecdotes*

That brute, who hated everybody that he hoped would get him a mitre, and did not.
Horace Walpole, Letter to George Montagu, 20 June 1766

Swift has sailed into his rest; / Savage indignation there / Cannot lacerate his breast. / Imitate him if you dare, / World-besotted traveller; he / Served human liberty. /
William Butler Yeats, *Swift's Epitaph*

*See also* Lord Mansfield, Duke of Marlborough, Alexander Pope

## SWINBURNE, ALGERNON CHARLES

1837–1909 Poet

Having Mr Swinburne's defence of his prurient poetics, *Punch* hereby gives him his royal license to change his name to what is evidently its true form – Swine-born.

Anon., Review of *Poems and Ballads*, in *Punch*, 1866

I attempt to describe Mr Swinburne; and lo! the Bacchanal screams, the sterile Dolores sweats, serpents dance, men and women wrench, wriggle, and form in an endless alliteration of heated and meaningless words, the veriest garbage of Baudelaire flowered over with the epithets of the Della Cruscans.

Robert Buchanan, in *Contemporary Review*, October 1871

It is probable that there is not much to be gained by an absolute system of prosody; by the erudite complexities of Swinburnian metre. With Swinburne, once the trick is perceived and the scholarship appreciated, the effect is somewhat diminished. When the unexpectedness, due to the unfamiliarity of the metres to English ears, wears off and is understood, one ceases to look for what one does not find in Swinburne; the inexplicable line with the music that can never be recaptured in other words. Swinburne mastered his technique, which is a great deal, but he did not master it to the extent of being able to take liberties with it, which is everything.

T. S. Eliot, *Reflections on 'Vers Libre'*

The words of condemnation are words which express his qualities. You may say 'diffuse'. But the diffuseness is essential; had Swinburne practised greater concentration his verse would be, not better in the same kind, but a different thing. His diffuseness is one of his glories.

T. S. Eliot, *The Sacred Wood*

[Emerson] condemned Swinburne severely as a perfect leper and a mere sodomite, which criticism recalls Carlyle's scathing description of that poet – as a man standing up to his neck in a cesspool, and adding to its contents.

Interview with Ralph Waldo Emerson, in *Frank Leslie's Illustrated Newspaper*, 3 January 1874

It was important, at meals, to keep the wine or beer or spirits out of Swinburne's reach. If this were not done, as often by hosts or hostesses not aware of his weakness, he would gradually fix his stare upon the bottle as if he wished to fascinate it, and then, in a moment, flash or pounce upon it, like a mongoose on a snake, drawing it towards him as though it resisted and had to be struggled with. Then, if no one had the presence of mind to interfere, a tumbler was filled in a moment, and Swinburne had drained it to the last drop, sucking-in the liquid with a sort of fiery gluttony, tilting the glass into his shaking lips, and violently opening and shutting his eyelids. It was an extraordinary sight, and one which never failed to fill me with alarm, for after that the Bacchic transition might come at any moment.

Edmund Gosse, Manuscript notes on Swinburne

Take him at his best he is by far the best – finest poet; truest artist – of the young lot – when he refrains from pointing a hand at the genitals.

George Meredith, Letter to Frederick Greenwood, 1 January 1873

A sea blown to storm by a sigh.

George Meredith, in Siegfried Sassoon, *George Meredith*

A mind all aflame with the feverish carnality of a schoolboy over the dirtiest passages in Lemprière.

John Morley, reviewing *Poems and Ballads*, in *Saturday Review*, 1866

Swinburne . . . expresses in verse what he finds in books as passionately as a poet expresses what he finds in life.

George Bernard Shaw, in *Saturday Review*, 11 July 1896

He is a reed through which all things blow into music.

Alfred, Lord Tennyson (in conversation), in Hallam Tennyson, *Alfred Tennyson, A Memoir*

Isn't he the damnedest simulacrum!

Walt Whitman, attributed

Mr Swinburne is already the Poet Laureate of England. The fact that his appointment to this high post has not been degraded by official confirmation renders his position all the more unassailable.

Oscar Wilde, in *Idler*, April 1895

You know, Watts is a solicitor, and the business of a solicitor is to conceal crime. Swinburne's genius has been killed, and Watts is doing his best to conceal it.

Oscar Wilde (of Swinburne's retirement to Putney with Theodore Watts-Dunton), in Vincent O'Sullivan, *Aspects of Wilde*

*See also* Robert Browning, Rudyard Kipling

## SYDENHAM, THOMAS

1624–89 Physician

Strange things have been said in jest, or in earnest, concerning the studies necessary to form a physician. Sydenham advised Sir Richard Blackmore to read Don Quixote. He probably spoke in jest. But it is impossible to read Sydenham and not perceive that his mind did in truth hardly admit any auxiliary to the exercise of its own observation.

P. M. Latham, *Lectures on Subjects Connected with Clinical Medicine*

He was famous for his cool regimen in the smallpox, which his greatest adversaries have been since forc'd to take up and follow. He was also famous for his method of giving the bark after the paroxysm in agues, and for his laudanum.

Anthony à Wood, *Athenae Oxonienses*

## SYNGE, JOHN MILLINGTON

1871–1909 Dramatist

When I was writing 'The Shadow of the Glen' I got more aid than any learning could have given me from a chink in the floor of the old Wicklow house where I was staying, that let me hear what was being said by the servant girls in the kitchen.

On himself, Preface to *The Playboy of the Western World*

Synge has just had an operation on his throat and has come through it all right . . . When he woke out of the ether sleep, his first words, to the great delight of the doctor, who knows his plays, were: 'May God damn the English, they can't even swear without vulgarity.' This tale delights the Company, who shudder at the bad language they have to speak in his plays.

William Butler Yeats, Letter to John Quinn, 4 October 1907

And that enquiring man John Synge comes next, / That dying chose the living world for text / And never could have rested in the tomb / But that, long travelling, he had come / Towards nightfall upon certain set apart / In a most desolate stony place, / Towards

nightfall upon a race / Passionate and simple like his heart. /
William Butler Yeats, *In Memory of Major Robert Gregory*

He was the only man I have ever known incapable of a political thought or of a humanitarian purpose.
William Butler Yeats, *Autobiographies*

In Paris, Synge once said to me, 'We should unite stoicism, asceticism, and ecstasy. Two of them have often come together, but the three, never.'
*Ibid.*

# 'T'

## TAFT, ROBERT ALPHONSO

1889–1953 Politician

[The] Dagwood Bumstead of American Politics.

Anon., in *Time*, 1940

. . . he has a positive genius for being wrong. He is an authentic living representative of the old Bourbons of whom it was said that they 'learned nothing and forgot nothing.'

Marvin Harrison, *Robert A. Taft, Our Illustrious Dunderhead*

*See also* Dwight Eisenhower

## TAFT, WILLIAM HOWARD

1857–1930 Twenty-Seventh United States President

The amiable, goodnatured, subthyroid Taft had the misfortune to follow the crusading, club-brandishing, hyper-thyroid Roosevelt, much as a dim star follows a blazing comet. The Nation felt let down.

Thomas A. Bailey, *Presidential Greatness*

Taft had served so long under Theodore Roosevelt as a trouble shooter and yes-man that he never recovered from the subordinate experience . . . When someone addressed him as 'Mr President', he would instinctively turn around to see where Roosevelt was.

*Ibid.*

. . . He loathed being President and being Chief Justice was all happiness for him. He fought against being President and yielded to the acceptance of that heritage because of the insistence of Mrs Taft – very ambitious in that direction. It had always been the ambition of his life to be on the Supreme Court. Taft once said that the Supreme Court was his notion of what heaven must be like.

Felix Frankfurter, *Reminiscences*

He was a bad President, but a good sport.

Felix Frankfurter, in *The New Republic*

[A president who] meant well but meant well feebly.

Theodore Roosevelt, 1912, in *The American Heritage Pictorial History of the Presidents of the United States*

When I suggested to him that he occupy a Chair of Law at the University he said that he was afraid that a chair would not be adequate, but that if we would provide a Sofa of Law, it might be all right.

Anson Phelps Stokes, 1912, in F. C. Hicks, *William Howard Taft: Yale Professor of Law and New Haven Citizen*

Will was then at his stoutest. He sat down in the very small theater seat and seemed to overflow. He looked at me smilingly and said: 'Horace, if this theater burns, it has got to burn around me.'

Horace Dutton Taft, *Memories and Opinions*

*See also* Chauncey Depew

## TALLIS, THOMAS

*circa* 1510–85 Composer

Ye sacred muses, race of Jove / Whom Musick's love delighteth / Come down from Christ all heavens above / To Earth where sorrow dwelleth. / In mourning weeds, with tears in eyes, / Tallis is dead and Musick dies. /

Anon., set to music by William Byrd, 1585

## TARBELL, IDA MINERVA

1857–1944 Author, Journalist

The only reason I am glad that I am a woman is that I will not have to marry one.

On herself, in Mary E. Tomkins, *Ida M. Tarbell*

Muckraking crusader for the middle class, liberated New Woman who yet remained womanly, promoter of the values of Old America, and a person of unquestioned integrity, she was a sort of national maiden aunt.

Mary E. Tomkins, *ibid.*

## TARLTON, RICHARD

– d. 1588 Actor

The partie nowe is gone, / and closlie clad in claye, / Of all the jesters in the lande, / he bare the praise awaie. /

John Scottowe, British Library MS Harley 3885, f. 19

## TAYLOR, JEREMY, BISHOP

1613–67 Religious Author

Jer. Taylor's discursive intellect dazzle-darkened his intuition. The principle of becoming all things to all men, if by *any* means he might save *any*, with him as with Burke, thickened the protecting epidermis of the tact-nerve of truth into something like a callus. But take him all in all, such a miraculous combination of erudition, broad, deep, and omnigenous; of logic subtle as well as acute, and as robust as agile; of psychological insight, so fine yet so secure! of public prudence and practical *sageness* that one ray of *creative Faith* would have lit up and transfigured into wisdom, and of genuine imagination, with its streaming face unifying all at one moment like that of the setting sun when through an interspace of blue sky no larger than itself, it emerges from the cloud to sink behind the mountain, but a face seen only at *starts*, when some breeze from the higher air scatters, for a moment, the cloud of butterfly fancies, which flutter round him like a morning-garment of ten thousand colours – (now how shall I get out of this sentence? the tail is too big to be taken up into the coilers mouth) – well, as I was saying, I believe such a complete man hardly shall we meet again.

Samuel Taylor Coleridge, Letter to John Kenyon, 3 November 1814

## TAYLOR, ZACHARY

1784–1850 Twelfth United States President

I think I hear his cheerful voice, / 'On column! Steady! Steady!' / So handy and so prompt was he / We called him Rough and Ready. /

Anon. soldier's ditty, composed during the Seminole Wars, *circa* 1837

Jesus is the most respectable person in the United States. Jesus sits on the President's chair. Zachary Taylor sits there, which is the same thing, for he believes in war, and in the Jesus who gave the Mexicans hell.

William Lloyd Garrison, in Russel B. Nye, *William Lloyd Garrison and the Humanitarian Reformers*

## TELFORD, THOMAS

1757–1834 Engineer

Telford it was, by whose presiding mind / The whole great work was plann'd and perfected; / Telford, who o'er the vale of Cambrian Dee, / Aloft in air, at giddy height upborne, / Carried his navigable road, and hung /

High o'er Menaï's straits the bending bridge. /

Robert Southey, *Inscriptions for the Caledonian Canal*

## TEMPLE, HENRY JOHN, *see under* PALMERSTON, VISCOUNT

## TENNYSON, ALFRED, LORD

1809–92 Poet

Baron Alfred T. de T. / Are we at last in sweet accord? / I learn – excuse the girlish glee – / That you've become a noble lord; / So now that time to think you've had / Of what makes charming girls, / Perhaps you find they're not so bad – / Those daughters of a hundred earls. /

Anon., *The Vere de Vere to Tennyson*

The real truth is that Tennyson, with all his temperament and artistic skill, is deficient in intellectual power; and no modern poet can make very much of his business unless he is pre-eminently strong in this.

Matthew Arnold, Letter to his Sister, 1860

He had a large, loose-limbed body, a swarthy complexion, a high, narrow forehead, and huge bricklayer's hands; in youth he looked like a gypsy; in age like a dirty old monk; he had the finest ear, perhaps, of any English poet; he was also undoubtedly the stupidest; there was little about melancholia that he didn't know; there was little else that he did.

W. H. Auden, Introduction to *A Selection from the Poems of Alfred Lord Tennyson*

He could not think up to the height of his own towering style.

G. K. Chesterton, *The Victorian Age in Literature*

Tennyson is a great poet, for reasons that are perfectly clear. He has three qualities which are seldom found together except in the greatest poets: abundance, variety, and complete competence. We therefore cannot appreciate his work unless we read a good deal of it. We may not admire his aims: but whatever he sets out to do, he succeeds in doing, with a mastery that gives us the sense of confidence that is one of the major pleasures of poetry . . . He had the finest ear of any English poet since Milton.

T. S. Eliot, Introduction to Tennyson's *Poems*

I remember him well, a sort of Hyperion.

Edward Fitzgerald (describing Tennyson at Cambridge), in Hallam Tennyson, *Tennyson, A Memoir*

No, you cannot read the *Idylls of the King* except in minute doses because of the sub-nauseating sissiness – there is no other convenient word – of the points of view of both Lord Tennyson and the characters that he projects . . . and because of the insupportable want of skill in the construction of sentences, the choice of words and the perpetual ampliation of images.

Ford Madox Ford, *The March of Literature*

Tennyson had the British Empire for God, and Queen Victoria for Virgin Mary.

Lady Gregory, in William Butler Yeats, Journal, 17 March 1909

You call Tennyson 'a great outsider'; you mean, I think, to the soul of poetry. I feel what you mean, though it grieves me to hear him depreciated, as of late years has often been done. Come what may he will be one of our greatest poets. To me his poetry appears 'chryselephantine'; always of precious mental material and each verse a work of art, no botchy places, not only so but no half-wrought or low-toned ones, no drab, no brown-holland; but the form, though fine, not the perfect artist's form, not equal to the material.

Gerard Manley Hopkins, Letter to R. W. Dixon, 1879

Tennyson was not Tennysonian.

Henry James, *The Middle Years*

Tennyson, while affecting to dread observation, was none the less no little vain, a weakness of which Meredith gave me this amusing illustration. Tennyson and William Morris were once walking together on a road in the Isle of Wight. Suddenly in the distance appeared two cyclists wheeling towards them. Tennyson immediately took alarm, and, turning to Morris, growled out, 'Oh, Morris, what shall I do. Those fellows are sure to bother me!' Thereupon Morris drew him protectively to his side. 'Keep close to me,' he said, 'I'll see that they don't bother you.' The cyclists came on, sped by without a sign, and presently disappeared on the horizon. There was a moment or two of silence, and then Tennyson, evidently huffed that he had attracted no attention, once more growled out, 'They never even looked at me!'

Richard Le Gallienne, *The Romantic '90s*

The great length of his mild fluency: the yards of linen-drapery for the delight of women.

George Meredith, in Frank Harris, *My Life and Loves*

Brahms is just like Tennyson, an extraordinary musician, with the brains of a third rate village policeman.

George Bernard Shaw, Letter to Pakenham Beatty, 4 April 1893

Tennyson, who was nothing if not a virtuoso, never produced a success that will bear reading after Poe's failures.

George Bernard Shaw, *Pen Portraits and Reviews*

Tennyson's knowledge of nature – nature in every aspect – was simply astonishing. His passion for 'star-gazing' has often been commented upon by readers of his poetry. Since Dante no poet in any land has so loved the stars. He had an equal delight in watching the lightning; and I remember being at Aldworth once during a thunder-storm when I was alarmed at the temerity with which he persisted, in spite of all remonstrances, in gazing at the blinding lightning. For moonlight effects he had a passion equally strong, and it is especially pathetic to those who know this to remember that he passed away in the light he so much loved – in a room where there was no artificial light – nothing to quicken the darkness but the light of the full moon.

Theodore Watts-Dunton, *Impressions of Tennyson*

*See also* Matthew Arnold

## TERRY, DAME (ALICE) ELLEN

1847–1928 Actress

Do you know, I have no weight on the stage; unless I have heavy robes I can't keep on the ground.

On herself, Letter to George Bernard Shaw

E. T. was persuadable – especially on Mondays – less so on Tuesdays. On Wednesday, people around her found it difficult to make her understand what it was they were trying to say – but by the time Thursday arrived she could be counted on to do the very thing they didn't expect. Friday she devoted to telling them that it didn't hurt, and that they must be brave and not cry – Saturday was always a half-holiday, spent in promising her advisers that she would be good next week – and on Sunday she generally drove away to Hampton Court with Irving, waving her lily white hand.

Edward Gordon Craig, *Ellen Terry and Her Secret Self*

Miss Ellen Terry is 'aesthetic'; not only her garments but her features themselves bear the stamp of the new enthusiasm. She has a charm, a great deal of a certain amateurish, angular grace, a total lack of what the French call *chic*, and a countenance very happily adapted to the expression of pathetic emotion. To this last effect her voice also contributes; it has a sort of monotonous, husky thickness which is extremely touching, though it gravely interferes with the modulation of many of her speeches.

Henry James, in *Nation*, 12 June 1879

One may say that her marriages were adventures and her friendships enduring.

George Bernard Shaw, in C. St J. Constable ed., *Ellen Terry and Bernard Shaw, A Correspondence*

She was an extremely beautiful girl and as innocent as a rose. When Watts kissed her, she took for granted she was going to have a baby.

George Bernard Shaw, in Stephen Winston, *Days with Bernard Shaw*

Judging from the banquet, Lady Macbeth seems an economical housekeeper and evidently patronises local industries for her husband's clothes and the servants' liveries, but she takes care to do all her own shopping in Byzantium.

Oscar Wilde, on Ellen Terry in Irving's revival of *Macbeth*, 29 December 1888

## THACKERAY, WILLIAM MAKEPEACE

1811–63 Novelist

William Makepeace Thackeray / Wept into his daiquiri, / When he heard St John's Wood / Thought he was no good. /

W. H. Auden, *Academic Graffiti*

He dissects his victims with a smile; and performs the cruellest of operations on their self-love with a pleasantry which looks provokingly very like good-nature.

Robert Bell, Review of *Vanity Fair*, in *Fraser's Magazine*, 1848

Thackeray is unique. I *can* say no more, I *will* say no less.

Charlotte Brontë, Letter to W. S. Williams, 29 March 1848

George Smythe said that, as they say novelists always draw their own characters, he wished Thackeray would draw his own – that would be a character! The Cynic Parasite!

Benjamin Disraeli, *Reminiscences*

If Mr Thackeray falls short of Fielding, much of whose peculiar power and more of whose manner he has inherited or studiously acquired, it is because an equal amount of large cordiality has not raised him entirely above the region of the sneering, into that of simple uncontaminated human affection. His satiric pencil is dipped in deeper colours than that of his prototype. Not Vanity Fair so properly as Rascality Fair is the scene he lays open to our view; and he never wholly escapes from his equivocal associations, scarcely ever lays aside for a whole page his accustomed sneer. His is a less comfortable, and on the whole therefore, let us add, a less true view of society than Fielding's.

John Forster, Review of *Vanity Fair*, in *Examiner*, July 1848

As a satirist, it is his business to tear away the mask from life, but as an artist and a teacher he grievously errs when he shows us *everywhere* corruption underneath the mask. His scepticism is pushed too far. While trampling on cant, while exposing what is base and mean, and despicable, he is not attentive enough to honour, and to paint what is high, and generous, and noble in human nature.

G. H. Lewes, in *Morning Chronicle*, March 1848

Thackeray settled like a meat-fly on whatever one had got for dinner, and made one sick of it.

John Ruskin, *Fors Clavigera*

It is a terrible thing to be taught by a master of his craft that in life there is little to excite admiration – nothing to inspire enthusiasm. It is fearful to have insight into the human heart, and to detect in that holy of holies not even one solitary spark of the once pure flame ... Guilt is among us – crime abounds – falsehood is around and about us; but, conscious as we are of these facts, we know that man may yet trust to his fellow man, and that evil is not permitted to outweigh good. A series of novels, based upon the principle which Mr Thackeray delights to illustrate would utterly destroy this knowledge and render us a race of unbelievers – animals less happy than the brutes who, dumb and unreasoning as they are, can still consort together and derive some consolation from their companionship.

*The Times*, 22 December 1852

Among all our novelists his style is the purest, as to my ear it is also the most harmonious. Sometimes it is disfigured by a slight touch of affectation, by little conceits which smell of the oil; – but the language is always lucid. The reader, without labour, knows what he means, and knows all that he means.

Anthony Trollope, *Autobiography*

*See also* Tobias Smollett

## THOMAS À BECKET

1118?–70 Archbishop of Canterbury, Statesman

. . . For three hundred years, he was accounted one of the greatest saints in heaven, as may appear from the accounts in the ledger-books of the offerings made to the three greatest altars in Christ's Church in Canterbury. The one was to Christ, the other to the Virgin, and the third to St Thomas. In one year there was offered at Christ's altar, 31.2s.6d; to the Virgin's altar, 631.5s.6d; but to St Thomas's altar, 8321.12s.3d.

Gilbert Burnet, *History of the Reformation*

. . . your Becket was a noisy egoist and hypocrite; getting his brains spilt on the floor of Canterbury Cathedral, to secure the main chance, – somewhat uncertain how!

Thomas Carlyle, *Past and Present*

You are the Archbishop in revolt against the King; / in rebellion to the King and the law of the land; / You are the Archbishop who was made by the King; / whom he set in your place to carry out his command. / You are his servant, his tool and his jack, / You wore his favours on your back, / You had your honours all from his hand; from him you had the power, the seal and the ring. / This is the man who was the tradesman's son: the backstairs brat who was born in Cheapside; / This is the creature that crawled upon the King; swollen with blood and swollen with pride. / Creeping out of the London dirt, / Crawling up like a louse on your shirt, / The man who cheated, swindled, lied; broke his oath and betrayed his King. /

T. S. Eliot, *Murder in the Cathedral* (the four knights accuse Becket)

Will no one free me of this turbulent priest?

Henry II, attributed

A bearer of the iniquity of the clergy.
Henry VIII, Royal Proclamation of November 1538

Other saints had borne testimony by their sufferings to the general doctrine of Christianity; but Becket had sacrificed his life to the power of the clergy; and this peculiar merit challenged, and not in vain, a suitable acknowledgement of his memory.
David Hume, *History of England*

A minister of iniquity.
John of Salisbury, *Entheticus II*

There is probably no hour in medieval history of which the details are so well known, and so revealing of character, as is the last hour of the archbishop's life, from about half-past two to half-past three on that dark December afternoon.
David Knowles, *Archbishop Thomas Becket: A Character Study*

In the seven years (1155–62) in which he held that office, the Angevin chancery became the most perfect piece of administrative machinery that Europe had yet known.
T. F. Tout, on Becket's service as Lord Chancellor, *The Place of St Thomas of Canterbury in History: a Centenary Study*

## THOMAS, DYLAN MARLAIS

1914–53 Poet

It is typical of the physically weak to emphasize the strength of life (Nietzsche): of the apprehensive and complex-ridden to emphasize its naivete and dark wholesomeness (D. H. Lawrence); of the naked-nerved and blood-timid to emphasize its brutality and horror (Me!).
On himself, Letter to Pamela Hansford Johnson, 1933

I should say I wanted to write poetry in the beginning because I had fallen in love with words. The first poems I knew were nursery rhymes, and before I could read them for myself I had come to love just the words of them, the words alone. What the words stood for, symbolised, or meant, was of very secondary importance; what mattered was the *sound* of them as I heard them for the first time on the lips of the remote and incomprehensible grown-ups who seemed, for some reason, to be living in my world. And these words were, to me, as the notes of bells, the sounds of musical instruments, the noises of wind, sea, and rain, the rattle of milkcarts, the clopping of hooves on cobbles, the fingering of branches on a window pane, might be to someone, deaf from birth, who has miraculously found his hearing. I did not care what the words said, overmuch, nor what happened to Jack & Jill & the Mother Goose rest of them; I cared for the shapes of sound that their names, and the words describing their actions, made in my ears; I cared for the colours the words cast on my eyes.
On himself, quoted in *Texas Quarterly*, Winter 1961

Myself, I believe it possible that if one kept one's ear close to the dirt of Dylan Thomas's grave in Wales, one might overhear that fruity voice murmuring ironically to itself a variation on the last words of the dying Vespasian: 'I think I am becoming a near myth.'
George Barker, in *Listener*, 4 December 1965

In America, visiting British writers are greeted at cocktail parties by faculty wives with 'Can you screw as good as Dylan?'
Anthony Burgess, *Urgent Copy*

Dylan wore a green porkpie hat pulled down level with his slightly bulging eyes: like the agate marbles we used as Alley Taws when I was a boy in France, but a darker brown. His full lips were set low in a round full face, a fag-end stuck to the lower one. His nose was bulbous and shiny. He told me afterwards that he used to rub it up with his fist before the mirror every morning until it shone satisfactorily; as a housewife might polish her doorknob or I the silver-topped malacca cane that I affected in those days.

Julian Maclaren-Ross, *Memoirs of the Forties*

. . . Young and gay / A bulbous Taliessin, a spruce and small / Bow-tied Silenus roistering his way / Through lands of fruit and fable, well aware / That even Dionysus has his day. /

Louis MacNeice, *Autumn Sequel*

There is a story of the friend in the funeral parlour, who looked down at the poet's painted face, loud suit and carnation in his buttonhole, only to declare, 'He would never have been seen dead in it.'

Andrew Sinclair, *Dylan Thomas*

I think it was Whitman who said that 'even in religious fervor there is always a touch of animal heat.' Both religious fervour and animal heat were in his poetry, to the highest degree. His poetry was the 'pure fire compressed into holy forms' of which one of Porphyry's Oracles spoke. The generation of those poems was attended by 'the great heat' that Aristotle said 'attended the generation of lions.' To him, blood was spirit.

Edith Sitwell, *Taken Care Of*

The great thing to remember about Dylan was that he was a complete chameleon and could adapt himself to any company and play any role. He was, in fact, a natural born actor . . . His favourite role was that of a Welsh country gentleman for which in later days he dressed in hairy tweeds and carried a knobbed walkingstick. Alternatively he could be a B.B.C. actor and verse reader, for which he wore a light grey smooth tweed suit. The role of the drunken Welsh poet with 'fag in the corner of the mouth, and dirty raincoat, and polo sweater' sometimes lasted for a week or more, but not longer.

Donald Taylor, in Constantine Fitzgibbon, *Life of Dylan Thomas*

## THOMAS, NORMAN MATTOON

1884–1968 Socialist, Politician

*Roosevelt*: Norman, I'm a damn sight better politician than you. *Thomas*: Certainly Mr President, you're on that side of the desk and I'm on this.

On himself, *Autobiography*

I would rather be right than be president but I am perfectly willing to be both.

On himself, 'The Dissenter's Role in a Totalitarian Age', in *New York Times Magazine*, 20 November 1949

It is not often in this great Republic that one hears a political hullabaloo that is also a work of art.

H. L. Mencken, in *Baltimore Sun*, 18 October 1948

. . . called himself a Socialist as a result of misunderstanding.

Leon Trotsky, in Harry Fleischman, *Norman Thomas, a biography*

## THOMSON, JAMES

1700–48 Poet

Dr Johnson said that Thomson had a true poetical genius, the power of viewing everything in a poetical light. That his fault was such a cloud of words sometimes that the sense could hardly peep through. He said Shiels, who compiled Cibber's *Lives of the Poets*, was one day with him. He took down Thomson and read a good portion to Shiels, and then asked if this was not very fine. Shiels was high in admiration. 'Well,' said Dr Johnson, 'I have missed every other line.'

James Boswell, *Journal*, 11 April 1776

Remembrance oft shall haunt the shore / When Thames in summer wreaths is drest / And oft suspend the dashing oar / To bid his gentle spirit rest. /

William Collins, *Ode on the Death of Mr Thomson*

Among his peculiarities was a very unskilful and inarticulate manner of pronouncing any lofty or solemn composition. He was once reading to Doddington, who, being himself a reader eminently elegant, was so much provoked by his odd utterance, that he snatched the paper from his hand, and told him that he did not understand his own verses.

Samuel Johnson, *Lives of the Poets*

## THOMSON, SIR WILLIAM, BARON KELVIN

1824–1907 Scientist, Inventor

Thirty years later another undergraduate of Peterhouse, named William Thomson, better known to fame as Lord Kelvin, was so certain he would be top of the [examination] list that he sent his servant to find out who was second. (It was William Thomson.)

B. V. Bowden, *Faster than Thought*

Lord Kelvin appeared to have the unique power of carrying on two trains of thought, or attending to two things at a time. At meals or in company his eyes at times had an abstracted or far-away look as if his mind was 'voyaging o'er strange seas of thought alone,' but yet he could still attend apparently to what was going on around him. At lunch I remember one day when his mind had apparently been pondering some abstruse scientific question, and Lady Thomson had been discussing plans for an afternoon excursion, Sir William suddenly looked up and said, 'At what times does the dissipation of energy begin?'

Sir Ambrose Fleming, *Memories of a Scientific Life*

## THOREAU, HENRY DAVID

1817–62 Essayist, Poet, Transcendentalist

I should not talk so much about myself if there were anybody else whom I knew as well.

On himself, in *Walden*

I would rather sit on a pumpkin and have it all to myself than be crowded on a velvet cushion.

On himself, in *ibid.*

My life hath been the poem I would have writ, / But I could not both live and utter it. /

On himself, in Walter Harding, *The Days of Henry Thoreau*

When a pious visitor inquired sweetly, 'Henry, have you made your peace with God?' he replied 'We have never quarrelled.'

Brooks Atkinson, *Henry Thoreau, the Cosmic Yankee*

He liked to administer doses of moral quinine, and he never thought of sugaring his pills.

Van Wyck Brooks, *The Flowering of New England 1815–1865*

He was bred to no profession; he never married; he lived alone; he never went to church; he never voted; he refused to pay a tax to the state; he ate no flesh, he drank no wine, he never knew the use of tobacco; and, though a naturalist, he used neither trap nor gun.

Ralph Waldo Emerson, in Mark Van Doren, *Henry David Thoreau, A Critical Study*

. . . the nullifier of civilization, who insisted on nibbling his asparagus at the wrong end.

Oliver Wendell Holmes, in Jay B. Hubbell, *Who Are the Major American Writers?*

He was imperfect, unfinished, inartistic; he was worse than provincial – he was parochial.

Henry James, *Life of Nathaniel Hawthorne*

He seems to me to have been a man with so high a conceit of himself that he accepted without questioning, and insisted on our accepting, his defects and weaknesses of character as virtues and powers peculiar to himself.

James Russell Lowell, 'Thoreau', in Edmund Wilson ed., *The Shock of Recognition*

By creating a classic image of the cynic hermit in ideal solitude Thoreau has demonstrated some of the meannesses of the demands of Time and Matter, and furnished the spirit and will for social criticism; he has made men acute critics, if not sensible shepherds, of their own sentiments.

Mark Van Doren, *Henry David Thoreau, A Critical Study*

## THURBER, JAMES GROVER

1894–1961 Cartoonist, Writer, Playwright

With sixty staring me in the face, I have developed inflammation of the sentence structure and a definite hardening of the paragraphs.

On himself, in *New York Post*, 30 June 1955

I do not have a psychiatrist and I do not want one, for the simple reason that if he listened to me long enough, he might become disturbed.

On himself, *Credos and Curios*

The mistaken exits and entrances of my thirties have moved me several times to some thought of spending the rest of my days wandering aimlessly around the South Seas, like a character out of Conrad, silent and inscrutable. But the necessity for frequent visits to my oculist and dentist have prevented this.

On himself, *My Life and Hard Times*

My theories and views of literature vary with the lateness of the hour, the quality of my companions, and the quantity of liquor.

On himself, in Fred B. Millet, *Contemporary American Authors*

Freud discovered the Id, and Thurber named it Walter Mitty.

Larry Adler, in *Sunday Times*, 5 October 1975

Helen [Mrs Thurber] said some drunk dame told Jim at a party that she would like to have a baby by him. Jim said, 'Surely you don't mean by unartificial insemination!'

Nunnally Johnson, Letter to Groucho Marx, 9 October 1961

To Thurber and [E. B.] White it seemed that, the way things were going, sex as nature intended it was on the way out. After a while people would just sit around and read sex books. Boldly they undertook to save the human race from extinction. They also hoped to make some money.

Dale Kramer, *Ross and the New Yorker*

Above the still cool lake of marriage he saw rising the thin mist of Man's disparity with Woman. In his drawings one finds not only the simple themes of love and misunderstanding, but also the rarer and tenderer insupportabilities.

E. B. White, in Charles S. Holmes, *The Clocks of Columbus, The Literary Career of James Thurber*

## TOKLAS, ALICE BABETTE

1877–1967 Author, Literary Figure

I wish to God we had gone together as I always so fatuously thought we would

– a bomb – shipwreck – just anything but this.

On herself, referring to Gertrude Stein's death, in Margo Jefferson, 'Passionate Friends', in *Newsweek*, 7 January 1974

Miss Toklas was incredibly ugly, uglier than almost anyone I had ever met. A thin, withered creature, she sat hunched in her chair, in her heavy tweed suit and her thick lisle stockings, impregnable and indifferent. She had a huge nose, a dark moustache, and her dark-dyed hair was combed into absurd bangs over her forehead.

Otto Friedrich, 'The Grave of Alice B. Toklas', in *Esquire*, January 1968

I like a view but I like to sit with my back turned to it.

Gertrude Stein, impersonating Miss Toklas

## TOOKE, JOHN HORNE

1736–1812 Radical, Philologist

Sir Francis Burdett told us that Horne Tooke, when advised to take a wife said, 'With all my heart; whose wife shall it be?'

Lord Broughton, *Recollections of a Long Life*

The fellow who looks like a half-and-half person.

James Fenimore Cooper, *Gleanings in Europe: England*

He wanted effect and *momentum.* Each of his sentences told very well of itself, but they did not altogether make a speech. He left off where he began. His eloquence was a succession of drops, not a stream. His arguments, though subtle and new, did not affect the main body of the question. The coldness and pettiness of his manner did not warm the hearts or expand the understandings of his hearers. Instead of encouraging, he checked the ardour of his friends; and teazed, instead of overpowering his antagonists.

William Hazlitt, considering Tooke as a Parliamentary speaker, in *The Spirit of the Age*

*See also* Richard Porson

## TOSCANINI, ARTURO

1867–1957 Conductor

After I die, I shall return to earth as a gatekeeper of a bordello and I won't let any of you – not a one of you [in the entire orchestra] – enter!

On himself, in Howard Taubman, *The Maestro: The Life of Arturo Toscanini*

Any *asino* can conduct – but to make music... eh? Is *difficile*!

On himself, in Samuel Antek, *This Was Toscanini*

A glorified bandmaster!

Thomas Beecham, in Neville Cardus, *Sir Thomas Beecham*

The man was supercharged; and it permeated the atmosphere, creating an aura of excitement that we didn't feel with other conductors. A concert can be a concert, or it can be a concert plus an event; and with Toscanini we had the double feature. But it was the dress rehearsals that were absolutely extraordinary: in that atmosphere of quiet and intense concentration we were hypnotized, and the ninety-five men functioned as one.

Bernard H. Haggin, *The Toscanini Musicians Knew*

*See also* Thomas Beecham

## TOWNSHEND, CHARLES

1725–67 Politician

Protective poverty of heart was the contrived shield of his stricken, vulnerable self; gifted enough to be aware, however dimly, of its ugliness and purpose, he consistently disguised or veiled it.

Sir Lewis Namier and John Brooke, *Charles Townshend*

Charles Townshend is dead. All those parts and fire are extinguished; those volatile salts are evaporated; that first eloquence of the world is dumb; that duplicity is fixed; that cowardice terminated heroically.

Horace Walpole, Letter to Sir Horace Mann, 27 September 1767

## TRACY, SPENCER

1900–67

Spence is the best we have, because you don't see the mechanism at work. He covers up, never overacts, gives the impression he isn't acting at all. I try to do it, and I succeed, but not the way Spence does. He has direct contact with an audience he never sees.

Humphrey Bogart, in Larry Swindell, *Spencer Tracy*

Spence was the kind of actor about whom you thought 'I've got a lot of things I could say to you, but I don't say them because you *know*', and next day everything I'd thought of telling him would be there in the rushes. Also, I was never sure whether Spence was really listening when I talked to him. He was one of those naturally original actors who did it but never let you see him doing it.

George Cukor, in Gavin Lambert, *On Cukor*

The guy's good and there's nobody in this business who can touch him, so you're a fool to try. And don't fall for that humble stuff either; the bastard knows it!

Clark Gable, in Larry Swindell, *Spencer Tracy*

The face was unforgettable. It was craggy, freckled and roughhewn. It was tough and sturdy and sunburned and later seamed with a network of wrinkles. Someone once said the lines would hold two days of rain. He himself said his face reminded him of a beat-up barn door.

David Zinman, *Fifty Classic Motion Pictures*

## TREE, SIR HERBERT BEERBOHM

1853–1917 Actor-manager

It is difficult to live up to one's posters ... When I pass my name in such large letters I blush, but at the same time instinctively raise my hat.

On himself, in Hesketh Pearson, *Beerbohm Tree*

It was characteristic of his complexity that he was greatly amused at his own naivete. He once handed me a letter from a stranger who had seen him act on the previous night. 'That's very nice,' I said after reading it. 'Very,' said he, 'I can stand any amount of flattery so long as it's fulsome enough.'

Max Beerbohm, *From a Brother's Standpoint*

With the amount of personal attention, Mr Tree, which you give to all your presentations, and the care you bestow on every detail, I really don't think you need an actual producer. Nor, with the constant supervision you so thoroughly exercise, have you any use for a stage-manager. What you really require are a couple of *tame, trained echoes*!

Hugh Moss, after an engagement, in Joe Graham, *An Old Stock-Actor's Memories*

[He] turned to Shakespeare as to a forest out of which ... scaffolding could be hewn without remonstrance from the landlord ... As far as I could discover, the notion that a play could succeed without any further help from the actor than a simple impersonation

of his part, never occurred to Tree.
George Bernard Shaw, *From the Point of View of a Playwright*

A charming fellow, and so clever: he models himself on me.
Oscar Wilde, in Hesketh Pearson, *Beerbohm Tree*

## TROLLOPE, ANTHONY

1815–82 Novelist

I was thinking today that nature intended me for an American rather than an Englishman. I think I should have made a better American yet I hold it higher to be a bad Englishman, than a good American, as I am not.
On himself, in C. P. Snow, *Trollope*

Of all novelists in any country, Trollope best understands the role of money. Compared with him, even Balzac is too romantic.
W. H. Auden, *Forewords and Afterwords.*

Have you ever read the novels of Anthony Trollope? They precisely suit my taste, – solid and substantial, written on the strength of beef and through the inspiration of ale, and just as real as if some giant had hewn a great lump out of the earth, and put it under a glass case, with all its inhabitants going about their daily business, and not suspecting that they were being made a show of. And these books are just as English as a beef-steak.
Nathaniel Hawthorne, Letter to Joseph M. Field

He has a gross and repulsive face and manner, but appears *bon enfant* when you talk with him. But he is the dullest Briton of them all.
Henry James, Letter to the James family, 1 November 1875

His first, his inestimable merit was a complete appreciation of the usual.
Henry James, *Partial Portraits*

A big, red-faced, rather underbred Englishman of the bald-with-spectacles type. A good roaring positive fellow who deafened me till I thought of Dante's Cerberus.
James Russell Lowell, Letter, 20 September 1861

*See also* A. E. Housman

## TRUMAN, HARRY S.

1884–1972 Thirty-Third United States President

I don't know whether you fellows ever had a load of hay or a bull fall on you. But last night the moon, the stars and all the planets fell on me. If you fellows ever pray, pray for me.
On himself to newspapermen on becoming President, in Jonathan Daniels, *The Man of Independence*

I never gave them hell, I just tell the truth and they think it's hell.
On himself, in *Look*, 3 April 1956

The buck stops here.
On himself, notice on his presidential desk

If somebody throws a brick at me I can catch it and throw it back. But when somebody awards a decoration to me, I am out of words.
On himself, on receiving the Grand Cross of Merit of Austria, 7 May 1964

I don't give a damn about *The Missouri Waltz* but I can't say it outloud because it's the song of Missouri. It's as bad as *The Star-Spangled Banner* so far as music is concerned.
On himself, in *Time*, 10 February 1958

Among President Truman's many weaknesses was his utter inability to discriminate between history and histrionics.
Anon., in Douglas MacArthur, *Reminiscences*

Mr Truman was unable to make the simple complex in the way so many men in public life tend to do. For very understandable reasons, of course. If one makes something complex out of something simple, then one is able to delay making up one's mind. And that was something that never troubled Mr Truman.

Dean Acheson, in Merle Miller, *Plain Speaking, An Oral Biography of Harry S. Truman*

Truman . . . seemed to stand for nothing more spectacular than honesty in war contracting, which was like standing for virtue in Hollywood or adequate rainfall in the Middle West.

George E. Allen, *Presidents Who Have Known Me*

Truman was nominated by men speculating beyond the death of Roosevelt who knew what they wanted but did not know what they were getting.

Jonathan Daniels, *The Man of Independence*

He is a man totally unfitted for the position. His principles are elastic, and he is careless with the truth. He has no special knowledge of any subject, and he is a malignant, scheming sort of an individual who is dangerous not only to the United Mine Workers, but dangerous to the United States of America.

John L. Lewis, United Mine Workers Convention, 1948

. . . was not able to make peace, because politically he was too weak at home. He was not able to make war because the risks were too great. President Eisenhower signed an armistice which accepted the partition of Korea and a peace victory because being himself the victorious commander in World War II and a Republican, he could not be attacked as an appeaser. President Truman and Secretary Acheson, on the other hand, never seemed able to afford to make peace on the only terms which the Chinese would agree to.

Walter Lippmann, in Bert Cochran, *Harry Truman and the Crisis Presidency*

Truman had been sent to Washington by a man criticized throughout the country as a crook. I didn't see any future in an association like that. He was a guy – a punk – set up by gangsters.

Victor Messall, when offered the post of Senator Truman's chief assistant, in *ibid.*

He was liked, he was admired, he evoked steadfast loyalty in many, but he could not inspire.

Cabell Phillips, *The Truman Presidency*

. . . right on all the big things, wrong on most of the little ones.

Sam Rayburn, attributed

He was distressingly petty in petty things; he was gallantly big in big things.

Clinton Rossiter, in Thomas A. Bailey, *Presidential Greatness*

Mr Truman believes other people should be 'free to govern themselves as they see fit' – so long as they see fit to see as we see fit.

I. F. Stone, 'With Malice Toward None – Except Half Mankind,' in *The Truman Era*

Harry Truman proves the old adage that any man can become President of the United States.

Norman Thomas, in Murray B. Seidler, *Norman Thomas, Respectable Rebel*

President Truman cannot prevent the tide from coming in or the sun from rising. But once America stands for opposition to change we are lost.

America will become the most hated nation in the world.

Henry Wallace, in *New York Times*, 14 March 1947

*See also* John F. Kennedy

## TUCKER, SOPHIE (SOPHIE ABUZA)

1884–1966 Entertainer

The Last of the Red-Hot Mamas.

On herself, publicity introduction coined by her

## TURNER, JOSEPH MALLORD WILLIAM

1775–1851 Painter

Turner's one dream, the extraordinarily high aspiration of his life, was to gain a complete knowledge of light in all its phases.

E. Chesneau, *The English School of Painting*

He seems to paint with tinted steam, so evanescent, and so airy. The public think he is laughing at them, and so they laugh at him in return.

John Constable, Letter to George Constable, 12 May 1836

The Philosopher of Art and the Newton of Painting.

J. Elmes, *Sir Christopher Wren*

[Benjamin] West has spoken in the highest manner of a picture in the Exhibition painted by Turner, that is what Rembrandt thought of but could not do.

Joseph Farington, Diary, 17 April 1801

Shortly before the end, Dr Price, of Margate, who had attended Turner when he had been ill there, was summoned to London for a consultation with Mr Bartlett. He is said to have told the patient that death was near. 'Go downstairs,' Turner said to the doctor, 'take a glass of sherry and then look at me again.' The doctor did so, but his opinion remained unchanged.

A. J. Finsberg, *The Life of J. M. W. Turner R.A.*

In the gallery was a gorgeous display of haunted dreams thrown on the canvas, rather in the way of hints and insinuations than real pictures, and yet the effect of some was most fascinating. The colouring almost Venetian, the imagination of some almost as grand as they were vague; but I think one great pleasure in them is the opportunity they give for trying to find out what he can possibly mean, and then you hug your own creative ingenuity, whilst you pretend to be astonished at Turner's. This especially refers to the Deluge and the Brazen Serpent.

Caroline Fox, Journals, May 1849

At a dinner when I was present, a salad was offered to Turner, who called the attention of his neighbour at the table ... to it in the following words: 'Nice cool green that lettuce, isn't it? and the beetroot pretty red – not quite strong enough; and the mixture, delicate tint of yellow that. Add some mustard, and then you have one of my pictures.'

William P. Frith, *My Autobiography and Reminiscences*

I wonder whether Turner ever did have any distinctive personal experience before nature. He seems to me to have had so intense a desire to create, to do, to be so busy about picture-making that he never had the time for that.

Roger Fry, *Reflections on British Painting*

All the taste and all the imagination being borrowed, his powers of eye, hand, and memory, are equal to any thing. In general, his pictures are a waste of morbid strength. They give pleasure only by the excess of power triumphing over the barrenness of the subject.

William Hazlitt, in *Morning Chronicle*, 5 February 1814

If you have ever in your life had one opportunity, with your eyes and heart open, of seeing the dew rise from a hill pasture, or the storm gather on a sea-cliff, and if you yet have no feeling for the glorious passages of mingled earth and heaven which Turner calls up before you into breathing tangible being, there is indeed no hope for your apathy, art will never touch you, nor nature inform.

John Ruskin, *Modern Painters*

Turner made drawings of mountains and clouds which the public said were absurd. I said, on the contrary, they were the only true drawings of mountains and clouds ever made yet: and I proved this to be so, as only it could be proved, by steady test of physical science: but Turner had drawn his mountains rightly, long before their structure was known to any geologist in Europe; and has painted perfectly truths of anatomy in clouds which I challenge any meteorologist in Europe to explain to this day.

John Ruskin, *The Eagle's Nest*, vol. 3

Views on the Thames, crude blotches, nothing could be more vicious.

Benjamin West, in Joseph Farington, Diary, 5 May 1807

I have often heard my father describe the lectures. He declared you could hardly hear anything Turner said, he rambled on in such a very indistinct way which was most difficult to follow. My father said that at the General Assemblies he would make long speeches in an equally confused and rambling manner, and if interrupted or called to order for not confining himself to the subject in question, he would become angry and say, 'Nay, nay, if you make an abeyance of it I will sit down.' But though the subject matter of his lectures was neither listened to nor understood, they were well attended as he used to display beautiful drawings of imaginary buildings with fine effects of light and shade, on the wall behind his rostrum.

William T. Whitley, *Art in England 1800–20*

*See also* John Constable

## TURPIN, (BERNARD) BEN

1869–1940 Motion Picture Comedian

We paid Turpin $1500 a week at the height of his powers. He invested all his money, bought apartment houses, and became a rich man. He always saved a few dollars a week by personally doing the janitor work at all his apartment houses.

He seldom drove an automobile – a frantic thought at that; who knows how many directions he would have tried to drive at once? He preferred to save money by travelling by streetcar. As he would enter the trolley, he would draw his wren-like physique up to full strut and squeak, at the top of his voice, 'I'm Ben Turpin. Three thousand dollars a week!'

Mack Sennett, *King of Comedy*

## TWAIN, MARK (SAMUEL LANGHORNE CLEMENS)

1835–1910 Writer

I am different from Washington. I have a higher and grander standard of principle. Washington could not lie. I *can* lie but I won't.

On himself, in *Chicago Tribune*, 20 December 1871

I have noticed my conscience for many years, and I know it is more trouble and bother to me than anything else I started with.

On himself, in A. K. Adams, *The Home Book of Humorous Quotations*

Twenty-four years ago, Madam, I was incredibly handsome. The remains of it are still visible through the rift of time. I was so handsome that women became spellbound when I came in view. In San Francisco, in rainy seasons, I was frequently mistaken for a cloudless day.

*Ibid.*

The reports of my death are greatly exaggerated.

*Ibid.*, when learning of his reported demise

I don't mind what the opposition say of me, so long as they don't tell the truth about me; but when they descend to telling the truth about me, I consider that that is taking an unfair advantage.

On himself, Speech delivered at Hartford, Connecticut, 26 October 1880

I have never taken any exercise, except sleeping and resting, and I never intend to take any. Exercise is loathsome. And it cannot be any benefit when you are tired; and I am always tired.

On himself, in Maxwell Geismar, *Mark Twain, An American Prophet*

My books are water; those of the great geniuses are wine. Everybody drinks water.

On himself, May 1886 entry in his notebook, in Frederick Anderson ed., *Mark Twain, The Critical Heritage*

His wife not only edited his works but edited him.

Van Wyck Brooks, *The Ordeal of Mark Twain*

... a hack writer who would not have been considered fourth rate in Europe, who tricked out a few of the old proven 'sure fire' literary skeletons with sufficient local color to intrigue the superficial and the lazy.

William Faulkner, in Michael Millgate, *The Achievement of William Faulkner*

He glimmered at you from the narrow slits of fine blue-greenish eyes, under branching brows, which with age grew more and more like a sort of plumage, and he was apt to smile into your face with a subtle but amiable perception, and yet with a sort of remote absence; you were all there for him, but he was not all there for you.

William Dean Howells, in Edward Wagenknecht, *Mark Twain: The Man and His Work*

I love to think of the great and godlike Clemens. He is the biggest man you have on your side of the water by a damn sight, and don't you forget it. Cervantes was a relation of his.

Rudyard Kipling, Undated letter to Frank Doubleday

But who is this in sweeping Oxford gown / Who steers the raft, or ambles up and down, / Or throws his gown aside, and there in white / Stands gleaming like a pillar of the night? / The lion of high courts, with hoary mane, / Fierce jester that this boyish court will gain – / Mark Twain! / The bad world's idol: / Old Mark Twain. /

Vachel Lindsay, *The Raft*

Mark Twain and I are in very much the same position. We have to put things in such a way as to make people, who would otherwise hang us, believe that we are joking.

George Bernard Shaw, remark to Archibald Henderson

## TWEED, WILLIAM MARCY

1823–78 Politician

This is / BOSS TWEED / The Tammany Atlas who all sustains / (A Tammany

Samson perhaps for his pains), / Who rules the city where Oakey reigns, / The master of Woodward and Ingersoll / And all of the gang on the City Roll, / And formerly lord of 'Slippery Dick.' / Who controll'd the plastering laid on so thick / By the comptroller's plasterer, Garvey by name, / The Garvey whose fame is the little game / Of laying on plaster and knowing the trick / Of charging as if he himself were a brick / Of the well-plaster'd House / That TWEED built. /

Anon., *The House that Tweed built*

It is better to be one of Mr Tweed's horses than a poor taxpayer of this city.

Anon., in *New York Times*, 28 September 1870

Mr Tweed is inspired to all high and noble aims, by the contemplation of personal beauty and innocence as imbedded in a photograph of himself.

*Ibid.*, 26 January 1871

One of the most suave, sleek and oleaginous persons on earth is the New York professional politician, when things are going his way ... Had there been any doubt of his identity, it might have been easily determined by the size of his diamond and the conspicuous position it occupied upon his person ... The politician who had not got a diamond on his bosom was of little account among his fellows, and was looked upon as having neglected his opportunities ... But the days of the politicians' diamond glory are well nigh gone ... They went out with Boss Tweed, who set the political fashion, and who wore the most brilliant diamond of all.

Matthew Breen, *Thirty Years of New York Politics*

Skilled to pull wires, he baffles Nature's hope / Who sure intended him to stretch a rope.

James Russell Lowell, *The Boss*

## TWINING, RICHARD

1749–1824 Merchant

It seems as if Nature had curiously plann'd / That men's names with their trades should agree; / There's Twining the Tea-Man, who lives in the Strand, / Would be *whining*, if robb'd of his T. /

Theodore Hook, *Epigram*

## TYE, CHRISTOPHER

*circa* 1497–1572 Musician

Dr Tye was a peevish and humoursome man, especially in his latter days, and sometimes playing on the organ in the chapel of Qu. Eliz. which contained much music, but little delight to the ear, she would send the verger to tell him that he played out of tune, whereupon he sent word that her ears were out of tune.

Anthony à Wood, *Fasti Oxonienses*

# 'V'

## VALENTINO, RUDOLPH (RUDOLPHO DI VALENTINA D'AUTONGUOLLA)

1895–1926 Actor

Valentino had silently acted out the fantasies of women all over the world. Valentino and his world were a dream. A whole generation of females wanted to ride off into a sandy paradise with him. At thirteen I had been such a female.

Bette Davis, *The Lonely Life*

He had more sheer animal magnetism than any actor before or since. *The Sheik* and *Blood and Sand* placed Valentino on a pinnacle of adoration before he knew the *a b c*'s of screen acting. He became a far more accomplished actor later on, but women didn't attend his pictures to see him act. They went to swoon.

Jesse Lasky, *I Blow My Own Horn*

Catnip to women.

H. L. Mencken, Appendix from Moronia', *Prejudices*, sixth series

I began to observe Valentino more closely. A curiously naive and boyish young fellow, certainly not much beyond thirty, and with a disarming air of inexperience. To my eye, at least, not handsome, but nevertheless rather attractive. There was an obvious fineness in him; even his clothes were not precisely those of his horrible trade. He began talking of his home, his people, his early youth. His words were simple and yet somehow very eloquent. I could still see the mime before me, but now and then, briefly and darkly, there was a flash of something else. That something else, I concluded, was what is commonly called, for want of a better name, a gentleman.

*Ibid.*

*See also* Elinor Glyn

## VANBRUGH, SIR JOHN

1664–1726 Dramatist, Architect

Under this stone, reader, survey / Dead Sir John Vanbrugh's house of clay. / Lie heavy on him earth! for he / Laid heavy loads on thee. /

Abel Evans, *Epitaph*

He never faltered in his career; and from first to last – at Blenheim and Castle Howard, as at Seaton Delaval and Grimsthorpe – there is one principle runs through all his designs, and it was a worthy one – a lofty aspiration after grandeur and eternity.

James Fergusson, *History of the Modern Styles of Architecture*

He discovers the utmost dramatic generalship in bringing off his characters at a pinch, and by an instantaneous *ruse de guerre*, when the case seems hopeless in any other hands. The train of his associations, to express the same thing in metaphysical language, lies in following the suggestions of his fancy into every possible combination of cause and effect, rather than into every possible combination of likeness or difference.

William Hazlitt, *Lectures on the English Comic Writers*

Vanbrugh used his weighty materials as a pigment, and the sky his canvas, with a brush too wide to allow any niceties of detail. Surely Mammon was his Zeus.

Sir Edwin Lutyens, in C. Hussey, *The Life of Sir Edwin Lutyens*

To speak then of Vanbrugh in the language of a painter, he had originality of invention, he understood light and shadow, and had great skill in composition. To support his principal object, he produced his second and third groups or masses; he perfectly understood in his art what is the most difficult in ours, the conduct of the back-ground; by which the design and invention is set off to the greatest advantage. What the back-ground is in painting, in architecture is the real ground on which the building is erected; and no architect took greater care than he that his work should not appear crude and hard; that is, it did not abruptly start out of the ground without expectation or preparation.

Sir Joshua Reynolds, *Discourse XIII*, December 1786

Heaviness was the lightest of his faults . . . The Italian style . . . which he contrived to caricature . . . is apparent in all his works; he helped himself liberally to its vices, contributed many of his own, and by an unfortunate misfortune adding impurity to that which was already greatly impure, left it disgusting and often odious.

Sir Robert Smirke, *Manuscript Notes*

Van's Genius without Thought or Lecture / Is hugely turnd to Architecture. /

Jonathan Swift, *The History of Vanbrug's House*

From such deep Rudiments as these, / *Van* is become by due Degrees, / For building fam'd; and justly reckon'd / At Court, *Vitruvius* the *Second.* / No Wonder; since wise *Authors* show, / That *best Foundations* must be *low.* / And now the *Duke* has wisely ta'en him / To be his *Architect* at *Blenheim.* / But Raillery for once apart, / If this Rule holds in ev'ry Art; / Or if his Grace were no more skill'd in / The Art of battering Walls than Building; / We might expect to see next Year / A *Mouse-trap* Man chief Engineer. /

*Ibid.*

Sir John was a man of Pleasure, and likewise a Poet, and an Architect. The general Opinion is, that he is as sprightly in his Writings as he is heavy in his Buildings. 'Tis he who rais'd the famous Castle of *Blenheim*, a ponderous and lasting Monument of our unfortunate Battle of Hochstet. Were the Apartments but as spacious as the walls are thick, this Castle would be commodious enough.

Voltaire, *Letters Concerning the English Nation*

Vanbrugh dealt in quarries, and Kent in lumber.

Horace Walpole, Letter to Sir Horace Mann, 22 April 1775

His humour was broad like his keystones, though not so heavy.

Lawrence Whistler, *Sir John Vanbrugh*

Vanbrugh . . . was neither nursed nor tutored; he sprang into power like Athene, fully armed with imagination, and so great was the impression he made, that at once a new manner appeared in the chief works.

*Ibid.*

*See also* Nicholas Hawksmoor

## VAN BUREN, MARTIN

1782–1862 Eighth United States President

The Red Fox of Kinderhook.

Anon., common nickname for Van Buren

[a] service dough-face . . . Madison had none of his obsequiousness, his sycophancy, his profound dissimulation and duplicity. In the last of these he much more resembles Jefferson though with

very little of his genius. The most disgusting part of his character, his fawnng servility, belonged neither to Jefferson nor to Madison.

John Quincy Adams, in L. Falkner, *The President Who Wouldn't Retire*

Van Buren was not reelected, but his campaign was so hilarious that he was popularly acclaimed the Panic of 1837.

Richard Armour, *It All Started With Columbus*

He stood on the dividing-line between the mere politician and the statesman – perfect in the arts of the one, possessing largely the comprehensive powers of the other.

James G. Blaine, *Twenty Years of Congress*

He is not ... of the race of the lion or the tiger; he belonged to a lower order – the fox.

John C. Calhoun, in Louis W. Koenig, *The Rise of the Little Magician*

He rowed to his object with muffled oars.

John Randolph of Roanoke, in Edward Boykin ed., *The Wit and Wisdom of Congress*

When he enters the Senate chamber in the morning, he struts and swaggers like a crow in the gutter. He is laced up in corsets, such as women in a town wear and, if possible, tighter than the best of them. It would be difficult to say from his personal appearance whether he was man or woman, but for his large red and gray whiskers. [He is] as opposite to General Jackson as dung is to a diamond ... secret, sly, selfish, cold, calculating, distrustful, treacherous ... It is said that ... he could laugh on one side of his face and cry on the other at one and the same time.

Senator White, in A. Steinberg, *The First Ten*

## VANDERBILT, CORNELIUS

1794–1879 Financier, Capitalist

Vanderbilt made his money in ships thus, while others became captains of industry, he became a commodore ... One of his favorite expressions, which endeared him to everyone, was 'The public be damned.'

Richard Armour, *It All Started With Columbus*

## VANE, SIR HENRY

1613–62 Statesman, Author

There never was such a prostitute sight, / That ere profaned this purer light / A hocus-pocus juggling Knight, / Which nobody can deny. /

His cunning state tricks and oracles, / His lying wonders and miracles, / Are turned at last into Parliament shackles / Which nobody can deny. /

Anon., *Vanity of Vanities or Sir Henry Vane's Picture*, before 1662

So much dissimulation and enthusiasm, such vast parts and such strong delusions, good sense and madness, can hardly be believed to meet in one man. He was successively a Presbyterian, Independent, Anabaptist, and Fifth Monarchy Man. In sum, he was the Proteus of his times, a mere hotch-potch of religion, chief ring-leader of all the frantic sectarians, of a turbulent spirit and working brain, of a strong composition of choler and melancholy, an inventor not only of whimseys in religion, but of crotchets in the state.

Baker, Jones and Reed eds., *Biographia Britannica*

Vane, young in years but in sage counsel old / Than whom a better senator ne'er held / The helm of Rome, when gowns not arms repell'd / The fierce Epirot and the African bold, – / Whether to settle peace or to unfold / The drift of hollow states hard to be spell'd, – / Then to advise how war may, best upheld, / Move by her two main nerves, iron and gold, / In all her equipage! – besides to know / Both spiritual pow'r and civil what each means / What severs each, thou hast learn'd, which few have done. / The bounds of either sword to thee we owe: / Therefore on thy firm hand Religion leans / In peace, and reckons thee her eldest son. /

John Milton, *To Sir Henry Vane the Younger*

*See also* Lord Strafford

## VAUGHAN, HENRY

1622–95 Poet

Above the voiceful windings of a river / An old green slab of simply graven stone / Shuns notice, overshadowed by a yew. / Here Vaughan lies dead, whose name flows on for ever / Through pastures of the spirit washed with dew / And starlit with eternities unknown. / Here sleeps the Silurist; the loved physician; / The face that left no portraiture behind; / The skull that housed white angels and had vision / Of daybreak through the gateways of the mind. /

Siegfried Sassoon, *At the Grave of Henry Vaughan*

Made his first entry into *Jesus* Coll. in *Mich.* Term 1638, aged 17 years: where spending two Years or more in Logicals under a noted Tutor, was taken thence and designed by his Father for the obtaining of some knowledge in the municipal Laws at *London*. But soon after the Civil War beginning, to the horror of all good Men, he was sent for home, followed the pleasant Paths of Poetry and Philology, became noted for his ingenuity, and published several Specimens thereof . . . Afterwards applying his Mind to the study of Physic, became at length eminent in his own Country for the practice thereof, and was esteemed by Scholars *an ingenious Person, but proud and humorous*.

Anthony à Wood, *Athenae Oxonienses*

## VAUGHAN WILLIAMS, SIR RALPH

1872–1958 Composer

[C.V.] Stanford would sometimes sigh deeply when I brought him my week's work and say he was hoping against hope.

On himself, at the Composers' Concourse, 1957

*Reporter*: Tell me, Dr Vaughan Williams, what do you think about music?
*RVW*: It's a Rum Go!

Leslie Ayre, *The Wit of Music*

In a work like Vaughan Williams's *Pastoral Symphony* it is no exaggeration to say that the creation of a particular type of grey, reflective, English-landscape mood has outweighed the exigencies of symphonic form. To those who find this mood sympathetic, their intense and personal emotional reaction will more than compensate for the monotony of texture and the lack of form, of which a less well-disposed listener might perhaps be unduly conscious.

Constant Lambert, *Music Ho!*

## VEBLEN, THORSTEIN BUNDE

1857–1929 Economist, Social Theorist

We may now leave him in peace, remote and aloof in his Olympian privacy; whence may his stinging phrases continue to puncture our cherished illusions or to goad our lethargic minds.

Paul T. Homan, 'Thorstein Veblen', in Howard W. Odum ed., *American Masters of Social Science*

The man who shook the world with his irony, and who opened the way to a new social system for the generation which should find the wit to resolve the conflicts he had pointed out, went slowly out of life, lonely, trivial, unappeased and disagreeable. But that was probably all in the character he had chosen out of those available to him.

Rexford Guy Tugwell, 'Veblen and Business Enterprise', in Malcolm Cowley and Bernard Smith eds, *Books That Changed Our Minds*

He was likewise a master of devious implication, pungent epigram, and adhesive phrases that clung like leeches to the bloated form of capitalism.

George F. Whicher, 'The Twentieth Century', in Arthur Hobson Quinn ed., *The Literature of the American People*

## VICTORIA, QUEEN

1819–1901

. . . they wished to treat me like a girl, but I will show them that I am Queen of England.

On herself, Letter to Lord Melbourne on the Bedchamber Question, May 1839

Lord John Russell may resign, and Lord Aberdeen may resign, but I *can't* resign.

On herself, speaking to Lord Clarendon on the formation of a government, January 1855

The Queen herself, though it was tried in all ways, *never* could *before* her accession take the slightest interest in public affairs; but, the moment she felt the responsibility, she bent her neck to the yoke and worked hard, though she *hates* it *all* as much now as she did as a girl.

On herself, Memorandum to Sir Henry Ponsonby, 9 July 1872

Oh if the Queen were a man, she would like to go and give those horrid Russians whose word one cannot trust such a beating.

On herself, Letter to Disraeli, January 1878

Others but herself *may submit* to his [Gladstone's] democratic rule but *not the Queen.*

On herself, Memorandum to Sir Henry Ponsonby, 4 April 1880

As I get older, I cannot understand the world. I cannot comprehend its littlenesses. When I look at the frivolities and littlenesses, it seems to me as if they were all a little mad.

On herself, Diary, *circa* 1885

We are not amused.

On herself, attributed, remark probably made after she saw a horseguard attempting to imitate her, 1889

How different, how very different, from the home life of our own dear Queen!

Anon., Comment of a contemporary woman after a performance of *Antony and Cleopatra*, in Irvin S. Cobb, *A Laugh a Day*

How shall we speak of an infinite loss . . . the unimaginable touch of fate that extinguishes an epoch, that removes the central figure of all the world . . . The golden reign is closed. The supreme woman of the world, best of the highest, greatest of the good, is gone. The Victorian age is over. Never, never was loss like this, so inward and profound that only the slow years can reveal its true reality. The Queen is dead.

Anon., in *Daily Telegraph*, 23 January 1901

It is indeed a pity that you find no consolation in the company of your children. The root of the trouble lies in the mistaken notion that, the function of a mother is to be always correcting, scolding, ordering them about and organising their activities. It is not possible to be on

happy friendly terms with people you have just been scolding.
Prince Albert, Letter to Victoria, 1 October 1856

'I will have no melancholy in this house' is her formula – and not a bad one either in moments of anxiety.
A. J. Balfour, Letter to Lord Salisbury, 19 December 1899

She was the greatest of Englishwomen – I had almost said of Englishmen – for she added the highest of manly qualities to the personal delicacy of the woman.
Joseph Chamberlain, Letter to Lord Milner, 25 January 1901

Your Majesty's life has been passed in constant communion with great men, and the knowledge and management of important transactions. Even if your Majesty were not gifted with those great abilities, which all must now acknowledge, this rare and choice experiment must give your Majesty an advantage in judgment, which few living persons, and probably no living Prince, can rival.
Benjamin Disraeli, Letter to Queen Victoria, 26 February 1868

Murmurings of children in a dream. The royal project of gracious interposition with our rivals is a mere phantom. It pleases the vanity of a court deprived of substantial power.
Benjamin Disraeli, Letter to Lord Derby concerning the Queen's offer to mediate with the Liberals, 21 October 1866

Her chief fault (in little things and great) seems to be impatience; in Sea phrase, She always wants to *go ahead*; she can't bear contradiction nor to be thwarted.
Adolphus Fitzclarence, in Charles Greville, Diary, 23 September 1842

To speak in rude and general terms, the Queen is invisible, and the Prince of Wales is not respected. With the Queen, who abounds beyond all necessity in private and personal kindnesses to those having relations with her, it is a matter of great and ever increasing difficulty to arrange for any part of those formal ceremonial duties to the public, which in an ordinary state of things would go as matters of course. These parts of business are among the most difficult, and are the most painful, of the duties of my place; and it would be a relief to me if I could lay the blame upon the unhandy manner in which I perform them. The Queen's reluctance grows, and will grow, with age.
William Ewart Gladstone, Letter to Earl Granville, December 1870

It was so awfully pathetic seeing Her drawn on a gun carriage by the eight cream coloured horses of Jubilee renown – but I never at any funeral felt so strongly before, that She Herself was not on the bier but watching it all from somewhere and rejoicing in Her people's loyalty.
Kathleen Isherwood, Letter, 3 February 1901

She's more of a man than I expected.
Henry James (after reading the Queen's *Letters*), in E. M. Forster, Diary, 1908

'Ave you 'eard o' the Widow at Windsor/ With a hairy gold crown on 'er 'ead? / She 'as ships on the foam – she 'as millions at 'ome, / An' she pays us poor beggars in red. /
Rudyard Kipling, *The Widow at Windsor*

Walk wide o' the Widow at Windsor, / For 'alf o' Creation she owns: / We 'ave bought 'er the same with the sword an' the flame, / An' we've salted it down with our bones. /
*Ibid.*

The finest & most poetic thing that can be said about the Queen, is . . . that her virtues and powers are *not* those of a great woman, like Elizabeth or Catherine II ... but are the virtues and powers of an ordinary woman: things that any person, however humble, can appreciate and imitate ... an example inestimably precious to the whole world.

Alfred Munby, Letter to Austin Dobson, 4 July 1897

You never saw anybody so entirely taken up with military affairs as she is.

Lord Panmure, Letter to Lord Raglan, 1855

Dear dead Victoria / Rotted cosily; / *In excelsis gloria,* / And R.I.P. / And her shroud was buttoned neat, / And her bones were clean and round, / And her soul was at her feet / Like a bishop's marble hound. /

Dorothy Parker, *Victoria*

Her court was pure; her life serene; / God gave her peace; her land reposed; / A thousand claims to reverence closed / In her as Mother, Wife and Queen. /

Alfred, Lord Tennyson, *To The Queen*

*See also* Prince Albert, Richard Burton, Duke of Cumberland, Duke of Marlborough, Lord Melbourne, D. G. Rossetti, Alfred, Lord Tennyson, Oscar Wilde

## VILLIERS, BARBARA, COUNTESS OF CASTLEMAINE, DUCHESS OF CLEVELAND

1641–1709 Mistress to Charles II, Court Figure

But ere I part, I Cleveland must behold – / The Amazon gamester with her keeper's gold, / Hedged in by rooks and sharpers to prove true / The proverb, 'lightly come and lightly go', / She for her soul cant give the dice-box o'er / 'Till she's as poor and wretched as Jane Shore; / And she'll by sad experience find it worse / Than broke in visage to be broke in purse. /

Anon., *Tunbridge Satire*

The Empress Massalina tir'd in lust at least, / But you could never satisfy this beast. / Cleveland I say, was much to be admir'd / For she was never satisfied or tired. / Full forty men a day have swived the whore, / Yet like a bitch she wags her tail for more. /

John Lacy, *Satire*

Endeed I can never enough admire her beauty.

Samuel Pepys, Diary, 7 September 1661

Young Harry Killigrew is banished the Court lately for saying that my Lady Castlemayne was a little lecherous girl when she was young, and used to rub her thing with her fingers or against the end of forms, and that she must be rubbed with something else. This she complained to the King of – and he sent to the Duke of York, whose servant he is, to turn him away. The Duke of York hath done it, but takes it ill of my Lady that he was not complained to first. She attended him to excuse it, but ill blood was made by it.

*Ibid.*, 21 October 1666

It seems she is with child, and the King says he did not get it; with that she made a slighting 'puh' with her mouth, and went out of the house, and never came in again till the King sent to Sir Dan. Harvey's to pray her ... But it seems she hath told the King that whoever did get it, he should own it; and the bottom of the quarrel is this; she is fallen in love with young Jermin, who hath of late lain with her oftener than the King and is now going to marry my Lady Falmouth. The King, he is mad at her entertaining Jermin, and she is mad at Jermin's going to marry from her, so they are all mad, and thus the Kingdom is governed.

*Ibid.*, 29 July 1667

Thy strumpets Charles, have 'scaped no nation's ear; / Cleveland the van, and Portsmouth led the rear; / A brace of cherubs of as vile a breed / As ever was produced of human seed. / To all but thee the punks were ever kind, / Free as loose air, and gen'rous as the wind; / Both steer'd thy pego and the nations helm / And both betray'd thy pintle and thy realm.

Thomas Sackville, Earl of Dorset (?), *A Faithful Catalogue of our Most Eminent Ninnies*

If the Church of Rome has got by her no more than the Church of England has lost, the Matter is not much.

Bishop Stillingfleet, on Castlemaine's conversion, 1663, in J. Oldmixon, *History of England*

Libell on the countess of Castlemayne's doore in Merton Coll [January 1666] . . . The reason why she is not ducked 'Cause by Caesar she is ——.

Anthony à Wood, *Life and Times*

## VILLIERS, GEORGE, *see under* BUCKINGHAM, DUKES OF

## VON STERNBERG, JOSEF

1894–1969 Film Director

Instead of the Elinor Glyn plots of the day, I had in mind a visual poem. Instead of flat lighting, shadows. In the place of pasty masks, faces in relief, plastic and deep-eyed. Instead of scenery which meant nothing, an emotionalised background that would transfer itself into my foreground. Instead of saccharine characters, sober figures moving in rhythm.

On himself, of his first film *The Salvation Hunters*

When they ask me what elements are necessary for a director, I propose some absolutely horrible qualifications. I tell them he must know all the languages, he must know the history of the theatre from its beginnings, he must be an expert in psychoanalysis and must have had some psychiatric training. He must know every emotion. And they ask me 'Did you know all this?' And I say 'No – but I never asked anyone how to become a director.'

On himself, Interview, December 1964, in Kevin Brownlow, *The Parade's Gone By*

The only way to succeed is to make people hate you. That way they remember you.

On himself, to Clive Brook, in Kevin Brownlow, *ibid.*

Von Sternberg could film the telephone directory and make it exciting, mysterious and sensuous.

Kevin Brownlow, in *ibid.*

Critical historians have evaluated Von Sternberg's pictures as things of beauty but not a joy forever. His artistry with a camera was rarely surpassed, but he sometimes allowed pictorial effects to overshadow the story he was telling.

Jesse Lasky, *I Blow My Own Horn*

Jo has been his usual obnoxious, brilliant self; refusing to concede the merit of suggestions and then acting upon them: making changes that would be aggravating in any other director that turn out all right. As with all his pictures, he makes silly things look great.

David O. Selznick, Letter to Bud Schulberg, in Rudy Behlmer, *Memo from David O. Selznick*

## VON STROHEIM, ERICH (OSWALD VAN NORDENWALL)

1885–1957 Film Director, Actor

Genius! In talking of films, what meaning can we give this word so devalued by hypocrisy and confused standards? An artist of genius is one who creates without imitating, and who draws out of the depths of his own being the least predictable part of his work. How many in the history of the cinema fit this definition? Whatever their number, Erich von Stroheim is at their head. He owed nothing to anyone. Yet it is to this man, who died in poverty, that every one of us is in debt.

René Clair, introducing a retrospective of von Stroheim's work at the Venice Film Festival, 1958

'This is a true honor' said [Billy] Wilder by way of introduction. 'In my opinion, you were twenty years ahead of your time.' 'Thirty' replied von Stroheim without smiling.

Thomas Quinn Curtis, *Von Stroheim*

He told me that if he should die tomorrow, there would be sorrow only in one group in Hollywood, the workmen, the laborers, the artisans. 'I had no trouble with them; never! I got on well with them for the plain reason that I was one of them. I have always stood with them better than I have with the wealthy and the powerful. I could *never* get on with vice-presidents.'

Lloyd Lewis, in *ibid.*

Von Stroheim was the greatest director in the world. That's a fact, and no one who knows pictures would dispute it. But he was impossible, a crazy artist. If he had only been ten percent less himself and ten percent more reasonable, we would still be making pictures together.

Louis B. Mayer, in *ibid.*

Some Hollywood flack, in a burst of inspiration, dubbed him the Man You Love to Hate. He was a short man, almost squat, with a vulpine smirk that told you, the moment his image flashed on the screen, that no wife or bank roll must be left unguarded. The clean-shaven bullet head, the glittering monocle, and the ram rod back (kept rigid by a corset it was whispered) were as familiar and as dear to the moviegoing public as the Pickford curls or Eugene O'Brien's pompadour. No matter what the background of the picture was – an English drawing room, a compartment on the Orient Express, the legation quarter of Peiping – he always wore tight-fitting military tunics, flaunted an ivory cigarette holder, and kissed ladies' hands profusely, betraying them in the next breath with utter impartiality. For sheer menace, he made even topnotch vipers like Lew Cody, Ivan Lebedeff, and Rockliffe Fellowes seem rank stumblebums by comparison. He was the ace of cads, a man without a single redeeming feature, the embodiment of Prussian Junkerism, and the greatest heavy of the silent film, and his name, of course, was Erich von Stroheim.

S. J. Perelman, 'Cloudland Revisited: Vintage Swine', in *The Most of S. J. Perelman*

# 'W'

## WALLACE, HENRY AGARD
1888–1965 Politician

Much of what Mr Wallace calls his global thinking is, no matter how you slice it, still Globaloney.
Claire Booth Luce, Speech in the House of Representatives, 9 February 1943

## WALLER, EDMUND
1606–87 Poet

One of the first refiners of our English language and poetrey. When he was a brisque young sparke, and first studyed Poetry; me thought, sayd he, I never sawe a good copie of English verses; they want smoothness; then I began to essay. I have severall times heard him say that he cannot versify when he will: but when the Fitt comes upon him, he does it easily, i.e. in plaine terms, when his Mercurius and Venus are well aspected.
John Aubrey, *Brief Lives*

Unless he had written, none of us could write.
John Dryden, Preface to William Walsh, *A Dialogue Concerning Women*

Waller belonged to the same class as Suckling – the sportive, the sparkling, the polished, with fancy, wit, elegance of style, and easiness of versification at his command. Poetry was the plaything of his idle hours – the mistress, to whom he addressed his verses, was his real Muse.
William Hazlitt, 'A Critical List of Authors', in *Select British Poets*

The general character of his poetry is elegance and gaiety. He is never pathetic, and very rarely sublime. He seems neither to have had a mind much elevated by nature nor amplified by learning. His thoughts are such as a liberal conversation and large acquaintance with life would easily supply. They had however then, perhaps, that grace of novelty which they are now often supposed to want by those who, having already found them in later books, do not know or inquire who produced them first. This treatment is unjust. Let not the original author lose by his imitators.
Samuel Johnson, *Lives of the Poets*

His importation of the French theory of the couplet as a kind of thought-coop did nothing but mischief.
James Russell Lowell, 'Essay on Dryden', in *My Study Windows*

## WALPOLE, HORACE, FOURTH EARL OF ORFORD
1717–97 Author

It is charming to totter into vogue.
On himself, Letter to G. A. Selwyn, December 1765

He was a witty, sarcastic, ingenious, deeply-thinking, highly-cultivated, quaint, though evermore gallant and romantic, though very mundane, old bachelor of other days.
Fanny Burney, *Memoirs of Dr Burney*

Walpole deserves his place as the central figure in every account of eighteenth-century medievalism. He was not an originator. To give a new direction to taste, to furnish men's minds with a new Utopia, requires more imagination and independence than Walpole could command. But to catch and intensify new ideas as they float from mind to mind requires gifts too; and these gifts Walpole had. Wit, curiosity, a graceful style, and a good social position were more valuable assets than passionate conviction or massive learning.

Kenneth Clark, *The Gothic Revival*

The conformation of his mind was such that whatever was little seemed to him great, and whatever was great seemed to him little.

T. B. Macaulay, 'Walpole', in *Edinburgh Review*, October 1833

Walpole ought never to be confused with Walpole, who was quite different; it was Walpole who lived in a house called Strawberry Jam and spent his time writing letters to famous men (such as the Prime Minister, Walpole, etc.). Walpole is memorable for inventing the new policy of letting dogs go to sleep.

W. C. Sellar and R. J. Yeatman, *1066 and All That*

He was mischievous and obscene; he gibbered and mocked and pelted the holy shrines with nutshells. And yet with what a grace he did it – with what ease and brilliancy and wit! ... He is the best company in the world – the most amusing, the most intriguing – the strangest mixture of ape and Cupid that ever was.

Virginia Woolf, *Essays*: 'The Death of the Moth'

A queer sort of imagination haunted the seemingly prosaic edifice of Walpole's mind. What but imagination gone astray and vagrant over pots and pans instead of firmly held in place was his love of knick-knacks and antiquities, Strawberry hills and decomposing royalties?

*Ibid.*, 'Granite and Rainbow'

## WALPOLE, SIR HUGH SEYMOUR

1884–1941 Author

I was a young man in a hurry, ambitious, greedy, excitable. I was not really vain. When he [Henry James] told me gently that I was an idiot and that my novels were worthless, I believed that, from his point of view, it must be so, and that if the world had been peopled with Henry Jameses I should certainly never publish a line. The world was not.

On himself, *The Apple Trees*

You bleat and jump like a white lambkin on the vast epistolary green which stretches before you co-extensive with life ... I positively invite and applaud your gambols.

Henry James, Letter to Walpole, *circa* 1909

I have little doubt that he would have given all his popularity to gain the esteem of the intelligentsia. He knocked humbly at their doors and besought them to let him in, and it was a bitterness to him that they only laughed.

Somerset Maugham, *A Writer's Notebook*

How *cooold* he be ainy goood? He knows naaaathing about saix!

Robertson Nicoll, in Frank Swinnerton, *The Georgian Literary Scene*

## WALPOLE, SIR ROBERT, FIRST EARL OF ORFORD

1676–1745 Prime Minister

Who killed Cock Robin? / I, said the Sparrow, / With my bow and arrow, / I killed Cock Robin. /

Nursery rhyme, *circa* 1744, traditionally held to refer to Walpole's fall

All the birds of the air / Fell a-sighing and a-sobbing / When they heard the bell toll / For poor Cock Robin. /

*Ibid.*

He would frequently ask young fellows at their first appearance in the world, while their honest hearts were yet untainted, 'Well, are you to be an old

Roman? a patriot? You will soon come off of that and grow wiser.' And thus he was more dangerous to the morals than to the liberties of his country, to which I am persuaded he meant no ill in his heart.

Lord Chesterfield, *Letters and Characters*, vol. 2

I think 'tis thought a fault to wish anybody dead, but I hope 'tis none to wish he might be hanged, having brought to ruin so great a country as this might have been.

Sarah Churchill, *Opinions of Sarah, Duchess of Marlborough*

When Sir Robert Walpole was dismissed from all his employments he retired to Houghton and walked into the Library; when, pulling down a book and holding it some minutes to his eyes, he suddenly and seeming sullenly exchanged it for another. He held that about half as long, and looking out a third returned it instantly to its shelf and burst into tears. 'I have led a life of business so long,' said he, 'that I have lost my taste for reading, and now – what shall I do?'

Mrs Piozzi (Hester Lynch Thrale), *Memoirs*

He had a heightened awareness both of the world and of men. From this sprang both his exquisite taste and his finesse in human relations. He could live outside his own character. He possessed *empathy*, the quality to get, as it were, into the skin of other human beings, to feel with them; an intuitive quality which, of course, could err, but more often brilliantly clarified a common situation.

J. H. Plumb, *Sir Robert Walpole*

Seen him I have, but in his happier hour / Of Social Pleasure, ill-exchang'd for Pow'r; / Seen him, uncumber'd with the venal tribe, / Smile without Art, and win without a bribe. / Would he oblige me? Let me only find / He does not think me what he thinks mankind. / Come, come, at all I laugh he laughs, no doubt, / The only diff'rence is, I dare laugh out. /

Alexander Pope, *Epilogue to the Satires*, dialogue 1

With favour and fortune fastidiously blest, / He's loud in his laugh, and he's coarse in his jest: / Of favour and fortune unmerited, vain, / A sharper in trifles, a dupe in the main. / Achieving of nothing – still promising wonders – / By dint of experience improving in blunders. / Oppressing true merit, exalting the base, / And selling his country to purchase his place. / A jobber of stocks by retailing false news – / A prater at court in the style of the stews: / Of virtue and worth by profession a giber, / Of juries and senates the bully and briber. / Though I name not the wretch, yet you know whom I mean – / 'Tis the cur-dog of Britain, and spaniel of Spain. /

Jonathan Swift, *A Character of Sir Robert Walpole*

*See also* H. H. Asquith, Lord Chatham, Lord Melbourne, Horace Walpole

## WALSINGHAM, SIR FRANCIS

1530?–90 Statesman

He outdid the Jesuits in their own bowe and overreached them in their own equivocation, and mental reservation; never setling a lye, but warily drawing out and discovering truth.

D. Lloyd, *State Worthies*

. . . the great Maecenas of this age, / As wel to al that civil artes professe, / As those that are inspired with martial rage. /

Edmund Spenser, *Sonnet to Walsingham Prefatory to the Faery Queen*

*See also* Sir Martin Frobisher

## WALTON, IZAAK

1593–1683 Author

And angling, too, that solitary vice, / Whatever Izaak Walton sings or says: / The quaint, old, cruel coxcomb, in his gullet / Should have a hook, and a small trout to pull it.

Lord Byron, *Don Juan*, canto xiii

What Walton saw in angling was not that delight in the consciousness of accomplishment and intelligence which sends the true fisherman to the river and keeps him there, rejoicing in his strength, whether he kill or go away empty. It was rather the pretext – with a worm and perhaps a good supper at one end and a contemplative man at the other – of a day in the fields.

W. E. Henley, *Walton*

## WALWYN, WILLIAM

*fl.* 1649 Leveller

. . . the complexion also of many of them being like the bellei of a toad, and to speak the truth, Worley was one of the properest gentlemen amongst them all, as he was the most remarkable and taken notice of, by reason of his habit and busie diligence; he went that day in a great white and brown basket-hilted beard, and with a set of teeth in his head much like a potfish, all staring and standing at some distance one from another, as if they had not been good friends. It may be conjectured he picks them twice a day with a bed-staffe, they looke so white and cleare; he was mighty diligent about the Commonwealthe that day, and the privileges of the subject, and all the fraternity came flocking about him on all occasions, as a company of turkeys do about a frogge, wondering at him as at a strange sight.

John Bastwick, *A Just Defence of John Bastwick*

## WARBURTON, WILLIAM, BISHOP OF GLOUCESTER

1698–1779 Scholar

Orthodoxy is my doxy – heterodoxy is another man's doxy.

On himself, in Joseph Priestley, *Memoirs*

I am well informed, that Warburton said of Johnson, 'I admire him, but I cannot bear his style': and that Johnson being told of this, said, 'That is exactly my case as to him.'

James Boswell, *Life of Johnson*

The manner in which he [Dr Johnson] expressed his admiration of the fertility of Warburton's genius and of the variety of his materials, was, 'The table is always full, Sir. He brings things from the north, and the south, and from every quarter . . . He carries you round and round, without carrying you forward to the point; but then you have no wish to be carried forward.'

*Ibid.*

W. is a sneaking Parson, & I told him he flatterd.

Alexander Pope, Letter to Martha Blount, August 1743

## WARD, ARTEMUS (CHARLES FARRAR BROWNE)

1834–67 Humorist

I am happiest when I am idle. I could live for months without performing any kind of labour, and at the expiration of that time I should feel fresh and vigorous enough to go right on in the same way for numerous more months.

On himself, *Pyrotechny*

## WARD, JOHN WILLIAM, EARL DUDLEY OF CASTLE DUDLEY

1781–1833 Politician

Ward has no heart, they say; but I

deny it: / He has a heart, and gets his speeches by it. /
Samuel Rogers, *Epigram*

## WARD, WILLIAM GEORGE

1812–82 Theologian

Farewell, whose living like I shall not find, / Whose Faith and Work were bells of full accord, / My friend, the most unworldly of mankind, / Most generous of all Ultramontanes, Ward, / How subtle at tierce and quart of mind with mind, / How loyal in the following of thy Lord. /
Alfred, Lord Tennyson, *In Memoriam, W. G. Ward*

## WASHINGTON, GEORGE

1732–99 First United States President

I can't tell a lie, Pa; you know I can't tell a lie. I did cut it with my hatchet.
On himself, when asked by his father how a cherry tree had come to be destroyed, in Mason Locke Weems, *Life of Washington*

I am so hackneyed to the touches of the painter's pencils that I am now altogether at their beck . . . at first I was as impatient and as restive under the operation as a colt is of the saddle. The next time I submitted very reluctantly, but with less flouncing. Now no dray horse moves more readily to his thill than I do to the painter's chair.
On himself, Letter to Francis Hopkinson, 1785

My movements to the chair of Government will be accompanied by feelings not unlike those of a culprit who is going to the place of his execution.
On himself, Letter to Henry Knox, 1 April 1789

Perhaps the reason little folks / Are sometimes great when they grow taller / Is just because, like Washington, / They do their best when they are smaller. /
Anon., in James Morton Smith ed., *George Washington, A Profile*

Instead of adoring a Washington, mankind should applaud the nation which educated him . . . I glory in the character of a Washington, because I know him to be only an exemplification of the American character.
John Adams, 1785, in Marcus Cunliffe, *George Washington, Man and Monument*

. . . is a soldier, – a warrior; he is a modest man; sensible; speaks little; in action cool, like a bishop of his prayers.
Roger Atkinson, in Moses Coit Tyler, *Patrick Henry*

Where may the wearied eye repose / When gazing on the Great, / Where neither guilty glory glows, / Nor despicable state? / Yes-one-the first-the last-the best- / The Cincinnatus of the West / Whom Envy cannot hate, / Bequeathed the name of Washington, / To make men blush there was but one. /
Lord Byron, *Ode to Napoleon Buonaparte*

He has become entombed in his own myth – a metaphorical Washington Monument that hides from us the lineaments of the real man.
Marcus Cunliffe, *George Washington, Man and Monument*

If, among all the pedestals supplied by history for public characters of extraordinary nobility and purity, I saw one higher than all the rest, and if I were required, at a moment's notice, to name the fittest occupant for it, I think my choice, at any time during the last forty-five years, would have lighted, and would now light upon Washington!
William Ewart Gladstone, in *ibid.*

Did anyone ever see Washington nude? It is inconceivable. He had no nakedness, but I imagine he was born with his clothes on, and his hair powdered, and made a stately bow on his first appearance in the world.

Nathaniel Hawthorne, in Daniel Boorstin, 'The Mythologizing of George Washington', in James Morton Smith ed., *George Washington, A Profile*

. . . A Citizen, first in war, first in peace, first in the hearts of his countrymen.

Henry (Light Horse Harry) Lee, Resolution proposed to Congress on the death of Washington, 26 December 1799

Washington is the mightiest name of earth – long since the mightiest in the cause of civil liberty, still mightiest in moral reformation . . . To add brightness to the sun or glory to the name of Washington is alike impossible. Let none attempt it. In solemn awe pronounce the name and in its naked deathless splendor leave it shining on.

Abraham Lincoln, 1842, in James Morton Smith ed., *George Washington, A Profile*

Virginia gave us this imperial man / Cast in the massive mould / Of those high-statured ages old / Which into grander forms our mortal metal ran; / She gave us this unblemished gentleman: / What shall we give her back but love and praise / As in the dear old unestranged days / Before the inevitable wrong began? / Mother of states and undiminished men, / Thou gavest us a country, giving him. /

James Russell Lowell, *Under the Old Elm*

A simple gentleman of Virginia with no extraordinary talents had so disciplined himself that he could lead an insubordinate and divided people into ordered liberty and enduring union.

Samuel Eliot Morison, 'The Young Man Washington', in James Morton Smith ed., *George Washington, A Profile*

Advice to a statuary who is to execute the statue of Washington.
Take from the mine the coldest, hardest stone, / It needs no fashion: it is Washington, / But if you chisel, let the stroke be rude, / And on his heart engrave – Ingratitude. /

Thomas Paine, in Dixon Wecter, 'President Washington and Parson Weems', in *ibid.*

G. Washington was abowt the best man this world sot eyes on . . . He never slept over! . . . He luved his country dearly. He wasn't after the spiles. He was a human angil in a 3 kornered hat and knee britches.

Artemus Ward (Charles Farrar Browne), in *ibid.*

The crude commercialism of America, its materialising spirit . . . are entirely due to the country having adopted for its national hero a man who was incapable of telling a lie.

Oscar Wilde, *The Decay of Lying*

*See also* John Adams, John Quincy Adams, John Brown, Robert E. Lee, Mark Twain, Noah Webster

## WATSON-WENTWORTH, CHARLES, *see under* ROCKINGHAM, MARQUESS OF

## WATT, JAMES

1736–1819 Engineer

He devoured every kind of learning. Not content with chemistry and natural philosophy, he studied anatomy, and was one day found carrying home for dissection the head of a child that had died of some hidden disorder.

Henry, Lord Brougham, *Lives of Men of Letters and Science who flourished in the time of George III*

His peculiar achievement was to make use of science, for the first time in history, in conceiving a major invention, which has had the unique effect of giving mankind a dynamic outlook, in place of the ancient static belief that nothing very fundamentally changes.

J. G. Crowther, *Scientists of the Industrial Revolution*

I am sure that James Watt had no desire to establish a matriarchal family; yet by making it possible for men to sleep in places distant from those in which they work he has had this effect upon a great part of our urban populations.

Bertrand Russell, *Why I am Not a Christian: The New Generation*

Many distinguished inventors are found comparatively helpless in the conduct of business, which demands the exercise of different qualities, – the power of organizing the labour of large numbers of men, promptitude of action in emergencies, and sagacious dealing with the practical affairs of life. Thus Watt hated that jostling with the world, and contact with men of many classes, which are usually encountered in the conduct of any extensive industrial operation. He declared that he would rather face a loaded cannon than settle an account or make a bargain; and there is every probability that he would have derived no pecuniary advantage whatever from his great invention [i.e. the steam engine], nor been able to defend it against the repeated attacks of the mechanical pirates who fell upon him in Cornwall, London, and Lancashire, had he not been so fortunate as to meet, at the great crisis of his career, with the illustrious Matthew Boulton, 'the father of Birmingham'.

Samuel Smiles, *Self-help*

## WAUGH, EVELYN ARTHUR ST JOHN

1903–66 Novelist

My 39th birthday. A good year. I have begotten a fine daughter; published a successful book; drunk over 300 bottles of wine and smoked 300 Havana cigars. I get steadily worse as a soldier with the passage of time but more humble and patient – as far as soldiering is concerned; I have about £900 in hand and no grave debts except to the government; health excellent except when impaired by wine; a wife I love; agreeable work in surroundings of great beauty. Well that is as much as one can hope for.

On himself, Diary, October 1942

I regard writing not as investigation of character but as an exercise in the use of language, and with this I am obsessed. I have no technical psychological interest. It is drama, speech, and events that interest me.

On himself, in *Paris Review*, 1962

He had the sharp eye of a Hogarth alternating with that of the Ancient Mariner.

Harold Acton, *Adam*, 1966

Evelyn was attracted by the foibles of those who lived in large, aristocratic houses. He . . . fostered a fascination, though in many ways despising it, for the higher echelons of the Army and military etiquette. He drank port and put on weight, and attempted to behave in the manner of an Edwardian aristocrat. He was very conscious of what a gentleman should or should not do: no gentleman looks out of a window, no gentleman wears a brown suit. In fact, Evelyn's abiding complex and the source of much of his misery was that he was not a six-foot tall, extremely handsome and rich duke.

Cecil Beaton, *The Strenuous Years*

In literary calendars 1945 is marked as the year Waugh ended. It was the year of *Brideshead Revisited* . . . After that it was clear he had been conclusively eaten by his successor, Mr Evelyn Waugh, English novelist, officer (ret.) and gentleman. Mr Waugh writes a prose as fluent, lovely and lacking in intellectual content as a weeping willow: Waugh had written – and, almost as much as written, *omitted* – in fragments and ellipses, like a fiercer Firbank.

Brigid Brophy, *Don't Never Forget*

The satire of Evelyn Waugh in his early books was derived from his ignorance of life. He found cruel things funny because he did not understand them and he was able to communicate that fun.

Cyril Connolly, *Enemies of Promise*

One phrase from 'Pinfold' is a true heartcry from Evelyn Waugh: 'Why does everybody except me find it so easy to be nice?' At times, when remonstrated with for not being 'nice', he would retort, 'You don't know how much nastier I would be if I hadn't become a Catholic.'

Tom Driberg, in *Observer Colour Magazine*, 20 May 1973

If Mr Waugh would sternly root out the sentimentalities and adolescent values which have, so deplorably as it seems to many of us, coiled themselves about the enchanting comic spirit which is his supreme asset as a writer, and return to being the drily ironic narrator of the humours of his world and of his lavish inventive fancy, he would thereby increase his stature . . . There is in nearly every writer . . . a soft-headed romantic, who will, if allowed, get out of hand . . . In Mr Waugh's case, this romantic being, kept well under in earlier life, would seem to have temporarily seized the pen. An unhappy and unsuitable partnership, overdue for dissolution.

Rose Macaulay, in *Horizon*, December 1946

Despite all Waugh's efforts to appear to be an irascible, deaf old curmudgeon, a sort of inner saintliness kept breaking through.

Malcolm Muggeridge, in M. Gross, *The World of George Orwell*

W's driving forces. Snobbery. Catholicism . . . One cannot really be a Catholic & grown-up. Conclude. Waugh is *abt.* as good a novelist as one can be (i.e. as novelists go today) while holding untenable opinions.

George Orwell, 'Manuscript Notebook', in *Collected Essays*

*See also* Nancy Mitford

## WEBB, MARTHA BEATRICE, LADY PASSFIELD

1858–1943 Economist, Socialist

That she was a superior person is clear. But she was also insular because she was keenly aware of her own superiority. She is reported to have said once, when asked if she had ever felt shy, 'Oh, no. If I ever felt inclined to be scared going into a room full of people I would say to myself, "You're the cleverest member of one of the cleverest families in the cleverest class of the cleverest nation of the world, so what have you got to be frightened of?"' Such assurance stunted her potential stature.

David A. Shannon, Introduction to Beatrice Webb, *American Diary*

There's no more mysticism in Beatrice than in a steam engine.

H. G. Wells, in Desmond MacCarthy, 'The Webbs as I saw them' (essays)

. . . beneath the metallic façade and the surface of polished certainty, there was a neurotic turmoil of doubt and discontent, suppressed or controlled, an ego tortured in the old-fashioned religious way almost universal among the wise and good in the nineteenth century . . . She had, too, the temperament strongly suppressed, the passion and imagination of an artist, though she would herself have denied this. Her defence against these psychological stresses was a highly personal form of mysticism.

Leonard Woolf, *Beginning Again*

## WEBB, SIDNEY JAMES, LORD PASSFIELD

1859–1947 Economist, Socialist

Lord Passfield, he says, is utterly useless, vacillating and weak. Lord Passover he calls him.

Sir Donald Cameron, in Margery Perham, *East African Journey*

Sidney is simply unconscious of all the little meanness which turns social intercourse sour; he is sometimes tired, occasionally bored, but never unkindly or anxious to shine, or be admired, and wholly unaware of the absence of, or presence of, social consideration. I verily believe that if he were thrown . . . into a company of persons all of whom wanted to snub him, he would take up the first book and become absorbed in it, with a sort of feeling that they were good-natured enough not to claim his attention, or that they did not perceive that he was reading on the sly. And the greater personages they happened to be, the more fully satisfied he would be at the arrangement; since it would relieve him of any haunting fear that he was neglecting his social duty and making others uncomfortable. On the other hand, whether in his own house or in another's, if some person is neglected or out of it, Sidney will quite unconsciously drift to them and be seen eagerly talking to them.

Beatrice Webb, *Our Partnership*

. . . all the way through exactly what he appeared to be on the surface. He had no doubts or hesitations . . . for he knew accurately what could be known about important subjects or, if he did not actually know about it, he knew that he could obtain accurate knowledge about it with the aid of a secretary and an index card.

Leonard Woolf, *Beginning Again*

## WEBB, BEATRICE AND SIDNEY

(dates as above)

Old people are always absorbed in something, usually themselves; we prefer to be absorbed in the Soviet Union.

On themselves, in Kingsley Martin, 'The Webbs in Retirement', in Margaret Cole (ed.), *The Webbs and their Work*

Only once do I remember the Webbs going gay.

Blanche Patch, *Thirty Years with GBS*

He did the work. She kept him at it.

J. H. Plumb, Lecture at Cambridge, *circa* 1965

Sidney and Beatrice Webb . . . were the most completely married couple I have ever known. They were, however, very averse from any romantic view of love or marriage. Marriage was a social institution designed to fit instinct into a legal framework. During the first ten years of their marriage, Mrs Webb would remark at intervals, 'as Sidney always says, marriage is the waste-paper basket of the emotions'.

Bertrand Russell, *Autobiography*, vol. 1

How did the idea enter into your head that their relationship was frigid and inhuman? I used to live with them, and work with them a good deal, and you may take it from me that you couldn't be more wrong. Though Sidney, when they were working together, could stick it out almost indefinitely, Beatrice would suddenly reach the end of her tether, jump up, throw her pen away, fling herself on her husband, and half smother him with kisses. This might happen two or three times in a morning; and after each outbreak she would return to work with new vigour, and grind away like a slave until the need for a similar stimulant became imperative.

George Bernard Shaw, in Hesketh Pearson, *Bernard Shaw, a Postscript*

## WEBSTER, DANIEL

1782–1852 Statesman

A living lie, because no man on earth could be so great as he looked.

Anon., in John F. Kennedy, *Profiles in Courage*

. . . the gigantic intellect, the envious temper, the ravenous ambition, and the rotten heart of Daniel Webster.

John Quincy Adams, in R. N. Current, *Daniel Webster and the Rise of National Conservatism*

As a logic fencer, or parliamentary Hercules, one would incline to back him at first sight against all the extant world. The tanned complexion; that amorphous crag-like face; the dull black eyes under the precipice of brows, the dull anthracite furnaces needing only to be *blown*; the mastiff mouth accurately closed.

Thomas Carlyle, Letter to Ralph Waldo Emerson, in Henry Cabot Lodge, *Daniel Webster*

The word 'honor' in the mouth of Mr Webster is like the word 'love' in the mouth of a whore.

Ralph Waldo Emerson, in Ray Gingers, *Joke Book about American History*

A single look would be enough to wither up a whole volume of bad logic.

Thomas Hamilton, in Bertha M. Rothe ed., *Daniel Webster Reader*

. . . remembered best as the quasi-official rhapsodist of American nationalism.

Richard Hofstadter, *The American Political Tradition*

Mr Webster appeared like a great seventy-four gun ship, which required deeper water, larger space, and stronger wind to be set in motion.

Benjamin Perry, in N. D. Brown, *Daniel Webster and the Politics of Availability*

I would not attempt to vie with the honorable gentleman from Massachusetts in a field where every nigger is his peer and every billy-goat his master.

John Randolph of Roanoke, believing that Webster had accused him of impotence

Daniel Webster struck me much like a steam engine in trousers.

Sydney Smith, in Lady Holland, *Memoirs*, vol. 1

God is only the president of the day, and Webster is his orator.

Henry David Thoreau, *Walden*

## WEBSTER, JOHN

1580?–1625? Dramatist

Webster was not, in the special sense of the word, a great dramatist, but was a great poet who wrote haphazard dramatic or melodramatic romances for an eagerly receptive but semi-barbarous public.

William Archer, 'Webster, Lamb, and Swinburne', in *New Review*, 1893

A play of Webster's is full of the feverish and ghastly turmoil of a nest of maggots

Rupert Brooke, *John Webster and the Elizabethan Drama*

I suppose you could define a pessimist as a man who thinks John Webster's *Duchess of Malfi* a great play; an optimist as one who believes it actable.

Ronald Bryden, 'Blood Soaked Circus', in *Observer*, 18 July 1971

Webster was much possessed by death / And saw the skull beneath the skin; / And breastless creatures under ground / Leaned backward with a lipless grin. / Daffodil bulbs instead of balls / Stared from the sockets of the eyes! / He knew that thought clings round dead limbs / Tightening its lusts and luxuries. /

T. S. Eliot, *Whispers of Immortality*

To move a horror skilfully, to touch a soul to the quick, to lay upon fear as much as it can bear, to wean and weary a life till it is ready to drop and then step in with mortal instruments to take its last forfeit: this only a Webster can do.

Charles Lamb, *Specimens of English Dramatic Poets*

The vices and the crimes which he delights to paint, all partake of an extravagance which, nevertheless, makes them impressive and terrible, and in the retribution and the punishment, there is a character of corresponding wildness. But our sympathies, suddenly awakened, are allowed as suddenly to subside. There is nothing of what Wordsworth calls 'a mighty stream of tendency' in the events of his dramas.

'H.M.', in *Blackwood's Edinburgh Magazine*, 1818

Webster, it may be said, was as it were a limb of Shakespeare: but that limb, it might be replied, was the right arm.

Algernon C. Swinburne, *The Age of Shakespeare*

As to our Countryman *Webster*, tho' I am to confess obligations to him, I am not oblig'd to be blind to all his Faults. He is not without his incidents of *Horror*, almost as extravagant as those of the *Spaniard*. He had a strong and impetuous Genius, but withal a most wild and indigested one: He sometimes conceived nobly, but did not always express with clearness; and if he now and then soars handsomely, he as often rises into the Region of Bombast: his Conceptions were so eccentric, that we are not to wonder why we cannot ever trace him. As for Rules, he either knew them not, or thought them too servile a restraint. Hence it is, that he skips over *years* and *kingdoms* with an equal Liberty.

Lewis Theobald, Preface to *The Fatal Secret*

Webster is not concerned with humanity. He is the poet of bile and brainstorm, the sweet singer of apoplexy; ideally, one feels, he would have had all his characters drowned in a sea of cold sweat. His muse drew nourishment from Bedlam, and might, a few centuries later, have done the same from Belsen. I picture him plagued with hypochondria, probably homosexual, and consumed by feelings of persecution – an intensely neurotic mind, in short, at large in the richest, most teeming vocabulary that any age ever offered to a writer.

Kenneth Tynan, 'A Sea of Cold Sweat', in *Observer*, 18 December 1960

*See also* Thomas Dekker

## WEBSTER, NOAH

1758–1843 Lexicographer

If my name's a terror to evil doers, mention it.

On himself, in Harry R. Warfel, *Noah Webster, Schoolmaster to America*

I have contributed, in a small degree, to the instruction of at least four million of the rising generation; and it is not unreasonable to expect that a few seeds of improvement planted by my hand, may germinate and grow and ripen nto valuable fruit, when my remains shall be mingled with the dust.

On himself, Letter to Timothy Pickering, 1817

By the time he was a little over 30, this son of a New England farmer had hobnobbed with Washington and Franklin, pamphleteered for the adoption of the Constitution, gained renown as a lecturer on the English language and education, and hustled his books like an 18th-century Jacqueline Susann.

E. Jennifer Monaghan, 'Noah Webster', in *New York Times Book Review*, 21 September 1975

The ease with which Webster walked about the Jericho of English lexicography, blowing his trumpet of destruction, was an American ease, born of a sense that America was a continent and not a province.

Horace E. Scudder, *Noah Webster*

He had no conception of the enormous weight of the English language and literature, when he undertook to shovel it out of the path of American civilization.

*Ibid.*

## WEDGWOOD, JOSIAH

1730–95 Potter, Designer, Manufacturer

Whether, O Friend of Art! your gems derive / Fine forms from Greece, and fabled Gods revive; / Or bid from modern life the portrait breathe, / And bind round Honour's brow the laurel wreath; / Buoyant shall sail, with Fame's historic page, / Each fair medallion o'er the wrecks of age; / Nor Time shall mar, nor Steel, nor Fire, nor Rust / Touch the hard polish of the immortal bust. /

Erasmus Darwin, *The Loves of the Plants*

## WELLES, GIDEON

1802–78 Politician

As a sop to New England, Mr Lincoln had made Gideon Welles of Connecticut, his Secretary of the Navy. He was tall and 'venerably insignificant', with a flowing beard and a huge gray wig. Welles had been a newspaperman in Hartford, and did not know the stem from the stern of a ship, but he was an industrious and capable administrator. He was also very irritable, and those who under valued him did not know that, with pen dipped in gall, he kept a diary. In one respect, Welles was unique among the Cabinet members – he did not think himself a better man than the President.

Margaret Leech, *Reveille in Washington*

## WELLESLEY, ARTHUR, *see under* WELLINGTON, DUKE OF

## WELLINGTON, DUKE OF (ARTHUR WELLESLEY)

1769–1852 Soldier, Prime Minister

I like to walk alone.

On himself, Letter to Henry Wellesley, 7 July 1801

It is a bad thing always to be fighting. While in the thick of it I am too much occupied to feel anything; but it is wretched just after. It is quite impossible to think of glory. Both mind and feelings are exhausted. I am wretched even at the moment of victory, and I always say that next to a battle lost, the greatest misery is a battle gained.

On himself, in Lady Frances Shelley, Diary

The only thing I am afraid of is fear.

On himself, in Philip Henry Stanhope, *Conversations with the Duke of Wellington*

To Stop The Duke Go For Gold.

A slogan widely used in 1830, probably the inspiration of Francis Place

The Duke of Wellington had exhausted nature and exhausted glory. His career was one unclouded longest day.

Anon., Obituary in *The Times*, September 1852

You are 'the best of cut-throats': – do not start; / The phrase is Shakespeare's, and not misapplied: / War's a brain-spattering, windpipe-slitting art, / Unless her cause by Right be sanctified. / If you have acted *once* a generous part, / The World, not the World's masters, will decide, / And I shall be delighted to learn who, / Save you and yours, have gained by Waterloo? /

Lord Byron, *Don Juan*, canto ix

Never had mortal Man such opportunity, / Except Napoleon, or abused it more: / You might have freed fall'n Europe from the Unity / Of Tyrants, and been blest from shore to shore: / And *now* – What *is* your fame? Shall the muse tune it ye? / Now that the rabble's first vain shouts are o'er? / Go – hear it in your famish'd Country's cries! / Behold the world! and curse your victories! /

*Ibid.*

The Duke's government – a dictatorship of patriotism.

Benjamin Disraeli, *Endymion*

The Duke of Wellington brought to the post of first minister immortal fame; a quality of success which would almost seem to include all others.

Benjamin Disraeli, *Sybil*

The Duke said '[Count] D'Orsay is the only painter who ever made me look like a gentleman.' Calling on D'Orsay one day in his studio, the Duke's portrait being on an easel, & that of the Marquess Wellesley, his brother, framed and suspended, D'Orsay said, looking from the easel to the framed picture 'Cock pheasant & Hen pheasant!'

Benjamin Disraeli, *Reminiscences*

The Duke of Wellington said, that going to the Opera in state (8 carriages & state liveries) he, as Master of the Horse, sitting in the same carriage as the Queen & the Prince Consort, the Duke said, 'How very ill men look when they smile.'

'Much worse when they frown' replied Albert.

*Ibid.*

We would rather see his long nose in a fight than a reinforcement of 10,000 men a day.

Captain John Kincaid, in Michael Glover, *Wellington as Military Commander*

Great Chieftain, who takest such pains / To prove – what is granted *nem con.* / With how mod'rate a portion of brains / Some heroes contrive to get on. /

Thomas Moore, *Dog Day Reflections*

Great in council and great in war, / Foremost captain of his time, / Rich in saving common-sense, / And, as the greatest only are, / In his simplicity sublime.

Alfred, Lord Tennyson, *Ode on the Death of the Duke of Wellington*

He was the pride and the *bon genie*, as it were of this country! He was the GREATEST man this country ever produced, and the most *devoted* and *loyal* subject, and the staunchest supporter the Crown ever had... Albert is much grieved.

Queen Victoria, *Letters*

If England should require her army again, and I should be with it, let me have 'Old Nosey' to command. Our interests would be sure to be looked into, we should never have occasion to fear an enemy. There are two things we should be certain of. First, we should always be as well supplied with rations as the nature of the service would admit. The second is we should be sure to give the enemy a d----d good thrashing. What can a soldier desire more?

Private Wheeler, *Letters*

You are the only subject I shake hands with.

William IV, Conversation with Wellington, in Lady Salisbury, Diary, 10 July 1835

Him the mighty deed / Elates not, brought far nearer the grave's rest, / As shows that time-worn face, for he such seed / Has sown as yields, we trust, the fruit of fame / In Heaven; hence no one blushes for thy name, / Conqueror, 'mid some sad thoughts, divinely blest! /

William Wordsworth, *On a Portrait of the Duke of Wellington*

*See also* John Abernethy, Charles Dickens, George IV, C. J. Napier

## WELLS, HERBERT GEORGE

1866–1946 Author

I had rather be called a journalist than an artist, that is the essence of it.

On himself, Letter to Henry James, 1915

Every one of us who started writing in the nineties, was discovered to be 'a second' – somebody or other. In the course of two or three years I was welcomed as a second Dickens, a second Bulwer-Lytton and a second Jules Verne. But also I was a second Barrie, though J. M. B. was hardly more than my contemporary, and, when I turned to short stories, I became a second Kipling ... Later on I figured as a second Diderot, a second Carlyle and a second Rousseau.

On himself, *Experiment in Autobiography*

I launched the phrase 'The war to end war' – and that was not the least of my crimes.

On himself, in Geoffrey West, *H. G. Wells*

All Wells' characters are as flat as a photograph. But the photographs are agitated with such vigour that we forget their complexities lie on the surface and would disappear if it was scratched or curled up.

E. M. Forster, *Aspects of the Novel*

Wells impressed me as about the best mind that I had met in my many years in England: a handsome body and fine head. I had hoped extraordinary things from him, but the Great War seems to have shaken him, and his latest attempt to write a natural history of the earth chilled me. A history of humanity to the present time in which Shakespeare is not mentioned and Jesus is dismissed in a page carelessly, if not with contempt, shocks me.

Frank Harris, *My Life and Loves*

Your big feeling for life, your capacity for chewing up the thickness of the world in such enormous mouthfuls, while you fairly slobber, so to speak, with the multitudinous taste – this constitutes for me a rare and wonderful and admirable exhibition.

Henry James, Letter to Wells, 3 March 1911

Whatever Wells writes is not only alive, but kicking.

Henry James, in G. K. Chesterton, *Autobiography*

A whole generation of cocky, iconoclastic young men and women came into being ... You were the most energetic and intimate of our fathers. You opened so many doors. You delighted and excited and angered us. You offered us all the world in tempting cans with lively labels: Socialism, Free Love, Marriage,

Education, World Organization, and H. G. Wells's Patent Feminism – Very Perishable. Down they went. And gradually, on this varied if not always digestible diet, the children grew older.

Freda Kirchwey, 'A Private Letter to H. G. Wells', in *Nation* (New York), 28 November 1928

I like Wells, he is so warm, such a passionate declaimer or reasoner or whatever you like. But, ugh! – he hurts me. He always seems to be looking at life as a cold and hungry little boy in the street stares at a shop where there is hot pork.

D. H. Lawrence, Letter to A. D. McLeod, April 1913

Mr Wells's directing idea – 'the reorientation of loyalties through a realisation of the essential unity of our species' – is not trivial. To this he has devoted his life with a noble disinterestedness... We may find it hard to like or respect him, but he is doing work that needs doing and that at the moment seems terribly urgent. Yet we must also remind ourselves that the more his kind of influence seems likely to prevail ... the more urgent is drastic criticism. If he belongs to the past it is only in the sense that it has long been impossible to discuss him seriously except as a case, a type, a portent. As such, he matters.

F. R. Leavis, in *Scrutiny*, May 1932

His death on August 13, 1946, at the age of 79, came with a shock. England without H. G. Wells, to many of us, will hardly be England. 'Heavens, *what* a bourgeois!' Lenin exclaimed of him after a long and famous interview. Translated out of Marxian into English that reads: 'Heavens, *what* an Englishman!'

John Middleton Murry, in *Adelphi*, October–December 1946

Back in the nineteen-hundreds it was a wonderful experience for a boy to discover H. G. Wells. There you were, in a world of pedants, clergymen and golfers, with your future employers exhorting you to 'get on or get out', your parents systematically warping your sexual life, and your dull-witted schoolmasters sniggering over their Latin tags; and here was this wonderful man who could tell you about the inhabitants of the planets and the bottom of the sea, and who *knew* that the future was not going to be what respectable people imagined.

George Orwell, in *Horizon*, August 1941

The connecting link is Wells's belief in Science. He is saying all the time, if only the small shopkeeper could acquire a scientific outlook, his troubles would be ended. And of course he believes that this is going to happen, probably in the quite near future. A few more million pounds for scientific research, a few more generations scientifically educated, a few more superstitions shovelled into the dustbin, and the job is done.

George Orwell, *Essays*: 'The Rediscovery of Europe'

I stopped thinking about him when he became a thinker.

Lytton Strachey, in conversation with Hesketh Pearson, May 1921

Wells never learnt how to write a novel which was a work of art. When advised of this, he bluffed after the manner of the defendant in an English Law Court charged with libel. This defendant answers the charge by saying that the words were never uttered, or alternatively that they do not bear the meaning put upon them, or again alternatively that they are in fact true, and legitimate comment. Wells, charged with being unaesthetic, replied that he never said he was, and alternatively that the aesthetes can't prove it, and anyway, Yah!

Frank Swinnerton, *The Georgian Literary Scene*

The tragedy of H. G.'s life – his aptitude for 'fine thinking' and even 'good feeling' and yet his total incapacity for decent conduct. He says in so many words that directly you leave your study you inevitably become a cad and are indeed mean and dishonourable and probably cruel.

Beatrice Webb, Diary (commenting on *The New Machiavelli*), 5 November 1910

The Old Maid among novelists; even the sex-obsession that lay clotted on *Ann Veronica* and *The New Machiavelli* like cold white sauce was merely Old Maid's mania, the reaction towards the flesh of a mind too long absorbed in airships and colloids.

Rebecca West, Review of Wells's novel *Marriage*, in *Freewoman*, 19 September 1912

*See also* G. K. Chesterton, George Bernard Shaw

## WENTWORTH, THOMAS, *see under* STRAFFORD, EARL OF

## WESLEY, CHARLES

1707–88 Methodist

Not unfrequently he has come to the house in the City Road, and having left the pony in the garden in front, he would enter, crying out, 'Pen and ink! pen and ink!' These being supplied, he wrote the hymn he had been composing. When this was done, he would look round on those present and salute them with much kindness, ask after their health, give out a short hymn, and thus put all in mind of eternity.

Thomas Jackson, *Life of the Rev. Charles Wesley*

## WESLEY, JOHN

1703–91 Founder of Methodism

I look upon all the world as my parish.

On himself, Journal, June 1739

Though I am always in haste, I am never in a hurry.

On himself, Letter, December 1777

To live for God while in this vale of tears, / He rose at four o'clock for threescore years; / Then spent the live-long day in something great and good; / Nor loung'd one hour away, nor ever ling'ring stood. /

That this is no romance, one instance hear, / And may it rend in twain each sluggard's ear! / His last day's work but one he plann'd, and thought to ride / A HUNDRED MILES AND EIGHT, and preach and write beside. /

Thomas Olivers, in Maldwyn Edwards, *The Astonishing Youth*

The Emperor Charles V, and his rival of France, appear at this day infinitely insignificant, if we compare them with Luther and Loyola; and there may come a time when the name of Wesley will be more generally known, and in remoter regions of the globe, than that of Frederick or of Catherine.

Robert Southey, *Life of John Wesley*

## WESLEY, SAMUEL SEBASTIAN

1810–76 Composer

His crabbedness and eccentricity, of which many stories are told, were chiefly due to an abnormal sensitiveness of ear.

Sir Henry Hadow, *English Music*

He has the gift, possessed by those alone who stand in the inner courts, of making music which first surprises us by its novelty and afterwards convinces us that it was inevitable; he leads us into paths hitherto untrodden and opens the way by which we can follow.

*Ibid.*

As Wesley played the pedals much more than his predecessors, and was also much fuller in his harmonical combinations, the old [organ] blower felt that he would soon be unable to discharge the extra amount of work imposed upon him; and one evening, when Samuel Sebastian had been laying it on rather stronger than usual, the old man let out the wind, and turning to me with tears in his eyes, said – 'O Master William, I can't abide him; he'll be the death of me if he goes on like this long.'

And so it proved, for three weeks afterwards poor old Glen, the organ-blower, was carried to his last home, and died, if not of a broken heart, at least of insufficient wind.

William Spark, *Musical Memories*

## WEST, BENJAMIN

1738–1820 Painter

Mr West's name stands deservedly high in the annals of art in this country – too high for him to condescend to be his own puffer, even at second-hand. He comes forward, in the present instance, as the painter and the showman of the piece; as the candidate for public applause, and the judge who awards himself the prize; as the idol on the altar, and the priest who offers up the grateful incense of praise. He places himself, as it were, before his own performance, with a *Catalogue Raisonné* in his hand, and, before the spectator can form a judgement on the work itself, dazzles him with an account of the prodigies of art which are there conceived and executed.

William Hazlitt, on West's exhibiting of *Death on the Pale Horse*, in *Edinburgh Review*, December 1817

WEST, let me whisper in thy ear / Snug as a thief within a mill, / From me thou has no cause to fear; / To panegyric will I turn my skill; / And if thy *picture* I am forc'd to blame, / I'll say most handsome things about the *frame*.

Peter Pindar (John Wolcot), *Lyric Odes to the Royal Academicians*, 1783, ode 2

The beauties of the art, his converse shows; / His *canvass*, almost ev'ry thing that's bad! / Thus at th'Academy, we must suppose, / A man more useful never could be had; / Who in himself, a host, so much can do; / Who is both precept and example too.

Peter Pindar (John Wolcot), *Farewell Odes*, for 1786, ode 5

We have an American, West, who deals in high history, and is vastly admired, but he is heavier than Guercino, and has still less grace, and is very inferior.

Horace Walpole, Letter to Sir Horace Mann, 22 April 1775

*See also* J. M. W. Turner

## WHARTON, EDITH NEWBOLD JONES

1862–1937 Author

Mrs Wharton at her best was an analyst of the paralysis that attends success. Hers was not a world where romance was apt to flourish.

Louis Auchincloss, 'Edith Wharton and Her New York', in Irving Howe ed., *Edith Wharton, A Collection of Critical Essays*

Mrs Wharton, do you know what's the matter with you? You don't know anything about life.

F. Scott Fitzgerald, upon first meeting Mrs Wharton, in Grace Kellogg, *The Two Lives of Edith Wharton*

In the novels written during the last fifteen years of her life, Mrs Wharton's intellectual conservatism hardened into an embittered and querulous disdain for modern life; she no longer really knew what was happening in America; and she lost what had once been her main gift: the accurate location of the target she wished to destroy.

Irving Howe, 'The Achievement of Edith Wharton', in Irving Howe ed., *Edith Wharton, A Collection of Critical Essays*

... I take to her very kindly as regards her diabolical little cleverness, the quantity of intention and intelligence in her style and her sharp eye for an interesting *kind* of subject ... I want to get hold of the little lady and pump the pure essence of my wisdom and experience into her.

Henry James, Letter to Mary Cadwalader Jones, 1902

She was herself a novel of his, no doubt in his earlier manner.

Percy Lubbock, referring to Edith Wharton and Henry James, in Millicent Bell, *Edith Wharton and Henry James, The Story of Their Friendship*

She is as finished as a Sheraton sideboard, and with her poise, grace, high standards, and perfect breeding, she suggests as inevitably old wine and slender decanters.

Vernon L. Parrington, *Our Literary Aristocrat*, in Irving Howe ed., *Edith Wharton, A Collection of Critical Essays*

## WHARTON, THOMAS, MARQUIS OF WHARTON

1648–1715 Statesman

Unheard, came creeping out sly *Cataline*, / Father of *Faction*; who with Force unseen / Rowls on with steddy pace, the *Great Machine*. / Of antient Stock, in covert *Saw-pits* bold, / In Plots consummate and in tricks grown old, / Since among Knaves he holds the foremost place, / Old *Ferguson*'s footsteps, who so well can trace; / Tho' twice his marriage-bed has been betray'd / Good reasons still his Vengeance have allay'd. / The injury his former Spouse has done / The large Estate she left did well attone. / He is content his present Spouse should strole / To gain young Cully's to the Kit-Kat Bowl. /

Anon., *The Seven Wise Men*

He was a man of great wit and versatile cleverness, and cynically ostentatious in his immorality, having the reputation of being the greatest rake and the truest Whig of his time.

*Encyclopaedia Britannica*, 13th edition.

It is for your honour that those who are now your enemies were always so.

Joseph Addison, Dedication to fifth volume of *Spectator*

In small things and great his devotion to his party constantly appeared. He had the finest stud in England; and his delight was to win plates from Tories. Sometimes when, in a distant county, it was fully expected that the horse of a High Church squire would be first on the course, down came, on the very eve of the race, Wharton's Careless, who had ceased to run at Newmarket merely for want of competitors, or Wharton's Gelding, for whom Lewis the Fourteenth had in vain offered a thousand pistoles. A man whose mere sport was of this description was not likely to be easily beaten in any serious contest.

T. B. Macaulay, *History of England*

The superiority of his genius consists in nothing else but an inexhaustible fund of political lies, which he plentifully speaks, and by an unparalleled generosity forgets, and consequently contradicts, the next hour.

Jonathan Swift, in *Examiner*, no. 15, 1710

## WHEWELL, WILLIAM

1794–1866 Academic

Someone having said of Whewell that his *forte* was science, 'Yes,' assented Sydney Smith, 'and his foible is omniscience.'

Sydney Smith, in Walter Jerrold, *A Book of Famous Wits*

*See also* Herbert Spencer

## WHISTLER, JAMES ABBOTT MCNEILL

1834–1903 Artist

I have hardly a warm personal enemy left.

On himself, in Joseph and Elizabeth Robins Pennell, *The Whistler Journal*

I have also executed a good deal of distemper.

On himself, *The Gentle Art of Making Enemies*

To the question: 'Do you think genius is hereditary?' he replied: 'I can't tell you; heaven has granted me no offspring.'

On himself, in Hesketh Pearson, *Lives of the Wits*

'What!' exclaimed the examiner: 'you do not know the date of the Battle of Buena Vista? Suppose you were to go out to dinner, and the company began to talk of the Mexican war, and you, a West Point man, were asked the date of the battle, what would you do?' 'Do? Why, I should refuse to associate with people who could talk of such things at dinner!'

On himself, in *ibid.*

A suppositious conversation in *Punch* brought about the following interchange of telegrams: –
From Oscar Wilde, Exeter, to J. McNeill Whistler, Tite St – *Punch* too ridiculous – when you and I are together we never talk about anything except ourselves.
From Whistler, Tite St, to Oscar Wilde, Exeter. – No, no, Oscar, you forget – when you and I are together, we never talk about anything except me.

On himself, *The Gentle Art of Making Enemies*

Art should be independent of all claptrap – should stand alone, and appeal to the artistic sense of eye or ear, without confounding this with emotions entirely foreign to it, as devotion, pity, love, patriotism, and the like. All these have no kind of concern with it; and that is why I insist on calling my works 'arrangements' and 'harmonies.'

Take the picture of my mother, exhibited at the Royal Academy as an 'Arrangement in Grey and Black.' Now that is what it is. To me it is interesting as a picture of my mother; but what can or ought the public to care about the identity of the portrait?

On himself, Letter to *World*, 22 May 1878

Whistler once made London a half-way house between New York and Paris and wrote rude things in the visitors' book.

Max Beerbohm, in Katherine Lyon Mix, *Max and the Americans*

No man ever preached the impersonality of art so well; no man ever preached the impersonality of art so personally.

G. K. Chesterton, reviewing *The Gentle Art of Making Enemies*

Like the white lock of Whistler, / That lit our aimless gloom, / Men showed their own white feather / As proudly as a plume. /

G. K. Chesterton, 'To Edmund Clerihew Bentley', *The Man Who Was Thursday*

Mr. Whistler's experiments have no relation whatever to life; they have only a relation to painting.
Henry James, 'The Picture Season in London', in *Galaxy*, August 1877

The effect of Whistler at his best is exactly to give to the place he hangs in – or perhaps I should say to the person he hangs for – something of the sense, of the illusion, of a great museum.
Henry James, 'The Grafton Galleries', in *Harper's Weekly*, 26 June 1897

Lost in over-subtlety.
Augustus John, *Chiaroscuro*

Respect for the great traditions of art always remained his standard: 'What is not worthy of the Louvre is not worthy of art,' he said again and again.
Elizabeth and Joseph Pennell, *The Life of James McNeill Whistler*

You had your searches, your uncertainties, / And this is good to know – for us, I mean, / Who bear the brunt of our America / And try to wrench her impulse into art. /
Ezra Pound, *To Whistler, American*

There's a combative Artist named Whistler / Who is, like his own hog-hairs, a bristler: / A tube of white lead / And a punch on the head / Offer varied attractions to Whistler. /
Dante Gabriel Rossetti, in Elizabeth and Joseph Pennell, *The Life of James McNeill Whistler*

I have seen, and heard much of Cockney impudence before now; but never expected to hear a coxcomb ask two hundred guineas for flinging a pot of paint in the public's face.
John Ruskin, *Fors Clavigera*

'I only know of two painters in the world,' said a newly introduced feminine enthusiast to Whistler, 'yourself and Velasquez.' 'Why,' answered Whistler in dulcet tones, 'why drag in Velasquez?'
D. C. Seitz, *Whistler Stories*

Fly away, butterfly, back to Japan / Tempt not a pinch at the hand of a man, / And strive not to sting ere you die away. / So pert and so painted, so proud and so pretty, / To brush the bright down from your wings were a pity – / Fly away, butterfly, fly away. /
Algernon C. Swinburne, in Stanley Weintraub, *Whistler: a biography*

I never saw any one so feverishly alive as this little old man, with his bright, withered cheeks, over which the skin was drawn tightly, his darting eyes, under their prickly bushes of eyebrow, his fantastically-creased black and white curls of hair, his bitter and subtle mouth, and, above all, his exquisite hands never at rest.
Arthur Symons, *Studies in Seven Arts*

A miniature Mephistopheles, mocking the majority.
Oscar Wilde, in *Pall Mall Gazette*, 21 February 1885

As for borrowing Mr Whistler's ideas about art, the only thoroughly original ideas I have ever heard him express have had reference to his own superiority as a painter over painters greater than himself.
Oscar Wilde, in *Truth*, January 1890.

With our James vulgarity begins at home, and should be allowed to stay there.
Oscar Wilde, Letter to *World*

Mr Whistler in pointing out that the power of the painter is to be found in his powers of vision, not in his cleverness of hand, has expressed a truth which needed expression, and which, coming from the lord of form and colour, cannot fail to have its influence. His lecture, the Apocrypha though it be for the people, yet remains from this time as the Bible for the painter, the masterpiece of masterpieces, the song of songs. It is true he has pronounced the panegyric of the Philistine, but I can fancy Ariel praising Caliban for a jest: and in that he has read the Commination Service over the critics, let all men thank him, the critics themselves indeed most of all, for he has now relieved them from the necessity of a tedious existence.

Oscar Wilde, in Stanley Weintraub, *Whistler: a biography*

All his life Whistler committed the unpardonable offence of being himself; sprung of a nation where the *vox populi* is the *vox dei*, he hated the *vox populi*.

John Butler Yeats, in *ibid.*

*See also* Ezra Pound, Oscar Wilde

## WHITEFIELD, GEORGE

1714–70 Calvinist Methodist

I love those that thunder out the word! The Christian world is in a deep sleep. Nothing but a loud voice can waken them out of it!

On himself, in Arnold A. Dallimore, *George Whitefield*

I had rather wear out than rust out.

On himself, attributed

He looked as if he was cloathed with authority from ye great God and a sweet collome solemnity sat upon his brow and my hearing him preach gave me a heart wound by gods blessing.

Anon., in William Warren Sweet, *Religion in Colonial America*

In the dreadfullest winter I ever saw, people wallowed in the snow day and night, for the benefit of his beastly brayings.

Dr Timothy Cutler, in *ibid.*

His eloquence had a wonderful Power over the Hearts and Purses of his Hearers.

Benjamin Franklin, *The Autobiography of Benjamin Franklin*

I never treated Whitefield's ministry with contempt; I believe he did good. He had devoted himself to the lower classes of mankind, and among them he was of use. But when familiarity and noise claim the praise due to knowledge, art and elegance, we must beat down such pretensions.

Samuel Johnson, in James Boswell, *Life of Johnson*

## WHITEHEAD, ALFRED NORTH

1861–1947 Mathematician, Philosopher

He was a very modest man, and his most extreme boast was that he did try to have the qualities of his defects.

Bertrand Russell, *Portraits From Memory*

## WHITGIFT, JOHN

1530–1604 Archbishop of Canterbury

Of all the Bishops that ever were in that place, (I mean, in the see of Canterbury), none did ever so much hurt unto the Church of God, as he hath done, since his coming. No Bishop had ever such an aspiring and ambitious mind as he: no, not Stephen Gardiner of Winchester. None so tyrannous as he: no, not Bonner.

'Martin Marprelate', *Dialogue of Tyrannical Dealing*

Every year he entertained the queen [Elizabeth I] at one of his houses, so long as he was archbishop; and some years twice or thrice, where all things were performed in so seemly an order, that she went thence always exceedingly well pleased. And besides many public and gracious favours done unto him, she would salute him, and bid him farewell by the name of Black Husband; calling also his men her servants, as a token of her good contentment with their attendance and pains.

Sir George Paule, *Life of Whitgift*

## WHITMAN, WALT

1819–92 Poet

I celebrate myself, and sing myself, / And what I assume you shall assume. /

On himself, *Song of Myself*

Do I contradict myself? / Very well then I contradict myself, / (I am large, I contain multitudes). /

*Ibid.*

There is something in my nature furtive like an old hen! You see a hen wandering up and down a hedgerow, looking apparently quite unconcerned, but presently she finds a concealed spot, and furtively lays an egg, and comes away as though nothing had happened! That is how I felt in writing *Leaves of Grass.*

On himself, in Edgar Lee Masters, *Whitman*

I am as bad as the worst, but thank God I am as good as the best.

*Ibid.*

In Whitman's works the elemental parts of a man's mind and the fragments of imperfect education may be seen merging together, floating and sinking in a sea of insensate egotism and rhapsody, repellent, divine, disgusting, extraordinary.

John Jay Chapman, 'Walt Whitman', in Francis Murphy ed., *Walt Whitman, A Critical Anthology*

... we do not want to plant corn, to hoe it, to drive the crows away, to gather it, husk it, grind it, sift it, bake it, and butter it, before eating it, and then take the risk of its being at last moldy in our mouths. And this is what you have to do in reading Mr Whitman's rhythm.

William Dean Howells, review of 'Drum-Taps', in *ibid.*

It exhibits the effort of an essentially prosaic mind to lift itself, by a prolonged muscular strain, into poetry.

Henry James, referring to *Leaves of Grass*, 'Mr Walt Whitman', in Edwin Haviland Miller ed., *A Century of Whitman Criticism*

This awful Whitman. This post-mortem poet. This poet with the private soul leaking out of him all the time. All his privacy leaking out in a sort of dribble, oozing into the universe.

D. H. Lawrence, *Studies in Classic American Literature*

Whitman was like a prophet straying in a fog and shouting half-truths with a voice of great trumpets. He was seeking something, but he never knew quite what, and he never found it. He vanishes in the mist, and his words float back, dim, superb, to us behind him.

Amy Lowell, 'Walt Whitman and The New Poetry', in Francis Murphy ed., *Walt Whitman, A Critical Anthology*

Whitman, despite his cosmic consciousness and mysticism, sang the seen – not the unseen. He sat at a loom throwing the shuttle and guiding the threads without any pattern other than that the fabric should be unmistakably American.

Edgar Lee Masters, *Whitman*

He *is* America. His crudity is an exceeding great stench but it *is* America. He is a hollow place in the rock that echoes with his time. He *does* 'chant the crucial stage' and he is the 'voice triumphant.' He is disgusting. He is an exceedingly nauseating pill, but he accomplishes his mission ...

I honor him for he prophesied me while I can only recognize him as a forebear of whom I ought to be proud . . . It is a great thing, reading a man to know not 'His tricks are as yet my tricks, but I can easily make them mine' but 'His message is my message. We will see that men hear [it].'

Ezra Pound, *What I feel about Walt Whitman*, 1 February 1909

The absence of any principle of selection or of a sustained style enables him to render aspects of things and of emotion which would have eluded a trained writer. He is, therefore, interesting even where he is grotesque or perverse.

George Santayana, *The Poetry of Barbarism*

. . . he is a writer of something occasionally like English, and a man of something occasionally like genius.

Algernon C. Swinburne, 'Whitmania', in Edwin Haviland Miller ed., *A Century of Whitman Criticism*

*See also* Thomas Hardy, Rudyard Kipling, George Meredith, Dylan Thomas

## WHITTIER, JOHN GREENLEAF

1807–92 Poet, Author

Phrenologically, I have too much self-esteem to be troubled by the opinions of others – and I love my friends too well to deny them the gratification (if it be one) of abusing me to their hearts' content.

On himself, in Edward Wagenknecht, *John Greenleaf Whittier, A Portrait in Paradox*

There is Whittier, whose swelling and vehement heart / Strains the strait-breasted drab of the Quaker apart, / And reveals the live Man, still supreme and erect, / Underneath the bemummying wrappers of sect. /

James Russell Lowell, 'A Fable for Critics', in Edmund Wilson ed., *The Shock of Recognition*

. . . a sort of minor saint in outmoded Quaker dress.

Robert Penn Warren, *John Greenleaf Whittier's Poetry*

## WHITTINGTON, RICHARD (DICK)

–d. 1423 Lord Mayor of London

He travelled as far as Holloway, and there sat down on a stone to consider what course he should take; but while he was thus ruminating, Bow Bells, of which there were only six, began to ring; and he thought their sounds addressed him in this manner:

'Turn again, Whittington,
Thrice Lord Mayor of London.'

'Lord Mayor of London!' said he to himself; 'what would not one endure to be Lord Mayor of London, and ride in such a fine coach? Well, I'll go back again, and bear all the pummelling and ill-usage of Cicely rather than miss the opportunity of being Lord Mayor!'

Andrew Lang, 'The History of Whittington', in *The Blue Fairy Book*

## WILBERFORCE, WILLIAM

1759–1833 Philanthropist, Abolitionist

God Almighty has set before me two great objects, the suppression of the Slave Trade and the reformation of manners.

On himself, Diary, 1787

They charge me with fanaticism. If to be feelingly alive to the sufferings of my fellow-creatures is to be a fanatic, I am one of the most incurable fanatics ever permitted to be at large.

On himself, in the House of Commons, 19 June 1816

I saw what seemed a mere shrimp mount upon the table; but, as I listened, he grew, and grew, until the shrimp became a whale.

James Boswell, Letter to Dundas on Wilberforce at a public meeting in York on 25 March 1784

Go, W—, with narrow skull, / Go home and preach away at Hull. / No longer to the Senate cackle / In strains that suit the tabernacle; / I hate your little wittling sneer, / Your pert and self-sufficient leer. / Mischief to trade sits on your lip, / Insects will gnaw the noblest ship. / Go, W—, begone, for shame, / Thou dwarf with big resounding name. /

James Boswell, in J. Wesley Bready, *England: Before and After Wesley*

O Wilberforce! thou man of black renown, / Whose merit none enough can sing or say, / Thou hast struck one immense Colossus down, / Thou moral Washington of Africa! / But there's another little thing, I own, / Which you should perpetrate some summer's day, / And set the other half of earth to rights; / You have freed the *blacks* – now pray shut up the whites.

Lord Byron, *Don Juan*, canto xiv

Your friend, Mr Wilberforce, will be very happy any morning to hand your Ladyship to the guillotine.

Lord Grenville, comment to Lady Spencer on Wilberforce's pacificist amendment, January 1795

He has two strings to his bow: – he by no means neglects his worldly interests, while he expects a bright reversion in the skies. Mr Wilberforce is far from being a hypocrite; but he is . . . as fine a specimen of *moral equivocation* as can well be conceived.

William Hazlitt, *The Spirit of the Age*

If I were called upon to describe [him] in one word, I should say he was the most 'amusable' man I ever met with in my life. Instead of having to think what subjects will interest him, it is perfectly impossible to hit one that does not. I never saw any one who touched life at so many points; and this the more remarkable in a man who is supposed to live absorbed in the contemplations of a future state.

Sir James Mackintosh, 1829, in R. I. and S. Wilberforce, *Life of Wilberforce*

If this is madness, I hope that he will bite us all.

Mrs Sykes, comment to his mother on Wilberforce's 'conversion', Summer 1786

## WILDE, OSCAR FINGAL O'FLAHERTIE WILLS

1854–1900 Author, Dramatist, Wit

I rise sometimes after six, but don't do much but bathe, and although always feeling slightly immortal when in the sea, feel sometimes slightly heretical when good Roman Catholic boys enter the water with little amulets and crosses round their necks and arms that the good S. Christopher may hold them up.

I am now off to bed after reading a chapter of S. Thomas à Kempis. I think half-an-hour's warping of the inner man daily is greatly conducive to holiness.

On himself, Letter to William Ward, 26 July 1876

I am so glad you like that strange coloured book of mine: it contains much of me in it. Basil Hallward is what I think I am; Lord Henry what the world thinks me; Dorian what I would like to be – in other ages, perhaps.

On himself, on *The Picture of Dorian Gray*, Letter to Ralph Payne, 12 February 1894

What the paradox was to me in the sphere of thought, perversity became to me in the realm of passion.

On himself, *De Profundis*

The two great turning points of my life were when my father sent me to Oxford, and when society sent me to prison.

*Ibid.*

The Gods had given me almost everything. I had genius, a distinguished name, high social position, brilliancy, intellectual daring: I made art a philosophy, and philosophy an art: I altered the minds of men and the colours of things: there was nothing I said or did that did not make people wonder: I took the drama, the most objective form known to art, and made it as personal a mode of expression as the lyric or the sonnet, at the same time I widened its range and enriched its characterisation: drama, novel, poem in rhyme, poem in prose, subtle or fantastic dialogue, whatever I touched I made beautiful in a new mode of beauty: to truth itself I gave what is false no less than what is true as its rightful province, and showed that the false and the true are merely forms of intellectual existence. I treated art as the supreme reality, and life as a mere mode of fiction: I awoke the imagination of my century so that it created myth and legend around me: I summed up all systems in a phrase, and all existence in an epigram.

On himself, Letter to Lord Alfred Douglas, *De Profundis*, January–March 1897

The prisoner looks to liberty as an immediate return to all his ancient energy, quickened into more vital forces by long disuse. When he goes out he finds he still has to suffer. His punishment as far as its effects go, lasts intellectually and physically, just as it lasts socially. He has still to pay. One gets no receipt for the past when one walks out into the beautiful air.

On himself, Letter to Frank Harris, June 1897

It is curious how vanity helps the successful man and wrecks the failure. In old days half of my strength was my vanity.

On himself, Letter to Robert Ross, 16 November 1897

My writing has gone to bits – like my character. I am simply a self-conscious nerve in pain.

*Ibid.*

The three women I have most admired are Queen Victoria, Sarah Bernhardt, and Lily Langtry. I would have married any one of them with pleasure.

On himself, in Vincent O'Sullivan, *Letters of Oscar Wilde*, footnote

Alas I am dying beyond my means.

On himself, last words, attributed

Mr Oscar Wilde is no poet, but a cleverish man who has an infinite contempt for his readers, and thinks he can take them in with a little mouthing verse.

Anon., Review in *Spectator*, 13 August 1881

He has made of infamy a new Thermopylae.

Anon., in William Butler Yeats, *Autobiographies*

From the beginning Wilde performed his life and continued to do so even after fate had taken the plot out of his hands.

W. H. Auden, *Forewords and Afterwords*

Of his poems not one has survived, for he was totally lacking in a poetic voice of his own; what he wrote was an imitation of poetry-in-general.

*Ibid.*

The solution that, deliberately or accidentally, he found was to subordinate every other dramatic element to dialogue for its own sake and create a verbal universe in which the characters are determined by the kinds of things they say, and the plot is nothing but a succession of opportunities to say them.

*Ibid.*, on Wilde's plays

He sipped at a weak hock and seltzer / As he gazed at the London skies / Through the Nottingham lace of the curtains / Or was it his bees-winged eyes? /

John Betjeman, *The Arrest of Oscar Wilde at the Cadogan Hotel*

That sovereign of insufferables.

Ambrose Bierce, *Wasp* (San Francisco), 1882

He . . . was really a charlatan. I mean by a charlatan one sufficiently dignified to despise the tricks that he employs . . . Wilde and his school professed to stand as solitary artistic souls apart from the public. They professed to scorn the middle class, and declared that the artist must not work for the bourgeois. The truth is that no artist so really great ever worked so much for the bourgeois as Oscar Wilde. No man, so capable of thinking about truth and beauty ever thought so constantly about his effect on the middle classes. He studied the Surbiton school-mistress with exquisite attention, and knew exactly how to shock, and how to please her . . . He descended below himself to be on top of others. He became purposely stupider than Oscar Wilde that he might seem cleverer than the nearest curate. He lowered himself to superiority; he stooped to conquer.

G. K. Chesterton, in *Daily News*, 19 October 1909

Queerly enough, it was the very multitude of his falsities that prevented him from being entirely false. Like a many-coloured humming top, he was at once a bewilderment and a balance. He was so fond of being many-sided that among his sides he even admitted the right side. He loved so much to multiply his souls that he had among them one soul at least that was saved.

*Ibid.*

His gaze was constantly fixed on himself; yet not on himself, but on his reflection in the looking-glass . . . Introspection of the genuine kind he never achieved . . . while Whistler was a prophet who liked to play Pierrot, Wilde grew into a Pierrot who liked to play the prophet.

Harold Child, in *Times Literary Supplement*, 18 June 1908

*Wilde*: I wish I had said that.
*Whistler*: You will, Oscar, you will.

L. C. Ingleby, *Oscar Wilde*

He was, on his plane, as insufferable as a Methodist is on his.

H. L. Mencken, Introduction to Wilde's *A House of Pomegranates*

Oscar Wilde's talent seems to me essentially rootless, something growing in a glass in a little water.

George Moore, Letter to Frank Harris, in *Pearson's Magazine*, New York, March 1918

'Have you anything to declare?' asked the customs official. 'No. I have nothing to declare'; he paused: 'except my genius.'

Hesketh Pearson, on Wilde's arrival in New York, *Life of Oscar Wilde*

The nineties, the early nineties when Wilde's talent was in full fruition, seem now, at least in literature, to be coloured by the personality of Wilde, and the movement foolishly called decadent. But in the nineties when Wilde was writing, he had a very few silent friends, and a very great number of vociferous enemies. His books were laughed at, his poetry parodied, his person not kindly caricatured, and even when his plays won popular applause, this hostility against him was only smothered, not choked. His disaster ungagged it, and few men have been sent to perdition with a louder cry of hounds behind them.

Arthur Ransome, *Oscar Wilde, A Critical Study*

Men lived more vividly in his presence, and talked better than themselves.

*Ibid.*

Too many of Wilde's paragraphs are perorations.

*Ibid.*

His tasks were always too easy for him, he never strained for achievement, and nothing requires more generosity to forgive than success without effort . . . He pawned much of himself to the moment, and was never able to redeem it.

*Ibid.*

It was the very element of his tragedy that it could not be shared or alleviated; on the path he had henceforth to tread there could be no comrade; his offence was one at which charity itself stood embarrassed, and compassion felt the fear of compromise.

E. T. Raymond, *Portraits of the Nineties*

He was never quite sure himself where and when he was serious.

Robert Ross, Letter to Adela Schuster, 23 December 1900

There was also in Queen Victoria's reign a famous inventor and poet called Oscar Wilde who wrote very well but behaved rather beardsley; he made himself memorable by inventing Art, Asceticism, etc., and was the leader of a set of disgusting old gentlemen called 'the naughty nineties'.

W. C. Sellar and R. J. Yeatman, *1066 and All That*

Mr Wilde, an arch-artist, is so colossally lazy that he trifles even with the work by which an artist escapes work.

George Bernard Shaw, on *An Ideal Husband*, in *Saturday Review*, 12 January 1895

Mr Wilde has written scenes in which there is hardly a speech which could conceivably be uttered by one real person at a real at-home; but the deflection from common sense is so subtle that it is evidently produced as a tuner tunes a piano: that is, he first tunes a fifth perfectly, and then flattens it a shade. If he could not tune the perfect fifth, he could not produce the practicable one.

George Bernard Shaw, in *Saturday Review*, 4 May 1895

When Oscar came to join his God, / Not earth to earth, but sod to sod, / It was for sinners such as this / Hell was created bottomless.

Algernon C. Swinburne, *Oscar Wilde*

What has Oscar in common with art, except that he dines at our tables and picks from our platters the plums for the pudding that he peddles in the provinces? Oscar – the amiable, irresponsible, esurient Oscar – with no more sense of a picture than he has of the fit of a coat – has the courage of the opinions . . . of others!

James McNeill Whistler, Letter to *World*, 1885

Bourgeois malgré lui.

James McNeill Whistler, attributed

I think his fate is rather like Humpty Dumpty's, quite as tragic and quite as impossible to put right.

Constance Wilde, Letter to her brother, 26 March 1897

Wilde had arrived in Dieppe, and Dowson pressed upon him the necessity of acquiring 'a more wholesome taste.' They emptied their pockets onto the café table, and though there was not much, there was enough, if both heaps were put into one. Meanwhile the news had spread, and they set out accompanied by a cheering crowd. Arrived at their destination, Dowson and the crowd remained outside, and presently Wilde returned. He said in a low voice to Dowson, 'The first these ten years, and it will be the last. It was like cold mutton' . . . and then aloud, so that the crowd might hear him, 'But tell it in England, for it will entirely restore my character.'

William Butler Yeats,
*Autobiographies*, describing Wilde's visit to a brothel after his release from prison

*See also* Shakespeare, James McNeill Whistler

## WILDER, THORNTON NIVEN

1897–1975 Author, Playwright

I constantly rewrite, discard and replace the cycle of plays. Some are on the stove, some are in the oven, some are in the waste-basket. There are no first drafts in my life. An incinerator is a writer's best friend.

On himself, *New York Times*,
6 November 1961

Whenever I'm asked what college I attended, I'm tempted to reply Thornton Wilder!

Garson Kanin, *Washington Star*,
12 August 1975

Thornton Wilder . . . posed the same questions as Euripides, Sophocles and the other classic Greeks whose works fascinated and comforted him. And the reason that he couldn't answer the questions lay in the very face of literature; the writer, being mortal, doesn't know the answers any more than anyone else does. But he has the wit to keep on asking.

Rod MacLeish, *Washington Post*,
11 December 1975

## WILDMAN, SIR JOHN

1621?–93 Politician

And where's my old friend & fellow rebel Johnee Wildman? Mount Atlas stand on tiptoes where art thee? And behold a mighty stone fell from the skies into the bottom of the sea, and gave a mighty plump, and great was the fall of that stone, and so farewell, Johnee Wildman.

Richard Overton, July 1649, in
Maurice Ashley, *John Wildman*

## WILKES, JOHN

1727–97 Radical

Give me a grain of truth . . . and I will mix it up with a great mass of falsehood, so that no chemist shall ever be able to separate them.

On himself, in Henry Crabb
Robinson, Diary

Nothing has been so obnoxious to me through life as a dead calm.

On himself, in Horace Bleackley,
*Life of John Wilkes*

I scarcely ever met with a better companion, he has inexhaustible spirits, infinite wit and humour, and a great deal of knowledge; but a thorough profligate in principle as in practice, his life is stained with every vice, and his conversation full of blasphemy and indecency. These morals he glories in; for shame is a weakness he has long since surmounted.

Edward Gibbon, in O. A. Sherard,
*A Life of John Wilkes*

Wilkes had his revenge one night at Carlton House when the prince called for toasts. He gave 'The King – long life to him'. The prince, who detested his father and rejoiced in his illness, resented the words. 'Since when have you been so anxious over my parent's health?' he said. 'Since I had the pleasure of your royal highness's acquaintance,' answered Wilkes with a bow.

Raymond Postgate, *That Devil Wilkes*

Wilkes telling stories against himself – as that of the old lady looking up at the signboard of one of the numerous Wilkes's Head Taverns, and muttering, 'Aye, he swings everywhere but where he ought.'

O. A. Sherard, *A Life of John Wilkes*

*See also* Sir Philip Francis, John Glynn

## WILKIE, SIR DAVID

1785–1841 Painter

When he has made a sketch for a picture & settled his design, He then walks about looking for a person proper to be a model for completing each character in his picture, & He then paints *everything from the life* . . . He sometimes walks abt. for a *week* before He can meet with the character of head &c. that will suit him.

Joseph Farington, Diary, 12 December 1807

January 2. Out on business. Called on Newton, who mentioned a saying of Wilkie's, which for his servility is a touch. 'To be acquainted with a Nobleman on pleasant terms is a good thing, but it is a great thing to be acquainted with one on any terms.' Up with your flap, David, and boo as you are kicked.

Benjamin R. Haydon, Diary. 1830

## WILKINS, TIMOTHY

–d. 1671 Epicurean

Timothy Wilkins died; lived and died an epicure; some men are soon chosen.

Anthony à Wood, *Life and Times*, October 1671

## WILKINSON, TATE

1739–1803 Actor-Manager

During his career as manager, if any member of his company had obstinately neglected to listen to his advice on any particular point of acting, or the like, he would mount, on some future night, into the gallery, and hiss most strenuously – an expedient which presently brought the trifler to his senses. On one occasion, being more than usually indignant at some very slovenly exhibition on the stage, his hiss was remarkably audible. The delinquent actor, however, seemed to have friends around him, for, on a cry of 'Turn him out', poor Wilkinson was unceremoniously handed down from his own gallery, and ejected into the street. Notwithstanding, he still maintained this useful and very disinterested experiment.

George Raymond, *Memoirs of R. W. Elliston*

## WILLIAM I ('THE CONQUEROR')

1027–87

When the famous William, 'the Conqueror' of England . . . had brought under his sway the farthest limits of the island, and had tamed the minds of the rebels by awful examples, to prevent error from having free course in fortune, he decided to bring the conquered people under the rule of written law. So, setting out before him the English Laws in their threefold versions, namely, Mercian law, Dane law and Wessex law, he repudiated some of them, approved others and added those Norman laws from overseas which seemed to him most effective in preserving the peace. Lastly, to give the finishing touch of all this forethought, after taking counsel he sent his most skilful councillors in circuit throughout the realm. By these a careful survey of the whole country was made, of its woods, its pastures and meadows, as well as of arable land, and was set down in common language and drawn up into a book; in order, that is, that every man may be content with his own rights, and not encroach unpunished on those of others.

Richard FitzNeal, attributed, *Dialogus Scaccario*, translated by Charles Johnson (on William's legislation and Domesday Book)

William, indeed, seems to have been astute without wisdom, resolute without foresight, powerful without ultimate purpose, a man of very limited aims and very limited vision, narrow, ignorant and superstitious.

R. G. Richardson and G. O. Sayles, *The Governance of Mediaeval England*

To receive the oath, he caused a parliament to be called. It is commonly said that it was in Bayeux that he had his great council assembled. He sent for all the holy bodies thither, and put so many of them together as to fill a whole chest, and then covered them with a pall; but Harold neither saw them, nor knew of their being there; for naught was shewn or told to him about it; and over all was a philactery, the best that he could select; OIL DE BOEF, as I have heard it called. When Harold placed his hand upon it, the hand trembled, and the flesh quivered; but he swore and promised upon his oath, to take Ele to wife, and to deliver up England to the duke: and thereunto to do all in his power, according to his might and wit, after the death of Edward, if he should live, so help him God and the holy relics there! Many cried 'God grant it!' and when Harold had kissed the saints, and had risen upon his feet, the duke led him to the chest, and made him stand near it; and took off the chest the pall that had covered it, and showed Harold upon what holy relics he had sworn: and he was sorely alarmed at the sight.

Robert Wace, *Roman de Rou*, translated by Edgar Taylor (describing the ruse by which William tricked the future King Harold)

Seeing a large part of the hostile host pursuing his own troops, the prince thrust himself in front of those in flight, shouting at them and threatening them with his spear. Staying their retreat, he took off his helmet, and standing before them bare-headed, he cried: 'Look at me well. I am still alive and by the grace of God I shall yet prove victor. What is this madness which makes you fly, and what way is open for your retreat? You are allowing yourselves to be pursued and killed by men whom you could slaughter like cattle. You are throwing away victory and lasting glory, rushing into ruin and incurring lasting disgrace. And all for naught since by flight none of you can escape destruction.' With these words he restored their courage, and leaping to the front and wielding his death-dealing sword, he defied the enemy who merited death for their disloyalty to him their prince.

William of Poitiers, *Life of William I*, translated by D. C. Douglas and G. W. Greenaway

*See also* Edward I, Hereward the Wake

## WILLIAM II

–d. 1100

There exists no proof as / To who shot William Rufus / But shooting him would seem / To have been quite a sound scheme. /

E. C. Bentley, *More Biography*

Then was there flowing hair and extravagant dress; and then was invented the fashion of shoes with curved points; then the model for young men was to rival women in delicacy of person, to mince their gait, to walk with loose gesture, and half-naked. Enervated and effeminate, they unwillingly remained what nature had made them; the assailers of others' chastity, prodigal of their own. Troops of pathics and droves of harlots followed the court.

William of Malmesbury, describing William's court, in *Chronicle of the Kings of England*, translated by J. A. Giles

A few countrymen conveyed the body, placed on a cart, to the cathedral at Winchester, the blood dripping from it all the way. Next year the tower fell; though I forbear to mention the different opinions on this subject, lest I should seem to assent too readily to unsupported trifles, more especially as the building might have fallen, through imperfect structure, even though he had never been buried there.

*Ibid.*

*See also* George II

## WILLIAM III
1650–1702

There is one certain means by which I can be sure never to see my country's ruin: I will die in the last ditch.

On himself, to the Duke of Buckingham, attributed

What is the rhyme for porringer? / What is the rhyme for porringer? / The king he had a daughter fair / And gave the Prince of Orange her. /

Anon., Nursery rhyme, traditional

King William thinks all / Queen Mary talks all / Prince George drinks all / And Princess Anne eats all. /

Anon., shortly after the Glorious Revolution of 1688

He has gotten in part the shape of a man, / But more of a monkey, deny it who can; / He has the tread of a goose, and the legs of a swan, / A dainty fine king indeed. /

Anon., *Coronation Ballad*, 1689

Have you not seen on the stage come tell ho / A strutting thing called a Punchinello? / Of all things I know 'tis likest this fellow / A dainty fine king indeed. /

*Ibid.*

He had not a trace of that second sight of the battlefield which is the mark of military genius. He was no more than a resolute man of good common sense whom the accident of birth had carried to the conduct of war. It was in the sphere of politics that his inspiration lay. Perhaps he has never been surpassed in the sagacity, patience, and discretion of his statecraft. The combinations he made, the difficulties he surmounted, the adroitness with which he used the time factor, or played upon the weakness of others, the unerring sense of proportion and power of assigning to objectives their true priorities, all mark him for the highest fame.

Winston Churchill, *Marlborough, His Life and Times*

Rejoice you sots, your idol's come again / To pick your pockets and kidnap your men. / Give him your moneys and his Dutch your lands / Ring not your bells ye fools, but wring your hands. /

Henry Hall, ascribed, *Upon the King's Return from Flanders*

Hail happy William, thou art strangely great! / What is the cause, thy virtue, or thy fate? / For thee the child the parent's heart will sting; / For thee the Favorite will desert his King; / For thee the Patriot will subvert the laws; / For thee the Judge will still decide the cause; / For thee the Prelate will his church betray; / For thee the Soldier fights without his pay; / For thee the Freeman mortgages his hold; / For thee the Miser lavishes his gold; / For thee the Merchant loses all his store; / For thee the tradesman is content and poor; / For thee the sailor's pressed and starves on shore; / For thee the Senate our best laws suspend / And will make any new to serve thy end... / And that this wonder may more wondrous seem / Thou never yet did'st one kind thing for them. / Rebels like witches, having signed the rolls / Must serve their Masters, though they damn their souls. /

Henry Hall, or John Grubham Howe, *A Panegyric*

His most illustrious antagonist, the great Condé, remarked, after the bloody day of Seneff, that the Prince of Orange had in all things borne himself like an old general, except in exposing himself like a young soldier.

T. B. Macaulay, *History of England*

He praised and reprimanded, rewarded and punished, with the stern tranquillity of a Mohawk chief.

*Ibid.*

He was in truth far better qualified to save a nation than to adorn a court... He seldom came forth from his closet, and when he appeared in the public rooms, he stood among the crowd of courtiers and ladies, stern and abstracted, making no jest, and smiling at none. His freezing look, his silence, the dry and concise answers which he uttered when he could keep silence no longer, disgusted noblemen and gentlemen who had been accustomed to be slapped on the back by their royal masters... He spoke our language, but not well. His accent was foreign: his diction was inelegant; and his vocabulary seems to have been no larger than was necessary for the transaction of business.

*Ibid.*

That character, almost devoid of the humanity and kindliness which we appreciate most of all in kings, seemed like a grim edifice or institution, divided into separate, independent compartments, connected by few corridors, and known to the world only from its cold, forbidding antechamber.

David Ogg, *England in the Reigns of James II and William III*

He was the first English King who was a good European. The least forthcoming and the most inscrutable of monarchs, he nevertheless familiarized men with a new type of kingship, detached, dignified, and, in all impersonal matters, essentially just.

*Ibid.*

I do not doubt but King William came over with a view to the crown. Nor was he called upon by patriotism, for he was not an Englishman, to assert our liberties. No; his patriotism was of a higher rank. He aimed not at the crown of England for ambition, but to employ its forces and wealth against Louis XIV for the common cause of the liberties of Europe. The Whigs did not understand the extent of his views, and the Tories betrayed him. He has been thought not to have understood us; but the truth was he took either party as it was predominant, that he might sway the parliament to support his general plan.

Horace Walpole, Letter to William Mason, *circa* 1792

## WILLIAM IV

1765–1837

... he is an immense improvement on the last unforgiving animal [George IV]. This man at least *wishes* to make everybody happy.

Emily Eden, Letter, August 1830

Etiquette is a thing he cannot comprehend.

Charles Greville, Diary, 24 July 1830

Of political dexterity and artifice he was altogether incapable, and although if he had been false, able, and artful, he might have caused more perplexity to his Whig Government and have played a better party game, it is perhaps fortunate for the Country, and certainly happy for his own reputation, that his virtues thus predominated over his talents.

*Ibid.*, 25 June 1837

They gave William IV a lovely funeral. It took six men to carry the beer.

Louis Untermeyer, *A Treasury of Laughter*

*See also* Duke of Wellington

## WILLIAMS, WILLIAM CARLOS

1883–1963 Author, Physician

I don't play golf, am not a joiner. I vote Democratic, read as much as my eyes will stand, and work at my trade day in and day out. When I can find nothing better to do, I write.

On himself, in Stanley J. Kunitz and Howard Haycraft eds, *Twentieth Century Authors*

Among the poets of his own illustrious generation, William Carlos Williams was the man on the margin, the incorrigible maverick, the embattled messiah.

John Malcolm Brinnin, 'William Carlos Williams', in Leonard Unger ed., *Seven Modern American Poets*

I think he wouldn't make so much of the great American language if he were judicious about everything. And that is the beauty of it – he is willing to be reckless, and if you can't be that, what's the point of the whole thing?

Marianne Moore, in an interview with Donald Hall, in Charles Tomlinson ed., *Marianne Moore: A Collection of Critical Essays*

. . . at any rate he has not in his ancestral endocrines the arid curse of our nation. None of his immediate forebears burnt witches in Salem, or attended assemblies for producing prohibitions.

Ezra Pound, in Noel Stock, *The Life of Ezra Pound*

## WILLKIE, WENDELL LEWIS

1892–1944 Lawyer, Politician

Trying to give Willkie advice is just as effective as giving castor oil to the sphinx.

Anon., in Mary Earhart Dillon, *Wendell Willkie*

The rich man's Roosevelt; the simple, barefoot boy from Wall Street.

Harold L. Ickes, in Leon A. Harris, *The Fine Art of Political Wit*

He seemed to us like a man who had set out on a mule to defeat a German Panzer division, confident of his star, sure that he needed nothing more to rout the mechanized political forces against him. If it's an act, it's a good one.

Arthur Korck, *Memoirs*

## WILMOT, JOHN, EARL OF ROCHESTER

1647–80 Poet, Libertine

Were I (who to my cost already am / One of those strange prodigious Creatures *Man*) / A Spirit free, to choose for my own share, / What Case of Flesh, and Blood, I pleas'd to weare, / I'd be a *Dog*, a *Monkey*, or a *Bear*. / Or any thing but that vain *Animal*, / Who is so proud of being rational. /

On himself, *A Satyr Against Mankind*

Talking of Rochester's Poems, he [Johnson] said, he had given them to Mr Steevens to castrate for the edition of the Poets for which he was to write Prefaces. Dr Taylor (the only time I ever heard him say any thing witty) observed, that 'if Rochester had been castrated himself, his exceptionable poems would not have been written.' I asked if Burnet had not given a good Life of Rochester. *Johnson*: 'We have a good *Death*; there is not much *Life.*'

James Boswell, *Life of Johnson*

I find it is not for me to contend any way with your Lordship, who can write better on the meanest subject than I can on the best.

John Dryden, Letter to Wilmot, 1673

The very name of Rochester is offensive to modest ears; yet does his poetry discover such energy of style and such poignancy of satire, as give ground to imagine what so fine a genius, had he fallen in a more happy age, and had followed better models, was capable of producing. The ancient satirists often used great liberty in their expressions; but their freedom no more resembles the licentiousness of Rochester than the nakedness of an Indian does that of a common prostitute.

David Hume, *History of England*

His Sins were like his Parts, (for from them corrupted they sprang), all of them high and extraordinary. He seem'd to affect something singular and paradoxical in his Impieties, as well as in his Writings, above the reach and thought of other men ... For this was the heightening and amazing circumstance of his sins, that he was so diligent and industrious to recommend and propagate them ... Nay, so confirm'd was he in Sin, that he lived, and oftentimes almost died, a Martyr for it.

Robert Parsons, *A Sermon preached at the Earl of Rochester's Funeral*

With no poetick ardors fir'd, / I press the bed where *Wilmot* lay; / That here he lov'd, or here expir'd, / Begets no numbers grave or gay. /

Alexander Pope, *On Lying in the Earl of Rochester's Bed at Atterbury.*

Rail on, poor feeble scribbler, speak of me / In as ill terms as the world speaks of thee. / Sit swelling in thy hole like a vex'd toad, / And all thy pox and malice spit abroad. / Thou canst blast no man's name by thy ill word; / Thy pen is full as harmless as thy sword. /

Sir Car Scroope, *The Author's Reply*

A Man whom the Muses were fond to inspire, and ashamed to avow.

Horace Walpole, *Catalogue of Royal and Noble Authors*

Lord Rochester's poems have much more obscenity than wit, more wit than poetry, more poetry than politeness.

*Ibid.*

*See also* Samuel Richardson

## WILSON, EDMUND

1895–1972 Critic

It is so damned easy for such as he, born into easy means, graduated from a fashionable university into a critical chair overlooking Washington Square, etc., to sit tight and hatch little squibs of advice to poets not to be so 'professional' as he claims they are, as though all the names he has just mentioned had been as suavely nourished as he.

Hart Crane, Undated letter to Yvor Winters

... the man in the iron necktie.

e.e. cummings, in Joseph Epstein, 'The Twenties', in *New York Times Book Review*, 15 June 1975

Wilson is not like other critics; some critics are boring even when they are original; he fascinates even when he is wrong.

Alfred Kazin, in Max J. Herzberg,

*The Reader's Encyclopedia of American Literature*

... quiet, reticent, and rather shy, his friends appropriately call him 'Bunny'!

Stanley J. Kunitz and Howard Haycraft eds, *Twentieth Century Authors*

## WILSON, HARRIETTE

1789–1846 Courtesan

I shall not say why and how I became, at the age of fifteen, the mistress of the Earl of Craven. Whether it was love, or the severity of my father, or the winning arts of the noble lord, which induced me to leave my parental roof and place myself under his protection, does not now much signify; or, if it does, I am not in the humour to gratify curiosity in this matter.

On herself, *Memoirs*

## WILSON, (THOMAS) WOODROW

1856–1924 Twenty-Eighth United States President

Here's to Woodrow, King Divine, / Who rules this place along with Fine / We hear he's soon to leave this town / To take on Teddy Roosevelt's crown. /

Anon., Princeton students' song, *circa* 1908

Mr Wilson's name among the Allies is like that of the rich uncle, and they have accepted his manners out of respect for his means.

Anon., in *London Morning Post*, 1919, in Thomas A. Bailey, *Woodrow Wilson and the Lost Peace*

An idealist, a philosopher, a moralist, a religionist, he was born, as someone has well said, halfway between the Bible and the dictionary, and he never lost his faith in the power of words.

Thomas A. Bailey, *Woodrow Wilson and the Peacemakers*

He wore a sterilized, disinfected expression, yet he could suddenly confront a person or a camera with a momentary expression of almost lover-like understanding and affection.

William C. Bullitt, Introduction to William C. Bullitt and Sigmund Freud, *Thomas Woodrow Wilson: Twenty-eighth President of the United States – A Psychological Study*

Mr Wilson bores me with his Fourteen Points; why, God Almighty has only ten.

Georges Clemenceau, in *The American Heritage Pictorial History of the Presidents*

Lloyd George believes himself to be Napoleon but President Wilson believes himself to be Jesus Christ.

Georges Clemenceau, in Thomas A. Bailey, *Woodrow Wilson and the Lost Peace*

How can I talk to a fellow who thinks himself the first man in two thousand years to know anything about peace on earth?

*Ibid.*

They say Wilson has blundered. Perhaps he has, but I notice he usually blunders forward.

Josephus Daniels, in S. B. McKinley, *Woodrow Wilson: A Biography*

Like Odysseus, he looked wiser when seated.

John Maynard Keynes, in Robert L. Heilbroner, *The Worldly Philosophers*

William Allen White had a Kansan's suspicion of anyone with a handshake 'like a ten-cent pickled mackerel in brown paper.'

Walter Lord, *The Good Years*

The University president who cashiered every professor unwilling to support Woodrow Wilson for the first vacancy in the Trinity.

H. L. Mencken, 'Star Spangled Men', in *New Republic*, 29 September 1920

Byzantine logothete.

Theodore Roosevelt, in D. H. Elletson, *Roosevelt and Wilson: A Comparative Study*

I feel certain that he would not recognize a generous impulse if he met it on the street.

William Howard Taft, in Alpheus Thomas Mason, *William Howard Taft*

## WINCHELL, WALTER

1897–1972 Journalist

If only when my epitaph is readied, they will say, 'Here is Walter Winchell – with his ear to ground – as usual.'

On himself, in Ed Weiner, *Let's Go to Press*

When you are in the brick-throwing racket, you must expect to get hit with one occasionally. My greatest thrill has been surviving my imitators.

*Ibid.*

He is more like some freak of climate – a tornado, say, or an electric storm that is heard whistling and roaring far away, against which everybody braces himself; and then it strikes and does its whirling damage.

Alistair Cooke, 'Walter Winchell: "an American Myth"', in *Listener*, 20 November 1947

The three of us are all in the same business – libel – but Winchell seems to know where to stop.

H. L. Mencken, to George Jean Nathan, in Bob Thomas, *Winchell*

Poor Walter. He's afraid he'll wake up some day and discover he's not Walter Winchell.

Dorothy Parker, in *ibid.*

## WINSTANLEY, GERRARD

*fl.* 1648–52 Leveller, Digger

Sometimes my heart hath been full of deadness and uncomfortableness, wading like a man in the dark and slabby weather; and within a little time I have been filled with such peace, light, life and fulness, that if I had two pairs of hands, I had matter enough revealed to have kept them writing a long time.

On himself, Preface to *Several Pieces Gathered into One Volume*

Being a friend to love wading through the bondage of the world.

On himself, Dedication to *Fire in the Bush*

## WITHER, GEORGE

1588–1667 Poet, Pamphleteer

To Him-selfe G. W. wisheth all happiness.

On himself, *Dedication of Abuses Stript and Whipt*

Wither seems to have contemplated to a degree of idolatry his own possible virtue. He is for ever anticipating persecution and martyrdom; fingering, as it were, the flames, to try how he can bear them.

Charles Lamb, *On the Poetical Works of George Wither*

Worthy Withers.

Alexander Pope, *Dunciad*, book i

*Wither's* motto. *Nec habeo, nec careo, nec curo.* Nor have I, nor want I, nor care I.

Anthony à Wood, *Athenae Oxonienses*

This our Author ... sided with the Presb. in the beginning of the Civil Wars rais'd by them, *an.* 1642, became an Enemy to the King and Regality, sold the Estate he had, and with the Moneys received for it rais'd a Troop of

Horse for the Parliament, was made a Captain and soon after a Major, having this motto on his Colours, *Pro Rege, Lege, Grege*: but being taken Prisoner by the Cavaliers, Sir *Jo. Denham* the Poet (some of whose land at *Egham* in *Surry Wither* had got into his clutches) desired his Majesty not to hang him, *because that so long as* Wither *lived,* Denham *would not be accounted the worst Poet in* England.

*Ibid.*

## WITTGENSTEIN, LUDWIG JOSEF JOHANN

1889–1951 Philosopher

. . . Wittgenstein, picking up a poker to emphasize a point, asked: 'Give me an example of a moral rule.' [Karl] Popper replied with: 'Not to threaten visiting lecturers with pokers.' Whereupon, Popper has written, 'Wittgenstein, in a rage, threw the poker down and stormed out of the room, banging the door behind him.' But not, according to some accounts, before Russell had pulled himself up in his chair and roared out: 'Wittgenstein, it is you who is creating all the confusion.'

Ronald W. Clark, describing a philosophical meeting at Cambridge in 1946, in *The Life of Bertrand Russell*

The fundamental thing about human languages is that they can and should be used to describe something; and this something is, somehow, the world. To be constantly and almost exclusively interested in the medium – in spectacle-cleaning – is a result of a philosophical mistake. This philosophical mistake can quite easily be traced in Wittgenstein.

Karl Popper, in Bryan Magee, *Modern British Philosophy*

My German engineer, I think is a fool. He thinks nothing empirical is knowable – I asked him to admit that there was not a rhinoceros in the room, but he wouldn't.

Bertrand Russell, Letter to Lady Ottoline Morrell, November 1911

You know the best remark [G. E.] Moore ever made? I asked him one time who his best pupil was, and he said, 'Wittgenstein.' I said, 'Why?' 'Because, Bertrand, he is my only pupil who always looks puzzled.'

Bertrand Russell, in Ved Mehta, *Fly and the Fly-Bottle*

## WODEHOUSE, SIR PELHAM GRENVILLE

1881–1975 Writer

One great advantage in being historian to a man like Jeeves is that his mere personality prevents one selling one's artistic soul for gold. In recent years I have had lucrative offers for his services from theatrical managers, motion-picture magnates, the proprietors of one or two widely advertised commodities, and even the editor of the comic supplement of an American newspaper, who wanted him for a 'comic strip'. But, tempting though the terms were, it only needed Jeeves' deprecating cough and his murmured 'I would scarcely advocate it, sir,' to put the jack under my better nature.

On himself, Introduction to *Jeeves Omnibus*

With Sean O'Casey's statement that I am 'English literature's performing flea', I scarcely know how to deal. Thinking it over, I believe he meant to be complimentary, for all the performing fleas I have met have impressed me with their sterling artistry and that indefinable something which makes the good trouper.

On himself, *Performing Flea*

If my analysis of Wodehouse's mentality is accepted, the idea that in 1941 he consciously aided the Nazi propaganda machine becomes untenable and even ridiculous ... His moral outlook has remained that of a public-school boy, and according to the public-school code, treachery in time of war is the most unforgivable of all sins. But how could he fail to grasp that what he did would be a big propaganda score for the Germans and would bring a torrent of disapproval on his head? To answer this one must take ... into consideration ... Wodehouse's complete lack – so far as one can judge from his printed works – of political awareness. It is nonsense to talk of 'Fascist tendencies' in his books. There are no post-1918 tendencies at all.

George Orwell, *In Defence of P. G. Wodehouse*

It was in the Edwardian epoch that he began to develop the style which has made him a national institution. But his stories use ancient devices of comedy. Some of his comic routines are as old as Aristophanes. Jeeves, like Sherlock Holmes, now belongs to folk-lore. He derives ultimately from the clever slaves of ancient literature.

W. W. Robson, *Modern English Literature*

I confess I find myself slightly shocked when anybody admits to not liking Wodehouse, although I can see that this is an unreasonable reaction. But I think I can be dogmatic on a few points from my own observation; that Wodehouse has been more read than any other English novelist by his fellow novelists; that nobody with any genuine feeling for the English language has failed to recognise at least an element of truth in Belloc's judgment of 1934, that Wodehouse was 'the best writer of English now alive, the head of my profession'; that the failure of academic literary criticism to take any account of Wodehouse's supreme mastery of the English language or the profound influence he has had on every worthwhile English novelist in the past 50 years demonstrates in better and conciser form than anything else how the Eng. Lit. industry is divorced from the subject it claims to study.

Auberon Waugh, in *New Statesman*, 21 February 1975

## WOFFINGTON, MARGARET (PEG)

*circa* 1714–60 Actress

This agreable Actress in the Part of Sir *Harry* coming into the Greenroom said pleasantly, *In my Conscience, I believe half the Men in the House take me for one of their own Sex.* Another Actress reply'd, *It may be so, but in my Conscience! the other half can convince them to the Contrary.*

W. R. Chetwood, *A General History of the Stage*

## WOLFE, JAMES

1727–59 Soldier

Wolfe, where'er he fought, / Put so much of his heart into his act / That his example had a magnet's force, / And all were swift to follow whom all loved. /

William Cowper, *The Task*, book 2

Mad, is he? then I hope he will *bite* some of my other generals.

George II, in Beckles Wilson, *Life and Letters of James Wolfe*

The sons of earth, the proud giants of old, / Have broke from their darksome abodes; / And such is the news, that in heaven 'tis told, / They're marching to war with the gods. / A council was held in the chamber of Jove, / And this was the final decree, / That Wolfe should be call'd to the armies above, / And the charge was intrusted to me. /

To the plains of Quebec with the orders I flew, / He begg'd for a moment's delay; / And cried, O forbear! Let me victory hear, / And then the command I'll obey. / With a darkening film I encompass'd his eyes, / And convey'd him away in an urn, / Lest the fondness he bore for his own native shore, / Should tempt him again to return.

Thomas Paine, 'Death of General Wolfe', in *Pennsylvania Magazine*, March 1775

What he accomplished was done in the years when the ordinary mortal is learning his business; he was to war what William Pitt, the son of the great commoner who sent him to Quebec, was later to politics, what Keats was to literature.

Edward Salmon, *General Wolfe*

## WOLFE, THOMAS CLAYTON

1900–38 Author

I will go everywhere and do everything. I will meet all the people I can. I will think all the thoughts, feel all the emotions I am able, and I will write, write, write.

On himself, in Malcolm Cowley, *A Second Flowering*

His persistent immaturity – still another fault that is often urged against him – was not so much a weakness of character as it was a feature of his literary policy. He had to play the part of an innocent in the great world. He had to have illusions, then lose them painfully, then replace them with others, because that repeated process was the story he wanted to tell.

Malcolm Cowley, *ibid.*

He thought of himself as writing the last great epic of American nationality, certainly the last great American romance, as he perhaps did; but the epic was a personal quarrel, and the romance a vast inchoate yearning to the end.

Alfred Kazin, *On Native Grounds*

He wrote one book all his life, as all the volumes he produced were chapters in it.

*Ibid.*

The merits of Wolfe's work are probably more apparent at a first reading; its defects emerge with overpowering insistence on subsequent reflection and further acquaintance. It is hardly likely that the four unwieldy novels can long survive in a world which has proved itself too difficult for dinosaurs.

George F. Whicher, 'The Twentieth Century', in Arthur Hobson Quinn ed., *The Literature of the American People*

## WOLLSTONECRAFT, MARY (MARY GODWIN)

1759–97 Advocate of Women's Rights

I know what you are thinking of, but I have nothing to communicate on the subject of religion.

On herself, attributed last words, spoken to her husband

In all probability had she been married well in early life, she had then been a happy woman and universally respected.

Anon., in *Monthly Visitor*, February 1798

Her works will be read with disgust by every female who has any pretensions to delicacy; with detestation by everyone attached to the interests of religion and morality, and with indignation by anyone who might feel any regard for the unhappy woman, whose frailties should have been buried in oblivion.

Anon., in *Historical Magazine*, 1799

Whilom this dame the Rights of Women writ, / That is the title to the book she places, / Exhorting bashful womankind to quit / All foolish modesty and coy grimaces, / And name their backsides as it were their faces; / Such licence loose-tongued liberty adores, / Which adds to female speech exceeding graces; / Lucky the maid that on her volume pores, / A scripture archly fram'd for propagating whores. /

Anon., in the *Anti-Jacobin*, vol. 9, 1801

For Mary verily would wear the breeches / God help poor silly men from such usurping b-----s. /

*Ibid.*

The strength of her mind lay in intuition. She was often right, by this means alone, in matters of mere speculation. Yet though perhaps in the strict sense of the term, she reasoned little, it is surprising what a degree of soundness is to be found in her determination. But if this quality was of use to her in topics that seem the proper province of reasoning, it was much more so in matters directly appealing to the intellectual taste. In a robust and unwavering judgement of this sort, there is a kind of witchcraft.

William Godwin, *Memoirs of the Author of 'A Vindication of the Rights of Woman'*

Fierce passion's slave, she veer'd with every gust, / Love, Rights, and Wrongs, Philosophy, and Lust. /

T. J. Mathias, *The Shade of Alexander Pope on the Banks of the Thames*

Hard was thy fate in all the scenes of life, / As daughter, sister, mother, friend, and wife; / But harder still thy fate in death we own, / Thus mourned by Godwin with a heart of stone. /

William Roscoe, in Elizabeth Robins Pennell, *Mary Wollstonecraft Godwin*

A philosophizing serpent ... that hyena in petticoats.

Horace Walpole, *Letters*

*See also* Mary Shelley

## WOLSEY, THOMAS, CARDINAL

1475?–1530 Archbishop, Statesman

Had I but served God as diligently as I have served the King, he would not have given me over in my gray hairs.

On himself, addressed to Sir William Kingston

Little Boy Blue, / Come blow your horn, / The sheep's in the meadow, / The cow's in the corn; / But where is the boy / Who looks after the sheep? / He's under a haycock, / Fast asleep. / Will you wake him? / No, not I, / For if I do, / He's sure to cry. /

Nursery rhyme, traditionally taken to refer to Wolsey

Item, that he, having the French pox, presumed to come and breathe on the king.

*The Articles of Parliament Against Wolsey*, 1529

Thomas Wolsey, Cardinal, was a butcher's son, of Ipswych, in Suffolke. He was a fellowe of Magdalen Colledge in Oxford, where he was tutor to a young gentleman of Limmington, near Ilchester, *in com.* Somerset, in whose guift the presentation of that church is, worth the better part of 200 *li. per annum*, which he gave to his tutor, Wolsey. He had committed hereabout some debauchery (I thinke, drunke: no doubt he was of a high rough spirit), and spake derogatorily of Sir Amias Paulet (a Justice of Peace in the neighbourhood) who putt him into the stockes ... which, when he came to be Cardinall, he did not forget; he layed a fine upon Sir Amias to build the gate of the Middle Temple.

John Aubrey, *Brief Lives*

The once proud Cardinal was soon further disgraced, and wrote the most abject letters to his vile sovereign; who humbled him one day and encouraged him the next, according to his humour, until he was at last ordered to go and reside in his diocese of York. He said he was too poor; but I don't know how he made that out, for he took a hundred and sixty servants with him, and seventy-two cartloads of furniture, food, and wine.

Charles Dickens, *A Child's History of England*

King Henry took just offence that the cardinal set his own arms above the king's on the gatehouse, at the entrance into the college. This was no verbal but a real *ego et rex meus*, excusable by no plea in manners or grammar; except only that, (which is rather fault than figure), a harsh down-right hysterosis. But, to humble the cardinal's pride, some afterwards set up, on a window, a painted mastiff-dog, gnawing the spade-bone of a shoulder of mutton, to mind the cardinal of his extraction, being the son of a butcher; it being utterly improbable, (that some have fancied), that that picture was placed there by the cardinal's own appointment, to be to him a monitor of humility.

Thomas Fuller, *Church History of Britain*

Their heads will catch cold who wait bare for a dead pope's triple crown. Wolsey may be an instance hereof, who, on every avoidance of St Peter's chair, was sitting down therein, when suddenly someone or other clapt in before him!

*Ibid.*

In full-blown dignity, see Wolsey stand, / Law in his voice, and fortune in his hand: / To him the church, the realm, their pow'rs consign, / Thro' him the rays of regal bounty shine, / Turn'd by his nod the stream of honour flows, / His smile alone security bestows, / Still to new heights his restless wishes tow'r, / Claim leads to claim, and pow'r advances pow'r; / Till conquest unresisted ceas'd to please, / And rights submitted left him none to seize.

Samuel Johnson, *Vanity of Human Wishes*

*Katharine*: ... he was a man / Of an unbounded stomach, ever ranking / Himself with princes; one that by suggestion / Tied all the kingdom; simony was fair play: / His own opinion was his law: i' the presence / He would say untruths, and be ever double / Both in his words and meaning. He was never, / (But where he meant to ruin) pitiful: / His promises were, as he then was, mighty, / But his performances, as he is now, nothing: / Of his own body he was ill, and gave / The clergy ill example. /

William Shakespeare, *Henry VIII*, Act IV, Scene ii

*Griffith*: He was a scholar, and a ripe and good one; / Exceeding wise, fair-spoken, and persuading; / Lofty and sour to them that lov'd him not, / But to those men that sought him sweet as summer.

*Ibid.*

*See also* Lord Melbourne

## WOOD, ANTHONY (À)

1632–95 Antiquary, Historian

Merton Wood, with his Antiquitie, / Will live to all Eternitie. /

Anon., contemporary

A little silly fellow who hath an ill designe to libell honest men.

Gilbert Burnet, remark reported to Wood, and noted in his *Life and Times*

Just as naturally as a cuttle fish ejects poisonous ink, so did Mr Wood eject spite.

Llewelyn Powys ed., *Life and Times of Anthony à Wood*

His indefatigable industry was so high, that through earnestness he would burst out of bleeding suddenly, insomuch that he had a bason frequently held under him that he might not spoil his papers.

Richard Rawlinson, *Memoranda Relating to Wood*

## WOOD, EDWARD FREDERICK LINDLEY, EARL OF HALIFAX

1881–1959 Statesman

I have had enough obloquy for one life-time.

On himself, 1938, on his vice-regal period, in A. J. P. Taylor, *English History 1914–1945*

... he always appears a sort of Jesus in long boots. The long boots are needed because he has had to wade through the mud. But he was not responsible for the mud, oh, dear no! Edward Wood could never make anything so dirty as mud, and the last thing he would think of, would be to throw it at others.

Lord Beaverbrook, Letter to Arthur Brisbane, 28 May 1930

He fascinates and bamboozles everyone. Is he saint turned worldling, or worldling become saint?

Henry Channon, Diary, 16 February 1939

It appears that during the Halifax reign in India someone asked 'What is the Viceroy thinking?' and the answer was 'Whom did he see last?'

*Ibid.*, 24 May 1939

## WOOD, SIR HENRY JOSEPH

1869–1944 Conductor

A hundred seasons may elapse / Ere timber reach its prime. / Small wonder, then, we hope our Wood / Will go on beating time. /

Anon., heard at the Savage Club, 1944

It would not be true to say that Henry Wood ... ever really walked on to a concert platform. His progress was more in the nature of an eager little trot, rather as though he were anxious that his reputation for punctuality should not be marred.

Leslie Ayre, *The Proms*

No one could have called him a great conductor: but he carried 'usefulness' to the point of genius.

Victor Gollancz, *Journey Towards Music*

He has been burning the candle at both ends & in the middle too & now he is a wreck.

A. J. Jaeger, Letter to Edward Elgar, 16 October 1902

It was generous-minded Sir Henry Wood who first started mixed bathing in the sea of music.

Dame Ethel Smyth, *An Open Secret*

I cannot imagine a situation in which he would fail to hit on the one kindly thing that can be said without verging on humbug. Once I remarked: 'What amazes me is the way you contrive to turn on the warm tap if it is humanly possible.'

'Well you don't want people to *catch cold*, do you?'

Dame Ethel Smyth, *A Final Burning of Boats*

## WOOLF, LEONARD SIDNEY

1880–1969 Author

I don't think he is an 'idiot', rather a perverse, partially-educated alien German, who has thrown in his lot violently with Bolshevism and Mr Joyce's 'Ulysses' and 'the great sexual emancipation' and all the rest of the nasty fads of the hour. It is no use for us to strive with such a man.

Edmund Gosse, Letter to Sidney Colvin, 1924

There's a story that a week or two before the engagement he proposed in a train, and she accepted him, but owing to the rattling of the carriage he didn't hear, and took up a newspaper, saying 'What?' On which she had a violent revulsion and replied 'Oh, nothing!'

Lytton Strachey, Letter to Lady Ottoline Morrell, 12 June 1912

## WOOLF, (ADELINE) VIRGINIA

1882–1941 Novelist

People, like Arnold Bennett, say I can't create, or didn't in *Jacob's Room*, characters that survive. My answer is – but I leave that to the *Nation*: it's only the old argument that character is dissipated into shreds now; the old post-Dostoievsky arguments. I daresay it's true, however, that I haven't that 'reality' gift. I insubstantise, wilfully to some extent, distrusting reality – its cheapness.

On herself, *A Writer's Diary*, 19 June 1923

I do not know how Virginia Woolf is thought of by the younger literary generation; I do know that by my own, even in the palmiest days of social consciousness, she was admired and loved much more than she realized. I do not know if she is going to exert an influence on the future development of the novel – I rather suspect that her style and her vision were so unique that influence would only result in tame imitation – but I cannot imagine a time, however bleak, or a writer, whatever his school, when and for whom her devotion to her art, her industry, her severity with herself – above all, her passionate love, not only or chiefly for the big moments of life but also for its daily humdrum 'sausage-and-haddock' details – will not remain an example that is at once an inspiration and a judge.

W. H. Auden, *Forewords and Afterwords*

Great novels are devastatingly particular. Virginia Woolf's novels are too devastatingly vague. I lost patience when I discovered (from the luncheon in *Between the Acts* ...) that she thought you need a corkscrew to open a bottle of champagne. For evocation, subtlety of mood, atmosphere – all the qualities the Lupians praise – the sensitive Mrs Woolf can be shamed by an old toughy like Simenon, who has the literary good sense to approach the intangible through the concrete.

Brigid Brophy, *Don't Never Forget*

Virginia Woolf seemed to have the worst defect of the Mandarin style, the ability to spin cocoons of language out of nothing. The history of her literary style has been that of a form at first simple, growing more and more elaborate, the content lagging far behind, then catching up, till ... she produced a masterpiece in *The Waves*.

Cyril Connolly, *Enemies of Promise*

She is like a plant which is supposed to grow in a well-prepared garden bed – the bed of esoteric literature – and then pushes up suckers all over the place, through the gravel of the front drive, and even through the flagstones of the kitchen yard. She was full of interests, and their number increased as she grew older, she was curious about life, and she was tough, sensitive but tough.

E. M. Forster, *Virginia Woolf* (Reid Lecture)

Virginia had this reputation of being a rather malicious person – deservedly so, I think. Adrian – Virginia's brother, Vanessa and Clive and several others suddenly discovered they were no longer on speaking terms. So Adrian called on them and said 'Something's wrong between us – it must be the Goat' – that was Virginia's nickname. He got everyone to write down what Virginia had said about the others. We met a month later and read the notes aloud – and from that time, Virginia's power was broken for ever.

David Garnett, in *Observer Colour Supplement*, 5 March 1972

Her works are very strange. They're very beautiful, aren't they? but one gets such a curious feeling from them. She sees with incredible clarity, but always as though through a sheet of plate glass. Her books are not immediate. They're very puzzling to me.

Aldous Huxley, in *Paris Review*

The reader not prepared to readjust himself to the technique of *Mrs Dalloway* or *To the Lighthouse* will get very little return for the energy he must lay out in wrestling with those involved periods. He is repaid by none of the obvious satisfactions he expects from a novel – no friendly characters, no reassuring conviction that life is as he wants it to be, no glow of companionship or stirring relation of action... He is dimly aware of having missed the point and feels cheated, or at best impressed but irritated.

Q. D. Leavis, *Fiction and the Reading Public*

She was extremely beautiful, with an austere intellectual beauty of bone and outline, with large melancholy eyes under carved lids, and the nose and lips, the long narrow cheek of a Gothic Madonna. Her voice, light, musical, with a throaty note in it, was one of her great charms. She was tall and thin, and her hands were astonishingly exquisite. She used to spread them out to the fire, and they were so transparent one fancied one saw the long fragile bones through the fine skin. There was something about her that made one think of William Morris and the New Age and the Emancipation of Women.

Rosamond Lehmann, *Penguin New Writing*, no. 7

In Strachey, because there is no *Sturm und Drang* ... there is no joy. And on this plane of judgement I may as well agree with you that Virginia Woolf is not a figure of sufficient importance to warrant a difference of opinion between us. She does not face the problem, and it may be that ... I may have to put her down along with Strachey and Garnett among the forces which are imposing a premature and hardening limitation on contemporary literature – fencing it off into a small perfection which is a denial of further progress.

Edwin Muir, Letter to Stephen Hudson, 8 May 1925

Virginia Woolf, I enjoyed talking to her, but thought *nothing* of her writing. I considered her 'a beautiful little knitter'.

Edith Sitwell, Letter to Geoffrey Singleton, 11 July 1955

I am now in the middle of Virginia's [*To the Lighthouse*] – which I like, so far, much better than Mrs Dalloway. It really is most unfortunate that she rules out copulation – not the ghost of it visible – so that her presentation of things becomes little more, it seems to me, than an arabesque – an exquisite arabesque, of course.

Lytton Strachey, Letter to E. B. C. Lucas, 7 May 1927

For me, this work seems very clever, very ingenious, but creatively unimportant. It was done – as so much modern un-creative writing is done – with the superficial wits; there was nothing in it for those who did not pride themselves upon intellectual superiority to the herd.

Frank Swinnerton, *The Georgian Literary Scene*

*See also* Lytton Strachey, Leonard Woolf

## WOOLLCOTT, ALEXANDER HUMPHREYS

1887–1943 Author, Critic

To all things clergic / I am allergic. /
On himself, in Samuel Hopkins Adams, *Alexander Woollcott, His Life and His World*

You must have suspected more than once that I'm a pretty trivial, rootless person, a fellow of motley and diffused affections, permanently adrift.
On himself, Letter to Robert Rudd

. . . the smartest of Alecs.
Heywood Broun, in Robert E. Drennan ed., *Wit's End*

His life was what the marquees describe as a 'continuous performance.'
John Mason Brown, Introduction to *The Portable Woollcott*

. . . a New Jersey Nero who mistook his pinafore for a toga.
Edna Ferber, in Edwin P. Hoyt, *Alexander Woollcott: The Man Who Came to Dinner*

I want to be alone on this trip. I don't expect to talk to a man or woman – just Aleck Woollcott.
Edna Ferber, in Robert E. Drennan ed., *Wit's End*

. . . a persnickety fellow with more fizz than brain.
Ben Hecht, in *ibid.*

He looked like something that had gotten loose from Macy's Thanksgiving Day Parade.
Harpo Marx, in Edwin P. Hoyt, *Alexander Woollcott: The Man Who Came to Dinner*

Just a big dreamer with a sense of double entry.
Harpo Marx, in Samuel Hopkins Adams, *Alexander Woollcott, His Life and His World*

. . . a fat duchess with the emotions of a fish.
Harold Ross, in Robert E. Drennan ed., *Wit's End*

Old Vitriol and Violets.
James Thurber, in *ibid.*

*See also* Robert Benchley

## WORDSWORTH, WILLIAM

1770–1850 Poet

The principal object, then, proposed in these Poems was to choose incidents and situations from common life, and to relate or describe them, throughout, as far as was possible in a selection of language really used by men, and, at the same time, to throw over them a certain colouring of imagination, whereby ordinary things should be presented to the mind in an unusual aspect; and further, and above all, to make these incidents and situations interesting by tracing in them, truly though not ostentatiously, the primary laws of our nature: chiefly, as far as regards the manner in which we associate ideas in a state of excitement.
On himself, Preface to the *Lyrical Ballads*

No poet, perhaps, is so evidently filled with a new and sacred energy when the inspiration is upon him; no poet, when it fails him, is so left 'weak as is a breaking wave' . . . Wordsworth's poetry, when he is at his best, is inevitable, as inevitable as Nature herself. It might seem that Nature not only gave him the matter for his poem, but wrote his poem for him. He has no style . . . When he seeks to have a style he falls into ponderosity and pomposity.
Matthew Arnold, *Wordsworth*

Just for a handful of silver he left us, / Just for a riband to stick in his coat – / Found the one gift of which fortune bereft us, / Lost all the others she lets us devote; / They, with the gold to give, doled him out silver, / So much was theirs who so little allowed: / How all our copper had gone for his service! / Rags – were they purple, his heart had been proud! / We that had loved him so, followed him, honoured him, / Lived in his mild and magnificent eye, / Learned his great language, caught his clear accents, / Made him our pattern to live and to die! / Shakespeare was of us, Milton was for us, / Burns, Shelley, were with us, – they watch from their graves! / He alone breaks from the van and the freemen, / He alone sinks to the rear and the slaves! /

Robert Browning, *The Lost Leader*

Next comes the dull disciple of thy school, / That mild apostate from poetic rule, / The simple Wordsworth, framer of a lay, / As soft as evening in his favourite May, / Who warns his friend 'to shake off toil and trouble, / And quit his books for fear of growing double', / Who, both by precept and example, shows / That prose is verse, and verse is merely prose; / Convincing all, by demonstration plain, / Poetic souls delight in prose insane / And Christmas stories tortured into rhyme / Contain the essence of the true sublime. /

Lord Byron, *English Bards and Scotch Reviewers*

And Wordsworth, in a rather long *Excursion* / (I think the quarto holds five hundred pages), / Has given a sample from the vasty version / Of his new system to perplex the sages; / 'Tis poetry – at least by his assertion, / And may appear so when the Dog Star rages – / And he who understands it would be able / To add a story to the Tower of Babel. /

Lord Byron, Dedication to *Don Juan*

The great Metaquizzical poet.

Lord Byron, Letter to John Murray, 19 January 1821

He is himself, and, I dare affirm, that he will hereafter be admitted as the first and greatest philosophical poet, the only man who has effected a complete and constant synthesis of thought and feeling and combined them with poetic forms, with the music of pleasurable passion, and with Imagination or the *modifying* power in that highest sense of the word... Wordsworth is a poet, and I feel myself a better poet, in knowing how to honour *him* than in all my own poetic compositions, all I have done or hope to do.

Samuel Taylor Coleridge, Letter to Richard Sharp, 1804

He strides on so far before you, that he dwindles in the distance.

Samuel Taylor Coleridge, quoted by William Hazlitt, in *Examiner*, 12 January 1817

Wordsworth is really the first, in the unsettled state of affairs in his time, to annex new authority for the poet, to meddle with social affairs, and to offer a new kind of religious sentiment which it seemed the peculiar prerogative of the poet to interpret.

T. S. Eliot, *The Use of Poetry and the Use of Criticism*

Is Wordsworth a bell with a wooden tongue?

Ralph Waldo Emerson, *Journal*, 1863

I have been poring over Wordsworth lately: which has had much effect in bettering my Blue Devils: for his philosophy does not abjure melancholy, but puts a pleasant countenance upon it, and connects it with humanity. It is very well, if the sensibility that makes us fearful of ourselves is diverted to become a cause of sympathy and interest with Nature and mankind: and this I think Wordsworth tends to do.

Edward Fitzgerald, Letter to John Allen, 1832

He evidently loves the monologue style of conversation, but shows great candour in giving due consideration to any remarks which others may make. His manner is simple, his general appearance that of the abstract thinker, whom his subject gradually warms into poetry.

Caroline Fox, *Journals*, June 1842

Wordsworth had quite the figure and air of a sturdy mountaineer in search of a stray sheep or goat. We had a scorching ramble of more than two hours in which Wordsworth *expanded* amazingly . . . There were no bursts of information but a gradual development of it. He looked round, as we ascended, from time to time, at the prospect up and down and beyond the river; and he talked of painting, sketching, and many other subjects suggested by the scene. But he did not after all talk like a painter or a philosopher, and not one bit like a poet. There was an inflexible matter-of-fact manner and spirit in all he said, which came out in a rather hoarse and harsh *burr* that made it disagreeable as well as unimpressive. I could hardly believe in the man's identity, or be convinced that I walked beside the author so remarkable for his imaginative and vapoury abstractions.

Thomas Colley Grattan, *Beaten Paths and Those Who Trod Them*

Once as I was walking with Wordsworth in Pall Mall we ran into Christie's, where there was a very good copy of the Transfiguration, which he abused through thick and thin. In the corner stood the group of Cupid and Psyche kissing. After looking some time he turned round to me with an expression I shall never forget, and said, 'The Dev-ils!'

Benjamin Robert Haydon, *Autobiography*

He has produced a deeper impression, and on a smaller circle, than any other of his contemporaries. His powers have been mistaken by the age, nor does he exactly understand them himself. He cannot form a whole. He has not the constructive faculty. He can give only the fine tones of thought, drawn from his mind by accident or nature, like the sounds drawn from the Aeolian harp by the wandering gale. – He is totally deficient in all the machinery of poetry.

William Hazlitt, *Lectures on the English Poets*

The most original poet now living, and the one whose writings could the least be spared; for they have no substitutes elsewhere. The vulgar do not read them; the learned, who see all things through books, do not understand them; the great, despite the fashionable, may ridicule them; but the author has created himself an interest in the heart of the retired and lonely student of nature, which can never die.

William Hazlitt, *The Spirit of the Age*

Coleridge has told me that he himself liked to compose in walking over uneven ground, or breaking through the straggling branches of a copsewood; whereas Wordsworth always wrote (if he could) walking up and down a straight gravel-walk, or in some spot where the continuity of his verse met with no collateral interruption.

William Hazlitt, in *Examiner*, 12 January 1817

A modern Moses who sits on Pisgah with his back obstinately turned to that promised land, the Future; he is only fit for those old maid tabbies, the Muses.

Douglas Jerrold, Review of Wordsworth's Poems

It may be said that we ought to read our contemporaries: that Wordsworth, etc., ought to have their due from us. But for the sake of a few fine imaginative or domestic passages, are we to be bullied into a certain Philosophy engendered in the whims of an Egotist? Every man has his speculations, but every man does not brood and peacock over them till he makes a false coinage and deceives himself.

John Keats, Letter to John H. Reynolds, 3 February 1818

Separate from the pleasure of your company, I don't much care if I never see another mountain in my life.

Charles Lamb, Letter to Wordsworth, 30 January 1801

I needed to be made to feel that there was real, permanent happiness in tranquil contemplation. Wordsworth taught me this not only without turning away from, but with a greatly increased interest in the common feelings and common destiny of human beings.

John Stuart Mill, *Autobiography*

Compared with the greatest poets, he may be said to be the poet of unpoetical natures, possessed of quiet and contemplative tastes. But unpoetical natures are precisely those which require poetic cultivation. This cultivation Wordsworth is much more fitted to give than poets who are intrinsically far more poets than he.

*Ibid.*

Is Wordsworth sleeping in peace on his bed of mud in the profundity of Pathos, or will he ever again wake to dole out a lyrical ballad?

Thomas Love Peacock, Letter, 1808

Perhaps 'alive' is scarcely the word one would apply to the 'luminary' of the Lake District. Wordsworth drew his first orderly and deliberate breath in 1770, and continued the alternative processes of inhalation and exhalation until 1850.

Ezra Pound, in *Future*, September 1913

Mr Wordsworth, a stupid man, with a decided gift for portraying nature in vignettes, never yet ruined anyone's morals, unless, perhaps, he has driven some susceptible persons to crime in a very fury of boredom.

*Ibid.*, November 1917

He had a mind which was somehow / At once circumference and centre / Of all he might or feel or know; / Nothing went ever out, although / Something did ever enter. /

He had as much imagination / As a pint-pot; – he never could / Fancy another situation, / From which to dart his contemplation / Than that wherein he stood. /

Percy Bysshe Shelley, *Peter Bell the Third*

Wordsworth was a tea-time bore, the great Frost of literature, the verbose, the humourless, the platitudinary reporter of Nature in her dullest moods. Open him at any page: and there lies the English language not, as George Moore said of Pater, in a glass coffin, but in a large, sultry, and unhygienic box.

Dylan Thomas, Letter to Pamela Hansford Johnson, 1933

He found in stones the sermons he had already hidden there.

Oscar Wilde, *The Decay of Lying*

Wordsworth is so often flat and heavy partly because his moral sense has no theatrical elements, it is an obedience, a discipline which he has not created. This increases his popularity with the better sort of journalists, the *Spectator* writers, for instance, with all who are

part of the machine and yet care for poetry.
William Butler Yeats, *Memoirs*

*See also* Lord Byron, John Cavanagh, Samuel Taylor Coleridge, George Crabbe, Rudyard Kipling, W. S. Landor, Alexander Pope, Sir Walter Scott, Robert Louis Stevenson, John Webster

## WOTTON, SIR HENRY

1568–1639 Poet, Diplomat

His good old genially pious life.
Thomas Carlyle, *Frederick the Great*

What shall we say, since silent now is he, / Who when he spoke, all things would silent be! / Who had so many languages in store, / That only Fame shall speak of him in more. / Whom England now no more returned must see; / He's gone to heav'n, on his fourth embassy. /
Abraham Cowley, *An Elegy on Sir Henry Wotton*

## WREN, SIR CHRISTOPHER

1632–1723 Architect, Mathematician

Sir Christopher Wren / Said, 'I am going to dine with some men. / If anybody calls / Say I am designing St Paul's.' /
Edmund Clerihew Bentley, *Biography for Beginners*

Wren's mind was finely balanced between cognition and inspiration. In science, he was capable of devising the theoretical formula to solve a problem but not bothering to proceed to the solution; on the other hand he found congenial the emphasis of post-Baconian science on experiment, because he needed visible results to maintain his interest . . . This need may explain his involvement first with anatomy and then with architecture.
K. Downes, *Nicholas Hawksmoor*

That miracle of a youth.
John Evelyn, Diary, 10 July 1654

Wren's solutions are not adopted as the only possible ones; his architectural music is latitudinarian; his preferences are never exclusive to alternatives.
V. Fürst, *The Architecture of Sir Christopher Wren*

There scarce ever met in one man, in so great a perfection, such a Mechanical Hand, and so Philosophical a Mind.
Robert Hooke, Preface to *Micrographia*

Thro' several reigns we have patiently seen the noblest publick buildings perish (if I may say so) under the hand of one single court-architect; who, if he had been able to profit by experience, wou'd long since at our expense, have prov'd the greatest master in the world.
The First Earl of Shaftesbury, *A Letter Concerning Design*

Generally, the City churches give a wonderful picture of Wren's mind during the central period of his career. It is an energetic, adventurous mind, proceeding by intellectual argument rather than by the intuitive conceptions of aesthetic entities to which all argument must be subordinated. Wren was, through and through, an empiricist. A design of his never *grows*: it is stated at once, then abruptly altered or wholly superseded.
J. Summerson, *Architecture in Britain 1530–1830*

*See also* Inigo Jones

## WRIGHT, FRANK LLOYD

1867–1959 Architect

Early in life I had to choose between honest arrogance and hypocritical humility. I chose honest arrogance and have seen no occasion to change.
On himself, in Herbert Jacobs, *Frank Lloyd Wright*

My grandfather, Frank Lloyd Wright, wore a red sash on his wedding night. That is glamour.

Anne Baxter, in *Time*, 5 May 1952

I agree that non-critical estimates of Frank Lloyd Wright are rather meaningless now. I would go further and say that critical estimates of Wright are also meaningless now. Sometime Frank Lloyd Wright will be re-evaluated – and his great concept of architecture where everything is all one organism, all one thing, will be appreciated.

Eero Saarinen, *Eero Saarinen, on His Work*

## WRIGHT, JOSEPH (OF DERBY)

1734–97 Painter

But see far off the modest Wright retire! / Alone he rules his Element of Fire: / Like Meteors darting through the gloom of Night, / His sparkles flash upon the dazzled sight; / Our eyes with momentary anguish smart, / And Nature trembles at the power of Art. / May the bold colours, claiming endless praise, / For ages shine with undiminish'd blaze, / And when the fierce VESUVIO burns no more, / May his red deluge down thy canvass pour. /

William Hayley, *An Essay on Painting*, epistle 2

The Man Of Night! / O'er *woollen* hills, where gold and silver moons / Now mount like sixpences, and now balloons; / Where sea-reflections, nothing nat'ral tell ye, / So much like fiddle-strings, or vermicelli; / Where ev'ry thing exclaimeth, how severe! / 'What *are* we?' and 'what business have we here?' /

Peter Pindar (John Wolcot), *Lyric Odes for 1783*, ode 5

## WRIGHT, ORVILLE, and WRIGHT, WILBUR

1871–1948 and 1867–1912 Pioneer Aviators

This biplane is the shape of human flight. / Its name might better be First Motor Kite. / Its makers' name – Time cannot get that wrong, / For it was writ in heaven doubly Wright. /

Robert Frost, *The Wrights' Biplane*

## WYCHERLEY, WILLIAM

1640?–1716 Dramatist

Mr Wycherley being indeed almost the only man alive, who has made Comedy instructive in its Fable; almost all the rest being contented to instruct by their characters.

John Dennis, *The Usefulness of the Stage*

I must confess that I have no great Opinion of that which Men generally call Humility: in most Men, Humility is want of Heat; 'tis Phlegm, 'tis Impotence, 'tis a wretched Necessity, of which they who lie under it vainly endeavour to make a Virtue. But in a Man of Mr Wycherley's Make, 'tis Choice, 'tis Force of Mind, 'tis a Good, 'tis a generous Condescension, and what Force of Mind is there not requisite to bend back a Soul by perpetual Reflection, which would be always rising and eternally aspiring by virtue of its inborn Fire?

John Dennis, *The Select Works*

He appears to have led, during a long course of years, that most wretched life, the life of a vicious old boy about town.

T. B. Macaulay, *Essays*: 'On the Comic Dramatists of the Restoration'

In truth, Wycherley's indecency is protected against the critics as a skunk is protected against the hunters. It is safe because it is too filthy to handle, and too noisome even to approach.

*Ibid.*

*Pope*: His memory did not carry above a sentence at a time. These single sentences were good, but the whole was without connection and good for nothing but to be flung into maxims. *Spence*: In spite of his good sense, I could never read his plays with true pleasure, from the general stiffness of his style. *Pope*: Ay, that was occasioned by his being always studying for antitheses.

Joseph Spence, *Anecdotes*

*See also* Alexander Pope, Thomas Shadwell

## WYCLIFFE, JOHN

–d. 1384 Religious and Social Reformer

John Wycleve was a grand dissembler, a man of little conscience, and what he did as to religion, was more out of vaine glory, and to obtaine unto him a name, than out of honestie.

Dr John Fell, in Anthony à Wood, *Life and Times*, June 1672

To Lutterworth they come, – Sumner, Commissary, Official, Chancellor, Proctors, Doctors, and the servants (so that the remnant of the body would not hold out a bone, amongst so many hands) take what was left out of the grave, and burnt them to ashes, and cast them into Swift, a neighbouring brook running hard by. Thus this brook hath conveyed his ashes into Avon, Avon into Severn, Severn into the narrow seas, they, into the main ocean. And thus the ashes of Wickliffe are the emblem of his doctrine, which now, is dispersed all the world over.

Thomas Fuller, *Church History of Britain* (on the disinterment, burning and dispersal of Wycliffe's remains in accordance with a decree of the Council of Constance)

He was a master of irony, and no account of him is balanced which omits his elephantine playfulness.

Bernard L. Manning, in *The Cambridge Medieval History*, vol. 7, 1932

Not least art thou, thou little Bethlehem / In Judah, for in thee the Lord was born; / Nor thou in Britain, little Lutterworth, / Least for in thee the word was born again. /

Alfred, Lord Tennyson, *To Sir John Oldcastle*

The devil's instrument, church's enemy, people's confusion, heretics' idol, hypocrites' mirror, schism's broacher, hatred's sewer, lies' forger, flatteries' sink; who at his death despaired like Cain, and, stricken by the horrible judgment of God, breathed forth his wicked soul to the dark mansion of the black devil!

Thomas Walsingham, *Ypodigma Neustriae*, translated by Thomas Fuller

# 'Y'

## YATES, MARY ANN

1728–87 Actress

Mrs Yates, to a very fine figure joins a very handsome face, though not now in her *première jeunesse*: but the expression of her face is infinitely haughty and hard. With an *overdone* civility, as soon as our names were spoken, she rose from her seat hastily, and rather *rushed* towards, than meerly advanced to meet us; but I doubt not it was meant as the very *pink of politeness.*

Fanny Burney, Diary, 1774

Too much stumping about, and too much flumping about.

Kitty Clive, in W. Clark Russell, *Representative Actors*

On Mrs Yates rehearsing one morning at Drury-Lane Theatre a new part of a tragic princess, where at her death a *flourish of trumpets* was necessary, Hopkins the prompter, doubtful whether it was proper to go through the whole ceremony at that time, walked up softly to her as she lay seemingly dead upon the stage, and whispered, 'Madam! Madam!' – 'Well, what does the man want?' – 'Only, Madam, to know whether you would have the *flourish* now, or *wait for it till night.*'

Samuel Foote, in William Cooke, *Memoirs of Samuel Foote*

## YEATS, WILLIAM BUTLER

1865–1939 Poet

No people hate as we [the Irish] do in whom that past is always alive, there are moments when hatred poisons my life and I accuse myself of effeminacy because I have not given it adequate expression. It is not enough to have put it into the mouth of a rambling peasant poet. Then I remind myself that though mine is the first English marriage I know of in the direct line, all my family names are English and that I owe my soul to Shakespeare, to Spenser and to Blake, perhaps to William Morris, and to the English language in which I think, speak and write, that everything I love has come to me through English, my hatred tortures me with love, my love with hate. I am like the Tibetan monk who dreams at his initiation that he is eaten by a wild beast and learns on waking that he himself is eater and eaten.

On himself, *A General Introduction for my Work*

We were the last romantics – chose for theme / Traditional sanctity and loveliness; / Whatever's written in what poets name / The book of the people; whatever most can bless / The mind of man or elevate to rhyme; / But all is changed, that high horse riderless, / Though mounted in that saddle Homer rode / Where the swan drifts upon a darkening flood. /

On himself, addressing Lady Gregory, *Coole Park and Ballylee*

Under bare Ben Bulben's head / In Drumcliff churchyard Yeats is laid. / An ancestor was rector there / Long years ago, a church stands near, / By the road an ancient cross. / No marble, no conventional phrase; / On limestone quarried near the spot / By his command these words are cut: / Cast a cold eye / On life, on death. / Horseman, pass by! /

On himself, *Under Ben Bulben*

You were silly like us; your gift survived it all: / The parish of rich women, physical decay, / Yourself. Mad Ireland hurt you into poetry. /

W. H. Auden, *In Memory of W. B. Yeats*

To get the Last Poems of Yeats / You need not mug up on dates; / All a reader requires / Is some knowledge of gyres / And the sort of people he hates. /

W. H. Auden, *Academic Graffiti*

'Yeats claimed,' said Sargent, 'that he could be a chancellor or the ruler of a nation, if he chose! He boasted that he could quell mobs! When he sat for me he wore a velvet coat and a huge loose bow tie, and a long lock of hair fell across his brow. He told me that he did these things to remind himself of his own importance as an artist!' 'Why,' quietly interrupted Fox, 'didn't he tie a string around his finger?'

Martin Birnbaum, *John Singer Sargent; A Conversation Piece*

Against this drab background of dreary modern materialism, Willie Yeats was calmly walking about as the Man Who Knew the Fairies. Yeats stood for enchantment . . . But I very specially rejoiced in the fighting instinct which made the Irishman so firm and positive about it. He was the real original rationalist who said that the fairies stand to reason. He staggered the materialists by attacking their abstract materialism with a completely concrete mysticism.

G. K. Chesterton, *Autobiography*

Your omission of my work from the absurdly-named Oxford Book of Modern Verse is exactly typical of the attitude of the minor to the major poet. For example Thomas Moore, the Yeats of the 19th century, would undoubtedly have excluded Keats and Shelley from any anthology he had compiled.

Lord Alfred Douglas, Telegram to Yeats on the publication of *The Oxford Book of Modern Verse* (edited by Yeats)

He hammered on truth's anvil till he made / Such images as must endure, / Immortalised the house that has decayed, / The fallen lintel, rotted roof and floor; / Became what he created in his blood / Through years of thinking in the marrowbone – / Man and poet contracted into God / Beyond the certainties in book and stone. /

Brendan Kennelly, *Yeats*

Yeats in spite of his paunch was elegant in a smooth light suit and a just sufficiently crooked bow tie. His manner was hierophantic, even when he said: 'This afternoon I have been playing croquet with my daughter.' . . . He confined the conversation to spiritualism and the phases of the moon . . . He talked a great deal about the spirits to whom his wife, being a medium, had introduced him. 'Have you ever seen them?' Dodds asked . . . Yeats was a little piqued. No, he said grudgingly, he had never actually seen them . . . but – with a flash of triumph – he had often *smelt* them.

Louis MacNeice, *The Strings are False*

Translated into political terms, Yeats's tendency is Fascist. Throughout most of his life, and long before Fascism was ever heard of, he had the outlook of those who reach Fascism by its aristocratic route. He is a great hater of democracy, of the modern world, science, machinery, the concept of progress – above all, of the idea of human equality. Much of the imagery in his work is feudal, and it is clear that he was not altogether free from ordinary snobbishness. Later these tendencies took clearer shape and led him to 'the exultant acceptance of authoritarianism as the only solution.'

George Orwell, in *Horizon*, January 1943

My stay at Stone Cottage [Yeats's home] will not be in the least profitable.

I detest the country. Yeats will amuse me part of the time and bore me to death with psychical research the rest. I regard the visit as a duty to posterity.

Ezra Pound, in Charles Norman, *Ezra Pound*

Yeats, in spite of his desire to be a public figure, was more apolitical than any fully responsible person alive.

Arland Ussher, *Three Great Irishmen*

*See also* Mrs Patrick Campbell, Ford Madox Ford, Andrew Marvell, Edith Sitwell

## YORK AND ALBANY, DUKE OF (FREDERICK AUGUSTUS)

1763–1827 Soldier

Oh, the brave old Duke of York, / He had ten thousand men; / He marched them up to the top of the hill, / And he marched them down again. / And when they were up, they were up, / And when they were down, they were down, / And when they were only half-way up, / They were neither up nor down. /

Nursery rhyme, traditional

The Duke of York was spoken of, as a well meaning and an honest man, but as one scarcely on a level with the ordinary scale of human intellect. Neither he nor his brother [George IV], however, had any proper knowledge of *meum* and *tuum*, a fault that was probably as much owing to the flatterers that surrounded them, and to defective education, as to natural tendencies.

James Fenimore Cooper, *Gleanings in Europe: England*

## YOUNG, BRIGHAM

1801–77 Mormon Leader

Their leader in the early days in Utah was Bigamy Young. When he arrived in Salt Lake City he said to his followers, 'This is the place,' although he had never been there before. It was uncanny.

Richard Armour, *It All Started With Columbus*

He is dreadfully married. He's the most married man I ever saw in my life.

Artemus Ward (Charles Farrar Browne), *Artemus Ward's Lecture*

## YOUNG, EDWARD

1683–1765 Poet

When Young was writing a tragedy Grafton is said by Spence to have sent him a human skull, with a candle in it, as a lamp; and the poet is reported to have used it.

Herbert Croft, in Samuel Johnson, *Life of Young*

A sort of cross between a sycophant and a psalmist.

George Eliot, in *Westminster Review*, January 1857

Of Young's poems it is difficult to give any general character, for he has no uniformity of manner: one of his pieces has no great resemblance to another. He began to write early and continued long, and at different times had different modes of poetical excellence in view. His numbers are sometimes smooth and sometimes rugged; his style is sometimes concatenated and sometimes abrupt, sometimes diffusive and sometimes concise. His plan seems to have started in his mind at the present moment, and his thoughts appear the effects of chance, sometimes adverse and sometimes lucky, with very little operation of judgement.

Samuel Johnson, *Life of Young*

*See also* George Crabbe

## YOUNG, THOMAS

1773–1829 Physician, Physicist, Egyptologist

When I was a boy, I thought myself a man; now I am a man, I find myself a boy.

On himself, in George Peacock, *Life of Thomas Young*

It is recorded of Young that, when requested by an acquaintance, who presumed somewhat upon his youthful appearance, to exhibit a specimen of his handwriting, he very delicately rebuked the inquiry by writing a sentence in his best style in fourteen different languages.

John Tyndall, *New Fragments*

Immediately after his return to England he became a fellow-commoner of Emanuel College, Cambridge. When the master of the college introduced him to those who were to be his tutors he jocularly said, 'I have brought you a pupil qualified to read lectures to his tutors'.

*Ibid.*

# 'Z'

## ZIEGFELD, FLORENZ

1869–1932 Impresario

He was the kind of fellow who made people feel honored to have him owe them money.

Buddy de Sylva, in Eddie Cantor, *Take My Life*

Florenz Ziegfeld was a man with an engaging smile and a hawklike nose and all the charm in the world when he wanted to have it, and show it. He had considerably more temperament than anybody he ever managed, all the way from Sandow the Strong Man and Anna Held to W. C. Fields and Marilyn Miller. He squandered money on his productions, his whims, his affectations. He wore imported lavender shirts, went in for 500-word conversations by long-distance telephone, sent to South Africa for baby elephants and often sent special messengers to Baltimore for terrapin.

Ward Morehouse, in 'The Ziegfeld Follies: A Formula With Class', in *Theatre Arts*, May 1956

# Index of Persons Quoted

## MORE ABOUT PENGUINS AND PELICANS

For further information about books available from Penguins please write to Dept EP, Penguin Books Ltd, Harmondsworth, Middlesex UB7 0DA.

*In the U.S.A.*: For a complete list of books available from Penguins in the United States write to Dept CS, Penguin Books, 625 Madison Avenue, New York, New York 10022.

*In Canada*: For a complete list of books available from Penguins in Canada write to Penguin Books Canada Ltd, 2801 John Street, Markham, Ontario L3R 1B4.

*In Australia*: For a complete list of books available from Penguins in Australia write to the Marketing Department, Penguin Books Australia Ltd, P.O. Box 257, Ringwood, Victoria 3134.

*In New Zealand*: For a complete list of books available from Penguins in New Zealand write to the Marketing Department, Penguin Books (N.Z.) Ltd, P.O. Box 4019, Auckland 10.

## PENGUIN REFERENCE BOOKS

'Penguin Reference books are becoming indispensable; they are easy to travel with and, if they wear out, cheap to replace' – Cyril Connolly in the *Sunday Times*

### THE PENGUIN DICTIONARY OF QUOTATIONS

*J. M. and M. J. Cohen*

The reader, the writer, the after-dinner speaker, the crossword-solver and the browser will find what they want among the 12,000 or so quotations which include the immortal lines from Shakespeare, the Bible or Paradise Lost side by side with remarks and stray lines by almost unknown writers.

### THE PENGUIN DICTIONARY OF MODERN QUOTATIONS

*J. M. and M. J. Cohen*

This companion to *The Penguin Dictionary of Quotations* ranges from the wit of the Goon Show to the declarations of statesmen and the most memorable sayings of the famous and infamous.

### THE INTERNATIONAL THESAURUS OF QUOTATIONS

*Rhoda Thomas Tripp*

'I hate quotations. Tell me what you know' – Emerson

This reference book does for quotations what Roget did for words and phrases. It contains 16,000 of the most penetrating, provocative and witty quotations from the last 2,500 years and from six continents, grouped strictly by their meaning rather than by author or key words. In more than 1,000 subject categories, carefully selected for their relevance to today's world, the reader will find endless stimulation and thought-provoking amusement.